Psychology

EIGHTH EDITION IN MODULES

Custom Edition for Psychology 106
Brookdale Community College

Psychology

EIGHTH EDITION IN MODULES

David G. Myers

Hope College
Holland, Michigan

—WORTH—
Custom Publishing

ISBN-13: 978-1-4292-1176-5
ISBN-10: 1-4292-1176-8

Printed in the United States of America

Custom Publishing Division
Worth Publishers
41 Madison Avenue
New York, NY 10010

www.worthpublishers.com/custompub

About the Author

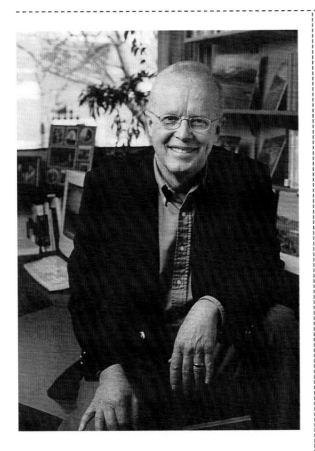

David Myers received his psychology Ph.D. from the University of Iowa. He has spent his career at Hope College, Michigan, where he is the John Dirk Werkman Professor of Psychology and has taught dozens of introductory psychology sections. Hope College students have invited him to be their commencement speaker and voted him "outstanding professor."

Myers' scientific articles have, with support from National Science Foundation grants, appeared in more than two dozen scientific periodicals, including *Science, American Scientist, Psychological Science,* and the *American Psychologist.* In addition to his scholarly writing and his textbooks for introductory and social psychology, he also digests psychological science for the general public. His writings have appeared in three dozen magazines, from *Today's Education* to *Scientific American.* He also has authored five general audience books, including *The Pursuit of Happiness* and *Intuition: Its Powers and Perils.*

David Myers has chaired his city's Human Relations Commission, helped found a thriving assistance center for families in poverty, and spoken to hundreds of college and community groups. He bikes to work year-round and plays daily pick-up basketball. David and Carol Myers have raised two sons and a daughter.

Brief Contents

Brookdale Community College Psychology Club

The Psychology Club is one of the important activities of the Psychology Department. Under the guidance of a faculty advisor, students meet about twice a month. Activities including field trips, research projects and guest lectures are arranged for students. Students will get opportunities to work with faculty, the members of the Psychology Honor Society, and the Human Services Club. This is an excellent resource for students to take their interest of psychology beyond the classroom.

An opportunity for working on research projects, under the guidance of faculty members, is a great experience. Students from Brookdale have been presenting papers at major professional conferences, and such activities are recommended for students who are planning to pursue the study of psychology. Membership and participation in academic club activities is given special credit when you transfer to institutions of higher learning.

There is no fee or any special requirement to be members of this club. You can contact Professor David Stout of the Psychology Department for more details at 732-224-2340, or email him at dstout@brookdalecc.edu.

JOIN THE HUMAN SERVICES CLUB!!!

The Brookdale Community College Human Services Club meets together every other week.

Meetings include:
Community Service Idea Sharing, Socializing, Free Food, and Fun Discussion Activities

For details about our meetings, contact Professor David Stout of the Psychology Department at 732-224-2340, or email him at dstout@brookdalecc.edu.

Psi Beta
Psychology Honor Society at Brookdale Community College

What is Psi Beta?

Psi Beta is the national honor society in psychology, for community and junior colleges, and was founded in 1981 to recognize the scholastic achievements and interests in psychology of two year students.

How can I become a member?

To become a member of the Brookdale chapter of Psi Beta you must:

- Be enrolled as a full- or part-time student at Brookdale, have earned a cumulative GPA of 3.17 or better and completed 12 college credits.
- Have earned no less than a "B" average in psychology courses, beginning with Introductory Psychology.
- Have demonstrated a genuine interest in psychology and demonstrate high standards of personal behavior and integrity.

Signing up for the Brookdale Community College chapter of Psi Beta is simple:
- Complete a registration card
- Provide the chapter Advisor with a copy of your student transcript which can easily be obtained from WebAdvisor, "List of Courses Completed".
- Submit a check made out to ASBCC in the amount of $55.00. Please include student ID number and phone number in "memo" line. This is a one time/lifetime fee.

Faculty Advisors

Prof. Joel Morgovsky
jmorgovsky@brookdalecc.edu
Phone: 732-224-2846

Prof. Rajkumari Wesley
rwesley@brookdalecc.edu
Phone: 732-224-2170

Brookdale Community College Positive Psychology Center (BCCPPC)
Mission Statement

Dr. Elaine H. Olaoye, Director
bccppc@brookdalecc.edu

- The BCCPPC is an initiative under the auspices of the Social Sciences Division.
- The mission is consistent with the activities of Positive Psychology Center as defined by Seligman and Csikzentmihalyi (2000) that "challenges psychology to shift more of its intellectual energy to the study of the positive aspects of human experience."
- Specifically BCCPPC will provide students with a research perspective that allows them to better explore and understand 'normality'.
- BCCPPC will support and encourage a positive perspective and 'normality' in the local community.
- BCCPPC will define and encourage the use of two epistemologies in research: hypothetico-deductive and metaphorical-abductive methods of knowing.
- BCCPPC will be interdisciplinary and international, exploring complementary relations between disciplines and cultures.
- It is recognized that psychology in the 20th century has had an almost exclusive focus on pathology and this has affected
    - Chosen methodologies
    - Chosen areas of study
    - Perspectives on human behavior

BCCPPC is focused on addressing the above through research and critical thinking. Seligman & Peterson's character strengths and virtues are a major focus of research aimed at exploring and defining normality. The power and responsibility of individuals and of psychologists, is the focus of research, debate, expressive writing and publication. BCCPPC is a registered node in the University of Pennsylvania's Positive Psychology network.

- BCCPPC's email: bbcppc@brookdalecc.edu
- BCCPPC has a website and conducts internet research.
- BCCPPC shares space used by the Addictions Center.
- The staffing of BCCPPC consists of volunteers, all unpaid.
- BCCPPC will expand its Board of Advisors
- BCCPPC seeks to reimburse students for one credit of PSY 295 if they fulfill specified research requirement in hours and training.
- Students can register for a course in Positive Psychology with Professor Joel Morgovsky, jmorgovsky@brookdalecc.edu
- BCCPCC can offer an honors research option for interested students.
- PSY 245 students are invited to participate in research activities.
- BCCPPC welcomes community involvement in research and other activities.

NEED HELP IN PSYCHOLOGY?

Come see the Psychology Learning Assistants!

Help is available for all Psychology courses.

We are located on the first floor of MAN in Room 127.

This is where YOU, the student, can come for all questions concerning study groups, tutoring, re-testing, study guides, etcetera...Please come see us if you are concerned about your progress in a class or of you need help with the proper APA (American Psychological Association) format for writing papers.

Critical thinking: metacognitive and epistemological issues in arising in 21st century psychology

by
Elaine H. Olaoye, Ph.D.
Professor, Psychology
Director, Brookdale Positive Psychology Center

This article looks at the major schism in psychology that manifests itself, for example, in the tensions between scientists and practitioners in the discipline. The article suggests that addressing this divide is important for the future of psychology. It identifies some trends that suggest that this might be narrowing and presents examples of the methods and content of poetry, that can provide critical complements to the limitations imposed by the scientific method and operational definitions that do not always address what is truly human. Students' responses are presented as evidence of the complementary relationship that psychology and poetry can have in the classroom.

"For over twenty-five years
Gathering the fragments of an ancient
A broken dream
The pieces
Lisping a language
Elusive... dance
Dazzling the mind
Weaving loops of excitement"
From ***Rethinking Psychology***, (Olaoye, 2002, p.73)

Psychology in moving forward as a science has had to sacrifice important information about human beings in order to fit in the celebrated and higher status scientific paradigm. Students develop concerns about the physiological models and the behavioral responses that scientifically dictated limitations and statistical abstractions impose on the discipline.

Carol Tavris in an article published in the Chronicle of Higher Education (Tavris, 2003) entitled "Mind Games: Psychological Warfare Between Therapists and Scientists" detailed some of the differences that exist between these two areas of psychology. The article was so troublesome that it prompted a response from the current president of the American

Psychological Association, Robert Sternberg, in the following issue. In his response Sternberg attempted to bridge the gap by pointing to psychologists who see themselves as 'Scientist-Practitioners'. Whether one takes sides or does not, there can be little doubt that there is a chasm, however small or large between these two areas of functioning. As psychology looks to the 21st century it must address the underpinnings of the scientist-practitioner division.

The new editor of **The Counseling Psychologist**, Robert Carter, professor at Columbia University writes :

> " One bridge we have to the past that affects our future is our professional identity. While making significant contributions to psychology over the years, we have struggled with our own identity as a specialty area. Some of us have not always felt part of the core of psychology and some of us proclaim ourselves to be outsiders in one way or another" (Carter, 2003 p.6).

A repeated insight that is so often missed, even by psychologists, is that the struggle with this professional identity is a source of strength, not just for the professionals involved but also for the discipline of psychology: In a growing discipline it is important to engage a creative tension between practices of the past and the unfolding demands of the future, a creative tension between weaknesses identified in the past and strengths that need to be built in the future, as well as creative tensions between populations and subjects excluded in the past and populations and subjects that need to be included in the future.

As we look back on the history of psychology from the 1600s to the 1950s, we see a narrowing of the domain. Thus, in teaching the history of psychology, I triumphantly make critical statements like, "With Descartes, psychology lost its soul" (1600s). "With Watson, psychology lost its mind" (1920s) and "Psychology is first and foremost the study of behavior" (1940s). The progress of psychology has been dependent upon a critical epistemic factor: The willingness to allow psychology to be authentic, to be licensed to treat people with psychological disorders, even though it is able to research, to study only limited abstractions in particular areas with regard to its understanding of human nature.

In the 1950s supported by technological advances that allowed more accurate physiological exploration of the brain, we witnessed a rebirth of cognitive psychology. While for some psychologists this is new, for many students it is so obvious that this has always been important. Still more recently, we are seeing more acknowledgement of a neglected area of psychology, emotions, and in particular positive emotions (Seligman & Csikszentmihalyi, 2000, Myers 2000).

For most of the century of its existence, psychology has focused on behavior, cognition and negative emotions such as anxiety, depression and anger. From a metacognition standpoint, psychology has privileged these areas of functioning and ignored and unwittingly marginalized other equally critical areas of human functioning: thus the practitioners experience tensions with the scientists whose studies are limited to very specific variables that do not always provide much direction or knowledge,for dealing with the many broad and unfolding variables that characterize modern life.

As we focus on building bridges to a productive future in psychology, we also need to look at what we need to start incorporating in the classroom. We identify below two epistemic factors that need greater acknowledgement:

(i)   The acknowledgement that human beings in living their lives have to deal cognitively and emotionally with areas of human functioning that the discipline of scientific psychology has had to ignore.

(ii)   The acknowledgement that recognition and mastery of these two parallel modes of operation (as opposed to one at the expense of the other) releases energy, insight and ideas that help to point psychology towards its next major step in understanding human nature and functioning.

The recognition of these two epistemic factors and their relationship to each other does much to restructure the traditional view of the domain of psychology and, consequently, our approaches to teaching and understanding it. The introduction of poetry into the objectives is an attempt to be more inclusive, an attempt to allow students to respond to their feelings as well as their cognitions, and also engage in the process of not only balancing these two energies, but being enriched by them also.

Below are excerpts from a student's paper "An Exploration of the Processes of Human Learning" Psy 105, June 30, 1998 that demonstrates the inclusion of emotional factors.

What is learning? According to Weiten, learning is defined as "the relatively durable change in behavior or knowledge that is due to experience." There are many stimuli in today's world that promote this process of change in a body of knowledge or skill. One stimuli that provokes personal insights about the learning process is the poem. *On Learning* (Olaoye, 20002, p.44). *On Learning* is an insightful poem that discusses the emotions associated with the discovery or new information.

Upon reading *On Learning* I experienced many different emotions. One of the many emotions that I encountered was that of affirmation. I felt affirmed for many reasons. I have always had an innate desire to learn. I enjoy any hobby that will contribute to the body of knowledge that I have. I feel that in today's society, one is not seen as normal if they have this desire to learn. Many people feel that doing minimal amounts of work and achieving minimal amounts of knowledge are adequate. I do not agree. Many times I feel alone in this notion. This is especially when I am away at school...

When I take a class that interests me, I am fascinated by the information that I have learned. I too "love the delicate dawning of fresh thoughts scarcely spawning" (Olaoye).The feelings conveyed in this poem made me realize that I am not alone in my desire to learn. Another emotion that I experienced while reading the poem *On Learning* was that of curiosity. I felt that on a superficial level, this poem was merely about a person who enjoys learning. When exploring the poem further, I became curious about the convoluted text it contained. "With tireless time and gentle cultivation, weaver from doubt and elusive contradictions, profound and poignant integrations." (Olaoye)... After contemplating the meaning of these phrases it became more real to me. To me this particular phase meant that with time and effort any complicated body of knowledge can be understood. This message is quite positive. I can apply my life and studies to the "tireless time and cultivation" of knowledge (Olaoye)...

I love learning about many things. I love the feeling of satisfaction that comes over me when I have grasped a difficult concept. It makes me feel as if I am on top of the world and that I can learn anything. My favorite disciplines to learn about are those dealing with science and math...

Every student should have a passion for learning. I consider myself to be lucky because I have discovered my passion for learning at such a young age. Reading poems such as "On Learning" proliferates my desire to learn. Knowing that *On Learning* has been written shows me that there are others with a similar passion to mine.

The above represents an important and frequent experience of students who are invited to reflect on emotionally as well as cognitively based readings. Students are invited to develop an appreciation for these two epistemologies. This perspective does not diminish psychology, *au contraire* it allows psychology to contribute to knowledge and practice, what it has empirical evidence of, without leading to the assumption that this is all there is to know.

As a psychologist who has taught psychology fulltime for over twenty years and who teaches physiological psychology as well as statistics each semester and recognizes them to be critical areas for understanding and growth in psychology, I felt that something was missing. As I stacked all this knowledge from these various sources against the complexities and dynamics going on in students' lives as well as the world around us, I noticed that psychology was still not doing enough to command the respect of truly discerning students. For psychologists who are aware of this discrepancy, initiating strategies that help address this limitation becomes a critical part of their mission of being a psychologist. By permitting, recognizing, honoring and sharing deeper expressions of the human spirit, poetry has been part of a strategy offered for the last four years as a method of helping a new generation take advantage of knowledge and methods across disciplines that are relevant and have been available.

As a psychologist who writes poetry and recognizes the transforming powers of poetry, using poetry is a decision to honor the subjectivity that poetry represents along with the objectivity that scientific psychology attempts to achieve. To acknowledge the importance of subjectivity is to emphasize that first, no one has a vantage point outside their personal and cultural history. Second, the test of subjectivity, whether it is primarily collectivistic, narcissistic or individualistic is whether it makes sense to others. As I wrote in **Passions of the Soul**:

> "Today in an age of skepticism, we tend to appreciate poets more for the questions they raise than the answers they might proffer. We read poetry less to receive some objective truth and more to understand how a particular person struggles to find out what is true for herself." (Olaoye, 2002, p.6)

Finally the use of poetry honors a contrasting epistemology to the one used in psychology: While psychology emphasizes the use of operational definitions and empirical facts, poetry emphasizes a metaphorical approach to knowing. This requires that the listener simultaneously affirm and negate: x is y and x is not y. Metaphors and similes require that the listener use what is familiar as a bridge to understanding what is new. Metaphors and similes also have multiple associations or meanings which allow the richness that characterizes them, and that allows them to create a different resonance across people and over time. These all point to important ways in which humans discern what is true in contrast to what is factual. Unfortunately, too many scientifically trained individuals have become tone deaf to the beauty, complexity and truth of metaphors and similes with the result that a particular epistemology (a way of knowing) becomes ontology (what is real). For example in the poem "I want" (Olaoye 2002) love is compared to spring:

"I want
To reconsummate Spring
With you
Until
My love becomes like
The seeds and bulbs and buds of spring
And grow and open
With infinite grace and beauty
Seeking and kissing life
Until we are enjoined, entwined,
In an eternally fertile and fragrant flowering"(Olaoye, 2002, p.39).

A factual/literal way of knowing would focus on the impossibility of a person being spring and therefore dismiss this statement and demand instead an operational or measurable definition of love. Thus Zimbardo, Weber & Johnson, authors of a 3rd edition, introductory psychology text wrote:

"You take the first step in understanding psychological process by *describing* it as precisely and objectively as possible. Consider *love*. We would begin to construct a description of love by identifying exactly what we mean when we use this term: Can we define it in terms of objective, observable behaviors? Social psychologist Zick Rubin says that many objective behaviors signify love. For example one way to tell when two people are in love is to measure how much time they spend looking into each other's eyes (Rubin 1973). Lovers he has observed, spend much more time gazing at each other than do mere acquaintances. Such a *behavioral* description of an otherwise fuzzy concept, like love is an operational definition. Observations made of these behaviors become the "facts" of psychology, known as data.' (Zimbardo et. al., 2000, p.5)

Using the methodology associated with similes and metaphors, while knowing that a person cannot be spring (x is not y), there is an acceptance that some of the attributes of spring can make more visible aspects of love that are latent, desired, and real but unexpressed (x is y). While operational definitions narrow options, limit imagination, similes and metaphors stimulate the imagination and open up relevant possibilities. In this instance instead of limiting love to only verifiable physiological, behavioral and social dimensions, understandings of love move beyond these obvious features to reach for the less visible but more powerful growth and spiritual dimensions: the manifest cycles, energy and beauty of spring are used to increase appreciation and awareness of these non-empirical dimensions of love.

How do students respond to opportunities to compare these two epistemologies? Below are some excerpts that address the juxtaposition of these two approaches to knowing.

On homeostatis (Perry, 2003):
> The poem Angry One (Olaoye,2000, p.42) is a complement to homeostatis. The poem shows the various faces of anger. Through the poem's progression it demonstrates how the mind goes through several emotions that renders the angry one spent. When that moment of rest comes the mind is able to become sane once more. Our mind is able to return to its natural condition. "This is our moment of surrender, Oh angry one, when spent and weary, we signal involuntary cessation, when softened and sober, we embrace, glad that we are sane again."(Olaoye, 2002, p.42).

On ego functioning (Perry, 2003):
> "Zimbardo, Weber & Johnson (2003) describe the ego as the conscious, rational part of the Personality charged with keeping the peace between the superego and the id (p.428). Olaoye (2002) describes the tension between the two in stanza two, "Unlocking and opening the doors of perception wide, 'Til I reach a space murkier than cheerless night where vision is blinded by darkness and by light, 'Til I reach a space unbounded by breadth and length where colossal powers can be ensnared by weakness and by strength"(Olaoye, 2002, p.20-21).

On prejudice and discrimination (Perry, 2003):

> When I read Zimbardo's text on prejudice and discrimination it explained in detail what the words meant, and the differences between the two. However, it does not reach a person on a personal or emotional level. Zimbardo's text is dry and boring but it does explain thoroughly. The problem is that it is exactly what he explains as the least effective way to overcome prejudice and discrimination…Olaoye on the other hand, uses an inspirational tone. She reaches the reader on a personal and emotional level. *"On becoming an Afro-American"* (Olaoye, 2002, p.53) was energized with the constant call to "Breakout, Breakfree"…The reader is touched with the emotion not with definitions. It made you think and feel"

On attribution theory:

> "The principles maintained in "To Look at Anyone" (Olaoye, 2002, p.25) complement those of attribution theory… it would be most ideal of all the aspirations in the poem were reachable; but its worth is recognized. Attribution theory is the extremely watered-down mundane version of the sentiment reflected by the poem."

The results of including this type of content and process in introductory level psychology courses include increased self-affirmation, improved affect with regard to learning, increased appreciation for the complementary contributions of two epistemologies, clearer understanding of the contributions and limitations of current psychology, increased motivation to develop new ideas related to the expansion of psychology and a keener enjoyment of psychology and life.

"Looking at the next twenty-five years
Gathering fragments
Of a radiant, of a powerful vision
The pieces
Whispering transcendent tales
Sparkle and play along new ways…"

From ***Rethinking Psychology***, (Olaoye, 2002, p. 73)

References

Fowler, R.D. The healing arts, *APA Monitor*, 29 (March) 3, 1998

Myers, G., (2000), The funds, friends and faith of happy people. *American Psychologist* 55, 56-67

Olaoye, Elaine H. (2002) Passions of the Soul. Red Bank, New Jersey: Northwind Publishers

Olaoye, Elaine, H 'Reconnecting with the emotional domain in analyzing research in psychology: The role of informal and poetic writing in psychology'. Paper presented to the

Second National Conference on "Writing Across the Curriculum", Charleston, South Carolina, February 1995.

Rubin, Z. (1973) Liking and Loving: An invitation to social psychology. New York: Holt, Rinehart and Winston

Seligman, M. & Csikszentmihalyi, M (2000), Positive Psychology. *American Psychologist* 55, 5-14.

Tavris, Carol (2003), Mind games: psychological warfare between therapists and scientists, Chronicle of Higher Education

Zimbardo, P., Weber, A., Johnson, R (2000) Psychology (3rd ed.) Boston: Allyn and Bacon

Zimbardo, P., Weber, A, Johnson, R (2003) Psychology (4th ed.) Boston: Allyn and Bacon

Keep the "Secret"

By Lynne Schmelter-Davis
Assistant Professor, Psychology
Psychology Department Chair
Brookdale Community College (County College of Monmouth)
Lincroft, New Jersey 07740
lschmelterdavis@brookdalecc.edu
732-224-2581: office
732-580-9210: cell
March, 2007

Many of the students in my Psychology classes, both in-person and online, have been reading a book by Rhonda Byrne, called, "The Secret". Some of the students have been confusing the book with our course in Positive Psychology and with the seminars being offered by Community Development on "Happiness". This is alarming and the record needs to be set straight. "The Secret" has made the best seller lists and was featured twice on "Oprah". There are over 3 million copies in print and 1.5 million DVD's of "The Secret" have been sold to people who don't like to read. What is it about? It purports to be the secret of life supposedly known by historically and currently famous and successful people (knowing "the Secret" is how they became famous and successful). This book is dangerous, simplistic and a bunch of claptrap.

First, let me tell you the "Secret". By reading the "Secret" here you will save $23.95 at the bookstore just in case you were tempted to buy the book to learn what people were talking about. Not buying the book will get it off best seller lists and off television and hopefully its thesis will ebb until the next resurrection of this dumb idea.

Okay, here is the "Secret": In the universe "like attracts like" and "thoughts become things". That's it. Think you can own a brand new Mercedes and believe it and the universe will give it to you. The book is heavy on materialism, and it stresses not to worry about the world running out of new luxury cars because the universe has enough material goods to come across for all of us. Now, that's not the dangerous and evil part. It's the reverse of the "new Mercedes" thoughts that get us humans into trouble. Remember, "like attracts like and thoughts become things". Being afraid of getting cancer (thinking of cancer!) will urge the universe to give you cancer. Thoughts of losing your job, your spouse, your hair or your home will cause disaster in your life. If bad things happen to good people (like drowning or a being killed while at work) it's because they thought they could be in the wrong place at the wrong time and so the universe gave them a tsunami or a terrorist crashing an airplane into their building. There is no such thing as fate that you didn't bring upon yourself. Don't feel sorry for those poor saps that lose their homes and loved ones in an earthquake. It's obvious they lacked positive thoughts about the solidness of the earth and imagined catastrophe on a huge scale. I wouldn't send money to the N.Y. Times Neediness Cases either because now that I know "The Secret" it is clear to me that they asked the universe for their hardships and it's up to them to ask for better stuff from now on.

You might say, so who cares about a stupid book? Millions of people are reading (and believing) in this blame-the-victim, mean spirited idea. They carry this idea into some areas of public policy as well. Some politicians want to cut funding for welfare and subsidized housing because they believe that the recipients have caused their own poverty and that they could earn a living if they "had" to. Believers in the "The Secret" blame poverty on negative thoughts and failure to use positive visualization to get the universe to get these poor folks some good stuff. Once you know "The Secret" there is no failure. Everything good will come to you as long as you're patient and thinking ("thoughts become things") of what you want and not letting negative thoughts get in the way. Negative thoughts might come from reading the newspaper or watching television, not that you would consciously court this kind of negativity but stuff happens and it wouldn't be your fault but it could postpone your new home or promotion at work. The book states that even your obesity is the fault of your thoughts (the universe gave you fat!) and has nothing to do with what you eat. Next time when you eat that strawberry short cake think hard that it is celery to avoid weight gain.

It's interesting to note that all the wealthy, successful people who give testimony to the efficacy of using "The Secret" who are quoted in the book earned their money in the same way. They give workshops, seminars and consultations on how to use "The Secret" to get everything you want (especially new cars and boats). Several of the students in my psychology classes have read "The Secret" and have told me that they think only of getting "As on papers and exams." Unfortunately, their thinking does not include studying the material and doing their homework and I have been thinking that students who do not do their work will receive an "F". I can't write a bestseller because my "secret" for success is too boring. You know the one…work hard, pay attention, stay in school and eat healthy. Oh, yeah, don't forget to avoid bad luck and get plenty of good luck.

IQ AND INTELLIGENCE
Can they, should they be the same?
Students wonder...

by
Elaine H. Olaoye, Ph.D.

Copyright 2007 Elaine H. Olaoye

This activity is designed to help students wonder about if there are differences between IQ and intelligence. It brings together two different approaches to help the student explore the question of whether what is measured by IQ tests is the totality of intelligence.

Students will have an opportunity to do a reflection essay at the end of the exercise.

Psychologists do not agree on what is intelligence but they are learning more about the brain each day. Some of the unresolved differences center around whether intelligence should be defined as a single general factor (Spearman's g) or whether it should be defined as multiple factors (Sternberg's 3 or Gardener's 7)?

After reading about how psychologists define intelligence pages 430 - 440, read and reflect on Dickinson's metaphors of the brain on page 48 in Meyer's 8th Edition.

Now you are ready to reflect on your feelings and thoughts about what you read. Some guiding questions follow.

How do you feel after reading about the differences psychologists have in defining intelligence? *Check below which apply to you*
1. ___ I feel that it should be singular and hierarchical
2. ___ I feel that it should in be three types with Sternberg
3. ___ I feel it should be different and complex with Gardener.
4. ___ I feel it should very detailed as with Guilford
5. ___ I feel confused
6. ___ I am on the fence, undecided.

How do you feel after reading about how Dickinson has defined intelligence?
Check below which apply

1. ___I feel wide and deep with Dickinson
2. ___I feel overwhelmed, I reject Dickinson's . . . images
3. ___I feel confused by these images
4. ___I am stimulated by the images
5. ___I feel unmoved

What do you think after reading about how psychologists have defined intelligence?
Check below which apply

- ___I think that intelligence can and should measured on a single dimension.
- ___I think that intelligence can and should be measured on multiple dimensions.
- ___I think the structure of intelligence remains unclear.
- ___I think it is not possible to take a position.

What do you think after reading about how Dickinson has defined intelligence?
Check below which apply

1. ___I think it is silly to liken intelligence to the sky and sea
2. ___I think it is energizing to expand my images of intelligence by seeing it as . . . wider than the sky and deeper than the sea.
3. ___I think these images are irrelevant
4. ___I think metaphors miss the point

Which definitions seem to reflect that intelligence could be larger than what it measures? *Check below which apply*

1. ___Spearman's 'g'
2. ___Sternberg's '3'
3. ___Gardener's '8'
4. ___Guilford's '120'
5. ___No model does this

Which definition seems to have something in common with the breadth and depth of Dickinson's images? *Check below which apply*

1. ___Spearman's 'g'
2. ___Sternberg's '3'
3. ___Gardener's '8'
4. ___Guilford's '120"
5. ___No model does this

How are your observations and questions about differences between IQ and intelligence now? *Check below which apply*

- __Clearer
- __More complex
- __Confused
- __Stimulated
- __Unchanged

Reaction Essay Option

1. Describe your cognitive and emotional responses to each phase of this exercise.
2. Try and describe not only your thoughts but the images that came to your mind.
3. How do feel about IQ tests, do they measure intelligence accurately? Have they improved? Are they likely to improve still more with the new research on the brain? How useful are they? Who benefits most from IQ tests?
4. How do you feel about your intelligence, can it be measured completely by psychologists? How important are IQ tests to your understanding of yourself?
5. What did you think, how did you feel reading about intelligence as described by Emily Dickinson? Do images and metaphors increase your understanding?
6. Did using the two approaches to intelligence stimulate your psychological imagination and/or increase your understanding? Is using one only, better?

Timeline

The Story of Psychology: A Timeline

by Charles L. Brewer, Furman University

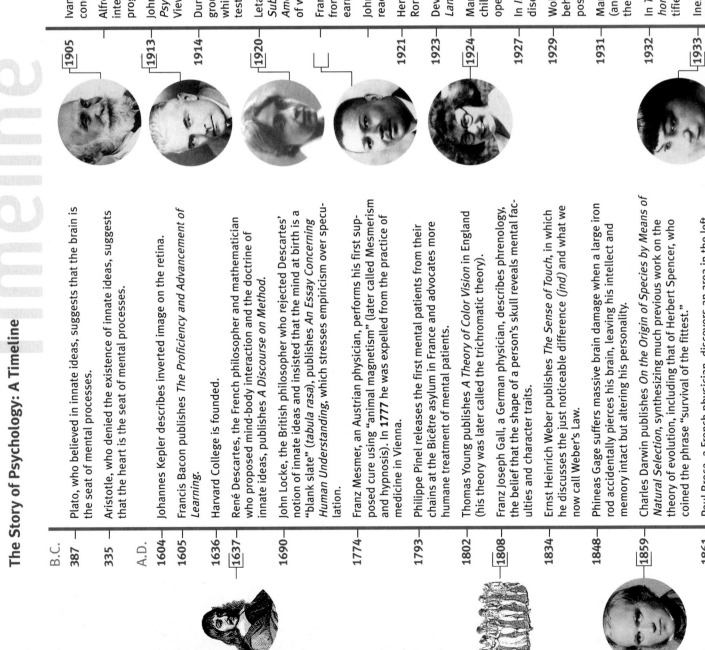

B.C.

387 — Plato, who believed in innate ideas, suggests that the brain is the seat of mental processes.

335 — Aristotle, who denied the existence of innate ideas, suggests that the heart is the seat of mental processes.

A.D.

1604 — Johannes Kepler describes inverted image on the retina.

1605 — Francis Bacon publishes *The Proficiency and Advancement of Learning*.

1636 — Harvard College is founded.

1637 — René Descartes, the French philosopher and mathematician who proposed mind-body interaction and the doctrine of innate ideas, publishes *A Discourse on Method*.

1690 — John Locke, the British philosopher who rejected Descartes' notion of innate ideas and insisted that the mind at birth is a "blank slate" (*tabula rasa*), publishes *An Essay Concerning Human Understanding*, which stresses empiricism over speculation.

1774 — Franz Mesmer, an Austrian physician, performs his first supposed cure using "animal magnetism" (later called Mesmerism and hypnosis). In **1777** he was expelled from the practice of medicine in Vienna.

1793 — Philippe Pinel releases the first mental patients from their chains at the Bicêtre asylum in France and advocates more humane treatment of mental patients.

1802 — Thomas Young publishes *A Theory of Color Vision* in England (his theory was later called the trichromatic theory).

1808 — Franz Joseph Gall, a German physician, describes phrenology, the belief that the shape of a person's skull reveals mental faculties and character traits.

1834 — Ernst Heinrich Weber publishes *The Sense of Touch*, in which he discusses the just noticeable difference (*jnd*) and what we now call Weber's Law.

1848 — Phineas Gage suffers massive brain damage when a large iron rod accidentally pierces his brain, leaving his intellect and memory intact but altering his personality.

1859 — Charles Darwin publishes *On the Origin of Species by Means of Natural Selection*, synthesizing much previous work on the theory of evolution, including that of Herbert Spencer, who coined the phrase "survival of the fittest."

1861 — Paul Broca, a French physician, discovers an area in the left

1905 — Ivan Petrovich Pavlov begins publishing studies of conditioning in animals.

— — Alfred Binet and Théodore Simon produce the first intelligence test for assessing the abilities and academic progress of Parisian schoolchildren.

1913 — John B. Watson outlines the tenets of behaviorism in a *Psychological Review* article, "Psychology as the Behaviorist Views It."

1914 — During World War I, Robert Yerkes and his staff develop a group intelligence test for evaluating U.S. military personnel, which increases the U.S. public's acceptance of psychological testing.

1920 — Leta Stetter Hollingworth publishes *The Psychology of Subnormal Children*, an early classic. In **1921** she was cited in *American Men of Science* for her research on the psychology of women.

— — Francis Cecil Sumner receives a Ph.D. degree in psychology from Clark University, becoming the first African-American to earn a psychology doctorate.

— — John B. Watson and Rosalie Rayner report conditioning a fear reaction in a child called "Little Albert."

1921 — Hermann Rorschach, a Swiss psychiatrist, introduces the Rorschach inkblot test.

1923 — Developmental psychologist Jean Piaget publishes *The Language and Thought of the Child*.

1924 — Mary Cover Jones reports reconditioning a fear reaction in a child (Peter), a forerunner of systematic desensitization developed by Joseph Wolpe.

1927 — In *Introduction to the Technique of Child Analysis*, Anna Freud discusses psychoanalysis in the treatment of children.

1929 — Wolfgang Köhler publishes *Gestalt Psychology*, which criticizes behaviorism and outlines essential elements of the Gestalt position and approach.

1931 — Margaret Floy Washburn becomes the first female psychologist (and the second female scientist in any discipline) elected to the U.S. National Academy of Sciences.

1932 — In *The Wisdom of the Body*, Walter B. Cannon coins the term *homeostasis*, discusses the fight-or-flight response, and identifies hormonal changes associated with stress.

1933 — Inez Beverly Prosser becomes the first African-American psychoanalysis.

1936 — Egas Moniz, Portuguese physician, publishes work on the first frontal lobotomies performed on humans.

1938 — B. F. Skinner publishes *The Behavior of Organisms*, which describes operant conditioning of animals.

In *Primary Mental Abilities*, Louis L. Thurstone proposes seven such abilities.

Ugo Cerletti and Lucino Bini use electroshock treatment with a human patient.

1939 — David Wechsler publishes the Wechsler-Bellevue intelligence test, forerunner of the Wechsler Intelligence Scale for Children (WISC) and the Wechsler Adult Intelligence Scale (WAIS).

Mamie Phipps Clark receives a master's degree from Howard University. In collaboration with Kenneth B. Clark, she later extended her thesis, "The Development of Consciousness of Self in Negro Preschool Children," providing joint research cited in the U.S. Supreme Court's **1954** decision to end racial segregation in public schools.

Edward Alexander Bott helps found the Canadian Psychological Association. He becomes its first president in **1940.**

World War II provides many opportunities for psychologists to enhance the popularity and influence of psychology, especially in applied areas.

1943 — Psychologist Starke Hathaway and physician J. Charnley McKinley publish the Minnesota Multiphasic Personality Inventory (MMPI).

1945 — Karen Horney, who criticized Freud's theory of female sexual development, publishes *Our Inner Conflicts.*

1946 — Benjamin Spock's first edition of *The Commonsense Book of Baby and Child Care* appears; the book will influence child rearing in North America for several decades.

1948 — Alfred Kinsey and his colleagues publish *Sexual Behavior in the Human Male.*

B. F. Skinner's novel, *Walden Two,* describes a Utopian community based on positive reinforcement, which becomes a clarion call for applying psychological principles in everyday living, especially communal living.

Ernest R. Hilgard publishes *Theories of Learning,* which was required reading for several generations of psychology students in North America.

1949 — Raymond B. Cattell publishes the Sixteen Personality Factor Questionnaire (16PF).

Continued

1876 ne coined the expression "nature and nurture" to correspond with "heredity and environment."

1874 — Carl Wernicke, a German neurologist and psychiatrist, shows that damage to a specific area in the left temporal lobe (now called Wernicke's area) disrupts ability to comprehend or produce spoken or written language.

1878 — G. Stanley Hall receives from Harvard University the first Ph.D. degree in psychology awarded in the United States.

1879 — Wilhelm Wundt establishes at the University of Leipzig, Germany, the first psychology laboratory, which becomes a Mecca for psychology students from all over the world.

1883 — G. Stanley Hall, student of Wilhelm Wundt, establishes the first formal U.S. psychology laboratory at Johns Hopkins University.

1885 — Hermann Ebbinghaus publishes *On Memory,* summarizing his extensive research on learning and memory, including the "forgetting curve."

1889 — Alfred Binet and Henri Beaunis establish the first psychology laboratory in France at the Sorbonne, and the first International Congress of Psychology meets in Paris.

1890 — William James, Harvard University philosopher and psychologist, publishes *The Principles of Psychology,* describing psychology as "the science of mental life."

1891 — James Mark Baldwin establishes the first psychology laboratory in the British Commonwealth at the University of Toronto.

1892 — G. Stanley Hall spearheads the founding of the American Psychological Association (APA) and becomes its first president.

1893 — Mary Whiton Calkins (pictured) and Christine Ladd-Franklin are the first women elected to membership in the APA.

1894 — Margaret Floy Washburn is the first woman to receive a Ph.D. degree in psychology (Cornell University).

Harvard University denies Mary Whiton Calkins admission to doctoral candidacy because of her gender, despite Hugo Münsterberg's claim that she was the best student he had ever had there.

1896 — John Dewey publishes "The Reflex Arc Concept in Psychology," helping to formalize the school of psychology called functionalism.

1898 — In "Animal Intelligence," Edward L. Thorndike, Columbia University, describes his learning experiments with cats in "puzzle boxes." In **1905**, he proposed the "law of effect."

1900 — Sigmund Freud publishes *The Interpretation of Dreams,* his major theoretical work on psychoanalysis.

1901 — Ten founders establish the British Psychological Society.

1905 — Mary Whiton Calkins becomes the first woman president of the APA.

The Story of Psychology: A Timeline   (continued)

1949 In *The Organization of Behavior: A Neuropsychological Theory*, Canadian psychologist Donald O. Hebb outlines a new and influential conceptualization of how the nervous system functions.

1950 Solomon Asch publishes studies of effects of conformity on judgments of line length.

In *Childhood and Society*, Erik Erikson outlines his stages of psychosocial development.

1951 Carl Rogers publishes *Client-Centered Therapy*.

1952 The American Psychiatric Association publishes *Diagnostic and Statistical Manual of Mental Disorders*, an influential book that will be updated periodically.

1953 Eugene Aserinski and Nathaniel Kleitman describe rapid eye movements (REM) that occur during sleep.

Janet Taylor's Manifest Anxiety Scale appears in the *Journal of Abnormal Psychology*.

1954 In *Motivation and Personality*, Abraham Maslow proposes a hierarchy of motives ranging from physiological needs to self-actualization.

James Olds and Peter Milner, McGill University neuropsychologists, describe rewarding effects of electrical stimulation of the hypothalamus in rats.

Gordon Allport publishes *The Nature of Prejudice*.

1956 In his *Psychological Review* article titled "The Magical Number Seven, Plus or Minus Two: Some Limits on Our Capacity for Processing Information," George Miller coins the term *chunk* for memory researchers.

1957 Robert Sears, Eleanor Maccoby, and Harry Levin publish *Patterns of Child Rearing*.

Charles Ferster and B. F. Skinner publish *Schedules of Reinforcement*.

1959 Noam Chomsky's critical review of B. F. Skinner's *Verbal Behavior* appears in the journal *Language*.

Eleanor Gibson and Richard Walk report their research on infants' depth perception in "The Visual Cliff."

Harry Harlow outlines "The Nature of Love," his work on attachment in monkeys.

Lloyd Peterson and Margaret Peterson in the *Journal of Experimental Psychology* article, "Short-Term Retention of Individual Verbal Items," highlight the importance of rehearsal in memory.

John Thibaut and Harold Kelley publish *The Social Psychology*

1969 In his APA presidential address, "Psychology as a Means of Promoting Human Welfare," George Miller emphasizes the importance of "giving psychology away."

1971 Kenneth B. Clark becomes the first African-American president of the American Psychological Association.

Albert Bandura publishes *Social Learning Theory*.

Allan Paivio publishes *Imagery and Verbal Processes*.

B. F. Skinner publishes *Beyond Freedom and Dignity*.

1972 Elliot Aronson publishes *The Social Animal*.

Fergus Craik and Robert Lockhart's "Levels of Processing: A Framework for Memory Research" appears in the *Journal of Verbal Learning and Verbal Behavior*.

Robert Rescorla and Allan Wagner publish their associative model of Pavlovian conditioning.

Under the leadership of Derald Sue and Stanley Sue, the Asian-American Psychological Association is founded.

1973 Ethologists Karl von Frisch, Konrad Lorenz, and Nikolaas Tinbergen receive the Nobel Prize for their research on animal behavior.

1974 APA's Division 2 first publishes its journal, *Teaching of Psychology*, with Robert S. Daniel as editor.

Eleanor Maccoby (pictured) and Carol Jacklin publish *The Psychology of Sex Differences*.

1975 Biologist Edward O. Wilson's *Sociobiology* appears; it will be a controversial precursor to evolutionary psychology.

1976 Sandra Wood Scarr and Richard A. Weinberg publish "IQ Test Performance of Black Children Adopted by White Families" in *American Psychologist*.

1978 Psychologist Herbert A. Simon, Carnegie-Mellon University, wins a Nobel Prize for pioneering research on computer simulations of human thinking and problem solving.

1979 James J. Gibson publishes *The Ecological Approach to Visual Perception*.

Elizabeth Loftus publishes *Eyewitness Testimony*.

Ellen Langer is the first woman to be granted tenure in Harvard University's Department of Psychology.

1981 David Hubel and Torsten Wiesel receive a Nobel Prize for research on single-cell recordings that identified feature detector cells in the visual cortex.

Roger Sperry receives a Nobel Prize for research on split-brain nation of intelligence.

1984 The American Psychological Association creates Division 44 (Society for the Psychological Study of Lesbian and Gay Issues).

1986 In *Intelligence Applied*, Robert Sternberg proposes the triarchic theory of intelligence.

1987 Elizabeth Scarborough and Laurel Furumoto (pictured) publish *Untold Lives: The First Generation of American Women Psychologists.*

Fluoxetine (Prozac) is introduced as a treatment for depression.

Wilbert J. McKeachie, University of Michigan, receives the first APA Award for Distinguished Career Contributions to Education and Training in Psychology.

1988 The American Psychological Society is founded. It changes its name to Association of Psychological Science in 2006.

1990 Psychiatrist Aaron Beck receives the Distinguished Scientific Award for the Applications of Psychology for advancing understanding and treatment of psychopathology, including pivotal contributions to the development of cognitive therapy.

1990 B. F. Skinner receives APA's first Citation for Outstanding Lifetime Contributions to Psychology and presents his last public address, "Can Psychology Be a Science of Mind?" (He died a few days later at age 86.)

1991 The U.S. National Conference on Enhancing the Quality of Undergraduate Education in Psychology is held at St. Mary's College of Maryland, and suggestions from participants produce many salutary changes in numerous psychology programs.

Martin Seligman publishes *Learned Optimism,* which foreshadows the "positive psychology" movement.

1992 Teachers of Psychology in Secondary Schools (TOPSS) is established as part of the APA.

About 3,000 U.S. secondary school students take the first Advanced Placement Examination in Psychology, hoping to earn exemption from an introductory psychology course at the post-secondary level.

1993 Psychologist Judith Rodin is elected president of the University of Pennsylvania, becoming the first female president of an Ivy League school.

In his *Frames of Mind,* Howard Gardner outlines his theory of multiple intelligences.

2002 New Mexico becomes the first U.S. state to allow qualified clinical psychologists to prescribe certain drugs.

The first International Conference on Education in Psychology is held in St. Petersburg, Russia, with Wilbert J. McKeachie and Charles L. Brewer as keynote speakers.

Psychologist Daniel Kahneman, Princeton University, receives a Nobel Prize for research on decision making.

1961 Georg von Békésy receives a Nobel Prize for research on the physiology of hearing.

David McClelland publishes *The Achieving Society.*

1962 Jerome Kagan and Howard Moss publish *Birth to Maturity.*

Stanley Schachter and Jerome Singer publish findings that support the two-factor theory of emotion.

Albert Ellis' *Reason and Emotion in Psychotherapy* appears; it is a milestone in the development of rational-emotive therapy (RET).

1963 Raymond B. Cattell distinguishes between *fluid* and *crystallized* intelligence.

Stanley Milgram's "Behavioral Study of Obedience" appears in the *Journal of Abnormal and Social Psychology.*

1965 Canadian researcher Ronald Melzack and British researcher Patrick Wall propose the gate control theory of pain.

Robert Zajonc's "Social Facilitation" is published in *Science.*

1966 Nancy Bayley becomes the first woman to receive the APA's Distinguished Scientific Contribution Award.

Jerome Bruner and colleagues at Harvard University's Center for Cognitive Studies publish *Studies in Cognitive Growth.*

William Masters and Virginia Johnson publish results of their research in *Human Sexual Responses.*

Allen Gardner and Beatrix Gardner begin training a chimpanzee (Washoe) in American Sign Language at the University of Nevada, Reno.

John Garcia (pictured) and Robert Koelling publish a study on taste aversion in rats.

David M. Green and John A. Swets publish *Signal Detection Theory and Psychophysics.*

Julian Rotter publishes research on locus of control.

1967 Ulric Neisser's *Cognitive Psychology,* helps to steer psychology away from behaviorism and toward cognitive processes.

Martin Seligman and Steven Maier publish the results of their research with "learned helplessness" in dogs.

1968 Richard Atkinson and Richard Shiffrin's influential three-stage memory model appears in *The Psychology of Learning and Motivation.*

Neal E. Miller's article in *Science,* describing instrumental conditioning of autonomic responses, stimulates research on biofeedback.

1969 Albert Bandura publishes *Principles of Behavior Modification.*

ANOTHER VOICE ON: THE HISTORY AND SCIENCE OF PSYCHOLOGY

MAYA ANGELOU (b. 1928), FROM "HUMAN FAMILY," 1994, *THE COMPLETE COLLECTED POEMS OF MAYA ANGELOU*

I note the obvious differences
in the human family.
Some of us are serious,
some thrive on comedy.

Some declare their lives are lived
as true profundity,
and others claim they really live
the real reality.

The variety of our skin tones
can confuse, bemuse, delight,
brown and pink and beige and purple,
tan and blue and white.

I've sailed upon the seven seas
and stopped in every land,

I've seen the wonders of the world,
not yet one common man.

I know ten thousand women
called Jane and Mary Jane,
but I've not seen any two
who really were the same.

Mirror twins are different
although their features jibe,
and lovers think quite different thoughts
while lying side by side.

We love and lose in China,
we weep on England's moors,
and laugh and moan in Guinea,
and thrive on Spanish shores.

We seek success in Finland,
are born and die in Maine,
In minor ways we differ,
in major we're the same.

I note the obvious differences
between each sort and type,
but we are more alike, my friends,
than we are unalike.

We are more alike, my friends,
than we are unalike.

We are more alike, my friends,
than we are unalike.

Introduction to the History and Science of Psychology

"What's it like being married to a psychologist?" people occasionally ask my wife. "Does he use his psychology on you?"

"So, does your Dad, like, analyze you?" my children have been asked many times.

"What do you think of me?" asked one barber, hoping for a personality analysis after learning that I am a psychologist.

For most people whose exposure to psychology comes from popular books, magazines, and TV, psychologists analyze personality, offer counseling, and dispense childrearing advice.

Do they? Yes, and much more. Consider some of psychology's questions that from time to time you may wonder about:

Have you ever found yourself reacting to something just as one of your biological parents would—perhaps in a way you vowed you never would—and then wondered how much of your personality you inherited? *To what extent is personality predisposed by one's genes? To what extent by one's environments?*

Have you ever wondered why a baby finds a game of peekaboo so delightful? The infant reacts as if, when you move behind a door, you disappear—only to reappear later out of thin air. *What do babies actually perceive and think?*

Have you ever awakened from a nightmare and, with great relief, wondered why you had such a crazy dream? *How often, and why, do we dream?*

Have you ever wondered what leads to success? Are some people just born smarter? *Does sheer intelligence explain why some people get richer, think more creatively, or relate more sensitively?*

Have you ever become depressed or anxious and wondered whether you'll ever feel "normal"? *What triggers our bad moods—and our good ones?*

Have you ever worried about how to act among people of a different culture, race, or gender? *In what ways are we alike as members of the human family? How do we differ?*

Such questions provide grist for psychology's mill because psychology is a science that seeks to answer all sorts of questions about us all: how we think, feel, and act. In Module 1, we trace psychology's roots and survey its scope. In Module 2, we consider how psychological science can help you to think critically in everyday life and to understand some dangers in relying too heavily on intuition and common sense. In Module 3, we survey psychology's methods—how psychologists ask and answer questions.

A smile is a smile the world around
Throughout this book, you will see examples not only of our cultural and gender diversity but also of the similarities that define our shared human nature. People in different cultures vary in when and how often they smile, but a smile *means* the same thing anywhere in the world.

© Stock Image/Alamy

Sally Cassidy/The Picture Cube/Index Stock Imagery

Robert Caputo/Stock, Boston

1

The History and Scope of Psychology

Psychology's Roots

OBJECTIVE **1-1** | Define *psychology.*

Once upon a time, on a planet in your neighborhood of the universe, there came to be people. Soon thereafter, these creatures became intensely interested in themselves and in one another. They wondered, *"Who are we? From where come our thoughts? Our feelings? Our actions? And how are we to understand—and to master or manage—those around us?"* Psychology's answers to these wonderings have developed from international roots in philosophy and biology into a science that aims to describe and explain how we think, feel, and act. Today we define **psychology** as *the scientific study of behavior and mental processes.* Let's unpack this definition. *Behavior* is anything an organism *does*—any action we can observe and record. Yelling, smiling, blinking, sweating, talking, and questionnaire marking are all observable behaviors. *Mental processes* are the internal, subjective experiences we infer from behavior—sensations, perceptions, dreams, thoughts, beliefs, and feelings.

The key word in psychology's definition is *science. Psychology is less a set of findings than a way of asking and answering questions.* As science, psychology evaluates competing ideas with careful observation and rigorous analysis. In its attempt to describe and explain human nature, psychological science welcomes hunches and plausible-sounding theories. And it puts them to the test. If a theory works—if the data support its predictions—so much the better for that theory. If the predictions fail, the theory will be revised or rejected.

My aim in this text, then, is not merely to report results but also to show you how psychologists play their game. You will see how researchers evaluate conflicting opinions and ideas. And you will learn how all of us, whether scientists or simply curious people, can think smarter when describing and explaining the events of our lives.

But first, let's consider the roots of today's psychology to help us appreciate psychologists' varied perspectives.

Prescientific Psychology

OBJECTIVE **1-2** | Trace psychology's prescientific roots, from early understandings of mind and body to the beginnings of modern science.

We can trace many of psychology's current questions back through human history. These early thinkers wondered: How do our minds work? How do our bodies relate to our minds? How much of what we know comes built in? How much is acquired through experience? In India, for example, Buddha pondered how sensations and perceptions combine to form ideas. In China, Confucius stressed the power of ideas and of an educated mind. In ancient Israel, Hebrew scholars anticipated today's psychology by linking mind and emotion to the body; people were said to think with their hearts and feel with their bowels.

In ancient Greece, the philosopher-teacher Socrates (469–399 B.C.) and his student Plato (428–348 B.C.) concluded that mind is separable from body and continues after the body dies, and that knowledge is innate—born within us. As Socrates lay

Throughout the text, important concepts are boldfaced. As you study, you can find these terms with their definitions in a nearby margin and in the Glossary at the end of the book.

Throughout the text you will find Objectives that preview my aims for the section ahead, and that help focus your reading. At the end of each module, the Learning Outcomes will help you review what you've read.

dying, Plato's future student, a teenager named Aristotle (384–322 B.C.), was developing a sharp mind in another part of Greece. Aristotle's love of data distinguished him from Socrates and Plato, who derived principles by logic. An intellectual ancestor of today's scientists, Aristotle derived principles from careful observations. His observations told him that "the soul is not separable from the body, and the same holds good of particular parts of the soul" (*De Anima*). Moreover, he said knowledge is *not* preexisting (sorry, Socrates and Plato); instead, it grows from the experiences stored in our memories.

The next 2000 years brought few enduring new insights into human nature, but that changed in the 1600s, when modern science began to flourish. With it came new theories of human behavior, and new versions of the ancient debates. A frail but brilliant Frenchman named René Descartes (1595–1650) agreed with Socrates and Plato about the existence of innate ideas and the mind's being "entirely distinct from the body" and able to survive its death. Descartes' concept of mind forced him to conjecture, as people have ever since, how the immaterial mind and physical body communicate. A scientist as well as a philosopher, Descartes dissected animals and concluded that the fluid in the brain's cavities contained "animal spirits." These spirits, he surmised, flowed from the brain through what we call the nerves (which he thought were hollow) to the muscles, provoking movement. Memories formed as experiences opened pores in the brain, into which the animal spirits also flowed.

Descartes was right that nerve paths are important and that they enable reflexes. Yet, genius though he was, and standing upon the knowledge accumulated from 99+ percent of our human history, he hardly had a clue of what today's average 12-year-old knows. Indeed, most of the scientific story of our self-exploration—the story told in this book's modules—has been written in but the last historical eyeblink of human time.

Meanwhile, across the English channel in Britain, science was taking a more down-to-earth form, centered on experiment, experience, and common-sense judgment. Francis Bacon (1561–1626) became one of the founders of modern science, and his influence lingers in the experiments of today's psychological science. Bacon also was fascinated by the human mind and its failings. Anticipating what we have come to appreciate about our mind's hunger to perceive patterns even in random events, he wrote that "the human understanding, from its peculiar nature, easily supposes a greater degree of order and equality in things than it really finds" (*Novum Organuum*). He also foresaw research findings on our noticing and remembering events that confirm our beliefs: "All superstition is much the same whether it be that of astrology, dreams, omens . . . in all of which the deluded believers observe events which are fulfilled, but neglect and pass over their failure, though it be much more common."

Some 50 years after Bacon's death, John Locke (1632–1704), a British political philosopher, sat down to write a one-page essay on "our own abilities" for an upcoming discussion with friends. After 20 years and hundreds of pages, Locke had completed one of history's latest and greatest late papers (*An Essay Concerning Human Understanding*), in which he famously argued that the mind at birth is a blank slate—a "white paper"—on which experience writes. This idea, adding to Bacon's ideas, helped form modern **empiricism,** the view that knowledge originates in experience and that science should, therefore, rely on observation and experimentation.

Psychological Science Is Born

OBJECTIVE **1-3** | Explain how the early psychologists sought to understand the mind's structure and functions, and identify some leading psychologists who worked in these areas.

Philosophers' thinking about thinking continued until the birth of psychology as we know it, on a December day in 1879, in a small room on the third floor of a shabby building at Germany's University of Leipzig. There, two young men were helping an

Bettmann/Corbis

A seventeenth-century view of nerves
In his *Treatise of Man*, Descartes proposed the hydraulics of a simple reflex.

■ **psychology** the scientific study of behavior and mental processes.

■ **empiricism** the view that (a) knowledge comes from experience via the senses, and (b) science flourishes through observation and experiment.

Wilhelm Wundt
Wundt (far left) established the first psychology laboratory at the University of Leipzig, Germany.

Information sources are cited in parentheses, with name and date, then provided fully in the References section at the book's end.

austere, middle-aged professor, Wilhelm Wundt, create an experimental apparatus. Their machine measured the time lag between people's hearing a ball hit a platform and their pressing a telegraph key. Later, the researchers compared this lag with the time required for slightly more complex tasks. Curiously, people responded in about one-tenth of a second when asked to press the key as soon as the sound occurred—and in about two-tenths of a second when asked to press the key as soon as they were consciously aware of perceiving the sound. (To be aware of one's awareness takes a little longer.) Wundt was seeking to measure "atoms of the mind"—the fastest and simplest mental processes (Hunt, 1993). Thus began what many consider psychology's first experiment, launching the first psychological laboratory, staffed by Wundt and psychology's first graduate students.

Before long this new science of psychology became organized into different branches, or schools of thought, each promoted by pioneering thinkers. These early schools included *structuralism* and *functionalism,* described here, and Gestalt psychology, behaviorism, and psychoanalysis, described in other modules.

Thinking About the Mind's Structure

Soon after receiving his Ph.D. in 1892, Wundt's student Edward Bradford Titchener joined the Cornell University faculty and introduced **structuralism.** As physicists and chemists discerned the structure of matter, so Titchener aimed to discover the elements of mind. His method was to engage people in self-reflective *introspection* (looking inward), training them to report elements of their experience as they looked at a rose, listened to a metronome, smelled a scent, or tasted a substance. What were their immediate sensations, their images, their feelings? And how did these relate to one another? Titchener shared with the English essayist C. S. Lewis (1960, pp. 18–19) the view that "there is one thing, and only one in the whole universe which we know more about than we could learn from external observation." That one thing, Lewis said, is ourselves. "We have, so to speak, inside information."

Alas, structuralism waned as introspection waned. Introspection required smart, verbal people. It also proved somewhat unreliable, its results varying from person to person and experience to experience. Moreover, recent studies indicate that people's recollections frequently err. So do their self-reports about what, for example, has caused them to help or hurt another (Myers, 2002). Often we just don't know why we feel what we feel and do what we do.

Edward Bradford Titchener
Used introspection to search for the mind's structural elements.

"The rose is smooth-petaled, sweetly aromatic,..."

"You don't know your own mind."
Jonathan Swift, *Polite Conversation,* 1738

Thinking About the Mind's Functions

Unlike those hoping to assemble the structure of mind from simple elements—which was rather like trying to understand a car by examining its disconnected parts—philosopher-psychologist William James thought it more fruitful to consider the evolved *functions* of our thoughts and feelings. Smelling is what the nose does; thinking is what the brain does. But why do the nose and brain do these things? Under the influence of evolutionary theorist Charles Darwin, James assumed that thinking, like smelling, developed because it was adaptive—it contributed to our ancestors' survival. Consciousness serves a function. It enables us to consider our past, adjust to our present circumstances, and plan our future. As a **functionalist,** James encouraged explorations of down-to-earth emotions, memories, will power, habits, and moment-to-moment streams of consciousness.

James' greatest legacy, however, came less from his laboratory than from his Harvard teaching and his writing. When not plagued by ill health and depression, James was an impish, outgoing, and joyous man, who once recalled that "the first lecture on psychology I ever heard was the first I ever gave." During one of his wise-cracking lectures, a student interrupted and asked him to get serious (Hunt, 1993). He was reportedly one of the first American professors to solicit end-of-course student evaluations of his teaching. He loved his students, his family, and the world of ideas, but tired of painstaking chores such as proofreading. "Send me no proofs!" he once told an editor. "I will return them unopened and never speak to you again" (Hunt, 1993, p. 145).

James displayed the same spunk in 1890, when—over the objections of Harvard's president—he admitted Mary Calkins into his graduate seminar (Scarborough & Furumoto, 1987). When Calkins joined, all the other students dropped. (In those years women lacked even the right to vote.) So James tutored her alone. Later she finished all the requirements for a Harvard Ph.D., outscoring all the male students on the qualifying exams. Alas, Harvard denied her the degree she had earned, offering her instead a degree from Radcliffe College, its undergraduate sister school for women. Calkins resisted the unequal treatment and refused the degree. More than a century later, psychologists and psychology students were lobbying Harvard to posthumously award the Ph.D. she earned (*Feminist Psychologist,* 2002).

Calkins nevertheless became a distinguished memory researcher and the American Psychological Association's (APA's) first female president in 1905. What a different world from the recent past—1996 to 2005—when women claimed two-thirds or more of new psychology Ph.D.s and were 5 of the 10 elected presidents of the science-oriented American Psychological Society. In Canada and Europe, too, most recent psychology doctorates have been earned by women.

When Harvard denied Calkins the claim to being psychology's first female psychology Ph.D., that honor fell to Margaret Floy Washburn, who later wrote an influential book, *The Animal Mind,* and became the second female APA president in 1921. Although Washburn's thesis was the first foreign study Wundt published in his journal, her gender meant she was barred from joining the organization of experimental psychologists founded by Titchener, her own graduate adviser (Johnson, 1997).

James' influence reached even further through his dozens of well-received articles, which moved the publisher Henry Holt to offer a contract for a textbook of the new science of psychology. James agreed and began work in 1878, with an apology for requesting two years to finish his writing. The work proved an unexpected chore and actually took him 12 years. (Why am I not surprised?) More than a century later, people still read the resulting *Principles of Psychology* and marvel at the brilliance and elegance with which James introduced psychology to the educated public.

William James and Mary Whiton Calkins
James, legendary teacher-writer, mentored Calkins, who became a pioneering memory researcher and American Psychological Association president.

■ **structuralism** an early school of psychology that used introspection to explore the elemental structure of the human mind.

■ **functionalism** a school of psychology that focused on how mental and behavioral processes function—how they enable the organism to adapt, survive, and flourish.

Margaret Floy Washburn
The first woman to receive a psychology Ph.D.; synthesized animal behavior research in *The Animal Mind.*

Sigmund Freud
Famed personality theorist and therapist, whose controversial ideas influenced humanity's self-understanding.

Psychological Science Develops

OBJECTIVE 1-4 | Describe the evolution of psychology as defined from the 1920s through today.

This young science of psychology developed from the more established fields of philosophy and biology. Wundt was both a philosopher and a physiologist. James was an American philosopher. Ivan Pavlov, who pioneered the study of learning, was a Russian physiologist. Sigmund Freud, who developed an influential theory of personality, was an Austrian physician. Jean Piaget, the last century's most influential observer of children, was a Swiss biologist. This list of pioneering psychologists—"Magellans of the mind," as Morton Hunt (1993) has called them—illustrates psychology's origins in many disciplines and countries.

The rest of the story of psychology—the subject of this book—develops at many levels. With activities ranging from psychotherapy to the study of nerve cell activity, *psychology* is not easily defined. Wundt and Titchener focused on *inner* sensations, images, and feelings. James, too, engaged in introspective examination of the stream of consciousness and of emotion. Freud emphasized the ways emotional responses to childhood experiences and our unconscious thought processes affect our behavior. Thus, until the 1920s, *psychology* was defined as "the science of mental life."

From the 1920s into the 1960s, American psychologists, initially led by flamboyant and provocative John B. Watson and later by the equally provocative B. F. Skinner, dismissed introspection and redefined *psychology* as "the scientific study of observable behavior." After all, said these *behaviorists,* science is rooted in observation. You cannot observe a sensation, a feeling, or a thought, but you *can* observe and record people's *behavior* as they respond to different situations.

Humanistic psychology was a softer, 1960s response to Freudian psychology and to behaviorism, which pioneers Carl Rogers and Abraham Maslow found too mechanistic. Rather than calling up childhood memories or focusing on learned behaviors, Rogers and Maslow both emphasized the importance of current environmental influences on our growth potential, and the importance of meeting our needs for love and acceptance.

In the 1960s, psychology began to recapture its initial interest in mental processes through studies of how our mind processes and retains information. This *cognitive*

■ **humanistic psychology** historically significant perspective that emphasized the growth potential of healthy people; used personalized methods to study personality in hopes of fostering personal growth.

John B. Watson and Rosalie Rayner
Working with Rayner, Watson championed psychology as the science of behavior and demonstrated conditioned responses on a baby who became famous as "Little Albert."

B. F. Skinner
A leading behaviorist, who rejected introspection and studied how consequences shape behavior.

revolution supported ideas developed by earlier psychologists, such as the importance of considering internal thought processes, but it expanded upon those ideas to explore scientifically the ways we perceive, process, and remember information. Cognitive psychology and more recently *cognitive neuroscience* (the study of the interaction of thought processes and brain function) have been especially beneficial in expanding the understanding and treatment of disorders such as depression.

To encompass psychology's concern with observable behavior *and* with inner thoughts and feelings, we define *psychology* today as the scientific study of behavior *and* mental processes.

Contemporary Psychology

Like its pioneers, today's psychologists are citizens of many lands. The International Union of Psychological Science has 69 member nations, from Albania to Zimbabwe. Nearly everywhere, membership in psychological societies is mushrooming—from 4183 American Psychological Association members and affiliates in 1945 to more than 160,000 today, with similarly rapid growth in Britain (from 1100 to 34,000). In China, five universities had psychology departments in 1985; by the century's end, there were 50 (Jing, 1999). Worldwide, some 500,000 people have been trained as psychologists, and 130,000 of them belong to European psychological organizations (Tikkanen, 2001). Moreover, thanks to international publications, joint meetings, and the Internet, collaboration and communication cross borders more now than ever: "We are moving rapidly towards a single world of psychological science," reports Robert Bjork (2000). Psychology is *growing* and it is *globalizing*.

Today's psychologists debate some enduring issues and view behavior from differing perspectives. They also teach, work, and do research in many different subfields.

Psychology's Big Debate

OBJECTIVE **1-5** | Summarize the nature-nurture debate in psychology, and describe the principle of natural selection.

During its short history, psychology has wrestled with some issues that will reappear throughout this book. The biggest and most persistent issue concerns *the relative contributions of biology and experience*. As we have seen, the origins of this **nature-nurture** debate are ancient. Do our human traits develop through experience, or do we come equipped with them? The ancient Greeks debated this, with Plato assuming that character and intelligence are largely inherited and that certain ideas are also inborn, and Aristotle countering that there is nothing in the mind that does not first come in from the external world through the senses. In the 1600s, philosophers rekindled the debate. Locke rejected the notion of inborn ideas, offering his notion that the mind is a blank sheet on which experience writes. Descartes disagreed, believing that some ideas are innate.

Two centuries later, Descartes' views gained support from a curious naturalist. In 1831, an indifferent student but ardent collector of beetles, mollusks, and shells set sail on what was to prove a historic round-the-world journey. The 22-year-old voyager was Charles Darwin, and for some time afterward, he pondered the incredible species variation he had encountered, including tortoises on one island that differed from those on other islands of the region. Darwin's 1859 *Origin of Species* explained this diversity of life by proposing an evolutionary process. From among chance variations in organisms, he believed, nature selects those that best enable an organism to survive and reproduce in a particular environment. Darwin's principle of **natural selection**—"the single best idea anyone has ever had," says philosopher Daniel Dennett (1996)—is still with us nearly 150 years later as an organizing principle of biology. Evolution also has become an important principle for twenty-first century psychology. This would surely have pleased Darwin, for he believed his theory

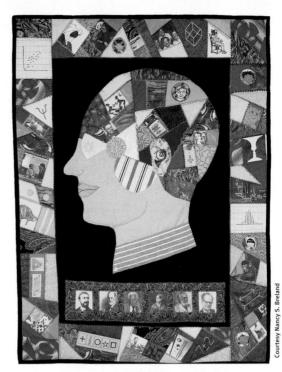

Courtesy Nancy S. Breland

Psychology's scope and history
In her quilt, "Crazy About Psychology," Nancy S. Breland, a psychology professor at the College of New Jersey, captures images and people from psychology's first century.

■ **nature-nurture issue** the longstanding controversy over the relative contributions that genes and experience make to the development of psychological traits and behaviors.

■ **natural selection** the principle that, among the range of inherited trait variations, those contributing to reproduction and survival will most likely be passed on to succeeding generations.

Charles Darwin
Argued that natural selection shapes behaviors as well as bodies.

Monika Suteski

A nature-made nature-nurture experiment
Because identical twins have the same genes, they are ideal participants in studies designed to shed light on hereditary and environmental influences on temperament, intelligence, and other traits. Studies of identical and fraternal twins provide a rich array of findings that underscore the importance of both nature and nurture.

explained not only animal structures (such as why polar bear coats are white) but also animal behaviors (such as the emotional expressions associated with lust and rage).

The nature-nurture debate weaves a thread from the distant past to our time. Today's psychologists have continued the debate by asking:

- How are differences in intelligence, personality, and psychological disorders influenced by heredity and by environment?
- Is children's grammar mostly innate or formed by experience?
- Are sexual behaviors more "pushed" by inner biology or "pulled" by external incentives?
- Should we treat depression as a disorder of the brain or a disorder of thought—or both?
- How are we humans alike (because of our common biology and evolutionary history) and different (because of our differing environments)?
- Are gender differences biologically predisposed or socially constructed?

The debate continues. Yet over and over again we will see that in contemporary science the nature-nurture tension dissolves: *Nurture works on what nature endows.* Our species is biologically endowed with an enormous capacity to learn and adapt. Moreover, every psychological event (every thought, every emotion) is simultaneously a biological event. Thus depression can be *both* a thought disorder and a brain disorder.

Psychology's Three Main Levels of Analysis

OBJECTIVE **1-6** | Identify the three main levels of analysis in the biopsychosocial approach, and explain why psychology's varied perspectives are complementary.

Each of us is a complex system that is part of a larger social system, but each of us is also composed of smaller systems, such as our nervous system and body organs, which are composed of still smaller systems—cells, molecules, and atoms.

These different systems suggest different **levels of analysis,** which offer complementary outlooks. It's like explaining why grizzly bears hibernate. Is it because hibernation enhanced their ancestors' survival and reproduction? Because their inner physiology drives them to do so? Because cold environments hinder food gathering during winter? Such perspectives are complementary, because "everything is related to everything else" (Brewer, 1996). Together, different levels of analysis form an integrated **biopsychosocial approach,** which considers the influences of biological, psychological, and social-cultural factors (**FIGURE 1.1**). Each level provides a valuable vantage point for looking at behavior, yet each by itself is incomplete.

FIGURE 1.1
Biopsychosocial approach
This integrated viewpoint incorporates various levels of analysis and offers a more complete picture of any given behavior or mental process.

Biological influences:
- genetic predispositions
- genetic mutations
- natural selection of adaptive physiology and behaviors
- genes responding to the environment

Psychological influences:
- learned fears and other learned expectations
- emotional responses
- cognitive processing and perceptual interpretations

Behavior or mental process

Social-cultural influences:
- presence of others
- cultural, societal, and family expectations
- peer and other group influences
- compelling models (such as the media)

TABLE **1.1**

PSYCHOLOGY'S CURRENT PERSPECTIVES

Perspective	Focus	Sample Questions
Neuroscience	How the body and brain enable emotions, memories, and sensory experiences	How are messages transmitted within the body? How is blood chemistry linked with moods and motives?
Evolutionary	How the natural selection of traits promotes the perpetuation of one's genes	How does evolution influence behavior tendencies?
Behavior genetics	How much our genes and our environment influence our individual differences	To what extent are psychological traits such as intelligence, personality, sexual orientation, and vulnerability to depression attributable to our genes? To our environment?
Psychodynamic	How behavior springs from unconscious drives and conflicts	How can someone's personality traits and disorders be explained in terms of sexual and aggressive drives or as the disguised effects of unfulfilled wishes and childhood traumas?
Behavioral	How we learn observable responses	How do we learn to fear particular objects or situations? What is the most effective way to alter our behavior, say, to lose weight or stop smoking?
Cognitive	How we encode, process, store, and retrieve information	How do we use information in remembering? Reasoning? Solving problems?
Social-cultural	How behavior and thinking vary across situations and cultures	How are we—as Africans, Asians, Australians, or North Americans—alike as members of one human family? As products of different environmental contexts, how do we differ?

Consider, for example, how psychology's varied perspectives described in **TABLE 1.1** can supplement one another and shed light on anger.

- Someone working from a *neuroscience perspective* might study brain circuits that produce the physical state of being "red in the face" and "hot under the collar."
- Someone working from the *evolutionary perspective* might analyze how anger facilitated the survival of our ancestors' genes.
- Someone working from the *behavior genetics perspective* might study how heredity and experience influence our individual differences in temperament.
- Someone working from the *psychodynamic perspective* might view an outburst as an outlet for unconscious hostility.
- Someone working from the *behavioral perspective* might study the facial expressions and body gestures that accompany anger, or might attempt to determine which external stimuli result in angry responses or aggressive acts.
- Someone working from the *cognitive perspective* might study how our interpretation of a situation affects our anger and how our anger affects our thinking.
- Someone working from the *social-cultural perspective* might explore which situations produce the most anger, and how expressions of anger vary across cultural contexts.

This important point—that different perspectives can complement one another—is also true of the different academic disciplines. Each academic perspective has its questions and its limits. A perfume manufacturer needs chemistry to create its products, psychology to know what will sell, and marketing and business to turn a profit. Differing academic perspectives are like different two-dimensional views of a three-dimensional object. Each two-dimensional perspective is helpful, but by itself fails to reveal the whole picture.

So bear in mind psychology's limits. Don't expect it to answer the ultimate questions, such as those posed by Russian novelist Leo Tolstoy (1904): "Why should I live? Why should I do anything? Is there in life any purpose which the inevitable death that awaits me does not undo and destroy?" Instead, expect that psychology will help you understand why people think, feel, and act as they do. Then you should find the study of psychology fascinating and useful.

Gabe Palmer/Corbis

Views of anger
How would each of psychology's levels of analysis (see Figure 1.1) explain what's going on here?

Want to learn more? See Appendix A, Careers in Psychology, at the end of this book for more information about psychology's subfields and to learn about the many interesting options available to those with bachelor's, master's, and doctoral degrees in psychology.

■ **levels of analysis** the differing complementary views, from biological to psychological to social-cultural, for analyzing any given phenomenon.

■ **biopsychosocial approach** an integrated perspective that incorporates biological, psychological, and social-cultural levels of analysis.

■ **basic research** pure science that aims to increase the scientific knowledge base.

■ **applied research** scientific study that aims to solve practical problems.

■ **counseling psychology** a branch of psychology that assists people with problems in living (often related to school, work, or marriage) and in achieving greater well-being.

■ **clinical psychology** a branch of psychology that studies, assesses, and treats people with psychological disorders.

■ **psychiatry** a branch of medicine dealing with psychological disorders; practiced by physicians who sometimes provide medical (for example, drug) treatments as well as psychological therapy.

Psychology's Subfields

OBJECTIVE 1-7 | Identify some of psychology's subfields, and explain the difference between clinical psychology and psychiatry.

Psychology is a collection of diverse subfields. Some psychologists do basic research, some do applied research, and some provide professional services. Picturing a chemist at work, you probably envision a white-coated scientist surrounded by glassware and high-tech equipment. Picture a psychologist at work and you would be right to envision

- a white-coated scientist probing a rat's brain.
- an intelligence researcher measuring how quickly an infant becomes bored with (looks away from) a familiar picture.
- an executive evaluating a new "healthy life-styles" training program for employees.
- someone at a computer keyboard analyzing data on whether adopted teens' temperaments more closely resemble those of their adoptive parents or those of their biological parents.
- a therapist listening carefully to a client's depressed thoughts.
- a traveler en route to another culture to collect data on variations in human values and behaviors.
- a teacher or writer sharing the joy of psychology with others.

The cluster of subfields we call psychology has less unity than most other sciences. But there is a payoff: Psychology is a meeting ground for different disciplines and is thus a perfect home for those with wide-ranging interests. In their diverse activities, from biological experimentation to cultural comparisons, a common quest unites the tribe of psychology: to describe and explain behavior and the mind underlying it.

Some psychologists conduct **basic research** that builds psychology's knowledge base. In the pages that follow we will meet a wide variety of such researchers:

- *Biological psychologists* exploring the links between brain and mind
- *Developmental psychologists* studying our changing abilities from womb to tomb
- *Cognitive psychologists* experimenting with how we perceive, think, and solve problems
- *Personality psychologists* investigating our persistent traits
- *Social psychologists* exploring how we view and affect one another

These psychologists also may conduct **applied research** that tackles practical problems. So do other psychologists, such as *industrial/organizational psychologists* as they study and advise on behavior in the workplace. They use psychology's concepts and methods to help organizations and companies select and train employees more effectively, to boost morale and productivity, to design products, and to implement systems.

Although most psychology textbooks focus on psychological science, psychology is also a helping profession devoted to such practical issues as how to have a happy marriage, how to overcome anxiety or depression, and how to raise thriving children. **Counseling psychologists** help people cope with challenges (including academic, vocational, and marital issues) by recognizing their strengths and resources. **Clinical psychologists** assess and treat mental, emotional, and behavior disorders (APA, 2003). Both counseling and clinical psychologists administer and interpret tests, provide counseling and therapy, and sometimes conduct basic and applied research. By contrast, **psychiatrists,** who also often provide psychotherapy, are medical doctors licensed to prescribe drugs and otherwise treat physical causes of psychological disorders. (Some clinical psychologists are lobbying for a similar right to prescribe mental health–related drugs, and in 2002 New Mexico was the first state to grant that right to specially trained and licensed psychologists.)

With perspectives ranging from the biological to the social, and with settings from the laboratory to the clinic, psychology relates to many disciplines. More and more, psychology connects with fields ranging from mathematics to biology to sociology to philosophy. And more and more, psychology's methods and findings aid other disciplines.

"I'm a social scientist, Michael. That means I can't explain electricity or anything like that, but if you ever want to know about people I'm your man."

Michael Newman/Photo Edit

Jeff Greenberg/PhotoEdit

Psychologists teach in medical schools, law schools, and theological seminaries, and they work in hospitals, factories, and corporate offices. They engage in interdisciplinary studies, such as psychohistory (the psychological analysis of historical characters), psycholinguistics (the study of language and thinking), and psychoceramics (the study of crackpots).[1]

Psychology also influences modern culture. Knowledge transforms us. Learning about the solar system and the germ theory of disease alters the way people think and act. Learning psychology's findings also changes people: They less often judge psychological disorders as a moral failing, treatable by punishment and ostracism. They less often regard and treat women as men's mental inferiors. They less often view and rear children as ignorant, willful beasts in need of taming. "In each case," notes Morton Hunt (1990, p. 206), "knowledge has modified attitudes, and, through them, behavior." Once aware of psychology's well-researched ideas—about how body and mind connect, how a child's mind grows, how we construct our perceptions, how we remember (and misremember) our experiences, how people across the world differ (and are alike)—your mind may never again be quite the same.

[1]Confession time: I wrote the last part of this sentence on April Fools' Day.

Michael Newman/Photo Edit

Psychology:
A science and a profession
Psychologists experiment with, observe, test, and treat behavior. Here we see psychologists testing a child, recording children's behavior through a two-way mirror, and doing face-to-face therapy.

"Once expanded to the dimensions of a larger idea, [the mind] never returns to its original size."

Oliver Wendell Holmes, 1809–1894

Laura Dwight

I see you!
A biological psychologist might view this child's delighted response as evidence of brain maturation. A cognitive psychologist might see it as a demonstration of the baby's growing knowledge of his surroundings. For a cross-cultural psychologist, the role of grandparents in different societies might be the issue of interest. As you will see throughout this book, these and other perspectives offer complementary views of behavior.

CLOSE-UP:

YOUR STUDY OF PSYCHOLOGY

OBJECTIVE 1-8 | **Describe some effective study techniques.**

The investment you are making in studying psychology should enrich your life and enlarge your vision. Although many of life's significant questions are beyond psychology, some very important ones are illuminated by even a first psychology course. Through painstaking research, psychologists have gained insights into brain and mind, depression and joy, dreams and memories. Even the unanswered questions can enrich us, by renewing our sense of mystery about "things too wonderful" for us yet to understand. What is more, your study of psychology can help teach you *how to ask and answer important questions*—how to think critically as you evaluate competing ideas and claims.

Having your life enriched and your vision enlarged (and getting a decent grade) requires effective study. To master information you must *actively process* it. Your mind is not like your stomach, something to be filled passively; it is more like a muscle that grows stronger with exercise. Countless experiments reveal that people learn and remember material best when they put it in their own words, rehearse it, and then review and rehearse it again.

A simple study method incorporates these principles. You can remember it as SQ3R: *Survey, Question, Read, Review,* and *Reflect.*

First, *survey* what you're about to read, including module outlines and section heads. Note a section's main topic, as indicated by the learning objective at the beginning. This will focus your reading and study.

Keep the learning objective in mind as a *question* you will attempt to answer as you *read* the section. Usually a single module—sometimes just a main section within a module—will be as much as you can absorb without tiring. Read actively and critically. Ask questions. Make notes. Consider implications: How does what you've read support or challenge your assumptions? How convincing is the evidence? How does it relate to your own life?

Finally, *review* and *reflect*. To root a module's organization more deeply in your memory, rescan the module and the marginal definitions of key terms. Study the Learning Outcomes at the end of each module. Quiz yourself with the end-of-module Test Yourself questions and, perhaps, by taking quizzes in the book's accompanying study guide and on-line learning resources (at www.worth publishers.com/myers). Glance over your notes or highlighting. Then stop and let it all sink in. Better yet, summarize the material for a friend or lecture about it to an imaginary audience.

Survey, question, read, review, reflect. I have organized the modules to facilitate your using the SQ3R study method. Each module begins with an outline that helps you survey what is upcoming, and each main section begins with a learning objective. I have divided modules into shorter sections of readable length. To assist your reviewing, each module ends with a Learning Outcomes narrative summary, followed by an organized reminder of key terms and a big-picture Test Yourself question. Finally, an Ask Yourself question is designed to help you reflect—applying what you've learned to your own life to make the material more meaningful and memorable. Survey, question, read, review, reflect.

Five additional study hints may further boost your learning:

Distribute your study time: One of psychology's oldest findings is

Learning how to ask and answer important questions
The basic study tips in this box are beneficial to students at all levels and in all places, including these children at a village school in Niger.

Oliver Strewe/Getty Images

that spaced practice promotes better retention than massed practice. You'll remember material better if you space your time over several study periods—perhaps one hour a day, six days a week—rather than cram it into one long study blitz. Spacing your study sessions requires a disciplined approach to managing your time. (Richard O. Straub explains time management in the helpful *Study Guide* that accompanies this text.)

In class, listen actively: As psychologist William James urged some 100 years ago, *"No reception without reaction, no impression without . . . expression."* Listen for the main idea and sub-ideas in lectures. *Write them down.* Ask questions during and after class. In class, as in your private study, process the information actively and you will understand and retain it better.

Overlearn. Psychology tells us that "overlearning improves retention." The more often students read assigned material and the fewer classes they miss, the better their exam scores are (Woehr & Cavell, 1993). Students frequently stop short of overlearning and overestimate how much they know. Really *learning* something requires more than momentarily understanding it. You may understand a module as you read it, but if you devote extra study time to rereading, to testing yourself, and to reviewing what you think you know, you will actually *learn* the material and retain your new knowledge longer.

Focus on the big ideas. It helps to step back periodically and see the big picture so that you know how all the facts and research fit together. To understand and appreciate psychology's lessons, for example, it's important to read about the research that informs them, but it is also important to watch for the bigger concepts and themes that psychologists construct from these smaller findings. Among this book's big ideas are these:

- Critical thinking and scientific scrutiny help us think smarter about many things.

- We gain understanding by viewing a phenomenon from the biological, psychological, and social-cultural levels. Everything psychological is simultaneously biological. Yet our behavior is often influenced by our environment and our culture.

- Nature (our genes and our biological makeup) and nurture (our environment, our culture, and the world around us) work together in forming our traits and behaviors.

- We are creatures of our culture and gender, yet we are far more alike than different.

- Much of our human information processing is unconscious, below the radar screen of our awareness.

Be a smart test-taker. If a test contains both multiple-choice questions and an essay question, turn first to the essay. Read the question carefully, noting exactly what the instructor is asking. On the back of a page, pencil in a list of points you'd like to make, and then organize them. Before writing, put the essay aside and work through the multiple-choice questions. (As you do so, you may continue to mull over the essay question. Sometimes the objective questions will bring pertinent thoughts to mind.) Then reread the essay question, rethink your answer, and start writing. When you finish, proofread your work to eliminate spelling and grammatical errors that make you look less competent than you are.

When reading multiple-choice questions, don't confuse yourself by trying to imagine how each choice might be the right one. Try instead to answer the question as if it were a fill-in-the-blank. First, cover the answers, recall what you know, and complete the sentence in your mind. Then read the answers on the test and find the alternative that best matches your own answer.

As you read psychology, you will learn much more than effective study techniques. Psychology teaches us how to ask important questions—how to think critically as we evaluate competing ideas and popular claims. It deepens our appreciation for how we humans perceive, think, feel, and act. By so doing, it informs our living and enlarges our compassion. Through this book I hope to help guide you toward that end. As educator Charles Eliot said a century ago, "Books are the quietest and most constant of friends, and the most patient of teachers."

>> LEARNING OUTCOMES

The History and Scope of Psychology

OBJECTIVE 1-1 | Define *psychology.*

Psychology is the scientific study of behavior (anything an organism does) and mental processes (subjective experiences inferred from behavior). The key word in this definition is *science.*

OBJECTIVE 1-2 | Trace psychology's prescientific roots, from early understandings of mind and body to the beginnings of modern science.

Psychology traces its roots back through recorded history to India, China, the Middle East, and Europe, where scholars tried to understand how our minds work and how our bodies relate to our minds. More than 2000 years ago, Buddha and Confucius focused on the powers and origin of ideas. The ancient Hebrews, Socrates, his student Plato, and Plato's student Aristotle pondered whether mind and body are connected or distinct, and whether human ideas are innate or result from experience. In the 1600s, René Descartes and John Locke reengaged aspects of those ancient debates, and Locke coined his famous description of the mind as a "white paper." The ideas of Francis Bacon and John Locke were important ingredients in the development of modern *empiricism,* the view that knowledge comes from experience through the senses and that science should rely on observation and experimentation.

OBJECTIVE 1-3 | Explain how the early psychologists sought to understand the mind's structure and functions, and identify some leading psychologists who worked in these areas.

In Germany in the late 1800s, Wilhelm Wundt ran the first true experiments in psychology's first lab. Soon, the new discipline formed branches. Edward Bradford Titchener and other *structuralists* searched for the basic elements of the mind by training people to look inward and describe the smallest units of their experiences. Focusing on how mental and behavioral processes help us to adapt, survive, and flourish, William James and other functionalists tried to explain why we do what we do. James also wrote a popular text for the new discipline.

OBJECTIVE 1-4 | Describe the evolution of psychology as defined from the 1920s through today.

Until the 1920s, psychology was a "science of mental life" studied through introspection. Then American behaviorists, led by John B. Watson and later by B. F. Skinner, changed psychology's focus to the study of observable behavior. In the 1960s, humanistic psychologists drew attention to the importance of environmental influences, personal growth, and the needs for love and acceptance. Also in the 1960s, the cognitive revolution began to refocus psychology's interest in mental processes, with special attention to perception, information processing, and memory. Cognitive neuroscientists are broadening our understanding of these and other processes in today's psychology, which views itself as a "science of behavior and mental processes."

OBJECTIVE 1-5 | Summarize the nature-nurture debate in psychology, and describe the principle of natural selection.

Psychology's biggest and most enduring issue concerns the balance between the influences of nature (genes) and nurture (all other influences, from conception to death). A great deal of research, including studies of identical and fraternal twins, sheds light on the relative importance of these two sets of influences on such traits as personality and intelligence. Psychologists now believe that in most cases, every psychological event is simultaneously a biological event. Charles Darwin proposed a mechanism—the principle of natural selection—by which nature selects chance variations that enable organisms to survive and reproduce in particular environments.

OBJECTIVE 1-6 | Identify the three main levels of analysis in the biopsychosocial approach, and explain why psychology's varied perspectives are complementary.

The biopsychosocial approach integrates information from the biological, psychological, and social-cultural levels of analysis. Psychologists study human behaviors and mental processes from many different perspectives (including the neuroscientific, evolutionary, behavior genetics, psychodynamic, behavioral, cognitive, and social-cultural perspectives). Melding the information gathered from these many lines of research creates a more complete understanding of behaviors and mental processes than would be available from any one viewpoint alone.

OBJECTIVE 1-7 | Identify some of psychology's subfields, and explain the difference between clinical psychology and psychiatry.

Psychology's subfields encompass basic research (often done by biological, developmental, cognitive, personality, and social psychologists), applied research (sometimes conducted by industrial/organizational psychologists), and clinical applications (the work of counseling and clinical psychologists). Clinical psychologists study, assess, and treat (with psychotherapy) people with psychological disorders; psychiatrists also study, assess, and treat people with disorders, but they are medical doctors who can prescribe medication as well as offer psychotherapy.

OBJECTIVE 1-8 | Describe some effective study techniques.

SQ3R is an effective study method in which you *survey* material before reading it, keep in mind a *question* you will try to answer as you *read,* and then *review* the material you have read, and *reflect* on it to make it meaningful and memorable. Five additional tips are to distribute study time, listen actively in class, overlearn, focus on big ideas, and be a smart test-taker.

TERMS AND CONCEPTS TO REMEMBER

psychology, p. 1-0	levels of analysis, p. 1-6
empiricism, p. 1-1	biopsychosocial approach, p. 1-7
structuralism, p. 1-2	basic research, p. 1-8
functionalism, p. 1-3	applied research, p. 1-8
humanistic psychology, p. 1-4	counseling psychology, p. 1-8
nature-nurture issue, p. 1-5	clinical psychology, p. 1-8
natural selection, p. 1-5	psychiatry, p. 1-8

TEST YOURSELF*

1. What events defined the founding of scientific psychology?

2. What are psychology's major levels of analysis?

ASK YOURSELF**

1. How do you think psychology might change as more people from non-Western countries contribute their ideas to the field?

2. When you signed up for this course, what did you think psychology would be all about?

> **WEB**

Multiple-choice *self-tests* and more may be found at www.worthpublishers.com/myers.

*The Test Yourself questions offer you a handy self-test on the material you have just read. Answers to these questions can be found in Appendix B at the back of the book.

**The Ask Yourself questions will help you reflect on key issues and connect them to your own life. Making these issues personally meaningful will make them memorable.

MODULE

The Need for Psychological Science

Frequently Asked Questions About Psychology

2

Thinking Critically With Psychological Science

What good fortune for those in power that people do not think.

Adolf Hitler, 1889–1945

Hoping to satisfy their curiosity about people and to remedy their own woes, millions turn to "psychology." They listen to talk-radio counseling, read articles on psychic powers, attend stop-smoking hypnosis seminars, and absorb self-help books on the meaning of dreams, the path to ecstatic love, and the roots of personal happiness.

Others, intrigued by claims of psychological truth, wonder: Do mothers and infants bond in the first hours after birth? Should we trust childhood sexual abuse memories that get "recovered" in adulthood—and prosecute the alleged predators? Are first-born children more driven to achieve? Does handwriting offer clues to personality? Does psychotherapy heal?

In working with such questions, how can we separate uninformed opinions from examined conclusions? *How can we best use psychology to understand why people think, feel, and act as they do?*

The Need for Psychological Science

As we familiarize ourselves with psychological science's strategies and incorporate its underlying principles into our daily thinking, our thinking becomes smarter. Two phenomena—hindsight bias and judgmental overconfidence—illustrate why we cannot rely solely on intuition and common sense. The critical inquiry that flows from a scientific approach—undergirded by curiosity, skepticism, and humility—helps winnow sense from nonsense.

The Limits of Intuition and Common Sense

Some people think psychology merely documents what people already know and dresses it in jargon: "So what else is new—you get paid for using fancy methods to prove what my grandmother knew?" Others scorn a scientific approach because of their faith in human intuition. Advocates of "intuitive management" urge us to distrust statistical predictors and tune into our hunches when hiring, firing, and investing. Like *Star Wars'* Luke Skywalker, should we trust the force within?

Actually, notes writer Madeleine L'Engle, "The naked intellect is an extraordinarily inaccurate instrument" (1972). Our intuition can lead us astray.

- Imagine (or ask someone to imagine) folding a sheet of paper on itself 100 times. Roughly how thick would it then be?
- A rope is placed around the Earth at the equator. How much more rope would have to be added for the rope to be 1 foot above the Earth all the way around? (See this module's final page for the answers.)

Our notions of common sense similarly err. We're all wise after the fact, presuming that we could have foreseen what happened.

The limits of intuition
Personnel interviewers tend to be overconfident of their gut feelings about job applicants. Their confidence stems partly from their recalling cases where their favorable impression proved right, and partly from their ignorance about rejected applicants who succeeded elsewhere.

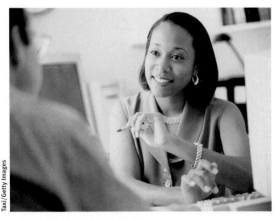

Taxi/Getty Images

Did We Know It All Along? Hindsight Bias

OBJECTIVE **2-1** | Describe *hindsight bias,* and explain how it can make research findings seem like mere common sense.

How easy it is to seem astute when drawing the bull's eye after the arrow has struck. *After* each stock market downswing—after the bursting of the dot-com bubble, for example—investment gurus say "the market was obviously overdue for a correction." After the first World Trade Center tower in New York was hit on September 11, 2001 (9/11), commentators said people in the second tower *should* have immediately evacuated (it became obvious only later that it was not an accident). And after physicians receive case information *plus* an autopsy report, they find the cause of death to be self-evident—something they presume they easily could have foreseen, knowing the symptoms. But *before* the arrow strikes, the stock market drops, the terrorists attack, and death occurs, these results are anything but obvious. Causes of death, for example, are not so clear to doctors told the same symptoms without the autopsy report (Dawson & others, 1988). Finding that something has happened makes it seem inevitable. Psychologists Paul Slovic and Baruch Fischhoff (1977) have called this 20/20 hindsight vision **hindsight bias,** also known as the *I-knew-it-all-along phenomenon.*

This phenomenon is easy to demonstrate: Give half the members of a group some purported psychological finding, and the other half an opposite result. Tell the first group, "Psychologists have found that separation weakens romantic attraction. As the saying goes, 'Out of sight, out of mind.'" Ask them to imagine why this might be true. Most people can, and nearly all will then regard this true finding as unsurprising.

Tell the second group just the opposite—that "psychologists have found that separation strengthens romantic attraction. As the saying goes, 'Absence makes the heart grow fonder.'" People given this untrue result can also easily explain it, and they overwhelmingly see it as unsurprising common sense. Obviously, when both a supposed finding and its opposite seem like common sense, there is a problem.

Such errors in our recollections and explanations show why we need psychological research. Just asking people how and why they felt or acted as they did can sometimes be misleading—*not* because common sense is usually wrong, but because it is after the fact. Common sense describes what has happened more easily than it predicts what will happen. As physicist Neils Bohr reportedly said, "Prediction is very difficult, especially about the future."

The phenomenon is widespread. Some 100 studies have observed hindsight bias in various countries and among both children and adults (Bernstein & others, 2004; Guilbault & others, 2004). Nevertheless, Grandmother is often right. As Yogi Berra once said, "You can observe a lot by watching." (We have Berra to thank for other gems, such as "Nobody ever comes here—it's too crowded," and "If the people don't want to come out to the ballpark, nobody's gonna stop 'em.") Because we're all

> "Life is lived forwards, but understood backwards."
>
> Philosopher Søren Kierkegaard, 1813–1855

> "History is written through a rearview mirror, but it unfolds through a foggy windshield."
>
> Samuel Berger, President Clinton's national security adviser, in testimony before the 9/11 Commission, 2004

> "Anything seems commonplace, once explained."
>
> Dr. Watson to Sherlock Holmes

Non Sequitur

■ **hindsight bias** the tendency to believe, after learning an outcome, that one would have foreseen it. (Also known as the *I-knew-it-all-along phenomenon.*)

TABLE 2.1

TRUE OR FALSE?

Psychological research has either confirmed or refuted each of these statements (adapted, in part, from Furnham & others, 2003).

1. If you want to teach a habit that persists, reward the desired behavior every time, not just intermittently.

2. Patients whose brains are surgically split down the middle survive and function much as they did before the surgery.

3. Traumatic experiences, such as sexual abuse or surviving the Holocaust, are typically "repressed" from memory.

4. Most abused children do *not* become abusive adults.

5. Most infants recognize their own reflection in a mirror by the end of their first year.

6. Adopted siblings tend not to develop similar personalities, even though reared by the same parents.

7. Fears of harmless objects, such as flowers, are just as easy to acquire as fears of potentially dangerous objects, such as snakes.

8. Lie detection tests often lie.

(For answers, see this module's final page.)

Hindsight bias *After* the horror of 9/11, it seemed obvious that the U.S. intelligence analysts should have taken advance warnings more seriously, that airport security should have anticipated box-cutter–wielding terrorists, that occupants of the second World Trade Center tower should have known to play it safe and leave. With 20/20 hindsight, everything seems obvious. Thus we now spend billions to protect ourselves against what the terrorists did last time.

Tim Boyle/Getty Images

behavior watchers, it would be surprising if many of psychology's findings had *not* been foreseen. Many people believe that love breeds happiness, and they are right, according to researchers who have found we have a deep "need to belong" to others. Indeed, note Daniel Gilbert, Brett Pelham, and Douglas Krull (2003), "Good ideas in psychology usually have an oddly familiar quality, and the moment we encounter them we feel certain that we once came close to thinking the same thing ourselves and simply failed to write it down."

But sometimes Grandmother's intuition has it wrong. Informed by countless casual observations, our intuition may tell us that familiarity breeds contempt, that dreams predict the future, and that emotional reactions coincide with menstrual phase. The available evidence suggests that these common-sense ideas are wrong, wrong, and wrong. Do you know which of the popular ideas in **TABLE 2.1** have been confirmed by psychology's research, and which have been refuted? Throughout this book we will see how research has both inspired and overturned popular ideas—about aging, about sleep and dreams, about personality. And we will also see how it has surprised us with discoveries about how the brain's chemical messengers control our moods and memories, about animal abilities, and about the effects of stress on our capacity to fight disease.

Overconfidence

OBJECTIVE 2-2 | Describe how overconfidence contaminates our everyday judgments.

Our everyday thinking is limited not only by our after-the-fact common sense but also by our human tendency toward overconfidence—we tend to think we know more than we do. Asked how sure we are of our answers to factual questions (Is Boston north or south of Paris?), we tend to be more confident than correct.[1]

---

[1]Boston is south of Paris.

Or consider these three anagrams, which Richard Goranson (1978) asked people to unscramble:

WREAT → WATER
ETRYN → ENTRY
GRABE → BARGE

Reflect for a moment: About how many seconds do you think it would have taken you to unscramble each of these?

Once people know the target word, hindsight makes it seem obvious—so much so that they become overconfident. They think they would have seen the solution in only 10 seconds or so, when in reality the average problem solver spends 3 minutes, as you also might, given a similar anagram without the solution: OCHSA (see this module's final page to check your answer).

Are we any better at predicting our social behavior? To find out, Robert Vallone and his associates (1990) had students predict at the beginning of the school year whether they would drop a course, vote in an upcoming election, call their parents more than twice a month, and so forth. On average, the students felt 84 percent confident in making these self-predictions. Later quizzes about their actual behavior showed their predictions were correct only 71 percent of the time. Even when they were 100 percent sure of themselves, their self-predictions erred 15 percent of the time.

It's not just collegians. For a dozen years, Ohio State University psychologist Philip Tetlock (1998) collected experts' predictions of political, economic, and military situations. In the late 1980s, for example, he invited expert professors, think-tank analysts, government experts, and journalists to project the governance of the Soviet Union or of South Africa five years later, and to rate how confident they felt. Others did the same for the future of Canada in 1992. After the five years had elapsed (and Communism had collapsed in the Soviet Union, South Africa had become a multiracial democracy, and the Canadian constitution continued), Tetlock invited the experts to recall and reflect on their predictions—which, as in laboratory studies, were far more confident than correct. Experts who had felt more than 80 percent confident were right less than 40 percent of the time.

Despite their lackluster predictions, those who erred were nearly as likely as those who got it right to convince themselves that their initial analysis was *still basically right*. I was "almost right," many of them felt. "The hardliners almost succeeded in their coup attempt against Gorbachev." "The Quebecois separatists almost won the secessionist referendum." "But for the coincidence of de Klerk and Mandela, the transition to black majority rule in South Africa would have been a lot bloodier." The overconfidence of political experts (and stock market forecasters and sports prognosticators) is therefore hard to dislodge, no matter what the outcome.

The point to remember: Hindsight bias and overconfidence often lead us to overestimate our intuition. But scientific inquiry, fed by curious skepticism and by humility, can help us sift reality from illusions.

The Scientific Attitude

OBJECTIVE 2-3 | Explain how the scientific attitude encourages critical thinking.

Underlying all science is, first, a hard-headed *curiosity,* a passion to explore and understand without misleading or being misled. Some questions (Is there life after death?) are beyond science. To answer them in any way requires a leap of faith. With many other ideas (Can some people demonstrate ESP?), the proof is in the pudding. No matter how sensible or crazy-sounding an idea, the hard-headed question is, Does it work? When put to the test, can its predictions be confirmed?

Fun anagram solutions from Wordsmith.org:
Elvis = lives
Dormitory = dirty room
Slot machines = cash lost in 'em

"We don't like their sound. Groups of guitars are on their way out."
Decca Records, in turning down a recording contract with the Beatles in 1962

"Computers in the future may weigh no more than 1.5 tons."
Popular Mechanics, 1949

"The telephone may be appropriate for our American cousins, but not here, because we have an adequate supply of messenger boys."
British expert group evaluating the invention of the telephone

"They couldn't hit an elephant at this dist—."
General John Sedgwick's last words, uttered during a U.S. Civil War battle, 1864

The amazing Randi The magician James Randi exemplifies skepticism. He has tested and debunked a variety of psychic phenomena.

This scientific approach has a long history. As ancient a figure as Moses used such an approach. How do you evaluate a self-proclaimed prophet? His answer: Put the prophet to the test. If the predicted event "does not take place or prove true," then so much the worse for the prophet (*Deuteronomy* 18:22). Magician James Randi uses Moses' approach when testing those claiming to see auras around people's bodies:

Randi:	Do you see an aura around my head?
Aura-seer:	Yes, indeed.
Randi:	Can you still see the aura if I put this magazine in front of my face?
Aura-seer:	Of course.
Randi:	Then if I were to step behind a wall barely taller than I am, you could determine my location from the aura visible above my head, right?

Randi has told me that no aura-seer has agreed to take this simple test.

When subjected to such scrutiny, crazy-sounding ideas sometimes find support. During the 1700s, scientists scoffed at the notion that meteorites had extraterrestrial origins. When two Yale scientists dared to deviate from the conventional opinion, Thomas Jefferson jeered, "Gentlemen, I would rather believe that those two Yankee Professors would lie than to believe that stones fell from heaven." Sometimes scientific inquiry refutes skeptics.

More often, science relegates crazy-sounding ideas to the mountain of forgotten claims of perpetual motion machines, miracle cancer cures, and out-of-body travels into centuries past. To sift reality from fantasy, sense from nonsense, therefore requires a scientific attitude: being skeptical but not cynical, open but not gullible.

As scientists, psychologists approach the world of behavior with a *curious skepticism.* They persistently ask two questions: What do you mean? How do you know? In business, the motto is "Show me the money." In science, it is "Show me the evidence."

Do parental behaviors determine their children's sexual orientation? Can astrologers analyze your character and predict your future based on the position of the planets at your birth? As you will see in the pages that follow, putting such claims to the test has led most psychologists to doubt them. In the arena of competing ideas, skeptical testing can reveal which ones best match the facts. "To believe with certainty," says a Polish proverb, "we must begin by doubting."

Putting a scientific attitude into practice requires not only skepticism but also *humility,* because we may have to reject our own ideas. In the last analysis, what matters is not my opinion or yours, but the truths nature reveals in response to our questioning. If people don't behave as our ideas predict, then so much the worse for our ideas. This is the humble attitude expressed in one of psychology's early mottos: "The rat is always right."

Historians of science tell us that these attitudes of curiosity, skepticism, and humility helped make modern science possible. Many of its founders, including Copernicus and Newton, were people whose religious convictions made them humble before nature and skeptical of mere human authority (Hooykaas, 1972; Merton, 1938). Today's deeply religious people sometimes view science, especially psychological science, as a threat. Yet, notes sociologist Rodney Stark (2003a,b), the scientific revolution was led mostly by deeply religious people acting on the religious idea that "in order to love and honor God, it is necessary to fully appreciate the wonders of his handiwork."

Of course, scientists, like anyone else, can have big egos and may cling to their preconceptions. We all view nature through the spectacles of our preconceived ideas. Nevertheless, the ideal that unifies psychologists with all scientists is the curious, skeptical, humble scrutiny of competing ideas. As a community, scientists check and recheck one another's findings and conclusions.

This scientific attitude prepares us to think smarter. Smart thinking, called **critical thinking,** examines assumptions, discerns hidden values, evaluates evidence, and assesses conclusions. Whether reading a news report or listening to a conversation, critical thinkers ask questions. Like scientists, they wonder, How do they know that?

What is this person's agenda? Is the conclusion based on anecdote and gut feelings, or on evidence? Does the evidence justify a cause-effect conclusion? What alternative explanations are possible? Carried to an extreme, healthy skepticism can degenerate into a negative cynicism that scorns any unproven idea. Better to have a critical attitude that produces humility—an awareness of our own vulnerability to error and an openness to surprises and new perspectives.

Has psychology's critical inquiry been open to surprising findings? The answer is plainly yes. Believe it or not . . .

- massive losses of brain tissue early in life may have minimal long-term effects.
- within days, newborns can recognize their mother's odor and voice.
- brain damage can leave a person able to learn new skills, yet be unaware of such learning.
- diverse groups—men and women, old and young, rich and working class, those with disabilities and without—report roughly comparable levels of personal happiness.
- electroconvulsive therapy (delivering an electric shock to the brain) is often a very effective treatment for severe depression.

And has critical inquiry convincingly debunked popular presumptions? The answer is again yes. The evidence indicates that . . .

- sleepwalkers are *not* acting out their dreams and sleeptalkers are *not* verbalizing their dreams.
- our past experiences are *not* all recorded verbatim in our brains; with brain stimulation or hypnosis, one *cannot* simply "play the tape" and relive long-buried or repressed memories.
- most people do *not* suffer from unrealistically low self-esteem, and high self-esteem is not all good.
- opposites do *not* generally attract.

In each of these instances and more, what has been learned is not yet what is widely believed.

The Scientific Method

OBJECTIVE 2-4 | Describe how psychological theories guide scientific research.

Psychologists arm their scientific attitude with the *scientific method:* They make observations, form theories, and then refine their theories in the light of new observations. In everyday conversation, we tend to use *theory* to mean "mere hunch." In science, however, *theory* is linked with observation. A scientific **theory** *explains* through an integrated set of principles that *organizes* and *predicts* behaviors or events. By organizing isolated facts, a theory simplifies things. There are too many facts about behavior to remember them all. By linking facts and bridging them to deeper principles, a theory offers a useful summary. When we connect the observed dots, we may discover a coherent picture.

A good theory of depression, for example, helps us organize countless observations concerning depression into a short list of principles. Imagine we observe over and over that people with depression describe their past, present, and future in gloomy terms. We might therefore theorize that low self-esteem contributes to depression. So far so good: Our self-esteem principle neatly summarizes a long list of facts about people with depression.

Yet no matter how reasonable a theory may sound—and low self-esteem seems a reasonable explanation of depression—we must put it to the test. A good theory doesn't just sound appealing. It must produce testable predictions, called **hypotheses.** By enabling us to test and reject or revise the theory, such predictions give direction to research. They specify what results would support the theory and what results would disconfirm it. To test our self-esteem theory of depression, we might assess people's self-esteem by having them indicate their agreement to statements such as "I

> " The real purpose of the scientific method is to make sure Nature hasn't misled you into thinking you know something you don't actually know."
>
> Robert M. Pirsig, *Zen and the Art of Motorcycle Maintenance,* 1974

■ **critical thinking** thinking that does not blindly accept arguments and conclusions. Rather, it examines assumptions, discerns hidden values, evaluates evidence, and assesses conclusions.

■ **theory** an explanation using an integrated set of principles that organizes and predicts observations.

■ **hypothesis** a testable prediction, often implied by a theory.

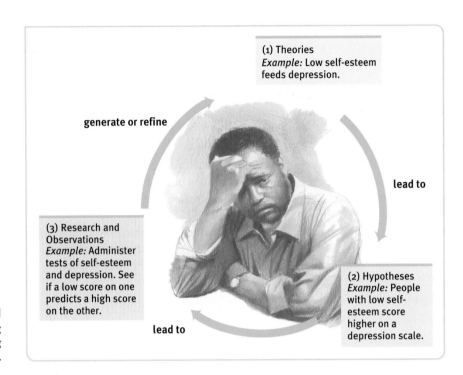

FIGURE 2.1

The scientific method A self-correcting process for asking questions and observing nature's answer.

Good theories explain by
1. organizing and linking observed facts.
2. implying hypotheses that offer testable predictions and, sometimes, practical applications.

have good ideas" and "I am fun to be with." Then we could see whether, as we hypothesized, people who report poorer self-images also score higher on a depression scale (**FIGURE 2.1**).

In testing our theory, we should be aware that it can bias subjective observations. Having theorized that depression springs from low self-esteem, we may see what we expect. We may perceive depressed people's neutral comments as self-disparaging. The urge to see what we expect is an ever-present temptation for all of us. For example, according to the bipartisan U.S. Senate Select Committee on Intelligence (2004), preconceived expectations that Iraq had weapons of mass destruction led intelligence analysts to wrongly interpret ambiguous observations as confirming that theory, and this theory-driven conclusion then led to the preemptive U.S. invasion of Iraq.

As a check on their biases, psychologists report their research—with precise **operational definitions** of concepts that allow anyone to **replicate** (repeat) their observations. If other researchers re-create a study with different participants and materials and get similar results, then our confidence in the finding's reliability grows. The first study of hindsight bias aroused psychologists' curiosity. Now, after many successful replications with differing people and questions, we feel sure of the phenomenon's power.

In the end, our theory will be useful if it (1) effectively *organizes* a range of self-reports and observations and (2) implies clear *predictions* that anyone can use to check the theory or to derive practical applications. (If we boost people's self-esteem, will their depression lift?) Eventually, our research will probably lead to a revised theory that better organizes and predicts what we know about depression.

Frequently Asked Questions About Psychology

You are now prepared to think critically about psychological matters. Yet, even knowing this much, you may still be approaching psychology with a mixture of curiosity and apprehension. So before we move ahead, let's address some frequently asked questions.

Can Laboratory Experiments Illuminate Everyday Life?

OBJECTIVE 2-5 | Explain the value of simplified laboratory conditions in discovering general principles of behavior.

When you see or hear about psychological research, do you ever wonder whether people's behavior in the lab will predict their behavior in real life? For example, does detecting the blink of a faint red light in a dark room have anything useful to say about flying a plane at night? Does our tendency to remember best the first and last items in a list of unrelated words tell us anything about why we remember the names of certain people we meet at a party? After viewing a violent, sexually explicit film, does an aroused man's increased willingness to push buttons that he thinks will electrically shock a woman really say anything about whether violent pornography makes a man more likely to abuse a woman?

Before you answer, consider: The experimenter *intends* the laboratory environment to be a simplified reality—one that simulates and controls important features of everyday life to allow focused study of one or two specific behaviors. Laboratory experiments have the advantage of allowing researchers to rule out effects from other factors. Just as an aeronautical wind tunnel enables an engineer to re-create atmospheric forces under controlled conditions, a laboratory experiment enables a psychologist to re-create psychological forces under controlled conditions.

People in the lab are not different creatures from their out-of-lab selves. For example, Cecilia Cheng (2001) observed that Hong Kong adults who coped flexibly with laboratory stresses also coped flexibly with stress in their marriages. In aggression studies, deciding whether to push a button that delivers a shock may not be the same as slapping someone in the face, but the *principle* is the same. And the experiment's purpose, notes Douglas Mook (1983), is not to re-create the exact behaviors of everyday life but to test theoretical principles. *It is the resulting principles—not the specific findings—that help explain everyday behaviors.*

When psychologists apply laboratory research on aggression to actual violence, they are applying theoretical *principles* of aggressive behavior, principles they have refined through many experiments. Similarly, it is the principles of the visual system, developed from experiments in artificial settings (such as looking at red lights in the dark), that we apply to more complex behaviors such as night flying. And many investigations show that principles derived in the laboratory *do* typically generalize to the everyday world (Anderson & others, 1999).

The point to remember: As psychologists, our concerns lie less with particular behaviors than with the general principles that help explain many behaviors.

Does Behavior Depend on One's Culture?

OBJECTIVE 2-6 | Discuss whether psychological research can be generalized across cultures and genders.

If culture shapes behavior, what can psychological studies done in one culture, often with white Europeans or North Americans, really tell us about people in general? As we will see time and again, **culture**—shared ideas and behaviors that one generation passes on to the next—matters. Our culture influences our standards of promptness and frankness, our attitudes toward premarital sex and varying body shapes, our tendency to be casual or formal, our eye contact, our conversational distance, and much, much more. Being aware of such differences, we can restrain our assumptions that others will think and act as we do. Given the growing mixing and clashing of cultures, our need for such awareness is urgent.

■ **operational definition** a statement of the procedures (operations) used to define research variables. For example, *human intelligence* may be operationally defined as what an intelligence test measures.

■ **replication** repeating the essence of a research study, usually with different participants in different situations, to see whether the basic finding extends to other participants and circumstances.

■ **culture** the enduring behaviors, ideas, attitudes, and traditions shared by a large group of people and transmitted from one generation to the next.

A cultured greeting Because culture shapes people's understanding of social behavior, actions that seem ordinary to us may seem quite odd to visitors from far away. Yet underlying these differences are powerful similarities. Supporters of newly elected leaders everywhere typically greet them with pleased deference, though not necessarily with bows and folded hands, as in India. Here influential and popular politician Sonia Gandhi greets some of her constituents shortly after her election.

Ami Vitale/Getty Images

Our shared biological heritage does, however, unite us as a universal human family. The same underlying processes guide people everywhere:

- People diagnosed with dyslexia, a reading disorder, exhibit the same brain malfunction whether they are Italian, French, or British (Paulesu & others, 2001).
- Variation in languages—spoken and gestured—may impede communication across cultures. Yet all languages share deep principles of grammar, and people from opposite hemispheres can communicate with a smile or a frown.
- People in different cultures do vary in feelings of loneliness. But across cultures, loneliness is magnified by shyness, low self-esteem, and being unmarried (Jones & others, 1985; Rokach & others, 2002).
- Most Japanese prefer their fish raw and most North Americans prefer theirs cooked. But the same principles of hunger and taste influence all of us when we sit down to a meal. We are each in certain respects like all others, like some others, and like no other. Studying people of all races and cultures helps us discern our similarities and our differences, our human kinship and our diversity.

The point to remember: Even when specific attitudes and behaviors vary across cultures, as they often do, the underlying processes are much the same.

Does Behavior Vary With Gender?

At your birth, friends and family immediately wondered which of the two human types you were: male or female. Given how important gender is to our identity and to others' perceptions of us, do we need a different psychology for women and for men?

You will see throughout this book that gender issues permeate psychology. Researchers report gender differences in what we dream, in how we express and detect emotions, and in our risk for alcoholism, depression, and eating disorders. Not only is studying such differences interesting, it also is potentially beneficial. For example, many researchers believe that women carry on conversations more readily to build relationships, while men talk more to give information and advice (Tannen, 1990). Knowing this difference can help us prevent conflicts and misunderstandings in everyday relationships.

Nevertheless, it's important to remember that psychologically as well as biologically, women and men are overwhelmingly similar. Whether female or male, we learn to walk at about the same age. We experience the same sensations of light and sound. We feel the same pangs of hunger, desire, and fear. We exhibit similar overall intelligence and well-being. We also tend to exhibit and perceive the very behaviors our culture expects of males and females.

So, gender matters. Biology determines our sex, and then culture further bends the genders. Yet in many ways female and male are similarly human.

Why Do Psychologists Study Animals?

OBJECTIVE 2-7 | Explain why psychologists study animals, and discuss the ethics of experimentation with both animals and humans.

Many psychologists study animals because they find them fascinating. They want to understand how different species learn, think, and behave. Psychologists also study animals to learn about people, by doing experiments that are permissible only with animals. Human physiology resembles that of many other animals. We humans are not *like* animals; we *are* animals. Animal experiments have therefore led to treatments for human diseases—insulin for diabetes, vaccines to prevent polio and rabies, transplants to replace defective organs.

Likewise, the same processes by which humans see, exhibit emotion, and become obese are present in rats and monkeys. To discover more about the basics of human learning, researchers even study sea slugs. To understand how a combustion engine

"All people are the same; only their habits differ."

Confucius, 551–479 B.C.

"Rats are very similar to humans except that they are not stupid enough to purchase lottery tickets."

Dave Barry, July 2, 2002

Animal research benefiting animals Thanks partly to research on the benefits of novelty, control, and stimulation, these Bronx Zoo gorillas are enjoying improved quality of life.

works, you would do better to study a lawn mower's engine than a Mercedes'. Like Mercedes engines, humans are complex. But the simplicity of the sea slug's nervous system is precisely what makes it so revealing of the neural mechanisms of learning.

Is It Ethical to Experiment on Animals?

If we share important similarities with other animals, then should we not respect them? "We cannot defend our scientific work with animals on the basis of the similarities between them and ourselves and then defend it morally on the basis of differences," noted Roger Ulrich (1991). The animal protection movement protests the use of animals in psychological, biological, and medical research. Researchers remind us that the world's 30 million mammals used each year in research are but a fraction of 1 percent of the billions of animals killed annually for food (which means the average person eats 20 animals a year). While researchers each year conduct experiments on some 200,000 dogs and cats cared for under humane regulations, humane animal shelters are forced to kill 50 times that many (Goodwin & Morrison, 1999).

Animal protection organizations, such as Psychologists for the Ethical Treatment of Animals, advocate naturalistic observation of animals rather than laboratory manipulation. Animal researchers have responded that the issue is not the morality of good versus evil but of compassion for animals versus compassion for people. How many of us would have attacked Pasteur's experiments with rabies, which caused some dogs to suffer but led to a vaccine that spared millions of people (and dogs) from agonizing death? And would we really wish to have deprived ourselves of the animal research that led to effective methods of training children with mental disorders; of understanding aging; of relieving fears and depression; and of controlling obesity, alcoholism, and stress-related pain and disease? The answers to such questions vary by culture. In Gallup surveys in Canada and the United States, about 6 in 10 adults deem medical testing on animals "morally acceptable." In Britain, only 37 percent do (Mason, 2003).

Out of this heated debate, two issues emerge. The basic one is whether it is right to place the well-being of humans above that of animals. In experiments on stress and cancer, is it right that mice get tumors in hopes that people might not? Should some monkeys be exposed to an HIV-like virus in the search for an AIDS vaccine? Is our use of other animals as natural as the behavior of carnivorous hawks, cats, and whales? Defenders of research on animals argue that anyone who has eaten a hamburger, worn leather shoes, tolerated hunting and fishing, or supported the extermination of crop-destroying or plague-carrying pests has already agreed that, yes, it is sometimes permissible to sacrifice animals for the sake of human well-being.

Scott Plous (1993) notes, however, that our compassion for animals varies, as does our compassion for people—based on their perceived similarity to us. We feel more attraction, give more help, and act less aggressively toward similar others. Likewise,

> "I believe that to prevent, cripple, or needlessly complicate the research that can relieve animal and human suffering is profoundly inhuman, cruel, and immoral."
> Psychologist Neal Miller, 1983

> "Please do not forget those of us who suffer from incurable diseases or disabilities who hope for a cure through research that requires the use of animals."
> Psychologist Dennis Feeney (1987)

we value animals according to their perceived kinship with us. Thus, primates and companion pets get top priority. (Western people raise or trap mink and foxes for their fur, but not dogs or cats.) Other mammals occupy the second rung on the privilege ladder, followed by birds, fish, and reptiles on the third rung, with insects at the bottom. In deciding which animals have rights, we each draw our own cut-off line somewhere across the animal kingdom.

If we give human life first priority, the second issue is the priority we give to the well-being of animals in research. What safeguards should protect them? Most researchers today feel ethically obligated to enhance the well-being of captive animals and protect them from needless suffering. In one survey of animal researchers, 98 percent or more supported government regulations protecting primates, dogs, and cats, and 74 percent supported regulations providing for the humane care of rats and mice (Plous & Herzog, 2000). Many professional associations and funding agencies now have guidelines for the humane use of animals. For example, British Psychological Society guidelines call for housing animals under reasonably natural living conditions, with companions for social animals (Lea, 2000). American Psychological Association (2002) guidelines mandate ensuring the "comfort, health, and humane treatment" of animals, and of minimizing "infection, illness, and pain of animal subjects." Humane care also leads to more effective science, because pain and stress would distort the animals' behavior during experiments.

Animals have themselves benefited from animal research. One Ohio team of research psychologists measured stress hormone levels in samples of millions of dogs brought each year to animal shelters, and they devised methods of handling and stroking them that reduced stress and eased their transition to adoptive homes (Tuber & others, 1999). Thanks to animal behavior studies, formerly idle Bronx Zoo animals are now staving off listless boredom by working for their supper, as would their counterparts in the wild (Stewart, 2002). Other studies have helped improve care and management in animals' natural habitats. By revealing our behavioral kinship with animals and the remarkable intelligence of chimpanzees, gorillas, and other animals, experiments have also led to increased empathy and protection for them. At its best, a psychology concerned for humans and sensitive to animals serves the welfare of both.

Is It Ethical to Experiment on People?

If the image of animals or people receiving supposed electric shocks troubles you, you may be relieved to know that most psychological research involves no such stress. With people, blinking lights, flashing words, and pleasant social interactions are more common.

Occasionally, though, researchers do temporarily stress or deceive people, but only when they believe it is essential to a justifiable end, such as understanding and controlling violent behavior or studying mood swings. Such experiments wouldn't work if the participants knew all there was to know about the experiment beforehand. Either the procedures would be ineffective or the participants, wanting to be helpful, might try to confirm the researchers' predictions.

Ethical principles developed by the American Psychological Association (1992) and the British Psychological Society (1993) urge investigators to (1) obtain the informed consent of potential participants, (2) protect them from harm and discomfort, (3) treat information about individual participants confidentially, and (4) fully explain the research afterward. Moreover, most universities today screen research proposals through an ethics committee that safeguards the well-being of every participant.

Much research, however, occurs outside of university laboratories, in places where there may be no ethics committees. For example, retail stores routinely survey people, photograph their purchasing behavior, track their buying patterns, and test the effectiveness of advertising. Curiously, such research attracts less attention than the scientific research done to advance human understanding.

> "The righteous know the needs of their animals."
>
> Proverbs 12:10

> "The greatness of a nation can be judged by the way its animals are treated."
>
> Mahatma Gandhi, 1869–1948

Is Psychology Free of Value Judgments?

OBJECTIVE 2-8 | Describe how personal values can influence psychologists' research and its application, and discuss psychology's potential to manipulate people.

Psychology is definitely not value-free. Values affect what we study, how we study it, and how we interpret results. Consider: Researchers' values influence their choice of research topics—whether to study worker productivity or worker morale, sex discrimi- nation or gender differences, con- formity or independence. Values can also color "the facts." As we noted earlier, our preconceptions can bias our observations and in- terpretations; sometimes we see what we want or expect to see (FIGURE 2.2).

Even the words we use to de- scribe a phenomenon can reflect our values. Labeling the sex acts we do not practice as "perver- sions" or as "sexual variations" conveys a value judgment. The same holds true in everyday speech, when one per- son's "rigidity" is another's "consistency," or one person's "faith" is another's "fa- naticism." Our labeling someone as "firm" or "stubborn," "careful" or "picky," "discreet" or "secretive" reveals our feelings. Both in and out of psychology, labels describe and labels evaluate.

Popular applications of psychology also contain hidden values. If you defer to "professional" guidance about how to live—how to raise children, how to achieve self- fulfillment, what to do with sexual feelings, how to get ahead at work—you are ac- cepting value-laden advice. A science of behavior and mental processes can certainly help us reach our goals, but it cannot decide what those goals should be. (See Think- ing Critically About Desegregation and the Death Penalty, on the next page.)

FIGURE 2.2

What do you see? People interpret ambiguous information to fit their precon- ceptions. Did you see a duck or a rabbit? Before showing some friends this image, ask them if they can see the duck lying on its back (or the bunny in the grass). (From Shepard, 1990.)

"It is doubtless impossible to approach any human problem with a mind free from bias."

Simone de Beauvoir, *The Second Sex*, 1953

Is Psychology Potentially Dangerous?

If some people see psychology as merely common sense, others have a different con- cern—that it is becoming dangerously powerful. Is it an accident that astronomy is the oldest science and psychology the youngest? Exploring the external universe is one thing, but exploring our own inner universe seems more dangerous and threat- ening. Might psychology be used to manipulate people?

Knowledge, like all power, can be used for good or evil. Nuclear power has been used to light up cities—and to demolish them. Persuasive power has been used to ed- ucate people—and to deceive them. The power of mind-altering drugs has been used to restore sanity—and to destroy it.

Although psychology does indeed have the power to deceive, its purpose is to en- lighten. Every day, psychologists are exploring ways to enhance learning, creativity, and compassion. Psychology also speaks to many of our world's great problems—war, overpopulation, prejudice, family dysfunction, crime—all of which involve attitudes and behaviors. And psychology speaks to our deepest longings—for nourishment, for love, for happiness. True, psychology cannot address all of life's great questions, but it speaks to some mighty important ones.

DESEGREGATION AND THE DEATH PENALTY— WHEN BELIEFS COLLIDE WITH PSYCHOLOGICAL SCIENCE

An influential modern viewpoint, ironically called *postmodernism*, questions scientific objectivity. Rather than mirroring the real world, say postmodernists, scientific concepts are socially constructed fictions. Like all knowledge, they reflect the culture that formed them. "Intelligence," for instance, is a concept psychologists created and defined. Because personal values guide theory and research, "truth" is said to be personal and subjective. (What behaviors shall we call "intelligent"?) In our quest for truth, we cannot help following our hunches, our biases, our cultural bent.

Psychological scientists agree that many important questions lie beyond the reach of science. And they agree that personal beliefs often shape perceptions. But they also believe that there is a real world out there, and that we advance truth by checking our hunches against it. Marie Curie did not just construct the concept of radium, she *discovered* radium. It really exists. In the behavioral sciences, pure objectivity, like pure love, may be unattainable. Yet most would argue that it is better to humble ourselves before reliable evidence than to cling to untested presumptions.

Humbling itself before the evidence is what the U.S. Supreme Court did in making its historic 1954 decision declaring segregated schools unconstitutional. This was the Court's first case in which social psychologists participated actively. They did so as expert witnesses and as authors, led by Kenneth Clark (1952), of an influential social science brief that formed part of the case presented. The Court found it noteworthy that when Kenneth Clark and Mamie Phipps Clark

Psychologists Mamie Phipps Clark and Kenneth B. Clark
Their work was cited in the historic U.S. Supreme Court school desegregation decision in 1954.

Office of Public Affairs at Columbia University

(1947) gave African-American children a choice between Black dolls and White dolls, most chose the White, which suggested that under segregation Black children were internalizing anti-Black prejudice.

This social science success inspired hundreds more studies that researchers hoped would inform future judicial decisions. More recently, however, the Court has joined postmodernists in discounting behavioral science research. In deciding whether the death penalty falls under the Constitution's ban on "cruel and unusual punishment," the Court wrestled with whether society defines execution as cruel and unusual, whether courts inflict the penalty arbitrarily, whether they apply it with racial bias, and whether execution deters crime more than all other available punishments. The behavioral science answers to each of these questions, note psychologists Mark Costanzo (1997) and Craig Haney and Deana

Logan (1994), could hardly be clearer. And yet, on two of these issues—the fairness of the death penalty and its effectiveness—the Court has disregarded social science research.

Is the death penalty applied fairly? Studies show that those eligible to serve as jurors in capital punishment cases—namely, those who accept the death penalty—do not represent the greater population. Compared with people excluded by virtue of their qualms about capital punishment, those chosen as jurors are less likely to be minorities and women. They are also more likely to believe the prosecution's arguments, and they are more conviction-prone.

Does the death penalty work—does it deter crime? The evidence is consistent: States with a death penalty do not have lower homicide rates. After instituting the death penalty, these states did not see their rates drop. And homicide has not risen in states that have abandoned the death penalty. A person committing a crime of passion doesn't pause to calculate the consequences (and, if she or he did, would likely consider life in a prison cell an ample deterrent). Yet the Court persists in its belief that "the death penalty undoubtedly is a significant deterrent."

Beliefs guide perceptions. And that, say psychological scientists responding to postmodernists, is why we *need* to think smarter—to restrain our hunches, our biases, and our cultural leanings by checking them against available evidence. Why not put our testable beliefs to the test? If they find support, so much the better for them. If they collide against a wall of observation, so much the worse for them. These ideals of skeptical scrutiny and humility fuel all scientific endeavor.

Thinking Critically With Psychological Science

OBJECTIVE 2-1 | Describe *hindsight bias*, and explain how it can make research findings seem like mere common sense.

Hindsight bias (also called the *I-knew-it-all-along phenomenon*) is the tendency to believe, after learning an outcome, that we would have foreseen it. Thus, learning the outcome of a study can make it seem like obvious common sense. Scientific inquiry and critical thinking can help us overcome this tendency to overestimate our unaided intuition.

OBJECTIVE 2-2 | Describe how overconfidence contaminates our everyday judgments.

We are routinely *overconfident* of our judgments, thanks partly to our bias to seek information that confirms them. Science, with its procedures for gathering and sifting evidence, restrains error by taking us beyond the limits of our intuition and common sense.

OBJECTIVE 2-3 | Explain how the scientific attitude encourages critical thinking.

Although limited by the testable questions it can address, a scientific approach helps us sift reality from illusion. Scientific inquiry begins with an attitude—a curious eagerness to *skeptically* scrutinize competing ideas and an open-minded *humility* before nature. This attitude carries into everyday life as *critical thinking,* which examines assumptions, discerns hidden values, evaluates evidence, and assesses outcomes. Putting ideas, even crazy-sounding ideas, to the test helps us winnow sense from nonsense.

OBJECTIVE 2-4 | Describe how psychological theories guide scientific research.

Psychological *theories* organize *observations* and imply predictive *hypotheses.* After constructing precise operational definitions of their procedures, researchers test their hypotheses (predictions), validate and refine the theory, and, sometimes, suggest practical applications. If other researchers can replicate the study with similar results, we can then place greater confidence in the conclusion.

OBJECTIVE 2-5 | Explain the value of simplified laboratory conditions in discovering general principles of behavior.

Researchers test theoretical principles by creating a controlled, simplified environment in the lab. Their concern is not the particular behavior being studied, but rather the underlying principles that help explain many behaviors.

OBJECTIVE 2-6 | Discuss whether psychological research can be generalized across cultures and genders.

Behaviors, ideas, attitudes, and traditions vary across cultures, but the principles that underlie them are shared, in part because of our common biological heritage. Biology also determines our sex, but our culture sets up expectations about what it means to be male or female. Males and females do differ in some ways, but they are biologically and psychologically much more alike than different.

OBJECTIVE 2-7 | Explain why psychologists study animals, and discuss the ethics of experimentation with both animals and humans.

Some psychologists study animals out of an interest in animal behavior. Others do so because knowledge of other animals' physiological and psychological processes helps them understand similar human processes.

Under ethical and legal guidelines, animals used in psychological experiments rarely experience pain. Nevertheless, animal rights groups raise an important issue: Even if it leads to the relief of human suffering, is an animal's temporary suffering justified?

Occasionally researchers temporarily stress or deceive people to learn something important. Professional ethical standards, enforced by university ethics committees, safeguard research participants' well-being.

OBJECTIVE 2-8 | Describe how personal values can influence psychologists' research and its application, and discuss psychology's potential to manipulate people.

Psychologists' own values influence their choice of research topics, their theories and observations, their labels for behavior, and their professional advice. Psychology has the power to deceive, but so far, applications of psychology's principles have been overwhelmingly for the good. Psychology can help us reach our goals, but it cannot decide what those goals should be.

TERMS AND CONCEPTS TO REMEMBER

hindsight bias, p. 2-1
critical thinking, p. 2-4
theory, p. 2-5
hypothesis, p.2-5

operational definition, p. 2-6
replication, p. 2-6
culture, p. 2-7

TEST YOURSELF

1. What is the scientific attitude, and why is it important for critical thinking?

2. How are human and animal research subjects protected?

(Answers in Appendix B.)

ASK YOURSELF

1. How might the scientific method help us understand the roots of terrorism?

2. Were any of the Frequently Asked Questions your questions? Do you have other questions or concerns about psychology?

ANSWERS TO QUESTIONS WITHIN THE MODULE

Q. Which of the popular ideas in Table 2.1 have been confirmed or refuted by psychological research?

A. The odd-numbered statements have been refuted. The even-numbered statements have been confirmed.

Q. Roughly how thick would a sheet of paper be if you folded it on itself 100 times?

A. Given a 0.1-millimeter-thick sheet, the thickness after 100 folds would be 800 trillion times the distance between the Earth and the Sun (Gilovich, 1991).

Q. If a rope were placed around the Earth at the equator, how much additional rope would be needed for the rope to be 1 foot above the Earth all the way around?

A. About 6 more feet of rope. The circumference of a circle, or of the Earth, is $2\pi r$. The circumference of a rope elevated one foot is $2\pi(r + 1)$. Thus the added length is $2\pi(r + 1) - 2\pi r = 2\pi$, or about 6 feet.

Q. Can you unscramble this anagram? OCHSA.

A. Did you figure it out? The answer is CHAOS.

>WEB

Multiple-choice **self-tests** and more may be found at www.worthpublishers.com/myers.

MODULE

3

Description

Correlation

Experimentation

Statistical Reasoning

Research Strategies: How Psychologists Ask and Answer Questions

Description

The starting point of any science is description. In everyday life, all of us observe and describe people, often drawing conclusions about why they behave as they do. Professional psychologists do much the same, though more objectively and systematically.

The Case Study

OBJECTIVE 3-1 | Identify an advantage and a disadvantage of using case studies to study behavior.

Among the oldest research methods is the **case study,** in which psychologists study one individual in great depth in the hope of revealing things true of us all. Some examples: Much of our early knowledge about the brain came from case studies of individuals who suffered a particular impairment after damage to a certain brain region. Jean Piaget taught us about children's thinking after carefully observing and questioning but a few children. Studies of only a few chimpanzees have revealed their capacity for understanding and language. Intensive case studies are sometimes very revealing.

Case studies can suggest hypotheses for further study. They also show us what *can* happen. In everyday life, however, individual cases sometimes mislead us: An individual may be atypical. Unrepresentative information can lead to mistaken judgments and false conclusions. Indeed, anytime a researcher mentions a finding ("Smokers die younger: 95 percent of men over 85 are nonsmokers") someone is sure to offer a contradictory case ("Well, I have an uncle who smoked two packs a day and lived to be 89"). Anecdotal cases—dramatic stories, personal experiences, even psychological case examples—have a way of overwhelming general truths. Highly publicized school shootings can raise alarm about school violence even while school violence rates are subsiding. Numbers can be numbing (in one study [Murray & Wheeler, 1937] of 1300 dream reports concerning a kidnapped child, only 5 percent correctly envisioned the child as dead). Anecdotes are often more startling. ("But I know a man who dreamed his sister was in a car accident, and two days later she was.") As psychologist Gordon Allport (1954, p. 9) said, "Given a thimbleful of [dramatic] facts we rush to make generalizations as large as a tub."

The point to remember: Individual cases can suggest fruitful ideas. What's true of all of us can be glimpsed in any one of us. But to discern the general truths that cover individual cases, we must answer questions with other methods.

> 'Well my dear,' said Miss Marple, 'human nature is very much the same everywhere, and of course, one has opportunities of observing it at closer quarters in a village.'"
>
> Agatha Christie, *The Tuesday Club Murders*, 1933

The case of the conversational chimpanzee In intensive case studies of chimpanzees, psychologists have explored the intriguing question of whether language is uniquely human. Here Nim Chimpsky signs *hug* as his trainer, psychologist Herbert Terrace, shows him the puppet Ernie. But is Nim really capable of using language? Cognitive theorists continue to debate that issue.

Susan Kuklin/Photo Researchers

The Survey

OBJECTIVE 3-2 | Identify the advantages and disadvantages of using surveys to study behavior and mental processes, and explain the importance of wording effects and random sampling.

The **survey** method looks at many cases in less depth. A survey asks people to report their behavior or opinions. Questions about everything from sexual practices to political opinions get put to the public. It's hard to think of a significant question that survey researchers have not asked. For example, Harris and Gallup polls have revealed that 72 percent of Americans think there is too much TV violence, 84 percent favor equal job opportunities for homosexual people, 89 percent say they face high stress, 95 percent believe in God, and 96 percent would like to change something about their appearance. In Britain, seven in ten 18- to 29-year-olds support gay marriage; among those over 50, about the same percentage oppose it (a generation gap found in many Western countries). But asking questions is tricky, and the answers may well depend on your wording and your choice of respondents.

Wording Effects

Even subtle changes in the order or wording of questions can have major effects. Should cigarette ads or pornography be allowed on television? People are much more likely to approve "not allowing" such things than "forbidding" or "censoring" them. In one national survey, only 27 percent of Americans approved of "government censorship" of media sex and violence, though 66 percent approved of "more restrictions on what is shown on television" (Lacayo, 1995). People are similarly much more approving of "aid to the needy" than of "welfare," of "affirmative action" than of "preferential treatment," and of "revenue enhancers" than of "taxes." Because wording is such a delicate matter, critical thinkers will reflect on how the phrasing of a question might have affected the opinions respondents expressed.

Random Sampling

In our everyday experience we spend most of our time with a biased sample of people—mostly those who share our attitudes and habits. Thus, when we wonder how many people hold a particular belief, those who think as we do come to mind most readily. This tendency to overestimate others' agreement with us is the **false consensus effect** (Ross & others, 1977). Vegetarians will think more people are vegetarians than will meat-eaters, and conservatives will perceive more support for conservative views than will liberals.

You can describe human experience using your estimates of others, perhaps supplemented by dramatic anecdotes and personal experience. But for an accurate picture of the experiences and attitudes of a whole population, there's only one game in town—the representative sample.

We can extend this point to everyday thinking, as we generalize from samples we observe, especially vivid cases. Given (a) a statistical summary of a professor's student evaluations and (b) the vivid comments of two irate students, an administrator's impression of the professor may be influenced as much by the two unhappy students as by the many favorable evaluations in the statistical summary. Standing in the checkout line at the supermarket, George sees the woman in front of him pay with government-provided food stamps and then watches with dismay as she drives away in a fancy car. In both situations, the temptation to generalize from a few vivid but unrepresentative cases is nearly irresistible.

The point to remember: The best basis for generalizing is from a representative sample of cases.

If you wish to survey the students at your college or university, how could you survey a representative sample of the total student **population**—the whole group you want to study and describe? Typically, you would choose a **random sample,** one in which every person in the entire group has an equal chance of participating.

■ **case study** an observation technique in which one person is studied in depth in the hope of revealing universal principles.

■ **survey** a technique for ascertaining the self-reported attitudes or behaviors of people, usually by questioning a representative, random sample of them.

■ **false consensus effect** the tendency to overestimate the extent to which others share our beliefs and behaviors.

■ **population** all the cases in a group, from which samples may be drawn for a study. (*Note:* Except for national studies, this does *not* refer to a country's whole population.)

■ **random sample** a sample that fairly represents a population because each member has an equal chance of inclusion.

This Modern World by Tom Tomorrow © 1991.

With very large samples, estimates become quite reliable. *E* is estimated to represent 12.7 percent of the letters in written English. *E*, in fact, is 12.3 percent of the 925,141 letters in Melville's *Moby Dick*, 12.4 percent of the 586,747 letters in Dickens' *A Tale of Two Cities*, and 12.1 percent of the 3,901,021 letters in 12 of Mark Twain's works (*Chance News*, 1997).

To sample the students randomly, you would *not* send each of them a questionnaire. (The conscientious people who return it would not be a random sample.) Rather, you would aim for a representative sample by, say, using a table of random numbers to pick participants from a student listing and then making sure you involve as many as possible. Large representative samples are better than small ones, but a small representative sample of 100 is better than an unrepresentative sample of 500.

The point to remember: Before believing survey findings, think critically: Consider the sample. You cannot compensate for an unrepresentative sample by simply adding more people.

The random-sampling principle also works in national surveys. Imagine that you had a giant barrel containing 60 million white beans mixed with 40 million red beans. A scoop that randomly sampled 1500 of them would contain about 60 percent white and 40 percent red beans, give or take 2 or 3 percent. Sampling voters in a national election survey is like sampling the beans; 1500 randomly sampled people, drawn from all areas of a country, provide a remarkably accurate snapshot of the opinions of a nation. Without random sampling, large samples—including call-in phone samples and TV Web site polls—often merely give misleading results.

Naturalistic Observation

OBJECTIVE 3-3 | Identify an advantage and a disadvantage of using naturalistic observation to study behavior.

A third descriptive research method involves watching and recording the behavior of organisms in their natural environment. These **naturalistic observations** range from watching chimpanzee societies in the jungle, to unobtrusively videotaping (and later systematically analyzing) parent-child interactions in different cultures, to recording students' self-seating patterns in the lunchrooms of multiracial schools.

Naturalistic observation
For more than 20 years, psychologist Gilda Morelli has lived among and observed the Efe people of Central Africa, including the man and baby shown here, studying paternal and maternal care and observing children's development.

Courtesy of Gilda Morelli

Like the case study and survey methods, naturalistic observation does not *explain* behavior. It *describes* it. Nevertheless, descriptions can be revealing. We once thought, for example, that only humans use tools. Then naturalistic observation revealed that chimpanzees sometimes insert a stick in a termite mound and withdraw it, eating the stick's load of termites. Such unobtrusive naturalistic observations, recalls chimpanzee observer Jane Goodall (1998), paved the way for later studies of animal thinking, language, and emotion: "Observations, made in the natural habitat, helped to show that the societies and behavior of animals are far more complex than previously supposed," thus expanding our understanding of our fellow animals. We later learned that chimps and baboons also use deception to achieve their aims. Psychologists Andrew Whiten and Richard Byrne (1988) repeatedly saw one young baboon pretending to have been attacked by another as a tactic to get its mother to drive the other baboon away from its food.

Naturalistic observations are also done with humans. Here are three examples I think you will enjoy.

- *A funny finding.* We humans laugh 30 times more often in social situations than in solitary situations. (Have you noticed how seldom you laugh when alone?) When we do laugh, 17 muscles contort our mouth and squeeze our eyes, and we emit a series of 75-millisecond vowel-like sounds that are spaced about one-fifth of a second apart (Provine, 2001).

- *Sounding out students.* What, really, are introductory psychology students saying and doing during their everyday lives? To find out, Matthias Mehl and James Pennebaker (2003) equipped 52 such University of Texas students with a belt-worn tape recorder that, for up to four days, captured 30 seconds of their waking hours every 12.5 minutes—thus enabling the researchers to eavesdrop on more than 10,000 half-minute life slices. On what percentage of the slices do you suppose they found the students talking with someone? What percentage captured the students at a computer keyboard? The answers: 28 and 9 percent, respectively. (What percentage of *your* waking hours are spent in these activities?)

- *Culture, climate, and the pace of life.* Naturalistic observation also enabled Robert Levine and Ara Norenzayan (1999) to compare the pace of life in 31 countries. By operationally defining *pace of life* as walking speed, the speed with which postal clerks completed a simple request, and the accuracy of public clocks, they concluded that life is fastest paced in Japan and Western Europe, and slower paced in economically less-developed countries. People in colder climates also tend to live at a faster pace (and are more prone to die from heart disease). Naturalistic observation describes behavior more than it explains it. But this study illustrates how naturalistic observation can also be used with correlational research, our next topic.

"How would you like me to answer that question? As a member of my ethnic group, educational class, income group, or religious category?"

■ **naturalistic observation** observing and recording behavior in naturally occurring situations without trying to manipulate and control the situation.

■ **correlation** a measure of the extent to which two factors vary together, and thus of how well either factor predicts the other. The *correlation coefficient* is the mathematical expression of the relationship, ranging from –1 to +1.

■ **scatterplot** a graphed cluster of dots, each of which represents the values of two variables. The slope of the points suggests the direction of the relationship between the two variables. The amount of scatter suggests the strength of the correlation (little scatter indicates high correlation). (Also called a *scattergram* or *scatter diagram*.)

Correlation

OBJECTIVE 3-4 | Describe positive and negative correlations, and explain how correlational measures can aid the process of prediction.

Describing behavior is a first step toward predicting it. When surveys and naturalistic observations reveal that one trait or behavior accompanies another, we say the two **correlate.** The *correlation coefficient* is a statistical measure of a relationship (FIGURE **3.1**): It reveals how closely two things vary together and thus how well either one *predicts* the other. Knowing how much aptitude test scores *correlate* with school success tells us how well the scores *predict* school success.

Throughout this book we will often ask how strongly two things are related: For example, how closely related are the personality scores of identical twins? How well do intelligence test scores predict achievement? How closely is stress related to disease?

FIGURE 3.2 on the next page illustrates perfect positive and negative correlations, which rarely occur in the "real world." These graphs are called **scatterplots,** because each point *plots* the value of two variables. A positive correlation means that two sets of scores, such as height and weight, tend to rise or fall together. A correlation's being negative has nothing to do with its strength or weakness; a negative correlation means two things relate inversely (one set of scores goes up as the other goes down). As toothbrushing goes up from zero, tooth decay goes down; brushing and decay correlate (negatively). A weak correlation, indicating little or no relationship, has a coefficient near zero.

FIGURE 3.1
How to read a correlation coefficient

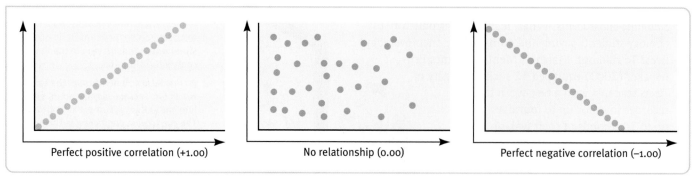

Perfect positive correlation (+1.00)   No relationship (0.00)   Perfect negative correlation (−1.00)

FIGURE 3.2

Scatterplots, showing patterns of correlation Correlations can range from +1.00 (scores on one measure increase in direct proportion to scores on another) to −1.00 (scores on one measure decrease precisely as scores rise on the other).

Here are some recent news reports of correlational research. Can you spot which are reporting positive correlations, which negative?

- The more TV is on in the homes of young children, the less time they spend reading (Kaiser, 2003).
- The more sexual content teens see on TV, the more likely they are to have sex (Collins & others, 2004).
- The longer children are breast-fed, the greater their later academic achievement (Horwood & Fergusson, 1998).
- The more income rose among a sample of poor families, the fewer psychiatric symptoms their children experienced (Costello & others, 2003).

(These are negative, positive, positive, and negative correlations, respectively.)

Statistics can help us see what the naked eye sometimes misses. To demonstrate this for yourself, try an imaginary project. Wondering if tall men are more or less easygoing, you collect two sets of scores: men's heights and men's temperaments. You measure the heights of 20 men, and have someone else independently assess their temperaments (from zero for extremely calm to 100 for highly reactive).

With all the relevant data (**TABLE 3.1**) right in front of you, can you tell whether there is (1) a positive correlation between height and reactive temperament, (2) very little or no correlation, or (3) a negative correlation?

Comparing the columns in Table 3.1, most people detect very little relationship between height and temperament. In fact, the correlation in this imaginary example is moderately positive, +0.63, as we can see if we display the data as a scatterplot. In **FIGURE 3.3**, moving from left to right, the upward, oval-shaped slope of the cluster of points shows that our two imaginary sets of scores (height and reactivity) tend to rise together.

If we fail to see a relationship when data are presented as systematically as in Table 3.1, how much less likely are we to notice them in everyday life? To see what is right in front of us, we sometimes need statistical illumination. We can easily see evidence of gender discrimination when given statistically summarized information about job level, seniority, performance, gender, and salary. But we often see no discrimination when the same information dribbles in, case by case (Twiss & others, 1989).

Though informative, psychology's correlations usually leave most of the variation among individuals unpredicted. For example, research shows there is a correlation between parents' abusiveness and their children's later abusiveness when they become parents. But this does not mean that most abused children become abusive. The correlation simply indicates a statistical relationship: Although most abused children do not grow into abusers, nonabused children are even less likely to become abusive.

The point to remember: A correlation coefficient helps us see the world more clearly by revealing the extent to which two things relate.

TABLE 3.1

HEIGHT AND TEMPERAMENT OF 20 MEN

Height	Height in Inches	Temperament
1	80	75
2	63	66
3	61	60
4	79	90
5	74	60
6	69	42
7	62	42
8	75	60
9	77	81
10	60	39
11	64	48
12	76	69
13	71	72
14	66	57
15	73	63
16	70	75
17	63	30
18	71	57
19	68	84
20	70	39

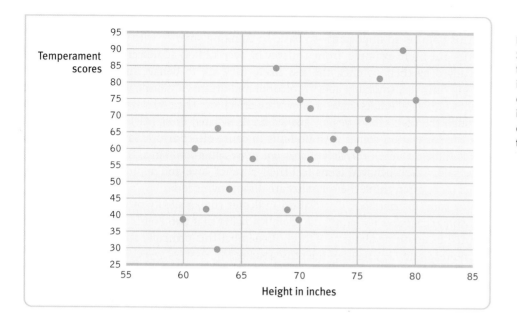

FIGURE **3.3**
Scatterplot for height and temperament This display of data from 20 imagined people (each represented by a data point) reveals an upward slope, indicating a positive correlation. The considerable scatter of the data indicates the correlation is much lower than +1.0.

Correlation and Causation

OBJECTIVE 3-5 | Explain why correlational research fails to provide evidence of cause-effect relationships.

Correlations help us predict, and they restrain the illusions of our flawed intuition. Watching violence correlates with (and therefore predicts) aggression. But does that mean it *causes* aggression? Does low self-esteem *cause* depression? If, based on the correlational evidence, you assume that they do, you have much company. A nearly irresistible thinking error is assuming that correlation proves causation. But no matter how strong the relationship, it does not!

For example, what about the negative correlation between self-esteem and depression? Perhaps low self-esteem does cause depression. But as **FIGURE 3.4** suggests, we'd get the same correlation between low self-esteem and depression if depression caused people to be down on themselves, or if something else—a third factor such as heredity or brain chemistry—caused both low self-esteem and depression. Among men, length of marriage correlates positively with hair loss—because both are associated with a third factor, age. And people who wear hats are *more* likely to suffer skin cancer—because both are associated with fair-skinned people (who are vulnerable to skin cancer and more likely to wear protective hats).

Correlation need not mean causation Length of marriage correlates with hair loss in men. Does this mean that marriage causes men to lose their hair (or that balding men make better husbands)? In this case, as in many others, a third factor obviously explains the correlation: Golden anniversaries and baldness both accompany aging.

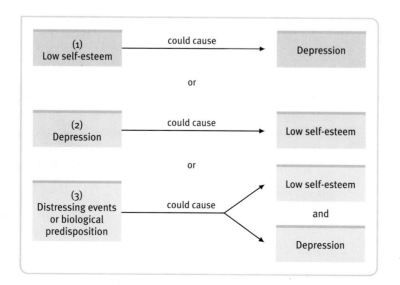

FIGURE **3.4**
Three possible cause-effect relationships People low in self-esteem are more likely to report depression than are those high in self-esteem. One possible explanation of this negative correlation is that a bad self-image causes depressed feelings. But, as the diagram indicates, other cause-effect relationships are possible.

This point is so important—so basic to thinking smarter with psychology—that it merits one more example, from a survey of over 12,000 adolescents: The more teens feel loved by their parents, the less likely they are to behave in unhealthy ways—having early sex, smoking, abusing alcohol and drugs, exhibiting violence (Resnick & others, 1997). "Adults have a powerful effect on their children's behavior right through the high school years," gushed an Associated Press (AP) story on the study. But the correlation comes with no built-in cause-effect arrow. Said differently (turn the volume up here), *correlation does not prove causation.* Thus, the AP could as well have said, "Well-behaved teens feel their parents' love and approval; out-of-bounds teens more often think their parents are disapproving jerks."

The point to remember: Correlation indicates the *possibility* of a cause-effect relationship, *but it does not prove causation.* Knowing that two events are correlated need not tell us anything about causation. Remember this principle and you will be wiser as you read and hear news of scientific studies.

Illusory Correlations

OBJECTIVE 3-6 | Describe how people form illusory correlations.

Correlations make visible the relationships we might otherwise miss. They also restrain our "seeing" relationships that actually do not exist. A perceived nonexistent correlation is an **illusory correlation.** When we *believe* there is a relationship between two things, we are likely to *notice* and *recall* instances that confirm our belief (Trolier & Hamilton, 1986).

Illusory correlations help explain many a superstitious belief, such as the presumption that more babies are born when the moon is full or that infertile couples who adopt become more likely to conceive (Gilovich, 1991). Those who conceive after adopting capture our attention. We're less likely to notice those who adopt and never conceive, or those who conceive without adopting. In other words, illusory correlations occur when we over-rely on the top left cell of **FIGURE 3.5**, ignoring equally essential information in the other cells.

Such illusory thinking helps explain why for so many years people believed (and many still do) that sugar made children hyperactive, that getting cold and wet caused one to catch a cold, and that weather changes trigger arthritis pain. Physician Donald Redelmeier, working with psychologist Amos Tversky (1996), followed 18 arthritis patients for 15 months. The researchers recorded both the patients' pain reports and the daily weather—temperature, humidity, and barometric pressure. Despite patients' beliefs, the weather was uncorrelated with their discomfort, either on the same day or up to two days earlier or later. Shown columns of random numbers labeled "arthritis pain" and "barometric pressure," even college students saw a correlation where there was none. We seem prone to perceiving patterns, whether they're there or not.

A *New York Times* writer reported a massive survey showing that "adolescents whose parents smoked were 50 percent more likely than children of nonsmokers to report having had sex." He concluded (would you agree?) that the survey indicated a causal effect—that "to reduce the chances that their children will become sexually active at an early age" parents might "quit smoking" (O'Neil, 2002).

FIGURE 3.5
Illusory correlation in everyday life
Many people believe infertile couples become more likely to conceive a child after adopting a baby. This belief arises from their attention being drawn to such cases. The many couples who adopt without conceiving or conceive without adopting grab less attention. To determine whether there actually is a correlation between adoption and conception, we need data from all four cells in this figure. (From Gilovich, 1991)

	Conceive	Do not conceive
Adopt	confirming evidence	disconfirming evidence
Do not adopt	disconfirming evidence	confirming evidence

Michael Newman Jr./PhotoEdit

Because we are sensitive to dramatic or unusual events, we are especially likely to notice and remember the occurrence of two such events in sequence—say, a premonition of an unlikely phone call followed by the call. When the call does not follow the premonition, we are less likely to note and remember the nonevent.

Likewise, instances of positive-thinking people being cured of cancer impress those who believe that positive attitudes counter disease. But to assess whether positive thinking actually affects cancer, we need three more types of information. We need an estimate of how many positive thinkers were *not* cured. Then we need to know how many cancer patients were and were not cured among those not using positive thinking. Without these comparison figures, the positive examples of a few tell us nothing about the actual correlation between attitudes and disease.

The point to remember: When we notice random coincidences, we may forget that they are random and instead see them as correlated. Thus, we can easily deceive ourselves by seeing what is not there.

Perceiving Order in Random Events

OBJECTIVE 3-7 | Explain the human tendency to perceive order in random sequences.

Illusory correlations arise from our natural eagerness to make sense of our world—what poet Wallace Stevens called our "rage for order." Given even random data, we look for order, for meaningful patterns. And we usually find such, because *random sequences often don't look random.* Consider a random coin flip: If someone flipped a coin six times, which of the following sequences of heads (H) and tails (T) would be most likely: HHHTTT or HTTHTH or HHHHHH?

Daniel Kahneman and Amos Tversky (1972) found that most people believe HTTHTH would be the most likely random sequence. Actually, all three are equally likely (or, you might say, equally unlikely) to occur. A bridge or poker hand of 10 through Ace, all of hearts, would seem extraordinary; actually, it would be no more or less likely than any other specific hand of cards (**FIGURE 3.6**).

In actual random sequences, patterns and streaks (such as repeating digits) occur more often than people expect. To demonstrate this phenomenon for myself (as you can do), I flipped a coin 51 times, with these results:

1. H	11. T	21. T	31. T	41. H	51. T
2. T	12. H	22. T	32. T	42. H	
3. T	13. H	23. H	33. T	43. H	
4. T	14. T	24. T	34. T	44. H	
5. H	15. T	25. T	35. T	45. T	
6. H	16. H	26. T	36. H	46. H	
7. H	17. T	27. H	37. T	47. H	
8. T	18. T	28. T	38. T	48. T	
9. T	19. H	29. H	39. H	49. T	
10. T	20. H	30. T	40. T	50. T	

Looking over the sequence, patterns jump out: Tosses 10 to 22 provided an almost perfect pattern of pairs of tails followed by pairs of heads. On tosses 30 to 38 I had a "cold hand," with only one head in eight tosses. But my fortunes immediately reversed with a "hot hand"—seven heads out of the next nine tosses. Similar streaks happen, about as often as one would expect in random sequences, in basketball shooting, baseball hitting, and mutual fund stock pickers' selections (Gilovich & others, 1985; Malkiel, 1989, 1995; Myers, 2002). Whether flipping coins, watching basketball, or monitoring investment adviser performance, random sequences often don't look random, and so get overinterpreted ("When you're hot, you're hot—give her the ball!").

■ **illusory correlation** the perception of a relationship where none exists.

FIGURE 3.6
Two random sequences Your chances of being dealt either of these hands are precisely the same: 1 in 2,598,960.

BIZARRE SEQUENCE OF COMPUTER-GENERATED RANDOM NUMBERS

Bizarre-looking, perhaps. But actually no more unlikely than any other number sequence.

Given enough random events, something weird will happen Angelo and Maria Gallina were the beneficiaries of one of those extraordinary chance events when they won two California lottery games on the same day.

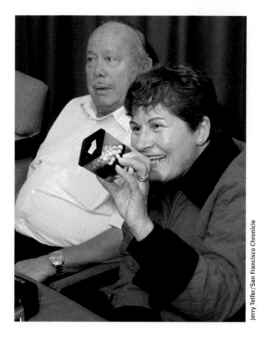

Jerry Telfer/San Francisco Chronicle

On March 11, 1998, Utah's Ernie and Lynn Carey gained three new grandchildren when three of their daughters gave birth—on the same day (*Los Angeles Times*, 1998).

What explains these streaky patterns? Was I exercising some sort of paranormal control over my coin? Did I snap out of my tails funk and get in a heads groove? No such explanations are needed, for these are the sorts of streaks found in any random data. Comparing each toss to the next, 24 of the 50 comparisons yielded a changed result—just the sort of near 50-50 result we expect from coin tossing. Despite the seeming patterns in these data, the outcome of one toss gives no clue to the outcome of the next toss.

However, some happenings seem so extraordinary that we struggle to conceive an ordinary, chance-related explanation (as applies to our coin-tosses). In such cases, statisticians often are less mystified. When Evelyn Marie Adams won the New Jersey lottery *twice*, newspapers reported the odds of her feat as 1 in 17 trillion. Bizarre? Actually, 1 in 17 trillion are the odds that a given person who buys a single ticket for two New Jersey lotteries will win both times. But statisticians Stephen Samuels and George McCabe (1989) report that, given the millions of people who buy U.S. state lottery tickets, it was "practically a sure thing" that someday, somewhere, someone would hit a state jackpot twice. Indeed, say fellow statisticians Persi Diaconis and Frederick Mosteller (1989), "with a large enough sample, any outrageous thing is likely to happen." "The really unusual day would be one where nothing unusual happens," adds Diaconis (2002). An event that happens to but one in 1 billion people every day occurs about six times a day, 2000 times a year.

Experimentation

Happy are they, remarked the Roman poet Virgil, "who have been able to perceive the causes of things." We endlessly wonder and debate *why* we act as we do. Why do people smoke? Have babies while they are still children? Do stupid things when drunk? Become troubled teens and open fire on their classmates? Though psychology cannot answer these questions directly, it has helped us to understand what influences drug use, sexual behaviors, thinking when drinking, and aggression.

Exploring Cause and Effect

OBJECTIVE 3-8 | Explain how experiments help researchers isolate cause and effect.

Many factors influence our everyday behavior. To isolate cause and effect—say, in looking for causes of depression—psychologists statistically control for other factors. For example, many studies have found that breast-fed infants grow up with somewhat higher intelligence scores than those of infants bottle-fed with cow's milk (Angelsen & others, 2001; Mortensen & others, 2002; Quinn & others, 2001). Mother's milk correlates modestly but positively with later intelligence. But does this mean that smarter mothers (who more often breast-feed) have smarter children? Or, as some researchers believe, do the nutrients of mother's milk contribute to brain development? To help answer this question, researchers have "controlled for" (statistically removed differences in) maternal age, education, and intelligence. Still, breast-fed infants exhibit slightly higher intelligence as young children.

The clearest and cleanest way to isolate cause and effect is, however, to **experiment.** Experiments enable a researcher to focus on the possible effects of one or more factors by (1) *manipulating the factors of interest* and (2) *holding constant ("controlling") other factors*. Knowing that correlations of infant nutrition and later intelligence can't possibly control for all other possible factors, a British research team led by Alan Lucas (1998) decided to experiment, using 424 hospital preterm infants. With parental permission, the researchers randomly assigned some infants to the usual infant formula feedings and others to donated breast milk feedings. When given intelligence tests at age 8, the children nourished with breast milk had significantly higher intelligence scores than their formula-fed counterparts. No single experiment is conclusive, of course, but by randomly assigning infants to a feeding condition, these researchers were able to hold constant all factors except nutrition. This eliminated alternative explanations and supported the conclusion that, so far as the developing intelligence of preterm infants is concerned, breast is best. (*Note:* The other infants were not harmed by the experiment, because they received the standard feeding.)

If a behavior (such as test performance) changes when we vary an experimental factor (such as infant nutrition), then we know the factor is having an effect. *The point to remember:* Unlike correlational studies, which uncover naturally occurring relationships, an experiment manipulates a factor to determine its effect.

Understanding experimentation is central to thinking critically with psychological science. So, let's consider further how we experiment.

Evaluating Therapies

OBJECTIVE *3-9* | Explain why the double-blind procedure and random assignment build confidence in research findings.

Our tendency to seek new remedies when we are ill or emotionally down can produce misleading testimonies. If three days into a cold we start taking vitamin C tablets and find our cold symptoms lessening, we may credit the pills rather than the cold naturally subsiding. If, after nearly failing the first exam, we listen to a "peak learning" subliminal tape and then improve on the next exam, we may credit the tape rather than conclude that our performance has returned to our average. In the 1700s, blood-letting *seemed* effective. Sometimes people improved after the treatment; when they didn't, the practitioner inferred the disease was just too advanced to be reversed. (We, of course, now know that blood-letting is a *bad* treatment.) So, whether or not a remedy is truly effective, enthusiastic users will probably endorse it. To find out whether it actually is effective, we must experiment.

And that is precisely how new drug treatments and new methods of psychological therapy are evaluated. In many of these studies, the participants are *blind* (uninformed) about what treatment, if any, they are receiving. One group receives the treatment. Others receive a pseudotreatment—an inert *placebo* (perhaps a pill with no drug in it). Often, neither the participant nor the research assistant collecting the data knows whether the participant's group is receiving the treatment. This **double-blind procedure** enables researchers to check a treatment's actual effects apart from the research participants' (and their own) enthusiasm for it and from the healing power of belief. The **placebo effect** is well documented in reducing pain, depression, and anxiety (Kirsch & Sapirstein, 1998). Just *believing* you are getting a treatment can boost your spirits, relax your body, and relieve your symptoms.

The double-blind procedure is one way to create an **experimental condition** in which people receive the treatment and a contrasting **control condition** without the treatment. By **randomly assigning** people to these conditions, researchers can be

■ **experiment** a research method in which an investigator manipulates one or more factors (independent variables) to observe the effect on some behavior or mental process (the dependent variable). By random assignment of participants, the experimenter aims to control other relevant factors.

■ **double-blind procedure** an experimental procedure in which both the research participants and the research staff are ignorant (blind) about whether the research participants have received the treatment or a placebo. Commonly used in drug-evaluation studies.

■ **placebo** [pluh-SEE-bo; Latin for "I shall please"] **effect** experimental results caused by expectations alone; any effect on behavior caused by the administration of an inert substance or condition, which is assumed to be an active agent.

■ **experimental condition** the condition of an experiment that exposes participants to the treatment, that is, to one version of the independent variable.

■ **control condition** the condition of an experiment that contrasts with the experimental condition and serves as a comparison for evaluating the effect of the treatment.

■ **random assignment** assigning participants to experimental and control conditions by chance, thus minimizing preexisting differences between those assigned to the different groups.

■ **independent variable** the experimental factor that is manipulated; the variable whose effect is being studied.

■ **dependent variable** the outcome factor; the variable that may change in response to manipulations of the independent variable.

fairly certain the two groups are otherwise identical. Random assignment roughly equalizes the two groups in age, attitudes, and every other characteristic. With random assignment, as occurred with the infants in the breast milk experiment, we also can know that any later differences between people in the experimental and control conditions will usually be the result of the treatment.

Another example: On the advice of their physicians, millions of postmenopausal women turned to hormone replacement therapy after correlational studies found that women on replacement hormones had lower rates of heart disease, stroke, and colon cancer. But these women may also have been more likely to receive medical care, to exercise, and to eat well. So, did the hormones make women healthy or did healthy women take the hormones? In 2002, the National Institutes of Health announced the surprising results of a massive experiment that randomly assigned 16,608 healthy women to either replacement hormones or a placebo. The shocking result: Compared with women in the control condition, women receiving the hormones had *more* health problems (Love, 2002).

Independent and Dependent Variables

OBJECTIVE 3-10 | Explain the difference between an independent and a dependent variable.

Here is an even more potent example: The drug Viagra was approved for use after 21 clinical trials, including an experiment in which researchers randomly assigned 329 men with impotence to either an experimental condition (Viagra) or a control condition (a placebo). It was a double-blind procedure—neither the men nor the person who gave them the pills knew which drug they were receiving. The result: At peak doses, 69 percent of Viagra-assisted attempts at intercourse were successful, compared with 22 percent for men receiving the placebo (Goldstein & others, 1998). Viagra had an effect.

This simple experiment manipulated just one drug factor. We call this experimental factor the **independent variable** because we can vary it independently of other factors, such as the men's age, weight, and personality (which random assignment should control). Experiments examine the effect of one or more independent variables on some measurable behavior, called the **dependent variable** because it can vary *depending* on what takes place during the experiment. Both variables are given precise operational definitions, which specify the procedures that manipulate the independent variable (the precise drug dosage and timing in this study) or measure the dependent variable (the questions that assessed the men's responses). These definitions answer the "What do you mean?" question with a level of precision that enables others to repeat the study. (See **FIGURE 3.7** for another experiment's design.)

FIGURE 3.7
Experimentation To discern causation, psychologists may randomly assign some participants to an experimental treatment, others to a control condition. Measuring the dependent variable (child's intelligence score) will determine the effect of the independent variable (type of milk received in first 12 months).

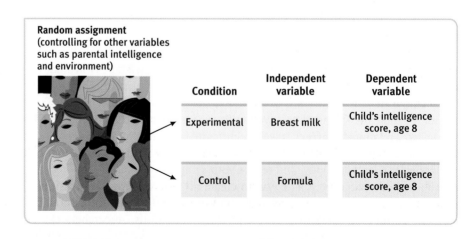

TABLE 3.2

COMPARING RESEARCH METHODS

Research Method	Basic Purpose	How Conducted	What Is Manipulated	Weaknesses
Descriptive	To observe and record behavior	Do case studies, surveys, or naturalistic observations	Nothing	No control of variables; single cases may be misleading
Correlational	To detect naturally occurring relationships; to assess how well one variable predicts another	Compute statistical association, sometimes among survey responses	Nothing	Does not specify cause and effect
Experimental	To explore cause and effect	Manipulate one or more factors; use random assignment	The independent variable(s)	Sometimes not feasible; results may not generalize to other contexts; not ethical to manipulate certain variables

Experiments can also help us evaluate social programs. Do early childhood education programs boost impoverished children's chances for success? What are the effects of different anti-smoking campaigns? Do school sex-education programs reduce teen pregnancies? To answer these questions, we can experiment: If an intervention is welcomed but resources are scarce, we could use a lottery to randomly assign some people (or regions) to experience the new program and others to a control condition. If later the two groups differ, the intervention's effect will be confirmed (Passell, 1993).

Let's recap. A variable is anything that can vary (infant nutrition, intelligence, TV exposure—anything within the bounds of what is feasible and ethical). Experiments aim to *manipulate* an *independent* variable, *measure* the *dependent* variable, and *control* all other variables. An experiment has at least two different conditions: an experimental condition and a comparison or control condition. Random assignment works to equate the conditions before any treatment effects. In this way, an experiment tests the effect of at least one independent variable (what we manipulate) on at least one dependent variable (the outcome we measure). **TABLE 3.2** compares the features of psychology's research methods.

Note the distinction between random *sampling* (typically associated with surveys) and random *assignment* in experiments. Random sampling helps us generalize to a larger population. Random assignment controls extraneous influences, which helps us infer cause and effect.

Statistical Reasoning

OBJECTIVE **3-11** | Explain the importance of statistical principles, and give an example of their use in everyday life.

Having gathered data, we must next organize, summarize, and make inferences from it, using statistics. Today's statistics are tools that help us see and interpret what the unaided eye might miss.

Off-the-top-of-the-head estimates often misread reality and then mislead the public. Someone throws out a big round number. Others echo it and before long the big round number becomes public misinformation. A few examples:

- *One percent of Americans (2.7 million) are homeless.* Or is it 300,000, an earlier estimate by the federal government? Or 600,000, an estimate by the Urban Institute (Crossen, 1994)?
- *Ten percent of people are lesbians or gay men.* Or is it 2 to 3 percent, as suggested by various national surveys?
- *We ordinarily use but 10 percent of our brain.* Or is it closer to 100 percent? (Which 90 percent, or even 10 percent, would you be willing to sacrifice?)

"Figures can be misleading—so I've written a song which I think expresses the real story of the firm's performance this quarter."

■ **mode** the most frequently occurring score(s) in a distribution.

■ **mean** the arithmetic average of a distribution, obtained by adding the scores and then dividing by the number of scores.

■ **median** the middle score in a distribution; half the scores are above it and half are below it.

■ **range** the difference between the highest and lowest scores in a distribution.

■ **standard deviation** a computed measure of how much scores vary around the mean score.

• *We remember 10 percent of what we read, 20 percent of what we hear, 30 percent of what we see, and 80 percent of what we say.* So reported the British Audio Visual Society (Genovese, 2004). Or is it, as a book on accelerated learning declares, 20 percent of what we read, 30 percent of what we hear, 40 percent of what we see, and 50 percent of what we say?

The point to remember: Doubt big, round, undocumented numbers. Rather than swallow top-of-the-head estimates, focus on thinking smarter by applying simple statistical principles to everyday reasoning.

Describing Data

OBJECTIVE **3-12** | Explain how bar graphs can misrepresent data.

Once researchers have gathered their data, their first task is to *organize* them. One way is to use a simple *bar graph,* as in **FIGURE 3.8**, which displays a distribution of trucks of different brands still on the road after a decade. When reading statistical graphs such as this, take care. As you can see, people can design a graph to make a difference look small or big, depending on what they want to emphasize.

The point to remember: Think smart. When viewing figures in magazines and on television, read the scale labels and note their range.

Measures of Central Tendency

OBJECTIVE **3-13** | Describe the three measures of central tendency, and tell which is most affected by extreme scores.

The next step is to summarize the data using some *measure of central tendency,* a single score that represents a whole set of scores. The simplest measure is the **mode,** the most frequently occurring score or scores. The most commonly reported is the **mean,** or arithmetic average—the total sum of all the scores divided by the number of scores. On a divided highway, the median is the middle. So, too, with data: The **median** is the midpoint—the 50th percentile. If you arrange all the scores in order from the highest to the lowest, half will be above the median and half will be below it.

FIGURE 3.8 Read the scale labels An American truck manufacturer offered a graph (a)—with actual brand names included—to suggest the much greater durability of its trucks. Note, however, how the apparent difference shrinks as the vertical scale changes (graph b).

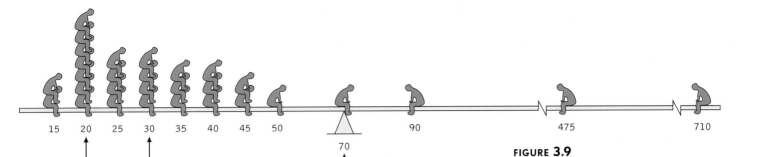

15   20   25   30   35   40   45   50   90   475   710

Mode   **Median**   70
                                          Mean

One family   Income per family in thousands of dollars

FIGURE 3.9

A skewed distribution This graphic representation of the distribution of incomes illustrates the three measures of central tendency—mode, median, and mean. Note how just a few high incomes make the mean—the fulcrum point that balances the incomes above and below—deceptively high.

Measures of central tendency neatly summarize data. But consider what happens to the mean when a distribution is lopsided or *skewed*. With income data, for example, the mode, median, and mean often tell very different stories (**FIGURE 3.9**). This happens because the mean is biased by a few extreme scores. When Microsoft founder Bill Gates sits down in an intimate cafe, its average (mean) patron instantly becomes a billionaire. Understanding this, you can see how a British newspaper could accurately run the headline "Income for 62% Is Below Average" (Waterhouse, 1993). Because the bottom *half* of British income earners receive only a *quarter* of the national income cake, most British people, like most people everywhere, make less than the mean.

In the United States, advocates and critics described the 2003 tax cut with different statistics, both true. The White House explained that "92 million Americans will receive an average tax cut of $1083." Critics agreed, but also noted that 50 million taxpayers got no cut, and half of the 92 million who did benefit received less than $100 (Krugman, 2003). Mean and median tell different true stories.

The point to remember: Always note which measure of central tendency is reported. Then, if it is a mean, consider whether a few atypical scores could be distorting it.

The average person has one ovary and one testicle.

Measures of Variation

OBJECTIVE 3-14 | Describe two measures of variation.

Knowing the value of an appropriate measure of central tendency can tell us a great deal. But it also helps to know something about the amount of *variation* in the data—how similar or diverse the scores are. Averages derived from scores with low variability are more reliable than averages based on scores with high variability. Consider a basketball player who scored between 13 and 17 points in each of her first 10 games in a season. Knowing this, we would be more confident that she would score near 15 points in her next game than if her scores had varied from 5 to 25 points.

The **range** of scores—the gap between the lowest and highest scores—provides only a crude estimate of variation because a couple of extreme scores in an otherwise uniform group, such as the $475,000 and $710,000 incomes in Figure 3.9, will create a deceptively large range.

The more useful standard for measuring how much scores deviate from one another is the **standard deviation.** It better gauges whether scores are packed together or dispersed, because it uses information from each score (**TABLE 3.3** on the next page). (The computation assembles information about how much individual scores differ from the mean.) If your college or university attracts students of a certain ability level, their intelligence scores will have a smaller standard deviation than the one found in the more diverse community population outside your school.

"The poor are getting poorer, but with the rich getting richer it all averages out in the long run."

TABLE 3.3

STANDARD DEVIATION IS MUCH MORE INFORMATIVE THAN MEAN ALONE

Note that the test scores in Class A and Class B have the same mean (80), but very different standard deviations, which tell us more about how the students in each class are really faring.

Test Scores in Class A			Test Scores in Class B		
Score	Deviation From the Mean	Squared Deviation	Score	Deviation From the Mean	Squared Deviation
72	−8	64	60	−20	400
74	−6	36	60	−20	400
77	−3	9	70	−10	100
79	−1	1	70	−10	100
82	+2	4	90	+10	100
84	+4	16	90	+10	100
85	+5	25	100	+20	400
87	+7	49	100	+20	400

Total = 640
Mean = 640 ÷ 8 = 80   Sum of (deviations)² = 204

Total = 640
Mean = 640 ÷ 8 = 80   Sum of (deviations)² = 2000

Standard deviation =

$$\sqrt{\frac{\textit{Sum of (deviations)}^2}{\textit{Number of scores}}} = \sqrt{\frac{204}{8}} = 5.0$$

Standard deviation =

$$\sqrt{\frac{\textit{Sum of (deviations)}^2}{\textit{Number of scores}}} = \sqrt{\frac{2000}{8}} = 15.8$$

Making Inferences

Data are "noisy." One group's average score (breast-fed babies' intelligence scores) could conceivably differ from another's (the formula-fed babies) not because of any real difference but merely because of chance fluctuations in the people sampled. How confidently, then, can we infer that an observed difference accurately estimates the true difference?

When Is an Observed Difference Reliable?

OBJECTIVE **3-15** | Identify three principles for making generalizations from samples.

In deciding when it is safe to generalize from a sample, we should keep three principles in mind. Let's look at each in turn.

1. ***Representative samples are better than biased samples.*** The best basis for generalizing is not from the exceptional and memorable cases one finds at the extremes (remember Bill Gates' income?) but from a representative sample of cases. No research involves a representative sample of the whole human population. Thus, it pays to keep in mind what population a study has sampled.

2. ***Less-variable observations are more reliable than those that are more variable.*** As we noted in the example of the basketball player whose points scored were consistent, an average is more reliable when it comes from scores with low variability.

3. ***More cases are better than fewer.*** An eager prospective university student visits two college campuses, each for a day. At the first, the student randomly attends two classes and discovers both instructors to be witty and engaging. At the next campus, the two sampled instructors seem dull and uninspiring. Returning home, the student (discounting the small sample size of only two teachers at each institution) tells friends about the "great teachers" at the first school, and the "bores" at the second. Again, we know it but we ignore it: *Averages based on many cases are more reliable* (less variable) than averages based on only a few cases.

The point to remember: Don't be overly impressed by a few anecdotes. Generalizations based on a few unrepresentative cases are unreliable.

When Is a Difference Significant?

OBJECTIVE 3-16 | Explain how psychologists decide whether differences are meaningful.

■ **statistical significance** a statistical statement of how likely it is that an obtained result occurred by chance.

Statistical tests also help us determine whether differences are meaningful. Here is the underlying logic: When *averages* from two samples are each *reliable* measures of their respective populations (as when each is based on many observations that have small variability), then their difference (sometimes even a very small difference) is likely to be reliable as well. (The less the variability in women's and in men's aggression scores, the more confidence we would have that any observed gender difference is reliable.) But when the *difference* between the sample averages is *large,* we have even more confidence that the difference between them reflects a real difference in their populations.

In short, *when the sample averages are reliable and the difference between them is relatively large,* we say the difference has **statistical significance.** This simply means that the difference we observed is probably not due to chance variation between the samples.

In judging statistical significance, psychologists are conservative. They are like juries who must presume innocence until guilt is proven. For most psychologists, proof beyond a reasonable doubt means not making much of a finding unless the odds of its occurring by chance are less than 5 percent (an arbitrary criterion).

Given large enough or homogeneous enough samples, a difference between them may be "statistically significant" yet have little practical significance. For example, comparisons of intelligence test scores among hundreds of thousands of first-born and later-born individuals indicate a highly significant tendency for first-born individuals to have higher average scores than their later-born siblings (Zajonc & Markus, 1975). But because the scores differ by only one or two points, the difference has little practical importance. Such findings have caused some psychologists to advocate alternatives to significance testing (Hunter, 1997). Better, they say, to use other ways to express a finding's "effect size"—its magnitude and reliability.

The point to remember: Statistical significance indicates the *likelihood* that a result will happen by chance. It does not indicate the *importance* of the result.

Using the principles we have discussed here will help us to think critically—to see more clearly what we might otherwise miss or misinterpret, and to generalize more accurately from our observations. We do think smarter when we understand and use the principles of research methods and statistics (Fong & others, 1986; Lehman & others, 1988; VanderStoep & Shaughnessy, 1997). It requires training and practice, but developing clear and critical thinking abilities is part of becoming an educated person. The report of the Project on Redefining the Meaning and Purpose of Baccalaureate Degrees (1985) eloquently asserts why there are few higher priorities in a college education:

> If anything is paid attention to in our colleges and universities, thinking must be it. Unfortunately, thinking can be lazy. It can be sloppy. . . . It can be fooled, misled, bullied. . . . Students possess great untrained and untapped capacities for logical thinking, critical analysis, and inquiry, but these are capacities that are not spontaneous: They grow out of wide instruction, experience, encouragement, correction, and constant use.

PEANUTS

>> LEARNING OUTCOMES

Research Strategies: How Psychologists Ask and Answer Questions

OBJECTIVE 3-1 | **Identify an advantage and a disadvantage of using case studies to study behavior.**

Researchers using case studies focus in depth on one individual, in the hope of revealing universal principles. Case studies describe behavior. They can suggest hypotheses, but studying an unrepresentative individual may lead to false conclusions.

OBJECTIVE 3-2 | **Identify the advantages and disadvantages of using surveys to study behavior and mental processes, and explain the importance of wording effects and random sampling.**

Surveys describe behavior by gathering information from a large number of people. This technique relies on people giving accurate self-reports of their attitudes or behaviors. Wording effects—subtle influences in the sequence or phrasing of questions—can affect responses. Random sampling helps researchers achieve a sample that fairly represents the population under study. Because random sampling chooses people by chance, each person in the entire group has an equal chance of participating.

OBJECTIVE 3-3 | **Identify an advantage and a disadvantage of using naturalistic observation to study behavior.**

Naturalistic observation gives researchers an opportunity to watch and record behavior in naturally occurring situations. Like other forms of description, naturalistic observation cannot explain behaviors, but it can expand our understanding and lead to hypotheses that can be studied by other methods.

OBJECTIVE 3-4 | **Describe positive and negative correlations, and explain how correlational measures can aid the process of prediction.**

A *correlation coefficient* is a statistical measure of the strength and duration of the relationship between two factors. In a *positive correlation* (ranging from 0 to +1.00), the two factors rise or fall together. In a *negative correlation* (ranging from 0 to −1.00), one item rises as the other falls. Scatterplots and the correlations they reveal help us to see relationships that the naked eye might miss.

OBJECTIVE 3-5 | **Explain why correlational research fails to provide evidence of cause-effect relationships.**

A correlation indicates the *possibility* of a cause-effect relationship, but it does not prove causation or, if causation exists, the direction of the influence. A third factor may be the cause of the correlation.

OBJECTIVE 3-6 | **Describe how people form illusory correlations.**

Illusory correlations are random (often dramatic or unusual) events that we notice and falsely assume are related. Once we believe two things are related, we tend to notice and recall instances that confirm this belief.

OBJECTIVE 3-7 | **Explain the human tendency to perceive order in random sequences.**

We search for patterns in an attempt to make sense of the world around us. Patterns or sequences occur naturally in sets of random data, but we tend to interpret these patterns as meaningful connections.

OBJECTIVE 3-8 | **Explain how experiments help researchers isolate cause and effect.**

To discover cause-effect relationships, psychologists conduct *experiments*. By manipulating one or more factors of interest, and controlling other factors, experimenters can determine the effect on some behavior or mental process.

OBJECTIVE 3-9 | **Explain why the double-blind procedure and random assignment build confidence in research findings.**

In a *double-blind procedure*, neither the researchers nor the participants know whether participants are receiving the treatment or a placebo. This counteracts the possibility that a placebo effect or researchers' expectations will unintentionally influence the study's results. *Random assignment* minimizes preexisting differences between the groups by selecting people by chance for the *experimental condition* (the group exposed to the treatment) or the *control condition* (a group that experiences no treatment or a different version of the treatment).

OBJECTIVE 3-10 | **Explain the difference between an independent and a dependent variable.**

The *independent variable* is the factor you manipulate to study its effect. The *dependent variable* is the factor you measure to discover any changes that occur in response to these manipulations.

OBJECTIVE 3-11 | **Explain the importance of statistical principles, and give an example of their use in everyday life.**

Statistics help us to organize, summarize, and make inferences from data. We need not remember complicated formulas to think more clearly and critically about the data we encounter in everyday life. For example, understanding statistical concepts teaches us the importance of doubting big, round, undocumented numbers.

OBJECTIVE 3-12 | **Explain how bar graphs can misrepresent data.**

Scale labels and ranges used in bar graphs can be designed to minimize or maximize differences. When looking at statistical graphs in books and magazines and on TV and the Internet, think critically.

OBJECTIVE 3-13 | **Describe the three measures of central tendency, and tell which is most affected by extreme scores.**

The *median* is the middle score in a group of data. The *mode* is the most frequently occurring score. The *mean*, the arithmetic average, is most easily distorted by a few very high or very low scores.

OBJECTIVE 3-14 | **Describe two measures of variation.**

Measures of variation tell us how similar or diverse data are. A *range* describes the gap between the highest and lowest scores. The more useful measure, the *standard deviation,* states how much scores vary around the mean, or average, score.

OBJECTIVE 3-15 | **Identify three principles for making generalizations from samples.**

1. Representative samples are better than biased samples.
2. Less-variable observations are more reliable than those that are more variable.
3. More cases are better than fewer.

OBJECTIVE **3-16** | **Explain how psychologists decide whether differences are meaningful.**

When averages from two samples are each reliable measures of their own populations, and the difference between them is relatively large, we can assume the difference is *significant*—that the result did not occur by chance alone. Statistical significance indicates the likelihood of a result's occurring, not the importance of the result.

TERMS AND CONCEPTS TO REMEMBER

case study, p. 3-0	experimental condition, p. 3-9
survey, p. 3-1	control condition, p. 3-9
false consensus effect, p. 3-1	random assignment, p. 3-9
population, p. 3-1	independent variable, p. 3-10
random sample, p. 3-1	dependent variable, p. 3-10
naturalistic observation, p. 3-2	mode, p. 3-12
correlation, p. 3-3	mean, p. 3-12
scatterplot, p. 3-3	median, p. 3-12
illusory correlation, p. 3-6	range, p. 3-13
experiment, p. 3-9	standard deviation, p. 3-13
double-blind procedure, p. 3-9	statistical significance, p. 3-15
placebo effect, p. 3-9	

TEST YOURSELF

1. What are the strengths and weaknesses of the three different methods psychologists use to describe behavior—case studies, surveys, and naturalistic observation?

2. Here are some recently reported correlations, with interpretations drawn by journalists. Further research, often including experiments, has clarified cause and effect in each case. Knowing just these correlations, can you come up with other possible explanations for each of these?

   a. Alcohol use is associated with violence. (One interpretation: Drinking triggers or unleashes aggressive behavior.)

   b. Educated people live longer, on average, than less-educated people. (One interpretation: Education lengthens life and enhances health.)

   c. Teens engaged in team sports are less likely to use drugs, smoke, have sex, carry weapons, and eat junk food than are teens who do not engage in team sports. (One interpretation: Team sports encourage healthy living.)

   d. Adolescents who frequently see smoking in movies are more likely to smoke. (One interpretation: Movie stars' behavior influences impressionable teens.)

3. Why, when testing a new drug for blood pressure, would we learn more about its effectiveness from giving it to half of the participants in a group of 1000 than to all 1000 participants?

4. Consider a question posed by Christopher Jepson, David Krantz, and Richard Nisbett (1983) to University of Michigan introductory psychology students:

   The registrar's office at the University of Michigan has found that usually about 100 students in Arts and Sciences have perfect marks at the end of their first term at the University. However, only about 10 to 15 students graduate with perfect marks. What do you think is the most likely explanation for the fact that there are more perfect marks after one term than at graduation?

(Answers in Appendix B.)

ASK YOURSELF

1. Can you recall examples of misleading surveys you have experienced or read about? What principles for a good survey did they violate?

2. Can you think of an example of correlational research that you recently heard about from a friend or on the news? Was an unwarranted conclusion drawn?

3. If you were to become a research psychologist, what questions would you like to explore with experiments?

4. Find a graph in a popular magazine ad. How does the advertiser use (or abuse) statistics to make a point?

>WEB

Multiple-choice *self-tests* and more may be found at www.worthpublishers.com/myers.

ANOTHER VOICE ON: NEUROSCIENCE AND BEHAVIOR

FROM "THE BRAIN IS WIDER THAN THE SKY," *THE COMPLETE POEMS OF EMILY DICKINSON*. BOSTON: LITTLE, BROWN, 1924.

The brain is wider than the sky,
For, put them side by side,
The one the other will include
With ease, and you beside.

The brain is deeper than the sea,
For, hold them, blue to blue,
The one the other will absorb,
As sponges, buckets do.

Neuroscience and Behavior

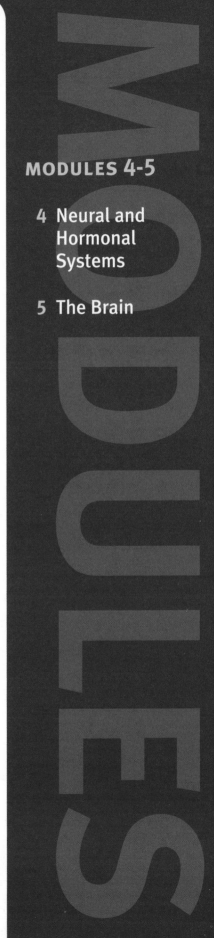
OBJECTIVE **4-1** | Describe the ill-fated phrenology theory's contribution to the study of the brain's functions.

No principle is more central to today's psychology, or to this book, than this: *Everything psychological is simultaneously biological.* Your every idea, every mood, every urge is a biological happening. You love, laugh, and cry with your body. Without your body—your genes, your brain, your appearance—you are, indeed, nobody. Although we find it convenient to talk separately of biological and psychological influences on behavior, we need to remember: To think, feel, or act without a body would be like running without legs.

Today's science is riveted on our body's most amazing parts—the brain, its component neural systems, and their genetic instructions. The brain's ultimate challenge? To understand itself. How does our brain organize and communicate with itself? How do our heredity and our experience together wire our brain? How does the brain process the information we need to shoot a basketball? To delight in a guitarist's notes? To remember our first kiss?

Our understanding of how the brain gives birth to the mind has come a long way. The ancient philosopher Plato correctly located the mind in the spherical head—his idea of the perfect form. His student, Aristotle, believed the mind was in the heart, which pumps warmth and vitality to the body. The heart remains our symbol for love, but science has long overtaken philosophy on this issue. It's your brain, not your heart, that falls in love.

We have come far since the early 1800s, when the German physician Franz Gall invented *phrenology,* a popular but ill-fated theory that claimed bumps on the skull could reveal our mental abilities and our character traits. At one point, Britain had 29 phrenological societies, and phrenologists traveled North America giving skull readings (Hunt, 1993). Humorist Mark Twain put one famous phrenologist to the test when he came, using a pseudonym, for a skull-reading. "He found a cavity [and] startled me by saying that that cavity represented the total absence of the sense of humor!" Three months later, Twain sat for a second reading, this time identifying himself. Now "the cavity was gone, and in its place was . . . the loftiest bump of humor he had ever encountered in his life-long experience!" (Lopez, 2002). Phrenology did, however, correctly focus attention on the idea that various brain regions have particular functions.

Within little more than the last century, we have also realized, as we will see in Module 4, that the body is composed of cells; that among these are nerve cells that conduct electricity and "talk" to one another by sending chemical messages across a tiny gap that separates them. We have also learned, as we will see in Module 5, that specific brain systems serve specific functions (though not the functions Gall supposed); and that from the information processed in these different brain systems, we construct our experience of sights and sounds, meanings and memories, pain and passion. You and I are privileged to live in a time when discoveries about the interplay of our biology and our behavior and mental processes are occurring at an exhilarating pace.

4

Neural and Hormonal Systems

Neural Communication

OBJECTIVE 4-2 | Explain how viewing each person as a biopsychosocial system helps us understand human behavior, and discuss why researchers study other animals in search of clues to human neural processes.

The body's information system is built from billions of interconnected cells called *neurons.* To fathom our thoughts and actions, memories and moods, we must first understand how neurons work and communicate.

We are each a system composed of subsystems that are in turn composed of even smaller subsystems. Tiny cells organize to form such body organs as the stomach, heart, and brain. These organs in turn form larger systems for digestion, circulation, and information processing. And those systems are part of an even larger system—the individual, who in turn is a part of a family, culture, and community. We are *biopsychosocial* systems. To understand our behavior, we need to study how these biological, psychological, and social-cultural systems work and interact.

Throughout this book you will find examples of this interplay. By studying the links between biological activity and psychological events, **biological psychologists** are gaining a better understanding of sleep and dreams, depression and schizophrenia, hunger and sex, stress and disease. We therefore begin our study of psychology with a look at its biological roots. We will start small and build from the bottom up—from nerve cells in this module to the environmental and cultural influences that interact with our biology in later modules. We will also work from the top down as we consider how our thinking and emotions influence our brain and our health. At all levels, psychologists examine how we process information—how we take in information; how we organize, interpret, and store it; and how we use it.

For scientists, it is a happy fact of nature that the information systems of humans and other animals operate similarly—so similarly, in fact, that you could not distinguish between small samples of brain tissue from a human and a monkey. This similarity allows researchers to study relatively simple animals, such as squids and sea slugs, to discover how our neural systems operate. It allows them to study other mammals' brains to understand the organization of our own. Cars differ, but all have engines, accelerators, steering wheels, and brakes. A Martian could study any one of them and grasp the operating principles. Likewise, animals differ, yet their nervous systems operate similarly. Though the human brain is more complex than a rat's, both follow the same principles.

Neurons

OBJECTIVE 4-3 | Describe the parts of a neuron, and explain how its impulses are generated.

Our body's neural information system is complexity built from simplicity. Its building blocks are neurons, or nerve cells. There are many different types of **neurons,** but all are variations on the same theme (**FIGURE 4.1**). Each consists of a cell body and its branching fibers. The bushy **dendrite** fibers receive information and conduct it toward the cell body. From there, **axon** fibers pass the message along to other neurons or to muscles or glands. Axons speak. Dendrites listen.

■ **biological psychology** a branch of psychology concerned with the links between biology and behavior. (Some biological psychologists call themselves *behavioral neuroscientists, neuropsychologists, behavior geneticists, physiological psychologists,* or *biopsychologists.*)

■ **neuron** a nerve cell; the basic building block of the nervous system.

■ **dendrite** the bushy, branching extensions of a neuron that receive messages and conduct impulses toward the cell body.

■ **axon** the extension of a neuron, ending in branching terminal fibers, through which messages pass to other neurons or to muscles or glands.

■ **myelin** [MY-uh-lin] **sheath** a layer of fatty tissue segmentally encasing the fibers of many neurons; enables vastly greater transmission speed of neural impulses as the impulse hops from one node to the next.

■ **action potential** a neural impulse; a brief electrical charge that travels down an axon. The action potential is generated by the movement of positively charged atoms in and out of channels in the axon's membrane.

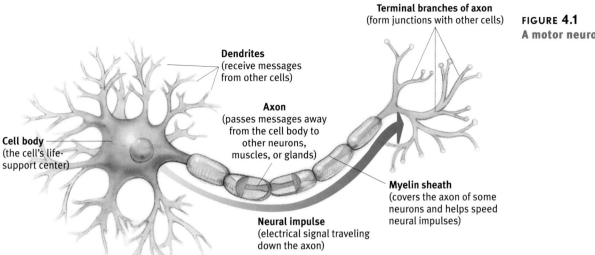

Terminal branches of axon
(form junctions with other cells)

FIGURE 4.1
A motor neuron

Dendrites
(receive messages
from other cells)

Axon
(passes messages away
from the cell body to
other neurons,
muscles, or glands)

Cell body
(the cell's life-
support center)

Myelin sheath
(covers the axon of some
neurons and helps speed
neural impulses)

Neural impulse
(electrical signal traveling
down the axon)

Unlike the short dendrites, axons are sometimes very long, projecting several feet through the body. *Motor neurons,* which control muscles, are the neural system's giant redwoods. A neuron carrying orders to a leg muscle has a cell body and axon roughly on the scale of a basketball attached to a rope 4 miles long. A layer of fatty tissue, called the **myelin sheath,** insulates the axons of some neurons and helps speed their impulses. The myelin sheath's importance is evident in multiple sclerosis, a disease in which the myelin sheath degenerates. The result is a slowing of all communication to muscles and the eventual loss of muscle control.

Depending on the type of fiber, the neural impulse travels at speeds ranging from a sluggish 2 miles per hour to a breakneck 200 or more miles per hour. But even this top speed is 3 million times slower than that of electricity through a wire. We measure brain activity in milliseconds (thousandths of a second) and computer activity in nanoseconds (billionths of a second). That helps to explain why, unlike the nearly instantaneous reactions of a high-speed computer, your reaction to a sudden event, such as a child darting in front of your car, may take a quarter-second or more. Your brain is vastly more complex than a computer, but not faster at executing simple responses.

A neuron fires an impulse when it receives signals from sense receptors stimulated by pressure, heat, or light, or when it is stimulated by chemical messages from neighboring neurons. The impulse, called the **action potential,** is a brief electrical charge that travels down the axon.

Neurons, like batteries, generate electricity from chemical events. The chemistry-to-electricity process involves the exchange of electrically charged atoms, called *ions.* The fluid interior of a resting axon has an excess of negatively charged ions, while the fluid outside the axon membrane has more positively charged ions. This positive-outside/negative-inside state is called the *resting potential.* Like a tightly guarded facility, the axon's surface is very selective about what it allows in. We say the axon's surface is *selectively permeable.* For example, a resting axon has gates that block positive sodium ions.

When a neuron fires, however, the security parameters change: The first bit of the axon opens its gates, rather like sewer covers flipping open, and the positively charged sodium ions flood through the membrane (**FIGURE 4.2** on the next page). This *depolarizes* that part of the axon, causing the axon's next channel to open, and then the next, like dominoes falling, each one tripping the next. During a resting pause (the *refractory period,* rather like a camera flash pausing to recharge), the neuron pumps the positively charged sodium ions back outside. Then it can fire again. (In myelinated neurons, as in Figure 4.1, the action potential speeds up by hopping from one

"I sing the body electric."
Walt Whitman, "Children of Adam," 1855

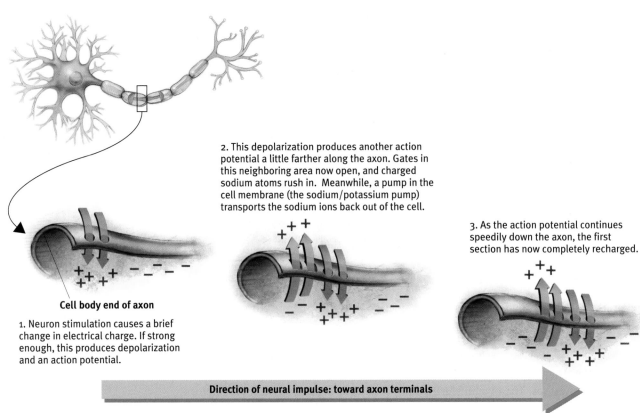

2. This depolarization produces another action potential a little farther along the axon. Gates in this neighboring area now open, and charged sodium atoms rush in. Meanwhile, a pump in the cell membrane (the sodium/potassium pump) transports the sodium ions back out of the cell.

3. As the action potential continues speedily down the axon, the first section has now completely recharged.

Cell body end of axon

1. Neuron stimulation causes a brief change in electrical charge. If strong enough, this produces depolarization and an action potential.

Direction of neural impulse: toward axon terminals

FIGURE 4.2
Action potential

> "What one neuron tells another neuron is simply how much it is excited."
> Francis Crick, *The Astonishing Hypothesis*, 1994

■ **threshold** the level of stimulation required to trigger a neural impulse.

■ **synapse** [SIN-aps] the junction between the axon tip of the sending neuron and the dendrite or cell body of the receiving neuron. The tiny gap at this junction is called the *synaptic gap* or *cleft.*

■ **neurotransmitters** chemical messengers that traverse the synaptic gaps between neurons. When released by the sending neuron, neurotransmitters travel across the synapse and bind to receptor sites on the receiving neuron, thereby influencing whether that neuron will generate a neural impulse.

myelin "sausage" to the next.) The mind boggles when imagining this electrochemical process repeating up to 100 or even 1000 times a second. But this is just the first of many astonishments.

The neuron is a miniature decision-making device that performs some complex calculations. From hundreds, even thousands, of other neurons, it receives signals on its dendrites and cell body. Most of these signals are *excitatory,* somewhat like pushing a neuron's accelerator. Other signals are *inhibitory,* more like pushing its brake. If excitatory signals minus inhibitory signals exceed a minimum intensity, called the **threshold,** the combined signals trigger an action potential. (Think of it this way: If the excitatory party animals outvote the inhibitory party poopers, the party's on.) The action potential transmits down the axon, which branches into junctions with hundreds or thousands of other neurons and with the body's muscles and glands.

Increasing the stimulus above the threshold, however, will not increase the action potential's intensity. The neuron's reaction is an *all-or-none response:* Like guns, neurons either fire or they don't. How then do we detect the intensity of a stimulus? How do we distinguish a gentle touch from a big hug? A strong stimulus—a slap rather than a tap—can trigger more neurons to fire, and to fire more often. But it does not affect the action potential's strength or speed. Squeezing a trigger harder won't make a bullet go faster.

How Neurons Communicate

OBJECTIVE 4-4 | Describe how nerve cells communicate.

Neurons interweave so intricately that even with a microscope it is hard to see where one neuron ends and another begins. Scientists once believed that the branching axon of one cell fused with the dendrites of another in an uninterrupted fabric. Then a Spanish anatomist, Santiago Ramon y Cajal (1852–1934), described gaps between individual nerve cells and concluded that the individual neurons must function as independent agents within the nervous system. At the same time, the British physiologist Sir Charles Sherrington (1857–1952) noticed that neural impulses were taking an unexpectedly long time to travel a neural pathway. Sherrington inferred there must be a brief interruption in the transmission.

We now know that the axon terminal of one neuron is in fact separated from the receiving neuron by a gap less than a millionth of an inch wide. Sherrington called this junction the **synapse,** and the gap is called the *synaptic gap* or *cleft*. To Cajal, these near-unions of neurons—"protoplasmic kisses," he called them—were another of nature's marvels. "Like elegant ladies air-kissing so as not to muss their makeup, dendrites and axons don't quite touch," notes Diane Ackerman (2004). How do the neurons execute this protoplasmic kiss? How does information cross the tiny synaptic gap? The answer is one of the important scientific discoveries of our age.

When the action potential reaches the knoblike terminals at an axon's end, it triggers the release of chemical messengers, called **neurotransmitters** (FIGURE **4.3**). Within 1/10,000th of a second, the neurotransmitter molecules cross the synaptic gap and bind to receptor sites on the receiving neuron—as precisely as a key fits a lock. For an instant, the neurotransmitter unlocks tiny channels at the receiving site. This allows ions to enter the receiving neuron, thereby either exciting or inhibiting its readiness to fire. Excess neurotransmitters are reabsorbed by the sending neuron in a process called *reuptake*.

> "All information processing in the brain involves neurons 'talking to' each other at synapses."
>
> Neuroscientist Solomon H. Snyder (1984)

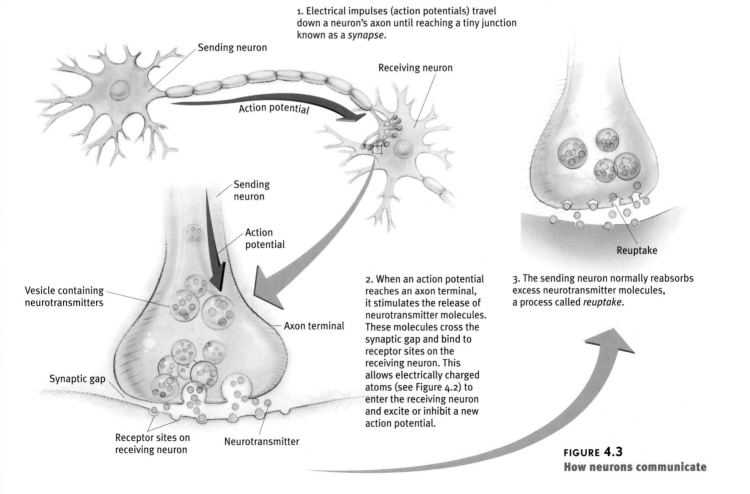

1. Electrical impulses (action potentials) travel down a neuron's axon until reaching a tiny junction known as a *synapse*.

Sending neuron

Receiving neuron

Action potential

Sending neuron

Action potential

Vesicle containing neurotransmitters

Axon terminal

Synaptic gap

Receptor sites on receiving neuron

Neurotransmitter

2. When an action potential reaches an axon terminal, it stimulates the release of neurotransmitter molecules. These molecules cross the synaptic gap and bind to receptor sites on the receiving neuron. This allows electrically charged atoms (see Figure 4.2) to enter the receiving neuron and excite or inhibit a new action potential.

Reuptake

3. The sending neuron normally reabsorbs excess neurotransmitter molecules, a process called *reuptake*.

FIGURE 4.3
How neurons communicate

How Neurotransmitters Influence Us

OBJECTIVE 4-5 | Explain how neurotransmitters affect behavior, and outline the effects of acetylcholine and the endorphins.

As researchers discovered dozens of different neurotransmitters, they also encountered new questions: Are certain neurotransmitters found only in specific places? How do they affect our moods, memories, and mental abilities? Can we boost or diminish these effects through drugs or diet?

Elsewhere in this text, we will examine neurotransmitter influences on depression and euphoria, hunger and thinking, addictions and therapy. Here, we will focus on how neurotransmitters influence our motions and our emotions. We now know that a particular neural pathway in the brain may use only one or two neurotransmitters (**FIGURE 4.4**), and that particular neurotransmitters may have particular effects on behavior and emotions. (**TABLE 4.1** offers examples.)

Acetylcholine (ACh) is one of the best-understood neurotransmitters. In addition to its role in learning and memory, ACh is the messenger at every junction between a motor neuron and skeletal muscle. When ACh is released to our muscle cells, the muscle contracts. If ACh transmission is blocked, the muscles cannot contract.

An exciting discovery about neurotransmitters occurred when Candace Pert and Solomon Snyder (1973) attached a radioactive tracer to morphine, showing them where it was taken up in an animal's brain. Their discovery: The morphine, an opiate drug that elevates mood and eases pain, bound to receptors in areas linked with mood and pain sensations.

Serotonin pathways

Dopamine pathways

Both photos from *Mapping the Mind*, Rita Carter, © 1989 University of California Press

FIGURE 4.4
Neurotransmitter pathways
Each of the brain's differing chemical messengers has designated pathways where it operates, as shown here for serotonin and dopamine (Carter, 1998).

Stanley Chou/Getty Images

TABLE 4.1

SOME NEUROTRANSMITTERS AND THEIR FUNCTIONS

Neurotransmitter	Function	Examples of Malfunctions
Acetylcholine (ACh)	Enables muscle action, learning, and memory.	With Alzheimer's disease, ACh-producing neurons deteriorate.
Dopamine	Influences movement, learning, attention, and emotion.	Excess dopamine receptor activity linked to schizophrenia. Starved of dopamine, the brain produces the tremors and decreased mobility of Parkinson's disease.
Serotonin	Affects mood, hunger, sleep, and arousal.	Undersupply linked to depression; Prozac and some other antidepressant drugs raise serotonin levels.
Norepinephrine	Helps control alertness and arousal.	Undersupply can depress mood.
GABA (gamma-aminobutyric acid)	A major inhibitory neurotransmitter.	Undersupply linked to seizures, tremors, and insomnia.
Glutamate	A major excitatory neurotransmitter; involved in memory.	Oversupply can overstimulate brain, producing migraines or seizures (which is why some people avoid MSG, monosodium glutamate, in food).

It was hard to imagine why the brain would contain these "opiate receptors" unless it had its own naturally occurring opiates. Why would the brain have a chemical lock, unless it also had a corresponding key? Researchers soon confirmed that the brain does indeed contain several types of neurotransmitter molecules similar to morphine. Named **endorphins** (short for *end*ogenous [produced within] *morphine*), these natural opiates are released in response to pain and vigorous exercise. They may therefore help explain good feelings such as the "runner's high," the painkilling effects of acupuncture, and the indifference to pain in some severely injured people, such as David Livingstone reported in his 1857 *Missionary Travels:*

> I heard a shout. Starting, and looking half round, I saw the lion just in the act of springing upon me. I was upon a little height, he caught my shoulder as he sprang, and we both came to the ground below together. Growling horribly close to my ear, he shook me as a terrier does a rat. The shock produced a stupor similar to that which seems to be felt by a mouse after the first shake of the cat. It caused a sort of dreaminess in which there was no sense of pain nor feeling of terror, though [I was] quite conscious of all that was happening. . . . This peculiar state is probably produced in all animals killed by the carnivora; and if so, is a merciful provision by our benevolent Creator for lessening the pain of death.

How Drugs and Other Chemicals Alter Neurotransmission

OBJECTIVE 4-6 | Explain how drugs and other chemicals affect neurotransmission, and describe the contrasting effects of agonists and antagonists.

If indeed the endorphins lessen pain and boost mood, why not flood the brain with artificial opiates, thereby intensifying the brain's own "feel-good" chemistry? One problem is that when flooded with opiate drugs such as heroin and morphine, the brain may stop producing its own natural opiates. When the drug is withdrawn, the brain may then be deprived of any form of opiate. For a drug addict, the result is discomfort that persists until the brain resumes production of its natural opiates or receives more artificial opiates. Mood-altering drugs, from alcohol to nicotine to heroin, share a common effect: They trigger unpleasant, lingering aftereffects. For suppressing the body's own neurotransmitter production, nature charges a price.

Various drugs affect communication at the synapse, often by either exciting or inhibiting neurons' firing. *Agonists* excite. An agonist molecule may be similar enough to the neurotransmitter to mimic its effects (**FIGURE 4.5b** on the next page) or it may block the neurotransmitter's reuptake. Some opiate drugs, for example, produce a temporary "high" by amplifying normal sensations of arousal or pleasure. Not so pleasant are the effects of black widow spider venom, which floods synapses with ACh. The result? Violent muscle contractions, convulsions, and possible death.

Antagonists inhibit. An antagonist can be a drug molecule that inhibits a neurotransmitter's release. Botulin, a poison that can form in improperly canned food, causes paralysis by blocking ACh release from the sending neuron. (Injections of botulin—Botox—smooth wrinkles by paralyzing the underlying facial muscles.) Or it may be enough like the natural neurotransmitter to occupy its receptor site and block its effect, as in **FIGURE 4.5c,** but not similar enough to stimulate the receptor (rather like foreign coins that fit into, but won't operate, a soda or candy machine). Curare, a poison that certain South American Indians apply to the tips of their hunting darts, occupies and blocks ACh receptor sites, leaving the neurotransmitter unable to affect the muscles. Struck by one of these darts, an animal becomes paralyzed.

" Physician Lewis Thomas, on the endorphins: "There it is, a biologically universal act of mercy. I cannot explain it, except to say that I would have put it in had I been around at the very beginning, sitting as a member of a planning committee."

The Youngest Science, 1983

■ **acetylcholine** [ah-seat-el-KO-leen] **(ACh)** a neurotransmitter that enables learning and memory and also triggers muscle contraction.

■ **endorphins** [en-DOR-fins] "morphine within"—natural, opiatelike neurotransmitters linked to pain control and to pleasure.

FIGURE 4.5
Agonists and antagonists

Vesicles containing neurotrans-mitters

Sending neuron

Action potential

Synaptic gap

Neurotransmitter molecule

Receptor sites

Receiving neuron

Neurotransmitters carry a message from a sending neuron across a synapse to receptor sites on a receiving neuron.

This neurotransmitter molecule fits the receptor site on the receiving neuron, much as a key fits a lock.

This agonist molecule excites. It is similar enough in structure to the neurotransmitter molecule to mimic its effects on the receiving neuron. Morphine, for instance, mimics the action of endorphins.

This antagonist molecule inhibits. It has a structure similar enough to the neurotransmitter to occupy its receptor site and block its action, but not similar enough to stimulate the receptor. Curare poisoning paralyzes its victims by blocking ACh receptors involved in muscle movement.

Neurotransmitter molecule

Receiving cell membrane

Receptor site on receiving neuron

(a)

Agonist mimics neurotransmitter

(b)

Antagonist blocks neurotransmitter

(c)

Neurotransmitter research is leading to new therapeutic drugs to alleviate depression, schizophrenia, and other disorders. But designing a drug can be harder than it sounds. A *blood-brain barrier* enables the brain to fence out unwanted chemicals circulating in the blood. Scientists know, for example, that the tremors of Parkinson's disease result from the death of nerve cells that produce dopamine. Giving the patient dopamine doesn't help, because dopamine cannot cross the blood-brain barrier. But some chemicals can slither through this barrier. One, L-dopa, a raw material the brain can convert to dopamine, enables many patients to regain better muscular control.

The Nervous System

OBJECTIVE 4-7 | Describe the nervous system's two major divisions, and identify the three types of neurons that transmit information through the system.

To live is to take in information from the world and the body's tissues, to make decisions, and to send back information and orders to the body's tissues. Neurons are the elementary components of our **nervous system,** our body's speedy electrochemical information network (**FIGURE 4.6**). The brain and spinal cord form the **central nervous system (CNS).** The **peripheral nervous system (PNS)** links the central nervous system with the body's sense receptors, muscles, and glands. The axons carrying this PNS information are bundled into the electrical cables that we know as **nerves.** The optic nerve, for example, bundles a million axon fibers

■ **nervous system** the body's speedy, electrochemical communication network, consisting of all the nerve cells of the peripheral and central nervous systems.

■ **central nervous system (CNS)** the brain and spinal cord.

■ **peripheral nervous system (PNS)** the sensory and motor neurons that connect the central nervous system (CNS) to the rest of the body.

■ **nerves** neural "cables" containing many axons. These bundled axons, which are part of the peripheral nervous system, connect the central nervous system with muscles, glands, and sense organs.

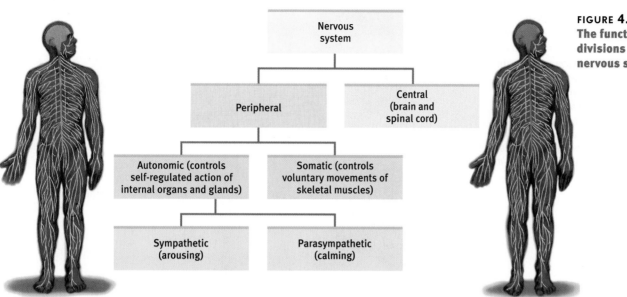

FIGURE **4.6**
The functional divisions of the human nervous system

into a single cable carrying the information that each eye sends to the brain (Mason & Kandel, 1991).

Information travels in the nervous system through three types of neurons. The **sensory neurons** send information from the body's tissues and sensory organs inward to the central nervous system's brain and spinal cord, which process the information. The central nervous system then sends instructions out to the body's tissues via the **motor neurons.** In between the sensory input and motor output, information is processed by the central nervous system's internal communication via its **interneurons**. Our complexity resides mostly in our interneuron systems. Our nervous system has a few million sensory neurons, a few million motor neurons, and billions and billions of interneurons.

The Peripheral Nervous System

OBJECTIVE 4-8 | Identify the subdivisions of the peripheral nervous system, and describe their functions.

Our peripheral nervous system has two components—somatic and autonomic. The **somatic nervous system** enables voluntary control of our skeletal muscles. As you reach the bottom of this page, the somatic nervous system will report to your brain the current state of your skeletal muscles and carry instructions back, triggering your hand to turn the page.

Our **autonomic nervous system** controls the glands and the muscles of our internal organs. Like an automatic pilot, this system may be consciously overridden. But usually it operates on its own (autonomously) to influence our internal functioning, including our heartbeat, digestion, and glandular activity.

The autonomic nervous system is a dual system (**FIGURE 4.7** on the next page). The **sympathetic nervous system** arouses. If something alarms, enrages, or challenges you (such as a longed-for job interview), the sympathetic system will accelerate your heartbeat, raise your blood pressure, slow your digestion, raise your blood sugar, and cool you with perspiration, making you alert and ready for action. (Lie-detection machines measure such stress responses, which sometimes also accompany lies.) When the stress subsides, the **parasympathetic nervous system** produces opposite effects. It conserves energy as it calms you by decreasing your heartbeat, lowering your blood sugar, and so forth. In everyday situations, the sympathetic and parasympathetic nervous systems work together to keep us in a steady internal state.

■ **sensory neurons** neurons that carry incoming information from the sense receptors to the central nervous system.

■ **motor neurons** neurons that carry outgoing information from the central nervous system to the muscles and glands.

■ **interneurons** central nervous system neurons that internally communicate and intervene between the sensory inputs and motor outputs.

■ **somatic nervous system** the division of the peripheral nervous system that controls the body's skeletal muscles. Also called the *skeletal nervous system*.

■ **autonomic** [aw-tuh-NAHM-ik] **nervous system** the part of the peripheral nervous system that controls the glands and the muscles of the internal organs (such as the heart). Its sympathetic division arouses; its parasympathetic division calms.

■ **sympathetic nervous system** the division of the autonomic nervous system that arouses the body, mobilizing its energy in stressful situations.

■ **parasympathetic nervous system** the division of the autonomic nervous system that calms the body, conserving its energy.

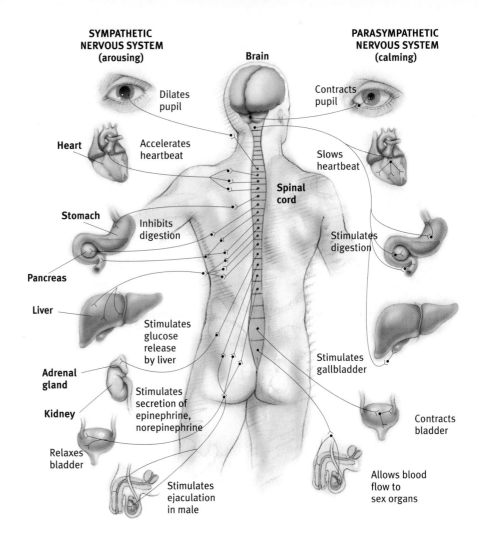

SYMPATHETIC NERVOUS SYSTEM (arousing)

PARASYMPATHETIC NERVOUS SYSTEM (calming)

Brain

Dilates pupil — Contracts pupil

Heart — Accelerates heartbeat — Slows heartbeat

Spinal cord

Stomach — Inhibits digestion — Stimulates digestion

Pancreas

Liver — Stimulates glucose release by liver — Stimulates gallbladder

Adrenal gland — Stimulates secretion of epinephrine, norepinephrine

Kidney

Relaxes bladder — Contracts bladder

Stimulates ejaculation in male — Allows blood flow to sex organs

The Central Nervous System

OBJECTIVE 4-9 | Contrast the simplicity of the reflex pathways with the complexity of neural networks.

"You are your synapses."
Joseph Le Doux, *The Synaptic Self*, 2002

From the simplicity of neurons "talking" to other neurons arises the complexity of the central nervous system that enables our humanity—our thinking, feeling, and acting. Tens of billions of neurons, each communicating with thousands of other neurons, yield an ever-changing wiring diagram that dwarfs a powerful computer. One of the great remaining scientific mysteries is how this neural machinery organizes itself into complex circuits capable of learning, feeling, and thinking.

The Spinal Cord and Reflexes

The central nervous system's spinal cord is an information highway connecting the peripheral nervous system to the brain. Ascending neural fibers send up sensory information, and descending fibers send back motor-control information.

The neural pathways governing our **reflexes,** our automatic responses to stimuli, illustrate the spinal cord's work. A simple spinal reflex pathway is composed of a single sensory neuron and a single motor neuron. These often communicate through an interneuron. The knee-jerk response, for example, involves one such simple pathway; a headless warm body could do it.

Another such pathway enables the pain reflex (**FIGURE 4.8**). When your finger touches a flame, neural activity excited by the heat travels via sensory neurons to interneurons in your spinal cord. These interneurons respond by activating motor neurons to the muscles in your arm. That's why it feels as if your hand jerks away not by your choice, but on its own.

■ **reflex** a simple, automatic, inborn response to a sensory stimulus, such as the knee-jerk response.

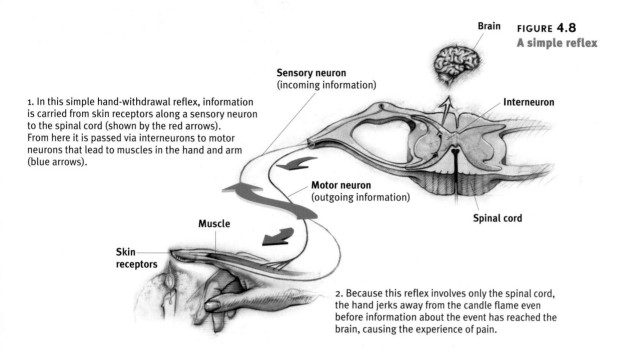

FIGURE 4.8
A simple reflex

Brain

Sensory neuron
(incoming information)

Interneuron

1. In this simple hand-withdrawal reflex, information is carried from skin receptors along a sensory neuron to the spinal cord (shown by the red arrows). From here it is passed via interneurons to motor neurons that lead to muscles in the hand and arm (blue arrows).

Motor neuron
(outgoing information)

Spinal cord

Muscle

Skin receptors

2. Because this reflex involves only the spinal cord, the hand jerks away from the candle flame even before information about the event has reached the brain, causing the experience of pain.

Because the simple pain reflex pathway runs through the spinal cord and out, your hand jerks from the candle's flame *before* your brain receives and responds to the information that causes you to feel pain. Information travels to and from the brain by way of the spinal cord. Were the top of your spinal cord severed, you would not feel such pain. Nor would you feel pleasure. Your brain would literally be out of touch with your body. You would lose all sensation and voluntary movement in body regions whose sensory and motor neurons connect with the spinal cord below its point of injury. You would exhibit the knee-jerk without feeling the tap. With the severing of the brain center that keeps the brakes on erections, men paralyzed below the waist are often capable of an erection (a simple reflex) if their genitals are stimulated (Goldstein, 2000). Females similarly paralyzed may respond with vaginal lubrication. But, depending on where and how completely the spinal cord is severed, they may be genitally unresponsive to erotic images and have no genital feeling (Kennedy & Over, 1990; Sipski & Alexander, 1999). To produce bodily pain or pleasure, the sensory information must reach the brain.

The Brain and Neural Networks

The other part of your central nervous system, your brain, receives information, interprets it, and decides responses. In doing so, the brain functions rather like a computing machine. It receives slightly differing images of an object from the two eyes, computes their difference, and instantly infers how far away the object must be to project such a difference. As basketball star LeBron James releases his falling-away jump shot, his agile brain performs an incredible number of instant computations, adjusting for body position and movement, distance, and angle.

How does James' brain perform such computations? First, each neuron connects with thousands of others. To get a feel for the complexity of these interconnections, consider: You could join two 8-studded Lego bricks 24 ways, and six bricks nearly 103 million ways. With some 40 billion neurons, each having roughly 10,000 contacts with other neurons, we end up with perhaps 400 trillion synapses—places where neurons meet and greet their neighbors (de Courten-Myers, 2005). A grain-of-sand–sized speck of your brain contains 100,000 neurons and one billion "talking" synapses (Ramachandran & Blakeslee, 1998). Being human takes a lot of nerve.

> "If the nervous system be cut off between the brain and other parts, the experiences of those other parts are nonexistent for the mind. The eye is blind, the ear deaf, the hand insensible and motionless."
>
> William James, *Principles of Psychology*, 1890

"The body is made up of millions and millions of crumbs."

Neurons in the brain connect
with one another to form networks

Inputs   Outputs

The brain learns by modifying
certain connections in response to feedback

FIGURE 4.9
A simplified neural network
Neurons network with nearby neurons.
Encoded in these networks of interrelating
neurons is your own enduring identity, your
sense of self that extends across the years.

Neurons cluster into work groups called **neural networks.** To understand why neurons tend to connect with nearby neurons, Stephen Kosslyn and Olivier Koenig (1992, p. 12) invite us to "think about why cities exist; why don't people distribute themselves more evenly across the countryside?" Like people networking with people, neurons network with nearby neurons with which they can have short, fast connections. As in **FIGURE 4.9,** the cells in each layer of a neural network connect with various cells in the next layer. Learning occurs as feedback strengthens connections that produce certain results. Piano practice, for example, builds neural connections. Neurons that fire together wire together.

New computer models simulate neural networks, complete with excitatory and inhibitory connections that gain strength with experience—and mimic the brain's capacity for learning. Of course, our own neural networks are more complicated than the networks depicted in Figure 4.9. In our brains, one neural network is interconnected with other networks that do different things. Open the brain and you will see no arrows that tell you where one network ends and the next begins; what distinguishes them is their specific functions. Each is a subnetwork, contributing its little bit of information to the whole information-processing system that we call the brain.

The Endocrine System

OBJECTIVE 4-10 | Describe the nature and functions of the endocrine system and its interaction with the nervous system.

So far we have focused on the body's speedy electrochemical information system. There is, however, another communication system. Interconnected with the nervous system is the second of the body's communication systems, the **endocrine system** (**FIGURE 4.10**). The endocrine system's glands secrete another form of chemical messengers, **hormones.** Hormones originate in one tissue, travel through the bloodstream, and affect other tissues, including the brain. When they act on the brain, they influence our interest in sex, food, and aggression.

Some hormones are chemically identical to neurotransmitters (those chemical messengers that diffuse across a synapse and excite or inhibit an adjacent neuron). The endocrine system and nervous system are therefore kindred systems: They both secrete molecules that activate receptors elsewhere. But unlike the speedy nervous system, zipping messages from eyes to brain to hand in a fraction of a second, endocrine messages trudge along. If the nervous system's communication delivers messages rather like e-mail, the endocrine system is the body's snail mail. Several seconds or more may elapse before the bloodstream carries a hormone from an endocrine

■ **neural networks** interconnected neural cells. With experience, networks can learn, as feedback strengthens or inhibits connections that produce certain results. Computer simulations of neural networks show analogous learning.

■ **endocrine** [EN-duh-krin] **system** the body's "slow" chemical communication system; a set of glands that secrete hormones into the bloodstream.

■ **hormones** chemical messengers, mostly those manufactured by the endocrine glands, that are produced in one tissue and affect another.

■ **adrenal** [ah-DREEN-el] **glands** a pair of endocrine glands just above the kidneys. The adrenals secrete the hormones epinephrine (adrenaline) and norepinephrine (noradrenaline), which help to arouse the body in times of stress.

■ **pituitary gland** the endocrine system's most influential gland. Under the influence of the hypothalamus, the pituitary regulates growth and controls other endocrine glands.

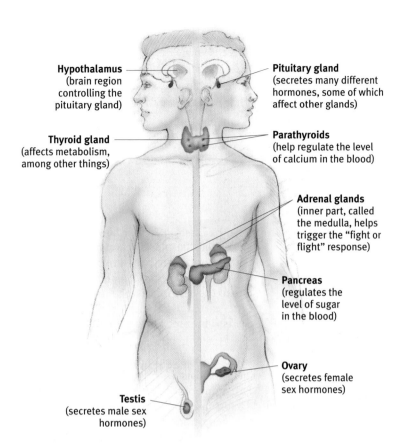

FIGURE 4.10
The endocrine system

Hypothalamus (brain region controlling the pituitary gland)

Pituitary gland (secretes many different hormones, some of which affect other glands)

Thyroid gland (affects metabolism, among other things)

Parathyroids (help regulate the level of calcium in the blood)

Adrenal glands (inner part, called the medulla, helps trigger the "fight or flight" response)

Pancreas (regulates the level of sugar in the blood)

Ovary (secretes female sex hormones)

Testis (secretes male sex hormones)

gland to its target tissue. But these endocrine messages are often worth the wait because their effects usually outlast the effects of a neural message. And that helps explain why sometimes, after our conscious mind is distracted from some mildly stressful news, we may have a lingering feeling that something isn't quite right. Under the influence of hormones and nonverbal brain areas, the feeling outlasts the thought—until we recapture the awareness and perhaps feel relief at recalling the reason for our discomfort.

The endocrine system's hormones influence many aspects of our lives—growth, reproduction, metabolism, mood—working to keep everything in balance while we respond to stress, exertion, and our own thoughts. In a moment of danger, for example, the autonomic nervous system orders the **adrenal glands** on top of the kidneys to release *epinephrine* and *norepinephrine* (also called *adrenaline* and *noradrenaline*). These hormones increase heart rate, blood pressure, and blood sugar, providing us with a surge of energy. When the emergency passes, the hormones—and the feelings of excitement—linger a while.

The most influential endocrine gland is the **pituitary gland,** a pea-sized structure located in the core of the brain, where it is controlled by an adjacent brain area called the *hypothalamus*. The pituitary releases hormones that influence growth, and its secretions also influence the release of hormones by other endocrine glands. The pituitary, then, is really a sort of master gland (whose own master is the hypothalamus). For example, under the brain's influence, the pituitary triggers your sex glands to release sex hormones. These in turn influence your brain and behavior.

This feedback system (brain → pituitary → other glands → hormones → brain) reveals the intimate connection of the nervous and endocrine systems: the nervous system directing endocrine secretions, which then affect the nervous system. In fact, the two systems so closely interconnect that the distinction between them sometimes blurs. Researchers have discovered that neurotransmitters can drift in the brain's fluid to nerve receptors at distant sites, thereby affecting overall alertness or mood (Agnati & others, 1992; Pert, 1986). In such cases, the distinction between certain neurotransmitters and their chemical twins—which are called hormones when released by glands—is no longer so clear. Conducting and coordinating this whole electrochemical orchestra is that maestro we call the brain.

>> LEARNING OUTCOMES

Neural and Hormonal Systems

OBJECTIVE 4-1 | Describe the ill-fated phrenology theory's contribution to the study of the brain's functions.

Franz Gall did not subject his beliefs about phrenology to scientific tests, but this early theory did help scientists to begin thinking about links among our biology, behavior, and mental processes.

OBJECTIVE 4-2 | Explain how viewing each person as a biopsychosocial system helps us understand human behavior, and discuss why researchers study other animals in search of clues to human neural processes.

For convenience, we may talk separately about biological or psychological influences on behavior, but in reality, everything psychological is simultaneously biological. Viewing each person as a biopsychosocial system lets us study behavior from multiple levels of analysis. At the biological level, neurons and other cells comprise organs, which form larger systems (digestion, circulation, information processing). At the social-cultural level, people live in specific times and places and are subject to specific environmental and social-cultural influences. At the psychological level, people's thoughts and emotions interact with their biology and personal history to produce that unique individual. Scientists study neural processes in other mammals and in relatively simple animals because humans and other animals have similar neural systems.

OBJECTIVE 4-3 | Describe the parts of a neuron, and explain how its impulses are generated.

The billions of neurons in the nervous system send signals through their *axons,* which are sometimes encased in a myelin sheath. Neurons receive signals from other cells through their branching *dendrites* and their *cell body.* If the combined signals are strong enough, the neuron fires, transmitting an electrical impulse (the action potential) down its axon, by means of a chemistry-to-electricity process in which ions are exchanged. The neuron's reaction is an all-or-none response.

OBJECTIVE 4-4 | Describe how nerve cells communicate.

When action potentials reach the end of an axon (the axon terminals), they stimulate the release of neurotransmitters. These chemical messengers carry a message from the sending neuron across a synapse to receptor sites on a receiving neuron. The sending neuron, in a process called *reuptake,* then normally absorbs the excess neurotransmitter molecules in the synaptic gap. The receiving neuron, if the signals from that neuron and others are strong enough, generates its own action potential and relays the message to other cells.

OBJECTIVE 4-5 | Explain how neurotransmitters affect behavior, and outline the effects of acetylcholine and the endorphins.

Each neurotransmitter travels a designated path in the brain and has a particular effect on behavior and emotions. Acetylcholine, one of the best-understood neurotransmitters, affects muscle action, learning, and memory. The endorphins are natural opiates released in response to pain and exercise.

OBJECTIVE 4-6 | Explain how drugs and other chemicals affect neurotransmission, and describe the contrasting effects of agonists and antagonists.

Drugs and other chemicals affect communication at the synapse. *Agonists,* such as some of the opiates, excite by mimicking particular neurotransmitters or by blocking their reuptake. *Antagonists,* such as curare, inhibit a particular neurotransmitter's release or block its effect.

OBJECTIVE 4-7 | Describe the nervous system's two major divisions, and identify the three types of neurons that transmit information through the system.

One major division of the nervous system is the *central nervous system (CNS),* which consists of the brain and spinal cord. The other is the *peripheral nervous system (PNS),* which consists of the neurons that connect the CNS to the rest of the body by means of nerves (bundled axons of the sensory and motor neurons). *Sensory neurons* carry incoming information from sense receptors to the CNS, and *motor neurons* carry information from the CNS out to the muscles and glands. *Interneurons* communicate within the CNS and between sensory and motor neurons.

OBJECTIVE 4-8 | Identify the subdivisions of the peripheral nervous system, and describe their functions.

The PNS has two main divisions. The *somatic nervous system* enables voluntary control of the skeletal muscles. The *autonomic nervous system,* through its sympathetic and parasympathetic divisions, controls involuntary muscles and glands.

OBJECTIVE 4-9 | Contrast the simplicity of the reflex pathways with the complexity of neural networks.

Reflexes are automatic inborn responses to stimuli, and they do not rely on conscious decisions made in the brain. A single sensory neuron, excited by some stimulus (such as a flame), passes a message to an interneuron in the spinal cord. The interneuron activates a motor neuron, causing some muscle reaction (such as jerking away from the heat source). *Neural networks,* found in the brain, are clusters of neurons that share some special task and strengthen with use, learning from experience. Each neural network connects with other networks performing different tasks.

OBJECTIVE 4-10 | **Describe the nature and functions of the endocrine system and its interaction with the nervous system.**

The endocrine system is a set of glands that secrete *hormones,* chemical messengers that travel through the bloodstream and affect other tissues, including the brain. Some hormones are chemically identical to neurotransmitters. The endocrine system's master gland, the pituitary, influences hormone release by other glands. In a feedback system, the brain's hypothalamus influences the pituitary gland, which influences other glands, which release hormones, which in turn influence the brain.

TERMS AND CONCEPTS TO REMEMBER

biological psychology, p. 4-0
neuron, p. 4-0
dendrite, p. 4-0
axon, p. 4-0
myelin [MY-uh-lin] sheath, p. 4-1
action potential, p. 4-1
threshold, p. 4-2
synapse [SIN-aps], p. 4-3
neurotransmitters, p. 4-3
acetylcholine [ah-seat-el-KO-leen] (ACh), p. 4-4
endorphins [en-DOR-fins], p. 4-5
nervous system, p. 4-6
central nervous system (CNS), p. 4-6
peripheral nervous system (PNS), p. 4-6

nerves, p. 4-6
sensory neurons, p. 4-7
motor neurons, p. 4-7
interneurons, p. 4-7
somatic nervous system, p. 4-7
autonomic [aw-tuh-NAHM-ik] nervous system, p. 4-7
sympathetic nervous system, p. 4-7
parasympathetic nervous system, p. 4-7
reflex, p. 4-8
neural networks, p. 4-10
endocrine [EN-duh-krin] system, p. 4-10
hormones, p. 4-10
adrenal [ah-DREEN-el] glands, p. 4-11
pituitary gland, p. 4-11

TEST YOURSELF

1. How do neurons communicate with one another?

2. How does information flow through your nervous system as you pick up a fork? Can you summarize this process?

3. Why is the pituitary gland called the "master gland"?

(Answers in Appendix B.)

ASK YOURSELF

1. Can you recall a time when the endorphin response may have protected you from feeling extreme pain?

2. Does our nervous system's design—with its synaptic gaps that chemical messenger molecules cross in an imperceptibly brief instant—surprise you? Would you have designed yourself differently?

3. Can you remember feeling an extended period of discomfort after some particularly stressful event? How long did those feelings last?

>WEB

Multiple-choice *self-tests* and more may be found at www.worthpublishers.com/myers.

5

The Brain

In a jar on a display shelf in Cornell University's psychology department resides the well-preserved brain of Edward Bradford Titchener, a great turn-of-the-century experimental psychologist and proponent of the study of consciousness. Imagine yourself gazing at that wrinkled mass of grayish tissue, wondering if in any sense Titchener is still in there.[1]

You might answer that, without the living whir of electrochemical activity, there could be nothing of Titchener in his preserved brain. Consider then an experiment about which the inquisitive Titchener himself might have daydreamed. Imagine that just moments before his death, someone removed Titchener's brain from his body and kept it alive by floating it in a tank of cerebral fluid while feeding it enriched blood. Would Titchener now still be in there? Further imagine that someone then transplanted the still-living brain into the body of a person with severe brain damage. To whose home should the recovered patient return?

That we can imagine such questions illustrates how convinced we are that we live in our heads. And for good reason: The brain enables the mind—seeing, hearing, smelling, feeling, remembering, thinking, speaking, dreaming. The brain is what poet Diane Ackerman (2004, p. 3) calls "that shiny mound of being . . . that dream factory . . . that huddle of neurons calling all the plays . . . that fickle pleasuredrome."

Moreover, it is the brain that self-reflectively analyzes the brain. When we're thinking about our brain, we're thinking *with* our brain—by firing countless millions of synapses and releasing billions of neurotransmitter molecules. Indeed, say neuroscientists, the *mind is what the brain does*. But precisely where and how are the mind's functions tied to the brain? Let's first see how scientists explore such questions.

The Tools of Discovery

OBJECTIVE **5-1** | Describe several techniques for studying the brain.

For centuries, we had no tools high-powered yet gentle enough to explore the living human brain. Now, within a lifetime, all that has changed. The known universe's most amazing organ is being probed and mapped by a new generation of neural cartographers. Whether in the interests of science or medicine, we can selectively **lesion** (destroy) tiny clusters of normal or defective brain cells, leaving their surroundings unharmed. We can probe the brain with tiny electrical pulses. We can snoop on the messages of individual neurons and eavesdrop on the chatter of billions of neurons. We can see color representations of the brain's energy-consuming activity. These techniques for peering into the thinking, feeling brain are doing for psychology what the microscope did for biology and the telescope did for astronomy.

Clinical Observation

The oldest method of studying brain-mind connections is to observe the effects of specific brain diseases and injuries. Such observations were first recorded some 5000 years ago. But it was not until the last two centuries that physicians began systemati-

"I am a brain, Watson. The rest of me is a mere appendix."

Sherlock Holmes, in Arthur Conan Doyle's "The Adventure of the Mazarin Stone"

Remember: *Neurons* (the nervous system's basic building blocks) communicate electrochemically by transmitting *neurotransmitters* (chemical messengers) across the *synapses* (tiny gaps) that separate them.

"You're certainly a lot less fun since the operation."

■ **lesion** [LEE-zhuhn] tissue destruction. A brain lesion is a naturally or experimentally caused destruction of brain tissue.

[1]Carl Sagan's *Broca's Brain* (1979) inspired this question.

Banking brains
Francine Benes, director of McLean Hospital's Brain Bank, sees the collection as a valuable database.

cally recording the results of damage to specific brain areas. Some noted that damage to one side of the brain often caused numbness or paralysis on the body's opposite side, suggesting that the right side of the body is wired to the brain's left side, and vice versa. Others noticed that damage to the back of the brain disrupted vision, and that damage to the left-front part of the brain produced speech difficulties. Gradually, these early explorers were mapping the brain. Today, records of more than 1500 brain-injured patients have been assembled by University of Iowa researchers into the largest-ever brain-damage registry. The Harvard Brain Bank at Boston's McLean Hospital stores 3000 brains from both "normal" people and those who suffered various psychiatric or neurological disorders. Their stories provide clues to our own brains' inner workings.

■ **electroencephalogram (EEG)** an amplified recording of the waves of electrical activity that sweep across the brain's surface. These waves are measured by electrodes placed on the scalp.

Manipulating the Brain

Today's scientists do not need to await brain injuries. They can electrically, chemically, or magnetically *stimulate* various parts of the brain and note the effects. They can also surgically lesion tissue in specific brain areas in animals. For example, a lesion in one area of the hypothalamus in a rat's brain reduces eating, causing the rat to starve unless force-fed. A lesion in another area produces *over*eating.

Recording the Brain's Electrical Activity

Right now, your mental activity is giving off telltale electrical, metabolic, and magnetic signals that would enable neuroscientists to observe your brain at work. The tips of modern microelectrodes are so small they can detect the electrical pulse in a single neuron, providing some astonishingly precise findings. For example, we can now detect exactly where the information goes in a cat's brain when someone strokes its whisker.

Electrical activity in the brain's billions of neurons sweeps in regular waves across its surface. The **electroencephalogram (EEG)** is an amplified read-out of such waves. Studying an EEG of the brain's activity is like studying a car engine by listening to its hum. However, by presenting a stimulus repeatedly and having a computer filter out brain activity unrelated to the stimulus, one can identify the electrical wave evoked by the stimulus (**FIGURE 5.1**).

FIGURE 5.1
An electroencephalograph providing amplified tracings of waves of electrical activity in the brain
Here it is displaying the brain activity of this 4-year-old who has epilepsy.

Courtesy of Brookhaven National Laboratories

FIGURE 5.2
The PET scan
To obtain a PET scan, researchers inject volunteers with a low and harmless dose of a short-lived radioactive sugar. Detectors around the subject's head pick up the release of gamma rays from the sugar, which has concentrated in active brain areas. A computer then processes and translates these signals into a map of the brain at work.

Neuroimaging Techniques

Newer windows into the brain give us a Supermanlike ability to see inside the living brain. One such tool, the **PET (positron emission tomography) scan** (**FIGURE 5.2**), depicts brain activity by showing each brain area's consumption of its chemical fuel, the sugar glucose (see Figure 5.22). Active neurons are glucose hogs. A person is given a temporarily radioactive form of glucose, and the PET scan locates and measures the radioactivity, thereby detecting where this "food for thought" goes. PET scans show that the brain areas that light up when people silently say the name of an animal differ from those that light up when they say the name of a tool (Martin & others, 1996). Rather like weather radar showing rain activity, PET scan "hot spots" show which brain areas are most active as the person performs mathematical calculations, listens to music, or daydreams.

Another new way of having one's head examined exploits the fact that the centers of atoms, including those in our brains, spin like tops. In **MRI (magnetic resonance imaging)** scans, the head is put in a strong magnetic field, which aligns the spinning atoms. Then a brief pulse of radio waves disorients the atoms momentarily. When the atoms return to their normal spin, they release signals that provide images of their concentrations, resulting in a detailed picture of the brain's (and the body's) soft tissues. MRI scans reveal a larger-than-average neural area in the left brain of musicians who display perfect pitch (Schlaug & others, 1995). MRI scans can also reveal enlarged fluid-filled brain areas in some patients who have schizophrenia, a disabling psychological disorder (**FIGURE 5.3**).

Both photos from Daniel Weinberger, M.D., CBDB, NIMH

FIGURE 5.3
MRI scan of a healthy individual (left) and a person with schizophrenia (right)
Note the enlarged fluid-filled brain region in the image on the right.

A special application of MRI, **fMRI (functional MRI),** can reveal the brain's functioning as well as its structure. Where the brain is especially active, blood goes. By comparing MRI scans taken less than a second apart, researchers can watch the brain light up (with increased oxygen-laden bloodflow) as a person performs different mental functions. As the person looks at a face, for example, the fMRI machine detects blood rushing to the back of the brain, which processes visual information (see Figure 5.17). Such snapshots of the brain's changing activity provide new insights into how the brain divides its labor.

In one intriguing study, neuroscientist Daniel Langleben and his colleagues (2002) discovered that fMRI scans located increased brain activity associated with lying. When participants lied about a playing card they held in their hand, the telltale fMRI revealed increased activity in two brain regions (**FIGURE 5.4**). One was the anterior cingulate cortex, an area typically active when we experience conflicting urges. Some researchers speculate that more portable methods of measuring brain activity might someday detect lies in real-life situations.

To be learning about the neurosciences now is like studying world geography while Magellan was exploring the seas. The number of explorers grows: The growing membership of the interdisciplinary Society for Neuroscience, founded in 1969, surpassed

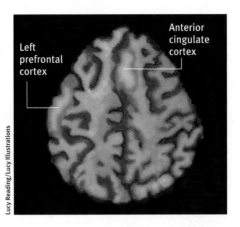

Left prefrontal cortex

Anterior cingulate cortex

FIGURE 5.4
Brain reading
An fMRI scan identified two brain areas that became especially active when a participant lied about holding a five of clubs.

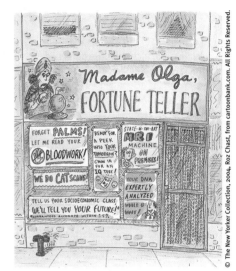

38,000 in 2006. Every year the explorers announce new discoveries, which also generate new interpretations of old discoveries.

Researchers are assembling this wealth of new information in computer databases. This brain cartography will give all researchers instant access through electronic networks to PET or MRI studies that reveal activity in a particular brain area while a person, for example, solves math problems. Clearly, this is the golden age of brain science.

Older Brain Structures

OBJECTIVE 5-2 | Describe the components of the brainstem, and summarize the functions of the brainstem, thalamus, and cerebellum.

If you could open the skull and look inside, the first thing you might note is the brain's size. In dinosaurs, the brain represents 1/100,000th of the body's weight, in whales 1/10,000th, in elephants 1/600th, in humans 1/45th. It looks as though a principle is emerging. But keep on. In mice the brain is 1/40th the body's weight, and in marmosets 1/25th. So there are exceptions to the rule that the ratio of brain to body weight provides a clue to a species' intelligence.

More useful indicators about an animal's capacities come from its brain structures. In primitive vertebrate (backboned) animals, such as sharks, the brain primarily regulates basic survival functions: breathing, resting, and feeding. In lower mammals, such as rodents, a more complex brain enables emotion and greater memory. In advanced mammals, such as humans, the brain processes more information, so we are able to act with foresight.

To enable this increasing complexity, species have elaborated new brain systems on top of the old, much as the Earth's landscape covers the old with the new. Digging down, one discovers the fossil remnants of the past—brainstem components still performing much as they did for our distant ancestors. Starting with the brainstem and working up to the newer systems, let's now explore the brain.

The Brainstem

The brain's basement—its oldest and innermost region—is the **brainstem.** It begins where the spinal cord enters the skull and swells slightly, forming the **medulla.** Here lie the controls for your heartbeat and breathing. If the top of a cat's brainstem is severed from the rest of the brain above it, the animal will still breathe and live—and even run, climb, and groom (Klemm, 1990). But cut off from the brain's higher region, it won't purposefully run or climb to get food. Just above the medulla sits the *pons,* which helps coordinate movements.

■ **PET (positron emission tomography) scan** a visual display of brain activity that detects where a radioactive form of glucose goes while the brain performs a given task.

■ **MRI (magnetic resonance imaging)** a technique that uses magnetic fields and radio waves to produce computer-generated images that distinguish among different types of soft tissue; allows us to see structures within the brain.

■ **fMRI (functional magnetic resonance imaging)** a technique for revealing blood flow and, therefore, brain activity by comparing successive MRI scans. MRI scans show brain anatomy; fMRI scans show brain function.

■ **brainstem** the oldest part and central core of the brain, beginning where the spinal cord swells as it enters the skull; the brainstem is responsible for automatic survival functions.

■ **medulla** [muh-DUL-uh] the base of the brainstem; controls heartbeat and breathing.

FIGURE 5.5
The brainstem and thalamus
The brainstem, including the pons and medulla, is an extension of the spinal cord. The thalamus is attached to its top. The reticular formation passes through both structures.

■ **reticular formation** a nerve network in the brainstem that plays an important role in controlling arousal.

■ **thalamus** [THAL-uh-muss] the brain's sensory switchboard, located on top of the brainstem; it directs messages to the sensory receiving areas in the cortex and transmits replies to the cerebellum and medulla.

■ **cerebellum** [sehr-uh-BELL-um] the "little brain" attached to the rear of the brainstem; its functions include processing sensory input and coordinating movement output and balance.

■ **limbic system** a doughnut-shaped system of neural structures at the border of the brainstem and cerebral hemispheres; associated with emotions such as fear and aggression and drives such as those for food and sex. Includes the hippocampus, amygdala, and hypothalamus.

■ **amygdala** [uh-MIG-duh-la] two lima bean-sized neural clusters that are components of the limbic system and are linked to emotion.

The brainstem is also the crossover point, where most nerves to and from each side of the brain connect with the body's opposite side. This peculiar cross-wiring is but one of many surprises the brain has to offer.

Inside the brainstem, between your ears, lies the **reticular** ("netlike") **formation,** a finger-shaped network of neurons that extends from the spinal cord right up to the thalamus (**FIGURE 5.5**). As the spinal cord's sensory input travels up to the thalamus, some of it travels through the reticular formation, which filters incoming stimuli and relays important information to other areas of the brain.

In 1949, Giuseppe Moruzzi and Horace Magoun discovered that electrically stimulating the reticular formation of a sleeping cat almost instantly produced an awake, alert animal. When Magoun *severed* a cat's reticular formation from higher brain regions, without damaging the nearby sensory pathways, the effect was equally dramatic: The cat lapsed into a coma from which it never awakened. Magoun could clap his hands by the cat's ear, even pinch it; still, no response. The conclusion? The reticular formation is involved in arousal. Later researchers discovered that elsewhere in the brainstem are neurons whose activity is needed for sleep.

The Thalamus

Atop the brainstem sits the brain's sensory switchboard, a joined pair of egg-shaped structures called the **thalamus** (Figure 5.5). It receives information from all the senses except smell and routes it to the brain regions that deal with seeing, hearing, tasting, and touching. Think of the thalamus as being to sensory input what London is to England's trains: a hub through which traffic passes en route to various destinations. The thalamus also receives some of the higher brain's replies, which it then directs to the medulla and to the cerebellum.

The Cerebellum

Extending from the rear of the brainstem is the baseball-sized **cerebellum,** meaning "little brain," which is what its two wrinkled halves resemble (**FIGURE 5.6**). The cerebellum enables one type of nonverbal learning and memory. New studies reveal that it also helps us judge time, modulate our emotions, and discriminate sounds and textures (Bower & Parsons, 2003). In addition to processing sensory information, the cerebellum coordinates voluntary movement. When soccer great David Beckham fires the ball into the net with a perfectly timed kick, give his cerebellum some credit.

If you injured your cerebellum, you would have difficulty walking, keeping your balance, or shaking hands. Your movements would be jerky and exaggerated.

Note: These older brain functions all occur without any conscious effort. This illustrates another of our recurring themes: *Our brain processes most information outside of our awareness.* We are aware of the *results* of our brain's labor (say, our current visual experience) but not of *how* we construct the visual image. Likewise, whether we are asleep or awake, our brainstem manages its life-sustaining functions, freeing our newer brain regions to dream, think, talk, or savor a memory.

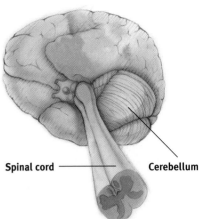

FIGURE 5.6
The brain's organ of agility
Hanging at the back of the brain, the cerebellum coordinates our movements, as when David Beckham directs the ball precisely.

The Limbic System

OBJECTIVE 5-3 | Describe the structures and functions of the limbic system, and explain how one of these structures controls the pituitary gland.

At the border ("limbus") of the brain's older parts and the cerebral hemispheres is the doughnut-shaped **limbic system** (**FIGURE 5.7**). One limbic system component, the *hippocampus,* processes memory. (If animals or humans lose their hippocampus to surgery or injury, they become unable to process new memories of facts and episodes.) The limbic system also has important links to emotions such as fear and anger, and to basic motives such as those for food and sex.

The Amygdala

In the limbic system, two lima bean-sized neural clusters, called the **amygdala,** influence aggression and fear (**FIGURE 5.8**). In 1939, psychologist Heinrich Klüver and neurosurgeon Paul Bucy surgically lesioned the part of a rhesus monkey's brain that included the amygdala. The result? The normally ill-tempered monkey turned into the most mellow of creatures. Poke it, pinch it, do virtually anything that normally would trigger a ferocious response, and still the animal remained placid. In later studies with other wild animals, including the lynx, wolverine, and wild rat, researchers noted the same effect. What then might happen if we electrically stimulated the amygdala in a normally placid domestic animal, such as a cat? Do so in one spot and the cat prepares to attack, hissing with its back arched, its pupils dilated, its hair on end. Move the electrode only slightly within the amygdala, cage the cat with a small mouse, and now it cowers in terror.

FIGURE 5.7 The limbic system
Limbic structures form a doughnut-shaped neural system between the brain's older parts and its cerebral hemispheres. Although part of the hormonal (endocrine) system, not the brain, the pituitary gland is controlled by the limbic system's hypothalamus, just above it.

FIGURE 5.8
The amygdala

Aggression as a brain state
Back arched and fur fluffed, this fierce cat is ready to attack. Electrical stimulation of a cat's amygdala provokes reactions such as the one shown here, suggesting its role in emotions like rage. Which division of the autonomic nervous system is activated by such stimulation? (See the final page of this module.)

hypothalamus [hi-po-THAL-uh-muss] a neural structure lying below (*hypo*) the thalamus; it directs several maintenance activities (eating, drinking, body temperature), helps govern the endocrine system via the pituitary gland, and is linked to emotion.

cerebral [seh-REE-bruhl] **cortex** the intricate fabric of interconnected neural cells that covers the cerebral hemispheres; the body's ultimate control and information-processing center.

FIGURE 5.9
The hypothalamus
This small but important structure, colored yellow/orange in this MRI scan photograph, helps keep the body's internal environment in a steady state by regulating thirst, hunger, and body temperature. Its activity also influences experiences of pleasurable reward.

> " If you were designing a robot vehicle to walk into the future and survive, . . . you'd wire it up so that behavior that ensured the survival of the self or the species—like sex and eating—would be naturally reinforcing."
> Candace Pert (1986)

These experiments confirm the amygdala's role in rage and fear, not to mention the perception of such emotions and the processing of emotional memories (Anderson & Phelps, 2000; Poremba & Gabriel, 2001). Still, we must be careful. The brain is *not* neatly organized into structures that correspond to our categories of behavior. Actually, both aggressive and fearful behavior involve neural activity in all levels of the brain, not solely in the amygdala. Even within the limbic system, stimulating neural structures other than the amygdala can evoke such behavior. If you put a charge to your car's dead battery, you can activate the engine. Yet the battery is merely one link in an integrated system.

Given that amygdala lesions can transform violent monkeys into mellow ones, might such lesions do the same in violent humans? You might think so. But such *psychosurgery* has produced varied results (Mark & Ervin, 1970; Valenstein, 1986). In a few cases involving patients who suffered brain abnormalities, it reduced fits of rage, though sometimes with devastating side effects on the patient's everyday functioning. For ethical reasons, and because of the uncertainties involved, drastic psychosurgery is rarely used. Perhaps, though, as we learn more about how the brain controls behavior, we will learn to alleviate brain disorders without creating new ones.

The Hypothalamus

Another of the limbic system's fascinating structures lies just below (*hypo*) the thalamus, and so is called the **hypothalamus** (**FIGURE 5.9**). By either lesioning or stimulating different areas, neuroscientists have identified hypothalamic neural networks that perform specific bodily maintenance duties. Some neural clusters influence hunger; others regulate thirst, body temperature, and sexual behavior.

The hypothalamus both monitors blood chemistry and takes orders from other parts of the brain. For example, thinking about sex (in your brain's cerebral cortex) can stimulate your hypothalamus to secrete hormones. Through these hormones, the hypothalamus controls the adjacent "master gland," the pituitary (see Figure 5.7), which in turn influences hormone release by other glands. (Note the interplay between the nervous and hormone systems: The brain influences the hormone system, which in turn influences the brain.)

The story of a remarkable discovery about the hypothalamus illustrates how progress in scientific research often occurs—when curious, open-minded investigators make an unexpected observation. Two young McGill University neuropsychologists, James Olds and Peter Milner (1954), were trying to implant electrodes in the reticular formations of white rats when they made a magnificent mistake. In one rat, they incorrectly placed an electrode in what was later discovered to be a region of the hypothalamus (Olds, 1975). Curiously, the rat kept returning to the place on its tabletop enclosure where it had been stimulated by this misplaced electrode, as if seeking more stimulation. Upon discovering their mistake, Olds and Milner alertly recognized that they had stumbled upon a brain center that provides a pleasurable reward.

In a meticulous series of experiments, Olds (1958) went on to locate other "pleasure centers," as he called them. (What the rats actually experience only they know, and they aren't telling. Rather than attribute human feelings to rats, today's scientists refer to *reward centers,* not "pleasure centers.") When allowed to trigger their own stimulation in these areas by pressing a pedal, rats would sometimes do so at a feverish pace—up to 7000 times per hour—until they dropped from exhaustion. Moreover, they would do anything to get this stimulation, even cross an electrified floor that a starving rat would not cross even to reach food (**FIGURE 5.10**).

Similar reward centers in or near the hypothalamus were later discovered in many other species, including goldfish, dolphins, and monkeys. In fact, animal research has revealed both a general reward system that triggers the release of the neurotransmitter dopamine and specific centers associated with the pleasures of eating, drinking, and sex. Animals, it seems, come equipped with built-in systems that reward activities essential to survival.

FIGURE 5.10
Rat with an implanted electrode
With an electrode implanted in a reward center of its hypothalamus, the rat readily crosses an electrified grid, accepting the painful shocks, to press a lever that sends electrical impulses to its "pleasure centers."

More recent experiments have found new ways of using limbic stimulation to control animals' actions. By using brain stimulation to reward rats for turning left or right, Sanjiv Talwar and his colleagues (2002) trained rats that had never been outdoors to navigate natural environments (**FIGURE 5.11**). By pressing buttons on a laptop, the researchers can direct a rat—which carries a receiver, power source, and video camera on a backpack—to turn on cue, climb trees, scurry along branches, and turn around and come back down. Their work suggests future applications in search-and-rescue operations.

Dramatic findings like these have led people to wonder whether humans, too, might have limbic centers for pleasure. Indeed we do. One neurosurgeon used electrodes to calm violent patients. Stimulated patients reported mild pleasure; however, unlike Olds' rats, they were not driven to a frenzy (Deutsch, 1972; Hooper & Teresi, 1986). Some researchers believe that addictive disorders, such as alcoholism, drug abuse, and binge eating, may stem from a *reward deficiency syndrome*—a genetically disposed deficiency in the natural brain systems for pleasure and well-being that leads people to crave whatever provides that missing pleasure or relieves negative feelings (Blum & others, 1996).

Sanjiv Talwar, SUNY Downstate

FIGURE 5.11
Ratbot on a pleasure cruise
When stimulated by remote control, this rat could be guided to navigate across a field and even up a tree.

The Cerebral Cortex

OBJECTIVE 5-4 | Define *cerebral cortex*, and explain its importance for the human brain.

Older brain networks sustain basic life functions and enable memory, emotions, and basic drives. Newer neural networks within the cerebral hemispheres form specialized work teams that enable our perceiving, thinking, and speaking. Your **cerebral cortex** is an intricate covering of interconnected neural cells that, like bark on a tree, forms a thin surface layer on your cerebral hemispheres. It is your body's ultimate control and information-processing center. (**FIGURE 5.12** on the next page locates the cerebral cortex as well as other brain areas discussed in this module.)

With the expansion of the cerebral cortex, tight genetic controls relax and the organism's adaptability increases. Frogs and other amphibians have a small cortex and operate extensively on preprogrammed genetic instructions. The larger cortex of

The people who first dissected and labeled the brain used the language of scholars—Latin and Greek. Their words are actually attempts at graphic description: For example, *cortex* means "bark," *cerebellum* is "little brain," and *thalamus* is "inner chamber."

FIGURE 5.12
Brain structures and their functions

Right hemisphere

Left hemisphere

Corpus callosum: axon fibers connecting two cerebral hemispheres

Thalamus: relays messages between lower brain centers and cerebral cortex

Hypothalamus: controls maintenance functions such as eating; helps govern endocrine system; linked to emotion and reward

Pituitary: master endocrine gland

Reticular formation: helps control arousal

Medulla: controls heartbeat and breathing

Spinal cord: pathway for neural fibers traveling to and from brain; controls simple reflexes

Cerebellum: coordinates voluntary movement and balance

Cerebral cortex: ultimate control and information-processing center

Amygdala: neural centers in the limbic system linked to emotion

Hippocampus: a structure in the limbic system linked to memory

■ Cerebral cortex   ■ Limbic system   ■ Brainstem

mammals offers increased capacities for learning and thinking, enabling them to be more adaptable. What makes us distinctively human mostly arises from the complex functions of our brain's thinking crown, its cerebral cortex.

Structure of the Cortex

OBJECTIVE 5-5 | Identify the four lobes of the cerebral cortex.

If you opened a human skull, exposing the brain, you would see a wrinkled organ, shaped somewhat like the meat of an oversized walnut. Eighty percent of the brain's weight lies in the ballooning left and right cerebral hemispheres, which are mostly filled with axon connections between the brain's surface and its other regions. The cerebral cortex—the brain hemispheres' thin surface layer—contains some 20 to 23 billion nerve cells (an estimate projected by sampling square-millimeter columns of cortical tissue [de Courten-Myers, 2002]).

Supporting these billions of nerve cells are nine times as many spidery **glial cells**— "glue cells" that guide neural connections, provide nutrients and insulating myelin, and mop up ions and neurotransmitters. Neurons are like queen bees; on their own they cannot feed or sheathe themselves. Glial cells are neural nannies. New evidence suggests they may also play a role in learning and thinking. By "chatting" with neurons they may participate in information transmission and memory (Travis, 1994). Moving up the ladder of animal life, the proportion of glia to neurons increases. A recent post-mortem analysis of Einstein's brain did not find more or larger-than-usual neurons, but it did reveal a much greater concentration of glia than found in an average Albert's head (Fields, 2004).

Looking at a human brain, the first thing you would notice about the cerebral cortex is its wrinkled surface, only about one-third of which would be visible. These folds

■ **glial cells (glia)** cells in the nervous system that support, nourish, and protect neurons.

■ **frontal lobes** the portion of the cerebral cortex lying just behind the forehead; in volved in speaking and muscle movements and in making plans and judgments.

■ **parietal** [puh-RYE-uh-tuhl] **lobes** the portion of the cerebral cortex lying at the top of the head and toward the rear; receives sensory input for touch and body position.

■ **occipital** [ahk-SIP-uh-tuhl] **lobes** the portion of the cerebral cortex lying at the back of the head; includes the visual areas, which receive visual information from the opposite visual field.

■ **temporal lobes** the portion of the cerebral cortex lying roughly above the ears; includes the auditory areas, each of which receives auditory information primarily from the opposite ear.

FIGURE 5.13

The cerebral cortex
If flattened, a human cortex would cover about four pages of this book. A chimpanzee's would cover one page, a monkey's a postcard, and a rat's a postage stamp (Calvin, 1996).

greatly increase the brain's surface area. If flattened, the brain's surface would be roughly the size of a large pizza. (To fit a thin pizza crust inside a skull, we would need to crumple it up.) In rats and other lower mammals, the cortex surface is smoother, with less neural fabric (**FIGURE 5.13**).

Each brain hemisphere is divided into four *lobes,* geographic subdivisions separated by prominent *fissures,* or folds (**FIGURE 5.14**). Starting at the front of your brain and going around over the top, there are the **frontal lobes** (behind your forehead), the **parietal lobes** (at the top and to the rear), the **occipital lobes** (at the back of your head), and the **temporal lobes** (on the sides of your head, just above your ears). Each lobe carries out many functions, and many functions require the interplay of several lobes.

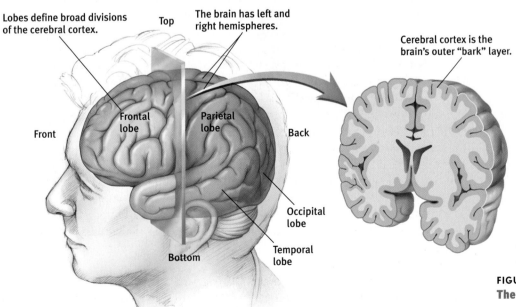

FIGURE 5.14
The cortex and its basic subdivisions

■ **motor cortex** an area at the rear of the frontal lobes that controls voluntary movements.

■ **sensory cortex** the area at the front of the parietal lobes that registers and processes body touch and movement sensations.

Functions of the Cortex

OBJECTIVE 5-6 | Summarize some of the findings on the functions of the motor cortex and the sensory cortex, and discuss the importance of the association areas.

More than a century ago, autopsies of people partially paralyzed or speechless revealed damaged cortical areas. But this rather crude evidence did not convince researchers that specific parts of the cortex perform specific functions. After all, if control of speech and movement were diffused across the cortex, damage to almost any area might produce the same effect. A television would go dead with its power cord cut, but we would be deluding ourselves if we thought we had "localized" the picture in the cord.

This analogy reminds us how easy it is to err when trying to localize brain functions. Complex activities such as speaking, drawing, and shooting pool involve many brain areas. For example, our experience of vocal music integrates brain activity in areas involved in speech and music processing. Mereille Besson and colleagues (1998) discovered this when recording electrical activity in the brains of French musicians listening to unaccompanied operatic solos. The musicians' brains processed the lyrics and tunes in separate brain areas en route to their experiencing "the exquisite unity of vocal music." Moreover, the spine-tingling thrills that music lovers enjoy appear to activate the same brain reward systems that are stimulated by sex and pleasing foods (Weinberger, 2004). As with other complex activities and experiences, music engages multiple brain areas.

Motor Functions

Scientists have, however, localized simpler brain functions. For example, in 1870, when German physicians Gustav Fritsch and Eduard Hitzig applied mild electrical stimulation to the cortexes of dogs, they made an important discovery: They could make different body parts move. The effects were selective: Stimulation caused movement only when applied to an arch-shaped region at the back of the frontal lobe, running roughly from ear to ear across the top of the brain. This arch we now call the **motor cortex** (**FIGURE 5.15**). Moreover, when the researchers stimulated specific parts of this region in the left or right hemisphere, specific body parts moved on the *opposite* side of the body.

FIGURE 5.15
Left hemisphere tissue devoted to each body part in the motor cortex and the sensory cortex
As you can see from this classic though inexact representation, the amount of cortex devoted to a body part is not proportional to that part's size. Rather, the brain devotes more tissue to sensitive areas and to areas requiring precise control. Thus, the fingers have a greater representation in the cortex than does the upper arm.

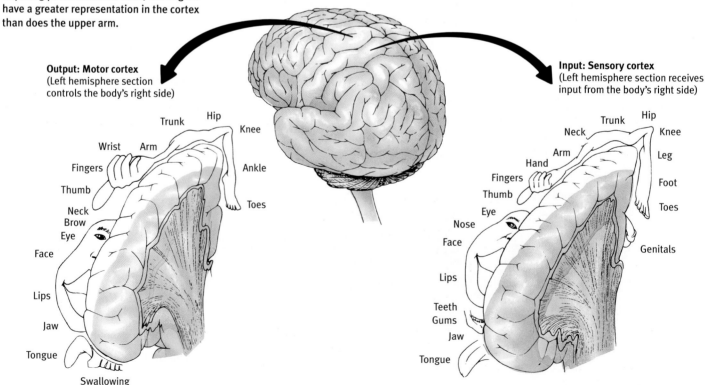

Output: Motor cortex
(Left hemisphere section controls the body's right side)

Input: Sensory cortex
(Left hemisphere section receives input from the body's right side)

Mapping the Motor Cortex A half-century ago, neurosurgeons Otfrid Foerster in Germany and Wilder Penfield in Montreal mapped the motor cortex in hundreds of wide-awake patients. Before putting the knife to the brain, the surgeons needed to know the possible side effects of removing different parts of the cortex. They painlessly (the brain has no sensory receptors) stimulated different cortical areas and noted the body responses. Like Fritsch and Hitzig, they found that when they stimulated different areas of the motor cortex at the back of the frontal lobe, different body parts moved. (Kids, don't try this without parental supervision.) They were now able to map the motor cortex according to the body parts it controlled (Figure 5.15). Interestingly, those areas of the body requiring precise control, such as the fingers and mouth, occupied the greatest amount of cortical space.

Neuroscientist José Delgado repeatedly demonstrated the mechanics of motor behavior. In one human patient, he stimulated a spot on the left motor cortex that triggered the right hand to make a fist. Asked to keep the fingers open during the next stimulation, the patient, whose fingers closed despite his best efforts, remarked, "I guess, Doctor, that your electricity is stronger than my will" (Delgado, 1969, p. 114). Scientists have also been able to predict a monkey's arm motion a tenth of a second before it moves—by repeatedly measuring motor cortex activity preceding specific arm movements (Gibbs, 1996).

Neural Prosthetics By similarly eavesdropping on the brain, could we enable someone—perhaps a paralyzed person—to move a robotic limb or command a cursor to write e-mail or surf the Web? To find out, Brown University brain researchers implanted 100 tiny recording electrodes in the motor cortexes of three monkeys (Nicolelis & Chapin, 2002; Serruya & others, 2002). As the monkeys used a joystick to move a cursor to follow a moving red target (to gain rewards), the researchers matched the brain signals with the arm movements. Then they let their computer operate the joystick. When a monkey merely thought about a move, the mind-reading computer moved the cursor with nearly the same proficiency as the monkey.

Newer research has recorded messages not from the motor neurons that directly control a monkey's arm, but from a brain area involved in planning and intention (Musallam & others, 2004). While the monkeys awaited a cue that told them to reach toward a spot (to get a juice reward) that had flashed on a screen in one of up to eight locations, a computer program recorded their neural activity. By matching the brain activity to a monkey's subsequent pointing, the mind-reading researchers could now program a cursor to move in response to the monkey's thinking (**FIGURE 5.16**). Monkey think, computer do.

In 2004, the U.S. Food and Drug Administration approved the first clinical trial of neural prosthetics with paralyzed humans (Pollack, 2004). The first patient, a paralyzed 25-year-old man, is now able to mentally control a television, draw shapes on a computer screen, and play video games—all thanks to an aspirin-sized chip with 100 microelectrodes recording activity in his motor cortex (Patoine, 2005).

Sensory Functions

If the motor cortex sends messages out to the body, where does the cortex receive the *incoming* messages? Penfield identified a cortical area that specializes in receiving information from the skin senses and from the movement of body parts. This area, parallel to the motor cortex and just behind it at the front of the parietal lobes, we now call the **sensory cortex** (Figure 5.15). Stimulate a point on the top of this band of tissue, and a person may report being touched on the shoulder; stimulate some point on the side, and the person may feel something on the face.

The more sensitive a body region, the larger the area of the sensory cortex devoted to it; your supersensitive lips project to a larger brain area than do your toes (Figure 5.15). (That's one reason we kiss with our lips rather than touch toes.) Similarly, rats have a large area of the brain devoted to their whisker sensations, owls to their hearing sensations, and so forth.

Demonstration: Try moving your right hand in a circular motion, as if polishing a table. Now start your right foot doing the same motion synchronized with the hand. Now reverse the foot motion (but not the hand). Tough, huh? But easier if you try moving the *left* foot opposite to the right hand. The left and right limbs are controlled by opposite sides of the brain. So their opposed activities interfere less with one another.

FIGURE 5.16
Mind over matter
Can just thinking make something happen? A California Institute of Technology research team led by Sam Musallam implanted electrodes in a parietal lobe region and recorded neural activity as a monkey planned to reach. When programmed into a computer's memory, this activity then enabled the monkey to move a cursor merely by thinking about it.

FIGURE 5.17
New technology shows the brain in action
This functional MRI scan shows the visual cortex—the occipital lobes—activated (color representation of increased bloodflow) as the subject looks at faces. When the person stops looking at faces, the region instantly calms down.

Courtesy of V. P. Clark, K. Keill, J. Ma. Maisog, S. Courtney, L. G. Ungerleider, and J. V. Haxby, National Institute of Mental Health

Scientists have identified other areas where the cortex receives input from senses other than touch. At this moment, you are receiving visual information in the occipital lobes at the very back of your brain (**FIGURE 5.17**). A bad enough bash there would make you blind. Stimulated there, you might see flashes of light or dashes of color. (In a sense, we *do* have eyes in the back of our head!) From your occipital lobes, visual information goes to other areas that specialize in tasks such as identifying words, detecting emotions, and recognizing faces.

Any sound you now hear is processed by the auditory areas in your temporal lobe (**FIGURE 5.18**). (If you think of your clenched fist as a brain, and hold it in front of you, your thumb would roughly correspond to the temporal lobe.) Most of this auditory information travels a circuitous route from one ear to the auditory receiving area above your opposite ear. If you were stimulated there, you might hear a sound. The sound needn't be real. MRI scans of people with schizophrenia reveal that auditory areas of the temporal lobe are active during auditory hallucinations (Lennox & others, 1999). Even the phantom ringing sound experienced by people with hearing loss is—if heard in one ear—associated with activity in the temporal lobe on the brain's opposite side (Muhlnickel, 1998).

Association Areas

So far, we have pointed out small areas of the cortex that either receive sensory input or direct muscular output. In humans, that leaves a full three-fourths of the thin wrinkled layer, the cerebral cortex, uncommitted to sensory or muscular activity. What then goes on in this vast region of the brain? Neurons in these **association areas** (the peach-colored areas in **FIGURE 5.19**) integrate information. They associate various sensory inputs with stored memories—a very important part of thinking.

Electrically probing the association areas doesn't trigger any observable response. So, unlike the sensory and motor areas, we can't so neatly specify the functions of the association areas. Their silence seems to have led to one of pop psychology's most widespread falsehoods: that we ordinarily use only 10 percent of our brains (as if the odds are 90 percent that a bullet to your brain would land in an area you don't use). This fabrication—"one of the hardiest weeds in the garden of psychology," writes Donald McBurney (1996, p. 44)—implies that if we could activate our whole brain, we would be far smarter than those who drudge along on 10 percent brain power. But surgically lesioned animals and brain-damaged humans bear witness that the association areas are not dormant. (The brain has no appendix—no apparently purposeless tissue. Moreover, given that brain tissue demands a lot of energy, nature would not

Rat
Cat

FIGURE 5.18
The visual cortex and auditory cortex
The occipital lobes at the rear of the brain receive input from the eyes. An auditory area of the temporal lobes receives information from the ears.

Visual cortex
Auditory cortex

FIGURE 5.19
Areas of the cortex in four mammals
More intelligent animals have increased "uncommitted" or association areas of the cortex. These vast areas of the brain are responsible for integrating and acting on information received and processed by sensory areas.

■ Motor areas
■ Sensory areas
■ Association areas

Chimpanzee
Human

squander resources on unused brain.) Rather, these areas interpret, integrate, and act on information processed by the sensory areas.

Association areas are found in all four lobes. In the frontal lobes, these areas enable us to judge, plan, and process new memories. People with damaged frontal lobes may have intact memories, score high on intelligence tests, and be able to bake a cake—yet be unable to plan ahead to *begin* baking the cake for the birthday party.

Frontal lobe damage also can alter personality, removing a person's inhibitions. Consider the classic case of railroad worker Phineas Gage. One afternoon in 1848, Gage, then 25 years old, was packing gunpowder into a rock with a tamping iron. A spark ignited the gunpowder, shooting the rod up through his left cheek and out the top of his skull, leaving his frontal lobes massively damaged (**FIGURE 5.20**). To everyone's amazement, Gage was immediately able to sit up and speak, and after the wound healed he returned to work.

Although his mental abilities and memories were intact, his personality was not. The affable, soft-spoken Phineas Gage was now irritable, profane, and dishonest. He eventually lost his job and ended up earning his living as a fairground exhibit. This person, said his friends, was "no longer Gage." With his frontal lobes ruptured, Gage's moral compass became disconnected from his behavior.

The same loss of moral compass was recently discovered to be true of two people who as young children had experienced frontal lobe damage similar to Gage's. Both of these individuals recovered, but they also matured as morally deficient—stealing, lying, and abusing and neglecting their out-of-wedlock children without remorse (Dolan, 1999). Although raised in good homes, they seemingly didn't know right from wrong.

Other association areas also perform mental functions. For example, the parietal lobes, parts of which were large and unusually shaped in Einstein's normal-weight brain, enable mathematical and spatial reasoning (Witelson & others, 1999). An area on the underside of the right temporal lobe enables us to recognize faces. If a stroke or head injury destroyed this area of your brain, you would still be able to describe facial features and to recognize someone's gender and approximate age, yet be strangely unable to identify the person as, say, Britney Spears or even your grandmother. But by and large, complex mental functions such as learning and memory don't reside in any one place. There is no one spot in a rat's small association cortex that, when damaged, will obliterate its ability to learn or remember a maze. Complex human abilities, such as memory and language, result from the intricate coordination of many brain areas.

Language

OBJECTIVE 5-7 | Describe the five brain areas that would be involved if you read this sentence aloud.

Consider this curious finding: Damage to any one of several cortical areas can cause **aphasia,** an impaired use of language. It is even more curious that some people with aphasia can speak fluently but cannot read (despite good vision), while others can comprehend what they read but cannot speak. Still others can write but not read, read but not write, read numbers but not letters, or sing but not speak. This is puzzling, because we think of speaking and reading, or writing and reading, or singing and speaking as merely different examples of the same general ability. So, how did researchers solve the mystery of how we use language? Consider these clues, which fit together as neatly as Lego blocks in a toy house.

Clue 1 In 1865, French physician Paul Broca reported that after damage to a specific area of the left frontal lobe (later called **Broca's area**) a person would struggle to speak words while still being able to sing familiar songs and comprehend speech.

FIGURE 5.20
Phineas Gage reconsidered
Using measurements of his skull (which was kept as a medical record) and modern neuroimaging techniques, researcher Hanna Damasio and her colleagues (1994) have reconstructed the probable path of the rod through Gage's brain.

■ **association areas** areas of the cerebral cortex that are not involved in primary motor or sensory functions; rather, they are involved in higher mental functions such as learning, remembering, thinking, and speaking.

■ **aphasia** impairment of language, usually caused by left hemisphere damage either to Broca's area (impairing speaking) or to Wernicke's area (impairing understanding).

■ **Broca's area** controls language expression—an area of the frontal lobe, usually in the left hemisphere, that directs the muscle movements involved in speech.

■ **Wernicke's area** controls language reception—a brain area involved in language comprehension and expression; usually in the left temporal lobe.

■ **plasticity** the brain's capacity for modification, as evident in brain reorganization following damage (especially in children) and in experiments on the effects of experience on brain development.

Clue 2 In 1874, German investigator Carl Wernicke discovered that after damage to a specific area of the left temporal lobe (**Wernicke's area**) people could speak only meaningless words. Asked to describe a picture that showed two boys stealing cookies behind a woman's back, one patient responded: "Mother is away her working her work to get her better, but when she's looking the two boys looking the other part. She's working another time" (Geschwind, 1979).

Clue 3 It was later discovered that reading aloud involves a third brain area. The *angular gyrus* receives the visual information from the visual area and recodes it into the auditory form, which Wernicke's area uses to derive its meaning.

Clue 4 Nerve fibers interconnect these brain areas.

Norman Geschwind assembled these clues into an explanation of how we use language (**FIGURES 5.21** and **5.22**). When you read aloud, the words (1) register in the visual area, (2) are relayed to a second brain area, the *angular gyrus,* which transforms the words into an auditory code that is (3) received and understood in the nearby Wernicke's area and (4) sent to Broca's area, which (5) controls the motor cortex as it creates the pronounced word. Depending on which link in this chain is damaged, a different form of aphasia occurs. Damage to the angular gyrus leaves the person able to speak and understand but unable to read. Damage to Wernicke's area disrupts understanding. Damage to Broca's area disrupts speaking. The now-familiar principle bears repeating: *Complex abilities result from the intricate coordination of many brain areas.*

Said another way, the brain operates by dividing its mental functions—speaking, perceiving, thinking, remembering—into subfunctions. Our conscious experience *seems* indivisible. Right now, assuming you have sight, you are experiencing a whole visual scene as if your eyes were video cameras projecting the scene into your brain. Actually, researchers have discovered that the brain breaks vision into specialized subtasks, such as discerning color, depth, movement, and form. (After a localized stroke that destroys one of these neural work teams, people may lose just one aspect of vision, such as the ability to perceive movement.) Each of these specialized neural networks, having simultaneously done its own thing, then feeds its information to "higher-level" networks that combine the atoms of experience and relay them to progressively higher-level association areas, enabling us to recognize a face as "Grandmother."

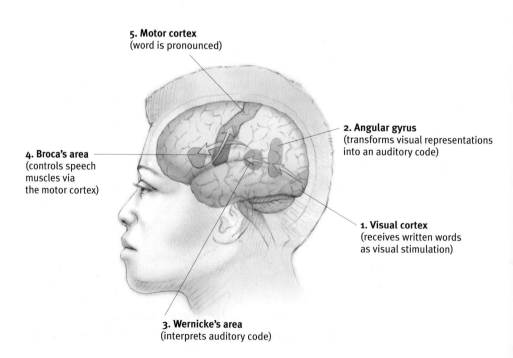

5. Motor cortex
(word is pronounced)

2. Angular gyrus
(transforms visual representations into an auditory code)

4. Broca's area
(controls speech muscles via the motor cortex)

1. Visual cortex
(receives written words as visual stimulation)

3. Wernicke's area
(interprets auditory code)

FIGURE 5.21
Specialization and integration in language

(a)
Hearing words
(auditory cortex and
Wernicke's area)

(b)
Seeing words
(visual cortex and
angular gyrus)

(c)
Speaking words
(Broca's area and
the motor cortex)

FIGURE 5.22
Brain activity when hearing, seeing, and speaking words
PET scans such as these detect the activity of different areas of the brain.

The same is true of reading a word: The brain computes the word's form, sound, and meaning using different neural networks (Posner & Carr, 1992). Thus fMRI scans show that jokes playing on meaning ("Why don't sharks bite lawyers? . . . Professional courtesy") are processed in a different brain area than jokes playing on words ("What kind of lights did Noah use on the ark? . . . Flood lights") (Goel & Dolan, 2001). Think about it: *What you experience as a continuous, indivisible stream of perception is actually but the visible tip of the information-processing iceberg, most of which lies beneath the surface of your conscious awareness.*

To sum up, the mind's subsystems are localized in particular brain regions, yet the brain acts as a unified whole. Moving your hand; recognizing faces; even perceiving color, motion, and depth—all depend on specific neural networks. Yet complex functions such as listening, learning, and loving involve the coordination of many brain areas. Together, these two principles—specialization and integration—describe the brain's functioning.

The Brain's Plasticity

OBJECTIVE 5-8 | Discuss the brain's plasticity following injury or illness.

The brain is sculpted not only by our genes but also by our experiences. Let's focus now on some evidence from studies of the brain's **plasticity,** its ability to modify itself after some types of damage.

Most severed neurons will not regenerate (if your spinal cord were severed, you likely would be permanently paralyzed). And some brain functions seem preassigned to particular areas. A newborn who suffered damage to the facial recognition areas on both temporal lobes never regained a normal ability to recognize faces (Farah & others, 2000). But some neural tissue can *reorganize* in response to damage. It happens within all of us, as the brain repairs itself after little mishaps. Plasticity is especially evident after serious damage. Lose a finger and the sensory cortex that received its input will begin to receive input from the adjacent fingers, which then become more sensitive (Fox, 1984). MRI scans show that well-practiced pianists likewise have a larger-than-usual auditory cortex area that encodes piano sounds (Bavelier & others, 2000; Pantev & others, 1998). Our brains are most plastic when we are young children (Kolb, 1989; see **FIGURE 5.23**).

The brain's plasticity is good news for those blind or deaf. If a blind person uses one finger to read Braille, the brain area dedicated to that finger expands as the sense of touch invades the visual cortex that normally helps people see (Barinaga, 1992a; Sadato & others, 1996). Temporarily "knock out" the visual cortex with magnetic stimulation, and a lifelong-blind person will make more errors on a *language* task (Amedi & others, 2004). In deaf people whose native language is sign, the temporal lobe area normally dedicated to auditory information waits in vain for stimulation.

FIGURE 5.23
Brain plasticity
If an injury or a surgical procedure destroys one part of a child's brain or, as in the case of this 6-year-old, even an entire *hemisphere* (to eliminate seizures), the brain will compensate by putting other surplus areas to work. One Johns Hopkins medical team, reflecting on the 58 child hemispherectomies they had performed, reported being "awed" by how well children retain their memory, personality, and humor after removal of either brain hemisphere (Vining & others, 1997).

Finally, it looks for other signals to process, such as those from the visual system. That helps explain why some studies find that deaf people have enhanced peripheral vision (Bosworth & Dolkins, 1999).

If a body part is amputated, sensory fibers that terminate on adjacent areas of the sensory cortex may invade the brain tissue that's no longer receiving sensory input. As Figure 5.15 shows, the hand is between the face and the arm regions on the sensory cortex. This explains a mysterious phenomenon: When stroking the face of someone whose hand had been amputated, V. S. Ramachandran found the person felt the sensations not only on his face but also on his nonexistent ("phantom") fingers. Ditto when stroking the arm, whose sensory fibers had also invaded the brain area vacated by the hand. Note, too, that the toes region is adjacent to the genitals. So what do you suppose was the sexual intercourse experience of another Ramachandran patient whose lower leg had been amputated? "I actually experience my orgasm in my foot. And there it's much bigger than it used to be because it's no longer just confined to my genitals" (Ramachandran & Blakeslee, 1998, p. 36).

Although brain modification often takes the form of reorganization, new evidence suggests that, contrary to long-held belief, adult mice and humans can also, in two older brain regions, generate new brain cells (Kempermann & Gage, 1999; Van Praag & others, 2002). Moreover, monkey brains form thousands of new neurons each day. These baby neurons originate deep in the brain and may then migrate to the thinking frontal lobe and form connections with neighboring neurons (Gould & others, 1999). Master stem cells that can develop into any type of brain cell have also been discovered in the human embryo. If mass-produced in a lab and injected into a damaged brain, might neural stem cells turn themselves into replacements for lost brain cells? Might we someday be able to rebuild damaged brains, much as we reseed damaged lawns? Might new drugs spur the production of new nerve cells? Stay tuned. Today's biotech companies are hard at work on such possibilities (Gage, 2003).

Our Divided Brain

OBJECTIVE 5-9 | Describe split-brain research, and explain how it helps us understand the functions of our left and right hemispheres.

For more than a century, clinical evidence has shown that the brain's two sides serve differing functions. Accidents, strokes, and tumors in the left hemisphere generally impair reading, writing, speaking, arithmetic reasoning, and understanding. Similar lesions in the right hemisphere seldom have such dramatic effects.

By 1960 the left hemisphere was therefore described as the "dominant" or "major" hemisphere, and its silent companion to the right as the "subordinate" or "minor" hemisphere. Then researchers found that the "minor" right hemisphere was not so limited after all. The story of this discovery is a fascinating chapter in psychology's history.

Splitting the Brain

In 1961, two Los Angeles neurosurgeons, Philip Vogel and Joseph Bogen, speculated that major epileptic seizures were caused by an amplification of abnormal brain activity that reverberated between the two cerebral hemispheres. They wondered whether they could reduce seizures in their patients with uncontrollable epilepsy by cutting communication between the hemispheres. To do this, Vogel and Bogen knew they would have to sever the **corpus callosum,** the wide band of axon fibers connecting the two hemispheres (**FIGURE 5.24**).

The surgeons had reason to believe such an operation would not be incapacitating. Psychologists Roger Sperry, Ronald Myers, and Michael Gazzaniga had divided the brains of cats and monkeys in this manner with no serious ill effects. So Vogel and

"You wouldn't want to have a date with the right hemisphere."

Michael Gazzaniga (2000)

■ **corpus callosum** [KOR-pus kah-LOW-sum] the large band of neural fibers connecting the two brain hemispheres and carrying messages between them.

■ **split brain** a condition in which the two hemispheres of the brain are isolated by cutting the connecting fibers (mainly those of the corpus callosum) between them.

Corpus callosum

Martin M. Rother

Courtesy of Terence Williams, University of Iowa

FIGURE 5.24
The corpus callosum
This large band of neural fibers connects the two brain hemispheres. To photograph the half brain shown at left, the hemispheres were separated by cutting through the corpus callosum and lower brain regions. In the view on the right, a surgeon has cut back brain tissue to expose the corpus callosum and bundles of fibers coming out from it.

Bogen operated. The result? The seizures were all but eliminated and the patients with these **split brains** were surprisingly normal, their personality and intellect hardly affected. Waking from the surgery, one patient even managed to quip that he had a "splitting headache" (Gazzaniga, 1967).

Only a decade earlier, neuropsychologist Karl Lashley had jested that maybe the corpus callosum served only "to keep the hemispheres from sagging." The ingenious experiments of Sperry and Gazzaniga revealed that this broad band of more than 200 million nerve fibers, capable of transferring more than a billion bits of information per second between the hemispheres, has a more significant purpose. Their studies of split-brain people—"the most fascinating people on Earth"—provided a key to understanding the two hemispheres' complementary functions.

As **FIGURE 5.25** explains, the peculiar nature of our visual wiring enabled the researchers to send information to the patient's left or right brain—by having the patient stare at a spot and then flashing a stimulus to its right or left. They could do this with you, too, but in your intact brain the hemisphere that received the information would instantly pass the news to its partner across the valley. The split-brain surgery severed the phone cables—the corpus callosum—across the valley, enabling the researchers to quiz each hemisphere separately.

In an early experiment, Gazzaniga (1967) asked split-brain patients to stare at a dot as he flashed HE•ART on a screen (**FIGURE 5.26** on the next page). Thus, HE appeared in their left visual field (which transmits to the right brain) and ART in the right field (which transmits to the left brain). When he then asked what they had seen, the patients *said* they had seen ART. But when asked to *point* to the word, they were startled when their left hand (controlled by the right brain) pointed to HE. Given an opportunity to express itself, each hemisphere reported only what it had seen. The right brain (controlling the left hand) intuitively knew what it could not verbally report.

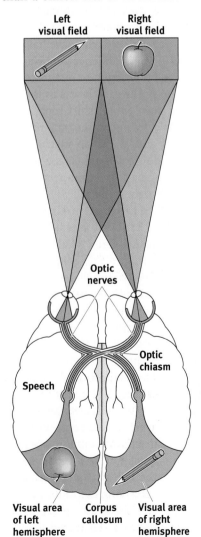

Left visual field   Right visual field

Optic nerves

Optic chiasm

Speech

Visual area of left hemisphere   Corpus callosum   Visual area of right hemisphere

FIGURE 5.25
The information highway from eye to brain
Information from the left half of your field of vision goes to your right hemisphere, and information from the right half of your visual field goes to your left hemisphere, which usually controls speech. (Note, however, that each eye receives sensory information from both the right and left visual fields.) The data received by either hemisphere are quickly transmitted to the other across the corpus callosum. In a person with a severed corpus callosum, this information sharing does not take place.

FIGURE 5.26

Testing the divided brain
When an experimenter flashes the word HEART across the visual field, the split-brain person reports seeing the portion of the word transmitted to her left hemisphere. However, if asked to indicate with her left hand what she saw, she points to the portion of the word transmitted to her right hemisphere. (From Gazzaniga, 1983.)

"Look at the dot."

Two words separated by a dot are momentarily projected.

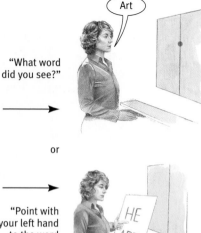

Art

"What word did you see?"

or

"Point with your left hand to the word you saw."

"Do not let your left hand know what your right hand is doing."

Matthew 6:3

Question: If we flashed a red light to the right hemisphere of a split-brain patient and flashed a green light to the left hemisphere, would each observe its own color? Would the person be aware that the colors differ? What would the person verbally report seeing? (Answers on this module's final page.)

FIGURE 5.27

Try this!
Joe, a split-brain patient, can simultaneously draw two different shapes.

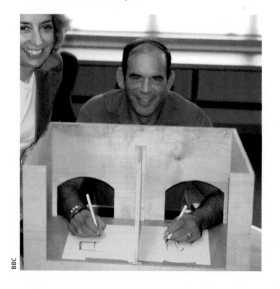

When a picture of a spoon was flashed to their right hemisphere, the patients could not say what they had viewed. But when asked to identify what they had viewed by feeling an assortment of hidden objects with their left hand, they readily selected the spoon. If the experimenter said, "Right!" the patient might reply, "What? Right? How could I possibly pick out the right object when I don't know what I saw?" It is, of course, the left hemisphere doing the talking here, bewildered by what the nonverbal right hemisphere knows.

A few people who have had split-brain surgery have been for a time bothered by the unruly independence of their left hand, which might unbutton a shirt while the right hand buttoned it, or put grocery store items back on the shelf after the right hand put them in the cart. It was as if each hemisphere was thinking "I've half a mind to wear my green (blue) shirt today." Indeed, said Sperry (1964), split-brain surgery leaves people "with two separate minds." With a split brain, both hemispheres can comprehend and follow an instruction to copy—*simultaneously*—different figures with the left and right hand (Franz & others, 2000; see **FIGURE 5.27**). (Reading these reports, I fantasize a split-brain person enjoying a solitary game of "rock, paper, scissors"—left versus right hand.)

When the "two minds" are at odds, the left hemisphere does mental gymnastics to rationalize reactions it does not understand. If a patient follows an order sent to the right hemisphere ("Walk"), the interpretive left hemisphere will offer a ready explanation ("I'm going into the house to get a Coke"). Thus, Michael Gazzaniga (1988) concludes that the conscious left hemisphere is an "interpreter" that instantly constructs theories to explain our behavior. Unlike the unconscious mind that runs our lives rather like the autopilot that operates a jumbo jet, the conscious mind acts like the pilot who occasionally takes control of the jet. It also acts as the mind's press secretary (and sometimes its storyteller), by explaining decisions made behind closed doors (Wegner, 2002; Wilson, 2002). These reports illustrate a core concept we will re-visit throughout this book: *The unconscious brain can control our behavior without our conscious effort or will.*

These experiments demonstrate that the left hemisphere is more active when a person deliberates over decisions (Rogers, 2003). The right hemisphere understands simple requests, easily perceives objects, and is more engaged when quick, intuitive responses are needed. The right side of the brain also surpasses the left at copying drawings and at recognizing faces, perceiving differences, perceiving emotion, and expressing emotion through the more expressive left side of the face. Right-hemisphere damage therefore more greatly disrupts emotion processing and social conduct (Tranel & others, 2002).

Most of the body's paired organs—kidneys, lungs, breasts—perform identical functions, providing a backup system should one side fail. Not so the brain's two halves, which can simultaneously carry out different functions with minimal duplication of effort. The result is a biologically odd but smart couple, each seemingly with a mind of its own.

Which one is happier?
Look at the center of one face, then the other. Does one appear happier? Most people say the right face does. Some researchers think this is because the right hemisphere, which is skilled in emotion processing, receives information from the left half of each face (when looking at its center).

Studying Hemispheric Differences in the Intact Brain

So, what about the 99.99+ percent of us with undivided brains? Have scientists found *our* hemispheres to be similarly specialized? With a warning that these findings are not meant to be overestimated (see Thinking Critically About Left Brain/Right Brain), the answer is yes.

When a person performs a *perceptual* task, for example, brain waves, bloodflow, and glucose consumption reveal increased activity in the *right* hemisphere; when a person speaks or calculates, activity increases in the *left* hemisphere. On occasion, hemispheric specialization (called *lateralization*) has been dramatically shown by using magnetic stimulation to temporarily disrupt left- or right-brain activity (Knecht & others, 2002), or by briefly sedating an entire hemisphere. To check for the locus of language before surgery, a physician may inject a sedative into the neck artery that feeds blood to the hemisphere on its side of the body. Before the drug is injected, the patient is lying down, arms in the air, conversing easily. You can likely predict what happens when the drug flows into the artery going to the left hemisphere: Within seconds, the person's right arm falls limp. If the left hemisphere controls language, the patient also becomes speechless until the drug wears off. When the drug enters the artery to the right hemisphere, the *left* arm falls limp, but the person can still speak. With the right rather than left hemisphere asleep, people also have difficulty recognizing themselves in an altered photo (Keenan, 2001).

Other tests confirm hemispheric specialization. For example, most people recognize a picture faster and more accurately when it is flashed (via the left visual field) to the right hemisphere. But they recognize a word faster and more accurately when it is flashed to the left hemisphere. If a word is flashed to your right hemisphere, perception takes a fraction of a second longer—the length of time it takes to send the information through the corpus callosum to the more verbal left hemisphere.

Which hemisphere would you suppose enables sign language among deaf people? The right, because of its visual-spatial superiority? Or the left, because of its processing language? Studies reveal that, just as hearing people usually use the left hemisphere to process speech, deaf people use the left hemisphere to read signs (Corina & others, 1992; Hickok & others, 2001). A stroke in the left hemisphere will disrupt a deaf person's signing, much as it would disrupt a hearing person's speaking. Broca's area is similarly involved in both spoken and signed speech production (Corina, 1998). To the brain, language is language, whether spoken or signed.

Although the left hemisphere is adept at making quick, literal interpretations of language, the right hemisphere excels in making subtle inferences (Beeman & Chiarello, 1998; Bowden & Beeman, 1998; Mason & Just, 2004). If primed with the flashed word *foot*, the left hemisphere will be especially quick to then recognize the closely associated word *heel*. But if primed with *foot*, *cry*, and *glass*, the right hemisphere will more quickly recognize another word that is distantly related to all three (*cut*). And if given an insightlike problem—what word goes with *boot*, *summer*, and *ground*?—the right hemisphere more quickly than the left recognizes that the solution is *camp*. As one patient explained after suffering right-hemisphere stroke damage, "I understand words, but I'm missing the subtleties." The right hemisphere also helps us modulate our speech to make meaning clear—as when we ask "What's that in the road ahead?" instead of "What's that in the road, a head?" (Heller, 1990).

THINKING CRITICALLY ABOUT :

LEFT BRAIN/RIGHT BRAIN

You've heard or read it many times: Some people are "left-brained," others "right-brained." But neuroscientists raise a caution flag: Beware the fad of locating complex human abilities such as science or art in either hemisphere. "The left-right dichotomy in cognitive mode is an idea with which it is very easy to run wild," warned Roger Sperry (1982).

Why do the popularizations of brain research so greatly exaggerate the findings? In *The Left-Hander Syndrome,* University of British Columbia psychologist Stanley Coren (1993) illustrates how journalism often oversimplifies and embellishes science. He recalls hearing a convention talk by Doreen Kimura, a psychologist then at the University of Western Ontario in London, Ontario. Kimura reported that melodies fed to the left ear were more easily recognized than melodies fed to the right ear. Knowing that the left ear sends most of its information to the right hemisphere, she concluded that, among her right-handed student volunteers, the right brain was better at recognizing melodies.

A few days later, the *New York Times* reported that "Doreen Kimura, a psychologist from London, Ontario, has found that *musical ability* is controlled by the right side of the brain" (italics highlight the embellishment). Apparently drawing from the *Times* story, a syndicated newspaper story then reported that "London psychologist, Dr. Doreen Kimura, claims that musicians are right-brained!" (But Kimura studied

university students, not musicians.) Later, a follow-up newspaper article further distorted the study: "An English psychologist has finally explained why there are so many great left-handed musicians."

Knowing that Kimura is not English, did not study musicians, and did not study left-handers, Coren recalled the words of an American editor: "Everything you read in the newspaper is absolutely true, except for the rare story of which you happen to have first-hand knowledge."

What can happen is this: As information flows from scientist to reader, it gets simplified as well as embellished, much as gossip does

Left brain/right brain
Is the artist a "right-brained" person? Such notions distort scientific findings regarding the cerebral hemispheres. While some areas of each hemisphere specialize in different tasks, the brain's two sides cooperate to enable whatever we do.

Robert Brenner/PhotoEdit

in passing from one person to the next. A TV network picks up an interesting finding, then reduces it to a 30-second report with an 11-second sound bite from the researcher. This alerts a major newspaper to a story angle, which in turn gets picked up by popular science magazines and, eventually, by supermarket magazines and tabloids.

At each step, notes Coren, "Ideas become more speculative and more distant from the actual research. . . . After a while, the neuropsychologist is no longer even visible in the communication chain." The rumors grow, accumulate, and evolve into scientific misinformation that becomes "'accepted truths,' which show up in conversation and writing in sentences that begin with, 'As everybody knows . . . ,' or 'Scientists have shown that. . . .'" In the end, sighs Coren, the public myth drowns out the voices of dissenting scientists.

The moral is not to discount everything you read, but to beware. Reporters want their stories to be newsworthy. When at their best, their ideal (and mine, in writing this book) is to extract the essence—to simplify without becoming simplistic. When at their worst, they distort a pretzel-shaped finding into a breadstick-shaped story: Some people are left-brained, others right-brained. . . .

From simply looking at the two hemispheres, which appear alike to the naked eye, who would suppose that they contribute so uniquely to the harmony of the whole? Yet a variety of observations—of people with split brains and people with normal brains—converge beautifully, leaving little doubt that we have unified brains with specialized parts.

Brain Organization and Handedness

Objective 5-10 | Discuss the relationships among brain organization, handedness, and mortality.

Nearly 90 percent of us are primarily right-handed (Medland & others, 2004). Some 10 percent of us (somewhat more among males, somewhat less among females) are left-handed. (A few people write with their right hand and throw a ball with their left, or vice versa.) Almost all (95 percent) right-handers process speech primarily in the left hemisphere, which tends to be the slightly larger hemisphere (Springer & Deutsch, 1985). Left-handers are more diverse. More than half process speech in the left hemisphere, as right-handers do. About a quarter process language in the right hemisphere; the other quarter use both hemispheres.

Is Handedness Inherited?

Judging from prehistoric human cave drawings, tools, and hand and arm bones, this veer to the right occurred long ago (Corballis, 1989; Steele, 2000). Right-handedness prevails in all human cultures. Moreover, it appears prior to culture's impact. Ultrasound observations of fetal thumb-sucking reveal that more than 9 in 10 fetuses suck the right hand's thumb (Hepper & others, 1990, 2004). This bias for the right hand is unique to humans and to the primates most like us: chimpanzees (Hopkins & others, 2005) and gorillas—only about 35 percent of whom are left-handed. Other primates are more evenly divided between lefties and righties.

Observing 150 human babies during the first two days after their birth, George Michel (1981) found that two-thirds consistently preferred to lie with their heads turned to the right. When he again studied a sample of these babies at age 5 months, almost all of the "head-right" babies reached for things with their right hands, and almost all of the "head-left" babies reached with their left hands. Such findings, along with the universal prevalence of right-handers, indicate that either genes or some prenatal factors influence handedness.

So, Is It All Right to Be Left-Handed?

Judging by our everyday conversation, left-handedness is not all right. To be "coming out of left field" or to offer a "left-handed compliment" is hardly better than to be "gauche" or "sinister" (words derived from the French and Latin for "left"). On the other hand, right-handedness is "right on," which any "righteous" "right-hand man" "in his right mind" usually is.

Left-handers are more numerous than usual among those with reading disabilities, allergies, and migraine headaches (Geschwind & Behan, 1984). But in Iran, where students report which hand they write with when taking the university entrance exam, lefties outperform righties in all subjects (Noroozian & others, 2003). Left-handedness is also more common among musicians, mathematicians, professional baseball and cricket players, architects, and artists, including such luminaries as Michelangelo, Leonardo da Vinci, and Picasso.[2] Although left-handers must tolerate elbow jostling at dinner parties, right-handed desks, and awkward scissors, the pros and cons of being a lefty seem roughly equal. But researchers have turned up one con that deserves more attention: Left-handers seem to disappear with age!

A Scientific Mystery: The Case of the Disappearing Southpaws

While studying handedness, psychologist Stanley Coren (1993) stumbled upon a rather stunning fact: With age, the percentage of left-handers declines dramatically. In his initial sample of 5147 people, he found that 15 percent of 10-year-olds, 5 percent of 50-year-olds, and less than 1 percent of those over age 80 were left-handers (**FIGURE 5.28** on the next page). Other researchers around the world have confirmed Coren's finding.

Most people also kick with their right foot, look through a microscope with their right eye, and (had you noticed?) kiss with their head and nose tilted to the right (Güntürkün, 2003).

Evidence that challenges a genetic explanation of handedness: Handedness is one of but a few traits that genetically identical twins aren't especially likely to share (Halpern & Coren, 1990).

---

[2]Strategic factors explain the higher-than-normal percentage of lefties in sports. For example, it helps a soccer team to have left-footed players play the left side of the field (Wood & Aggleton, 1989). In golf, however, no left-hander won the American Masters tournament until Canadian Mike Weir did so in 2003.

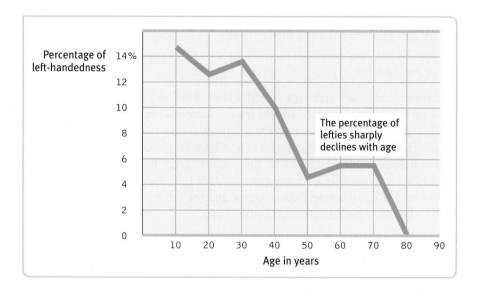

FIGURE **5.28**
The disappearing southpaws
The percentage of left-handers decreases sharply in samples of older people. (Adapted from Coren, 1993b.)

Percentage of left-handedness

The percentage of lefties sharply declines with age

Age in years

> "Truth is arrived at by the painstaking process of eliminating the untrue. When you have eliminated the impossible, whatever remains, *however improbable,* must be the truth."
>
> Sherlock Holmes in Arthur Conan Doyle's "The Sign of the Four," 1890

Intrigued, Coren and fellow sleuth Diane Halpern (1991; Halpern & Coren, 1988, 1991, 1993) set out in search of an answer. (If you were one of them, what explanations might have come to mind?)

Perhaps, Coren and Halpern first thought, childhood coercion causes natural lefties to become right-handed as they age. (Many older people can recall having their left hand slapped, tied down, or even balled into a fist with surgical tape when they tried to use it.) If today's parents and teachers are more accepting of left-handedness than were those of earlier times, the result might be more young left-handers. But North American and European studies suggest that during the twentieth century, left-handers increased only from about 6 percent of the population to 10 percent (Porac & others, 1980), too little to explain the much greater percentage of left-handers among the very young. Coren and his colleagues found further support for the stability of left-handedness in art works dated from 15,400 to 3000 B.C., where 10 percent of the people were depicted as left-handed. In modern art works, 11 percent are left-handers.

Might simple learning explain the slow and gradual disappearance of left-handers? Might the world's being designed for right-handers make it easier for lefties to learn *gradually* to use their right hands? But again, no. Preschoolers who switch handedness complete the process before adolescence. Handedness rarely switches after age 8 or 9, and even before then it occurs only for specific coerced actions (such as eating or writing).

What else remains? Coren and Halpern dared to think the unthinkable: that left-handers die younger. "That can't be true," skeptical colleagues replied when Coren first voiced the idea. "If true, surely someone would have noticed by now. Besides, my paternal grandmother was left-handed and lived to 91." But vivid anecdotes ("I know a person who . . .") are no substitute for conclusions based on large and representative samples. Neither examples nor counterexamples prove a generality.

So to explore their morbid idea, Coren and Halpern first reflected on the lefties' known health risks. Left-handers are more likely to have experienced birth stress, such as prematurity or the need for assisted respiration. They also endure more headaches, have more accidents (partly because of right-handed equipment; see **FIGURE 5.29**), have more knee and joint problems, use more tobacco and alcohol, and suffer more immune system problems (including allergies such as asthma, eczema, and hay fever).

These handedness differences aren't huge (individual differences are much greater). But might they, like gender differences in health risks, add up to differing life spans? When Coren and Halpern studied a random sample of recently deceased people of all ages they found that, on average, right-handers did live eight or nine

FIGURE 5.29
The southpaw's hazardous life
In the book *The Left-Hander Syndrome*, Stanley Coren illustrates risks posed by a world made for right-handers. When left-handers use a drill press, their left arm may obscure their view.

years longer. This difference dwindled a bit when Coren, Halpern, and other researchers excluded children. By comparing left-handed and right-handed former baseball and cricket players, they found the life-span difference reduced—three years, Coren estimated—but still apparent (Aggleton & others, 1993; Rogerson, 1994).

This stunning finding triggered an avalanche of publicity, much of it distorted, which in turn triggered nasty responses: "Dear professor . . . we strongly suggest that you beware of sinister lefties bearing grudges—and chain saws," and "You right-handers think that you'll live longer than left-handers but you won't if we kill you first" (Halpern & others, 1996). The finding also stimulated some follow-up research that produced no life-expectancy advantage for right-handers (Harris, 1993). One National Institute on Aging research team followed 3800 East Boston adults for six years and found that, at any age, left-handers were *not* more likely to die (Salive & others, 1993). Coren (1993) responded that six years is not long enough to catch a statistically significant handedness effect in a sample this small.

The unfinished case of the disappearing southpaws illustrates the very heart of science—how it dares to ask researchable questions, even those with unsettling implications. In the court of scientific judgment, researchers are welcome to state new ideas but they must expose themselves to counterexamination from opposing views and to heated debate. Over time, science has a way of unmasking error, taking us closer to truth, and often to an improved world. As it explains the absence of elder left-handers, it may also point the way to safer, more comfortable environments for left-handed people.

Long-lived left-handers:
- Benjamin Franklin (84)
- Charlie Chaplin (88)
- Pablo Picasso (92)
- The Queen Mother (101)

Short-lived left-handers:
- Babe Ruth (53)
- Marilyn Monroe (36)
- Alexander the Great (33)
- Kurt Cobain (27)

Reflections on the Biological Revolution in Psychology

We have glimpsed the truth of an overriding principle: Everything psychological is simultaneously biological. We have focused on how our thoughts, feelings, and actions arise from our specialized yet integrated brain. Elsewhere in this text, we will further explore the significance of the biological revolution in psychology. We will see, for example, how

- genes and experience jointly influence our personality, emotions, and intelligence.
- brain development underlies a child's mental development.
- our sense organs and our brain enable us to see and hear.
- the brain stores memories.
- our brain and body work to create our experiences of hunger and sexuality, anger and fear, sleep and dreams.
- mind and body together influence our vulnerability to disease and our capacity for healing.
- aberrant brain anatomy and chemistry influence depression and schizophrenia;

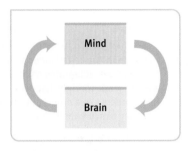

Mind and brain as holistic system
In Roger Sperry's view, the brain creates and controls the emergent mind, which in turn influences the brain. (Think vividly about biting into a lemon and you may salivate.)

"If I were a college student today, I don't think I could resist going into neuro-science."
—Novelist Tom Wolfe, 2004

and we'll see how biological treatments can alleviate these conditions.

- our species' evolutionary history may predispose us to hurt, help, or love certain others.

Today's neuroscience has come a long way, yet what is unknown still dwarfs what is known. We can describe the brain. We can learn the functions of its parts. We can study how the parts communicate. But how do we get mind out of meat? How does the electrochemical whir in a hunk of tissue the size of a head of lettuce give rise to elation, a creative idea, or that memory of Grandmother?

Much as gas and air can give rise to something different—fire—so also, believed Roger Sperry, does the complex human brain give rise to something different: consciousness. The mind, he argued, emerges from the brain's dance of ions, yet is not reducible to it. Cells cannot be fully explained by the actions of atoms, nor minds by the activity of cells. Psychology is rooted in biology which is rooted in chemistry which is rooted in physics. Yet psychology is more than applied physics. As Jerome Kagan (1998) reminds us, the meaning of the Gettysburg Address is not reducible to neural activity. Sexual love is more than blood flooding to the genitals. Morality and responsibility become possible when we understand the mind as a "holistic system," said Sperry (1992). We are not mere jabbering robots.

The mind seeking to understand the brain—that is indeed among the ultimate scientific challenges. And so it will always be. To paraphrase cosmologist John Barrow, a brain simple enough to be understood is too simple to produce a mind able to understand it.

>> LEARNING OUTCOMES

The Brain

OBJECTIVE 5-1 | Describe several techniques for studying the brain.
Clinical observations have long revealed the general effects of damage to various areas of the brain. But *MRI scans* now reveal brain structures, and *EEG, PET,* and *fMRI (functional MRI) recordings* reveal brain activity. By surgically lesioning or electrically stimulating specific brain areas, by recording the brain's surface electrical activity, and by displaying neural activity with computer-aided brain scans, neuroscientists explore the connections among brain, mind, and behavior.

OBJECTIVE 5-2 | Describe the components of the brainstem, and summarize the functions of the brainstem, thalamus, and cerebellum.
The brainstem is the oldest part of the brain and is responsible for automatic survival functions. Its components are the *medulla* (which controls heartbeat and breathing), the *pons* (which helps coordinate movements), and the *reticular formation* (which affects arousal). The *thalamus,* the brain's sensory switchboard, sits above the brainstem. The *cerebellum,* attached to the rear of the brainstem, coordinates muscle movement and helps process sensory information.

OBJECTIVE 5-3 | Describe the structures and functions of the limbic system, and explain how one of these structures controls the pituitary gland.
Between the brainstem and cerebral cortex is the limbic system, which is linked to emotions, memory, and drives. One of its neural centers, the *amygdala,* is involved in responses of aggression and fear. Another, the *hypothalamus,* is involved in various bodily maintenance functions, pleasurable rewards, and the control of the hormonal system. The hypothalamus sits just above the *pituitary* (the "master gland") and controls it by stimulating it to trigger the release of hormones. The *hippocampus,* also part of the limbic system, processes memory.

OBJECTIVE 5-4 | Define *cerebral cortex,* and explain its importance for the human brain.
The *cerebral cortex* is the thin layer of interconnected neurons covering the brain's hemispheres. The human brain's cortex enables learning, thinking, and other complex forms of information processing that make us uniquely human.

OBJECTIVE 5-5 | Identify the four lobes of the cerebral cortex.
Each cerebral hemisphere has four geographic areas. The *frontal lobes,* just behind the forehead, are involved in speaking, muscle movements, and planning and judgments. The *parietal lobes,* at the top of the head and toward the rear, receive sensory input for touch and body position. The *occipital lobes,* at the back of the head, include visual areas. The *temporal lobes,* just above the ears, include auditory areas. Each lobe performs many functions and interacts with other areas of the cortex.

OBJECTIVE 5-6 | Summarize some of the findings on the functions of the motor cortex and the sensory cortex, and discuss the importance of the association areas.
Some brain areas serve specific functions (see Figure 5.12). One is the *motor cortex,* an arch-shaped region at the rear of the

frontal lobes that controls voluntary movements. Another is the sensory cortex, a region at the front of the parietal lobes that registers and processes body sensations. Body parts that require precise control (in the motor cortex) or that are especially sensitive (in the sensory cortex) occupy the most space. The major portion of each of the four lobes, however, is devoted to uncommitted association areas, which integrate information involved in learning, remembering, thinking, and other higher-level functions.

OBJECTIVE 5-7 | **Describe the five brain areas that would be involved if you read this sentence aloud.**

Language depends on the integration of many specific neural networks performing specialized subtasks. As you read aloud, your *visual cortex* registers words as visual stimuli, the *angular gyrus* transforms those visual representations into auditory codes, *Wernicke's area* interprets those codes and sends the message to *Broca's area,* which controls the *motor cortex* as you pronounce words.

OBJECTIVE 5-8 | **Discuss the brain's plasticity following injury or illness.**

If one hemisphere is damaged early in life, the other will pick up many of its functions. This plasticity diminishes later in life, although nearby neurons may partially compensate for damaged ones after a stroke or other brain injury.

OBJECTIVE 5-9 | **Describe split-brain research, and explain how it helps us understand the functions of our left and right hemispheres.**

Split-brain research (experiments on people with a severed corpus callosum) has confirmed that in most people the left hemisphere is the more verbal, and that the right hemisphere excels in visual perception and the recognition of emotion. Studies of healthy people with intact brains confirm that each hemisphere makes unique contributions to the integrated functioning of the brain.

OBJECTIVE 5-10 | **Discuss the relationships among brain organization, handedness, and mortality.**

Almost all right-handers process speech in the left hemisphere, as do more than half of all left-handers. The remainder of left-handers split about evenly in processing language in the right hemisphere or in both hemispheres. The percentage of lefties decreases sharply with age, from about 15 percent at age 10 to less than 1 percent at age 80. This decline may reflect a higher risk of accidents.

TERMS AND CONCEPTS TO REMEMBER

lesion [LEE-zhuhn], p. 5-0
electroencephalogram (EEG), p. 5-1
PET (positron emission tomography) scan, p. 5-2
MRI (magnetic resonance imaging), p. 5-2
fMRI (functional MRI), p. 5-2
brainstem, p. 5-3
medulla [muh-DUL-uh], p. 5-3
reticular formation, p. 5-4
thalamus [THAL-uh-muss], p. 5-4
cerebellum [sehr-uh-BELL-um], p. 5-4
limbic system, p. 5-5
amygdala [uh-MIG-duh-la], p. 5-5
hypothalamus [hi-po-THAL-uh-muss], p. 5-6
cerebral [seh-REE-bruhl] cortex, p. 5-7
glial cells (glia), p. 5-8
frontal lobes, p. 5-9
parietal [puh-RYE-uh-tuhl] lobes, p. 5-9
occipital [ahk-SIP-uh-tuhl] lobes, p. 5-9
temporal lobes, p. 5-9
motor cortex, p. 5-10
sensory cortex, p. 5-11
association areas, p. 5-12
aphasia, p. 5-13
Broca's area, p. 5-13
Wernicke's area, p. 5-14
plasticity, p. 5-15
corpus callosum [KOR-pus kah-LOW-sum], p. 5-16
split brain, p. 5-17

TEST YOURSELF

1. Within what brain region would damage be most likely to disrupt your ability to skip rope? Your ability to sense tastes or sounds? In what brain region would damage perhaps leave you in a coma? Without the very breath and heartbeat of life?

(Answer in Appendix B.)

ASK YOURSELF

1. How might you feel with two separate brain hemispheres, both of which controlled your thought and action but one of which dominated your consciousness and speech? How might that affect your sense of self, as one indivisible person?

ANSWERS TO QUESTIONS WITHIN THE MODULE

Q. If you electrically stimulated a cat's amygdala, which division of the cat's nervous system would be aroused?
A. Its sympathetic nervous system.
Q. If we flashed a red light to the right hemisphere of a split-brain patient and flashed a green light to the left hemisphere, would each observe its own color?
A. Yes.
Q. Would the person be aware that the colors differ?
A. No.
Q. What would the person verbally report seeing?
A. Green.

>WEB

Multiple-choice *self-tests* and more may be found at www.worthpublishers.com/myers.

ANOTHER VOICE ON: NATURE, NURTURE, AND HUMAN DIVERSITY

JUDITH ORTIZ COFER (b. 1952), FROM "THE CHANGELING," 1992

As a young girl
vying for my father's attention,
I invented a game that made him look up
from his reading and shake his head
as if both baffled and amused.

In my brother's closet, I'd change
into his dungarees––the rough material
molding me into boy shape; hide
my long hair under an army helmet
he'd been given by Father, and emerge

transformed into the legendary Che
of grown-up talk.

Strutting around the room,
I'd tell of life in the mountains,
of carnage and rivers of blood,
and of manly feasts with rum and music
to celebrate victories para la libertad.
He would listen with a smile
to my tales of battles and brotherhood
until Mother called us to dinner.

She was not amused
by my transformations, sternly
   forbidding me
from sitting down with them as a man.
She'd order me back to the dark cubicle
that smelled of adventure, to shed
my costume, to braid my hair furiously
with blind hands, and to return invisible,
   as myself,
to the real world of her kitchen.

TEST YOURSELF

1. As society succeeds in creating equality of opportunity, it will also increase the heritability of ability. The heritability of intelligence scores will be greater in a society marked by equal opportunity than in a society of peasants and aristocrats. Why?

(Answer in Appendix B.)

ASK YOURSELF

1. How have genetic and environmental influences shaped *your* intelligence?

ANSWERS TO QUESTIONS WITHIN THE MODULE

Q. If environments became more equal, the heritability of intelligence would

a. increase.

b. decrease.

c. be unchanged.

A. Heritability—variations explained by genetic influences—will *increase* as environmental variation decreases.

Q. In prosperous country X everyone eats all they want. In country Y the rich are well fed, but the semistarved poor are often thin. In which country will the heritability of body weight be greater?

A. Heritability—differences due to genes—will be greater in country X, where environmental differences in nutrition are minimal.

Q. Which two responses in Figure 33.5 (repeated below) show a different view of the standard? (From Vandenberg & Kuse, 1978.)

Standard   **Responses**

A. The first and fourth alternatives are different views of the standard.

>WEB

Multiple-choice *self-tests* and more may be found at www.worthpublishers.com/myers.

YANN MARTEL, FROM *THE LIFE OF PI*, 2000

As the cartons of survival rations diminished, I reduced my intake, holding myself to only two biscuits every eight hours. I was continuously hungry. I thought about food obsessively. The less I had to eat, the larger became the portions I dreamed of. My fantasy meals grew to be the size of India. A Ganges of dhal soup. Hot chapattis the size of Rajasthan. Bowls of rice as big as Uttar Pradesh. Sambars to flood all of Tali Nadu. Ice cream heaped as high as the Himalayas. My dreaming became quite expert: All ingredients for my dishes were always in fresh and plentiful supply; the oven or frying pan was always at just the right temperature; the proportion of things was always bang on; nothing was ever burnt or undercooked, nothing too hot or too cold. Every meal was simply perfect—only just beyond the reach of my hands.

By the time the last of the biscuits had disappeared, anything was good to eat, no matter the taste. I could put anything in my mouth, chew it, and swallow it—delicious, foul, or plain—so long as it wasn't salty. My body developed a revulsion for salt that I still experience to this day.

Motivation and Work

"What's my motivation?" the actor asks the director. In our everyday conversation, "What motivated you to do *that?*" is a way of asking "What *caused* your behavior?" To psychologists, a *motivation* is a need or desire that *energizes* behavior and *directs* it toward a goal. Experienced mountaineer Aron Ralston understands the extent to which motivation can energize and direct behavior. Having bagged nearly all of Colorado's tallest peaks, many of them solo and in winter, Ralston, on a Saturday spring morning in 2003, ventured to do some solo canyon hiking that seemed so risk-free he did not bother to tell anyone where he was going. In Utah's narrow Bluejohn Canyon, just 150 yards above his final rappel, he was climbing over an 800-pound rock when it shifted and pinned his right wrist and arm. He was, as the title of his recent book says, caught *Between a Rock and a Hard Place.*

Realizing no one would be rescuing him, Ralston tried with all his might to dislodge the rock. Then with his dull pocket knife he tried chipping away at the rock. When that, too, failed, he rigged up ropes to lift the rock. Alas, nothing worked. Hour after

Motivation personified
Aron Ralston's motivation to live and belong energized and directed his sacrificing half of his arm.

hour, then cold night after cold night, he was stuck. By Tuesday, he had run out of food and water. On Wednesday, as thirst and hunger gnawed, he began saving and sipping his own urine. Using his video recorder, he said his good-byes to family and friends, for whom he now felt intense love: "So again love to everyone. Bring love and peace and happiness and beautiful lives into the world in my honor. Thank you. Love you."

On Thursday, surprised to find himself still alive, Ralston had a seemingly divine insight into his reproductive future, a vision of a preschool boy being scooped up by a one-armed man. With this inspiration, he summoned his remaining strength and his enormous will to live and, over the next hour, willfully broke his bones and then proceeded to use that dull knife to cut off his arm. The moment after putting on a tourniquet, chopping the last piece of skin, and breaking free—and before rappelling with his bleeding half-arm down a 65-foot cliff and hiking 5 miles till finding someone—he was, in his own words, "just reeling with this euphoria . . . having been dead and standing in my grave, leaving my last will and testament, etching 'Rest in peace' on the wall, all of that, gone and then replaced with having my life again. It was undoubtedly the sweetest moment that I will ever experience" (Ralston, 2004).

Aron Ralston's thirst and hunger, his sense of belonging to others, and his underlying will to live and become a father highlight motivation's energizing and directing power. In Modules 35 through 37, we explore motivation by focusing on four motives—hunger, sex, the need to belong, and achievement at work. Although other identifiable motives exist (including thirst and curiosity), a close look at these four reveals the interplay between nature (the physiological "push") and nurture (the cognitive and cultural "pulls"). Before considering specific motivations, we'll take time in Module 34 to see how psychologists have approached the study of motivation.

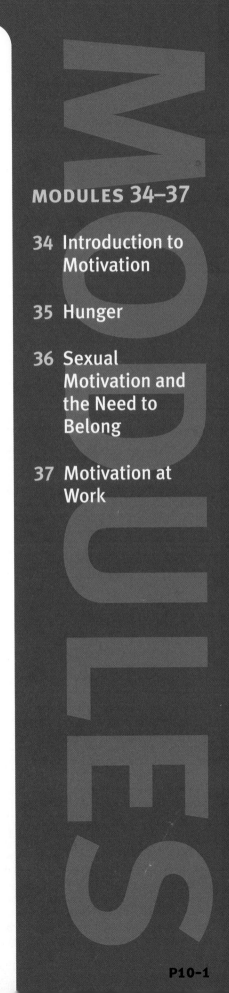

MODULE

Instincts

Drives and Incentives

Optimum Arousal

A Hierarchy of Motives

34

Introduction to Motivation

OBJECTIVE 34-1 | Define *motivation* as psychologists use the term today, and name four perspectives useful for studying motivated behaviors.

Psychologists today define **motivation** as a need or desire that energizes and directs behavior. In their attempt to understand motivated behaviors, psychologists have used four perspectives. These include instinct theory (now replaced by the research on genetic predispositions and evolutionary influences), drive-reduction theory (emphasizing the interaction between inner pushes and external pulls), and arousal theory (emphasizing the urge for an optimum level of stimulation). The fourth perspective, Abraham Maslow's hierarchy of needs, describes how some motives are, if unsatisfied, more basic and compelling than others.

Instincts

OBJECTIVE 34-2 | Discuss instinct theory and its misuses.

Early in the twentieth century, as the influence of Charles Darwin's evolutionary theory grew, it became fashionable to classify all sorts of behaviors as instincts. If people criticized themselves, it was because of their "self-abasement instinct." If they boasted, it reflected their "self-assertion instinct." After scanning 500 books, one sociologist compiled a list of 5759 supposed human instincts! Before long, this fad for naming instincts collapsed under its own weight. Rather than *explaining* human behaviors, the early instinct theorists were simply *naming* them. It was like "explaining" a bright child's low grades by labeling the child an "underachiever." To name a behavior is *not* to explain it.

To qualify as an **instinct,** a complex behavior must have a fixed pattern throughout a species and be unlearned (Tinbergen, 1951). Such behaviors are common in other species. Newly hatched ducks and geese form attachments to the first moving object they see. And mature salmon swim hundreds of miles upstream to reach the

"What do you think . . . should we get started on that motivation research or not?"

Same motive, different wiring
The more complex the nervous system, the more adaptable the organism. Both the woman and the weaverbird satisfy their need for shelter in ways that reflect their inherited capacities. The woman's behavior is flexible; she can learn whatever skills she needs to build a house. The bird's behavior pattern is fixed; it can build only this kind of nest.

place they were born, where they will mate and then die. Human behavior, too, exhibits certain innate tendencies, including simple fixed patterns such as an infant's rooting and sucking. Most psychologists, though, view human behavior as directed by physiological needs *and* by psychological wants.

Although instinct theory failed to explain human motives, the underlying assumption that genes predispose species-typical behavior remains as strong as ever. Psychologists may apply this perspective, for example, in explanations of our human similarities, animals' biological predispositions to learn certain behaviors, and the influence of evolution on our phobias, our helping behaviors, and our romantic attractions.

Drives and Incentives

OBJECTIVE 34-3 | Explain how drive-reduction theory views human motivation.

When the original instinct theory of motivation collapsed, it was replaced by **drive-reduction theory**—the idea that a physiological need creates an aroused state that *drives* the organism to reduce the need by, say, eating or drinking. With few exceptions, when a physiological need increases, so does a psychological drive—an aroused, motivated state.

The physiological aim of drive reduction is **homeostasis**—the maintenance of a steady internal state. An example of homeostasis (literally "staying the same") is the body's temperature-regulation system, which works like a thermostat. Both systems operate through feedback loops. Sensors feed room temperature to a control device. If the room temperature cools, the control device switches on the furnace. Likewise, if our body temperature cools, blood vessels constrict to conserve warmth, and we feel driven to put on more clothes or seek a warmer environment. Similarly, if the water level in our cells drops, sensors detect our need for water and we feel thirsty (**FIGURE 34.1**).

Not only are we *pushed* by our "need" to reduce drives, we also are *pulled* by **incentives**—positive or negative stimuli that lure or repel us. This is one way our individual learning histories influence our motives. Depending on our learning, the aroma of good food, whether fresh roasted peanuts or toasted ants, can motivate our behavior. So can the sight of someone we find attractive or the threat of disapproval from family or friends.

When there is both a need and an incentive, we feel strongly driven. The food-deprived person who smells baking bread feels a strong hunger drive. In the presence of that drive, the baking bread becomes a compelling incentive. For each motive, we can therefore ask, "How is it pushed by our inborn physiological needs and pulled by incentives in the environment?"

Optimum Arousal

OBJECTIVE 34-4 | Discuss the contribution of arousal theory to the study of motivation.

We are much more than homeostatic systems, however. Some motivated behaviors actually *increase* arousal. Well-fed animals will leave their shelter to explore, seemingly in the absence of any need-based drive. From taking such risks, animals gain information and resources (Renner, 1992).

Curiosity drives monkeys to monkey around trying to figure out how to unlock a latch that opens nothing or how to open a window that allows them to see outside

■ **motivation** a need or desire that energizes and directs behavior.

■ **instinct** a complex behavior that is rigidly patterned throughout a species and is unlearned.

■ **drive-reduction theory** the idea that a physiological need creates an aroused tension state (a drive) that motivates an organism to satisfy the need.

■ **homeostasis** a tendency to maintain a balanced or constant internal state; the regulation of any aspect of body chemistry, such as blood glucose, around a particular level.

■ **incentive** a positive or negative environmental stimulus that motivates behavior.

FIGURE 34.1
Drive-reduction theory

Driven by curiosity

Baby monkeys and small children are fascinated by things they've never handled before. Their drive to explore the relatively unfamiliar is one of several motives that do not fill any immediate physiological need.

their room (Butler, 1954). It drives the 9-month-old infant who investigates every accessible corner of the house. It drives the scientists whose work this text discusses. And it drives explorers and adventurers such as Aron Ralston. Asked why he wanted to climb Mount Everest, George Mallory answered, "Because it is there." Those who, like Mallory and Ralston, enjoy high arousal are most likely to enjoy intense music, novel foods, and risky behaviors (Zuckerman, 1979).

So, human motivation aims not to eliminate arousal but to seek optimum levels of arousal. Having all our biological needs satisfied, we feel driven to experience stimulation. Lacking stimulation, we feel bored and look for a way to increase arousal to some optimum level. However, with too much stimulation comes stress, and we then look for a way to decrease arousal.

A Hierarchy of Motives

OBJECTIVE **34-5** | Describe Maslow's hierarchy of needs.

Some needs take priority over others. At this moment, with your needs for air and water satisfied, other motives—such as your desire to achieve—are energizing and directing your behavior. Let your need for water go unsatisfied and your thirst will preoccupy you. But if you were deprived of air, your thirst would disappear.

Abraham Maslow (1970) described these priorities as a **hierarchy of needs** (**FIGURE 34.2**). At the base of this pyramid are our physiological needs, such as those for food and water. Only if these needs are met are we prompted to meet our need for safety, and then to satisfy the uniquely human needs to give and receive love and to enjoy self-esteem. Beyond this, said Maslow (1971), lies the highest of human needs: to actualize one's full potential.

FIGURE 34.2

Maslow's hierarchy of needs

Once our lower-level needs are met, we are prompted to satisfy our higher-level needs. While struggling to meet their basic needs for water, food, safe shelter, and medical attention, these survivors of the 2005 New Orleans hurricane were probably not immediately concerned with the higher-level needs on Maslow's hierarchy, such as esteem and self-actualization. (From Maslow, 1970.)

Self-actualization needs
Need to live up to one's fullest and unique potential

Esteem needs
Need for self-esteem, achievement, competence, and independence; need for recognition and respect from others

Belongingness and love needs
Need to love and be loved, to belong and be accepted; need to avoid loneliness and alienation

Safety needs
Need to feel that the world is organized and predictable; need to feel safe, secure, and stable

Physiological needs
Need to satisfy hunger and thirst

Maslow's hierarchy is somewhat arbitrary; the order of such needs is not universally fixed. People have starved themselves to make a political statement. Nevertheless, the simple idea that some motives are more compelling than others provides a framework for thinking about motivation, and life-satisfaction surveys in 39 nations support this basic idea (Oishi & others, 1999). In poorer nations that lack easy access to money and the food and shelter it buys, financial satisfaction more strongly predicts subjective well-being. In wealthy nations, where most are able to meet basic needs, home-life satisfaction is a better predictor. Self-esteem matters most in individualist nations, whose citizens tend to focus more on personal achievements than on family and community identity. So what motives preoccupy you depend on your situation.

■ **hierarchy of needs** Maslow's pyramid of human needs, beginning at the base with physiological needs that must first be satisfied before higher-level safety needs and then psychological needs become active.

" Hunger is the most urgent form of poverty."

Alliance to End Hunger, 2002

>> LEARNING OUTCOMES

Introduction to Motivation

OBJECTIVE 34-1 | **Define *motivation* as psychologists use the term today, and name four perspectives useful for studying motivated behavior.**
Motivation is the energizing and directing of behavior. The *instinct, drive-reduction, arousal,* and *hierarchy of needs* perspectives offer insights into motivated behaviors.

OBJECTIVE 34-2 | **Discuss instinct theory and its misuses.**
Instincts are rigidly patterned, complex behaviors found throughout a species. Early instinct theorists, influenced by Darwin's theory of natural selection, tried but failed to classify human behaviors as though they were propelled by such instincts. The underlying idea—that genes predispose species-typical behavior—is still influential.

OBJECTIVE 34-3 | **Explain how drive-reduction theory views human motivation.**
Drive-reduction theory proposes that physiological needs create aroused psychological states that drive us to reduce or satisfy those needs. The physiological aim of drive reduction is internal stability, or *homeostasis*. We are most strongly driven when pushed by the need to reduce a drive (such as satisfying hunger) and pulled by an external incentive (the smell of cooking food, for example). Depending on our personal and cultural histories, we respond more to some stimuli than to others.

OBJECTIVE 34-4 | **Discuss the contribution of arousal theory to the study of motivation.**
Arousal theory helps explain the motivation for behaviors that do not reduce immediate physiological needs or tension states. Curiosity-driven behaviors, for example, suggest that too little stimulation can motivate people to seek a higher level of arousal.

OBJECTIVE 34-5 | **Describe Maslow's hierarchy of needs.**
Maslow's hierarchy of needs proposes a pyramid-shaped sequence in which lower-level needs, such as hunger and thirst, are more compelling than higher-level needs, such as the need to love or to be respected. Maslow's sequence of needs is not universal, but his hierarchy provides a framework for thinking about motivated behaviors.

TERMS AND CONCEPTS TO REMEMBER

motivation, p. 34-0	homeostasis, p. 34-1
instinct, p. 34-0	incentive, p. 34-1
drive-reduction theory, p. 34-1	hierarchy of needs, p. 34-2

TEST YOURSELF

1. While on a long road trip, you suddenly feel very lonely and want to pull over and call a loved one. But the dark, deserted stretch of road is intimidating, so you keep on driving. What motivational perspective would most easily explain this behavior and why?

(Answer in Appendix B.)

ASK YOURSELF

1. Consider your own experiences with Maslow's hierarchy of needs. Have you ever experienced true hunger or thirst that displaced your concern for other, higher-level needs? Do you usually feel safe? Loved? Confident? How often do you feel you are able to address what Maslow called your "self-actualization" needs?

>WEB

Multiple-choice *self-tests* and more may be found at www.worthpublishers.com/myers.

The Physiology of Hunger

The Psychology of Hunger

35

Hunger

A vivid demonstration of the supremacy of physiological needs came from starvation experiences in World War II prison camps. David Mandel (1983), a Nazi concentration camp survivor, recalled how a starving "father and son would fight over a piece of bread. Like dogs." One father, whose 20-year-old son stole his bread from under his pillow while he slept, went into a deep depression, asking over and over how his son could do such a thing. The next day the father died. "Hunger does something to you that's hard to describe," Mandel explained. In this module, we look at both the physiology and the psychology of hunger.

"Never get a tattoo when you're drunk and hungry."

The Physiology of Hunger

OBJECTIVE 35-1 | Describe the physiological determinants of hunger.

To learn more about the results of semistarvation, scientist Ancel Keys and his colleagues (1950) fed 36 male volunteers—all conscientious objectors to the war—just enough to maintain their initial weight. Then, for six months, they cut this food level in half. The effects soon became visible. Without thinking about it, the men began conserving energy; they appeared listless and apathetic. Their body weights dropped rapidly, eventually stabilizing at about 25 percent below their starting weights. But the psychological effects were especially dramatic. Consistent with Maslow's idea of a needs hierarchy, the men became obsessed with food. They talked food. They daydreamed food. They collected recipes, read cookbooks, and feasted their eyes on delectable forbidden foods. At the same time, they lost interest in sex and social activities. They became preoccupied with their unfulfilled basic need. As one participant reported, "If we see a show, the most interesting part of it is contained in scenes where people are eating. I couldn't laugh at the funniest picture in the world, and love scenes are completely dull."

"Nobody wants to kiss when they are hungry."

Dorothea Dix, 1801–1887

GARFIELD

THE TV ADVERTISERS DIDN'T WASTE ANY TIME

I'VE BEEN ON A DIET ONE DAY AND THEY'RE ALREADY RUNNING MORE FOOD COMMERCIALS

Washburn swallows balloon, which measures stomach contractions.

Washburn presses key each time he feels hungry.

Stomach contractions

Hunger pangs

0 1 2 3 4 5 6 7 8 9 10
Time in minutes

FIGURE 35.1
Monitoring stomach contractions
Using this procedure, Washburn showed that stomach contractions (transmitted by the stomach balloon) accompany our feelings of hunger (indicated by a key press). (From Cannon, 1929.)

Keys' semistarved volunteers felt their hunger in response to a homeostatic system designed to maintain normal body weight and an adequate nutrient supply. But what precisely triggers hunger? Is it the pangs of an empty stomach? That is how it feels. And so it seemed after A. L. Washburn, working with Walter Cannon (Cannon & Washburn, 1912), intentionally swallowed a balloon. When inflated in his stomach, the balloon transmitted his stomach contractions to a recording device (**FIGURE 35.1**). While his stomach was being monitored, Washburn pressed a key each time he felt hungry. The discovery: Washburn was indeed having stomach contractions whenever he felt hungry.

Would hunger persist without stomach pangs? Researchers answered that question early in the twentieth century, when they removed some rats' stomachs and attached their esophagi to their small intestines (Tsang, 1938). Did the rats continue to eat? Indeed they did. Some hunger persists similarly in humans whose ulcerated or cancerous stomachs have been removed. You and I can feel some hunger even on a full stomach. So can animals that fill their stomachs by eating low-calorie food; they will eat more than animals that consume a less-filling, high-calorie diet (McHugh & Moran, 1978).

If the pangs of an empty stomach are not the only source of hunger, what else matters? Body chemicals and brain states offer some insights.

Body Chemistry and the Brain

People and other animals automatically regulate their caloric intake to prevent energy deficits and maintain a stable body weight. This suggests that the body is somehow, somewhere, keeping tabs on its available resources. One such resource is the blood sugar **glucose.** Increases in the hormone *insulin* (secreted by the pancreas) diminish blood glucose, partly by converting it to stored fat. Your body is normally adept at maintaining its blood glucose level. But if that level drops, your hunger increases.

You do not consciously feel this change in your blood chemistry. Rather, your brain is automatically monitoring your body's internal state. Signals from your stomach, intestines, and liver (indicating whether glucose is being deposited or withdrawn) all signal your brain to motivate eating or not. But where in the brain are these messages integrated? During the 1940s and 1950s, researchers located hunger controls within the hypothalamus, a small but complex neural traffic intersection buried deep in the brain (**FIGURE 35.2**).

■ **glucose** the form of sugar that circulates in the blood and provides the major source of energy for body tissues. When its level is low, we feel hunger.

"The full person does not understand the needs of the hungry."

Irish proverb

Pix* Elation from Fran Heyl Associates

FIGURE 35.2
The hypothalamus
The hypothalamus (colored red) performs various body maintenance functions, including control of hunger. Blood vessels supply the hypothalamus, enabling it to respond to our current blood chemistry as well as to incoming neural information about the body's state.

Evidence for the brain's control of eating
A lesion near the middle (ventromedial) area of the hypothalamus caused this rat's weight to triple.

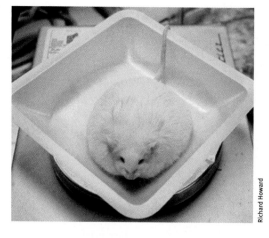

Richard Howard

Actually, two distinct hypothalamic centers help control eating. Experiments during the 1960s suggested that activity along the sides of the hypothalamus (the *lateral hypothalamus*) brings on hunger. When electrically stimulated there, well-fed animals would begin to eat; when the area was destroyed, even starving animals had no interest in food. Late-twentieth-century research helped explain this behavior. If a rat is deprived of food and its blood sugar levels wane, the lateral hypothalamus will churn out the hunger-triggering hormone *orexin*. When given orexin, rats become ravenously hungry (Sakurai & others, 1998).

Activity in the second center—the lower mid-hypothalamus (the *ventromedial hypothalamus*)—depresses hunger. Stimulate this area and an animal will stop eating; destroy it and the animal's stomach and intestines will process food more rapidly, causing it to become extremely fat (Duggan & Booth, 1986; Hoebel & Teitelbaum, 1966). After these mid-hypothalamus lesions, rats eat more often, produce more fat, and use less fat for energy, rather like a miser who runs every bit of extra money to the bank and resists taking any out (Pinel, 1993). This discovery also explains why some patients with tumors near the base of the brain (in what we now realize is the hypothalamus) eat excessively and become very overweight (Miller, 1995).

The hypothalamus monitors levels of the body's appetite hormones (**FIGURE 35.3**). One interesting line of research is focusing on *ghrelin,* a hunger-arousing hormone secreted by an empty stomach. When people with severe obesity undergo bypass surgery that seals off part of the stomach, the remaining stomach then produces much less ghrelin, and their appetite lessens (Lemonick, 2002).

Experimental manipulation of appetite hormones has raised hopes for an appetite-reducing medication. Such a pill might counteract the body's hunger-producing chemicals, such as ghrelin, and hunger-dampening chemicals such as *leptin,* which is secreted by fat cells. Or perhaps it might increase levels of *PYY,* a digestive hormone that *suppresses* appetite. The recent ups and downs of excitement over PYY illustrate the intense search for a substance that might someday be a treatment, if not a magic bullet, for obesity. The initial report that PYY suppresses appetite in mice was followed by a skeptical statement from 12 laboratories reporting a big fat disappointment: The PYY finding did not replicate. But a few months later, this was followed by newer studies using different methods that *did* find at least a temporary appetite-suppressing effect (Gura, 2004).

An older hunger theory proposes that manipulating the lateral and ventromedial hypothalamus alters the body's "weight thermostat," predisposing us to keep our body at a particular weight

"To put it simply, PYY is the fullness hormone and ghrelin is the hunger hormone."
Hunger researcher Stephen R. Bloom (2002)

FIGURE 35.3
The appetite hormones
Insulin: Hormone secreted by pancreas; controls blood glucose.
Leptin: Protein secreted by fat cells; when abundant, causes brain to increase metabolism and decrease hunger.
Orexin: Hunger-triggering hormone secreted by hypothalamus.
Ghrelin: Hormone secreted by empty stomach; sends "I'm hungry" signals to the brain.
PYY: Digestive tract hormone; sends "I'm *not* hungry" signals to the brain.

level, called its **set point** (Keesey & Corbett, 1983). When semistarved rats fall below their normal weight, biological pressures act to restore the lost weight: Hunger increases and energy expenditure decreases. If body weight rises—as happens when rats are force-fed—hunger decreases and energy expenditure increases. This stable weight toward which semistarved and overstuffed rats return is their set point. In rats and humans, heredity influences body type and set point.

Human bodies regulate weight through the control of food intake, energy output, and **basal metabolic rate**—the rate of energy expenditure for maintaining basic body functions when the body is at rest. By the end of their 24 weeks of semistarvation, the men who participated in Key's experiment had stabilized at three-quarters of their normal weight—while eating half of what they previously did. The stabilization resulted from reduced energy expenditure, achieved partly by physical lethargy and partly by a 29 percent drop in their basal metabolic rate. In a reverse experiment—in which volunteers were overfed 1000 calories a day for eight weeks—those who gained the least weight tended to spend the extra caloric energy by fidgeting more (Levine & others, 1999). Under normal circumstances, those who fidget most (and burn more calories) weigh less than more inactive obese people, report James Levine and his colleagues (2005). (The researchers outfitted people with undergarments that for 10 days monitored their movements every half second.)

Some researchers, however, doubt that the body has a precise set point that drives hunger. They believe that slow, sustained changes in body weight can, for example, alter one's set point. This casts doubt on the idea that our bodies have a preset tendency to maintain optimum weight (Assanand & others, 1998). Psychological factors also sometimes drive our feelings of hunger. Given unlimited access to a wide variety of tasty foods, people and other animals tend to overeat and gain weight. For all these reasons, some researchers have abandoned the idea of a biologically fixed *set point*. They prefer the term *settling point* to indicate the level at which a person's weight settles in response to caloric intake and expenditure (which is influenced by environment as well as biology).

> Over the next 40 years you will eat about 20 tons of food. If during those years you increase your daily intake by just .01 ounce more than required for your energy needs, you will gain 24 pounds (Martin & others, 1991).

The Psychology of Hunger

OBJECTIVE 35-2 | Discuss psychological and cultural influences on hunger.

Our eagerness to eat is indeed pushed by our physiological state—our body chemistry and hypothalamic activity. Yet there is more to hunger than meets the stomach. This was strikingly apparent when Paul Rozin and his trickster colleagues (1998) tested two patients with amnesia who had no memory for events occurring more than a minute ago. If, 20 minutes after eating a normal lunch, the patients were offered another, both readily consumed it . . . and usually a third meal offered 20 minutes after the second was finished. This suggests that part of knowing when to eat is our memory of our last meal. As time accumulates since we last ate, we anticipate eating again and start feeling hungry.

Taste Preference: Biology or Culture?

Body chemistry and environmental factors together influence not only when we feel hunger, but what we feel hungry for—our taste preference. When feeling tense or depressed, do you crave starchy, carbohydrate-laden foods? Carbohydrates help boost levels of the neurotransmitter serotonin, which has calming effects.

Our preferences for sweet and salty tastes are genetic and universal. Other taste preferences are conditioned, as when people given highly salted foods develop a liking for excess salt (Beauchamp, 1987), or when people develop an aversion to a food eaten before becoming violently ill. (The frequency of children's illnesses provides many chances for them to learn food aversions.)

■ **set point** the point at which an individual's "weight thermostat" is supposedly set. When the body falls below this weight, an increase in hunger and a lowered metabolic rate may act to restore the lost weight.

■ **basal metabolic rate** the body's resting rate of energy expenditure.

An acquired taste
For Alaskan natives (left), but not for most other North Americans, whale blubber is a tasty treat. For these Campa Indians in Peru (right), roasted ants are similarly delicious. People everywhere learn to enjoy the fatty, bitter, or irritating foods prescribed by their culture.

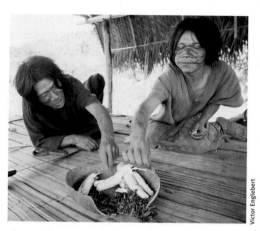

Culture affects taste, too. Bedouins enjoy eating the eye of a camel, which most North Americans would find repulsive. Similarly, most North Americans and Europeans shun dog, rat, and horse meat, all of which are prized elsewhere.

Our natural wariness of things unfamiliar extends to novel foods (especially novel animal-based rather than vegetarian foods). In experiments, people have tried novel fruit drinks or ethnic foods. With repeated exposure, their appreciation for the new taste typically increases; moreover, exposure to one set of novel foods increases our willingness to try another (Pliner, 1982; Pliner & Pelchat, 1993). Rats, too, tend to avoid unfamiliar foods (Sclafani, 1995). This *neophobia* surely was adaptive for our ancestors, protecting them from potentially toxic substances.

Other taste preferences are also adaptive. For example, the spices most commonly used in the recipes of hot climates, where food—especially meat—spoils more quickly, inhibit the growth of bacteria (**FIGURE 35.4**). Pregnancy-related nausea is another example of adaptive taste preferences. Food aversions stemming from this nausea peak about the tenth week, when the developing embryo is most vulnerable to toxins.

FIGURE 35.4
Hot cultures like hot spices
Countries with hot climates, in which food historically spoiled more quickly, feature recipes with more bacteria-inhibiting spices (Sherman & Flaxman, 2001). India averages nearly 10 spices per meat recipe, Finland 2 spices.

Eating Disorders

OBJECTIVE 35-3 | Explain how the eating disorders anorexia nervosa and bulimia nervosa demonstrate the influence of psychological forces on physiologically motivated behaviors.

Psychological influences on eating behavior are strikingly evident when a motive for abnormal thinness overwhelms normal homeostatic pressures. Two such eating disorders are anorexia nervosa and bulimia.

Anorexia nervosa always begins as a weight-loss diet. People with this disorder drop significantly below normal weight (typically, by 15 percent or more) yet feel fat and remain obsessed with losing weight. Even when emaciated, the person—usually an adolescent and 9 times out of 10 a female—continues to limit food intake.

Bulimia nervosa nearly always begins after a dieter has broken diet restrictions and gorged. Those with bulimia have repeated episodes of overeating followed by compensatory vomiting, laxative use, fasting, or excessive exercise. Most binge-purge

■ **anorexia nervosa** an eating disorder in which a normal-weight person (usually an adolescent female) diets and becomes significantly (15 percent or more) underweight, yet, still feeling fat, continues to starve.

■ **bulimia nervosa** an eating disorder characterized by episodes of overeating, usually of high-calorie foods, followed by vomiting, laxative use, fasting, or excessive exercise.

Dying to be thin
Anorexia was identified and named in the 1870s, when it appeared among affluent adolescent girls (Brumberg, 2000). This 1930s photo illustrates the physical condition (left). Many modern-day celebrities have struggled publicly with eating disorders, including teen actress Mary-Kate Olsen (right).

eaters are women in their late teens or early twenties. They eat the way some people with alcoholism drink—in spurts, sometimes influenced by friends who are bingeing (Crandall, 1988). Preoccupied with food (craving sweet and high-fat foods), and fearful of becoming overweight, people with bulimia experience bouts of depression and anxiety, most severe during and following binges (Hinz & Williamson, 1987; Johnson & others, 2002). About half of those with anorexia also display the binge-purge-depression symptoms of bulimia. Unlike anorexia, bulimia is marked by weight fluctuations within or above normal ranges, making the condition easy to hide.

Eating disorders do *not* provide (as some have speculated) a telltale sign of childhood sexual abuse (Smolak & Murnen, 2002; Stice, 2002). Families may provide a fertile ground for the growth of eating disorders in another way, however. Mothers of girls with eating disorders are themselves often focused on their own weight and on their daughters' weight and appearance (Pike & Rodin, 1991). The families of bulimia patients have a higher-than-usual incidence of childhood obesity and negative self-evaluation (Jacobi & others, 2004). Anorexia patients also tend to have low self-evaluations and often come from families that are competitive, high-achieving, and protective (Pate & others, 1992; Yates, 1989, 1990). Sufferers set perfectionist standards, fret about falling short of expectations, and are intensely concerned with how others perceive them (Polivy & Herman, 2002; Striegel-Moore & others, 1993). Some of these factors also predict teen boys' pursuit of unrealistic muscularity (Ricciardelli & McCabe, 2004).

Genetics, too, may influence susceptibility to eating disorders. If twins are identical rather than fraternal, the chances of the other twin's sharing the disorder are somewhat greater (Fairburn & others, 1999; Kaplan, 2004). Evolution may have predisposed such genes, suggests Shan Guisinger (2004). Faced with famine, our ancestors who denied their starvation and became hyperactive rather than hunkering down may have been more likely to search for food.

There is, however, a cultural explanation for the fact that anorexia and bulimia occur mostly in women and mostly in weight-conscious cultures. Body ideals vary across culture and time. In India, women students rate their ideals as close to their actual shape. In much of Africa—where thinness can signal poverty, AIDS, and hunger, and the prosperous are plump—bigger is better (Knickmeyer, 2001). In Western cultures, however, the rise in eating disorders over the last 50 years has coincided with a dramatic increase in women having a poor body image, according to a recent analysis of 222 studies of 141,000 people (Feingold & Mazzella, 1998).

"Thanks, but we don't eat."

"Gee, I had no idea you were married to a supermodel."

Other research confirms that those vulnerable to eating disorders are those who most idealize thinness and have the greatest body dissatisfaction (Stice, 2002; Thompson & Stice, 2001; Vohs & others, 2001). Not surprisingly, those people are most often women. In one national survey, nearly one-half of U.S. women reported feeling negative about their appearance and preoccupied with being or becoming overweight (Cash & Henry, 1995). And in a turn-of-the-century British survey of 3500 bank and university staff, men were more likely to *be* overweight and women were more likely to *perceive* themselves as overweight (Emslie & others, 2001).

Similar gender differences appeared in an experiment led by Barbara Fredrickson (1998), who had University of Michigan men and women put on a sweater or a swim suit and complete a math test while alone in a changing room. For the women but not the men, wearing the swimsuit triggered self-consciousness and shame that disrupted their math performance. In one informal survey with 60,000 respondents, 9 in 10 women said they would rather have a perfect body than have a mate with a perfect body; 6 of 10 men preferred the reverse (Lever, 2003).

Part of the cultural pressure is surely transmitted by the "thin-ideal" exemplified in fashion magazines, advertisements, and even in some toys. What do you suppose happens when young women repeatedly encounter doctored magazine images of fashion models, who appear to be unnaturally thin (Tovee & others, 1997)? Eric Stice and Heather Shaw (1994) and Heidi Posavac and colleagues (1998) report that women often feel ashamed, depressed, and dissatisfied with their own bodies—the very attitudes that predispose eating disorders. When Stice and his colleagues (2001) gave some adolescent girls (but not others) a 15-month subscription to a teen fashion magazine (*Seventeen*), vulnerable girls (who were already dissatisfied, idealizing thinness, and lacking social support) exhibited increased body dissatisfaction and eating disorder tendencies. But even ultra-thin models do not reflect the impossible standard of the classic Barbie doll. Adjusted to a height of 5 feet 7 inches, her 32–16–29 figure (in centimeters, 82 bust, 41 waist, and 73 hips) defines a body shape approximated by fewer than 1 in 100,000 women (Norton & others, 1996).

It seems clear that the sickness of today's eating disorders lies not just within the victims but also within our weight-obsessed culture—a culture that says, in countless ways, "Fat is bad," that motivates millions of women to be "always dieting," and that encourages eating binges by pressuring women to live in a constant state of semistarvation. As compelling as our biological motives are, eating behavior is clearly also affected by psychological and social-cultural factors (**FIGURE 35.5**).

FIGURE 35.5
Levels of analysis for our hunger motivation
Clearly, we are biologically driven to eat, yet psychological and social-cultural factors strongly influence what, when, and how much we eat.

Biological influences:
- mid-hypothalamic centers in the brain monitoring appetite
- appetite hormones
- stomach pangs
- set/settling point weight
- universal attraction to sweet and salty
- adaptive wariness toward novel foods

Psychological influences:
- sight and smell of food
- variety of foods available
- memory of time elapsed since last meal
- mood

Eating behavior

Social-cultural influences:
- culturally learned taste preferences
- learned restraint in cultures idealizing thinness

>> LEARNING OUTCOMES

Hunger

OBJECTIVE 35-1 | **Describe the physiological determinants of hunger.**

Washburn and Cannon showed that hunger's inner push corresponds to the stomach's contractions, but hunger has other causes. Variations in body chemistry that influence our feelings of hunger include those of *insulin* (secreted by the pancreas; controls blood glucose), *leptin* (secreted by fat cells; signals brain to increase metabolism and decrease hunger), *orexin* (secreted by the hypothalamus; triggers hunger), *ghrelin* (secreted by empty stomach; sends hunger signals to brain), and *PYY* (secreted by digestive tract; sends not-hungry signals to brain). All this information is integrated in two areas of the hypothalamus, which regulates the body's weight by affecting our feelings of hunger and satiety. Researchers differ on whether the body has a precise *set point* (a biologically fixed tendency to maintain an optimum weight) or a *settling point* (an environmentally and biologically influenced level at which weight settles in response to caloric intake and output).

OBJECTIVE 35-2 | **Discuss psychological and cultural influences on hunger.**

Our hunger is influenced not only by our physical state but also by our memory of when we last ate and our expectation of when we should eat again. Humans prefer certain tastes (such as sweet and salty) but learn from family and culture to satisfy those preferences with specific foods. Some taste aversions (to new foods or foods that have made us ill) have survival value.

OBJECTIVE 35-3 | **Explain how the eating disorders anorexia nervosa and bulimia nervosa demonstrate the influence of psychological forces on physiologically motivated behaviors.**

In the past half-century, a dramatic increase in poor body image has coincided with a rise in eating disorders among women in Western cultures. People with *anorexia nervosa* (usually adolescent females) starve themselves but continue to diet because they view themselves as fat; those with *bulimia nervosa* (primarily females in their teens and twenties) binge and purge in secret. These eating disorders may have a genetic component, but cultural pressures, low self-esteem, and negative emotions seem to interact with stressful life experiences to produce these conditions.

TERMS AND CONCEPTS TO REMEMBER

glucose, p. 35-1

set point, p. 35-3

basal metabolic rate, p. 35-3

anorexia nervosa, p. 35-4

bulimia nervosa, p. 35-4

TEST YOURSELF

1. You are traveling and have not eaten anything in eight hours. As your long-awaited favorite dish is placed in front of you, your mouth waters. Even imagining this may set your mouth to watering. What triggers this anticipatory drooling?

(Answer in Appendix B.)

ASK YOURSELF

1. Do you feel in touch with your body's hunger signals? Do you eat when your body needs food? Or do you tend to be more externally influenced by enticing foods even when you're full?

>WEB

Multiple-choice **self-tests** and more may be found at www.worthpublishers.com/myers.

36

Sexual Motivation and the Need to Belong

Sex is part of life. Had this not been so for all your ancestors, you would not be reading this book. Sexual motivation is nature's clever way of making people procreate, thus enabling our species' survival. When two people feel attracted, they hardly stop to think of themselves as guided by their genes. As the pleasure we take in eating is nature's inventive method of getting our body nourishment, so the pleasure of sex is our genes' way of preserving and spreading themselves. Our human need to belong—to connect in close relationships—enhances our chance of leaving a genetic legacy.

Our first descriptions of sexual behavior in the United States came from Indiana University biologist Alfred Kinsey and his colleagues (1948, 1953). Unable to answer his students' questions about people's sexual practices, Kinsey set out to find some answers. His controversial research was shocking to a 1940s audience. Social scientists were quick to point out what Kinsey readily acknowledged—that his nonrandom sample contained an overrepresentation of well-educated white urbanites. Nevertheless, his statistics-laden volumes became bestsellers. Here readers learned the surprising news that most of the men and nearly half the women reported having had premarital sexual intercourse; that most women and virtually all men reported having masturbated; and that women who reported masturbating to orgasm before marriage seldom had difficulties experiencing orgasm after marriage. Kinsey's books also revealed enormously varied sexual behavior, some men and women saying they had never had an orgasm and others reporting they had four or more a day. For those who evaluate themselves by comparisons with others, Kinsey's nonrandom sample—and other more reliable findings showing wide variations in "normal" sexual behavior around the world—are reassuring. Given the range of sex drives and the variety of sexual behaviors, our own sexual interests probably fall well within the definition of "normal."

> " Maybe . . . it starts with a kiss."
> Prenatal photographer Lennart Nilsson, answering the question "When does life begin?"

In a British survey of 18,876 people, 1 percent reported having "never felt sexually attracted to anyone at all" (Bogaert, 2004).

The Physiology of Sex

Sexual arousal depends on the interplay of internal and external stimuli. To understand sexual motivation, we must consider both.

The Sexual Response Cycle

OBJECTIVE 36-1 | Describe the human sexual response cycle, and discuss some causes of sexual disorders.

The headlines created by Kinsey's 1940s surveys reappeared in the 1960s after other scientists recorded the physiological responses of volunteers who masturbated or had intercourse. With the help of 382 female and 312 male volunteers—a somewhat atypical sample, consisting only of people able and willing to display arousal and orgasm while being observed in a laboratory—gynecologist-obstetrician William Masters and his collaborator Virginia Johnson (1966) monitored or filmed more than 10,000 sexual "cycles."

Their description of the **sexual response cycle** identified four stages, similar in men and women. During the initial *excitement phase,* the genital areas become engorged with blood, a woman's vagina expands and secretes lubricant, and her breasts and nipples may enlarge.

"I love the idea of there being two sexes, don't you?"

In the *plateau phase,* excitement peaks as breathing, pulse, and blood pressure rates continue to increase. The penis becomes fully engorged and some fluid—frequently containing enough live sperm to enable conception—may appear at its tip. Vaginal secretion continues to increase, the clitoris retracts, and orgasm feels imminent.

Masters and Johnson observed muscle contractions all over the body during *orgasm;* these were accompanied by further increases in breathing, pulse, and blood pressure rates. A woman's arousal and orgasm facilitate conception by helping propel semen from the penis, positioning the uterus to receive sperm, and drawing the sperm further inward. A woman's orgasm therefore not only reinforces intercourse, which is essential to natural reproduction, it also increases retention of deposited sperm (Furlow & Thornhill, 1996). In the excitement of the moment, men and women are hardly aware of all this as their rhythmic genital contractions create a pleasurable feeling of sexual release.

The feeling apparently is much the same for both sexes. In one study, a panel of experts could not reliably distinguish between descriptions of orgasm written by men and those written by women (Vance & Wagner, 1976). University of Groningen neuroscientist Gerg Holstege and his colleagues (2003a,b) understand why. They discovered that when men and women undergo PET scans while having orgasms, the same subcortical brain regions glow. And when people who are passionately in love undergo fMRI scans while viewing photos of their beloved or of a stranger, men's and women's brain responses to their partner are pretty similar (Fisher & others, 2002).

After orgasm, the body gradually returns to its unaroused state as the engorged genital blood vessels release their accumulated blood—relatively quickly if orgasm has occurred, relatively slowly otherwise. (It's like the nasal tickle that goes away rapidly if you have sneezed, slowly otherwise.) During this *resolution phase,* the male enters a **refractory period,** lasting from a few minutes to a day or more, during which he is incapable of another orgasm. The female's much shorter refractory period may enable her to have another orgasm if restimulated during or soon after resolution.

Masters and Johnson sought not only to describe the human sexual response cycle but also to understand and treat the inability to complete it. **Sexual disorders** are problems that consistently impair sexual functioning. Some involve sexual motivation, especially lack of sexual energy and arousability. Others include, for men, *premature ejaculation* and *erectile dysfunction* (inability to have or maintain an erection), and, for women, *orgasmic disorder* (infrequently or never experiencing orgasm).

What causes such problems? The idea that personality disorders are to blame has been largely discounted. Most women who experience sexual distress relate it to their emotional relationship with the partner during sex, not to physical aspects of the activity (Bancroft & others, 2003). Men or women with sexual disorders can often be helped by receiving behaviorally oriented therapy where, for example, men may learn ways to control their urge to ejaculate, and women are trained to bring themselves to orgasm. Starting with the introduction of Viagra in 1998, erectile disorder has been routinely treated by taking a pill.

Hormones and Sexual Behavior

OBJECTIVE 36-2 | Discuss the impact of hormones on sexual motivation and behavior.

Sex hormones have two effects: They direct the physical development of male and female sex characteristics, and (especially in nonhuman animals) they activate sexual behavior. In most mammals, nature neatly synchronizes sex with fertility. The female becomes sexually receptive ("in heat") when production of the female hormone **estrogen** peaks at ovulation. In experiments, researchers can stimulate receptivity by injecting female animals with estrogen. Male hormone levels are more constant, and

A nonsmoking 50-year-old male has about a 1-in-a-million chance of a heart attack during any hour. This increases to merely 2-in-a-million during the hour following sex (with no increase for those who exercise regularly). Compared with risks associated with heavy exertion or anger, this risk seems not worth losing sleep (or sex) over (Muller & others, 1996).

■ **sexual response cycle** the four stages of sexual responding described by Masters and Johnson—excitement, plateau, orgasm, and resolution.

■ **refractory period** a resting period after orgasm, during which a man cannot achieve another orgasm.

■ **sexual disorder** a problem that consistently impairs sexual arousal or functioning.

■ **estrogen** a sex hormone, secreted in greater amounts by females than by males. In nonhuman female mammals, estrogen levels peak during ovulation, promoting sexual receptivity.

"Fill'er up with testosterone."

researchers cannot so easily manipulate the sexual behavior of male animals with hormones (Feder, 1984). Nevertheless, castrated male rats—having lost their testes, which manufacture the male sex hormone **testosterone**—gradually lose much of their interest in receptive females. They gradually regain it if injected with testosterone.

In humans, hormones more loosely influence sexual behavior, although sexual desire rises slightly at ovulation among women with mates (Pillsworth & others, 2004). One study invited partnered women who were not at risk for pregnancy to keep a diary of their sexual activity. (These women were either using intrauterine devices or had undergone surgery to prevent pregnancy.) On the days around ovulation, intercourse was 24 percent more frequent (Wilcox & others, 2004). But women's sexuality also differs from that of other mammalian females in being more responsive to testosterone level than to estrogen level (Meston & Frohlich, 2000; Reichman, 1998). If a woman's natural testosterone level drops, as happens with removal of the ovaries or adrenal glands, her sexual interest may wane. But testosterone-replacement therapy can often restore diminished sexual appetite, as it did for 549 naturally menopausal women who found that a testosterone-replacement patch restored sexual activity, arousal, and pleasure more than did a placebo (Davis & others, 2003; Kroll & others, 2004).

In men, normal fluctuations in testosterone levels, from man to man and hour to hour, have little effect on sexual drive (Byrne, 1982). Indeed, fluctuations in male hormones are partly a *response* to sexual stimulation. When James Dabbs and his colleagues (1987, 2000) had heterosexual male collegians converse separately with another male student and with a female student, the men's testosterone levels rose with the social arousal, but especially after talking with the female. Thus, sexual arousal can be a cause as well as a consequence of increased testosterone levels.

Although normal short-term hormonal changes have little effect on men's and women's desire, large hormonal shifts over the life span have a greater effect. A person's interest in dating and sexual stimulation usually increases with the pubertal surge in sex hormones, as happens with male testosterone levels during puberty.

If the hormonal surge is precluded—as it was during the 1600s and 1700s for prepubertal boys who were castrated to preserve their soprano voices for Italian opera—the normal development of sex characteristics and sexual desire does not occur (Peschel & Peschel, 1987). Among adult men who suffer castration, sex drive typically falls as testosterone levels decline (Hucker & Bain, 1990). Male sex offenders similarly lose much of their sexual urge when voluntarily taking Depo-Provera, a drug that reduces testosterone level to that of a prepubertal boy (Money & others, 1983). In later life, as sex hormone levels decline, the frequency of sexual fantasies and intercourse declines as well (Leitenberg & Henning, 1995). For men with abnormally low testosterone levels, testosterone-replacement therapy often increases sexual desire and also energy and vitality (Yates, 2000).

To summarize: We might compare human sex hormones, especially testosterone, to the fuel in a car. Without fuel, a car will not run. But if the fuel level is minimally adequate, adding more fuel to the gas tank won't change how the car runs. The analogy is imperfect, because the interaction between hormones and sexual motivation is two-way. However, the analogy correctly suggests that biology is a necessary but not sufficient explanation of human sexual behavior. The hormonal fuel is essential, but so are the psychological stimuli that turn on the engine, keep it running, and shift it into high gear.

■ **testosterone** the most important of the male sex hormones. Both males and females have it, but the additional testosterone in males stimulates the growth of the male sex organs in the fetus and the development of the male sex characteristics during puberty.

The Psychology of Sex

OBJECTIVE 36-3 | Describe the role of external stimuli and fantasies on sexual motivation and behavior.

Hunger and sex are different sorts of motivations. Hunger responds to a *need*. If we do not eat, we die. Sex is not in this sense a need. If we do not have sex, we may feel like dying, but we do not. Nevertheless, there are similarities between hunger and sexual motivation. Both depend on internal physiological factors. And both are influenced by external and imagined stimuli, as well as cultural expectations (FIGURE 36.1).

<blockquote>"Ours is a society which stimulates interest in sex by constant titillation. . . . Cinema, television, and all the formidable array of our marketing technology project our very effective forms of titillation and our prejudices about man as a sexy animal into every corner of every hovel in the world."

Germaine Greer, 1984</blockquote>

Biological influences:
• sexual maturity
• sex hormones, especially testosterone
• sexual orientation

Psychological influences:
• exposure to stimulating conditions
• sexual fantasies

Sexual motivation

Social-cultural influences:
• family and society values
• religious and personal values
• cultural expectations

FIGURE 36.1
Levels of analysis for sexual motivation
Compared with our motivation for eating, our sexual motivation is less influenced by biological factors. Psychological and social-cultural factors play a bigger role.

External Stimuli

Many studies confirm that men become aroused when they see, hear, or read erotic material. Surprising to many (because sexually explicit materials are sold mostly to men) is that most women—at least the less-inhibited women who volunteer to participate in such studies—report or exhibit nearly as much arousal to the same stimuli (Heiman, 1975; Stockton & Murnen, 1992). (Their brains do, however, respond differently, with fMRI scans revealing a more active amygdala in men viewing erotica [Hamann & others, 2004].)

People may find such arousal either pleasing or disturbing. (Those who find it disturbing often limit their exposure to such materials, just as those wishing to control hunger limit their exposure to tempting cues.) With repeated exposure, the emotional response to any erotic stimulus often *habituates* (lessens). During the 1920s, when Western women's hemlines first reached the knee, an exposed leg was a mildly erotic stimulus, as were modest (by today's standards) two-piece swimsuits and movie scenes of a mere kiss.

Can sexually explicit material have adverse effects? Research indicates that it can. Depictions of women being sexually coerced—and enjoying it—tend to increase viewers' acceptance of the false idea that women enjoy rape and tend to increase male viewers' willingness to hurt women (Malamuth & Check, 1981; Zillmann, 1989). Images of sexually attractive women and men may also lead people to devalue their own partners and relationships. After male collegians watch TV or magazine depictions of sexually attractive women, they often find an average woman, or their own girlfriends or wives, less attractive (Kenrick & Gutierres, 1980; Kenrick & others, 1989; Weaver & others, 1984). Viewing X-rated sex films similarly tends to diminish people's satisfaction with their own sexual partners (Zillmann, 1989). Some sex researchers suspect that reading or watching erotica may create expectations that few men and women can fulfill.

Sexually explicit TV programs also divert attention from TV ads, making the ads more forgettable. Ads embedded in nonsexual and nonviolent programs more often produce memory for the products (Bushman & Bonacci, 2002).

Imagined Stimuli

The brain, it has been said, is our most significant sex organ. The stimuli inside our heads—our imagination—can influence sexual arousal and desire. People who, because of a spinal cord injury, have no genital sensation, can still feel sexual desire (Willmuth, 1987). Consider, too, the erotic potential of dreams. Sleep researchers have discovered that genital arousal accompanies all types of dreams, even though most dreams have no sexual content. But in nearly all men and some 40 percent of women (Wells, 1986), dreams sometimes do contain sexual imagery that leads to orgasm. In men, nighttime orgasm and nocturnal emissions ("wet dreams") are more likely when orgasm has not occurred recently.

Wide-awake people become sexually aroused not only by memories of prior sexual activities but also by fantasies. In one survey of masturbation-related fantasies (Hunt, 1974), 19 percent of women and 10 percent of men reported imagining being taken by someone overwhelmed with desire for them. Fantasy is not reality, however. To paraphrase Susan Brownmiller (1975), there's a big difference between fantasizing that Brad Pitt just won't take no for an answer and having a hostile stranger actually force himself on you.

About 95 percent of both men and women say they have had sexual fantasies. But men (whether gay or straight) fantasize about sex more often, more physically, and less romantically—and prefer less personal and faster-paced sex content in books and videos (Leitenberg & Henning, 1995). Fantasizing about sex does *not* indicate a sexual problem or dissatisfaction. If anything, sexually active people have more sexual fantasies.

> "There is no difference between being raped and being run over by a truck except that afterward men ask if you enjoyed it."
>
> Marge Piercy, "Rape Poem," 1976

Adolescent Sexuality

OBJECTIVE 36-4 | Discuss some of the forces that influence teen pregnancy and teen attitudes toward contraception.

Adolescents' physical maturation fosters a sexual dimension to their emerging identity. Yet sexual expression varies dramatically with time and culture. Among American women born before 1900, a mere 3 percent had experienced premarital sex by age 18 (Smith, 1998). In the United States today, about half of ninth-to twelfth-graders report having had sexual intercourse, as do 42 percent of Canadian 16-year-olds (Boroditsky & others, 1995; CDC, 2004). Teen intercourse rates are higher in Western Europe but much lower in Arab and Asian countries and among North Americans of Asian descent (McLaughlin & others, 1997). In one survey, only 2.5 percent of 4688 unmarried Chinese students entering Hong Kong's six universities reported having had sexual intercourse (Meston & others, 1996).

An increase in teen sexual activity in Western countries led to a twentieth-century increase in the adolescent pregnancy rate. The often-impoverished futures of teen mothers and of children in father-absent homes have in turn prompted new research on teen sexuality, adolescents' use of contraceptives, and teens' risk of contracting *sexually transmitted infections* (STIs).

Teen Pregnancy

Compared with European teens, American teens have lower rates of intercourse, but they also have lower rates of contraceptive use and thus higher rates of teen pregnancy and abortion (Call & others, 2002). (Only one-third of sexually active male teens use condoms consistently [Sonenstein, 1992]). Why?

Ignorance Half of sexually active Canadian teen girls have mistaken ideas about which birth control methods will protect them from pregnancy and STIs (Immen, 1995). Most teens also overestimate their peers' sexual activity, and that misperception may influence their own behavior (Child Trends, 2001).

Guilt related to sexual activity In one survey, 72 percent of 12- to 17-year-old American girls who have had sex said they regretted it (Reuters, 2000). Sexual inhibitions can reduce sexual activity, but they may also reduce attempts at birth control if passion overwhelms intentions (Gerrard & Luus, 1995). Not wanting to appear deliberately sexual or promiscuous, teens may hesitate to carry and produce a condom. The result may be conception.

Minimal communication about birth control Many teenagers are uncomfortable discussing contraception with their parents, partners, and peers (Kotva & Schneider, 1990; Milan & Kilmann, 1987). Teens who talk freely with friends or parents and are in an exclusive relationship with a partner with whom they communicate openly are more likely to use contraceptives.

Alcohol use Sexually active teens are typically alcohol-using teens (Albert & others, 2003; National Research Council, 1987), and those who use alcohol prior to sex are less likely to use condoms (Kotchick & others, 2001). By depressing the brain centers that control judgment, inhibition, and self-awareness, alcohol tends to break down normal restraints, a phenomenon well known to sexually coercive males.

Mass media norms of unprotected promiscuity An average hour of prime-time television on the three major U.S. networks contains approximately 15 sexual acts, words, and innuendos. Nearly all of these instances involve unmarried partners, about half have no prior romantic relationship or have just met, and few communicate any concern for birth control or STIs (Brown & others, 2002; Kunkel, 2001; Sapolsky & Tabarlet, 1991). TV and movie portrayals of unsafe sex without consequence, contends Planned Parenthood, amounts to a campaign of sex disinformation.

Sexually Transmitted Infections

OBJECTIVE 36-5 | Describe trends in the spread of sexually transmitted infections.

Unprotected sex has led to increased rates of STIs (also called *STD* for *sexually transmitted disease*). Two-thirds of new infections occur in persons under 25 (ASHA, 2003). Teenage girls, because of their less mature biological development and lower levels of protective antibodies, seem especially vulnerable to STIs (Guttmacher, 1994; Morell, 1995). To comprehend the mathematics of sexually transmitted infection, imagine this scenario: Over the course of a year, Pat has sex with 9 people, each of whom over the same period has sex with 9 other people, who in turn have sex with 9 others. How many "phantom" sex partners (past partners of partners) will Pat have? Laura Brannon and Timothy Brock (1994) report that the actual number—511—is more than five times the estimate given by the average student.

Given these odds, the rapid spread of STIs is not surprising. Condoms offer no protection against certain skin-to-skin STIs—notably the human papilloma virus, which is responsible for most genital cancers (Medical Institute, 1994; NIH, 2001). Condoms do, however, reduce tenfold the risk of contracting HIV (human immunodeficiency virus—the virus that causes AIDS) from an infected partner (Pinkerton & Abramson, 1997).

One response to these facts of life has been a greater emphasis on teen abstinence within some comprehensive sex education programs. A National Longitudinal Study of Adolescent Health among 12,000 teens found several predictors of sexual restraint:

High intelligence Teens with high rather than average intelligence test scores more often delay sex, evidently because they appreciate possible negative consequences and are more focused on future achievement than on here-and-now pleasures (Halpern & others, 2000).

Religiosity Actively religious teens and adults more often reserve sex for marital commitment (Rostosky & others, 2004; Smith, 1998).

"Will your child learn to multiply before she learns to subtract?"
Anti–teen-pregnancy poster, Children's Defense Fund

"Condoms should be used on every conceivable occasion."
Anonymous

"All of us who make motion pictures are teachers, teachers with very loud voices."
Film producer George Lucas, Academy Award ceremonies, 1992

■ **sexual orientation** an enduring sexual attraction toward members of either one's own sex (homosexual orientation) or the other sex (heterosexual orientation).

Father presence In studies that followed hundreds of New Zealand and U.S. girls from age 5 to 18, a father's absence was linked to sexual activity before age 16 and teen pregnancy (Ellis & others, 2003). These associations held even after adjusting for other adverse influences such as poverty.

Participation in service learning programs In several experiments, teens who volunteer as tutors or teachers' aides or take part in community projects have lower pregnancy rates than other comparable teens randomly assigned to control conditions (Kirby, 2002; O'Donnell & others, 2002). Researchers are unsure why. Does service learning promote a sense of personal competence, control, and responsibility? Does it encourage more future-oriented thinking? Or does it simply reduce opportunities for unprotected sex?

In recent history, the pendulum of sexual values has swung from the European eroticism of the early 1800s to the conservative Victorian era of the late 1800s, from the libertine flapper era of the 1920s to the family values period of the 1950s. The pendulum may have begun a new swing toward commitment in the twenty-first century, with declining teen birth rates since 1991, and virgins (54 percent in 2002) now outnumbering nonvirgins (46 percent) among U.S. 15- to 19-year-olds (CDC, 2004; Mohn & others, 2003).

Sexual Orientation

OBJECTIVE 36-6 | Summarize current views on the number of people whose sexual orientation is homosexual, and discuss the research on environmental and biological influences on sexual orientation.

To motivate is to energize and direct behavior. So far, we have considered the energizing of sexual motivation but not its direction. We express the direction of our sexual interest in our **sexual orientation**—our enduring sexual attraction toward members of our own sex (homosexual orientation) or the other sex (heterosexual orientation). Cultures vary in their attitudes toward homosexuality. But as far as we know, all cultures in all times have been predominantly heterosexual (Bullough, 1990). Whether a culture condemns or accepts homosexuality, heterosexuality prevails and homosexuality survives.

Gay men and lesbians often recall childhood play preferences like those of the other sex (Bailey & Zucker, 1995). But most homosexual people report not becoming aware of same-sex attraction until during or shortly after puberty, and not thinking of themselves as gay or lesbian until around age 20 (Garnets & Kimmel, 1990).

Sexual Orientation Statistics

How many people are exclusively homosexual? Until recently, the popular press assumed a homosexuality rate of 10 percent. In a 2002 Gallup survey, the average American estimated that 21 percent of men are gay and 22 percent of women are lesbian (Robinson, 2002). But in both Europe and the United States, more than a dozen national surveys in the early 1990s explored sexual orientation, using methods that protected the respondent's anonymity. Their results agree in suggesting that a more accurate figure is about 3 or 4 percent of men and 1 or 2 percent of women (Laumann & others, 1994; National Center for Health Statistics, 1991; Smith, 1998). Estimates derived from the sex of unmarried partners reported in the 2000 U.S. Census suggest that 2.5 percent of the population is gay or lesbian (Tarmann, 2002). Fewer than 1 percent of survey respondents—for example, 12 people out of 7076 Dutch adults in one recent survey (Sandfort & others, 2001)—reported being actively bisexual. (Studies indicate that men who describe themselves as bisexual tend to respond like homosexual men; they typically have genital arousal to same-sex erotic stimuli [Rieger & others, 2005].) In the Dutch study, a larger number of adults reported having had an isolated homosexual experience. And most people report having had an

> "It has been maintained for years that we each use only about 10 percent of our brain capacity; that the condom failure rate is 10 percent; and until just last year, that 10 percent of Americans are homosexual. Such statistics are partly artifacts, I suspect, of our decimal system; in a base 12 system, we'd no doubt show a similar affinity for statistics that were multiples of 8.333 percent."
>
> John Allen Paulos, "Counting on Dyscalculia," 1993

occasional homosexual fantasy. Health experts find it helpful to know sexual statistics, but numbers do not decide issues of human rights.

What does it feel like to be homosexual in a heterosexual culture? If you are heterosexual, one way to understand is to imagine how you would feel if you were ostracized or fired for openly admitting or displaying your feelings toward someone of the other sex; if you overheard people making crude jokes about heterosexual people; if most movies, TV shows, and advertisements portrayed (or implied) homosexuality; and if your family members were pleading with you to change your heterosexual lifestyle and to enter into a homosexual marriage.

Facing such reactions, homosexual people often struggle with their sexual orientation. They may at first try to ignore or deny their desires, hoping they will go away. But they don't. Then they may try to change, through psychotherapy, willpower, or prayer. But the feelings typically persist, as do those of heterosexual people—who are similarly incapable of becoming homosexual (Haldeman, 1994, 2002; Myers & Scanzoni, 2005). Most of today's psychologists therefore view sexual orientation as neither willfully chosen nor willfully changed. Sexual orientation in some ways is like handedness: Most people are one way, some the other. A very few are truly ambidextrous. Regardless, the way one is endures.

Women's sexual orientation tends to be less strongly felt and potentially more fluid and changeable than men's (Diamond, 2000, 2003; Peplau & Garnets, 2000). Men's lesser sexual variability is apparent in many ways, notes Roy Baumeister (2000). Across time, across cultures, across situations, and across differing levels of education, religiosity, and peer influence, adult women's sexual drive and interests are more flexible and varying than are adult men's. Women, more than men, for example, prefer to alternate periods of high sexual activity with periods of almost none, and are somewhat more likely than men to feel bisexual attractions. Baumeister calls this phenomenon the gender difference in *erotic plasticity*.

Gays and lesbians suffer elevated rates of depression and risk of suicide attempts, which researchers suspect result from their experiences with bullying, harassment, and discrimination (Sandfort & others, 2001; Warner & others, 2004). Most people, whether straight or gay, accept their orientation—by electing celibacy, by engaging in promiscuous sex (a choice more commonly made by gay men than by lesbian women), or by entering into a committed, long-term love relationship (a choice more often made by lesbians than by gays) (Kulkin & others, 2000; Peplau, 1982; Remafedi, 1999; Weinberg & Williams, 1974). Mental health professionals are now more accepting of clients' sexual orientation. The American Psychiatric Association dropped homosexuality from its list of "mental illnesses" in 1973, as did the World Health Organization in 1993, and Japan's and China's psychiatric associations in 1995 and 2001.

Origins of Sexual Orientation

If our sexual orientation is indeed something we do not choose and seemingly cannot change, then where do these preferences come from? How do we move toward either a heterosexual or a homosexual orientation? See if you can anticipate the consensus that has emerged from hundreds of research studies by responding yes or no to the following questions:

1. Is homosexuality linked with problems in a child's relationships with parents, such as with a domineering mother and an ineffectual father, or a possessive mother and a hostile father? *Yes?*

2. Does homosexuality involve a fear or hatred of people of the other gender, leading individuals to direct their sexual desires toward members of their own sex? *No*

3. Is sexual orientation linked with levels of sex hormones currently in the blood?

4. As children, were many homosexuals molested, seduced, or otherwise sexually victimized by an adult homosexual?

Personal values affect sexual orientation less than they affect other forms of sexual behavior. Compared with people who rarely attend religious services, for example, those who attend regularly are one-third as likely to have cohabited before marriage, and they report having had many fewer sex partners. But (if male) they are just as likely to be homosexual (Smith, 1998).

Note that the scientific question is not "What causes homosexuality?" (or "What causes heterosexuality?") but "What causes differing sexual orientation?" In pursuit of answers, psychological science compares the backgrounds and physiology of people whose sexual orientations *differ*.

The answer to all these questions appears to be no (Storms, 1983). Consider the findings of lengthy Kinsey Institute interviews with nearly 1000 homosexuals and 500 heterosexuals (Bell & others, 1981; Hammersmith, 1982). The investigators assessed nearly every imaginable psychological cause of homosexuality—parental relationships, childhood sexual experiences, peer relationships, dating experiences. Their findings: Homosexuals were no more likely than heterosexuals to have been smothered by maternal love, neglected by their father, or sexually abused. And consider this: If "distant fathers" were more likely to produce homosexual sons, then shouldn't boys growing up in father-absent homes more often be gay? (They are not.) And shouldn't the rising number of such homes have led to a noticeable increase in the gay population? (It has not.)

Homosexual people do, however, appear more often in certain populations. One study (Ludwig, 1995) of the biographies of 1004 eminent people found homosexual and bisexual people overrepresented (11 percent of the sample), especially among poets (24 percent), fiction writers (21 percent), and artists and musicians (15 percent). Men who have older brothers are also somewhat more likely to be gay, report Ray Blanchard (1997, 2001) and Anthony Bogaert (2003). Assuming the odds of homosexuality are roughly 3 percent among first sons, they rise to about 4 percent among second sons, 5 percent or a little more for third sons, and so on for each additional older brother. The reason for this curious phenomenon—the *fraternal birth-order effect*—is unclear. Blanchard suspects a defensive maternal immune response to foreign substances produced by male fetuses. The maternal antibodies may become stronger after each pregnancy with a male fetus and may prevent the fetus' brain from developing in a male-typical pattern. Women with older sisters, and women who were womb-mates of twin brothers, exhibit no such sibling effect (Rose & others, 2002).

So, what else might influence sexual orientation? One theory proposes that people develop same-sex erotic attachments if segregated by gender at the time their sex drive matures (Storms, 1981). Indeed, gay men tend to recall going through puberty somewhat earlier, when peers are more likely to be all males (Bogaert & others, 2002). But even in tribal cultures in which homosexual behavior is expected of all boys before marriage, heterosexuality prevails (Money, 1987). (As this illustrates, homosexual *behavior* does not always indicate a homosexual *orientation*.)

The bottom line from a half-century's theory and research: If there are environmental factors that influence sexual orientation, we do not yet know what they are. This reality has motivated researchers to consider more carefully the possible biological influences on orientation, including evidence of homosexuality in the animal world, and the influences of differing brain centers, genetics, and prenatal hormone exposure.

Same-Sex Attraction in Animals

At Coney Island's New York Aquarium, Wendell and Cass spent several years as devoted same-sex partners. So, also, are the Central Park Zoo penguins Silo and Roy. Biologist Bruce Bagemihl (1999) identifies several hundred species in which at least occasional same-sex relations have been observed. Grizzlies, gorillas, monkeys, flamingos, and owls are all on the long list. Among rams, for example, some 6 to 10 percent—to sheep-breeding ranchers, the "duds"—display same-sex attraction by shunning ewes and seeking to mount other males (Perkins & Fitzgerald, 1997). So, some degree of homosexuality seems to be a natural part of the animal world as well.

The Brain and Sexual Orientation

Researcher Simon LeVay (1991) studied sections of the hypothalamus taken from deceased heterosexual and homosexual people. As a gay scientist, LeVay wanted to do "something connected with my gay identity." He knew he had to avoid biasing the results, so he did the study *blind,* without knowing which donors were gay. For

Genetic study of sexual orientation: Are you in (or do you know of) a family with two or more gay brothers? If so, a nationwide study being conducted by a Chicago-area university research team welcomes your visit to www.gaybros.com.

"Gay" penguins
New York Aquarium penguins Wendell and Cass have company in the animal kingdom.

David Hecker/AFP/Getty Images

nine months he peered through his microscope at a cell cluster he thought might be important. Then one morning, LeVay sat down and broke the codes. His discovery: The cell cluster was reliably larger in heterosexual men than in women and homosexual men. As the brain difference became apparent, LeVay said(1994), "I was almost in a state of shock. . . . I took a walk by myself on the cliffs over the ocean. I sat for half an hour just thinking what this might mean."

It should not surprise us that brains differ with sexual orientation. Remember our maxim: *Everything psychological is simultaneously biological.* The critical question is, when did the brain difference begin? At conception? In the womb? During childhood or adolescence? Did experience produce the difference? Or did genes or prenatal hormones (or genes via prenatal hormones)?

LeVay does not view this neural center as a sexual orientation center; rather, he sees it as an important part of the neural pathway engaged in sexual behavior. He acknowledges that sexual behavior patterns may influence the brain's anatomy. In fish, birds, rats, and humans, brain structures vary with experience—including sexual experience, reports sex researcher Marc Breedlove (1997). But LeVay believes it more likely that brain anatomy influences sexual orientation. His hunch seems confirmed by the discovery of a similar hypothalamic difference between the 6 to 10 percent of male sheep that display same-sex attraction and the 90+ percent attracted to females (Larkin & others, 2002; Roselli & others, 2002). Moreover, report University of London psychologists Qazi Rahman and Glenn Wilson (2003), "The neuroanatomical correlates of male homosexuality differentiate very early postnatally, if not prenatally."

A functional hypothalamus difference surfaced in recent reports of brain responses to hormone-derived sexual scents. Swedish researchers (Savic & others, 2005) reported that when straight women are given a whiff of a scent derived from men's sweat, their hypothalamus lights up in an area governing sexual arousal. Gay men's brains responded similarly to the men's scent, but straight men's brains showed the arousal response only to a female hormone derivative. It's not surprising, then, that another research team has since reported that gays and lesbians differ from their straight counterparts in their preferences for sex-related sweat odors (Martins & others, 2005). Odors taken from gay men, for example, are liked by other gay men but not by heterosexual men.

Laura Allen and Roger Gorski (1992) also concluded that brain anatomy influences sexual orientation after discovering that a section of the anterior commissure (the fibers that, like the corpus callosum, connect right and left hemispheres) is one-third larger in homosexual men than in heterosexual men.

> "Gay men simply don't have the brain cells to be attracted to women."
> Simon LeVay, *The Sexual Brain*, 1993

Genes and Sexual Orientation

There is evidence to suggest a genetic influence on sexual orientation. "First, homosexuality does appear to run in families," note Brian Mustanski and Michael Bailey (2003). "Second, twin studies have established that genes play a substantial role in explaining individual differences in sexual orientation." Although results vary, an identical twin is somewhat more likely than a fraternal twin to share a co-twin's homosexual orientation. However, in many identical twin pairs (especially female twins), the twin and co-twin's orientations differ, indicating that other factors besides genes are at work. And third, experimenters have, by genetic manipulations, managed to create female fruit flies that during courtship act like males (pursuing other females) and males that act like females (Demir & Dickson, 2005). "We have shown that a single gene in the fruit fly is sufficient to determine all aspects of the flies' sexual orientation and behavior," explained Barry Dickson (2005).

But why, many people wonder, would "gay genes" exist? Given that same-sex couples cannot reproduce, how could genes that predispose homosexuality have survived in the human gene pool? Researchers have speculated about possible reasons. Perhaps, for example, kin selection is at work. Evolutionary psychologists remind us that many of our genes also reside in our biological relatives. Perhaps, then, gay people's genes live on through their supporting the survival and reproductive success of their nieces, nephews, and other relatives (who also carry many of the same genes). Or perhaps maternal genetics are at work. A recent Italian study (Camperio-Ciani & others, 2004) confirms what others have found—that homosexual men have more homosexual relatives on their mother's side than on their father's. It also finds that, compared with the maternal relatives of heterosexual men, the maternal relatives of homosexual men produce more offspring. Perhaps, surmised the researchers, genes that convey a reproductive advantage in mothers and aunts somehow influence the sexual orientation of their sons and nephews.

Prenatal Hormones and Sexual Orientation

There are elevated rates of homosexual orientation in identical *and* fraternal twins, which suggests that not just shared genetics but also a shared prenatal environment may be a factor. In animals and some exceptional human cases, abnormal prenatal hormone conditions have altered a fetus' sexual orientation. German researcher Gunter Dorner (1976, 1988) pioneered this research by manipulating a fetal rat's exposure to male hormones, thereby "inverting" its sexual orientation. Similarly, when pregnant sheep are injected with testosterone during a critical period of fetal development, their female offspring will later show homosexual behavior (Money, 1987).

In humans, a critical period for the brain's neural-hormonal control system may exist between the middle of the second and fifth months after conception (Ellis & Ames, 1987; Gladue, 1990; Meyer-Bahlburg, 1995). Exposure to the hormone levels typically experienced by female fetuses during this time appears to predispose the person (whether female or male) to be attracted to males in later life.

Some research reveals that homosexual individuals of both sexes have many traits that are intermediate between heterosexual females and males (**TABLE 36.1**). For example, in some (but not all) studies, gay men have had fingerprint patterns rather like those of heterosexual women (Mustanski & others, 2002; Sanders & others,

---

TABLE 36.1

BIOLOGICAL CORRELATES OF SEXUAL ORIENTATION

On average (the evidence is strongest for males), various biological and behavioral traits of gays and lesbians fall between those of straight men and straight women. Tentative findings—some in need of replication—include these:

Brain differences
- One hypothalamic cell cluster is larger in straight men than in women and gay men; same difference is found in male sheep displaying other-sex versus same-sex attraction.
- Anterior commissure is larger in gay men than in women or straight men.
- Gay men's hypothalamus reacts as does a woman's to the smell of sex-related hormones.

Genetic influences
- Shared sexual orientation is higher among identical twins than among fraternal twins.
- Sexual attraction in fruit flies can be genetically manipulated.

Prenatal hormonal influences
- Altered prenatal hormone exposure may lead to homosexuality in humans and other animals.
- Men with several older brothers are more likely to be gay.

These brain differences and genetic and prenatal influences may contribute to observed gay-straight differences in
- spatial abilities.
- fingerprint ridge counts.
- auditory system development.
- handedness.
- occupational preferences.
- relative finger lengths.
- gender nonconformity.
- age of onset of puberty in males.
- male body size.
- sleep length.

2002). Most people have more fingerprint ridges on their right hand than on their left. Jeff Hall and Doreen Kimura (1994) first observed that this difference was greater for heterosexual males than for females and gay males. Given that fingerprint ridges are complete by the sixteenth fetal week, the researchers suspected the difference was due to prenatal hormones. Prenatal hormones also are a possible explanation for why data from 20 studies revealed that "homosexual participants had 39 percent greater odds of being non–right-handed" (Lalumière & others, 2000).

Lesbians likewise have some male-typical traits. For example, their cochlea and hearing system develop in a way that is intermediate between those of heterosexual females and heterosexual males, and which seems attributable to prenatal hormonal influence (McFadden, 2002).

Another striking illustration of gay-straight differences appears in studies showing that homosexual men's spatial abilities resemble those typical of heterosexual women (Cohen, 2002; Gladue, 1994; McCormick & Witelson, 1991; Sanders & Wright, 1997). On mental rotation tasks such as the one illustrated in **FIGURE 36.2,** for example, heterosexual men tend to outscore women. A study by Qazi Rahman and colleagues (2003) found that, as on a number of other measures, the scores of both homosexual males and females fall between those of heterosexual males and heterosexual females.

Because the physiological evidence is preliminary and controversial, some scientists remain skeptical. Rather than specifying sexual orientation, they suggest, biological factors may predispose a temperament that influences sexuality "in the context of individual learning and experience" (Byne & Parsons, 1993). Daryl Bem (1996, 1998, 2000) has theorized that genes code for prenatal hormones and brain anatomy, which predispose *temperaments* that lead children to prefer gender-typical or gender-atypical activities and friends. These preferences may later lead children to feel attracted to whichever sex feels different from their own. The dissimilar-seeming sex (whether or not it conforms to one's own anatomy) becomes associated with anxiety and other forms of arousal, which are eventually transformed into romantic arousal. The exotic becomes erotic.

Regardless of the process, the consistency of the genetic, prenatal, and brain findings has swung the pendulum toward a biological explanation of sexual orientation (Rahman & Wilson, 2003). Nature more than nurture, most psychiatrists now believe, predisposes orientation (Vreeland & others, 1995). This helps explain why sexual orientation is so difficult to change.

Still, some people wonder: Should the cause of sexual orientation matter? Perhaps it shouldn't, but people's assumptions matter. Those who believe, as do 40 percent of Americans (up from 13 percent in 1977 [Gallup, 2002]) and most gays and lesbians, that sexual orientation is biologically

Gay more than straight men express interest in occupations that attract many women, such as decorator, florist, and flight attendant (Lippa, 2002). (Given that some 96 percent of men are not gay, most men in such occupations may nevertheless be straight.)

"Modern scientific research indicates that sexual orientation is … partly determined by genetics, but more specifically by hormonal activity in the womb."

Glenn Wilson and Qazi Rahman, *Born Gay: The Psychobiology of Sex Orientation,* 2005

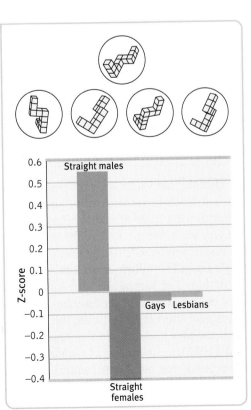

FIGURE 36.2

Spatial abilities and sexual orientation

Which of the four figures can be rotated to match the target figure at the top? Straight males tend to find this an easier task than do straight females, with gays and lesbians intermediate. (From Rahman, Wilson, & Abrahams, 2004, with 60 people tested in each group.)

disposed, express more accepting attitudes toward homosexual people (Allen & others, 1996; Furnham & Taylor, 1990; Kaiser, 2001; Whitley, 1990). Consider:

- Between 1977 and 2002, American Gallup surveys found that support for equal job rights for gays and lesbians rose from 56 to 85 percent, and agreement that "homosexuality should be an acceptable alternative life-style" rose from 34 to 52 percent.
- In Canadian Gallup surveys between 1992 and 2001, support for same-sex marriages nearly doubled—from 24 to 46 percent (Mazzuca, 2002), and will likely rise further, now that Canada has begun allowing same-sex marriage.
- Acceptance is most common among women, among those with a gay or lesbian friend or relative, and among younger adults (Altmeyer, 2001; Herek & Capitanio, 1996; Kaiser, 2001; Kite & Whitley, 1996; Whitley, 2002). In 2001 surveys by the Gallup Organization and by the Kaiser Family Foundation, 60 to 65 percent of 18- to 29-year-olds supported gay/lesbian marriage or legal relationships—double the support expressed by those 65 and older (Carlson, 2002; Kaiser, 2001). Moreover, among entering collegians, support for laws prohibiting homosexual relationships has plummeted since 1987 (**FIGURE 36.3**).

These dramatic attitude shifts do not represent a liberalization of all sex-related attitudes. For example, in periodic U.S. national surveys, agreement that extramarital sex is "always wrong" *increased* from 69.6 percent in 1973 to 79.4 percent in 2000 (NORC, 2002).

To gay and lesbian activists, the new biological research is a double-edged sword (Diamond, 1993). If sexual orientation, like skin color and sex, is genetically influenced, that offers a further rationale for civil rights protection. Moreover, it may alleviate parents' concerns about their children being unduly influenced by gay teachers and role models. It does, however, raise the troubling possibility that genetic markers of sexual orientation could someday be identified through fetal testing, and a fetus could be aborted simply for being predisposed to an unwanted orientation.

FIGURE 36.3
Changing attitudes
(Source: Annual UCLA/American Council on Education surveys of some 7 million entering collegians.)

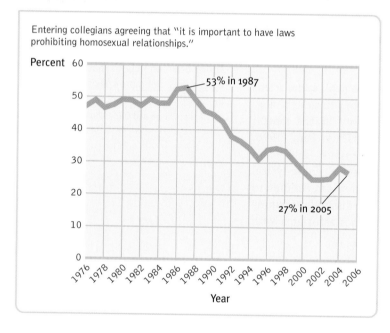

Entering collegians agreeing that "it is important to have laws prohibiting homosexual relationships."

53% in 1987

27% in 2005

Sex and Human Values

OBJECTIVE 36-7 | Discuss the place of values in sex research.

Recognizing that values are both personal and cultural, most sex researchers and educators strive to keep their writings on sexuality value-free.

But can the study of sexual behavior and what motivates it ever be free of values? The very words we use to describe behavior often reflect our personal values, as when sex researchers label sexually restrained individuals as "erotophobic" and as having "high sex guilt." Whether we label sexual acts we do not practice as "perversions," "deviations," or part of an "alternative sexual life-style" depends on our attitude toward the behaviors. Labels describe, but they also evaluate.

Sex education separated from the context of human values may also give some students the idea that sexual intercourse is simply a recreational activity. Diana Baumrind (1982), a University of California child-rearing expert, has observed that an implication that adults are neutral about adolescent sexual activity is unfortunate, because "promiscuous recreational sex poses certain psychological, social, health, and moral problems that must be faced realistically."

Perhaps we can agree that the knowledge provided by sex research is preferable to ignorance, and yet also agree that researchers' values should be stated openly, enabling us to debate them and to reflect on our own values. We should remember that scientific research on sexual motivation does not aim to define the personal meaning of sex in our own lives. You could know every available fact about sex—that the initial spasms of male and female orgasm come at 0.8-second intervals, that the female nipples expand 10 millimeters at the peak of sexual arousal, that systolic blood pressure rises some 60 points and the respiration rate to 40 breaths per minute—but fail to understand the human significance of sexual intimacy.

Surely one significance of sexual intimacy is its expression of our profoundly social nature. Sex is a socially significant act. Men and women can achieve orgasm alone, yet most people find greater satisfaction while embracing their loved one. There is a yearning for closeness in sexual motivation. Sex at its human best is life-uniting and love-renewing.

A sharing of love
For most adults, a sexual relationship fulfills not only a biological motive, but a social need for intimacy.

The Need to Belong

OBJECTIVE 36-8 | Describe the adaptive value of social attachments, and identify both healthy and unhealthy consequences of our need to belong.

Separated from friends or family—isolated in prison, alone at a new school, living in a foreign land—most people feel keenly their lost connections with important others. We are what Aristotle called the *social animal.* "Without friends," wrote Aristotle in his *Nichomachean Ethics,* "no one would choose to live, though he had all other goods." We have a need to affiliate with others, even to become strongly attached to certain others in enduring, close relationships. Human beings, contended the personality theorist Alfred Adler, have an "urge to community" (Ferguson, 1989). Roy Baumeister and Mark Leary (1995) have assembled evidence for this deep *need to belong.*

Aiding Survival

Social bonds boosted our ancestors' survival rate. By keeping children close to their caregivers, attachments served as a powerful survival impulse. As adults, those who formed attachments were more likely to come together to reproduce and to stay together to nurture their offspring to maturity. To be "wretched" literally means, in its Middle English origin (*wrecche*), to be without kin nearby.

Cooperation in groups also enhanced survival. In solo combat, our ancestors were not the toughest predators. But as hunters they learned that six hands were better than two. And as foragers, they gained protection from predators and enemies by traveling in groups. Those who felt a need to belong survived and reproduced most successfully, and their genes now predominate. We are innately social creatures. People in every society on Earth belong to groups and prefer and favor "us" over "them."

Wanting to Belong

The need to belong colors our thoughts and emotions. We spend a great deal of time thinking about actual and hoped-for relationships. When relationships form, we often feel joy. Falling in mutual love, people have been known to feel their cheeks ache from their irrepressible grins. Asked, "What is necessary for your happiness?" or "What is it that makes your life meaningful?" most people mention—before anything else—close, satisfying relationships with family, friends, or romantic partners (Berscheid, 1985). Happiness hits close to home.

Pause a moment to consider: What was your most satisfying moment in the past week? Kennon Sheldon and his colleagues (2001) asked that

Separation amplifies the felt need to belong

In the film *Cast Away*, Chuck Noland (played by Tom Hanks) combats social starvation by talking with his girlfriend's snapshot and a volleyball he named Wilson.

question of American and South Korean collegians, then asked them to rate how much this peak experience had satisfied various needs. In both countries, the satisfaction of self-esteem and relatedness-belonging needs were the top two contributors to the peak moment. Another study found that *very* happy university students are not distinguished by their money but by their "rich and satisfying close relationships" (Diener & Seligman, 2002). The need to belong runs deeper, it seems, than any need to be rich.

South Africans have a word for these human bonds that define us all. *Ubuntu* (oo-BOON-too), explains Desmond Tutu (1999), expresses the fact that "my humanity is caught up, is inextricably bound up, in yours." A Zulu maxim captures the idea: *Umuntu ngumuntu ngabantu*—"a person is a person through other persons."

Acting to Increase Social Acceptance

When we feel included, accepted, and loved by those important to us, our self-esteem rides high. Indeed, say Mark Leary and his colleagues (1998), self-esteem is a gauge of how valued and accepted we feel. Much of our social behavior therefore aims to increase our belonging—our social acceptance and inclusion. To avoid rejection, we generally conform to group standards and seek to make favorable impressions. To win friendship and esteem, we monitor our behavior, hoping to create the right impressions. Seeking love and belonging, we spend billions on clothes, cosmetics, and diet and fitness aids—all motivated by our quest for acceptance.

Like sexual motivation, which feeds both love and exploitation, the need to belong feeds both deep attachments and menacing threats. Out of our need to define a "we" come loving families, faithful friendships, and team spirit, but also teen gangs, ethnic rivalries, and fanatic nationalism.

Maintaining Relationships

For most of us, familiarity breeds liking, not contempt. We resist breaking social bonds. Thrown together at school, at summer camp, on a vacation cruise, people resist the group's dissolution. Hoping to maintain our relationships, we promise to call, to write, to come back for reunions. Parting, we feel distress. Attachments can even keep people in abusive relationships if the fear of being alone seems worse than the pain of emotional or physical abuse. Even when bad relationships break, people suffer. In one 16-nation survey, separated and divorced people were only half as likely as married people to say they were "very happy" (Inglehart, 1990). After such separations, feelings of loneliness and anger—and sometimes even a strange desire to be near the former partner—are commonplace.

The need to connect
Six days a week, women from the Philippines work as "domestic helpers" in 154,000 Hong Kong households. On Sundays, they throng to the central business district to picnic, dance, sing, talk, and laugh. "Humanity could stage no greater display of happiness," reported one observer (*Economist*, 2001).

AP/Wide World Photos

The fear of being alone has some basis in reality. Children who move through a series of foster homes, with repeated disruption of budding attachments, may come to have difficulty forming deep attachments. And children reared in institutions without a sense of belonging to anyone, or locked away at home under extreme neglect, become pathetic creatures—withdrawn, frightened, speechless.

When something threatens or dissolves our social ties, negative emotions—anxiety, loneliness, jealousy, guilt—overwhelm us. The bereaved often feel life is empty, pointless. Even the first weeks living on a college campus away from home can be distressing. For immigrants and refugees who move alone to new places, the stress and loneliness can be depressing. But if feelings of acceptance and connection build, so do self-esteem, positive feelings, and desires to help rather than hurt others (Buckley & Leary, 2001). After years of placing individual refugee and immigrant families in isolated communities, U.S. policies today encourage *chain migration* (Pipher, 2002). The second refugee Sudanese family settling in a town generally has an easier adjustment than the first.

Avoiding the Pain of Ostracism

Sometimes, though, the need to belong is denied. Perhaps you can recall such a time, when you felt excluded or ignored or shunned. Perhaps you received the silent treatment. Perhaps others avoided you, or averted their eyes in your presence, or even mocked you behind your back.

Social psychologist Kipling Williams (2002) and his colleagues have studied such experiences of *ostracism*—of social exclusion—in both natural and laboratory settings. Worldwide, humans use ostracism to control social behavior, with punishing effects. For children, even a brief time-out in isolation can be punishing. For adults, ostracism can be even more painful. Exile, imprisonment, and solitary confinement are progressively more severe forms of punishment. Even to be shunned—given the cold shoulder or the silent treatment, with others' eyes avoiding yours—is to have one's need to belong threatened, observe Kipling Williams and Lisa Zadro (2001). "It's the meanest thing you can do to someone, especially if you know they can't fight back. I never should have been born," said Lea, a lifelong victim of the silent treatment by her mother and grandmother. Like Lea, people often respond to ostracism with depressed moods, initial efforts to restore their acceptance, and then withdrawal. "I came home every night and cried. I lost 25 pounds, had no self-esteem and felt that I wasn't worthy," reported Richard, after two years of silent treatment by his employer.

Williams and his colleagues were surprised to discover a toll even from "cyber-ostracism" by strangers. (Perhaps you can recall the feeling from being ignored in a chat room or having an e-mail go unanswered.) Such ostracism, they discovered, elicits increased activity in a brain area, the *anterior cingulate cortex,* that also activates in response to physical pain (Eisenberger & others, 2003). Psychologically, too, we experience social pain with the same emotional unpleasantness that marks physical pain (MacDonald & Leary, 2005). To experience ostracism is to experience real pain. And pain, whatever its source, focuses our attention and motivates corrective action.

If rejected and unable to remedy the situation, people sometimes turn nasty. In a series of studies, Jean Twenge and her collaborators (2001, 2002; Baumeister & others, 2002) either told people (based on a personality test) that they were "the type likely to end up alone later in life" or that others whom they had met didn't want them in a group that was forming. The researchers told other participants that they would have "rewarding relationships throughout life" or that "everyone chose you as someone they'd like to work with." Those excluded became much more likely to engage in self-defeating behaviors and underperform on aptitude tests. They also exhibited more antisocial behavior, such as disparaging or aggressing against (with a blast of noise) those who had insulted them. "If intelligent, well-adjusted, successful university students can turn aggressive in response to a small laboratory experience of

Social exclusion fosters freaking out
Most socially excluded teens do not commit violence, but some do. Charles "Andy" Williams, described by a classmate as someone his peers derided as "freak, dork, nerd, stuff like that," went on a shooting spree at his suburban California high school, killing 2 and wounding 13 (Bowles & Kasindorf, 2001).

AP/Wide World Photos

social exclusion," noted the research team, "it is disturbing to imagine the aggressive tendencies that might arise from a series of important rejections or chronic exclusion from desired groups in actual social life."

Fortifying Health

Do you have close friends—people with whom you freely disclose your ups and downs? People who have close friends tend to be happier. Those who feel supported by close relationships also live with better health and at lower risk for psychological disorder and premature death than do those who lack social support. Married people, for example, are less at risk for depression, suicide, and early death than are unattached people. All this evidence affirms Baumeister and Leary's (1995) contention that "human beings are fundamentally and pervasively motivated by a need to belong."

>> LEARNING OUTCOMES

Sexual Motivation and the Need to Belong

OBJECTIVE 36-1 | Describe the human sexual response cycle, and discuss some causes of sexual disorders.

Masters and Johnson described four stages in the human sexual response cycle: *excitement, plateau, orgasm* (which seems to involve similar feelings and brain activity in males and females), and *resolution*. During the resolution phase, males experience a refractory period, when renewed arousal and orgasm are impossible. Sexual disorders (problems that consistently impair sexual arousal or functioning, such as premature ejaculation, female orgasmic disorder, and erectile dysfunction) are being successfully treated by behaviorally oriented therapy, which assumes that people learn and can modify their sexual responses, or with drug therapy.

OBJECTIVE 36-2 | Discuss the impact of hormones on sexual motivation and behavior.

The sex hormones *testosterone* and *estrogen* are present in both males and females, but males have a higher level of testosterone and females a higher level of estrogen. These hormones help our bodies develop and function as either male or female. In nonhuman animals, they also help stimulate sexual activity. In women with mates, desire does rise slightly at ovulation, but women's sexuality is more responsive to testosterone level than to estrogen level. Short-term shifts in testosterone level are normal in men.

OBJECTIVE 36-3 | Describe the role of external stimuli and fantasies on sexual motivation and behavior.

Erotic material and other external stimuli can trigger sexual arousal in both men and women, although the activated brain areas differ somewhat. Sexually explicit material may lead people to perceive their partners as comparatively less appealing and to devalue their relationships. Sexually coercive material tends to increase viewers' acceptance of rape and violence toward women. In combination with the internal hormonal push and the external pull of sexual stimuli, fantasies (imagined stimuli) influence sexual arousal.

OBJECTIVE 36-4 | Discuss some of the forces that influence teen pregnancy and teen attitudes toward contraception.

Adolescents' physical maturation fosters a sexual dimension to their emerging identity, but rates of teen intercourse vary from culture to culture. In the twentieth century, teen sexual activity increased in North America. Factors contributing to increased rates of teen pregnancy include ignorance about conception; guilt related to sexual activity; minimal communication about contraception with parents, partners, and peers; alcohol use; and mass media norms of unprotected promiscuity.

OBJECTIVE 36-5 | Describe trends in the spread of sexually transmitted infections.

STIs—sexually transmitted infections, such as the human papilloma virus, AIDS, and others—have spread rapidly, especially among people under the age of 25. Teen girls seem especially vulnerable because of their less mature bodies and lower levels of protective antibodies. Comprehensive sex-education programs often emphasize teen abstinence. High intelligence, religiosity, father presence, and participation in service learning programs tend to be predictors of teen sexual restraint.

OBJECTIVE 36-6 | Summarize current views on the number of people whose sexual orientation is homosexual, and discuss the research on environmental and biological influences on sexual orientation.

Studies indicate that about 3 or 4 percent of men and 1 or 2 percent of women are homosexual, and that sexual orientation is enduring. Research does not support cause-effect links between homosexuality and a child's relationships with parents, father-absent homes, fear or hatred of people of the other gender, childhood sexual experiences, peer relationships, or dating experiences. The likelihood of a biological component of homosexuality is indicated by the existence of same-sex behavior in several hundred species; straight-gay differences in body and brain characteristics; genetic studies of family members and twins; and the effect of exposure to certain hormones during critical periods of prenatal development. The increasing public perception that sexual orientation is biologically influenced is reflected in increasing acceptance of gays and lesbians and their relationships.

OBJECTIVE 36-7 | **Discuss the place of values in sex research.**
Scientific research on sexual motivation does not attempt to define the personal meaning of sex in our lives. Sex research and education are not value-free, and some believe that researchers and educators should therefore openly acknowledge their sex-related values.

OBJECTIVE 36-8 | **Describe the adaptive value of social attachments, and identify both healthy and unhealthy consequences of our need to belong.**
Our need to *affiliate*—to feel connected and identified with others—boosted our ancestors' chances for survival, which may explain why humans in every society live in groups. When *ostracized* (excluded or shunned by others), people suffer from stress and depression—a real pain that increases activity in the same brain areas that respond to physical pain. Those who are socially secure in their friendships, families, or marriages tend to be healthier and to have lower levels of depression, suicide, and early death. When socially excluded, people may engage in self-defeating or antisocial behaviors.

TERMS AND CONCEPTS TO REMEMBER

sexual response cycle, p. 36-0
refractory period, p. 36-1
sexual disorder, p. 36-1
estrogen, p. 36-1
testosterone, p. 36-2
sexual orientation, p 36-6

TEST YOURSELF

1. How might the evolutionary psychology perspective explain sexual motivation and our need to affiliate?

(Answer in Appendix B.)

ASK YOURSELF

1. What do you think would be an effective strategy for reducing teen pregnancy?

2. Have there been times when you felt "out of the loop" with family and friends, or even ostracized by them? How did you respond?

>WEB

Multiple-choice *self-tests* and more may be found at www.worthpublishers.com/myers.

37

Motivation at Work

OBJECTIVE 37-1 | Discuss the importance of flow, and identify the three subfields of industrial-organizational psychology.

The healthy life, said Sigmund Freud, is filled by love and by work. For most of us, work is life's biggest single waking activity. To live is to work. Work helps satisfy several levels of need. Work supports us. Work connects us. Work defines us. Meeting someone for the first time, and wondering "Who are you?" we may ask, "So, what do you do?"

If we feel dissatisfied with our work-related pay, relationships, or identity, we may change where or for whom we work, as 16 percent of Australians did in just the year 2000 (Trewin, 2001). Most people therefore have neither a single vocation nor a predictable career path. Two decades from now, most of you reading this book will be doing work you cannot now imagine. To prepare you and others for this unknown future, many colleges and universities focus less on training your job skills and more on enlarging your capacities for understanding, thinking, and communicating in any work environment.

Amy Wrzesniewski and her colleagues (1997, 2001) have identified person-to-person variations in people's attitudes toward their work. Across various occupations, some people view their work as a *job,* a necessary way to make money but not a positive and fulfilling activity. Others view their work as a *career,* an opportunity to advance from one position to a better position. The rest—those who view their work as a *calling,* a fulfilling and socially useful activity—report the highest satisfaction with their work and their lives.

This finding would not surprise Mihaly Csikszentmihalyi (1990, 1999), who has observed that people's quality of life increases when they are purposefully engaged. Between the anxiety of being overwhelmed and stressed, and the apathy of being underwhelmed and bored, lies a zone in which people experience **flow.** Csikszentmihalyi (chick-SENT-me-hi) formulated the flow concept after studying artists who spent hour after hour painting or sculpting with enormous concentration. Immersed in a project, they worked as if nothing else mattered, and then promptly forgot about it once they finished. The artists seemed driven less by the external rewards of producing art—money, praise, promotion—than by the intrinsic rewards of creating the work. Recognizing that e-mail and other Internet-related distractions can disrupt such flow, Microsoft is developing an *attentional user interface* that aims to "detect when users are available for communication, or when the user is in a state of flow" (Ullman, 2005).

Csikszentmihalyi's later observations—of dancers, chess players, surgeons, writers, parents, mountain climbers, sailors, and farmers; of Australians, North Americans, Koreans, Japanese, and Italians; of people from their teens to their golden years—confirmed an overriding principle: It's exhilarating to flow with an activity that fully engages our skills. Flow experiences boost our sense of self-esteem, competence, and well-being. When the researchers beeped people at random intervals and asked them to report what they were doing and how much they were enjoying themselves, those who were vegetating usually reported little sense of flow and little satisfaction. People reported more positive feelings when interrupted while doing something active, something that engaged their skills, be it play or work. And other research (Inglehart, 1990) indicates that in almost every industrialized nation, people have reported markedly lower well-being if unemployed (**FIGURE 37.1**). Idleness may sound like bliss, but purposeful work enriches our lives.

Sometimes, notes Gene Weingarten (2002), a humor writer knows "when to just get out of the way." Here are some sample job titles from the U.S. Department of Labor *Dictionary of Occupational Titles:* Animal impersonator, human projectile, banana ripening-room supervisor, impregnator, impregnator helper, dope sprayer, finger waver, rug scratcher, egg smeller, bottom buffer, cookie breaker, brain picker, hand pouncer, bosom presser, mother repairer, and breaker repairer.

Have you ever noticed that when you are immersed in an activity, time flies? And that when you are watching the clock, it seems to move more slowly? French researchers have confirmed that the more we attend to an event's duration, the longer it seems to last (Couli & others, 2004).

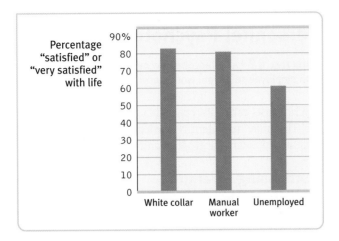

FIGURE 37.1
The bane of unemployment
To want work but not have it is to feel less satisfied with life. Data from 169,776 adults in 16 nations (Inglehart, 1990).

In industrialized nations, work has been changing, from farming to manufacturing to "knowledge work." More and more work is *outsourced* to temporary employees and consultants who communicate electronically from virtual workplaces in remote locations. (This book and its teaching package are developed and produced by a team of people in a dozen cities, from Alaska to Florida.) As work changes, will our attitudes toward our work also change? Will our satisfaction with work increase or decrease? Will the *psychological contract*—the subjective sense of mutual obligations between workers and employers—become more or less trusting and secure? These are among the questions that fascinate psychologists who study work-related behavior.

Industrial-organizational (I/O) psychology is a fast-growing profession that applies psychology's principles to the workplace (see Close-Up: I/O Psychology at Work). Here we consider two subfields: **personnel psychology,** which applies psychology's methods and principles to selecting and evaluating workers, and **organizational psychology,** which considers how work environments and management styles influence worker motivation, satisfaction, and productivity. Personnel psychologists match people with jobs, by identifying and placing well-suited candidates. Organizational psychologists modify jobs and supervision in ways that boost morale and productivity. (A third subfield, *human factors psychology,* explores how machines and environments can be optimally designed to fit human abilities.)

■ **flow** a completely involved, focused state of consciousness, with diminished awareness of self and time, resulting from optimal engagement of one's skills.

■ **industrial-organizational (I/O) psychology** the application of psychological concepts and methods to optimizing human behavior in workplaces.

■ **personnel psychology** a subfield of I/O psychology that focuses on employee recruitment, selection, placement, training, appraisal, and development.

■ **organizational psychology** a subfield of I/O psychology that examines organizational influences on worker satisfaction and productivity and facilitates organizational change.

CLOSE-UP:

I/O PSYCHOLOGY AT WORK

As scientists, consultants, and management professionals, industrial-organizational psychologists are found working in varied areas:

PERSONNEL PSYCHOLOGY

Selecting and placing employees
- Developing and validating assessment tools for selecting, placing and promoting workers
- Analyzing job content
- Optimizing worker placement

Training and developing employees
- Identifying needs

- Designing training programs
- Evaluating training programs

Appraising performance
- Developing criteria
- Measuring individual performance
- Measuring organizational performance

ORGANIZATIONAL PSYCHOLOGY

Developing organizations
- Analyzing organizational structures
- Maximizing worker satisfaction and productivity
- Facilitating organizational change

Enhancing quality of worklife
- Expanding individual productivity
- Identifying elements of satisfaction
- Redesigning jobs

HUMAN FACTORS (ENGINEERING) PSYCHOLOGY
- Designing optimum work environments
- Optimizing person-machine interactions
- Developing systems technologies

Adapted from the Society of Industrial and Organizational Psychology (siop.org)

Personnel Psychology

OBJECTIVE 37-2 | Describe how personnel psychologists help organizations with employee selection, work placement, and performance appraisal.

Psychologists can assist organizations at various stages of selecting and assessing employees. They may help identify needed job skills, decide upon selection methods, recruit and evaluate applicants, introduce and train new employees, and appraise their performance.

Harnessing Strengths

As a new AT&T human resource executive, psychologist Mary Tenopyr (1997) was assigned to solve a problem: Customer service representatives were failing at a high rate. After concluding that many of the hires were ill-matched to the demands of their new job, Tenopyr developed a new selection instrument:

1. She asked new applicants to respond to various questions (without as yet making any use of their responses).
2. She followed up later to assess which of the applicants excelled on the job.
3. She identified the individual items on the earlier test that best predicted who would succeed.

The happy result of her data-driven work was a new test that enabled AT&T to identify likely-to-succeed customer representatives.

As this illustrates, personnel selection aims to match people's strengths with work that enables them and their organizations to flourish. Marry the strengths of people with the tasks of organizations and the result is often prosperity and profit.

Your strengths are any enduring qualities that can be productively applied. Are you naturally curious? Persuasive? Charming? Persistent? Competitive? Analytical? Empathic? Organized? Articulate? Neat? Mechanical? Any such trait, if matched with suitable work, can function as a strength. (See Close-Up: Discovering Your Strengths.)

Marcus Buckingham and Donald Clifton (2001) argued that the first step to a stronger organization is instituting a strengths-based selection system. Thus, as a manager, you would first identify a group of the most effective people in any role—

Artistic strengths

At age 21, Henri Matisse was a sickly and often depressed lawyer's clerk. When his mother gave him a box of paints to cheer him up one day, he felt the darkness lift and his energy surge. He began to fill his days with painting and drawing and went on to art school and a life as one of the world's great painters. For Matisse, doing art felt like "a comfortable armchair." That is how exercising our strengths often feels.

CLOSE-UP:

DISCOVERING YOUR STRENGTHS

You can use some of the techniques personnel psychologists have developed to identify your own strengths and pinpoint types of work that will likely prove satisfying and successful. Buckingham and Clifton (2001) have suggested asking yourself:

- What activities give me pleasure? (Bringing order out of chaos? Playing host? Helping others? Challenging sloppy thinking?)
- What activities leave me wondering, "When can I do this again?" (Rather than "When will this be over?")
- What sort of challenges do I relish? (And which do I dread?)

- What sorts of tasks do I learn easily? (And which do I struggle with?)

Some people find themselves in flow—their skills engaged and time flying—when teaching or selling or writing or cleaning or consoling or creating or repairing. If an activity feels good, if it comes easily, if you look forward to it, then look deeper and see your strengths at work.

Satisfied and successful people devote far less time to correcting their deficiencies than to accentuating their strengths. Top performers are "rarely well rounded," Buckingham and Clifton found (p. 26). Instead, they have sharpened their existing skills.

Given the persistence of our traits and temperaments, we should focus not on our deficiencies, but rather on identifying and employing our talents. Better to recognize the activities we quickly learn and become absorbed in—and to further develop those strengths—than to sign up for assertiveness training if shy, for public speaking courses if nervous and soft-spoken, or for drawing classes if we express our artistic side in stick figures.

As Robert Louis Stevenson said in *Of Men and Books* (1882), "To be what we are, and to become what we are capable of becoming, is the only end of life."

the ones you would want to hire more of—and compare their strengths with those of a group of the least effective people in that role. In defining these groups, you would try to measure performance as objectively as possible. In one Gallup study of more than 5000 telecommunications customer-service representatives, those evaluated most favorably by their managers were strong in "harmony" and "responsibility," while those actually rated most effective by customers were strong in energy, assertiveness, and eagerness to learn. So, for example, if you needed to hire new people in software development, and you had discovered that your best software developers are analytical, disciplined, and eager to learn, you would focus employment ads less on experience than on the identified strengths: "Do you take a logical and systematic approach to problem solving [analytical]? Are you a perfectionist who strives for timely completion of your projects [disciplined]? Do you want to learn to use Java, C++, and PHP [eager to learn]? If you can say yes to these questions, then please call. . . ."

Identifying people's strengths and matching strengths to work is a first step toward workplace effectiveness. To assess applicants' strengths and decide who is best-suited to the job, personnel managers use various tools, including ability tests, personality tests, and behavioral observations in "assessment centers" that simulate job tasks. Here we focus on job interviews.

Do Interviews Predict Performance?

Interviewers tend to feel confident in their ability to predict long-term job performance from an unstructured, get-acquainted interview. What's therefore shocking is how error-prone those predictions are. Whether predicting job or graduate school success, interviewers' judgments are weak predictors. From their review of 85 years of personnel-selection research, I/O psychologists Frank Schmidt and John Hunter (1998; Schmidt, 2002) determined that for all but less-skilled jobs, general mental ability best predicts on-the-job performance. Subjective overall evaluations from informal interviews are more useful than handwriting analysis (which is worthless). But informal interviews are less informative than aptitude tests, work samples, job knowledge tests, and past job performance. If there's a contest between what our gut tells us about someone and what test scores, work samples, and past performance tell us, we should distrust our gut.

The Interviewer Illusion

Interviewers often overrate their discernment, a phenomenon psychologist Richard Nisbett (1987) has labeled the *interviewer illusion*. "I have excellent interviewing skills, and so don't need reference checking as much as someone who doesn't have my ability to read people," is a comment sometimes heard by I/O consultants. Four factors explain this gap between interviewers' intuition and the resulting reality:

- *Interviews disclose the interviewee's good intentions, which are less revealing than habitual behaviors* (Ouellette & Wood, 1998). Intentions matter. People can change. But the best predictor of the person we will be is the person we have been. Wherever we go, we take ourselves along.
- *Interviewers more often follow the successful careers of those they have hired than the successful careers of those they have rejected and lost track of.* This missing feedback prevents interviewers from getting a reality check on their hiring ability.
- *Interviewers presume that people are what they seem to be in the interview situation.* When meeting others, we discount the enormous influence of varying situations and mistakenly presume that what we see is what we will get. But mountains of research on everything from chattiness to conscientiousness reveals that how we behave reflects not only our enduring traits, but the details of the particular situation (wanting to impress in a job interview).
- *Interviewers' preconceptions and moods color how they perceive interviewees' responses* (Cable & Gilovich, 1998; Macan & Dipboye, 1994). If interviewers instantly like a

"Between the idea and reality . . . falls the shadow."

T. S. Eliot, *The Hollow Men*, 1925

■ **structured interviews** interview process that asks the same job-relevant questions of all applicants, each of whom is rated on established scales.

■ **achievement motivation** a desire for significant accomplishment: for mastery of things, people, or ideas; for attaining a high standard.

person who perhaps is similar to themselves, they may interpret the person's assertiveness as indicating "confidence" rather than "arrogance." If told certain applicants have been prescreened, interviewers are disposed to judge them more favorably.

An unstructured interview does provide a sense of someone's personality—their expressiveness, warmth, and verbal ability, for example. But this information reveals less about the person's behavior toward others in different situations than most people suppose. Hoping to improve prediction and selection, personnel psychologists have put people in simulated work situations, scoured sources for information on past performance, aggregated evaluations from multiple interviews, administered tests, and developed job-specific interviews.

Structured Interviews

Unlike casual conversation aimed at getting a feel for someone, **structured interviews** offer a disciplined method of collecting information. A personnel psychologist may analyze a job, script questions, and train interviewers. The interviewers then put the same questions, in the same order, to all applicants, and rate each applicant on established scales.

In an *unstructured* interview, someone might ask, "How organized are you?" "How well do you get along with people?" or "How do you handle stress?" Street-smart applicants know how to score high: "Although I sometimes drive myself too hard, I handle stress by prioritizing and delegating, and by making sure I leave time for sleep and exercise."

By contrast, structured interviews pinpoint strengths (attitudes, behaviors, knowledge, and skills) that distinguish high performers in a particular line of work. The process includes describing job-specific situations and asking candidates to explain how they would handle them, and how they handled similar situations in their prior employment. "Tell me about a time when you were caught between conflicting demands, without time to accomplish both. How did you handle that?"

To reduce memory distortions and bias, the interviewer takes notes and makes ratings as the interview proceeds and avoids irrelevant and follow-up questions. The structured interview therefore feels less warm, but that can be explained to the applicant: "This conversation won't typify how we relate to each other in this organization."

A review of 150 findings revealed that structured interviews had double the predictive accuracy of unstructured seat-of-the-pants interviews (Schmidt & Hunter, 1998; Wiesner & Cronshaw, 1988). Thanks partly to its greater reliability and partly to its job-analysis focus, the predictive power of one structured interview is roughly equal to that of the average judgment from three or four unstructured interviews (Huffcutt & others, 2001; Schmidt & Zimmerman, 2004).

If, instead, we let our intuitions bias the hiring process, notes Malcolm Gladwell (2000), then "all we will have done is replace the old-boy network, where you hired your nephew, with the new-boy network, where you hire whoever impressed you most when you shook his hand. Social progress, unless we're careful, can merely be the means by which we replace the obviously arbitrary with the not so obviously arbitrary."

To recap, personnel psychologists assist organizations in analyzing jobs, recruiting well-suited applicants, selecting and placing employees, and appraising their performance (**FIGURE 37.2**)—the topic we turn to next.

FIGURE 37.2
Personnel psychologists' tasks
Personnel psychologists consult in human resource activities, from job definition to employee appraisal.

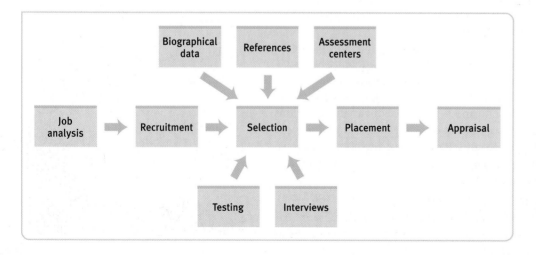

Appraising Performance

Performance appraisal serves organizational purposes: It helps decide who to retain, how to appropriately reward and pay people, and how to better harness employee strengths, sometimes with job shifts or promotions. Performance appraisal also serves individual purposes: Feedback affirms workers' strengths and helps motivate needed improvements.

Performance appraisal methods include

- *checklists* on which supervisors simply check behaviors that describe the worker ("always attends to customers' needs," "takes long breaks").
- *graphic rating scales* on which a supervisor checks the extent to which a worker is dependable, productive, and so forth.
- *behavior rating scales* on which a supervisor checks behaviors that best describe a worker's performance. If rating the extent to which a worker "follows procedures," the supervisor might mark the employee somewhere between "often takes shortcuts" and "always follows established procedures" (Levy, 2003).

In some organizations, performance feedback comes not only from supervisors but also from all organizational levels. If you join an organization that practices *360-degree feedback* (**FIGURE 37.3**) you will rate yourself, your manager, and your other colleagues, and you will be rated by your manager, other colleagues, and customers (Green, 2002). The net result is often more open communication and more complete appraisal.

Performance appraisal, like other social judgments, is vulnerable to bias (Murphy & Cleveland, 1995). *Halo errors* occur when one's overall evaluation of an employee, or of a trait such as their friendliness, biases ratings of their specific work-related behaviors, such as their reliability. *Leniency* and *severity errors* reflect evaluators' tendencies to be either too easy or too harsh on everyone. *Recency errors* occur when raters focus only on easily remembered recent behavior. By encouraging multiple raters and developing objective, job-relevant performance measures, personnel psychologists seek to support their organizations while also helping employees perceive the appraisal process as fair.

Organizational Psychology: Motivating Achievement

OBJECTIVE 37-3 | Define *achievement motivation,* and explain why organizations would employ an I/O psychologist to help motivate employees and foster employee satisfaction.

The appraisal of work and the matching of talents to work matter, but so does overall motivation. Before considering how organizational psychologists assist with efforts to motivate employees and keep them engaged, let's take a closer look at why any employee might want to pursue high standards or difficult goals.

Think of someone you know who strives to succeed by excelling at any task where evaluation is possible. Now think of someone who is less driven. Psychologist Henry Murray (1938) defined the first person's **achievement motivation** as a desire for significant accomplishment, for mastering skills or ideas, for control, and for rapidly attaining a high standard.

As you might expect from their persistence and eagerness for realistic challenges, people with high achievement motivation do achieve more. One study followed the lives of 1528 California children whose intelligence test scores were in the top 1 percent. Forty years later, when researchers compared those who were most and least successful professionally, they found a motivational difference. Those most successful were more ambitious, energetic, and persistent. As children, they had more active hobbies. As adults, they participated in more groups and favored being

FIGURE 37.3
360-degree feedback
With multisource 360-degree feedback, one's knowledge, skills, and behaviors are rated by self and surrounding others. Professors, for example, may be rated by their department chairs, their students, and their colleagues. After receiving all these ratings, professors discuss the 360-degree feedback with their department chair.

Disciplined motivation feeds achievement
Aware that he was far behind other students when beginning his graduate education in psychology, B. F. Skinner devised a daily discipline of rising at 6:00 A.M., studying until breakfast, then going to classes, labs, and the library. After dinner he studied some more, leaving no more than 15 unscheduled minutes each day, and later continued a disciplined daily routine as he became one of the twentieth century's most influential psychologists.

a sports participant to being a spectator (Goleman, 1980). In other studies of both secondary school and university students, self-discipline has been a better predictor of school performance, attendance, and graduation honors than intelligence scores have been. "Discipline outdoes talent," concluded researchers Angela Duckworth and Martin Seligman (2005). By their early twenties, for example, top violinists have accumulated some 10,000 lifetime practice hours—double the practice time of other violin students aiming to be teachers (Ericsson & others, 1993, 2001). From his studies, Herbert Simon (1998), a psychologist who won the Nobel prize for economics, estimates that world-class experts in a field typically have invested "at least 10 years of hard work—say, 40 hours a week for 50 weeks a year."

Similarly, a study of outstanding scholars, athletes, and artists found that all were highly motivated and self-disciplined, willing to dedicate hours every day to the pursuit of their goals (Bloom, 1985). These superstar achievers were distinguished not so much by their extraordinary natural talent as by their extraordinary daily discipline. Great achievement, it seems, mixes a teaspoon of inspiration with a gallon of perspiration.

What distinguishes extremely successful individuals from their equally talented peers, note Duckworth and Seligman, is *grit*—passionate dedication to an ambitious, long-term goal. Although intelligence is distributed like a bell curve, achievements are not. That tells us that achievement involves much more than raw ability. And that is why organizational psychologists seek ways to engage and motivate ordinary people doing ordinary jobs.

Satisfaction and Engagement

Because work is such a big part of life, employee satisfaction is a priority concern for I/O psychologists. Satisfaction with work feeds satisfaction with life (see Close-Up: Doing Well While Doing Good). Moreover, studies confirm that decreased job stress feeds improved health.

Does employee satisfaction also contribute to successful organizations? Positive moods at work do contribute to creativity, persistence, and helpfulness (Brief & Weiss, 2002). But are engaged, happy workers also less often absent? Less likely to quit? Less prone to theft? More punctual? More productive? Conclusive evidence of satisfaction's benefits is, some have said, the holy grail of I/O psychology. Statistical digests of prior research have found a modest positive correlation between individual job satisfaction and performance (Judge & others, 2001; Parker & others, 2003). In one recent analysis of 4500 employees at 42 British manufacturing companies, the most productive workers tended to be those in satisfying work environments (Patterson & others, 2004).

Engaged employees facilitate organizational success
Best Buy's 400 electronic goods stores have nearly identical product layout and operations manuals. Yet some stores have much more engaged employees—and more profitable performance. The store with the highest worker-engagement scores is in the top tenth of stores in having profits beyond budget. And the store with the least-engaged employees is in the bottom tenth (Buckingham, 2001).

Capital-Journal/David Eulitt/AP/Wide World Photos

CLOSE-UP:

DOING WELL WHILE DOING GOOD: "THE GREAT EXPERIMENT"

At the end of the 1700s, the more than 1000 workers in the cotton mill at New Lanark, Scotland—many of them children drawn from nearby Glasgow poorhouses—worked 13-hour days and lived in grim conditions, with education and sanitation neglected, theft and drunkenness commonplace, and most families occupying just one room.

On a visit to Glasgow, Welsh-born Robert Owen—an idealistic young cotton-mill manager—chanced to meet and fall in love with the mill owner's daughter. After their marriage, Owen, with several partners, purchased the mill and on the first day of the 1800s took control as its manager. Before long, he began what he said was "the most important experiment for the happiness of the human race that had yet been instituted at any time in any part of the world" (Owen, 1814). The exploitation of child and adult labor was, he observed, producing unhappy and inefficient workers. Believing that better working and living conditions could pay economic dividends, he undertook (with some resistance from his partners, whom he ultimately bought out) numerous innovations: a nursery for preschool

Courtesy of New Lanark World Heritage Site

The great experiment
New Lanark Mills, now preserved as a World Heritage Site (www.newlanark.org), provided an influential demonstration of how industries could do well while doing good. In its heyday, New Lanark was visited by many European royals and reformers who came to observe its vibrant workforce and prosperous business.

children, education (with encouragement rather than corporal punishment), Sundays off, health care, paid sick days, unemployment pay for days when the mill could not operate, and a company store selling goods at reduced prices.

Owen also innovated a goals and worker-assessment program that included detailed records of daily productivity and costs. By each employee's workstation, one of four colored boards indicated that person's performance for the previous day. Owen could walk through the mill and at a glance see how individuals were performing. There was, he said, "no beating, no abusive language. . . . I merely looked at the person and then at the color. . . . I could at once see by the expression [which color] was shown."

The commercial success that followed was essential to sustaining what became a movement toward humanitarian reforms. By 1816, with decades of profitability still ahead, Owen believed he had demonstrated "that society may be formed so as to exist without crime, without poverty, with health greatly improved, with little if any misery, and with intelligence and happiness increased a hundredfold." Although his Utopian vision has not been fulfilled, Owen's great experiment did lay the groundwork for employment practices that have today become accepted in much of the world.

In the United States, the *Fortune* "100 Best Companies to Work For" have also produced markedly higher than average returns for their investors (Fulmer & others, 2003). Other positive data come from the biggest-ever study, a recent analysis of Gallup data from more than 198,000 employees (**TABLE 37.1** on the next page) in nearly 8000 business units of 36 large companies (including some 1100 bank branches, 1200 stores, and 4200 teams or departments). James Harter, Frank Schmidt, and Theodore Hayes (2002) explored correlations between various measures of organizational success and *employee engagement*—the extent of workers' involvement, satisfaction, and enthusiasm. They found that engaged workers know what's expected of them, have what they need to do their work, feel fulfilled in their work, have regular opportunities to do what they do best, perceive that they are part of something significant, and have opportunities to learn and develop. They also found that business units with engaged employees have more loyal customers, less

Three types of employees (Crabtree, 2005):
Engaged: working with passion and feeling a profound connection to their company or organization.
Not-engaged: putting in the time, but investing little passion or energy into their work.
Actively disengaged: unhappy workers undermining what their colleagues accomplish.

TABLE 37.1

THE GALLUP WORKPLACE AUDIT

Overall satisfaction—On a 5-point scale, where 5 is extremely satisfied and 1 is extremely dissatisfied, how satisfied are you with *(name of company)* as a place to work? _____

On a scale of 1 to 5, where 1 is strongly disagree and 5 is strongly agree, please indicate your agreement with the following items.

1. I know what is expected from me at work.

2. I have the materials and equipment I need to do my work right.

3. At work, I have the opportunity to do what I do best every day.

4. In the last seven days, I have received recognition or praise for doing good work.

5. My supervisor, or someone at work, seems to care about me as a person.

6. There is someone at work who encourages my development.

7. At work, my opinions seem to count.

8. The mission/purpose of my company makes me feel my job is important.

9. My associates (fellow employees) are committed to doing quality work.

10. I have a best friend at work.

11. In the last six months, someone at work has talked to me about my progress.

12. This last year, I have had opportunities at work to learn and grow.

Note: These statements are proprietary and copyrighted by The Gallup Organization. They may not be printed or reproduced in any manner without the written consent of The Gallup Organization. Reprinted here by permission.

turnover, higher productivity, and greater profits: "Business units above the median on employee engagement had a 70 percent higher success rate than those below the median." Business units in the top quarter on employee engagement averaged about $100,000 more in monthly revenue. A separate analysis for a company with 275 retail stores found that annual turnover was 55 percent among stores whose employee engagement was in the top quarter, and 75 percent among stores with employees in the bottom quarter (Harter, 2000).

Managing Well

OBJECTIVE 37-4 | Describe some effective management techniques.

Every leader dreams of managing in ways that enhance people's satisfaction, engagement, and productivity and their organization's success. Effective leaders harness job-relevant strengths, set goals, and choose an appropriate leadership style.

Harnessing Job-Relevant Strengths

"The major challenge for CEOs over the next 20 years will be the effective deployment of human assets," observes Marcus Buckingham (2001). That challenge is "about psychology. It's about getting [individuals] to be more productive, more focused, more fulfilled than [they were] yesterday." To do so, he and others maintain, effective leaders want first to select the right people. Then, they aim to discern their employees' natural talents, adjust their work roles to suit their talents, and develop those talents into great strengths (**FIGURE 37.4**). For example, should every college professor at a given school be expected to teach the same load, advise the same number of students, serve on the same number of committees, and engage in the same amount of research? Or should each job description be tailored to harness a specific person's unique strengths?

FIGURE 37.4
On the right path
The Gallup Organization path to organizational success (adapted from Fleming, 2001).

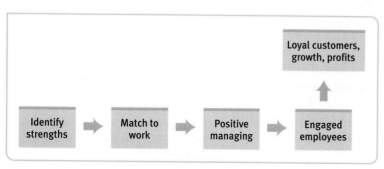

Managers who excel spend less time trying to instill talents that are not there and more time developing and drawing out what is there. Kenneth Tucker (2002) notes that great managers

- start by helping people identify and measure their talents.
- match tasks to talents and then give people freedom to do what they do best.
- care how their people feel about their work.
- reinforce positive behaviors through recognition and reward.

Thus, rather than focusing on weaknesses and packing people off to training seminars to fix those problems, good managers focus training time on educating people about their strengths and building upon them (which means not promoting people into roles ill-suited to their strengths).

Celebrating engaged and productive employees in every organizational role builds upon a basic principle of operant conditioning: To teach a behavior, catch a person doing something right and reinforce it. These principles also apply to reinforcing employees. It sounds simple, but many managers are like parents who, when a child returns home with perfect scores, except for that one troublesome biology class, focus on the biology score and ignore the rest. "Sixty-five percent of Americans received NO praise or recognition in the workplace last year," reported the Gallup Organization (2004).

Positive coaching
Larry Brown, an adviser to "The Positive Coaching Alliance," has been observed during practices to offer his players 4 to 5 positive comments for every negative comment (Insana, 2005). In 2004, his underdog Detroit Pistons won the National Basketball Association championship.

Setting Specific, Challenging Goals

In study after study, people merely asked to do their best do not do so. But more specific, challenging goals do motivate higher achievement, especially when combined with progress reports (Locke & Latham, 2002). Specific, measurable objectives, such as "finish gathering information for the history paper by Friday," serve to direct attention, promote effort, motivate persistence, and stimulate creative strategies. When people share in setting a goal and find the goal challenging yet attainable, reaching it boosts their self-evaluation (White & others, 1995). Moreover, when people state not only goals but also *implementation intentions*—action plans that specify when, where, and how they will march toward achieving those goals—they become more focused in their work and on-time completion becomes more likely (Burgess & others, 2004; Koestner & others, 2002; Koole & Spijker, 2000). (Before beginning each new edition of this book, my editor, my associates, and I *manage by objectives*—we agree on target dates for the completion of each chapter draft.) So, to motivate high productivity, effective leaders work with people to define explicit goals, elicit commitments to implementation plans, and provide feedback on progress.

Choosing an Appropriate Leadership Style

Leadership varies from a boss-focused directive style to a democratic style that empowers workers in setting goals and strategies. Which works best may depend on the situation and the leader. The best leadership style for leading a discussion may not be the best style for leading troops on a charge (Fiedler, 1981). Moreover, different leaders are suited to different styles. Some excel at **task leadership**—setting standards, organizing work, and focusing attention on goals. Being goal-oriented, task leaders are good at keeping a group centered on its mission. Typically, they have a directive style, which can work well if the leader is bright enough to give good orders (Fiedler, 1987).

Other managers excel at **social leadership**—mediating conflicts and building high-achieving teams (Evans & Dion, 1991). Social leaders often have a democratic style: They delegate authority and welcome the participation of team members. Many experiments show that social leadership is good for morale. Subordinates usually feel more satisfied and motivated when they can participate in decision making (Burger, 1987; Spector, 1986).

■ **task leadership** goal-oriented leadership that sets standards, organizes work, and focuses attention on goals.

■ **social leadership** group-oriented leadership that builds teamwork, mediates conflict, and offers support.

> "Good leaders don't ask more than their constituents can give, but they often ask—and get—more than their constituents intended to give or thought it was possible to give."
>
> John W. Gardner, *Excellence,* 1984

Sharing vision and decisions
As CEO, Jeffrey Bleustein helped Harley-Davidson thrive, in part by replacing the organization's command-and-control management style with one based on companywide consensus planning and decision making.

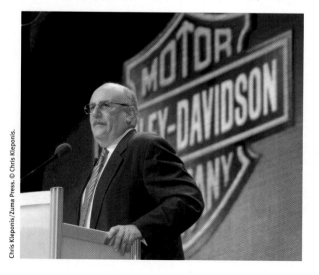

Because effective leadership styles vary with the situation and the person, the once-popular *great person theory of leadership*—that all great leaders share certain traits—now seems overstated. But a leader's personality does matter. Effective leaders of laboratory groups, work teams, and large corporations tend to exude a self-confident *charisma* (House & Singh, 1987; Shamir & others, 1993). Their charisma is a mix of a *vision* of some goal, an ability to *communicate* it clearly and simply, and enough optimism and faith in their group to *inspire* others to follow. In one study of 50 Dutch companies, the highest morale was at those firms with chief executives who most inspired their colleagues "to transcend their own self-interests for the sake of the collective" (de Hoogh & others, 2004). Leadership of this kind—*transformational leadership*—motivates others to identify with and commit themselves to the group's mission. Transformational leaders, many of whom are natural extraverts, articulate high standards, inspire people to share their vision, and offer personal attention (Bono & Judge, 2004). The frequent result is more engaged, trusting, and effective workers (Turner & others, 2002).

Peter Smith and Monir Tayeb (1989) compiled data from studies in India, Taiwan, and Iran indicating that effective managers—whether in coal mines, banks, or government offices—often exhibit a high degree of *both* task and social leadership. As achievement-minded people, effective managers certainly care about how well work is done, yet at the same time they are sensitive to their subordinates' needs. In one national survey of American workers, those in family-friendly organizations offering flexible-time hours reported feeling greater loyalty to their employers (Roehling & others, 2001).

Many successful businesses have also increased employee participation in making decisions, a management style common in Sweden and Japan and increasingly elsewhere (Naylor, 1990; Sundstrom & others, 1990). Although managers often think better of work they have directly supervised, studies reveal a *voice effect*: If given a chance to voice their opinion during a decision-making process, people will respond more positively to the decision (van den Bos & Spruijt, 2002). And as we noted earlier, positive engaged employees are a mark of thriving organizations.

The rags-to-riches Harley-Davidson story illustrates the potential of inviting workers to participate in decision making (Teerlink & Ozley, 2000). In 1987, the struggling company began transforming its *command-and-control* management process to a *joint-vision* process. The aim: "To push decision-making, planning, and strategizing from a handful of people at the top, down throughout the organization. We wanted all the employees to think every day about how to improve the company," reported CEO Jeffrey Bleustein (2002). In the mid-1990s, Harley signed a cooperative agreement with its unions that included them "in decision-making in virtually every aspect of the business." Consensus decision-making can take longer, but "when the decision is made, it gets implemented quickly and the commitment is by the group," says Bleustein. The result has been more engaged workers and also more satisfied stockholders. Every $1 of Harley-Davidson stock purchased at the beginning of 1988 was worth $125 by mid-2005.

Identifiable physiological mechanisms drive some motives, such as hunger (though learned tastes and cultural expectations matter, too). Achievement at work is more obviously driven by psychological factors, such as an intrinsic quest for mastery and the external rewards of recognition. But what unifies these and all other motives is their common effect: the energizing and directing of behavior.

>> LEARNING OUTCOMES

Motivation at Work

OBJECTIVE 37-1 | Discuss the importance of flow, and identify the three subfields of industrial-organizational psychology.

People may view their work as a job, a career, or a calling. Those in the last group report the highest satisfaction—a feeling consistent with *flow*, the involved focused state of consciousness in which we have a diminished awareness of ourselves and of passing time. *Industrial-organizational (I/O) psychology* studies behavior in the workplace through the three subfields of *personnel psychology, organizational psychology,* and *human factors psychology.*

OBJECTIVE 37-2 | Describe how personnel psychologists help organizations with employee selection, work placement, and performance appraisal.

Personnel psychologists work with organizations to devise selection methods (such as structured interviews) for new employees, to recruit and evaluate applicants, and to design and evaluate training programs. Personnel psychologists also help organizations identify people's strengths, analyze job content, appraise individual and organizational performance, and avoid forms of bias that can affect performance appraisal.

OBJECTIVE 37-3 | Define *achievement motivation,* and explain why organizations would employ an I/O psychologist to help motivate employees and foster employee satisfaction.

Achievement motivation is the desire for significant accomplishment; for mastery of things, people, or ideas; and for attaining a high standard. Organizations turn to I/O psychologists because research shows that the most productive and engaged workers are those working in satisfying environments. Employee satisfaction also tends to translate into higher profits, higher productivity, lower turnover, and more loyal customers.

OBJECTIVE 37-4 | Describe some effective management techniques.

Effective managers focus training on developing people's strengths, not overcoming their weaknesses. They attempt to "catch the employee doing something right" and reward that behavior. Effective managers also work with employees to set specific, challenging, and measurable objectives and to outline detailed paths to achieving those goals. *Task leadership* sets standards, organizes work, and focuses attention on goals. *Social leadership* builds teamwork, mediates conflict, and offers support. Managers' personalities do matter, and some may be better suited to one leadership style than to the other, or to some combination of the two.

TERMS AND CONCEPTS TO REMEMBER

flow, p. 37-0

industrial-organizational psychology, p. 37-1

personnel psychology, p. 37-1

organizational psychology, p. 37-1

structured interviews, p. 37-4

achievement motivation, p. 37-5

task leadership, p. 37-9

social leadership, p. 37-9

TEST YOURSELF

1. A human resources director explains to you that "I don't bother with tests or references. I can pick employees by my gut." Based on I/O research, what concerns does this raise?

(Answer in Appendix B.)

ASK YOURSELF

1. Are you highly motivated, or not highly motivated, to achieve in school? How has this affected your academic success? How might you improve upon your own achievement levels?

>WEB

Multiple-choice *self-tests* and more may be found at www.worthpublishers.com/myers.

ANOTHER VOICE ON: EMOTION

ADMIRAL DENNIS BLAIR, COMMANDER OF U.S. PACIFIC FORCES (USCINCPAC),
REMARKS AT PACIFIC ISLANDS CONFERENCE OF LEADERS, JANUARY 31, 2001, EAST-WEST CENTER, HONOLULU

On a recent trip to one of your beautiful islands . . . , I had the opportunity to take a break and go fishing, and I overheard a conversation between a Harvard businessman on vacation, and one of the local fishermen. The fisherman had a small boat with several large yellowfin tuna. . . . The businessman complimented the man on the quality of his fish, and asked how long it took to catch them. The fisherman replied only a little while. The businessman asked . . . why didn't he stay out longer and catch more fish? The fisherman said he had enough to support his family's immediate needs.

The businessman then asked, "But what do you do with the rest of your time?"

The fisherman said, "I sleep late, fish a little, play with my children, take a nap with my wife, stroll into the village each evening where I drink a beer and play the ukelele with my friends. I have a full and wonderful life."

The businessman scoffed, "I'm a Harvard MBA, and I could help you. You should spend more time fishing, and with the proceeds, you could buy a bigger boat. With the money from the bigger boat, you could buy several boats. Eventually, you'd own a fleet of fishing boats . . . . You'd make millions of dollars!"

"But what then?" asked the fisherman.

The businessman said, "Then you could retire—move to a small fishing village where you could sleep late . . . fish a little . . . play with your kids . . . take a nap with your wife . . . stroll down to the village in the evenings . . . where you could drink a beer . . . and play the ukelele with your friends!"

Emotion

No one needs to tell you that feelings add color to your life, or that in times of stress they can disrupt your life or save it. Of all the species, we seem the most emotional (Hebb, 1980). More often than any other creature, we express fear, anger, sadness, joy, and love.

We all can recall times when we have been overcome with emotion. I retain a flashbulb memory for the day I went to a huge store to drop off film and brought along Peter, my toddler first-born child. As I set Peter down on his feet and prepared to complete the paperwork, a passerby warned, "You'd better be careful or you'll lose that boy!" Not more than a few breaths later, after dropping the film in the slot, I turned and found no Peter beside me.

With mild anxiety, I peered around one end of the counter. No Peter in sight. With slightly more anxiety, I peered around the other end. No Peter there, either. Now, with my heart accelerating, I circled the neighboring counters. Still no Peter anywhere. As anxiety turned to panic, I began racing up and down the store aisles. He was nowhere to be found. Apprised of my alarm, the store manager used the public-address system to ask customers to assist in looking for a missing child. Soon after, I passed the customer who had warned me. "I told you that you were going to lose him!" he said scornfully. With visions of kidnapping (strangers routinely adored that beautiful child), I braced for the possibility that my negligence had caused me to lose what I loved above all else, and—dread of all dreads—that I might have to return home and face my wife without our only child.

But then, as I passed the customer service counter yet again, there he was, having been found and returned by some obliging customer! In an instant, the arousal of dread spilled into the elation of ecstasy. Clutching my son, with tears suddenly flowing, I found myself unable to speak my thanks and stumbled out of the store awash in joy.

So, how do psychologists think about and study such emotions? In Module 38, we examine three classic theories of emotion that explore the interplay of physiological activation, expressive behavior, and conscious experience. Module 39 then turns to the topic of how we experience and express our emotions. In Module 40, we'll take an in-depth look at fear, anger, and happiness.

MODULE

38

Introduction to Emotion

OBJECTIVE **38-1** | Identify the three components of emotions, and contrast the James-Lange, Cannon-Bard, and two-factor theories of emotion.

Where do emotions come from? Why do we have them? What are they made of? Emotions are our body's adaptive response. They exist not to give us interesting experiences but to enhance our survival. When we face challenges, emotions focus our attention and energize our action. Our heart races. Our pace quickens. All our senses go on high alert. Receiving unexpected good news, we may find our eyes tearing. We raise our hands triumphantly. We feel exuberance and a newfound confidence. **Emotions** are a mix of (1) physiological arousal (heart pounding), (2) expressive behaviors (quickened pace), and (3) conscious experience, including thoughts (is this a kidnapping?) and feelings (a sense of fear, and later joy). The puzzle for psychologists has been figuring out how these three pieces fit together.

Not only emotion, but most psychological phenomena (vision, sleep, memory, sex, and so forth) can be approached these three ways—physiologically, behaviorally, and cognitively.

Theories of Emotion

There are two controversies over the interplay of our physiology, expressions, and experience in emotions. The first, a chicken-and-egg debate, is old: Does your physiological arousal precede or follow your emotional experience? (Did I first notice my heart racing and my faster step, and then feel anxious dread about losing Peter? Or did my sense of fear come first, stirring my heart and legs to respond?) The second controversy concerns the interaction between thinking and feeling: Does cognition always precede emotion? (Was I required to make a conscious appraisal of the kidnapping threat before I could react emotionally?)

Common sense tells most of us that we cry because we are sad, lash out because we are angry, tremble because we are afraid. First comes conscious awareness, then the physiological trimmings. But to pioneering psychologist William James, this commonsense view of emotion was 180 degrees out of line. According to James, "We feel sorry because we cry, angry because we strike, afraid because we tremble" (1890, p. 1066). Perhaps you can recall a time when your car skidded on slick pavement. As it careened crazily you hit your brakes and regained control. Just after the fishtail ended, you noticed your racing heart and *then,* shaking with fright, you felt the whoosh of emotion. Your feeling of fear *followed* your body's response. James' idea, also proposed by Danish physiologist Carl Lange, is called the **James-Lange theory.**

The James-Lange theory struck U.S. physiologist Walter Cannon (1871–1943) as implausible. Cannon thought the body's responses were not distinct enough to evoke the different emotions. Does a racing heart signal fear, anger, or love? Also, changes in heart rate, perspiration, and body temperature seemed too slow to trigger sudden emotion. Cannon, and later another physiologist, Philip Bard, concluded that physiological arousal and our emotional experience occur simultaneously: The emotion-triggering stimulus is routed simultaneously to the brain's cortex, causing the subjective awareness of emotion, and to the sympathetic nervous system, causing the body's arousal. This **Cannon-Bard theory** implies that your heart begins pounding *as* you experience fear; one does not cause the other.

The joys of friendship
According to the James-Lange theory, we don't just smile because we share a friend's joy. We also share the joy because we are smiling with them.

Digital Vision/Getty Images

Let's check your understanding of the James-Lange and Cannon-Bard theories. Imagine that your brain could not sense your heart pounding or your stomach churning. According to each theory, how would this affect your experienced emotions?

Cannon and Bard would have expected you to experience emotions normally, because they believed emotions occur separately from (though simultaneously with) the body's arousal. James and Lange would have expected greatly diminished emotions because they believed that to experience emotion you must first perceive your body's arousal.

Stanley Schachter and Jerome Singer (1962) proposed a third theory: that our physiology and our cognitions—perceptions, memories, and interpretations—together create emotion. In their **two-factor theory,** emotions therefore have two ingredients: physical arousal and a cognitive label (**FIGURE 38.1**). Like James and Lange, Schachter and Singer presumed that our experience of emotion grows from our awareness of our body's arousal. Yet like Cannon and Bard, Schachter and Singer also believed that emotions are physiologically similar. Thus, in their view, an emotional experience requires a conscious interpretation of the arousal.

To assess the James-Lange, Cannon-Bard, and two-factor theories, we'll consider in the next section the answers researchers have gleaned to three questions:

- Does physiological arousal always precede emotional experience?
- Are different emotions marked by distinct physiological responses?
- What is the connection between what we *think* and how we *feel?*

■ **emotion** a response of the whole organism, involving (1) physiological arousal, (2) expressive behaviors, and (3) conscious experience.

■ **James-Lange theory** the theory that our experience of emotion is our awareness of our physiological responses to emotion-arousing stimuli.

■ **Cannon-Bard theory** the theory that an emotion-arousing stimulus simultaneously triggers (1) physiological responses and (2) the subjective experience of emotion.

■ **two-factor theory** Schachter-Singer's theory that to experience emotion one must (1) be physically aroused and (2) cognitively label the arousal.

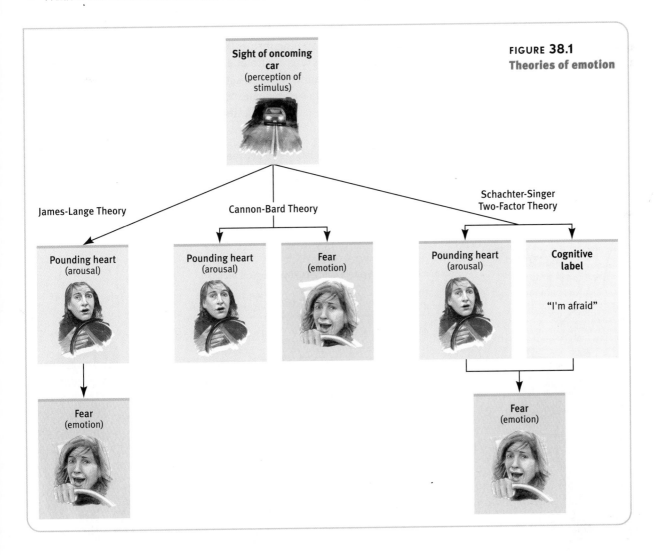

FIGURE 38.1
Theories of emotion

Sight of oncoming car (perception of stimulus)

James-Lange Theory

Cannon-Bard Theory

Schachter-Singer Two-Factor Theory

Pounding heart (arousal)

Pounding heart (arousal)

Fear (emotion)

Pounding heart (arousal)

Cognitive label

"I'm afraid"

Fear (emotion)

Fear (emotion)

Embodied Emotion

Whether you are eagerly anticipating a long-awaited vacation, falling in love, or grieving the death of a loved one, you need little convincing that emotions involve the body. Feeling without a body is like breathing without lungs. Some physical responses are easy to notice, others—many taking place at the level of neurons in your brain—happen without your awareness. As you hear a motorcycle slowing down behind you on a dark street, your muscles tense, your stomach develops butterflies, your mouth becomes dry.

Emotions and the Autonomic Nervous System

OBJECTIVE **38-2** | Describe the role of the autonomic nervous system during emotional arousal.

As your *autonomic nervous system* mobilizes for action, your body also responds for action in less noticeable ways. To provide energy, your liver pours extra sugar into your bloodstream. To help burn the sugar, your respiration increases to supply needed oxygen. Your digestion slows, diverting blood from your internal organs to your muscles. With blood sugar driven into the large muscles, running becomes easier. Your pupils dilate, letting in more light. To cool your stirred-up body, you perspire. If wounded, your blood would clot more quickly. After your next crisis, think of this: Without any conscious effort, your body's response to danger was wonderfully coordinated and adaptive—preparing you to fight or flee.

The autonomic nervous system controls our arousal (**FIGURE 38.2**). Its *sympathetic division* directs the adrenal glands atop the kidneys to release the stress hormones epinephrine (adrenaline) and norepinephrine (noradrenaline). This hormonal surge increases heart rate, blood pressure, and blood sugar levels. When the crisis passes, the parasympathetic neural centers become active, calming the body. Even after the *parasympathetic division* inhibits further release of stress hormones, those already in the bloodstream linger awhile, so arousal diminishes gradually.

Arousal and Performance

OBJECTIVE **38-3** | Discuss the relationship between arousal and performance.

Prolonged arousal taxes the body. But in many situations arousal is adaptive. Too little arousal (say, sleepiness) can be as disruptive as extremely high levels. When you're taking an exam, it pays to be moderately aroused—alert but not trembling with nervousness.

"Fear lends wings to his feet."

Virgil, Aeneid, 19 B.C.

One explanation of sudden death caused by a voodoo "curse" is that the terrified person's parasympathetic nervous system, which calms the body, overreacts to the extreme arousal by slowing the heart to a stop (Seligman, 1974).

FIGURE 38.2
Emotional arousal
Emotional arousal involves autonomic nervous system activation.

Autonomic Nervous System Controls Physiological Arousal		
Sympathetic division (arousing)		Parasympathetic division (calming)
Pupils dilate	EYES	Pupils contract
Decreases	SALIVATION	Increases
Perspires	SKIN	Dries
Increases	RESPIRATION	Decreases
Accelerates	HEART	Slows
Inhibits	DIGESTION	Activates
Secrete stress hormones	ADRENAL GLANDS	Decrease secretion of stress hormones

Although we usually perform best when we feel moderately aroused, the level of arousal for optimal performance varies for different tasks. With easy or well-learned tasks, peak performance comes with relatively high arousal. With more difficult or unrehearsed tasks, optimal arousal is somewhat lower (**FIGURE 38.3**). Runners, who are performing a well-learned task, usually achieve their peak performances when highly aroused by competition. Basketball players shooting free throws—a less automatic skill—may not perform quite as well if a packed fieldhouse makes them hyperaroused (Sokoll & Mynatt, 1984). Likewise, students who feel great anxiety during exams perform more poorly than those equally able but more confident. Teaching anxious students how to relax before an exam often enables them to perform better (Hembree, 1988).

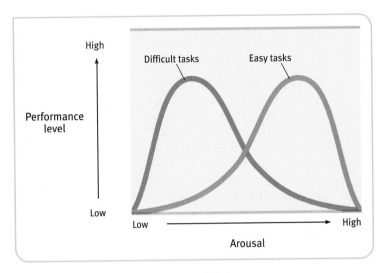

FIGURE 38.3
Arousal and performance
Performance peaks at lower levels of arousal for difficult tasks, and at higher levels for easy or well-learned tasks.

Physiological Similarities Among Specific Emotions

OBJECTIVE 38-4 | Name three emotions that involve similar physiological arousal.

Imagine conducting an experiment measuring the physiological responses of emotion. In each of four rooms, you have someone watching a movie: In the first, the person is viewing a horror show; in the second, an anger-provoking film; in the third, a sexually arousing film; in the fourth, an utterly boring movie. From the control center you monitor each person's physiological responses, measuring perspiration, breathing, and heart rates. Do you think you could tell who is frightened? Who is angry? Who is sexually aroused? Who is bored?

With training, you could probably pick out the bored viewer. But discerning physiological differences among fear, anger, and sexual arousal would be much more difficult (Cacioppo & others, 1997; Zillmann, 1986).

To you and me, sexual arousal, fear, and anger nevertheless *feel* different. If sexually stimulated, you will experience a genital response. If afraid, you may feel a clutching, sinking sensation in your chest and a knot in your stomach. If angry, you may feel "hot under the collar" and experience a pressing inner tension. And, despite similar arousal, fear and anger not only feel different, they also *look* different. People may appear "paralyzed with fear" or "ready to explode." So, does research pinpoint any distinct physiological or brain pattern indicators of each emotion? Sometimes. Read on.

> "No one ever told me that grief felt so much like fear. I am not afraid, but the sensation is like being afraid. The same fluttering in the stomach, the same restlessness, the yawning. I keep on swallowing."
>
> C. S. Lewis, *A Grief Observed*, 1961

Emotional arousal
Elated excitement and panicky fear involve similar physiological arousal. That allows us to flip rapidly between the two emotions.

Physiological Differences Among Specific Emotions

OBJECTIVE 38-5 | Describe some physiological and brain pattern indicators of specific emotions.

The finger temperatures and hormone secretions that accompany fear and rage do sometimes differ (Ax, 1953; Levenson, 1992). And, though fear and joy can prompt similar increased heart rate, they stimulate different facial muscles. During fear, brow muscles tense. During joy, muscles in the cheek and under the eye pull into a smile (Witvliet & Vrana, 1995).

LIE DETECTION

The creators and users of the *lie detector,* or **polygraph** have believed that our physical indicators of emotion can provide a telltale equivalent of Pinocchio's nose. Polygraphs do not literally detect lies, and their accuracy has been increasingly questioned as our understanding of physiological measures of emotion has grown.

Rather, they measure several physical responses that accompany emotion, such as changes in breathing, cardiovascular activity, and perspiration. While you try to relax, an examiner monitors these responses as you answer questions. Some items, called control questions, aim to make anyone a little nervous. If asked, "In the last 20 years, have you ever taken something that didn't belong to you?" many people will tell a white lie and say no, causing arousal the polygraph will detect. If your physiological reactions to critical questions ("Did you ever steal anything from your previous employer?") are weaker than to control questions, the examiner infers you are telling the truth. The assumption has been that only a thief becomes agitated when denying a theft.

Can polygraph tests like this identify liars?

To learn more, read on.

But there are two problems: First, as you have seen, our physiological arousal is much the same from one emotion to another—anxiety, irritation, and guilt all prompt similar physiological reactivity. Second, these tests err about one-third of the time, especially when innocent people respond with heightened tension to the accusations implied by the relevant questions (**FIGURE 38.4**). Many rape victims, for example, "fail" lie detector tests when reacting emotionally while telling the truth about their assailant (Lykken, 1991). Good advice, then, would be never to take a lie detector test if you are innocent.

A 2002 U.S. National Academy of Sciences report noted that "no spy has ever been caught [by] using the polygraph." It is not for lack of trying. The FBI, CIA, and Departments of Defense and Energy in the United States have spent millions of dollars testing tens of thousands of employees. Meanwhile Aldrich Ames, who enjoyed an unexplained lavish life-style as a Russian spy within the CIA, went undetected. Ames "took scores of polygraph tests and passed them all," notes Robert Park (1999). "Nobody thought to investigate the source of his sudden wealth—after all, he was passing the lie detector tests." The truth is, lie detectors can lie.

In one survey, more than 9 in 10 psychophysiologists and research psychologists agreed that savvy criminals and spies could beat the test by augmenting their arousal to control questions, such as by biting their tongues (Iacono & Lykken, 1997). Serial rapist and killer Gary Ridgway, who admitted to 48 Seattle-area murders ("I killed so many women I have a hard time keeping them straight"), was an

In 1966, a young man named Charles Whitman killed his wife and mother and then climbed to the top of a tower at the University of Texas and shot 38 people. An autopsy later revealed a tumor pressing against his amygdala, which may have contributed to his violence.

Given the physical indicators of emotion, might we, like Pinocchio, give some telltale sign whenever we lie? **See Thinking Critically About: Lie Detection.**

Emotions differ much more in the brain circuits they use (Kalin, 1993; Panksepp, 1982). Observers watching (and subtly mimicking) fearful faces show more amygdala brain activity than do those watching angry faces (Whalen & others, 2001). The power of the amygdala is also apparent in other research. Stimulate one area of a cat's amygdala and it will pull back in terror at the sight of a mouse. Stimulate another amygdala area and the cat will look enraged—pupils dilated, fur and tail erect, claws out, hissing furiously.

Emotions also activate different areas of the brain's cortex. Experiencing negative emotions such as disgust, people show more activity in the right prefrontal cortex than in the left. Depression-prone people, and those with generally negative personalities also show more right frontal activity (Harmon-Jones, Abramson, & others, 2002). One man, having lost part of his right frontal lobe in brain surgery, became (his not-unhappy wife reported) less irritable and more affectionate (Goleman, 1995). My father, after a right-hemisphere stroke at age 92, lived the last two years of his life with happy gratitude and nary a complaint or negative emotion.

When people experience positive moods—when they are enthusiastic, energized, and happy—brain scans and EEG recordings reveal more left frontal lobe activity.

early suspect but had been cleared after passing a polygraph test (Johnson, 2003).

A more effective approach to lie detection uses the *guilty knowledge test*, which assesses a suspect's physiological responses to crime-scene details known only to the police and the guilty person (Ben-Shakhar & Elaad, 2003). If a camera and computer had been stolen, for example, presumably only one guilty of the crime would react strongly to the specific brand name of these items. Given enough such specific probes, an innocent person will seldom be wrongly accused.

Several twenty-first century research teams are exploring new ways to nab liars. Some are developing computer software that compares the language of truth-tellers and liars (who use fewer first-person pronouns and more negative-emotion words). Other software analyzes facial microexpressions linked with lying (Adelson, 2004; Newman

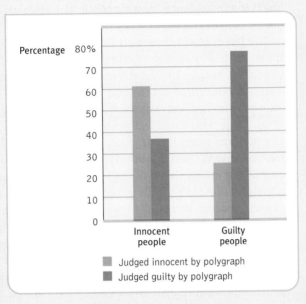

FIGURE 38.4

How often do lie detectors lie?
Benjamin Kleinmuntz and Julian Szucko (1984) had polygraph experts study the polygraph data of 50 theft suspects who later confessed to being guilty and 50 suspects whose innocence was later established by someone's confession. Had the polygraph experts been the judges, more than one-third of the innocent would have been declared guilty, and almost one-fourth of the guilty would have been declared innocent.

& others, 2003). Psychologist Paul Ekman (2003) runs training seminars that teach law enforcement officers to detect the fleeting signals of deceit in facial expressions.

Other researchers are going straight to the seat of deceit—the brain. EEG recordings have revealed a brain wave that indicates familiarity with a crime scene, and fMRI scans have shown liars' brains lighting up in places that honest people's brains do not (Faro & others, 2004; Farwell & Smith, 2001; Langleben & others, 2002, 2005). Given the cumbersome and expensive nature of such assessments, researchers are also testing a portable "near-infrared light" that similarly detects brain blood-flow patterns associated with lying (Izzetoglu & others, 2003). Pinocchio's giveaway signal of lying may be not the length of his nose, but rather the telltale activity in places such as his left frontal lobe and anterior cingulate cortex. Skeptics, however, note that we are a long way from commercial reality (Illes, 2004).

People with positive personalities—exuberant infants and alert, energetic, and persistently goal-directed adults—also show more activity in the left frontal lobe than in the right (Davidson, 2000, 2003; Urry & others, 2004). Indeed, the more a person's baseline frontal lobe activity tilts left, the more upbeat the person typically is. (When you're happy and you know it, your brain will surely show it.)

The left frontal lobe's rich supply of dopamine receptors may help explain why a peppy left hemisphere predicts a perky disposition. A neural pathway that increases dopamine levels runs from the frontal lobes to a nearby cluster of neurons, the *nucleus accumbens*. This small region lights up when people experience natural or drug-induced pleasures. In case studies, electrical stimulation of the nucleus accumbens of depressed patients has triggered smiling, laughter, and giddy euphoria (Okun & others, 2004).

To return to our assessment of the James-Lange, Cannon-Bard, and two-factor theories of emotion, we have seen that emotions as varied as fear, joy, and anger involve a similar general autonomic arousal (as in similar heart rate). But we have also seen that real, if subtle, physiological and brain differences help explain why we experience them so differently. As long as the evidence suggested that our physiological

■ **polygraph** a machine, commonly used in attempts to detect lies, that measures several of the physiological responses accompanying emotion (such as perspiration and cardiovascular and breathing changes).

reactions to different emotions were much the same, the James-Lange assumption that we experience our emotions through differing body states seemed improbable. But this new evidence showing subtle physiological distinctions among the emotions makes the James-Lange theory plausible.

The James-Lange theory also finds support in observations of people with severed spinal cords. Psychologist George Hohmann (1966) interviewed 25 soldiers who suffered such injuries in World War II. He asked them to recall emotion-arousing incidents that occurred before and after their spinal injuries. Those with lower-spine injuries, who had lost sensation only in their legs, reported little change in their emotions. Those who could feel nothing below the neck reported a considerable decrease in emotional intensity (as James and Lange would have expected). The anger, as one man confessed, "just doesn't have the heat to it that it used to. It's a mental kind of anger." But emotions expressed mostly in body areas above the neck are felt more intensely by those with high spinal-cord injury. Virtually all the men Hohmann interviewed reported increases in weeping, lumps in the throat, and getting choked up when saying good-bye, worshipping, or watching a touching movie.

Such evidence has breathed new life into the James-Lange theory and has led some researchers to view feelings as "mostly shadows" of our bodily responses and behaviors (Damasio, 2003). But most researchers agree with Cannon and Bard that our experienced emotions also involve cognition (Averill, 1993). Whether we fear the man behind us on the dark street depends entirely on whether we interpret his actions as threatening or friendly. So, with James and Lange we can say that our body's reactions are an important ingredient of emotion. And with Cannon and Bard we can say that there is more to the experience of emotion than reading our body's responses.

> "Every moment is more intense."
> Christopher Reeve (1952–2004) after his paralysis

Cognition and Emotion

What is the connection between what we *think* and how we *feel?* Which is the chicken and which the egg?

We know that our emotions affect our thinking. When we *feel* like singing "Oh, what a beautiful morning!" we *see* the world and the people around us as wonderful. If the following day we find ourselves singing the blues, we perceive the same world and the same people as less than wonderful.

Can we experience emotion apart from thinking? Or do we become what we think? The issue has practical implications for self-improvement: Can we change our emotions by changing our thinking?

Cognition Can Define Emotion

OBJECTIVE 38-6 | Explain how the spillover effect influences our experience of emotions.

Sometimes our arousal response to one event spills over into our response to the next event. Imagine arriving home after an invigorating run and finding a message that you got a longed-for job. With arousal lingering from the run, would you feel more elated than if you received this news after awakening from a nap?

To find out whether this *spillover effect* exists, Stanley Schachter and Jerome Singer (1962) aroused college men with injections of the hormone epinephrine. Picture yourself as one of their participants: After receiving the injection, you go to a waiting room, where you find yourself with another person (actually an accomplice of the experimenters) who is acting either euphoric or irritated. As you observe this person, you begin to feel your heart race, your body flush, and your breathing become more rapid. If told to expect these effects from the injection, what would you feel? Schachter's and Singer's volunteers felt little emotion—because they attributed their arousal to the drug. But if told the injection would produce no effects, what would you feel? Perhaps you would react, as another group of participants did, by "catching" the apparent emotion of the person you are with—becoming happy if the accomplice is acting euphoric, and testy if the accomplice is acting irritated.

This discovery—that a stirred-up state can be experienced as one emotion or another very different one, depending on how we interpret and label it—has been replicated in dozens of experiments. Insult people who have just been aroused by pedaling an exercise bike or watching rock videos and they will find it easy to misattribute their arousal to the provocation. Their feelings of anger will be greater than those of people who were similarly provoked but not previously aroused. Likewise, sexually aroused people react with more hostility in anger-provoking situations. And, vice versa—the arousal that lingers after an intense argument or a frightening experience may intensify sexual passion (Palace, 1995). Just as the Schachter-Singer two-factor theory predicts, arousal + label = emotion. As we have seen, emotional arousal is not as undifferentiated as Schachter and Singer believed. But arousal—from emotions as diverse as anger, fear, and sexual excitement—can indeed spill from one emotion to another (Reisenzein, 1983; Sinclair & others, 1994; Zillmann, 1986). *The point to remember:* Arousal fuels emotion; cognition channels it.

Cognition Does Not Always Precede Emotion

OBJECTIVE 38-7 | Distinguish the two alternative pathways that sensory stimuli may travel when triggering an emotional response.

Reuters/Corbis

AP Photo/Nati Harnik

The spillover effect
Arousal from a soccer match (top photo) or a political protest (bottom photo) can fuel anger, which can descend into rioting or other violent confrontations.

To experience an emotion, must we first label our arousal? Sometimes we experience unlabeled emotion. Imagine receiving some unsettling news. There's a deadline you've forgotten about, or you discover that you've hurt someone's feelings. As the ongoing conversation distracts your attention, you lose awareness of the bad news. Yet as its bodily effects linger, the now-unlabeled feeling still churns. You feel a little bad. You know there's a reason. But for the moment you can't put your finger on it. Robert Zajonc (pronounced ZI-yence; 1980, 1984a) has contended that we actually have many emotional reactions apart from, or even before, our interpretations of a situation. For example, when people repeatedly view stimuli flashed too briefly for them to perceive and recall, they nevertheless come to prefer those stimuli. Without being consciously aware of having seen the stimuli, they rather like them. A subliminally flashed smiling or angry face can also prime us to feel better or worse about a follow-up stimulus (Murphy & others, 1995). In one set of experiments, thirsty people drank about 50 percent more fruit-flavored drink after viewing a subliminally flashed (thus unperceived) happy rather than neutral face (Berridge & Winkielman, 2003). If flashed an angry face, they drank substantially less. Research on neurological processes shows how we can experience emotion unconsciously, before cognition.

Like speedy reflexes that operate apart from the brain's thinking cortex, some emotions take the "low road," via neural pathways that bypass the cortex (which offers the alternative "high road" pathway). One low-road pathway runs from the eye or ear via the thalamus to the *amygdala,* an emotional control center (**FIGURE 38.5** on the next page). This amygdala shortcut, bypassing the cortex, enables our greased-lightning emotional response before our intellect intervenes. So speedy is the amygdala response

Can you recall liking something or someone immediately, without knowing why?

"Oh! ye'll take the high road and I'll take the low road, And I'll be in Scotland afore ye."
Bonnie Banks O' Loch Lomond

FIGURE 38.5

The brain's shortcut for emotions
Sensory input may be routed (a) directly to the amygdala (via the thalamus) for an instant emotional reaction and (b) to the cortex for analysis.

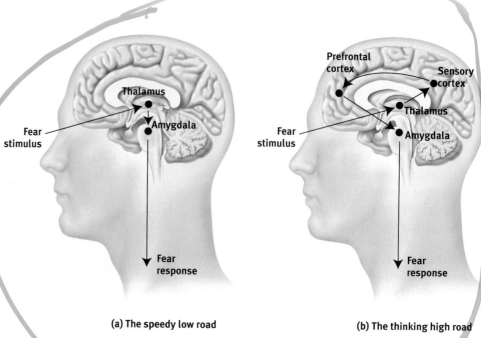

(a) The speedy low road

(b) The thinking high road

The amygdala, notes biologist Robert Sapolsky (2003), "is also central to aggression, underlining the fact that aggression can be rooted in fear—an observation that can explain much sociopolitical behavior."

that we may be unaware of what's transpired (Dimberg & others, 2000). In one fascinating experiment, Paul Whalen and his colleagues (2004) used fMRI scans to observe the amygdala's response to subliminally presented fearful eyes (**FIGURE 38.6**). Compared with a control condition that presented the whites of happy eyes, the fearful eyes triggered increased amygdala activity (despite no one's being aware of seeing them).

The amygdala sends more neural projections up to the cortex than it receives back. This makes it easier for our feelings to hijack our thinking than for our thinking to rule our feelings, note Joseph LeDoux and Jorge Armony (1999). In the forest, we jump at the sound of rustling bushes nearby, leaving the cortex to decide later whether the sound was made by a predator or just the wind. Such an experience supports Zajonc's belief that *some* of our emotional reactions involve no deliberate thinking and that cognition is not always necessary for emotion. The heart is not always subject to the mind.

Emotion researcher Richard Lazarus (1991, 1998) conceded that our brains process and react to vast amounts of information without our conscious awareness, and he willingly granted that some emotional responses do not require *conscious* thinking. But, he noted, even instantaneously felt emotions require some sort of cognitive appraisal of the situation; otherwise, how would we *know* what we are reacting to? The appraisal may be effortless and we may not be conscious of it, but it is still a mental function. Emotions arise when we *appraise* an event as beneficial or harmful to our well-being, whether we truly know it is or not. We appraise the sound of the rustling bushes as the presence of a threat. Later, we learn that it was "just the wind."

FIGURE 38.6

The brain's sensitivity to threats
Even when fearful eyes (left) were flashed too briefly for people to consciously perceive them, fMRI scans revealed that their hypervigilant amygdala was alerted (Whalen & others, 2004).

Complex emotions such as guilt, happiness, and love most clearly arise from our interpretations and expectations. Highly emotional people are intense partly because of their interpretations. They may *personalize* events as being somehow directed at them, and they may *generalize* their experiences by blowing single incidents out of proportion (Larsen & others, 1987). We may attribute a bad exam grade to an unfair exam and feel angry, to our own inability and feel depressed, or to lack of preparation and feel accepting (Weiner, 1985).

To sum up, as Zajonc and LeDoux have demonstrated, some emotional responses—especially simple likes, dislikes, and fears—involve no conscious thinking (**FIGURE 38.7**). We may fear the spider, even if we "know" it is harmless. Such responses are difficult to alter by changing our thinking.

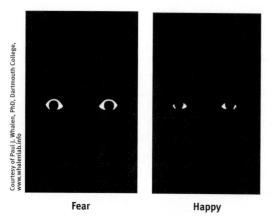

Courtesy of Paul J. Whalen, PhD, Dartmouth College, www.whalenlab.info

Fear   Happy

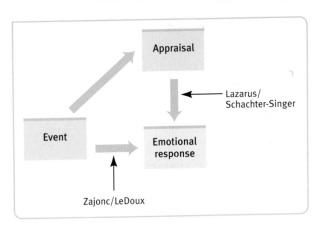

FIGURE 38.7
Two routes to emotion
Zajonc and LeDoux emphasize that some emotional responses are immediate, before any conscious appraisal. Lazarus, Schachter, and Singer emphasized that our appraisal and labeling of events also determines our emotional responses.

Other emotions—including moods such as depression and complex feelings such as hatred and love—are, as Lazarus, Schachter, and Singer predicted, greatly affected by our interpretations, memories, and expectations. For these emotions, learning to *think* more positively about ourselves and the world around us helps us *feel* better.

>> LEARNING OUTCOMES

Introduction to Emotion

OBJECTIVE 38-1 | Identify the three components of emotions, and contrast the James-Lange, Cannon-Bard, and two-factor theories of emotion.

Emotion's three components are (1) physiological arousal, (2) expressive behaviors, and (3) conscious experience. William James and Carl Lange proposed that we feel emotion *after* we notice our physiological responses. Walter Cannon and Philip Bard believed that we feel emotion *at the same time* that our bodies respond. Stanley Schachter and Jerome Singer's two-factor theory of emotion focused on the interplay of thinking and feeling, not on the timing of feelings. They proposed that emotions have two components, physical arousal and a cognitive label.

OBJECTIVE 38-2 | Describe the role of the autonomic nervous system during emotional arousal.

The autonomic nervous system (ANS) controls arousal. Its *sympathetic division* mobilizes us for action by directing the adrenals to release stress hormones, which in turn increase heart rate, blood pressure, and blood sugar levels, and by triggering other defensive physical reactions. The *parasympathetic division* calms us after a crisis has passed, though arousal diminishes gradually.

OBJECTIVE 38-3 | Discuss the relationship between arousal and performance.

Very high or very low arousal can be disruptive. We perform best when arousal is moderate, though this varies with the difficulty of the task. For easy or well-learned tasks, best performance is linked to high arousal. For difficult tasks, performance peaks at lower levels.

OBJECTIVE 38-4 | Name three emotions that involve similar physiological arousal.

We display similar physiological arousal during fear, anger, and sexual arousal, though our emotional experiences (and sometimes our facial expressions) differ during these three states.

OBJECTIVE 38-5 | Describe some physiological and brain pattern indicators of specific emotions.

Some emotions are associated with minute movements of muscles in the brow (during fear) and cheeks (during joy) and under the eyes (during joy). Brain scans also show increased activity in the amygdala during fear. Negative emotions (disgust, for example) trigger more activity in the right prefrontal cortex; positive moods (enthusiasm, for example) register in the left frontal lobe, which has many dopamine receptors.

OBJECTIVE 38-6 | Explain how the spillover effect influences our experience of emotions.

The *spillover effect* occurs when our arousal from one event influences our response to other events. Emotional arousal is sometimes general enough to require us to define the emotion we are experiencing. Arousal fuels emotion; cognition channels it.

OBJECTIVE 38-7 | Distinguish the two alternative pathways that sensory stimuli may travel when triggering an emotional response.

When sensory input goes directly to the amygdala via the thalamus, bypassing the cortex, it triggers an immediate emotional response that may be outside our conscious awareness. Responses to complex emotions (such as guilt, happiness, and love) require interpretation and are routed along the slower route to the cortex for analysis.

TERMS AND CONCEPTS TO REMEMBER

emotion, p. 38-0

James-Lange theory, p. 38-0

Cannon-Bard theory, p. 38-0

two-factor theory, p. 38-1

polygraph, p. 38-4

TEST YOURSELF

1. Christine is holding her 8-month-old baby when a fierce dog appears out of nowhere and, with teeth bared, leaps for the baby's face. Christine immediately ducks for cover to protect the baby, screams at the dog, then notices that her heart is banging in her chest and she's broken out in a cold sweat. How would the James-Lange, Cannon-Bard, and two-factor theories explain Christine's emotional reaction?

2. How do the two divisions of the autonomic nervous system help us respond to and recover from a crisis, and why is this relevant to the study of emotions?

(Answers in Appendix B.)

ASK YOURSELF

1. Can you remember a time when you began to feel upset or uneasy and only later labeled those feelings?

2. Can you think of a recent time when you noticed your body's reactions to an emotionally charged situation, such as a difficult social setting or perhaps even a test or game you were worrying about in advance? Did you perceive the situation as a challenge or a threat? How well did you do?

>WEB

Multiple-choice *self-tests* and more may be found at www.worthpublishers.com/myers.

39

Expressed Emotion

There is a simple method of deciphering people's emotions: We read their bodies, listen to their tone of voice, and study their faces. People's expressive behavior reveals their emotion. Does this nonverbal language vary with culture, or is it universal? And do our expressions influence our experienced emotions?

Nonverbal Communication

OBJECTIVE 39-1 | Describe some of the factors that affect our ability to decipher nonverbal cues.

All of us communicate nonverbally as well as verbally. To Westerners, a firm handshake immediately conveys an outgoing, expressive personality (Chaplin & others, 2000). With a gaze, an averted glance, or a stare we can communicate intimacy, submission, or dominance (Kleinke, 1986). Among those passionately in love, gazing into one another's eyes is typically prolonged and mutual (Rubin, 1970). Joan Kellerman, James Lewis, and James Laird (1989) wondered if intimate gazes would stir such feelings between strangers. To find out, they asked unacquainted male-female pairs to gaze intently for two minutes either at each other's hands or into each other's eyes. After separating, the eye-gazers reported feeling a tingle of attraction and affection. What if you do not want people to know how you feel, or if you do not even want to feel that way in the first place? Can we suppress our emotional expressions? Sometimes. But as Jane Richards and James Gross (2000) discovered, suppressing expression comes at a cost. Compared with those who simply watched a distressing film, those who diverted mental energy and attention into suppressing their emotional expressions remembered its details less well.

Most of us are good enough at reading nonverbal cues to decipher the emotions in an old silent film. We are especially good at detecting nonverbal threats. When hearing emotions conveyed in another language, people most readily detect anger (Scherer & others, 2001). When viewing subliminally flashed words, we more often sense the presence of a negative word, such as *snake* or *bomb* (Dijksterhuis & Aarts, 2003). In a crowd of faces, a single angry face (**FIGURE 39.1**) will "pop out" faster than a single happy one (Fox & others, 2000; Hansen & Hansen, 1988).

> "Your face, my thane, is a book where men may read strange matters."
>
> Lady Macbeth to her husband, in William Shakespeare's *Macbeth*

Injected as part of the war on wrinkles, Botox paralyzes facial muscles that create wrinkles, allowing the overlying skin to relax and smooth. By erasing the subtle expressions of frown lines or twinkling eyes, might this cosmetic procedure hide subtle emotions?

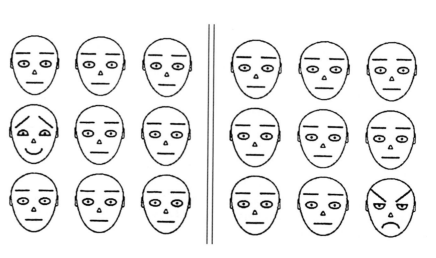

FIGURE 39.1
Radar for threats: An angry face pops out
Our emotion-detecting radar excels at detecting threats, and thus an angry face. Using stimuli such as these, Arne Öhman and his Stockholm colleagues (2001) found that people more speedily detect an angry face than a happy one. In other "Where's Waldo?"-like experiments, people more readily spotted images of threat-relevant snakes than of flowers (Öhman & others, 2001).

Used by permission of S. D. Pollak, D. J. Kistler and the National Academy of Sciences

FIGURE 39.2

Experience influences how we perceive emotions

Shown one of the morphed middle faces, evenly mixing fear or sadness with anger, physically abused children were more likely than nonabused children to perceive the face as angry (Pollak & Kistler, 2002; Pollak & Tolley-Schell, 2003).

By exposing different parts of emotion-laden faces, Robert Kestenbaum (1992) discovered that we read fear and anger mostly from the eyes, and happiness from the mouth. Fleeting *changes* in expression also help us read a face (Ambadar & others, 2005). Some of us are more sensitive than others to such cues. Robert Rosenthal, Judith Hall, and their colleagues (1979) discovered this by showing hundreds of people brief film clips of portions of a person's emotionally expressive face or body, sometimes accompanied by a garbled voice. For example, after a 2-second scene revealing only the face of an upset woman, the researchers would ask whether the woman was criticizing someone for being late or was talking about her divorce. Rosenthal and Hall reported that, given such "thin slices," some people are much better than others at detecting emotion. Introverts tend to do better at reading others' emotions, although extraverts are themselves easier to read (Ambady & others, 1995).

Experience can sensitize us to particular emotions. Shown a series of faces that morphed from sadness or fear to anger, physically abused children are much quicker than other children to see anger (**FIGURE 39.2**). Shown a face that is 60 percent fear and 40 percent anger, they are as likely to perceive anger as fear. Their perceptions become sensitively attuned to glimmers of danger signals that nonabused children miss.

Gender, Emotion, and Nonverbal Behavior

OBJECTIVE 39-2 | Describe some gender differences in perceiving and communicating emotions.

Is women's intuition, as so many believe, superior to men's? Consider: As Jackie Larsen left her Grand Marais, Minnesota, church prayer group one April 2001 morning, she encountered Christopher Bono, a clean-cut, well-mannered youth. Bono's car had broken down, and he said he was looking for a ride to meet friends in Thunder Bay. When Bono later appeared in Larsen's shop, where she had promised to help him phone his friends, she felt a pain in her stomach. Intuitively sensing that something was very wrong with this young man, she insisted that they talk outside on the sidewalk. "I said, 'I am a mother and I have to talk to you like a mother. . . . I can tell by your manners that you have a nice mother.'" At the mention of his mother, Bono's eyes fixed on her. "I don't know where my mother is," he said.

As the conversation ended, Larsen directed Bono back to the church to meet the pastor. She also called the police and suggested that they trace his license plates. The car was registered to his mother in southern Illinois. When police went to her apartment, they found blood all over and Lucia Bono dead in the bathtub. Christopher Bono, 16, was charged with first-degree murder (Biggs, 2001).

Was it a coincidence that Larsen, who saw through Bono's calm exterior, was a woman? Some psychologists would say no. In her analysis of 125 studies of sensitivity to nonverbal cues, Judith Hall (1984, 1987) discerned that women generally surpass men at reading people's emotional cues. Women's nonverbal sensitivity also gives them an edge in spotting lies (DePaulo, 1994). And women have surpassed men in discerning whether a male-female couple is a genuine romantic couple or a posed phony couple, and in discerning which of two people in a photo is the other's supervisor (Barnes & Sternberg, 1989).

Women's nonverbal sensitivity helps explain their greater emotional literacy. Invited by Lisa Feldman Barrett and her colleagues (2000) to describe how they would feel in certain situations, men described simpler emotional reactions. You might like to try this yourself: Ask some people how they might feel when saying good-bye to friends after graduation. Barrett's work suggests you are more likely to hear men say, simply, "I'll feel bad," and to hear women express more complex emotions: "It will be bittersweet; I'll feel both happy and sad."

Women's skill at decoding others' emotions may also contribute to their greater emotional responsiveness in both positive and negative situations (Grossman & Wood, 1993; Sprecher & Sedikides, 1993; Stoppard & Gruchy, 1993). In studies of 23,000 people from 26 cultures around the world, women more than men reported themselves open to feelings (Costa & others, 2001). That helps explain the extremely strong perception that emotionality is "more true of women"—a perception expressed by nearly 100 percent of 18- to 29-year-old Americans (Newport, 2001).

When surveyed, women are also far more likely than men to describe themselves as empathic. If you have *empathy,* you identify with others and imagine what it must be like to walk in their shoes. You rejoice with those who rejoice and weep with those who weep. Physiological measures of empathy, such as one's heart rate while seeing another's distress, reveal a much smaller gender gap than is reported in surveys (Eisenberg & Lennon, 1983). Nevertheless, females are more likely to *express* empathy—to cry and to report distress when observing someone in distress. Ann Kring and Albert Gordon (1998) observed this gender difference in videotapes of men and women students watching film clips that were sad (children with a dying parent), happy (slapstick comedy), or frightening (a man nearly falling off the ledge of a tall building). As **FIGURE 39.3** shows, the women reacted more visibly to each film type. Women also tend to experience emotional events (such as viewing pictures of mutilation) more deeply—with more brain activation in areas sensitive to emotion—and then to remember the scenes better three weeks later (Canli & others, 2002).

In another exploration of gender and facial expression, Harold Hill and Alan Johnston (2001) animated an image of an average head with expressions (smirks, head tosses, raised eyebrows) that had been digitally captured from the faces of London University students as they read a joke. Despite having no anatomical clues to gender, observers could usually detect gender in the telltale expressions.

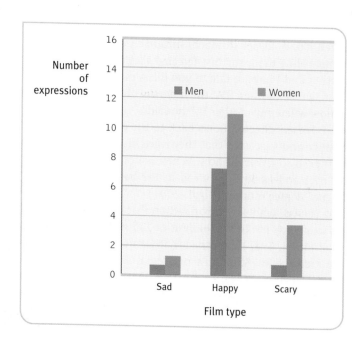

FIGURE 39.3
Gender and expressiveness
Although male and female students did not differ dramatically in self-reported emotions or physiological responses while viewing emotional films, the women's faces *showed* much more emotion. (From Kring & Gordon, 1998.)

Ekman & Matsumoto, Japanese and Caucasian Facial Expression of Emotion

FIGURE 39.4
Culture-specific or culturally universal expressions?
As people of differing cultures and races, do our faces speak differing languages? Which face expresses disgust? Anger? Fear? Happiness? Sadness? Surprise? The answers are on this module's final page. (From Matsumoto and Ekman, 1989.)

Do people from different cultures share these similarities because they share experiences, such as American movies, the BBC, and CNN? Apparently not. Ekman and his team asked isolated people in New Guinea to display various emotions in response to such statements as, "Pretend your child has died." When the researchers showed videotapes of the New Guineans' facial reactions to North American collegians, the students read them easily.

Facial expressions do contain some nonverbal accents that provide clues to one's culture (Marsh & others, 2003). So it is not surprising that data from 182 studies show slightly enhanced accuracy when people judge emotions from their own culture (Elfenbein & Ambady, 2002, 2003a,b). Still, the telltale signs of emotion generally cross cultures.

Children's facial expressions—even those of blind children who have never seen a face—are also universal (Eibl-Eibesfeldt, 1971). People blind from birth spontaneously exhibit the common facial expressions associated with such emotions as joy, sadness, fear, and anger (Galati & others, 1997). The world over, children cry when distressed, shake their heads when defiant, and smile when they are happy.

The discovery that facial muscles speak a fairly universal language would not have surprised pioneering emotion researcher Charles Darwin (1809–1882). He speculated that in prehistoric times, before our ancestors communicated in words, their ability to convey threats, greetings, and submission with facial expressions helped them survive. That shared heritage, he believed, is why all humans express the basic emotions with similar facial expressions. A sneer, for example, retains elements of an animal's baring its teeth in a snarl.

Smiles, too, are social phenomena as well as emotional reflexes. Bowlers don't smile when they score a strike—they smile when they turn to face their companions (Jones & others, 1991; Kraut & Johnston, 1979). Even euphoric winners of Olympic gold medals typically don't smile when they are awaiting their ceremony but do when interacting with officials and facing the crowd and cameras (Fernández-Dols & Ruiz-Belda, 1995).

It has also been adaptive for us to interpret faces in particular contexts. People judge an angry face set in a frightening situation as afraid. They judge a fearful face set in a painful situation as pained (Carroll & Russell, 1996). Movie directors harness this phenomenon by creating contexts and soundtracks that amplify our perceptions of particular emotions.

Emotional expressions may enhance our survival in other ways, too. Surprise raises the eyebrows and widens the eyes, enabling us to take in more information. Disgust wrinkles the nose, closing it from foul odors.

> "For news of the heart, ask the face."
> Guinean proverb

While weightless, astronauts' fluids move toward their upper body and their faces become puffy. This makes nonverbal communication more difficult, increasing the risks of misunderstanding, especially among multinational crews (Gelman, 1989).

Although cultures share a universal facial language for basic emotions, they differ in how much emotion they express. In cultures that encourage individuality, as in Western Europe, Australia, New Zealand, and North America, emotional displays often are intense and prolonged. People focus on their own goals and attitudes and express themselves accordingly. Watching a film of someone's hand being cut, Americans grimace (whether alone or with other viewers). Japanese viewers hide their emotions when in the presence of others (Triandis, 1994). Cultural differences exist both between and within nations. The Irish and their Irish-American descendants tend to be more expressive than Scandinavians and their Scandinavian-American descendants (Tsai & Chentsova-Dutton, 2003). And that reminds us of a familiar lesson: Like most psychological events, emotion is best understood not only as a biological and cognitive phenomenon, but also as a social-cultural phenomenon.

The Effects of Facial Expressions

OBJECTIVE 39-5 | Discuss the facial feedback and behavior feedback phenomena, and give an example of each.

> "Whenever I feel afraid
> I hold my head erect
> And whistle a happy tune."
> Richard Rodgers and Oscar Hammerstein,
> *The King and I,* 1958

As William James struggled with feelings of depression and grief, he came to believe that we can control emotions by going "through the outward movements" of any emotion we want to experience. "To feel cheerful," he advised, "sit up cheerfully, look around cheerfully, and act as if cheerfulness were already there."

Recent findings concerning the emotional effects of facial expressions are precisely what James might have predicted. Expressions not only communicate emotion, they also amplify and regulate it. In his 1872 book, *The Expression of the Emotions in Man and Animals,* Darwin contended that "the free expression by outward signs of an emotion intensifies it. . . . He who gives way to violent gestures will increase his rage."

Was Darwin right? I was driving in my car one day when the song "Put On a Happy Face" came on the radio. How phony, I thought. But I tested Darwin's hypothesis anyway, as you can, too. Fake a big grin. Now scowl. Can you feel the "smile therapy" difference?

Participants in dozens of experiments have felt a difference. For example, James Laird and his colleagues (1974, 1984, 1989) subtly induced students to make a frowning expression by asking them to "contract these muscles" and "pull your brows together" (supposedly to help the researchers attach facial electrodes). The results? The students reported feeling a little angry. Students similarly induced to smile felt happier, found cartoons funnier, and recalled happier memories than did the frowners. People instructed to mold their faces in ways that express other basic emotions also experienced those emotions. For example, they reported feeling more fear than anger, disgust, or sadness when made to construct a fearful expression: "Raise your eyebrows. And open your eyes wide. Move your whole head back, so that your chin is tucked in a little bit, and let your mouth relax and hang open a little" (Duclos & others, 1989). The face is more than a billboard that displays our feelings; it also feeds our feelings.

> "Refuse to express a passion and it dies. . . . If we wish to conquer undesirable emotional tendencies in ourselves, we must . . . go through the outward movements of those contrary dispositions which we prefer to cultivate."
> William James, *Principles of Psychology,* 1890

In the absence of competing emotions, this *facial feedback* effect is subtle yet detectable. Consider these findings:

- If manipulated into furrowing their brows (**FIGURE 39.5**), people feel sadder while looking at sad photos.
- Saying the phonemes *e* and *ah,* which activate smiling muscles, puts people—believe it or not—in a better mood than saying the German *ü* (rather like saying the English *e* and *u* together), which activates muscles associated with negative emotions (Zajonc & others, 1989).

Courtesy of Louis Schakel/Michael Kausman/The New York Times Pictures

FIGURE 39.5

How to make people frown without telling them to frown

Randy Larsen, Margaret Kasimatis, and Kurt Frey's (1992) solution: Attach two golf tees above the eyebrows and ask people to make the tee tips touch. Research participants felt sad while viewing scenes of war, sickness, and starvation, and even sadder with their "sad face" muscles activated.

- Just activating one of the smiling muscles by holding a pen in the teeth (rather than with the lips, which activates a frowning muscle) is enough to make cartoons seem more amusing (Strack & others, 1988). A heartier smile—made not just with the mouth but with raised cheeks that crinkle the eyes—enhances positive feelings even more when you are reacting to something pleasant or funny (Soussignan, 2001). Looking at yourself in a mirror further amplifies the effect (Kleinke & others, 1998). Smile warmly on the outside and you feel better on the inside. Scowl and the whole world seems to scowl back.

Sara Snodgrass and her associates (1986) observed the *behavior feedback* phenomenon with walking. You can duplicate the participants' experience: Walk for a few minutes while taking short, shuffling steps, keeping your eyes downcast. Now walk around taking long strides, with your arms swinging and your eyes looking straight ahead. Can you feel your mood shift? Going through the motions awakens the emotions.

Better yet, report William Flack and his team (1999), manipulate *both* face and posture. To generate an angry feeling, for example, follow the instructions they gave their research participants:

> Push your eyebrows together and down. Clench your teeth tightly and push your lips together. Put your feet flat on the floor directly below your knees, and put your forearms and elbows on the arms of the chair. Now clench your fists tightly and lean your upper body slightly forward.

But let's leave you feeling happier:

> Push the corners of your mouth up and back, letting your mouth open a little. Sit up as straight as you can in your chair. Put your hands at the ends of the armrests, and make sure that your legs are straight in front of you, knees bent, and feet right below your knees.

If assuming emotional expressions and postures triggers a feeling, then would imitating others' expressions help us feel what they are feeling? Again, the laboratory evidence is supportive. Kathleen Burns Vaughn and John Lanzetta (1981) asked some students but not others to make a pained expression whenever an electric shock was apparently delivered to someone they were watching. With each apparent shock, the grimacing observers perspired more and had a faster heart rate than observers who didn't imitate the expression. Just seeing a loved one wince at a light electrical shock also activates a pain-related brain region. This suggests a neural basis for empathy—for literally feeling the other's pain (Singer & others, 2004). So one small way to become more empathic—to feel what others feel—is to let your own face mimic the other person's expression. Acting as another acts helps us feel what another feels. Indeed, natural mimicry of others' emotions helps explain why emotions are contagious (Dimberg & others, 2000; Newmann & Strack, 2000).

A request from your author: Smile often as you read this book.

>> LEARNING OUTCOMES

Expressed Emotion

OBJECTIVE 39-1 | **Describe some of the factors that affect our ability to decipher nonverbal cues.**

Most people can detect nonverbal cues, and we are especially sensitive to nonverbal threats. Experience contributes to our sensitivity to cues, as studies of abused children show.

OBJECTIVE 39-2 | **Describe some gender differences in perceiving and communicating emotions.**

Women generally surpass men at reading deception and other emotional cues, giving detailed descriptions of their emotional reactions, describing themselves as emotional, expressing empathy in words and facial expressions, and conveying happiness. Men communicate anger better.

OBJECTIVE 39-3 | **Discuss the research results on reading and misreading facial and behavioral indicators of emotion.**

Facial muscles reveal signs of emotion. But lie detection methods based on facial expressions don't yet exist, and most of us have difficulty detecting expressions of deceit. The absence of verbal or emotional cues in e-mails deprives us of an important source of information.

OBJECTIVE 39-4 | **Discuss the culture-specific and culturally universal aspects of emotional expression, and explain how emotional expressions could enhance survival.**

Many facial expressions, such as those of happiness and fear, are found all over the world (and among children blind from birth), indicating that they are culturally universal aspects of emotion. Cultures differ, however, in the amount of emotional expression they consider acceptable. In prelinguistic, prehistoric times, emotional expressions could have enhanced survival by enabling communication of threats, greetings, and submission. Some emotional expressions help us to take in more sensory information or to avoid taking in toxic substances.

OBJECTIVE 39-5 | **Discuss the facial feedback and behavior feedback phenomena, and give an example of each.**

The *facial feedback hypothesis* proposes that expressions amplify our emotions by activating muscles associated with specific states (such as happiness) and the muscles signal the body to respond as though we were experiencing those states. Similarly, the *behavior feedback hypothesis* assumes that if we move our body as we would when experiencing some emotion (shuffling along with downcast eyes, as when sad), we are likely to feel that emotion to some degree.

TEST YOURSELF

1. Who tends to express more emotion—men or women? How do we know the answer to that question?

(Answer in Appendix B.)

ASK YOURSELF

1. Can you think of one situation in which you would like to change the way you feel, and create a simple plan for doing so? For instance, if you would like to feel more cheerful on your way to class tomorrow morning rather than dragging yourself there, you might try walking briskly—with head held high and a pleasant expression on your face.

ANSWER TO QUESTION WITHIN THE MODULE

Q. Which of the faces in Figure 39.4 expresses disgust? Anger? Fear? Happiness? Sadness? Surprise?

A. The photos in Figure 39.4, from left to right and top to bottom, express happiness, surprise, fear, sadness, anger, and disgust.

>WEB

Multiple-choice *self-tests* and more may be found at www.worthpublishers.com/myers.

40

Experienced Emotion

OBJECTIVE 40-1 | Name several basic emotions, and describe two dimensions psychologists use to differentiate emotions.

How many distinct emotions are there? Carroll Izard (1977) isolated 10 such basic emotions (joy, interest-excitement, surprise, sadness, anger, disgust, contempt, fear, shame, and guilt), most of which are present in infancy (**FIGURE 40.1**). Jessica Tracey and Richard Robins (2004) believe that pride is also a distinct emotion, signaled by a small smile, head slightly tilted back, and an open posture. And Phillip Shaver and his colleagues (1996) believe that love, too, may be a basic emotion. But Izard has argued that other emotions are combinations of these 10. Love, he says, is a mixture of joy and interest-excitement.

The ingredients of emotion include not only physiology and expressive behavior but also our conscious experience. We sometimes experience feelings as "obscure and confused," noted Benjamin Constant de Rebecque in 1816. To cut through the obscurity, psychologists have asked people to describe their emotions. Varied people, including Estonians, Poles, Greeks, Chinese, and Canadians, place emotions along the two dimensions illustrated in **FIGURE 40.2** (on the next page)—pleasant (or positive) *valence* and low versus high *arousal* (Russell & others, 1989, 1999a,b; Watson & others, 1999).

Successful Olympic gymnasts and high-performing students taking exams label arousal as energizing, as giving them an edge (Raglin, 1992). For them arousal has

(d) Disgust (nose wrinkled, upper lip raised, tongue pushed outward)

(a) Joy (mouth forming smile, cheeks lifted, twinkle in eye)

(e) Surprise (brows raised, eyes widened, mouth rounded in oval shape)

(b) Anger (brows drawn together and downward, eyes fixed, mouth squarish)

(c) Interest (brows raised or knitted, mouth softly rounded, lips may be pursed)

(f) Sadness (brow's inner corner raised, mouth corners drawn down)

(g) Fear (brows level, drawn in and up, eyelids lifted, mouth corners retracted)

FIGURE 40.1
Infants' naturally occurring emotions
To identify the emotions present from birth, Carroll Izard analyzed the facial expressions of very young infants.

FIGURE 40.2
Two dimensions of emotion
James Russell, David Watson, Auke Tellegen, and others describe emotions as variations on two dimensions—arousal (low versus high) and valence (pleasant versus unpleasant feeling).

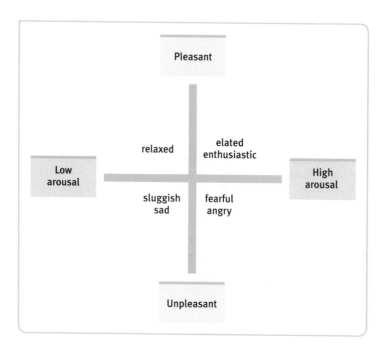

positive valence, while for those suffering stage fright it has negative valence. Experienced professors and public speakers similarly welcome prelecture arousal as meaning they are "up" or "on" rather than flat. On the valence and arousal dimensions, terrified is more frightened (more unpleasant and aroused) than afraid, enraged is angrier than angry, delighted is happier than happy.

Let's take a closer look at three of these emotions: fear, anger, and happiness. What functions do they serve? What influences our experience of each?

Fear

Fear can be poisonous. It can torment us, rob us of sleep, and preoccupy our thinking. People can be literally scared to death. Fear can also be contagious. In 1903, someone yelled "Fire!" as a fire broke out in Chicago's Iroquois Theater. Eddie Foy, the comedian on stage at the time, tried to reassure the crowd by calling out, "Don't get excited. There's no danger. Take it easy!" Alas, the crowd panicked. During the 10 minutes it took the fire department to arrive and quickly extinguish the flames, more than 500 people perished, most of them trampled or smothered in a stampede. Bodies were piled 7 or 8 feet deep in the stairways, and many of the faces bore heel marks (Brown, 1965).

More often, fear is adaptive. It's an alarm system that prepares our bodies to flee from danger. Fear of real or imagined enemies binds people together as families, tribes, and nations. Fear of injury can protect us from harm. Fear of punishment or retaliation can constrain us from harming one another. Fear helps us focus on a problem and rehearse coping strategies.

Learning Fear

OBJECTIVE 40-2 | State two ways we learn our fears.

People can be afraid of almost anything—"afraid of truth, afraid of fortune, afraid of death, and afraid of each other," observed Ralph Waldo Emerson. Why so many fears? Behaviorists John B. Watson and Rosalie Rayner (1920) showed that infants can learn to fear furry objects associated with frightening noises. Child development researchers now know that when infants begin to crawl, they learn from their falls and near-falls—and become increasingly afraid of heights (Campos & others, 1992). Through such conditioning, the short list of naturally painful and frightening events can multiply into a long list of human fears—fear of driving or flying, fear of mice or cockroaches, fear of closed or open spaces, fear of failure or of success, fear of another race or nation.

Learning by observation extends the list. Susan Mineka (1985) sought to explain why nearly all monkeys reared in the wild fear snakes, yet lab-reared monkeys do not. Surely, most wild monkeys do not actually suffer snake bites. Do they learn their fear through observation? To find out, Mineka experimented with six monkeys reared in the wild (all strongly fearful of snakes) and their lab-reared offspring (virtually none of which feared snakes). After repeatedly observing their parents or peers refusing to reach for food in the presence of a snake, the younger monkeys developed a similar strong fear of snakes. When retested three months later, their learned fear persisted, suggesting that our fears may reflect not only our own past traumas but also the fears we learn from our parents and friends.

It did not take direct experience for people to become more fearful after observing the trauma of 9/11. Within New York City, a school system study found tens of thousands of children experiencing nightmares and fears of public places (Goodnough, 2002). Nationally, women responded to the attacks with greater fear, men with greater anger (Lerner & others, 2002). Four weeks after the attack, 27 percent of women and 10 percent of men reported being afraid to fly (ICR, 2001).

The Biology of Fear

OBJECTIVE **40-3** | Discuss some of the biological components of fear.

We may be biologically prepared to learn some fears more quickly than others. Monkeys learn to fear snakes even by watching videotapes of monkeys reacting fearfully to a snake; but they *don't* learn to fear flowers when video splicing transposes the seemingly feared stimulus into a flower (Cook & Mineka, 1991). We humans quickly learn to fear snakes, spiders, and cliffs—fears that probably helped our ancestors survive (Öhman & Mineka, 2003). But our Stone Age fears leave us unprepared for high-tech dangers—cars, electricity, bombs, and global warming—all of which are now far more dangerous (Lumsden & Wilson, 1983; McNally, 1987).

One key to fear learning lies in the amygdala, that limbic system neural center deep in the brain (**FIGURE 40.3**). The amygdala plays a key role in associating various emotions, including fear, with certain situations (Barinaga, 1992b). Rabbits learn to react with fear to a tone that predicts an impending small shock—unless their amygdala is damaged. If rats have their amygdala deactivated by a drug that blocks the strengthening of neural connections, they, too, show no fear learning. The amygdala receives input from regions such as the *anterior cingulate cortex,* a higher-level center for processing emotion. And it sends output to all the parts of the brain that produce the bodily symptoms of extreme fear, such as diarrhea and shortness of breath.

The amygdala is similarly involved in human fears. If an experimenter repeatedly blasts people with a blaring horn after showing a blue slide, they will begin to react emotionally to the slide (as measured by their perspiring skin conducting electricity). If they have suffered damage to the nearby hippocampus, they still show the emotional reaction but won't be able to remember why. If they have suffered amygdala damage, they will remember the conditioning but will show no emotional effect of it (Schacter, 1996).

FIGURE 40.3

The amygdala—a neural key to fear learning

Nerves running out from these knots of neural tissue, one on either side of the brain's center, carry messages that control heart rate, sweating, stress hormones, attention, and other engines that rev up in threatening situations.

Courtesy of National Geographic Magazine and Laboratory of Neuro Imaging (LONI) at UCLA. Art and brain modeling by Amanda Hammond, Jacopo Annese, and Arthur Toga. LONI; spider art by Joon-Hyuck Kim.

Hard-wired fears
Entertainment businesses exploit our survival circuits. Although we can *know* that amusement park deaths are extremely rare, our fear alarm system nevertheless gives us an adrenaline rush and sweaty palms during a free-flying fair ride.

Researchers have been mapping these circuits, showing which activate as humans and other animals learn fears. If people are subjected to an aversive sound while viewing faces, amygdala fear pathways will become active on future viewings of the face (Buchel & others, 1998; Morris & others, 1998). Patients who have lost use of the amygdala are unusually trusting of scary-looking people (Adolphs & others, 1998).

Of course, there are people whose fears seem to fall outside the average range. Some, with *phobias,* have intense fears of specific objects (such as bugs) or situations (such as public speaking) that disrupt their ability to cope. They may be very fearful of threatening or embarrassing situations. To be ever-attentive to potential threats is to be chronically anxious (Mineka & Sutton, 1992). But others—courageous heroes and remorseless criminals—are less fearful than most of us. Astronauts and adventurers who have "the right stuff"—who can keep their wits and function coolly and effectively in times of severe stress—seem to thrive on risk. So, too, do con artists and killers who charm their intended victims without a hint of nervousness. In laboratory tests, they exhibit little fear of a tone that predictably precedes a painful electric shock.

Experience helps shape such fearfulness or fearlessness, but so do our genes. Genes influence our temperament—our emotional reactivity. Among identical twins, one twin's level of fearfulness is similar to the other's—even when they have been reared separately (Lykken, 1982). Scientists have isolated a gene that influences the amygdala's response to frightening situations (Hariri & others, 2002). People with a short version of this gene have less of a protein that speeds the reuptake of the neurotransmitter serotonin. With more serotonin available to activate their amygdala neurons, people with this short gene exhibit a revved-up amygdala response to frightening pictures.

Anger

OBJECTIVE 40-4 | Identify some common triggers and consequences of anger, and assess the catharsis hypothesis.

"I thought it would be nice if we had a forum where we could get together and have screaming tantrums."

"Anger will never disappear so long as thoughts of resentment are cherished in the mind."

The Buddha, 500 B.C.

Anger, the sages have said, is "a short madness" (Horace, 65-8 B.C.) that "carries the mind away" (Virgil, 70-19 B.C.) and can be "many times more hurtful than the injury that caused it" (Thomas Fuller, 1654-1734). But they have also said, "noble anger" (William Shakespeare, 1564-1616) "makes any coward brave" (Cato, 234-149 B.C.) and "brings back . . . strength" (Virgil).

What makes us angry? To find out, James Averill (1983) asked people to recall or keep careful records of their experiences with anger. Most reported becoming at least mildly angry several times a week, some several times a day. The anger was often a response to friends' or loved ones' perceived misdeeds and was especially common when another person's act seemed willful, unjustified, and avoidable. But blameless annoyances—foul odors, high temperatures, a traffic jam, aches and pains—also have the power to make us angry (Berkowitz, 1990).

What do we do with our anger? And what *should* we do with our anger? In a Gallup survey of teens, boys more than girls reported walking away from the situation or working it off with exercise; girls more often reported talking with a friend, listening to music, or writing (Ray, 2005).

When anger fuels physically or verbally aggressive acts we later regret, it becomes maladaptive. Anger also primes prejudice, and after 9/11, Americans who responded with anger more than fear also displayed intolerance for immigrants and Muslims (DeSteno & others, 2004; Skitka & others, 2004). And anger can harm us—chronic hostility is linked to heart disease (Smith & Ruiz, 2002; Williams, 1993). But controlled expressions of anger are more adaptive than either hostile outbursts or pent-up angry feelings. Participants in Averill's research recalled that when they were angry they often reacted assertively rather than hurtfully. Their anger frequently led them to talk things over with the offender, thereby lessening the aggravation.

Popular books and articles on aggression at times advise that even releasing angry feelings as hostile outbursts can be better than internalizing them. When irritated, should we lash out at the offender? Was Ann Landers (1969) right that "youngsters should be taught to vent their anger"? Are "recovery" therapists right in encouraging us to rage at our dead parents, imaginatively curse the boss, or confront our childhood abuser?

Such encouragement to vent our rage is typical in individualized cultures, but it would seldom be heard in cultures where people's identity is centered more on the group. People who keenly sense their *inter*dependence see anger as a threat to group harmony (Markus & Kitayama, 1991). In Tahiti, for instance, people learn to be considerate and gentle. In Japan, from infancy on, anger expressions are less common than in Western cultures.

The Western "vent your anger" advice presumes that through aggressive action or fantasy we can achieve emotional release, or **catharsis.** Experimenters report that *sometimes* when people retaliate against a provoker, they may indeed calm down. But this tends to be true only *if* their counterattack is directed against the provoker, *if* their retaliation seems justifiable, and *if* their target is not intimidating (Geen & Quanty, 1977; Hokanson & Edelman, 1966). In short, expressing anger can be *temporarily* calming *if* it does not leave us feeling guilty or anxious.

However, despite the afterglow—people sometimes feel better for hours afterward—catharsis usually fails to cleanse one's rage. More often, expressing anger breeds more anger. For one thing, it may provoke further retaliation, thus escalating a minor conflict into a major confrontation. For another, expressing anger can magnify anger. Ebbe Ebbesen and his colleagues (1975) saw this when they interviewed 100 frustrated engineers and technicians just laid off by an aerospace company. They asked some of the workers questions that released hostility, such as, "What instances can you think of where the company has not been fair with you?" When these people later filled out a questionnaire that assessed their attitudes toward the company, did this opportunity to "drain off" their hostility reduce it? Quite the contrary. Compared with those who had not vented their anger, those who had let it all out exhibited *more* hostility. Even when provoked people hit a punching bag *believing* it will be cathartic, the effect is the opposite—leading them to exhibit *more* cruelty (Bushman & others, 1999). And when they wallop a punching bag while ruminating about the person who angered them, they become even more aggressive when given a chance for revenge. "Venting to reduce anger is like using gasoline to put out a fire," concluded the researcher, Brad Bushman (2002).

Ironically, when angry outbursts do temporarily calm us, they may be reinforcing and therefore habit forming. If stressed managers find they can drain off some of their tension by berating an employee, then the next time they feel irritated and tense they may be more likely to explode again. Think about it: The next time you are angry you are likely to do whatever has relieved your anger in the past.

What, then, is the best way to handle our anger? Experts offer two suggestions. First, wait. You can bring down the level of physiological arousal of anger by waiting. "It is true of the body as of arrows," noted Carol Tavris (1982), "what goes up must come down. Any emotional arousal will simmer down if you just wait long enough." Second, deal with anger in a way that involves neither being chronically angry over every little annoyance nor passively sulking, merely rehearsing your reasons for your anger. Ruminating inwardly about the causes of your anger serves only to increase it (Rusting & Nolen-Hoeksema, 1998). Don't join those who stifle their feelings over a series of provocations and then suddenly overreact to a single incident (Baumeister & others, 1990). Calm yourself in other ways, such as by exercising, playing an instrument, or talking it through with a friend.

SIX CHIX

The catharsis myth: Is it true?

■ **catharsis** emotional release. In psychology, the catharsis hypothesis maintains that "releasing" aggressive energy (through action or fantasy) relieves aggressive urges.

A cool culture
Domestic violence is rare in Micronesia. This photo of community life on Pulap Island suggests one possible reason: Family life takes place in the open on this island. Relatives and neighbors who witness angry outbursts can step in before the emotion escalates into child, spouse, or elder abuse.

Anger does communicate strength and competence (Tiedens, 2001). It can benefit a relationship when it expresses a grievance in ways that promote reconciliation rather than retaliation. Civility means not only keeping silent about trivial irritations but also communicating important ones clearly and assertively. A nonaccusing statement of feeling—perhaps letting one's housemate know that "I get irritated when you leave your dirty dishes for me to clean up"—can help resolve the conflicts that cause anger.

What if someone else's behavior really hurts you? Research suggests that the age-old response of forgiveness may be what the doctor ordered. Without letting the offender off the hook or inviting further harm, forgiveness releases anger and can calm the body. To explore the bodily effects of forgiveness, Charlotte Witvliet and her co-researchers (2001) invited college students to recall an incident where someone had hurt them. As the students mentally rehearsed forgiveness, their negative feelings—and their perspiration, blood pressure, heart rate, and facial tension—all were lower than when they rehearsed their grudges.

Happiness

OBJECTIVE 40-5 | Describe how the feel-good, do-good phenomenon works, and discuss the importance of research on subjective well-being.

"How to gain, how to keep, how to recover happiness is in fact for most men at all times the secret motive for all they do," observed William James (1902, p. 76). People everywhere—in 48 countries on six continents in one study—also desire happiness for their children (Diener & Lucas, 2004). Understandably so, for one's state of happiness or unhappiness colors everything. People who are happy perceive the world as safer, make decisions more easily, rate job applicants more favorably, are more cooperative, and live healthier and more energized and satisfied lives (Lyukomirsky & others, 2005; Myers, 1993). When your mood is gloomy and your thinking preoccupied, life as a whole seems depressing. Let your mood brighten and your thinking broadens and becomes more playful and creative (Fredrickson, 2002, 2003). Your relationships, your self-image, and your hopes for the future also seem more promising. Positive emotions fuel upward spirals.

Moreover—and this is one of psychology's most consistent findings—when we feel happy we are more willing to help others. In study after study, a mood-boosting experience (finding money, succeeding on a challenging task, recalling a happy event) has made people more likely to give money, pick up someone's dropped papers, volunteer time, and do other good deeds. Psychologists call it the **feel-good, do-good phenomenon** (Salovey, 1990). Happiness doesn't just feel good, it does good.

■ **feel-good, do-good phenomenon** people's tendency to be helpful when already in a good mood.

■ **subjective well-being** self-perceived happiness or satisfaction with life. Used along with measures of objective well-being (for example, physical and economic indicators) to evaluate people's quality of life.

Gender differences also appear in the emotions women and men express best. After asking students to recall and talk about times when they were happy, sad, and angry, Erik Coats and Robert Feldman (1996) showed silent 5-second videos of the students' recollections to other participants acting as judges. Nearly two-thirds of the time, the judges correctly discerned women's recall of being happy, but they were able to spot happy recollections less than half the time when observing men. Men, however, slightly surpassed women in conveying their anger.

Detecting and Computing Emotion

OBJECTIVE **39-3** | Discuss the research results on reading and misreading facial and behavioral indicators of emotion.

Hard-to-control facial muscles reveal signs of emotions you may be trying to conceal. Lifting just the inner part of your eyebrows, which few people do consciously, reveals distress or worry. Eyebrows raised and pulled together signal fear. Activated muscles under the eyes and raised cheeks suggest a natural smile. A feigned smile, such as one we make for a photographer, often continues for more than 4 or 5 seconds. Most authentic expressions have faded by that time. Feigned smiles are also switched on and off more abruptly than is a genuine happy smile (Bugental, 1986).

Most people find it difficult to detect deceiving expressions. In one digest of 186 studies of discerning lies from truths, people were just 54 percent accurate—barely better than a coin toss (Bond & DePaulo, 2005). Can we learn how to better detect deceit? Paul Ekman and Maureen O'Sullivan (1991) found that by teaching researchers to watch for telltale signs of lying, such as a rise in voice pitch, they could boost accuracy rates. They had university students watch either a nature film or an upsetting gruesome film. Regardless, the students were instructed to talk and act as if they were watching and enjoying the nature film. Training enabled the researchers to discern lying versus truth-telling with 86 percent accuracy. Using our intuition, could the rest of us do as well? Not likely. Ekman and O'Sullivan challenged 39 college students, 67 psychiatrists, 110 court judges, 126 police officers, and 90 federal polygraphers to spot the liars. All five groups' guesses were, as we noted from other research, near chance (50 percent). Only a sixth group of experienced crowd-scanners—U.S. Secret Service agents—beat chance. But even they were only 64 percent correct.

In a follow-up study, the Ekman team (1999) found three more groups of skilled lie-catchers. When viewing videotapes of people stating their opinions—or the opposite of their opinions—on issues such as the death penalty, federal law officers (mostly CIA agents) spotted the liars 73 percent of the time. Clinical psychologists interested in lying research did so 68 percent of the time, and street-smart Los Angeles County sheriff's interrogators scored an almost equal 67 percent. Experienced British police interrogators exhibit similar accuracy (Mann & others, 2004). With experience—trained intuition—people can often catch the liar's leaking microexpressions of guilt, despair, and fear.

When people aren't seeking to deceive us, we do much better. As we noted earlier, our brains are rather amazing detectors of subtle expressions. Elisha Babad, Frank Bernieri, and Robert Rosenthal (1991) discovered just *how* amazing after videotaping teachers talking to unseen schoolchildren. A mere 10-second clip of either the teacher's voice or face provided enough clues for both young and old viewers to determine whether the teacher liked and admired the child he or she was addressing. Teachers may think they can conceal their feelings and stay objective, but their students can sense what their expressive tones and gestures reveal.

Which of Paul Ekman's smiles is feigned, which natural?
The smile on the right engages the facial muscles of a natural smile.

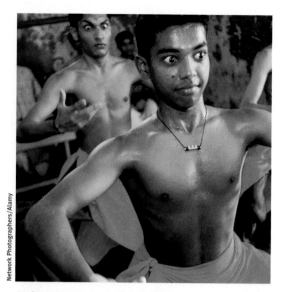

A silent language of emotion
Hindu classic dance uses the face and body to effectively convey 10 different emotions (Hejmadi & others, 2000).

The growing awareness that we communicate through the body's silent language has led to studies of how job applicants and interviewers communicate (or miscommunicate) nonverbally. Popular guidebooks and articles offer advice on how to interpret nonverbal signals when negotiating a business deal, selling a product, or flirting. It pays to be able to read feelings that leak through via subtle facial expressions, body movements, and postures. Fidgeting, for example, may reveal anxiety or boredom. More specific interpretations of postures and gestures are risky, because different expressions may convey the same emotion: Either a cold stare or the avoidance of eye contact may signify hostility. And a single gesture can convey very different emotions: Folded arms, for example, can signify either irritation or relaxation.

Such gestures, facial expressions, and tones of voice are all absent in computer-based communication. E-mail communications sometimes include sideways *emoticons,* such as ;-) for a knowing wink and :-(for a frown. But e-mail letters and Internet discussions otherwise lack nonverbal cues to status, personality, and age. Nobody knows what you look or sound like, or anything about your background; you are judged solely on your words. When first meeting an e-mail pen pal face to face, people are often surprised at the person they encounter.

It's also easy to misread e-mailed communications, where the absence of expressive e-motion can make for ambiguous emotion. So can the absence of those vocal nuances by which we signal that a statement is serious, kidding, or sarcastic. Research by Justin Kruger and his colleagues (1999) shows that communicators often think their "just kidding" intent is equally clear, whether e-mailed or spoken. But they commonly exhibit egocentrism by not foreseeing misinterpretations in the absence of nonverbal cues.

Culture and Emotional Expression

OBJECTIVE 39-4 | Discuss the culture-specific and culturally universal aspects of emotional expression, and explain how emotional expressions could enhance survival.

The meaning of gestures varies with the culture. Some years ago, psychologist Otto Klineberg (1938) observed that in Chinese literature people clapped their hands to express worry or disappointment, laughed a great "Ho-Ho" to express anger, and stuck out their tongues to show surprise. Similarly, the North American "thumbs up" and "A-OK" signs would be insults in certain other cultures. (When former U.S. President Richard Nixon made the latter sign in Brazil, he didn't realize he was saying "Let's have sex.") Just how important cultural definitions of gestures can be was demonstrated in 1968, when North Korea publicized photos of supposedly happy officers from a captured U.S. Navy spy ship. In the photo, three of the men raised their middle fingers; they had told captors it was a "Hawaiian good luck sign" (Fleming & Scott, 1991).

Do facial expressions also have different meanings in different cultures? To find out, two investigative teams—one led by Paul Ekman, Wallace Friesen, and others (1975, 1987, 1994), the other by Carroll Izard (1977, 1994)—showed photographs of different facial expressions to people in different parts of the world and asked them to guess the emotion. You can try this matching task yourself by pairing the six emotions with the six faces of **FIGURE 39.4**.

Regardless of your cultural background, you probably did pretty well. A smile's a smile the world around. Ditto for anger, and to a lesser extent the other basic expressions (Elfenbein & Ambady, 1999). (There is no culture where people frown when they are happy.) Despite some differences, cultures and languages share many similarities in the ways they categorize emotions—as anger, fear, and so on.

(Doing good also promotes good feeling, a phenomenon harnessed by some happiness coaches and instructors as they assign people to perform a daily "random act of kindness" and to record the results.)

Despite the significance of happiness, psychology throughout its history has more often focused on negative emotions. Since 1887, *Psychological Abstracts* (a guide to psychology's literature) has included, as of this writing, 12,876 articles mentioning anger, 82,297 mentioning anxiety, and 103,840 mentioning depression. For every 17 articles on these topics, only one dealt with the positive emotions of joy (1450), life satisfaction (5263), or happiness (4727). There is, of course, good reason to focus on negative emotions; they can make our lives miserable and drive us to seek help. But researchers are becoming increasingly interested in **subjective well-being,** assessed either as feelings of happiness (sometimes defined as a high ratio of positive to negative feelings) or as a sense of satisfaction with life. A new *positive psychology* is on the rise.

On this subject, as on so many others, whatever psychological research reveals will have been anticipated by someone. We have inherited many contradictory maxims concerning happiness: that it comes from knowing the truth, or from preserving illusions; from living for the present, or from living for the future; from being with others, or from living in peaceful solitude (Tatarkiewicz, 1976). The list goes on, making the scientific task clear: to ask which of these competing ideas fit reality. Sifting the actual predictors of happiness from the plausible hunches requires research.

The Short Life of Emotional Ups and Downs

OBJECTIVE 40-6 | Discuss some of the daily and longer-term variations in the duration of emotions.

In their happiness research, psychologists have studied influences on both our temporary moods and our long-term life satisfaction. When studying people's hour-by-hour moods, David Watson (2000) and Daniel Kahneman and his colleagues (2004) discovered that positive emotion rises over the early to middle part of most days (**FIGURE 40.4**). Studying people's reports of day-to-day moods confirms that stressful events—an argument, a sick child, a car problem—trigger bad moods. No surprise there. But by the next day, the gloom nearly always lifts (Affleck & others, 1994; Bolger & others, 1989; Stone & Neale, 1984). If anything, people tend to rebound from bad days to a *better*-than-usual good mood the following day. When in a bad mood, can you usually depend on rebounding within a day or two? Are your times of elation similarly hard to sustain? Over the long run, our emotional ups and downs tend to balance.

Apart from prolonged grief over the loss of a loved one or lingering anxiety after a trauma (such as child abuse, rape, or the terrors of war), even tragedy is not permanently depressing. Learning that one is HIV-positive is devastating. But after five weeks of adapting to the grim news, those who tested positive felt less emotionally distraught than they had expected (Sieff & others, 1999). Kidney dialysis patients recognize that their health is relatively poor, yet in their moment-to-moment experiences they report being just as happy as healthy nonpatients (Riis & others, 2005). People who become blind or paralyzed also usually recover near-normal levels of day-to-day happiness (Gerhart & others, 1994; Myers, 1993). Among a sample of Germans incapacitated by ALS (amyotrophic lateral sclerosis, a progressive neurological disease that leads to paralysis), a striking 85 percent rated their quality of life as "satisfactory," "good," or "very good." Moreover, their ratings were not much affected by

FIGURE 40.4

Moods across the day

When psychologist David Watson (2000) sampled nearly 4500 mood reports from 150 people, he found this pattern of variation from the average levels of positive and negative emotions.

Human resilience
Seven weeks after her 1994 wedding, Anna Putt of South Midlands, England, shown here with her husband, Des, suffered a brain-stem stroke that left her "locked-in." For months afterward, she recalls, "I was paralyzed from the neck down and was unable to communicate. These were VERY frightening times. But with encouragement from family, friends, faith, and medical staff, I tried to keep positive." In the ensuing three years, she became able to "talk" (by nodding at letters), to steer an electric wheelchair with her head, and to use a computer (by nodding while wearing spectacles that guide a cursor). Despite her paralysis, she reports that "I enjoy going out in the fresh air. My motto is 'Don't look back, move forward.' God would not want me to stop trying and I have no intention of doing so. Life is what you make of it!"

Courtesy of Anna Putt

"Weeping may tarry for the night, but joy comes with the morning."

Psalms 30:5

"I have a 'fortune cookie maxim' that I'm very proud of: Nothing in life is quite as important as you think it is while you are thinking about it. So, nothing will ever make you as happy as you think it will."

Nobel Laureate psychologist Daniel Kahneman, Gallup interview, "What Were They Thinking?" 2005

whether they were or were not on ventilators or feeding tubes (Kübler & others, 2005). "If you are a paraplegic," explains Daniel Kahneman (2005), "you will gradually start thinking of other things, and the more time you spend thinking of other things the less miserable you are going to be." A major disability often leaves people somewhat less happy than the average person (Lucas, 2005). Yet they reportedly express considerably more happiness than able-bodied people with depression (Schwartz & Estrin, 2004; Kübler & others, in press). Even patients "locked-in" a motionless body "rarely want to die," report Eimar Smith and Mark Delargy (2005), which "counters a popular misconception that such patients would have been better off dead."

In less life-threatening contexts, the pattern continues. Faculty members up for tenure expect their lives would be deflated by a negative decision. Actually, 5 to 10 years later, those denied are not noticeably less happy than those who were awarded tenure, report Daniel Gilbert and colleagues (1998). The same is true of romantic breakups, which feel devastating. The surprising reality: *We overestimate the duration of emotions and underestimate our capacity to adapt.*

Wealth and Well-Being

OBJECTIVE 40-7 | Summarize the findings on the relationship between affluence and happiness.

The emotional impact of dramatically positive events also dissipates sooner than we might expect. Once their rush of euphoria wears off, state lottery winners typically find their overall happiness unchanged (Brickman & others, 1978). Other research confirms that there is much more to well-being than being well-off. Many people (including most German citizens, and most new American collegians, as **FIGURE 40.5** suggests) believe they would be happier if they had more money (Csikszentmihalyi, 1999).

They probably would be—temporarily. Consider:

- Within most affluent countries, people with lots of money are somewhat happier than those who struggle to afford life's basic needs (Di Tella & others, 2001).
- People in rich countries are also somewhat happier than those in poor countries (Steel & Ones, 2002).
- Those who have experienced a recent windfall from a lottery, an inheritance, or a surging economy typically feel some elation (Diener & Oishi, 2000; Gardner & Oswald, 2001). *Losing* money has even more emotional impact (Hobfoll & others, 2003; Kahneman & Tversky, 1979). This illustrates a basic principle, note Roy Baumeister and his colleagues (2001): "Bad is stronger than good." Losses loom larger than gains, cruel words linger longer than kind ones, a bad reputation is more easily acquired than a good one, and pain produces misery more than health produces joy.

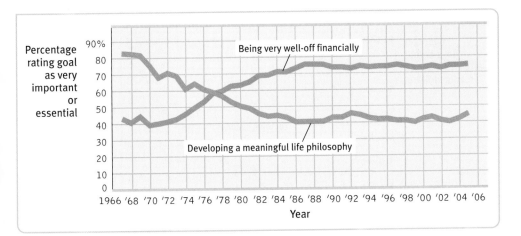

FIGURE 40.5

The changing materialism of entering college students

From 1970 through most of the 1980s, annual surveys of more than 200,000 entering U.S. college students revealed an increasing desire for wealth. (From *The American Freshman* surveys, UCLA, 1966 to 2005.)

Yet in the long run, increased affluence hardly affects happiness. Even in Pakistani and Indian slums, people "are more satisfied than one might expect" (Biswas-Diener & Diener, 2001; Suhail & Chaudry, 2004). Wealth is like health: Its utter absence can breed misery, yet having it is no guarantee of happiness. Growing up poor puts one at risk for certain problems, but so does growing up rich. Children of affluence are at greater-than-normal risk for substance abuse, anxiety, and depression (Luthar & Latendresse, 2005). What matters more than money (assuming one can afford life's necessities with a sense of security) is how you feel about what you have. Those who live with a sense of gratitude—or who cultivate their gratitude by each day writing down what they are grateful for—enjoy greater happiness (McCullough & others, 2004; Watkins, 2004).

Most people agree that money can't buy happiness, but they do believe that a *little* more money would make them a *little* more happy, secure, and comfortable. So, over time, does our happiness grow, little by little, with our paychecks? If his government achieves its 4 percent economic growth-rate goal, noted Australian researcher Richard Eckersley (2001), its people will be twice as rich in 20 years, "and 10 times richer than we were 100 years ago. Can we be sure that this increasing wealth creation is beneficial to personal and social well-being?"

No, we cannot. During the last four decades, the average U.S. citizen's buying power more than doubled. The 1957 after-tax income, inflated to 1995 dollars, was $8500 per person; by 2005, thanks partly to the rich getting richer and to women's increasing employment, it was well above $20,000. Did this more-than-doubled wealth—enabling twice as many cars per person, not to mention iPods, laptops, and camera cell phones—also buy more happiness? Are those of us who enjoy the abundance of the affluent Western world happier with its little levers we can adjust to heat and cool our homes to precisely the desired degree, to release clean water for a warm shower or a cold drink, and to microwave our plentiful food? As **FIGURE 40.6** on the next page shows, the average American, though certainly richer, is not a bit happier. In 1957, some 35 percent said they were "very happy," as did slightly fewer—34 percent—in 2004.

Indeed, if we can judge from statistics—including doubled divorce and teen suicide rates, and mushrooming depression—contemporary Americans seem to be more often miserable. Much the same has been true of the European countries, Australia, and Japan: In these countries, people enjoy better nutrition, health care, education, and science, and they are somewhat happier than those in very poor countries (Diener & Biswas-Diener, 2002; Eckersley, 2000). Yet their increasing real incomes have *not* produced increasing happiness. Such findings lob a bombshell at modern materialism: *Economic growth in affluent countries has provided no apparent boost to morale or social well-being.*

"**Money won't make you happy, Waldron. So instead of a raise, I'm giving a Prozac.**"

" Australians are three times richer than their parents and grandparents were in the 1950s, but they are not happier."

A Manifesto for Well-Being, 2005

" Americans say that money doesn't bring happiness. But it helps you to live with misery in comfort."

Farah Pahlavi, exiled widow of the wealthy Shah of Iran, 2004

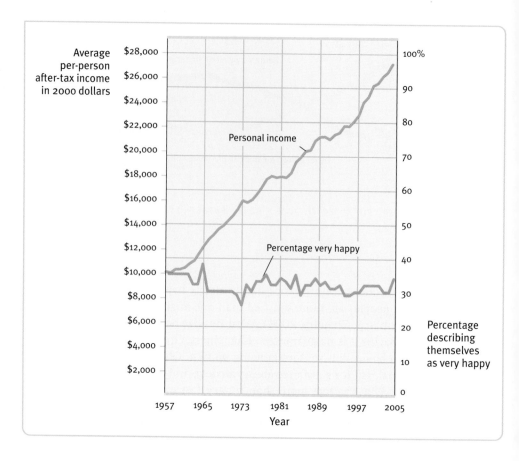

The wealthier-but-no-happier phenomenon even appears in China, which in the decade after 1994 enjoyed a dramatic economic advance. Average household incomes more than doubled, enabling households with a color TV to soar from 40 to 82 percent, those with a landline phone to jump from 10 to 63 percent, and those with cell phones to skyrocket from near zero to 48 percent. Despite this dramatic growth in income and consumption, nationwide Gallup surveys revealed that the proportion of Chinese expressing satisfaction with their lives simultaneously *declined* (Burkholder, 2005a,b). Moreover, the better-off urban Chinese were more likely to feel dissatisfaction than were the poorer rural Chinese. And in the latest World Values Surveys of well-being in 82 countries, the happiest two—Puerto Rico and Mexico—were far from the richest (though the unhappiest, mostly in Eastern Europe, were economically stressed—see **TABLE 40.1**).

Equally interesting are studies showing that individuals who strive hardest for wealth tend to live with lower well-being, a finding that "comes through very strongly in every culture I've looked at," reports Richard Ryan (1999). This is especially so for those seeking money to prove themselves, gain power, or show off rather than support their families (Srivastava & others, 2001). Ryan's collaborator, Tim Kasser (2000, 2002), concludes from their studies that those who instead strive for "intimacy, personal growth, and contribution to the community" experience a higher quality of life. This echoes an earlier finding by H. W. Perkins (1991): Among 800 college alumni surveyed, those preferring a high income and occupational success and prestige to having very close friends and a close marriage were twice as likely as their former classmates to describe themselves as "fairly" or "very" *un*happy. A similar correlation appears among 7167 college students

TABLE 40.1

SUBJECTIVE WELL-BEING (COMBINED HAPPINESS AND SATISFACTION) IN 82 SOCIETIES

The Top 10	The Bottom 10
1. Puerto Rico	73. Bulgaria
2. Mexico	74. Belarus
3. Denmark	75. Georgia
4. Ireland	76. Romania
5. Iceland	77. Moldova
6. Switzerland	78. Russia
7. Northern Ireland	79. Armenia
8. Colombia	80. Ukraine
9. Netherlands	81. Zimbabwe
10. Canada	82. Indonesia

(The United States and Australia were in a virtual tie for fifteenth place.)

Source: Ronald Inglehart and others (2004)

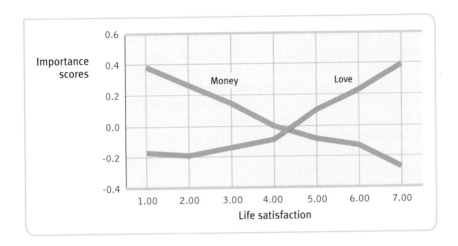

Values and life satisfaction
Among college and university students worldwide, those who report high life satisfaction give priority to love over money. (From Diener & Oishi, 2000.)

surveyed in 41 countries. Those who value love more than money report much higher satisfaction with life than do their money-hungry peers (**FIGURE 40.7**).

If we are both richer and healthier, but no happier, than our grandparents were at our age, should our national priorities focus more on advancing psychological well-being? In Bhutan, says King Jigme Singye Wangchuk, "gross national happiness is more important than gross national product." Bhutan's prime minister frames his annual report in terms of Bhutan's four pillars of progress toward national happiness: "The promotion of equitable and sustainable socio-economic development, preservation and promotion of cultural values, conservation of the natural environment, and establishment of good governance" (Esty, 2004). Ed Diener and Martin Seligman (2004) have proposed ways in which the U.S. Census Bureau and other national organizations might measure national well-being. "If high well-being is the overarching goal of all nations, national indicators of well-being are crucial to assessing the impact of national and corporate policies," they note.

"But on the positive side, money can't buy happiness—so who cares?"

Two Psychological Phenomena: Adaptation and Comparison

OBJECTIVE **40-8** | Describe how adaptation and relative deprivation affect our appraisals of our achievements.

Two psychological principles explain why, for all but the very poor, more money buys no more than a temporary surge of happiness and why our emotions seem attached to elastic bands that pull us back from highs or lows. In its own way, each principle suggests that happiness is relative.

Happiness and Prior Experience

The **adaptation-level phenomenon** describes our tendency to judge various stimuli relative to those we have previously experienced. As psychologist Harry Helson (1898–1977) explained, we adjust our *neutral* levels—the points at which sounds seem neither loud nor soft, temperatures neither hot nor cold, events neither pleasant nor unpleasant—based on our experience. We then notice and react to variations up or down from these levels.

"No happiness lasts for long."
Seneca, Agamemnon, A.D. 60

adaptation-level phenomenon our tendency to form judgments (of sounds, of lights, of income) relative to a neutral level defined by our prior experience.

HI & LOIS

"Continued pleasures wear off. . . . Pleasure is always contingent upon change and disappears with continuous satisfaction."

Dutch psychologist Nico Frijda (1988)

"Shortly after I realized I had plenty, I realized there was plenty more."

"I have also learned why people work so hard to succeed: It is because they envy the things their neighbors have. But it is useless. It is like chasing the wind. . . . It is better to have only a little, with peace of mind, than be busy all the time with both hands, trying to catch the wind."

Ecclesiastes 4:4

"Our poverty became a reality. Not because of our having less, but by our neighbors having more."

Will Campbell, *Brother to a Dragonfly*, 1977

■ **relative deprivation** the perception that one is worse off relative to those with whom one compares oneself.

Thus, if our current condition—our income, academic average, or social prestige—increases, we feel an initial surge of pleasure. We then adapt to this new level of achievement, come to consider it as normal, and require something even better to give us another surge of happiness. From my childhood, I can recall the thrill of watching my family's first 12-inch, black-and-white TV. Now, if the color goes out on our 27-inch TV, I feel deprived. Having adapted upward, I perceive as negative what I once experienced as positive. *The point to remember:* Satisfaction and dissatisfaction, success and failure—all are relative to our recent experience. Satisfaction, as Ryan (1999) says, "has a short half-life."

So, could we ever create a permanent social paradise? Social psychologist Donald Campbell (1975) answered no: If you woke up tomorrow to your utopia—perhaps a world with no bills, no ills, perfect scores, someone who loves you unreservedly—you would feel euphoric, for a time. But then you would gradually recalibrate your adaptation level. Before long you would again sometimes feel gratified (when achievements surpass expectations), sometimes feel deprived (when they fall below), and sometimes feel neutral. That helps explain why material wants can be insatiable—why many a child "needs" just one more Nintendo game. When the victor belongs to the spoils and the possessor is possessed by possessions, adaptation level has run amuck.

Seeking happiness through material achievement requires an ever-increasing abundance of things (which means depletion of the Earth's resources). At the end of his *Chronicles of Narnia*, C. S. Lewis depicts heaven as a place where good things do continually increase, where life is a never-ending story "in which every chapter is better than the one before." Here on Earth the unavoidable ups and downs of real life preclude a perpetual high.

Happiness and Others' Attainments

Happiness is relative not only to our past experience but also to our comparisons with others (Lyubomirsky, 2001). We are always comparing ourselves with others. And whether we feel good or bad depends on who those others are. We are slow-witted or clumsy only when others are smart or agile.

Two examples: To explain the frustration expressed by U.S. Air Corps soldiers during World War II, researchers formulated the concept of **relative deprivation**—the sense that we are worse off than others with whom we compare ourselves. Despite a relatively rapid promotion rate for the group, many soldiers were frustrated about their own promotion rates (Merton & Kitt, 1950). Apparently, seeing so many others being promoted inflated the soldiers' expectations. And when expectations soar above attainments, the result is disappointment. Alex Rodriguez's $252 million, 10-year baseball contract surely made him temporarily happy, but it also diminished other star players' satisfaction with their lesser, multimillion-dollar contracts. Likewise, the economic surge that has made some urban Chinese newly affluent may have fueled among others a sense of relative deprivation.

Such comparisons help us understand why the middle- and upper-income people in a given country, who can compare themselves with the relatively poor, tend to be slightly more satisfied with life than their less fortunate compatriots. Nevertheless, once people reach a moderate income level, further increases do little to increase their happiness. Why? Because as people climb the ladder of success they mostly compare themselves with peers who are at or above their current level (Gruder, 1977; Suls & Tesch, 1978). "Beggars do not envy millionaires, though of course they will envy other beggars who are more successful," noted Bertrand Russell (1930, p. 90). Thus, "Napoleon envied Caesar, Caesar envied Alexander, and Alexander, I daresay, envied Hercules, who never existed. You cannot, therefore, get away from envy by means of success alone, for there will always be in history or legend some person even more successful than you are" (pp. 68–69).

Just as comparing ourselves with those who are better off creates envy, so counting our blessings as we compare ourselves with those less well off boosts our contentment. Marshall Dermer and his colleagues (1979) demonstrated this by asking University of Wisconsin-Milwaukee women to study others' deprivation and suffering. After viewing vivid depictions of how grim life was in Milwaukee in 1900, or after imagining and then writing about various personal tragedies, such as being burned and disfigured, the women expressed greater satisfaction with their own lives. Similarly, when mildly depressed people read about someone who is even more depressed, they feel somewhat better (Gibbons, 1986). "I cried because I had no shoes," states a Persian saying, "until I met a man who had no feet."

The effect of comparison with others helps explain why students of a given level of academic ability tend to have a higher academic self-concept if they attend a school where most other students are not exceptionally able (Marsh & Parker, 1984). If you were near the top of your high school class, you might feel inferior upon entering a college where everyone was near the top of their class.

Predictors of Happiness

OBJECTIVE 40-9 | Summarize the ways that we can influence our own levels of happiness.

If, as the adaptation-level phenomenon implies, our emotions tend to balance around normal, why do some people seem so filled with joy and others so gloomy day after day? What makes one person normally happy and another less so? The answers vary somewhat by culture. Self-esteem matters more to individualistic Westerners, social acceptance matters more to those in communal cultures (Diener & others, 2003). But across many countries, research does reveal several predictors of happiness (TABLE **40.2**)

"I could cry when I think of the years I wasted accumulating money, only to learn that my cheerful disposition is genetic."

Although tasks and relationships affect our happiness, genes matter, too. From their study of 254 identical and fraternal twins, David Lykken and Auke Tellegen (1996) estimated that 50 percent of the difference among people's happiness ratings is heritable. Even identical twins raised apart are often similarly happy. Depending on our outlook and recent experiences, our happiness seems to fluctuate around our "happiness set point," which disposes some people to be ever upbeat and others more negative. But when researchers have followed thousands of lives over two decades, they observe that people's satisfaction with life is not fixed (Fujita & Diener, 2005; Mroczek & Spiro, 2005). Satisfaction may rise or fall, and happiness can be influenced by factors that are under our control. (See Close-Up: How to Be Happier, on the next page.)

Studies of chimpanzees in zoos reveal that happiness in chimpanzees, as rated by 200 employees, is also genetically influenced (Weiss & others, 2000, 2002).

TABLE **40.2**

HAPPINESS IS . . .

Researchers Have Found That Happy People Tend To	However, Happiness Seems Not Much Related to Other Factors, Such As
Have high self-esteem (in individualistic countries).	Age.
Be optimistic, outgoing, and agreeable.	Gender (women are more often depressed, but also more often joyful).
Have close friendships or a satisfying marriage.	Education levels.
Have work and leisure that engage their skills.	Parenthood (having children or not).
Have a meaningful religious faith.	Physical attractiveness.
Sleep well and exercise.	

Source: Summarized from DeNeve & Cooper (1998), Diener & others (2003), Lucas & others (2004), Myers (1993, 2000), and Myers & Diener (1995, 1996).

"Researchers say I'm not happier for being richer, but do you know how much researchers make?"

HOW TO BE HAPPIER

Happiness, like cholesterol level, is genetically influenced. Yet as cholesterol is also influenced by diet and exercise, so our happiness is to some extent under our personal control. Here are some research-based suggestions for improving your mood and increasing your satisfaction with life.

1. ***Realize that enduring happiness doesn't come from financial success.*** People adapt to changing circumstances—even to wealth or a disability. Thus wealth is like health: Its utter absence breeds misery, but having it (or any circumstance we long for) doesn't guarantee happiness.

2. ***Take control of your time.*** Happy people feel in control of their lives, often aided by mastering their use of time. It helps to set goals and break them into daily aims. Although we often overestimate how much we will accomplish in any given day (leaving us frustrated), we generally *underestimate* how much we can accomplish in a year, given just a little progress every day.

3. ***Act happy.*** We can sometimes act ourselves into a frame of mind. Manipulated into a smiling expression, people feel better; when they scowl, the whole world seems to scowl back. So put on a happy face. Talk *as if* you feel positive self-esteem, are optimistic, and are outgoing. Going through the motions can trigger the emotions.

4. ***Seek work and leisure that engage your skills.*** Happy people often are in a zone called "flow"—absorbed in a task that challenges them without overwhelming them. The most expensive forms of leisure (sitting on a yacht) often provide less flow experience than gardening, socializing, or craft work.

5. ***Join the "movement" movement.*** An avalanche of research reveals that aerobic exercise not only promotes health and energy, it also is an antidote for mild depression and anxiety. Sound minds reside in sound bodies. Off your duffs, couch potatoes.

6. ***Give your body the sleep it wants.*** Happy people live active vigorous lives yet reserve time for renewing sleep and solitude. Many people suffer from sleep debt, with resulting fatigue, diminished alertness, and gloomy moods.

7. ***Give priority to close relationships.*** Intimate friendships with those who care deeply about you can help you weather difficult times. Confiding is good for soul and body. Resolve to nurture your closest relationships: to *not* take those closest to you for granted, to display to them the sort of kindness that you display to others, to affirm them, to play together and share together.

8. ***Focus beyond self.*** Reach out to those in need. Happiness increases helpfulness (those who feel good do good). But doing good also makes one feel good.

9. ***Be grateful.*** People who keep a gratitude journal—who pause each day to reflect on some positive aspect of their lives (their health, friends, family, freedom, education, senses, natural surroundings, and so on) experience heightened well-being.

10. ***Nurture your spiritual self.*** For many people, faith provides a support community, a reason to focus beyond self, and a sense of purpose and hope. That helps explain why people active in faith communities report greater than average happiness and often cope well with crisis.

Digested from David G. Myers, *The Pursuit of Happiness* (Avon Books)

FIGURE 40.8
Levels of analysis for the study of emotion
As with other psychological phenomena, researchers explore emotion at biological, psychological, and social-cultural levels.

Our studies of happiness, regardless of their source and duration, remind us that emotions combine physiological activation (left hemisphere especially), expressive behaviors (huge smile), and conscious experience, including thoughts (I was so ready for that test) and feelings (pride, satisfaction). Fear, anger, happiness, and so much else have this in common: They are biopsychosocial phenomena (**FIGURE 40.8**). Our genetic predispositions, brain activity, outlooks, experiences, relationships, and cultures jointly form us.

>> LEARNING OUTCOMES

Experienced Emotion

OBJECTIVE 40-1 | Name several basic emotions, and describe two dimensions psychologists use to differentiate emotions.

Izard's list of 10 basic emotions includes joy, interest-excitement, surprise, sadness, anger, disgust, contempt, fear, shame, and guilt. Other psychologists include pride and love. Emotions can be placed along two dimensions: *arousal* (high versus low) and *valence* (pleasant, or positive, versus unpleasant, or negative).

OBJECTIVE 40-2 | State two ways we learn our fears.

We learn specific fears through *conditioning* (associating emotions with specific situations) and through *observational learning* (watching others display fear in response to certain events or surroundings).

OBJECTIVE 40-3 | Discuss some of the biological components of fear.

We are biologically prepared to learn some fears (snakes, spiders) but not others (fast driving, electricity). The amygdala plays a key role in fear learning, associating fear with specific situations. The amygdala receives information from cortical areas that process emotion, and it sends information to other areas that produce the bodily symptoms of fear. We may be genetically predisposed to be fearful or fearless.

OBJECTIVE 40-4 | Identify some common triggers and consequences of anger, and assess the catharsis hypothesis.

Frustrating or insulting actions we interpret as willful, unjustified, and avoidable may evoke anger. Research does not support the *catharsis hypothesis*—the idea that releasing negative energy will calm aggressive tendencies. Venting rage may calm us temporarily, but in the long run it may actually amplify anger. Anger is better handled by waiting until the level of physical arousal diminishes, calming oneself, and expressing grievances in ways that promote reconciliation. When reconciliation fails, forgiveness can reduce one's anger and its physical symptoms.

OBJECTIVE 40-5 | Describe how the feel-good, do-good phenomenon works, and discuss the importance of research on subjective well-being.

The *feel-good, do-good phenomenon* is our increased willingness to help others when we are in a good mood. Research on the causes and consequences of subjective well-being (self-perceived happiness or satisfaction with life) is supplementing psychology's traditional focus on negative emotions.

OBJECTIVE 40-6 | Discuss some of the daily and longer-term variations in the duration of emotions.

Negative emotion is highest just after we wake up and before we go to sleep. Positive emotion rises gradually, peaking about seven hours after we rise, then falls gradually. The moods triggered by the day's good or bad events seldom last beyond that day. Even significant bad events, such as a serious illness, seldom destroy happiness permanently.

OBJECTIVE 40-7 | Summarize the findings on the relationship between affluence and happiness.

Money can help us avoid pain (and thereby increase happiness) by enabling better nutrition, health care, education, and science. Increases in wealth can also increase happiness in the short term, but in the longer term, affluence does not increase happiness at either the individual or national level.

OBJECTIVE 40-8 | Describe how adaptation and relative deprivation affect our appraisals of our achievements.

The *adaptation-level phenomenon* is our tendency to assess stimuli (including material possessions) by contrasting them with a neutral level that changes with our experience. The *relative-deprivation principle* is our perception that we are less well off than others with whom we compare ourselves. Thus, happiness is relative to both our past experience and our comparisons with others.

OBJECTIVE 40-9 | Summarize the ways that we can influence our own levels of happiness.

Happiness is in part genetically influenced, and in part under our own control. Research-based suggestions for improving our own happiness are (1) realizing that enduring happiness doesn't come from financial success; (2) taking control of one's time; (3) acting happy; (4) seeking work and leisure that engage one's skills; (5) exercising regularly; (6) getting adequate sleep; (7) giving priority to close relationships; (8) focusing beyond oneself; (9) being grateful for what we have; and (10) nurturing our spiritual selves.

TERMS AND CONCEPTS TO REMEMBER

catharsis, p. 40-5

feel-good, do-good phenomenon, p. 40-6

subjective well-being, p. 40-7

adaptation-level phenomenon, p. 40-11

relative deprivation, p. 40-12

TEST YOURSELF

1. What things do (and do not) predict self-reported happiness?

(Answer in Appendix B.)

ASK YOURSELF

1. If we learn our emotional responses, we may be able to learn new responses to replace old ones. Would you like to change any of your emotional responses? Do you feel you are too easily provoked to anger or fear, for instance? How might you go about changing your behavior or your thinking in order to change your emotional reactions?

>WEB

Multiple-choice *self-tests* and more may be found at www.worthpublishers.com/myers.

ANOTHER VOICE ON: STRESS AND HEALTH

AUDRE LORDE (1934–1992), "LATER," FROM *THE CANCER JOURNALS*, 1980

October 5, 1978

If I said this all didn't matter I would be lying. I see this as a serious break in my work/living, but also as a serious chance to learn something that I can share for use. And I mourn the women who limit their loss to the physical loss alone, who do not move into the whole terrible meaning of mortality as both weapon and power. After all, what could we possibly be afraid of after having admitted to ourselves that we had dealt face to face with death and not embraced it? For once we accept the actual existence of our dying, who can ever have power over us again? Now I am anxious for more living—to sample and partake of the sweetness of each moment . . .

Stress and Health

OBJECTIVE 41-1 | Identify some behavior-related causes of illness and death, and describe health psychology's contribution to the field of behavioral medicine.

No one needs to be told that psychological states cause physical reactions. Nervous about an important encounter, we feel stomach butterflies. Anxious over speaking in public, we frequent the bathroom. Smoldering over a conflict with a family member, we get a splitting headache.

If such stress endures, it may also bring on (in those physiologically predisposed) skin rashes, asthma attacks, or high blood pressure. This mind-body connection was strikingly apparent in an inadvertent experiment conducted by British Airways on an April 23, 1999, flight from San Francisco to London. Three hours after takeoff, a mistakenly played message told passengers the plane was about to crash into the sea. Although the flight crew immediately recognized the error and tried to calm the terrified passengers, several required medical assistance (Associated Press, 1999).

Prolonged stress—together with unhealthy behaviors—can put us at serious risk. Centers for Disease Control researchers have attributed half of the deaths in the United States to people's behavior—to cigarette smoking, alcohol abuse, unprotected sex, ignoring doctors' orders, insufficient exercise, illicit drugs, and poor nutrition (Mokdad & others, 2004). Modify these behavioral sources of illness and we might lessen suffering, increase life expectancy, and enhance quality of life. To pursue these goals, psychologists and physicians created the interdisciplinary field of **behavioral medicine,** integrating behavioral and medical knowledge.

Health psychology provides psychology's contribution to behavioral medicine. Its numbers include many of the 3900 psychologists who were recently counted on the faculties of Canadian and U.S. medical schools (Williams & Kohut, 1999). In the early 1950s, the average medical school had 2 faculty psychologists; at the century's end, each averaged about 30 (Sheridan, 1999).

For psychologists, health is more than "merely the slowest possible rate at which one can die" (Prairie Home Companion, 1999). Health psychologists ask: How do our emotions, personality, attitudes, and behaviors influence our risk of disease (Module 41)? How can we better cope with stress to prevent illness and promote health and well-being, and how do our perceptions of a situation determine the stress we feel (Module 42)? How can we reduce our vulnerability to stress- and behavior-related health problems (Module 43)?

■ **behavioral medicine** an interdisciplinary field that integrates behavioral and medical knowledge and applies that knowledge to health and disease.

■ **health psychology** the application of psychological concepts and research to illness prevention and treatment and to health advancement.

41

Stress and Illness

Walking along the path toward his mountain campsite, Karl hears a rustle at his feet. As he glimpses a rattlesnake, his body mobilizes: His muscles tense, his adrenaline flows, his heart pounds, and he flees, racing to the security of camp. Once there, Karl's muscles gradually relax and his heart rate and breathing ease.

At about the same time, Karen leaves her suburban apartment and, delayed by road construction, arrives at the parking lot of the commuter train station just in time to see the 8:05 pull away. Catching the next train, she arrives in the city late and elbows her way through crowds of rush-hour pedestrians. Once at her bank office, she apologizes to her first client, who wonders where Karen has been and why his quarterly investment report is not ready. Karen does her best to mollify the client. Afterward, she notices her tense muscles, clenched teeth, and churning stomach.

Karl's response to stress saved his life; Karen's, if chronic, could increase her risk of serious illness or stress-linked health problems. Moreover, feeling under pressure, she might sleep and exercise less and smoke and drink more, further endangering her long-term health.

Stress and Stressors

OBJECTIVE 41-2 | Discuss the role of appraisal in the way we respond to stressful events.

Four in 10 people frequently report experiencing stress (Saad, 2001). What are they talking about? Stress is a slippery concept. It sometimes describes threats or challenges ("Karen was under a lot of stress"), other times our responses ("When Karl saw the rattler, he experienced acute stress"). Karen's missed train was a *stressor,* Karl's physical and emotional responses were a *stress reaction,* and the process by which Karen and Karl related to their environments was *stress.*

Thus, **stress** is not just a stimulus or a response. It is the process by which we appraise and cope with environmental threats and challenges (**FIGURE 41.1**). Stress arises less from events themselves than from how we appraise them (Lazarus, 1998). One person, alone in a house, dismisses its creaking sounds and experiences no stress; someone else suspects an intruder and becomes alarmed. One person regards a new job as a welcome challenge; someone else appraises it as risking failure.

FIGURE 41.1

Stress appraisal

The events of our lives flow through a psychological filter. How we appraise an event influences how much stress we experience and how effectively we respond.

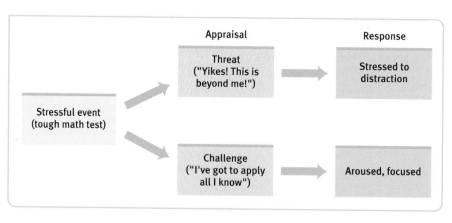

When short-lived, or when perceived as challenges, stressors can have positive effects. A momentary stress can mobilize the immune system for fending off infections and healing wounds (Segerstrom & Miller, 2004). Stress also arouses and motivates us to conquer problems. Championship athletes, successful entertainers, and great teachers and leaders all thrive and excel when aroused by a challenge (Blascovich & others, 2004). Having conquered cancer or rebounded from a lost job, some people emerge with stronger self-esteem and a deepened spirituality and sense of purpose. Indeed, some stress early in life is conducive to later emotional resilience and physical growth (Landauer & Whiting, 1979). Adversity can beget growth. The Chinese character for *crisis*, note Virginia O'Leary and Jeannette Ickovics (1995), combines the symbols for *danger* and *opportunity*.

But stressors can also threaten us. And experiencing severe or prolonged stress may harm us. Children's physiological responses to severe child abuse put them at later risk of chronic disease (Repetti & others, 2002). Those who had post-traumatic stress reactions to heavy combat in the Vietnam War went on to suffer greatly elevated rates of circulatory, digestive, respiratory, and infectious diseases (Boscarino, 1997).

The Stress Response System

OBJECTIVE 41-3 | Describe the dual-track system by which our body responds to stress, and identify the three phases of the general adaptation syndrome.

Medical interest in stress dates back to Hippocrates (460–377 B.C.). But it was not until the 1920s that physiologist Walter Cannon (1929) confirmed that the stress response is part of a unified mind-body system. He observed that extreme cold, lack of oxygen, and emotion-arousing incidents all trigger an outpouring of the stress hormones epinephrine and norepinephrine from the adrenal glands. This outpouring is but one part of the sympathetic nervous system's response. When alerted by any of a number of brain pathways, the sympathetic nervous system increases heart rate and respiration, diverts blood from digestion to the skeletal muscles, dulls pain, and releases sugar and fat from the body's stores—all to prepare the body for the wonderfully adaptive response that Cannon called *fight or flight*.

Since Cannon's time, physiologists have identified an additional stress response system. On orders from the cerebral cortex (via the hypothalamus and pituitary gland), the outer part of the adrenal glands secretes *glucocorticoid* stress hormones such as *cortisol*. The two stress hormone systems work at different speeds, explains biologist Robert Sapolsky (2003): "In a fight-or-flight scenario, epinephrine is the one handing out guns; glucocorticoids are the ones drawing up blueprints for new aircraft carriers needed for the war effort" (FIGURE 41.2).

There are alternatives to fight-or-flight. One is a common response to the stress of a loved one's death: Withdraw. Pull back. Conserve energy. Another, especially common among women, report Shelley Taylor and her colleagues (2000), is to seek and give support: "Tend and befriend."

■ **stress** the process by which we perceive and respond to certain events, called *stressors*, that we appraise as threatening or challenging.

FIGURE 41.2
Two-track stress response system
Our body responds to stress with a two-track system. (1) The sympathetic nervous system prompts the release of the stress hormones epinephrine and norepinephrine from nerve endings in the *inner* part of the adrenal glands. (2) The cerebral cortex, by way of the hypothalamus and pituitary gland, directs the release of glucocorticoid stress hormones from the *outer* part of the adrenal glands. Both systems trigger fight-or-flight physiological effects in our bodies, such as faster breathing and tense muscles.

(2) Cerebral cortex orchestrates release of glucocorticoids

Cerebral cortex (perceives stressor)

Hypothalamus
Amygdala
Pituitary gland

(1) Sympathetic nervous system triggers release of epinephrine and norepinephrine.

Arteries widen

Lungs work faster

Heart beats faster

Muscles tense

Adrenal glands release hormones

Stomach, digestion shuts down

Canadian scientist Hans Selye's (1936, 1976) 40 years of research on stress extended Cannon's findings and helped make stress a major concept in both psychology and medicine. The story of how Selye arrived at his concept of the stress response is one worth remembering in times of intellectual discouragement. Hoping to discover a new sex hormone, Selye injected rats with ovarian hormone extract. He detected three effects: enlargement of the adrenal cortex, shrinkage of the thymus gland (which contains disease-fighting white blood cells), and bleeding ulcers. Because no known hormone had ever produced such symptoms, Selye was elated: "At the age of 28, I seemed to be already on the track of a new hormone."

Before long, Selye's elation turned to disappointment. When he injected the rats with other fluids, he observed the same effects: adrenal enlargement, thymus shrinkage, and bleeding ulcers. Alas, he concluded, the effects were *not* due to a new hormone:

> All my dreams of discovering a new hormone were shattered. All the time and all the materials that went into this long study were wasted. . . . I became so depressed that for a few days I could not do any work at all. I just sat in my laboratory, brooding. . . . The ensuing period of introverted contemplation turned out to be the decisive factor in my whole career; it pointed the way for all my subsequent work. . . . As I repetitiously continued to go over my ill-fated experiments and their possible interpretation, it suddenly struck me that one could look at them from an entirely different angle. If there was such a thing as a single nonspecific reaction of the body to damage of any kind, . . . the general medical implications of the syndrome would be enormous! (1976, pp. 24–26)

To verify his hunch, Selye studied animals' reactions to various other stressors, such as electric shock, surgical trauma, and immobilizing restraint. He discovered that the body's adaptive response to stress was so general—like a single burglar alarm that sounds no matter what intrudes—that he called it the **general adaptation syndrome (GAS).**

Selye saw the GAS as having three phases (**FIGURE 41.3**). Let's say you suffer a physical or emotional trauma. In Phase 1, you experience an *alarm reaction* due to the sudden activation of your sympathetic nervous system. Your heart rate zooms. Blood is diverted to your skeletal muscles. You feel the faintness of shock. With your resources mobilized, you are now ready to fight the challenge during Phase 2, *resistance.* Your temperature, blood pressure, and respiration remain high, and there is a sudden outpouring of hormones. If persistent, the stress may eventually deplete your body's

FIGURE 41.3
Selye's general adaptation syndrome
This girl being carried to freedom and medical attention managed to escape her terrorist captors in a 2004, three-day Chechnya school holdup. Experiencing such a trauma, the body enters an alarm phase of temporary shock. From this it rebounds, as stress resistance rises. If the stress is prolonged, as it was for the 400 school hostages and their waiting loved ones, wear and tear may lead to exhaustion.

EPA/Yuri Kochetkov/Landov

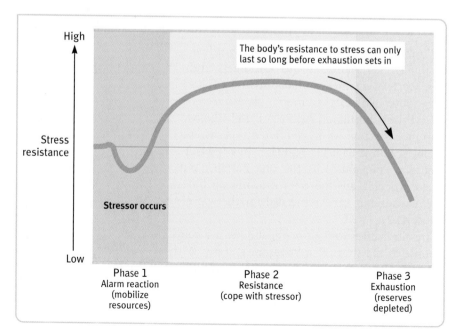

reserves during Phase 3, *exhaustion*. With exhaustion, you are more vulnerable to illness or even, in extreme cases, collapse and death.

Few medical experts today quarrel with Selye's basic point: Although the human body comes designed to cope with temporary stress, prolonged stress can produce physical deterioration. In one recent study, women who suffered enduring stress as caregivers for children with serious disorders displayed a symptom that is a normal part of the aging process—shorter bits of DNA at the ends of their chromosomes (Epel & others, 2004). When these DNA pieces, called *telomeres*, get too short, the cell can no longer divide, and it ultimately dies. The most stressed women had cells that looked a decade older than their chronological age, which may help explain why severe stress seems to age people. Even fearful, easily stressed rats have been found to die sooner (after about 600 days) than their more confident siblings, which average 700-day life spans (Cavigelli & McClintock, 2003).

Other studies have taken MRI brain scans of people who have experienced a prolonged flood of stress hormones, due to sustained child abuse, combat, or an endocrine disease (Sapolsky, 1999). Most have a shrunken *hippocampus*, the inner brain structure vital to laying down explicit (declarative) memories. In animals, too, various stresses—being subordinate in a group, being physically restrained, being isolated—can cause hippocampal tissue to shrink (McEwen, 1998, 2002). Such findings serve as further incentives to today's *health psychologists*, who have joined with physicians to create the interdisciplinary field of *behavioral medicine*. Health psychologists are actively exploring such questions as What causes stress? And how does stress affect us?

Stressful Life Events

OBJECTIVE 41-4 | Discuss the health consequences of catastrophes, significant life changes, and daily hassles.

Research has focused on our responses to three types of stressors: catastrophes, significant life changes, and daily hassles.

Catastrophes

Catastrophes are unpredictable large-scale events, such as war and natural disasters, that nearly everyone appraises as threatening. Although people often provide one another with aid as well as comfort after such events, the health consequences can be significant. In the three weeks after the 9/11 terrorist attacks, two-thirds of Americans surveyed by University of Michigan researchers said they were having some trouble concentrating and sleeping (Wahlberg, 2001). In another national survey, New Yorkers were especially likely to report such symptoms (NSF, 2001). Sleeping pill prescriptions rose by a reported 28 percent in the New York area (HMHL, 2002).

■ general adaptation syndrome (GAS) Selye's concept of the body's adaptive response to stress in three stages—alarm, resistance, exhaustion.

Les Stone/Corbis

Toxic stress

On the day of its 1994 earthquake, Los Angeles experienced a fivefold increase in sudden-death heart attacks—especially in the first two hours after the quake and near its epicenter. Physical exertion (running, lifting debris) was a factor in only 13 percent of the deaths, leaving stress as the likely trigger for the others (Muller & Verier, 1996).

■ **coronary heart disease** the clogging of the vessels that nourish the heart muscle; the leading cause of death in many developed countries.

Do other community disasters usually produce effects this great? After digesting data from 52 studies of catastrophic floods, hurricanes, and fires, Anthony Rubonis and Leonard Bickman (1991) found the typical effect more modest but nonetheless genuine. In disaster's wake, rates of psychological disorders such as depression and anxiety rose an average 17 percent. Refugees fleeing their homeland also suffer increased rates of psychological disorder. Their stress stems from the trauma of uprooting and family separation, and from the challenges of adjusting to a foreign culture's new language, ethnicity, climate, and social norms (Pipher, 2002; Williams & Berry, 1991).

Significant Life Changes

The second type of life-event stressor is a significant personal life change—leaving home, the death of a loved one, the loss of a job, a marriage, a divorce. Life transitions and insecurities are often keenly felt during young adulthood. That helps explain why, when 15,000 Canadian adults were asked whether "You are trying to take on too many things at once," responses indicated highest stress levels among the youngest adults (**FIGURE 41.4**). The same is true of Americans: Half of adults under age 50 report "frequent" stress, as do fewer than 30 percent of those over 50 (Saad, 2001).

Some psychologists study the health effects of life changes by following people over time to see if such events precede illnesses. Others compare the life changes recalled by those who have or have not suffered a specific health problem, such as a heart attack. A review of these studies commissioned by the U.S. National Academy of Sciences revealed that people recently widowed, fired, or divorced are more vulnerable to disease (Dohrenwend & others, 1982). A Finnish study of 96,000 widowed people confirmed the phenomenon: Their risk of death doubled in the week following their partner's death (Kaprio & others, 1987). Experiencing a cluster of crises puts one even more at risk.

Daily Hassles

Our happiness stems less from enduring good fortune than from our response to daily events—a perfect exam score, a gratifying e-mail, your team's winning the big game. This principle works for negative events, too. Everyday annoyances—rush-hour traffic, aggravating housemates, long lines at the store, too many things to do, e-mail spam, and obnoxious cell-phone talkers—may be the most significant sources of stress (Kohn & Macdonald, 1992; Lazarus, 1990; Ruffin, 1993). Although some people can simply shrug off such hassles, others are "driven up the wall" by them.

FIGURE 41.4
Chronic stress, by age
As Canadians age, feelings of chronic stress tend to subside. (Data from Statistics Canada, 1999.)

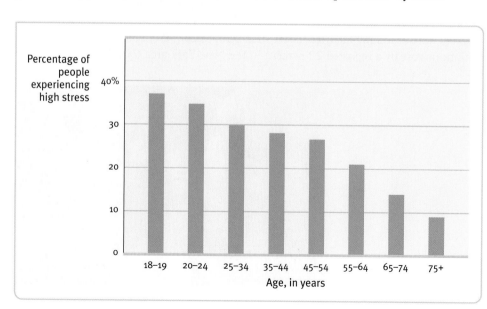

Over time, these little stressors can add up and take a toll on our health and well-being. Hypertension (high blood pressure) rates are high among residents of urban ghettos, where the stresses that accompany poverty, unemployment, solo parenting, and overcrowding are part of daily life for some people. And these daily pressures may be compounded by racism, which—like other stressors—can have both psychological and physical consequences. Thinking that some of the people you encounter each day will distrust you, dislike you, or doubt your abilities makes daily life stressful. Rodney Clark and his colleagues (1999) found that this stress took a toll on the health of many African-Americans, driving up blood pressure levels.

> "It's not the large things that send a man to the madhouse . . . no, it's the continuing series of small tragedies . . . not the death of his love but the shoelace that snaps with no time left."
>
> Charles Bukowski, cited by Lazarus in Wallis, 1983

Stress and the Heart

OBJECTIVE 41-5 | Discuss the role of stress in causing coronary heart disease, and contrast Type A and Type B personalities.

In the past century, behavior-related illnesses have emerged as the major causes of death. Stress, it seems, can put us at risk for one of today's four leading causes of serious illness and death: heart disease, cancer, stroke, and chronic lung disease (FIGURE 41.5).

Elevated blood pressure is just one of the factors that increase the risk of **coronary heart disease,** the closing of the vessels that nourish the heart muscle. Although infrequent before 1900, this condition became by the 1950s North America's leading cause of death, and it remains so today. In addition to hypertension and a family history of the disease, many behavioral and physiological factors—smoking, obesity, a high-fat diet, physical inactivity, and an elevated cholesterol level—increase the risk of heart disease. The psychological factors of stress and personality also play a big role.

In 1956, cardiologists Meyer Friedman, Ray Rosenman, and their colleagues stumbled upon an indication of how big that role is (Friedman & Ulmer, 1984). While studying the eating behavior of San Francisco Junior League women and their husbands, Friedman and Rosenman discovered that the women consumed as much cholesterol and fat as their husbands did, yet they were far less susceptible to heart disease. Was it because of their female sex hormones? No, the researchers surmised, because African-American women (with the same sex hormones but facing more stress than the white Junior Leaguers) were as prone to heart disease as their husbands.

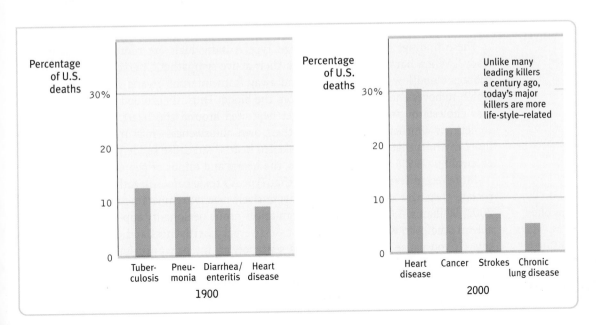

FIGURE 41.5

The four leading causes of death in the United States in 1900 and 2000 With the conquering of the major infectious diseases, diseases influenced by behavior have now emerged as the major causes of death. The story is much the same in Canada, Australia, New Zealand, and most European countries. (From National Center for Health Statistics, *World Health Statistics Annual,* and Statistics Canada, 2002.)

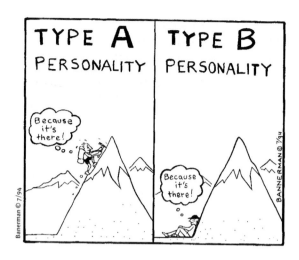

In both India and America, Type A bus drivers are literally hard-driving: They brake, pass, and honk their horns more often than their more easygoing Type B colleagues (Evans & others, 1987).

" The fire you kindle for your enemy often burns you more than him."

Chinese proverb

The Junior League president thought she knew the answer: "It's the stress they have to face in their businesses, day in, day out," she said sadly. "Why, when my husband comes home at night, it takes at least one martini just to unclench his jaws."

To test the idea that stress increases vulnerability to heart disease, Friedman and Rosenman measured the blood cholesterol level and clotting speed of 40 tax accountants. From January through March, both of these coronary warning indicators were completely normal. Then, as the accountants began scrambling to finish their clients' tax returns before the April 15 filing deadline, their cholesterol and clotting measures rose to dangerous levels. In May and June, with the deadline past, the measures returned to normal. The researchers' hunch had paid off: Stress predicted heart attack risk.

The stage was set for Friedman and Rosenman's classic nine-year study of more than 3000 healthy men aged 35 to 59. At the start of the study, they interviewed each man for 15 minutes about his work and eating habits. During the interview, they noted the man's manner of talking and other behavioral patterns. Those who seemed the most reactive, competitive, hard-driving, impatient, time-conscious, supermotivated, verbally aggressive, and easily angered they called **Type A.** The roughly equal number who were more easygoing they called **Type B.** Which group do you suppose turned out to be the most coronary-prone?

By the time the study was complete, 257 men had suffered heart attacks; 69 percent of them were Type A. Moreover, not one of the "pure" Type Bs—the most mellow and laid-back of their group—had suffered a heart attack.

As often happens in science, this exciting discovery provoked enormous public interest. But after the honeymoon period, in which the finding seemed definitive and revolutionary, other researchers began asking: Is the finding reliable? If so, what is the toxic component of the Type A profile: Time-consciousness? Competitiveness? Anger?

In relaxed situations, the arousal of Type As and Type Bs is no different. But when harassed, given a challenge, or threatened with a loss of control, Type A individuals are more physiologically reactive. Their hormonal secretions, pulse rate, and blood pressure soar, while Type Bs remain calm (Lyness, 1993). For example, when Redford Williams (1989) asked Duke University men to do simple math problems (with a prize for the fastest), the Type A students' stress-hormone levels rose to more than double those of their Type B classmates. These hormones accelerate the buildup of plaque (scarlike masses formed by cholesterol deposits) on the artery walls. And that produces atherosclerosis ("hardening" of the arteries), high blood pressure, and increased risk of strokes and heart attacks (Schneiderman & others, 1989).

These findings suggest that reactive Type A individuals are more often "combat ready." When harassed or challenged, their active sympathetic nervous system redistributes bloodflow to the muscles and away from internal organs such as the liver, which removes cholesterol and fat from the blood. Thus, their blood may contain excess cholesterol and fat that later get deposited around the heart. Further stress— sometimes conflicts brought on by their own abrasiveness—may trigger the altered heart rhythms that, in those with weakened hearts, can cause sudden death (Kamarck & Jennings, 1991). In important ways, the hearts and minds of people interact.

More recent research has revealed that Type A's toxic core is negative emotions—especially the anger associated with an aggressively reactive temperament (Smith & Ruiz, 2002; Williams, 1993). The effect of an anger-prone personality appears most noticeably in studies in which interviewers assess verbal assertiveness and emotional intensity. (If you pause in the middle of a sentence, an intense, anger-prone person may jump in and finish it for you.) Among young and middle-aged adults, those who react with anger over little things are the most coronary-prone. One study followed 13,000 middle-aged people for five years. Among those with normal blood pressure, people who had scored high on anger were three times more likely to have had heart attacks, even after researchers controlled for smoking and weight (Williams & others, 2000). Another study followed 1055 male medical students over an average of 36 years. Those who had reported being hot-tempered were five times more likely to have had a heart at-

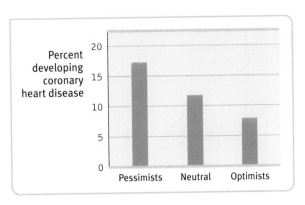

FIGURE 41.6
Pessimism and heart disease
A Harvard School of Public Health team found pessimistic adult men at doubled risk of developing heart disease over a 10-year period. (From Kubzansky & others, 2001.)

tack by age 55 (Chang & others, 2002). As Charles Spielberger and Perry London (1982) put it, rage "seems to lash back and strike us in the heart muscle."

Pessimism seems to be similarly toxic. Laura Kubzansky and her colleagues (2001) studied 1306 initially healthy men who a decade earlier had scored as optimists, pessimists, or neither. Over the decade, pessimists were more than twice as likely as optimists to develop heart disease, even after other risk factors such as smoking had been ruled out (**FIGURE 41.6**).

Depression, too, can be lethal. The accumulated evidence from 57 studies suggests that "depression substantially increases the risk of death, especially death by unnatural causes and cardiovascular disease" (Wulsin & others, 1999). One study of 7406 women age 67 or older found that among those with no depressive symptoms, 7 percent died within six years, as did 24 percent of those with six or more depressive symptoms (Whooley & Browner, 1998). In the years following a heart attack, people with high scores for depression are four times likelier than their low-scoring counterparts to develop further heart problems (Frasure-Smith & Lespérance, 2005). Depression is disheartening.

> "A cheerful heart is a good medicine, but a downcast spirit dries up the bones."
> Proverbs 17:22

Stress and Susceptibility to Disease

OBJECTIVE 41-6 | Distinguish between a psychophysiological illness and hypochondriasis.

Not so long ago, the term *psychosomatic* described psychologically caused physical symptoms. To laypeople, the term implied that the symptoms were unreal—"merely" psychosomatic. To avoid such connotations and to better describe the genuine physiological effects of psychological states, most experts today refer instead to stress-related **psychophysiological illnesses,** such as hypertension and some headaches. Let's take a closer look at some ways stress also affects our resistance to disease.

Stress and the Immune System

OBJECTIVE 41-7 | Describe the effect of stress on immune system functioning.

Hundreds of new experiments reveal the nervous and endocrine systems' influence on the immune system (Sternberg, 2001). Your immune system is a complex surveillance system that defends your body by isolating and destroying bacteria, viruses, and other foreign substances. This system includes two types of white blood cells, called **lymphocytes.** *B lymphocytes* form in the *bone marrow* and release antibodies that fight bacterial infections. *T lymphocytes* form in the *thymus* and other lymphatic tissue and attack cancer cells, viruses, and foreign substances—even "good" ones, such as transplanted organs. Another agent of the immune system is the *macrophage* ("big eater"), which identifies, pursues, and ingests harmful invaders (**FIGURE 41.7** on the next page). Age, nutrition, genetics, body temperature, and stress all influence the immune system's activity.

■ **Type A** Friedman and Rosenman's term for competitive, hard-driving, impatient, verbally aggressive, and anger-prone people.

■ **Type B** Friedman and Rosenman's term for easygoing, relaxed people.

■ **psychophysiological illness** literally, "mind-body" illness; any stress-related physical illness, such as hypertension and some headaches. *Note:* This is distinct from *hypochondriasis*—misinterpreting normal physical sensations as symptoms of a disease.

■ **lymphocytes** the two types of white blood cells that are part of the body's immune system: *B lymphocytes* form in the *bone marrow* and release antibodies that fight bacterial infections; *T lymphocytes* form in the *thymus* and other lymphatic tissue and attack cancer cells, viruses, and foreign substances.

FIGURE 41.7
The immune system in action

A large macrophage (at top) is about to trap and ingest a tiny bacterium (lower right). Macrophages constantly patrol our bodies in search of invaders—such as this *Escherichia coli* bacterium—and debris, such as worn-out red blood cells.

"In the eyes of God or biology or what have you, it is just very important to have women."

Immunologist Normal Talal (1995)

Your immune system can err in two directions. Responding too strongly, it may attack the body's own tissues, causing arthritis or an allergic reaction. Underreacting, it may allow a dormant herpes virus to erupt or cancer cells to multiply. Women are immunologically stronger than men (Morell, 1995), making them less susceptible to infections. But this very strength also makes them more susceptible to self-attacking diseases, such as lupus and multiple sclerosis.

Your immune system is not a headless horseman. The brain regulates the secretion of stress hormones, which suppress the disease-fighting lymphocytes. Thus, when animals are physically restrained, given unavoidable electric shocks, or subjected to noise, crowding, cold water, social defeat, or maternal separation, their immune systems become less active (Maier & others, 1994). One study monitored immune responses in 43 monkeys over six months (Cohen & others, 1992). Twenty-one were stressed by being housed with new roommates—three or four new monkeys—each month. (To empathize with the monkeys, recall the stress of leaving home to attend school or summer camp, and imagine having to repeat this experience monthly.) Compared with monkeys left in stable groups, the socially disrupted monkeys experienced weakened immune systems. Stress similarly depresses the immune system of humans. Consider:

- Surgical wounds heal more slowly in stressed animals and humans. In one experiment, dental students received *punch wounds* (precise small holes punched in the skin). Compared with wounds placed during summer vacation, those placed three days before a major exam healed 40 percent more slowly. In fact, report Janice Kiecolt-Glaser and her co-researchers (1998), "no student healed as rapidly during this stressful period as during vacation."

- In another experiment, 47 percent of participants living stress-filled lives developed colds after a virus was dropped in their noses, as did only 27 percent of those living relatively free of stress (**FIGURE 41.8**). In follow-up research, the happiest and most relaxed people were likewise markedly less vulnerable to an experimentally delivered cold virus (Cohen & others, 2003).

FIGURE 41.8
Stress and colds

In an experiment by Sheldon Cohen and colleagues (1991), people with the highest life stress scores were also most vulnerable when exposed to an experimentally delivered cold virus.

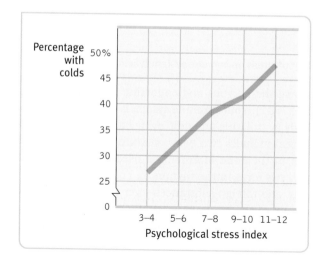

- Data combined from 23 studies reveal that family caregivers of people with dementia exhibit a 15 percent below-normal immune antibody response and a 23 percent increase in stress hormones (Vitaliano & others, 2003). Other data, assembled from 293 studies, confirm that chronic stress causes wear and tear on the immune system (Segerstrom & Miller, 2004).
- Managing stress may be life-sustaining. The one personality trait shared by 169 centenarians (people over 100) was their ability to manage stress well (Perls & others, 1999).

The stress effect on immunity makes physiological sense (Maier & others, 1994). It takes energy to fight infections, produce inflammations, and maintain fevers. Thus, when diseased, our bodies reduce muscular energy output by inactivity and increased sleep. But stress creates a competing energy need. Stress triggers an aroused fight-or-flight response, diverting energy from the disease-fighting system to the muscles and brain, rendering us more vulnerable to illness. The bottom line: Stress does not make us sick, but it does restrain our immune functioning, making us more vulnerable to foreign invaders.

> "When the heart is at ease, the body is healthy."
>
> Chinese proverb

Stress and AIDS

OBJECTIVE 41-8 | Discuss the findings on the link between stress and AIDS.

AIDS has become the world's fourth leading cause of death and the number one killer in Africa. AIDS, as its name tells us, is an immune disorder—an *acquired immune deficiency syndrome* caused by the *human immunodeficiency virus (HIV)*, which is spread by the exchange of bodily fluids, primarily semen and blood. If a disease spread by human contact kills slowly, as does HIV, it ironically can be lethal to more people: Those who carry the disease have time to spread it, often without realizing they are infected. When the HIV infection manifests itself as AIDS, some years after the initial infection, the person has difficulty fighting off other diseases, such as pneumonia. Worldwide, reports the United Nations, more than 25 million people have died of AIDS, including 3.1 million in 2005 (UNAIDS, 2005). (In the United States, where "only" a half-million of these fatalities have occurred, AIDS has killed more people than did combat in all the twentieth-century wars.) In 2005, some 40 million—half of them women—were infected with HIV, often without their awareness (UNAIDS, 2005). In Africa, which is ground zero for AIDS, UNAIDS (2005) warns, more than 80 million AIDS deaths are possible by 2025.

So if stress serves to suppress immune functioning, could it also exacerbate the course of AIDS? Researchers have found that stress and negative emotions do correlate with a progression from HIV infection to AIDS and with the speed of decline in those infected (Bower & others, 1998; Kiecolt-Glaser & Glaser, 1995; Leserman & others, 1999). HIV-infected men faced with stressful life circumstances, such as the loss of a partner, exhibit somewhat greater immune suppression and a faster disease progression.

Would efforts to reduce stress help control the disease? Although the benefits are small compared with available drug treatments, the answer appears again to be yes. Educational initiatives, bereavement support groups, cognitive therapy, and exercise programs that reduce distress have all had positive consequences for HIV-positive individuals (Baum & Posluszny, 1999; Schneiderman, 1999). Better yet is preventing HIV infection, which is the focus of many educational programs, such as the ABC (abstinence, being faithful, condom use) program used in many countries, with notable success in Uganda (Altman, 2004; USAID, 2004).

In North America and Western Europe, 75 percent of people with AIDS are men. In sub-Saharan Africa, 60 percent of people with AIDS are women (and among 15- to 24-year-olds, 75 percent are women). Girls' thin layer of cervical cells makes them especially vulnerable (Altman, 2004; UNAIDS, 2005).

Africa is ground zero for AIDS
Lesotho and other African countries have publicized the "ABC" campaign—Abstinence, Be Faithful, and use Condoms.

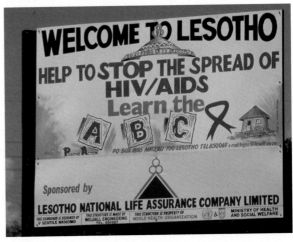

UNAIDS/G. Pirozzi

Stress and Cancer

OBJECTIVE 41-9 | Discuss the findings on the link between stress and cancer.

Stress and negative emotions have also been linked to cancer's rate of progression. To explore a possible connection between stress and cancer, experimenters have implanted tumor cells into rodents or given them *carcinogens* (cancer-producing substances). Those rodents also exposed to uncontrollable stress, such as inescapable shocks, were more prone to cancer (Sklar & Anisman, 1981). In rodents with immune systems weakened by stress, tumors developed sooner and grew larger.

Some investigators have reported that people are at increased risk for cancer within a year after experiencing depression, helplessness, or bereavement. One large Swedish study revealed that people with a history of workplace stress had 5.5 times greater risk of colon cancer than those who reported no such problems, a difference not attributable to differing age, smoking, drinking, or physical characteristics (Courtney & others, 1993). Other researchers have found no link between stress and human cancer (Edelman & Kidman, 1997; Fox, 1998; Petticrew & others, 1999, 2002). Concentration camp survivors and former prisoners of war, for example, have not exhibited elevated cancer rates.

One danger in hyping reports on attitudes and cancer is that some patients may be led to blame themselves for their illness—"If only I had been more expressive, relaxed, and hopeful." A corollary danger is a "wellness macho" among the healthy, who take credit for their "healthy character" and lay a guilt trip on the ill: "She has cancer? That's what you get for holding your feelings in and being so nice." Dying thus becomes the ultimate failure.

The emerging view seems to be that stress does not create cancer cells. At worst, it may affect their growth by weakening the body's natural defenses against a few proliferating, malignant cells. Although a relaxed, hopeful state may enhance these defenses, we should be aware of the thin line that divides science from wishful thinking. The powerful biological processes at work in advanced cancer or AIDS are not likely to be derailed by avoiding stress or maintaining a relaxed but determined spirit (Anderson, 2002; Kessler & others, 1991).

> "I didn't give myself cancer."
>
> Mayor Barbara Boggs Sigmund, 1939–1990, Princeton, New Jersey

When organic causes of illness are unknown, it is tempting to invent psychological explanations. Before the germ that causes tuberculosis was discovered, personality explanations of TB were popular (Sontag, 1978).

Conditioning the Immune System

OBJECTIVE 41-10 | Describe the impact of learning on immune system functioning.

A seasonal allergy sufferer sees a flower on a restaurant table and, not realizing it is plastic, begins to sneeze. Such experiences hint that stress is not the only psychological influence on the body's ailments. Simple classical conditioning may be an added influence. This raises an intriguing question: If conditioning affects the body's overt physiological responses, might it affect the immune system as well?

Psychologist Robert Ader and immunologist Nicholas Cohen (1985) discovered that the answer is yes. Ader came upon this discovery while researching taste aversion in rats. He paired the rats' drinking of saccharin-sweetened water with injections of a drug that suppresses immune functioning. After repeated pairings, sweetened water alone triggered immune suppression, as if the drug had been given (**FIGURE 41.9**). Such conditioned immune suppression can triple an animal's likelihood of growing a tumor when fed a carcinogen (Blom & others, 1995).

Many questions about the role of the immune system and ways to harness its healing potential remain unanswered. If it is possible to condition the immune system's suppression, should it not also be possible to condition its enhancement? Might this be one way in which *placebos*—treatments that have no biochemical effect—sometimes promote healing? Might negative beliefs—expecting the worst—have an opposite ("nocebo") effect, as people get what they expect? Although results have been mixed, researchers are hoping to answer such questions (Hróbjartsson & Gøtzsche, 2001).

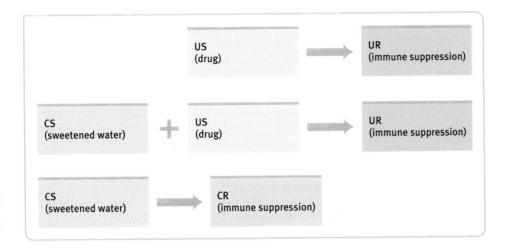

FIGURE 41.9
The conditioning of immune suppression
After Ader and Cohen (1985) associated sweetened water with a drug that causes immune suppression in rats, the inert substance alone triggered the conditioned immune response.

For now, we can view the stress effect on our disease resistance as a price we pay for the benefits of stress (**FIGURE 41.10**). Stress invigorates our lives by arousing and motivating us. An unstressed life would hardly be challenging or productive. Moreover, it pays to spend our resources in fighting or fleeing an external threat. But we do so at the cost of diminished resources for fighting internal threats to health. When the stress is momentary, the cost is negligible. When uncontrollable aggravations persist, the cost may become considerable.

This behavioral medicine research provides yet another reminder of one of contemporary psychology's overriding themes: *Mind and body interact; everything psychological is simultaneously physiological.* Psychological states are physiological events that influence other parts of our physiological system. Just pausing to *think* about biting into an orange section—the sweet, tangy juice from the pulpy fruit flooding across your tongue—can trigger salivation. As the Indian sage Santi Parva recognized more than 4000 years ago, "Mental disorders arise from physical causes, and likewise physical disorders arise from mental causes." There is an interplay between our heads and our health. We are biopsychosocial systems.

FIGURE 41.10
Stress can have a variety of health-related consequences
This is especially so when experienced by "disease-prone" angry, depressed, or anxious persons.

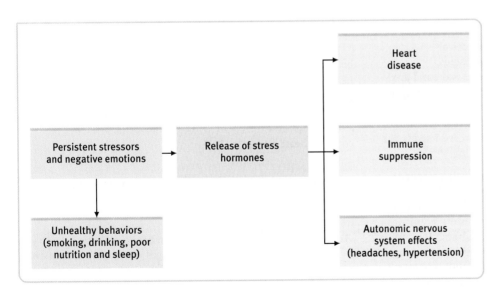

Stress and Illness

OBJECTIVE 41-1 | **Identify some behavior-related causes of illness and death, and describe health psychology's contribution to the field of behavioral medicine.**

Unhealthy behaviors (such as smoking, abuse of alcohol and other drugs, too little exercise, and poor nutrition) and exposure to prolonged stress can make us more vulnerable to some illnesses. *Behavioral medicine* is based on the idea that mind and body interact. *Health psychology* studies the ways our attitudes, emotions, behaviors, and personality influence our health, well-being, and risk of disease.

OBJECTIVE 41-2 | **Discuss the role of appraisal in the way we respond to stressful events.**

Stress is the *process* by which we respond to stressful events (stressors). An important part of that process is our appraisal of an event as threatening, challenging, or unimportant. Our appraisals help determine whether our response will be healthy feelings of energized and directed arousal, or overwhelming feelings of distress.

OBJECTIVE 41-3 | **Describe the dual-track system by which our body responds to stress, and identify the three phases of the general adaptation syndrome.**

The first (and faster) track of the stress-response system is the *fight-or-flight response,* in which the sympathetic nervous system responds to a stressor on several fronts: The inner parts of the adrenal glands pour out epinephrine and norepinephrine, heart and respiration rates increase, blood flows away from digestive organs and toward skeletal muscles, sensations of pain diminish, and the body releases stored sugar and fat. On the slower track of the system, the cerebral cortex, perceiving a stressor, stimulates the hypothalamus and the pituitary gland to trigger the release of glucocorticoid stress hormones, such as cortisol, from the outer part of the adrenals. The three stages of the general adaptation syndrome are *alarm* (temporary shock state in which the body mobilizes resources), *resistance* (period of coping with the stressor), and *exhaustion* (depletion of reserves following prolonged stress).

OBJECTIVE 41-4 | **Discuss the health consequences of catastrophes, significant life changes, and daily hassles.**

Large-scale catastrophic events can increase depression and anxiety and cause problems with concentrating and sleeping. Significant life events, such as personal losses or even changes, may leave people vulnerable to disease. But daily hassles—small, everyday stressors—are the most significant sources of stress for most people and can damage health and well-being.

OBJECTIVE 41-5 | **Discuss the role of stress in causing coronary heart disease, and contrast Type A and Type B personalities.**

Stress can increase the risk of coronary heart disease, a leading cause of death in the United States and other Western countries. The vital link in this stress-disease path is negative emotions—depression, pessimism, but especially anger. Under stress, people with *Type A personalities* (competitive, hard-driving, impatient, and anger-prone) are physiologically more reactive, with an outpouring of hormones that accelerate the buildup of plaque on artery walls, leading to high blood pressure and increased risk of strokes and heart attacks. People with *Type B personalities* (easygoing and relaxed) are at lower risk for these conditions.

OBJECTIVE 41-6 | **Distinguish between a psychophysiological illness and hypochondriasis.**

Psychophysiological illnesses are stress-related physical illnesses, such as hypertension (high blood pressure) and some headaches. *Hypochondriasis* is misinterpreting normal physical sensations as symptoms of a disease.

OBJECTIVE 41-7 | **Describe the effect of stress on immune system functioning.**

The immune system's *B lymphocytes* (formed in bone marrow) release antibodies that fight bacterial infections. The *T lymphocytes* (formed in the thymus and lymphatic tissue) fight cancer cells, viruses, and foreign substances. Other immune-system agents, the *macrophages,* ingest harmful invaders, worn-out cells, and other internal debris. Stress does not directly cause disease, but it can divert energy away from immune system activities and make us more vulnerable to infections and disease.

OBJECTIVE 41-8 | **Discuss the findings on the link between stress and AIDS.**

AIDS is caused by the HIV virus, not by stress. But stress and negative emotions may accelerate the progression from viral infection to actual AIDS. HIV-positive individuals benefit more from drug treatments, but programs that reduce stress do seem to help somewhat.

OBJECTIVE 41-9 | **Discuss the findings on the link between stress and cancer.**

Stress does not create cancer cells. Researchers disagree on whether stress influences the disease's progression, but they do agree that avoiding stress and maintaining a hopeful and determined attitude cannot reverse the destructive processes under way in advanced cancer.

OBJECTIVE 41-10 | **Describe the impact of learning on immune system functioning.**

Researchers have conditioned immune system suppression in laboratory experiments and are working on ways to condition immune-system enhancement.

TERMS AND CONCEPTS TO REMEMBER

behavioral medicine, p. P12-1
health psychology, p. P12-1
stress, p. 41-0
general adaptation syndrome (GAS), p. 41-2
coronary heart disease, p. 41-5

Type A, p. 41-6
Type B, p. 41-6
psychophysiological illness, p. 41-7
lymphocytes, p. 41-7

TEST YOURSELF

1. What are the basic links in our stress response system?

(Answer in Appendix B.)

ASK YOURSELF

1. What are the stresses of your own life? How intensely do you respond to them? Are there changes you could make to avoid the persistent stressors in your life?

>WEB

Multiple-choice *self-tests* and more may be found at www.worthpublishers.com/myers.

Coping With Stress

Promoting health begins with implementing strategies that prevent illness and enhance wellness. Traditionally, people have thought about their health only when something goes wrong—visiting a physician for diagnosis and treatment. That, say health psychologists, is like ignoring a car's maintenance and going to a mechanic only when the car breaks down. Now that we realize that our attitudes and behaviors affect our health, attention is turning to health maintenance—ways of coping with stress, preventing illness, and promoting well-being.

Strategies for Alleviating Stress

OBJECTIVE 42-1 | Contrast problem-focused coping and emotion-focused coping.

Stressors are unavoidable. This fact, coupled with the growing awareness that persistent stress correlates with heart disease, lowered immunity, and other bodily ailments, gives us a clear message. We need to learn to **cope** with the stress in our lives by finding emotional, cognitive, or behavioral ways to alleviate it. We address some stressors directly, with **problem-focused coping.** For example, if our impatience leads to a family fight, we may go directly to that family member to work things out. If, despite our best efforts, we cannot get along with that family member, we may also incorporate an **emotion-focused strategy,** such as reaching out to friends to help address our own emotional needs.

We tend to use problem-focused strategies when we feel a sense of control over a situation and think we can change the circumstances, or at least change ourselves to more capably deal with the circumstances. We turn to emotion-focused strategies when we cannot—or *believe* we cannot—change a situation. Sometimes these strategies are movements toward better long-term health, as when we attempt to gain emotional distance from a damaging, discontinued relationship or keep busy with active hobbies to avoid thinking about an old addiction. Emotion-focused strategies can be nonadaptive, however, as when students worried about not keeping up with the reading in class go out to party to get it off their mind. Sometimes a problem-focused strategy (catching up with the reading) more effectively reduces stress and promotes long-term health and satisfaction.

Several factors affect our ability to cope successfully, including our feelings of personal control, our explanatory style, and our supportive connections.

Perceived Control

OBJECTIVE 42-2 | Describe how a perceived lack of control can affect health.

If two rats receive simultaneous shocks, but one can turn a wheel to stop the shocks, the helpless rat becomes more susceptible to ulcers and lowered immunity to disease (Laudenslager & Reite, 1984) (**FIGURE 42.1** on the next page). In humans, too, uncontrollable threats trigger the strongest stress responses (Dickerson & Kemeny, 2004). For example, a bacterial infection often combines with uncontrollable stress to produce the most severe ulcers (Overmier & Murison, 1997). To cure the ulcer, kill the bug with antibiotics and control the acid secretions with reduced stress.

■ **coping** alleviating stress using emotional, cognitive, or behavioral methods.

■ **problem-focused coping** attempting to alleviate stress directly—by changing the stressor or the way we interact with that stressor.

■ **emotion-focused coping** attempting to alleviate stress by avoiding or ignoring a stressor and attending to emotional needs related to one's stress reaction.

FIGURE 42.1

Health consequences of a loss of control

The "executive" rat at the left can switch off the tail shock by turning the wheel. Because it has control over the shock, it is no more likely to develop ulcers than is the unshocked control rat on the right. The "subordinate" rat in the center receives the same shocks as the executive rat, but with no control over the shocks, it is more likely to develop ulcers. (Adapted from Weiss, 1977.)

Perceiving a loss of control, we become vulnerable to ill health. Elderly nursing home residents who have little perceived control over their activities tend to decline faster and die sooner than do those given more control over their activities (Rodin, 1986). Workers given control over their work environment—by being able to adjust office furnishings and control interruptions and distractions—also experience less stress (O'Neill, 1993). This helps explain why British civil service workers at the executive grades outlive those at clerical or laboring grades, and why Finnish workers with low job stress are less than half as likely to die of cardiovascular disease (strokes or heart disease) as those with a demanding job and little control. The more control workers have, the longer they live (Bosma & others, 1997, 1998; Kivimaki & others, 2002; Marmot & others, 1997).

Control may also help explain a well-established link between economic status and longevity. In one study of 843 grave markers in an old graveyard in Glasgow, Scotland, those with the costliest, highest pillars (indicating the most affluence) tended to live the longest (Carroll & others, 1994). Likewise, Scottish regions with the least overcrowding and unemployment have the greatest longevity. There and elsewhere, high economic status predicts a lower risk of heart and respiratory diseases (Sapolsky, 2005). Wealthy predicts healthy among children, too (Chen, 2004). With higher economic status comes lower risks of infant mortality, low birth weight, smoking, and violence. Even among other primates, those at the bottom of the social pecking order are more likely than their higher-status companions to become sick when exposed to a coldlike virus (Cohen & others, 1997). But for those high-status baboons and monkeys who frequently have to physically defend their dominant position, high status also entails stress (Sapolsky, 2005).

Why does perceived loss of control predict health problems? Animal studies show—and human studies confirm—that losing control provokes an outpouring of stress hormones. When rats cannot control shock or when primates or humans feel unable to control their environment, stress hormone levels rise, blood pressure increases, and immune responses drop (Rodin, 1986; Sapolsky, 2005). Captive animals therefore experience more stress and are more vulnerable to disease than are wild animals (Roberts, 1988). The crowding that occurs in high-density neighborhoods, prisons, and college dorms is another source of diminished feelings of control—and of elevated levels of stress hormones and blood pressure (Fleming & others, 1987; Ostfeld & others, 1987).

Explanatory Style

OBJECTIVE 42-3 | Discuss the links among explanatory style, stress, and health.

Another influence on our coping with stress is whether our basic outlook is optimistic or pessimistic. Psychologists Michael Scheier and Charles Carver (1992) report that optimists—people who agree with statements such as, "In uncertain times, I usually expect the best"—perceive more control, cope better with stressful events, and enjoy better health. During the last month of a semester, students previously identified as optimistic report less fatigue and fewer coughs, aches, and pains. And during the stressful first few weeks of law school, those who are optimistic ("It's unlikely that I will fail") enjoy better moods and stronger infection-thwarting immune systems (Segerstrom & others, 1998). Optimists also respond to stress with smaller increases in blood pressure, and they recover more quickly from heart bypass surgery.

One study that followed 2428 middle-aged Finnish men for up to 10 years discovered that the number of deaths among men with a bleak, hopeless outlook was more than double that found among their optimistic counterparts. Another study asked 795 Americans aged 64 to 79 years if they were "hopeful about the future." When the researchers checked up on these folks about five years later, 29 percent of those answering "No" had died—more than double the 11 percent of deaths among those who said "Yes" (Stern & others, 2001). Mayo Clinic research similarly finds that optimists tend to outlive pessimists (Maruta & others, 2002).

Those with a hopeful outlook live longer. At least that was so among 180 Catholic nuns who at about 22 years of age wrote brief autobiographies. Despite living thereafter with similar life-styles and status, those who had expressed happiness, love, and other positive feelings lived an average seven years longer than their more dour counterparts (Danner & others, 2001). By age 80, some 54 percent of those expressing few positive emotions had died, as had only 24 percent of the most positive-spirited.

Those who manage to find humor in life's daily events also seem to benefit. Laughter arouses us, massages muscles, and then leaves us feeling relaxed (Robinson, 1983). There is not yet enough consistent evidence to suggest that "laughter is the best medicine" (Martin, 2001, 2002). But some recent studies suggest that mirthful humor (not hostile sarcasm) may defuse stress and strengthen immune activity (Berk & others, 2001; Kimata, 2001). People who laugh a lot also have exhibited a lower incidence of heart disease (Clark & others, 2001). In one experiment, laughter in response to a hilarious movie clip caused the blood vessels' inner lining to respond with improved tone and increased blood flow, the opposite of what happened after people viewed a stressful movie clip (Miller, 2005). Perhaps future experiments will show that, indeed, those who laugh, last.

> "There ain't much fun in medicine, but there's a heck of a lot of medicine in fun."
> Humorist Josh Billings, 1818–1885

Social Support

OBJECTIVE 42-4 | Describe some of the ways that social support acts as a stress buffer.

Social support also matters. Consider Linda and Emily. When interviewed for a study conducted by UCLA social psychologist Shelley Taylor (1989), both Los Angeles women had married, raised three children, suffered comparable breast tumors, and recovered from surgery and six months of chemotherapy. But there was a difference. Linda, a widow in her early fifties, was living alone, her children scattered in Atlanta, Boston, and Europe. "She had become odd in ways that people sometimes do when they are isolated," reported Taylor. "Having no one with whom to share her thoughts on a daily basis, she unloaded them somewhat inappropriately with strangers, including our interviewer."

CLOSE-UP:

PETS ARE FRIENDS, TOO

Jonathan Cavendish /Corbis

Have you ever wished for a friend who would love you just as you are, who is nonjudgmental, and who is always there for you, no matter your mood? For many tens of millions of people that friend exists, and it is a loyal dog or a friendly cat.

Many people describe their pet as a cherished family member who helps them feel calm, happy, and valued. Can pets also help people handle stress? If so, might pets have a

healing power? From her review of research, Karen Allen (2003) reports that, yes, pets have been found to increase the odds of survival after a heart attack, to relieve depression among AIDS patients, and to lower the level of blood lipids that contribute to cardiovascular risk. As nursing pioneer Florence Nightingale (1860) foresaw, "A small pet animal is often an excellent companion for the sick." Allen reports from her own research that women's blood pressure rises as they struggle with challenging math problems in the presence of a best friend or even a spouse, but much less so when accompanied by their dog.

So would pets be good medicine for people who do not have pets? To find out, Allen studied a group of stockbrokers who lived alone, described their work as stressful, and

had high blood pressure. She randomly selected half to adopt an animal shelter cat or dog. When later facing stress, these new pet owners exhibited less than half the blood pressure increase of their counterparts without pets. The effect was greatest for those with few social contacts or friends. Her conclusion: For lowering blood pressure, pets are no substitute for effective drugs and exercise, but they are, for those who enjoy animals and live alone, a healthy pleasure.

Pet Ownership Statistics (in millions)

	Dogs	Cats
Australia	4.0	3.5
Canada	3.5	4.5
United States	65	75
United Kingdom	6.1	7.5

Sources: petnet.com.au, Statistics Canada, U.S. Humane Society, U.K. Cats Protection League

---

Interviewing Emily was difficult in a different way. Phone calls interrupted. Her children, all living nearby, were in and out of the house, dropping things off with a quick kiss. Her husband called from his office for a brief chat. Two dogs roamed the house, greeting visitors enthusiastically. All in all, Emily "seemed a serene and contented person, basking in the warmth of her family."

Three years later, the researchers tried to reinterview the women. Linda, they learned, had died two years before. Emily was still lovingly supported by her family and friends and was as happy and healthy as ever.

No two cancers are identical, so we cannot be certain that different social situations led to Linda's and Emily's fates. But they do illustrate a conclusion drawn from several large studies: Social support—feeling liked, affirmed, and encouraged by intimate friends and family—promotes not only happiness, but also health. Humans aren't the only source of stress-buffering comfort. After stressful events, Medicare patients who have a dog or other companionable pet are less likely to visit their doctor (Siegel, 1990). (See Close-Up: Pets Are Friends, Too.)

Relationships can sometimes be stressful, especially in crowded living conditions lacking privacy (Evans & others, 1989). "Hell is others," wrote Jean-Paul Sartre. Peter Warr and Roy Payne (1982) asked a representative sample of British adults what, if anything, had emotionally strained them the day before. Their most frequent answer? "Family."

But asked what prompted yesterday's times of pleasure, the same British sample, by an even larger margin, again answered, "Family." For most of us, family relationships provide not only our greatest heartaches (even when well-meaning, family intrusions can be stressful) but also our greatest comfort and joy. Moreover, seven massive investigations, each following thousands of people for several years, revealed that close relationships predict health. Compared with those having few social ties, people are less likely to die prematurely if supported by close relationships with friends, family, fellow workers, members of a faith community, or other support groups (Cohen, 1988; House & others, 1988; Nelson, 1988). Leukemia and heart disease patients also have enjoyed markedly increased survival rates if married or supported by family or friends (Case & others, 1992; Colon & others, 1991; Williams & others, 1992).

Carefully controlled studies indicate that married people live longer, healthier lives than the unmarried (Murray, 2000; Wilson & Oswald, 2002). The National Center for Health Statistics (2004) reports that regardless of people's age, sex, race, and income, they tend to be healthier if married. Married folks experience less pain from headaches and backaches, suffer less stress, drink and smoke less, and, despite being slightly more overweight, are generally healthier. A seven-decades-long Harvard study found that a good marriage at age 50 predicts healthy aging better than does a low cholesterol level at 50 (Vaillant, 2002). But marital functioning also matters. Conflict-laden marriages are not conducive to health; positive, happy, supportive ones are (Kiecolt-Glaser & Newton, 2001). One five-year study following 1532 older married adults found it was even better to give than to receive. After controlling for preexisting health and personality differences, researchers observed a markedly lower risk of dying during the five-year period among those who frequently reached out to help friends and neighbors and who made their spouse feel loved and cared for (Brown & others, 2003).

How can we explain this link between social support and health? Is it just that healthy people are more likely to support others and to marry and stay married? Actually, the research suggests that people with supportive friends and marriage partners eat better, exercise more, sleep better, and smoke less, and therefore cope with stress more effectively (Helgeson & others, 1998).

Environments that support our need to belong also foster stronger immune functioning. Given ample social support, spouses of cancer patients exhibit stronger immune functioning (Baron & others, 1990). Social ties and positive sociability even confer resistance to cold viruses. Sheldon Cohen and his colleagues (1997, 2004) demonstrated this by putting 276 healthy volunteers in quarantine for five days after administering nasal drops laden with a cold virus, and then repeating the experiment with 334 more volunteers. (In both experiments, the volunteers were paid $800 each to endure this experience.) The cold fact is that the effect of social ties is nothing to sneeze at. Age, race, sex, smoking, and other health habits being equal, those with the most social ties were least likely to catch a cold and they produced less mucus. More sociability meant less susceptibility. More than 50 studies further reveal that social support calms the cardiovascular system, lowering blood pressure and stress hormones (Uchino & others, 1996, 1999).

Close relationships also provide the opportunity to *confide* painful feelings, a social support component that has now been extensively studied. In one study, health psychologists James Pennebaker and Robin O'Heeron (1984) contacted the surviving spouses of people who had committed suicide or died in car accidents. Those who bore their grief alone had more health problems than those who could express it openly. Talking about our troubles can be "open heart therapy."

Older people, many of whom have lost a spouse and close friends, are somewhat less likely to enjoy such confiding (**FIGURE 42.2** on the next page), and suppressing emotions is sometimes detrimental to our physical health. When Pennebaker surveyed more than 700 undergraduate women, he found that about 1 in 12 reported a traumatic sexual experience in childhood. Compared with women who had experienced nonsexual traumas, such as parental death or divorce, the sexually abused women—especially those who had kept their secret to themselves—reported more headaches and stomach ailments. Another study, of 437 Australian ambulance drivers, confirmed the ill effects of suppressing one's emotions after witnessing traumas (Wastell, 2002).

"Woe to one who is alone and falls and does not have another to help."
Ecclesiastes 4:10

Bob Daemmrich/Stock, Boston

Friendships are good medicine
Several long-term studies of thousands of people have found that individuals with close supportive relationships are less likely than socially isolated people to die prematurely.

"I get by with a little help from my friends."
John Lennon and Paul McCartney, *Sgt. Pepper's Lonely Hearts Club Band*, 1967

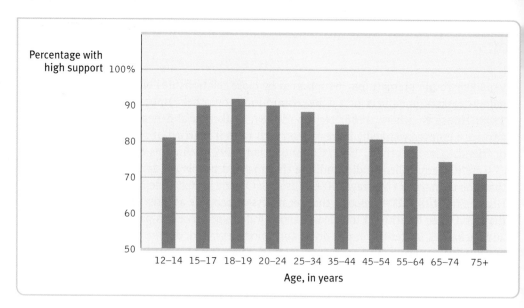

Percentage with
high support

FIGURE 42.2

Social support across the life span

Do you have someone you can confide in? Someone to count on in a crisis? Someone to count on for advice? Someone who makes you feel loved and cared for? In a national health survey, 9 in 10 young adult Canadians, but only 7 in 10 over the age of 75, indicated high social support by answering yes to all four questions. (Data from Statistics Canada, 1999, p. 133.)

■ **aerobic exercise** sustained exercise that increases heart and lung fitness; may also alleviate depression and anxiety.

Actively suppressing thoughts can cause them to bubble up intrusively, preoccupying the person (Wegner, 1990). (In the next five seconds, please *do not* picture a white bear.) Disclosing suppressed thoughts may stop the cycle. In a simulated confessional, Pennebaker asked volunteers to share with a hidden experimenter some upsetting events that had been preying on their minds. He asked some of the volunteers to describe a trivial event before they divulged the troubling one. Physiological measures revealed that their bodies remained tense the whole time they talked about the trivial event; they relaxed only when they later confided the cause of their turmoil.

Writing about personal traumas in a diary can also help (Hemenover, 2003; Lyubomirsky & others, 2006). When volunteers in one experiment did this, they had fewer health problems during the ensuing four to six months (Pennebaker, 1990). As one participant explained, "Although I have not talked with anyone about what I wrote, I was finally able to deal with it, work through the pain instead of trying to block it out. Now it doesn't hurt to think about it."

Pennebaker and his colleagues (1989) also invited 33 Holocaust survivors to spend two hours recalling their experiences. Many did so in intimate detail never before disclosed. In the weeks following, most watched a videotape of their recollections and showed it to family and friends. Those who were most self-disclosing had the most improved health 14 months later. Talking about a stressful event can temporarily arouse people, but in the long run it calms them (Mendolia & Kleck, 1993). Confiding is good for the soul.

Managing Stress

Having a sense of control, developing a more optimistic explanatory style, and building our base of social support can help us *experience* less stress and thus improve our health. But sometimes we cannot alleviate stress and simply need to *manage* our stress in a healthful way. Aerobic exercise, biofeedback, relaxation, meditation, and spirituality may help us gather inner strength and lessen stress.

Aerobic Exercise

OBJECTIVE 42-5 | Discuss the advantages of aerobic exercise as a technique for managing stress and fostering well-being.

Aerobic exercise is sustained exercise that increases heart and lung fitness. Jogging, swimming and biking are common examples. Such exercise strengthens the body. Does it also boost the spirit?

"Is there anyone here who specializes in stress management?"

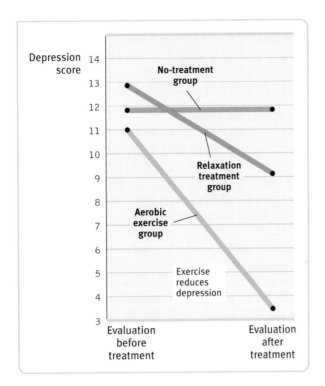

FIGURE 42.3
Aerobic exercise and depression
Mildly depressed college women who participated in an aerobic exercise program showed markedly reduced depression, compared with those who did relaxation exercises or received no treatment. (From McCann & Holmes, 1984).

Exercise and Mood

Many studies suggest that aerobic exercise can reduce stress, depression, and anxiety. For example, 3 in 10 American and Canadian, and 2 in 10 British people who do aerobic exercise three times a week or more also manage stressful events better, exhibit more self-confidence, feel more vigor, and feel depressed and fatigued less often than those who exercise less (McMurray, 2004). In a 2002 Gallup survey, nonexercisers were twice as likely as exercisers to report being "not too happy" (Brooks, 2002). But if we state this observation the other way around—that stressed and depressed people exercise less—cause and effect become unclear.

Experiments have resolved this ambiguity by randomly assigning stressed, depressed, or anxious people either to aerobic exercise or to other treatments. In one such experiment, Lisa McCann and David Holmes (1984) assigned one third of a group of mildly depressed female college students to a program of aerobic exercise and another third to a treatment of relaxation exercises; the remaining third, a control group, received no treatment. As **FIGURE 42.3** shows, 10 weeks later the women in the aerobic exercise program reported the greatest decrease in depression. Many of them had, quite literally, run away from their troubles. Vigorous exercise provides a "substantial" immediate mood boost, reports David Watson (2000) from his monitoring of university students. Even a 10-minute walk stimulates two hours of increased well-being by raising energy levels and lowering tension (Thayer, 1987, 1993).

More than 150 other studies confirm that exercise reduces depression and anxiety and is therefore a useful adjunct to antidepressant drugs and psychotherapy (Arent & others, 2000; Berger & Motl, 2000; Dunn & others, 2005). Not only is exercise about as effective as drugs, some research suggests it better prevents symptom recurrence (Babyak & others, 2000; Salmon, 2001). Researchers are now wondering *why* aerobic exercise alleviates negative emotions. They know that exercise:

- orders up mood-boosting chemicals from our body's internal pharmacy—neurotransmitters such as norepinephrine, serotonin, and the endorphins (Jacobs, 1994; Salmon, 2001).
- modestly enhances cognitive abilities, such as memory (Etnier & others, 1997).
- promotes the growth of new brain cells in mice exercising daily on a running-wheel regimen (Kempermann & Gage, 1999).

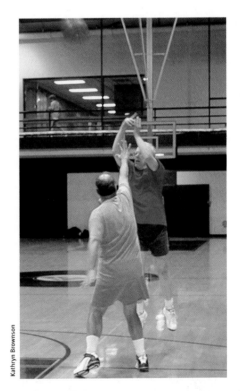

The mood boost
When one's energy or spirits are sagging, few things reboot the day better than exercising (as I can vouch from my daily noontime basketball). Aerobic exercise appears to counteract depression partly by increasing arousal (replacing depression's low-arousal state) and by doing naturally what Prozac does—increasing the brain's serotonin activity.

Perhaps the emotional benefits of exercise are also a side effect of increased warmth and body arousal (counteracting depression's low arousal state), or of the muscle relaxation and sounder sleep that occur afterward. Or perhaps a sense of accomplishment and an improved physique enhance one's emotional state.

Exercise and Health

Other research reveals that exercise not only boosts our mood, but also strengthens the heart, increases blood flow, keeps blood vessels open, and lowers both blood pressure and the blood pressure reaction to stress (Ford, 2002; Manson, 2002). And being physically healthy may make us stronger and better able to manage our stress. Compared with inactive adults, people who exercise suffer half as many heart attacks (Powell & others, 1987). Exercise makes the muscles hungry for the "bad fats" that, if not used by the muscles, contribute to clogged arteries (Barinaga, 1997). One study following adult Finnish twins for nearly 20 years revealed that, other things being equal, occasional exercise reduced the risk of death by 29 percent, compared with no exercise. Daily conditioning exercise reduced death risk by 43 percent (Kujala & others, 1998).

The genes passed down to us from our distant ancestors were those that enabled the physical activity essential to hunting, foraging, and farming. In muscle cells, those genes, when activated by exercise, respond by producing proteins. In the modern inactive person, note biologists Frank Booth and Darrell Neufer (2005), these genes produce lower quantities of proteins and leave us susceptible to more than 20 chronic diseases, such as type-2 diabetes, cardiovascular disease, and cancer. Inactivity is thus potentially toxic.

By one estimate, moderate exercise adds two years to one's expected life. "Perhaps God does not subtract the time spent exercising from your allotted time on Earth," jests Martin Seligman (1994, p. 193).

Biofeedback, Relaxation, and Meditation

OBJECTIVE 42-6 | Compare the benefits of biofeedback and relaxation training as stress-management techniques, and discuss meditation as a relaxation technique.

Knowing the damaging effects of stress, could we train people to bring their heart rate and blood pressure under conscious control? When a few psychologists started experimenting with this idea, many of their colleagues thought them foolish. After all, these functions are controlled by the autonomic ("involuntary") nervous system. Then, in the late 1960s, experiments by respected psychologists made the skeptics wonder. Neal Miller, for one, found that rats could modify their heartbeat if given pleasurable brain stimulation when their heartbeat increased or decreased. Later research revealed that some paralyzed humans could also learn to control their blood pressure (Miller & Brucker, 1979).

Miller was experimenting with **biofeedback,** a system of recording, amplifying, and feeding back information about subtle physiological responses. Biofeedback instruments mirror the results of a person's own efforts, thereby allowing the person to learn techniques for controlling a particular physiological response (**FIGURE 42.4**).

After a decade of study, however, researchers decided the initial claims for biofeedback were overblown and oversold (Miller, 1985). A 1995 National Institutes of Health panel declared that biofeedback works best on tension headaches. Many have since turned to alternative medicine (for further discussion, turn the page and see Thinking Critically About: Alternative Medicine—New Ways to Health, or Old Snake Oil?) in search of quick relief from stress and illnesses, but simple methods of relaxation, which require no expensive equipment, produce many of the same results biofeedback once promised.

Sixty studies find that relaxation procedures can help alleviate headaches, hypertension, anxiety, and insomnia (Stetter & Kupper, 2002). Such findings would not

■ **biofeedback** a system for electronically recording, amplifying, and feeding back information regarding a subtle physiological state, such as blood pressure or muscle tension.

surprise Meyer Friedman and his colleagues. To find out whether teaching
Type A heart attack victims (Type A people are, by definition, competitive, hard-
driving, impatient, and anger-prone) to
relax might reduce their risk of another
attack, the researchers randomly assigned
hundreds of middle-aged, male heart-
attack survivors to one of two groups. The
first group received standard advice from
cardiologists concerning medications,
diet, and exercise habits. The second group received similar advice
plus continuing counseling on modifying their life-styles—how to
slow down and relax by walking, talking, and eating more slowly;
by smiling at others and laughing at themselves; by admitting mis-
takes; by taking time to enjoy life; and by renewing their religious faith. As **FIGURE**
42.5 indicates, during the ensuing three years, the second group experienced half as
many repeat heart attacks as the first group. This, wrote the exuberant Friedman, is
an unprecedented, spectacular reduction in heart-attack recurrence. A smaller-scale
British study similarly divided heart-attack–prone people into control and life-style
modification groups (Eysenck & Grossarth-Maticek, 1991). During the next 13
years, it also found a 50 percent reduction in death rate among those trained to alter
their thinking and life-style.

Cardiologist Herbert Benson (1996) became intrigued with meditative relaxation
when he found that experienced meditators could decrease their blood pressure, heart
rate, and oxygen consumption and raise their fingertip temperature. You can experience the essence of this *relaxation response,* as Benson calls it, right now: Assume a
comfortable position, breathe deeply, and relax your muscles from foot to face. Now,
close your eyes and focus on a single word or a phrase. (About 80 percent of Benson's
patients choose to focus on a favorite prayer.) When other thoughts intrude, let them
drift away as you silently repeat your phrase continually for 10 to 20 minutes. Tibetan
Buddhists deep in meditation and Franciscan nuns deep in centering prayer report a
diminished sense of self, space, and time. Brain scans reveal the neural footprints of
such spiritual feelings during these mystical experiences: A part of the parietal lobe
that tracks where we are in space is less active than usual, and a frontal lobe area involved in focused attention is more active (Newberg & D'Aquili, 2001).

System receives signal   Amplifies signal   Processes signal

Displays signal   Feedback

Patient observes signal

FIGURE 42.4
Biofeedback systems
Biofeedback systems—such as this one,
which records tension in the forehead muscle of a headache sufferer—allow people to
monitor their subtle physiological responses. As this man relaxes his forehead muscle,
the pointer on the display screen (or a tone)
may go lower.

Meditation is a modern phenomenon with
a long history: "Sit down alone and in
silence. Lower your head, shut your eyes,
breathe out gently, and imagine yourself
looking into your own heart. . . . As you
breathe out, say 'Lord Jesus Christ, have
mercy on me.' . . . Try to put all other
thoughts aside. Be calm, be patient, and
repeat the process very frequently"
(Gregory of Sinai, died 1346).

FIGURE 42.5
**Recurrent heart attacks and life-style
modification**
The San Francisco Recurrent Coronary
Prevention Project offered counseling from a
cardiologist to survivors of heart attacks.
Those who were also guided in modifying
their Type A life-style suffered fewer repeat
heart attacks. (From Friedman & Ulmer, 1984.)

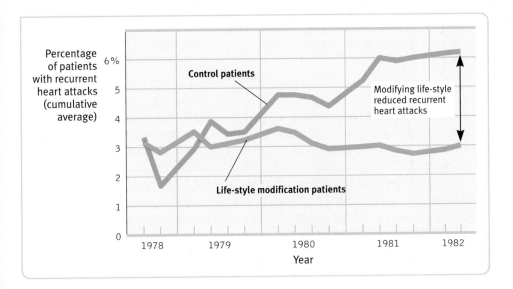

Percentage
of patients
with recurrent
heart attacks
(cumulative
average)

Control patients

Modifying life-style
reduced recurrent
heart attacks

Life-style modification patients

6%

5

4

3

2

1

0

1978   1979   1980   1981   1982
Year

Ghislain and Marie David De Lossy/Getty Images

THINKING CRITICALLY ABOUT :

ALTERNATIVE MEDICINE—NEW WAYS TO HEALTH, OR OLD SNAKE OIL?

One health care growth market is **complementary and alternative medicine**, which encompasses such methods as acupuncture, massage therapy, homeopathy, spiritual healing, herbal remedies, chiropractic, and aromatherapy. In Germany, herbal remedies and homeopathy are enormously popular. In China, herbal therapies have long flourished, as have acupuncture and acupressure therapies that claim to correct "imbalances of energy flow" (called *Qi* or *Chi*) at identifiable points close to the skin. Andrew Weil's many books on alternative medicine have sold millions of copies, putting him on the cover of *Time* magazine. Facing political pressure to explore such things, the U.S. National Institutes of Health established the National Center for Complementary and Alternative Medicine, which the center defines as health care treatments not taught widely in medical schools, not usually reimbursed by insurance companies, and not used in hospitals (**TABLE 42.1**).

So what shall we make of alternative medicine? Some aspects, such as life-style changes and stress management, have acknowledged validity. Do the other aspects offer, as some believe, a new medical paradigm? Or do they represent, as others maintain, a retreat from rationality and science?

Supporters of alternative medicine offer inspirational cases, such as these from Andrew Weil's books (Relman, 1998):

- A young woman diagnosed with bone cancer starts a vigorous exercise program (biking 500 miles and running 60 miles weekly), becomes vegetarian (consuming fresh fruit, juices, and whole grains), and shucks the alleged cancer.
- A woman uses "respiratory biofeedback" to end her Parkinson's-induced seizures.
- A man with scleroderma, a progressive and fatal disease of the skin and internal organs, cures himself with vinegar, lemons, aloe vera juice, and vitamin E.

Critics point out that people consult physicians for diagnosable, curable diseases and employ alternative medicine when they are either incurably ill or well but feeling subpar. Thus, an otherwise healthy person with a cold may try an herbal remedy and then credit the subsequent return to good health to alternative medicine, rather than to the body's natural return to normal. (Of course, the same may happen when people take traditional medicine for a cold.) Alternative medicine will seem especially effective with cyclical diseases, such as arthritis and allergies, as people seek therapy during the downturn and presume its effectiveness during the ensuing upturn. Add to this the healing power of belief—the placebo effect—plus the natural disappearance (*spontaneous remission*) of many diseases, and alternative medicine practices are bound to seem effective, whether they are or not. One study of 302 migraine headache patients in Germany found that 51 percent of those receiving acupuncture treatment found relief, as did only 15 percent of those in a waiting list control group. But among a third group that received "sham acupuncture" (needles inserted at nonacupuncture points), 53 percent enjoyed relief. Such results, the investigators suspected, may indicate "a powerful placebo effect" (Linde & others, 2005).

The National Council Against Health Fraud and the editors of leading medical journals and of the *Scientific Review of Alternative Medicine* doubt the efficacy of alternative medicine therapies. "After more than ten years and $200 million," contends Kimball Atwood (2003), government-funded alternative medicine research "has not demonstrated efficacy" for any of the alternative medicine treatments studied.

" Sickness is the manifestation of evil in the body."

Andrew Weil, *Health and Healing*, 1998

Psychologist Richard Davidson reports that Buddhist monks who are experienced in meditation display elevated levels of the left frontal lobe activity associated with positive emotions. To explore whether such activity is a *result* of meditation, Davidson and his colleagues (2003) ran baseline brain scans of all volunteers and then randomly assigned them either to a control group or to an eight-week course in "mindfulness meditation." Compared with both the control group and their own baseline, the meditation participants exhibited noticeably more left-hemisphere activity, and also improved immune functioning, after the training. Such effects may help explain the astonishing results of a study that randomly assigned 73 residents of homes for the elderly either to daily meditation or to none. After three years, one-fourth of the nonmeditators had died, but all the meditators were still alive (Alexander & others, 1989).

TABLE 42.1

SUBFIELDS OF ALTERNATIVE MEDICINE

Alternative Systems of Medical Practice	Health Care Ranging From Self-Care Following Popular Beliefs to Treatments Based on Alternative Traditions or Practices
Bioelectromagnetic applications	The study of how living organisms interact with electromagnetic (EM) fields
Diet, nutrition, life-style changes	The knowledge of how to prevent illness, maintain health, and reverse the effects of chronic disease through dietary or nutritional intervention
Herbal medicine	Employing plant and plant products from folk medicine traditions for pharmacological use
Manual healing	Using touch and manipulation with the hands as a diagnostic and therapeutic tool
Mind-body control	Exploring the mind's capacity to affect the body, based on traditional medical systems that make use of the interconnectedness of mind and body
Pharmacological and biological treatments	Drugs and vaccines not yet accepted by mainstream medicine

Source: Offered without endorsement by the National Center for Complementary and Alternative Medicine (nccam.nih.gov)

"In God we trust. All others must have data."

George Lundberg, Editor, *Journal of the American Medical Association*, 1998

In November 1998, the *Journal of the American Medical Association* published seven new alternative medicine research studies. Three explored treatments that proved useless (chiropractic manipulation for tension headaches, a popular herb for weight loss, and acupuncture to control nerve pain caused by HIV). Four other treatments, however—an herb mixture for inflammatory bowel syndrome, an herbal remedy for bladder problems, yoga for carpal tunnel syndrome pain, and a Chinese method for inducing fetuses in the breech position to turn—showed some benefits. As always, the way to discern what works and what does not is to experiment: Randomly assign patients to receive the therapy or a placebo control. Then ask the critical question: When neither the therapist nor the patient knows who is getting the real therapy, is the real therapy effective?

Much of today's mainstream medicine began as yesterday's alternative medicine. Natural botanical life has given us digitalis (from purple foxglove), morphine (from the opium poppy), and penicillin (from penicillium mold). In each case, the active ingredient was verified in controlled trials. We have medical and public health science to thank for the antibiotics, vaccines, surgical procedures, sanitation, and emergency medicine that helped lengthen our life expectancy by three decades during the last century. If you have acute chest pain, find a lump in your chest, cough up blood, or develop a high fever, you would do well to seek out someone trained in medical science—someone undergirded by research on what treatments really work best for what ailments at what doses for what lengths of time.

Indeed, said *New England Journal of Medicine* editors Marcia Angell and Jerome Kassirer (1998), "There cannot be two kinds of medicine—conventional and alternative. There is only medicine that has been adequately tested and medicine that has not, medicine that works and medicine that may or may not work. Once a treatment has been tested rigorously, it no longer matters whether it was considered alternative at the outset."

■ **complementary and alternative medicine** Unproven health care treatments not taught widely in medical schools, not used in hospitals, and not usually reimbursed by insurance companies.

A more recent study found that hypertension patients assigned to meditation training had (compared with other treatment groups) a 30 percent lower cardiovascular death rate over the ensuing 19-year study period (Schneider & others, 2005).

Spirituality and Faith Communities

OBJECTIVE 42-7 | Discuss the correlation between religiosity and longevity, and offer some possible explanations for this link.

As humans suffered ills and sought healing throughout history, two healing traditions—religion and medicine—have joined hands in caring for them. Often those hands belonged to the same person—the spiritual leader was also the healer. Maimonides was a twelfth-century rabbi and a renowned physician. Hospitals, which were first established in monasteries and then spread by missionaries, often carry the names of saints or faith communities.

As medical science matured, healing and religion diverged. Rather than asking God to spare their children from smallpox, people were able to vaccinate them. Rather than seeking a spiritual healer when burning with bacterial fever, they were able to use antibiotics. Recently, however, religion and healing are converging once again:

- Of America's 135 medical schools, 101 offered spirituality and health courses in 2005, up from 5 in 1992 (Koenig, 2002; Puchalski, 2005).
- Since 1995, Harvard Medical School has annually attracted 1000 to 2000 health professionals to its Spirituality and Healing in Medicine conferences.
- Duke University has established a Center for Spirituality, Theology, and Health.
- A Yankelovich survey (1997) found 94 percent of U.S. HMO professionals and 99 percent of family physicians agreeing that "personal prayer, meditation, or other spiritual and religious practices" can enhance medical treatment.
- Booksellers are featuring such titles as *The Healing Power of Faith* (Simon & Schuster, 1999), *Religion and Health* (Oxford University Press, 2000), and *Faith, Medicine, and Science* (Haworth, 2005).

Is there fire underneath all this smoke? More than a thousand studies have sought to correlate the *faith factor* with health and healing. For example, Jeremy Kark and his colleagues (1996) compared the death rates for 3900 Israelis either in one of 11 religiously orthodox or in one of 11 matched, nonreligious collective settlements (kibbutz communities). The researchers reported that over a 16-year period, "belonging to a religious collective was associated with a strong protective effect" not explained by age or economic differences. In every age group, religious community members were about half as likely to have died as were their nonreligious counterparts. This is roughly comparable to the gender difference in mortality.

In response to such findings, Richard Sloan and his skeptical colleagues (1999, 2000, 2002, 2005) remind us that mere correlations can leave many factors uncontrolled. Consider one obvious possibility: Women are more religiously active than men, and women outlive men. So perhaps religious involvement is merely an expression of the gender effect on longevity.

However, several new studies find the religiosity-longevity correlation among men alone, and even more strongly among women (McCullough & others, 2000, 2005). One study that followed 5286 Californians over 28 years found that, after controlling for age, gender, ethnicity, and education, frequent religious attenders were 36 percent less likely to have died in any year (**FIGURE 42.6**).

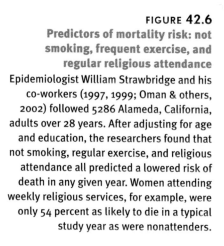

FIGURE 42.6

Predictors of mortality risk: not smoking, frequent exercise, and regular religious attendance
Epidemiologist William Strawbridge and his co-workers (1997, 1999; Oman & others, 2002) followed 5286 Alameda, California, adults over 28 years. After adjusting for age and education, the researchers found that not smoking, regular exercise, and religious attendance all predicted a lowered risk of death in any given year. Women attending weekly religious services, for example, were only 54 percent as likely to die in a typical study year as were nonattenders.

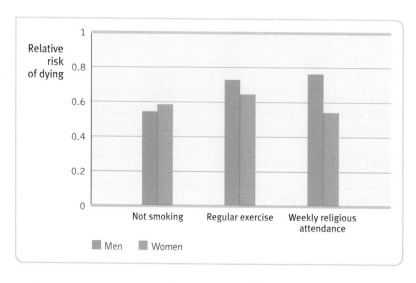

A U.S. National Health Interview Survey (Hummer & others, 1999) followed 21,204 people over 8 years. After controlling for age, sex, race, and region, researchers found that nonattenders were 1.87 times more likely to have died than were those attending more than weekly. This translated into a life expectancy at age 20 of 83 years for frequent attenders and 75 years for infrequent attenders (**FIGURE 42.7**).

These correlational findings do not indicate that nonattenders who start attending services and change nothing else will live 8 years longer. But they do indicate that as a *predictor* of health and longevity, religious involvement rivals nonsmoking and exercise effects. Such findings demand explanation. Can you imagine what intervening variables might account for the correlation?

First, religiously active people have healthier life-styles; for example, they smoke and drink less (Lyons, 2002; Strawbridge & others, 2001). Health-oriented, vegetarian Seventh Day Adventists have a longer-than-usual life expectancy (Berkel & de Waard, 1983). Religiously orthodox Israelis eat less fat than do their nonreligious compatriots. But such differences are not great enough to explain the dramatically reduced mortality in the religious kibbutzim, argued the Israeli researchers. In the recent American studies, too, about 75 percent of the longevity difference remains after controlling for unhealthy behaviors such as inactivity and smoking (Musick & others, 1999).

Social support is another variable that helps explain the faith factor (George & others, 2002). For Judaism, Christianity, and Islam, faith is not solo spirituality but a communal experience that helps satisfy the need to belong. The more than 350,000 faith communities in North America and the millions more elsewhere provide support networks for their active participants—people who are there for one another when misfortune strikes. Moreover, religion encourages another predictor of health and longevity. In the religious kibbutzim, for example, divorce has been almost nonexistent.

But even after controlling for gender, unhealthy behaviors, social ties, and preexisting health problems, the mortality studies find much of the mortality reduction remaining (George & others, 2000; Powell & others, 2003). Researchers therefore speculate that a third set of intervening variables is the stress protection and enhanced well-being associated with a coherent worldview, a sense of hope for the long-term future, feelings of ultimate acceptance, and the relaxed meditation of prayer or Sabbath observance (**FIGURE 42.8**). These variables might also help to explain other recent findings among the religiously active, such as healthier immune functioning

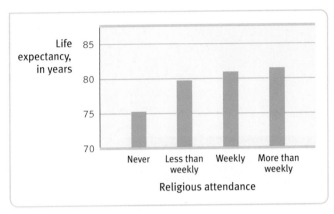

FIGURE 42.7
Religious attendance and life expectancy
In a national health survey financed by the U.S. Centers for Disease Control and Prevention, religiously active people had longer life expectancies. (Data from Hummer & others, 1999.)

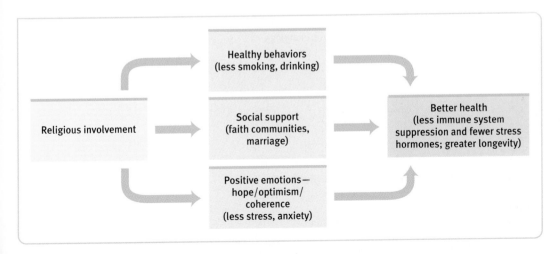

FIGURE 42.8
Possible explanations for the correlation between religious involvement and health/longevity

and fewer hospital admissions and, for AIDS patients, fewer stress hormones and longer survival (Ironson & others, 2002; Koenig & Larson, 1998; Lutgendorf & others, 2004).

Although the religion-health correlation is yet to be fully explained, Harold Pincus (1997), deputy medical director of the American Psychiatric Association, believes these findings "have made clear that anyone involved in providing health care services . . . cannot ignore . . . the important connections between spirituality, religion, and health."

Let's summarize: Sustained emotional reactions to stressful events can be debilitating. However, we can cope with stressors by problem-solving or emotional coping, and we can manage stress by making ourselves emotionally and physically stronger (**FIGURE 42.9**).

FIGURE 42.9
Managing stress
Life events can be debilitating or not. It all depends on how we appraise them and whether the stresses are buffered by a stress-resistant disposition, healthy habits, enduring social support, and spiritual engagement.

>> LEARNING OUTCOMES

Coping With Stress

OBJECTIVE 42-1 | **Contrast problem-focused coping and emotion-focused coping.**

When we use *problem-focused coping,* we attempt to reduce stress directly by changing the events that trigger stress reactions or by changing the way we react to those events. We tend to use *emotion-focused coping* (putting distance between ourselves and a stressor, or attending to our own emotional needs) when we believe—rightly or wrongly—that we cannot change a stressful situation.

OBJECTIVE 42-2 | **Describe how a perceived lack of control can affect health.**

A perceived lack of control has been associated with higher than normal susceptibility to bacterial infections, cardiovascular disease, and, possibly, a shorter life span due to elevated levels of stress hormones and diminished immune system responses.

OBJECTIVE 42-3 | **Discuss the links among explanatory style, stress, and health.**

Compared with people with a pessimistic explanatory style, optimists tend to feel they have more control over stressors, cope better with stressful events, enjoy better moods, have stronger immune systems, and live longer than pessimists.

OBJECTIVE 42-4 | **Describe some of the ways that social support acts as a stress buffer.**

Supportive family members, marriage partners, close friends, and companionable pets help people cope with stressful events. Social support fosters stronger immune functioning, calms the cardiovascular system, and lowers blood pressure.

OBJECTIVE 42-5 | **Discuss the advantages of aerobic exercise as a technique for managing stress and fostering well-being.**

Aerobic exercise (sustained exercise that increases heart and lung fitness) can raise energy levels, increase self-confidence, lower tension, and alleviate depression and anxiety. Studies have linked aerobic exercise to lowered blood pressure, increased arousal, higher levels of neurotransmitters that boost moods (such as norepinephrine, serotonin, and the endorphins), enhanced cognitive abilities, and (in mice) the growth of new brain cells.

OBJECTIVE 42-6 | **Compare the benefits of biofeedback and relaxation training as stress-management techniques, and discuss meditation as a relaxation technique.**

Biofeedback techniques have helped control tension headaches, but simple relaxation exercises have been equally effective in combating hypertension, anxiety, and insomnia, and in lowering rates of recurring heart attacks. Some search for relief from stress and illnesses in complementary and alternative medicine. While meditating, people have shown increased left frontal lobe activity and improved immune functioning, compared with those in control groups.

OBJECTIVE 42-7 | **Discuss the correlation between religiosity and longevity, and offer some possible explanations for this link.**

Regular religious attendance has been a reliable predictor of a longer life span. Researchers have isolated three possible influences: (1) Religiously active people have healthy life-styles. (2) Faith communities often function as social support networks and often encourage marriage (which, when happy, is associated with better health and longer life span). (3) Religious attendance—with its accompanying coherent worldview, sense of hope for the future, feelings of acceptance, and relaxed meditative state—may foster positive emotions and decrease feelings of stress and anxiety.

TERMS AND CONCEPTS TO REMEMBER

coping, p. 42-1

problem-focused coping, p. 42-1

emotion-focused coping, p. 42-1

aerobic exercise, p. 42-6

biofeedback, p. 42-8

complementary and alternative medicine, p. 42-10

TEST YOURSELF

1. What are some ways that social support can help us cope with stress?

(Answer in Appendix B.)

ASK YOURSELF

1. In the past month, have you tended toward using more problem-focused or more emotion-focused strategies for coping with stress? Have your methods been effective, or do you think you need to modify your approach?

>WEB

Multiple-choice *self-tests* and more may be found at www.worthpublishers.com/myers.

Smoking

Obesity

43

Modifying Illness-Related Behaviors

Researchers are persuaded that health-promotion programs would cost far less than many countries now spend to treat diseases (**TABLE 43.1**). (U.S. Bureau of the Census, 2004). Moreover, among patients visiting their primary care physicians with such typical complaints as fatigue, headache, chest or abdominal pain, dizziness, constipation, and insomnia, fewer than 20 percent have a clear organic problem (Kroenke & Mangelsdorff, 1989). Medical researchers presume many of the rest involve *psychosocial factors*. It is clear that even modestly successful health-promotion programs could save more money than they cost.

What makes health-promoting programs successful? Let's take a closer look at smoking, and at obesity and weight control.

TABLE 43.1

HEALTH-CARE COSTS AND LONGEVITY

More than health-care expenditures are at issue when it comes to predicting longevity—one measure of a nation's overall health.

	Health Care as Percentage of GDP (gross domestic product)	Life Expectancy (in years) for Those Born in 2003
United States	14%	77.1
United Kingdom	8%	78.2
Canada	9%	79.8
Australia	9%	80.1

Source: U.S. Bureau of the Census, 2004

Smoking

The Risks of Smoking

OBJECTIVE 43-1 | Explain why people smoke.

Imagine that cigarettes were harmless—except, once in every 25,000 packs, an occasional innocent-looking one is filled with dynamite instead of tobacco. Not such a bad risk of having your head blown off. But with 250 million packs a day consumed worldwide, we could expect more than 10,000 gruesome daily deaths (more than three times the 9/11 fatalities each and every day)—surely enough to have cigarettes banned everywhere.[1]

The lost lives from these dynamite-loaded cigarettes approximate those from today's actual cigarettes. Each year throughout the world, tobacco kills nearly 5 million of its 1.3 billion customers, reports the World Health Organization ([WHO] 2005). (Imagine the outrage if terrorists took down an equivalent of 25 loaded jumbo jets today, let alone tomorrow and every day thereafter.) And the worst is yet to come.

"There is an overwhelming medical and scientific consensus that cigarette smoking causes lung cancer, heart disease, emphysema, and other serious diseases in smokers. Smokers are far more likely to develop serious diseases, like lung cancer, than nonsmokers."

Philip Morris Companies Inc., 1999

[1] This analogy, adapted here with world-based numbers, was suggested by mathematician Sam Saunders, as reported by K. C. Cole (1998).

Given present trends, according to the WHO, the death rate will soon grow to 10 million annually, meaning that *half a billion* (say that number slowly) people alive today will be killed by tobacco (Lopez, 1999). A teen-to-the-grave smoker has a 50 percent chance of dying from the habit, and the death is often agonizing and premature, as the Philip Morris company acknowledged in 2001. Responding to Czech Republic complaints about the health-care costs of tobacco, Philip Morris reassured the Czechs that there was actually a net "health-care cost savings due to early mortality" and the resulting savings on pensions and elderly housing (Herbert, 2001). Smoke a cigarette and nature will charge you 12 minutes—ironically, just about the length of time you spend smoking it (*Discover*, 1996). Eliminating smoking would increase life expectancy more than any other preventive measure (**FIGURE 43.1**).

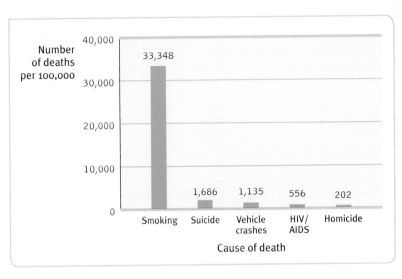

FIGURE 43.1
Premature deaths per 100,000 Canadians who were smoking by age 15
Smoking-related early deaths will eventually claim nine times more Canadian teen smokers than will suicide, car accidents, AIDS, and homicide combined (Statistics Canada, 1999).

The risks of smoking are hardly well-guarded secrets. Indeed, reports the World Health Organization (2005), "evidence shows that smoking harms nearly every organ of the body." The type of smoker who doesn't know about smoking's hazards, comic Dave Barry notes, is the "type of smoker whose brain has been removed with a melon scoop." The "Smoking Can Be Harmful to Your Health" warning is on every pack sold in the United States, and 97 percent of Americans believe that smoking is harmful (Blizzard, 2004). In Canada, 97 percent of adults and teens agree that smoking is associated with lung cancer, and nearly as many acknowledge smoking's links with respiratory ailments and heart disease (Statistics Canada, 1999).

Nevertheless, the statistics of smoking risks fail to persuade many teens (which brings to mind Joseph Stalin's reputed saying, "A single death is a tragedy; a million deaths is a statistic"). Asked to consider a 16-year-old smoker, 4 in 10 adolescent smokers agree that "although smoking may eventually harm this person's health, the very next single cigarette he/she smokes will probably not cause any harm" (Slovic, 2000). (The next one and the next and the next also, individually, do not matter; but the 300,000 smoked before age 60 by today's pack-a-day teens do, of course.)

Nonsmokers not only live healthier, they live happier. Smoking correlates with higher rates of depression, chronic disabilities, and divorce (Doherty & Doherty, 1998; Vita & others, 1998). For example, nondepressed teens who smoke suffer a quadrupled risk of developing depression (Goodman, 2000). Healthy living seems to add both years to life and life to years.

When and Why Do People Start Smoking?

Smoking is a *pediatric disease*. It usually begins during early adolescence and is especially common among those who get low grades, who drop out of school, who feel less competent and in control of their future, and whose friends, parents, and siblings smoke (Chassin & others, 1987; Schulenberg & others, 1994). If you are in college or university, and if by now the cigarette manufacturers haven't attracted your business, they almost surely never will.

We learn behaviors through the models we imitate and the social rewards we receive, which largely explains an adolescent's vulnerability to the allure of smoking. Adolescents are self-conscious and often think the world is watching their every move. So, they may begin smoking to imitate cool models, to get the social reward of being accepted by other smokers, and to project a mature image (Covington & Omelich, 1988). Cigarette companies, mindful that people decide on smoking and establish their brand loyalty during their teens, have effectively modeled smoking

SNAPSHOTS

© Jason Love

FIGURE 43.2
Peer influence
Kids don't smoke if their friends don't (Philip Morris, 2003).

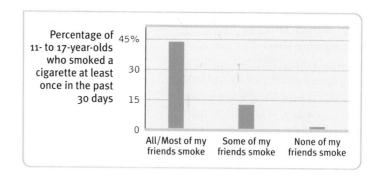

Percentage of 11- to 17-year-olds who smoked a cigarette at least once in the past 30 days

45%
30
15
0

All/Most of my friends smoke   Some of my friends smoke   None of my friends smoke

A correlation–causation question: Does the close link between teen smoking and friends' smoking reflect peer influence? Teens seeking similar friends? Or both?

Nic-a-teen
Aware that virtually all smokers start as teenagers—and that sales would plummet if no teens were enticed to smoke—cigarette companies target teens. By portraying tough, appealing, socially adept smokers, they entice teens to imitate. They are supported by the resurgence of Hollywood's modeling of smoking. With such stars as Vanessa Williams, Gwyneth Paltrow, Sharon Stone, Julia Roberts, Brad Pitt, Jim Carrey, Bruce Willis, and Arnold Schwarzenegger all looking cool or rebellious while dragging on a cigarette or cigar, teens in the mid-1990s were getting the message and becoming addicted in increasing numbers.

"A cigarette in the hands of a Hollywood star on screen is a gun aimed at a 12- or 14-year-old."

Screenwriter Joe Eszterhas, 2002

Asked "If you had to do it all over again, would you start smoking?" more than 85 percent of adult smokers answer No (Slovic & others, 2002).

with themes that appeal to youths: independence, adventure-seeking, social approval, sophistication. Typically, teens who start smoking also have friends who smoke, who suggest its pleasures, and who offer them cigarettes (Eiser, 1985; Evans & others, 1988; Rose & others, 1999). Among teens whose parents and best friends are non-smokers, the smoking rate is close to zero (Moss & others, 1992, and see **FIGURE 43.2**).

After smoking's toxicity became known, smoking in movies declined to about once every 12 minutes, on average, during the 1970s and 1980s, but then returned to about every 4 minutes during the 1990s (Brody, 2001). Smoking was modeled in films for teens, and by popular stars such as Julia Roberts, Gwyneth Paltrow, Jim Carrey, and Brad Pitt. Moreover, the more teens watch smoking in films, the more likely they are to experiment with tobacco (Dalton & others, 2002). Joe Eszterhas (2002), a screenwriter for 14 of the recent movies that often glamorized smoking, and a throat-cancer patient after a lifetime of smoking, says, "I find it hard to forgive myself. I have been an accomplice to the murders of untold numbers of human beings. . . . I don't wish my fate upon anyone in Hollywood, but I beg that Hollywood stop imposing it upon millions of others."

Why Do People Not Stop Smoking?

Once addicted to nicotine we find it very hard to quit. Tobacco products are as addictive as heroin and cocaine. Indeed, some who have kicked the heroin habit have been unable to also stop smoking. Surveys in Britain and the United States show that at least one in three of those who try cigarettes become hooked—a higher addiction rate than for heroin and cocaine (Anthony & others, 1994; Heishman & others, 1997).

As with other addictions, a smoker becomes *dependent;* each year fewer than one of every seven smokers who want to quit will do so. A smoker also develops *tolerance,* eventually needing larger and larger doses to get the same effect. A sad irony is that those who are initially most sensitive to nicotine—and most likely to feel sick or dizzy on first smoking—tend to develop a tolerance quickly and to become most strongly addicted (Pomerleau & others, 1993). Quitting causes *nicotine-withdrawal* symptoms, including craving, insomnia, anxiety, and irritability. And all it takes to relieve these aversive states is a cigarette—a portable nicotine dispenser.

As with all addictive drugs, nicotine use is not only compulsive and mood-altering, it is also reinforcing. Smoking delivers its hit of nicotine within 7 seconds, triggering the release of epinephrine and norepinephrine, which in turn diminish appetite and boost alertness and mental efficiency (**FIGURE 43.3**). At the same time, nicotine stimulates the central nervous system to release neurotransmitters that calm anxiety and reduce sensitivity to pain. For example, nicotine stimulates dopamine, and, like heroin and morphine, stimulates opioid release (Nowak, 1994; Scott & others, 2004). These rewards keep people smoking even when they wish they could stop (as do four in five smokers)—indeed, even when they know they are committing slow-motion suicide (Saad, 2002). Even if given low-nicotine cigarettes, smokers end up smoking more of them to maintain a roughly constant level of nicotine in the blood.

Consistent with the biopsychosocial perspective, genes influence one's propensity to cigarette addiction (**FIGURE 43.4**). A meta-analysis of twin studies indicates a 60 percent heritability (Heath & Madden, 1995). Two recent studies have further discovered that smokers and nonsmokers tend to differ in a gene that influences responses to the neurotransmitter dopamine (Lerman & others, 1999; Sabol & others, 1999).

1. Arouses the brain to a state of increased alertness

2. Increases heart rate and blood pressure

3. At high levels, relaxes muscles and triggers the release of neurotransmitters that may reduce stress

4. Reduces circulation to extremities

5. Suppresses appetite for carbohydrates

FIGURE 43.3
Where there's smoke . . . : The physiological effects of nicotine
Nicotine reaches the brain within 7 seconds, twice as fast as intravenous heroin. Within minutes, the amount in the blood soars.

FIGURE 43.4
Biopsychosocial approach to studying smoking behavior

Biological influences:
• genetic influences on nicotine addiction
• physiological addiction

Psychological influences:
• adolescent response to "cool" smoker models

Smoking behavior

Social-cultural influences:
• persuasive tobacco company efforts to convince teens to start smoking
• friends and family members who smoke

Helping Smokers Quit

OBJECTIVE 43-2 | Discuss ways of helping smokers to quit smoking—or preventing young people from ever starting.

The efforts to help people stop smoking include public health warnings, counseling, drug treatments, hypnosis, aversive conditioning (for example, having people sicken themselves by rapidly smoking cigarette after cigarette), operant conditioning, cognitive therapy, and support groups. The good news is that these treatments are often

CLOSE-UP:

FOR THOSE WHO WANT TO STOP SMOKING

Most smokers want to quit, and nearly half try each year, but fewer than one in seven succeed permanently, reports an expert panel appointed by the U.S. Agency for Health Care Policy and Research. The panel's smoking-cessation guidelines do, however, offer some helpful pointers (Wetter & others, 1998).

1. Set a quit date.
2. Inform family and friends.
3. Remove all cigarettes.
4. Review things you learned from previous attempts to quit and anticipate challenges.
5. Use a nicotine patch or gum.
6. Be totally abstinent—not even a single puff.

7. Abstain from or greatly limit alcohol (which facilitates relapse).
8. If other smokers live or work with you, quit together.
9. Avoid places where others are likely to smoke.
10. Exercise. In controlled experiments, quitters assigned to regular exercise had higher success rates (Bock & others, 1999).

> "To cease smoking is the easiest thing I ever did; I ought to know because I've done it a thousand times."
>
> Mark Twain, 1835–1910

"There's no shooting—we just make you keep smoking."

effective in the short run. But the bad news is that all but one-fifth of the participants eventually succumb to the habit again (Schelling, 1992). For those quitting solo, the odds are even lower. With a pack of cigarettes seldom more than minutes away, a single moment of weakness, often while experiencing stress or a negative mood, can be enough to break the resolve (Kassel & others, 2003).

Better news comes from a Centers for Disease Control report that half of Americans who have ever smoked have quit. More than 90 percent did so on their own, often after repeated attempts. For those who endure, the acute craving and withdrawal symptoms gradually dissipate over the ensuing six months (Ward & others, 1997). Because so many people have stopped or not started smoking, the percentage of American, Canadian, and British smokers has dropped sharply over the last 30 years (**FIGURE 43.5**). By 2004, 6 in 10 survey respondents in America, 7 in 10 in Britain, and almost 8 in 10 in Canada favored bans on workplace and restaurant smoking (Mason, 2004). And in 2005, the World Health Organization announced that 57 countries (including Australia, Britain, and Canada, but not the United States) had committed themselves to a global tobacco treaty that ensures strong tobacco warnings and bans on tobacco advertising, promotion, and sponsorship.

Still, among high school dropouts and those of lower socioeconomic levels, smoking rates remain high. It's among college students and graduates that smoking has become gauche rather than cool. In the United States, Canada, and Britain, smoking has become rare among the highly educated or in the upper socioeconomic level, but two to three times as common among the least educated (Halsey & Webb, 2000; Statistics Canada, 1999). The drop has been most pronounced in the male smoking rate, which now barely exceeds that of women. Thanks in part to such trends, the death rate due to coronary heart disease has declined by about 30 percent since the mid-1960s. Smoking-related cancer deaths have also been declining, especially among men (Wingo & others, 1999). If you, or someone you love, would like to stop smoking, see the Close-Up: For Those Who Want to Stop Smoking.

FIGURE 43.5 Smoking trends Gallup surveys reveal sharp drops in population smoking rates in Canada, the United States, and Britain since 1974 (McMurray, 2004).

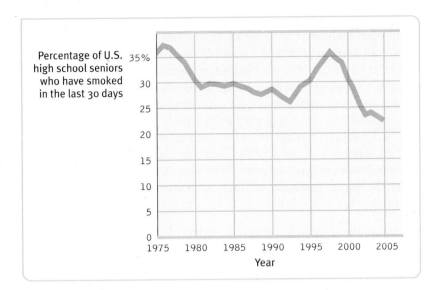

Percentage of U.S. high school seniors who have smoked in the last 30 days

FIGURE 43.6
The ups and downs of U.S. teen smoking
Adult smoking has dropped sharply over the last quarter-century, especially among educated people. But smoking made a temporary comeback among U.S. teens in the 1990s as Hollywood modeled smoking. (Data from Johnston & others, 2005.)

Smoking rebounded among U.S. teens during the mid-1990s, before falling again (**FIGURE 43.6**). A similar 1990s comeback occurred among Canadian teens (Brooke, 2000). And despite the declining cigarette sales among educated Western adults and new cigarette advertising restrictions, per-person cigarette consumption is near an all-time high worldwide.

Smoking has skyrocketed in Asia. In China, where most men but no more than 1 in 10 women smoke and where one-third of men are destined to be killed by tobacco, cigarette consumption soared from 100 billion cigarettes a year in the early 1950s to 1.8 trillion at the century's end (Cheng, 1999; Schwartz & Pomfret, 1998). In Japan, 35 percent (50 percent of men) are smokers (Coleman, 1997). Countries such as Kenya and Zimbabwe, with their relatively low per-person consumption rates, are prime targets for British and U.S. tobacco companies, which are putting hundreds of millions of unsuspecting people at risk for ill health and premature death. The World Health Organization has predicted that in the next three decades, 70 percent of tobacco-related deaths will occur in developing countries where many people are unaware of the dangers of smoking (Lopez, 1999; Schwartz & Pomfret, 1998).

How Can We Prevent Smoking?

It is vastly easier never to begin smoking than, once addicted, to stop. Social psychological analyses of why adolescents start smoking have helped generate curricular programs teachers can implement easily and inexpensively. According to a National Cancer Institute panel, the key ingredients of such programs are

* information about the effects of smoking.
* information about peer, parent, and media influences.
* training in refusal skills, through modeling and role playing.

The informational ingredients can also be offered through the mass media, which Australia has effectively used to discourage smoking across educational levels (Macaskill & others, 1992). In 1998, Florida initiated a massive youth-oriented media campaign to reduce the allure of smoking, and by early 1999, the number of 12- to 14-year-olds who reported smoking had dropped 19 percent from that of the previous year (*MMWR*, 1999).

There is one other way to discourage smoking: Make it more immediately costly. The most effective rewards and punishments are immediate. When the delayed rewards of exercise compete with the

Effective prevention
The state of Florida directed a huge, youth-oriented anti-smoking campaign in 1998, which had reduced rates of smoking by 1999.

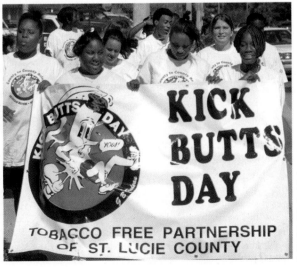

Paul J. Milette/Palm Beach Post

immediate discomfort of doing so, the immediate consequences may win out. Likewise, even *knowing* that in the long run smoking is often suicidal, many continue to smoke. If we could only raise the immediate costs, consumption would surely decline. The U.S. Centers for Disease Control (Brown & others, 1993) reports that raising cigarette taxes (and therefore prices) cuts consumption by about 4 percent for each 10 percent rise. The effect is doubly great among smokers in developing countries and among teenagers—the age when 90 percent of smokers start their habit (de Beyer, 2005). Many U.S. states sharply increased cigarette taxes—producing a 70 percent cigarette price increase between 1997 and 2001—and, sure enough, teen smoking began declining, especially in states also having vigorous smoking-prevention programs (Manning, 2002; Robison & Mason, 2002).

Obesity

Obesity and Weight Control

OBJECTIVE **43-3** | Discuss the adaptive advantages and modern-day disadvantages of a body that stores fat.

Why do some people gain weight while others eat the same amount and seldom add a pound? And why do so few overweight people win the battle of the bulge? Is there weight-loss hope for the 65 percent of Americans who, according to the Centers for Disease Control, are overweight?

Our bodies store fat for good reasons. Fat is an ideal form of stored energy—a high-calorie fuel reserve to carry the body through periods when food is scarce—a common occurrence in the feast-or-famine existence of our prehistoric ancestors. (Think of that spare tire around the middle as an energy storehouse—biology's counterpart to a hiker's waist-borne snack pack.) No wonder that in most developing societies today, as in Europe in earlier centuries—in fact, wherever people face famine—obesity signals affluence and social status (Furnham & Baguma, 1994).

In those parts of the world where food and sweets are now abundantly available, the rule that once served our hungry distant ancestors (When you find energy-rich fat or sugar, eat it!) has become dysfunctional. Being slightly overweight poses only modest health risks (Gibbs, 2005). Fitness matters more than being a little overweight. But significant obesity (**FIGURE 43.7**), especially among children, increases the risk of diabetes, high blood pressure, heart disease, gallstones, arthritis, and certain types of cancer, thus shortening life expectancy (Olshansky & others, 2005). The risks are greater for apple-shaped people who carry their weight in pot bellies than for pear-shaped people with ample hips and thighs (Greenwood, 1989). New research also has linked women's obesity to their risk of late-life Alzheimer's disease and brain tissue loss (Gustafson & others, 2003, 2004).

Cultures without a thin-ideal for women are also cultures without eating disorders. Ghanians, for example, idealize a larger body size than do Americans—and experience fewer eating disorders (Cogan & others, 1996). The same is true of African-American women compared with European-American women (Parker & others, 1995).

The Garden of Love (detail), Peter Paul Rubens, The Prado, Madrid/The Bridgeman Art Library/Superstock

Rubens' *The Garden of Love*
In other times and places, plumper bodies have been idealized. When food is scarce, plump seems beautiful; where food is plentiful, slender seems beautiful.

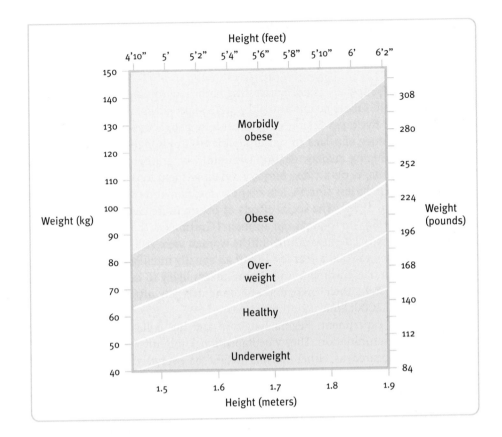

FIGURE **43.7**

Obesity measured as body mass index (BMI)

U.S. government guidelines encourage a body mass index (BMI) under 25. The World Health Organization and many countries define obesity as a BMI of 30 or more. The shading in this graph is based on BMI measurements for these heights and weights. BMI is calculated by using the following formula:

$$\frac{\text{Weight in kg (pounds} \times .45)}{\text{Squared height in meters (inches} \div 39.4)^2} = \text{BMI}$$

Not surprisingly, then, one study (Calle & others, 1999) that followed more than 1 million Americans over 14 years revealed that being significantly overweight can cut life short (**FIGURE 43.8**). Those overweight at age 40 die three years earlier than their slim counterparts, reports another long-term study (Peeters & others, 2003). The death rate is especially high among very overweight men. Understandably, in 2004 the U.S. Medicare system began recognizing obesity as an illness.

Yearly health care expenditures per U.S. woman, age 35 to 44 (Wee & others, 2005). As economist Paul Krugman (2005) says, "Fat is a fiscal issue."

Normal weight:	$2127
BMIs 25 to 29.9:	$2358
BMIs 30 to 34.9:	$2873
BMIs 35 to 39.9:	$3058
BMIs 40 and up:	$3506

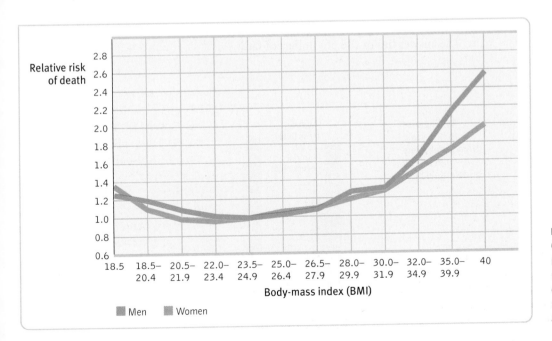

FIGURE **43.8**

Obesity and mortality

Relative risk of death among healthy nonsmokers rises with extremely high or low body mass index. (Data from 14-year study of 1.05 million Americans, Calle & others, 1999.)

The Social Effects of Obesity

OBJECTIVE **43-4** | Describe some of the social effects of obesity.

"The [obesity lawsuit] bill says, 'Don't run off and file a lawsuit if you are fat.' It says, 'Look in the mirror because you're the one to blame.'"

U.S. Representative F. James Sensenbrenner, 2004

Obesity can also be socially toxic, by affecting both how you are treated and how you feel about yourself. Obese people know the stereotype: slow, lazy, and sloppy (Crandall, 1994, 1995; Ryckman & others, 1989). Many people see obesity as a matter of choice or as evidence of a lack of self-discipline or a personality problem—a maladjusted way of reducing anxiety, dealing with guilt, or gratifying an "oral fixation." Widen people's images on a video monitor (making them look fatter) and observers suddenly rate them as less sincere, less friendly, meaner, and more obnoxious (Gardner & Tockerman, 1994). The social effects of obesity were clear in a study that followed 370 obese 16- to 24-year-old women (Gortmaker & others, 1993). When restudied seven years later, two-thirds of the women were still obese. They also were making less money—$7000 a year less—than an equally intelligent comparison group of some 5000 nonobese women. And they were less likely to be married. In personal ads, men often state their preference for, and women often advertise, slimness (Miller & others, 2000; Smith & others, 1990).

In one clever experiment, Regina Pingitore and her colleagues (1994) demonstrated weight discrimination. They videotaped mock job interviews in which professional actors appeared as either normal-weight or overweight applicants. In one condition, actors wore makeup and prostheses that made them look 30 pounds heavier. When appearing overweight, the same person, using the same lines, intonation, and gestures, was rated less worthy of hiring. The weight bias was especially strong against women applicants (**FIGURE 43.9**). Other studies reveal that weight discrimination, though hardly discussed, is greater than race and gender discrimination. It occurs at every stage of the employment cycle—hiring, placement, promotion, compensation, discipline, and discharge (Roehling, 1999). Experiments show that anti-fat prejudice even extends to applicants who are *seen* with an obese person (Hebl & Mannix, 2003).

"For fat students, the school experience is one of almost constant harassment."

Report on Size Discrimination, National Education Association, 1994

Weight discrimination takes its toll at home, too. In studies of patients who were especially unhappy with their weight—those who had lost an average of 100 pounds after short-cutting digestion with intestinal bypass surgery—4 in 5 said their children had asked them not to attend school functions. And 9 in 10 said they would rather have a leg amputated than be obese again (Rand & Macgregor, 1990, 1991).

Why don't obese people drop their excess baggage and free themselves of all this pain? The answer lies in the physiology of fat.

FIGURE 43.9
Gender and weight discrimination
When women applicants were made to look overweight, university students were less willing to think they would hire them. Among men applicants, weight mattered less. (Data from Pingitore & others, 1994.)

The Physiology of Obesity

OBJECTIVE 43-5 | Discuss some research findings on the role of heredity and environment in determining body weight.

Research on the physiology of obesity challenges the stereotype of severely overweight people being weak-willed gluttons. First, consider the arithmetic of weight gain: People get fat by consuming more calories than they expend. The energy equivalent of a pound of fat is 3500 calories; therefore, dieters have been told they will lose a pound for every 3500-calorie reduction in their diet. Surprise: This conclusion is false. Why? Read on.

Fat Cells

The immediate determinants of body fat are the size and number of fat cells. A typical adult has 30 to 40 billion of these miniature fuel tanks, half of which lie near the skin's surface. A fat cell can vary from relatively empty, like a deflated balloon, to overly full. In an obese person, fat cells may swell to two or three times their normal size and then divide or trigger nearby immature fat cells to divide—resulting in up to 75 billion fat cells (Hirsch, 2003). Once the number of fat cells increases—due to genetic predisposition, early childhood eating patterns, or adult overeating—it never decreases (**FIGURE 43.10**). On a diet, fat cells may shrink, but they never disappear (Sjöstrum, 1980).

Set Points and Metabolism

Once we become fat, we require less food to maintain our weight than we did to attain it. Why? Because compared with other tissue, fat has a lower metabolic rate—it takes less food energy to maintain. The "weight thermostat" of an obese person's body is set to maintain body weight within a higher-than-average range. When weight drops below this *set-point* (often considered a *settling-point* range of weight rather than a precise number of pounds), the person's hunger increases and metabolism decreases. Thus, the body adapts to starvation by burning off fewer calories, and to extra calories by burning off more.

In a classic month-long experiment (Bray, 1969), obese patients whose daily food intake was reduced from 3500 to 450 calories lost only 6 percent of their weight—partly because their bodies reacted as though they were being starved—their metabolic rates dropped about 15 percent (**FIGURE 43.11**). That is why reducing your food intake by 3500 calories may not reduce your weight by 1 pound. That is also why further weight loss comes slowly following the rapid losses during the initial three weeks or so of a rigorous diet. And that is why amounts of food that worked to maintain weight before a diet began may increase it when a diet ends—the body is still conserving energy.

Never obese   Obese   Reduced obese

FIGURE 43.10
Fat cells
We store energy in fat cells, which become larger and more numerous if we are obese, and smaller (but still more numerous) if we then lose weight. (Adapted from Jules Hirsch, 2003.)

FIGURE 43.11
The effects of a severe diet on obese patients' body weight and metabolism
After seven days on a 3500-calorie diet, six obese patients were given only 450 calories a day for the next 24 days. Body weight declined only 6 percent and then leveled off, because metabolism dropped about 15 percent. (From Bray, 1969.)

Phyllis Picardi/Stock, Boston

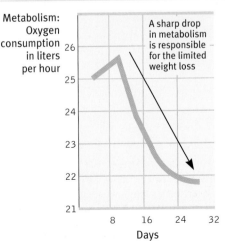

Individual differences in resting metabolism also explain why two people of the same height, age, and activity level can maintain the same weight, even if one of them eats much less than the other does. Lean people are naturally disposed to fidget and move about more than are energy-conserving overweight people who tend to sit still longer (Levine & others, 2005). Most overweight people are just normal people whose bodies predispose them to weigh more. This appears true despite findings that people—obese people, especially—tend to overestimate their physical activity and underestimate their caloric intake (Brownell & Wadden, 1992; Lichtman & others, 1992).

The Genetic Factor

Studies reveal a genetic influence on body weight. Consider:

- Despite shared family meals, adoptive siblings' body weights are uncorrelated with one another or with those of their adoptive parents. Rather, people's weights resemble those of their biological parents (Grilo & Pogue-Geile, 1991).
- Identical twins have closely similar weights, even when reared apart (Plomin & others, 1997; Stunkard & others, 1990). Across studies, their weight correlates +.74. The much lower +.32 correlation among fraternal twins suggests that genes explain two-thirds of our varying body mass (Maes & others, 1997). Being overweight is therefore *not* simply a matter of scarfing too many hot fudge sundaes. And losing weight is not merely a matter of mind over platter.
- Given an obese parent, a boy is three times, and a girl six times, more likely to be obese than their counterparts with normal-weight parents (Carrière, 2003).

So, the specifics of our genes predispose the size of our jeans. But the genetic influence is surely complex, with different genes, like differing band members, making music by playing together. Some genes might influence when our intestines signal "full," with others dictating how efficiently we burn calories or convert extra calories to fat, and still others prompting us to fidget or sit still. But recent experiments do detail one genetic mechanism for weight control. As a normal mouse's fat cells become bloated, its genes produce the protein leptin, which is monitored by the brain. When researchers injected obese mice with daily doses of leptin, the mice then ate less, became more active, and lost weight. So, might injections of leptin similarly serve as virtual fat for humans, fooling the brain into making a fat body trimmer? Although initial hopes for this magic-bullet obesity drug have been dashed, more than 100 obesity drugs were in the testing pipeline at the end of 2004. One of the more promising blocks the same brain receptors tickled by marijuana, which stimulates appetite (*Science*, 2004). By the time you read this, some of these drugs may be reaching the market.

Fat-signaling hormone

The obese mouse at left has a defective gene for producing the fat-signaling hormone, leptin. When the genetically similar mouse at right was treated with leptin, it shed 40 percent of its body weight.

Courtesy of John Soltis, The Rockefeller University, New York, NY

The Food and Activity Factors

Genes aren't the whole story behind obesity, however. Genes cannot explain why obesity is six times more common in women in lower socioeconomic classes, more common among Americans than among Europeans, and more common among Americans today than in 1900, and less common among recent immigrants (Goel & others, 2004). Western cultures have become like animal feedlots—places where farmers fatten animals by restricting their exercise and offering abundant fattening food. In a massive long-term study of 50,000 nurses, researchers found—even after controlling for exercise, smoking, age, and diet—that each two-hour increase in daily TV watching predicted a 23 percent obesity increase and a 7 percent diabetes increase (Hu & others, 2003). Among Ontario's Old Order Amish, where farming and gardening is labor intensive and pedometers reveal that men walk nine miles a day and women seven miles, the obesity rate is one-seventh the U.S. rate (Bassett & others, 2004). People living in walking-dependent communities such as Manhattan tend to weigh less than more sedentary folks in car-dependent suburbs (Ewing & others, 2003).

Survival of the fattest

Lack of exercise and high-calorie foods are compounded by larger serving sizes (Double Whoppers) and a tripled percentage of meals eaten at fast-food restaurants since 1997 (Farley & Cohen, 2001). Compared with 1971, today's women are eating 300 more calories a day and today's men nearly 200 more (O'Connor, 2004). For example, on most North American college campuses, yesterday's cafeteria line with limited choices has been replaced by today's food buffet, with multiple serving stations offering all-you-can-eat entrees and make-your-own waffles washed down with limitless soft drinks (Brody, 2003). For many, the understandable result is the "freshman 15." And compared with their counterparts in the early 1900s, people are eating a higher-fat, higher-sugar diet, expending fewer calories, and suffering higher rates of diabetes at younger ages (Brody, 2003; Thompson, 1998). Taken together, Big Macs, sugar-laden soft drinks, inactivity, and tobacco form a weapon of mass destruction. Obese smokers die, on average, 13.5 years sooner than their normal-weight nonsmoking neighbors (Peeters & others, 2003).

Your parents and grandparents at age 30 likely weighed less than you did or will. Since 1960, the average American has grown one inch and gained 23 pounds (**TABLE 43.2**). In Britain, the average woman's dress size has increased from size 12 in 1951 to size 16 today; just since 1980, adult obesity rates have nearly tripled, to 21 percent (Hawkes, 2002; Merriman, 1999). And over the last 40 years, as health experts have cajoled Americans to lose weight, the adult obesity rate has more than doubled to over 30 percent (CDC, 2004; and see **FIGURE 43.12**). Just since 1986, the number of obese Americans who were more than 100 pounds overweight has quadrupled (Sturm, 2003).

And so it goes, pretty much everywhere this book is being read. Worldwide, 60 percent of people are overweight, estimates the World Health Organization (Booth & Neufer, 2005). Australia, similar to Britain and America, classifies some 60 percent of its population as overweight or obese (Australian Bureau of Statistics, 1999; Halsey &

TABLE 43.2

AVERAGE U.S. BODY WEIGHT (POUNDS), 1960 TO 2002

	1960–1962	1971–1974	1988–1994	1999–2002
19-year-olds				
Men	–	160	161	172
Women	–	131	139	149
20- to 74-year-olds				
Men	166	173	182	189
Women	140	144	153	163

Source: Centers for Disease Control and Prevention report by C. L. Ogden & others (2004).

In Gallup surveys from 1990 to 2001, the average American's reported body weight rose 10 pounds (Saad, 2002). That comes to a collective weight gain of well over a billion pounds. The extra 10 pounds per person cost airlines $275 million in 2000 to burn the extra fuel needed to lift that weight (Dannenberg & others, 2004).

FIGURE **43.12**
Trading risks
As smoking, which kills some 400,000 Americans a year, has been dropping, obesity, which also contributes to many deaths, has been increasing. (Source: Centers for Disease Control and Prevention.)

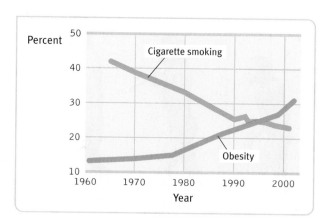

Webb, 2000; Healey, 2004). In Canada, the proportion of people classified as overweight has increased by 60 percent since 1985 (Statistics Canada, 1999). Commenting on a reported tripling of child obesity over the past 15 years, Canadian National Institute of Nutrition president, Anne Kennedy, noted, "The trend is mimicking the United States. We're five years behind, but catching up" (Krauss, 2002).

The "bottom" line: New stadiums, theaters, and subway cars are offering wider seats to accommodate this population growth (Hampson, 2000). The Washington State Ferries abandoned its 50-year-old standard of 18 inches per person. "Eighteen-inch butts are a thing of the past," explained a spokesperson (Shepherd, 1999). New York City, facing a large problem with Big Apple bottoms, has mostly replaced its 17.5-inch bucket-style subway seats with bucketless seats (Hampson, 2000). In the end, today's people need more room.

Note how these findings reinforce a familiar lesson from our earlier study of intelligence: There can be high levels of heritability (genetic influence on individual differences) without heredity explaining group differences. Genes mostly determine why one person today is heavier than another. Environment mostly determines why people today are heavier than their counterparts 50 years ago.

Losing Weight

OBJECTIVE 43-6 | Discuss the chances of success for an overweight person who wants to lose weight.

Perhaps you are shaking your head: "Slim chance we have of becoming and staying thin. If we lose weight on a diet, our metabolism slows and our hungry fat cells cry out, 'Feed me!' We're fated for fat!" Indeed, the condition of an obese person's body reduced to average weight is much like that of a semistarved body. Held under normal set point, each body "thinks" it is starving. Having lost weight, formerly obese people look normal, but their fat cells may be abnormally small, their metabolism slowed, and their minds obsessed with food.

All this explains why, short of drastic surgery to tie off part of the stomach and small intestine, most people who succeed on a weight-loss program eventually regain most of the weight (Garner & Wooley, 1991; Jeffery & others, 2000). (Millions of people can vouch that it is possible to lose weight; they have done it lots of times.) Some people do manage to keep pounds off, especially with programs that modify their life-style and ongoing eating behavior. But for most people, the only long-term result of this losing battle is a thinner wallet.

Yet, the battle of the bulge rages on as intensely as ever, and it is most intense among those with two X chromosomes. Fighting obesity is an enormous business. Americans spend $40 billion a year on diet foods and drinks (Kolata, 2004).

"We've been active in this field for 35 years, and our enthusiasm for dieting, especially dieting based on unrealistic expectations, has not yet been kindled."
University of Toronto researchers C. Peter Herman and Janet Polivy (2003)

Two-thirds of women and half of men say they want to lose weight; about half of those women and men say they are "seriously trying" (Moore, 2003). Asked if they would rather "be five years younger or weigh 15 pounds less," 29 percent of men and 48 percent of women said they would prefer losing the weight (*Responsive Community,* 1996).

With fat cells, set points, metabolism, and genetic factors all tirelessly conspiring against shedding excess pounds, what advice can psychology offer? For some helpful hints, see Close-Up: For Those Who Want to Lose Weight on the next page.

"It works as well as most other diet plans. . . . I've lost over $200 in less than three weeks."

Psychologist Kelly Brownell (2002) proposes altering the environments that put people at risk for obesity.

- Slap an extra tax on calorie-laden junk food and soft drinks. We're reducing smoking with increased cigarette taxes. Why not, for the same reason, institute a "Twinkie Tax"?
- Use the revenues to subsidize healthy foods and to finance health-supportive nutritional advertising.
- Establish a fast-food–free zone around schools.
- Ban the advertising of junk foods to kids.
- Encourage activity by designing communities with walks, bike paths, and residences near workplaces.

Although mindful that preserving weight loss is a constant challenge, Stanley Schachter (1982) was less pessimistic than most of today's obesity researchers about the dieter's chances of success. He recognized the overwhelming rate of failure among those in structured weight-loss programs, but he also noted that these people are a special group who probably have been unable to help themselves. Moreover, the failure rates recorded for these programs are based on single attempts at weight loss. Perhaps when people try repeatedly to lose weight, more of them do eventually succeed. When Schachter interviewed people, he found that one-fourth had at one time been significantly overweight and had tried to slim down.

A hard-won success story
Tammy and Jeffrey Munson—two volunteers in the National Weight Control Registry—shown before and after she lost 147 pounds and he lost 100 pounds.

Joe R. Liuzzo

CLOSE-UP:

FOR THOSE WHO WANT TO LOSE WEIGHT

People struggling with obesity are well advised to seek medical evaluation and guidance. For others who wish to take off a few pounds, researchers have offered these tips.

Begin only if you feel motivated and self-disciplined. For most people, permanent weight loss requires making a career of staying thin—a lifelong change in eating habits combined with gradually increased exercise.

Minimize exposure to tempting food cues. Keep tempting foods out of the house or out of sight. Go to the supermarket only on a full stomach, and avoid the sweets and chips aisles. Eat simple meals, with only a few different foods; given more variety, people consume more (Raynor & Epstein, 2001).

Take steps to boost your metabolism. Inactive people are often overweight (**FIGURE 43.13**). One of the few predictors of successful long-term weight loss is exercise,

both during and after changing your eating patterns (Jeffery & others, 2000; McGuire & others, 1999; Wadden & others, 1998). Exercise, such as brisk walking, running, and swimming, not only empties fat cells, builds muscle, and makes you feel better, it also temporarily speeds up metabolism and can help lower your set point (Bennett, 1995; Kolata, 1987; Thompson & others, 1982). Even brief bouts of exercise—four 10-minute walks a day—provide benefits (Jakicic & others, 1999). Lack of exercise helps explain why many fail to lose weight permanently. In a Centers for Disease Control study of 107,000 adults, only one in five of those trying to lose weight were following the government recommendation to both count calories and exercise 150 minutes weekly (Serdula & others, 1999).

Be realistic and moderate. Being moderately heavy is less risky than being extremely thin (Ernsberger

"I looked at you and thought, I bet this man runs marathons."

& Koletsky, 1999). Permanent weight loss is not easy. Set a realistic goal and take it gradually. "A reasonable time line for a 10 percent reduction in body weight is six months," advises the National Institutes of Health (1998).

Eat healthy foods. Whole grains, fruits, vegetables, and healthy fats such as those found in olive oil and fish help regulate appetite and artery-clogging cholesterol (Taubes, 2001, 2002). Better crispy greens than Krispy Kremes.

Don't starve all day and eat one big meal at night. This eating pattern, common among overweight people, slows metabolism. Moreover, those who eat a balanced breakfast are, by late morning, more alert and less fatigued (Spring & others, 1992).

Beware of the binge. Among people who consciously restrain their eating, drinking alcohol or feeling anxious or depressed can unleash the urge to eat (Herman & Polivy, 1980). So can being distracted from monitoring your eating (Ward & Mann, 2000). (Ever notice that you eat more when out with friends?) Once the diet is broken, the person often thinks "what the heck" and then binges (Polivy & Herman, 1985, 1987). A lapse need not become a full collapse: Remember, most people occasionally lapse. Remind yourself that you've succeeded before, and continue with your plan, which may require lifelong self-control.

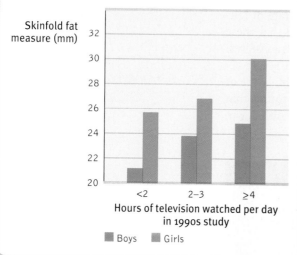

Skinfold fat measure (mm)

Hours of television watched per day in 1990s study

■ Boys ■ Girls

FIGURE 43.13

American idle: Couch potatoes beware— TV watching correlates with obesity

In a 1980s study of 6671 young people 12 to 17 years old, and in a 1990s follow-up study of 4063 individuals 8 to 16 years old, obesity was more common among those who watched the most television (Andersen & others, 1998; Dietz & Gortmaker, 1985). Of course, overweight people may avoid activity, preferring to sit and watch TV. But the association between TV watching and obesity remained when many other factors were controlled, suggesting that inactivity and snacking while watching TV do contribute to obesity. Also, as lifestyles have become more sedentary and TV watching has increased, so has the percentage of overweight people in Britain, North America, and elsewhere. When California children were placed in a TV-reduction educational program, they watched less—and lost weight (Robinson, 1999).

Of these, 6 out of 10 had *succeeded*: They weighed at least 10 percent less than their maximum prediet weight (an average loss of 35 pounds) and were no longer obese. A 1993 survey of 90,000 *Consumer Reports* readers found 25 percent of dieters claiming an enduring weight loss. Aided by media publicity, the National Weight Control Registry has identified more than 4000 people who have maintained significant weight loss for at least one year and are being studied over time. On average, these people have lost 60 pounds and kept it off for five years, virtually always with continued diet and exercise.

These findings hint that prospects for losing weight may be somewhat brighter than the dismal conclusions drawn from following patients who undergo a single weight-loss program. If all this has a familiar ring, recall that stop-smoking programs tend to be (1) effective in the short run and (2) ineffective in the long run, but that (3) many people are former smokers.

There is another option for overweight people, and one chosen by 13 percent of the people Schachter interviewed: to accept one's weight. We all do well to note that researchers have *not* identified guilt, hostility, oral fixation, or any similar personality maladjustment as causes of obesity. Nor is obesity simply a matter of a lack of willpower. Dieters are more likely to binge when under stress or after breaking their diets, which may be largely a consequence of their constant dieting. Indeed, the relentless pursuit of thinness puts people at risk not only for binge eating and food obsession, but also for weight fluctuations, malnutrition, smoking, depression, and harmful side effects of weight-loss drugs (Cogan & Ernsberger, 1999).

"Fat is not a four-letter word," proclaims the National Association to Advance Fat Acceptance, so "a waist is a terrible thing to mind." Such statements discount the health risks linked with significant obesity, but they do convey a valid point: It is surely better to accept oneself as a bit heavy than to diet and binge and feel continually out of control and guilty. Fans loved Oprah Winfrey before she lost 67 pounds. They loved her after she put them back on. They loved her when she shed them again. And they will love her still, chubby or not.

While working to clarify the precise relationships among diet, behavior, and health (**FIGURE 43.14**), health psychologists continue their efforts to persuade us

"Fat! So?"

Popular T-shirt at the 1999 convention of the National Association to Advance Fat Acceptance

FIGURE 43.14
A biopsychosocial approach to health

to adopt healthier life-styles. Such persuasion is a challenge. Happy people tend to see themselves as relatively invulnerable to health problems, especially those that might arise from their own actions (Salovey & Birnbaum, 1989; Weinstein, 1987). They also typically believe their own life-style is healthier than other people's—that they drink less alcohol, consume less fat and cholesterol, and get more exercise. Often they are fooling themselves. Most smokers—even most of those who have smoked for 20 years or tried quitting 10 or more times—think they will successfully quit within the next year (Slovic, 2001). Few young adults expect to gain weight, yet most do. When buying clothes, we prefer snug fits over loose fits, telling ourselves we will soon be taking off a few pounds. (Store clerks never hear, "I'll take that sweater in an extra large, because people my age usually put on more weight.")

Furthermore, many individuals who admit to risky behaviors will deny that the behaviors actually make them personally more vulnerable to illness or injury. Unlike people who are told they have normal blood pressure, those told they have high blood pressure tend to dismiss its seriousness (Croyle & Ditto, 1990). And smokers may delude themselves by saying that their exercising counteracts smoking's effects.

Because of our tendency to deny health risks, the first hurdle health-promotion programs must surmount is to get us to realize our vulnerability to stress- and behavior-related health problems. Only then will we make an effort to control stress, stop smoking, moderate our drinking, eat wisely, exercise regularly, and even buckle our seat belts.

>> Learning Outcomes

Modifying Illness-Related Behaviors

OBJECTIVE 43-1 | **Explain why people smoke.**

Teen smoking comes in part from social rewards—identifying with or being accepted by "cool" people. Depending on their genetic inheritance, one in three early smokers will develop a physiological addiction to nicotine. By triggering a release of epinephrine, norepinephine, dopamine, and the opioids, nicotine takes away unpleasant cravings and delivers rewards.

OBJECTIVE 43-2 | **Discuss ways of helping smokers to quit smoking—or preventing young people from ever starting.**

Helpful pointers include setting a quit date, informing family and friends of the decision, removing all cigarettes, reviewing successful strategies learned in previous attempts, using a nicotine patch or gum, abstaining totally from smoking, abstaining from alcohol, avoiding places where others are likely to smoke, and exercising. Programs that successfully discourage young people from smoking (1) provide information about the effects of smoking; (2) educate young people about peer, parent, and media influences; and (3) use modeling and role playing to train young people in refusal skills. Raising cigarette taxes effectively cuts consumption.

OBJECTIVE 43-3 | **Discuss the adaptive advantages and modern-day disadvantages of a body that stores fat.**

Fat is a concentrated fuel reserve that can be used during times of famine. This once-adaptive tendency is maladaptive for modern humans in a world of easily accessible food. A lack of exercise and an abundance of high-calorie food have led to high rates of obesity (defined as a body mass index of 30 or more), with increased risks of diabetes, high blood pressure, heart disease, and other health problems.

OBJECTIVE 43-4 | **Describe some of the social effects of obesity.**

Obese people, particularly obese women, may encounter bias in hiring, placement, promotion, compensation, discipline, and discharge in the workplace; in searching for a romantic relationship; and in interactions with family and others.

OBJECTIVE 43-5 | **Discuss some research findings on the role of heredity and environment in determining body weight.**

Studies of twins and adopted children indicate that being overweight is at least in part an inherited trait. People differ in the number and size of their fat cells, and in their resting metabolic rates. Once someone gains weight, however, fat cells multiply, and less energy is needed to maintain fat tissue than is needed to maintain muscle tissue. Environmental factors, such as frequently eating high-calorie foods and living a sedentary life, also matter. Genes mostly determine why one man is heavier than another, but environment mostly determines why the same man is heavier than his grandfather was at the same age.

OBJECTIVE 43-6 | **Discuss the chances of success for an overweight person who wants to lose weight.**

People who fail to lose weight in structured programs may represent a group at especially high risk. Many people who were once significantly overweight have successfully lost weight and kept it off for at least one year. Some overweight people, realizing that obesity is not a matter of willpower, choose to accept their weight. Others who want to lose weight can improve their chances by beginning a weight-loss program only when feeling motivated and self-disciplined; minimizing exposure to tempting food cues; boosting energy expenditure through exercise; setting realistic and moderate goals; eating healthy foods; spacing small meals throughout the day; and remembering that occasional lapses will occur when making a lifelong change in eating patterns.

TEST YOURSELF

1. Nonsmokers, the text reports, are less likely to become depressed and get divorced. What type of research finding is this, and what explanations might it have?

(Answer in Appendix B.)

ASK YOURSELF

1. To promote health by discouraging smoking, many governments now heavily tax cigarettes. Would you concur with the suggestion of Kelly Brownell (1997), director of Yale's Center for Eating and Weight Disorders, to slap a similar tax on unhealthy foods to decrease their consumption? Explain your perspective on this issue.

>WEB

Multiple-choice **self-tests** and more may be found at www.worthpublishers.com/myers.

JAMES BALDWIN (1924–1987), FROM "SONNY'S BLUES," 1957, *GOING TO MEET THE MAN*

So, we drove along, between the green of the park and the stony, lifeless elegance of hotels and apartment buildings, toward the vivid, killing streets of our childhood. These streets hadn't changed, though housing projects jutted up out of them now like rocks in the middle of a boiling sea. Most of the houses in which we had grown up had vanished. . . . Houses exactly like the houses of our past yet dominated the landscape, boys exactly like the boys we once had been found themselves smothering in these houses, came down into the streets for light and air and found themselves encircled by disaster. Some escaped the trap, most didn't. Those who got out always left something of themselves behind, as some animals amputate a leg and leave it in the trap. It might be said, perhaps, that I had escaped, after all, I was a school teacher, or that Sonny had, he hadn't lived in Harlem for years. Yet, as the cab moved uptown through streets which seemed, with a rush, to darken with dark people, . . . it came to me that what we both were seeking through our separate cab windows was that part of ourselves which had been left behind. It's always at the hour of trouble and confrontation that the missing member aches.

Personality

OBJECTIVE 44-1 | Define *personality*.

Lord of the Rings hobbit-hero Frodo Baggins knew that throughout his harrowing journey there was one who would never fail him—his loyal and ever-cheerful companion, Sam Gamgee. Even before they left their beloved hometown, Frodo warned Sam that the journey would not be easy:

> "It is going to be very dangerous, Sam. It is already dangerous. Most likely neither of us will come back."
>
> "If you don't come back, sir, then I shan't, that's certain," said Sam. "[The Elves told me] 'Don't you leave him!' Leave him! I said. I never mean to. I am going with him, if he climbs to the Moon; and if any of those Black Riders try to stop him, they'll have Sam Gamgee to reckon with." (Tolkien, *The Fellowship of the Ring*, p. 96)

And so they did! Later in the story, when it became clear that Frodo had to venture into the dreaded land of Mordor without the rest of the company, it was Sam who insisted he would accompany Frodo, come what may. It was Sam who lifted Frodo's flagging spirits with songs and stories from their boyhood, and Sam upon whom Frodo leaned when he could barely take another step. When Frodo was overcome by the evil of the ring he bore, it was Sam who saved Frodo from completely succumbing to it. And in the end, it was Sam who enabled Frodo to successfully reach the end of his journey. Sam Gamgee—the cheerful, conscientious, emotionally stable optimist—never faltered in his faithfulness or his belief that they could overcome the threatening darkness.

J. R. R. Tolkien's character Sam Gamgee, as he appears and reappears throughout the trilogy, exhibits the distinctiveness and consistency that define **personality**—an individual's characteristic pattern of thinking, feeling, and acting. Other modules in this book emphasize our similarity—how we all develop, perceive, learn, remember, think, and feel. Modules 44 through 46 emphasize our individuality.

Actually, much of psychology deals with personality. Across the field, psychologists study biological influences on personality; personality development across the life span; personality-related aspects of learning, motivation, emotion, and health; disorders of personality; and social influences on personality.

We begin with two grand theories—historically significant perspectives that helped establish the field of personality psychology and raised key issues still being addressed in today's research and clinical work and that became part of our cultural legacy.

- Sigmund Freud's psychoanalytic theory (Module 44) proposed that childhood sexuality and unconscious motivations influence personality.
- The *humanistic* approach (Module 45) focused on our inner capacities for growth and self-fulfillment.

These historic theories, which offer sweeping perspectives on human nature, are complemented by what Module 46 goes on to explore: today's more focused and down-to-earth scientific research of specific aspects of personality.

Today's personality researchers engage in focused analyses of the basic dimensions of personality and their impact on behavior; on the biological roots of these basic dimensions; on the interaction of persons and environments; and on studies of self-esteem, self-serving bias, and cultural influences on one's sense of self. Along the way, we'll survey some contemporary findings about the unconscious mind—findings that probably would have surprised Freud himself.

■ **personality** an individual's characteristic pattern of thinking, feeling, and acting.

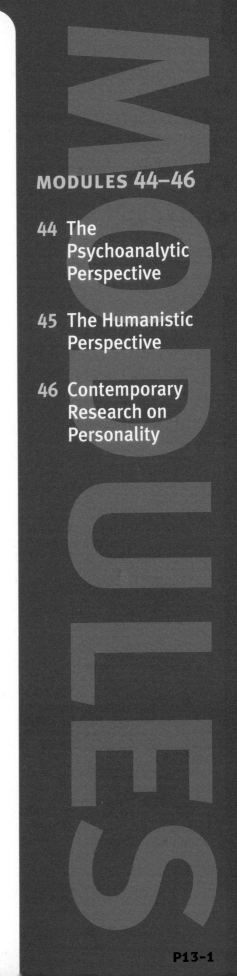

44

The Psychoanalytic Perspective

OBJECTIVE 44-2 | Explain how Freud's experiences in private practice led to his theory of psychoanalysis.

"Sigmund Freud has left an important—and I believe indelible—mark on human self-understanding," observes Drew Westen (1998). Others disagree, noting that Freud's current influence in psychological science has diminished (Robins & others, 1999). But love him or hate him, Freud has profoundly influenced Western culture. Ask 100 people on the street to name a notable deceased psychologist, suggests Keith Stanovich (1996, p. 1), and "Freud would be the winner hands down." In the popular mind, he is to psychology's history what Elvis is to rock music's history. Freud's influence lingers in literary and film interpretation, psychiatry, and clinical psychology. So, who was this early personality theorist, and what did he teach?

Long before entering the University of Vienna in 1873, a youthful Sigmund Freud showed signs of independence and brilliance. He had a prodigious memory and so loved reading plays, poetry, and philosophy that he once ran up a bookstore debt beyond his means. As a teen he often took his evening meal in his tiny bedroom in order to lose no time from his studies.

Sigmund Freud, 1856–1939
"I was the only worker in a new field."

Freud went to medical school and after graduation set up a private practice, specializing in nervous disorders. Before long, however, he faced patients whose disorders made no neurological sense. For example, a patient might have lost all feeling in a hand—yet there is no sensory nerve that, if damaged, would numb the entire hand and nothing else. Freud's search for a cause for such disorders set his mind running. His views, which evolved as he treated patients and analyzed himself, eventually filled 24 volumes published between 1888 and 1939. Following his first solo book, *The Interpretation of Dreams* (1900), his ideas gradually began to attract both dedicated followers and intense criticism. For now, let's reserve judgment on Freud's theory and instead try to see things as he did. It is impossible to summarize 24 volumes in these few pages, but we can highlight Freud's *psychoanalytic theory*—the first comprehensive theory of personality, which included ideas about an unconscious region of the mind, psychosexual stages, and defense mechanisms for holding anxiety at bay.

Exploring the Unconscious

OBJECTIVE 44-3 | Discuss Freud's view of the mind as an iceberg, and explain how he used this image to represent conscious and unconscious regions of the mind.

Might some neurological disorders have psychological rather than physiological causes? Observing patients led Freud to his "discovery" of the unconscious. He decided that the peculiar loss of feeling in one's hand might be caused by a fear of touching one's genitals; that unexplained blindness or deafness might be caused by

■ **free association** in psychoanalysis, a method of exploring the unconscious in which the person relaxes and says whatever comes to mind, no matter how trivial or embarrassing.

■ **psychoanalysis** Freud's theory of personality that attributes thoughts and actions to unconscious motives and conflicts; the techniques used in treating psychological disorders by seeking to expose and interpret unconscious tensions.

■ **unconscious** according to Freud, a reservoir of mostly unacceptable thoughts, wishes, feelings, and memories. According to contemporary psychologists, information processing of which we are unaware.

not wanting to see or hear something that aroused intense anxiety. Initially, Freud thought hypnosis might unlock the door to the unconscious, but patients displayed an uneven capacity for hypnosis. He then turned to **free association**—in which he merely told the patient to relax and say whatever came to mind, no matter how embarrassing or trivial. Freud assumed that a line of mental dominoes had fallen from his patients' distant past to their troubled present. Free association, he believed, allowed him to retrace that line, following a chain of thought leading into the patient's unconscious, where painful unconscious memories, often from childhood, could be retrieved and released. Freud called his theory of personality and the associated treatment techniques **psychoanalysis.**

"Good morning, beheaded—uh, I mean beloved."

Basic to Freud's theory was his belief that the mind is like an iceberg—mostly hidden (**FIGURE 44.1**). Our conscious awareness is the part of the iceberg that floats above the surface. Below the surface is the much larger, **unconscious** region containing thoughts, wishes, feelings, and memories, of which we are unaware. Some of these thoughts we store temporarily in a *preconscious* area, from which we can retrieve them into conscious awareness. Of greater interest to Freud was the mass of unacceptable passions and thoughts that he believed we *repress,* or forcibly block from our consciousness because they would be too unsettling to acknowledge. Freud believed that, although we are not consciously aware of them, these troublesome feelings and ideas powerfully influence us, sometimes gaining expression in disguised forms—the work we choose, the beliefs we hold, our daily habits, our troubling symptoms.

For Freud the determinist, nothing was ever accidental. He believed he could glimpse the unconscious seeping not only into people's free associations, beliefs, habits, and symptoms but also into slips of the tongue and pen. He illustrated with a financially stressed patient who, not wanting any large pills, said, "Please do not give me any bills, because I cannot swallow them." Similarly, Freud viewed jokes as expressions of repressed sexual and aggressive tendencies, and dreams as the "royal road to the unconscious." The remembered content of dreams (their *manifest content*) he believed to be a censored expression of the dreamer's unconscious wishes (the dream's *latent content*). In his analysis of dreams, Freud searched for the nature of patients' inner conflicts and their release from inner tensions.

"I know how hard it is for you to put food on your family."

George W. Bush, 2000

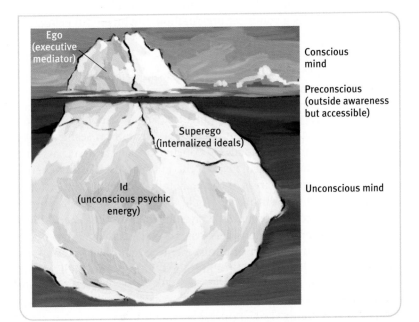

Ego (executive mediator)

Superego (internalized ideals)

Id (unconscious psychic energy)

Conscious mind

Preconscious (outside awareness but accessible)

Unconscious mind

FIGURE 44.1
Freud's idea of the mind's structure
Consciousness is like an iceberg's visible tip. Note that the id is totally unconscious, but ego and superego operate both consciously and unconsciously. (Adapted from Freud, 1933, p. 111.)

"Fifty is plenty."   "Hundred and fifty."

The ego struggles to reconcile the demands of superego and id, said Freud.

Personality Structure

OBJECTIVE 44-4 | Describe Freud's view of personality structure, and discuss the interactions of the id, ego, and superego

In Freud's view, human personality—including its emotions and strivings—arises from a conflict between our aggressive, pleasure-seeking biological impulses and the internalized social restraints against them. Freud believed personality is the result of our efforts to resolve this basic conflict—to express these impulses in ways that bring satisfaction without also bringing guilt or punishment. To understand the mind's dynamics during this conflict, Freud proposed three interacting systems: the *id, ego,* and *superego* (see Figure 44.1).

The **id** has a reservoir of unconscious psychic energy constantly striving to satisfy basic drives to survive, reproduce, and aggress. The id operates on the *pleasure principle:* If not constrained by reality, it seeks immediate gratification. To envision an id-dominated person, think of newborn infants, crying out for satisfaction the moment they feel a need, caring nothing for the outside world's conditions and demands. Or think of people with a present rather than future time perspective—those who often use tobacco, alcohol, and other drugs, and would sooner party now than sacrifice today's pleasure for future success and happiness (Keough & others, 1999).

As the **ego** develops, the young child learns to cope with the real world. The ego, operating on the *reality principle,* seeks to gratify the id's impulses in realistic ways that will bring long-term pleasure rather than pain or destruction. (Imagine what would happen if, lacking an ego, we expressed our unrestrained sexual or aggressive impulses whenever we felt them.) The ego contains our partly conscious perceptions, thoughts, judgments, and memories.

Beginning around age 4 or 5, Freud theorized, a child's ego recognizes the demands of the newly emerging **superego,** the voice of conscience that forces the ego to consider not only the real but the ideal, and that focuses solely on how one *ought* to behave. The superego strives for perfection, judging actions and producing positive feelings of pride or negative feelings of guilt. Someone with an exceptionally strong superego may be virtuous yet, ironically, guilt-ridden; another with a weak superego may be wantonly self-indulgent and remorseless.

Because the superego's demands often oppose the id's, the ego struggles to reconcile the two. It is the personality "executive," mediating the impulsive demands of the id, the restraining demands of the superego, and the real-life demands of the external world. If chaste Jane feels sexually attracted to John she may satisfy both id and superego by joining a volunteer organization to which John belongs.

Personality Development

OBJECTIVE 44-5 | Identify Freud's psychosexual stages of development, and describe the effects of fixation on behavior.

Analysis of his patients' histories convinced Freud that personality forms during life's first few years. Again and again his patients' symptoms seemed rooted in unresolved conflicts from early childhood. He concluded that children pass through a series of **psychosexual stages,** during which the id's pleasure-seeking energies focus on distinct pleasure-sensitive areas of the body called *erogenous zones* (**TABLE 44.1**).

Freud believed that during the *phallic stage* boys seek genital stimulation, and they develop both unconscious sexual desires for their mother and jealousy and hatred for their father, whom they consider a rival. Given these feelings, boys supposedly also feel guilt and a lurking fear of punishment, perhaps by castration, from their father. Freud called this collection of feelings the **Oedipus complex** after the Greek legend of Oedipus, who unknowingly killed his father and married his mother. Some psychoanalysts in Freud's era believed that girls experienced a parallel *Electra complex.* Freud's own thinking seemed to vary on this issue.

■ **id** contains a reservoir of unconscious psychic energy that, according to Freud, strives to satisfy basic sexual and aggressive drives. The id operates on the *pleasure principle,* demanding immediate gratification.

■ **ego** the largely conscious, "executive" part of personality that, according to Freud, mediates among the demands of the id, superego, and reality. The ego operates on the *reality principle,* satisfying the id's desires in ways that will realistically bring pleasure rather than pain.

■ **superego** the part of personality that, according to Freud, represents internalized ideals and provides standards for judgment (the conscience) and for future aspirations.

■ **psychosexual stages** the childhood stages of development (oral, anal, phallic, latency, genital) during which, according to Freud, the id's pleasure-seeking energies focus on distinct erogenous zones.

■ **Oedipus** [ED-uh-puss] **complex** according to Freud, a boy's sexual desires toward his mother and feelings of jealousy and hatred for the rival father.

■ **identification** the process by which, according to Freud, children incorporate their parents' values into their developing superegos.

■ **fixation** according to Freud, a lingering focus of pleasure-seeking energies at an earlier psychosexual stage, in which conflicts were unresolved.

TABLE 44.1

FREUD'S PSYCHOSEXUAL STAGES

Stage	Focus
Oral (0–18 months)	Pleasure centers on the mouth—sucking, biting, chewing
Anal (18–36 months)	Pleasure focuses on bowel and bladder elimination; coping with demands for control
Phallic (3–6 years)	Pleasure zone is the genitals; coping with incestuous sexual feelings
Latency (6 to puberty)	Dormant sexual feelings
Genital (puberty on)	Maturation of sexual interests

Children eventually cope with threatening feelings, said Freud, by repressing them and by identifying with (trying to become like) the rival parent. It's as though something inside the child decides, "If you can't beat 'em [the parent of the same sex], join 'em." Through this **identification** process, children's superegos gain strength as they incorporate many of their parents' values. Freud believed that identification with the same-sex parent provides what psychologists now call our *gender identity*—our sense of being male or female. This illustrates what both Freud and today's *object relations theorists* have presumed: that our early childhood relations with parents, caregivers, and everything else influences our developing identity, personality, and frailties.

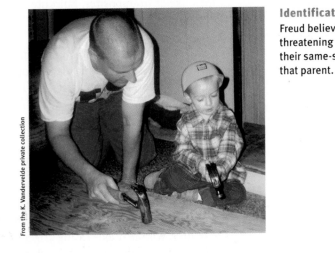

From the K. Vandervelde private collection

Identification
Freud believed that children cope with threatening feelings of competition with their same-sex parent by identifying with that parent.

In Freud's view, conflicts unresolved during earlier psychosexual stages could surface as maladaptive behavior in the adult years. At any point in the oral, anal, or phallic stages, strong conflict could lock, or **fixate,** the person's pleasure-seeking energies in that stage. A person who had been either orally overindulged or deprived (perhaps by abrupt, early weaning) might fixate at the oral stage, for example. This orally fixated adult could exhibit either passive dependence (like that of a nursing infant) or an exaggerated denial of this dependence—perhaps by acting tough and uttering biting sarcasm. Or the person might continue to seek oral gratification by smoking and eating excessively. In such ways, Freud suggested, the twig of personality is bent at an early age.

Defense Mechanisms

OBJECTIVE 44-6 | Describe the function of defense mechanisms, and identify six of them.

Anxiety, said Freud, is the price we pay for civilization. As members of social groups, we must control our sexual and aggressive impulses, not act them out. But sometimes the ego fears losing control of this inner war between the demands of the id and the superego, and the result is a dark cloud of unfocused anxiety, which leaves us feeling unsettled but unsure why.

"Oh, for goodness' sake! Smoke!"

Freud proposed that the ego protects itself with **defense mechanisms,** tactics that reduce or redirect anxiety by distorting reality. Here are six examples.

- **Repression** banishes anxiety-arousing thoughts and feelings from consciousness. According to Freud, *repression underlies all the other defense mechanisms,* each of which disguises threatening impulses and keeps them from reaching consciousness. Freud believed that repression explains why we do not remember our childhood lust for our parent of the other sex. However, he also believed that repression is often incomplete, that repressed urges seep out in dream symbols and slips of the tongue.

- **Regression** allows us to retreat to an earlier, more infantile stage of development. Facing the anxious first days of school, a child may regress to the oral comfort of thumb-sucking. Juvenile monkeys, when anxious, retreat to infantile clinging to their mothers or to one another (Suomi, 1987). Even homesick new college students may long for the security and comfort of home.

- In **reaction formation,** the ego unconsciously makes unacceptable impulses look like their opposites. En route to consciousness, the unacceptable proposition "I hate him" becomes "I love him." Timidity becomes daring. Feelings of inadequacy become bravado.

- **Projection** disguises threatening impulses by attributing them to others. Thus, "He doesn't trust me" may be a projection of the actual feeling "I don't trust him" or "I don't trust myself." An El Salvadoran saying captures the idea: "The thief thinks everyone else is a thief."

- **Rationalization** occurs when we unconsciously generate self-justifying explanations to hide from ourselves the real reasons for our actions. Thus, habitual drinkers may say they drink with their friends "just to be sociable." Students who fail to study may rationalize, "All work and no play makes Jack [or Jill] a dull person."

- **Displacement** diverts sexual or aggressive impulses toward an object or person that is psychologically more acceptable than the one that aroused the feelings. Children who fear expressing anger against their parents may displace it by kicking the family pet. Students upset over an exam may snap at a roommate.

Note that all these defense mechanisms function indirectly and unconsciously. They reduce anxiety by disguising our threatening impulses. Just as the body unconsciously defends itself against disease, so also, believed Freud, does the ego unconsciously defend itself against anxiety.

> "For seven and a half years I've worked alongside President Reagan. We've had triumphs. Made some mistakes. We've had some sex . . . uh . . . setbacks."
>
> George H. W. Bush, 1988

> "The lady doth protest too much, methinks."
>
> William Shakespeare, *Hamlet*, 1600

■ **defense mechanisms** in psychoanalytic theory, the ego's protective methods of reducing anxiety by unconsciously distorting reality.

■ **repression** in psychoanalytic theory, the basic defense mechanism that banishes anxiety-arousing thoughts, feelings, and memories from consciousness.

■ **regression** psychoanalytic defense mechanism in which an individual faced with anxiety retreats to a more infantile psychosexual stage, where some psychic energy remains fixated.

■ **reaction formation** psychoanalytic defense mechanism by which the ego unconsciously switches unacceptable impulses into their opposites. Thus, people may express feelings that are the opposite of their anxiety-arousing unconscious feelings.

Regression
Faced with a mild stressor, children and young monkeys will regress, retreating to the comfort of earlier behaviors.

David Young-Wolff / Photo Edit

Harlow Primate Laboratory, University of Wisconsin

The Neo-Freudian and Psychodynamic Theorists

OBJECTIVE 44-7 | Contrast the views of the neo-Freudians and psychodynamic theorists with Freud's original theory.

Freud's writings were controversial, but they soon attracted followers, mostly young, ambitious physicians who formed an inner circle around their strong-minded leader. These pioneering psychoanalysts and others, whom we now call *neo-Freudians,* accepted Freud's basic ideas: the personality structures of id, ego, and superego; the importance of the unconscious; the shaping of personality in childhood; and the dynamics of anxiety and the defense mechanisms. But they veered away from Freud in two important ways. First, they placed more emphasis on the conscious mind's role in interpreting experience and in coping with the environment. And second, they doubted that sex and aggression were all-consuming motivations. Instead, they tended to emphasize loftier motives and social interactions. The following examples illustrate.

Alfred Adler and Karen Horney [HORN-eye] agreed with Freud that childhood is important. But they believed that childhood *social,* not sexual, tensions are crucial for personality formation. Adler (who had proposed the still-popular idea of the *inferiority complex*) himself struggled to overcome childhood illnesses and accidents, and he believed that much of our behavior is driven by efforts to conquer childhood feelings of inferiority, feelings that trigger our strivings for superiority and power. Horney said childhood anxiety, caused by the dependent child's sense of helplessness, triggers our desire for love and security. Horney countered Freud's assumptions that women have weak superegos and suffer "penis envy," and she attempted to balance the bias she detected in this masculine view of psychology.

Unlike other neo-Freudians, Carl Jung—Freud's disciple-turned-dissenter—placed less emphasis on social factors and agreed with Freud that the unconscious exerts a powerful influence. But to Jung (pronounced Yoong), the unconscious contains more than our repressed thoughts and feelings. He believed we also have a **collective unconscious,** a common reservoir of images derived from our species' universal experiences. Jung said that the collective unconscious explains why, for many people, spiritual concerns are deeply rooted and why people in different cultures share certain myths and images, such as mother as a symbol of nurturance. (Today's psychologists discount the idea of inherited experiences. But many do believe that our shared evolutionary history shaped some universal dispositions.)

■ **projection** psychoanalytic defense mechanism by which people disguise their own threatening impulses by attributing them to others.

■ **rationalization** defense mechanism that offers self-justifying explanations in place of the real, more threatening, unconscious reasons for one's actions.

■ **displacement** psychoanalytic defense mechanism that shifts sexual or aggressive impulses toward a more acceptable or less threatening object or person, as when redirecting anger toward a safer outlet.

■ **collective unconscious** Carl Jung's concept of a shared, inherited reservoir of memory traces from our species' history.

> The female . . . acknowledges the fact of her castration, and with it, too, the superiority of the male and her own inferiority; but she rebels against this unwelcome state of affairs."
>
> Sigmund Freud, *Female Sexuality,* 1931

Alfred Adler
"The individual feels at home in life and feels his existence to be worthwhile just so far as he is useful to others and is overcoming feelings of inferiority" (*Problems of Neurosis,* 1964).

Karen Horney
"The view that women are infantile and emotional creatures, and as such, incapable of responsibility and independence is the work of the masculine tendency to lower women's self-respect" (*Feminine Psychology,* 1932).

Carl Jung
"We can keep from a child all knowledge of earlier myths, but we cannot take from him the need for mythology" (*Symbols of Transformation,* 1912).

■ **projective test** a personality test, such as the Rorschach or TAT, that provides ambiguous stimuli designed to trigger projection of one's inner dynamics.

■ **Thematic Apperception Test (TAT)** a projective test in which people express their inner feelings and interests through the stories they make up about ambiguous scenes.

■ **Rorschach inkblot test** the most widely used projective test, a set of 10 inkblots, designed by Hermann Rorschach; seeks to identify people's inner feelings by analyzing their interpretations of the blots.

Freud died in 1939. Since then, some of his ideas have been incorporated into *psychodynamic theory*. "Most contemporary dynamic theorists and therapists are not wedded to the idea that sex is the basis of personality," notes Drew Westen (1996). They "do not talk about ids and egos, and do not go around classifying their patients as oral, anal, or phallic characters." What they do assume, with Freud, is that much of our mental life is unconscious, that we often struggle with inner conflicts among our wishes, fears, and values, and that childhood shapes our personalities and ways of becoming attached to others. For example, Freud's idea that early childhood experiences with caregivers were key to the developing personality laid the groundwork for later theory and research on infant attachment and on its long-term consequences.

Assessing Unconscious Processes

OBJECTIVE 44-8 | Describe two projective tests used to assess personality, and discuss some criticisms of them.

Those who study personality or provide therapy need ways to evaluate personality characteristics. Methods of assessment differ because they are tailored to different personality theories. So what might be the tool of choice for clinicians working in the Freudian tradition?

Evaluating personality from this perspective would require a road into the unconscious mind, which contains residues from early childhood experiences. (Recall that Freud believed free association and dream interpretation could reveal the unconscious.) Objective assessment tools, such as agree-disagree or true-false questionnaires would be inadequate because they would merely tap the conscious surface. The tool of choice would be a sort of psychological x-ray—a test that sees through our surface pretensions and reveals our hidden conflicts and impulses.

Projective tests aim to provide such a view by presenting an ambiguous stimulus and then asking test-takers to describe it or tell a story about it. The stimulus has no inherent significance, so any meaning people read into it presumably is a projection of their interests and conflicts. Henry Murray (1933) demonstrated a possible basis for such a test at a party hosted by his 11-year-old daughter. Murray engaged the children in a frightening game called "Murder." When shown some photographs after the game, the children perceived the photos as more malicious than they had before the game. These children, it seemed to Murray, had *projected* their inner feelings into the pictures. A few years later, Murray introduced the **Thematic Apperception Test (TAT),** in which people view ambiguous pictures and then make up stories about them (**FIGURE 44.2**). One use of storytelling has been to assess achievement motivation. Shown a daydreaming boy, those who imagine he is fantasizing about an achievement are presumed to be projecting their own goals. "As a rule," said Murray, "the subject leaves the test happily unaware that he has presented the psychologist with what amounts to an x-ray of his inner self" (quoted by Talbot, 1999).

Other projective tests ask test-takers to draw a person, to complete sentences ("My mother . . ."), or to provide the first word that comes to mind after the examiner says a test word. Most widely used is the famous **Rorschach inkblot test,** introduced in 1921 by Swiss psychiatrist Hermann Rorschach [ROAR-shock]. The test assumes that what we see in its 10 inkblots reflects our inner feelings and conflicts (**FIGURE 44.3**). If we see predatory animals or weapons, the examiner may infer we have aggressive tendencies.

Is this a reasonable assumption? If so, can a psychologist use the Rorschach to understand one's personality and diagnose an emotional disorder? The two primary criteria of a good test are *reliability* (consistency of

> "We don't see things as they are; we see things as we are."
>
> The Talmud

FIGURE 44.2
The TAT
This clinician presumes that the hopes, fears, and interests expressed in this boy's descriptions of a series of ambiguous pictures in the Thematic Apperception Test (TAT) are projections of his inner feelings.

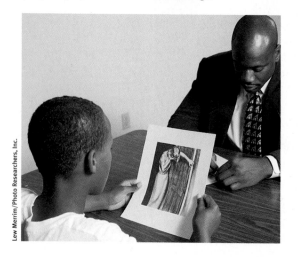

Lew Merrim/Photo Researchers, Inc.

results) and *validity* (predicting what it's supposed to). On those criteria, how good is the Rorschach?

By the second half of the twentieth century, critics had pointed out that no universally accepted system existed for scoring and interpreting the Rohrschach tests (Sechrest & others, 1998). Two raters who had been trained in different scoring systems would display only minimal agreement on the results of a given test. Nor was the test very successful at predicting behavior or at discriminating between groups (for example, identifying who is suicidal and who is not). The Rorschach is not an emotional MRI.

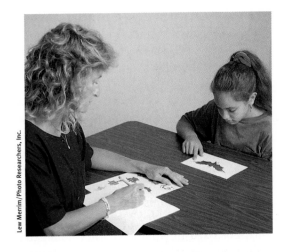

With all the criticisms, the Rorschach remains "simultaneously, the most cherished and the most reviled of all psychological assessment tools" (Hunsley & Bailey, 1999). Clinicians—82 percent of whom report administering it at least occasionally—often cherish the Rorschach (Watkins & others, 1995; Lilienfeld & others, 2000). Some offer judges Rorschach-based assessments of criminals' violence potential. Other clinicians view it as a diagnostic tool, a source of suggestive leads, or an icebreaker and a revealing interview technique. Edward Aronow and his colleagues (1995) report the example of a woman who found "four pink geese" in a Rorschach card, and then, under prompting, recalled that her uncle, a farmer, had molested her, that he had four daughters, and that his white geese became pink when slaughtered. There is now a research-based, computer-aided coding and interpretation tool that aims to improve agreement among raters and enhance the test's validity (Erdberg, 1990; Exner, 2003). For example, a person's seeing lots of reflections in the blots is said to indicate self-centeredness. The Society for Personality Assessment acknowledges that one should not "use Rorschach findings alone to draw a legal conclusion" or to decide whether, for example, child sexual abuse has occurred. But the society contends that "the Rorschach possesses documented reliability and validity" and that its use in personality assessment is "appropriate and justified."

But the evidence is insufficient to its revilers, who argue that the test has very limited validity and who note that inkblot assessments diagnose many normal adults as pathological (Wood & others, 2003, 2006). They argue that only a few of the many Rorschach-derived scores, such as ones for hostility and anxiety, have demonstrated validity. Other critics find "no scientific basis for justifying the use of Rorschach scales in psychological assessments" (Hunsley & Bailey, 1999) and even propose a moratorium on its clinical and forensic use (Garb & others, 2005). "If psychologists used tea leaves instead of the Rorschach, we'd probably be better off," suggests psychologist-critic James Wood (2003), "because then, at least, no one would take the results seriously."

Alternative projective assessment techniques, such as the TAT and the Draw-a-Person test fare little better, conclude Scott Lilienfeld, James Wood, and Howard Garb (2001). "Even seasoned professionals," they warn, "can be fooled by their intuitions and their faith in tools that lack strong evidence of effectiveness. When a substantial body of research demonstrates that old intuitions are wrong, it is time to adopt new ways of thinking." Freud himself probably would have been uncomfortable with trying to diagnose patients based on tests and would have been more interested in the therapist–patient interactions that take place during the test.

FIGURE 44.3

The Rorschach test

In this projective test, people tell what they see in a series of symmetrical inkblots. Some who use this test are confident that the interpretation of ambiguous stimuli will reveal unconscious aspects of the test-taker's personality. Others use it as an icebreaker or to supplement other information.

"If a professional psychologist is 'evaluating' you in a situation in which you are at risk and asks you for responses to ink blots . . . walk out of that psychologist's office."
Robyn Dawes, *House of Cards: Psychology and Psychotherapy Based on Myth*, 1994

"The forward thrust of the antlers shows a determined personality, yet the small sun indicates a lack of self-confidence. . . ."

"The Rorschach Inkblot Test has been resoundingly discredited . . . I call it the Dracula of psychological tests, because no one has been able to drive a stake through the cursed thing's heart."
Carol Tavris, "Mind Games: Psychological Warfare Between Therapists and Scientists," 2003

"Dawkins' law of adversarial debate: 'When two incompatible beliefs are advocated with equal intensity, the truth does not lie halfway between them.'"
Richard Dawkins, 2004

Evaluating the Psychoanalytic Perspective

OBJECTIVE 44-9 | Summarize psychology's current assessment of Freud's theory of psychoanalysis.

Contradictory Evidence from Modern Research

We critique Freud from an early twenty-first–century perspective, a perspective that itself will be subject to revision. Freud did not have access to neurotransmitter or DNA studies, or to all that we have since learned about human development, thinking, and emotion. Thus, to criticize his theories by comparing them with current concepts, some say, is like comparing Henry Ford's Model T with today's Mustang.

But Freud's admirers and his critics agree that recent research contradicts many of his specific ideas. Today's developmental psychologists see our development as life-long, not fixed in childhood. They doubt that infants' neural networks are mature enough to sustain as much emotional trauma as Freud assumed. Some think Freud overestimated parental influence and underestimated peer influence (and abuse). They also doubt that conscience and gender identity form as the child resolves the Oedipus complex at age 5 or 6. We gain our gender identity earlier and become strongly masculine or feminine even without a same-sex parent present. And they note that Freud's ideas about childhood sexuality arose from his rejection of stories of childhood sexual abuse told by his female patients—stories that some scholars believe he suggested, coerced, or later misremembered and then attributed to their own childhood sexual wishes and conflicts (Esterson, 2001; Powell & Boer, 1994). Today, we understand how Freud's questioning might have created false memories, and we also know that childhood sexual abuse does happen.

New ideas about why we dream dispute Freud's belief that dreams disguise and fulfill wishes. And slips of the tongue can be explained as competition between similar verbal choices in our memory network. Someone who says "I don't want to do that—it's a lot of brothel" may simply be blending *bother* and *trouble* (Foss & Hakes, 1978). Researchers find little support for Freud's idea that defense mechanisms disguise sexual and aggressive impulses (though our cognitive gymnastics do indeed work to protect our self-esteem). History also has failed to support another of Freud's ideas—that suppressed sexuality causes psychological disorders. From Freud's time to ours, sexual inhibition has diminished; psychological disorders have not.

Is Repression a Myth?

Freud's entire psychoanalytic theory rests on his assumption that the human mind often *represses* painful experiences, banishing them into the unconscious until, with the help of a guide, we somehow uncover them, finding them intact, like long-lost books in a dusty attic. Recover and resolve the painful repressed memories of our childhood and emotional healing would follow. Under Freud's influence, repression became a widely accepted concept, used to explain hypnotic phenomena, psychological disorders, and apparent lost and recovered memories of childhood traumas (Cheit, 1998). In one survey, 88 percent of university students believed that painful experiences commonly get pushed out of awareness and into the unconscious (Garry & others, 1994).

Actually, contend many of today's researchers, repression, if it ever occurs, is a rare mental response to terrible trauma. "Repression folklore is . . . partly refuted, partly untested, and partly untestable," says Elizabeth Loftus (1995). Consider: If the human mind indeed commonly banishes painful experiences, how do we explain these odd findings?

- Shouldn't we expect children who have witnessed a parent's murder to repress the experience? A study of sixteen 5- to 10-year-old children who had this horrific experience found that not one repressed the memory (Malmquist, 1986).

"Many aspects of Freudian theory are indeed out of date, and they should be: Freud died in 1939, and he has been slow to undertake further revisions."

Psychologist Drew Westen (1998)

"I remember your name perfectly but I just can't think of your face."

Oxford professor W. A. Spooner, 1844–1930, famous for his linguistic flip-flops (*spoonerisms*). Spooner rebuked one student for "fighting a liar in the quadrangle" and another who "hissed my mystery lecture," adding "You have tasted two worms."

- Shouldn't survivors of Nazi death camps have banished the atrocities from consciousness? With rare exceptions, they remember all too well—although many do benefit from disclosing and talking through their experiences (Helmreich, 1992, 1994; Pennebaker, 1990).
- Shouldn't battle-scarred veterans suffer amnesia for their worst experiences? In one neurological unit in a British hospital, 35 percent of military patients arrived with amnesia after severe combat during World War II (Arrigo & Pezdek, 1997; Karon & Widener, 1997, 1998). But such cases often appear to be either concussion-related or a *false amnesia* tactic for escaping intolerable situations (Holmes, 1990, 1994). Folklore regarding recovered battlefield memories is either unconfirmed or related to therapists' use of suggestive techniques.

There are exceptions—one death camp survivor reportedly forgot for more than 30 years the snatching and shooting of her infant son (Kraft, 1996). Some researchers believe that extreme, prolonged stress, such as the stress some severely abused children experience, might disrupt memory by damaging the hippocampus (Schacter, 1996). But the far more common reality is that high stress (and associated stress hormones) enhances memory. Powerfully negative emotional events are therefore remembered well (Alexander & others, 2005; Shobe & Kihlstrom, 1997).

In fact, too well: Traumatic events, such as rape and torture, haunt survivors, who experience unwanted flashbacks. They are seared onto the soul. "You see the babies," said Holocaust survivor Sally H. (1979). "You see the screaming mothers. You see hanging people. You sit and you see that face there. It's something you don't forget."

The Modern Unconscious Mind

Freud was right about at least one thing: We indeed have limited access to all that goes on in our minds (Erdelyi, 1985, 1988; Kihlstrom, 1990). In fact, our capacity for unconscious learning is quite sophisticated. Pawel Lewicki and his colleagues (1992, 1997) at the University of Tulsa's Nonconscious Information Processing Laboratory discovered that people's nonconscious learning can anticipate patterns "too complex and too confusing to be consciously noticed." In one study, some students watched (others did not) as the numeral 6 jumped around a computer screen from quadrant to quadrant. Although the movement seemed to be in random order—no one consciously detected any rule—it was based on a complex, hidden pattern. And those who had seen the earlier presentations were quicker to find the next 6 when it was hidden among a screen full of numbers. Without knowing how they did it, their ability to track the number from one quadrant to another was improving. When the number's movement became truly random, their performance declined.

Lewicki repeated the experiment with his quick-witted psychology professor colleagues, who knew he was studying nonconscious learning. They, too, gained speed in locating the target's next position, and they, too, did not know why. When the experimenters switched to a random sequence and performance declined, the professors conjectured reasons for the decline (threatening subliminal messages, perhaps?). To students who had displayed nonconscious learning, Lewicki even offered $100 if they could uncover the hidden pattern. Some spent hours trying to decipher the sequence. None succeeded.

Other researchers have confirmed the reality of nonconscious *implicit learning* (Fletcher & others, 2005; Frensch & Rünger, 2003). Such experiments point to a vast realm of out-of-sight information. Nevertheless, the "iceberg" notion held by today's research psychologists differs from Freud's—so much so, argues Anthony Greenwald (1992), that it is time to abandon Freud's view of the unconscious. Many psychologists now think of the unconscious not as seething passions and repressive censoring

> "Warning. Despite 70 years of research, there is no objective evidence to support the concept of repression."
>
> Psychologist David S. Holmes (1994)

> "During the Holocaust, many children . . . were forced to endure the unendurable. For those who continue to suffer [the] pain is still present, many years later, as real as it was on the day it occurred."
>
> Eric Zillmer, Molly Harrower, Barry Ritzler, and Robert Archer, *The Quest for the Nazi Personality*, 1995

■ **terror-management theory** proposes that faith in one's worldview and the pursuit of self-esteem provide protection against a deeply rooted fear of death.

> Two passengers leaned against the ship's rail and stared at the sea. 'There sure is a lot of water in the ocean,' said one. 'Yes,' answered his friend, 'we've only seen the top of it.'"
>
> Psychologist George A. Miller (1962)

> I don't want to attain immortality through my work; I want to attain immortality by not dying."
>
> Woody Allen

but as cooler information processing that occurs without our awareness. To these researchers, the unconscious also involves

- the schemas that automatically control our perceptions and interpretations.
- the priming by stimuli to which we have not consciously attended.
- the right-hemisphere activity that enables the split-brain patient's left hand to carry out an instruction the patient cannot verbalize.
- the parallel processing of different aspects of vision and thinking.
- the implicit memories that operate without conscious recall, even among those with amnesia.
- the emotions that activate instantly, before conscious analysis.
- the self-concept and stereotypes that automatically and unconsciously influence how we process information about ourselves and others.

More than we realize, we fly on autopilot. Our lives are guided by off-screen, out-of-sight, nonconscious information processing. The nonconscious mind is huge. This understanding of nonconscious information processing is more like the pre-Freudian view of an underground stream of thought from which spontaneous creative ideas surface.

Recent history has supported Freud's idea that we defend ourselves against anxiety. Again, however, the contemporary idea differs from Freud's. Jeff Greenberg, Sheldon Solomon, and Tom Pyszczynski (1997) believe that one source of anxiety is "the terror resulting from our awareness of vulnerability and death." More than 130 studies testing their **terror-management theory** show that thinking about one's mortality—for example, by writing a short essay on dying and its associated emotions—provokes enough anxiety to intensify prejudices. Death anxiety motivates contempt for others and esteem for oneself.

Faced with a threatening world, people act not only to enhance their self-esteem but also to adhere more strongly to worldviews that answer questions about life's meaning. Moreover, they cleave to close relationships (Mikulincer & others, 2003). The events of 9/11—a striking experience of the terror of death—led trapped World Trade Center occupants to spend their last moments calling loved ones, and led most Americans to reach out to family and friends.

Recent research has also provided some support for Freud's idea of defense mechanisms (even if they don't work exactly as Freud supposed). For example, Roy Baumeister and his colleagues (1998) found that people tend to see their foibles and attitudes in others, a phenomenon that Freud called projection and that today's researchers call the *false consensus effect,* the tendency to overestimate the extent to which others share our beliefs and behaviors. People who cheat on their taxes or break speed limits tend to think many others do likewise. People falsely told they are high in repressed anger or dishonesty tend more to see such in others (Schimel & others, 2003). Moreover, when trying to suppress thinking about our own faults we become more likely to see them in others (Newman & others, 1997). Supportive evidence is, however, meager for other defenses, such as displacement, that are tied to instinctual energy. More evidence exists for defenses, such as reaction formation, that defend self-esteem. Defense mechanisms, Baumeister concludes, are motivated less by the seething impulses that Freud presumed than by our need to protect our self-image.

Freud's Ideas as Scientific Theory

Psychologists also criticize Freud's theory for its scientific shortcomings, for falling short of the standard that good scientific theories explain observations and offer testable hypotheses. Freud's theory rests on few objective observations and parts of it offer few hypotheses to verify or reject. (For Freud, his own recollections and interpretations of patients' free associations, dreams, and slips were evidence enough.)

What is the most serious problem with Freud's theory? It offers after-the-fact explanations of any characteristic (of one person's smoking, another's fear of horses,

> We are arguing like a man who should say, 'If there were an invisible cat in that chair, the chair would look empty; but the chair does look empty; therefore there is an invisible cat in it.'"
>
> C. S. Lewis, *Four Loves,* 1958

another's sexual orientation) yet fails to *predict* such behaviors and traits. If you feel angry at your mother's death, you illustrate his theory because "your unresolved childhood dependency needs are threatened." If you do not feel angry, you again illustrate his theory because "you are repressing your anger." That, said Calvin Hall and Gardner Lindzey (1978, p. 68), "is like betting on a horse after the race has been run." A good theory makes testable predictions.

For such reasons, some of Freud's critics offer harsh words. They see a decaying Freudian edifice built on the swamplands of childhood sexuality, repression, dream analysis, and after-the-fact speculation. "When we stand on [Freud's] shoulders, we only discover that we're looking further in the wrong direction," says John Kihlstrom (1997). Freud's most searing critic, Frederick Crews (1998), likens Freud to Peter Sellers' bumbling Inspector Clouseau, albeit with a unique talent for bamboozling an entire century. What is original about Freud's ideas is not good, and what is good is not original (the unconscious mind is an idea that dates back to Plato).

So, should psychology post a "Do Not Resuscitate" order on this old theory? Freud's supporters object. To criticize Freudian theory for not making testable predictions is, they say, like criticizing baseball for not being an aerobic exercise, something it was never intended to be. Freud never claimed that psychoanalysis was predictive science. He merely claimed that, looking back, psychoanalysts could find meaning in our state of mind (Rieff, 1979).

Freud's supporters also note that some of his ideas *are* enduring. It was Freud who drew our attention to the unconscious and the irrational, to our self-protective defenses, to the importance of human sexuality, and to the tension between our biological impulses and our social well-being. It was Freud who challenged our self-righteousness, punctured our pretensions, and reminded us of our potential for evil.

In science, Darwin's legacy lives while Freud's is waning (Bornstein, 2001). In the popular culture, Freud's legacy lives on. Some ideas that many people assume to be true—that childhood experiences mold personality, that dreams have meaning, that many behaviors have disguised motives—are part of that legacy. His early twentieth-century concepts penetrate our twenty-first-century language. Without realizing their source, we may speak of *ego, repression, projection, complex* (as in "inferiority complex"), *sibling rivalry, Freudian slips,* and *fixation.* "Freud's premises may have undergone a steady decline in currency within academia for many years," noted Martin Seligman (1994), "but Hollywood, the talk shows, many therapists, and the general public still love them."

>> LEARNING OUTCOMES

The Psychoanalytic Perspective

OBJECTIVE 44-1 | Define *personality*.

Psychologists define *personality* as an individual's characteristic pattern of thinking, feeling, and acting. The early grand theories of personality tried to explain human nature, but current theories tend to focus on specific aspects of personality, such as our traits, uniqueness, sense of personal control, and concept of self.

OBJECTIVE 44-2 | Explain how Freud's experiences in private practice led to his theory of psychoanalysis.

As a physician specializing in nervous disorders, Freud encountered patients whose complaints could not be explained in terms of purely physical causes. His attempt to understand these conditions led to his theory of psychoanalysis, the first comprehensive theory of personality.

OBJECTIVE 44-3 | Discuss Freud's view of the mind as an iceberg, and explain how he used this image to represent conscious and unconscious regions of the mind.

Freud believed that most of the mind—the *unconscious*—is hidden from view (as most of an iceberg is hidden below water) because we repress the thoughts, wishes, feelings, and memories that create feelings of anxiety. In his view, this repression is never fully successful, and the troublesome thoughts and feelings express themselves in disguised forms unless we retrieve them into conscious awareness and free ourselves from the tensions they create. He sought to analyze these unconscious dynamics through *free association* and *dream interpretation*.

OBJECTIVE 44-4 | Describe Freud's view of personality structure, and discuss the interactions of the id, ego, and superego.

Freud saw personality as the product of a conflict between our biological impulses and our internalized social restraints on these impulses. Three systems (id, ego, and superego) interact in this conflict. The *id,* which wants immediate gratification, operates in the unconscious and attempts to satisfy basic sexual and aggressive drives. The *superego,* our internalized set of ideals, is the voice of our conscience, judging our actions and producing feelings of pride or guilt. The *ego,* the largely conscious, reality-oriented executive, attempts to reconcile the impulses of the id with the demands of the superego and those of the external world.

OBJECTIVE 44-5 | Identify Freud's psychosexual stages of development, and describe the effects of fixation on behavior.

Freud believed that children develop through psychosexual stages—*oral, anal, phallic, latency,* and *genital*—in which the id is focused on a particular erogenous zone. During the phallic stage, for example, boys may desire their mother and fear punishment for these feelings from their father—a set of reactions Freud called the Oedipus complex. A person who fails to resolve the conflicts associated with a psychosexual stage may remain locked into that stage. This fixation would appear in maladaptive behavior focused on the erogenous zone dominant at that stage.

OBJECTIVE 44-6 | Describe the function of defense mechanisms, and identify six of them.

Freud believed the ego uses defense mechanisms to protect itself from anxiety, the byproduct of the conflict between the id and the superego. The basic defense mechanism, according to Freud, is *repression* (banishing troublesome ideas and feelings into the unconscious); others include *regression* (retreating to an infantile stage), *reaction formation* (transforming unacceptable impulses into acceptable opposites), *projection* (attributing one's unacceptable impulses to others), *rationalization* (explaining one's behavior in terms of self-justifying rather than unacceptable motives), and *displacement* (focusing sexual or aggressive impulses on a person more acceptable than the one who aroused the emotion).

OBJECTIVE 44-7 | Contrast the views of the neo-Freudians and psychodynamic theorists with Freud's original theory.

The *neo-Freudians* accepted many of Freud's basic ideas (the id-ego-superego structure, the importance of the unconscious, the shaping of personality in childhood, and the dynamics of anxiety and the defense mechanisms). But they proposed motives other than sex and aggression, and viewed the ego's conscious control as greater than Freud supposed. Alfred Adler (who coined the term *inferiority complex*) and Karen Horney (who refuted Freud's view of the inferiority of women) argued that social, not sexual, tensions are critical in personality formation. Carl Jung proposed a human collective unconscious containing memory traces from our species' history. Contemporary *psychodynamic* theorists and therapists refute some aspects of Freud's theory, such as the idea that sexual tensions are central to personality formation. They share with Freud the view that much of our mental life is unconscious, that childhood shapes our personality and attachment styles, and that we experience inner conflicts among our wishes, fears, and values.

OBJECTIVE 44-8 | Describe two projective tests used to assess personality, and discuss some criticisms of them.

The *Thematic Apperception Test (TAT)* is a series of ambiguous pictures used to elicit a story in which test-takers express their own inner feelings and interests. The *Rorschach inkblots* are similarly used to evoke test-takers' hidden feelings. Neither test is noted for *reliability* (consistency of results) or *validity* (predicting what it's supposed to predict).

OBJECTIVE 44-9 | Summarize psychology's current assessment of Freud's theory of psychoanalysis.

Recent research has contradicted many of Freud's basic ideas, including the overriding importance of childhood experiences, degree of parental influence, timing of gender-identity formation, importance of sexuality during childhood, existence of hidden content in dreams, frequency of repressed memories, and the existence of the unconscious mind as a reservoir of repressed thoughts and emotions. Critics note that Freud's ideas are not verifiable by scientific methods, and that his theory offers only after-the-fact explanations. Freud's supporters reply that he never viewed psychoanalysis as a predictive science, and that he drew psychology's attention to the unconscious and to the struggle to cope with anxiety. A vast amount of unconscious information processing does occur without our awareness. Current research does not support the concept of defense mechanisms closely tied to defense of the unconscious, but it does support some defenses that protect self-esteem. Finally, Freud is credited with focusing attention on the conflict between biological impulses and social restraints. And without question, his cultural impact has been enormous.

TERMS AND CONCEPTS TO REMEMBER

personality, p. P13-1

free association, p. 44-1

psychoanalysis, p. 44-1

unconscious, p. 44-1

id, p. 44-2

ego, p. 44-2

superego, p. 44-2

psychosexual stages, p. 44-2

Oedipus [ED-uh-puss] complex, p. 44-2

identification, p. 44-3

fixation, p. 44-3

defense mechanisms, p. 44-4

repression, p. 44-4

regression, p. 44-4

reaction formation, p. 44-4

projection, p. 44-4

rationalization, p. 44-4

displacement, p. 44-4

collective unconscious, p. 44-5

projective test, p. 44-6

Thematic Apperception Test (TAT), p. 44-6

Rorschach inkblot test, p. 44-6

terror-management theory, p. 44-10

TEST YOURSELF

1. What, according to Freud, were some of the important defense mechanisms, and what do they defend against? How many of these find support in modern research?

(Answer in Appendix B.)

ASK YOURSELF

1. How would you describe *your* personality? What characteristics make up your typical patterns of thinking, feeling, and acting?

2. What understanding and impressions of Freud did you bring to this chapter? Have they changed in any way after reading this section?

>WEB

Multiple-choice *self-tests* and more may be found at www.worthpublishers.com/myers.

45

The Humanistic Perspective

By the 1960s, some personality psychologists had become discontented with the negativism of Sigmund Freud's psychoanalytic theory and the mechanistic psychology of B. F. Skinner's behaviorism. In contrast to Freud's study of the base motives of "sick" people, these *humanistic psychologists* focused on the ways "healthy" people strive for self-determination and self-realization. In contrast to behaviorism's scientific objectivity, they studied people through their own self-reported experiences and feelings.

Two pioneering theorists—Abraham Maslow (1908–1970) and Carl Rogers (1902–1987)—offered a *third-force perspective* that emphasized human potential and seeing the world through the person's (not the researcher's) eyes.

Abraham Maslow's Self-Actualizing Person

OBJECTIVE 45-1 | Summarize Abraham Maslow's concept of self-actualization, and explain how his ideas illustrate the humanistic perpective.

Maslow proposed that we are motivated by a hierarchy of needs. If our physiological needs are met, we become concerned with personal safety; if we achieve a sense of security, we then seek to love, to be loved, and to love ourselves; with our love needs satisfied, we seek self-esteem. Having achieved self-esteem, we ultimately seek **self-actualization,** the process of fulfilling our potential.

Ted Polumbaum/Time Pix/Getty Images

Abraham Maslow

"Any theory of motivation that is worthy of attention must deal with the highest capacities of the healthy and strong person as well as with the defensive maneuvers of crippled spirits" (*Motivation and Personality*, 1970).

Maslow (1970) developed his ideas by studying healthy, creative people rather than troubled clinical cases. He based his description of self-actualization on a study of those who seemed notable for their rich and productive lives—among them, Abraham Lincoln, Thomas Jefferson, and Eleanor Roosevelt. Maslow reported that these people shared certain characteristics: Self-aware and self-accepting, open and spontaneous, loving and caring, not paralyzed by others' opinions, they were secure in their sense of who they were. Their interests were problem-centered rather than self-centered. They focused their energies on a particular task, one they often regarded as their mission in life. Most enjoyed a few deep relationships rather than many superficial ones. Many had been moved by spiritual or personal *peak experiences* that surpassed ordinary consciousness.

These, said Maslow, are mature adult qualities, ones found in those who have learned enough about life to be compassionate, to have outgrown their mixed feelings toward their parents, to have found their calling, to have "acquired enough courage to be unpopular, to be unashamed about being openly virtuous, etc." Maslow's work with college students led him to speculate that those likely to become self-actualizing adults were likable, caring, "privately affectionate to those of their elders who deserve it," and "secretly uneasy about the cruelty, meanness, and mob spirit so often found in young people."

Carl Rogers' Person-Centered Perspective

OBJECTIVE 45-2 | Discuss Carl Rogers' person-centered perspective, and explain the importance of unconditional positive regard.

Fellow humanistic psychologist Carl Rogers agreed with much of Maslow's thinking. Rogers believed that people are basically good and are endowed with self-actualizing tendencies. Unless thwarted by an environment that inhibits growth, each of us is like an acorn, primed for growth and fulfillment. Rogers (1980) believed that a growth-promoting climate required three conditions—genuineness, acceptance, and empathy.

According to Rogers, people nurture our growth by being *genuine*—by being open with their own feelings, dropping their facades, and being transparent and self-disclosing.

People also nurture our growth by being *accepting*—by offering us what Rogers called **unconditional positive regard.** This is an attitude of grace, an attitude that values us even knowing our failings. It is a profound relief to drop our pretenses, confess our worst feelings, and discover that we are still accepted. In a good marriage, a close family, or an intimate friendship, we are free to be spontaneous without fearing the loss of others' esteem.

Finally, people nurture our growth by being *empathic*—by sharing and mirroring our feelings and reflecting our meanings. "Rarely do we listen with real understanding, true empathy," said Rogers. "Yet listening, of this very special kind, is one of the most potent forces for change that I know."

Genuineness, acceptance, and empathy are the water, sun, and nutrients that enable people to grow like vigorous oak trees, according to Rogers. For "as persons are accepted and prized, they tend to develop a more caring attitude toward themselves" (Rogers, 1980, p. 116). As persons are empathically heard, "it becomes possible for them to listen more accurately to the flow of inner experiencings."

Rogers believed that genuineness, acceptance, and empathy nurture growth not only in the relationship between therapist and client but also between parent and child, leader and group, teacher and student, administrator and staff member—in fact, between any two human beings.

For Maslow, and even more for Rogers, a central feature of personality is one's **self-concept**—all the thoughts and feelings we have in response to the question, "Who am I?" If our self-concept is positive, we tend to act and perceive the world positively. If it is negative—if in our own eyes we fall far short of our *ideal self*—said Rogers, we feel dissatisfied and unhappy. A worthwhile goal for therapists, parents, teachers, and friends is therefore, he said, to help others know, accept, and be true to themselves.

Assessing the Self

OBJECTIVE 45-3 | Explain how humanistic psychologists assessed personality.

Humanistic psychologists sometimes assessed personality by asking people to fill out questionnaires that would evaluate self-concept. One questionnaire, inspired by Carl Rogers, asked people to describe themselves both as they would *ideally* like to be and as they *actually* are. When the ideal and the actual self are nearly alike, said Rogers, the self-concept is positive. Assessing his clients' personal growth during therapy, he looked for successively closer ratings of actual and ideal self.

Some humanistic psychologists believed that any standardized assessment of personality, even a questionnaire, is depersonalizing. Rather than forcing the person to respond to narrow categories, these humanistic psychologists presumed that interviews and intimate conversation would provide a better understanding of each person's unique experiences.

■ **self-actualization** according to Maslow, the ultimate psychological need that arises after basic physical and psychological needs are met and self-esteem is achieved; the motivation to fulfill one's potential.

■ **unconditional positive regard** according to Rogers, an attitude of total acceptance toward another person.

■ **self-concept** all our thoughts and feelings about ourselves, in answer to the question, "Who am I?"

The picture of empathy
Being open and sharing confidences is easier when the listener shows real understanding. Within such relationships people can relax and fully express their true selves.

Mark Antman/The Image Works

© The New Yorker Collection, 2001, Pat Byrnes from cartoonbank.com. All Rights Reserved

"Just remember, son, it doesn't matter whether you win or lose—unless you want Daddy's love."

A father *not* offering unconditional positive regard.

Evaluating the Humanistic Perspective

OBJECTIVE 45-4 | State the major criticisms of the humanistic perspective on personality.

One thing said of Freud can also be said of the humanistic psychologists: Their impact has been pervasive. Their ideas have influenced counseling, education, child-rearing, and management.

They have also influenced—sometimes in ways they did not intend—much of today's popular psychology. Many people have absorbed Maslow's and Rogers' ideas—that a positive self-concept is the key to happiness and success, that acceptance and empathy help nurture positive feelings about oneself, and that people are basically good and capable of self-improvement. One study found that, by a four-to-one margin, Americans believe "human nature is basically good" rather than "fundamentally perverse and corrupt" (NORC, 1985). Humanistic psychologists can also take satisfaction in the changed response to one item on the MMPI (the most widely used personality test): Among those in the 1930s normal standardization sample, only 9 percent agreed that "I am an important person"; by the mid-1980s, more than half agreed (Holden, 1986b). Responding to a 1989 Gallup poll, 85 percent of Americans rated "having a good self-image or self-respect" as *very* important; 0 percent rated it unimportant. And 89 percent of people responding to a 1992 *Newsweek* Gallup poll rated self-esteem as very important for "motivating a person to work hard and succeed." Humanistic psychology's message has been heard.

Perhaps one reason that message has been so well received is that its emphasis on the individual self reflects and reinforces Western cultural values. Movie plots feature rugged individualists who, true to themselves, buck social convention or take the law into their own hands. Popular songs have proclaimed "I Did It My Way" and reminded us that to love yourself is "The Greatest Love of All" (Schoeneman, 1994).

The prominence of the humanistic perspective set off a backlash of criticism. First, said the critics, its concepts are vague and subjective. Consider the description of self-actualizing people as open, spontaneous, loving, self-accepting, and productive. Is this a scientific description? Isn't it merely a description of Maslow's personal values and ideals? Maslow, noted M. Brewster Smith (1978), offered impressions of his own personal heroes. Imagine another theorist who began with a different set of heroes—perhaps Napoleon, Alexander the Great, and John D. Rockefeller, Sr. This theorist would likely describe self-actualizing people as "undeterred by the needs of others," "motivated to achieve," and "obsessed with power."

Critics also objected to the idea that, as Carl Rogers put it, "The only question which matters is, 'Am I living in a way which is deeply satisfying to me, and which truly expresses me?'" (quoted by Wallach & Wallach, 1985). The individualism encouraged by humanistic psychology—trusting and acting on one's feelings, being true to oneself, fulfilling oneself—can, the critics have said, lead to self-indulgence, selfishness, and an erosion of moral restraints (Campbell & Specht, 1985; Wallach & Wallach, 1983). Indeed, it is those who focus beyond themselves who are most likely to experience social support, to enjoy life, and to cope effectively with stress (Crandall, 1984).

Humanistic psychologists have countered that a secure, nondefensive self-acceptance is actually the first step toward loving others. Indeed, people who feel intrinsically liked and accepted—for who they are, not just for their achievements—exhibit less-defensive attitudes (Schimel & others, 2001).

A final accusation leveled against humanistic psychology is that it fails to appreciate the reality of our human capacity for evil. Faced with global warming, overpopulation, terrorism, and the spread of nuclear weapons, we may become apathetic from either of two rationalizations. One is a naive optimism that denies the threat ("People are basically good; everything will work out."). The other is a dark despair ("It's hopeless; why try?"). Action requires enough

"We do pretty well when you stop to think that people are basically good."

realism to fuel concern and enough optimism to provide hope. Humanistic psychology, say the critics, encourages the needed hope but not the equally necessary realism about evil.

Even within humanistic psychology there has been debate over whether people are basically good. Carl Rogers clearly thought so. Although aware of the "incredible amount" of cruel, destructive behavior in the world, he did "not find that this evil is inherent in human nature." He stated that he had never known an individual who—given growth-promoting conditions—had chosen "the cruel or destructive path" (Rogers, 1981). Evil, in his view, springs not from human nature but from toxic cultural influences, including "the constricting, destructive influence of our educational system, the injustice of our distribution of wealth, [and] our cultivated prejudices against individuals who are different."

Fellow humanistic psychologist Rollo May dissented. Of course the cultural context matters, he said. But "who makes up the culture except persons like you and me? The culture is evil as well as good because we, the human beings who constitute it, are evil as well as good." May agreed with the critics who saw people joining the humanistic movement as seekers of "a community of like-minded persons who also are playing possum to the evils about us." Accepting the reality of human evil requires "the age-old religious truths of mercy and forgiveness," he said, "and it leaves no place for self-righteousness" (May, 1982).

>> LEARNING OUTCOMES

The Humanistic Perspective

OBJECTIVE 45-1 | **Summarize Abraham Maslow's concept of self-actualization, and explain how his ideas illustrate the humanistic perspective.**

Maslow proposed a hierarchy of needs, with physiological needs at the base. He believed that after fulfilling other needs (physiological; safety; belongingness and love; self-esteem), people will be motivated to achieve their highest potential, self-actualization. Maslow typifies humanistic psychology's attempt to turn psychology's attention from baser motives and environmental conditioning to the growth potential of healthy people, believed to be basically good.

OBJECTIVE 45-2 | **Discuss Carl Rogers' person-centered perspective, and explain the importance of unconditional positive regard.**

Like Maslow, Rogers believed that unless thwarted by their environment, people will grow and realize their self-actualizing tendencies. He advised treating others in a way that is genuine, accepting, and empathic, with an attitude of unconditional positive regard—total acceptance toward the other person. In Rogers' view, a central feature of personality is our self-concept, our thoughts and feelings in response to the question "Who am I?"

OBJECTIVE 45-3 | **Explain how humanistic psychologists assessed personality.**

Some assessed personality through questionnaires on which people reported their self-concept, for example, by comparing their actual self with their ideal self. Others believed that we could understand a person's subjective personal experiences only through interviews and intimate conversations.

OBJECTIVE 45-4 | **State the major criticisms of the humanistic perspective on personality.**

Although humanistic psychology helped renew psychology's interest in the self, its critics argue that its concepts were vague and subjective, its values individualist and self-centered, and its assumptions naively optimistic.

TERMS AND CONCEPTS TO REMEMBER

self-actualization, p. 45-0   self-concept, p. 45-1
unconditional positive regard,
   p. 45-1

TEST YOURSELF

1. What does it mean to be "empathic"? To be "self-actualized"?

(Answer in Appendix B.)

ASK YOURSELF

1. Have you had someone in your life who accepted you unconditionally? Do you think this person helped you to know yourself better and to develop a better image of yourself?

> **WEB**

Multiple-choice *self-tests* and more may be found at www.worthpublishers.com/myers.

The Trait Perspective

The Social-Cognitive Perspective

Exploring the Self

46

Contemporary Research on Personality

The Trait Perspective

OBJECTIVE 46-1 | Cite the main difference between the trait and psychoanalytic perspectives on personality.

Trait researchers attempt to define personality in terms of stable and enduring behavior patterns, such as Sam Gamgee's loyalty and optimism. The trait perspective can be traced in part to a remarkable meeting in 1919, when Gordon Allport, a curious 22-year-old psychology student, interviewed Sigmund Freud in Vienna. Allport soon discovered just how preoccupied the founder of psychoanalysis was with finding hidden motives.

> Soon after I had entered the famous red burlap room with pictures of dreams on the wall, he summoned me to his inner office. He did not speak to me but sat in expectant silence, for me to state my mission. I was not prepared for silence and had to think fast to find a suitable conversational gambit. I told him of an episode on the tram car on my way to his office. A small boy about 4 years of age had displayed a conspicuous dirt phobia. He kept saying to his mother, "I don't want to sit there . . . don't let that dirty man sit beside me." To him everything was *schmutzig* (filthy). His mother was a well-starched *Hausfrau,* so dominant and purposive looking that I thought the cause and effect apparent.
>
> When I finished my story Freud fixed his kindly therapeutic eyes upon me and said, "And was that little boy you?" Flabbergasted and feeling a bit guilty, I contrived to change the subject. While Freud's misunderstanding of my motivation was amusing, it also started a deep train of thought (1967, pp. 7–8).

That train of thought ultimately led Allport to do what Freud did not do—to describe personality in terms of fundamental **traits**—people's characteristic behaviors and conscious motives (such as the professional curiosity that actually motivated Allport to see Freud). Meeting Freud, said Allport, "taught me that [psychoanalysis], for all its merits, may plunge too deep, and that psychologists would do well to give full recognition to manifest motives before probing the unconscious." Allport came to define personality in terms of identifiable behavior patterns. He was concerned less with *explaining* individual traits than with *describing* them. How, then, can theorists use traits to describe and classify personalities? One way is describing people using broad personality "types" that signal one's most noteworthy trait and its associated characteristics. An analogy may help. Imagine that you want to describe and classify apples. Someone might correctly say that every apple is unique. Still, you might find it useful to begin by classifying apples as distinct *types*—Granny Smith, MacIntosh, Red or Golden Delicious, and so forth. That is precisely how the ancient Greeks described personality—by classifying people according to four types. Depending on which of one's bodily "humors," or fluids, they believed to predominate, they declared people melancholic (depressed), sanguine (cheerful), phlegmatic (unemotional), or choleric (irritable).

A more recent classification, written by Isabel Briggs Myers (1987) and her mother, Kathleen Briggs, attempts to sort people according to Carl Jung's personality types, based on their responses to 126 questions. The *Myers-Briggs Type Indicator,*

trait a characteristic pattern of behavior or a disposition to feel and act, as assessed by self-report inventories and peer reports.

which has been taken by 2.5 million Americans a year and used by 89 of the 100 largest corporations, is quite simple (Gladwell, 2004). It offers choices, such as "Do you usually value sentiment more than logic, or value logic more than sentiment?" Then it counts the test-taker's preferences, labels them as indicating, say, a "feeling" or "thinking" type, and feeds them back to the person in complimentary terms. Feeling types, for example, are told they are sensitive to values and "sympathetic, appreciative, and tactful"; thinking types are told they "prefer an objective standard of truth" and are "good at analyzing." (Every type has its strengths, so everyone gets flattered.)

Most people agree with their announced type profile. It mirrors their declared preferences and leaves them feeling good. They may also accept their label as a basis for being matched with work partners and tasks that supposedly suit their temperaments. A National Research Council report noted, however, that despite the test's popularity in business and career counseling, its initial use outran research on its value as a predictor of job performance, and "the popularity of this instrument in the absence of proven scientific worth is troublesome" (Druckman & Bjork, 1991, p. 101; see also Pittenger, 1993). Since those cautionary words, research on the Myers-Briggs has been accumulating, thanks to periodicals such as the *Journal of Psychological Type.*

Exploring Traits

OBJECTIVE 46-2 | Describe some of the ways psychologists have attempted to compile a list of basic personality traits.

Classifying people as one or another distinct personality type fails to capture their full individuality. We are each a unique complex of multiple traits. So how else could we describe our personalities? To return to our apple analogy, we might describe an apple by placing it along several trait dimensions—relatively large or small, red or yellow, sweet or sour. By placing people on several trait dimensions simultaneously, psychologists can describe countless individual personality variations, much as researchers can describe thousands of colors in terms of their variations on just three color dimensions—hue, saturation, and brightness.

What trait dimensions describe personality? If you had an upcoming blind date, what personality traits might give you an accurate sense of the person? Allport and his associate H. S. Odbert (1936) literally counted all the words in an unabridged dictionary with which one could describe people. How many were there? Almost 18,000! How, then, could psychologists condense the list to a manageable number of basic traits?

Factor Analysis

One way has been to propose traits, such as anxiety, that some theory regards as basic. A newer technique is *factor analysis,* a statistical procedure that has been used to identify clusters of related items. Imagine that people who describe themselves as outgoing also tend to say that they like excitement and practical jokes and dislike quiet reading. Such a statistically correlated cluster of behaviors reflects a basic factor, or trait—in this case, *extraversion.*

British psychologists Hans Eysenck and Sybil Eysenck [EYE-zink] believed that we can reduce many of our normal individual variations to two or three dimensions, including *extraversion-introversion* and *emotional stability-instability* (**FIGURE 46.1** on the next page). People in 35 countries around the world, from China to Uganda to Russia, have taken the *Eysenck Personality Questionnaire,* and when their answers are analyzed, the extraversion and emotionality factors inevitably emerged as basic personality dimensions (Eysenck, 1990, 1992). The Eysencks believed that these factors are genetically influenced and recent research supports this belief.

Chris Rock: the extravert
Trait labels such as *extraversion* can describe our temperament and typical behaviors.

AP Photo/Julie Jacobson

FIGURE 46.1

Two personality factors

Mapmakers can tell us a lot by using two axes (north-south and east-west). Hans Eysenck and Sybil Eysenck use two primary personality factors—extraversion–introversion and stability–instability—as axes for describing personality variation. Varying combinations define other, more specific traits. (From Eysenck & Eysenck, 1963.)

UNSTABLE

Moody · Touchy
Anxious · Restless
Rigid · Aggressive
Sober · Excitable
Pessimistic · Changeable
Reserved · Impulsive
Unsociable · Optimistic
Quiet · Active

INTROVERTED — **EXTRAVERTED**

Passive · Sociable
Careful · Outgoing
Thoughtful · Talkative
Peaceful · Responsive
Controlled · Easygoing
Reliable · Lively
Even-tempered · Carefree
Calm · Leadership

STABLE

Biology and Personality

Brain-activity scans of extraverts add to the growing list of traits and mental states that have been explored with brain-imaging procedures. (At this writing, that list includes intelligence, impulsivity, addictive cravings, sexual attraction, aggressiveness, empathy, spiritual experience, and even racial and political attitudes [Olson, 2005]). Such studies indicate that extraverts seek stimulation because their normal *brain arousal* is relatively low. For example, PET scans show that a frontal lobe area involved in behavior inhibition is less active in extraverts than in introverts (Johnson & others, 1999).

Our biology influences our personality in other ways as well. Our *genes* have much to say about the *temperament*—our emotional reactivity—and the behavioral style that help define our personality. Jerome Kagan, for example, attributes differences in children's shyness and inhibition to their *autonomic nervous system* reactivity. Given a reactive autonomic nervous system, we respond to stress with greater anxiety and inhibition. The fearless, curious child may become the rock-climbing or fast-driving adult. And studies comparing identical and fraternal twins, comparing identical twins reared apart, and comparing adoptees with their adoptive and biological parents all remind us: Personality forms under the influence of genes.

That fact of life also appears in animal personalities. Samuel Gosling and his colleagues (2003) report that personality differences among dogs (in energy, affection, reactivity, and curious intelligence) are as evident, and as consistently judged, as personality differences among humans. Even birds have stable personalities. Among a European relative of the chickadee, bold birds more quickly inspect new objects and explore trees (Groothuis & Carere, 2005; Verbeek & others, 1994). By selective breeding, researchers can produce bold or shy birds. Both have their place in natural history. In lean years, bold birds are more likely to find food; in abundant years, shy birds feed with less risk.

Assessing Traits

OBJECTIVE 46-3 | Explain how psychologists use personality inventories to assess traits, and discuss the most widely used personality inventory

If stable and enduring traits guide our actions, can we devise valid and reliable tests of them? Several trait assessment techniques exist. Some profile a person's behavior patterns—often providing quick assessments of a single trait, such as extraversion, anxiety, or self-esteem. **Personality inventories**—longer questionnaires covering a wide range of feelings and behaviors—are designed to assess several traits at once.

The most extensively researched personality inventory is the **Minnesota Multiphasic Personality Inventory (MMPI).** Although it assesses "abnormal" personality tendencies rather than normal personality traits, the MMPI illustrates a good way of developing a personality inventory. One of its creators, Starke Hathaway (1960), compared his effort to that of Alfred Binet, who developed the first intelligence test by

■ **personality inventory** a questionnaire (often with true-false or agree-disagree items) on which people respond to items designed to gauge a wide range of feelings and behaviors; used to assess selected personality traits.

■ **Minnesota Multiphasic Personality Inventory (MMPI)** the most widely researched and clinically used of all personality tests. Originally developed to identify emotional disorders (still considered its most appropriate use), this test is now used for many other screening purposes.

■ **empirically derived test** a test (such as the MMPI) developed by testing a pool of items and then selecting those that discriminate between groups.

selecting items that discriminated children who would have trouble progressing normally in French schools. The MMPI items, too, were **empirically derived.** That is, from a large pool of items, Hathaway and his colleagues selected those on which particular diagnostic groups differed. They then grouped the questions into 10 clinical scales.

Hathaway and others initially gave hundreds of true-false statements ("No one seems to understand me"; "I get all the sympathy I should"; "I like poetry") to groups of psychologically disordered patients and to "normal" people. They retained any statement—no matter how silly it sounded—on which the patient group's answer differed from that of the normal group. "Nothing in the newspaper interests me except the comics" may seem senseless, but it just so happened that depressed people were more likely to answer "true." (Nevertheless, people have had fun spoofing the MMPI with their own mock items: "Weeping brings tears to my eyes," "Frantic screams make me nervous," and "I stay in the bathtub until I look like a raisin" [Frankel & others, 1983].) Today's MMPI-2 also has newer scales assessing, for instance, work attitudes, family problems, and anger.

In contrast to the subjectivity of most projective tests favored by psychoanalysts, personality inventories are scored objectively—so objectively that a computer can administer and score them. (The computer can also provide descriptions of people who previously responded similarly.) Objectivity does not, however, guarantee validity. For example, individuals taking the MMPI for employment purposes can give socially desirable answers to create a good impression. But in so doing they may also score high on a "lie scale" that assesses faking (as when people respond "false" to a universally true statement such as "I get angry sometimes"). For better or worse, the objectivity of the MMPI contributes to its popularity and to its translation into more than 100 languages.

The Big Five Factors

OBJECTIVE 46-4 | Identify the Big Five personality factors, and discuss some of the strengths of this approach to studying personality.

Today's trait researchers believe that earlier trait dimensions, such as the Eysencks' introverted-extraverted and unstable-stable dimensions, are important. But they do not tell the whole story. A slightly expanded set of factors—dubbed the *Big Five*—does a better job (John & Srivastava, 1999; McCrae & Costa, 1999). If a test specifies where you are on the five dimensions (conscientiousness, agreeableness, neuroticism, openness, and extraversion; see TABLE **46.1**), it has said

TABLE 46.1

THE "BIG FIVE" PERSONALITY FACTORS (Adapted from McCrae & Costa (1986, p. 1002)

(*Memory tip:* Picturing a CANOE will help you recall these.)

Trait Dimension	Endpoints of the Dimension		
Conscientiousness	Organized	←——→	Disorganized
	Careful	←——→	Careless
	Disciplined	←——→	Impulsive
Agreeableness	Soft-hearted	←——→	Ruthless
	Trusting	←——→	Suspicious
	Helpful	←——→	Uncooperative
Neuroticism (emotional stability vs. instability)	Calm	←——→	Anxious
	Secure	←——→	Insecure
	Self-satisfied	←——→	Self-pitying
Openness	Imaginative	←——→	Practical
	Preference for variety	←——→	Preference for routine
	Independent	←——→	Conforming
Extraversion	Sociable	←——→	Retiring
	Fun-loving	←——→	Sober
	Affectionate	←——→	Reserved

HOW TO BE A "SUCCESSFUL" ASTROLOGER OR PALM READER

Can we discern people's traits from the alignment of the stars and planets at the time of their birth? From their handwriting? From lines on their palms?

Astronomers scoff at the naiveté of astrology—the constellations have shifted in the millennia since astrologers formulated their predictions (Kelly, 1997, 1998). Humorists mock it: "No offense," writes Dave Barry, "but if you take the horoscope seriously your frontal lobes are the size of Raisinets." Psychologists instead ask questions: Does it work? Can astrologers surpass chance when given someone's birth date and asked to identify the person from a short lineup of different personality descriptions? Can people pick out their own horoscopes from a lineup of horoscopes?

The consistent answers have been: No, no, and no (British Psychological Society, 1993; Carlson, 1985; Kelly, 1997). Graphologists, who make predictions from handwriting samples, have similarly been found to do no better than chance when trying to discern people's occupations from examining several pages of their handwriting (Beyerstein & Beyerstein, 1992; Dean & others, 1992). Nevertheless, graphologists—and introductory psychology students—will often *perceive* correlations between personality and handwriting even where there are none (King & Koehler, 2000).

If all these perceived correlations evaporate under close scrutiny, how do astrologers and the like persuade thousands of newspapers and millions of people worldwide to buy

© 2000 by Rob Pudim

their advice? Ray Hyman (1981), palm reader turned research psychologist, has revealed the suckering methods of astrologers, palm readers, and crystal-ball gazers.

Their first technique, the "stock spiel," builds on the observation that each of us is in some ways like no one else and in other ways just like everyone. That some things are true of us all enables the "seer" to offer statements that seem impressively accurate: "I sense that you worry about things more than you let on, even to your best friends." A number of such generally true statements can be combined into a personality description. Imagine that you take a personality test and then receive the following character sketch:

> You have a strong need for other people to like and to admire you. You have a

tendency to be critical of yourself. . . . You pride yourself on being an independent thinker and do not accept other opinions without satisfactory proof. You have found it unwise to be too frank in revealing yourself to others. At times you are extraverted, affable, sociable; at other times you are introverted, wary, and reserved. Some of your aspirations tend to be pretty unrealistic (Davies, 1997; Forer, 1949).

In experiments, college students have received stock assessments like this one, drawn from statements in a newsstand astrology book. When they think the bogus, generic feedback was prepared just for them and when it is favorable, they nearly

much of what there is to say about your personality. Around the world, people describe others in terms roughly consistent with this list. But the Big Five is not the last word: Other factor analysis researchers and theorists wonder whether we should add dimensions such as self-consciousness, masculinity-femininity, intellect-imagination, religiosity, or positive-negative emotion (Ashton & others, always rate the description as either "good" or "excellent" (Davies, 1997). Even skeptics of astrology, when given a flattering description attributed to an astrologer, begin to think that "maybe there's something to this astrology stuff after all" (Glick & others, 1989). An astrologer, it has been said, is someone "prepared to tell you what you think of yourself" (Jones, 2000).

French psychologist Michael Gauguelin had similar results when he placed an ad in a Paris newspaper offering a free personal horoscope. Ninety-four percent of those receiving the horoscope praised the description as accurate. Whose horoscope had they all actually received? That of France's Dr. Petiot, a notorious mass murderer (Kurtz, 1983). This acceptance of stock, positive descriptions is called the *Barnum effect*, named in honor of master showman P. T. Barnum's dictum, "There's a sucker born every minute."

A second technique used by seers is to "read" our clothing, physical features, nonverbal gestures, and reactions to what they are saying. Imagine yourself as the character reader visited by a young woman in her late twenties or early thirties. Hyman described the woman as "wearing expensive jewelry, a wedding band, and a black dress of cheap material. The observant reader noted that she was wearing shoes which were advertised for people with foot trouble." Do these clues suggest anything?

Drawing on these observations, the character reader proceeded to amaze his client with his insights.

He assumed the woman had come to see him, as did most of his female customers, because of a love or financial problem. The black dress and the wedding band led him to reason that her husband had died recently. The expensive jewelry suggested she had been financially comfortable during the marriage, but the cheap dress suggested her

"Madame Zelinski can provide an even more accurate reading with your date of birth and Social Security number."

husband's death had left her impoverished. The therapeutic shoes signified she was now on her feet more than she had been used to, implying that she had been working to support herself since her husband's death. Based on these insights, the reader correctly guessed that the woman was wondering if she should remarry in hope of ending her economic hardship. No wonder, say the skeptics, that when mediums cannot see the person who has come to them, their clients cannot recognize the reading that was meant for them from among other readings (O'Keeffe & Wiseman, 2005).

If you are not as shrewd as this character reader, Hyman says it hardly matters. If people seek you out for a reading, start with some safe sympathy: "I sense you're having some problems lately. You seem unsure what to do. I get the feeling another person is involved." Then tell them what they want to hear. Memorize some Barnum statements from astrology and fortune-telling manuals and use them liberally. Tell people it is their responsibility to cooperate by relating your message to their specific experiences. Later they will recall that you predicted those specific details. Phrase statements as questions, and when you detect a positive response assert the statement strongly. Finally, be a good listener, and later, in different words, reveal to people what they earlier revealed to you. If you dupe them, they will come.

Better yet, beware of those who, by exploiting people with these techniques, are fortune takers rather than fortune tellers.

2004). For now, though, the winning number in the personality lottery is five. The Big Five—today's "common currency for personality psychology" (Funder, 2001)—has been the most active personality research topic since the early 1990s and is currently our best approximation of the basic trait dimensions (Endler & Speer, 1998).

The recent wave of Big Five research explores various questions:

- **How stable are these traits?** In adulthood, the Big Five traits are quite stable, with some tendencies (emotional instability, extraversion, and openness) waning a bit in the decades after college, and others (agreeableness and conscientiousness) rising (McCrae & others, 1999; Vaidya & others, 2002). Conscientiousness increases the most during people's twenties, as people mature and learn to manage their jobs and relationships. Agreeableness increases the most during people's thirties and continues to increase through their sixties (Srivastava & others, 2003).

- **How heritable are they?** Heritability of individual differences varies with the diversity of people studied, but it generally runs 50 percent or a tad more for each dimension (Loehlin & others, 1998).

- **How well do they apply to various cultures?** The Big Five dimensions describe personality in various cultures reasonably well (McCrae, 2001; Paunonen & others, 2000). "Features of personality traits are common to all human groups," infer Robert McCrae and 79 co-researchers (2005) from their recent 50-culture study.

- **Do the Big Five traits predict other personal attributes?** Yes again. Two examples: Highly conscientious people are more likely to be morning types (sometimes called "larks"); evening types ("owls") are marginally more extraverted (Jackson & Gerard, 1996). When one's partner scores lower on agreeableness, stability, and openness, marital and sexual satisfaction may suffer (Botwin & others, 1997; Donnellan & others, 2004).

By exploring such questions, Big Five research has sustained trait psychology and renewed appreciation for the importance of personality.

Evaluating the Trait Perspective

Are our personality traits stable and enduring? Or does our behavior depend on where and with whom we find ourselves? J. R. R. Tolkien created characters, like the loyal Sam Gamgee, whose personality traits were consistent across various times and places. The Italian playwright Luigi Pirandello had a different view. For him, personality was ever-changing, tailored to the particular role or situation. In one of Pirandello's plays, Lamberto Laudisi describes himself: "I am really what you take me to be; though, my dear madam, that does not prevent me from also being really what your husband, my sister, my niece, and Signora Cini take me to be—because they also are absolutely right!" To which Signora Sirelli responds, "In other words you are a different person for each of us."

The Person-Situation Controversy

OBJECTIVE 46-5 | Summarize the person-situation controversy, and explain its importance as a commentary on the trait perspective.

Who, then, typifies human personality, Tolkien's consistent Sam Gamgee or Pirandello's inconsistent Laudisi? Both. Our behavior is influenced by the interaction of our inner disposition with our environment. Still, the question lingers: Which is *more* important? Are we *more* as Tolkien or as Pirandello imagined us to be?

When we explore this *person-situation controversy,* we look for genuine personality traits that persist over time *and* across situations. Are some people dependably conscientious and others unreliable, some cheerful and others dour, some friendly and outgoing and others shy? If we are to consider friendliness a trait, friendly people must act friendly at different times and places. Do they? In considering research that has followed lives through time, some scholars (especially those who study infants) are impressed with personality change; others are struck by personality stability during adulthood. As

> "There is as much difference between us and ourselves, as between us and others."
>
> Michel de Montaigne, *Essays,* 1588

Roughly speaking, the temporary, external influences on behavior are the focus of social psychology, and the enduring, inner influences are the focus of personality psychology. In actuality, behavior always depends on the interaction of persons with situations.

FIGURE **46.2** illustrates, data from 152 long-term studies reveal that personality trait scores are positively correlated with scores obtained seven years later, and that as people grow older their personality stabilizes. Interests may change—the avid collector of tropical fish may become the avid gardener. Careers may change—the determined salesperson may become a determined social worker. Relationships may change—the hostile spouse may start over with a new partner. But most people recognize their traits as their own, note Robert McCrae and Paul Costa (1994), "and it is well that they do. A person's recognition of the inevitability of his or her one and only personality is . . . the culminating wisdom of a lifetime." So most people—including most psychologists—would probably side with Tolkien's assumption of stability of personality traits.

But the consistency of specific *behaviors* from one situation to the next is another matter. As Walter Mischel (1968, 1984, 2004) has pointed out, people do not act with predictable consistency. Mischel's studies of college students' conscientiousness revealed but a modest relationship between a student's being conscientious on one occasion (say, showing up for class on time) and being similarly conscientious on another occasion (say, turning in assignments on time). Pirandello would not have been surprised. If you've noticed how outgoing you are in some situations and how reserved you are in others, perhaps you're not surprised either (though for certain traits, Mischel reports, you may accurately assess yourself as more consistent).

This inconsistency in behaviors also makes personality test scores weak predictors of behaviors. People's scores on an extraversion test, for example, do not neatly predict how sociable they actually will be on any given occasion. If we remember such results, says Mischel, we will be more cautious about labeling and pigeonholing individuals. We will be more restrained when asked to predict whether someone is likely to violate parole, commit suicide, or be an effective employee. Years in advance, science can tell us the phase of the moon for any given date. A day in advance, meteorologists can often predict the weather. But we are much further from being able to predict how *you* will feel and act tomorrow.

In defense of traits, Seymour Epstein (1983a,b) maintained that trying to predict a specific act on the basis of a personality test result is like trying to predict your answer to a specific aptitude question on the basis of an intelligence test result. Your answer to any given question is unpredictable because it depends on so many variables (your intelligence, yes, but also your reading of the question, your momentary concentration, luck). Your *average* accuracy over many questions on several tests is more predictable. Similarly, people's *average* outgoingness, happiness, or carelessness over *many* situations is predictable, Epstein observed. When rating someone's shyness or agreeableness, this consistency enables people who know someone well to agree (Kenrick & Funder, 1988). As our best friends can verify, we *do* have personality traits—genetically influenced traits, we now know.

"Mr. Coughlin over there was the founder of one of the first motorcycle gangs."

Change and consistency can co-exist. If all people were to become somewhat less shy with age, there would be personality change, but also relative stability and predictability.

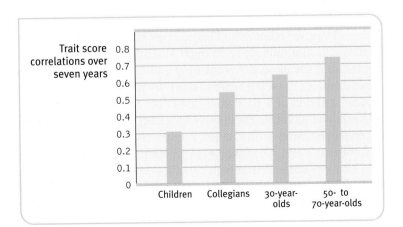

FIGURE **46.2**
Personality stability
With age, personality traits become more stable, as reflected in the correlation of trait scores with follow-up scores seven years later. (Data from Roberts & DelVecchio, 2000).

Our spaces express our personalities
Even at "zero acquaintance," people can discern something of others' personality from glimpsing their Web site, dorm room, or office. So, what is your read on University of Texas researcher Samuel Gosling?

John Langford Photography

Moreover, our traits are socially significant. They influence our health, our thinking, and our job performance (Deary & Matthews, 1993; Hogan, 1998). Our traits even lurk, report Samuel Gosling and his colleagues in a series of studies, in our

- *music preferences.* Classical, jazz, blues, and folk music lovers tend to be open to experience and verbally intelligent; country, pop, and religious music lovers tend to be cheerful, outgoing, and conscientious (Rentfrow & Gosling, 2003).
- *dorm rooms and offices.* Our personal spaces display our identity and leave a behavioral residue (in our scattered laundry or neat desktop). And that helps explain why just a few minutes' inspection of our living and working spaces can enable someone to assess with reasonable accuracy our conscientiousness, our openness to new experience, and even our emotional stability (Gosling & others, 2002).
- *personal Web sites.* Is a personal Web site also a canvas for self-expression? Or is it an opportunity for people to present themselves in false or misleading ways? It's more the former, report Simine Vazire and Gosling (2004). Visitors to personal Web sites quickly gain important clues to the owner's extraversion, conscientiousness, and openness to experience.

The bottom line: Traits exist. We differ. And our differences matter.

Consistency of Expressive Style

OBJECTIVE 46-6 | Explain why psychologists are interested in the consistency of the trait of expressiveness.

In unfamiliar, formal situations—perhaps as a guest in the home of a person from another culture—our traits may remain hidden as we attend carefully to social cues. In familiar, informal situations—just hanging out with friends—we feel less constrained, allowing our traits to emerge (Buss, 1989). In these informal situations, our expressive styles—our animation, manner of speaking, and gestures—are impressively consistent. Thus, we often form lasting impressions within a few moments of meeting someone. Nalini Ambady and Robert Rosenthal (1992, 1993) videotaped 13 Harvard University graduate students teaching undergraduate courses. Observers then viewed three *thin slices* of each teacher's behavior—mere 10-second clips from the beginning, middle, and end of a class—and rated each teacher's level of confidence, activeness, warmth, and so forth. These behavior ratings, based on 30 *seconds* of teaching from an entire semester, predicted amazingly well the teacher's average student ratings at the semester's end. Observing even thinner slices—three 2-second clips—yielded ratings that still correlated as high as +.72 with the student evaluations. Some people's first impressions, derived from expressive behavior, predicted other people's lasting impressions!

Mere glimpses of someone's behavior can be revealing because of the potency of traits such as expressiveness. In a study of physician malpractice suits, Ambady and her colleagues (2002) filtered four 10-second slices of surgeon-patient conversation, rendering the speech unintelligible while preserving its intonation, pitch, and rhythm. From those remaining clues, listeners were able to sense the surgeons' warmth, hostility, and dominance and to accurately assess which of them had been sued. Knowing nothing of a surgeon's skill or even what was being said, listeners could nonetheless derive from the tone of voice a feeling for whether the doctor was being empathic or overbearing, and that was enough to help predict the patients' responses.

Some people are naturally expressive (and therefore talented at pantomime and charades); others are less expressive (and therefore better poker players). To evaluate people's voluntary control over their expressiveness, Bella DePaulo and her colleagues (1992) asked people to *act* as expressive or inhibited as possible while stating opinions. Their remarkable findings: Inexpressive people, even when feigning expressiveness, were less expressive than expressive people acting naturally. Similarly, expressive people, even when trying to seem inhibited, were less inhibited than inexpressive people acting naturally. It's hard to be someone you're not, or not to be what you are.

The irrepressibility of expressiveness explains why we can size up how outgoing someone is within seconds. Picture this experiment by Maurice Levesque and David Kenny (1993). They seated groups of four university women around a table and asked each woman merely to state her name, year in school, hometown, and college residence. Judging from just these few seconds of verbal and nonverbal behavior, the women were then to guess one another's talkativeness. (How do you think you would do in guessing someone's talkativeness, based on such a small glimpse of their behavior?) When later correlated with how talkative each woman actually was during a series of one-on-one videotaped conversations, the snap judgments proved reasonably accurate. So did the judgments of Peter Borkenau and his co-workers (2004), who videotaped German adults as they engaged in varied behaviors, from making up a story to reading short sentences to introducing someone. Despite situational variations in behavior, personality came shining through. Someone who seemed smart or outgoing in one situation tended to seem (to someone else) smart or outgoing in another. When we judge an expressive trait such as outgoingness, thin slices of behavior can be revealing.

To sum up, we can say that at any moment the immediate situation powerfully influences a person's behavior, especially when the situation makes clear demands. We can better predict drivers' behavior at traffic lights from knowing the color of the lights than from knowing the drivers' personalities. Thus, professors may perceive certain students as subdued (based on their classroom behavior), but friends may perceive them as pretty wild (based on their party behavior). Averaging our behavior across many occasions does, however, reveal distinct personality traits. Moreover, we can, in a flash, perceive individual differences in some traits, such as expressiveness.

The Social-Cognitive Perspective

OBJECTIVE 46-7 | Describe the social-cognitive perspective, and explain how reciprocal determinism illustrates that perspective.

Today's psychological science, as we have noted so often, views persons as biopsychosocial organisms. People's biologically influenced psychological traits interact with their situations. The **social-cognitive perspective** on personality proposed by Albert Bandura (1986, 2001, 2005) emphasizes the interaction of persons and their situations. Much as nature and nurture always work together, so do persons and their situations.

■ **social-cognitive perspective** views behavior as influenced by the interaction between persons (and their thinking) and their social context.

Like learning theorists, social-cognitive theorists believe we learn many of our behaviors either through conditioning or by observing others and modeling our behavior after theirs. (That is the "social" part.) They also emphasize the importance of mental processes: What we *think* about our situations affects our behavior. (That is the "cognitive" part.) Instead of focusing solely on how our environment *controls* us (behaviorism), social-cognitive theorists focus on how we and our environment *interact:* How do we interpret and respond to external events? How do our schemas, our memories, and our expectations influence our behavior patterns?

Reciprocal Influences

Bandura (1986) called the process of interacting with our environment **reciprocal determinism**. "Behavior, internal personal factors, and environmental influences," he said, "all operate as interlocking determinants of each other" (**FIGURE 46.3**). For example, children's TV-viewing habits (past behavior) influence their viewing preferences (internal factor), which influence how television (environmental factor) affects their current behavior. The influences are mutual.

Consider three specific ways in which individuals and environments interact:

1. *Different people choose different environments.* The school you attend, the reading you do, the television programs you watch, the music you listen to, the friends you associate with—all are part of an environment you have chosen, based partly on your dispositions (Ickes & others, 1997). *You choose your environment and it then shapes you.*

2. *Our personalities shape how we interpret and react to events.* Anxious people, for example, are attuned to potentially threatening events (Eysenck & others, 1987). Thus, they perceive the world as threatening, and they react accordingly.

3. *Our personalities help create situations to which we react.* Many experiments reveal that how we view and treat people influences how they in turn treat us. If we expect someone to be angry with us, we may give the person a cold shoulder, touching off the very anger we expect. If we have an easygoing, positive disposition, we will likely enjoy close, supportive friendships (Donnellan & others, 2005; Kendler, 1997).

In such ways, we are both the products and the architects of our environments.

If all this has a familiar ring, it may be because it parallels and reinforces a pervasive theme in psychology and in this book: *Behavior emerges from the interplay of*

FIGURE 46.3
Reciprocal determinism
The social-cognitive perspective proposes that our personalities are shaped by the interaction of personal/cognitive factors (our feelings and thoughts), our environment, and our behaviors.

FIGURE **46.4**
**The biopsychosocial approach
to the study of personality**
As with other psychological phenomena,
personality is fruitfully studied at multiple
levels.

external and internal influences. Boiling water turns an egg hard and a potato soft. A threatening environment turns one person into a hero, another into a scoundrel. *At every moment,* our behavior is influenced by our biology, our social experiences, and our cognition and personality. And that, again, is why psychology benefits from these multiple levels of analysis (**FIGURE 46.4**).

Personal Control

OBJECTIVE 46-8 | Discuss the effects of a perception of internal or external control, and describe the concept of learned helplessness.

In studying how we interact with our environment, social-cognitive psychologists emphasize our sense of **personal control**—whether we learn to see ourselves as controlling, or as controlled by, our environment. Psychologists have two basic ways to study the effect of personal control (or any personality factor). One: *Correlate* people's feelings of control with their behaviors and achievements. Two: *Experiment,* by raising or lowering people's sense of control and noting the effects. Let's take these one at a time.

Internal Versus External Locus of Control

Consider your own feelings of control. Do you believe that your life is beyond your control? That the world is run by a few powerful people? That getting a good job depends mainly on being in the right place at the right time? Or do you more strongly believe that what happens to you is your own doing? That the average person can influence government decisions? That being a success is a matter of hard work, not luck?

Hundreds of studies have compared people who differ in their perceptions of control. On the one side are those who have what psychologist Julian Rotter called an **external locus of control**—the perception that chance or outside forces determine their fate. On the other are those who perceive an **internal locus of control** and believe that to a great extent they control their own destiny. In study after study, "internals" achieve more in school, act more independently, enjoy better health, and feel less depressed than do "externals" (Lachman & Weaver, 1998; Lefcourt, 1982; Presson & Benassi, 1996). Moreover, they are better able to delay gratification and cope with various stresses, including marital problems (Miller & others, 1986).

Self-control—the ability to control impulses and delay gratification—in turn predicts good adjustment, better grades, and social success, report June Tangney and her colleagues (2004). University students who plan their day's activities and then live out their day as planned are also at low risk for depression (Nezlek, 2001).

■ **reciprocal determinism** the interacting influences between personality and environmental factors.

■ **personal control** our sense of controlling our environment rather than feeling helpless.

■ **external locus of control** the perception that chance or outside forces beyond one's personal control determine one's fate.

■ **internal locus of control** the perception that one controls one's own fate.

RUBES

None of us experiences unvarying self-control. Self-control requires attention and energy. Like a muscle, self-control temporarily weakens after an exertion, replenishes with rest, and becomes stronger with exercise, report Roy Baumeister and Julia Exline (2000). Exercising willpower depletes mental energy. In one experiment, hungry people's resisting temptations to eat chocolate chip cookies led to their giving up sooner on a tedious task.

Learned Helplessness Versus Personal Control

People who feel helpless and oppressed often perceive control as external. This perception may then deepen their feelings of resignation. In fact, this is precisely what researcher Martin Seligman (1975, 1991) and others found in experiments with both animals and people. Dogs strapped in a harness and given repeated shocks, with no opportunity to avoid them, learned a sense of helplessness. Later placed in another situation where they *could* escape the punishment by simply leaping a hurdle, the dogs cowered as if without hope. People, too, when repeatedly faced with traumatic events over which they have no control, come to feel helpless, hopeless, and depressed. Psychologists call this passive resignation **learned helplessness** (FIGURE 46.5). In contrast, animals able to escape the shocks in the first situation learned personal control and easily escaped the shocks in the new situation.

Part of the shock we feel in an unfamiliar culture comes from a diminished sense of control when unsure how people in the new environment will respond (Triandis, 1994). Similarly, people given little control over their world in prisons, factories, colleges, and nursing homes experience lower morale and increased stress. Measures that increase control—allowing prisoners to move chairs and control room lights and the TV, having workers participate in decision making, offering nursing home patients choices about their environment—noticeably improve health and morale (Miller & Monge, 1986; Ruback & others, 1986; Wener & others, 1987). In one famous study of nursing home patients, 93 percent of those encouraged to exert more control became more alert, active, and happy (Rodin, 1986). As researcher Ellen Langer (1983, p. 291) concluded, "perceived control is basic to human functioning." She recommended that "for the young and old alike," it is important that we create environments that enhance our sense of control and personal efficacy. No wonder so many people like their iPods and TiVos, which give them control of the content and timing of their entertainment.

The verdict of these studies is reassuring: Under conditions of personal freedom and empowerment, people thrive. Small wonder that the citizens of stable democracies report higher levels of happiness (Inglehart, 1990). Shortly before the democratic revolution in the former East Germany, psychologists Gabriele Oettingen and Martin Seligman (1990) studied the telltale body language of working-class men in East and

FIGURE 46.5

Learned helplessness
When animals and people experience no control over repeated bad events, they often learn helplessness.

Peter Turnley/Corbis

Happy are those who choose their own path
These happy East Berliners, crossing over to West Berlin after the wall came down in 1989, seem to personify this sentiment, from the Roman philosopher Seneca.

West Berlin bars. Compared with their counterparts on the other side of the Wall, the empowered West Berliners much more often laughed, sat upright rather than slumped, and had upward- rather than downward-turned mouths.

Since these data were gathered, democracy movements have increased the personal control enjoyed by many Eastern Europeans. Not so for American collegians, who report feeling more and more *external* control. "The average college student in 2002 had a more external locus of control than 80 percent of college students in the early 1960s," report Jean Twenge and her collaborators (2004).

Some freedom and control is better than none, notes Barry Schwartz (2000, 2004). But does ever-increasing choice breed ever-happier lives? Apparently not. Schwartz notes that the "excess of freedom" in today's Western cultures contributes to decreasing life satisfaction, increased depression, and sometimes paralysis. (One reason I haven't replaced my rusty 12-year-old car is my dread of sorting through all the choices.) Increased consumer choices have not been an unmixed blessing. After choosing among 30 brands of jam or chocolate, people express less satisfaction than those choosing among a half-dozen options (Iyengar & Lepper, 2000). This *tyranny of choice* brings information overload and a greater likelihood that we will feel regret over some of the unchosen options.

Optimism Versus Pessimism

OBJECTIVE 46-9 | Discuss the link between performance and optimistic or pessimistic attributional style, and describe the goals of positive psychology.

One measure of how helpless or effective you feel is where you stand on optimism-pessimism. How do you characteristically explain negative and positive events? Perhaps you have known students whose *attributional style* is negative—who attribute poor performance to their lack of ability ("I can't do this") or to situations enduringly beyond their control ("There is nothing I can do about it"). Such students are more likely to persist in getting low grades than are students who adopt the more hopeful attitude that effort, good study habits, and self-discipline can make a difference (Noel & others, 1987; Peterson & Barrett, 1987). Although mere fantasies tend not to fuel motivation and success, realistic positive expectations do (Oettingen & Mayer, 2002).

In their study of professional achievement, Seligman and Peter Schulman (1986) compared sales made by new life insurance representatives who were more or less optimistic in their outlooks. Those who put an optimistic spin on their setbacks—seeing

learned helplessness the hopelessness and passive resignation an animal or human learns when unable to avoid repeated aversive events.

Positive expectations often motivate eventual success.

"We just haven't been flapping them hard enough."

them as flukes or as a means to learning a new approach—sold more policies during their first year and were half as likely to quit as were their more pessimistic peers. Seligman's finding came to life for him when Bob Dell, one of the optimistic recruits who began selling for Metropolitan Life after taking Seligman's optimism test, later dialed him up and sold him a policy.

Health, too, benefits from a basic optimism. A depressed hopelessness dampens the body's disease-fighting immune system. In repeated studies, optimists have outlived pessimists or lived with fewer illnesses. Such studies helped point Seligman toward proposing a more positive psychology (see Close-Up).

If positive thinking in the face of adversity pays dividends, so, too, can a dash of realism (Schneider, 2001). Self-disparaging explanations of past failures can depress ambition, but realistic anxiety over possible *future* failures can fuel energetic efforts to avoid the dreaded fate (Norem, 2001; Goodhart, 1986; Showers, 1992). If concerned about bombing the upcoming exam, students may study thoroughly and outperform their equally able but more confident peers. Edward Chang (2001) reports that, compared with European-American students, Asian-American students express somewhat greater pessimism—which he suspects helps explain their impressive academic achievements. Success requires enough optimism to provide hope and enough pessimism to prevent complacency.

Excessive optimism can blind us to real risks. Neil Weinstein (1980, 1982, 1996) has shown how our natural positive-thinking bias can promote "an unrealistic optimism about future life events." Most college students perceive themselves as less likely than their average classmate to develop drinking problems, drop out of school, or have a heart attack by age 40. Most late adolescents see themselves as much less vulnerable than their peers to the AIDS virus (Abrams, 1991).

Our natural positive-thinking bias does seem to vanish, however, when we are bracing ourselves for feedback, such as exam results (Taylor & Shepperd, 1998). (Have you ever noticed that, as a game nears its end, the outcome seems more in doubt when your team is ahead than when it is behind?) Positive illusions also vanish after a traumatic personal experience—as they did for California victims of a catastrophic earthquake, who had to give up their illusions of being less vulnerable than others to earthquakes (Helweg-Larsen, 1999).

Given illusory optimism, documented in some 200 research reports, people may fail to take sensible precautions. Most young Americans know that roughly half of U.S. marriages end in divorce, but they are confident that *theirs* will not (Lehman & Nisbett, 1985). Most cigarette smokers smoke high-tar brands, but only 17 percent believe their brand has a more hazardous tar level than most others (Segerstrom & others, 1993). Compared with other women at their university, sexually active undergraduate women—especially those who do *not* consistently use effective contraception—perceive themselves as *less* vulnerable to unwanted pregnancy (Burger & Burns, 1988). Those who optimistically venture into ill-fated relationships, deny the effects of smoking, or engage in unprotected sex remind us that, like pride, blind optimism may go before a fall.

Ironically, people often are most overconfident when most incompetent. That's because it often takes competence to recognize competence, note Justin Kruger and David Dunning (1999). They found that most students scoring at the low end of tests of grammar and logic believed they had scored in the top half. If you do not know what good grammar is, you may be unaware that your grammar is poor. This "ignorance of

"O God, give us grace to accept with serenity the things that cannot be changed, courage to change the things which should be changed, and the wisdom to distinguish the one from the other."

Reinhold Niebuhr, "The Serenity Prayer," 1943

"I didn't think it could happen to me."

Earvin "Magic" Johnson, *My Life*, 1993 (after contracting HIV)

"Ignorance more freely begets confidence than does knowledge."

Charles Darwin, *The Descent of Man*, 1871

CLOSE-UP:

TOWARD A MORE POSITIVE PSYCHOLOGY

During its first century, psychology understandably focused much of its attention on understanding and alleviating negative states. We have studied abuse and anxiety, depression and disease, prejudice and poverty. Since 1887, articles on selected negative emotions have outnumbered those on positive emotions by 17 to 1.

In ages past, notes 1998 American Psychological Association president Martin Seligman (2002), times of relative peace and prosperity have enabled cultures to turn their attention from repairing weakness and damage to promoting "the highest qualities of life." Prosperous fifth-century Athens nurtured philosophy and democracy. Flourishing fifteenth-century Florence nurtured great art. Victorian England, flush with the bounty of the British empire, nurtured honor, discipline, and duty. In this millennium, Seligman believes, thriving Western cultures have a parallel opportunity to create, as a "humane, scientific monument," a more **positive psychology**—a psychology concerned not only with weakness and damage but also with strength and virtue. Thanks to his own leadership and to some $30 million in new funding, the new positive psychology movement is gaining strength (Seligman, 2004).

Positive psychology shares with humanistic psychology an interest in advancing human fulfillment, but its methodology is scientific. From these roots have grown not only the new

Martin E. P. Seligman

"The main purpose of a positive psychology is to measure, understand, and then build the human strengths and the civic virtues."

Courtesy of Martin E.P. Seligman, Ph.D. Director, Positive Psychology Center/University of Pennsylvania

studies of happiness and health, but also the shift in emphasis from learned helplessness and depression to optimism and thriving. "Positive psychology," say Seligman and colleagues (2005) "is an umbrella term for the study of positive emotions, positive character traits, and enabling institutions."

Taken together, satisfaction with the past, happiness with the present, and optimism about the future define the movement's first pillar: *positive emotions*. Happiness, Seligman argues, is a by-product of a pleasant, engaged, and meaningful life.

Positive psychology is about building not just a pleasant life, says Seligman, but also a *good life* that engages one's skills, and a *meaningful life* that points beyond oneself.

Thus, the second pillar, *positive character,* focuses on exploring and enhancing virtues such as creativity, courage, compassion, integrity, self-control, leadership, wisdom, and spirituality. Current research examines the roots and fruits of such virtues, sometimes by studying individuals who exemplify them in extraordinary ways.

The third pillar, *positive groups, communities, and cultures,* seeks to foster a positive social ecology, including healthy families, communal neighborhoods, effective schools, socially responsible media, and civil dialogue.

Will psychology have a more positive mission in this century? Without slighting the need to repair damage and cure disease, positive psychology's proponents hope so. With *American Psychologist* and *British Psychologist* special issues devoted to positive psychology, with new books (*Authentic Happiness,* 2002; *A Psychology of Human Strengths,* 2003; *Character Strengths and Virtues,* 2004), with 150 networked scientists worldwide working in 50 research groups, and with prizes, research awards, summer institutes, and a new graduate program promoting positive psychology scholarship, these psychologists have reason to be positive.

■ **positive psychology** the scientific study of optimal human functioning; aims to discover and promote strengths and virtues that enable individuals and communities to thrive.

---

one's own incompetence" phenomenon has a parallel, as I can vouch, in hard-of-hearing persons' difficulty recognizing their own hearing loss. We're not so much "in denial" as we are simply unaware of what we don't hear. If I fail to hear my friend calling my name, the friend notices my inattention. But for me it's a nonevent. I hear what I hear—which, to me, seems pretty normal.

The difficulty in recognizing one's own incompetence helps explain why so many low-scoring students are dumbfounded after doing badly on an exam. If you don't know all the Scrabble word possibilities you've overlooked, you may feel pretty smart—until someone points them out. As Deanna Caputo and Dunning (2005) demonstrate in experiments that re-create this phenomenon, our ignorance of what we don't know helps sustain our confidence in our own abilities.

"The living-room [Scrabble] player is lucky. . . . He has no idea how miserably he fails with almost every turn, how many possible words or optimal plays slip by unnoticed."

Stephen Fatsis, *Word Freak*, 2001

DOONESBURY

Assessing Behavior in Situations

OBJECTIVE **46-10** | Explain why social-cognitive researchers assess behavior in realistic situations.

Social-cognitive psychologists explore how people interact with situations. To predict behavior, they often observe behavior in realistic situations.

The idea, though effective, is not new. One ambitious example was the U.S. Army's World War II strategy for assessing candidates for spy missions. Rather than using paper-and-pencil tests, army psychologists subjected the candidates to simulated undercover conditions. They tested their ability to handle stress, solve problems, maintain leadership, and withstand intense interrogation without blowing their covers. Although time-consuming and expensive, this assessment of behavior in a realistic situation helped predict later success on actual spy missions (OSS Assessment Staff, 1948).

Military and educational organizations and many Fortune 500 companies are adopting similar strategies in their evaluations of hundreds of thousands of people each year in assessment centers (Bray & Byham, 1991, 1997; Spychalski & others, 1997). AT&T has observed prospective managers doing simulated managerial work. Many colleges assess potential faculty members' teaching abilities by observing them teach, and assess graduate students' potentials via internships and student teaching.

Assessing behavior in situations Reality TV shows may take "show me" job interviews to the extreme, but they do illustrate a valid point. Seeing how a potential employee behaves in a job-relevant situation helps predict job performance.

Armies assess their soldiers by observing them during military exercises. Most American cities with populations of 50,000 or more use assessment centers in evaluating police and fire officers (Lowry, 1997).

These procedures exploit the principle that the best means of predicting future behavior is neither a personality test nor an interviewer's intuition. Rather, it is the person's past behavior patterns in similar situations (Mischel, 1981; Ouellette & Wood, 1998; Schmidt & Hunter, 1998). As long as the situation and the person remain much the same, the best predictor of future job performance is past job performance; the best predictor of future grades is past grades; the best predictor of future aggressiveness is past aggressiveness; the best predictor of drug use in young adulthood is drug use in high school. If you can't check the person's past behavior, the next-best thing is to create an assessment situation that simulates the task so you can see how the person handles it.

Evaluating the Social-Cognitive Perspective

OBJECTIVE 46-11 | State the major criticism of the social-cognitive perspective.

The social-cognitive perspective on personality sensitizes researchers to how situations affect, and are affected by, individuals. More than other perspectives, it builds from psychological research on learning and cognition.

Critics charge that the social-cognitive perspective focuses so much on the situation that it fails to appreciate the person's inner traits. Where is the person in this view of personality, ask the dissenters (Carlson, 1984), and where are human emotions? True, the situation does guide our behavior. But, say the critics, in many instances our unconscious motives, our emotions, and our pervasive traits shine through. Personality traits have been shown to predict behavior at work, love, and play. Our biologically influenced traits really do matter. Consider Percy Ray Pridgen and Charles Gill. Each faced the same situation: They had jointly won a $90 million lottery jackpot (Harriston, 1993). When Pridgen learned of the winning numbers, he began trembling uncontrollably, huddled with a friend behind a bathroom door while confirming the win, then sobbed. When Gill heard the news, he told his wife and then went to sleep.

Exploring the Self

OBJECTIVE 46-12 | Explain why psychology has generated so much research on the self, and give three examples of current research on the self.

Psychology's concern with people's sense of self dates back at least to William James, who devoted more than 100 pages of his 1890 *Principles of Psychology* to the topic. By 1943, Gordon Allport lamented that the self had become "lost to view." Although humanistic psychology's emphasis on the self did not instigate much scientific research, it did help renew the concept of self and keep it alive. Now, more than a century after James, the self is one of Western psychology's most vigorously researched topics. Every year, new studies galore appear on self-esteem, self-disclosure, self-awareness, self-schemas, self-monitoring, and so forth—more than 220,000 articles in all since 1967. Underlying this research is an assumption that the self, as organizer of our thoughts, feelings, and actions, is a pivotal center of personality.

One example of thinking about self is the concept of *possible selves* put forth by Hazel Markus and her colleagues (Cross & Markus, 1991; Markus & Nurius, 1986). Your possible selves include your visions of the self you dream of becoming—the rich self, the successful self, the loved and admired self. They also include the self you fear becoming—the unemployed self, the lonely self, the academically failed self.

A *New York Times* analysis of 100 rampage murders over the last half-century revealed that 55 of the killers had regularly exploded in anger and 63 had threatened violence (Goodstein & Glaberson, 2000). Most didn't, out of the blue, "just snap."

"The first step to better times is to imagine them."

Chinese fortune cookie

Possible selves

By giving them a chance to try out many possible selves, pretend games offer children important opportunities to grow emotionally, socially, and cognitively. This young boy may or may not grow up to be a physician, but playing adult roles will certainly bear fruit in terms of an expanded vision of what he might become.

Such possible selves motivate us by laying out specific goals and calling forth the energy to work toward them. University of Michigan students in a combined undergraduate/medical school program earn higher grades if they undergo the program with a clear vision of themselves as successful doctors. Dreams do often give birth to achievements.

Our self-focused perspective may motivate us, but it can also lead us to presume too readily that others are noticing and evaluating us. Thomas Gilovich (1996) demonstrated this **spotlight effect** by having individual Cornell University students don Barry Manilow T-shirts before entering a room with other students. Feeling self-conscious, the T-shirt wearers guessed that nearly half of their peers would take note of the shirt as they walked in. In reality, only 23 percent did. This absence of attention applies not only to our dorky clothes and bad hair but also to our nervousness, irritation, or attraction: Fewer people notice than we presume (Gilovich & Savitsky, 1999). Others are also less aware than we suppose of the variability—the ups and downs—of our appearance and performance (Gilovich & others, 2002). Even after a blunder (setting off a library alarm, showing up for dinner in the wrong clothes), we stick out like a sore thumb less than we imagine (Savitsky & others, 2001). Knowing about the spotlight effect can be empowering. Help public speakers to understand that their natural nervousness is not so apparent to their audience, and their speaking performance improves (Savitsky & Gilovich, 2003).

Self-focus affects our recall, too, but in a more constructive way: We remember information better if we encode it in terms of ourselves. Tory Higgins and John Bargh (1987) demonstrated this *self-reference* phenomenon by asking people to consider whether some specific words such as *friendly* described them, and whether the words described someone else. The participants better recalled words they had considered in relation to themselves.

The Benefits of Self-Esteem

OBJECTIVE 46-13 | Give two alternative explanations for the positive correlation between low self-esteem and personal problems.

How we feel about ourselves is also important. High **self-esteem**—a feeling of self-worth—pays dividends. People who feel good about themselves (who strongly agree with self-affirming questionnaire statements) have fewer sleepless nights, succumb less easily to pressures to conform, are more persistent at difficult tasks, are less shy and lonely, and are just plain happier (Crocker & Wolfe, 1999; Leary, 1999; Murray & others, 2002; Watson & others, 2002). Give high–self-esteem people happy news, and they are more likely than low–self-esteem people to savor it rather than dampen it (Wood & others, 2003).

Those whose self-esteem is low do not necessarily see themselves as worthless or wicked, but they seldom say good things about themselves. Low self-esteem often co-exists with unhappiness and despair, as psychotherapy researcher Hans Strupp (1982) noted: "As soon as one listens to a patient's story, one encounters unhappiness, frustration, and despair. . . . Basic to all these difficulties are impairments in self-acceptance and self-esteem." When low self-esteem signals social rejection, it may aid survival—by motivating people to behave in ways that restore their inclusion within a supportive group (Leary & others, 1995).

The correlational links between low self-esteem and personal problems have other possible interpretations. Psychologists Roy Baumeister and colleagues (2003, 2005), William Damon (1995), Robyn Dawes (1994), Mark Leary (1999), and Martin Seligman (1994, 2002) all doubt that high self-esteem is really "the armor that protects kids" from life's problems. Maybe self-esteem simply reflects reality. Maybe feeling good *follows* doing well. Maybe it's a side effect of meeting challenges and surmounting difficulties. Maybe self-esteem is a gauge that reads out the state of our relationships

Dear diary,
Sorry to bother you again.

LOW SELF-ESTEEM

with others. If so, isn't pushing the gauge artificially higher akin to forcing a car's low fuel gauge to display "full"? And if problems and failures cause low self-esteem, won't the best boost therefore come not so much from our repeatedly telling children how wonderful they are as from their own effective coping and hard-won achievements?

However, experiments do reveal an *effect* of low self-esteem. Temporarily deflate people's self-image (say, by telling them they did poorly on an aptitude test or by disparaging their personality) and they will be more likely to disparage others or to express heightened racial prejudice (Ybarra, 1999). Those who are negative about themselves also tend to be thin-skinned and judgmental (Baumgardner & others, 1989; Pelham, 1993). Some "love their neighbors as themselves"; others loathe their neighbors as themselves. In experiments, those made to feel insecure often become excessively critical, as if to impress others with their own brilliance (Amabile, 1983). Such findings are consistent with humanistic psychologists Abraham Maslow's and Carl Rogers' presumptions that a healthy self-image pays dividends. Accept yourself and you'll find it easier to accept others. Disparage yourself and you will be prone to the floccinaucinihilipilification[1] of others. Said more simply, people who are down on themselves tend to be down on other things and people.

Maintaining Self-Esteem

OBJECTIVE 46-14 | Discuss some ways that people maintain their self-esteem under conditions of discrimination or low status.

Is it true, as so many assume, that ethnic minorities, people with disabilities, and women live lives handicapped by impoverished self-esteem? The accumulated evidence says no. The National Institute of Mental Health's 1980s study of *Psychiatric Disorders in America* found rates of depression and alcoholism among African- and Hispanic-Americans roughly comparable with those of other Americans (if anything, America's ethnic minorities suffered slightly less depression. More recently, 261 comparisons of more than half a million people have revealed slightly *higher* self-esteem scores for black than for white children, adolescents, and young adults (Gray-Little & Hafdahl, 2000; Twenge & Crocker, 2002).

Some people wonder: How can this be? Some members of stigmatized groups (people of color, those with disabilities, women) have faced discrimination and lower status, yet, according to Jennifer Crocker and Brenda Major (1989), they maintain their self-esteem in three ways:

- They value the things at which they excel.
- They attribute problems to prejudice.
- They do as everyone does—they compare themselves to those in their own group.

These findings help us understand why, despite the realities of prejudice, such groups report levels of happiness roughly comparable to others.

Self-Serving Bias

OBJECTIVE 46-15 | Discuss self-serving bias, and contrast defensive and secure self-esteem.

Humanistic psychologist Carl Rogers (1958) once objected to the religious doctrine that humanity's problems arise from excessive self-love, or pride. He noted that most people he had known "despise themselves, regard themselves as worthless and unlovable." Mark Twain had a similar idea: "No man, deep down in the privacy of his heart, has any considerable respect for himself."

> "There's a lot of talk about self-esteem these days. It seems pretty basic to me. If you want to feel proud of yourself, you've got to do things you can be proud of."
>
> Oseola McCarty, Mississippi washerwoman, after donating $150,000 to the University of Southern Mississippi

---

[1] I couldn't resist throwing that in. But don't worry, you won't be tested on *floccinaucinihilipilification*, which is the act of estimating something as worthless (and was the longest nontechnical word in the first edition of the *Oxford English Dictionary*).

spotlight effect overestimating others' noticing and evaluating our appearance, performance, and blunders (as if we presume a spotlight shines on us).

self-esteem one's feelings of high or low self-worth.

PEANUTS

Actually, most of us have a good reputation with ourselves. In studies of self-esteem, even those who score low respond in the midrange of possible scores. (A low–self-esteem person responds to statements such as "I have good ideas" with qualifying adjectives such as *somewhat* or *sometimes*.) Moreover, one of psychology's most provocative and firmly established recent conclusions concerns our potent **self-serving bias**—our readiness to perceive ourselves favorably (Mezulis & others, 2004; Myers, 2005). Consider these findings:

People accept more responsibility for good deeds than for bad, and for successes than for failures. Athletes often privately credit their victories to their own prowess and their losses to bad breaks, lousy officiating, or the other team's exceptional performance. After receiving poor grades on an exam, most students in a half-dozen studies criticized the exam, not themselves. On insurance forms, drivers have explained accidents in such words as: "An invisible car came out of nowhere, struck my car, and vanished." "As I reached an intersection, a hedge sprang up, obscuring my vision, and I did not see the other car." "A pedestrian hit me and went under my car." The question "What have I done to deserve this?" is one we usually ask of our troubles, not our successes—those, we assume we deserve.

Most people see themselves as better than average. This is true for nearly any subjective and socially desirable dimension. In national surveys, most business executives say they are more ethical than their average counterpart. In several studies, 90 percent of business managers and more than 90 percent of college professors rated their performance as superior to that of their average peer. In Australia, 86 percent of people rate their job performance as above average, and only 1 percent as below average. The phenomenon, which reflects the overestimation of self rather than the underestimation of others (Epley & Dunning, 2000), is less striking in Asia, where people value modesty. Yet self-serving biases have been observed worldwide: among Dutch, Australian, and Chinese students; Japanese drivers; Indian Hindus; and French people of most walks of life. Ironically, people even see themselves as more immune than others to self-serving bias (Pronin & others, 2002). The world, it seems, is Garrison Keillor's Lake Wobegon writ large—a place where "all the women are strong, all the men are good-looking, and all the children are above average."

And who is at least "somewhat likely" to go to heaven? Of Americans surveyed by *U.S. News* (1997), 19 percent thought O. J. Simpson would make it. They were more optimistic about Bill Clinton (52 percent), Princess Diana (60 percent), and Michael Jordan (65 percent). The public figure closest to a perceived heavenly shoo-in was Mother Teresa (79 percent). But she was topped by the survey's respondents, 87 percent of whom believed *they* themselves were destined for eternal bliss.

Self-serving bias flies in the face of pop psychology. "All of us have inferiority complexes," wrote John Powell (1989, p. 15). "Those who seem not to have such a complex are only pretending." But additional findings remove any doubts (Myers, 2005):

- We remember and justify our past actions in self-enhancing ways.
- We exhibit an inflated confidence in our beliefs and judgments.
- We overestimate how desirably *we* would act in situations where most people behave less than admirably.

"To love oneself is the beginning of a life-long romance."

Oscar Wilde, *An Ideal Husband*, 1895

Three in four pet owners believe their pet is smarter than average (Nier, 2004).

"The [self-]portraits that we actually believe, when we are given freedom to voice them, are dramatically more positive than reality can sustain."

Shelley Taylor, *Positive Illusions*, 1989

- We often seek out favorable, self-enhancing information.
- We are quicker to believe flattering descriptions of ourselves than unflattering ones, and we are impressed with psychological tests that make us look good.
- We shore up our self-image by overestimating the commonality of our foibles and by *underestimating* the commonality of our strengths.
- We exhibit group pride—a tendency to see our group (our school, our country, our race) as superior.

Moreover, pride does often go before a fall. Self-serving perceptions underlie conflicts ranging from blaming one's spouse for marital discord to arrogantly promoting one's own ethnic superiority. "Aryan pride" fueled Nazi atrocities. No wonder religion and literature so often warn against the perils of excessive pride.

Finding their self-esteem threatened, people with large egos may do more than put others down; they may react violently. Among children, the recipe for frequent fighting mixes high self-esteem with social rejection. The most aggressive children tend to have high self-regard that gets punctured by other kids' dislike (van Boxtel, 2004). An adolescent or adult with a swelled head that gets deflated by insult is potentially dangerous. Brad Bushman and Roy Baumeister (1998) experimented with this "dark side of high self-esteem." They had 540 undergraduate volunteers write a paragraph, in response to which another supposed student gave them either praise ("Great essay!") or stinging criticism ("One of the worst essays I have read!"). Then the essay writers played a reaction-time game against the other student. After wins, they could assault their opponent with noise of any intensity for any duration.

Can you anticipate the result? After criticism, those with unrealistically high self-esteem were "exceptionally aggressive." They delivered three times the auditory torture of those with normal self-esteem. Threatened egotism, more than low self-esteem, it seems, predisposes aggression. "Encouraging people to feel good about themselves when they haven't earned it" poses problems, Baumeister (2001) concludes. "Conceited, self-important individuals turn nasty toward those who puncture their bubbles of self-love."

Despite the demonstrated perils of pride, many people reject the idea of self-serving bias, insisting it overlooks those who feel worthless and unlovable and seem to despise themselves. If self-serving bias prevails, why do so many people disparage themselves? For three reasons: Sometimes self-directed put-downs are *subtly strategic:* They elicit reassuring strokes. Saying "No one likes me" may at least elicit "But not everyone has met you!" Other times, such as before a game or an exam, self-disparaging comments *prepare us for possible failure.* The coach who extols the superior strength of the upcoming opponent makes a loss understandable, a victory noteworthy. And finally, self-disparagement also frequently pertains to one's *old self.* People are much more critical of their distant past selves than of their current selves—even when they have not changed (Wilson & Ross, 2001). "At 18, I was a jerk; today I'm more sensitive." In their own eyes, chumps yesterday, champs today.

Even so, it's true: All of us some of the time, and some of us much of the time, *do* feel inferior—especially when we compare ourselves with those who are a step or two higher on the ladder of status, looks, income, or ability. The deeper and more frequently we have such feelings, the more unhappy, even depressed, we are. But for most people, thinking has a naturally positive bias.

While recognizing the dark side of self-serving bias and self-esteem, some researchers prefer isolating the effects of two types of self-esteem—defensive and secure (Jordan & others, 2003; Kernis, 2003; Ryan & Deci, 2004). *Defensive self-esteem* is fragile. It focuses on sustaining itself, which makes failures and criticism feel threatening. Such egotism exposes one to perceived threats, which feed anger and disorder, note Jennifer Crocker and Lora Park (2004). Thus, like low self-esteem, defensive self-esteem correlates with aggressive and antisocial behavior (Donnellan & others,

■ **self-serving bias** a readiness to perceive oneself favorably.

> "The enthusiastic claims of the self-esteem movement mostly range from fantasy to hogwash. The effects of self-esteem are small, limited, and not all good."
>
> Roy Baumeister (1996)

> "If you compare yourself with others, you may become vain and bitter; for always there will be greater and lesser persons than yourself."
>
> Max Ehrmann, "Desiderata," 1927

2005). *Secure self-esteem* is less fragile, because it is less contingent on external evaluations. To feel accepted for who we are, and not for our looks, wealth, or acclaim, relieves pressures to succeed and enables us to focus beyond ourselves. By losing ourselves in relationships and purposes larger than self, Crocker and Park add, we may achieve a more secure self-esteem and greater quality of life.

Recognizing both the perils of self-righteousness and the dividends of secure self-esteem, psychologists Baumeister (1989), Jonathan Brown (1991), and Shelley Taylor (1989; Taylor & others, 2003) have all suggested that humans function best with modest self-enhancing illusions. Like the Japanese and European magnetic levitation trains, Brown notes, we function optimally when riding just off the rails—not so high that we gyrate and crash, yet not so in touch that we grind to a halt.

>> Learning Outcomes

Contemporary Research on Personality

OBJECTIVE 46-1 | Cite the main difference between the trait and psychoanalytic perspectives on personality.

Rather than explain personality in terms of childhood sexuality and unconscious motivations, as Sigmund Freud did, trait researchers have attempted to describe personality in terms of stable and enduring behavior patterns, or predispositions to feel and act. Some psychologists also have attempted to use dominant traits to describe personality "types."

OBJECTIVE 46-2 | Describe some of the ways psychologists have attempted to compile a list of basic personality traits.

Trait researchers attempt to describe personality by placing individuals at points on several trait dimensions simultaneously (sometimes by using *factor analysis*). Hans Eysenck and Sybil Eysenck proposed that two primary, genetically influenced dimensions (extraversion-introversion and emotional stability-instability) explain normal individual variations. Jerome Kagan believes that heredity, by influencing autonomic nervous system reactivity, also influences temperament and behavioral style, which help define personality.

OBJECTIVE 46-3 | Explain how psychologists use personality inventories to assess traits, and discuss the most widely used personality inventory.

Personality inventories are questionnaires on which people respond to items designed to gauge a wide range of feelings and behaviors. Items on the MMPI, the most widely used personality inventory, are empirically derived, and the tests are objectively scored. This does not guarantee *validity* (measuring what it is supposed to measure); people may answer questions in socially appropriate but untruthful ways.

OBJECTIVE 46-4 | Identify the Big Five personality factors, and discuss some of the strengths of this approach to studying personality.

The Big Five personality factors are *conscientiousness, agreeableness, neuroticism, openness,* and *extraversion*. These traits appear to be stable in adulthood, substantially heritable, applicable to all cultures, and good predictors of other personal attributes. Locating an individual on these five dimensions currently offers the most comprehensive picture of personality.

OBJECTIVE 46-5 | Summarize the person-situation controversy, and explain its importance as a commentary on the trait perspective.

Critics of the trait perspective point out that although people's general traits may persist over time, their specific behavior varies as their inner disposition interacts with a particular environment. Trait theorists reply that despite these variations, a person's *average* behavior across many different situations tends to be fairly consistent.

OBJECTIVE 46-6 | Explain why psychologists are interested in the consistency of the trait of expressiveness.

Expressive styles—animation, manner of speaking, and gestures—demonstrate how consistent traits can be, despite situational variations in behavior. Observers have been able to judge expressiveness in video snippets as short as 2 seconds long. We have little voluntary control over our expressiveness.

OBJECTIVE 46-7 | Describe the social-cognitive perspective, and explain how reciprocal determinism illustrates that perspective.

Reciprocal determinism is a term applied to the interacting influences between personality and environmental factors. This interaction is central to the social-cognitive perspective, which applies principles of learning (through conditioning and observation) and cognition (our thinking about our situations) to the study of personality. Such interactions occur when we choose an environment that then shapes us, when our personality shapes how we interpret and react to events, and when our personality helps create situations to which we react.

OBJECTIVE 46-8 | Discuss the effects of a perception of internal or external control, and describe the concept of learned helplessness.

People with an *internal locus of control* (who believe they control their own destiny) tend to experience higher school achievement, better health, less depression, and greater self-control than those with an *external locus of control* (who believe forces beyond their control determine their fate). *Learned helplessness* is an acquired response of hopelessness and passive resignation that animals and humans display after repeated exposure to traumatic events they cannot control.

OBJECTIVE 46-9 | Discuss the link between performance and optimistic or pessimistic attributional style, and describe the goals of positive psychology.

An optimistic or pessimistic *attributional style*—your way of explaining events—can be a window revealing how effective or helpless you feel. Students who express an attitude of hopeful optimism tend to get better grades than those who have a negative attributional style. But excessive optimism can foster feelings of invincibility that expose us to unnecessary risks.

Positive psychology uses scientific methods to study and foster (1) positive subjective well-being; (2) positive character; and (3) positive groups, communities, and cultures.

OBJECTIVE 46-10 | Explain why social-cognitive researchers assess behavior in realistic situations.

Social-cognitive researchers study how people's behaviors and beliefs affect, and are affected by, their surroundings. They observe people in realistic situations because the best way to predict someone's behavior in a given situation is to observe that person's behavior in similar situations.

OBJECTIVE 46-11 | State the major criticism of the social-cognitive perspective.

Critics fault the social-cognitive perspective for focusing so much on the situation that it loses sight of the importance of the influence of unconscious dynamics, emotions, and biologically influenced traits.

OBJECTIVE 46-12 | Explain why psychology has generated so much research on the self, and give three examples of current research on the self.

Psychological research on the self has been accumulating for more than a century. Many psychologists view the self—the organizer of our thoughts, feelings, and actions—as a critical part of personality. Recent research examples include the study of the influence of *possible selves* (the visions of the selves we dream of becoming or fear we may become), the concept of the *spotlight effect* (the assumption that we overestimate the extent to which others notice and evaluate our appearance, performance, and blunders), and the *self-reference effect* (the ability to better recall information if we relate it to our own person or life).

OBJECTIVE 46-13 | Give two alternative explanations for the positive correlation between low self-esteem and personal problems.

Abraham Maslow and Carl Rogers argued that a healthy self-image (high self-esteem) pays dividends in a personally fulfilling and successful life, and some experiments have shown the destructive power of a negative self-image. An alternative explanation of the link between low self-esteem and personal problems is that self-esteem, low or high, reflects reality, and that it is a side effect of one's success or failure in meeting challenges and surmounting difficulties.

OBJECTIVE 46-14 | Discuss some ways that people maintain their self-esteem under conditions of discrimination or low status.

Studies show that under conditions of discrimination or low status, people—often those of color, those with disabilities, and women—maintain their self-esteem by valuing the things at which they excel, by attributing problems to prejudice, and by comparing themselves with people in similar positions.

OBJECTIVE 46-15 | Discuss self-serving bias, and contrast defensive and secure self-esteem.

The *self-serving bias* (our readiness to perceive ourselves favorably) includes our tendencies (1) to more readily accept responsibility for good deeds and for successes than for bad deeds and failures, and (2) to see ourselves as better than average. *Defensive self-esteem* is fragile and takes the form of egotism focused on sustaining itself at any cost. *Secure self-esteem* is less fragile and less dependent on external evaluations.

TERMS AND CONCEPTS TO REMEMBER

trait, p. 46-0
personality inventory, p. 46-2
Minnesota Multiphasic Personality Inventory (MMPI), p. 46-2
empirically derived test, p. 46-3
social-cognitive perspective, p. 46-9
reciprocal determinism, p. 46-10

personal control, p. 46-11
external locus of control, p. 46-11
internal locus of control, p. 46-11
learned helplessness, p. 46-12
positive psychology, p. 46-15
spotlight effect, p. 46-18
self-esteem, p. 46-18
self-serving bias, p. 46-20

TEST YOURSELF

1. How many trait dimensions are currently used to describe personality, and what are those dimensions?

2. How do learned helplessness and optimism influence behavior?

3. In a 1997 Gallup poll, white Americans estimated 44 percent of their fellow white Americans to be high in prejudice (scoring them 5 or higher on a 10-point scale). How many rated themselves similarly high in prejudice? Just 14 percent. What phenomenon does this illustrate?

(Answers in Appendix B.)

ASK YOURSELF

1. Where would you place yourself on the five personality dimensions—stability, extraversion, openness, agreeableness, and conscientiousness? Where would your family and friends place you?

2. Are you a pessimist? Do you readily catastrophize, have low expectations, and attribute bad events to your inability or to circumstances beyond your control? Or are you an optimist, perhaps even someone who frequently exhibits "illusory optimism"? How did either tendency influence your choice of school or major?

3. What possible future selves do you envision? To what extent do these imagined selves motivate you now?

>WEB

Multiple-choice **self-tests** and more may be found at www.worthpublishers.com/myers.

ANOTHER VOICE ON: PSYCHOLOGICAL DISORDERS

CHRISTINE LINCOLN (b. 1966), FROM "SAP RISING"

We share the story about the women called maniacs. Women who lived a long time ago. They were just country women, really, who got tired of cookin' and cleanin', takin' care of their husband and chirrun. Got tired of everybody else usin' up what was supposed to be their lives.

So they met in the woods one night and had this dance. When the men found out, they got angry and tried to put an end to their women's foolishness. But they couldn't. The women rebelled. Started gatherin' every night. Before long, the men started callin' the women crazy, and

started treatin' them like they was, until the women began to believe it. Why is it when a man wants to be free, he's just being a man, but when a woman wants to live life from the position of the birds, the first thing folks say is that she's crazy?

Psychological Disorders

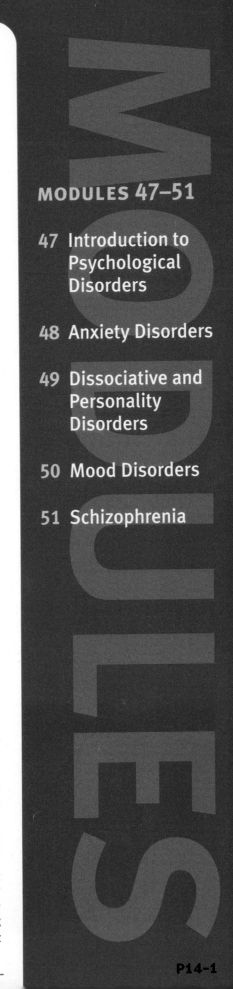
"We are all mad at some time or another."

Baptista Mantuanus, Eclogues, *1500*

I felt the need to clean my room at home in Indianapolis every Sunday and would spend four to five hours at it. I would take every book out of the bookcase, dust and put it back. At the time I loved doing it. Then I didn't want to do it anymore, but I couldn't stop. The clothes in my closet hung exactly two fingers apart. . . . I made a ritual of touching the wall in my bedroom before I went out because something bad would happen if I didn't do it the right way. I had a constant anxiety about it as a kid, and it made me think for the first time that I might be nuts.

Marc, diagnosed with
obsessive-compulsive disorder
(from Summers, 1996)

Whenever I get depressed it's because I've lost a sense of self. I can't find reasons to like myself. I think I'm ugly. I think no one likes me. . . . I become grumpy and short-tempered. Nobody wants to be around me. I'm left alone. Being alone confirms that I am ugly and not worth being with. I think I'm responsible for everything that goes wrong.

Greta, diagnosed with depression
(from Thorne, 1993, p. 21)

Voices, like the roar of a crowd came. I felt like Jesus; I was being crucified. It was dark. I just continued to huddle under the blanket, feeling weak, laid bare and defenseless in a cruel world I could no longer understand.

Stuart, diagnosed with
schizophrenia
(from Emmons & others, 1997)

People are fascinated by the exceptional, the unusual, the abnormal. "The sun shines and warms and lights us and we have no curiosity to know why this is so," observed Ralph Waldo Emerson, "but we ask the reason of all evil, of pain, and hunger, and [unusual] people." But why such fascination with disturbed people? Do we see in them something of ourselves? At various moments, all of us feel, think, or act the way disturbed people do much of the time. We, too, get anxious, depressed, withdrawn, suspicious, or deluded, just less intensely and more briefly. It's no wonder then that studying psychological disorders may at times evoke an eerie sense of self-recognition, one that illuminates the dynamics of our own personality. "To study the abnormal is the best way of understanding the normal," proposed William James (1842–1910).

Another reason for our curiosity is that so many of us have felt, either personally or through friends or family members, the bewilderment and pain of a psychological disorder that may bring unexplained physical symptoms, irrational fears, or a feeling that life is not worth living.

Module 47 introduces psychological disorders, explaining the major perspectives and categories and the risks of labeling, and the prevalence of the various disorders. Module 48 describes *anxiety disorders,* which are characterized by persistent distressing anxiety or maladaptive behaviors that reduce anxiety. Module 49 focuses on the rare and controversial *dissociative disorders,* and the problematic *personality disorders,* which impair social functioning. Module 50 examines in depth the emotional extremes of *mood disorders.* And Module 51 outlines the symptoms and characteristics of those suffering from *schizophrenia,* a frightening split from reality.

47

Introduction to Psychological Disorders

Most people would agree that someone who is too depressed to get out of bed for weeks at a time has a psychological disorder. But what about those who, having experienced a loss, are unable to resume their usual social activities? Where should we draw the line between sadness and depression? Between zany creativity and bizarre irrationality? Between normality and abnormality? Let's start with these questions:

- How should we *define* psychological disorders?
- How should we *understand* disorders—as sicknesses that need to be diagnosed and cured, or as natural responses to a troubling environment?
- How should we *classify* psychological disorders? And can we do so in a way that allows us to help people without stigmatizing them with *labels*?
- How *prevalent* are these disorders, and who is likely to experience them?

Defining Psychological Disorders

OBJECTIVE 47-1 | Identify the criteria for judging whether behavior is psychologically disordered.

■ **psychological disorder** deviant, distressful, and dysfunctional behavior patterns.

Mental health workers view **psychological disorders** as persistently harmful thoughts, feelings, and actions. When behavior is *deviant, distressful,* and *dysfunctional,* psychiatrists and psychologists label it disordered (Comer, 2004).

Being different (deviant) from most other people in one's culture is *part* of what it takes to define a psychological disorder. As the reclusive poet Emily Dickinson observed in 1862,

> Assent—and you are sane—
> Demur—you're straightaway dangerous—
> and handled with a Chain.

Standards for deviant behavior vary by culture and context. In some cultures, people routinely behave in ways (such as going about naked) that in other cultures would be grounds for arrest. In at least one cultural context—wartime—even mass killing may be viewed as normal and even heroic. Stuart claimed to hear voices and people presumed he was deranged. But others may claim to talk with the dead and not be seen as disordered because enough people find them rational (Friedrich, 1987).

Standards for deviance also vary with time. From 1952 through December 9, 1973, homosexuality was classified as an illness. By day's end on December 10, it was not. The American Psychiatric Association had dropped homosexuality as a disorder because more and more of its members no longer viewed being gay as a psychological problem. (Later research has revealed that the stigma and stresses associated with being gay do, however, increase the risk of mental health problems [Meyer, 2003].) In this new century, controversy swirls over the frequent diagnosing of children with *attention-deficit hyperactivity disorder* (see Thinking Critically About: ADHD—Pathologizing Rambunctiousness or Genuine Disorder?).

Culture and normality
Men of the West African Wodaabe tribe put on elaborate makeup and costumes to attract women. In Western society, the same behavior would break behavioral norms and might be judged abnormal.

Carol Beckwith

ADHD—PATHOLOGIZING RAMBUNCTIOUSNESS OR GENUINE DISORDER?

Eight-year-old Todd has always been energetic. At home, he darts from one activity to the next, rarely settling down to read a book or focus on play. At meals, he chatters away and often answers questions before they are fully asked. At play, he is reckless and overreacts to playmates who bump into him or take one of his toys. At school, his exasperated teacher complains that fidgety Todd won't listen or follow instructions and just can't seem to stay seated and do his lessons.

If taken to a psychologist or psychiatrist for an evaluation, Todd is much more likely today than two decades ago to be diagnosed with **attention-deficit hyperactivity disorder (ADHD).** According to the National Institute of Mental Health (2003), ADHD plagues some 4 percent of children who display one or more of its three key symptoms:

- *Inattention*—distractibility, forgetfulness, disorganization
- *Hyperactivity*—fidgeting, restlessness and not staying seated at school, excessive talking
- *Impulsivity*—difficulty taking turns, interrupting, blurting out answers while questions are being asked

To skeptics, being distractible, fidgety, and impulsive sounds like a "disorder" caused by a single genetic variation: a Y chromosome. And sure enough, ADHD is diagnosed two to three times more often in boys than in girls. Does energetic child + boring school = ADHD overdiagnosis? Is the label being applied to healthy schoolchildren who, in more natural outdoor environments, would seem perfectly normal?

Skeptics think so. In the decade after 1987, they note, the proportion of American children being treated for ADHD nearly quadrupled (Olfson & others, 2003). By 2005, a Gallup survey of 13- to 17-

year-olds found that 10 percent reported taking prescribed medication for ADHD (Mason, 2005). In some places, the diagnosis is commonplace, in others it is rare. Toddlers who watch lots of TV are, at age 7, more likely than average to display ADHD symptoms (Christakis & others, 2004). Some teachers refer lots of kids for ADHD assessment, others none. ADHD rates have varied by a factor of 10 in different counties of New York State (Carlson, 2000). Adults, too, now willingly accept the ADHD diagnosis for themselves and, contend the skeptics, find it a handy excuse for their past school failures, vocational difficulties, and lack of self-discipline.

Although acknowledging the diagnostic subjectivity and inconsistency—ADHD is not as objectively defined as is a broken arm—the World Federation for Mental Health (2003) has declared that "there is strong agreement among the international scientific community that ADHD is a real neurobiological disorder whose existence should no longer be debated." ADHD, agrees the National Institute of Mental Health (1999, 2003), is heritable. It is also marked in neuroimaging studies by telltale brain activity, notes a consensus statement by 75 researchers (Barkley & others, 2002). It is *not* caused by too much sugar or poor schools. It often coexists with a learning disorder or with defiant and temperprone behavior. It is treatable with nonaddictive medications such as Ritalin and Adderall, which are stimulants but help calm the hyperactivity and increase a person's ability to sit and focus on a task. Psychological therapies, such as those focused on shaping behaviors in the classroom and at home, have also helped address the distress of ADHD. And its more frequent diagnosis today may reflect increased

awareness of the disorder, especially in areas where the diagnosis is more common.

New research is seeking a more objective assessment of ADHD. Measures include a physical measure of fidgeting, an eye-tracking device that measures ability to focus on and follow spots of light, and more detailed brain imaging (Ashtari & others, 2004; Pavlidis, 2005; Teicher, 2002). Recognizing that about 80 percent of children medicated for ADHD still require medication as teens, as do 50 percent or more as adults, other researchers are exploring the long-term effects of taking stimulant drugs. People appear to tolerate long-term stimulant use with no increased risk of substance abuse (Biederman & others, 1999), but other possible effects are being investigated. In one study, rats were given prolonged exposure to Ritalin early in life, at a dosage comparable to that commonly prescribed for children. When the drug was withdrawn later in life, the rats (compared with others in a control group) were more prone to depressive symptoms and to giving up quickly when facing challenging tasks (Carlezon & others, 2003).

The bottom line: Extreme inattention, hyperactivity, and impulsivity can derail social, academic, and vocational achievements, and these symptoms can be treated with stimulant drugs. But the debate continues over whether normal rambunctiousness is too often diagnosed as a psychiatric disorder, and whether there is a cost to the long-term use of stimulant drugs in treating ADHD.

■ **attention-deficit hyperactivity disorder (ADHD)** a psychological disorder marked by the appearance by age 7 of one or more of three key symptoms: extreme inattention, hyperactivity, and impulsivity.

But there is more to a disorder than being deviant. Olympic gold medalists deviate from the norm in their physical abilities, and society honors them. To be considered disordered, deviant behavior must also cause the person *distress*.

Deviant and distressful behaviors are more likely to be considered disordered when also judged *dysfunctional*. By this measuring stick, even typical behaviors, such as the occasional despondency that many college students feel, may signal a psychological disorder *if* they become disabling. Dysfunction is key to defining a disorder: An intense fear of spiders may be deviant, but if it doesn't impair your life it is not a disorder.

Disordered behavior may also be dangerous. If depression deepens and people develop suicidal thoughts, they may be considered a danger to themselves.

Understanding Psychological Disorders

OBJECTIVE 47-2 | Contrast the medical model of psychological disorders with the biopsychosocial approach to disordered behavior.

To explain puzzling behavior, people in earlier times often presumed that strange forces— the movements of the stars, godlike powers, or evil spirits—were at work. "The devil made him do it," you might have said had you lived during the Middle Ages. The cure might have been to get rid of the evil force—by placating the great powers or exorcising the demon. Until the last two centuries, "mad" people were sometimes caged in zoolike conditions or given "therapies" appropriate to a demon: beatings, burning, or castration. In other times, therapy might have included pulling teeth, removing lengths of intestines, cauterizing the clitoris, or receiving transfusions of animal blood (Farina, 1982).

The Medical Model

In opposition to this brutal treatment, reformers such as Philippe Pinel (1745–1826) in France insisted that madness was not demon possession but a sickness of the mind caused by severe stresses and inhumane conditions. For Pinel and other reformers, "moral treatment" included boosting patients' morale by unchaining them and talking with them, and by replacing brutality with gentleness, isolation with activity, and filth with clean air and sunshine.

When physicians later discovered that syphilis infects the brain and distorts the mind, health reformers and medical workers refocused on physical causes for mental disorders and treatments that would cure them. By the 1800s, the assumption of this **medical model**—that psychological disorders are sicknesses—provided the impetus

John W. Verano

Yesterday's "therapy"
In other times and places, psychologically disordered people sometimes received brutal treatments, including the *trephination* evident in this Stone Age skull. Such skull holes may have been drilled in an attempt to release evil spirits and cure those with mental disorders. This patient may or may not have survived the "cure."

George Wesley Bellows, Dance in a Madhouse, 1907. © 1997 The Art Institute of Chicago

"Moral treatment"
Under Philippe Pinel's influence, hospitals sometimes sponsored patient dances, such as the "Lunatic Ball" depicted in this painting by George Bellows (*Dance in a Madhouse*).

for further reform as hospitals replaced asylums. Today, the medical perspective is recognizable in the terminology of the mental *health* movement: A mental *illness* (also called a psycho*pathology*) needs to be *diagnosed* on the basis of its *symptoms* and *cured* through *therapy*, which may include *treatment* in a psychiatric *hospital*.

The medical perspective has gained credibility from recent discoveries. Genetically influenced abnormalities in brain structure and biochemistry contribute to a number of disorders. "Mental illnesses are diagnosable disorders of the brain," declared a U.S. White House fact sheet on mental illness (1999). Two of the most troubling, depression and schizophrenia, often are treated medically. But psychological factors, such as traumatic stress, also play an important role.

The Biopsychosocial Approach

Today's psychologists contend that *all* behavior, whether called normal or disordered, arises from the interaction of nature (genetic and physiological factors) and nurture (past and present experiences). To presume that a person is "mentally ill" attributes the condition solely to an internal problem—to a "sickness" that must be found and cured. But maybe there is no deep, internal problem. Maybe instead there is a growth-blocking difficulty in the person's environment, in the person's current interpretations of events, or in the person's bad habits and poor social skills.

Evidence of environmental effects comes from links between disorder and culture. Some major disorders, such as depression and schizophrenia, occur worldwide. From Asia to Africa and across the Americas, schizophrenia symptoms often include irrationality and incoherent speech (Brislin, 1993; Draguns, 1990b). Other disorders are culture-bound (Beardsley, 1994; Castillo, 1997). Different cultures have different sources of stress, and they produce different ways of coping. Anorexia nervosa and bulimia, for example, are eating disorders that occur mostly in Western cultures. *Susto,* marked by severe anxiety, restlessness, and a fear of black magic, is found in Latin America. *Taijin-kyofusho,* which combines social anxiety about one's appearance with a readiness to blush and a fear of eye contact, appears in Japan. Such disorders may share an underlying dynamic (such as anxiety) while differing in the symptoms (an eating problem or a type of fear) manifested in a particular culture.

Today, most mental health workers assume that disorders are influenced by genetic predispositions and physiological states; by inner psychological dynamics; and by social and cultural circumstances. To get the whole picture, we need to use the biopsychosocial approach (**FIGURE 47.1**), which recognizes that mind and body are inseparable. Negative emotions contribute to physical illness, and physical abnormalities contribute to emotional malaise. We are mind embodied.

■ **medical model** the concept that diseases have physical causes that can be diagnosed, treated, and, in most cases, cured. When applied to psychological disorders, the medical model assumes that these *mental illnesses* can be diagnosed on the basis of their symptoms and cured through therapy, which may include treatment in a psychiatric hospital.

"Who in the rainbow can draw the line where the violet tint ends and the orange tint begins? Distinctly we see the difference of the colors, but where exactly does the one first blendingly enter into the other? So with sanity and insanity?"
Herman Melville, *Billy Budd, Sailor,* 1924

"It's no measure of health to be well adjusted to a profoundly sick society."
Krishnamurti, 1895–1986

FIGURE 47.1
The biopsychosocial approach to psychological disorders
Today's psychology studies how biological, psychological, and social-cultural factors interact to produce specific psychological disorders.

Biological influences:
• evolution
• individual genes
• brain structure and chemistry

Psychological influences:
• stress
• trauma
• learned helplessness
• mood-related perceptions and memories

Psychological disorder

Social-cultural influences:
• roles
• expectations
• definitions of *normality* and *disorder*

■ **DSM-IV** the American Psychiatric Association's *Diagnostic and Statistical Manual of Mental Disorders* (Fourth Edition), a widely used system for classifying psychological disorders. Presently distributed in an updated "text revision" (DSM-IV-TR).

Classifying Psychological Disorders

OBJECTIVE 47-3 | Describe the goals and content of the DSM-IV.

In biology and the other sciences, classification creates order. To classify an animal as a mammal says a great deal—that it is warm-blooded, has hair or fur, and nourishes its young with milk. In psychiatry and psychology, too, classification orders and describes symptoms. To classify a person's disorder as "schizophrenia" suggests that the person talks incoherently, hallucinates or has delusions (bizarre beliefs), shows either little emotion or inappropriate emotion, or is socially withdrawn. "Schizophrenia" provides a handy shorthand for describing a complex disorder.

In psychiatry and psychology, diagnostic classification aims not only to describe a disorder but also to predict its future course, imply appropriate treatment, and stimulate research into its causes. Indeed, to study a disorder we must first name and describe it. A current authoritative scheme for classifying psychological disorders is the American Psychiatric Association's *Diagnostic and Statistical Manual of Mental Disorders* (Fourth Edition), nicknamed **DSM-IV.** This 1994 volume, now updated as a 2000 "text revision" (DSM-IV-TR), will be more substantially revised as DSM-V, to appear about 2011. (A set of case illustrations accompanying DSM-IV provides several of this book's case examples.) DSM-IV was developed in coordination with the tenth edition of the World Health Organization's *International Classification of Diseases* (ICD-10), which covers both medical and psychological disorders.

The very idea of "diagnosing" people's problems in terms of their "symptoms" presumes a mental "illness." As a result, some practitioners are not enthralled with this medical terminology, but most find the classification to be a helpful and practical tool. It is also financially necessary: Most North American health insurance companies require an ICD diagnosis before they will pay for therapy.

DSM-IV defines a diagnostic process and 16 clinical syndromes (**TABLE 47.1**). Without presuming to explain their causes, it describes various disorders and lists their prevalence. To be helpful and useful, DSM-IV categories and diagnostic guidelines must be reliable, and they are. If one psychiatrist or psychologist diagnoses someone as having, say, catatonic schizophrenia, the chances are good that another mental health worker will independently give the same diagnosis. Following these guidelines, clinicians answer a series of objective questions about observable behaviors, such as, "Is the person afraid to leave home?" In one study, 16 psychologists used this structured-interview procedure to diagnose 75 psychiatric patients as suffering from (1) depression, (2) generalized anxiety, or (3) some other disorder (Riskind & others, 1987). Without knowing the first psychologist's diagnosis, another psychologist viewed a videotape of each interview and offered a second opinion. For 83 percent of the patients, the two opinions agreed.

Some critics have faulted the manual for casting too wide a net and bringing "almost any kind of behavior within the compass of psychiatry" (Eysenck & others, 1983). These critics point to behaviors ranging from irrational fear of humiliation and embarrassment (social phobia) to persistently breaking rules at home or school (conduct disorder). As the number of disorder categories has swelled (from 60 in the 1950s' DSM to 400 in today's), so has the number of adults who meet the criteria for at least one of them—nearly 30 percent in one recent year, according to a U.S. survey (Regier & others, 1998). As a complement to the DSM, some psychologists are offering a manual of human strengths and virtues (see Close-Up: The "un-DSM": A Diagnostic Manual of Human Strengths).

© 1992 by Sidney Harris.

"I'm always like this, and my family was wondering if you could prescribe a mild depressant."

TABLE **47.1**

HOW ARE PSYCHOLOGICAL DISORDERS DIAGNOSED?

Based on assessments, interviews, and observations, many clinicians diagnose by answering the following questions from the five levels, or *axes,* of the DSM-IV-TR.

Axis I Is a *Clinical Syndrome* present?
Using specifically defined criteria, clinicians may select none, one, or more syndromes from the following list:

- Disorders usually first diagnosed in infancy, childhood, and adolescence
- Delirium, dementia, amnesia, and other cognitive disorders
- Mental disorders due to a general medical condition
- Substance-related disorders
- Schizophrenia and other psychotic disorders
- Mood disorders
- Anxiety disorders
- Somatoform disorders
- Factitious disorders (intentionally feigned)
- Dissociative disorders
- Eating disorders
- Sexual disorders and gender identity disorder
- Sleep disorders
- Impulse-control disorders not classified elsewhere
- Adjustment disorders
- Other conditions that may be a focus of clinical attention

Axis II Is a *Personality Disorder* or *Mental Retardation* present?
Clinicians may or may not also select one of these two conditions.

Axis III Is a *General Medical Condition,* such as diabetes, hypertension, or arthritis, also present?

Axis IV Are *Psychosocial or Environmental Problems,* such as school or housing issues, also present?

Axis V What is the *Global Assessment* of this person's functioning?
Clinicians assign a code from 0–100. For example:

91–100 Superior functioning in a wide range of activities; life's problems never seem to get out of hand; is sought out by others because of his or her many positive qualities. No symptoms.
51–60 Moderate symptoms (for example, flat affect or occasional panic attacks) or moderate difficulty in social, occupational, or school functioning (for example, few friends, or conflicts with peers or coworkers).
1–10 Persistent danger of severely hurting self or others (for example, recurrent violence) or persistent inability to maintain minimal personal hygiene or serious suicidal act with clear expectation of death.

Labeling Psychological Disorders

OBJECTIVE 47-4 | Discuss the potential dangers and benefits of using diagnostic labels.

The DSM has other critics who register a more fundamental complaint—that these labels are at best arbitrary and at worst value judgments masquerading as science. Once we label a person, we view that person differently (Farina, 1982). Labels create preconceptions that guide our perceptions and our interpretations. It is better, some clinicians say, to study the roots of specific symptoms, such as distorted thoughts or perceptions, than to study catchall categories, such as "schizophrenia" (Persons, 1986).

In the most controversial demonstration of the biasing power of diagnostic labels, David Rosenhan (1973) and seven others went to mental hospital admissions offices, complaining of "hearing voices" that were saying "empty," "hollow," and "thud." Apart from this complaint and giving false names and occupations, they answered questions truthfully. All eight were diagnosed as mentally ill.

That these normal people were misdiagnosed is unsurprising. As one psychiatrist noted, if someone swallowed blood, went to an emergency room, and spat it up, would we fault the doctor for diagnosing a bleeding ulcer? What followed the

> " One of the unpardonable sins, in the eyes of most people, is for a man to go about unlabeled. The world regards such a person as the police do an unmuzzled dog, not under proper control."
>
> T. H. Huxley, *Evolution and Ethics,* 1893

CLOSE-UP:

THE "UN-DSM": A DIAGNOSTIC MANUAL OF HUMAN STRENGTHS

The fast-expanding positive psychology movement, which aims to discover and promote conditions that enable flourishing individuals and communities, has launched an effort, led by psychologists Christopher Peterson and Martin Seligman (2004), to create a classification system for human strengths and virtues. A manual that orders and defines harmful dysfunctions has been helpful, these researchers note. Why not also have a companion manual that would similarly order and define our human strengths—the thinking-feeling-action tendencies that contribute to the *good* life, for self and others?

Like the DSM-IV, *The Values in Action Classification of Strengths* draws insights from many researchers in proposing a common vocabulary that lends itself to cross-cultural understanding and to the budding science of strengths. Also like the DSM, the strengths manual offers assessment strategies and questionnaires that help researchers assess six clusters of 24 strengths:

Wisdom and Knowledge
- curiosity
- love of learning
- critical judgment and open-mindedness
- creativity
- perspective (wisdom)

Courage (overcoming opposition)
- bravery/valor
- industry and perseverance
- integrity and honesty
- vitality (zest and enthusiasm)

Love
- kindness
- intimate attachment
- social intelligence

Justice
- citizenship and teamwork
- fairness and equity
- leadership

Temperance
- humility
- self-control
- prudence and caution
- forgiveness and mercy

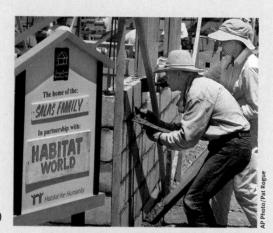

Building strengths
In their work for Habitat for Humanity, former U.S. President Jimmy Carter and First Lady Rosalynn Carter model strengths related to love and justice.

Transcendence
- appreciation of beauty, awe/wonder
- gratitude
- hope and optimism
- playfulness and humor
- spirituality and purpose

Labeling effect

Seeing *Asylum* on the shirts of this baseball team (from the State Homeopathic Asylum for the Insane in Middletown, New York), most observers of this 1890s photo will comment on the players' apparent depression or confusion. Actually, all the players were from the asylum's staff.

diagnosis *was* startling. Until being released (an average of 19 days later), the "patients" exhibited no further symptoms. Yet the clinicians were able to "discover" the causes of their disorders, such as reacting to mixed emotions about a parent, after analyzing their (quite normal) life histories. Even the routine behavior of taking notes was misinterpreted as a symptom.

Other studies confirm that labels affect how we perceive people. Ellen Langer and her colleagues (1974, 1980) had people watch a videotaped interview. Some were told the interviewee was normal (a job applicant). Others were told the person was out of the ordinary (a psychiatric or cancer patient). Those who watched unlabeled interviewees perceived them as normal; those who watched supposed patients perceived them as "different from most people." Therapists who thought they were evaluating a psychiatric patient perceived the interviewee as "frightened of his own aggressive impulses," a "passive, dependent type," and so forth. A label can, as Rosenhan discovered, have "a life and an influence of its own." (See Thinking Critically About: Insanity and Responsibility.)

INSANITY AND RESPONSIBILITY

My brain . . . my genes . . . my bad up-bringing made me do it. Such defenses were anticipated by Shakespeare's *Hamlet*. If I wrong someone when not myself, he explained, "then Hamlet does it not, Hamlet denies it. Who does it then? His madness." Such is the essence of a legal insanity defense, created in 1843 after a deluded Scotsman tried to shoot the prime minister (who he thought was persecuting him) but killed an assistant by mistake. Like U.S. President Reagan's near-assassin, John Hinckley, Scotsman Daniel M'Naughten was sent to a mental hospital rather than to prison.

In both cases, the public was outraged. "Hinckley Insane, Public Mad," declared one headline. And they were mad again when a deranged Jeffrey Dahmer in 1991 admitted murdering 15 young men and eating parts of their bodies. They were mad in 1998 when 15-year-old Kip Kinkel, driven by "those voices in my head," killed his parents and 2 fellow Springfield, Oregon, students and wounded 25 others. And they were mad in 2002 when Andrea Yates, after being taken off her antipsychotic medication, was tried in Texas for drowning her five children. All of these people were sent to jails, not hospitals, following their arrests.

These cases are not uncommon. A 1999 U.S. Justice Department study found that 283,000 jail and prison inmates had severe mental disorders. This is about 16 percent of the U.S. inmate population and considerably more than the 183,000 psychiatric inpatients in all types of U.S. hospitals (Bureau of the Census, 2004; Butterfield, 1999). Many

people who have been executed or are on death row have been limited by mental retardation or motivated by delusional voices. Larry Robison (1999) was twice hospitalized for paranoid schizophrenia, as were his

Elaine Thompson/AP Photo

Jail or hospital?
Unabomber Theodore Kaczynski lived in a shack for some 20 years, rarely bathed, sent bombs to strangers (killing 3 and injuring 23), and was diagnosed by his state-appointed psychiatrist with paranoid schizophrenia. One of his early letter bombs was addressed to the author of what was, at the time, psychology's most widely studied text. (The bomb was opened by his assistant, who recovered from injuries.) Should Kaczynski be jailed as a criminal or hospitalized (but also confined) as mentally ill?

brother, sister, uncle, and grandfather. When denied further treatment after insurance coverage ran out, Robison was discharged, killed five people, and was executed by the state of Texas. Four years later, another murderer with schizophrenia, Charles Singleton, was executed by the State of Arkansas after being forcibly medicated with antipsychotic drugs—in order to make him mentally competent, so that he could then be put to death.

Whom should we hold responsible? The people who commit such rare but terrible crimes or the "madness" that clouds their vision? Should we treat or should we punish executives who sexually harass their employees and then claim to have a sexual disorder? If a perpetrator's revolting crime is taken to indicate a disorder, does this create a social basis for evading responsibility (like the person who, having killed his parents, demands mercy because he is an orphan)? Some in Britain believed that is what happened when Brian Blackwell was allowed to plead guilty to a reduced charge of manslaughter after brutally killing his parents. Should he be credited with diminished responsibility because of his "narcissistic personality disorder," as the judicial system agreed, or was the disorder more a description than an explanation of his criminal behavior (*Psychologist*, 2005)? This much seems likely: If some superpsychologist were to understand the biological and environmental basis for everything—from generosity to vandalism—society would still wish to hold people responsible for their actions.

The stigmatizing power of labels was illustrated when a female associate of psychologist Stewart Page (1977) called 180 people in Toronto who were advertising furnished rooms for rent. When she merely asked if the room was still available, the answer was nearly always yes. When she instead said she was about to be released from a mental hospital, the answer three times out of four was no (as it was when

Coping With Disorder
"The only way I knew how to deal with it was to write a song about it," musician Billy Joe Armstrong of Green Day explained, referring to his song "Basket Case," which chronicles a personal struggle with anxiety disorders.

she said she was calling for her brother who was about to be released from jail). Some who said no room was available were later called by a second person who simply asked if the room was still available. Nearly always it was. Surveys in Western Europe have uncovered similar attitudes toward those labeled mentally ill. As we are coming to understand that many psychological disorders are diseases of the brain, not failures of character, the stigma seems to be lifting (Solomon, 1996). Public figures are feeling freer to "come out" and speak with candor about their struggles with disorders such as depression. And the more often people have contact with mental health patients, the more accepting their attitudes are (Kolodziej & Johnson, 1996).

But stereotypes linger. This is hardly surprising, given media images of psychological disorders. Movies sometimes offer reasonably accurate and sympathetic portrayals of disorders, as in the portrayal of mathematician John Nash's schizophrenia in *A Beautiful Mind*. But too often they stereotype mental health patients as homicidal (Hannibal Lecter in *Silence of the Lambs*) or as freaks (Hyler & others, 1991; Wahl, 1992). People with schizophrenia are more likely than others to commit violent crimes, especially if they also abuse alcohol (Citrome & Volavka, 1999; Tiihonen & others, 1997). However, at least 9 in 10 people with disorders are *not* dangerous; instead, they are anxious, depressed, or withdrawn. And *if* they steer clear of alcohol and drugs, those released from mental hospitals are no more prone to violence than are their neighbors (Steadman & others, 1998). Indeed, reports the U.S. Surgeon General's Office (1999, p. 7), "There is very little risk of violence or harm to a stranger from casual contact with an individual who has a mental disorder." (In fact, people with psychological disorders are more likely to be victims of violence, rather than perpetrators [Marley & Bulia, 2001].)

Not only can labels bias perceptions, they can also change reality. When teachers are told certain students are "gifted," when students expect someone to be "hostile," or when interviewers check to see whether someone is "extraverted," they may act in ways that elicit the very behavior expected (Snyder, 1984). Someone who was led to think you are nasty may treat you coldly, leading you to respond as a mean-spirited person would. Labels can serve as self-fulfilling prophecies.

But let us remember the benefits of diagnostic labels. Mental health professionals use labels to communicate about their cases, to comprehend the underlying causes, and to discern effective treatment programs.

Rates of Psychological Disorders

OBJECTIVE 47-5 | Discuss the prevalence of psychological disorders, and summarize the findings on the link between poverty and serious psychological disorders.

No known culture is free of two terrible maladies—depression and schizophrenia (Castillo, 1997; Draguns, 1990a,b, 1997). Some 450 million people worldwide suffer psychological disorders, according to the World Health Organization (WHO, 2004). The WHO also reports that, worldwide, mental disorders have accounted for 15.4 percent of the years of life lost due to death or disability—scoring slightly below cardiovascular conditions and slightly above cancer (Murray & Lopez, 1996). As members of the human family, few of us go through life unacquainted with the reality of psychological disturbance.

So how prevalent are the various disorders? Who is most vulnerable to them? At what times of life? To answer such questions, various countries have conducted lengthy, structured interviews with representative samples of thousands of their citizens. After asking hundreds of questions that probed for symptoms—"Has there ever been a period of two weeks or more when you felt like you wanted to die?"—the researchers have estimated the current, prior year, and lifetime prevalence of various disorders.

Does a full moon trigger "madness" in some people? James Rotton and I. W. Kelly (1985) examined data from 37 studies that related lunar phase to crime, homicides, crisis calls, and mental hospital admissions. Their conclusion: There is virtually no evidence of "moon madness." Nor does lunar phase correlate with suicides, assaults, emergency room visits, or traffic disasters (Martin & others, 1992; Raison & others, 1999).

TABLE 47.2

PERCENTAGE OF AMERICANS WHO HAVE EXPERIENCED SELECTED PSYCHOLOGICAL DISORDERS IN THE PRIOR YEAR

Disorder	Percentage
Alcohol abuse	5.2
Generalized anxiety	4.0
Phobias	7.8
Obsessive-compulsive disorder	2.1
Mood disorder	5.1
Schizophrenia	1.0
Antisocial personality	1.5
Any mental disorder	14.9

(Some people experience two or more of these disorders, such as depression and alcohol abuse, simultaneously.)

Source: Data from Narrow & others, 2002.

How many people suffer, or have suffered, a psychological disorder? More than most of us suppose:

- Summarizing a U.S. National Institute of Mental Health interview study and a follow-up survey, William Narrow and his colleagues (2002) estimated that 1 in 7 Americans had suffered a clinically significant mental disorder during the prior year (**TABLE 47.2**).
- Britain's Office of National Statistics (2002) recently reported a similar 1-in-6 disorder rate.
- An Australian government survey of 10,600 adults found that in any 12 months, slightly less than 1 in 6 "have a mental disorder" (Andrews & others, 1999). Another Australian government study of 4500 children and adolescents concluded that 1 in 7 had "mental health problems" (Sawyer & others, 2000).
- A twenty-first-century World Health Organization (2004) study—based on 90-minute interviews of 60,463 people—estimated the number of prior-year mental disorders in 20 countries. As **FIGURE 47.2** displays, the lowest rate of reported mental disorders was in Shanghai, the highest rate in the United States. Moreover, when people immigrate to the United States from Mexico and elsewhere, their mental health and their children's declines as they assimilate over time. For example, compared with people who have recently immigrated from Mexico, Mexican-Americans born in the United States are at greater risk of mental disorder (Grant & others, 2004; Vega & others, 1998).

One predictor of mental disorder is poverty. The incidence of serious psychological disorders is doubly high among those below the poverty line (Centers for Disease Control, 1992). Like so many other correlations, the poverty-disorder association raises a chicken-and-egg question: Does poverty cause disorders? Or do disorders cause poverty? It is both, though the answer varies with the disorder. Schizophrenia understandably leads to poverty. Yet the stresses and demoralization of poverty can also precipitate disorders, especially depression in women and substance abuse in men (Dohrenwend & others, 1992). In one natural experiment on the poverty-pathology link, researchers tracked rates of behavior problems in North Carolina Native American children as economic development enabled a dramatic reduction in their community's poverty rate. As the study began, children of poverty exhibited more deviant and aggressive behaviors. After four years, children whose families had moved above the poverty line exhibited a 40 percent decrease in

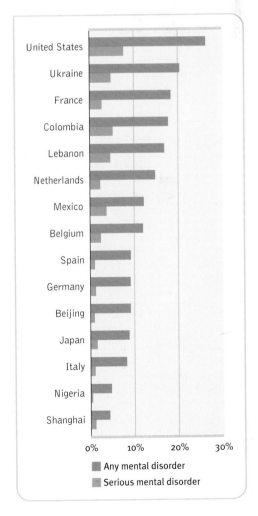

FIGURE 47.2
Prevalence of mental disorders during prior year From World Health Organization (2004) interviews in 20 countries.

TABLE **47.3**

RISK AND PROTECTIVE FACTORS FOR MENTAL DISORDERS

Risk Factors	Protective Factors
Academic failure	Aerobic exercise
Birth complications	Community offering empowerment, opportunity, and security
Caring for chronically ill or patients with dementia	Economic independence
Child abuse and neglect	Feelings of security
Chronic insomnia	Feelings of mastery and control
Chronic pain	Good parenting
Family disorganization or conflict	Literacy
Low birth weight	Positive attachment and early bonding
Low socioeconomic status	Positive parent-child relationships
Medical illness	Problem-solving skills
Neurochemical imbalance	Resilient coping with stress and adversity
Parental mental illness	Self-esteem
Parental substance abuse	Social and work skills
Personal loss and bereavement	Social support from family and friends
Poor work skills and habits	
Reading disabilities	
Sensory disabilities	
Social incompetence	
Stressful life events	
Substance abuse	
Trauma experiences	

Source: World Health Organization (2004a,b)

the behavior problems, while those who continued in their previous positions below or above the poverty line exhibited no change (Costello & others, 2003).

As **TABLE 47.3** indicates, there is a wide range of risk and protective factors for mental disorders. Those who experience a psychological disorder usually do so by early adulthood. "Over 75 percent of our sample with any disorder had experienced its first symptoms by age 24," reported Robins and Regier (1991, p. 331). The symptoms of antisocial personality disorder and of phobias are among the earliest to appear, at a median age of 8 and 10, respectively. Symptoms of alcohol abuse, obsessive-compulsive disorder, bipolar disorder (formerly called manic-depressive disorder), and schizophrenia appear at a median age near 20. Major depression often hits somewhat later, at a median age of 25. Such findings make clear the need for research and treatment to help the growing number of people, especially teenagers and young adults, who suffer the bewilderment and pain of a psychological disorder.

Although mindful of the pain, we can also be encouraged by the many successful people—including Leonardo da Vinci, Isaac Newton, and Leo Tolstoy—who pursued brilliant careers while enduring psychological difficulties. The bewilderment, fear, and sorrow caused by psychological disorders are real. But hope, too, is real, as our understanding of these disorders continues to grow.

>> LEARNING OUTCOMES

Introduction to Psychological Disorders

OBJECTIVE 47-1 | Identify the criteria for judging whether behavior is psychologically disordered.
Psychologists and psychiatrists consider behavior disordered when it is deviant, distressful, and dysfunctional. The definition of *deviant* varies with context and culture. It also varies with time; for example, some children who might have been judged rambunctious a few decades ago now are being diagnosed with attention-deficit hyperactivity disorder.

OBJECTIVE 47-2 | Contrast the medical model of psychological disorders with the biopsychosocial approach to disordered behavior.
The medical model assumes that psychological disorders are mental illnesses that can be diagnosed on the basis of their symptoms and cured through therapy, sometimes in a hospital. The biopsychosocial approach assumes that disordered behavior, like other behavior, arises from genetic predispositions and physiological states; inner psychological dynamics; and social-cultural circumstances.

OBJECTIVE 47-3 | Describe the goals and content of the DSM-IV.
The American Psychiatric Association's *Diagnostic and Statistical Manual of Mental Disorders,* Fourth Edition (DSM-IV), currently describes 400 disorders and their prevalence. The manual defines a structured interview technique, in which clinicians answer objective questions, posed at five different levels, or axes, about the individual's observable behaviors. The reliability of the classification is sufficiently high. DSM diagnoses are developed in coordination with International Classification of Diseases (ICD).

OBJECTIVE 47-4 | Discuss the potential dangers and benefits of using diagnostic labels.
Critics of the DSM-IV argue that diagnostic labels can stigmatize a person by biasing others' interpretations and perceptions of past and present behaviors and by affecting the ways people react to the labeled person. The benefits of diagnostic labels are that they establish a common vocabulary for mental health professionals giving therapy, and for researchers working on causes and treatments of disorders. Most North American health-care providers require an ICD diagnosis. One label, "sanity"—used in some legal defenses—raises questions a how a society should treat people with disorders who have committed crimes.

OBJECTIVE 47-5 | Discuss the prevalence of psychological disorders, and summarize the findings on the link between poverty and serious psychological disorders.
Research indicates that about 1 in 6 people has, or has had, a psychological disorder, usually by early adulthood. Poverty is a predictor of mental illness. Conditions and experiences associated with poverty contribute to the development of mental disorders, but some mental disorders, such as schizophrenia, can drive people into poverty.

TERMS AND CONCEPTS TO REMEMBER

psychological disorder, p. 47-0
attention-deficit hyperactivity
   disorder (ADHD), p. 47-1

medical model, p. 47-2
DSM-IV, p. 47-6

TEST YOURSELF

1. What is the biopsychosocial approach, and why is it important in our understanding of psychological disorders?
2. Does poverty cause psychological disorders? Explain.

(Answers in Appendix B.)

ASK YOURSELF

1. How would you draw the line between sending disturbed criminals to prisons or to mental hospitals? Would the person's history (for example, having suffered child abuse) influence your decisions?
2. Do you have a family member or friend who has experienced a psychological disorder? If so, has anything you have read in this chapter increased your understanding of the challenges that person has been facing?

>WEB

Multiple-choice *self-tests* and more may be found at www.worthpublishers.com/myers.

48

Anxiety Disorders

OBJECTIVE 48-1 | Define *anxiety disorders,* and explain how these conditions differ from normal feelings of stress, tension, or uneasiness.

Anxiety is part of life. Speaking in front of a class, peering down from a ledge, or waiting to play in a big game, any one of us might feel anxious. At times many of us feel enough anxiety that we fail to make eye contact or we avoid talking to someone— "shyness," we call it. Fortunately for most of us, our uneasiness is not intense and persistent. If it becomes so, we may have one of the **anxiety disorders,** marked by distressing, persistent anxiety or maladaptive behaviors that reduce anxiety. In this section we focus on four anxiety disorders:

- *Generalized anxiety disorder,* in which a person is unexplainably and continually tense and uneasy
- *Panic disorder,* in which a person experiences sudden episodes of intense dread
- *Phobias,* in which a person feels irrationally and intensely afraid of a specific object or situation
- *Obsessive-compulsive disorder,* in which a person is troubled by repetitive thoughts or actions

Generalized Anxiety Disorder and Panic Disorder

OBJECTIVE 48-2 | Contrast the symptoms of generalized anxiety disorder and panic disorder.

Tom, a 27-year-old electrician, complains of dizziness, sweating palms, heart palpitations, and ringing in his ears. He feels edgy and sometimes finds himself shaking. With reasonable success he hides his symptoms from his family and co-workers. Nevertheless, he has had few social contacts since the symptoms began two years ago. He occasionally has to leave work. His family doctor and a neurologist can find no physical problem.

Tom's unfocused, out-of-control, negative feelings suggest **generalized anxiety disorder.** The symptoms of this disorder are commonplace; their persistence is not. People with this condition (two-thirds are women), are continually tense and jittery, worried about various bad things that might happen, and plagued by muscular tension, agitation, and sleeplessness. The tension and apprehension may leak out through furrowed brows, twitching eyelids, trembling, perspiration, or fidgeting. Concentration is difficult, as attention switches from worry to worry. One of the worst characteristics of generalized anxiety disorder is that the person cannot identify, and therefore cannot deal with or avoid, its cause. To use Sigmund Freud's term, the anxiety is *free-floating.* Generalized anxiety disorder is often accompanied by depression, but even without depression it tends to be disabling (Hunt & others, 2004) and may lead to physical problems, such as ulcers and high blood pressure.

Panic disorder is to anxiety what a tornado is to a windy day. It strikes suddenly, wreaks havoc, and disappears. For the 1 person in 75 with this disorder, anxiety suddenly escalates into a terrifying *panic attack*—a minutes-long episode of intense fear that something horrible is about to happen. Heart palpitations, shortness of breath, choking sensations, trembling, or dizziness typically accompany the panic, which may

Gender and anxiety: Eight months after 9/11, more U.S. women (34 percent) than men (19 percent) told Gallup (2002) they were still less willing than before 9/11 to go into skyscrapers or fly on planes. In early 2003, more women (57 percent) than men (36 percent) were "somewhat worried" about becoming a terrorist victim (Jones, 2003).

be misperceived as a heart attack or other serious physical ailment. Smokers have a two- to fourfold risk of a first-time panic attack (Breslau & Klein, 1999; Goodwin & Hamilton, 2002; Insensee & others, 2003). Because nicotine is a stimulant, lighting up doesn't lighten up.

One woman recalled suddenly feeling "hot and as though I couldn't breathe. My heart was racing and I started to sweat and tremble and I was sure I was going to faint. Then my fingers started to feel numb and tingly and things seemed unreal. It was so bad I wondered if I was dying and asked my husband to take me to the emergency room. By the time we got there (about 10 minutes) the worst of the attack was over and I just felt washed out" (Greist & others, 1986). So unpredictable and frightening is this false-alarm experience that after several attacks, people come to fear the fear itself and to avoid situations where the panic has struck before.

Agoraphobia is fear or avoidance of situations in which escape might be difficult or help unavailable when panic strikes. Given such fear, people may avoid being outside the home, in a crowd, on a bus, or even on an elevator. After spending five years sailing the world, Charles Darwin began suffering panic disorder at age 28. Because of the attacks, he moved to the country, avoided social gatherings, and traveled only in his wife's company. But the relative seclusion did free him to focus on developing his evolutionary theory. "Even ill health," he reflected, "has saved me from the distraction of society and its amusements" (quoted in Ma, 1997).

Phobias

OBJECTIVE 48-3 | Explain how a phobia differs from the fears we all experience.

Phobias *focus* anxiety on a specific object, activity, or situation. (**Figure 48.1** ranks some common and less common fears and phobias.) A phobia is an irrational fear that disrupts behavior. Many people accept and live with this common psychological disorder, but some specific phobias can lead to incapacitating efforts to avoid the feared situation. Marilyn, a 28-year-old homemaker, is otherwise healthy and happy, but she so fears thunderstorms that she feels anxious as soon as a weather forecaster mentions possible storms later in the week. If her husband is away and a storm is forecast, she may stay with a close relative. During a storm, she hides from windows and buries her head to avoid seeing the lightning.

Other people suffer from irrational fears of specific animals, insects, heights, blood, or tunnels. Often they avoid the stimulus that arouses the fear, hiding during thunderstorms or avoiding high places. Potentially embarrassing social situations are difficult for those with a *social phobia,* an intense fear of being scrutinized by others. The anxious person may avoid speaking up, eating out, or going to parties—or will sweat, tremble, or have diarrhea when doing so. Social phobia is shyness taken to an extreme.

- **anxiety disorders** psychological disorders characterized by distressing, persistent anxiety or maladaptive behaviors that reduce anxiety.
- **generalized anxiety disorder** an anxiety disorder in which a person is continually tense, apprehensive, and in a state of autonomic nervous system arousal.
- **panic disorder** an anxiety disorder marked by unpredictable minutes-long episodes of intense dread in which a person experiences terror and accompanying chest pain, choking, or other frightening sensations.
- **phobia** an anxiety disorder marked by a persistent, irrational fear and avoidance of a specific object or situation.

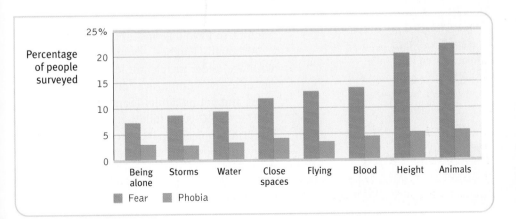

FIGURE 48.1
Some common and uncommon fears
This national interview study identified the commonality of various fears. A strong fear becomes a phobia if it provokes a compelling but irrational desire to avoid the dreaded object or situation.
(From Curtis & others, 1998.)

TABLE 48.1

COMMON OBSESSIONS AND COMPULSIONS AMONG CHILDREN AND ADOLESCENTS WITH OBSESSIVE-COMPULSIVE DISORDER

Thought or Behavior	Percentage Reporting Symptom
Obsessions (repetitive thoughts)	
Concern with dirt, germs, or toxins	40
Something terrible happening (fire, death, illness)	24
Symmetry, order, or exactness	17
Compulsions (repetitive behaviors)	
Excessive hand washing, bathing, tooth brushing, or grooming	85
Repeating rituals (in/out of a door, up/down from a chair)	51
Checking doors, locks, appliances, car brake, homework	46

Source: Adapted from Rapoport, 1989.

Snapshots

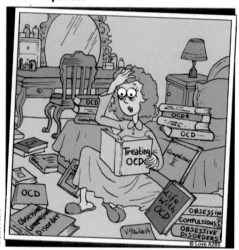

Obsessing about obsessive-compulsive disorder.

Obsessive-Compulsive Disorder

OBJECTIVE 48-4 | Describe the symptoms of obsessive-compulsive disorder.

As with generalized anxiety and phobias, we can see aspects of our own behavior in **obsessive-compulsive disorder (OCD).** We may at times be obsessed with senseless or offensive thoughts that will not go away. Or we may engage in compulsive behaviors, rigidly checking, ordering, and cleaning before guests arrive, or lining up books and pencils "just so" before studying.

Obsessive thoughts and compulsive behaviors cross the fine line between normality and disorder when they become so persistent that they interfere with everyday living and cause the person distress. Checking to see that the door is locked is normal; checking 10 times is not. Washing your hands is normal; washing so often that your skin becomes raw is not. (**TABLE 48.1** offers more examples.) At some time during their lives, often during their late teens or twenties, 2 to 3 percent of people cross that line from normal preoccupations and fussiness to debilitating disorder (Karno & others, 1988). The obsessive thoughts become so haunting, the compulsive rituals so senselessly time-consuming, that effective functioning becomes impossible.

One such person was billionaire aviator Howard Hughes. Hughes compulsively dictated the same phrases over and over again. Under stress, he developed a phobic fear of germs, which led to compulsive behaviors. Hughes became reclusive and insisted his assistants carry out elaborate hand-washing rituals and wear white gloves when handling any document he would later touch. He ordered tape around doors and windows and forbade his staff to touch or even look at him. "Everybody carries germs around with them," he explained. "I want to live longer than my parents, so I avoid germs" (Fowler, 1986).

Although Hughes' symptoms worsened with age, older people are less often plagued by obsessive-compulsive disorder than are teens and young adults (Samuels & Nestadt, 1997). A 40-year follow-up study of 144 Swedish people diagnosed around 1950 found that, for most, the obsessions and compulsions had gradually lessened, though only 1 in 5 had completely recovered (Skoog & Skoog, 1999).

The Aviator Howard Hughes, and his lifelong struggles with obsessive-compulsive disorder, were portrayed in this 2004 film starring Leonardo DiCaprio.

Post-Traumatic Stress Disorder

OBJECTIVE 48-5 | Describe the symptoms of post-traumatic stress disorder, and discuss survivor resiliency.

During the Iraq war, Jack's platoon was repeatedly under fire. In one ambush, his closest friend was killed while Jack stood a few feet away. Jack himself killed someone in an assault. Years later, images of these events intrude on him as flashbacks and nightmares. He still jumps at the sound of a firecracker or the backfire of a car. When annoyed by his family or friends, he lashes out in ways he seldom did before Iraq. To calm his continuing anxiety, he drinks more than he should.

Traumatic stress—experiencing or witnessing severely threatening, uncontrollable events with a sense of fear, helplessness, or horror—can produce **post-traumatic stress disorder (PTSD),** characterized by lingering symptoms including haunting memories and nightmares, a numbed social withdrawal, jumpy anxiety, and insomnia (Goodman & others, 1993; Kessler, 2000; Wilson & others, 1988). The more frequent and severe the assault experiences are, the more adverse the long-term outcomes tend to be (Golding, 1999). A sensitive limbic system that floods the body with stress hormones also increases vulnerability (Ozer & Weiss, 2004).

Many combat veterans, accident and disaster survivors, and sexual assault victims, including an estimated two-thirds of prostitutes, have experienced the symptoms of PTSD (Brewin & others, 1999; Farley & others, 1998; Taylor & others, 1998). After witnessing atrocities or living in life-threatening circumstances, children of the world's war zones and violent neighborhoods show similar symptoms (Garbarino, 1991, 1992). Their sense of basic trust erodes; many experience fearful wariness, troubled sleep, nightmares, and a sense of hopelessness about their future. This *learned helplessness* on the part of children who have repeatedly suffered abuse appears to make them more vulnerable to post-traumatic stress if assaulted as adults (Mineka & Zinbarg, 1996). Stretch a metal spring and it will snap back—unless stretched too far.

To pin down the frequency of PTSD, the U.S. Centers for Disease Control (1988) compared 7000 Vietnam combat veterans with 7000 noncombat veterans who served during the same years. Combat stress more than doubled a veteran's risk of alcohol abuse, depression, or anxiety. On average, 15 percent of all Vietnam veterans reported PTSD symptoms, but this rate was halved among those who had never seen combat and tripled among those who had experienced heavy combat. And among soldiers held captive in Vietnam, the more torture they suffered, the greater its psychological toll (Mollica & others, 1998). In the more recent Iraq war, one in six U.S. combat infantry has also reported symptoms of PTSD, depression, or severe anxiety in the months after returning home (Hoge & others, 2004).

Civilians, too, exhibit a stress *dose-response relationship.* PTSD rates vary from 4 percent among those who have experienced a natural disaster, to up to 50 percent among those who have been kidnapped, held captive, tortured, or raped (Brewin & others, 2000; Brody, 2000; Kessler, 2000). The greater one's emotional distress during a trauma, the higher the risk for post-traumatic symptoms (Ozer & others, 2003).

A month after the 9/11 terrorist attacks, a survey of Manhattan residents indicated that 8.5 percent were suffering PTSD, most as a result of the attack (Galea & others, 2002). Among those living near the World Trade Center, 20 percent reported such telltale signs as nightmares, severe anxiety, and fear of public places (Susser & others, 2002).

Some psychologists, however, believe that PTSD is overdiagnosed, due partly to a broadening definition of *trauma* (which originally meant direct exposure to serious threat, such as combat or rape [McNally, 2003]). PTSD is actually infrequent, say the

Bettmann/Corbis

Toxic trauma
Stressed soldiers, such as these in Northern Ireland, are at risk for being diagnosed with PTSD.

■ **obsessive-compulsive disorder (OCD)** an anxiety disorder characterized by unwanted repetitive thoughts (obsessions) and/or actions (compulsions).

■ **post-traumatic stress disorder (PTSD)** an anxiety disorder characterized by haunting memories, nightmares, social withdrawal, jumpy anxiety, and/or insomnia that lingers for four weeks or more after a traumatic experience.

critics, and no good purpose is served by pathologizing normal stress reactions (Wakefield & Spitzer, 2002). "Debriefing" survivors right after a trauma by getting them to revisit the experience and vent emotions has actually proven generally ineffective and sometimes harmful (McNally & others, 2003; Rose & others, 2003). Sometimes reliving the trauma exacerbates one's emotions.

Researchers also point to the impressive *survivor resiliency* most people display (Bonanno, 2004, 2005). About half of adults experience at least one traumatic event in their lifetime, but only about 1 in 10 women and 1 in 20 men develop PTSD (Ozer & Weiss, 2004). More than 9 in 10 New Yorkers, although understandably stunned and grief-stricken by 9/11, did *not* respond pathologically, and by the following January the stress symptoms of the rest had mostly subsided (Galea & others, 2002). Similarly, most combat-stressed veterans and most political dissidents who survive dozens of episodes of torture do *not* later exhibit PTSD (Mineka & Zinbarg, 1996).

Psychologist Peter Suedfeld (1998, 2000), who as a boy survived the Holocaust under conditions of privation while his mother died in Auschwitz, has documented the resilience of Holocaust survivors, most of whom have lived productive lives. The successes of southeast Asians who escaped war and emigrated to America in small boats further testify to the "hardiness and resilience of the survivors," notes Suedfeld. "It is not always true that 'What doesn't kill you makes you stronger,' but it is often true; and, in addition, what doesn't kill you may reveal to you just how strong you really are."

Indeed, suffering can lead to what Richard Tedeschi and Lawrence Calhoun (2004) call *post-traumatic growth*. Tedeschi and Calhoun have found that the struggle with challenging crises often leads people later to report an increased appreciation for life, more meaningful relationships, increased personal strength, changed priorities, and a richer spiritual life. An ancient idea common to Judaism, Christianity, Hinduism, Buddhism, and Islam—that suffering has transformative power—is, they say, borne out in the lives of cancer survivors who take fresh delight in their children and the joy of each new day, and even of bereaved people who report gaining new sensitivities. Reflecting on his son's death, Rabbi Harold Kushner (1986) observed that "I am a more sensitive person, a more effective pastor, a more sympathetic counselor because of Aaron's life and death than I would ever have been without it," though adding that, even so, "I would give up all of those gains in a second if I could have my son back."

Explaining Anxiety Disorders

OBJECTIVE 48-6 | Discuss the contributions of the learning and biological perspectives to our understanding of the development of anxiety disorders.

Anxiety is both a feeling and a cognition—a doubt-laden appraisal of one's safety or social skill. How do these anxious feelings and cognitions arise? Freud's psychoanalytic theory proposed that, beginning in childhood, people repress intolerable impulses, ideas, and feelings and that this submerged mental energy sometimes produces mystifying symptoms such as anxiety. Many of today's psychologists have turned to two contemporary perspectives—learning and biological—for a more complete understanding.

The Learning Perspective

Fear Conditioning

When bad events happen unpredictably and uncontrollably, anxiety often develops (Chorpita & Barlow, 1998). Researchers have linked general anxiety with classical conditioning of fear. In the laboratory, they have created chronically anxious, ulcer-prone rats by giving them unpredictable electric shocks (Schwartz, 1984). Like assault victims who report feeling anxious when returning to the scene of the crime, the rats become apprehensive in their lab environment. For many victims of PTSD, anxiety swells with any reminder of their trauma. Such experiences might help explain why anxious people are hyperattentive to possible threats, and how panic-prone people come to associate anxiety with certain cues (Bouton & others, 2001; Mineka & Zinbarg, 1996). In one survey, 58 percent of those with social phobia experienced their disorder after a traumatic event (Ost & Hugdahl, 1981).

Decades of research on conditioning show that dogs learn to fear neutral stimuli associated with shock, that infants come to fear furry objects associated with frightening noises, and that adults can become terrified of incidental stimuli linked with traumatic experiences. As infants become mobile they experience falls and near-falls—and become increasingly afraid of heights (Campos & others, 1992). Conditioned fears may remain long after we have forgotten the experiences that produced them (Jacobs & Nadel, 1985).

Through such conditioning, the short list of naturally painful and frightening events can multiply into a long list of human fears. My car was once struck by another whose driver missed a stop sign. For months afterward, I felt a twinge of unease when any car approached from a side street. Marilyn's phobia may have been similarly conditioned during a terrifying or painful experience associated with a thunderstorm. Two specific learning processes that might have contributed to her anxiety are stimulus generalization and reinforcement.

Stimulus generalization occurs, for example, when a person fears heights after a fall and later develops a fear of flying in an airplane without ever having flown. Once phobias and compulsions arise, *reinforcement* helps maintain them. Avoiding or escaping the feared situation reduces anxiety, thus reinforcing the phobic behavior. Feeling anxious or fearing a panic attack, a person may go inside and be reinforced by calmed anxiety (Antony & others, 1992). Compulsive behaviors similarly reduce anxiety. If washing your hands relieves your feelings of unease, you may wash your hands again when the feelings return.

Observational Learning

We might also learn fear through observational learning—by observing others' fears. As Susan Mineka (1985) demonstrated, wild monkeys transmit their fear of snakes to their watchful offspring. Human parents similarly transmit fears to their children. Moreover, just observing someone receiving a mild electric shock after a conditioned stimulus produces fear learning similar to that produced by direct experience (Olsson & Phelps, 2004).

The Biological Perspective

There is, however, more to anxiety than simple conditioning or observational learning, as evident from how few people develop lasting phobias after suffering traumas. The biological perspective can broaden our understanding of anxiety disorders. It cannot explain the sharp increase in the anxiety levels of both children and college students over the last half-century, which appears related to such things as fraying social support accompanying family breakup (Twenge, 2000). But the biological perspective does help explain why we learn some fears more readily and why some individuals are more vulnerable.

Natural Selection

We humans seem biologically prepared to fear threats faced by our ancestors. Most of our phobias focus on such objects: spiders, snakes, and other animals; closed spaces and heights; storms and darkness. (Those fearless about these occasional threats were less likely to survive and leave descendants.) It is easy to condition but hard to extinguish fears of such stimuli (Davey, 1995; Öhman, 1986). Many of our modern fears may also have an evolutionary explanation. For example, a fear of flying may also come from our biological past, which predisposes us to fear confinement and heights.

John Coletti/Stock, Boston

An emotional high
Although we humans seem biologically predisposed to fear heights—certainly an adaptive response—this construction worker seems fearless. The biological perspective helps us understand why most people would be terrified in this situation.

Moreover, consider what people tend *not* to learn to fear. World War II air raids produced remarkably few lasting phobias. As the air blitzes continued, the British, Japanese, and German populations became not more panicked, but rather more indifferent to planes outside of their immediate neighborhood (Mineka & Zinbarg, 1996). Evolution has not prepared us to fear bombs dropping from the sky.

Just as our phobias focus on dangers faced by our ancestors, our compulsive acts typically exaggerate behaviors that contributed to our species' survival. Grooming gone wild becomes hair pulling. Washing up becomes ritual hand washing. Checking territorial boundaries becomes checking and rechecking an already locked door (Rapoport, 1989).

Genes

Some people more than others seem genetically predisposed to particular fears and high anxiety. Pair a traumatic event with a sensitive, high-strung temperament and the result may be a new phobia. Among monkeys, fearfulness runs in families. Individual monkeys react more strongly to stress if their close biological relatives are anxiously reactive (Suomi, 1986). The power of genes appears in studies of humans, too. Vulnerability to anxiety disorder rises when the afflicted relative is an identical twin (Barlow, 1988; Hettema & others, 2001; Kendler & others, 1992, 1999, 2002a,b). Identical twins often develop similar phobias, in some cases even when raised separately (Carey, 1990; Eckert & others, 1981). One pair of 35-year-old female identical twins independently developed claustrophobia. They also became so afraid of water that each would gingerly wade backward into the ocean, and then only up to the knees.

The Brain

Generalized anxiety, panic attacks, and even obsessions and compulsions are biologically measurable as an overarousal of brain areas involved in impulse control and habitual behaviors. Brain scans of people with obsessive-compulsive disorder reveal elevated activity in specific brain areas associated with behaviors such as compulsive hand washing, checking, ordering, or hoarding (Mataix-Cols & others, 2004, 2005). As **FIGURE 48.2** shows, the *anterior cingulate cortex,* a brain region that monitors our actions and checks for errors, seems especially likely to be hyperactive in those with OCD (Ursu & others, 2003). When the disordered brain detects that something is amiss, it seems to generate a mental hiccup of repeating thoughts or actions (Gehring & others, 2000).

Fear-learning experiences can traumatize the brain, by creating fear circuits within the amygdala (Armony & others, 1998). Some antidepressant drugs dampen this fear-circuit activity and its associated obsessive-compulsive behavior. All in all, it is clear that biology is part of anxiety.

FIGURE 48.2

An obsessive-compulsive brain
Neuroscientist Stefan Ursu and his colleagues (2003) used functional magnetic resonance imaging (fMRI) scans to compare the brains of those with and without OCD as they engaged in a challenging cognitive task. The fMRI scans showed elevated activity in the anterior cingulate cortex of those with OCD.

S. Ursu, V. A. Stenger, M. K. Shear, M. R. Jones, & C. S. Carter (2003). Overactive action monitoring in obsessive-compulsive disorder. *Psychological Science, 14,* 347–353.

>> LEARNING OUTCOMES

Anxiety Disorders

OBJECTIVE 48-1 | Define *anxiety disorders,* and explain how these conditions differ from normal feelings of stress, tension, or uneasiness.

Anxiety is part of our everyday experience. It is classified as a psychological disorder only when it becomes distressing or persistent or is characterized by maladaptive behaviors intended to reduce it.

OBJECTIVE 48-2 | Contrast the symptoms of generalized anxiety disorder and panic disorder.

People with *generalized anxiety disorder* (two-thirds of whom are women) feel persistently and uncontrollably tense and apprehensive and are in a state of autonomic nervous system arousal. They are unable to identify, or avoid, the cause of these feelings. People with the more extreme *panic disorder* experience periodic minutes-long episodes of intense dread (which may include feelings of terror, chest pains, or choking) and may avoid situations where they have had panic attacks.

OBJECTIVE 48-3 | Explain how a phobia differs from the fears we all experience.

Phobias are more extreme and more disabling than normal fears. People with a *phobia* experience such persistent and irrational fears that they may be incapacitated by their attempts to avoid a specific object, animal, or situation.

OBJECTIVE 48-4 | Describe the symptoms of obsessive-compulsive disorder.

Persistent and repetitive thoughts and actions that characterize *obsessive-compulsive disorder* interfere with everyday living and cause the person distress. The *obsession* is a repetitive thought, such as a concern with dirt or germs; the *compulsion* is a repetitive action, such as excessive hand washing or bathing.

OBJECTIVE 48-5 | Describe the symptoms of post-traumatic stress disorder, and discuss survivor resiliency.

Four or more weeks of haunting memories, nightmares, social withdrawal, jumpy anxiety, and sleep problems are symptoms of *PTSD (post-traumatic stress disorder)*. Such symptoms appear following some traumatic event the individual witnessed or experienced but could not control. Some people are more resilient than others. Only about 10 percent of women and 20 percent of men react to trauma by developing PTSD. For those who survive a trauma, the experience can lead to a period of growth.

OBJECTIVE 48-6 | Discuss the contributions of the learning and biological perspectives to our understanding of the development of anxiety disorders.

Those working from the *learning perspective* view anxiety disorders as a product of fear conditioning, stimulus generalization, reinforcement of fearful behaviors, and observational learning of others' fear. Those working from the *biological perspective* consider the evolutionary survival value of fears of life-threatening animals, objects, or situations; inherited predispositions to emotional reactivity; and abnormal responses in the brain's fear circuits.

TERMS AND CONCEPTS TO REMEMBER

anxiety disorders, p. 48-0

generalized anxiety disorder, p. 48-0

panic disorder, p. 48-0

phobia, p. 48-1

obsessive-compulsive disorder (OCD), p. 48-2

post-traumatic stress disorder (PTSD), p. 48-3

TEST YOURSELF

1. How do generalized anxiety disorder, phobias, and obsessive-compulsive disorder differ?

(Answer in Appendix B.)

ASK YOURSELF

1. Can you recall a fear that you have learned? What role, if any, was played by fear conditioning and by observational learning?

>WEB

Multiple-choice **self-tests** and more may be found at www.worthpublishers.com/myers.

MODULE

49

Dissociative and Personality Disorders
Dissociative Disorders

OBJECTIVE 49-1 | Describe the symptoms of dissociative disorders, and explain why some critics are skeptical about dissociative identity disorder.

Among the most bewildering disorders are the rare **dissociative disorders,** in which a person appears to experience a sudden loss of memory or change in identity. When a situation becomes overwhelmingly stressful, people are said to dissociate themselves from it. Their conscious awareness becomes separated from painful memories, thoughts, and feelings. (Note that this explanation presumes the existence of repressed memories, which have recently been questioned.)

Certain symptoms of dissociation are not so rare. Now and then, many people may have a sense of being unreal, of being separated from their body, of watching themselves as if in a movie. Sometimes we may say, "I was not myself at the time." Perhaps you can recall getting in your car and driving to some unintended location while your mind was preoccupied elsewhere. Facing trauma, such detachment may actually protect a person from being overwhelmed by emotion. Only when such experiences are severe and prolonged do they suggest a dissociative disorder.

The king of dissociative disorders is the presumed massive dissociation of self from ordinary consciousness in those with **dissociative identity disorder (DID).** These people are said to have two or more distinct identities that alternately control the person's behavior, with memory impairment across the different personality states. The person with this disorder may be prim and proper one moment and loud and flirtatious the next. Each personality has its own voice and mannerisms, and the original one typically denies any awareness of the other(s).

Although people diagnosed as having multiple personalities are usually not violent, there have been cases in which the person reportedly became dissociated into a "good" and a "bad" (or aggressive) personality—a modest version of the Dr. Jekyll/Mr. Hyde split immortalized in Robert Louis Stevenson's story. One unusual case involved Kenneth Bianchi, who was on trial for the "Hillside Strangler" rapes and murders of 10 California women. During a hypnosis session with Bianchi, psychologist John Watkins (1984) "called forth" a hidden personality: "I've talked a bit to Ken, but I think that perhaps there might be another part of Ken that I haven't talked to, another part that maybe feels somewhat differently from the part that I've talked to. . . . Would you talk with me, Part, by saying, 'I'm here'?" Bianchi answered "Yes" and then claimed to be "Steve."

When speaking as Steve, Bianchi stated that he hated Ken because Ken was nice and that he (Steve), aided by a cousin, had murdered women. He also claimed that Ken knew nothing about his existence and that Ken was innocent of the murders. Was Bianchi's second personality a ruse, simply a way of disavowing responsibility for his actions? Indeed, Bianchi—a practiced liar who had read about multiple personality in psychology books—was later convicted.

Exploring our capacity for personality shifts, Nicholas Spanos (1986, 1994, 1996) asked college students to pretend they were accused murderers being examined by a psychiatrist. When given the same hypnotic treatment Bianchi received, most spontaneously expressed a second personality. This discovery made Spanos wonder: Are dissociative identities simply a more extreme version of our normal human capacity to vary the "selves" we present—as when we might display a goofy, loud self while hanging out with friends, and a subdued, respectful self around grandparents? Are clinicians who discover multiple personalities merely triggering role-playing by fantasy-prone people?

■ **dissociative disorders** disorders in which conscious awareness becomes separated (dissociated) from previous memories, thoughts, and feelings.

■ **dissociative identity disorder (DID)** a rare dissociative disorder in which a person exhibits two or more distinct and alternating personalities. Also called *multiple personality disorder.*

Multiple personalities

Chris Sizemore's story, *The Three Faces of Eve,* gave early visibility to what is now called *dissociative identity disorder.*

Lois Bernstein/Gamma Liaison

If so, can such people then convince themselves of the authenticity of their own role enactments? Are they like actors, who commonly report "losing themselves" in their roles? Spanos was no stranger to this line of thinking. In a related research area, he had also raised these questions about the hypnotic state. Given that most DID patients are highly hypnotizable, whatever explains one condition—dissociation or role playing—may help explain the other.

Those who accept DID as a genuine disorder find support in the distinct brain and body states associated with differing personalities (Putnam, 1991). Handedness, too, sometimes switches with personality (Henninger, 1992). Subtle memories of one personality's experience sometimes fail to transfer to another personality (Eich & others, 1997). In one study, ophthalmologists detected shifting visual acuity and eye-muscle balance as patients switched personalities. These changes did not occur among control subjects trying to simulate DID (Miller & others, 1991).

Skeptics nevertheless find it suspicious that the disorder became so popular in the late twentieth century. In North America, the number of diagnoses exploded from only 2 reported cases per decade from 1930 to 1960, to more than 20,000 in the 1980s—when the DSM contained the first formal code for this disorder (McHugh, 1995a). The average number of displayed personalities also mushroomed—from 3 to 12 per patient (Goff & Simms, 1993). How could such a dramatic disorder have gone unnoticed for so long? Many clinicians have never encountered a case of DID, and the disorder is much less prevalent outside North America, although in other cultures some people are said to be "possessed" by an alien spirit (Aldridge-Morris, 1989; Kluft, 1991). In Britain, the diagnosis—which some consider "a wacky American fad" (Cohen, 1995)—is rare. In India and Japan, it is essentially nonexistent.

To skeptics, these findings point to a cultural phenomenon—a disorder created by therapists in a particular social context (Merskey, 1992). Patients do not enter therapy saying "Allow me to introduce myselves." Rather, note skeptics, some therapists go fishing for multiple personalities: "Have you ever felt like another part of you does things you can't control? Does this part of you have a name? Can I talk to the angry part of you?" Once patients permit a therapist to talk, by name, "to the part of you that says those angry things" they have begun acting out the fantasy. The result may be a real phenomenon, which vulnerable patients may experience as another self. Yet, say skeptics, "It is no coincidence," that multiple personality studies began among practitioners of hypnosis and that symptoms are most dramatic *after* beginning therapy (Goff, 1993; Piper, 1998).

Both psychoanalytic and learning perspectives see the symptoms of dissociative disorders as ways of dealing with anxiety. Psychoanalysts view them as defenses against the anxiety caused by the eruption of unacceptable impulses; a wanton second personality enables the discharge of forbidden impulses. Learning theorists see dissociative disorders as behaviors reinforced by anxiety reduction.

Others view dissociative disorders as post-traumatic disorders—a natural, protective response to "histories of childhood trauma" (Putnam, 1995). Researchers debate whether most people with DID suffered physical, sexual, or emotional abuse as children (Gleaves, 1996; Kihlstrom, 2005; Lilienfeld & others, 1999). One study of 12 murderers diagnosed with DID did find that 11 of them had suffered severe, torturous child abuse (Lewis & others, 1997). One was set afire by his parents. Another was used in child pornography and was scarred from being made to sit on a stove burner. Perhaps, then, multiple personalities are the desperate efforts of the traumatized to detach from a horrific existence.

But then why, wonder the skeptics, did the children of the Holocaust, after enduring boxcars, concentration camps, and their parents' murders, not develop DID? Can the condition sometimes be contrived by fantasy-prone, emotionally vulnerable people, and constructed out of the therapist-patient interaction? If so, predicts psychiatrist Paul McHugh (1995b), "this epidemic will end in the way that the witch craze ended in Salem. The [multiple personality phenomenon] will be seen as manufactured."

"Would it be possible to speak with the personality that pays the bills?"

"Though this be madness, yet there is method in 't."
—William Shakespeare, *Hamlet*, 1600

■ **personality disorders** psychological disorders characterized by inflexible and enduring behavior patterns that impair social functioning.

■ **antisocial personality disorder** a personality disorder in which the person (usually a man) exhibits a lack of conscience for wrongdoing, even toward friends and family members. May be aggressive and ruthless or a clever con artist.

Personality Disorders

OBJECTIVE **49-2** | Contrast the three clusters of personality disorders, and describe the behaviors and brain activity associated with antisocial personality disorder.

Some maladaptive behavior patterns impair people's social functioning without anxiety, depression, or delusions. These disruptive patterns, called **personality disorders,** are inflexible and enduring patterns of behavior that impair one's social functioning. One cluster of disorders expresses anxiety, such as a fearful sensitivity to rejection that predisposes the withdrawn *avoidant personality disorder*. A second cluster expresses eccentric behaviors, such as the emotionless disengagement of the *schizoid personality disorder*.

A third cluster exhibits dramatic or impulsive behaviors. A person with a *histrionic personality disorder* displays shallow, attention-getting emotions and goes to great lengths to gain others' praise and reassurance. Those with self-focused *narcissistic personality disorder* exaggerate their own importance, aided by success fantasies. They find criticism hard to accept, often reacting with rage or shame. Those with *borderline personality disorder* have an unstable identity, unstable relationships, and unstable and impulsive emotions. If personality is one's enduring pattern of thinking, feeling, and acting, then a markedly unstable sense of self defines a borderline personality.

Antisocial Personality Disorder

The most troubling and heavily researched personality disorder is the **antisocial personality disorder.** The person (formerly called a *sociopath* or a *psychopath*) is typically a male whose lack of conscience becomes plain before age 15, as he begins to lie, steal, fight, or display unrestrained sexual behavior (Cale & Lilienfeld, 2002). About half of such children become antisocial adults—unable to keep a job, irresponsible as a spouse and parent, and assaultive or otherwise criminal (Farrington, 1991). When the antisocial personality combines a keen intelligence with amorality, the result may be a charming and clever con artist—or worse.

Despite their antisocial behavior, most criminals do not fit the description of antisocial personality disorder. Why? Because most criminals actually show responsible concern for their friends and family members. Antisocial personalities feel and fear little, and in extreme cases, the results can be horrifyingly tragic. Henry Lee Lucas reported that at age 13 he strangled a woman who refused to have sex with him. He at one time confessed to having bludgeoned, suffocated, stabbed, shot, or mutilated some 360 women, men, and children during his 32 years of crime. During the last 6 years of his reign of terror, Lucas teamed with Elwood Toole, who reportedly slaughtered about 50 people he "didn't think was worth living anyhow." It ended when Lucas confessed to stabbing and dismembering his 15-year-old common-law wife, who was Toole's niece.

The antisocial personality expresses little regret over violating others' rights. "Once I've done a crime, I just forget it," said Lucas. Toole was equally matter-of-fact: "I think of killing like smoking a cigarette, like another habit" (Darrach & Norris, 1984).

Understanding Antisocial Personality Disorder

Antisocial personality disorder is woven of both biological and psychological strands. No single gene codes for a complex behavior such as crime, but twin and adoption studies reveal that biological relatives of those with antisocial and unemotional tendencies are at increased risk for antisocial behavior (Rhee & Waldman, 2002; Viding & others, 2005). Their genetic vulnerability appears as a fearless approach to life. When they await aversive events, such as electric shocks or loud noises, they show little autonomic nervous system arousal (Hare, 1975). Even as youngsters, before committing any crime, they react with lower levels of stress hormones than do others their age (**FIGURE 49.1**).

Antisocial personality?

Dennis Rader, known as the "BTK killer" in Kansas, was convicted in 2005 of killing 10 people over a 30-year span. Rader exhibited the extreme lack of conscience that marks antisocial personality disorder.

EPA/Jeff Tuttle/Landow

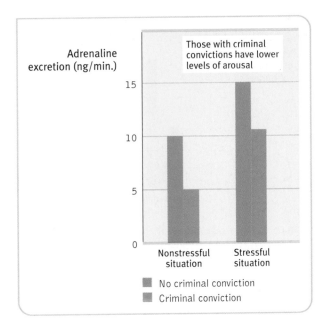

Adrenaline excretion (ng/min.)

Those with criminal convictions have lower levels of arousal

Nonstressful situation   Stressful situation

■ No criminal conviction
■ Criminal conviction

FIGURE 49.1
Cold-blooded arousability and risk of crime
Levels of the stress hormone adrenaline were measured in two groups of 13-year-old Swedish boys. In both stressful and non-stressful situations, those who were later convicted of a crime (as 18- to 26-year-olds) showed relatively low arousal. (From Magnusson, 1990.)

Some studies have detected the early signs of antisocial behavior in children as young as ages 3 to 6 (Caspi & others, 1996; Tremblay & others, 1994). Boys who later became aggressive or antisocial adolescents tended, as young children, to have been impulsive, uninhibited, unconcerned with social rewards, and low in anxiety. If channeled in more productive directions, such fearlessness may lead to courageous heroism, adventurism, or star-level athleticism (Poulton & Milne, 2002). Lacking a sense of social responsibility, the same disposition produces a cool con artist or killer (Lykken, 1995).

Genetic influences help wire the brain. Adrian Raine (1999) compared PET scans of 41 murderers' brains with those from people of similar age and sex. Raine found reduced activity in the murderers' frontal lobes, an area of the cortex that helps control impulses (**FIGURE 49.2**). This reduction was especially apparent in those who murdered impulsively. In a follow-up study, Raine and his team (2000) found that violent repeat offenders had 11 percent less frontal lobe tissue than normal. This helps explain why people with antisocial personality disorder exhibit marked deficits in frontal lobe cognitive functions, such as planning, organization, and inhibition (Morgan & Lilienfeld, 2000).

Perhaps a biologically based fearlessness, as well as early environment, helps explain the reunion of long-separated sisters Joyce Lott, 27, and Mary Jones, 29—in a South Carolina prison where both were sent on drug charges. After a newspaper story about their reunion, their long-lost half-brother Frank Strickland called. He explained it would be a while before he could come see them—because he, too, was in jail, on drug, burglary, and larceny charges (Shepherd & others, 1990).

Genetics alone is hardly the whole story of antisocial crime, however. Relative to 1960, the average American in 1995 (before the late 1990s crime decline) was twice as likely to be murdered, four times as likely to report being raped, four times as likely to report being robbed, and five times as likely to report being assaulted (FBI, *Uniform Crime Reports*). Violent crime was also surging in other Western nations. Yet the human gene pool had hardly changed. Or consider the British social experiment begun in 1787, exiling 160,000 criminals to Australia. The descendants of these exiles, carrying their ancestors' supposed "criminal genes," have helped create a civilized democracy whose crime rate is similar to Britain's. Genetic predispositions do put some individuals more at risk for antisocial conduct than others; biological as well as environmental influences explain why 5 to 6 percent of offenders commit 50 to 60 percent of crimes (Lyman, 1996). But we must look to sociocultural factors to explain the modern epidemic of violence.

FIGURE 49.2
Murderous minds
PET scans illustrate reduced activation (less red and yellow) in a murderer's frontal cortex—a brain area that helps brake impulsive, aggressive behavior. (From Raine, 1999.)

Normal   Murderer

FIGURE 49.3

Biopsychosocial roots of crime
Danish male babies whose backgrounds were marked *both* by obstetrical complications and social stresses associated with poverty were twice as likely to be criminal offenders by ages 20 to 22 as those in either the biological or social risk groups. (From Raine & others, 1996.)

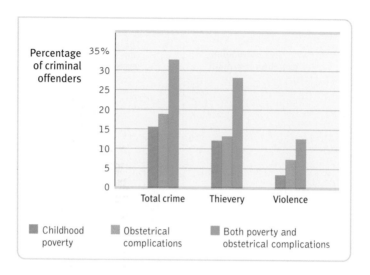

A study of criminal tendencies among young Danish men illustrates the usefulness of a complete biopsychosocial perspective. A research team led by Adrian Raine (1996) checked criminal records on nearly 400 men at ages 20 to 22, knowing that all had experienced either biological risk factors at birth, such as premature birth, or had come from family backgrounds marked by poverty and family instability. The researchers compared each of these groups with a *biosocial* group whose lives were marked by *both* the biological and social risk factors. The biosocial group had double the risk of committing crime (**FIGURE 49.3**). In one quarter-century study that followed 1037 children, two combined factors predicted antisocial problems: childhood maltreatment and a gene that altered neurotransmitter balance (Caspi & others, 2002). Neither "bad" genes nor a "bad" environment alone predisposed later antisocial behavior; rather, genes predisposed some children to be more sensitive to maltreatment. Within "genetically vulnerable segments of the population," environmental influences matter (Moffitt, 2005). With antisocial behavior, as with so much else, nature and nurture interact.

>> LEARNING OUTCOMES

Dissociative and Personality Disorders

OBJECTIVE 49-1 | Describe the symptoms of dissociative disorders, and explain why some critics are skeptical about dissociative identity disorder.

Dissociative disorders are conditions in which conscious awareness seems to become separated from previous memories, thoughts, and feelings. Skeptics note that the diagnosis of *dissociative identity disorder,* commonly known as multiple personality disorder, increased dramatically in the late twentieth century; that it is not found in many countries and is very rare in others; and that it may reflect role-playing by people who are very open to therapists' suggestions. This disorder may be a manifestation of feelings of anxiety or a response learned when behaviors are reinforced by reductions in feelings of anxiety.

OBJECTIVE 49-2 | Contrast the three clusters of personality disorders, and describe the behaviors and brain activity associated with antisocial personality disorder.

Personality disorders are inflexible and enduring patterns of behavior that impair social functioning. The main component of the first cluster is *anxiety;* of the second, *eccentric behaviors;* of the third, *dramatic or impulsive behaviors.* Antisocial personality disorder is characterized by a lack of conscience and, sometimes, aggressive and ruthless behavior. Brain scans of some murderers with this disorder have shown reduced activity in the frontal lobes, an area of control for impulsive, aggressive behavior. Genetic predisposition may interact with environmental influences to produce antisocial personality disorder.

TERMS AND CONCEPTS TO REMEMBER

dissociative disorders, p. 49-0

dissociative identity disorder (DID), p. 49-0

personality disorders, p. 49-2

antisocial personality disorder, p. 49-2

TEST YOURSELF

1. Is antisocial personality disorder an inherited condition?

(Answer in Appendix B.)

ASK YOURSELF

1. How would you evaluate the relative contributions of nature and nurture to antisocial personality disorder?

>WEB

Multiple-choice *self-tests* and more may be found at www.worthpublishers.com/myers.

50

MODULE

Mood Disorders

OBJECTIVE 50-1 | Define *mood disorders,* and contrast major depressive disorder and bipolar disorder.

The emotional extremes of **mood disorders** come in two principal forms: (1) *major depressive disorder,* in which the person experiences prolonged hopelessness and lethargy until usually rebounding to normality, and (2) *bipolar disorder* (formerly called *manic depressive disorder*), in which the person alternates between depression and *mania,* an overexcited, hyperactive state.

Major Depressive Disorder

Perhaps you know what depression feels like. If you are like most college students, at some time during this year—more likely the dark months of winter than the bright days of summer—you will probably experience a few of the symptoms of depression. You may feel deeply discouraged about the future, dissatisfied with your life, or isolated from others. You may lack the energy to get things done or even to force yourself out of bed; be unable to concentrate, eat, or sleep normally; or even wonder if you would be better off dead. Perhaps academic success came easily to you in high school, and now you find that disappointing grades jeopardize your goals. Maybe social stresses, such as feeling you don't belong or the breakup of a romance, have plunged you into despair. And maybe brooding has at times only worsened your self-torment.

You are not alone. Depression is the "common cold" of psychological disorders—an expression that effectively describes its pervasiveness but not its seriousness. Although phobias are more common, depression is the number one reason people seek mental health services. Moreover, it is the leading cause of disability worldwide (WHO, 2002). In any given year a depressive episode plagues 5.8 percent of men and 9.5 percent of women, reports the World Health Organization.

As anxiety is a response to the threat of future loss, depression is often a response to past and current loss. To feel bad in reaction to profoundly sad events (such as the death of a loved one) is to be in touch with reality. In such times, depression is like a car's low-oil-pressure light—a signal that warns us to stop and take protective measures. Biologically speaking, life's purpose is not happiness but survival and reproduction, and to this end, coughing, vomiting, and various forms of pain protect the body from dangerous toxins. Similarly, depression is a sort of psychic hibernation: It slows us down, defuses aggression, and restrains risk taking (Allen & Badcock, 2003). To grind temporarily to a halt and ruminate, as depressed people do, is to reassess one's life when feeling threatened, and to redirect energy in more promising ways. From this perspective, there is sense to suffering.

But when does this response become seriously maladaptive? The line separating life's normal "downs" from major depression is difficult to draw. Joy, contentment, sadness, and despair are different points on a continuum, points at which any of us may be found at any given moment.

For some people, recurring depression during winter's dark months constitutes a seasonal affective disorder. For others, winter darkness means more blue moods. When asked "Have you cried today?" Americans answered "yes" more often in the winter:

	Percentage answering yes	
	Men	Women
August	4%	7%
December	8%	21%

Source: Time/CNN survey, 1994

“ Depression . . . is well adapted to make a creature guard itself against any great or sudden evil.”

Charles Darwin, *The Life and Letters of Charles Darwin,* 1887

■ **mood disorders** psychological disorders characterized by emotional extremes. See *major depressive disorder, mania,* and *bipolar disorder.*

> "My life had come to a sudden stop. I was able to breathe, to eat, to drink, to sleep. I could not, indeed, help doing so; but there was no real life in me."
>
> Leo Tolstoy, *My Confession*, 1887

Major depressive disorder occurs when signs of depression (including lethargy, feelings of worthlessness, or loss of interest in family, friends, and activities) last two weeks or more and are not caused by drugs or a medical condition. The difference between a blue mood after bad news and a mood disorder is like the difference between gasping for breath for a few minutes after a hard run and being chronically short of breath. To sense what major depression feels like, suggest some clinicians, imagine combining the anguish of grief with the sluggishness of jet lag.

Between the temporary blue moods we all experience and the crushing impact of major depression is a condition called *dysthymic disorder*—a down-in-the-dumps mood that fills most of the day, nearly every day, for two years or more. Although less disabled than people with major depressions, those with dysthymic disorder tend to experience chronic low energy and self-esteem, have difficulty concentrating or making decisions, and sleep and eat too much or too little.

Bipolar Disorder

With or without therapy, episodes of major depression usually end, and people temporarily or permanently return to their previous behavior patterns. However, some people rebound to, or sometimes start with, the opposite emotional extreme—the euphoric, hyperactive, wildly optimistic state of **mania.** If depression is living in slow motion, mania is fast forward. Alternation between depression and mania signals **bipolar disorder.** During the manic phase of bipolar disorder, the person is typically overtalkative, overactive, and elated (though easily irritated if crossed); has little need for sleep; and shows fewer sexual inhibitions. Speech is loud, flighty, and hard to interrupt.

> "All the people in history, literature, art, whom I most admire: Mozart, Shakespeare, Homer, El Greco, St. John, Chekhov, Gregory of Nyssa, Dostoevsky, Emily Brontë: not one of them would qualify for a mental-health certificate."
>
> Madeleine L'Engle, *A Circle of Quiet*, 1972

One of mania's maladaptive symptoms is grandiose optimism and self-esteem, which may lead to reckless investments, spending sprees, and unsafe sex. Although people in a manic state find advice irritating, they need protection from their own poor judgment. In milder forms, however, the energy and free-flowing thinking of mania can fuel creativity. History offers many examples of creative bipolar people, from Walt Whitman and Ernest Hemingway to actress Margot Kidder. Bipolar disorder is especially common among creative artists and poets (Jamison, 1993, 1995; Kaufman & Baer, 2002). George Frideric Handel (1685–1759), who many believe suffered a mild form of bipolar disorder, composed his nearly four-hour-long *Messiah* during three weeks of intense, creative energy (Keynes, 1980). Robert Schumann composed 51 musical works during two years of mania (1840 and 1849) and none during 1844, when he was severely depressed (Slater & Meyer, 1959). Creative professionals who rely on precision and logic (architects, designers, journalists) less often suffer bipolar disorder than those who rely on emotional expression and vivid imagery (poets, novelists, entertainers), reports Arnold Ludwig (1995).

It is as true of emotions as of everything else: What goes up comes down. Before long, the elated mood either returns to normal or plunges into a depression. Though as maladaptive as major depression, bipolar disorder is much less common. Unlike major depression, it afflicts as many men as women.

Creativity and bipolar disorders
History has given us many creative artists, composers, and writers with bipolar disorder, including (left to right) Walt Whitman, Virginia Woolf, Samuel Clemens (Mark Twain), and Ernest Hemingway.

Explaining Mood Disorders

OBJECTIVE 50-2 | Discuss the facts that an acceptable theory of depression must explain.

Because depression profoundly affects so many people, it understandably has been t' subject of thousands of studies. Psychologists are working to develop a theory of m disorders that will suggest more effective ways to treat and prevent them. Resea Peter Lewinsohn and his colleagues (1985, 1998) summarized the facts that any theory of depression must explain. Among them are the following:

- *Many behavioral and cognitive changes accompany depression.* Depressed people are inactive and feel unmotivated. They are sensitive to negative happenings, expect negative outcomes, and more often recall negative information. In a depressed mood, we expect our team to lose, our grades to fall, our love to fail. When the depression lifts, these behavioral and cognitive accompaniments disappear. Nearly half the time, depressed people also exhibit symptoms of another disorder, such as anxiety or substance abuse.

- *Depression is widespread.* Its commonality suggests that its causes, too, must be common.

- *Compared with men, women are nearly twice as vulnerable to major depression* (**FIGURE 50.1**). In general, women are most vulnerable to disorders involving internalized states, such as depression, anxiety, and inhibited sexual desire. Men's disorders tend to be more external—alcohol abuse, antisocial conduct, lack of impulse control. When women get sad they often get sadder than men do. When men get mad, they often get madder than women do.

- *Most major depressive episodes self-terminate.* Therapy tends to speed recovery, yet most people suffering major depression eventually return to normal even without professional help. The plague of depression comes and, a few weeks or months later, it usually goes, though it sometimes recurs later.

- *Stressful events related to work, marriage, and close relationships often precede depression.* A family member's death, a job loss, a marital crisis, or a physical assault increase one's risk of depression. If stress-related anxiety is a "crackling, menacing brushfire," notes biologist Robert Sapolsky (2003), "depression is a suffocating heavy blanket thrown on top of it." One study followed 2000 people over time. It found that the risk of the onset of depression in the ensuing month ranged from less than 1 percent among those who had experienced no stressful life event to 24 percent among those with three such events (Kendler, 1998). The early loss of a parent due to death or separation also increases later vulnerability to depression (Agid & others, 1999).

- *With each new generation, the rate of depression is increasing, and the disorder is striking earlier (now often in the late teens).* This is true not only in Canada and the United States but also in Germany, Italy, France, Lebanon, New Zealand,

hope...
and the ove...
(Formerly called ...

About 50 percent of those who recover from depression will suffer another episode within two years. Recovery is more likely to be permanent the later the first episode strikes, the longer the person stays well, the fewer the previous episodes, the less stress experienced, and the more social support received (Belsher & Costello, 1988; Fergusson & Woodward, 2002; Kendler & others, 2001).

" I see depression as the plague of the modern era."

Lewis Judd, former chief, National Institute of Mental Health, 2000

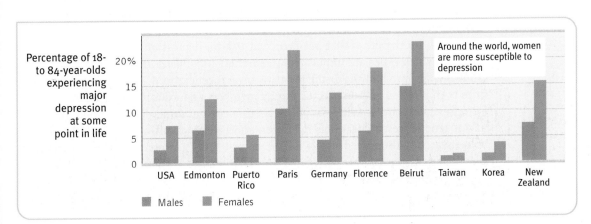

FIGURE 50.1
Gender and depression
Interviews with 38,000 adults in 10 countries confirm what many smaller studies have found: Women's risk of major depression is nearly double that of men's. Lifetime risk of depression also varies by culture—from 1.5 percent in Taiwan to 19 percent in Beirut. (Data from Weissman & others, 1996.)

Down Came the Rain
Actress Brooke Shields chronicled her disabling postpartum depression in this 2005 book.

Taiwan, and Puerto Rico (Cross-National Collaborative Group, 1992). In Australia, 12 percent of adolescents interviewed reported symptoms of depression. Most hid it from their parents; almost 90 percent of their parents perceived their depressed teen as *not* suffering depression (Sawyer & others, 2000). In North America, today's young adults are three times as likely as their grandparents to report having recently—or ever—suffered depression (despite the grandparents' many more years of being at risk). Asked "Have you ever felt that you were going to have a nervous breakdown?" 17 percent of Americans said "yes" in 1957, as did 24 percent in 1996 (Swindle & others, 2000). The increase appears partly authentic, but may also reflect today's young adults' greater willingness to disclose depression, as well as our tendency to forget many negative experiences over time.

As you might expect, researchers understand and interpret these facts in ways that reflect their different perspectives. Psychoanalytic theory, applying Sigmund Freud's ideas about the importance of early childhood experiences and unconscious impulses, suggested that depression occurs when significant losses evoke feelings associated with losses experienced in childhood. Loss of a romantic relationship or a job might evoke feelings associated with the loss of the intimate relationship with one's mother, for example. Alternatively, unresolved anger toward one's parents might be turned inward against the self. Today's biopsychosocial perspective is broadening our understanding with biological and cognitive explanations.

The Biological Perspective

OBJECTIVE 50-3 | Summarize the contributions of the biological perspective to the study of depression, and discuss the link between suicide and depression.

Most recent mental health research dollars have funded explorations of biological influences on mood disorders. Depression is a whole-body disorder. It involves genetic predispositions, biochemical imbalances, negative thoughts, and melancholy mood.

Genetic Influences

We have long known that mood disorders run in families. The risk of major depression and bipolar disorder increases if you have a depressed parent or sibling (Sullivan & others, 2000). If one identical twin is diagnosed with major depressive disorder, the chances are about 1 in 2 that at some time the other twin will be, too. If one identical twin has bipolar disorder, the chances are 7 in 10 that the other twin will at some point be diagnosed similarly. Among fraternal twins, the corresponding odds are just under 2 in 10 (Tsuang & Faraone, 1990). The greater similarity of identical twins' depressive tendencies also occurs among twins reared apart (DiLalla & others, 1996). Moreover, adopted people who suffer a mood disorder often have close biological relatives who suffer mood disorders, become dependent on alcohol, or commit suicide (Wender & others, 1986). (Turn the page and see Close-Up: Suicide for other research findings on suicide.)

A search for the genes that put people at risk for depression is now under way. To tease out which genes are implicated, researchers use *linkage analysis*. First, they find families that have had the disorder across several generations. Then they draw blood from both affected and unaffected family members and examine their DNA, looking for differences. Linkage analysis points us to a chromosome neighborhood, note behavior genetics researchers Robert Plomin and Peter McGuffin (2003); "a house-to-house search is then needed to find the culprit gene." *Association studies* search for correlations between more specific DNA variation and a population trait. One such DNA variation occurs, for example, in about 40 percent of people with late-onset Alzheimer's disease and about 15 percent of those without Alzheimer's (Plomin &

Explaining Mood Disorders

OBJECTIVE 50-2 | Discuss the facts that an acceptable theory of depression must explain.

Because depression profoundly affects so many people, it understandably has been the subject of thousands of studies. Psychologists are working to develop a theory of mood disorders that will suggest more effective ways to treat and prevent them. Researcher Peter Lewinsohn and his colleagues (1985, 1998) summarized the facts that any theory of depression must explain. Among them are the following:

- **Many behavioral and cognitive changes accompany depression.** Depressed people are inactive and feel unmotivated. They are sensitive to negative happenings, expect negative outcomes, and more often recall negative information. In a depressed mood, we expect our team to lose, our grades to fall, our love to fail. When the depression lifts, these behavioral and cognitive accompaniments disappear. Nearly half the time, depressed people also exhibit symptoms of another disorder, such as anxiety or substance abuse.

- **Depression is widespread.** Its commonality suggests that its causes, too, must be common.

- **Compared with men, women are nearly twice as vulnerable to major depression** (FIGURE 50.1). In general, women are most vulnerable to disorders involving internalized states, such as depression, anxiety, and inhibited sexual desire. Men's disorders tend to be more external—alcohol abuse, antisocial conduct, lack of impulse control. When women get sad they often get sadder than men do. When men get mad, they often get madder than women do.

- **Most major depressive episodes self-terminate.** Therapy tends to speed recovery, yet most people suffering major depression eventually return to normal even without professional help. The plague of depression comes and, a few weeks or months later, it usually goes, though it sometimes recurs later.

- **Stressful events related to work, marriage, and close relationships often precede depression.** A family member's death, a job loss, a marital crisis, or a physical assault increase one's risk of depression. If stress-related anxiety is a "crackling, menacing brushfire," notes biologist Robert Sapolsky (2003), "depression is a suffocating heavy blanket thrown on top of it." One study followed 2000 people over time. It found that the risk of the onset of depression in the ensuing month ranged from less than 1 percent among those who had experienced no stressful life event to 24 percent among those with three such events (Kendler, 1998). The early loss of a parent due to death or separation also increases later vulnerability to depression (Agid & others, 1999).

- **With each new generation, the rate of depression is increasing, and the disorder is striking earlier (now often in the late teens).** This is true not only in Canada and the United States but also in Germany, Italy, France, Lebanon, New Zealand,

■ **major depressive disorder** a mood disorder in which a person experiences, in the absence of drugs or a medical condition, two or more weeks of significantly depressed moods, feelings of worthlessness, and diminished interest or pleasure in most activities.

■ **mania** a mood disorder marked by a hyperactive, wildly optimistic state.

■ **bipolar disorder** a mood disorder in which the person alternates between the hopelessness and lethargy of depression and the overexcited state of mania. (Formerly called *manic-depressive disorder.*)

About 50 percent of those who recover from depression will suffer another episode within two years. Recovery is more likely to be permanent the later the first episode strikes, the longer the person stays well, the fewer the previous episodes, the less stress experienced, and the more social support received (Belsher & Costello, 1988; Fergusson & Woodward, 2002; Kendler & others, 2001).

" I see depression as the plague of the modern era."

Lewis Judd, former chief, National Institute of Mental Health, 2000

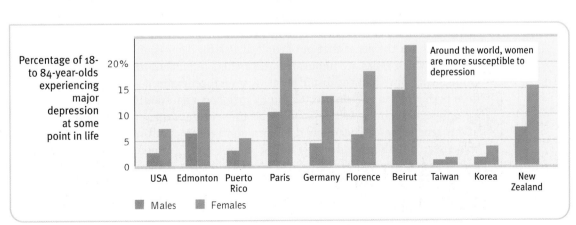

FIGURE **50.1**
Gender and depression
Interviews with 38,000 adults in 10 countries confirm what many smaller studies have found: Women's risk of major depression is nearly double that of men's. Lifetime risk of depression also varies by culture—from 1.5 percent in Taiwan to 19 percent in Beirut. (Data from Weissman & others, 1996.)

Down Came the Rain
Actress Brooke Shields chronicled her disabling postpartum depression in this 2005 book.

Taiwan, and Puerto Rico (Cross-National Collaborative Group, 1992). In Australia, 12 percent of adolescents interviewed reported symptoms of depression. Most hid it from their parents; almost 90 percent of their parents perceived their depressed teen as *not* suffering depression (Sawyer & others, 2000). In North America, today's young adults are three times as likely as their grandparents to report having recently—or ever--suffered depression (despite the grandparents' many more years of being at risk). Asked "Have you ever felt that you were going to have a nervous breakdown?" 17 percent of Americans said "yes" in 1957, as did 24 percent in 1996 (Swindle & others, 2000). The increase appears partly authentic, but may also reflect today's young adults' greater willingness to disclose depression, as well as our tendency to forget many negative experiences over time.

As you might expect, researchers understand and interpret these facts in ways that reflect their different perspectives. Psychoanalytic theory, applying Sigmund Freud's ideas about the importance of early childhood experiences and unconscious impulses, suggested that depression occurs when significant losses evoke feelings associated with losses experienced in childhood. Loss of a romantic relationship or a job might evoke feelings associated with the loss of the intimate relationship with one's mother, for example. Alternatively, unresolved anger toward one's parents might be turned inward against the self. Today's biopsychosocial perspective is broadening our understanding with biological and cognitive explanations.

The Biological Perspective

OBJECTIVE 50-3 | Summarize the contributions of the biological perspective to the study of depression, and discuss the link between suicide and depression.

Most recent mental health research dollars have funded explorations of biological influences on mood disorders. Depression is a whole-body disorder. It involves genetic predispositions, biochemical imbalances, negative thoughts, and melancholy mood.

Genetic Influences

We have long known that mood disorders run in families. The risk of major depression and bipolar disorder increases if you have a depressed parent or sibling (Sullivan & others, 2000). If one identical twin is diagnosed with major depressive disorder, the chances are about 1 in 2 that at some time the other twin will be, too. If one identical twin has bipolar disorder, the chances are 7 in 10 that the other twin will at some point be diagnosed similarly. Among fraternal twins, the corresponding odds are just under 2 in 10 (Tsuang & Faraone, 1990). The greater similarity of identical twins' depressive tendencies also occurs among twins reared apart (DiLalla & others, 1996). Moreover, adopted people who suffer a mood disorder often have close biological relatives who suffer mood disorders, become dependent on alcohol, or commit suicide (Wender & others, 1986). (Turn the page and see Close-Up: Suicide for other research findings on suicide.)

A search for the genes that put people at risk for depression is now under way. To tease out which genes are implicated, researchers use *linkage analysis*. First, they find families that have had the disorder across several generations. Then they draw blood from both affected and unaffected family members and examine their DNA, looking for differences. Linkage analysis points us to a chromosome neighborhood, note behavior genetics researchers Robert Plomin and Peter McGuffin (2003); "a house-to-house search is then needed to find the culprit gene." *Association studies* search for correlations between more specific DNA variation and a population trait. One such DNA variation occurs, for example, in about 40 percent of people with late-onset Alzheimer's disease and about 15 percent of those without Alzheimer's (Plomin &

McGuffin, 2003). The anticipated outcome of linkage and association studies in research on depression is a complex picture: Many genes have small effects that can combine with one another and with nongenetic factors to put some people at greater risk.

The Depressed Brain

Genes act by directing biochemical events that, down the line, influence behavior. The biochemical key is neurotransmitters, those messenger molecules that shuttle signals between nerve cells. *Norepinephrine,* a neurotransmitter that increases arousal and boosts mood, is scarce during depression and overabundant during mania. (Drugs that alleviate mania reduce norepinephrine.) Most people with a history of depression also have a history of habitual smoking. This may indicate an attempt to self-medicate with inhaled nicotine, which can temporarily increase norepinephrine and boost mood (HMHL, 2002).

A second neurotransmitter, *serotonin,* is also scarce during depression. Drugs that relieve depression tend to increase norepinephrine or serotonin supplies by blocking either their reuptake (as Prozac, Zoloft, and Paxil do with serotonin) or their chemical breakdown. Repetitive physical exercise, such as jogging, reduces depression as it increases serotonin (Jacobs, 1994).

Some of the genes under scrutiny provide codes for neurotransmitter systems such as serotonin (Plomin & McGuffin, 2003). One large study identified New Zealand young adults who had experienced several major stresses, such as a relationship breakup or a family death. These stressed individuals were much more likely to suffer depression if they carried a variation of a gene that codes for a protein that controls serotonin activity (Caspi & others, 2003). As we have seen so often throughout this book, genes and environments—nature and nurture—interact to form us.

People with depression have also recently been observed to have lower levels in their diet and blood of a "good" fat, *omega-3 fatty acid,* believed to enhance brain function (Edwards & others, 1998; Maes & others, 1999). Countries such as Japan, where people eat omega-3-rich fish, tend to have low depression rates (Hibbeln, 1998). Future research may determine whether eating more fish, walnuts, and other foods rich in omega-3 supports mental health.

Using modern scanning machines, researchers are also spotting neurological signs of depression. In many recent studies, the brain shows less activity during periods of depression, indicating a slowed-down state, and more activity during periods of mania (**FIGURE 50.2**). The left frontal lobe, which is active during positive emotions, is likely to be inactive during depressed states (Davidson & others, 2002). In one study of people with severe depression, MRI scans found their frontal lobes 7 percent smaller than normal (Coffey & others, 1993). The *hippocampus,* a memory-processing center linked with the brain's emotional circuitry, is vulnerable to stress-related damage. By boosting serotonin, which stimulates hippocampus neuron growth, antidepressant drugs may promote recovery from depression (Jacobs & others, 2000).

Gene-hunters' pursuit of bipolar-DNA links
Linkage studies seek to identify aberrant genes in family members suffering the disorder. These Pennsylvania Amish family members—an isolated population sharing a common life-style and some vulnerability to the disorder—have been among the volunteer participants.

Depressed state
(May 17)

Manic state
(May 18)

Depressed state
(May 27)

FIGURE 50.2
The ups and downs of bipolar disorder
PET scans show that brain energy consumption rises and falls with the patient's emotional switches. Red areas are where the brain rapidly consumes glucose.

CLOSE-UP:

SUICIDE

"But life, being weary of these worldly bars,
Never lacks power to dismiss itself."
—William Shakespeare, *Julius Caesar*, 1599

Each year some 1 million despairing people worldwide will say no to life by electing a permanent solution to what may be a temporary problem (Mann, 2003; WHO, 2004). Comparing the suicide rates of different groups, researchers have found

- **national differences:** The suicide rates of England, Italy, and Spain are little more than half those of Canada, Australia, and the United States; Austria and Finnish suicide rates are about double (WHO, 2002a). Within Europe, the most suicide-prone people (Lithuanians) have been 15 times more likely to kill themselves than the least (Portuguese).
- **racial differences:** White Americans are nearly twice as likely as black Americans to kill themselves (NIMH, 2002).
- **gender differences:** Women are much more likely than men to attempt suicide. But men are two to

four times more likely (depending on the country) to succeed (**FIGURE 50.3**). (An exception is China, where women account for most suicides [WHO, 2002c]). Men are more likely to use lethal methods, such as firing a bullet into the head, the method of choice in 6 of 10 U.S. suicides. The more lethal a suicide attempt, the more depressed the frontal lobe's serotonin-based activity often is (Mann, 2003).

- **age differences and trends:** The suicide rate surges among older men (Figure 50.2). Across the Western world, suicide rates have also surged since 1960 among older teens, especially males (Eckersley & Dear, 2002). For American, Australian, British, Canadian, and New Zealand 15- to 25-year-olds, suicide rates all doubled or more than doubled in the 30 years after 1960, paralleling the increasing late-teen and early-twenties rates of anxiety and depression.
- **other group differences:** Suicide rates are much higher among the rich, the nonreligious, and those

who are single, widowed, or divorced (Hoyer & Lund, 1993; Stack, 1992; Stengel, 1981). In both the United States and Australia, the teen suicide surge was almost entirely among males (Hassan & Carr, 1989). Gay and lesbian youth much more often suffer distress and attempt suicide than do their heterosexual peers (Goldfried, 2001).

Those who have been depressed have at least five times the general population's risk of suicide (Bostwick & Pankratz, 2000), but people seldom commit suicide while in the depths of depression, when energy and initiative are lacking. It is when they begin to rebound and become capable of following through that the risk increases. Teenage suicides may follow a traumatic event, such as a romantic breakup or a guilt-provoking antisocial act; they are often linked with drug and alcohol abuse (Fowler & others, 1986; Kolata, 1986). Compared with people who suffer no disorder, those addicted to alcohol are roughly 100 times more likely to commit suicide;

The Social-Cognitive Perspective

OBJECTIVE 50-4 | Summarize the contributions of the social-cognitive perspective to the study of depression, and describe the events in the cycle of depression.

Some people slide into depression for no obvious reason, even when life has been going well. But as we have noted, biological risk factors can predispose psychological reactions to stressful experiences (**FIGURE 50.4**). And the mind's negative thoughts somehow influence biological events that in a vicious cycle amplify depressing thoughts.

Depressed people view life through dark glasses. Their intensely negative assumptions about themselves, their situation, and their future lead them to magnify bad experiences and minimize good ones. Listen to Norman, a Canadian college professor, recalling his depression:

I [despaired] of ever being human again. I honestly felt subhuman, lower than the lowest vermin. Furthermore, I was self-deprecatory and could not understand why anyone would want to associate with me, let alone love me. . . . I was positive that I was a fraud and a phony and that I didn't deserve my Ph.D. I didn't deserve to have tenure; I didn't deserve to be a Full Professor. . . .

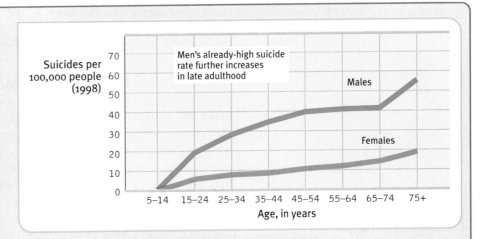

FIGURE 50.3

Suicide rates by gender and age

Worldwide suicide rates are higher among males than among females. The highest rates of all are found among older men. (From WHO, 2002a.)

some 3 percent of them do (Murphy & Wetzel, 1990). Even among people who have attempted suicide, those who abuse alcohol are five times more likely than others to kill themselves eventually (Beck & Steer, 1989).

Social suggestion may trigger the final act. Following highly publicized suicides and TV programs featuring suicide, known suicides increase. So do fatal auto "accidents" and private airplane crashes.

Suicide is not necessarily an act of hostility or revenge. The elderly sometimes choose death as an alternative to current or future suffering. In people of all ages, suicide may be a way of switching off unendurable pain and relieving the perceived burden on family members (Joiner & others, 2002; Shneidman, 1987).

In retrospect, families and friends may recall signs that they believe should have forewarned them—verbal hints, giving possessions away, or withdrawal and preoccupation with death. But few who talk of suicide or think suicidal thoughts (a number that includes one-third of all adolescents and college students) actually attempt suicide, and few of those who attempt it complete the act (Yip, 1998). The United States, for example, records about 30,000 suicides annually, but a half-million emergency room visits for attempted suicide (Surgeon General, 1999). One-third of those who kill themselves have tried to kill themselves previously. Most who do commit suicide have talked of it, and anyone who does threaten suicide is at least sending a signal of being desperate or feeling despondent. So, if a friend talks suicide, it's important to listen and to direct the friend to professional help.

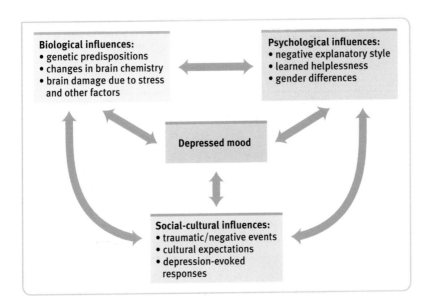

FIGURE 50.4

Biopsychosocial approach to depression

Seriously depressed moods result from a combination of factors, which affect each other. Altering any one component can alter the others.

I didn't deserve the research grants I had been awarded; I couldn't understand how I had written books and journal articles. . . . I must have conned a lot of people. (Endler, 1982, pp. 45–49)

Research reveals how *self-defeating beliefs* and a *negative explanatory style* feed depression's vicious cycle.

Negative Thoughts and Negative Moods Interact

Self-defeating beliefs may arise from *learned helplessness*. Both dogs and humans act depressed, passive, and withdrawn after experiencing uncontrollable painful events (Seligman, 1975, 1991). Gender differences in uncontrollable stress help explain why, beginning in their early teens, women are nearly twice as vulnerable to depression (Kessler, 2001). Women more often than men have been abused or made to feel helpless, and they may respond more strongly to stress (Hankin & Abramson 2001; Mazure & others, 2002; Nolen-Hoeksema, 2001, 2003). Thirty-six percent of women and 16 percent of men entering American colleges feel "frequently overwhelmed by all I have to do" (Sax & others, 2004). (Men report spending more of their time in "light anxiety" activities such as sports, TV watching, and partying, possibly avoiding activities that might make them feel overwhelmed.)

But why do life's unavoidable failures lead some people and not others to become depressed? The difference lies partly with people's *explanatory style.* We have some choice of whom or what to blame for our failures. If you fail a test and blame yourself, you may feel stupid and depressed. If you externalize the blame—perhaps attributing your failure to an unfair test—you are more likely to feel angry.

Depressed people tend to explain bad events in terms that are stable ("It's going to last forever"), global ("It's going to affect everything I do"), and internal ("It's all my fault") (**FIGURE 50.5**). Lyn Abramson, Gerald Metalsky, and Lauren Alloy (1989) theorized that the result of these pessimistic, overgeneralized, self-blaming attributions is a depressing sense of hopelessness. If you tend to see bad grades, social rejection, and work problems as inevitable and your own fault, and if you ruminate about such things, then when bad things happen you will probably experience the blues.

> "I have learned to accept my mistakes by referring them to a personal history which was not of my making."
>
> B. F. Skinner (1983)

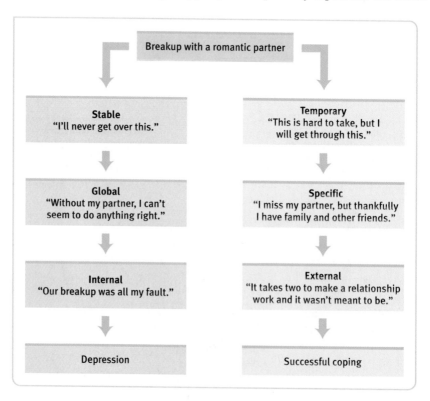

FIGURE 50.5
Explanatory style and depression

PEANUTS

Reprinted by permission of
United Feature Syndicate, Inc.

Might Charlie Brown be helped by an optimism-training program?

What might you expect of new college students who are not depressed but do exhibit a pessimistic explanatory style? Lauren Alloy and her collaborators (1999) monitored Temple University and University of Wisconsin students every 6 weeks for 2.5 years. Among those identified as having pessimistic thinking styles, 17 percent had a first episode of major depression, as did only 1 percent of those who began college with optimistic thinking styles. Follow-up research has found that students who exhibit optimism as they begin college develop more social support, which contributes to a lowered risk of depression (Brissette & others, 2002).

Martin Seligman (1991, 1995) argues that depression is common among young Westerners because of epidemic hopelessness stemming from the rise of individualism and the decline of commitment to religion and family. When facing failure or rejection, contends Seligman, the self-focused individual takes on personal responsibility for problems and has nothing to fall back on for hope. In non-Western cultures, where close-knit relationships and cooperation are the norm, major depression is less common and less tied to self-blame over personal failure. In Japan, for example, depressed people instead tend to report feeling shame over letting others down (Draguns, 1990a).

There is, however, a chicken-and-egg problem with the social-cognitive explanation of depression. Self-defeating beliefs, negative attributions, and self-blame surely do support depression. Peter Barnett and Ian Gotlib (1988) note that such cognitions *coincide* with a depressed mood and are *indicators* of depression. But do they *cause* depression, any more than a speedometer's reading 70 mph causes a car's speed? Before or after being depressed, people's thoughts are less negative. Perhaps this is because, in a phenomenon known as *state-dependent memory*, a depressed mood triggers negative thoughts. If you temporarily put people in a bad or sad mood, their memories, judgments, and expectations suddenly become more pessimistic.

Joseph Forgas and his associates (1984) provided a striking demonstration of the mood effect. First, they videotaped people talking to each other. The next day, they put those participants in a good or bad mood via hypnosis and had them watch the videotape of themselves. The happy participants detected in their screen selves more positive than negative behaviors; the unhappy participants more often saw themselves behaving negatively. Thus, even when watching themselves on videotape, mildly depressed people judge themselves more negatively.

Depression's Vicious Cycle

"A recipe for severe depression is preexisting pessimism encountering failure," notes Martin Seligman (1991, p. 78). Depression, as we have seen, is often brought on by stressful experiences—losing a job, getting divorced or rejected, suffering physical trauma—anything that disrupts your sense of who you are and why you are a worthy human being. We have also seen that depression can be adaptive, a time for lying low and gaining insights that can later lead to more effective strategies for interacting with the world. But depression-prone people respond to bad events in an especially self-focused, self-blaming way (Mor & Winquist, 2002; Pyszczynski & others, 1991; Wood & others, 1990a,b). Their self-esteem fluctuates more rapidly up with boosts and down

"Man never reasons so much and becomes so introspective as when he suffers, since he is anxious to get at the cause of his sufferings."
Luigi Pirandello, *Six Characters in Search of an Author*, 1922

Susan Nolen-Hoeksema
"This epidemic of morbid meditation is a disease that women suffer much more than men. Women can ruminate about anything and everything—our appearance, our families, our career, our health." (*Women Who Think Too Much: How to Break Free of Overthinking and Reclaim Your Life,* 2003)

FIGURE 50.6
The vicious cycle of depressed thinking
Cognitive therapists attempt to break this cycle by changing the way depressed people process events. Psychiatrists attempt to alter with medication the biological roots of persistently depressed moods.

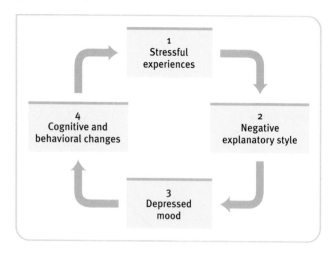

with threats (Butler & others, 1994). When down, their brooding amplifies their negative feelings, which in turn trigger depression's other cognitive and behavioral symptoms.

This cycle also helps explain women's doubled risk of depression. When trouble strikes, men tend to act, women tend to think—and often to *overthink,* as Susan Nolen-Hoeksema (2003) describes their rumination. Women often have vivid recall for both wonderful and horrid experiences; men more vaguely recall such experiences (Seidletz & Diener, 1998). This gender difference in emotional memory may feed women's greater rumination over negative events and explain why fewer men than women reported being "frequently overwhelmed on entering college."

None of us is immune to the dejection, diminished self-esteem, and negative thinking brought on by rejection or defeat. As Edward Hirt and his colleagues (1992) demonstrated, even small losses can temporarily sour our thinking. They studied some avid Indiana University basketball fans who seemed to regard the team as an extension of themselves. After the fans watched their team lose or win, the researchers asked them to predict the team's future performance and their own. After a loss, the morose fans offered bleaker assessments not only of the team's future, but also of their own likely performance at throwing darts, solving anagrams, and getting a date. When things aren't going our way, it may seem as though they never will.

But being withdrawn, self-focused, and complaining can elicit rejection (Furr & Funder, 1998; Gotlib & Hammen, 1992). In one study, researchers Stephen Strack and James Coyne (1983) noted that "depressed persons induced hostility, depression, and anxiety in others and got rejected. Their guesses that they were not accepted were not a matter of cognitive distortion." Weary of the person's fatigue, hopeless attitude, and lethargy, a spouse may threaten to leave or a boss may begin to question the person's competence. Indeed, people in the throes of depression are at high risk for divorce, job loss, and other stressful life events. (This provides another example of genetic–environmental interaction: People genetically disposed to depression more often experience depressing events.) The losses and stress only serve to compound the original depression. Rejection and depression feed each other. Misery may love another's company, but company does not love another's misery.

We can now assemble some of the pieces of the depression puzzle (**FIGURE 50.6**): (1) Negative, stressful events interpreted through (2) a ruminating, pessimistic explanatory style create (3) a hopeless, depressed state that (4) hampers the way the person thinks and acts. This, in turn, fuels (1) negative experiences such as rejection.

It is a cycle we can all recognize. Bad moods feed on themselves: When we *feel* down, we *think* negatively and remember bad experiences. On the brighter side, we can break the cycle of depression at any of these points—by moving to a different environment, by reversing our self-blame and negative attributions, by turning our attention outward, or by engaging in more pleasant activities and more competent behavior.

Winston Churchill called depression a "black dog" that periodically hounded him. Poet Emily Dickinson was so afraid of bursting into tears in public that she spent much of her adult life in seclusion (Patterson, 1951). Abraham Lincoln was so withdrawn and brooding as a young man that his friends feared he might take his own life (Kline, 1974). As each of these lives reminds us, people can and do struggle through depression. Most regain their capacity to love, to work, and even to succeed at the highest levels.

>> LEARNING OUTCOMES

Mood Disorders

OBJECTIVE 50-1 | **Define *mood disorders*, and contrast major depressive disorder and bipolar disorder.**

Mood disorders are characterized by emotional extremes. A person with *major depressive disorder* experiences two or more weeks of seriously depressed moods and feelings of worthlessness, takes little interest in most activities, and derives little pleasure from them. These feelings are not caused by drugs or a medical condition. People with the less common condition of *bipolar disorder* alternate between depression and *mania,* a hyperactive and wildly optimistic impulsive state.

OBJECTIVE 50-2 | **Discuss the facts that an acceptable theory of depression must explain.**

An acceptable theory of depression must account for the many behavioral and cognitive changes that accompany depression; its widespread occurrence; women's greater susceptibility to the disorder; the tendency of depressive episodes to self-terminate; the link between stressful events and the onset of depression; and the increasing rates and earlier age of onset of depression.

OBJECTIVE 50-3 | **Summarize the contributions of the biological perspective to the study of depression, and discuss the link between suicide and depression.**

The biological perspective on depression focuses on genetic influences (in part through *linkage analysis* and *association studies*) and on abnormalities in brain structure and function (including those found in neurotransmitter systems). Findings indicate that a predisposition to depression does run in some families, that the neurotransmitters norepinephrine and serotonin are scarce during depression, that activity in the left frontal lobes is slowed during depression, and that stress-related damage to the hippocampus increases the risk of depression. The risk of suicide is greatest when energy returns as depression begins to lift.

OBJECTIVE 50-4 | **Summarize the contributions of the social-cognitive perspective to the study of depression, and describe the events in the cycle of depression.**

The social-cognitive perspective stresses the power of self-defeating beliefs and negative explanatory styles that view bad events as stable, global, and internally caused. Critics note that these characteristics may coincide with, but not cause, depression. The cycle of depression consists of (1) negative stressful events (2) interpreted through a pessimistic explanatory style, creating a (3) hopeless depressed state, which (4) hampers the way the person thinks and acts, fueling more negative stressful events, such as rejection.

TERMS AND CONCEPTS TO REMEMBER

mood disorders, p. 50-1

major depressive disorder, p. 50-2

mania, p. 50-2

bipolar disorder, p. 50-2

TEST YOURSELF

1. What does it mean to say that "depression is the common cold of psychological disorders"?

(Answer in Appendix B.)

ASK YOURSELF

1. Has your entry into college life been a challenging time for you? What advice would you have for future collegians?

>WEB

Multiple-choice *self-tests* and more may be found at www.worthpublishers.com/myers.

51

Schizophrenia

If depression is the common cold of psychological disorders, chronic schizophrenia is the cancer. Nearly 1 in 100 people will develop schizophrenia, joining the estimated 24 million across the world who suffer one of humanity's most dreaded disorders (WHO, 2002d). It typically strikes as young people are maturing into adulthood, it knows no national boundaries, and it affects both males and females—though men tend to be struck earlier, more severely, and slightly more often (Aleman & others, 2003).

Symptoms of Schizophrenia

OBJECTIVE 51-1 | Describe the symptoms of schizophrenia, and differentiate delusions and hallucinations.

Literally translated, **schizophrenia** means "split mind." It refers not to a multiple-personality split but rather to a split from reality that shows itself in disorganized thinking, disturbed perceptions, and inappropriate emotions and actions.

Disorganized Thinking

Imagine trying to communicate with Maxine, a young woman whose thoughts spill out in no logical order. Her biographer, Susan Sheehan (1982, p. 25), observed her saying aloud to no one in particular, "This morning, when I was at Hillside [Hospital], I was making a movie. I was surrounded by movie stars . . . I'm Mary Poppins. Is this room painted blue to get me upset? My grandmother died four weeks after my eighteenth birthday."

As this strange monologue illustrates, the thinking of a person with schizophrenia is fragmented, bizarre, and distorted by false beliefs, called **delusions** ("I'm Mary Poppins"). Those with *paranoid* tendencies are particularly prone to delusions of persecution. Jumping from one idea to another may occur even within sentences, creating a sort of "word salad." One young man begged for "a little more allegro in the treatment," and suggested that "liberationary movement with a view to the widening of the horizon" will "ergo extort some wit in lectures."

Art by people diagnosed with schizophrenia
Commenting on the kind of artwork shown here, poet and art critic John Ashbery wrote: "The lure of the work is strong, but so is the terror of the unanswerable riddles it proposes."

August Natterer, *Witch's Head*. The Prinzhorn Collection, University of Heidelberg

L. Berthold, *Untitled*. The Prinzhorn Collection, University of Heidelberg

Photos of paintings by Kramert Museum, University of Illinois at Urbana-Champaign

Many psychologists believe disorganized thoughts result from a breakdown in selective attention. We normally have a remarkable capacity for selective attention—for, say, giving our undivided attention to one voice at a party while filtering out competing sensory stimuli. Those with schizophrenia cannot do this. Thus, an irrelevant stimulus or an extraneous part of the preceding thought easily distracts them. Minute stimuli, such as the grooves on a brick or the inflections of a voice, may distract their attention from the whole scene or from the speaker's meaning. As one former patient recalled, "What had happened to me . . . was a breakdown in the filter, and a hodge-podge of unrelated stimuli were distracting me from things which should have had my undivided attention" (MacDonald, 1960, p. 218). This selective attention difficulty is but one of dozens of cognitive differences associated with schizophrenia. Others range from deficiencies in working memory to the ability to smoothly follow a swinging pendulum with the eyes, a task that requires the coordination of several brain regions (Heinrichs, 2005).

Disturbed Perceptions

A person with schizophrenia may perceive things that are not there. Such *hallucinations* (sensory experiences without sensory stimulation) are usually auditory and often take the form of voices making insulting statements or giving orders. The voices may tell the patient that she is bad or that she must burn herself with a cigarette lighter. Less commonly, people see, feel, taste, or smell things that are not there. Hallucinations have been compared to dreams breaking into waking consciousness. When the unreal seems real, the resulting perceptions are at best bizarre, at worst terrifying.

Inappropriate Emotions and Actions

The emotions of schizophrenia are often utterly inappropriate. Maxine's emotions seemed split off from reality. She laughed after recalling her grandmother's death. On occasion, she became angry for no apparent reason or cried when others laughed. Other victims of schizophrenia sometimes lapse into *flat affect,* a zombielike state of apparent apathy.

Motor behavior may also be inappropriate. The person may perform senseless, compulsive acts, such as continually rocking or rubbing an arm. Those who exhibit *catatonia* may remain motionless for hours on end and then become agitated.

As you can imagine, such disorganized thinking, disturbed perceptions, and inappropriate emotions and actions profoundly disrupt social relationships and make it difficult to hold a job. During their most severe periods, people with schizophrenia live in a private inner world, preoccupied with illogical ideas and unreal images. Given a supportive environment, some eventually recover to enjoy a normal life or experience bouts of schizophrenia only intermittently. Others remain socially withdrawn and isolated throughout much of their lives, and their frequent hospitalizations help explain why many countries devote about 2 percent of their national health budget to care and treatment of those with schizophrenia (Knapp & others, 2004).

Subtypes of Schizophrenia

OBJECTIVE 51-2 | Distinguish the five subtypes of schizophrenia, and contrast chronic and acute schizophrenia.

We have thus far described schizophrenia as if it were a single disorder. Actually, it is a cluster of disorders. The subtypes share some common features, but they also have some distinguishing symptoms (**TABLE 51.1** on the next page). Schizophrenia patients

■ **schizophrenia** a group of severe disorders characterized by disorganized and delusional thinking, disturbed perceptions, and inappropriate emotions and actions.

■ **delusions** false beliefs, often of persecution or grandeur, that may accompany psychotic disorders.

TABLE 51.1

SUBTYPES OF SCHIZOPHRENIA

Paranoid:	Preoccupation with delusions or hallucinations, often with themes of persecution or grandiosity
Disorganized:	Disorganized speech or behavior, or flat or inappropriate emotion
Catatonic:	Immobility (or excessive, purposeless movement), extreme negativism, and/or parrotlike repeating of another's speech or movements
Undifferentiated:	Many and varied symptoms
Residual:	Withdrawal, after hallucinations and delusions have disappeared

with *positive symptoms* may experience hallucinations, talk in disorganized and deluded ways, and exhibit inappropriate laughter, tears, or rage. Those with *negative symptoms* have toneless voices, expressionless faces, or mute and rigid bodies. Thus, positive symptoms are the *presence* of inappropriate behaviors, and negative symptoms are the *absence* of appropriate behaviors. Because schizophrenia is a cluster of disorders, these varied symptoms could have more than one cause.

Sometimes, as in the case of Maxine, schizophrenia develops gradually, emerging from a long history of social inadequacy (which helps explain why those predisposed to schizophrenia often end up in the lower socioeconomic levels, or even homeless). Other times it appears suddenly, seemingly as a reaction to stress. One rule holds true around the world (World Health Organization, 1979): When schizophrenia is a slow-developing process (called *chronic,* or *process,* schizophrenia), recovery is doubtful. When a previously well-adjusted person develops schizophrenia rapidly (called *acute,* or *reactive,* schizophrenia) in reaction to particular life stresses, recovery is much more likely. Those with chronic schizophrenia often exhibit the negative symptom of withdrawal. Men, whose schizophrenia develops on average four years earlier than women's, more often exhibit negative symptoms and chronic schizophrenia (Räsänen & others, 2000). The outlook is better for those with positive symptoms—they more often have a reactive condition that responds to drug therapy (Fenton & McGlashan, 1991, 1994; Fowles, 1992).

> "When someone asks me to explain schizophrenia I tell them, you know how sometimes in your dreams you are in them yourself and some of them feel like real nightmares? My schizophrenia was like I was walking through a dream. But everything around me was real. At times, today's world seems so boring and I wonder if I would like to step back into the schizophrenic dream, but then I remember all the scary and horrifying experiences."
>
> Stuart Emmons, with Craig Geisler, Kalman J. Kaplan, and Martin Harrow, *Living With Schizophrenia*, 1997

Explaining Schizophrenia

Schizophrenia is not only the most dreaded psychological disorder but also one of the most heavily researched. Most of the new research studies link it with brain abnormalities and genetic predispositions. Schizophrenia is a disease of the brain exhibited in symptoms of the mind.

Brain Abnormalities

OBJECTIVE 51-3 | Outline some abnormal brain chemistry, functions, and structures associated with schizophrenia, and discuss the possible link between prenatal viral infections and schizophrenia.

Might imbalances in brain chemistry underlie schizophrenia? Scientists have long known that strange behavior can have strange chemical causes. The saying "mad as a hatter" refers to the psychological deterioration of British hatmakers whose brains, it was later discovered, were slowly poisoned as they moistened the brims of mercury-laden felt hats with their lips (Smith, 1983). Scientists are clarifying the mechanism by which chemicals such as LSD produce hallucinations. These discoveries hint that schizophrenia symptoms might have a biochemical key.

Dopamine Overactivity

Researchers discovered one such key when they examined schizophrenia patients' brains after death, and found an excess of receptors for *dopamine*—a sixfold excess for the so-called D4 dopamine receptor (Seeman & others, 1993; Wong & others, 1986). They speculate that such a high level may intensify brain signals in schizophrenia, creating positive symptoms such as hallucinations and paranoia. As we might therefore expect, drugs that block dopamine receptors often lessen these symptoms; drugs that increase dopamine levels, such as amphetamines and cocaine, sometimes intensify them (Swerdlow & Koob, 1987). Dopamine overactivity may underlie patients' overreactions to irrelevant external and internal stimuli.

Dopamine-blocking drugs have little effect on persistent negative symptoms of withdrawal. Researchers are now exploring another neurotransmitter, *glutamate,* which directs neurons to pass along an impulse. Impaired glutamate activity appears to be another source of schizophrenia symptoms (Javitt & Coyle, 2004). Drugs that interfere with glutamate receptors can produce schizophrenialike negative symptoms. Moreover, medications that neutralize the effect of such street drugs also seem to alleviate negative symptoms (HMHL, 2001).

Abnormal Brain Activity and Anatomy

Modern brain-scanning techniques reveal that many people with chronic schizophrenia have abnormal activity in multiple brain areas. Some have abnormally low brain activity in the frontal lobes, which are critical for reasoning, planning, and problem solving (Morey & others, 2005; Pettegrew & others, 1993; Resnick, 1992). People diagnosed with schizophrenia also display a noticeable decline in the brain waves that reflect synchronized neural firing in the frontal lobes (Spencer & others, 2004; Symond & others, 2005). Out-of-sync neurons may disrupt the integrated functioning of neural networks, possibly contributing to schizophrenia symptoms.

One study took PET scans of brain activity while people were hallucinating (Silbersweig & others, 1995). When participants heard a voice or saw something, their brains became vigorously active in several core regions, including the thalamus, a structure deep in the brain that filters incoming sensory signals and transmits them to the cortex. Another PET scan study of people with paranoia found increased activity in a fear-processing center, the amygdala (Epstein & others, 1998).

Many studies have found enlarged, fluid-filled areas and a corresponding shrinkage of cerebral tissue in people with schizophrenia (Wright & others, 2000), and one study even found such abnormalities in the brains of people who would *later* develop this disorder (Pantelis & others, 2002). The greater the shrinkage, the more severe the thought disorder (Collinson & others, 2003; Nelson & others, 1998; Shenton, 1992). One smaller-than-normal area is the cortex (**FIGURE 51.1** on the next page). Another is the thalamus, which may explain why people with schizophrenia have difficulty filtering sensory input and focusing attention (Andreasen & others, 1994). The bottom line of various studies, reports Nancy Andreasen (1997, 2001), is that schizophrenia involves not one isolated brain abnormality but problems with several brain regions and their interconnections.

Naturally, scientists wonder what causes these abnormalities. One possibility is some problem during prenatal development or delivery. Low birth weight and birth complications such as oxygen deprivation are known risk factors for schizophrenia (Buka & others, 1999; Zornberg & others, 2000). Famine is also a suspect. People conceived during the peak of the Dutch wartime famine later displayed a doubled rate of schizophrenia, as did those conceived during a 1959–1961 famine in eastern China (St. Clair & others, 2005; Susser & others, 1996).

About 60 percent of schizophrenia patients smoke, often heavily. Nicotine apparently stimulates certain brain receptors, which helps focus attention (Javitt & Coyle, 2004).

Studying the neurophysiology of schizophrenia
Psychiatrist E. Fuller Torrey is collecting the brains of hundreds of those who died as young adults and suffered disorders such as schizophrenia and bipolar disorder. Torrey is making tissue samples available to researchers worldwide.

Chris Usher

Paul Thompson and Arthur W. Toga, UCLA Laboratory of Neuro
Imaging and Judith L. Rapoport, National Institute of Mental Health

FIGURE 51.1

Schizophrenia and the shrinking brain.

Among adolescents who suffer a relatively rare childhood-onset schizophrenia, MRI scans by Paul Thompson and his colleagues (2001) revealed a much-greater-than-normal loss of cerebral cortex tissue between the ages of 13 and 18.

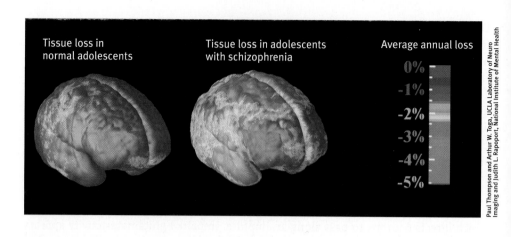

Maternal Virus During Midpregnancy

Another possible culprit is a midpregnancy viral infection that impairs fetal brain development. Can you imagine some ways to test this fetal-virus idea? Scientists exploring this possibility have asked the following questions:

- *Are people at increased risk of schizophrenia if, during the middle of their fetal development, their country experienced a flu epidemic?* The repeated answer is yes (Mednick & others, 1994; Murray & others, 1992; Wright & others, 1995).

- *Are people born in densely populated areas, where viral diseases spread more readily, at greater risk for schizophrenia?* The answer, confirmed in a study of 1.75 million Danes, is yes (Jablensky, 1999; Mortensen & others, 1999).

- *Are those born during the winter and spring months—after the fall-winter flu season—also at increased risk?* The answer is again yes, at 5 to 8 percent increased risk (Torrey & others, 1997, 2002).

- *In the Southern Hemisphere, where the seasons are the reverse of the Northern Hemisphere, are the months of above-average schizophrenia births similarly reversed?* Again, the answer is yes, though somewhat less so. In Australia, for example, people born between August and October are at greater risk—unless they migrated from the Northern Hemisphere, in which case their risk is greater if they were born between January and March (McGrath & others, 1995, 1999).

- *Are mothers who report being sick with influenza during pregnancy more likely to bear children who develop schizophrenia?* In one study of nearly 8000 women, the answer was yes. The schizophrenia risk increased from the customary 1 percent risk to about 2 percent—but only for infections during the second trimester (Brown & others, 2000).

- *Does blood drawn from pregnant women whose offspring develop schizophrenia show higher-than-normal levels of antibodies that suggest a viral infection?* In one study of 27 women whose children later developed schizophrenia, the answer was yes (Buka & others, 2001). One huge California study collected blood samples from some 20,000 pregnant women during the 1950s and 1960s, some of whose offspring were later diagnosed with schizophrenia. When antibodies in the blood indicated the mother was exposed to influenza during the first half of the pregnancy, the risk of the child's developing schizophrenia tripled. Flu during the second half of the pregnancy produced no such increase (Brown & others, 2004).

Schizophrenia has other causes (as genetics research makes plain). Moreover, the children of some 98 percent of women who catch the flu during their second trimester of pregnancy do *not* develop schizophrenia. Nevertheless, these converging lines of evidence suggest that prenatal viral infections play a contributing role. They also strengthen the U.S. Centers for Disease Control (2003) recommendation that "women who will be more than three months pregnant during the flu season" have a flu shot.

Why might a second-trimester maternal flu bout put fetuses at risk? Is it the virus itself? The mother's immune response to it? Medications taken? (Wyatt & others, 2001). Does the infection weaken the brain's supportive glial cells, leading to reduced synaptic connections (Moises & others, 2002)? In time, answers may become available.

Genetic Factors

OBJECTIVE 51-4 | Discuss the evidence for a genetic contribution to the development of schizophrenia.

Might people also inherit a predisposition to certain brain abnormalities? The evidence strongly suggests that, yes, some do. The nearly 1-in-100 odds of any person's being diagnosed with schizophrenia become about 1 in 10 among those whose sibling or parent has the disorder, and close to 1 in 2 if the affected sibling is an identical twin (FIGURE 51.2). Although there are barely more than a dozen such known cases, it appears that an identical twin of a person with schizophrenia retains that 1-in-2 chance when the twins are reared apart (Plomin & others, 1997).

Even with identical twins, there may be a prenatal environmental component. About two-thirds of identical twins share the same placenta and blood. (They usually also have opposite handedness to their co-twin.) If an identical twin has schizophrenia, the co-twin's chances of being similarly afflicted are 6 in 10 if they shared a single placenta, but only 1 in 10 if the twins had separate placentas (Davis & others, 1995a,b; Phelps & others, 1997). Twins who share a placenta are more likely to experience the same prenatal viruses. So it is possible that shared germs as well as shared genes produce identical twin similarities.

Adoption studies, however, confirm that the genetic link is real (Gottesman, 1991). Children adopted by someone who develops schizophrenia seldom "catch" the disorder. Rather, adopted children have an elevated risk if a biological parent is diagnosed with schizophrenia. One intriguing study of 87,907 Israelis also found that the older the biological father—and thus the more opportunities for the DNA in his sperm cells to have mutated—the greater the risk of offspring with schizophrenia (Malaspina & others, 2001).

With the genetic factor established, researchers are now sleuthing specific genes that, in some combination, might predispose schizophrenia-inducing brain abnormalities (Callicott & others, 2005; Egan & others, 2004). (It is not our genes but our brains that directly control our behavior.) Some of these genes provide the code for proteins involved in the brain's neurotransmission (including one that breaks down dopamine). Other important genes appear to code for proteins used to make the myelin that coats brain cells and influences their impulse transmission. Despite tantalizing findings, the culprit genes have proven elusive. The genetic contribution to schizophrenia is beyond question. But the genetic role is not as straightforward as the

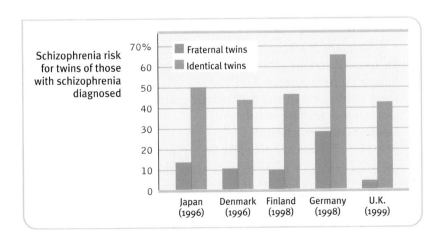

FIGURE 51.2
Risk of developing schizophrenia
The lifetime risk of developing schizophrenia varies with one's genetic relatedness to someone having this disorder. Across countries, barely more than 1 in 10 fraternal twins, but some 5 in 10 identical twins, share a schizophrenia diagnosis. (Adapted from Gottesman, 2001.)

No schizophrenia   Schizophrenia

Schizophrenia in identical twins

When twins differ, only the one afflicted with schizophrenia typically has enlarged, fluid-filled cranial cavities (right) (Suddath & others, 1990). The difference between the twins implies some nongenetic factor, such as a virus, is also at work.

The Genain quadruplets

The odds of any four people picked at random all being diagnosed with schizophrenia are 1 in 100 million. But genetically identical sisters Nora, Iris, Myra, and Hester Genain all have the disease. Two of the sisters have more severe forms of the disorder than the others, suggesting the influence of environmental as well as biological factors.

inheritance of eye color. A complex disorder such as schizophrenia is surely influenced by multiple genes with small effects.

Also remember that half the twins who share identical genes with a schizophrenia victim do *not* develop the disorder. Thus, behavior geneticists Susan Nicol and Irving Gottesman (1983) concluded that some people "have a genetic predisposition to the disorder but that this predisposition by itself is not sufficient for the development of schizophrenia." Other factors—including the prenatal viral infections, nutritional deprivation, and oxygen deprivation at birth mentioned earlier—may be ingredients for the disease.

Our knowledge of human genetics and of genetic influences on maladies such as schizophrenia is exploding, thanks partly to millions of new National Institute of Mental Health dollars focused on solving the schizophrenia riddle. So, can scientists develop genetic tests that reveal who is at risk? If so, will people in the future subject their embryos to genetic testing (and gene repair or abortion) if they are at risk for this or some other psychological or physical malady? Might they take their egg and sperm to the genetics lab for screening before combining them to produce an embryo? Or will children be tested for genetic risks and given appropriate preventive treatments? In this brave new twenty-first-century world, such questions await answers.

Psychological Factors

OBJECTIVE 51-5 | Describe some psychological factors that may be early warning signs of schizophrenia in children.

If genetically predisposed physiological abnormalities do not, by themselves, cause schizophrenia, neither do prenatal and psychological factors alone. It remains true, as Nicol and Gottesman (1983) noted more than two decades ago, that "no environmental causes have been discovered that will invariably, or even with moderate probability, produce schizophrenia in persons who are not related to" a person with schizophrenia. Psychologists long ago ceased blaming parents; no longer do they attribute schizophrenia to cold and capricious "refrigerator mothers."

Hoping to identify environmental triggers of schizophrenia, several investigators are now following the development of "high-risk" children, such as those born to a parent with schizophrenia or exposed to prenatal risks (Freedman & others, 1998; Olin & Mednick, 1996; Susser, 1999). One study followed 163 teens and early-twenties adults who had two relatives with schizophrenia. During the 2½-year study, the 20 percent who developed schizophrenia displayed some tendency to withdraw socially and behave oddly in advance of the onset of the disorder (Johnstone & others, 2005). By comparing the experiences of high-risk and low-risk children who do and do not develop schizophrenia, researchers have so far pinpointed the following possible early warning signs:

- A mother whose schizophrenia was severe and long-lasting
- Birth complications, often involving oxygen deprivation and low birth weight
- Separation from parents
- Short attention span and poor muscle coordination
- Disruptive or withdrawn behavior
- Emotional unpredictability
- Poor peer relations and solo play

Few of us can easily relate to the strange thoughts, perceptions, and behaviors of schizophrenia. Sometimes our thoughts do jump around, but we do not talk nonsensically. Occasionally we feel unjustly suspicious of someone, but we do not fear that the world is plotting against us. Often our perceptions err, but rarely do we see or hear things that are not there. We have felt regret after laughing at someone's misfortune, but we rarely giggle in response to bad news. At times we just want to be alone, but we do not live in social isolation. However, millions of people around the world do talk strangely, suffer delusions, hear nonexistent voices, see things that are not there, laugh or cry at inappropriate times, or withdraw into private imaginary worlds. The quest to solve the cruel puzzle of schizophrenia therefore continues, and more vigorously than ever.

>> LEARNING OUTCOMES

Schizophrenia

OBJECTIVE 51-1 | **Describe the symptoms of schizophrenia, and differentiate delusions and hallucinations.**
Schizophrenia is a group of disorders that typically strike during late adolescence, affect men very slightly more than women, and seem to occur in all cultures. Symptoms of schizophrenia are disorganized and delusional thinking (which may stem from a breakdown of selective attention), disturbed perceptions, and inappropriate emotions and actions. *Delusions* are false beliefs; *hallucinations* are sensory experiences without sensory stimulation.

OBJECTIVE 51-2 | **Distinguish the five subtypes of schizophrenia, and contrast chronic and acute schizophrenia.**
The subtypes of schizophrenia are *paranoid* (preoccupation with delusions or hallucinations, often of persecution or grandiosity), *disorganized* (disorganized speech or behavior, or flat affect or inappropriate emotions), *catatonic* (immobility, extreme negativism, and/or parrotlike repetition of another's speech or movements), *undifferentiated* (varied symptoms), and *residual* (withdrawal following hallucinations and delusions). *Chronic* (or *process*) *schizophrenia* emerges gradually, is often associated with negative symptoms (absence of appropriate behaviors), and carries a low chance of recovery. *Acute* (or *reactive*) schizophrenia develops rapidly (often in response to stress) in a previously well-adjusted person, may be associated with positive symptoms (presence of inappropriate behaviors), and carries a greater chance of recovery.

OBJECTIVE 51-3 | **Outline some abnormal brain chemistry, functions, and structures associated with schizophrenia, and discuss the possible link between prenatal viral infections and schizophrenia.**
People with schizophrenia have increased receptors for the neurotransmitter dopamine, which may intensify the positive symptoms of schizophrenia. Research is under way on a possible link between negative symptoms and impaired glutamate activity. Brain abnormalities associated with schizophrenia include enlarged, fluid-filled cerebral cavities and corresponding decreases in the cortex. Brain scans reveal abnormal activity in the frontal lobes, thalamus, and amygdala. Malfunctions in multiple brain regions and their connections apparently interact to produce the symptoms of schizophrenia. Research support is mounting for the causal effects of a virus suffered in mid-pregnancy.

OBJECTIVE 51-4 | **Discuss the evidence for a genetic contribution to the development of schizophrenia.**
The odds of developing schizophrenia are approximately 1 in 100 in the general population; 1 in 10 if a family member has it; and 1 in 2 if an identical twin has the disorder. Adoption studies show that an adopted child's chances of developing the disorder are greater if the biological parents have schizophrenia, but not if the adopted parents have it. But 50 percent of identical twins whose co-twin has schizophrenia do not develop the condition themselves, demonstrating that genetics is not the sole cause of this disorder.

OBJECTIVE 51-5 | **Describe some psychological factors that may be early warning signs of schizophrenia in children.**
No environmental event can by itself trigger schizophrenia, but some things may increase the risk in those genetically predisposed to the disorder. Early warning signs of schizophrenia include having a mother whose schizophrenia was severe and long-lasting; birth complications; separation from parents; short attention span and poor muscle coordination; disruptive or withdrawn behavior; emotional unpredictability; and poor peer relations and solo play.

TERMS AND CONCEPTS TO REMEMBER

schizophrenia, p. 51-0   delusions, p. 51-0

TEST YOURSELF

1. What are the five subtypes of schizophrenia?

(Answer in Appendix B.)

ASK YOURSELF

1. Civil libertarians defend the right of schizophrenia patients not to be hospitalized against their will. E. Fuller Torrey (1998), a psychiatrist who views schizophrenia as a brain disorder, objects: "If a person with Alzheimer's wanted to go outside with no shoes in the winter, we wouldn't say, 'That's fine, he should have free choice.'" Do you think patients with schizophrenia should be hospitalized and treated against their will? Or do they always have the right to live free, even if under bridges or in shelters?

>WEB

Multiple-choice *self-tests* and more may be found at www.worthpublishers.com/myers.

ANOTHER VOICE ON: THERAPY

JACK RIDL (b. 1944) FROM "THE HEALERS," POEMS FROM *THE SAME GHOST AND BETWEEN*

My father guessed at work.
He gave me things to do.
We strangled weeds from the flower bed,
Washed the car,
Walked the dog.

My mother guessed at a mother's love.
She went back to tucking sheets
Around me as I lay awake in bed.
She pulled her fingers through my hair.
She turned away. She held me.

My good friend guessed at leaving town.
So we lugged gravel, grinding gears
Up and down the western Pennsylvania
   hills.
We'd raise the bed and listen
To the gravel rush into a silent pile.

My preacher guessed at God.
He knew my answer; spread my sin;
Prayed; asked me to pray;
Sprinkled oil on my head;
Pronounced me of this world.

My doctor guessed at shock.
Strapped me down.
Hooked electrodes to my head.
Baptized me with volts.

I guessed at empty space
And all the breath
That I could spill to fill it up.

Therapy

Today we comprehend deep outer space and can state with certainty the chemical composition of Jupiter's atmosphere. But in understanding and treating the disturbances of deep inner space—the psychological disorders that continue to plague humankind—we are only beginning to make real progress. In the 2200 years since Eratosthenes correctly estimated the Earth's circumference, we have charted the heavens, explored our solar system, reconstructed the basic history of life, cracked the genetic code, and eliminated or found cures for all sorts of diseases. Meanwhile, we have treated psychological disorders with a bewildering variety of harsh and gentle methods: by cutting holes in the head and by giving warm baths and massages; by restraining, bleeding, or "beating the devil" out of people; by placing them in sunny, serene environments; by administering drugs and electric shocks; and by talking—talking about childhood experiences, about current feelings, about maladaptive thoughts and behaviors.

The transition from brutal to gentler treatments occurred thanks to the efforts of reformers such as Philippe Pinel in France and Dorothea Dix in the United States, Canada, and Scotland. Both advocated constructing mental hospitals to offer more humane methods of treatment. However, the introduction of therapeutic drugs and community-based treatment programs has largely emptied mental health hospitals since the mid-1950s.

Culver Pictures

Dorothea Dix (1802–1887)
"I . . . call your attention to the state of the Insane Persons confined within this Commonwealth, in cages."

Mental health therapies can be classified into two main categories: the psychological therapies (Modules 52 and 53) and the biomedical therapies (Module 54). Today, the favored treatment depends on both the disorder and the therapist's viewpoint.

The history of treatment

The engraving (below right) by William Hogarth (1697–1764) of London's St. Mary of Bethlehem hospital (commonly called Bedlam) depicts the treatment of mental disorders in the eighteenth century. Visitors paid to gawk at the patients as if they were viewing zoo animals. The chair on the left was designed by Benjamin Rush (1746–1813) "for the benefit of maniacal patients." Rush, a founder of the movement for more humane treatment of the mentally ill, believed they required restraint to regain their sensibilities.

The Granger Collection

The Granger Collection

52

The Psychological Therapies

OBJECTIVE 52-1 | Define *psychotherapy,* and explain what we mean by an *eclectic approach* to therapy.

Psychological therapy, or **psychotherapy** is "a planned emotionally charged, confiding interaction between a trained, socially sanctioned healer and a sufferer" (Frank, 1982). It is often the preferred treatment for disorders that researchers believe are learned, such as phobias. Among the dozens of types of psychotherapy, we will look at only the most influential. Each is built on one or more of psychology's major theories: psychoanalytic, humanistic, behavioral, and cognitive. We will also consider the use of some of these techniques in groups.

Depending on the client and the problem, some therapists—particularly the many using a biopsychosocial approach—draw from a variety of techniques. Indeed, half of all psychotherapists have described themselves as taking an **eclectic approach,** by using a blend of therapies (Beitman & others, 1989; Castonguay & Goldfried, 1994). Closely related to eclecticism is *psychotherapy integration.* Rather than picking and choosing methods, integration advocates aim to combine them into a single, coherent system.

Psychoanalysis

OBJECTIVE 52-2 | Define *psychoanalysis,* and discuss the aims of this form of therapy.

Although few clinicians today practice therapy as Sigmund Freud did, many of his techniques and assumptions survive, especially in the *psychodynamic therapies* (discussed later in this module). Freudian terminology has also crept into our modern vocabulary. Freud's **psychoanalysis** was the first of the psychological therapies.

Aims

Sigmund Freud assumed that many psychological problems are fueled by childhood's residue of repressed impulses and conflicts. It is therefore the psychoanalyst's job to bring these repressed feelings into conscious awareness where the patient can deal with them. By gaining insight into the origins of the disorder—by fulfilling the ancient imperative to "know thyself" in a deep way—patients work through the buried feelings and take responsibility for their own growth. Psychoanalytic theory presumes that healthier, less anxious living becomes possible when people release the energy they had previously devoted to id-ego-superego conflicts.

Freud's consulting room
Freud's office was rich with antiquities from around the world, including artwork related to his ideas about unconscious motives. His famous couch, piled high with pillows, placed patients in a comfortable reclining position facing away from him to help them focus inward.

Edmund Engelman

Methods

OBJECTIVE 52-3 | Describe some of the methods used in psychoanalysis, and list some criticisms of this form of therapy.

Psychoanalysis is historical reconstruction. It aims to unearth the past in hope of unmasking the present. But how?

When Freud discarded hypnosis as unreliable, he turned to *free association*. Imagine yourself as a patient using free association. First, you relax, perhaps by lying on a couch. To help you focus attention on your own thoughts and feelings, the psychoanalyst may sit out of your line of vision. You say aloud whatever comes to your mind from moment to moment, which may be a childhood memory, a dream, or a recent experience. It sounds easy, but soon you notice how often you edit your thoughts as you speak, omitting what seems trivial, irrelevant, or shameful. Even in the safe presence of the analyst, you may pause momentarily before uttering an embarrassing thought. You may make a joking remark or change the subject to something less threatening. Sometimes your mind goes blank or you find yourself unable to remember important details.

To the psychoanalyst, these blocks in the flow of your free associations indicate **resistance.** They hint that anxiety lurks and you are defending against sensitive material. The analyst will want to make you aware of your resistances and then **interpret** their meaning, providing *insight* into your underlying wishes, feelings, and conflicts. This interpretation—of, say, your not wanting to talk about your mother—may, if offered at the right moment, illuminate what you are avoiding and demonstrate how this resistance fits with other pieces of your psychological puzzle.

Freud believed that another clue to unconscious conflicts is your dreams' *latent content*—their underlying but censored meaning. Thus, after inviting you to report a dream, the analyst may offer a dream analysis, suggesting its meaning.

During many such sessions you will probably disclose to your analyst more of yourself than you have ever revealed to anyone else. Because psychoanalytic theory emphasizes the formative power of childhood experiences, much of what you reveal will pertain to your earliest memories. You may find yourself experiencing strong positive or negative feelings for your analyst. Freud would say you are **transferring** to the analyst your strongest feelings from earlier relationships with family members or other important people. Analysts and other therapists believe that transference exposes feelings that a person has previously defended against, such as dependency or mingled love and anger, giving you a belated chance to work through them with your analyst's help. But psychoanalysis is not just about excavating your childhood past. By examining your feelings toward the analyst you may also gain insight into your current relationships.

Critics point out that psychoanalysts' interpretations are hard to refute because they cannot be proven or disproven, a criticism psychoanalysts acknowledge. But they insist that interpretations often are a great help to patients. Psychoanalysis is therapy, not science.

Traditional psychoanalysis takes time, up to several years of several sessions a week, and it is expensive. (Three times a week for just two

- **psychotherapy** an emotionally charged, confiding interaction between a trained therapist and someone who suffers from psychological difficulties.
- **eclectic approach** an approach to psychotherapy that, depending on the client's problems, uses techniques from various forms of therapy.
- **psychoanalysis** Sigmund Freud's therapeutic technique. Freud believed the patient's free associations, resistances, dreams, and transferences—and the therapist's interpretations of them—released previously repressed feelings, allowing the patient to gain self-insight.
- **resistance** in psychoanalysis, the blocking from consciousness of anxiety-laden material.
- **interpretation** in psychoanalysis, the analyst's noting supposed dream meanings, resistances, and other significant behaviors and events in order to promote insight.
- **transference** in psychoanalysis, the patient's transfer to the analyst of emotions linked with other relationships (such as love or hatred for a parent).

> " I haven't seen my analyst in 200 years. He was a strict Freudian. If I'd been going all this time, I'd probably almost be cured by now."
>
> Woody Allen, after awakening from suspended animation in the movie *Sleeper*

"In the mental-health profession, we try to avoid negative labels, like 'a hundred and fifty bucks an hour—that's *crazy!*' or 'three fifty-minute sessions a week—that's *insane!*'"

years at more than $100 per hour comes to at least $30,000.) This helps explain why, outside of France, Germany, Quebec, and New York City, relatively few therapists offer it (Goode, 2003). Indeed, in the United States, managed health care has severely limited the types and length of mental health services that may be covered by insurance. This has contributed to a trend toward much shorter treatment periods and many fewer instances of in-patient care.

Psychodynamic Therapy

OBJECTIVE 52-4 | Contrast psychodynamic therapy and interpersonal therapy with traditional psychoanalysis.

Influenced by Freud, *psychodynamic* therapists try to understand a patient's current symptoms by focusing on themes across important relationships, including childhood experiences and the therapist relationship. They also help the person explore and gain perspective on defended-against thoughts and feelings. But these therapists may talk to the patient face to face (rather than out of the line of vision), once a week (rather than several times weekly), and for only a few weeks or months (rather than several years).

No brief excerpt can exemplify the way psychodynamic therapy interprets a patient's conflict. But we can illustrate psychodynamic therapists' goal of enabling insight by looking for common, recurring themes, especially in relationships. In the following interaction, therapist David Malan responds to all he has heard from a depressed patient by suggesting insights into her problems. Note how Malan interprets the woman's earlier remarks (when she did most of the talking) and suggests that her relationship with him reveals a characteristic pattern of behavior (1978, pp. 133–134).

Michael Newman/PhotoEdit, Inc.

Face-to-face therapy

In this type of therapy session, the couch has disappeared. But the influence of psychoanalytic theory may not have, especially if the therapist probes for the origin of the patient's symptoms by seeking information from the patient's childhood.

Malan: *I get the feeling that you're the sort of person who needs to keep active. If you don't keep active, then something goes wrong. Is that true?*

Patient: *Yes.*

Malan: *I get a second feeling about you and that is that you must, underneath all this, have an awful lot of very strong and upsetting feelings. Somehow they're there but you aren't really quite in touch with them. Isn't this right? I feel you've been like that as long as you can remember.*

Patient: *For quite a few years, whenever I really sat down and thought about it I got depressed, so I tried not to think about it.*

Malan: *You see, you've established a pattern, haven't you? You're even like that here with me, because in spite of the fact that you're in some trouble and you feel that the bottom is falling out of your world, the way you're telling me this is just as if there wasn't anything wrong.*

Interpersonal psychotherapy, a brief (12- to 16-session) variation of psychodynamic therapy, has been effective in treating depression (Weissman, 1999). Interpersonal psychotherapy aims to help people gain insight into the roots of their difficulties, but its goal is symptom relief in the here and now, not overall personality change. Rather than focusing mostly on undoing past hurts and offering interpretations, the therapist focuses primarily on current relationships and on helping people improve their relationship skills.

The case of Anna (not her real name), a 34-year-old married professional, illustrates these goals. Five months after receiving a promotion, with accompanying increased responsibilities and longer hours, Anna experienced increased tensions with her husband over his wish for a second child. She began feeling depressed, had trouble sleeping, became irritable, and was gaining weight. A typical psychodynamic therapist might have helped Anna gain insight into her angry impulses and her defenses against anger. An interpersonal therapist similarly wanted Anna to gain these insights, but also engaged her thinking on more immediate issues—how she could balance work and home, resolve the dispute with her husband, and express her emotions more effectively (Markowitz & others, 1998).

"You say, 'Off with her head' but what I'm hearing is, 'I feel neglected.'"

Humanistic Therapies

OBJECTIVE 52-5 | Identify the basic characteristics of the humanistic therapies, and describe the specific goals and techniques of Carl Rogers' client-centered therapy.

The humanistic perspective has emphasized people's inherent potential for self-fulfillment. Not surprisingly, humanistic therapists aim to boost self-fulfillment by helping people grow in self-awareness and self-acceptance. Like psychoanalytic therapies, humanistic therapies attempt to reduce the conflicts that are impeding natural developmental growth. But unlike many psychoanalytic therapists, humanistic therapists tend to focus on

- the *present* and *future* more than the past. They explore feelings as they occur, rather than achieving insights into the childhood origins of the feelings.
- *conscious* rather than unconscious thoughts.
- taking immediate *responsibility* for one's feelings and actions, rather than uncovering hidden determinants.
- promoting growth instead of curing illness. Thus, those in therapy became "clients" rather than "patients" (a label change that many therapists have followed).

One widely used humanistic technique has been Carl Rogers' (1961, 1980) **client-centered therapy.** A client-centered therapist focuses on the person's conscious self-perceptions rather than on the therapist's own interpretations. The therapist listens, without judging or interpreting, and refrains from directing the client toward certain insights, a strategy labeled *nondirective therapy.*

Believing that most people already possess the resources for growth, Rogers encouraged therapists to exhibit *genuineness, acceptance,* and *empathy.* When therapists drop their facades and genuinely express their true feelings, when they enable their

■ **client-centered therapy** a humanistic therapy, developed by Carl Rogers, in which the therapist uses techniques such as active listening within a genuine, accepting, empathic environment to facilitate clients' growth. (Also called *person-centered therapy.*)

Active listening
Carl Rogers (right) empathized with a client during this group therapy session.

■ **active listening** empathic listening in which the listener echoes, restates, and clarifies. A feature of Rogers' client-centered therapy.

"We have two ears and one mouth that we may listen the more and talk the less."

Zeno, 335–263 B.C., *Diogenes Laertius*

clients to feel unconditionally accepted, and when they empathically sense and reflect their clients' feelings, the clients may deepen their self-understanding and self-acceptance (Hill & Nakayama, 2000). As Rogers (1980, p. 10) explained,

> Hearing has consequences. When I truly hear a person and the meanings that are important to him at that moment, hearing not simply his words, but him, and when I let him know that I have heard his own private personal meanings, many things happen. There is first of all a grateful look. He feels released. He wants to tell me more about his world. He surges forth in a new sense of freedom. He becomes more open to the process of change.
>
> I have often noticed that the more deeply I hear the meanings of the person, the more there is that happens. Almost always, when a person realizes he has been deeply heard, his eyes moisten. I think in some real sense he is weeping for joy. It is as though he were saying, "Thank God, somebody heard me. Someone knows what it's like to be me."

"Hearing" refers to Rogers' technique of **active listening**—echoing, restating, and seeking clarification of what the person expresses (verbally or nonverbally) and acknowledging the expressed feelings. Active listening is now an accepted part of therapeutic counseling practices in many schools, colleges, and clinics. The counselor listens attentively and interrupts only to restate and confirm the client's feelings, to accept what the client is expressing, or to seek clarification. The following brief excerpt between Rogers and a male client illustrates how he sought to provide a psychological mirror that would help clients see themselves more clearly.

Client: *I just ain't no good to nobody, never was, and never will be.*

Rogers: *Feeling that now, hm? That you're just no good to yourself, no good to anybody. Never will be any good to anybody. Just that you're completely worthless, huh?—Those really are lousy feelings. Just feel that you're no good at all, hm?*

Client: *Yeah.* (Muttering in low, discouraged voice) *That's what this guy I went to town with just the other day told me.*

Rogers: *This guy that you went to town with really told you that you were no good? Is that what you're saying? Did I get that right?*

Client: *M-hm.*

Rogers: *I guess the meaning of that if I get it right is that here's somebody that—meant something to you and what does he think of you? Why, he's told you that he thinks you're no good at all. And that just really knocks the props out from under you.* (Client weeps quietly.) *It just brings the tears.* (Silence of 20 seconds)

Client: (Rather defiantly) *I don't care though.*

Rogers: *You tell yourself you don't care at all, but somehow I guess some part of you cares because some part of you weeps over it.* (1984, p. 167 Meador & Rogers)

Can a therapist be a perfect mirror, without selecting and interpreting what is reflected? Rogers conceded that one cannot be *totally* nondirective. Nevertheless, he believed that the therapist's most important contribution is to accept and understand the client. Given a nonjudgmental, grace-filled environment that provides *unconditional positive regard*, people may accept even their worst traits and feel valued and whole.

If you want to listen more actively in your own relationships, three hints may help:

1. *Paraphrase.* Check your understandings by summarizing the speaker's words in your own words.
2. *Invite clarification.* "What might be an example of that?" may encourage the speaker to say more.
3. *Reflect feelings.* "It sounds frustrating" might mirror what you're sensing from the speaker's body language and intensity.

Behavior Therapies

OBJECTIVE 52-6 | Explain how the basic assumption of behavior therapy differs from those of traditional psychoanalytic and humanistic therapies.

The therapies we have considered so far assume that many psychological problems diminish as self-awareness grows. Traditional psychoanalysts expect problems to subside as people gain insight into their unresolved and unconscious tensions. Humanistic therapists expect problems to abate as people get in touch with their feelings. Behavior therapists, however, doubt the healing power of self-awareness. They assume problem behaviors *are* the problems. For example, you can become aware of why you are highly anxious during exams and still be anxious. **Behavior therapy** applies learning principles to eliminate a troubling behavior. To treat phobias or sexual disorders, behavior therapists do not delve deeply below the surface looking for inner causes. They view maladaptive symptoms, such as anxiety, as learned behaviors that can be replaced with constructive behaviors.

Classical Conditioning Techniques

OBJECTIVE 52-7 | Define *counterconditioning*, and describe the techniques used in exposure therapies and aversive conditioning.

One cluster of behavior therapies derives from principles developed in Ivan Pavlov's early-twentieth-century conditioning experiments. As Pavlov and others showed, we learn various behaviors and emotions through classical conditioning. So, are maladaptive symptoms examples of conditioned responses? If so, might reconditioning be a solution? Learning theorist O. H. Mowrer developed one such conditioning therapy for chronic bed-wetters. The child sleeps on a liquid-sensitive pad connected to an alarm. Moisture on the pad triggers the alarm, waking the child. With sufficient repetition, this association of urinary relaxation with waking up stops the bed-wetting. In three out of four cases the treatment is effective, and the success provides a boost to the child's self-image (Christophersen & Edwards, 1992; Houts & others, 1994).

Another example: If a claustrophobic fear of elevators is a learned aversion to the stimulus of being in a confined space, then might one unlearn the fear by counterconditioning the fear response? **Counterconditioning** pairs the trigger stimulus with a new response that is incompatible with fear. And indeed, behavior therapists have successfully counterconditioned this fear by repeatedly pairing the enclosed space of the elevator with a relaxed response may displace the fear response. In such therapy, two specific counterconditioning techniques—*exposure therapies* and *aversive conditioning* may be used.

Exposure Therapies

Picture this scene reported in 1924 by Mary Cover Jones, an associate of the behaviorist John B. Watson: Three-year-old Peter is petrified of rabbits and other furry objects. Peter's fear arose during the course of his life at home and is quite intense. Jones aims to replace Peter's fear of rabbits with a conditioned response that is incompatible with fear. Her strategy is to associate the fear-evoking rabbit with the pleasurable, relaxed response associated with eating.

As Peter begins his midafternoon snack, Jones introduces a caged rabbit on the other side of the huge room. Peter, eagerly munching away on his crackers and drinking his milk, hardly notices. On succeeding days, she gradually moves the rabbit closer and closer. Within two months, Peter is tolerating the rabbit in his lap, even stroking it while he eats. Moreover, his

■ **behavior therapy** therapy that applies learning principles to the elimination of unwanted behaviors.

■ **counterconditioning** a behavior therapy procedure that conditions new responses to stimuli that trigger unwanted behaviors; based on classical conditioning. Includes *exposure therapy* and *aversive conditioning*.

What might a psychoanalyst say about this therapy for bed-wetting? How might a behavior therapist reply?

Hoping to fly free of fear
Some airlines offer programs that ease fear of flying through education and gradual exposure to simulated and actual air travel. Here a pilot explains the functions of the cockpit equipment to participants.

N. Rown/The Image Works

THE FAR SIDE® BY GARY LARSON

Professor Gallagher and his controversial technique of simultaneously confronting the fear of heights, snakes, and the dark.

fear of other furry objects subsides as well, having been "countered," or replaced, by a relaxed state that cannot coexist with fear (Fisher, 1984; Jones, 1924).

Unfortunately for those who might have been helped by her counterconditioning procedures, Jones' story of Peter and the rabbit did not immediately become part of psychology's lore. It was not until more than 30 years later that psychiatrist Joseph Wolpe (1958; Wolpe & Plaud, 1997) refined Jones' technique into what has become the most widely used method of behavior therapy: **exposure therapies,** which expose people to what they normally avoid. As people can habituate to the sound of a train passing their new apartment, so, with repeated exposure, can they become less anxiously responsive to things that once petrified them (Deacon & Abramowitz, 2004).

One widely used exposure therapy is **systematic desensitization.** Wolpe assumed, as did Jones, that you cannot be simultaneously anxious and relaxed. Therefore, if you can repeatedly relax when facing anxiety-provoking stimuli, you can gradually eliminate your anxiety. The trick is to proceed gradually.

Let's see how this might work with a common phobia. Imagine yourself afraid of public speaking. A behavior therapist might first ask for your help in constructing a hierarchy of anxiety-triggering speaking situations. Your anxiety hierarchy could range from mildly anxiety-provoking situations, such as speaking up in a small group of friends, to panic-provoking situations, such as having to address a large audience.

Using *progressive relaxation,* the therapist trains you to relax one muscle group after another, until you achieve a drowsy state of complete relaxation and comfort. Then the therapist asks you to imagine, with your eyes closed, a mildly anxiety-arousing situation: You are having coffee with a group of friends and are trying to decide whether to speak up. If imagining the scene causes you to feel any anxiety, you signal your tension by raising your finger, and the therapist instructs you to switch off the mental image and go back to deep relaxation. This imagined scene is repeatedly paired with relaxation until you feel no trace of anxiety.

The therapist progresses up the constructed anxiety hierarchy, using the relaxed state to desensitize you to each imagined situation. After several sessions, you practice what you had imagined in actual situations, beginning with relatively easy tasks and gradually moving to more anxiety-filled ones. Conquering your anxiety in an actual situation, not just in your imagination, raises your self-confidence (Foa & Kozak, 1986; Williams, 1987). Eventually, you may even become a confident public speaker.

When the anxiety-arousing situation is too expensive, difficult, or embarrassing to re-create, **virtual reality exposure therapy** offers an efficient middle ground. Wearing a head-mounted display unit that projects a three-dimensional virtual world, you would view a lifelike series of scenes. As your head turns, motion sensors adjust the scene. Experiments led by several research teams have treated people who fear flying, fear heights, fear particular animals, and fear public speaking (Gershon & others, 2002; Rothbaum & others, 2002). People who fear flying, for example, can peer out a virtual window of a simulated plane, feel vibrations, and hear the engine roar as the plane taxis down the runway and takes off. In initial experiments, those experiencing virtual reality exposure therapy have had greater relief from their fears—in real life—than have those in control groups (Hoffman, 2004; Krijn & others, 2004).

Virtual reality exposure therapy

Within the confines of a room, virtual reality technology exposes people to vivid simulations of feared stimuli, such as a plane's takeoff.

Aversive Conditioning

In systematic desensitization, the goal is substituting a positive (relaxed) response for a negative (fearful) response to a *harmless* stimulus. In **aversive conditioning,** the goal is substituting a negative (aversive) response for a positive response to a *harmful* stimulus (such as alcohol). Thus, aversive conditioning is the reverse of systematic desensitization—it seeks to condition an aversion to something the client *should* avoid.

The procedure is simple: It associates the unwanted behavior with unpleasant feelings. To treat nail biting, one can paint the fingernails with a yucky-tasting nail polish (Baskind, 1997). To treat alcoholism, an aversion therapist offers the client appealing drinks laced with a drug that produces severe nausea. By linking alcohol with violent nausea, the therapist seeks to transform the person's reaction to alcohol from positive to negative (**FIGURE 52.1**).

Does aversive conditioning work? In the short run it may. Arthur Wiens and Carol Menustik (1983) studied 685 patients with alcoholism who completed an aversion therapy program at a Portland, Oregon, hospital. One year later, after returning for several booster treatments of alcohol-sickness pairings, 63 percent were still successfully abstaining. But after three years, only 33 percent had remained abstinent.

The problem is that in therapy (as in research), cognition influences conditioning. People know that outside the therapist's office they can drink without fear of nausea. Their ability to discriminate between the aversive conditioning situation and all other situations can limit the treatment's effectiveness. Thus, aversive conditioning is often used in combination with other treatments.

Operant Conditioning

OBJECTIVE 52-8 | State the main premise of therapy based on operant conditioning principles, and describe the views of proponents and critics of behavior modification.

The work of B.F. Skinner and others teaches us a basic principle of operant conditioning: Voluntary behaviors are strongly influenced by their consequences. This simple fact enables behavior therapists to practice *behavior modification*—to reinforce desired behaviors and to withhold reinforcement for undesired behaviors or to punish them. Using operant conditioning to solve specific behavior problems has raised hopes for some cases thought to be hopeless. Children with mental retardation have been taught to care for themselves. Socially withdrawn children with autism have learned to interact. People with schizophrenia have been helped to behave more rationally in their hospital ward. In such cases, therapists use positive reinforcers to shape behavior in a step-by-step manner, rewarding closer and closer approximations of the desired behavior.

In extreme cases, treatment must be intensive. In one study, 19 withdrawn, uncommunicative 3-year-olds with autism participated in a 2-year program in which their parents spent 40 hours each week attempting to shape their behavior (Lovaas, 1987). The combination of positively reinforcing desired behaviors and ignoring or punishing aggressive and self-abusive behaviors worked wonders for some. By first grade, 9 of the 19 children were functioning successfully in school and exhibiting normal intelligence. In a group of 40 comparable children who did not undergo this treatment, only one showed similar improvement.

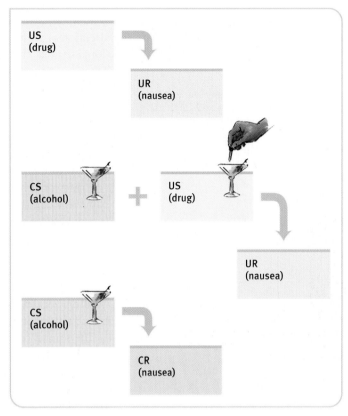

FIGURE **52.1**
Aversion therapy for alcoholism
After repeatedly imbibing an alcoholic drink mixed with a drug that produces severe nausea, some people with a history of alcohol abuse develop at least a temporary conditioned aversion to alcohol.

■ **exposure therapies** behavioral techniques, such as *systematic desensitization*, that treat anxieties by exposing people (in imagination or actuality) to the things they fear and avoid.

■ **systematic desensitization** a type of counterconditioning that associates a pleasant relaxed state with gradually increasing anxiety-triggering stimuli. Commonly used to treat phobias.

■ **virtual reality exposure therapy** An anxiety treatment that progressively exposes people to simulations of their greatest fears, such as airplane flying, spiders, or public speaking.

■ **aversive conditioning** a type of counterconditioning that associates an unpleasant state (such as nausea) with an unwanted behavior (such as drinking alcohol).

token economy an operant conditioning procedure in which people earn a token of some sort for exhibiting a desired behavior and can later exchange the tokens for various privileges or treats.

cognitive therapy therapy that teaches people new, more adaptive ways of thinking and acting; based on the assumption that thoughts intervene between events and our emotional reactions.

Rewards used to modify behavior vary. For some people, the reinforcing power of attention or praise is sufficient. Others require concrete rewards, such as food. In institutional settings, therapists may create a **token economy.** When people display appropriate behavior, such as getting out of bed, washing, dressing, eating, talking coherently, cleaning up their rooms, or playing cooperatively, they receive a token or plastic coin as a positive reinforcer. Later, they can exchange their accumulated tokens for various rewards, such as candy, watching television, trips to town, or better living quarters. Token economies have been successfully applied in various settings (homes, classrooms, hospitals, institutions for the delinquent) and among members of various populations (including disturbed children and people with schizophrenia and other mental disabilities).

Critics of behavior modification express two concerns. The first is practical: What happens when the reinforcers stop, as when the person leaves the institution? Could the person become so dependent on extrinsic rewards that the appropriate behaviors quickly disappear? If so, how can therapists make the appropriate behaviors durable? Proponents of behavior modification respond that they may wean patients from the tokens by shifting them toward other rewards, such as social approval, more typical of life outside the institution. They may also train people to behave in ways that are intrinsically rewarding. For example, as a withdrawn person becomes more socially competent, the intrinsic satisfactions of social interaction may help the person maintain the behavior.

The second concern is ethical: Is it right for one human to control another's behavior? Those who set up token economies may deprive people of something they desire and then decide which behaviors they will reinforce. To critics, the whole behavior modification process has an authoritarian taint. So why not reinforce adaptive behavior instead? They argue that treatment with positive rewards is more humane than being institutionalized or punished, and that the right to effective treatment and to an improved life justifies temporary deprivation. Advocates reply that some clients request the therapy. Moreover, control already exists; rewards and punishers are already maintaining destructive behavior patterns.

Cognitive Therapies

OBJECTIVE **52-9** | Contrast cognitive therapy and cognitive-behavior therapy, and give some examples of cognitive therapy for depression.

We have seen how behavior therapists treat specific fears and problem behaviors. But how do they deal with major depression? Or with general anxiety, in which anxiety has no focus and developing a hierarchy of anxiety-triggering situations is difficult? Behavior therapists treating these less clearly defined psychological problems have had help from the same *cognitive revolution* that has profoundly changed other areas of psychology during the last five decades.

Cognitive therapy for eating disorders aided by journaling
Cognitive therapists guide people toward new ways of explaining their good and bad experiences. By recording each day's positive events, and how one enabled them, for example, people may become more mindful of their self-control.

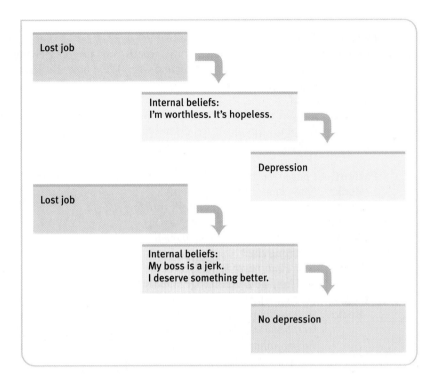

FIGURE 52.2
A cognitive perspective on psychological disorders
The person's emotional reactions are produced not directly by the event but by the person's thoughts in response to the event.

The **cognitive therapies** assume that our thinking colors our feelings (**FIGURE 52.2**), that between the event and our response lies the mind. Self-blaming and overgeneralized explanations of bad events are often an integral part of the vicious cycle of depression. The person experiencing depression interprets a suggestion as criticism, disagreement as dislike, praise as flattery, friendliness as pity. Ruminating on such thoughts sustains the bad mood. If depressed thinking patterns can be learned, then surely they can be replaced. Cognitive therapists therefore try in various ways to teach people new, more constructive ways of thinking. If people are miserable, they can be helped to change their minds.

> "Life does not consist mainly, or even largely, of facts and happenings. It consists mainly of the storm of thoughts that are forever blowing through one's mind."
> Mark Twain, 1835–1910

Cognitive Therapy for Depression

Cognitive therapist Aaron Beck was originally trained in Freudian techniques. As Beck analyzed the dreams of people with depression, he found recurring negative themes of loss, rejection, and abandonment that extended into their waking thoughts. Such negativity even extends into therapy, as clients recall and rehearse their failings and worst impulses (Kelly, 2000). So with cognitive therapy Beck and his colleagues (1979) instead have sought to reverse clients' catastrophizing beliefs about themselves, their situations, and their futures. With gentle questioning that aims to help people discover their irrationalities, they persuade depressed people to take off the dark glasses through which they view life (Beck & others, 1979, pp. 145–146):

Patient: *I agree with the descriptions of me but I guess I don't agree that the way I think makes me depressed.*

Beck: *How do you understand it?*

Patient: *I get depressed when things go wrong. Like when I fail a test.*

Beck: *How can failing a test make you depressed?*

Patient: *Well, if I fail I'll never get into law school.*

Beck: *So failing the test means a lot to you. But if failing a test could drive people into clinical depression, wouldn't you expect everyone who failed the test to have a depression? . . . Did everyone who failed get depressed enough to require treatment?*

Patient: *No, but it depends on how important the test was to the person.*

Beck: *Right, and who decides the importance?*

Patient:	*I do.*
Beck:	*And so, what we have to examine is your way of viewing the test (or the way that you think about the test) and how it affects your chances of getting into law school. Do you agree?*
Patient:	*Right.*
Beck:	*Do you agree that the way you interpret the results of the test will affect you? You might feel depressed, you might have trouble sleeping, not feel like eating, and you might even wonder if you should drop out of the course.*
Patient:	*I have been thinking that I wasn't going to make it. Yes, I agree.*
Beck:	*Now what did failing mean?*
Patient:	*(tearful) That I couldn't get into law school.*
Beck:	*And what does that mean to you?*
Patient:	*That I'm just not smart enough.*
Beck:	*Anything else?*
Patient:	*That I can never be happy.*
Beck:	*And how do these thoughts make you feel?*
Patient:	*Very unhappy.*
Beck:	*So it is the meaning of failing a test that makes you very unhappy. In fact, believing that you can never be happy is a powerful factor in producing unhappiness. So, you get yourself into a trap—by definition, failure to get into law school equals "I can never be happy."*

Another variety of cognitive therapy builds on the finding that depressed people do not exhibit the self-serving bias (seeing oneself as better than others) common in nondepressed people. Instead, they often attribute their failures to themselves and attribute their successes to external circumstances. Thus, Adele Rabin and her colleagues (1986) explained to 235 depressed adults the advantages of interpreting events as nondepressed people do. She then trained the participants to reform their habitually negative patterns of thinking and labeling. For example, she had them record each day's positive events and write down how they contributed to each. Compared with people who remained on a waiting list for therapy for depression, those who went through the positive-thinking exercises found their depression dropped dramatically (**FIGURE 52.3**). The more people change their negative thinking styles, the more their mood lifts (Seligman, 1991).

Here is another example: We often think in words. Therefore, getting people to change what they say to themselves is an effective way to change their thinking. Perhaps you can identify with the anxious students who before an exam make matters worse with self-defeating thoughts: "This exam's probably going to be impossible. All these other students seem so relaxed and confident. I wish I were better prepared. Anyhow, I'm so nervous I'll forget everything." To change such negative self-talk, Donald Meichenbaum (1977, 1985) has offered *stress inoculation training,* teaching people to restructure their thinking in stressful situations. Sometimes it may be enough simply to say more positive things to oneself: "Relax. The exam may be hard, but it will be hard for everyone else, too. I studied harder than most people. Besides, I don't need a perfect score to get a good grade." In experiments, depression-prone children and college students exhibit a halved rate of future depression after being trained to dispute their negative thoughts (Seligman, 2002). To a great extent, it *is* the thought that counts.

Knowing that there is two-way traffic between depressed mood and negative thinking, the Penn Optimism Program reached out to 9- to 13-year-old children targeted as at risk for depression. The program puts children through 12 small-group sessions, each lasting two hours, in which they learn to tune into their thoughts when facing tough situations and to imagine alternatives to negative thoughts. The leader might, for example,

FIGURE 52.3

Cognitive therapy for depression
Participants in a program that trained them to think more as nondepressed people do— noticing and taking personal credit for good events and not taking blame for, or overgeneralizing from, bad events—experienced dramatic declines in depression. (From Rabin & others, 1986.)

PEANUTS

present a cartoon depicting a child being called a name and invite the children to brain-storm positive ways to cope. In early experiments, the training halved the proportion of children suffering depression for up to two ensuing years (Gillham & others, 1995).

Cognitive therapists often combine the reversal of self-defeating thinking with efforts to modify behavior. This integrated therapy, called **cognitive-behavior therapy**, aims to alter the way people act (behavior therapy) and to alter the way they think (cognitive therapy). It seeks to make people aware of their irrational negative thinking, to replace it with new ways of thinking, *and* to practice the more positive approach in everyday settings.

In one study, for example, people with obsessive-compulsive behaviors learned to relabel their compulsive thoughts (Schwartz & others, 1996). Feeling the urge to wash their hands again, they would tell themselves, "I'm having a compulsive urge," and attribute it to their brain's abnormal activity, as shown in PET scans. Instead of giving in to the urge, they then engaged for 15 minutes in an enjoyable, alternative behavior, such as practicing an instrument, taking a walk, or gardening. This helped "unstick" the brain by shifting attention and engaging other parts of the brain. For two or three months, the weekly therapy sessions continued, with relabeling and re-focusing practice at home. By the study's end, most participants' symptoms had di-minished and their PET scans revealed normalized brain activity.

Group and Family Therapies

OBJECTIVE 52-10 | Discuss the rationale and benefits of group therapy, includ-ing family therapy.

Except for traditional psychoanalysis, the therapies we have considered may also occur in therapist-led small groups. Group therapy does not provide the same degree of thera-pist involvement with each client; however, it saves therapists' time and clients' money—and it often is no less effective than individual therapy (Fuhriman & Burlingame, 1994). Therapists frequently suggest group therapy for people experiencing family conflicts or those whose behavior is distressing to others. For up to 90 minutes a week, the therapist guides the interactions of 6 to 10 people as they engage issues and react to one another.

Group sessions also offer a unique benefit: The social context allows people both to discover that others have problems similar to their own and to receive feedback as they try out new ways of behaving. It can be a relief to find that you are not alone—to learn that others, despite their apparent composure, share your problems and your troublesome feelings. It can also be reassuring to hear that you yourself look poised even though you feel anxious and self-conscious.

One special type of group interaction, **family therapy,** assumes that no person is an island, that we live and grow in relation to others, especially our families. We struggle to differentiate ourselves from our families, but we also need to connect with them emotionally. Some of our problem behaviors arise from the tension between these two tendencies, which can create family stress. Clients often come to therapists seeking help in their relationships with family members.

■ **cognitive-behavior therapy** a popular integrated therapy that combines cognitive therapy (changing self-defeating thinking) with behavior therapy (changing behavior).

■ **family therapy** therapy that treats the family as a system. Views an individual's unwanted behaviors as influenced by or directed at other family members; attempts to guide family members toward positive relationships and improved communication.

Group therapy
This counselor works with troubled teens in groups, which enables the youths to feel less alone in their troubles and enables the counselor to assist more teens at lower cost.

With an estimated 1.8 million members worldwide, AA is said to be "the largest organization on Earth that nobody wanted to join" (Finlay, 2000).

Unlike most psychotherapy, which focuses on what happens inside the person's own skin, family therapists work with family groups to heal relationships and to mobilize family resources. Their aim is to help family members discover the role they play within their family's social system. A child's rebellion, for example, affects and is affected by other family tensions. Family therapists also attempt—usually with some success, research suggests (Hazelrigg & others, 1987; Shadish & others, 1993)—to open up communication within the family or to help family members discover new ways of preventing or resolving conflicts.

A wide range of people participate in self-help and support groups (Yalom, 1985). One analysis (Davison & others, 2000) of on-line support groups and more than 14,000 self-help groups reports that most support groups focus on stigmatized or hard-to-discuss illnesses. AIDS patients are 250 times more likely than hypertension patients to be in support groups. Those struggling with anorexia and alcoholism often join groups; those with migraines and ulcers do not. People with hearing loss have national organizations with local chapters; people with vision loss more often cope without such.

The grandparent of support groups, Alcoholics Anonymous (AA), reportedly has 87,000 groups worldwide (McKillop & others, 2003). Its famous 12-step strategy, emulated by many other self-help groups, asks members to admit their powerlessness, to seek help from a higher power and from one another, and (the twelfth step) to take the message to others in need of it. In one eight-year, $27 million investigation, people seeking treatment for alcoholism reduced their drinking sharply, although so did those assigned to cognitive-behavior therapy or to a "motivational therapy" (Project Match, 1997). The more AA meetings patients attend, the greater their alcohol abstinence. In one study of 2300 veterans who sought alcoholism treatment, a high level of AA involvement was followed by diminished alcohol problems (McKellar & others, 2003).

In an individualistic age, with more and more people living alone or feeling isolated, the popularity of support groups—for the addicted, the bereaved, the divorced, or simply those seeking fellowship and growth—seems to reflect a longing for community and connectedness. More than 100 million Americans belong to small religious, interest, or self-help groups that meet regularly—and 9 in 10 report that group members "support each other emotionally" (Gallup, 1994).

>> LEARNING OUTCOMES

The Psychological Therapies

OBJECTIVE 52-1 | Define *psychotherapy*, and explain what we mean by an *eclectic approach* to therapy.

Psychotherapy is an emotionally charged, confiding interaction between a trained therapist and someone suffering from psychological difficulties. An *eclectic approach* to psychotherapy uses techniques from various forms of therapy; psychotherapy integration attempts to combine a selection of assorted techniques into a single, coherent system.

OBJECTIVE 52-2 | Define *psychoanalysis*, and discuss the aims of this form of therapy.

Psychoanalysis is Sigmund Freud's therapeutic technique for helping people release previously repressed feelings and gain insight into current conflicts. Clinicians working from the psychoanalytic perspective try to help people gain insight into the unconscious origins of their disorders, work through the accompanying feelings, and take responsibility for their own growth.

OBJECTIVE 52-3 | Describe some of the methods used in psychoanalysis, and list some criticisms of this form of therapy.

Psychoanalysts may ask patients to *free associate* (saying aloud anything that comes to mind) and watch for pauses or diversions that may indicate *resistance* (the defensive blocking from consciousness of anxiety-laden material). Analysts may offer patients their interpretations of these instances of resistance, of dreams, and of other behaviors, such as *transference* (transferring to the therapist the strong feelings harbored against a family member or other significant person). Critics note that traditional psychoanalysis has relied on after-the-fact interpretations and repressed memories, and that it is time-consuming and very costly.

OBJECTIVE 52-4 | Contrast psychodynamic therapy and interpersonal therapy with traditional psychoanalysis.

Psychodynamic therapy has been influenced by traditional psychoanalysis but is briefer and less expensive. A psychodynamic therapist focuses on a patient's current conflicts and defenses by searching for themes common to many past and present important relationships, including (but not limited to) childhood experiences and interactions with the therapist. *Interpersonal therapy* (a brief 12- to 16-session form of psychodynamic therapy) deals primarily with current symptoms (such as depression) rather than the origins of unconscious conflicts.

OBJECTIVE 52-5 | **Identify the basic characteristics of the humanistic therapies, and describe the specific goals and techniques of Carl Rogers' client-centered therapy.**

Humanistic therapists focus on clients' present and future experiences, on conscious rather than unconscious thoughts, and on taking responsibility for one's feelings and actions. Carl Rogers' *client-centered therapy* proposed that therapists' most important contributions are to function as a psychological mirror through active listening and to provide a growth-fostering environment of unconditional positive regard, characterized by genuineness, acceptance, and empathy.

OBJECTIVE 52-6 | **Explain how the basic assumption of behavior therapy differs from those of traditional psychoanalytic and humanistic therapies.**

To help people alleviate current conflicts and problems, traditional psychoanalytic therapists attempt to explain the origin of behaviors, and humanistic therapists attempt to promote self-acceptance and self-awareness. Behavior therapists assume the problem behaviors *are* the problem, and they attempt to change them through new learning.

OBJECTIVE 52-7 | **Define *counterconditioning*, and describe the techniques used in exposure therapies and aversive conditioning.**

Counterconditioning uses classical conditioning techniques to pair new responses with old stimuli that have triggered maladaptive behaviors. *Exposure therapies* (including systematic desensitization and virtual reality exposure therapy) try to substitute a positive response (relaxation) for a negative one (fear). *Aversive conditioning* tries to substitute a negative response (such as nausea) for a positive one (pleasure) to a harmful stimulus (alcohol).

OBJECTIVE 52-8 | **State the main premise of therapy based on operant conditioning principles, and describe the views of proponents and critics of behavior modification.**

Operant conditioning therapies are based on the principle that voluntary behaviors are strongly influenced by their consequences. *Behavior modification* procedures thus enforce desired behaviors and withhold reinforcement for, or punish, undesired behaviors. In *token economies,* people receive tokens for desired behaviors and can later trade the tokens for privileges or treats. Critics object (1) on the practical grounds that these behaviors may disappear when the tokens are discontinued, and (2) on the ethical grounds that it is not right to control other people's behavior. Proponents counter that (1) social or intrinsic rewards can replace the tokens and continue to be reinforcing, and (2) with or without behavior modification, rewards and punishers already control people's behavior.

OBJECTIVE 52-9 | **Contrast cognitive therapy and cognitive-behavior therapy, and give some examples of cognitive therapy for depression.**

Cognitive therapy attempts to teach people to think in more adaptive ways, on the assumption that thoughts intervene between an event and our reactions to it. *Cognitive-behavior therapy* attempts to teach people to think in more adaptive ways but also to practice their new ways of thinking. In Aaron Beck's cognitive therapy for depression, therapists try to change self-defeating thinking by training clients to look at themselves in new, more positive ways. In *stress inoculation training,* people with depression learn to dispute their negative thoughts and to restructure their thinking in stressful situations.

OBJECTIVE 52-10 | **Discuss the rationale and benefits of group therapy, including family therapy.**

Group therapy sessions can help more people and cost less per person than individual therapy would. Clients may benefit from knowing others have similar problems and from getting feedback and reassurance. *Family therapy* views a family as an interactive system and attempts to help members discover the roles they play and to learn to communicate more openly and directly. Millions of people participate in self-help and support groups, such as Alcoholics Anonymous.

TERMS AND CONCEPTS TO REMEMBER

psychotherapy, p. 52-0
eclectic approach, p. 52-0
psychoanalysis, p. 52-0
resistance, p. 52-1
interpretation, p. 52-1
transference, p. 52-1
client-centered therapy, p. 52-3
active listening, p. 52-4
behavior therapy, p. 52-5
counterconditioning, p. 52-5
exposure therapies, p. 52-6

systematic desensitization, p. 52-6
virtual reality exposure therapy, p. 52-6
aversive conditioning, p. 52-7
token economy, p. 52-8
cognitive therapy, p. 52-9
cognitive-behavior therapy, p. 52-11
family therapy, p. 52-11

TEST YOURSELF

1. What is the major distinction between the underlying assumption in psychoanalytic and humanistic therapies and the underlying assumption in behavior therapies?

(Answer in Appendix B.)

ASK YOURSELF

1. Without trying to play therapist, how might you use the helping principles discussed in this module with a friend who is anxious?

>WEB

Multiple-choice *self-tests* and more may be found at www.worthpublishers.com/myers.

MODULE

53

Evaluating Psychotherapies

OBJECTIVE 53-1 | Define *psychotherapy*.

Advice columnist Ann Landers frequently advised her troubled letter writers to get professional help. One response urged the writer "not to give up. Hang in there until you find [a psychotherapist] who fills the bill. It's worth the effort." On the same day, she advised a second letter writer, "There are many excellent mental health facilities in your city. I urge you to make an appointment at once" (Farina & Fisher, 1982). Many share Ann Landers' confidence in **psychotherapy's** effectiveness.

Before 1950, the primary mental health providers were psychiatrists. Since then, demand has outgrown the psychiatric profession, and now most psychotherapy is done by clinical and counseling psychologists; clinical social workers; pastoral, marital, abuse, and school counselors; and psychiatric nurses. Thus, in addition to 55,000 clinical psychiatrists and 95,000 doctoral-level clinical psychologists in the United States, there are a quarter million other licensed therapists, many with social work training (Glenn, 2003). Much therapy is done through community mental health programs, which provide outpatient therapy, crisis phone lines, and halfway houses for those making the transition from hospitalization to independent living. With such an enormous outlay of time, money, effort, and hope, it is important to ask: Is the faith that Ann Landers and millions of others worldwide place in these therapists justified? And was the *Wall Street Journal* (1999) therefore wrong to suppose that including psychotherapy in health insurance plans would lead to "endless payments for dubious benefits of apparently marginal problems"?

Is Psychotherapy Effective?

The question, though simply put, is not simply answered. For one thing, measuring therapy's effectiveness is not like taking your body's temperature to see if your fever has gone away. If you and I were to undergo psychotherapy, how would we gauge its effectiveness? By how we feel about our progress? How our therapist feels about it? How our friends and family feel about it? How our behavior has changed?

Clients' Perceptions

OBJECTIVE 53-2 | Explain why clients tend to overestimate the effectiveness of psychotherapy.

If clients' testimonials were the only measuring stick, we could strongly affirm the effectiveness of psychotherapy. When 2900 *Consumer Reports* readers (1995; Kotkin & others, 1996; Seligman, 1995) related their experiences with mental health professionals, 89 percent said they were at least "fairly well satisfied." Among those who recalled feeling fair or very poor when beginning therapy, 9 in 10 now were feeling *very good, good,* or at least *so-so.* We have their word for it—and who should know better?

We should not dismiss these testimonials lightly. People enter therapy because they are suffering, and most leave feeling better about themselves. But there are several reasons why client testimonials do not persuade psychotherapy's skeptics:

- ***People often enter therapy in crisis.*** When, with the normal ebb and flow of events, the crisis passes, people may attribute their improvement to the therapy.

■ psychotherapy an emotionally charged, confiding interaction between a trained therapist and someone who suffers from psychological difficulties.

- *Clients may need to believe the therapy was worth the effort.* To admit investing time and money in something ineffective is like admitting to having one's car serviced repeatedly by a mechanic who never fixes it. Self-justification is a powerful human motive.
- *Clients generally speak kindly of their therapists.* Even if the clients' problems remain, say the critics, "they work hard to find something positive to say. The therapist had been very understanding, the client had gained a new perspective, he learned to communicate better, his mind was eased, anything at all so as not to have to say treatment was a failure" (Zilbergeld, 1983, p. 117).

Testimonials can be misleading. As research findings continue to document, we are prone to selective and biased recall and to making judgments that confirm our beliefs. Consider a massive experiment with over 500 Massachusetts boys, aged 5 to 13 years, many of whom seemed bound for delinquency. By the toss of a coin, half the boys were assigned to a five-year treatment program. Counselors visited the treated boys twice a month. The boys participated in community programs such as the Boy Scouts. As the need arose, they received academic tutoring, medical attention, and family assistance. Some 30 years after the end of the program, Joan McCord (1978, 1979) located 97 percent of the participants. To assess the treatment's impact, she sent them questionnaires and checked public records from courts, mental hospitals, and other sources.

Assessing the treatment program with client testimonials yielded encouraging results. Many of the men offered glowing reports. Some noted that had it not been for their counselors, "I would probably be in jail," "My life would have gone the other way," or "I think I would have ended up in a life of crime." The court records offered apparent support for these testimonials. Even among the "difficult" boys in the program, *66 percent* had no official juvenile crime record.

But recall psychology's most powerful tool for sorting reality from wishful thinking: the *control group*. For every boy who was counseled, there was a similar boy in a control group who was not. McCord tracked down these untreated people and found that among the predelinquent boys in the control group, *70 percent* had no juvenile record. Moreover, on some measures, such as a record of having committed a second crime, alcoholic tendencies, death rate, and job satisfaction, the untreated men exhibited slightly *fewer* problems. The glowing testimonials of those treated had been unintentionally deceiving.

This shocking finding—that testimonials can badly mislead—was confirmed in the 1990s. Delinquent boys put through "Scared Straight" programs (visiting jails, being taunted by prison inmates) said they were now more likely to be law-abiding. But they weren't. Compared with those not assigned to Scared Straight, boys who were in the program became *more* likely to commit new offenses (Dishion & others, 1999; Petrosino & others, 2000). Testimonials can and do mislead.

Clinicians' Perceptions

OBJECTIVE 53-3 | Give some reasons why clinicians tend to overestimate the effectiveness of psychotherapy, and describe two phenomena that contribute to clients' and clinicians' misperceptions in this area.

If clinicians' perceptions accurately reflected therapeutic effectiveness, we would have even more reason to celebrate. Case studies of successful treatment abound. Furthermore, every therapist treasures compliments from clients as they say good-bye or later express their gratitude. The problem is that clients justify entering psychotherapy by emphasizing their unhappiness, justify leaving therapy by emphasizing their well-being, and stay in touch only if satisfied. Therapists are aware of failures, but they are mostly the failures of *other* therapists—those whose clients, having experienced only temporary relief, are now seeking a new therapist for their recurring problems. Thus, the same person with the same recurring difficulty—the same old anxieties, depression, or marital difficulty—may be a "success" story in several therapists' files.

THINKING CRITICALLY ABOUT:

"REGRESSING" FROM UNUSUAL TO USUAL

Clients' and therapists' perceptions of therapy's effectiveness are vulnerable to inflation from two phenomena. One is the *placebo effect*—the power of *belief* in a treatment. An inert placebo is often used as a control treatment in drug experiments. If you *think* a treatment is going to be effective, it just may be (thanks to the healing power of your positive expectation).

The second phenomenon is **regression toward the mean**—the tendency for unusual events (or emotions) to "regress" (return) toward their average state. Thus, extraordinary happenings (feeling low) tend to be followed by more ordinary ones (a return to our more usual state). Because we returned to that more usual state, anything we tried in the interim may seem to

> The real purpose of [the] scientific method is to make sure Nature hasn't misled you into thinking you know something that you actually don't."
>
> Robert Pirsig, *Zen and the Art of Motorcycle Maintenence*, 1974

have been effective. Indeed, when things hit bottom, whatever we try—going to a psychotherapist, starting yoga, doing aerobic exercise—is more likely to be followed by improvement than by further descent.

The point may seem obvious, yet we regularly miss it: We sometimes attribute what may be a normal regression (the expected return to normal) to something we have done. Consider:

- Students who score much lower or higher on an exam than they usually do are likely, when retested, to return toward their average.
- Unusual ESP subjects who defy chance when first tested nearly always lose their "psychic powers" when retested (a phenomenon parapsychologists have called the "decline effect").
- Coaches often yell at their players after an unusually bad first half. They may then feel rewarded for having done so when the team's performance improves (returns to normal) during the second half.

> Once you become sensitized to it, you see regression everywhere."
>
> Psychologist Daniel Kahneman (1985)

- Scientists who win a Nobel prize—an extraordinary accomplishment—almost always experience diminished accomplishments thereafter, leading some to believe that winning a Nobel hinders creativity.

In each case, the cause-effect link may be genuine. More likely, however, is that each is an instance of the natural tendency for behavior to regress from the unusual to the more usual. And this defines a task for therapy-efficacy research: discerning whether troubled people's improvement following a particular therapy exceeds what we could expect from the placebo and regression effects, as shown in control groups not receiving the treatment.

■ **regression toward the mean** the tendency for extremes of unusual scores to fall back (regress) toward their average.

Because people enter therapy when they are extremely unhappy, and usually leave when they are less extremely unhappy, most therapists, like most clients, testify to therapy's success—regardless of the treatment (see Thinking Critically About: "Regressing" From Unusual to Usual). Although "treatments" have varied widely, from chains to counseling, every generation views its own approach as enlightened.

Outcome Research

OBJECTIVE 53-4 | Describe the importance of outcome studies in judging the effectiveness of psychotherapies, and discuss some of these findings.

How, then, can we objectively measure the effectiveness of psychotherapy? What types of people and problems are best helped, and by what type of psychotherapy? The questions have both academic and personal relevance. If you or someone you care about feels anxious or depressed, or suffers some psychological disorder, it is crucial for you to understand the likelihood of psychotherapy's being of help.

In hopes of better assessing psychotherapy's effectiveness, psychologists have turned to controlled research studies. Similar research in the 1800s transformed medicine from concocted treatments (bleeding, purging, infusions of plant and metal substances) into a science. The transformation occurred when skeptical physicians began to realize that many patients got better on their own, that most of the fashionable treatments were doing no good, and that sorting fact from superstition required following illnesses closely—with and without a particular treatment. Typhoid fever patients, for example, often improved after being bled, convincing most physicians that the treatment worked. Not until a control group was given mere bed rest—and 70 percent were observed to improve after five weeks of fever—did physicians learn, to their shock, that the blood-letting treatment was worthless (Thomas, 1992).

In psychology, the opening challenge in what became a spirited debate over such research was issued by British psychologist Hans Eysenck (1952). He summarized studies showing that two-thirds of those suffering nonpsychotic disorders improve markedly after undergoing psychotherapy. To this day, no one disputes that optimistic estimate.

So why then are we still debating psychotherapy's effectiveness? Because Eysenck also reported similar improvement among *untreated* persons, such as those who were on waiting lists. With or without psychotherapy, he said, roughly two-thirds improved noticeably. Time was a great healer.

The avalanche of criticism prompted by Eysenck's conclusions revealed shortcomings in his analyses. Also, in 1952 Eysenck could find only 24 studies of psychotherapy outcomes to analyze. Today, there are hundreds. The best of these *randomized clinical trials* randomly assign people on a waiting list to therapy or to no therapy. Afterward, researchers evaluate everyone, using tests and the reports of friends and family or of psychologists who don't know whether therapy was given. The results of many such studies are then digested by a technique called **meta-analysis,** a procedure for statistically combining the conclusions of a large number of different studies as if the results had come from one huge study with thousands of participants. Simply said, meta-analyses give us the bottom-line results of lots of studies.

In the first of more than five dozen meta-analyses of psychotherapy outcome studies, Mary Lee Smith and her colleagues (1980) combined the results of 475 investigations. For psychotherapists, the welcome result was that "the evidence overwhelmingly supports the efficacy of psychotherapy" (p. 183). **Figure 53.1** depicts their finding—that the average therapy client ends up better off than 80 percent of the untreated individuals on waiting lists. The claim is more modest than it first appears—by definition, about 50 percent of untreated people also are better off than the average untreated person. Nevertheless, Smith and her collaborators exulted that "psychotherapy benefits people of all ages as reliably as schooling educates them, medicine cures them, or business turns a profit" (p. 183).

■ **meta-analysis** a procedure for statistically combining the results of many different research studies.

"Fortunately, [psycho]analysis is not the only way to resolve inner conflicts. Life itself still remains a very effective therapist."

Karen Horney, *Our Inner Conflicts*, 1945

FIGURE 53.1
Treatment versus no treatment
These two normal distribution curves based on data from 475 studies show the improvement of untreated people and psychotherapy clients. The outcome for the average therapy client surpassed that for 80 percent of the untreated people. (Adapted from Smith & others, 1980.)

Newer research summaries confirm that psychotherapy works (Kopta & others, 1999; Shadish & others, 2000). In one ambitious study, the National Institute of Mental Health compared three depression treatments: cognitive therapy, interpersonal therapy, and a standard drug therapy. Twenty-eight experienced therapists at research sites in Norman, Oklahoma; Washington, DC; and Pittsburgh, Pennsylvania, were trained in one of the three methods and randomly assigned their share of the 239 participants suffering from depression. Clients in all three groups improved more than did those in a control group who received merely an inert medication and supportive attention, encouragement, and advice. Among people who completed a full 16-week treatment program, the depression had lifted for slightly more than half of those in each treatment group—but for only 29 percent of those in the control group (Elkin & others, 1989). This verdict echoes the results of the earlier outcome studies: *Those not undergoing therapy often improve, but those undergoing therapy are more likely to improve.*

Psychotherapy is also cost-effective when compared with the greater costs of medical care for psychologically related complaints. When people seek psychological treatment, their search for medical treatment drops—by 16 percent in one digest of 91 studies (Chiles & others, 1999).

The annual cost of psychological disorders and substance abuse—including crime, accidents, lost work, and treatment—is staggering. Thus, just as an investment in prenatal and well-baby care reduces long-term costs, so will an investment in almost any effective treatment for psychological problems. Anything that boosts employees' psychological well-being will reduce medical costs, improve work efficiency, and diminish absenteeism. Studies by health insurers show that mental health treatment can more than pay for itself with reduced medical costs (American Psychological Association, 1991).

But note that the claim—that psychotherapy, *on average*, is somewhat effective—refers to no one therapy in particular. It is like saying, "Surgery is somewhat effective," or reassuring lung-cancer patients that "on average," medical treatment of health problems is effective. What people want to know is not the average effectiveness of all therapy but the particular effectiveness of a treatment for their specific problems.

The Relative Effectiveness of Different Therapies

OBJECTIVE 53-5 | Summarize the findings on which psychotherapies are most effective for specific disorders.

So what can we tell people considering therapy, and those paying for it, about *which* psychotherapy will be most effective for their problem? Despite claims of superiority by advocates of different types of therapy, the meta-analysis conducted by Mary Lee Smith and her colleagues (1977, 1980) revealed no one type of therapy as generally superior. *Consumer Reports* readers, too, were equally satisfied, no matter what type of therapy they received and whether treated by a psychiatrist, psychologist, or social worker (Seligman, 1995). Moreover—and more astonishing—the group or individual context of the therapy made no discernible difference, nor did the level of training and experience of the therapist. Now, more than two decades after Smith's analysis, newer evidence indicates little if any connection between clinicians' experience, training, supervision, and licensing and their clients' outcomes (Bickman, 1999; Luborsky & others, 2002). Was the dodo bird in *Alice in Wonderland* right: "Everyone has won and all must have prizes"?

A Society of Clinical Psychology task force is answering that question by identifying treatments shown to be beneficial in controlled treatment studies (Chambless &

"Whatever differences in treatment efficacy exist, they appear to be extremely small, at best."

Bruce Wampold and colleagues (1997)

others, 1997; Norcross, 2002). The task force has pinpointed some elements of effective therapy, such as empathy. And it offers lists of *empirically supported therapies,* including, for example,

- cognitive therapy, interpersonal therapy, and behavior therapy for depression.
- cognitive therapy, exposure therapy, and stress inoculation training for anxiety.
- cognitive-behavior therapy for bulimia.
- behavior modification for bed-wetting.

Behavioral conditioning therapies have also achieved especially favorable results with specific behavior problems such as phobias, compulsions, marital problems, and sexual disorders (Bowers & Clum, 1988; Hunsley & DiGiulio, 2002; Shadish & Baldwin, 2005). And new studies confirm cognitive therapy's effectiveness in coping with depression and reducing suicide risk (Brown & others, 2005; DeRubeis & others, 2005; Hollon & others, 2005).

> "Different sores have different salves."
> English proverb

Moreover, therapy is most effective when the problem is clear-cut (Singer, 1981; Westen & Morrison, 2001). Those who experience phobias or panic, who are unassertive, or who are frustrated by sexual performance problems can hope for improvement. Those who suffer less-focused problems, such as depression and anxiety, usually benefit in the short term but often relapse later. Those who have chronic schizophrenia or who wish to change their whole personality are unlikely to benefit from psychotherapy alone (Zilbergeld, 1983). The more specific the problem, the greater the hope.

Meanwhile, controversy continues—some call it today's civil war in psychology—over the extent to which science should guide both clinical practice and the willingness of health care providers and insurers to pay for psychotherapy. On the one side are science-oriented psychologists working to extend the list of evidence-based practice, with well-defined and validated therapies for various disorders. On the other side are those who view therapy as more art than science, not something amenable to describing in a manual or testing in an experiment. People are too complex and therapy too intuitive for a cookie-cutter approach, say the nonscientist therapists. But by basing practice on evidence and making mental health professionals accountable for effectiveness, say the science-oriented clinicians, therapy stands to gain credibility. Moreover, the public will be protected from pseudotherapies, and therapists will be protected from accusations of sounding like snake-oil salesmen—"Trust me, I know it works, I've seen it work."

Evaluating Alternative Therapies

OBJECTIVE 53-6 | Evaluate the effectiveness of eye movement desensitization and reprocessing (EMDR) and light exposure therapies.

The tendency of abnormal states of mind to "regress" to normal, combined with the placebo effect, creates fertile soil for pseudotherapies. Bolstered by anecdotes, heralded by the media, praised on the Internet, alternative therapies can spread like wildfire. Princess Diana typified the modern fascination with alternative healers by seeking out spiritualists, a hypnotherapist, an "anger-release" therapist, reflexologists, aromatherapists, colonic irrigationists, and a "mind-body" therapist (Smith, 1999). She had much company. In one national survey, 57 percent of those with a history of anxiety attacks and 54 percent of those with a history of depression had used alternative treatments such as herbal medicine, massage, and spiritual healing (Kessler & others, 2001).

What can we say of such alternative therapies? Testimonials aside—every therapy, whether effective or not, will *seem* effective to some—what does the evidence say? Which are empirically validated?

TABLE 53.1

**COMPARISON OF SCIENTIFIC PSYCHOLOGY CITATIONS
AND UNFILTERED WEB SITES**

Topic	Psychology Journal Citations*	Web Sites**	Ratio
Systematic desensitization	2,301	56,800	1 to 25
Therapeutic touch	94	383,000	1 to 4,074
St. John's wort (herbal remedy)	200	2,590,000	1 to 12,950
Enneagram (personality typing)	32	775,000	1 to 24,218

*Using PsycINFO, January 2006
**Using Google, January 2006

About most, there is no evidence, because their proponents and devotees feel no need for controlled research. For them, personal experience is evidence enough. So which therapies do get systematically evaluated? To gauge scientific versus popular interest in various treatments and assessment techniques, clinical researcher Scott Lilienfeld (1998) suggests comparing the number of times each is mentioned in electronic searches of psychology's scientific literature and on unfiltered Web sources. As **TABLE 53.1** shows, some topics exist almost exclusively on the Web.

Let's now evaluate two alternative therapies—eye movement desensitization and reprocessing (EMDR) and light exposure therapy. As we do, remember that sifting sense from nonsense requires the scientific attitude: being skeptical but not cynical, open to surprises but not gullible.

Eye Movement Desensitization and Reprocessing

Walking in a park one day, Francine Shapiro (1989) observed that anxious thoughts vanished as her eyes spontaneously darted about. From this experience she developed a novel anxiety treatment: *eye movement desensitization and reprocessing (EMDR)*. While people imagined traumatic scenes, Shapiro triggered eye movements by waving her finger in front of their eyes, supposedly enabling them to unlock and reprocess previously frozen trauma memories. She tried this on 22 people haunted by old traumatic memories, and all reported marked reductions in their distress after just one therapeutic session. This extraordinary result evoked an enormous response from mental health professionals, 40,000 of whom from 52 countries have undergone training (EMDR, 2002). Not since the similarly charismatic Franz Anton Mesmer introduced *animal magnetism* (hypnosis) more than two centuries ago (also after feeling inspired by an outdoor experience) has a new therapy attracted so many devotees so quickly.

Does it work? For 84 to 100 percent of single-trauma victims participating in four recent studies, the answer is yes, reports Shapiro (1999, 2002). (When EMDR did not fare well in other trials, Shapiro argued that the therapists were not properly trained.) Moreover, the treatment need take no more than three 90-minute sessions. The Society of Clinical Psychology task force on empirically validated treatments acknowledges that the treatment is "probably efficacious" for the treatment of nonmilitary post-traumatic stress disorder (Chambless & others, 1997). Encouraged by their seeming successes, EMDR therapists are now applying the technique to other anxiety disorders, such as panic disorder, and, with Shapiro's (1995, 2002) encouragement, to a wide range of complaints, including pain, grief, paranoid schizophrenia, rage, and guilt.

EMDR is a therapy that thousands adore, and thousands more dismiss as a sham—"an excellent vehicle for illustrating the differences between scientific and pseudoscientific therapy techniques," suggest James Herbert and seven others (2000). Why,

" Meta-analyses [indicate that EMDR is] just as effective with fixed eyes. If that conclusion is right, what's useful in the therapy (chiefly behavioral desensitization) is not new, and what's new is superfluous."

Harvard Mental Health Letter, 2002

wondered skeptics, should rapidly moving one's eyes while recalling traumas be therapeutic? Indeed, eye movements, it seems, are not the therapeutic ingredient. When researchers tested the therapy without the eye movements—with finger tapping, for example, or with eyes fixed straight ahead while the therapist's finger wagged—the therapeutic results were the same (Devilly, 2003). What is therapeutic, the skeptics suspect, is the combination of exposure therapy—repeatedly reliving traumatic memories in a safe and reassuring context—and a robust placebo effect. Had Mesmer's pseudotherapy been compared with no treatment at all, notes Richard McNally (1999), it, too (thanks to the healing power of positive belief), could have been found "probably efficacious."

Light Exposure Therapy

Have you ever found yourself oversleeping, gaining weight, and feeling lethargic during the dark mornings and overcast days of winter? For some people, especially women and those living far from the equator, the wintertime blahs constitute a form of depression known as seasonal affective disorder, for which the appropriate acronym is SAD. To counteract these dark spirits, National Institute of Mental Health researchers in the early 1980s had a bright idea: Give SAD people a timed daily dose of intense light. When clinical experience indicated that light exposure could also relieve symptoms associated with wintertime depression, manufacturers produced light boxes that can now be rented or purchased from health supply and lighting stores.

Is this another placebo effect, attributable to people's expectations? Recent studies shed light on this therapy. One exposed some people with SAD to 90 minutes of bright light and others to a sham placebo treatment—a hissing "negative ion generator" about which the staff expressed similar enthusiasm (but which, unknown to the participants, was not turned on). After four weeks of exposure, 61 percent of those exposed to morning light had greatly improved, as had 50 percent of those exposed to evening light and 32 percent of those exposed to the placebo treatment (Eastman & others, 1998). Two other studies found that 30 minutes of light exposure produced relief for more than half the people receiving morning light therapy and for one-third receiving evening light therapy (Terman & Terman, 1998, 2001). From 20 carefully controlled trials we have a verdict (Golden & others, 2005): For many people, morning bright light does indeed dim SAD symptoms.

Light therapy
To counteract winter depression, some people spend time each morning in front of a box emitting intense light that mimics natural outdoor light.

Commonalities Among Psychotherapies

OBJECTIVE 53-7 | Describe the three benefits attributed to all psychotherapies.

Good therapists may have differing perspectives, yet share much in common, including compassion, sensitivity, and empathy. Jerome Frank (1982), Marvin Goldfried (Goldfried & Padawer, 1982), Hans Strupp (1986), and Bruce Wampold (2001) studied the common ingredients of various therapies and suggest they all offer at least three benefits: hope for demoralized people; a new perspective on oneself and the world; and an empathic, trusting, caring relationship. These nonspecific factors aren't all that therapy offers, but they are important (Barker & others, 1988; Jones & others, 1988; Roberts & others, 1993). They are part of what the growing numbers of self-help and support groups offer their members. And they have been part of what traditional healers offer (Jackson, 1992). Healers—special people to whom others disclose their suffering—have for centuries listened in order to understand and to empathize, reassure, advise, console, interpret, or explain. (For those thinking about seeking therapy, Close-Up: A Consumer's Guide to Psychotherapists on the next page offers some tips on when to seek help and how to start your search for a therapist.)

CLOSE-UP:

A Consumer's Guide to Psychotherapists

Life for everyone is marked by a mix of serenity and stress, blessing and bereavement, good moods and bad. So, when should a person seek the help of a mental health professional? When troubling thoughts and emotions interfere with your normal living, you might consider talking to a professional. The American Psychological Association offers these common trouble signals:

- Feelings of hopelessness
- Deep and lasting depression
- Self-destructive behavior, such as alcohol and drug abuse
- Disruptive fears
- Sudden mood shifts
- Thoughts of suicide
- Compulsive rituals, such as hand washing
- Sexual difficulties

In looking for a therapist, you may want to have a preliminary consultation with two or three. You can describe your problem and learn each therapist's treatment approach. You can ask questions about the therapist's values, credentials (TABLE **53.2**), and fees. And, knowing the importance of the emotional bond between therapist and client, you can assess your own feelings about each of them.

TABLE **53.2**

THERAPISTS AND THEIR TRAINING

Type	Description
Counselors	Marriage and family counselors specialize in problems arising from family relations. Pastoral counselors provide counseling to countless people. Abuse counselors work with substance abusers and with spouse and child abusers and their victims.
Clinical or psychiatric social workers	A two-year master of social work graduate program plus post-graduate supervision prepares some social workers to offer psychotherapy, mostly to people with everyday personal and family problems. About half have earned the National Association of Social Workers' designation of clinical social worker.
Clinical psychologists	Most are psychologists with a Ph.D. or Psy.D. and expertise in research, assessment, and therapy, supplemented by a supervised internship and, often, post-doctoral training. About half work in agencies and institutions, half in private practice.
Psychiatrists	Psychiatrists are physicians who specialize in the treatment of psychological disorders. Not all psychiatrists have had extensive training in psychotherapy, but as M.D.s they can prescribe medications. Thus, they tend to see those with the most serious problems. Many have their own private practice.

Hope for Demoralized People

People who seek therapy typically feel anxious, depressed, devoid of self-esteem, and incapable of turning things around. What any therapy offers is the expectation that, with commitment from the therapy seeker, things can and will get better. Apart from the particular therapeutic technique, this belief may itself function as a placebo, promoting improved morale, new feelings of self-efficacy, and diminished symptoms (Prioleau & others, 1983). Similar effects have been found in psychotherapy experiments in which the placebo treatment was listening to inspirational tapes or taking a fake pill.

The finding from meta-analyses that improvement is greater for placebo-treated people than for untreated people (although not as great as for those receiving actual psychotherapy) suggests that one reason therapies help is that they offer hope. Said another way, therapy outcomes vary with the attitude of the person seeking help—the person's motivation, confidence, and commitment. Each therapy, in its individual way, may harness the person's own healing powers. And that, says psychiatrist Jerome Frank, helps us understand why all sorts of treatments—including some folk healing rites that are powerless apart from the participants' belief—may in their own time and place produce cures.

A New Perspective

Every therapy offers people a plausible explanation of their symptoms and an alternative way of looking at themselves or responding to their world. Therapy can offer new experiences as well, ones that help people change their behaviors and their views of themselves. Armed with a believable fresh perspective, they may approach life with a new attitude.

"I utilize the best from Freud, the best from Jung, and the best from my Uncle Marty, a very smart fellow."

An Empathic, Trusting, Caring Relationship

To say that all therapies are about equally effective is not to say all *therapists* are equally effective. Regardless of their therapeutic technique, effective therapists are empathic people who seek to understand another's experience; who communicate their care and concern to the client; and who earn the client's trust and respect through respectful listening, reassurance, and advice. In a National Institute of Mental Health depression-treatment study, the most effective therapists were those who were perceived as most empathic and caring and who established the closest therapeutic bonds with their clients (Blatt & others, 1996). In another study, Marvin Gold-fried and his associates (1998) analyzed taped therapy sessions from 36 recognized master therapists. Some were cognitive-behavior therapists, others were psychodynamic-interpersonal therapists. Regardless, the striking finding was how *similar* the therapists were during the parts of their sessions they considered most significant. At key moments, the empathic therapists of both persuasions would help clients evaluate themselves, link one aspect of their life with another, and gain insight into their interactions with others. Indeed, some believe warmth and empathy are hallmarks of healers everywhere, whether psychiatrists, witch doctors, or shamans (Torrey, 1986). The emotional bond between therapist and client—the *therapeutic alliance*—is a key aspect of effective therapy (Klein & others, 2003; Wampold, 2001).

A caring relationship
Effective therapists form a bond of trust with their patients.

That all therapies offer *hope* through a *fresh perspective* offered by a caring person is supported by a meta-analysis of 39 studies. Each study compared treatment offered by professional therapists with treatment offered by laypeople: friendly professors, people who had had a few hours' training in empathic listening skills, and college students supervised by a professional clinician. The result? The *paraprofessionals,* as these and other briefly trained people are called, typically proved as effective as the professionals (Christensen & Jacobson, 1994). Although most of the problems they treated were mild, the trained paraprofessionals were—believe it or not—as effective as professionals even when dealing with more disturbed adults, such as those diagnosed with serious depression.

To recap, people who seek help usually improve. So do many of those who do not undergo psychotherapy, and that is a tribute to our human resourcefulness and our capacity to care for one another. Nevertheless, though the therapist's orientation and experience appear not to matter much, people who receive some psychotherapy usually improve more than those who do not. People with clear-cut, specific problems tend to improve the most.

Part of what all therapies offer is hope, a fresh way of looking at life, and an empathic, caring relationship. That may explain why the empathy and friendly counsel of paraprofessionals are often as helpful as professional psychotherapy. And that may also explain why people who feel supported by close relationships—who enjoy the fellowship and friendship of caring people--are less likely to need or seek therapy (Frank, 1982; O'Connor & Brown, 1984).

Culture and Values in Psychotherapy

OBJECTIVE 53-8 | Discuss the role of values and cultural differences in the therapeutic process.

All therapies offer hope, and nearly all therapists attempt to enhance their clients' sensitivity, openness, personal responsibility, and sense of purpose (Jensen & Bergin, 1988). But on certain matters of moral and cultural diversity, therapists may differ from one another and from their clients (Kelly, 1990). In Canada and the United States, for example, about 1 person in 25 is a self-proclaimed atheist or agnostic, as are (depending on the survey) one-fifth to one-half of psychiatrists and clinical psychologists (Gallup, 1993; Lukoff & others, 1992). In Britain, two-thirds of psychiatrists say they are atheists

CLOSE-UP:

PREVENTING PSYCHOLOGICAL DISORDERS BY TREATING THE SOCIAL CONTEXTS THAT BREED THEM

OBJECTIVE 53-9 | Explain the rationale of preventive mental health programs.

Psychotherapies and biomedical therapies tend to locate the cause of psychological disorders within the person with the disorder. We infer that people who act cruelly must be cruel and that people who act "crazy" must be "sick." We attach labels to such people, thereby distinguishing them from "normal" folks. It follows, then, that we try to treat "abnormal" people by giving them insight into their problems, by changing their thinking, and/or by helping them gain control with drugs.

There is an alternative viewpoint: We could interpret many psychological disorders as understandable responses to a disturbing and stressful society. According to this view, it is not just the person who needs treatment, but also the person's social context. Better to prevent a problem by reforming a sick situation and by developing people's coping competencies than to wait for a problem to arise and then treat it.

A story about the rescue of a drowning person from a rushing river illustrates this viewpoint: Having successfully administered first aid to the first victim, the rescuer spots another struggling person and pulls her out, too. After a half-dozen repetitions, the rescuer suddenly turns and starts running away while the river sweeps yet another floundering person into view. "Aren't you going to rescue that fellow?" asks a bystander. "Heck no," the rescuer replies. "I'm going upstream to find out what's pushing all these people in."

Preventive mental health is upstream work. It seeks to prevent psychological casualties by identifying and alleviating the conditions that cause them. George Albee (1986) believes there is abundant evidence that poverty, meaningless work, constant criticism, unemployment, racism, and sexism undermine people's sense of competence, personal control, and self-esteem. Such stresses increase their risk of depression, alcoholism, and suicide.

Albee contends that we who care about preventing psychological casualties should therefore support programs

> It is better to prevent than to cure."
>
> Peruvian folk wisdom

that alleviate poverty, discrimination, and other demoralizing situations. We eliminated smallpox not by treating the afflicted but by inoculating the unafflicted. We conquered yellow fever by controlling mosquitoes. Prevention of psychological problems means empowering those who have learned an attitude of helplessness, changing environments that breed loneliness, renewing the disintegrating family, and bolstering parents' and teachers' skills at nurturing children's achievements and resulting self-esteem. Indeed, "Everything aimed at improving the human condition, at making life more fulfilling and meaningful, may be considered part of primary prevention of mental or emotional disturbance" (Kessler & Albee, 1975, p. 557). That includes such programs as the cognitive training that promotes positive thinking in children at risk for depression.

There is, however, more to the story of psychological disorders than toxic environments and pessimism. Anxiety disorders, major depression, bipolar disorder, and schizophrenia are in part biological events. Yet Albee reminds us again of one of this book's themes: *A human being is an integrated*

Changing in China

These men are listening sympathetically to fellow patients, many of whom are HIV positive, at a support group meeting at a drug rehabilitation center in southwest China.

Michael Reynolds/EPA/SIPA

(Neeleman & Persaud, 1995). That raises an intriguing issue: What values prevail in psychotherapy? What values *should* prevail? Should it matter that highly religious people prefer religiously similar therapists (Worthington & others, 1996)?

Albert Ellis, a well-known therapist, and Allen Bergin, co-editor of the *Handbook of Psychotherapy and Behavior Change,* illustrate how sharply values can differ. Ellis (1980) assumes that "no one and nothing is supreme," that "self-gratification" should be encouraged, and that "unequivocal love, commitment, service, and . . . fidelity to any interpersonal commitment, especially marriage, leads to harmful consequences." Bergin (1980) assumes the opposite—that "because God is supreme, humility and the acceptance of divine authority are virtues," that "self-control and committed love and self-sacrifice are to be encouraged," and that "infidelity to any interpersonal commitment, especially marriage, leads to harmful consequences." Bergin and Ellis disagree more radically than most therapists on what values are healthiest. In so doing, however, they illustrate what they agree on: that psychotherapists' personal beliefs and values influence their practice. Knowing that clients tend to adopt

FIGURE 53.2

A biopsychosocial approach to therapy

Effective treatment of psychological disorders requires considering all possible influences—biological, psychological, and social-cultural—that may be contributing to a problem.

Biological considerations:
Biomedical techniques may be used to correct malfunctioning brain circuitry. *For example, a patient diagnosed with bipolar disorder (with moods swinging from depression to mania) might be given a prescription for drugs that would reduce her dramatic mood swings.*

Psychological considerations:
Therapy may help clients gain insight into patterns of thinking and behaving that are causing them distress and leading to dysfunction. *The client with bipolar disorder might be helped to recognize the patterns of relationship damage caused by her mood swings and to develop ways to improve her relationships with family and friends.*

Successful intervention

Social-cultural considerations:
Therapy can help people relearn more adaptive responses to the social and cultural influences in their environment. To be effective, all types of psychotherapy need to be sensitive to cultural differences in the clients being treated. *The client with bipolar disorder might be trained to recognize the settings and symptoms of her mood swings and to respond in ways that help her retain a healthier balance.*

biopsychosocial system (**FIGURE 53.2**). For years we have trusted our bodies to physicians and our minds to psychiatrists and psychologists. That neat separation no longer seems valid. Stress affects body chemistry and health. And chemical imbalances, whatever their cause, can produce schizophrenia and depression. *"Mens sana in corpore sano,"* says an ancient Latin adage: "A healthy mind in a healthy body."

Mental disorders arise from physical ones, and likewise physical disorders arise from mental ones."

The Mahabharata, c. A.D. 200

their therapists' values (Worthington & others, 1996), Bergin and Ellis also agree that therapists should divulge their values more openly.

Value differences also can become significant when a therapist from one culture meets a client from another. In North America, Europe, and Australia, for example, most therapists reflect their culture's individualism, which often gives priority to personal desires and identity. Clients who are immigrants from Asian countries, which expect people to be more mindful of others' expectations, may have trouble relating to therapies that require them to think only of their own well-being. Such differences help explain the reluctance of some minority populations to use mental health services (Sue, 1990). In one experiment, Asian-American clients matched with counselors who shared their cultural values (rather than mismatched with those who didn't) perceived more counselor empathy and felt more alliance with the counselor (Kim & others, 2005). Recognizing that therapists and clients may differ in their values, communication styles, and language, many therapy training programs now provide training in cultural sensitivity and recruit members of underrepresented cultural groups. (For a social-cultural perspective on disorders and therapy, see the Close-Up: Preventing Psychological Disorders by Treating the Social Contexts That Breed Them.)

>> Learning Outcomes

Evaluating Psychotherapies

OBJECTIVE 53-1 | **Define** *psychotherapy.*

Psychotherapy is an emotionally charged, confiding interaction between a trained therapist and someone who suffers from psychological difficulties.

OBJECTIVE 53-2 | **Explain why clients tend to overestimate the effectiveness of psychotherapy.**

Clients judge psychotherapy to be effective for three reasons: They tend to enter therapy in crisis, they need to believe their time and expense were justified, and they try to find something positive to say when asked to evaluate their therapist. Research has not upheld clients' views of therapy's effectiveness.

OBJECTIVE 53-3 | **Give some reasons why clinicians tend to overestimate the effectiveness of psychotherapy, and describe two phenomena that contribute to clients' and clinicians' misperceptions in this area.**

Clients enter therapy when they are unhappy, leave it when they are less unhappy, and stay in touch only if satisfied with the treatment they received. So clinicians are mostly aware of other therapists' failures, not their own. Both the *placebo effect* (the belief a treatment will work) and *regression toward the mean* (the tendency for extreme or unusual scores to fall back toward the mean) contribute to clients' and clinicians' misperceptions of the effectiveness of psychotherapy.

OBJECTIVE 53-4 | **Describe the importance of outcome studies in judging the effectiveness of psychotherapies, and discuss some of these findings.**

Outcome studies are randomized clinical trials in which people on a waiting list receive therapy or no therapy. Statistical digests (*meta-analyses*) of hundreds of these studies reveal that people who remain untreated often improve, but those who receive psychotherapy are more likely to improve and also to spend less time and money seeking other medical treatment later.

OBJECTIVE 53-5 | **Summarize the findings on which psychotherapies are most effective for specific disorders.**

Meta-analyses indicate that no one type of therapy is most effective overall, nor is there any connection between effectiveness and a therapist's training, experience, supervision, or licensing. Some therapies are particularly well-suited to specific disorders, such as cognitive, interpersonal, and behavior therapies for depression; cognitive, exposure, and stress-inoculation therapies for anxiety; cognitive-behavior therapy for bulimia; behavior modification for bed-wetting; and behavior conditioning therapies for phobias, compulsions, and sexual disorders. The more specific the problem, the greater the chances for effective treatment.

OBJECTIVE 53-6 | **Evaluate the effectiveness of eye movement desensitization and reprocessing (EMDR) and light exposure therapies.**

In *EMDR therapy,* a therapist attempts to unlock and reprocess previously frozen traumatic memories by waving a finger in front of the eyes of a person imagining traumatic scenes. EMDR has not held up under scientific testing, and its modest successes may be attributable to the placebo effect. In people with *seasonal affective disorder*, a form of depression linked to periods of decreased sunlight, *light exposure therapy* (exposure to daily timed doses of light that mimics outdoor light) has been proven effective by scientific research.

OBJECTIVE 53-7 | **Describe the three benefits attributed to all psychotherapies.**

All types of psychotherapy seem to offer *new hope* for demoralized people, a *fresh perspective,* and an *empathic, trusting, caring relationship.* The *therapeutic alliance*—the emotional bond between therapist and client—is an important part of effective therapy and may help explain why some paraprofessionals can be as helpful as professional psychotherapists.

OBJECTIVE 53-8 | **Discuss the role of values and cultural differences in the therapeutic process.**

Psychotherapists may differ in their personal beliefs, values, and cultural backgrounds. Such differences can affect the formation of a bond between therapist and client. People searching for a therapist should have preliminary consultations with two or three to find someone with whom they feel comfortable.

OBJECTIVE 53-9 | **Explain the rationale of preventive mental health programs.**

Advocates of preventive mental health argue that many psychological disorders are responses to social conditions. To prevent such disorders, we should change oppressive, esteem-destroying environments into more benevolent, nurturing environments that foster individual growth and self-confidence.

TERMS AND CONCEPTS TO REMEMBER

psychotherapy, p. 53-0
regression toward the mean, p. 53-2
meta-analysis, p. 53-3

TEST YOURSELF

1. How does the placebo effect bias clients' appraisals of the effectiveness of psychotherapies?

2. What are the influences to keep in mind for successful therapeutic intervention?

(Answers in Appendix B.)

ASK YOURSELF

1. Can you think of a time when your positive expectations for improvement may have been self-fulfilling?

2. Can you think of a specific way that improving the environment in your own community might prevent some psychological disorders among its residents?

>WEB

Multiple-choice *self-tests* and more may be found at www.worthpublishers.com/myers.

54

MODULE

The Biomedical Therapies

OBJECTIVE 54-1 | Discuss the goals of biomedical therapy, and explain how double-blind studies help researchers evaluate a drug's effectiveness.

The therapy often used to treat serious disorders is **biomedical therapy**—physically changing the brain's functioning by altering its chemistry with drugs, overloading its circuits with electroconvulsive shock, using magnetic impulses to stimulate or dampen its activity, or altering its circuits through psychosurgery.

Drug Therapies

By far the most widely used biomedical treatments today are the drug therapies. Since the 1950s, discoveries in **psychopharmacology** (the study of drug effects on mind and behavior) have revolutionized the treatment of people with severe disorders, liberating hundreds of thousands from hospital confinement. Thanks to drug therapy—and to efforts to minimize involuntary hospitalization and to support people with community mental health programs—the resident population of U.S. state and county mental hospitals is a fraction of what it was a half-century ago (**FIGURE 54.1**). For some unable to care for themselves, however, release from hospitals has meant homelessness, not liberation.

Almost any new treatment, including drug therapy, is greeted by an initial wave of enthusiasm as many people apparently improve. But that enthusiasm often diminishes after researchers subtract the rates of (1) normal recovery among untreated persons and (2) recovery due to the placebo effect, which arises from the positive expectations of patients and mental health workers alike. So, to evaluate the effectiveness of any new drug, researchers use the *double-blind technique*. Half the patients receive the drug, the other half a similar-appearing placebo (an inert substance, such as a suger pill). Neither the staff nor the patients know who gets which. The good news: In double-blind studies, several types of drugs have proven useful in treating psychological disorders.

"The mentally ill were out of the hospital, but in many cases they were simply out on the streets, less agitated but lost, still disabled but now uncared for."

Lewis Thomas, *Late Night Thoughts on Listening to Mahler's Ninth Symphony*, 1983

■ **biomedical therapy** prescribed medications or medical procedures that act directly on the patient's nervous system.

■ **psychopharmacology** the study of the effects of drugs on mind and behavior.

FIGURE 54.1

The emptying of U.S. mental hospitals

After the widespread introduction of antipsychotic drugs, starting in about 1955, the number of residents in state and county mental hospitals declined sharply. But in the rush to deinstitutionalize the mentally ill, many people who were ill-equipped to care for themselves were left homeless on city streets. (Data from the National Institute of Mental Health and Bureau of the Census, 2004.)

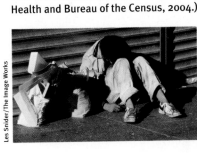

Les Snider/The Image Works

■ **tardive dyskinesia** involuntary movements of the facial muscles, tongue, and limbs; a possible neurotoxic side effect of long-term use of antipsychotic drugs that target D2 dopamine receptors.

Perhaps you can guess an occasional side effect of L-dopa, a drug that *raises* dopamine levels for Parkinson's patients: hallucinations.

Antipsychotic Drugs

OBJECTIVE 54-2 | Describe the characteristics of antipsychotic drugs, and discuss their use in treating schizophrenia.

The revolution in drug therapy for psychological disorders began with the accidental discovery that certain drugs, used for other medical purposes, calmed psychotic patients. These *antipsychotic* drugs, such as chlorpromazine (sold as Thorazine), dampened responsiveness to irrelevant stimuli. Thus they provided the most help to schizophrenia patients experiencing positive symptoms, such as auditory hallucinations and paranoia (Lehman & others, 1998; Lenzenweger & others, 1989). Patients exhibiting negative symptoms, such as apathy and withdrawal, often do not respond well to these antipsychotic drugs. A newer drug, clozapine (marketed since 1989 as Clozaril), does sometimes enable "awakenings" in such people. It also sometimes helps those who have positive symptoms but have not responded to other drugs. Those who take clozapine must have regular blood tests because in 1 percent of cases, it has a toxic effect on white blood cells.

The molecules of antipsychotic drugs are similar enough to molecules of the neurotransmitter dopamine to occupy its receptor sites and block its activity (Pickar & others, 1984; Taubes, 1994). (Clozapine blocks serotonin activity as well.) The finding that most antipsychotic drugs block dopamine receptors reinforces the idea that an overactive dopamine system contributes to schizophrenia.

Antipsychotics are powerful drugs. The first-generation dopamine-blocking drugs (such as Thorazine), which target D2 dopamine receptors, can produce sluggishness, tremors, and twitches similar to those of Parkinson's disease, which is marked by too little dopamine (Kaplan & Saddock, 1989). Long-term use of these medications can also produce **tardive dyskinesia,** a neurotoxic effect, involving involuntary movements of the facial muscles (such as grimacing), tongue, and limbs. In contrast, *new-generation antipsychotic drugs* (such as clozapine, Risperdal, and Zyprexa), which target D1 dopamine receptors, have fewer such side effects. However, these newer medications appear hardly more effective and seem to increase the risk of obesity and diabetes (Leberman & others, 2005). Another complication with both generations of these medications is that one person's effective dose may be another person's overdose or underdose. Only by carefully monitoring the dosage and its effects can psychiatrist and patient tread the fine line between symptom relief and extremely unpleasant side effects. But with the appropriate dosage, combined with life-skills programs and family support, hundreds of thousands of people with schizophrenia who had been consigned to the back wards of mental hospitals have returned to work and to near-normal lives, and relapse rates have been reduced (Leucht & others, 2003).

Antianxiety Drugs

OBJECTIVE 54-3 | Describe the characteristics of antianxiety drugs.

Like alcohol, *antianxiety* agents, such as Xanax or Ativan, depress central nervous system activity (and so should not be used in combination with alcohol). Used in combination with psychological therapy, an antianxiety drug can help a person learn to cope with frightening situations and fear-triggering stimuli.

The criticism sometimes made of the behavior therapies—that they reduce symptoms without resolving underlying problems—is also made of antianxiety drugs. Unlike the behavior therapies, however, these substances may be used as an ongoing treatment. "Popping a Xanax" at the first sign of tension can produce psychological dependence; the immediate relief reinforces a person's tendency to take drugs when anxious. Antianxiety drugs can also cause physiological dependence. When heavy users stop taking them, they may experience withdrawal symptoms, such as increased anxiety and insomnia.

Over the dozen years at the end of the twentieth century, the rate of outpatient treatment for anxiety disorders nearly doubled. The proportion of patients receiving medication during that time increased from 52 to 70 percent (Olfson & others, 2004). And the new standard drug treatment for anxiety disorders? Antidepressants.

Antidepressant Drugs

OBJECTIVE 54-4 | Describe the characteristics of antidepressant drugs, and discuss their use in treating specific disorders.

As the antianxiety drugs can calm people down from a state of anxiety, the *antidepressants* sometimes lift people up from a state of depression. (Their name is a bit of a misnomer now that these drugs are increasingly being used to successfully treat anxiety disorders such as obsessive-compulsive disorder.) This class of drugs works by increasing the availability of norepinephrine or serotonin, neurotransmitters that elevate arousal and mood and appear scarce during depression. Fluoxetine, which tens of million of users worldwide have known as Prozac, partially blocks the reabsorption and removal of serotonin from synapses (**FIGURE 54.2**). Because they slow the synaptic vacuuming up of serotonin, Prozac, and its cousins Zoloft and Paxil, are called *selective-serotonin-reuptake-inhibitors (SSRIs)*. Other dual-action antidepressants work by blocking the reabsorption or breakdown of both norepinephrine and serotonin. Though no less effective, the dual-action drugs have more potential side effects, such as dry mouth, weight gain, hypertension, or dizzy spells (Anderson, 2000; Mulrow, 1999). Administering them by means of a patch, bypassing the intestines and liver, helps reduce such side effects (Bodkin & Amsterdam, 2002).

The greater popularity of SSRI drugs helps explain why 89 percent of patients diagnosed with depression in 2001 received medication from their physicians, up from 70 percent in 1987, the year before SSRIs were introduced (Olfson & others, 2003; Stafford & others, 2001). And that, plus increasing numbers seeking help for depression and anxiety, helps explain a reported tripling in the total number of antidepressant prescriptions since 1992 (Goode, 2002). The drugs account for most of the $19.5 billion in worldwide antidepressant sales in 2000 (Sherman, 2004).

Be advised: Patients with depression who begin taking antidepressants do not wake up the next day singing "Oh, what a beautiful morning!" Although the influence of antidepressants on neurotransmission does occur within hours, their full psychological effect often requires four weeks. One possible reason for the delayed effect is that increased serotonin seems to promote *neurogenesis*—the birth of new brain cells, perhaps reversing stress-induced loss of neurons (Jacobs; 2004; Santarelli & others, 2003).

One side effect of SSRI drugs can be decreased sexual appetite, which has led to their occasional prescription to control sexual behavior (Slater, 2000).

On U.S. college campuses, the 9 percent of counseling center visitors taking psychiatric medication in 1994 nearly tripled, to 24.5 percent in 2004 (Duenwald, 2004).

FIGURE 54.2
Biology of antidepressants
Shown here is the action of Prozac, which partially blocks the reuptake of serotonin.

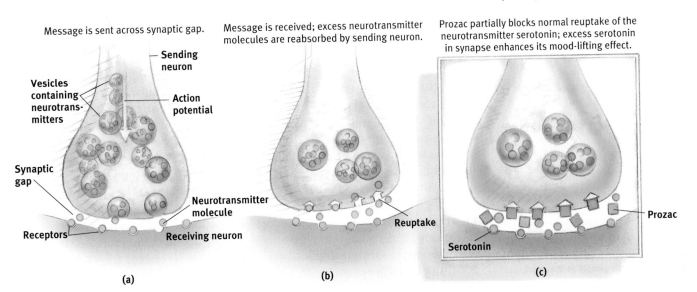

Message is sent across synaptic gap.

Message is received; excess neurotransmitter molecules are reabsorbed by sending neuron.

Prozac partially blocks normal reuptake of the neurotransmitter serotonin; excess serotonin in synapse enhances its mood-lifting effect.

Sending neuron

Vesicles containing neurotransmitters

Action potential

Synaptic gap

Neurotransmitter molecule

Receptors

Receiving neuron

Reuptake

Prozac

Serotonin

(a)   (b)   (c)

"If this doesn't help you don't worry, it's a placebo."

Antidepressant drugs are not the only way to give the body a lift. Aerobic exercise, which helps calm people who feel anxious and energize those who feel depressed, does about as much good for some people with mild to moderate depression, and has additional positive side effects. Cognitive therapy, by helping people reverse their habitual negative thinking style, can boost the drug-aided relief from depression and reduce the post-treatment risk of relapse (Hollon & others, 2002; Keller & others, 2000). Better yet, some studies suggest, is to attack depression from both above and below (Goldapple & others, 2004; TADS, 2004). Use antidepressant drugs (which work, bottom-up, on the emotion-forming limbic system) in conjunction with cognitive behavior therapy (which works, top-down, starting with changed frontal lobe activity).

Everyone agrees that people with depression often improve after a month on antidepressants. But after allowing for natural recovery (the regression to normal called *spontaneous recovery*) and the placebo effect, how big is the drug effect? Not big, report Irving Kirsch and his colleagues (1998, 2002) from their analyses of double-blind clinical trials: Placebos produced improvement comparable to 75 percent or so of the active drug's effect. Another research team analyzed data from 45 studies. Given antidepressants, 41 percent of participants improved; given placebos, 31 percent improved (Khan & others, 2000). Moreover, Kirsch reports, some of the 25 percent difference between the active drug and the placebo in the double-blind trials seems due to an additional placebo effect derived from the drug's side effects, which raise people's expectations because they know they're getting an active drug. Placebos that mimic the side effects of antidepressants are nearly as effective as the drugs themselves (Fisher & Greenberg, 1997).

Many who have witnessed or experienced the healing power of antidepressants question these findings. "It would be very miraculous if all the people I've seen getting better were getting better only by virtue of placebo," said the National Institute of Mental Health's director, Steven Hyman (1999). But this much seems assured: Our expectations have surprisingly powerful effects not only on our perceptions and our responses to such external stimuli as alcohol, hypnosis, and sexual situations (as we saw in earlier modules), but also on our biology and well-being (Kirsch & Lynn, 1999). The mind matters.

"No twisted thought without a twisted molecule."

Attributed to psychologist Ralph Gerard

Skeptics of the biomedical therapies are unsurprised. Yesterday, says neuroscientist Elliot Valenstein (1998), we blamed mothers and sought to heal their children's inner wounds. Today, hardly wiser, we blame brain chemistry and circuitry and pump in "molecules of the mind." But our knowledge of the biochemical roots of disorder and recovery is elementary, he contends. Psychotherapeutic drugs are not "'smart missiles' that can correct the precise biochemical error responsible for each mental illness" without side effects (1998, p. 5). The chemistry, brain circuitry, and life experiences that underlie behavior are too complex for that.

Although the effects of drug therapy are less exciting than many TV ads suggest, they also are less frightening than other stories have warned. Some people taking Prozac, for example, have committed suicide, but their numbers seem fewer than we would expect from the millions of people with depression who are now taking the medication. Prozac users who commit suicide are like cellular phone users who get brain cancer. Given the millions of people taking Prozac and using cellular phones, alarming anecdotes tell us nothing. The question critical thinkers want answered is this: Do these groups suffer an elevated *rate* of suicide and brain cancer? The answer in each case appears to be no (Paulos, 1995; Tollefson & others, 1993, 1994).

The suicide-risk concern resurfaced in the early twenty-first century with studies indicating that children and adults are at a temporary heightened risk of suicide just after beginning drug treatment (Wessely & Kerwin, 2004; Whittington & others, 2004). One explanation is that the drugs reduce one's lethargy before they lift one's feelings, thus giving formerly inert people enough energy to act on their depression. In Britain, where antidepressant prescriptions for children rose 70 percent from 1992 through 2001, the Department of Health warned against treating mild childhood depression

"I think the dosage needs adjusting. I'm not nearly as happy as the people in the ads."

with antidepressant drugs (Alvarez, 2004). In the United States, the Food and Drug Administration began requiring a warning label—that the drugs can cause suicidal behavior in children and teens. But other recent studies indicate that the long-term increase in antidepressant use correlates with a *decline* in the adolescent suicide rate (Grunebaum & others, 2004; Olfson & others, 2003). In U.S. Zip Code areas where antidepressant use increased during the 1990s, teen suicide was most likely to decrease. Such studies suggest that perhaps antidepressants increase suicide risk in the short run, but lower it in the long run.

"First of all I think you should know that last quarter's sales figures are interfering with my mood-stabilizing drugs."

Mood-Stabilizing Medications

OBJECTIVE 54-5 | Describe the use and effects of mood-stabilizing medications.

In addition to antipsychotic, antianxiety, and antidepressant drugs, psychiatrists have *mood-stabilizing drugs* in their arsenal. The simple salt *lithium* can be an effective mood stabilizer for those suffering the manic-depressive swings of bipolar disorder. Australian physician John Cade discovered this in the 1940s when he administered lithium to a patient with severe mania. Although his reason for doing so was misguided—he thought lithium had calmed excitable guinea pigs when actually it had made them sick—Cade found that in less than a week the patient became perfectly well (Snyder, 1986). With continued lithium use, emotional highs and lows typically stabilize. After suffering mood swings for years, about 7 in 10 people with bipolar disorder benefit from a long-term daily dose of this cheap salt (Solomon & others, 1995). Their risk of suicide is but one-sixth that of bipolar patients not taking lithium (Tondo & others, 1997). Although we do not fully understand why, lithium works. And so does Depakote, a drug originally used to treat epilepsy and more recently found effective in the control of manic episodes associated with bipolar disorder.

Brain Stimulation

Electroconvulsive Therapy

OBJECTIVE 54-6 | Describe the use of electroconvulsive therapy in treating severe depression, and discuss some possible alternatives to ECT.

A more controversial brain manipulation occurs through shock treatment, or **electroconvulsive therapy (ECT)** When ECT was first introduced in 1938, the wide-awake patient was strapped to a table and jolted with roughly 100 volts of electricity to the brain, producing racking convulsions and brief unconsciousness. ECT therefore gained a barbaric image, one that lingers still. Today, however, patients first receive a general anesthetic so they are not conscious, and a muscle relaxant to prevent injury from convulsions. Then a psychiatrist momentarily electrically shocks the unconscious patient's brain. Within 30 minutes, the patient awakens and remembers nothing of the treatment or of the hours preceding it (**FIGURE 54.3** on the next page).

Psychiatrists usually limit ECT to treatment of severe depression. (It tends to be ineffective in treating other psychological disorders.) After three such sessions each week for two to four weeks, 80 percent or more of people receiving ECT improve markedly, showing some memory loss for the treatment period but no discernible brain damage (Bergsholm & others, 1989; Coffey, 1993). "A miracle had happened in two weeks," reported noted research psychologist Norman Endler (1982) after ECT alleviated his deep depression. Study after study confirms that ECT is an effective treatment for severe depression in patients who have not responded to drug therapy (Consensus Conference, 1985; UK ECT Review Group, 2003). By 2001, confidence in ECT had further increased, with a *JAMA* (*Journal of the American Medical Association*) editorial concluding that "the results of ECT in treating severe depression are among the most positive treatment effects in all of medicine" (Glass, 2001).

The medical use of electricity is an ancient practice. Physicians treated the Roman Emperor Claudius (10 B.C.–A.D. 54) for headaches by pressing electric eels to his temples.

■ **electroconvulsive therapy (ECT)** a biomedical therapy for severely depressed patients in which a brief electric current is sent through the brain of an anesthetized patient.

FIGURE **54.3**
Electroconvulsive therapy
Although ECT is controversial, it is the preferred treatment for depression that does
not respond to drug therapy.

How does ECT work? After more than 50 years, no one knows for sure. One recip-
ient likened ECT to the smallpox vaccine, which was saving lives before we knew how
it worked. Perhaps the shock-induced seizures cause the brain to react by calming
neural centers where overactivity produces depression.

ECT reduces suicidal thoughts and is credited with saving many from suicide (Kellner & others, 2005). It is now administered with briefer pulses that disrupt memory
less (Fink, 1998; Kho & others, 2003). Yet its Frankensteinlike image continues. No
matter how impressive the results, the idea of electrically shocking people into convulsions still strikes many as barbaric, especially given our ignorance about why ECT
works. Moreover, ECT-treated patients, like other patients with a history of depression, are vulnerable to relapse. Nevertheless, electroconvulsive therapy is, in the
minds of many psychiatrists and patients, a lesser evil than severe depression's misery, anguish, and risk of suicide.

Alternatives to ECT

Hopes are now rising for gentler alternatives for jump-starting the depressed brain.
Some patients with chronic depression have found relief through a chest implant that
intermittently stimulates the vagus nerve, which sends signals to the brain's mood-
related limbic system (Marangell & others, 2002; Rush & others, 2005). In another
study of six patients who had failed to respond even to ECT, four gained "striking and
sustained remission of depression" following stimulation through electrodes planted
deep in their brains (Mayberg & others, 2005). The stimulation served to reduce activity in a region that is hyperactive in depression, and patients immediately experienced
such impressions as a "disappearance of the void" and a sense of "connectedness." This
finding will surely inspire further experiments to test the possibility of a brain pacemaker that can buzz people out of depression.

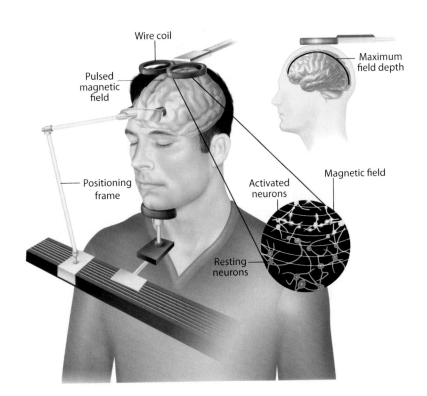

FIGURE **54.4**
Magnets for the mind
Repetitive transcranial magnetic stimulation (rTMS) sends a painless magnetic field through the skull to the cortical surface, where pulses can be used to stimulate or dampen activity in various areas (from George, 2003).

Depressed moods also seem to improve when repeated pulses surge through a magnetic coil held close to a person's skull (**FIGURE 54.4**). Unlike deep brain stimulation, the magnetic energy penetrates only to the brain's surface (though tests are under way with a higher energy field that penetrates more deeply). The painless procedure—called **repetitive transcranial magnetic stimulation (rTMS)**—is performed on wide-awake patients for 20 to 30 minutes for two to four weeks. Unlike ECT, the rTMS procedure produces no seizures, memory loss, or other side effects.

In one double-blind experiment, 67 Israelis with major depression were randomly assigned to two groups (Klein & others, 1999). One group received daily stimulations over a two-week period, while the other received sham treatments (without magnetic stimulation). At the end of the two weeks, half of the stimulated patients showed at least a 50 percent improvement in their scores on a depression scale, as did only a quarter of the placebo group. Newer studies confirmed the therapeutic effect, which inspired the beginning in 2005 of two large, multilocation clinical experiments on rTMS (Cohen & others, 2005; Janicak, 2005; Martin & others, 2003). One possible explanation of this effect is that the stimulation energizes depressed patients' relatively inactive left frontal lobe (Helmuth, 2001). When repeatedly stimulated, nerve cells can form functioning circuits through a process called *long-term potentiation (LTP)*. Before long, conclusive data from the clinical experiments should become available, indicating whether magnetic stimulation is, indeed, a valuable new treatment for depression.

Psychosurgery

OBJECTIVE 54-7 | Summarize the history of the psychosurgical procedure known as a lobotomy, and discuss the use of psychosurgery today.

Because its effects are irreversible, **psychosurgery**—surgery that removes or destroys brain tissue—is the most drastic and the least-used biomedical intervention for changing behavior. In the 1930s, Portuguese physician Egas Moniz developed what

■ **repetitive transcranial magnetic stimulation (rTMS)** the application of repeated pulses of magnetic energy to the brain; used to stimulate or suppress brain activity.

■ **psychosurgery** surgery that removes or destroys brain tissue in an effort to change behavior.

■ **lobotomy** a now-rare psychosurgical procedure once used to calm uncontrollably emotional or violent patients. The procedure cut the nerves that connect the frontal lobes to the emotion-controlling centers of the inner brain.

became the best-known psychosurgical operation: the **lobotomy.** Moniz found that cutting the nerves connecting the frontal lobes with the emotion-controlling centers of the inner brain calmed uncontrollably emotional and violent patients. After shocking the patient into a coma, a neurosurgeon would hammer an icepicklike instrument through each eye socket into the brain, then wiggle it to sever connections running up to the frontal lobes. The whole procedure was crude but easy and inexpensive, and it took only about 10 minutes. During the 1940s and 1950s, tens of thousands of severely disturbed people were "lobotomized," and Moniz was honored with a Nobel prize (Valenstein, 1986).

Although the intention was simply to disconnect emotion from thought, the effect was often more drastic: The lobotomy usually produced a permanently lethargic, immature, impulsive personality. During the 1950s, after some 35,000 people had been lobotomized in the United States alone, calming drugs became available and psychosurgery was largely abandoned. Today, lobotomies are history and other psychosurgery is used only in extreme cases. For example, if a patient suffers uncontrollable seizures, surgeons can deactivate the specific nerve clusters that cause or transmit the convulsions. MRI-guided precision surgery is also occasionally done to cut the circuits involved in severe obsessive-compulsive disorder (Sachdev & Sachdev, 1997). Because these procedures are irreversible, however, neurosurgeons perform them only as a last resort.

Mind-body interaction
The biomedical therapies assume that mind and body are a unit: Affect one and you will affect the other.

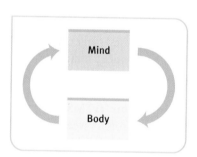

The effectiveness of the biomedical therapies reminds us of a fundamental lesson: We find it convenient to talk of separate psychological and biological influences, but everything psychological is also biological. Every thought and feeling depends on the functioning brain. Every creative idea, every moment of joy or anger, every period of depression emerges from the electrochemical activity of the living brain. The influence is two-way: When psychotherapy relieves obsessive-compulsive behavior, PET scans reveal a calmer brain (Schwartz & others, 1996).

>> LEARNING OUTCOMES

The Biomedical Therapies

OBJECTIVE 54-1 | **Discuss the goals of biomedical therapy, and explain how double-blind studies help researchers evaluate a drug's effectiveness.**

Biomedical therapy attempts to treat disorders with prescribed medications or medical procedures that act directly on a patient's nervous system. Since the 1950s, drug therapy has been used extensively to treat psychological disorders. *Double-blind studies,* in which neither the medical staff nor the patient knows whether the patient is taking the real drug or a placebo, eliminate the bias that can result from clinicians' and patients' expectations of improvement.

OBJECTIVE 54-2 | **Describe the characteristics of antipsychotic drugs, and discuss their use in treating schizophrenia.**

The antipsychotic drugs dampen responsiveness to irrelevant stimuli, and they have been used effectively to treat schizophrenia accompanied by positive symptoms (the presence of hallucinations and delusions). The first-generation antipsychotic drugs, which block D2 (dopamine) receptors, can produce *tardive dyskinesia,* (involuntary movements of facial muscles, the tongue, and arms and legs). Second-generation antipsychotics, which target D1 receptors, can affect metabolism, increasing the risk of obesity and diabetes.

OBJECTIVE 54-3 | **Describe the characteristics of antianxiety drugs.**

Antianxiety drugs, which depress central nervous system activity, are often used in combination with psychotherapy for treatment of anxiety disorders. These drugs can be psychologically and physically addictive.

OBJECTIVE 54-4 | **Describe the characteristics of antidepressant drugs, and discuss their use in treating specific disorders.**

Antidepressant drugs increase the availability of norepinephrine or serotonin, which elevate arousal and mood. *Selective-serotonin-reuptake-inhibitors (SSRIs)* block the reuptake of serotonin. Dual-action antidepressants block the reuptake or absorption of both norepinephrine and serotonin, but they have a greater risk of side effects. Antidepressants may be used to treat depression (often in combination with cognitive therapy) and the anxiety disorders. Their full psychological effects may not appear for several weeks.

OBJECTIVE 54-5 | **Describe the use and effects of mood-stabilizing medications.**

A few drugs, such as *lithium* for bipolar disorder, have proven very effective in stabilizing moods. Researchers do not yet understand how these medications work.

OBJECTIVE 54-6 | **Describe the use of electroconvulsive therapy in treating severe depression, and discuss some possible alternatives to ECT.**

In ECT, a brief electric current is sent through the brain of an anesthetized patient. Although controversial, ECT is an effective, last-resort treatment for many people with severe depression who have not responded to drug therapy. How ECT works is unknown. Depression has also been alleviated by some implanted devices that stimulate parts of the brain, and by repetitive transcranial magnetic stimulation (rTMS), in which pulses of magnetic energy sent through the skull to the surface of the cortex stimulate or dampen activity in various brain areas.

OBJECTIVE 54-7 | **Summarize the history of the psychosurgical procedure known as a lobotomy, and discuss the use of psychosurgery today.**

Lobotomy was a crude and irreversible procedure in which surgical instruments were inserted through a patient's eye sockets to sever connections running to the frontal lobes of the brain, with the intent of calming uncontrollably emotional or violent patients. This surgery disappeared in the 1950s, when its harmful effects (lethargy and an impulsive personality) became known and new and effective drug treatments were introduced. Today, neurosurgeons rarely perform brain surgery to treat psychological disorders.

TERMS AND CONCEPTS TO REMEMBER

biomedical therapy, p. 54-1
psychopharmacology, p. 54-1
tardive dyskinesia, p. 54-2
electroconvulsive therapy (ECT), p. 54-5

repetitive transcranial magnetic stimulation (rTMS), p. 54-7
psychosurgery, p. 54-7
lobotomy, p. 54-8

TEST YOURSELF

1. How do researchers evaluate the effectiveness of particular drug therapies?

(Answer in Appendix B.)

ASK YOURSELF

1. Have your feelings about therapy changed since you entered this course? If so, in what ways?

>WEB

Multiple-choice *self-tests* and more may be found at www.worthpublishers.com/myers.

SEKOU SUNDIATA (b. 1948), "BLINK YOUR EYES," 1995, *THE BLUE ONENESS DREAMS*

I could wake up in the morning
without a warning
and my world could change:

blink your eyes.
All depends, all depends on the skin,
all depends on the skin you're living in.

Social Psychology

OBJECTIVE 55-1 | Describe the three main focuses of social psychology.

On September 11, 2001, shortly after terrorists flew hijacked planes into the World Trade Center, I spoke by phone with my daughter, Laura. She was on the street in her Manhattan neighborhood, describing the tumultuous scene, when suddenly she yelled, "Oh my gosh! Oh my gosh!" as the second massive tower collapsed before her eyes. By almost anyone's definition, this catastrophic violence—accomplished by a mere 19 men with box cutters—was an evil act, to which the communal response was fear mixed with anger. A bully's single kick that collapses a nearly finished sandcastle triggers both fright and outrage. Likewise, for millions of stunned Americans, 9/11 evoked anxiety about what might come next and a lust for revenge.

But the cataclysm also triggered an outpouring of love and compassion. From around the country and the world, money and countless truckloads of food, clothing, and teddy bears—more than New Yorkers could possibly use—poured in. People in Toledo, Fargo, and Stockholm wept for those who wept. There on 6th Avenue and 24th Street, strangers hugged and talked, trying to make sense of senseless destruction. Although few transfusions would be needed, willing donors formed long lines at blood banks. "Everywhere I go I see concern," Laura wrote that evening.

> I see compassion. I see people with many differences united. I don't see violence. I don't see impatience. I don't see cruelty. Except when I look at that cloud of smoke, a constant backdrop all day. People are helping each other. People are desperate to do whatever they can.
>
> In the midst of this nightmare, I am utterly filled with love for the people of this city. It is incredible to witness their response. I am covered in goose bumps. My faith in humanity rises over that cloud and I see goodness and respect.

We watch and we wonder: What drives people to feel such hatred and to destroy so many innocent lives? And what motivates the heroic altruism of those who died trying to save others and of the many more who reached out to those coping with loss?

As the 9/11 horror so compellingly demonstrates, we are social animals. Depending on who or what influences our thinking, we may assume the best or the worst in others. And depending on our attitudes, we may approach them with closed fists or open arms.

"We cannot live for ourselves alone," remarked the novelist Herman Melville. "Our lives are connected by a thousand invisible threads." **Social psychologists** explore these connections by scientifically studying how we *think about, influence,* and *relate to* one another. In Modules 55 through 58, we consider these topics.

Social Thinking (Module 55) asks, How do we explain people's behavior? How do we form our beliefs and attitudes? What is the relationship between what we think and what we do? Social Influence (Module 56) asks, What invisible social threads pull us? How strong are they? How do they operate? Antisocial Relations (Module 57) asks, What makes us harm others? And in Prosocial Relations (Module 58): Why do we fall in love? And what can we do to transform the closed fists of aggression into the open arms of compassion?

■ **social psychology** the scientific study of how we think about, influence, and relate to one another.

MODULE

55

Social Thinking

Especially when the unexpected occurs, we analyze why people act as they do. Does her warmth reflect romantic interest, or is that how she relates to everyone? Does his absenteeism signify illness? Laziness? A stressful work atmosphere? Was the horror of 9/11 the work of crazed evil people, or of ordinary people corrupted by life events? Such questions intrigue social psychologists. Just as personality psychologists study the enduring, inner determinants of behavior that help to explain why different people act differently in a given situation, so *social psychologists* study the social influences that help explain why the same person will act differently in different situations.

Attributing Behavior to Persons or to Situations

OBJECTIVE 55-2 | Contrast dispositional and situational attributions, and explain how the fundamental attribution error can affect our analyses of behavior.

After studying how people explain others' behavior, Fritz Heider (1958) proposed an **attribution theory.** Heider noted that people usually attribute others' behavior either to their internal dispositions or to their external situations. A teacher, for example, may wonder whether a child's hostility reflects an aggressive personality (*a dispositional attribution*) or a reaction to stress or abuse (*a situational attribution*).

In class, we notice that Juliette seldom talks; over coffee, Jack talks nonstop. Attributing their behaviors to their personal dispositions, we decide Juliette is shy and Jack is outgoing. Because people do have enduring personality traits, such attributions are sometimes valid. However, we often fall prey to the **fundamental attribution error,** by overestimating the influence of personality and underestimating the influence of situations. In class, Jack may be as quiet as Juliette. Catch Juliette at a party and you may hardly recognize your quiet classmate.

An experiment by David Napolitan and George Goethals (1979) illustrates the phenomenon. They had Williams College students talk, one at a time, with a young woman who acted either aloof and critical or warm and friendly. Beforehand, they told half the students the woman's behavior would be spontaneous. They told the other half the truth—that she had been instructed to *act* friendly (or unfriendly). What do you suppose was the effect of being told the truth?

There was no effect. The students disregarded the information. If the woman acted friendly, they inferred she really was a warm person. If she acted unfriendly, they inferred she really was a cold person. In other words, they attributed her behavior to her personal disposition *even when told that her behavior was situational—* that she was merely acting that way for the purposes of the experiment. Although the fundamental attribution error occurs in all cultures studied, this tendency to attribute behavior to people's dispositions runs especially strong in individualistic Western countries. In East Asian cultures, for example, people are more sensitive to the power of the situation (Masuda & Kitayama, 2005).

As with other biases, people see themselves as less susceptible than others to the phenomenon (Pronin & others, 2004). The

The fundamental attribution error
If our new colleague at work acts grouchy, we may infer that she's a grouchy person, discounting her having lost sleep over a family worry, having a flat tire on the way to work, and being unable to find a parking place.

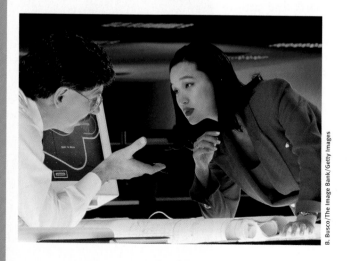

B. Busco/The Image Bank/Getty Images

fundamental attribution error is almost irresistible, though. In a high school play, I saw a talented 16-year-old convincingly play the part of a bitter old woman—so convincingly that, although I reminded myself of the fundamental attribution error, I still assumed that the young actress was typecast because she was well-suited for the part. Meeting her later at a cast party, I discovered she actually had a very pleasant disposition. I then remembered that several months earlier I had seen her play the part of a charming 10-year-old in *The Sound of Music*.

You, too, have surely committed the fundamental attribution error. In judging whether your psychology instructor is shy or outgoing, you have perhaps by now inferred that he or she has an outgoing personality. But you know your instructor only from the classroom, a situation that demands outgoing behavior. Catch the instructor in a different situation and you might be surprised (as some of my students have been when confronting me in a pick-up basketball game). Outside their assigned roles, professors seem less professorial, presidents less presidential, servants less servile.

The instructor, on the other hand, observes his or her own behavior in many different situations—in the classroom, in meetings, at home—and so might say, "Me, outgoing? It all depends on the situation. In class or with good friends, yes, I'm outgoing. But at conventions I'm really rather shy." So, when explaining *our own* behavior, or the behavior of those we know well and see in varied situations, we are sensitive to how behavior changes with the situations (Idson & Mischel, 2001).

When explaining *others'* behavior, particularly the behavior of strangers we have observed in only one type of situation, we often commit the fundamental attribution error: We disregard the situation and leap to unwarranted conclusions about their personality traits. Many people initially assumed that Nazi death camp commanders exhibited consistently vile behavior. Actually, many were unremarkable men who went home after the day's brutality and relaxed with a good book and the strains of classical music. Many of us initially assumed the 9/11 terrorists were obviously crazy, when actually they went unnoticed in their neighborhoods, health clubs, and favorite restaurants.

Researchers who have reversed the perspectives of actor and observer—by having each view a videotape replay of the situation from the other's perspective—have also reversed the attributions (Lassiter & Irvine, 1986; Storms, 1973). Seeing the world from the actor's perspective, the observers better appreciate the situation. Taking the observer's point of view, the actors better appreciate their own personal style.

The Effects of Attribution

In everyday life we often struggle to explain others' actions. A jury must decide whether a shooting was malicious or in self-defense. An interviewer must judge whether the applicant's geniality is genuine. When we make such judgments, our attributions—either to the person or to the situation—have important consequences (Fincham & Bradbury, 1993; Fletcher & others, 1990). Happily married couples attribute a spouse's tart-tongued remark to a temporary situation ("She must have had a bad day at work."). Unhappily married persons attribute the same remark to a mean disposition ("Why did I marry such a hostile person?").

Or consider the political effects of attribution: How do you explain poverty or unemployment? Researchers in Britain, India, Australia, and the United States (Furnham, 1982; Pandey & others, 1982; Wagstaff, 1982; Zucker & Weiner, 1993) report that political conservatives tend to attribute such social problems to the personal dispositions of the poor and unemployed themselves: "People generally get what they deserve. Those who don't work are often freeloaders. Anybody who takes the initiative can still get ahead." "Society is not to blame for

■ **attribution theory** suggests how we explain someone's behavior—by crediting either the situation or the person's disposition.

■ **fundamental attribution error** the tendency for observers, when analyzing another's behavior, to underestimate the impact of the situation and to overestimate the impact of personal disposition.

"Calling [9/11] *senseless, mindless, insane,* or the work of *madmen* is wrong . . . [it] fails to adopt the perspective of the perpetrators, as an act with a clearly defined purpose that we must understand in order to challenge it most effectively."
Psychologist Philip G. Zimbardo, "Fighting Terrorism by Understanding Man's Capacity for Evil," September 16, 2001

"Otis, shout at that man to pull himself together."

An attribution question
Some people blamed the New Orleans residents for not evacuating before the predicted Hurricane Katrina. Others attributed their inaction to the situation—to their not having cars or not being offered bus transportation.

Paul Buck/EPA/Landov

crime, criminals are," said one conservative U.S. presidential candidate (Dole, 1996). Political liberals (and social scientists) are more likely to blame past and present situations: "If you or I had to live with the same poor education, lack of opportunity, and discrimination, would we be any better off?" To understand and prevent terrorism, they say, consider the situations that breed terrorists. Better to drain the swamps than swat the mosquitoes.

Managers also have to make attributions. In evaluating employees, they are likely to attribute poor performance to personal factors, such as low ability or lack of motivation. But remember the actor's viewpoint: Workers doing poorly on a job recognize situational influences, such as inadequate supplies, poor working conditions, difficult co-workers, or impossible demands (Rice, 1985).

The point to remember: Our attributions—to individuals' dispositions or to their situations—have real consequences (**FIGURE 55.1**).

FIGURE 55.1
Attributions and reactions
How we explain someone's behavior affects how we react to it.

Negative behavior

Situational attribution
"Maybe that driver is ill."

Tolerant reaction
(proceed cautiously, allow driver a wide berth)

Dispositional attribution
"Crazy driver!"

Unfavorable reaction
(speed up and race past the other driver, craning to give a dirty look)

Attitudes and Actions

OBJECTIVE **55-3** | Define *attitude*.

Attitudes are feelings, based on our beliefs, that predispose our reactions to objects, people, and events. If we *believe* someone is mean, we may *feel* dislike for the person and *act* unfriendly. "Change the way people think," said South African civil rights martyr Steve Biko, "and things will never be the same." Such is the power of persuasion.

Attitudes Can Affect Actions

OBJECTIVE **55-4** | Describe the conditions under which attitudes can affect actions.

Our attitudes predict our behavior imperfectly because other factors, including the external situation, also influence behavior. Strong social pressures can weaken the attitude-behavior connection (Wallace & others, 2005). For example, the American public's overwhelming support for President George W. Bush's preparation to attack Iraq motivated Democratic leaders to vote to support Bush's war plan, despite their private reservations (Nagourney, 2002). Nevertheless, attitudes may indeed affect behavior when other influences are minimal, when the attitude is specific to the behavior, and when we are keenly aware of our attitudes.

Actions Can Affect Attitudes

OBJECTIVE **55-5** | Explain how the foot-in-the-door phenomenon, role-playing, and cognitive dissonance illustrate the influence of actions on attitudes.

Now consider a more surprising principle: Not only will people sometimes stand up for what they believe, they will also come to believe in what they have stood up for. Many streams of evidence confirm that *attitudes follow behavior* (**FIGURE 55.2**).

The Foot-in-the-Door Phenomenon

Convincing people to act against their beliefs can affect their attitude. During the Korean War, many captured U.S. soldiers were imprisoned in war camps run by Chinese communists. Without using brutality, the captors secured the collaboration of hundreds of their prisoners in various activities. Some merely ran errands or accepted favors. Others made radio appeals and false confessions. Still others informed on fellow prisoners and divulged military information. When the war ended, 21 prisoners chose to stay with the communists. More returned home "brainwashed"—convinced that communism was a good thing for Asia.

A key ingredient of the Chinese "thought-control" program was its effective use of the **foot-in-the-door phenomenon**—a tendency for people who agree to a small action to comply later with a larger one. The Chinese began with harmless requests but gradually escalated their demands on the prisoners (Schein, 1956). Having "trained" the prisoners to speak or write trivial statements, the communists then asked them to copy or create something more important, noting, perhaps, the flaws of capitalism. Then, perhaps to gain privileges, the prisoners participated in group discussions, wrote self-criticisms, or uttered public confessions. After doing so, they often adjusted their beliefs toward consistency with their public acts.

The point is simple, says Robert Cialdini (1993): To get people to agree to something big, "start small and build." And be wary of those who would exploit you with the tactic. This chicken-and-egg spiral, of actions-feeding-attitudes-feeding-actions, enables behavior to escalate. A trivial act makes the next act easier. Succumb to a temptation and you will find the next temptation harder to resist.

■ **attitude** feelings, often based on our beliefs, that predispose us to respond in a particular way to objects, people, and events.

■ **foot-in-the-door phenomenon** the tendency for people who have first agreed to a small request to comply later with a larger request.

FIGURE 55.2
Attitudes follow behavior
Cooperative actions, such as those performed by people on sports teams, feed mutual liking. Such attitudes, in turn, promote positive behavior.

D. MacDonald/PhotoEdit

Dozens of experiments have simulated part of the war prisoners' experience by coaxing people into acting against their attitudes or violating their moral standards. The nearly inevitable result: Doing becomes believing. When people are induced to harm an innocent victim—by making nasty comments or delivering electric shocks—they then begin to disparage their victim. If induced to speak or write on behalf of a position they have qualms about, they begin to believe their own words.

Fortunately, the attitudes-follow-behavior principle works as well for good deeds as for bad. The foot-in-the-door tactic has helped boost charitable contributions, blood donations, and product sales. In one experiment, researchers posing as safe-driving volunteers asked Californians to permit the installation of a large, poorly lettered "Drive Carefully" sign in their front yards. Only 17 percent consented. They approached other home owners with a small request first: Would they display a 3-inch-high "Be a Safe Driver" sign? Nearly all readily agreed. When reapproached two weeks later to allow the large, ugly sign in their front yards, 76 percent consented (Freedman & Fraser, 1966).

Racial attitudes likewise follow behavior. In the years immediately following the introduction of school desegregation in the United States and the passage of the Civil Rights Act of 1964, white Americans expressed diminishing racial prejudice. And as Americans in different regions came to act more alike—thanks to more uniform national standards against discrimination—they began to think more alike. Experiments confirm the observation: Moral action strengthens moral convictions.

Role-Playing Affects Attitudes

When you adopt a new role—when you become a college student, marry, or begin a new job—you strive to follow the social prescriptions. At first, your behaviors may feel phony, because you are *acting* a role. The first weeks in the military feel artificial—as if one is pretending to be a soldier. The first weeks of a marriage may feel like "playing house." Before long, however, what began as play-acting in the theater of life becomes *you*.

Researchers have confirmed this effect by assessing people's attitudes before and after they adopt a new role, sometimes in laboratory situations, sometimes in everyday situations, such as before and after taking a job. In one well-known laboratory study, male college students volunteered to spend time in a simulated prison devised by psychologist Philip Zimbardo (1972). Some he randomly designated as guards; he gave them uniforms, billy clubs, and whistles and instructed them to enforce certain rules. The remainder became prisoners; they were locked in barren cells and forced to wear humiliating outfits. After a day or two in which the volunteers self-consciously "played" their roles, the simulation became real—too real.

Most of the guards developed disparaging attitudes, and some devised cruel and degrading routines. One by one, the prisoners broke down, rebelled, or became passively resigned, causing Zimbardo to call off the study after only six days. More recently, similar situations have played themselves out in the real world—as in Iraq at the Abu Ghraib Prison (see Close-Up).

Greece's military junta during the early 1970s took advantage of the effects of role-playing to train men to become torturers (Staub, 1989). The men's indoctrination into their roles occurred in small steps. First, the trainee stood guard outside the interrogation cells—the "foot in the door." Next, he stood guard inside. Only then was he ready to become actively involved in the questioning and torture. As the nineteenth-century writer Nathaniel Hawthorne noted, "No man, for any considerable period, can wear one face to himself and another to the multitude without finally getting bewildered as to which may be true." What we do, we gradually become.

> "If the King destroys a man, that's proof to the King it must have been a bad man."
>
> Thomas Cromwell, in Robert Bolt's *A Man for All Seasons*, 1960

> "Fake it until you make it."
>
> Alcoholics Anonymous saying

The power of the situation
In Philip Zimbardo's Stanford Prison simulation, a toxic situation triggered degrading behaviors among those assigned to the guard role.

Philip G. Zimbardo, Inc.

CLOSE-UP:

ABU GHRAIB PRISON: AN "ATROCITY-PRODUCING SITUATION"?

As the first photos emerged in 2004 from Iraq's Abu Ghraib Prison, the civilized world was shocked. The photos showed U.S. military guards stripping prisoners naked, placing hoods on them, stacking them in piles, prodding them with electricity, taunting them with attack dogs, and subjecting them to sleep deprivation, humiliation, and extreme stress. Was the problem, as so many people initially supposed, a few bad apples—irresponsible or even sadistic guards? That was the U.S. Army's seeming verdict when it court-martialed and imprisoned some of the guards, and then cleared four of the five top commanding officers responsible for Abu Ghraib's policies and operations. The lower-level military guards were "sick bastards," explained the defense attorney for one of the commanding officers (Tarbert, 2004).

Many social psychologists, however, reminded us that a toxic situation can make even good apples go bad

Bad apples or bad barrels?
Both the Stanford Prison Experiment in 1972 and the real-life Abu Ghraib Prison fiasco in 2004 were powerfully toxic situations, contends social psychologist Philip Zimbardo.

Originally published in the New Yorker

(Fiske & others, 2004). "When ordinary people are put in a novel, evil place, such as most prisons, Situations Win, People Lose," offered Philip Zimbardo (2004), adding, "That is true for the majority of people in all the relevant social psychological research done over the past 40 years."

Consider the situation, explains Zimbardo. The guards, some of them model soldier-reservists with no prior criminal or sadistic history, were exhausted from working 12-hour shifts, seven days a week, for more than a month at a time. They were dealing with an enemy, and their prejudices were heightened by fears of lethal attacks and by the violent deaths of many fellow soldiers. They were put in an understaffed guard role, given minimal training and oversight, and encouraged to "soften up" for interrogation detainees who had been denied access to the Red Cross. "When you put that set of horrendous work conditions and external factors together, it creates an evil barrel. You could put virtually anybody in it and you're going to get this kind of evil behavior" (Zimbardo, 2005).

Cognitive Dissonance: Relief from Tension

So far we have seen that actions can affect attitudes, sometimes turning prisoners into collaborators, doubters into believers, mere acquaintances into friends, and compliant guards into abusers. But why? One explanation is that when we become aware that our attitudes and actions don't coincide, we experience tension, or *cognitive dissonance*. To relieve this tension, according to the **cognitive dissonance theory** proposed by Leon Festinger, we often bring our attitudes into line with our actions. It is as if we rationalize, "If I chose to do it (or say it), I must believe in it." The less coerced and more responsible we feel for a troubling act, the more dissonance we feel. The more dissonance we feel, the more motivated we are to find consistency, such as changing our attitudes to help justify the act.

The U.S. invasion of Iraq was mainly premised on the presumed threat of Saddam Hussein's weapons of mass destruction (WMD). As the war began, only 38 percent of Americans surveyed said the war was justified even if Iraq did not have WMD (Gallup, 2003), and nearly 80 percent believed such weapons would be found (Duffy, 2003; Newport & others, 2003). When no WMD were found, many Americans felt dissonance, which was heightened by their awareness of the war's financial and human costs, by scenes of chaos in Iraq, and by inflamed anti-American and pro-terrorist sentiments in some parts of the world.

To reduce dissonance, some people revised their memories of the main rationale for going to war, which now became liberating an oppressed people and promoting democracy in the Middle East. Before long, the once-minority opinion became the

■ **cognitive dissonance theory** the theory that we act to reduce the discomfort (dissonance) we feel when two of our thoughts (cognitions) are inconsistent. For example, when our awareness of our attitudes and of our actions clash, we can reduce the resulting dissonance by changing our attitudes.

"Look, I have my misgivings, too, but what choice do we have except stay the course?"

majority view: 58 percent of Americans said they supported the war even if there were no WMD (Gallup, 2003). "Whether or not they find weapons of mass destruction doesn't matter," explained Republican pollster Frank Luntz (2003), "because the rationale for the war changed." It was not until late 2004, when hopes for a flourishing peace waned, that Americans' support for the war dropped below 50 percent.

Dozens of experiments have explored cognitive dissonance by making people feel responsible for behavior that is inconsistent with their attitudes and that has foreseeable consequences. As a subject in one of these experiments, you might agree for a measly $2 to help a researcher by writing an essay that supports something you don't believe in (perhaps a tuition increase). Feeling responsible for the statements (which are not consistent with your attitudes), you would probably feel dissonance, especially if you thought an administrator would be reading your essay. How could you reduce the uncomfortable dissonance? One way would be to start believing your phony words. Your pretense would become your reality.

The attitudes-follow-behavior principle has another heartening implication: Although we cannot directly control all our feelings, we can influence them by altering our behavior. Facial expressions and body postures affect our emotions. If we are down in the dumps, we can do as cognitive therapists advise and talk in more positive, self-accepting ways with fewer self-put-downs. If we are unloving, we can become more loving by behaving as if we were so—by doing thoughtful things, expressing affection, giving affirmation. "Assume a virtue, if you have it not," says Hamlet to his mother. "For use can almost change the stamp of nature." *The point to remember:* Evil acts shape the self. But so do acts of good will. Act as though you like someone, and you soon will. Changing our behavior can change how we think about others and how we feel about ourselves.

" Sit all day in a moping posture, sigh, and reply to everything with a dismal voice, and your melancholy lingers. . . . If we wish to conquer undesirable emotional tendencies in ourselves, we must . . . go through the outward movements of those contrary dispositions which we prefer to cultivate."

William James, *Principles of Psychology,* 1890

>> LEARNING OUTCOMES

Social Thinking

OBJECTIVE 55-1 | Describe the three main focuses of social psychology.

Social psychology focuses on three broad topics: how people think about, influence, and relate to one another.

OBJECTIVE 55-2 | Contrast dispositional and situational attributions, and explain how the fundamental attribution error can affect our analyses of behavior.

We usually rely on *situational attributions,* stressing the influence of external events, to explain our own behavior (and often the behavior of those we know well and see in many different contexts). In explaining the actions of people we do not know well, we may resort to *dispositional attributions,* assuming their behavior stems from their personal traits. This *fundamental attribution error* (overestimating the influence of personal factors and underestimating the effect of context) can flaw our judgments of others.

OBJECTIVE 55-3 | Define *attitude.*

Attitudes are positive, negative, or mixed feelings, based on our beliefs, that predispose us to respond in a particular way to objects, people, and events.

OBJECTIVE 55-4 | Describe the conditions under which attitudes can affect actions.

Our attitudes are most likely to affect our behavior when social influences are minimal, the attitude is specific to the behavior, and we are very aware of the attitude.

OBJECTIVE 55-5 | Explain how the foot-in-the-door phenomenon, role-playing, and cognitive dissonance illustrate the influence of actions on attitudes.

The *foot-in-the-door phenomenon* describes people's willingness to agree to a large request after having agreed to a related small request. In *role-playing* studies, such as Philip Zimbardo's prison experiment, people who behaved in certain ways in scripted scenarios have adopted attitudes in keeping with those roles. Leon Festinger's *cognitive dissonance theory* proposes that we feel uncomfortable when we act in ways that conflict with our feelings and beliefs, and we reduce this discomfort by revising our attitudes to align them more closely with our behavior. In all three instances, attitudes adapt to behavior, rather than drive it.

TERMS AND CONCEPTS TO REMEMBER

social psychology, p. P16-1

attribution theory, p. 55-0

fundamental attribution error, p. 55-0

attitude, p. 55-3

foot-in-the-door phenomenon, p. 55-3

cognitive dissonance theory, p. 55-5

TEST YOURSELF

1. Driving to school one wintry day, Marco narrowly misses a car that slides through a red light. "Slow down! What a terrible driver," he thinks to himself. Moments later, Marco himself slips through an intersection and yelps, "Wow! These roads are awful. The city snow plows need to get out here." What social psychology principle has Marco just demonstrated? Explain.

(Answer in Appendix B.)

ASK YOURSELF

1. Do you have an attitude or tendency you would like to change? Using the attitudes-follow-behavior principle, how might you go about changing that attitude?

>WEB

Multiple-choice *self-tests* and more may be found at www.worthpublishers.com/myers.

Conformity and Obedience

Group Influence

56

Social Influence

Social psychology's great lesson is the enormous power of social influence. This influence can be seen in our conformity, our compliance, and our group behavior. Suicides, bomb threats, airplane hijackings, and UFO sightings all have a curious tendency to come in clusters. On campus, blue jeans are the dress code; on New York's Wall Street or London's Bond Street, dress suits are the norm. When we know how to act, how to groom, how to talk, life functions smoothly. Armed with principles of social influence, advertisers, fund-raisers, and campaign workers aim to sway our decisions to buy, to donate, to vote. Isolated with others who share their grievances, dissenters may gradually become rebels, and rebels may become terrorists. Let's examine the pull of these social strings. How strong are they? How do they operate?

Conformity and Obedience

OBJECTIVE 56-1 | Describe the chameleon effect, and give an example of it.

Behavior is contagious.

- One person laughs, coughs, or yawns, and others in the group soon do the same. Chimps, too, are more likely to yawn after observing another chimp yawn (Anderson & others, 2004).
- A cluster of people stand gazing upward, and passersby pause to do likewise.
- Bartenders and street musicians know to "seed" their tip containers with money to suggest that others have given.
- "Sickness" can also be psychologically contagious. In the anxious 9/11 aftermath, more than two dozen elementary and middle schools had outbreaks of children reporting red rashes, sometimes causing parents to wonder whether biological terrorism was at work (Talbot, 2002). Some cases may have been stress-related, but mostly, said health experts, people were just noticing normal early acne, insect bites, eczema, and dry skin from overheated classrooms.

We are natural mimics—an effect Tanya Chartrand and John Bargh (1999) call the *chameleon effect*. Unconsciously mimicking others' expressions, postures, and voice tones helps us feel what they are feeling. This helps explain why we feel happier around happy people than around depressed ones, and why studies of groups of British nurses and accountants reveal *mood linkage*—sharing up and down moods (Totterdell & others, 1998). Just hearing someone reading a neutral text in either a happy- or sad-sounding voice creates "mood contagion" in listeners (Neumann & Strack, 2000).

Chartrand and Bargh demonstrated the chameleon effect when they had students work in a room alongside a confederate working for the experimenter. Sometimes the confederates rubbed their face; on other occasions, they shook their foot. Sure enough, participants tended to rub their own face when they were with the face-rubbing person and shake their own foot when they were with the foot-shaking person. Such automatic mimicry is part of empathy. The most empathic people mimic—and are liked—the most. And those most eager to fit in with a group seem intuitively to know this, for they are especially prone to nonconscious mimicry (Lakin & Chartrand, 2003).

Niche conformity
Are these students asserting their individuality or identifying themselves with others of the same microculture?

Yuriko Nakao/Reuters/Corbis

NON SEQUITUR   by WILEY

Sometimes the effects of suggestibility are more serious. In the eight days following the 1999 shooting rampage at Colorado's Columbine High School, every U.S. state except Vermont experienced threats of copycat violence. Pennsylvania alone recorded 60 such threats (Cooper, 1999). Sociologist David Phillips and his colleagues (1985, 1989) found that suicides, too, sometimes increase following a highly publicized suicide. In the wake of Marilyn Monroe's suicide on August 6, 1962, the number of suicides in the United States exceeded the usual August count by 200. Although not all studies have confirmed the copycat suicide phenomenon, suicides have sometimes occurred in local clusters. Within an 18-day span, one 1500-student high school recorded 2 completed suicides, 7 attempted suicides, and 23 students with suicidal thoughts. Within a one-year period, one London psychiatric unit experienced 14 patient suicides (Joiner, 1999).

What causes suicide clusters? Do people act similarly because of their influence on one another? Or because they are simultaneously exposed to the same events and conditions? Seeking answers, social psychologists have conducted experiments on group pressure and conformity.

> ■ **conformity** adjusting one's behavior or thinking to coincide with a group standard.

Group Pressure and Conformity

OBJECTIVE **56-2** | Discuss Asch's experiments on conformity, and distinguish between normative and informational social influence.

Suggestibility is a subtle type of **conformity**—adjusting our behavior or thinking toward some group standard. To study conformity, Solomon Asch (1955) devised a simple test. As a participant in the study, you arrive at the experiment location in time to take a seat at a table where five people are already seated. The experimenter asks which of three comparison lines is identical to a standard line (**FIGURE 56.1**). You see clearly that the answer is Line 2 and await your turn to say so after the others. Your boredom with this experiment begins to show when the next set of lines proves equally easy.

FIGURE 56.1

Asch's conformity experiments

Which of the three comparison lines is equal to the standard line? What do you suppose most people would say after hearing five others say, "Line 3"? In this photo from one of Asch's experiments, the student in the center shows the severe discomfort that comes from disagreeing with the responses of other group members (in this case, confederates of the experimenter).

Standard line   Comparison lines

Now comes the third trial, and the correct answer seems just as clear-cut, but the first person gives what strikes you as a wrong answer: "Line 3." When the second person and then the third and fourth give the same wrong answer, you sit up straight and squint. When the fifth person agrees with the first four, you feel your heart begin to pound. The experimenter then looks to you for your answer. Torn between the unanimity of your five fellow respondents and the evidence of your own eyes, you feel tense and much less sure of yourself than you were moments ago. You hesitate before answering, wondering whether you should suffer the discomfort of being the oddball. What answer do you give?

In the experiments conducted by Asch and others after him, thousands of college students have experienced this conflict. Answering such questions alone, they erred less than 1 percent of the time. But the odds were quite different when several others—confederates working for the experimenter—answered incorrectly. Asch reports that more than one-third of the time, these "intelligent and well-meaning" college-student participants were then "willing to call white black" by going along with the group.

Conditions That Strengthen Conformity

Asch's procedure became the model for later investigations. Although experiments have not always found so much conformity, they do reveal that conformity increases when

- one is made to feel incompetent or insecure.
- the group has at least three people.
- the group is unanimous. (The dissent of just one other person greatly increases social courage.)
- one admires the group's status and attractiveness.
- one has made no prior commitment to any response.
- others in the group observe one's behavior.
- one's culture strongly encourages respect for social standards.

Thus, we might predict the behavior of Austin, an enthusiastic but insecure new fraternity member: Noting that the 40 other members appear unanimous in their plans for a fund-raiser, Austin is unlikely to voice his dissent.

Reasons for Conforming

Fish swim in schools. Birds fly in flocks. And humans, too, tend to go with their group, to think what it thinks and do what it does. But why? Why do we clap when others clap, eat as others eat, believe what others believe, even see what others see? Frequently, it is to avoid rejection or to gain social approval. In such cases, we are responding to what social psychologists call **normative social influence.** We are sensitive to social norms—understood rules for accepted and expected behavior—because the price we pay for being different may be severe.

Marco Lokar knows. During the 1991 Persian Gulf War, Lokar, an Italian, was the only Seton Hall University basketball player who chose not to display an American flag on his uniform. As the team traveled, the fans' abusive responses to his nonconforming behavior became unbearable, so he left the team and returned to Italy. Tony Smith also knows. In 2003, when the Manhattanville College basketball player likewise dissented from the impending war with Iraq—by turning sideways and not looking at the flag during the pregame national anthem—similar outrage resulted. In one game at another college, students stood and chanted "Leave the country!"

Respecting norms is not the only reason we conform: Groups may provide valuable information, and only an uncommonly stubborn person will *never* listen to others. When we accept others' opinions about reality, we are responding to **informational social influence.** "Those who never retract their opinions love themselves more than they love truth," observed the eighteenth-century French essayist, Joseph Joubert.

> "Have you ever noticed how one example—good or bad—can prompt others to follow? How one illegally parked car can give permission for others to do likewise? How one racial joke can fuel another?"
>
> Marian Wright Edelman,
> *The Measure of Our Success*, 1992

■ **normative social influence** influence resulting from a person's desire to gain approval or avoid disapproval.

■ **informational social influence** influence resulting from one's willingness to accept others' opinions about reality.

Slide 1

Slide 2

FIGURE 56.2
Informational influence
Sample task: After seeing Slides 1 and 2, participants judged which person in Slide 2 was the same as the person in Slide 1. (From Baron, Vandello, & Brunsman, 1996.)

As Rebecca Denton demonstrated in 2004, sometimes it pays to assume others are right and to follow their lead. Denton set a record for the furthest distance driven on the wrong side of a British divided highway—30 miles, with only one minor sideswipe, before the Welsh motorway ran out and police were able to puncture her tires. Denton later explained that she thought the hundreds of other drivers coming at her were all on the wrong side of the road (Woolcock, 2004).

Robert Baron and his colleagues (1996) cleverly demonstrated our openness to informational influence on tough, important judgments. They modernized the Asch experiment by showing University of Iowa students a slide of a stimulus person, followed by a slide of a four-person lineup (**FIGURE 56.2**). Their experiment made the task either easy (viewing the lineup for five seconds) or difficult (viewing the lineup for but half a second). It also led them to think their judgments as either unimportant (just a preliminary test of some eyewitness identification procedures) or as important (establishing norms for an actual police procedure, with a U.S. $20 award to the most accurate participants). When the accuracy of their judgments seemed important, people rarely conformed when the task was easy, but they conformed half the time when the task was difficult. If we are unsure of what is right, and if being right matters, we are receptive to others' opinions.

Our view of social influence as bad or good depends on our values. When influence supports what we approve, we applaud those who are "open-minded" and "sensitive" enough to be "responsive." When influence supports what we disapprove, we scorn the "submissive conformity" of those who comply with others' wishes. Cultural values also affect our tendency to conform to others' views. Cultures vary in the extent to which they value individualism or collectivism. Western Europeans and people in most English-speaking countries tend to prize individualism more than conformity and obedience. These values are reflected in social influence experiments that have been conducted in 17 countries: In individualist cultures, conformity rates are lower (Bond & Smith, 1996).

Obedience

OBJECTIVE 56-3 | Describe Milgram's experiments on obedience, and outline the conditions in which obedience was highest.

Social psychologist Stanley Milgram (1963, 1974) knew that people often comply with social pressures. But how would they respond to outright commands? To find out, he undertook what have become social psychology's most famous and controversial experiments. Imagine yourself as one of the nearly 1000 participants in Milgram's 20 experiments.

Stanley Milgram (1933–1984)
The late social psychologist's obedience experiments now "belong to the self-understanding of literate people in our age" (Sabini, 1986).

Responding to an advertisement, you come to Yale University's psychology department to participate in an experiment. Professor Milgram's assistant explains that the study concerns the effect of punishment on learning. You and another person draw slips from a hat to see who will be the "teacher" (which your slip says) and who will be the "learner." The learner is then led to an adjoining room and strapped into a chair that is wired through the wall to an electric shock machine. You sit in front of the machine, which has switches labeled with voltages. Your task: to teach and then test the learner on a list of word pairs. You are to punish the learner for wrong answers by delivering brief electric shocks, beginning with a switch labeled "15 Volts—Slight Shock." After each of the learner's errors, you are to move up to the next higher voltage. With each flick of a switch, lights flash, relay switches click on, and an electric buzzing fills the air.

If you comply with the experimenter's instructions, you hear the learner grunt when you flick the third, fourth, and fifth switches. After you activate the eighth switch (labeled "120 Volts—Moderate Shock"), the learner shouts that the shocks are painful. After the tenth switch ("150 Volts—Strong Shock"), he cries, "Get me out of here! I won't be in the experiment anymore! I refuse to go on!" When you hear these pleas, you draw back. But the experimenter prods you: "Please continue—the experiment requires that you continue." If you still resist, he insists, "It is absolutely essential that you continue," or "You have no other choice, you *must* go on."

If you obey, you hear the learner's protests escalate to shrieks of agony as you continue to raise the shock level with each succeeding error. After the 330-volt level, the learner refuses to answer and soon falls silent. Still, the experimenter pushes you toward the final, 450-volt switch, ordering you to ask the questions and, if no correct answer is given, to administer the next shock level.

How far do you think you would follow the experimenter's commands? In a survey Milgram conducted before the experiment, most people declared they would stop playing such a sadistic-seeming role soon after the learner first indicated pain and certainly before he shrieked in agony. This also was the prediction made by each of 40 psychiatrists whom Milgram asked to guess the outcome. When Milgram actually conducted the experiment with men aged 20 to 50, he was astonished to find that 63 percent complied fully—right up to the last switch. Ten later studies that included women found women's compliance rates were similar to men's (Blass, 1999).

Did the "teachers" figure out the hoax—that no shock was being delivered? Did they correctly guess the learner was a confederate who only pretended to feel the shocks? Did they realize the experiment was really testing their willingness to comply with commands to inflict punishment? No, the teachers typically displayed genuine distress: They perspired, trembled, laughed nervously, and bit their lips.

Milgram's use of deception and stress triggered a debate over his research ethics. In his own defense, Milgram pointed out that, after the participants learned of the deception and actual research purposes, virtually none regretted taking part (though perhaps by then the participants had reduced their dissonance). When 40 of the "teachers" who had agonized most were later interviewed by a psychiatrist, none appeared to be suffering emotional aftereffects. All in all, said Milgram, the experiments provoked less enduring stress than university students experience when facing and failing big exams (Blass, 1996).

Wondering whether the participants obeyed because the learners' protests were not convincing, Milgram repeated the experiment, with 40 new teachers. This time his confederate mentioned a "slight heart condition" while being strapped into the chair, and then he complained and screamed more intensely as the shocks became more punishing. Still, 65 percent of the new teachers complied fully (**FIGURE 56.3**).

"Drive off the cliff, James, I want to commit suicide."

Drawing by Mel Yauk.

© 1965 By Stanley Milgram, from the film *Obedience*, dist. by Penn State, Media Sales

FIGURE 56.3

Milgram's follow-up obedience experiment

In a repeat of the earlier experiment, 65 percent of the adult male "teachers" fully obeyed the experimenter's commands to continue. They did so despite the "learner's" earlier mention of a heart condition and despite hearing cries of protest after 150 volts and agonized protests after 330 volts. (Data from Milgram, 1974.)

In later experiments, Milgram discovered that subtle details of a situation powerfully influence people. When he varied the social conditions, the proportion of fully compliant participants varied from 0 to 93 percent. Obedience was highest when

- the person giving the orders was close at hand and was perceived to be a legitimate authority figure. (Such was the case in 2005 when Temple University's basketball coach sent a 250-pound bench player, Nehemiah Ingram, into a game with instructions to commit "hard fouls." Following orders, Ingram fouled out in four minutes after breaking an opposing player's right arm.)
- the authority figure was supported by a prestigious institution. Compliance was somewhat lower when Milgram dissociated his experiments from Yale University.
- the victim was depersonalized or at a distance, even in another room. (Similarly, in combat with an enemy they can see, many soldiers either do not fire their rifles or do not aim them properly. Such refusals to kill are rare among those who operate the more distant weapons of artillery or aircraft [Padgett, 1989].)
- there were no role models for defiance; that is, no other participants were seen disobeying the experimenter.

The power of legitimate, close-at-hand authorities is dramatically apparent in stories of those who complied with orders to carry out the atrocities of the Holocaust, and those who didn't. Obedience alone does not explain the Holocaust; anti-Semitic ideology produced eager killers as well (Mastroianni, 2002). But obedience was a factor. In the summer of 1942 nearly 500 middle-aged German reserve police officers were dispatched to Jozefow, Poland, in German-occupied territory. On July 13, the group's visibly upset commander informed his recruits, mostly family men, that they had been ordered to round up the village's Jews, who were said to be aiding the enemy. Able-bodied men were to be sent to work camps, and all the rest were to be shot on the spot. Given a chance to refuse participation in the executions, only about a dozen immediately did so. Within 17 hours, the remaining 485 officers killed 1500 helpless women, children, and elderly by shooting them in the back of the head as they lay face down. Hearing the pleadings of the victims, and seeing the gruesome results, some 20 percent of the officers did eventually dissent, managing either to miss their victims or to wander away and hide until the slaughter was over (Browning, 1992). But in real life, as in Milgram's experiments, the disobedient were the minority.

Standing up for democracy

Some individuals—roughly one in three in Milgram's experiments—resist social coercion, as did this unarmed man in Beijing, by single-handedly challenging an advancing line of tanks the day after the 1989 Tiananmen Square student uprising was suppressed.

Another story was being played out in the French village of Le Chambon, where French Jews destined for deportation to Germany were being sheltered by villagers who openly defied orders to cooperate with the "New Order." The villagers' ancestors had themselves been persecuted and their pastors had been teaching them to "resist whenever our adversaries will demand of us obedience contrary to the orders of the Gospel" (Rochat, 1993). Ordered by police to give a list of sheltered Jews, the head pastor modeled defiance: "I don't know of Jews, I only know of human beings." Without realizing how long and terrible the war would be, or how much punishment and poverty they would suffer, the resisters made an initial commitment to resist. Supported by their beliefs, their role models, their interaction with one another, and their own initial acts, they remained defiant to the war's end.

Lessons From the Conformity and Obedience Studies

OBJECTIVE 56-4 | Explain how the conformity and obedience studies can help us understand our susceptibility to social influence.

What do the Asch and Milgram experiments teach us about ourselves? How does judging the length of a line or flicking a shock switch relate to everyday social behavior? This research, like all psychological experiments, aimed not to re-create the literal behaviors of everyday life but to capture and explore the underlying processes that shape those behaviors. Asch and Milgram devised experiments in which the participants had to choose between adhering to their own standards and being responsive to others, a dilemma we all face frequently.

In Milgram's experiments, participants were also torn between what they should respond to—the pleas of the victim or the orders of the experimenter. Their moral sense warned them not to harm another, yet it also prompted them to obey the experimenter and to be a good research participant. With kindness and obedience on a collision course, obedience usually won.

Such experiments demonstrate that strong social influences can make people conform to falsehoods or capitulate to cruelty. "The most fundamental lesson of our study," Milgram noted, is that "ordinary people, simply doing their jobs, and without any particular hostility on their part, can become agents in a terrible destructive process" (1974, p. 6). Milgram did not entrap his "teachers" by asking them first to zap "learners" with enough electricity to make their hair stand on end. Rather, he exploited the foot-in-the-door effect, beginning with a little tickle of electricity and escalating step by step. In the minds of those throwing the switches, the small action became justified, making the next act tolerable. In Jozefow, in Le Chambon, and in Milgram's experiments, those who resisted usually did so early. After the first acts of compliance or resistance, attitudes began to follow and justify behavior.

So it happens when people succumb, gradually, to evil. In any society, great evils sometimes grow out of people's compliance with lesser evils. The Nazi leaders suspected that most German civil servants would resist shooting or gassing Jews directly, but they

"I was only following orders."
Adolf Eichmann, Director of Nazi deportation of Jews to concentration camps

found them surprisingly willing to handle the paperwork of the Holocaust (Silver & Geller, 1978). Likewise, when Milgram asked 40 men to administer the learning test while someone else did the shocking, 93 percent complied. Contrary to images of devilish villains, evil does not require monstrous characters; all it takes is ordinary people corrupted by an evil situation—ordinary soldiers who follow orders to torture prisoners, ordinary students who follow orders to haze initiates into their group, ordinary employees who follow orders to produce and market harmful products. Before leading the 9/11 attacks, Mohamed Atta reportedly was a sane, rational person who had been a "good boy" and an excellent student from a close-knit family—not someone who fits our image of evil monster.

> "The normal reaction to an abnormal situation is abnormal behavior."
>
> James Waller, *Becoming Evil: How Ordinary People Commit Genocide and Mass Killing*, 2006

Group Influence

How do groups affect our behavior? To find out, social psychologists study the various influences that operate in the simplest of groups—one person in the presence of another—and those that operate in more complex groups, such as families, teams, and committees.

Individual Behavior in the Presence of Others

OBJECTIVE 56-5 | Describe the conditions in which the presence of others is likely to result in social facilitation, social loafing, or deindividuation.

Appropriately, social psychology's first experiments focused on the simplest of all questions about social behavior: How are we influenced by the mere presence of others—by people watching us or joining us in various activities?

Social Facilitation

Having noticed that cyclists' racing times were faster when they competed against each other than when they competed with a clock, Norman Triplett (1898) hypothesized that the presence of others boosts performance. To test his hypothesis, Triplett had adolescents wind a fishing reel as rapidly as possible. He discovered that they wound the reel faster in the presence of someone doing the same thing. This phenomenon of stronger performance in others' presence is called **social facilitation.** For example, after a light turns green, drivers take about 15 percent less time to travel the first 100 yards when another car is beside them at the intersection than when they are alone (Towler, 1986).

Social facilitation
Skilled athletes often find they are "on" before an audience. What they do well, they do even better when people are watching.

But now things get tricky. On tougher tasks (learning nonsense syllables or solving complex multiplication problems), people perform *less* well when observers or others working on the same task are present. Further studies revealed why the presence of others sometimes helps and sometimes hinders performance (Guerin, 1986; Zajonc, 1965). When others observe us, we become aroused. This arousal strengthens the most *likely* response—the correct one on an easy task, an incorrect one on a difficult task. Thus, when we are being observed, we perform well-learned tasks more quickly and accurately, and unmastered tasks less quickly and accurately. James Michaels and his associates (1982) found that expert pool players who made 71 percent of their shots when alone made 80 percent when four people came to watch them. Poor shooters, who made 36 percent of their shots when alone, made only 25 percent when watched. The energizing effect of an enthusiastic audience probably contributes to the home advantage enjoyed by various sports teams. Studies of more than 80,000 college and professional athletic events in Canada, the United States, and England reveal that home teams win about 6 in 10

■ **social facilitation** stronger responses on simple or well-learned tasks in the presence of others.

Michelle Agins/NYT Pictures

TABLE 56.1

HOME ADVANTAGE IN MAJOR TEAM SPORTS

Sport	Games Studied	Home Team Winning Percentage
Baseball	23,034	53.5%
Football	2,592	57.3
Ice hockey	4,322	61.1
Basketball	13,596	64.4
Soccer	37,202	69.0

From Courneya & Carron, 1992

games (somewhat fewer for baseball and football, somewhat more for basketball and soccer—see **TABLE 56.1**).

The point to remember: What you do well, you are likely to do even better in front of an audience, especially a friendly audience; what you normally find difficult may seem all but impossible when you are being watched.

Social facilitation also helps explain a funny effect of crowding: Comedy records that are mildly amusing to people in an uncrowded room seem funnier in a densely packed room (Aiello & others, 1983; Freedman & Perlick, 1979). As comedians and actors know, a "good house" is a full one. The arousal triggered by crowding amplifies other reactions, too. If sitting close to one another, participants in experiments like a friendly person even more, an unfriendly person even less (Schiffenbauer & Schiavo, 1976; Storms & Thomas, 1977). The practical lesson: If choosing a room for a class or setting up chairs for a gathering, have barely enough seating.

Social Loafing

Social facilitation experiments test the effect of others' presence on performance on an individual task, such as shooting pool. But what happens to performance when people perform the task as a group? In a team tug-of-war, for example, do you suppose the effort a person puts forth would be more than, less than, or the same as the effort he or she would exert in a one-on-one tug-of-war? To find out, Alan Ingham and his fellow researchers (1974) asked blindfolded University of Massachusetts students to "pull as hard as you can" on a rope. When Ingham fooled the students into believing three others were also pulling behind them, they exerted only 82 percent as much effort as when they knew they were pulling alone.

To describe this diminished effort, Bibb Latané (1981; Jackson & Williams, 1988) coined the term **social loafing.** In 78 experiments conducted in the United States, India, Thailand, Japan, China, and Taiwan, social loafing occurred on various tasks, though it was especially common among men in individualistic cultures (Karau & Williams, 1993). In one of Latané's experiments, blindfolded people seated in a group clapped or shouted as loud as they could while listening through headphones to the sound of loud clapping or shouting. When told they were doing it with the others, the participants produced about one-third less noise than when they thought their individual efforts were identifiable.

Why this social loafing? First, people acting as part of a group feel less accountable and therefore worry less about what others think. Second, they may view their contribution as dispensable (Harkins & Szymanski, 1989; Kerr & Bruun, 1983). As many leaders of organizations know—and as you have perhaps observed on student group assignments—if group members share equally in the benefits regardless of how much they contribute, some may slack off. Unless highly motivated and identified with their group, they may free-ride on the other group members' efforts.

Deindividuation

So, the presence of others can arouse people (as in the social facilitation experiments) or can diminish their feelings of responsibility (as in the social loafing experiments). But sometimes the presence of others both arouses people *and* diminishes their sense of responsibility. The result can be uninhibited behavior ranging from a food fight in the dining hall or screaming at a basketball referee to vandalism or rioting. Abandoning normal restraints to the power of the group is termed **deindividuation.** To be deindividuated is to be less self-conscious and less restrained when in a group situation.

Deindividuation often occurs when group participation makes people feel aroused and anonymous. In one experiment, New York University women dressed in depersonalizing Ku Klux Klan-style hoods delivered twice as much electric shock to a victim as did identifiable women (Zimbardo, 1970). (As in all such experiments, the "victim" did not actually receive the shocks.) Similarly, tribal warriors who depersonalize

■ **social loafing** the tendency for people in a group to exert less effort when pooling their efforts toward attaining a common goal than when individually accountable.

■ **deindividuation** the loss of self-awareness and self-restraint occurring in group situations that foster arousal and anonymity.

■ **group polarization** the enhancement of a group's prevailing inclinations through discussion within the group.

themselves with face paints or masks are more likely than those with exposed faces to kill, torture, or mutilate captured enemies (Watson, 1973). Whether in a mob, at a rock concert, at a ballgame, or at worship, to lose self-consciousness (to become deindividuated) is to become more responsive to the group experience.

Effects of Group Interaction

OBJECTIVE 56-6 | Discuss how group interaction can facilitate group polarization and groupthink.

We have examined the conditions under which being in the *presence* of others can
- motivate people to exert themselves or tempt them to free-ride on the efforts of others.
- make easy tasks easier and difficult tasks harder.
- enhance humor or fuel mob violence.

Research shows that *interacting* with others can similarly have both bad and good effects.

Group Polarization

Educational researchers have noted that, over time, initial differences between groups of college students tend to grow. If the first-year students at College X tend to be more intellectually oriented than those at College Y, that difference will probably be amplified by the time they are seniors. Similarly, if the political conservatism of students who join fraternities and sororities is greater than that of students who do not, the gap in the political attitudes of the two groups will probably widen as they progress through college (Wilson & others, 1975). Likewise, notes Eleanor Maccoby (2002) from her decades of observing gender development, girls talk more intimately than boys do and play and fantasize less aggressively—and these gender differences widen over time as they interact mostly with their own gender.

This enhancement of a group's prevailing tendencies—called **group polarization**—occurs when people within a group discuss an idea that most of them either favor or oppose. Group polarization can have beneficial results, as when it amplifies a sought-after spiritual awareness or reinforces the resolve of those in a self-help group, or strengthens feelings of tolerance in a low-prejudice group. But it can also have dire consequences. George Bishop and I discovered that when high-prejudice students discussed racial issues, they became *more* prejudiced (**FIGURE 56.4**). (Low-prejudice students became even more accepting.) The experiment's ideological separation and polarization finds a seeming parallel in the growing polarization of American politics. The percentage of landslide counties—voting 60 percent or more for one presidential candidate—increased from 26 percent in 1976 to 48 percent in 2004 (Bishop, 2004). More and more, people are living near and learning from others who think as they do.

The polarizing effect of interaction among the like-minded applies not only to U.S. "red" and "blue" states, but also to suicide terrorists. After analyzing terrorist organizations around the world, psychologists Clark McCauley and Mary Segal (1987; McCauley, 2002) noted that the terrorist mentality does not erupt suddenly. Rather, it usually arises among people who get together because of a grievance and then become more and more extreme as they interact in isolation from any moderating influences. Increasingly, group members (who may be isolated with other "brothers" and "sisters" in camps) categorize the world as "us" and "them" (Moghaddam, 2005; Qirko, 2004). Suicide terrorism virtually never is done on a personal whim, reports researcher Ariel Merari (2002).

FIGURE 56.4
Group polarization
If a group is like-minded, discussion strengthens its prevailing opinions. Talking over racial issues increased prejudice in a high-prejudice group of high school students and decreased it in a low-prejudice group (Myers & Bishop, 1970).

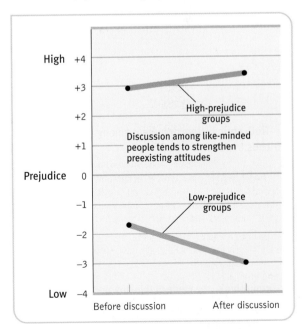

The Internet provides a medium for group polarization. Its tens of thousands of virtual groups enable bereaved parents, peacemakers, and teachers to find solace and support from kindred spirits. But the Internet also enables people who share interests in government cover-ups, extraterrestrial visitors, white supremacy, or citizen militias to find one another and to find support for their shared suspicions (McKenna & Bargh, 1998).

Groupthink

Does group interaction ever distort important decisions? Social psychologist Irving Janis began to think so as he read historian Arthur M. Schlesinger, Jr.'s account of how President John F. Kennedy and his advisers blundered into an ill-fated plan to invade Cuba with 1400 CIA-trained Cuban exiles. When the invaders were easily captured and soon linked to the U.S. government, Kennedy wondered in hindsight, "How could we have been so stupid?"

To find out, Janis (1982) studied the decision-making procedures that led to the fiasco. He discovered that the soaring morale of the recently elected president and his advisers fostered undue confidence in the plan. To preserve the good group feeling, any dissenting views were suppressed or self-censored, especially after President Kennedy voiced his enthusiasm for the scheme. Since no one spoke strongly against the idea, everyone assumed consensus support. To describe this harmonious but unrealistic group thinking, Janis coined the term **groupthink.**

Janis and others then examined other historical fiascos—the failure to anticipate the 1941 Japanese attack on Pearl Harbor, the escalation of the Vietnam War, the U.S. Watergate cover-up, the Chernobyl nuclear reactor accident (Reason, 1987), and the U.S. space shuttle *Challenger* explosion (Esser & Lindoerfer, 1989). They discovered that in these cases, too, groupthink was fed by overconfidence, conformity, self-justification, and group polarization.

Groupthink surfaced again, reported the U.S. Senate Intelligence Committee (2004), when "personnel involved in the Iraq WMD issue demonstrated several aspects of groupthink: examining few alternatives, selective gathering of information, pressure to conform within the group or withhold criticism, and collective rationalization." This groupthink led analysts to "interpret ambiguous evidence as conclusively indicative of a WMD program as well as ignore or minimize evidence that Iraq did not have [WMD] programs."

Despite such fiascos and tragedies, two heads are better than one in solving some types of problems. Knowing this, Janis also studied instances in which U.S. presidents and their advisers collectively made good decisions, such as when the Truman administration formulated the Marshall Plan, which offered assistance to Europe after World War II, and when the Kennedy administration worked to keep the Soviets from installing missiles in Cuba. In such instances—and in the business world, too, Janis believed—groupthink is prevented when a leader welcomes various opinions, invites experts' critiques of developing plans, and assigns people to identify possible problems. Just as the suppression of dissent bends a group toward bad decisions, so open debate often shapes good ones. None of us is as smart as all of us.

The Power of Individuals

OBJECTIVE 56-7 | Identify the characteristic common to minority positions that sway majorities.

In affirming the power of social influence, we must not overlook our power as individuals. *Social control* (the power of the situation) and *personal control* (the power of the individual) interact. People aren't billiard balls. When feeling pressured, we may react by doing the opposite of what is expected, thereby reasserting our sense of freedom (Brehm & Brehm, 1981).

"One's impulse to blow the whistle on this nonsense was simply undone by the circumstances of the discussion."

Arthur M. Schlesinger, Jr., *A Thousand Days*, 1965

"Truth springs from argument among friends."

Philosopher David Hume, 1711–1776

■ **groupthink** the mode of thinking that occurs when the desire for harmony in a decision-making group overrides a realistic appraisal of alternatives.

Such was the experience of three individual soldiers at the Abu Ghraib prison (O'Connor, 2004). Lt. David Sutton put an end to one incident, which he reported to his commanders. Navy dog-handler William Kimbro refused pressure to participate in improper interrogations using his attack dogs. Specialist Joseph Darby brought visual images of the horrors into the light of day, providing incontestable evidence of the atrocities. Each risked ridicule or even court-martial for not following orders.

As these three soldiers discovered, committed individuals can sway the majority and make social history. Were this not so, communism would have remained an obscure theory, Christianity would be a small Middle Eastern sect, and Rosa Parks' refusal to sit at the back of the bus would not have ignited the civil rights movement. Technological history, too, is often made by innovative minorities who overcome the majority's resistance to change. To many, the railroad was a nonsensical idea; some farmers even feared that train noise would prevent hens from laying eggs. People derided Robert Fulton's steamboat as "Fulton's Folly." As Fulton later said, "Never did a single encouraging remark, a bright hope, a warm wish, cross my path." Much the same reaction greeted the printing press, the telegraph, the incandescent lamp, and the typewriter (Cantril & Bumstead, 1960).

European social psychologists have sought to better understand *minority influence*—the power of one or two individuals to sway majorities (Moscovici, 1985). They investigated groups in which one or two individuals consistently expressed a controversial attitude or an unusual perceptual judgment. They repeatedly found that a minority that unswervingly holds to its position is far more successful in swaying the majority than is a minority that waffles. Holding consistently to a minority opinion will not make you popular, but it may make you influential. This is especially so if your self-confidence stimulates others to consider why you react as you do. Although people often follow the majority view publicly, they may privately develop sympathy for the minority view. Even when a minority's influence is not yet visible, it may be persuading some members of the majority to rethink their views (Wood & others, 1994). The powers of social influence are enormous, but so are the powers of the committed individual.

Margaret Bourke-White/Life Magazine. © 1946 Time Warner, Inc.

Gandhi

As the life of Mahatma Gandhi powerfully testifies, a consistent and persistent minority voice can sometimes sway the majority. The nonviolent appeals and fasts of the Hindu nationalist and spiritual leader were instrumental in winning India's independence from Britain in 1947.

>> LEARNING OUTCOMES

Social Influence

OBJECTIVE 56-1 | **Describe the chameleon effect, and give an example of it.**

The *chameleon effect* is our tendency to unconsciously mimic those around us, as when we pick up the mood of a happy or sad person. Automatic mimicry is an ingredient in the ability to empathize with others.

OBJECTIVE 56-2 | **Discuss Asch's experiments on conformity, and distinguish between normative and informational social influence.**

Solomon Asch found that people will conform to a group's judgment even when it is clearly incorrect. Conformity increases when we feel incompetent or insecure, admire the group's status and attractiveness, have made no prior commitment to a response, are being observed by members of the group, come from a culture that strongly encourages respect for group standards, and are in a group with at least three members, all unanimous in their decision. We may conform either to gain social approval (*normative social influence*—especially likely when we are unsure of what is right and being right matters) or because we welcome the information that others provide (*informational social influence*).

OBJECTIVE 56-3 | **Describe Milgram's experiments on obedience, and outline the conditions in which obedience was highest.**

In Stanley Milgram's experiments, people torn between obeying an experimenter and responding to another's pleas to stop the shocks usually chose to obey orders, even though obedience supposedly meant harming the other person. People were most likely to obey when the person giving orders was nearby and was perceived as a legitimate authority figure; the person giving orders was supported by a prestigious institution; the victim was depersonalized or at a distance; and no other person modeled defiance by disobeying.

OBJECTIVE 56-4 | **Explain how the conformity and obedience studies can help us understand our susceptibility to social influence.**

In the conformity studies, randomly chosen ordinary people conformed in spite of their own beliefs. In the obedience studies, randomly chosen people obeyed instructions to deliver punishments that, if real, would have harmed total strangers. People who resisted instructions did so early; after that, attitudes followed behavior. Understanding these tendencies could make us less susceptible to powerful social influences in our own lives.

OBJECTIVE 56-5 | **Describe the conditions in which the presence of others is likely to result in social facilitation, social loafing, or deindividuation.**

The presence of either observers or co-actors boosts arousal, strengthening our most likely response. This *social facilitation* tends to increase performance on easy or well-learned tasks but decrease it on difficult or newly learned ones. In the presence of others pooling their efforts toward a group goal, *social loafing* may occur, as some individuals ride free on the efforts of others. *Deindividuation,* a psychological state in which people become less self-aware and self-restrained, may result when a group experience arouses people and makes them feel anonymous.

OBJECTIVE 56-6 | **Discuss how group interaction can facilitate group polarization and groupthink.**

Discussion among like-minded people often produces *group polarization,* an enhancement of the group's prevailing opinions. This process fosters *groupthink,* as groups pressure members to conform, suppress dissenting information, and fail to consider alternatives. To prevent groupthink, leaders can welcome a variety of opinions, invite experts' critiques, and assign people to identify possible problems in developing plans.

OBJECTIVE 56-7 | **Identify the characteristic common to minority positions that sway majorities.**

Minorities that successfully sway group opinions usually express their views consistently.

TERMS AND CONCEPTS TO REMEMBER

conformity, p. 56-1

normative social influence, p. 56-1

informational social influence, p. 56-1

social facilitation, p. 56-7

social loafing, p. 56-8

deindividuation, p. 56-8

group polarization, p. 56-9

groupthink, p. 56-10

TEST YOURSELF

1. You are organizing a Town Hall–style meeting of fiercely competitive political candidates. To add to the fun, friends have suggested handing out masks of the candidates' faces for supporters to wear. What phenomenon might these masks engage?

(Answer in Appendix B.)

ASK YOURSELF

1. What two examples of social influence have you experienced this week? (Remember, influence may be informational.)

>WEB

Multiple-choice *self-tests* and more may be found at www.worthpublishers.com/myers.

57

Antisocial Relations

Social psychology studies how we think about and influence one another, and also how we *relate* to one another. What causes us to harm or to help or to fall in love? How can we transform the closed fists of aggression into the open arms of compassion? In this module we ponder insights into *antisocial* relations gleaned by researchers who have studied prejudice, aggression, and conflict.

Prejudice

OBJECTIVE 57-1 | Identify the three components of prejudice.

Prejudice means "prejudgment." It is an unjustifiable and usually negative attitude toward a group—often a different cultural, ethnic, or gender group. Like all attitudes, **prejudice** is a mixture of *beliefs* (called **stereotypes**), *emotions* (hostility, envy, or fear), and predispositions to *action* (to discriminate). To *believe* that overweight people are gluttonous, to *feel* antipathy for an overweight person, and to be hesitant to hire or date an overweight person is to be prejudiced. Prejudice is a negative *attitude;* **discrimination** is a negative *behavior.*

Like other forms of prejudgment, prejudices are schemas that influence how we notice and interpret events. In one 1970s study, most white participants perceived a white man shoving a black man as "horsing around." When they saw a black man shove a white man, they interpreted the act as "violent" (Duncan, 1976). Our preconceived ideas about people bias our impressions of their behavior. Prejudgments color perceptions.

How Prejudiced Are People?

OBJECTIVE 57-2 | Contrast overt and subtle forms of prejudice, and give examples of each.

To learn about levels of prejudice, we can assess what people say and what they do. To judge by what Americans say, gender and racial attitudes have changed dramatically in the last half-century. The one-third of Americans who in 1937 said they would vote for a qualified woman whom their party nominated for president soared to 87 percent in 2003 (Jones & Moore, 2003). Support for all forms of racial contact, including interracial marriage (**FIGURE 57.1** on the next page), has also dramatically increased. Nearly everyone agrees that children of all races should attend the same schools and that women and men should receive the same pay for the same job.

Yet as overt prejudice wanes, subtle prejudice lingers. Despite increased verbal support for interracial marriage, many people admit that in socially intimate settings (dating, dancing, marrying) they would feel uncomfortable with someone of another race. And in Western Europe, where many "guest workers" and refugees settled at the end of the twentieth century, "modern prejudice"—rejecting immigrant minorities as job applicants for supposedly nonracial reasons—has been replacing blatant prejudice (Jackson & others, 2001; Pettigrew, 1998). A slew of recent experiments illustrate that prejudice can be not only subtle but also automatic and unconscious (see Close-Up: Automatic Prejudice two pages from here).

■ **prejudice** an unjustifiable (and usually negative) attitude toward a group and its members. Prejudice generally involves stereotyped beliefs, negative feelings, and a predisposition to discriminatory action.

■ **stereotype** a generalized (sometimes accurate but often overgeneralized) belief about a group of people.

■ **discrimination** unjustifiable negative behavior toward a group or its members.

FIGURE 57.1
Prejudice over time
Americans' approval of interracial marriage has soared over the past half-century. (Gallup surveys reported by Ludwig, 2004.)

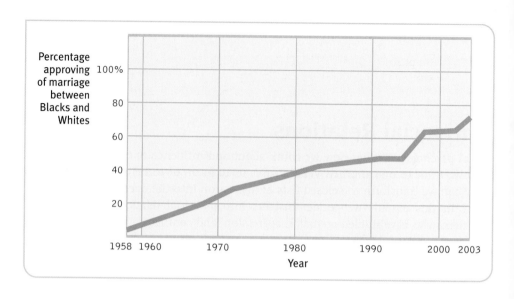

"Unhappily the world has yet to learn how to live with diversity."

Pope John Paul II, Address to the United Nations, 1995

But prejudice still surfaces in public settings. In a 2004 survey of Europeans, 6 in 10 people in both Britain and Germany said immigrants are a bad influence on their country (Lester, 2004). In most places in the world, gays and lesbians cannot comfortably acknowledge who they are and whom they love. In several U.S. states where black motorists are a minority of the drivers and speeders on interstate highways, they have been the majority of those stopped and searched by state police (Lamberth, 1998; Staples, 1999a,b). In one New Jersey turnpike study, African-Americans were 13.5 percent of the car occupants, 15 percent of the speeders, and 35 percent of the drivers stopped. Elmo Randolph, a New Jersey dentist, knew it all along. After being stopped more than 100 times over four years while driving his gold BMW from his home to his office, Dr. Randolph, guilty of nothing more than "driving while black," sold the car.

Gender prejudice and discrimination persist, too. Despite gender equality in intelligence scores, people tend to perceive their fathers as more intelligent than their mothers (Furnham & Rawles, 1995). In Saudi Arabia, women are not allowed to drive. In Western countries, we pay more to those (usually men) who drive machines that take care of our streets than to those (usually women) who take care of our children. Worldwide, women are more likely to live in poverty (Lipps, 1999), and their 69 percent literacy rate is well below men's 83 percent (PRB, 2002).

Female infants are no longer left out on a hillside to die of exposure, as was the practice in ancient Greece. Yet even today boys are often valued more than their sisters. During the 1970s Bangladesh famine, preschool girls were more malnourished than boys were, and in many developing countries death rates are higher for girls than for boys (Bairagi, 1987). With testing that enables sex-selective abortions, several south Asian countries, including certain regions of China and India, have experienced a shortfall in female births. Natural female mortality and the normal 105-to-100 male-to-female birth ratio hardly explains the world's estimated 101 million (say that number slowly) "missing women" (Sen, 2003). In 2005, China announced that the newborn sex ratio had reached 119 boys for every 100 girls (Yardley, 2005). With demographic predictions of 40 million Chinese bachelors unable to find mates, China has declared that sex-selective abortions—gender genocide—are now a criminal offense.

Suppose that you could only have one child. Would you prefer that it be a boy or a girl? When Gallup asked that question of Americans, two-thirds expressed a gender preference, and for two-thirds of those—in 2003 as in 1941—it was for a boy (Lyons, 2003). But the news isn't all bad for girls and women. Most people *feel* more positively about women in general than they do about men (Eagly, 1994;

CLOSE-UP:

AUTOMATIC PREJUDICE

As we have seen throughout this book, we process information on two levels: conscious and unconscious. To some extent, our thinking, our memories, and our attitudes are *explicit*—on the radar screen of our awareness. And to an even greater extent, today's researchers believe, they are *implicit*—below the radar, out-of-sight. Modern studies of implicit, automatic attitudes indicate that prejudice is often more of an unthinking knee-jerk response than a decision. Consider these findings on U.S. racial prejudice:

Implicit racial associations Anthony Greenwald and his colleagues (1998) showed that even people who deny harboring racial prejudice may carry negative associations. For example, 9 in 10 white respondents took longer to identify pleasant words (such as *peace* and *paradise*) as "good" when good was presented with black rather than white faces. Moreover, report Kurt Hugenberg and Galen Bodenhausen (2003), people who displayed the most *implicit prejudice* on this test also were the quickest to perceive anger and apparent threat in black faces.

Unconscious patronization Kent Harber (1998) asked white university women to evaluate a flawed essay said to be written by a black or a white fellow student. When they believed the writer was black, the women gave markedly *higher* ratings and never expressed the harsh criticisms they assigned to white-authored essays, such as "When I read college work this bad I just want to lay my head down on the table and cry." Did the evaluators calibrate their evaluations to their racial stereotypes, Harber wondered, leading them to patronize the black writers with less exacting standards? If used in real-world evaluations, such low expectations and the resulting "inflated praise and insufficient criticism" could hinder minority student achievement. (To preclude such bias, many teachers read essays while "blind" to their authors.)

Race-influenced perceptions Two research teams were curious about the shooting of an unarmed man in the doorway of his Bronx apartment building by officers who mistook his wallet for a gun. Each research team reenacted the situation, asking people to press buttons quickly to "shoot" or not shoot men who suddenly appeared on screen holding either a gun or a harmless object such as a flashlight or bottle (Correll & others, 2002; Greenwald & others, 2003). People (both Blacks and Whites, in one of the studies) more often mistakenly shot targets who were black.

Seeing black Several studies show that the more a person's features are perceived as typical of their racial category, the more likely they are to elicit race-based responding (Maddox, 2004). In one study of 182 police officers, Jennifer Eberhardt and her collaborators (2004) found that "black faces looked more criminal to police officers; the more black, the more criminal."

Reflexive bodily responses Today's biopsychosocial approach has stimulated neuroscience studies that measure people's instant responses to viewing white and black faces. These studies have detected implicit prejudice in people's facial-muscle responses and in the activation of their amygdala, an emotion-processing center (Cunningham & others, 2004; Eberhardt, 2005; Vanman & others, 2004). Even people who consciously express little prejudice may give off telltale signals as their body responds selectively to another's race.

If your own gut check sometimes reveals feelings you would rather not have about other people, be assured that you are not alone. It is what we do with our feelings that matters. By monitoring our feelings and actions, and by replacing old habits with new ones based on new friendships, we can free ourselves from prejudice.

Haddock & Zanna, 1994). People worldwide see women as having some traits, such as nurturance, sensitivity, and less aggressiveness, that most people prefer (Glick & others, 2004; Swim, 1994). That may explain why women tend to like women more than men like men (Rudman & Goodwin, 2004). And perhaps that is also why people prefer slightly feminized computer-generated faces—men's and women's—to slightly masculinized faces. Researcher David Perrett and his colleagues (1998) speculate that a slightly feminized male face connotes kindness, cooperativeness, and other traits of a good father. When the British Broadcasting Company invited 18,000 women to guess which of the men in **FIGURE 57.2** was most likely to place a personal ad seeking a "special lady to love and cherish forever," 66 percent guessed the slightly feminized face (b).

(a)

(b)

Professor Dave Perrett, St. Andrews University

FIGURE 57.2

Who do you like best? Which one placed an ad seeking a special lady to love and cherish forever? (See this module's final page.)

Social Roots of Prejudice

OBJECTIVE **57-3** | Discuss the social factors that contribute to prejudice.

Why does prejudice arise? Inequalities, social divisions, and emotional scapegoating are partly responsible.

Social Inequalities

When some people have money, power, and prestige and others do not, the "haves" usually develop attitudes that justify things as they are. In the extreme case, slave owners perceived slaves as innately lazy, ignorant, and irresponsible—as having the very traits that "justified" enslaving them. More commonly, women are perceived as unassertive but sensitive and therefore suited for the caretaking tasks they have traditionally performed (Hoffman & Hurst, 1990). In short, prejudice rationalizes inequalities.

Discrimination also increases prejudice through the reactions it provokes in its victims. In his classic 1954 book, *The Nature of Prejudice*, Gordon Allport noted that being a victim of discrimination can produce either self-blame or anger. Both reactions may create new grounds for prejudice through the classic *blame-the-victim* dynamic. If the circumstances of poverty breed a higher crime rate, someone can then use the higher crime rate to justify continuing the discrimination against those who live in poverty.

Us and Them: Ingroup and Outgroup

Thanks to our ancestral need to belong, we are a group-bound species. We cheer for our groups, kill for them, die for them. Indeed, we define who we are—our identities—partly in terms of our groups. Australian psychologists John Turner (1987) and Michael Hogg (1996) note that through our *social identities* we associate ourselves with certain groups and contrast ourselves with others. When Ian identifies himself as a man, an Aussie, a Labourite, a University of Sydney student, a Catholic, and a MacGregor, he knows who he is, and so do we.

The social definition of who you are also implies who you are not. Mentally drawing a circle that defines "us" (the **ingroup**) excludes "them" (the **outgroup**). Such group identifications typically promote an **ingroup bias**—a favoring of one's own group. Even arbitrarily creating an us-them distinction—by grouping people with the toss of a coin—leads people to show favoritism to their own group when dividing any rewards (Tajfel, 1982; Wilder, 1981).

The ingroup
Scotland's famed "Tartan Army" football fans, shown here during a match against archrival England, share a social identity that defines "us" (the Scottish ingroup) and "them" (the English outgroup).

Mike Hewitt/Getty Images

Eric Travers/EPA/Landov

The urge to distinguish enemies from friends and to have one's group be dominant predisposes prejudice against strangers (Whitley, 1999). To Greeks of the classical era, all non-Greeks were "barbarians." Most children believe their own school is better than the other schools in town. Many high school students form cliques—jocks, goths, skaters, gangsters, freaks, geeks—and disparage those outside their group. Even chimpanzees have been seen to wipe clean the spot where they were touched by a chimp from another group (Goodall, 1986).

Emotional Roots of Prejudice

OBJECTIVE 57-4 | Explain how scapegoating illustrates the emotional component of prejudice.

Prejudice springs not only from the divisions of society but also from the passions of the heart. Facing the terror of death tends to heighten patriotism and produce loathing and aggression toward "them"—those who threaten one's worldview (Pyszczynski & others, 2002). Recalling such terror may alter attitudes, as happened to participants when Mark Landau and eight others (2004) reminded them of their own mortality or of the terror of 9/11. This reminder of terror led to their expressing increased support for President Bush (a phenomenon harnessed by the president's 2004 campaign).

Prejudice may also express anger: When things go wrong, finding someone to blame can provide a target, a scapegoat, for one's anger. In the late 1600s, New England settlers, after suffering devastating losses at the hands of Native Americans and their French allies, lashed out by hanging people as supposed witches (Norton, 2002). Following 9/11, some outraged people lashed out at innocent Arab-Americans, about whom negative stereotypes blossomed. Calls to eliminate Saddam Hussein, whom Americans had been grudgingly tolerating, also increased. "Fear and anger create aggression, and aggression against citizens of different ethnicity or race creates racism and, in turn, new forms of terrorism," noted Philip Zimbardo (2001).

Evidence for this **scapegoat theory** of prejudice comes from high prejudice levels among economically frustrated people and from experiments in which a temporary frustration intensifies prejudice. In experiments, students who experience failure or are made to feel insecure will often restore their self-esteem by disparaging a rival school or another person (Cialdini & Richardson, 1980; Crocker & others, 1987). To boost our own sense of status, it helps to have others to denigrate. That is why a rival's misfortune sometimes provides a twinge of pleasure. By contrast, those made to feel loved and supported become more open to and accepting of others who differ (Mikulincer & Shaver, 2001).

> "All good people agree,
> And all good people say
> All nice people, like us, are We
> And everyone else is They.
> But if you cross over the sea
> Instead of over the way
> You may end by (think of it)
> Looking on We
> As only a sort of They."
> Rudyard Kipling, "We and They," 1926

> "If the Tiber reaches the walls, if the Nile does not rise to the fields, if the sky doesn't move or the Earth does, if there is famine, if there is plague, the cry is at once: 'The Christians to the lions!'"
> Tertullian, *Apologeticus*, A.D. 197

■ **ingroup** "Us"—people with whom one shares a common identity.

■ **outgroup** "Them"—those perceived as different or apart from one's ingroup.

■ **ingroup bias** the tendency to favor one's own group.

■ **scapegoat theory** the theory that prejudice offers an outlet for anger by providing someone to blame.

Cognitive Roots of Prejudice

OBJECTIVE 57-5 | Cite four ways that cognitive processes help create and maintain prejudice.

Prejudice springs from the divisions of society, the passions of the heart, and also from the mind's natural workings. Stereotyped beliefs are a by-product of how we cognitively simplify the world.

Do people of another race look alike?
Foreign sunbathers on Bali's beaches may think they do. Balinese masseuses wear identifying numbers on their hats, enabling visitors to recognize them easily.

Categorization

One way we simplify our world is to categorize. A chemist categorizes molecules as organic and inorganic. A mental health professional categorizes psychological disorders by types. In categorizing people into groups, however, we often stereotype them, biasing our perceptions of their diversity. We recognize how greatly we differ from other individuals in our groups. But we overestimate the similarity of those within other groups. "They"—the members of some other group—seem to look and act alike, but "we" are diverse (Bothwell & others, 1989). To those in one ethnic group, members of another often seem more alike in appearance, personality, and attitudes than they are. With experience, however, people get better at recognizing individual faces from another group. For example, people of European descent more accurately identify individual African faces if they have watched a great deal of basketball on television, exposing them to many African-heritage faces (Li & others, 1996).

Vivid Cases

We often judge the frequency of events by instances that readily come to mind. In a classic experiment, Myron Rothbart and his colleagues (1978) demonstrated this ability to overgeneralize from vivid, memorable cases. They divided University of Oregon student volunteers into two groups, then showed them information about 50 men. The first group's list included 10 men arrested for nonviolent crimes, such as forgery. The second group's list included 10 men arrested for violent crimes, such as assault. Later when both groups recalled how many men on their list had committed any sort of crime, the second group overestimated the number. Vivid (violent) cases are readily available to our memory and therefore influence our judgments of a group (**FIGURE 57.3**).

FIGURE 57.3
Vivid cases feed stereotypes
The 9/11 Muslim terrorists created, in many minds, an exaggerated stereotype of Muslims as terror-prone. Actually, reported a National Research Council panel on terrorism, when offering the inexact illustration at right, most terrorists are not Muslim and "the vast majority of Islamic people have no connection with and do not sympathize with terrorism" (Smelser & Mitchell, 2002).

Islam   Terrorism

The Just-World Phenomenon

As we noted earlier, people often justify their prejudice by blaming its victims. Bystanders, too, may blame victims by assuming the world is just and therefore "people get what they deserve." In experiments, merely observing someone receive painful shocks has led many people to think less of the victim (Lerner, 1980). This **just-world phenomenon** reflects an idea we commonly teach our children—that good is rewarded and evil is punished. From this it is but a short leap to assume that those who succeed must be good and those who suffer must be bad. Such reasoning enables the rich to see both their own wealth and the poor's misfortune as justly deserved. As one German civilian is said to have remarked when visiting the Bergen-Belsen concentration camp shortly after World War II, "What terrible criminals these prisoners must have been to receive such treatment."

Hindsight bias is also at work here (Carli & Leonard, 1989). Have you ever heard people say that rape victims, abused spouses, or people with AIDS got what they deserved? In some countries, women who have been raped have been sentenced to severe punishment for having violated a law against adultery (Mydans, 2002). An experiment by Ronnie Janoff-Bulman and her collaborators (1985) illustrates this phenomenon of blaming the victim. When given a detailed account of a date that ended with the woman's being raped, people perceived the woman's behavior as at least partly to blame. In hindsight, they thought, "She should have known better." (Blaming the victim also serves to reassure people that it couldn't happen to them.) Others, given the same account with the rape ending deleted, did not perceive the woman's behavior as inviting rape.

Aggression

OBJECTIVE 57-6 | Explain how psychology's definition of *aggression* differs from everyday usage.

The most destructive force in our social relations is aggression. In psychology, *aggression* has a more precise meaning than it does in everyday usage. The assertive, persistent salesperson is not aggressive. Nor is the dentist who makes you wince with pain. But the person who passes along a vicious rumor about you, the person who verbally assaults you, and the attacker who mugs you are aggressive. In psychology, **aggression** is any physical or verbal behavior intended to hurt or destroy, whether done reactively out of hostility or proactively as a calculated means to an end. Thus, murders and assaults that occurred as hostile outbursts are aggression. So were the 110 million war-related deaths that took place during the last century, many of which were cool and calculated.

Aggression research affirms that behavior emerges from the interaction of biology and experience. For a gun to fire, the trigger must be pulled; with some people, as with hair-trigger guns, it doesn't take much to trip an explosion. Let us look first at biological factors that influence our thresholds for aggressive behavior, then at the psychological factors that pull the trigger.

The Biology of Aggression

OBJECTIVE 57-7 | Describe three levels of biological influences on aggression.

Aggression varies too widely from culture to culture, era to era, and person to person to be considered an unlearned instinct. But biology does *influence* aggression. Stimuli that trigger aggressive behavior operate through our biological system. We can look for biological influences at three levels—genetic, neural, and biochemical. Our genes engineer our individual nervous systems, which operate electrochemically.

Genetic Influences

Animals have been bred for aggressiveness—sometimes for sport, sometimes for research. Twin studies suggest that genes influence human aggression as well (Miles & Carey, 1997; Rowe & others, 1999). If one identical twin admits to "having a violent temper," the other twin will often independently admit the same. Fraternal twins are much less likely to respond similarly. Researchers are now searching for genetic markers found in those who commit the most violence. (One is already well known and is carried by half the human race: the Y chromosome.)

In the last 25 years in the United States, guns have caused some 800,000 suicidal, homicidal, and accidental deaths. Compared with people of the same sex, race, age, and neighborhood, those who keep a gun in the home (ironically, often for protection) are nearly three times more likely to be murdered in the home—nearly always by a family member or close acquaintance. For every self-defense use of a gun in the home, there are 4 unintentional shootings, 7 criminal assaults or homicides, and 11 attempted or completed suicides (Kellermann & others, 1993, 1997, 1998).

■ **just-world phenomenon** the tendency of people to believe the world is just and that people therefore get what they deserve and deserve what they get.

■ **aggression** any physical or verbal behavior intended to hurt or destroy.

"It's a guy thing."

Neural Influences

Animal and human brains have neural systems that, when stimulated, either inhibit or produce aggressive behavior (Moyer, 1983). Consider:

- The domineering leader of a caged monkey colony had a radio-controlled electrode implanted in a brain area that, when stimulated, inhibits aggression. When researchers placed the button that activated the electrode in the colony's cage, one small monkey learned to push it every time the boss became threatening.
- A mild-mannered woman had an electrode implanted in her brain's limbic system (in the amygdala) by neurosurgeons seeking to diagnose a disorder. Because the brain has no sensory receptors, she was unable to feel the stimulation. But at the flick of a switch she snarled, "Take my blood pressure. Take it now," then stood up and began to strike the doctor.
- Intensive evaluation of 15 death-row inmates revealed that all 15 had suffered a severe head injury. Although most neurologically impaired people are not violent, researcher Dorothy Lewis and her colleagues (1986) inferred that unrecognized neurological disorders may be one ingredient in the violence recipe. Other studies of violent criminals have revealed diminished activity in the frontal lobes, which play an important role in controlling impulses (Amen & others, 1996; Davidson & others, 2000; Raine, 1999).

So, does the brain have a "violence center" that produces aggression when stimulated? Actually, no one spot in the brain controls aggression, because aggression is a complex behavior that occurs in particular contexts. Rather, the brain has neural systems that *facilitate* aggression, given provocation. And it has a frontal lobe system for inhibiting aggression, making aggression more likely if this system is damaged, inactive, disconnected, or not yet fully mature.

Biochemical Influences

Hormones, alcohol, and other substances in the blood influence the neural systems that control aggression. A raging bull will become a gentle Ferdinand when castration reduces its testosterone level. The same is true of castrated mice. When injected with testosterone, the castrated mice once again become aggressive.

Although humans are less sensitive to hormonal changes, violent criminals tend to be muscular young males with lower-than-average intelligence scores, low levels of the neurotransmitter serotonin, and higher-than-average testosterone levels (Dabbs & others, 2001a; Pendick, 1994). Drugs that sharply reduce their testosterone levels also subdue their aggressive tendencies. High testosterone correlates with irritability, low

> "We could avoid two-thirds of all crime simply by putting all able-bodied young men in cryogenic sleep from the age of 12 through 28."
>
> David T. Lykken, *The Antisocial Personalities*, 1995

A lean, mean fighting machine—the testosterone-laden female hyena
The hyena's unusual embryology pumps testosterone into female fetuses. The result is revved-up young female hyenas who seem born to fight.

tolerance for frustration, assertiveness, and impulsiveness—qualities that predispose somewhat more aggressive responses to provocation (Dabbs & others, 2001b; Harris, 1999). Among both teenage boys and adult men, high testosterone levels correlate with delinquency, hard drug use, and aggressive-bullying responses to frustration (Berman & others, 1993; Dabbs & Morris, 1990; Olweus & others, 1988). With age, testosterone levels—and aggressiveness—diminish.

The traffic between hormones and behavior is two-way. Testosterone heightens dominance and aggressiveness. But dominating behavior also boosts testosterone levels (Mazur & Booth, 1998). One study measured testosterone levels in the saliva of male college basketball fans before and after a big game. Testosterone levels swelled among the victorious fans and sank among the dejected ones (Bernhardt & others, 1998).

For both biological and psychological reasons, alcohol unleashes aggressive responses to frustration (Bushman, 1993; Ito & others, 1996; Taylor & Chermack, 1993). (Just *thinking* you've imbibed alcohol has some effect; but so, too, does unknowingly ingesting alcohol slipped into a drink.) Police data and prison surveys reinforce conclusions drawn from experiments on alcohol and aggression. Aggression-prone people are more likely to drink and to become violent when intoxicated (White & others, 1993). People who have been drinking commit 4 in 10 violent crimes and 3 in 4 acts of spousal abuse (Greenfeld, 1998).

The Psychology of Aggression

OBJECTIVE 57-8 | Outline four psychological triggers of aggression.

Biological factors influence the ease with which aggression is triggered. But what psychological factors pull the trigger?

Aversive Events

Although suffering sometimes builds character, it may also bring out the worst in us. Studies in which animals or humans experience unpleasant events reveal that those made miserable often make others miserable (Berkowitz, 1983, 1989).

Being blocked short of a goal also increases people's readiness to aggress. This phenomenon is called the **frustration-aggression principle:** Frustration creates anger, which may in some people generate aggression, especially in the presence of an aggressive cue, such as a gun. Organisms often respond to stress with a *fight-or-flight reaction*. After the frustration and stress of 9/11, Americans responded with a readiness to fight. Terrorism similarly may spring from a desire for revenge, sometimes after a friend or family member has been killed or injured.

Like frustration, other aversive stimuli—physical pain, personal insults, foul odors, hot temperatures, cigarette smoke, and a host of others—can also evoke hostility. For example, violent crime and spousal abuse rates are higher during hotter years, seasons, months, and days (**FIGURE 57.4** on the next page). When people are hotter than usual, they think, feel, and act more aggressively. From the available data, Craig Anderson and his colleagues (2000) project that, other things being equal, global warming of 4 degrees Fahrenheit (about 2 degrees centigrade) would induce more than 50,000 additional assaults and murders in the United States alone.

Ostracism can also be a real pain. In a series of studies, Jean Twenge and her collaborators (2001, 2002, 2003) told some people that others whom they had met didn't want them in their group, or that a personality test indicated they "were likely to end up alone later in life." Those led to feel socially excluded were later more likely to disparage or even deliver a blast of noise to someone who insulted

■ frustration-aggression principle the principle that frustration—the blocking of an attempt to achieve some goal—creates anger, which can generate aggression.

Recipe for aggression

When Indiana Pacers' Ron Artest attacked Detroit Pistons basketball fans, many influences appeared to create the perfect storm for aggression. The young male Pacer players, who were dominating the Pistons, were likely flush with testosterone. The Pistons' frustration had led one of its players to aggressively shove Artest. The high arousal level of the players and of the frustrated fans (many of whom were disinhibited by alcohol consumption) was easily channeled into aggression when one deindividuated fan threw a cup of beer at Artest.

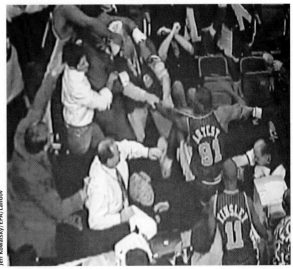

Jeff Kowalsky/EPA/Landov

FIGURE 57.4

Uncomfortably hot weather and aggressive reactions

Between 1980 and 1982 in Houston, murders and rapes were more common on days over 91 degrees Fahrenheit (33 degrees centigrade), as shown in the graph. This finding is consistent with those from laboratory experiments in which people working in a hot room react to provocations with greater hostility. (From Anderson & Anderson, 1984.)

> "Why do we kill people who kill people to show that killing people is wrong?"
> National Coalition to Abolish the Death Penalty, 1992

them. This rejection-induced aggression brings to mind various North American and European school shootings, committed by youth who had been shunned and mocked by peers. Other studies confirm that rejection often intensifies aggression (Catanese & Tice, 2005; Gaertner & Iuzzini, 2005).

Learning That Aggression Is Rewarding

Aggression may be a natural response to aversive events, but learning can alter natural reactions. Animals naturally eat when they are hungry. But if appropriately rewarded or punished, they can be taught either to overeat or to starve.

Our reactions are more likely to be aggressive in situations where experience has taught us that aggression pays. Children whose aggression successfully intimidates other children may become more aggressive. Animals that have successfully fought to get food or mates become increasingly ferocious.

Different cultures model, reinforce, and evoke different tendencies toward violence. For example, crime rates are higher (and average happiness is lower) in countries marked by a great disparity between rich and poor (Triandis, 1994). Richard Nisbett and Dov Cohen (1996) show how violence can vary by culture within a country. They analyzed violence among white Americans in southern U.S. towns settled by Scots-Irish herders whose tradition emphasized "manly honor," the use of arms to protect one's flock, and a history of coercive slavery. Their cultural descendants have triple the homicide rates and are more supportive of physically punishing children, of warfare initiatives, and of uncontrolled gun ownership than are their white counterparts in New England towns settled by Puritan, Quaker, and Dutch farmer-artisans.

Social influence also appears in high violence rates among cultures and families that experience minimal father care (Triandis, 1994). For example, the U.S. Bureau of Justice Statistics has reported that 70 percent of imprisoned juveniles did not grow up with two parents (Beck & others, 1988). (An absent parent is usually a father.) The correlation between father absence and violence in the United States holds for all races, income levels, and locations (Myers, 2000).

It is important, however, to note how many individuals are leading gentle, even heroic lives amid social stresses, reminding us again that individuals differ. The person matters. That people differ over time and place reminds us that environments differ. Yesterday's plundering Vikings have become today's peace-promoting Scandinavians. Situations matter. Like all behavior, aggression arises from the interaction of persons and situations.

Once established, however, aggressive behavior patterns are difficult to change. To foster a kinder, gentler world we had best model and reward sensitivity and cooperation from an early age, perhaps by training parents to discipline without modeling violence. Modeling violence—screaming and hitting—is precisely what exasperated parents often do. Parents of delinquent youngsters typically discipline with beatings, thus modeling aggression as a method of dealing with problems (Patterson & others, 1982, 1992). They also frequently cave into (reward) their children's tears and temper tantrums.

Parent-training programs advise a more positive approach. They encourage parents to reinforce desirable behaviors and to frame statements positively ("When you finish loading the dishwasher you can go play," rather than "If you don't load the dishwasher, there'll be no playing"). One *aggression-replacement program* that brought down re-arrest rates of juvenile offenders and gang members taught the youths and their parents communication skills, trained them in how to control anger, and encouraged more thoughtful moral reasoning (Goldstein & others, 1998).

Observing Models of Aggression

Parents are hardly the only aggression models. Observing TV violence tends to desensitize people to cruelty and prime them to respond aggressively when provoked. Does this media effect extend to sexual violence?

A woman's risk of rape has varied across cultures and times and was greater at the last century's end than half a century previous (Koss & others, 1994; Tjaden & Thoennes, 2000). In surveys, about one-fifth of women have reported that a man has forced them to do something sexually, about one-half have reported some form of unwanted sexual coercion, and most have reported experiencing verbal sexual harassment (Craig & others, 1989; Laumann & others, 1994; Sandberg & others, 1985). Similar levels of sexual coercion have been found in Canadian, Australian, and New Zealand surveys (Koss & others, 1994; Patton & Mannison, 1995).

What factors might explain this increased sexual aggression? Alcohol consumption—often linked with aggression—has not increased. We do know that sexually coercive men typically are sexually promiscuous and hostile in their relationships with women (**FIGURE 57.5**). Might changes in the media have contributed to such tendencies?

Coinciding with the increase in sexual aggression was the rise of the home video business, giving easier access to R-rated "slasher films" and X-rated films. Content analyses reveal that most X-rated films depict quick, casual sex between strangers, but that scenes of rape and sexual exploitation of women by men are also common (Cowan & others, 1988; NCTV, 1987; Yang & Linz, 1990). In just the United States, video, pay-per-view, and Internet pornography have combined to create a $10 billion- to $14-billion business—a bigger business than professional football, basketball, and baseball, put together," noted the *New York Times* (Rich, 2001). In one survey of collegians, 10 percent of women and 28.4 percent of men acknowledged accessing sexually explicit material on the Internet more often than "rarely" (Goodson & others, 2001). Although the explosion in Internet pornography has not been accompanied by a further increase in reported rapes, researchers nevertheless wonder whether images of sexual exploitation influence sexual aggression.

Rape scenes often portray the victim at first fleeing and resisting her attacker, but then becoming aroused and finally driven to ecstasy. In less graphic form, the same unrealistic script—she resists, he persists, she melts—is commonplace on TV and in romance novels. In *Gone With the Wind,* Scarlett O'Hara is carried to bed screaming and wakes up singing. Most rapists accept this *rape myth*—the idea that some women invite or enjoy rape and get "swept away" while being "taken" (Brinson, 1992). (In actuality, rape is traumatic, and it frequently harms women's reproductive and sexual health [Golding, 1996].)

FIGURE 57.5
Men who sexually coerce women
The recipe for coercion against women combines an impersonal approach to sex with a hostile masculinity. (Adapted from Malamuth, 1996.)

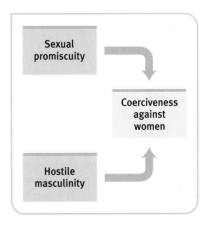

Pornography means different things to different people. Following Webster's dictionary, some define pornography as erotic depictions intended to excite sexual arousal. Others define it as sexual materials that exploit, degrade, or subordinate women.

In follow-up studies, Zillmann (1989) found that after massive exposure to X-rated sexual films, men and women became more accepting of extramarital sex, of women's sexual submission to men, and of a man's seducing a 12-year-old girl. As people heavily exposed to televised crime perceive the world as more dangerous, so people heavily exposed to pornography see the world as more sexual.

As U.S. First Lady, Hillary Rodham Clinton voiced concerns shared by many when she worried about media models of an "impulsive sexuality" that encourage uncommitted sex (a predictor of sexual violence) and father-absent families (a predictor of juvenile violence).

"What we're trying to do is raise the level of awareness of violence against women and pornography to at least the level of awareness of racist and Ku Klux Klan literature."
Gloria Steinem (1988)

When interviewed, Canadian and U.S. sex offenders (rapists, child molesters, and serial killers) do report a greater-than-usual appetite for sexually explicit and sexually violent materials—materials typically labeled as pornography (Marshall, 1989; Ressler & others, 1988; Oddone-Paolucci & others, 2000). For example, the Los Angeles Police Department has reported that pornography was "conspicuously present" in 62 percent of its extrafamilial child sexual abuse cases during the 1980s (Bennett, 1991). But are the sexual offenders merely, as sex researcher John Money (1988) suspected, using pornography "as an alibi to explain to themselves and their captors what otherwise is inexplicable"?

Laboratory experiments reveal that repeatedly watching X-rated films (even if nonviolent) later makes one's own partner seem less attractive, makes a woman's friendliness seem more sexual, and makes sexual aggression seem less serious (Harris, 1994). In one such experiment, Dolf Zillmann and Jennings Bryant (1984) showed undergraduates six brief, sexually explicit films each week for six weeks. A control group viewed nonerotic films during the same six-week period. Three weeks later, both groups read a newspaper report about a man convicted but not yet sentenced for raping a hitchhiker. When asked to suggest an appropriate prison term, those who had viewed sexually explicit films recommended sentences half as long as those recommended by the control group.

Experiments cannot elicit actual sexual violence, but they can assess a man's willingness to hurt a woman. Often the research gauges the effect of violent versus nonviolent erotic films on men's willingness to deliver supposed electric shocks to women who had earlier provoked the men. These experiments suggest that it's not the eroticism but rather the depictions of sexual *violence* (whether in R-rated slasher films or X-rated films) that most directly affect men's acceptance and performance of aggression against women. A conference of 21 social scientists, including many of the researchers who conducted these experiments, produced a consensus (Surgeon General, 1986): "Pornography that portrays sexual aggression as pleasurable for the victim increases the acceptance of the use of coercion in sexual relations." Contrary to much popular opinion, viewing such depictions does not provide an outlet for bottled-up impulses. Rather, "in laboratory studies measuring short-term effects, exposure to violent pornography increases punitive behavior toward women."

Acquiring Social Scripts

Significant behaviors, such as violence, usually have many determinants, making any single explanation an oversimplification. Asking what causes violence is therefore like asking what causes cancer. Those who study the effects of asbestos exposure on cancer rates may remind us that asbestos is indeed a cancer cause, albeit only one among many. Likewise, report Neil Malamuth and his colleagues (1991, 1995), several factors can create a predisposition to sexual violence. They include the media but also dominance motives, disinhibition by alcohol, and a history of child abuse. Still, if media depictions of violence can disinhibit and desensitize; if viewing sexual violence fosters hostile, domineering attitudes and behaviors; and if viewing pornography leads viewers to trivialize rape, devalue their partners, and engage in uncommitted sex, then media influence is not a minor issue.

Social psychologists attribute the media's influence partly to the *social scripts* (mental tapes for how to act, provided by our culture) they portray. When we find ourselves in new situations, uncertain how to act, we rely on social scripts. After so many action films, youngsters may acquire a script that gets played when they face real-life conflicts. Challenged, they may "act like a man" by intimidating or eliminating the threat. Likewise, after viewing multiple sexual innuendoes and acts in most prime-time TV hours—often involving impulsive or short-term relationships—youths may acquire sexual scripts they later enact in real-life relationships (Kunkel & others, 2001; Sapolsky & Tabarlet, 1991).

CLOSE-UP:

PARALLELS BETWEEN SMOKING EFFECTS AND MEDIA VIOLENCE EFFECTS

Researchers Brad Bushman and Craig Anderson (2001) note that the correlation between viewing violence and behaving aggressively nearly equals the correlation between smoking and lung cancer. They also note other parallels:

1. Not everyone who smokes gets lung cancer.
2. Smoking is only one cause of lung cancer, although an important one.
3. The first cigarette can nauseate, but the sickening effect lessens with repetition.
4. The short-term effect of one cigarette is minor and dissipates within an hour or so.
5. The long-term, cumulative effect of smoking can be severe.
6. Corporate interests have denied the smoking–lung cancer link.

1. Not everyone who watches violence becomes aggressive.
2. Viewing violence is only one cause of aggression, although an important one.
3. The first violence exposure can upset, but the upset lessens with repetition.
4. One violent TV program can prime aggressive thoughts and behaviors, but the effect dissipates within an hour or so.
5. The long-term, cumulative effect of viewing violence is increased likelihood of habitual aggression.
6. Corporate interests have denied the viewing violence–aggression link.

Might public consciousness be raised by making people aware of the information you have just been reading (see Close-Up: Parallels Between Smoking Effects and Media Violence Effects)? In the 1940s, movies often depicted African-Americans as childlike superstitious buffoons. Today, we would not tolerate such images. In the 1960s and 1970s, some rock music and movies glamorized drug use. Responding to a tidal change in cultural attitudes, the entertainment industry now more often portrays the dark side of drug use. In response to growing public concern about violence in the media, television violence levels declined in the early 1990s (Gerbner & others, 1993). The growing sensitivity to violence has raised hopes that entertainers, producers, and audiences might someday look back with embarrassment on the days when movies "entertained" people with scenes of torture, mutilation, and sexual coercion.

Densensitizing people to violence

Do Video Games Teach or Release Violence?

OBJECTIVE 57-9 | Discuss the effects of violent video games on social attitudes and behavior.

Violent video games became an issue for public debate after teen assassins in Paducah, Kentucky; Littleton, Colorado; and more than a dozen other places seemed to mimic the carnage in the splatter games they had so often played (Anderson, 2004). In 2002, two Grand Rapids, Michigan, teens and a man in his early twenties spent part of a night drinking beer and playing Grand Theft Auto III, using cars to run down simulated pedestrians, then beating them with fists, leaving a bloody body behind (Kolker, 2002). Then they went driving on a real drive, spotted a 38-year-old man on a bicycle, ran him down with their car, got out, stomped and punched him, and returned home to play the game some more. (The man, a father of three, died six days later.)

When youths play such games, do they learn social scripts? Interactive games transport the player into their own vivid reality. When youths play Grand Theft Auto: San

> "It'll be like the LA riots, the Oklahoma bombing, WWI, Vietnam, Duke, and Doom all mixed together."
>
> Journal entry by Columbine killer Eric Harris, 1998

> "We are what we repeatedly do."
>
> Aristotle

Andreas, they can carjack vehicles; run down pedestrians; do drive-by shootings; pick up a prostitute, have sex with her, and then kill her. What scripts are being learned?

Most abused children don't become abusive adults. And most youths who spend hundreds of hours in these mass murder simulators won't become teen assassins. Still, we wonder: If passively viewing violence elevates aggressive responses to provocation and lowers sensitivity to cruelty, what will be the effect of actively role-playing aggression? Although very few will commit slaughter, how many will become desensitized to violence and more open to violent acts?

Thirty-eight recent studies of more than 7000 people offer some answers (Anderson & others, 2004). Mary Ballard and Rose Wiest (1998) observed a rising level of arousal and feelings of hostility in college men as they played Mortal Kombat. Other studies have found that video games can prime aggressive thoughts and increase aggression. Consider this report from Craig Anderson and Karen Dill (2000): University men who have spent the most hours playing violent video games tend to be the most physically aggressive (for example, to acknowledge having hit or attacked someone else). In one experiment, people randomly assigned to play a game involving bloody murders with groaning victims (rather than to play nonviolent Myst) became more hostile. On a follow-up task, they also were more likely to blast intense noise at a fellow student.

Studies of young adolescents by Douglas Gentile and his co-researchers (2004) further reveal that kids who play a lot of violent video games see the world as more hostile, get into more arguments and fights, and get worse grades (those hours aren't spent reading or studying). Ah, but is this merely because naturally hostile kids are drawn to such games? No, says Gentile. Even among violent-game players who scored low in hostility, the 38 percent who had been in fights was nearly 10 times the 4 percent involved in fights among their nongaming counterparts. Moreover, over time, the nongamers become more likely to have fights only if they start playing the violent games. Anderson (2004a) believes that, due partly to the more repetitive and active participation of game play, violent video games have even greater effects "than the well-documented effects of exposure to violent television and movies."

Although much remains to be learned, these studies disconfirm the *catharsis hypothesis*—the idea that we feel better if we "blow off steam" by venting our emotions. Playing violent video games *increases* aggressive thoughts, emotions, and behaviors. One video game company's CEO rationalizes that we are "violent by nature [and] need release valves." "It's a way to process violent feelings and anxieties through a fantasy medium," adds a prominent civil liberties lawyer in explaining her hunch that playing violent games calms violent tendencies (Heins, 2004). Actually, expressing anger breeds more anger, and practicing violence breeds more violence. Tomorrow's games may have even greater effects. Social psychologists Susan Persky and Jim Blascovich (2005) created a violent video game for students to play on either a desktop computer or by putting on a headset and stepping into a virtual reality. As they predicted, the virtual reality more dramatically heightened aggressive feelings and behavior during and after the play.

To sum up, research reveals biological, psychological, and social influences on aggressive behavior. Like so much else, aggression is a biopsychosocial phenomenon (**FIGURE 57.6**).

FIGURE 57.6

Biopsychosocial understanding of aggression

Many factors contribute to aggressive behavior, but there are many ways to combat these influences, including learning anger management and communication skills, and avoiding violent media and video games.

Biological influences:
- genetic influences
- biochemical influences, such as testosterone and alcohol
- neural influences, such as severe head injuries

Psychological influences:
- dominating behavior (which boosts testosterone levels in the blood)
- believing you've drunk alcohol (whether you actually have or not)
- frustration
- aggressive role models
- rewards for aggressive behavior

Aggressive behavior

Social-cultural influences:
- deindividuation from being in a crowd
- challenging environmental factors, such as crowding, heat, and direct provocations
- parental models of aggression
- minimal father involvement
- being rejected from a group
- exposure to violent media

Conflict

OBJECTIVE 57-10 | Explain how social traps and mirror-image perceptions fuel social conflict.

We live in surprising times. With astonishing speed, late-twentieth-century democratic movements swept away totalitarian rule in Eastern European countries, and hopes for a new world order displaced the Cold War chill. And yet, the twenty-first century began with terrorist acts and war, and the world continued to spend $2 billion every day for arms and armies—money that could have been used for housing, nutrition, education, and health. Knowing that wars begin in human minds, psychologists have wondered: What in the human mind causes destructive conflict? How might the perceived threats of social diversity be replaced by a spirit of cooperation?

To a social psychologist, a **conflict** is a seeming incompatibility of actions, goals, or ideas. The elements of conflict are much the same at all levels, from nations at war, to cultural disputes within a society, to individuals in a marital dispute. In each situation, people become enmeshed in a potentially destructive social process that can produce results no one wants. Among the destructive processes are social traps and distorted perceptions.

Social Traps

In some situations, we support our collective well-being by pursuing our personal interests. As capitalist Adam Smith wrote in *The Wealth of Nations* (1776), "It is not from the benevolence of the butcher, the brewer, or the baker that we expect our dinner, but from their regard to their own interest." In other situations, we harm our collective well-being by pursuing our personal interests. Such situations are **social traps.**

Consider the simple game matrix in **FIGURE 57.7,** which is similar to those used in experiments with countless thousands of people. In this game, both sides can win or both can lose, depending on the players' individual choices. Pretend you are Person 1, and that you and Person 2 will each receive the amount shown after you separately choose either *A* or *B*. (You might invite someone to look at the matrix with you and take the role of Person 2.) Which do you choose—*A* or *B*?

As you ponder the game, you will discover that you and Person 2 are caught in a dilemma. If you both choose *A,* you both benefit, making $5 each. Neither of you benefits if you both choose *B,* for neither of you makes anything. Nevertheless, on any single trial you serve your own interests if you choose *B:* You can't lose, and you might make $10. But the same is true for the other person. Hence, the social trap: As long as you both pursue your own immediate best interest and choose *B,* you will both end up with nothing—the typical result—when you could have made $5.

Many real-life situations similarly pit our individual interests against our communal well-being. Individual whalers reasoned that the few whales they took would not threaten the species and that if they didn't take them other whalers would anyway. The result: Some species of whales became endangered. The individual car owner and home owner reasons, "It would cost me comfort or money to buy a more fuel-efficient car and furnace. Besides, the fossil fuels I burn don't noticeably add to the greenhouse gases." When enough others reason similarly, the collective result threatens disaster—global warming and the threat of rising seas and more extreme weather.

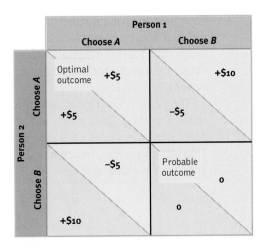

FIGURE 57.7
Social-trap game matrix
By pursuing our self-interest and not trusting others, we can end up losers. To illustrate this, imagine playing the game to the left. The pink triangles show the outcomes for Person 1, which depend on the choices made by both players. If you were Person 1, would you choose *A* or *B*? (This game is called a *non-zero-sum game* because the outcomes need not add up to zero; both sides can win or both can lose.)

- **conflict** a perceived incompatibility of actions, goals, or ideas.
- **social trap** a situation in which the conflicting parties, by each rationally pursuing their self-interest, become caught in mutually destructive behavior.

Not in my ocean!
Many people support alternative energy sources, including windmills. But proposals to construct windmill farms in real-world neighborhoods elicit less support. One such proposal, for locating windmills off the coast of Massachusetts' Nantucket Island, has produced heated debate over the future benefits of clean energy versus the costs of altering treasured ocean views and, possibly, migratory bird routes.

Social traps challenge us to find ways of reconciling our right to pursue our personal well-being with our responsibility for the well-being of all. Psychologists are therefore exploring ways to convince people to cooperate for their mutual betterment—through agreed-upon *regulations,* through better *communication,* and through promoting *awareness* of our responsibilities toward community, nation, and the whole of humanity (Dawes, 1980, Linder, 1982, Sato, 1987). Under such conditions, people more often cooperate, whether it be in playing a laboratory game or the real game of life.

Enemy Perceptions

Psychologists have noted that those in conflict have a curious tendency to form diabolical images of one another. These distorted images are ironically similar, so similar in fact that we call them *mirror-image perceptions:* As we see "them"—as untrustworthy and evil intentioned—so "they" see us. Each demonizes the other.

Mirror-image perceptions often feed a vicious cycle of hostility. If Juan believes Maria is annoyed with him, he may snub her, causing her to act in ways that justify his perception. As with individuals, so with countries. Perceptions can become self-fulfilling prophecies. They may confirm themselves by influencing the other country to react in ways that seem to justify them.

In the early twenty-first century, many Americans came to loathe Saddam Hussein. Like the "evil" Saddam Hussein, declared George W. Bush (2001), "some of today's tyrants are gripped by an implacable hatred of the United States of America. They hate our friends, they hate our values, they hate democracy and freedom and individual liberty. Many care little for the lives of their own people." Hussein (2002) reciprocated the perception, seeing the United States as "an evil tyrant" that, with Satan as its protector, lusted for oil and aggressively attacked those who "defend what is right."

The point is not that truth must lie midway between two such views (one may be more accurate). The point is that enemy perceptions often form mirror images. Moreover, as enemies change, so do perceptions. In American minds and media, the "bloodthirsty, cruel, treacherous" Japanese of World War II later became our "intelligent, hardworking, self-disciplined, resourceful allies" (Gallup, 1972).

>> LEARNING OUTCOMES

Antisocial Relations

OBJECTIVE 57-1 | Identify the three components of prejudice.

Prejudice is an attitude composed of *beliefs, emotions,* and *predispositions to action.* The beliefs are frequently *stereotypes* (sometimes accurate but often overgeneralized beliefs). The emotions are most often negative, and the action is usually *discrimination* (unjustifiable negative behavior).

OBJECTIVE 57-2 | Contrast overt and subtle forms of prejudice, and give examples of each.

Overt prejudice, such as denying a particular ethnic group the right to vote, is discrimination that *explicitly* (openly and consciously) expresses negative beliefs and emotions. *Subtle prejudice,* such as feeling fearful in the presence of a stranger with a particular ethnic background, is an *implicit* (often unconscious) expression of negative beliefs and emotions.

OBJECTIVE 57-3 | Discuss the social factors that contribute to prejudice.

One contributing factor is *inequality* (unequal distribution of money, power, and prestige) within a group; in such conditions, the "haves" usually develop negative attitudes toward the "have-nots" to justify their more privileged positions. Definitions of *social identity* ("we" the ingroup versus "they" the outgroup) are another source of prejudice because they promote ingroup bias (a tendency to favor one's own group) and discrimination.

OBJECTIVE 57-4 | Explain how scapegoating illustrates the emotional component of prejudice.

Troubled times, especially those that remind us of our own mortality, produce feelings of fear and anger. As in-group loyalty and out-group prejudice intensify, people may boost their self-esteem by searching for a *scapegoat*—someone to blame for the troubling event.

OBJECTIVE 57-5 | Cite four ways that cognitive processes help create and maintain prejudice.

We simplify the world around us by *creating categories,* but when we categorize people, we often stereotype them, overgeneralizing their characteristics and underestimating their differences. We also tend to judge the frequency of events by *vivid cases* that come to mind more readily than the long string of less vivid events involving the same group. We may justify people's less-privileged or punished position by the *just-world phenomenon,* assuming that the world is just and people get what they deserve. *Hindsight bias* (the tendency to believe, after learning an outcome, that we would have predicted it beforehand) may also contribute.

OBJECTIVE 57-6 | Explain how psychology's definition of *aggression* differs from everyday usage.

Psychology's definition of *aggression* as "any physical or verbal behavior intended to harm or destroy" includes behaviors (such as killing in combat) that might not be included in everyday usage.

OBJECTIVE 57-7 | Describe three levels of biological influences on aggression.

Genes influence aggression, for example by influencing temperament. *Neural systems* in the brain facilitate or inhibit aggression. Hormones (such as testosterone), alcohol (which releases inhibitions), and other substances are *biochemical influences* that contribute to aggression. Biological conditions set the threshold for aggressiveness, but psychological factors trigger aggressive behaviors.

OBJECTIVE 57-8 | Outline four psychological triggers of aggression.

Aversive events (such as environmental conditions or social rejection) can create frustration, leading to feelings of anger and hostility. *Reinforcement for aggressive behavior* can establish learned patterns of aggression that are difficult to change. People can also learn aggression and become desensitized to violence by *observing models act aggressively* in person or in the media. Media depictions of violence can also trigger aggression by providing *social scripts* (culturally sanctioned ways of acting in a given situation).

OBJECTIVE 57-9 | Discuss the effects of violent video games on social attitudes and behavior.

Playing violent video games can provide opportunities to observe modeled aggression and to role-play aggression; increase arousal and feelings of hostility; prime aggressive thoughts and increase aggression; and (in adolescents) lead to increased participation in arguments and fights and to falling grades. Virtual reality games may heighten these effects.

OBJECTIVE 57-10 | Explain how social traps and mirror-image perceptions fuel social conflict.

Social conflicts are situations in which people perceive their actions, goals, or ideas to be incompatible. In *social traps,* two or more individuals rationally pursue their own personal interests without regard for the well-being of others. People in conflict tend to perceive the worst in each other, producing *mirror-images* of identical demons. The perceptions can become self-fulfilling prophecies, triggering reactions that confirm the images. Helping people to agree on regulations, communicate better, and be more aware of responsibilities toward others can foster cooperation and avoid social traps.

TERMS AND CONCEPTS TO REMEMBER

prejudice, p. 57-1
stereotype, p. 57-1
discrimination, p. 57-1
ingroup, p. 57-4
outgroup, p. 57-4
ingroup bias, p. 57-4
scapegoat theory, p. 57-5

just-world phenomenon, p. 57-6
aggression, p. 57-7
frustration-aggression principle, p. 57-9
conflict, p. 57-15
social trap, p. 57-15

TEST YOURSELF

1. Horace says, "I have no prejudice within me toward anyone. I believe everyone deserves equal opportunity in housing and employment." Even if Horace indeed expresses no obvious prejudice, what sort of prejudice might nonetheless exist?

(Answer in Appendix B.)

ASK YOURSELF

1. Recent court rulings established that U.S. cities could seize private property and sell it to businesses that would increase taxes, benefiting the collective well-being. Do you agree with the ruling?

ANSWER TO QUESTION WITHIN THE MODULE

Q. Which face in Figure 57.2 do you like best? Which one placed an ad seeking a long-term relationship?

A. Research suggests that subtly feminized features convey a likeable image, which people tend to associate more with committed dads than with promiscuous cads. Thus, if you responded as others did to these questions, you would have picked computer-generated face (b) in response to both questions.

>WEB

Multiple-choice *self-tests* and more may be found at www.worthpublishers.com/myers.

58

MODULE

Prosocial Relations

Social psychology studies how we think about and influence one another, and also how we *relate* to one another. Social psychologists focus not only on the dark side of social relationships, but also on the bright side, by studying *prosocial* behavior—behavior that intends to help or benefit someone. Our positive behaviors toward others are evident from explorations of attraction, altruism, and peacemaking.

Attraction

Pause a moment and think about your relationships with two people—a close friend, and someone who stirs in you feelings of romantic love. What is the psychological chemistry that binds us together in these special sorts of attachments that help us cope with all other relationships? Social psychology suggests some answers.

The Psychology of Attraction

OBJECTIVE 58-1 | Describe the influence of proximity, physical attractiveness, and similarity on interpersonal attraction.

We endlessly wonder how we can win others' affection and what makes our own affections flourish or fade. Does familiarity breed contempt, or does it intensify our affection? Do birds of a feather flock together, or do opposites attract? Is beauty only skin deep, or does attractiveness matter greatly? Consider three ingredients of our liking for one another: proximity, physical attractiveness, and similarity.

Proximity

Before friendships become close, they must begin. *Proximity*—geographic nearness—is friendship's most powerful predictor. Proximity provides opportunities for aggression, but much more often it breeds liking. Study after study reveals that people are most likely to like, and even to marry, those who live in the same neighborhood, who sit nearby in class, who work in the same office, who share the same parking lot, who eat in the same dining hall. Look around.

Why is proximity so conducive to liking? Obviously, part of the answer is the greater availability of those we often meet. But there is more to it than that. For one thing, repeated exposure to novel stimuli—be they nonsense syllables, musical selections, geometric figures, Chinese characters, human faces, or the letters of our own name—increases our liking for them (Moreland & Zajonc, 1982; Zajonc, 2001; Nuttin, 1987). People are even somewhat more likely to marry someone whose first or last name resembles their own (Jones & others, 2004).

This phenomenon, exploited by advertisers, we call the **mere exposure effect.** Within certain limits (Bornstein, 1989, 1999), familiarity breeds fondness. Richard Moreland and Scott Beach (1992) demonstrated this by having four equally attractive women silently attend a 200-student class for zero, 5, 10, or 15 class sessions. At the end of the course, students were shown slides of each woman and asked to rate each one's attractiveness. The most attractive? The ones they'd seen most often. The phenomenon will come as no surprise to the young Taiwanese man who wrote more than 700 letters to his girlfriend, urging her to marry him. She did marry—the mail carrier (Steinberg, 1993).

■ **mere exposure effect** the phenomenon that repeated exposure to novel stimuli increases liking of them.

Familiarity breeds acceptance
When this rare white penguin was born in the Sydney, Australia, zoo, his tuxedoed peers ostracized him. Zookeepers thought they would need to dye him black to gain acceptance. But after three weeks of contact, the other penguins came to accept him.

Rex USA

The mere exposure effect
The mere exposure effect applies even to ourselves. Because the human face is not perfectly symmetrical, the face we see in the mirror is not the same as the one our friends see. Most of us prefer the familiar mirror image, while our friends like the reverse (Mita & others, 1977). The Prime Minister Junichiro Koizumi known to the Japanese people is shown at left. The person Koizumi sees in the mirror each morning is shown at right, and that's the photo he would probably prefer.

"I'm going to have to recuse myself."

No face is more familiar than one's own. And that explains why, when Lisa De-Bruine (2002) had McMaster University students play a social trap–type game with a supposed other player, they were more trusting and cooperative when the other person's image had some features of their own face morphed into it. In me I trust. In a follow-up study, DeBruine (2004) found that men also *liked* other men (and women liked other women) whose faces incorporated some morphed features of their own.

For our ancestors, the mere exposure phenomenon was adaptive. What was familiar was generally safe and approachable. What was unfamiliar was more often dangerous and threatening. Robert Zajonc (1998) concludes that evolution has hard-wired into us the tendency to bond with those who are familiar and to be wary of those who are unfamiliar. Gut-level prejudice against those culturally different may thus be a primitive, automatic emotional response (Devine, 1995).

Physical Attractiveness

Once proximity affords you contact, what most affects your first impressions: The person's sincerity? Intelligence? Personality? Hundreds of experiments reveal that it is something far more superficial: Appearance. For people taught that "beauty is only skin deep" and that "appearances can be deceiving," the power of physical attractiveness is unnerving. In one early study, Elaine Hatfield and her co-workers (Walster & others, 1966) randomly matched new University of Minnesota students for a Welcome Week dance. Before the dance, each student took a battery of personality and aptitude tests. On the night of the blind date, the couples danced and talked for more than two hours and then took a brief intermission to rate their dates. What determined whether they liked each other? As far as the researchers could determine, only one thing mattered: Physical attractiveness (which had been rated by the researchers

"Personal beauty is a greater recommendation than any letter of introduction."
Aristotle, *Apothegems,* 330 B.C.

Good looks help people get good jobs
In the 2004 presidential election, many Americans found the face on the left more likeable and trustworthy.

beforehand). Both the men and the women liked good-looking dates best. Although women are more likely than men to *say* that another's looks don't affect them, a man's looks do affect women's behavior (Feingold, 1990; Sprecher, 1989; Woll, 1986).

People's physical attractiveness has wide-ranging effects. It predicts their frequency of dating, their feelings of popularity, and others' initial impressions of their personalities. We perceive attractive people to be healthier, happier, more sensitive, more successful, and more socially skilled, though not more honest or compassionate (Eagly & others, 1991; Feingold, 1992; Hatfield & Sprecher, 1986).

When Neanderthals fall in love.

Attractive, well-dressed people are more likely to make a favorable impression on potential employers and to enjoy occupational success (Cash & Janda, 1984; Langlois & others, 2000; Solomon, 1987). Income analyses show a penalty for plainness or obesity and a premium for beauty (Engemann & Owyang, 2005).

An analysis of 100 top-grossing films since 1940 found that attractive characters were portrayed as morally superior to unattractive characters (Smith & others, 1999). But Hollywood modeling doesn't explain why, to judge from their gazing times, even babies prefer attractive over unattractive faces (Langlois & others, 1987). So do some blind people, discovered University of Birmingham professor John Hull (1990, p. 23) after going blind. A colleague's remarking on a woman's beauty would strangely affect his feelings. He finds this "deplorable . . . but I still feel it. . . . What can it matter to me what sighted men think of women . . . yet I do care what sighted men think, and I do not seem able to throw off this prejudice."

The importance of looks seems unfair and unenlightened. Why should it matter? Two thousand years ago the Roman statesman Cicero felt the same way: "The final good and the supreme duty of the wise person is to resist appearance." Cicero might be reassured by two other findings about attractiveness.

First, people's attractiveness is surprisingly unrelated to their self-esteem and happiness (Diener & others, 1995; Major & others, 1984). One reason may be that, except after comparing themselves with superattractive people, few people (thanks, perhaps, to the mere exposure effect) view themselves as unattractive (Thornton & Moore, 1993). Another reason is that strikingly attractive people are sometimes suspicious that praise for their work may simply be a reaction to their looks. When less attractive people are praised, they are more likely to accept it as sincere (Berscheid, 1981).

> Love comes in at the eye."
> William Butler Yeats, "A Drinking Song," 1909

Percentage of Men and Women Who "Constantly Think About Their Looks"

	Men	Women
Canada	18%	20%
United States	17	27
Mexico	40	45
Venezuela	47	65

From Roper Starch survey, reported by McCool (1999).

Extreme makeover

In affluent, beauty-conscious cultures, increasing numbers of people, such as this woman from the American TV show *Extreme Makeover,* have turned to cosmetic surgery to improve their looks. If money were no concern, might you ever do the same?

In the eye of the beholder
Conceptions of attractiveness vary by culture. Moreover, the current concept of attractiveness in Kenya, Morocco, and Scandinavia may well change in the future.

New York Times columnist Maureen Dowd on liposuction (January 19, 2000): "Women in the 50's vacuumed. Women in the 00's *are* vacuumed. Our Hoovers have turned on us!"

Cicero might also find comfort in knowing that attractiveness judgments are relative. The standards by which judges crown Miss Universe hardly apply to the whole planet. Rather, beauty is in the eye of the culture—beauty standards reflect one's place and time. Hoping to look attractive, people in different cultures have pierced their noses, lengthened their necks, bound their feet, and dyed or painted their skin and hair. They have gorged themselves to achieve a full figure or liposuctioned fat to achieve a slim one, applied chemicals hoping to rid themselves of unwanted hair or to regrow wanted hair, strapped on leather garments to make their breasts seem smaller or surgically filled their breasts with silicone and put on Wonder Bras to make them look bigger. In North America, the ultra-thin ideal of the Roaring Twenties gave way to the soft, voluptuous Marilyn Monroe ideal of the 1950s, only to be replaced by today's lean yet busty ideal. Americans now spend more on beauty supplies than on education and social services combined and, when still not satisfied, undergo millions of cosmetic medical treatments each year, including plastic surgery, Botox skin smoothing, teeth-capping or whitening, and laser hair removal (Wall, 2002). But the beauty race is like the arms race, with the result that since 1970 more and more women have become *un*happy with their appearance (Feingold & Mazella, 1998).

Some aspects of attractiveness, however, do cross place and time (Cunningham & others, 1995; Langlois & others, 2000). Men in 37 cultures, from Australia to Zambia, judge women as more attractive if they have a youthful appearance. Women feel attracted to healthy-looking men, but especially to those who seem mature, dominant, and affluent.

People everywhere also seem to prefer physical features—noses, legs, physiques—that are neither unusually large nor small. An averaged face is attractive (**FIGURE 58.1**). In one clever demonstration of this, Judith Langlois and Lori Roggman (1990) digitized the faces of up to 32 college students and used a computer to average them. Students judged the averaged, composite faces as more attractive than 96 percent of the individual faces. One reason is that averaged faces are symmetrical, and people with symmetrical faces and bodies are more sexually attractive (Rhodes & others, 1999; Singh, 1995; Thornhill & Gangestad, 1994). Merge either half of your face with its mirror image and your symmetrical new face would boost your attractiveness a notch.

FIGURE 58.1
Average is attractive
Which of these faces offered by University of St. Andrews psychologist David Perrett (2002) is most attractive? Most people say it's the face on the right—of a nonexistent person that is the average composite of these three plus 57 other actual faces.

Cultural standards aside, attractiveness also depends on our feelings about the person. In a Rodgers and Hammerstein musical, Prince Charming asks Cinderella, "Do I love you because you're beautiful, or are you beautiful because I love you?" Chances are it's both. As we see our loved ones again and again, their physical imperfections grow less noticeable and their attractiveness grows more apparent (Beaman & Klentz, 1983; Gross & Crofton, 1977). Shakespeare said it in *A Midsummer Night's Dream:* "Love looks not with the eyes, but with the mind." Come to love someone and watch beauty grow.

AP Photo/ Herman Miller Inc.

Beauty grows with mere exposure
Herman Miller, Inc.'s famed Aeron chair initially received high comfort ratings but abysmal beauty ratings. To some it looked like "lawn furniture" or "a giant prehistoric insect" (Gladwell, 2005). But then, with design awards, media visibility, and imitators, the ugly duckling came to be the company's best-selling chair ever and to be seen as beautiful. With people, too, beauty lies partly in the beholder's eye and can grow with exposure.

Similarity

Let's say that proximity has brought you into contact with someone and that your appearance has made a favorable first impression. What now influences whether acquaintances develop into friends? For example, as you get to know someone better, is the chemistry better if you are opposites or if you are alike?

It makes a good story—extremely different types living in harmonious union: Rat, Mole, and Badger in *The Wind in the Willows,* Frog and Toad in Arnold Lobel's books. The stories delight us by expressing what we seldom experience, for we tend *not* to like dissimilar people (Rosenbaum, 1986). In real life, opposites retract. Birds that flock together usually *are* of a feather. Friends and couples are far more likely to share common attitudes, beliefs, and interests (and, for that matter, age, religion, race, education, intelligence, smoking behavior, and economic status) than are randomly paired people. Much as you and I may dismiss such differences, seeing ourselves as one human family in a global village, we can't hang out with 6 billion people. Moreover, the more alike people are, the more their liking endures (Byrne, 1971). Journalist Walter Lippmann was right to suppose that love is best sustained "when the lovers love many things together, and not merely each other." That is also the assumption of one psychologist-founded Internet dating site, which claims to use the similarities that mark happy couples to match singles, some 10,000 of whom are known to have married (Carter & Snow, 2004; Warren, 2005). Similarity breeds content.

Proximity, attractiveness, and similarity are not the only determinants of attraction. We also like those who like us, especially when our self-image is low. When we believe someone likes us, we respond to them more warmly, which leads them to like us even more (Curtis & Miller, 1986). To be liked is powerfully rewarding.

Indeed, a simple *reward theory of attraction*—that we will like those whose behavior is rewarding to us and that we will continue relationships that offer more rewards than costs—can explain all the findings we have considered so far. When a person lives or works in close proximity with someone else, it costs less time and effort to develop the friendship and enjoy its benefits. Attractive people are aesthetically pleasing, and associating with them can be socially rewarding. Those with similar views reward us by validating our own.

Romantic Love

OBJECTIVE 58-2 | Describe the effect of physical arousal on passionate love, and identify two predictors of enduring companionate love.

Occasionally, people move quickly from initial impressions, to friendship, to the more intense, complex, and mysterious state of romantic love. Elaine Hatfield (1988) distinguishes two types of love: temporary passionate love and a more enduring companionate love.

"I can't wait to see what you're like on line."

HI & LOIS

Passionate Love

Noting that arousal is a key ingredient of **passionate love,** Hatfield suggests that Stanley Schachter's two-factor theory of emotion can help us understand this intense positive absorption in another. The theory assumes that (1) emotions have two ingredients—physical arousal plus cognitive appraisal—and that (2) arousal from any source can enhance one emotion or another, depending on how we interpret and label the arousal.

In tests of this theory, college men have been aroused by fright, by running in place, by viewing erotic materials, or by listening to humorous or repulsive monologues. They were then introduced to an attractive woman and asked to rate her (or their girlfriend). Unlike unaroused men, those who were stirred up attributed some of their arousal to the woman or girlfriend and felt more attracted to her (Carducci & others, 1978; Dermer & Pyszczynski, 1978; White & Kight, 1984).

Outside the laboratory, Donald Dutton and Arthur Aron (1974, 1989) went to two bridges across British Columbia's rocky Capilano River. One, a swaying footbridge, was 230 feet above the rocks; the other was low and solid. An attractive young female accomplice intercepted men coming off each bridge, sought their help in filling out a short questionnaire, and then offered her phone number in case they wanted to hear more about her project. Far more of those who had just crossed the high bridge—which left their hearts pounding—accepted the number and later called the woman. To be revved up and to associate some of that arousal with a desirable person is to feel the pull of passion. Adrenaline makes the heart grow fonder.

Companionate Love

Although the spark of romantic love often endures, the intense absorption in the other, the thrill of the romance, the giddy "floating on a cloud" feeling typically fades. Does this mean the French are correct in saying that "love makes the time pass and time makes love pass"? Or can friendship and commitment keep a relationship going after the passion cools? In Leo Tolstoy's *Family Happiness,* a young woman walks with a man she loves and realizes "that from that day he was mine, and I should never lose him now." Later, after their marriage, she reflects while sitting at home that their romantic courtship has been replaced by something quieter and more secure. "That day ended the romance of our marriage," she explains. "The old feeling became a precious irrecoverable remembrance; but a new feeling of love for my children and the father of my children laid the foundation of a new life and a quite different happiness; and that life and happiness have lasted to the present time."

Hatfield agrees, noting that as love matures it becomes a steadier **companionate love**—a deep, affectionate attachment. There may be adaptive wisdom to this change from passion to affection. Passionate love often produces children, whose survival is aided by the parents' waning obsession with one another. Social psychologist Ellen Berscheid and her colleagues (1984) noted that the failure to appreciate passionate love's limited half-life can doom a relationship: "If the inevitable odds against eternal passionate love in a relationship were better understood, more people might choose to be satisfied with the quieter feelings of satisfaction and contentment." Indeed, recognizing the short duration of passionate love, some societies have deemed such feelings an irrational reason for marrying.

> "When two people are under the influence of the most violent, most insane, most delusive, and most transient of passions, they are required to swear that they will remain in that excited, abnormal, and exhausting condition continuously until death do them part."
>
> George Bernard Shaw, "Getting Married," 1908

Better, such cultures say, to choose (or have someone choose for you) a partner with a compatible background and interests. Non-Western cultures, where people rate love less important for marriage, do have lower divorce rates (Levine & others, 1995).

One key to a gratifying and enduring relationship is **equity:** Both partners receive in proportion to what they give. When equity exists—when both partners freely give and receive, when they share decision making—their chances for sustained and satisfying companionate love are good (Gray-Little & Burks, 1983; Van Yperen & Buunk, 1990). Mutually sharing self and possessions, giving and getting emotional support, promoting and caring about one another's welfare are at the core of every type of loving relationship (Sternberg & Grajek, 1984). It's true for lovers, for parent and child, and for intimate friends.

Another vital ingredient of loving relationships is **self-disclosure,** the revealing of intimate details about ourselves—our likes and dislikes, our dreams and worries, our proud and shameful moments. "When I am with my friend," noted the Roman statesman Seneca, "me thinks I am alone, and as much at liberty to speak anything as to think it." Self-disclosure breeds liking, and liking breeds self-disclosure (Collins & Miller, 1994). As one person reveals a little, the other reciprocates, the first then reveals more, and on and on, as friends or lovers move to deeper intimacy. Each increase in intimacy rekindles passion (Baumeister & Bratslavsky, 1999).

One experiment marched pairs of volunteer students through 45 minutes of increasingly self-disclosing conversation—from "When did you last sing to yourself" to "When did you last cry in front of another person? By yourself?" By the experiment's end, those experiencing the escalating intimacy felt remarkably close to their conversation partner, much closer than others who had spent the time with small-talk questions, such as "What was your high school like?" (Aron & others, 1997). Given self-disclosing intimacy plus mutually supportive equality, the odds favor enduring companionate love.

MATRIMONY

Courtship and Matrimony (from the collection of Werner Nekes)

COURTSHIP

Sometimes passionate love becomes enduring companionate love, sometimes not *(invert the picture)*
What, in addition to similar attitudes and interests, predicts long-term loving attachment?

"When a match has equal partners then I fear not."
Aeschylus, *Prometheus Bound*, 478 B.C.

Altruism

OBJECTIVE **58-3** | Define *altruism,* and give an example.

Carl Wilkens, a Seventh Day Adventist missionary, was living with his family in Kigali, Rwanda, when Hutu militia began to slaughter the Tutsi in 1994. The U.S. government, church leaders, and friends all implored Wilkens to leave. He refused. After evacuating his family, and even after every other American had left Kigali, he alone stayed and contested the 800,000-person genocide. When the militia came to kill him and his Tutsi servants, his Hutu neighbors deterred them. Despite repeated death threats, he spent his days risking roadblocks to take food and water to orphanages and to negotiate, plead, and bully his way through the bloodshed, saving lives time and again. "It just seemed the right thing to do," he later explained (Kristof, 2004). Elsewhere in Kigali, Paul Rusesabagina, a Hutu married to a Tutsi

■ **passionate love** an aroused state of intense positive absorption in another, usually present at the beginning of a love relationship.

■ **companionate love** the deep affectionate attachment we feel for those with whom our lives are intertwined.

■ **equity** a condition in which people receive from a relationship in proportion to what they give to it.

■ **self-disclosure** revealing intimate aspects of oneself to others.

and the acting manager of a luxury hotel, was sheltering more than 1200 terrified Tutsis and moderate Hutus. When international peacemakers abandoned the city and hostile militia threatened his guests in the "Hotel Rwanda" (as it became called in a 2004 movie), the courageous Rusesabagina began cashing in past favors, bribing the militia, and telephoning influential persons abroad to bring pressure on local authorities, thereby sparing the lives of the hotel's occupants from the surrounding chaos.

Such selfless goodness exemplifies **altruism**—the unselfish regard for the welfare of others. Altruism became a major concern of social psychologists after an especially vile act of sexual violence. On March 13, 1964, a stalker repeatedly stabbed Kitty Genovese, then raped her as she lay dying outside her Queens, New York, apartment at 3:30 A.M. "Oh, my God, he stabbed me!" Genovese screamed into the early morning stillness. "Please help me!" Windows opened and lights went on as 38 of her neighbors heard her screams. Her attacker fled and then returned to stab her eight more times and rape her again. Not until he had fled for good did anyone so much as call the police, at 3:50 A.M.

> Probably no single incident has caused social psychologists to pay as much attention to an aspect of social behavior as Kitty Genovese's murder."
>
> R. Lance Shotland (1984)

Bystander Intervention

OBJECTIVE **58-4** | Describe the steps in the decision-making process involved in bystander intervention.

Reflecting on the Genovese murder and other such tragedies, most commentators were outraged by the bystanders' "apathy" and "indifference." Rather than blaming the onlookers, social psychologists John Darley and Bibb Latané (1968b) attributed their inaction to an important situational factor—the presence of others. Given certain circumstances, they suspected, most of us might behave similarly.

After staging emergencies under various conditions, Darley and Latané assembled their findings into a decision scheme: We will help only if the situation enables us first to *notice* the incident, then to *interpret* it as an emergency, and finally to *assume responsibility* for helping (**FIGURE 58.2**). At each step, the presence of other bystanders turns people away from the path that leads to helping. In the laboratory and on the street, people in a group of strangers are more likely than solitary individuals to keep their eyes focused on what they themselves are doing or where they are going. If they notice an unusual situation, they may infer from the blasé reactions of the other passersby that the situation is not an emergency. "The person lying on the sidewalk must be drunk," they think, and move on.

But sometimes, as with the Genovese murder, the emergency is unambiguous and people still fail to help. The witnesses looking out through their windows noticed the incident, correctly interpreted the emergency, and yet failed to assume responsibility. Why? To find out, Darley and Latané (1968a) simulated a physical emergency in their laboratory. University students participated in a discussion over an intercom.

FIGURE 58.2

The decision-making process for bystander intervention

Before helping, one must first notice an emergency, then correctly interpret it, and then feel responsible. (From Darley & Latané, 1968b.)

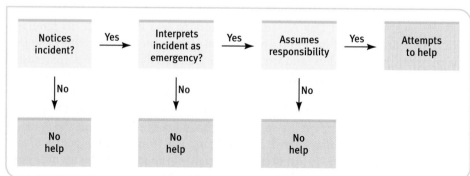

Akos Szilvasi/Stock, Boston

Each student was in a separate cubicle, and only the person whose microphone was switched on could be heard. One of the students was an accomplice of the experimenters. When his turn came, he made sounds as though he were having an epileptic seizure and called for help.

How did the other students react? As **FIGURE 58.3** shows, those who believed only they could hear the victim—and therefore thought they bore total responsibility for helping him—usually went to his aid. Those who thought others also could hear were more likely to react as did Kitty Genovese's neighbors. When more people shared responsibility for helping—when there was diffusion of responsibility—any single listener was less likely to help.

In hundreds of additional experiments, psychologists have studied the factors that influence bystanders' willingness to relay an emergency phone call, aid a stranded motorist, donate blood, pick up dropped books, contribute money, and give time. For example, Latané, James Dabbs (1975), and 145 collaborators took 1497 elevator rides in three cities and "accidentally" dropped coins or pencils in front of 4813 fellow passengers. The women coin droppers were more likely to receive help than were the men—a gender difference often reported by other researchers (Eagly & Crowley, 1986). But the major finding was the **bystander effect**—any particular bystander was less likely to give aid with other bystanders present. When alone with the person in need, 40 percent helped; in the presence of five other bystanders, only 20 percent helped.

From their observations of behavior in tens of thousands of such "emergencies," altruism researchers have discerned some additional patterns. The *best* odds of our helping someone occur when

- the victim appears to need and deserve help.
- the victim is in some way similar to us.
- we have just observed someone else being helpful.
- we are not in a hurry.
- we are in a small town or rural area.
- we are feeling guilty.
- we are focused on others and not preoccupied.
- we are in a good mood.

■ **altruism** unselfish regard for the welfare of others.

■ **bystander effect** the tendency for any given bystander to be less likely to give aid if other bystanders are present.

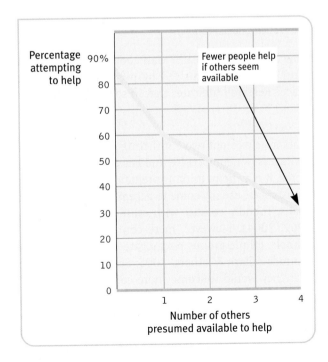

FIGURE 58.3
Responses to a simulated physical emergency
When people thought they alone heard the calls for help from a person they believed to be having an epileptic seizure, they usually helped. But when they thought four others were also hearing the calls, fewer than a third responded. (From Darley & Latané, 1968a.)

This last result, that happy people are helpful people, is one of the most consistent findings in all of psychology. No matter how people are cheered—whether by being made to feel successful and intelligent, by thinking happy thoughts, by finding money, or even by receiving a posthypnotic suggestion—they become more generous and more eager to help (Carlson & others, 1988).

The Norms for Helping

OBJECTIVE **58-5** | Explain altruistic behavior from the perspective of social exchange theory and social norms.

Why do we help? One widely held view is that self-interest underlies all human interactions, that our constant goal is to maximize rewards and minimize costs. Accountants call it cost-benefit analysis. Philosophers call it utilitarianism. Social psychologists call it **social exchange theory.** If you are pondering whether to donate blood, you may weigh the costs of doing so (time, discomfort, and anxiety) against the benefits (reduced guilt, social approval, good feelings). If you anticipate rewards from helping that exceed the costs, you help.

But why do we leave tips for people we will never see again and give directions to strangers? In part because we have been socialized to do so, through norms that prescribe how we *ought* to behave, often to our mutual benefit. Through socialization, we learn the **reciprocity norm,** the expectation that we should return help, not harm, to those who have helped us. In our relations with others of similar status, the reciprocity norm compels us to give (in favors, gifts, or social invitations) about as much as we receive. We also learn a **social-responsibility norm:** that we should help those who need our help—young children and others who cannot give as much as they receive—even if the costs outweigh the benefits. In repeated Gallup surveys, people who each week attend religious services often exhibit the social-responsibility norm: They report volunteering more than twice as many hours in helping the poor and infirm than do those who rarely or never attend religious services (Hodgkinson & Weitzman, 1992; Independent Sector, 2002). They also give away three times as much money.

Peacemaking

OBJECTIVE **58-6** | Discuss effective ways of encouraging peaceful cooperation and reducing social conflict.

How can we make peace? Can cooperation, communication, and conciliation transform the antagonisms fed by prejudice and conflicts into attitudes that promote peace? Research indicates that in some cases, they can.

Cooperation

Does it help to put two conflicting parties into close contact? It depends. When such contact is noncompetitive and between parties with equal status, such as fellow store clerks, it may help. Initially prejudiced co-workers of different races have, in such circumstances, usually come to accept one another. Among North Americans and Europeans, friendly contact with ethnic minorities has led to less prejudice (Pettigrew, 1969, 2004). However, mere contact is not always enough. In most desegregated schools, ethnic groups resegregate themselves in the lunchrooms and on the school grounds (Clark & others, 2005; Schofield, 1986). People in each group often think that they would welcome more contact with the other group, but they assume the other group does not reciprocate the wish (Shelton & Richeson, 2005). "I don't reach out to them, because I don't want to be rebuffed; they don't reach out to me, because they're just not interested." When such mirror-image misperceptions are corrected, friendships may then form and prejudices melt.

To see if enemies could overcome their differences, researcher Muzafer Sherif (1966) first instigated conflict. He placed 22 Oklahoma City boys in two separate areas of a Boy Scout camp. He then put the two groups through a series of competitive activities, with prizes going to the victors. Before long, each group became intensely proud of itself and hostile to the other group's "sneaky," "smart-alecky stinkers." Food wars broke out during meals. Cabins were ransacked. Fistfights had to be broken up by members of the camp staff. When Sherif brought the two groups together, they avoided one another, except to taunt and threaten.

Nevertheless, within a few days Sherif transformed these young enemies into jovial comrades. He gave them **superordinate goals**—shared goals that overrode their differences and that could be achieved only through cooperation. A planned disruption of the camp water supply necessitated that all 22 boys work together to restore water. Renting a movie in those pre-VCR days required their pooled resources. A stalled truck needed the combined force of all the boys pulling and pushing together to get it moving. Having used isolation and competition to make strangers into enemies, Sherif used shared predicaments and goals to reconcile the enemies and make them friends. What reduced conflict was not mere contact, but *cooperative* contact.

A shared predicament—a fearsome external threat and a superordinate desire to overcome it—likewise had a powerfully unifying effect in the weeks after 9/11. Nothing breeds solidarity quite like a common enemy. As suicide attacks in Israel can unify partisan Jews, and as Israeli military attacks on Palestinians can unify diverse Muslims, so Americans immediately felt that "we" were under attack. Gallup-surveyed approval of "our President" shot up from 51 percent the week before the attack to a highest-ever level of 90 percent 10 days after, just surpassing the previous approval-rating record of 89 percent enjoyed by his father, George Bush, at the climax of the 1991 Persian Gulf War (Newport, 2002). In chat groups and everyday speech, even the word *we* (relative to *I*) surged in the immediate aftermath (Pennebaker, 2002).

John Dovidio and Samuel Gaertner (1999) report that cooperation has especially positive effects when it leads people to define a new, inclusive group that dissolves their former subgroups. Seat the members of two groups not on opposite sides, but alternately around the table. Give them a new, shared name. Have them work together. Such experiences change "us and them" into "we." Those once perceived as being in another group now are seen as part of one's own group. One 18-year-old New Jersey man would not be surprised. After 9/11, he explained a shift in his social identity: "I just thought of myself as black. But now I feel like I'm an American, more than ever" (Sengupta, 2001). In one experiment by Dovidio and his colleagues (2004), white Americans who read a newspaper article about a terrorist threat against all Americans subsequently expressed reduced prejudice against African-Americans.

During the 1970s, several teams of educational researchers simultaneously wondered: If cooperative contacts between members of rival groups encourage positive attitudes, could we apply this principle in multicultural schools? Could we promote interracial friendships by replacing competitive classroom situations with cooperative ones? And could cooperative learning maintain or even enhance student achievement? Many experiments confirm that in all three cases, the answer is yes (Johnson & Johnson, 1989, 1994; Slavin & others, 2003). Members of interracial groups who work together on projects and play together on athletic teams typically come to feel friendly toward those of the other race. So do those who engage in cooperative classroom learning. So encouraging are these results that thousands of teachers have introduced interracial cooperative learning into their classrooms. Working with fellow students in all their diversity sets the stage, declared the Carnegie Council on Adolescent Development (1989), for "adult work life and for citizenship in a multicultural society."

social exchange theory the theory that our social behavior is an exchange process, the aim of which is to maximize benefits and minimize costs.

reciprocity norm an expectation that people will help, not hurt, those who have helped them.

social-responsibility norm an expectation that people will help those dependent upon them.

superordinate goals shared goals that override differences among people and require their cooperation.

"Most of us have overlapping identities which unite us with very different groups. We *can* love what we are, without hating what—and who—we are *not*. We can thrive in our own tradition, even as we learn from others."
U.N. Secretary General Kofi Annan, Nobel Prize Lecture, 2001

Superordinate goals override differences
Cooperative efforts to achieve shared goals are an effective way to break down social barriers.

Syracuse Newspapers/ The Image Works

> "I am prepared this day to declare myself a citizen of the world, and to invite everyone everywhere to embrace this broader vision of our interdependent world, our common quest for justice, and ultimately for Peace on Earth."
>
> Father Theodore Hesburgh, *The Human Imperative,* 1974

The power of cooperative activity to make friends of former enemies has led psychologists to urge increased international exchange and cooperation (Klineberg, 1984). As we engage in mutually beneficial trade, as we work to protect our common destiny on this fragile planet, and as we become more aware that our hopes and fears are shared, we can change misperceptions that lead to fragmentation and conflict into a solidarity based on common interests.

Working toward shared goals enables diverse peoples to discover unity in their common values and superordinate identity. "Common values," are what we need, declared the chair of Britain's Commission for Racial Equality as ethnic tensions recently flared (Phillips, 2004). And today's Rwandan government policy proclaims, "There is no ethnicity here. We are all Rwandan," as it seeks to resolve historic animosities between Tutsis and Hutus (Lacey, 2004). Western democracies have largely been spared ethnic tribal warfare because their different racial groups share so many of the very same goals, notes sociologist Amitai Etzioni (1999). In the United States, these shared goals include fair treatment for all, higher moral standards, and a wish that all high school graduates "understand the common history and ideas that tie all Americans together." Although diversity commands attention, we are—as working toward shared goals reminds us—more alike than different.

Communication

In experiments featuring a game known as the *social-trap*, distrusting people pursue their individual interests as a defense against exploitation. But when they are allowed to discuss the dilemma and negotiate, cooperation increases (Jorgenson & Papciak, 1981).

When real-life conflicts become intense, a third-party mediator—a marriage counselor, labor mediator, diplomat, community volunteer—may likewise facilitate much-needed communication (Rubin & others, 1994). Mediators help each party to voice its viewpoint and to understand the other's. By leading each side to think about the other's underlying needs and goals, the mediator aims to replace a competitive *win-lose* orientation with a cooperative *win-win* orientation that aims at a mutually beneficial resolution. A classic example: Two friends, after quarreling over an orange, agreed to split it. One squeezed his half for juice. The other used the peel from her half to make a cake. If only the two had understood each other's motives, they could have hit on the win-win solution of one having all the juice, the other all the peel.

Such understanding and cooperative resolution is most needed, yet least likely, in times of anger or crisis (Bodenhausen & others, 1994; Tetlock, 1988). When conflicts intensify, images become more stereotyped, communication more difficult, and judgments more rigid.

Conciliation

When tension and suspicion peak, cooperation and communication may become impossible. Each party is likely to threaten, coerce, or retaliate. In the weeks before the Persian Gulf War, President George Bush threatened, in the full glare of publicity, to "kick Saddam's ass." Saddam Hussein communicated in kind, threatening to make Americans "swim in their own blood."

Under such conditions, is there an alternative to war or surrender? Social psychologist Charles Osgood (1962, 1980) has advocated a strategy of "Graduated and Reciprocated Initiatives in Tension-Reduction," nicknamed **GRIT.** In applying GRIT, one side first announces its recognition of mutual interests and its intent to reduce tensions. It then initiates one or more small, conciliatory acts. Without weakening one's retaliatory capability, this modest beginning opens the door for reciprocation by the other party. Should the enemy respond with hostility, one reciprocates in kind. But so, too, with any conciliatory response. Thus, President Kennedy's gesture of stopping atmospheric nuclear tests began a series of reciprocated conciliatory acts that culminated in the 1993 atmospheric test-ban treaty.

In laboratory experiments, GRIT has been the most effective strategy known for increasing trust and cooperation (Lindskold & others, 1978, 1988). Even during intense personal conflict, when communication has been nonexistent, a small conciliatory gesture—a smile, a touch, a word of apology—may work wonders. Conciliations allow both parties to begin edging down the tension ladder to a safer rung where communication and mutual understanding can begin.

And how good that such can happen, for civilization advances not by cultural isolation—maintaining walls around ethnic enclaves—but by tapping the knowledge, the skills, and the arts that are each culture's legacy to the whole human race. Thomas Sowell (1991) observed that, thanks to cultural sharing, every modern society is enriched by a cultural mix. We have China to thank for paper and printing, and for the magnetic compass that opened the great explorations. We have Egypt to thank for trigonometry. We have the Islamic world and India's Hindus to thank for our Arabic numerals. While celebrating and claiming these diverse cultural legacies, we can also welcome the enrichment of today's social diversity. We can view ourselves as instruments in a human orchestra. And we can therefore affirm our own culture's heritage while building bridges of communication, understanding, and cooperation across cultural traditions as we think about, influence, and relate to one another.

"To begin with, I would like to express my sincere thanks and deep appreciation for the opportunity to meet with you. While there are still profound differences between us, I think the very fact of my presence here today is a major breakthrough."

GRIT Graduated and Reciprocated Initiatives in Tension-Reduction—a strategy designed to decrease international tensions.

>> LEARNING OUTCOMES

Prosocial Relations

OBJECTIVE 58-1 | **Describe the influence of proximity, physical attractiveness, and similarity on interpersonal attraction.**

Proximity—geographical nearness—promotes attraction, in part because it increases the opportunities for interaction and in part because of the mere exposure effect (repeated exposure to novel stimuli enhances liking). People prefer being with *physically attractive* people and perceive them as healthier, happier, more sensitive, more successful, and more socially skilled. Judgments of attractiveness vary by culture, and as time goes by we find those we care about to be more attractive. *Similarity of attitudes and interests* greatly increases liking after people make it past the first impression.

OBJECTIVE 58-2 | **Describe the effect of physical arousal on passionate love, and identify two predictors of enduring companionate love.**

Associating arousal with a desirable person is a key ingredient of *passionate love,* the intense absorption we cognitively label as love. Passionate love often matures into the deep affectionate attachment of *companionate love.* This transition is most likely in relationships characterized by *equality* and *intimate self-disclosure.*

OBJECTIVE 58-3 | **Define *altruism,* and give an example.**

Altruism is the unselfish regard for the welfare of others. Examples of altruism include helping victims of a natural disaster or giving blood with no expectation of personal reward.

OBJECTIVE 58-4 | **Describe the steps in the decision-making process involved in bystander intervention.**

The *bystander effect* is the tendency, identified by John Darley and Bibb Latané, for any given observer to be less likely to help if others are present. To offer help, a person must notice the incident, interpret it as an emergency, and assume responsibility for offering help. Diffusion of responsibility lowers the likelihood of helping. Odds of helping are highest when the victim is similar to us and appears to need and deserve help, and when we observe others helping, are feeling guilty, are not in a hurry or preoccupied, are in a small town or rural area, and are in a good mood.

OBJECTIVE 58-5 | **Explain altruistic behavior from the perspective of social exchange theory and social norms.**

Social exchange theory proposes that our social behaviors—even altruistic, helpful acts—are based on self-interest: maximizing our benefits (which may include our own good feelings) and minimizing our costs. *Social norms* influence altruistic behaviors by telling us how we *should* behave. The *reciprocity norm* is the expectation that we will help those who help us, and the *social-responsibility norm* is the expectation that we will help those who are dependent on us.

OBJECTIVE 58-6 | **Discuss effective ways of encouraging peaceful cooperation and reducing social conflict.**

Friendly contact between prejudiced people can change attitudes. But social conflict is most likely to be reduced when the circumstances favor cooperation to achieve superordinate goals (especially if subgroups disappear), understanding through communication (sometimes with the help of a third party), and reciprocated conciliatory gestures (such as the *GRIT* strategy).

TERMS AND CONCEPTS TO REMEMBER

mere exposure effect, p. 58-1
passionate love, p. 58-6
companionate love, p. 58-6
equity, p. 58-7
self-disclosure, p. 58-7
altruism, p. 58-8
bystander effect, p. 58-9

social exchange theory, p. 58-10
reciprocity norm, p. 58-10
social-responsibility norm, p. 58-10
superordinate goals, p. 58-11
GRIT, p. 58-13

TEST YOURSELF

1. Why didn't anybody help Kitty Genovese? What social relations principle did this incident illustrate?

(Answer in Appendix B.)

ASK YOURSELF

1. Do you regret not getting along with some friend or family members? How might you go about reconciling that relationship?

>WEB

Multiple-choice *self-tests* and more may be found at www.worthpublishers.com/myers.

Careers in Psychology

Jennifer Lento
University of San Diego

What can you do with a degree in psychology? Lots!

As a psychology major, you will graduate with a scientific mindset and an awareness of basic principles of human behavior (biological mechanisms, development, cognition, psychological disorders, social interaction). This background will prepare you for success in many areas, including business, helping professions, health services, marketing, law, sales, and teaching. You may even go on to graduate school for specialized training to become a psychology professional. This appendix describes the various levels of psychology education and some jobs available at those levels; psychology's specialized subfields; and ways you can improve your chances of admission to graduate school.[1]

Preparing for a Career in Psychology

Psychology is the second most popular major in the United States, second only to business (*Princeton Review,* 2005). More than 70,000 psychology majors graduate from U.S. colleges and universities each year. An undergraduate degree in psychology can prepare you for a broad array of jobs after graduation. For other jobs, you will need a graduate degree.

The Bachelor's Degree

Psychology majors graduate with a valuable skill set that increases their marketability in many fields. About 42 percent of U.S. psychology majors go on to graduate school in psychology (Fogg, Harrington, & Harrington, 2004). What happens to the rest? Most work in for-profit organizations after graduation, especially in management, sales, and administration. **TABLE A.1** on the next page shows the top 10 occupations that employ people with a bachelor's degree in psychology.

Clearly, psychology majors are marketable beyond the boundaries of psychology. Their sought-after skills and abilities include an ability to work and get along with others, a desire and willingness to learn new skills, adaptability to changing situations, and good critical-thinking and problem-solving skills (Landrum, 2001). There are some things that all psychology majors can do to maximize success in the job market. Employers that hire people with only a bachelor's degree tend to favor individuals with positive explanatory styles and practical experience as well as a good education (Cannon, 2005). Betsy Morgan and Ann Korschgen (1998) offer the following helpful tips for increasing your chances of getting a job after graduation:

1. Get to know your instructors.
2. Take courses that support your interests.

---

[1]Although this text covers the world of psychology for students in many countries, this appendix draws primarily from available U.S. data. Its description of psychology's subfields and its suggestions for preparing to enter the profession are, however, also applicable in many other countries.

TABLE **A.1**

TOP 10 U.S. OCCUPATIONS THAT EMPLOY PEOPLE WITH A BACHELOR'S DEGREE IN PSYCHOLOGY

1. Top- and mid-level managers, executives, administrators
2. Sales occupations, including retail
3. Social workers
4. Other management-related occupations
5. Personnel, training, labor relations specialists
6. Other administrative (record clerks, telephone operators)
7. Insurance, securities, real estate, business services
8. Other marketing and sales occupations
9. Registered nurses, pharmacists, therapists, physician assistants
10. Accountants, auditors, other financial specialists

Source: Fogg, Harrington, & Harrington (2004).

3. Familiarize yourself with available resources, such as campus career services and alumni.
4. Participate in at least one internship experience.
5. Volunteer some of your time and talent to campus or community organizations, such as Psi Chi or Psi Beta (psychology's national honor societies) or your school's psychology club.

Postgraduate Degrees

A graduate degree in psychology will give you proficiency in an area of psychological specialization. According to the U.S. Bureau of Labor Statistics (2004), psychologists with advanced degrees held approximately 139,000 jobs in 2000. Such jobs are expected to increase 21 to 35 percent (depending on the subfield of psychology) through 2012 because of the need for psychological services in a variety of settings. The work settings for psychologists vary somewhat by type of graduate degree. As shown in **FIGURE A.1,** psychologists with a doctorate work primarily in universities and colleges; most people with a master's degree work in other educational institutions (such as elementary and middle schools) and in for-profit companies. Among those seeking advanced training in psychology in the United States, 29 percent earn a master's degree, 7 percent earn a doctoral degree, and 6 percent earn some other professional degree (e.g., law or health professions) (Fogg, Harrington, & Harrington, 2004).

The Master's Degree

A master's degree in psychology requires at least two years of full-time graduate study in a specific subfield of psychology. In addition to specialized course work in psychology, requirements usually include practical experience in an applied setting and/or a master's thesis reporting on an original research project. You might acquire a master's degree to do specialized work in psychology. As a graduate with a master's degree, you might handle research and data collection and analysis in a university, government, or private industry setting. You might work under the supervision of a psychologist with a doctorate, providing some clinical service such as therapy or testing. Or you might find a job in the health, government, industry,

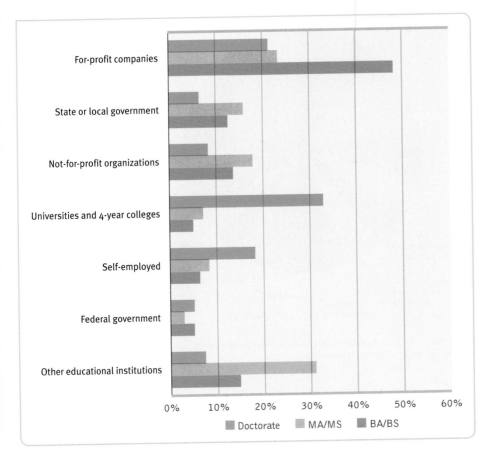

FIGURE A.1
Work settings for psychology-degree recipients
(Fogg, Harrington, & Harrington, 2004)

or education fields. You might also acquire a master's degree as a stepping stone for more advanced study in a doctoral program in psychology, which will considerably expand the number of employment opportunities available to you (Super & Super, 2001).

Doctoral Degrees

You will probably need five to seven years of graduate study in a specific subfield of psychology to get your doctoral degree. The *doctor of philosophy (Ph.D.)* in psychology culminates in a *dissertation* (an extensive research paper you will be required to defend orally) based on original research. Courses in quantitative research methods, which include the use of computer-based analysis, are an important part of graduate study and are necessary to complete the dissertation. The *doctor of psychology (Psy.D.)* may be based on clinical (therapeutic) work and examinations rather than a dissertation. If you pursue clinical and counseling psychology programs, you should expect at least a one-year internship in addition to the regular course work, clinical practice, and research.

FIGURE A.2 (on the next page) lists by subfield the Ph.D.s earned in the United States in a recent year. Clinical psychology is the most popular specialty area among holders of doctorates in psychology. The largest employment growth areas for doctoral graduates have been in the for-profit and self-employment sectors, including health services providers, industrial/organizational psychology, and educational psychology. About one-third of doctoral-level psychologists are employed in academic settings (Fogg, Harrington, & Harrington, 2004).

In 2001, a total of 73 percent of new doctoral respondents and 55 percent of new master's respondents indicated that their primary occupational position was their

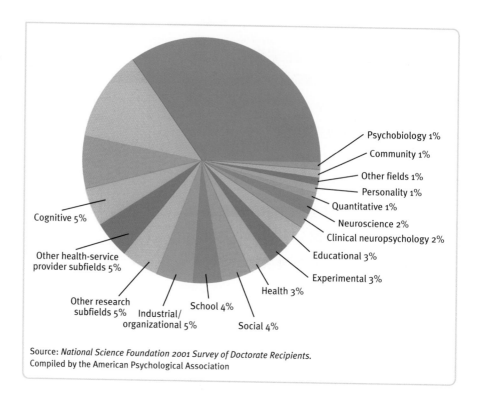

Psychobiology 1%
Community 1%
Other fields 1%
Personality 1%
Quantitative 1%
Neuroscience 2%
Clinical neuropsychology 2%
Educational 3%
Experimental 3%
Health 3%
Social 4%
School 4%
Industrial/ organizational 5%
Other research subfields 5%
Other health-service provider subfields 5%
Cognitive 5%

Source: *National Science Foundation 2001 Survey of Doctorate Recipients.*
Compiled by the American Psychological Association

Prescription privileges

Many psychologists would like the opportunity to prescribe therapeutic drugs in order to expand the scope of clinical practice and to meet the need for psychiatric services in many parts of the United States.
Psychologists in the U.S. military and in the states of New Mexico and Louisiana currently have prescription privileges.

first choice. Most new graduates with a master's degree or a Ph.D. are fairly satisfied with their current positions overall in terms of salary, benefits, opportunities for personal development, supervisors, colleagues, and working conditions (Kohout & Wicherski, 2004; Singleton, Tate, & Kohout, 2003).

Subfields of Psychology

If you are like most psychology students, you may be unaware of the wide variety of specialties and work settings available in psychology (Terre & Stoddart, 2000). To date, the American Psychological Association (APA) has 53 divisions (**TABLE A.2**). The following paragraphs (arranged alphabetically) describe some careers in the main specialty areas of psychology, most of which require a graduate degree in psychology.

Clinical psychologists promote psychological health in individuals, groups, and organizations. Some clinical psychologists specialize in specific psychological disorders. Others treat a range of disorders, from adjustment difficulties to severe psychopathology. Clinical psychologists might engage in research, teaching, assessment, and consultation. Some hold workshops and lectures on psychological issues for other professionals or for the public. Clinical psychologists work in a variety of settings, including private practice, mental health service organizations, schools, universities, industries, legal systems, medical systems, counseling centers, government agencies, and military services.

To become a clinical psychologist, you will need to earn a doctorate from a clinical psychology program. The APA sets the standards for clinical psychology graduate programs, offering *accreditation* (official recognition) to those who meet their standards. Unlike practitioners in most other subfields of psychology, clinical psychologists must, in all U.S. states, obtain a license to offer services such as therapy and testing.

Cognitive psychologists primarily do research to add to psychology's store of knowledge. Cognitive psychologists study thought processes and focus on such topics as

TABLE A.2

APA DIVISIONS BY NUMBER AND NAME

1. Society for General Psychology
2. Society for the Teaching of Psychology
3. Experimental Psychology
4. *There is no Division 4.*
5. Evaluation, Measurement, and Statistics
6. Behavioral Neuroscience and Comparative Psychology
7. Developmental Psychology
8. Society for Personality and Social Psychology
9. Society for the Psychological Study of Social Issues (SPSSI)
10. Society for the Psychology of Aesthetics, Creativity, and the Arts
11. *There is no Division 11.*
12. Society of Clinical Psychology
13. Society of Consulting Psychology
14. Society for Industrial and Organizational Psychology
15. Educational Psychology
16. School Psychology
17. Society of Counseling Psychology
18. Psychologists in Public Service
19. Society for Military Psychology
20. Adult Development and Aging
21. Applied Experimental and Engineering Psychology
22. Rehabilitation Psychology
23. Society for Consumer Psychology
24. Society for Theoretical and Philosophical Psychology
25. Behavior Analysis
26. Society for the History of Psychology
27. Society for Community Research and Action: Division of Community Psychology
28. Psychopharmacology and Substance Abuse

29. Psychotherapy
30. Society of Psychological Hypnosis
31. State, Provincial, and Territorial Psychological Association Affairs
32. Humanistic Psychology
33. Mental Retardation and Developmental Disabilities
34. Population and Environmental Psychology
35. Society for the Psychology of Women
36. Psychology of Religion
37. Child, Youth, and Family Services
38. Health Psychology
39. Psychoanalysis
40. Clinical Neuropsychology
41. American Psychology-Law Society
42. Psychologists in Independent Practice
43. Family Psychology
44. Society for the Psychological Study of Lesbian, Gay, and Bisexual Issues
45. Society for the Psychological Study of Ethnic Minority Issues
46. Media Psychology
47. Exercise and Sport Psychology
48. Society for the Study of Peace, Conflict, and Violence: Peace Psychology Division
49. Group Psychology and Group Psychotherapy
50. Addictions
51. Society for the Psychological Study of Men and Masculinity
52. International Psychology
53. Society of Clinical Child and Adolescent Psychology
54. Society of Pediatric Psychology
55. American Society for the Advancement of Pharmacotherapy

Source: American Psychological Association

Cognitive consulting
Cognitive psychologists may advise businesses on how to operate more effectively by understanding the human factors involved.

perception, language, attention, problem solving, memory, judgment and decision making, forgetting, and intelligence. Recent areas of research interest include designing computer-based models of thought processes and identifying biological correlates of cognition. As a cognitive psychologist, you might work as a professor, industrial consultant, or human factors specialist in an educational or business setting.

Community psychologists move beyond focusing on specific individuals or families and deal with broad problems of mental health in community settings. These psychologists believe that human behavior is powerfully influenced by the interaction between people and their physical, social, political, and economic environments. They seek to improve individual functioning by enhancing environmental settings that promote psychological health. Community psychologists focus on prevention, promotion of positive mental health, and crisis intervention, with special attention to the problems of underserved groups and ethnic minorities. As a community psychologist, your work settings could include federal, state, and local departments of mental health, corrections, and welfare. You might conduct research or help evaluate research in health service settings, serve as an independent consultant for a private or government agency, or teach and consult as a college or university faculty member.

Counseling psychologists help people adjust to life transitions or make life-style changes. This field is very similar to clinical psychology, except that counseling psychologists typically help people with adjustment problems rather than severe psychopathology. Like clinical psychologists, counseling psychologists conduct therapy and provide assessments to individuals and groups. As a counseling psychologist, you would emphasize your clients' strengths, helping clients cope during a transitional time using their own skills, interests, and abilities. You might find yourself working in an academic setting as a faculty member or administrator or in a university counseling center, community mental health center, business, or private practice. As with clinical psychology, you will need to obtain a state license to provide counseling services to the public.

Developmental psychologists conduct research in age-related behavioral changes and apply their scientific knowledge to educational, child care, policy, and related settings. As a developmental psychologist, you would investigate change across a broad range of topics, including the biological, social, psychological, and cognitive aspects of development. Developmental psychology informs a number of applied fields, including educational psychology, school psychology, child psychopathology, and gerontology. You will probably specialize in behavior during infancy, childhood, adolescence, or middle or late adulthood. Your work setting could be an educational institution, day-care center, youth group program, or senior center.

Educational psychologists study the relationship between learning and our physical and social environments. They study the psychological processes involved in learning and develop strategies for enhancing the learning process. As an educational psychologist, you might work in a university—in a psychology department or a school of education. You might conduct basic research on topics related to learning or develop innovative methods of teaching to enhance the learning process. You might be employed by a school or government agency or charged with designing and implementing effective employee-training programs in a business setting.

Experimental or *research psychologists* are a diverse group of scientists who investigate a variety of basic behavioral processes in research involving humans and/or other animals. Prominent areas of study in experimental research include motivation, thought, attention, learning, memory, perception, and language. As an experimental psychologist, you would most likely work in an academic setting, teaching courses and supervising students' research in addition to conducting your own research. Or you might be employed by a research institution, business, industry affiliate, or government agency.

Health psychologists are researchers and practitioners concerned with psychology's contribution to promoting health and preventing disease. As applied psychologists or clinicians, they may help individuals lead healthier lives by designing, conducting, and evaluating programs to stop smoking, lose weight, improve sleep, or prevent the spread of sexually transmitted diseases. As researchers and clinicians, they identify conditions and practices associated with health and illness to help create effective interventions. In public service, health psychologists study and work to improve government policies and health-care systems. As a health psychologist, you could be employed in a hospital, medical school, rehabilitation center, public health agency, college or university, or, if you are also a clinical psychologist, in private practice.

Forensic psychologists apply psychological principles to legal issues. They conduct research on the interface of law and psychology, help to create public policies related to mental health, and help law-enforcement agencies in criminal investigations. They also provide therapy and assessment to assist the legal community. Some forensic psychologists hold law degrees and provide clients with legal services as well. Although most forensic psychologists are clinical psychologists, they might have expertise in other areas of psychology, such as social or cognitive psychology. As a forensic psychologist, you might work in a university psychology department, law school, research organization, community mental health agency, law-enforcement agency, court, or correctional setting.

Industrial/organizational (I/O) psychologists study the relationship between people and their working environments. They may develop new ways to increase productivity, improve personnel selection, or promote job satisfaction in a business setting. Their interests include organizational structure and change, consumer behavior, and personnel selection and training. As an I/O psychologist, you might conduct workplace training or provide organizational analysis and development. You may find yourself working in business, industry, the government, or a college or university. Or you may be self-employed as a consultant or work for a management counseling firm.

Neuropsychologists investigate the relationship between neurological processes (structure and function of the brain) and behavior. As a neuropsychologist you might assess, diagnose, or treat disorders related to the central nervous system, such as Alzheimer's disease or stroke. If you are a *clinical neuropsychologist,* you might work in the neurology, neurosurgery, or psychiatric unit of a hospital. Neuropsychologists also work in academic settings, where they conduct research and teach.

Psychometric and *quantitative psychologists* study the methods and techniques used to acquire psychological knowledge. A psychometrician may update existing neurocognitive or personality tests or devise new tests for use in clinical and school settings or in business and industry. These psychologists also administer, score, and interpret such tests. Quantitative psychologists collaborate with researchers to design, analyze, and interpret the results of research programs. As a psychometric or quantitative psychologist, you will need to be well trained in research methods, statistics, and computer technology. You will most likely be employed by a university or college, testing company, private research firm, or government agency.

Rehabilitation psychologists are researchers and practitioners who work with people who have lost optimal functioning after an accident, illness, or other event. As a rehabilitation psychologist, you would probably work in a medical rehabilitation institution or hospital. You might also work in a medical school, university, state or federal vocational rehabilitation agency, or in private practice serving people with physical disabilities.

School psychologists are involved in the assessment of and intervention for children in educational settings. They diagnose and treat cognitive, social, and emotional

AP Photo/Jennifer Graylock

Criminal profiling
On the popular TV show *Law and Order, Special Victims Unit,* Dr. George Huang (played by B.D. Wong) is an FBI agent and psychiatrist who uses his background in forensic psychology to conduct criminal investigations.

problems that may negatively influence children's learning or overall functioning at school. As a school psychologist, you would collaborate with teachers, parents, and administrators, making recommendations to improve student learning. You would work in an academic setting, a mental health clinic, a federal or state government agency, a child guidance center, or a behavioral research laboratory.

Social psychologists are interested in our interactions with others. Social psychologists study how our beliefs, feelings, and behaviors are affected by and influence other people. They study topics such as attitudes, aggression, prejudice, interpersonal attraction, group behavior, and leadership. As a social psychologist, you might work in organizational consultation, marketing research, or other applied psychology fields. You would probably also be a college or university faculty member. Some social psychologists work for hospitals, federal agencies, or businesses performing applied research.

Sports psychologists are interested in how participation in sports and other physical activities can enhance personal development and well-being throughout the life span. As a sports psychologist, you would study the psychological factors that influence, and are influenced by, participation in sports and other physical activities, and you would apply this knowledge to everyday settings. You would most likely work as part of a team or organization, but you might also work in a private capacity.

Preparing Early for Graduate Study in Psychology

Competition for the openings for advanced degrees in psychology is keen. If you choose to go to graduate school, there a number of things you can do now to maximize your chances of gaining admission to the school of your choice.

If possible, begin preparing during your first year on campus to maximize opportunities and obtain the experience needed to gain admission to a competitive program. Kristy Arnold and Kelly Horrigan (2002) offer a number of suggestions to facilitate this process:

1. *Network.* Get to know faculty members and the psychology department by attending activities and meetings. Become involved in psychology clubs and in Psi Chi or Psi Beta, the national honor societies in psychology. These meetings connect students with similar interests and expose them to a broader study of the field.

2. *Become actively involved in research as early as possible.* Start by doing simple tasks such as data entry and data collection, and over time you will be prepared to conduct your own research project under the supervision of a research mentor.

3. *Volunteer or get a job in a psychology-related field.* Getting involved will show your willingness to apply psychological concepts to real-world settings. Further, it will showcase your ability to juggle a number of tasks successfully, such as work and school—an important skill for graduate school success.

4. *Maintain good grades.* Demonstrate the ability to do well in graduate school by demonstrating successful completion of challenging courses, especially those related to your interests in graduate school.

In your junior year, you should begin studying for the Graduate Record Exam (GRE), the standardized test that applicants to graduate school must complete. If you start preparing early, you will be ready for success in your graduate school application and study.

Membership benefits

Members of the Psi Chi Honor Society, such as those meeting here, enjoy educational and professional benefits. So do members of Psi Beta, the psychology honor society at two-year colleges. Members may attend special sessions at psychological conventions, apply for research grants and awards, and read about new findings and new opportunities in their society's newsletter.

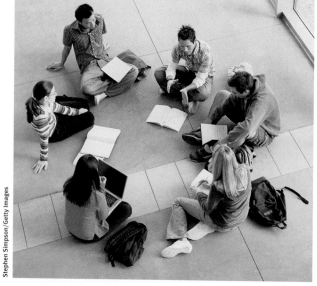

Stephen Simpson/Getty Images

So, the next time someone asks you what you will do with your psychology degree, tell them you have a lot of options. You might use your acquired skills and understanding to get a job and succeed in any number of fields, or you might pursue graduate school and then career opportunities in psychology or other associated professions. In any case, what you have learned about behavior and mental processes will surely enrich your life (Hammer, 2003).

For More Information

American Psychological Association (2003). *Careers for the twenty-first century*. Washington, DC.

American Psychological Association (2005). *Graduate study in psychology*. Washington, DC.

Appleby, D. C. (2002). *The savvy psychology major*. Dubuque, IA: Kendall/Hunt.

Arnold, K., & Horrigan, K. (2002). Gaining admission into the graduate program of your choice. *Eye on Psi Chi*, 30–33.

Actkinson, T. R. (2000). Master's and myths. *Eye on Psi Chi, 4*, 19–25.

Aubrecht, L. (2001). What can you do with a BA in psychology? *Eye on Psi Chi, 5*, 29–31.

Huss, M. (1996). Secrets to standing out from the pile: Getting into graduate school. *Psi Chi Newsletter*, 6–7.

Lammers, B. (2000). Quick tips for applying to graduate school in psychology. *Eye on Psi Chi, 4*, 40–42.

Landrum, E. (2001). I'm getting my bachelor's degree in psychology. What can I do with it? *Eye on Psi Chi, 6*, 22–24.

Morgan, B., & Korschgen, A. (2001). Psychology career exploration made easy. *Eye on Psi Chi*, 35–36.

Sternberg, R. (Ed.) (2002). *Career paths in psychology: Where your degree can take you*. Washington, DC: APA.

Answers to *Test Yourself* Questions

MODULE 1   The History and Scope of Psychology

1. What events defined the founding of scientific psychology?

ANSWER: The most outstanding event defining the founding of scientific psychology was Wilhelm Wundt's opening of the University of Leipzig psychology laboratory in 1879. The new science of psychology was soon organized into different schools of thought, including structuralism (founded by Edward Bradford Titchener, using introspection to explore the elemental structure of the human mind) and functionalism (founded by William James, focusing on how mental and behavioral processes enable organisms to adapt, survive, and flourish). James also wrote an important psychology textbook, completed in 1890.

2. What are psychology's major levels of analysis?

ANSWER: Psychology's three major levels of analysis are the biological, psychological, and social-cultural. The complementary insights of psychologists studying behavior and mental processes from the neuroscience, evolutionary, behavior genetics, psychodynamic, behavioral, cognitive, and social-cultural perspectives offer a richer understanding than could usually be gained from any one viewpoint alone.

MODULE 2   Thinking Critically With Psychological Science

1. What is the scientific attitude, and why is it important for critical thinking?

ANSWER: The scientific attitude combines *skeptical* testing of various claims and ideas with *humility* about ones' own unexamined presumptions. Examining assumptions, searching for hidden values, evaluating evidence, and assessing conclusions are essential parts of critical thinking.

2. How are human and animal research subjects protected?

ANSWER: Animal protection legislation, laboratory regulation and inspection, and local ethics committees serve to protect human and animal welfare.

MODULE 3   Research Strategies: How Psychologists Ask and Answer Questions

1. What are the strengths and weaknesses of the three different methods psychologists use to describe behavior—case studies, surveys, and naturalistic observation?

ANSWER: *Case studies* offer in-depth insights that may offer clues to what's true of others—or may, if the case is atypical, mislead. *Surveys* can accurately reveal the tendencies of large populations. But if the questions are leading, or if nonrandom samples are queried, the results can again mislead us. *Naturalistic observation* enables study of behavior undisturbed by researchers. But the lack of control may leave cause and effect ambiguous.

2. **Here are some recently reported correlations, with interpretations drawn by journalists. Further research, often including experiments, has clarified cause and effect in each case. Knowing just these correlations, can you come up with other possible explanations for each of these?**

   a. *Alcohol use is associated with violence. (One interpretation: Drinking triggers or unleashes aggressive behavior.)* Perhaps anger triggers drinking, or perhaps the same genes or rearing predispose both drinking and aggression. (Here researchers have learned that drinking does indeed trigger aggressive behavior.)

   b. *Educated people live longer, on average, than less-educated people. (One interpretation: Education lengthens life and enhances health.)* Perhaps richer people can afford more education *and* better health care. (Research supports *this* conclusion.)

   c. *Teens engaged in team sports are less likely to use drugs, smoke, have sex, carry weapons, and eat junk food than are teens who do not engage in team sports. (One interpretation: Team sports encourage healthy living.)* Perhaps some third factor explains this correlation—teens who use drugs, smoke, have sex, carry weapons, and eat junk food may be "loners" who do not enjoy playing on any team.

   d. *Adolescents who frequently see smoking in movies are more likely to smoke. (One interpretation: Movie stars' behavior influences impressionable teens.)* Perhaps adolescents who smoke and attend movies frequently have less parental supervision and more access to spending money than other adolescents.

3. **Why, when testing a new drug for blood pressure, would we learn more about its effectiveness from giving it to half of the participants in a group of 1000 than to all 1000 participants?**

   ANSWER: To determine whether this drug is medically effective, we must compare its effect on those randomly assigned to receive it (the experimental condition) with those who receive a placebo (the control condition). The only difference between the groups is whether they received the actual drug. So, if blood pressure is lower in the experimental group, then we know that the drug itself has produced this effect, not just the participants' knowledge that they are being treated (placebo effect).

4. **Consider a question posed by Christopher Jepson, David Krantz, and Richard Nisbett (1983) to University of Michigan introductory psychology students:**

   The registrar's office at the University of Michigan has found that usually about 100 students in Arts and Sciences have perfect marks at the end of their first term at the University. However, only about 10 to 15 students graduate with perfect marks. What do you think is the most likely explanation for the fact that there are more perfect marks after one term than at graduation?

   ANSWER: Most students in the study came up with plausible causes for the drop in marks, such as, "Students tend to work harder at the beginning of their college careers than toward the end." Fewer than a third recognized the statistical phenomenon clearly at work: Averages based on fewer courses are more variable, which guarantees a greater number of extremely low and high marks at the end of the first term.

MODULE 4 Neural and Hormonal Systems

1. **How do neurons communicate with one another?**

   ANSWER: A neuron fires when excitatory inputs exceed inhibitory inputs by a sufficient threshold. When the resulting impulse reaches the axon's end, it triggers the release of chemical neurotransmitters. After crossing a tiny gap, these molecules activate receptor sites on neighboring neurons. So, the brief answer to how neurons communicate with one another is *chemically*.

2. **How does information flow through your nervous system as you pick up a fork? Can you summarize this process?**

   ANSWER: Your central nervous system's hungry brain activates and guides the muscles of your arm and hand via your peripheral nervous system's motor neurons. As you pick up the fork, your brain processes the information from your sensory nervous system, enabling it to continue to guide the fork to your mouth. The functional circle starts with sensory input, continues with interneuron processing by the central nervous system, and finishes with motor output.

3. **Why is the pituitary gland called the "master gland"?**

ANSWER: The pituitary gland, responding to signals from the hypothalamus, releases hormones that act as triggers. In response, other endocrine glands release their own hormones, which in turn influence brain and behavior.

MODULE 5) The Brain

1. **Within what brain region would damage be most likely to disrupt your ability to skip rope? Your ability to sense tastes or sounds? In what brain region would damage perhaps leave you in a coma? Without the very breath and heartbeat of life?**

ANSWER: These regions are, respectively, the *cerebellum*, the *thalamus*, the *reticular formation*, and the *medulla*. These questions assess your understanding of the essential functions of the lower-level brain areas.

MODULE 6) Behavior Genetics and Evolutionary Psychology

1. **What is *heritability*?**

ANSWER: *Heritability* is the proportion of variation among individuals that we can attribute to genes. Note: Heritability is *not* the extent to which an *individual's* traits are genetically determined. Rather, it is the extent to which variation *among* individuals is due to their differing genes. For any trait, heritability can vary, depending on the population and range of environments studied.

2. **What are the three main criticisms of the evolutionary explanation of human sexuality?**

ANSWER: Critics of the evolutionary explanation of human sexuality point out that (1) it starts with an effect and works backward to propose an explanation; (2) unethical and immoral men could use such explanations to rationalize their behavior toward women; and (3) this explanation overlooks the effects of cultural expectations and socialization.

MODULE 7) Environmental Influences on Behavior

1. **To predict whether a teenager smokes, ask how many of the teen's friends smoke. One explanation for this correlation is peer influence. What's another?**

ANSWER: There may also be a *selection effect*. Adolescents tend to sort themselves into likeminded groups—the jocks, the geeks, the druggies, and so forth. Those who smoke may similarly seek out other teenagers who also smoke.

2. **How do individualist and collectivist cultures differ?**

ANSWER: A culture that favors individualism gives priority to personal goals over group goals; people in that culture will tend to define their identity in terms of their own personal attributes. A culture that favors collectivism gives priority to group goals over individual goals; people in collectivist cultures tend to define their identity in terms of group identifications. Cultures vary in the extent to which they favor individualism or collectivism.

3. **What are gender roles, and what do their variations tell us about our human capacity for learning and adaptation?**

ANSWER: *Gender roles* are social rules or norms for accepted and expected behavior for females and males. The norms associated with various roles, including gender roles, vary widely in different cultural contexts, which is proof that we are very capable of learning and adapting to the social demands of different environments.

MODULE 8 Prenatal Development and the Newborn

1. **Your friend—a heavy smoker—hopes to become pregnant soon and has stopped smoking. Why is this a good idea? What negative effects does smoking during pregnancy have on the fetus?**

   ANSWER: If a woman smokes during her pregnancy, the fetus may receive fewer nutrients and be born underweight and at risk for health problems. Your friend is wise to quit smoking before there is a chance that the pregnancy has begun. The most harmful effects of teratogens, such as cigarette smoke, occur during the first trimester of pregnancy—often before a woman even knows she is pregnant.

MODULE 9 Infancy and Childhood

1. **Use Piaget's first three stages of cognitive development to explain why young children are *not* just miniature adults in the way they think.**

   ANSWER: Infants in the *sensorimotor stage* tend to be focused only on their own perceptions of the world and may, for example, be unaware that objects continue to exist when unseen. A *preoperational* child is still egocentric and incapable of appreciating simple logic, such as the reversibility of operations. A preteen in the *concrete operational stage* is beginning to think logically about concrete events but not about abstract concepts.

MODULE 10 Adolescence

1. **How has the transition from childhood to adulthood changed in Western cultures in the last 100 years?**

   ANSWER: In the last 100 years, the transition to adulthood has started earlier and lasted longer, so that adolescence has lengthened from a period of about 7 years in 1890 to about 12 years in the 1990s.

MODULE 11 Adulthood, and Reflections on Developmental Issues

1. **Research has shown that living together before marriage predicts an increased likelihood of future divorce. Can you imagine two possible explanations for this correlation?**

   ANSWER: William Axinn and Arland Thornton (1992) report data that support two explanations. (1) The first explanation is an example of a *selection effect*—our tendency to seek out others who are similar to us. Cohabitation attracts people who are more open to terminating unsatisfying relationships. People who cohabit bring a more individualistic ethic to marriage, are more likely to see close relationships as temporary and fragile, are more accepting of divorce, and are about three times more likely after marriage to have an affair (Forste & Tanfer, 1996). (2) Axinn and Thornton's second explanation illustrates the *causal effect* of the experience of cohabitation. Over time, those who cohabit tend to become more approving of dissolving an unfulfilling union. This divorce-accepting attitude increases the odds of later divorce.

2. **What findings in psychology support the stage theory of development and the idea of stability in personality across the life span? What findings challenge these ideas?**

   ANSWER: Stage theory is supported by the work of Piaget (cognitive development), Kohlberg (moral development), and Erikson (psychosocial development), but it is challenged by findings that change is more gradual and less culturally universal than these theorists supposed. Some traits, such as temperament, do exhibit remarkable stability across many years. But we do change in other ways, such as in our social attitudes, especially during life's early years.

MODULE 12   Introduction to Sensation and Perception

1. **What is the rough distinction between sensation and perception?**

    ANSWER: *Sensation* is the bottom-up process by which the physical sensory system receives and represents stimuli. *Perception* is the top-down mental process of organizing and interpreting sensory input. But in our everyday experiences, sensation and perception are different aspects of one continuous process.

2. **Your friend insists that he *did* call you to dinner as you intently watched TV. What principle explains your not perceiving him?**

    ANSWER: This example illustrates *selective attention*—focusing conscious awareness on a particular stimulus. Your not perceiving the voice probably indicates that you were selectively focusing your attention on the TV.

MODULE 13   Vision

1. **What is the rapid sequence of events that occurs when you see and recognize someone you know?**

    ANSWER: Light waves reflect off the person and travel into your eye, where the rods and cones convert the light waves' energy into neural impulses sent to your brain. Your brain then processes the subdimensions of this visual input—including color, depth, movement, and form—separately but simultaneously, and integrates this information (along with previously stored information) into a conscious perception of the person you know.

MODULE 14   Hearing

1. **In a nutshell, how do we transform sound waves into perceived sound?**

    ANSWER: A simple figure offers a synopsis:

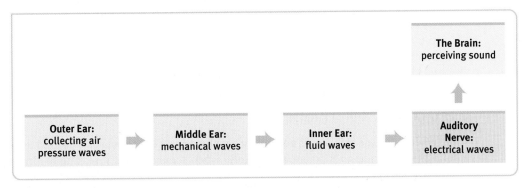

MODULE 15   Other Important Senses

1. **What does the biopsychosocial approach to pain teach us?**

    ANSWER: Considering the biological, psychological, and social-cultural influences on the perception of pain teaches us that our experience of pain is much more than neural messages sent to the brain.

2. **How does our system for sensing smell differ from our sensory systems for vision, touch, and taste?**

    ANSWER: We have three types of color receptors, four basic touch senses, and five taste sensations. But we have no basic smell receptors. Instead, 350 receptor proteins, individually and in combination, recognize some 10,000 discernible odors.

MODULE 16   Perceptual Organization

1. **How does the study of illusions inform our understanding of normal perceptions?**

    ANSWER: Perceptual illusions reveal the ways we organize and interpret sensory information. Our occasional misperceptions demonstrate the workings of our normally effective perceptual processes. For example, the perceived relationship between distance and size is generally valid, but under special circumstances it can lead us astray—as when it helps create the Moon illusion.

2. **What do we mean when we say that, in perception, the whole is greater than the sum of its parts?**

ANSWER: Gestalt psychologists used this saying to describe our perceptual tendency to organize clusters of sensations into meaningful forms or coherent groups.

MODULE 17 Perceptual Interpretation

1. **What type of evidence shows that, indeed, "there is more to perception than meets the senses"?**

ANSWER: We construct our perceptions based on both sensory input and—experiments show—on our assumptions, expectations, schemas, and perceptual sets, often influenced by the surrounding context.

MODULE 18 Waking and Sleeping Rhythms

1. **During psychology's history, what were the ups and downs of "consciousness"?**

ANSWER: Psychology began as the study of consciousness, but during the behaviorist era (for much of the first half of the twentieth century) psychologists focused on observations of behavior. After 1960, driven by discoveries in cognitive psychology and neuroscience, the study of consciousness (our awareness of ourselves and our environment) reemerged as a major topic in psychology.

2. **Are you getting enough sleep? What might you ask yourself to answer this question?**

ANSWER: You could start with the true/false questions in James Mass' sleep deprivation quiz in Table 18.1. Also, William Dement (1999, p. 73) invites you to consider these questions: "How often do you think about taking a quick snooze? How often do you rub your eyes and yawn during the day? How often do you feel like you really need some coffee?" Dement concludes that "each of these is a warning of a sleep debt that you ignore at your peril."

MODULE 19 Hypnosis

1. **When is the use of hypnosis potentially harmful, and when can hypnosis be used to help?**

ANSWER: Hypnosis is potentially harmful when some therapists, seeking to "hypnotically refresh" memories, plant false memories. But posthypnotic suggestions have helped alleviate some ailments, and hypnosis can also help control pain.

MODULE 20 Drugs and Consciousness

1. **A U.S. government survey of 27,616 current or former alcohol drinkers found that 40 percent of those who began drinking before age 15 grew dependent on alcohol. The same was true of only 10 percent of those who first imbibed at ages 21 or 22 (Grant & Dawson, 1998). What possible explanations might there be for this correlation between early use and later abuse?**

ANSWER: Possible explanations include (1) a biological predisposition to both early use and later abuse, (2) brain changes and taste preferences induced by early use, and (3) enduring habits, attitudes, activities, and/or peer relationships that are conducive to alcohol use.

2. **In what ways are near-death experiences similar to drug-induced hallucinations?**

ANSWER: Reports of near-death experiences and drug-induced hallucinations feature similar experiences: replay of old memories, out-of-body sensations, and visions of tunnels or funnels of bright light or beings of light.

MODULE 21 Classical Conditioning

1. **As we develop, we learn cues that lead us to expect and prepare for good and bad events. We learn to repeat behaviors that bring rewards. And we watch others and learn. What do psychologists call these three types of learning?**

   ANSWER: Through *classical conditioning,* we learn cues that lead us to expect and prepare for good and bad events. Through *operant conditioning,* we learn to repeat behaviors that bring rewards. Through *observational learning,* we watch others and learn.

2. **In slasher movies, sexually arousing images of women are sometimes paired with violence against women. Based on classical conditioning principles, what might be an effect of this pairing?**

   ANSWER: If viewing an attractive nude or semi-nude woman (a US) elicits sexual arousal (a UR), then pairing the US with a new stimulus (violence) could turn the violence into a conditioned stimulus (CS) that also becomes sexually arousing, a conditioned response (CR).

MODULE 22 Operant Conditioning

1. ***Positive reinforcement, negative reinforcement,* and *punishment* are tricky concepts for many students. Can you fit the right term in the four boxes in this table? (I've done the first one—positive reinforcement—for you.)**

Type of Stimulus	Give It	Take It Away
Desired (for example, a compliment):	**Positive** reinforcement	*Punishment (e.g., time-out)*
Undesired/aversive (for example, an insult):	*Punishment*	*Negative reinforcement*

MODULE 23 Learning by Observation

1. **Jason's parents and older friends all smoke, but they advise him not to. Juan's parents and friends don't smoke, but they say nothing to deter him from doing so. Will Jason or Juan be more likely to start smoking?**

   ANSWER: Although both saying and doing can influence people, experiments suggest that children more often do as others do and say as they say. Generalizing this finding to smoking, we can expect that Jason will be more likely to start smoking.

MODULE 24 Introduction to Memory

1. **Memory includes (in alphabetical order) long-term memory, sensory memory, and working/short-term memory. What's the correct order of these three memory stores?**

   ANSWER: Sensory memory, working/short-term memory, long-term memory.

MODULE 25 Encoding: Getting Information In

1. **What would be the most effective strategy to learn and retain a list of names of key historical figures for a week? For a year?**

   ANSWER: For a week: Make the names personally meaningful. For a year: Overlearn the list and space out rehearsals over the course of several weeks.

MODULE 26 Storage: Retaining Information

1. **Your friend tells you that her father experienced brain damage in an accident. She wonders if psychology can explain why he can still play checkers very well but has a hard time holding a sensible conversation. What can you tell her?**

ANSWER: Our *explicit* (declarable) memories differ from our *implicit* memories of skills and procedures, such as checkers. Our implicit memories are processed by more ancient brain areas, which apparently escaped damage during the accident.

MODULE 27   Retrieval: Getting Information Out

1. What is priming?

ANSWER: *Priming* is the activation (often without our awareness) of associations. Seeing a gun, for example, might temporarily predispose someone to interpret an ambiguous face as threatening or to recall a boss as nasty. Although the person might not consciously remember the gun, it may prime how that individual interprets or recalls events.

MODULE 28   Forgetting, Memory Construction, and Memory Improvement

1. Can you offer an example of proactive interference?

ANSWER: *Proactive* (forward-acting) interference occurs when earlier learning disrupts your recall of a later experience. Proactive interference has occurred if learning the names of new classmates in your first class makes it more difficult to learn the new names in your second class.

2. What—given the commonality of source amnesia—might life be like if we remembered all our waking experiences and all our dreams?

ANSWER: Real experiences would be confused with those we dreamed. When meeting someone, we might therefore be unsure whether we were reacting to something they previously had done or to something we dreamed they had done. William Dement (1999, p. 298) thinks this "would put a great burden on your sanity. . . . I truly believe that the wall of memory is a blessed protection."

3. What are the recommended memory strategies you just read about? (One advised rehearsing to-be-remembered material. What were the others?)

ANSWER: Study repeatedly to boost long-term recall. Spend more time rehearsing or actively thinking about the material. Make the material personally meaningful. To remember a list of unfamiliar items, use mnemonic devices. Refresh your memory by activating retrieval cues. Recall events while they are fresh, before you encounter possible misinformation. Minimize interference. Test your own knowledge, both to rehearse it and to help determine what you do not yet know.

MODULE 29   Thinking

1. The availability heuristic is a quick-and-easy but sometimes misleading guide to judging reality. What is the availability heuristic?

ANSWER: The *availability heuristic* is our tendency to judge the likelihood of an event by how easily we can recall instances of it. Like all heuristics, this guide is efficient. But it can mislead, as it does when we attempt to judge various risks (for example, of plane travel).

MODULE 30   Language and Thought

1. If children are not yet speaking, is there any reason to think they would benefit from parents and other caregivers reading to them?

ANSWER: Indeed there is, because well before age 1 children are learning to detect words among the stream of spoken sounds, and to discern grammatical rules. Before age 1, they also are babbling with the phonemes of their own language. More than many parents realize, their infants are soaking up language. As researcher Peter Jusczyk reminds us, "Little ears are listening."

2. **To say that "words are the mother of ideas" assumes the truth of what concept?**
   ANSWER: This phrase supports the linguistic determinism hypothesis, which asserts that language determines thought. Research indicates that this position is too extreme, but language does *influence* what we perceive and think.

3. **If your dog barks at a stranger at the front door, does this qualify as language? What if the dog yips in a telltale way to let you know she needs to go out?**
   ANSWER: These are definitely communications. But if language consists of words and the grammatical rules we use to combine them to communicate meaning, few scientists would label a dog's barking and yipping as language.

MODULE 31 Introduction to Intelligence

1. **Joseph is a straight-A student at Harvard Law School, writes a small column for the *Harvard Law Review*, and will be working for a Supreme Court justice next year. Judith is very proud of her grandson and says he is way more intelligent than she ever was. But Joseph is also very proud of his grandmother, who had been imprisoned by the Nazis. When the war ended, she walked out of Germany, contacted a relief agency, traveled to the United States, and began a new life. According to the definition of intelligence in this module, is Joseph the only intelligent person in this story? Why or why not?**
   ANSWER: Joseph is not the only intelligent person in this story. *Intelligence* is the ability to learn from experience, solve problems, and use knowledge to adapt to new situations. Judith certainly fits this description, given all that she accomplished after her release.

MODULE 32 Assessing Intelligence

1. **What was the purpose of Binet's pioneering intelligence test?**
   ANSWER: Binet's original test was designed to predict school achievement.

2. **The Smiths have enrolled their 2-year-old son in a special program that promises to assess his IQ and, if he places in the top 5 percent of test-takers, to create a plan that will guarantee his admission to a top university at age 18. Why is this endeavor of questionable value?**
   ANSWER: The Smiths would be wasting their time and money. Two years is too young an age for reliably predicting future intelligence.

MODULE 33 Genetic and Environmental Influences on Intelligence

1. **As society succeeds in creating equality of opportunity, it will also increase the heritability of ability. The heritability of intelligence scores will be greater in a society marked by equal opportunity than in a society of peasants and aristocrats. Why?**
   ANSWER: Perfect environmental equality would create 100 percent heritability—because genes alone would account for any remaining human differences.

MODULE 34 Introduction to Motivation

1. **While on a long road trip, you suddenly feel very lonely and want to pull over and call a loved one. But the dark, deserted stretch of road is intimidating, so you keep on driving. What motivational perspective would most easily explain this behavior and why?**
   ANSWER: *Drive-reduction theory*—the idea that physical needs create an aroused state that drives us to reduce the need—helps explain your behavior.

MODULE 35 Hunger

1. **You are traveling and have not eaten anything in eight hours. As your long-awaited favorite dish is placed in front of you, your mouth waters. Even imagining this may set your mouth to watering. What triggers this anticipatory drooling?**

ANSWER: You, like Pavlov's dogs, have learned through *classical conditioning* to respond to the cues—the sight and aroma—that signal the food about to enter your mouth. Both *physiological cues* (eight hours of deprivation have left you with low blood sugar) and *psychological cues* (the anticipation of the tasty meal) have heightened your experienced hunger.

MODULE 36 Sexual Motivation and the Need to Belong

1. **How might the evolutionary psychology perspective explain sexual motivation and our need to affiliate?**

   ANSWER: Evolutionary psychologists attempt to explain behaviors in terms of their survival value. From this perspective, sexual motivation and the need to affiliate can be interpreted as behaviors that help ensure the transmission (and therefore survival) of our DNA to future generations.

MODULE 37 Motivation at Work

1. **A human resources director explains to you that "I don't bother with tests or references. I can pick employees by my gut." Based on I/O research, what concerns does this raise?**

   ANSWER: Personnel interviewers feel very confident in their ability to predict long-term job performance from informal interviews. Unfortunately, this ability goes astray so often that I/O psychologists have labeled the gap between interviewers' intuition and workplace reality the *interviewer illusion*. Four factors contribute: (1) interviews disclose prospective workers' good intentions, not their habitual behaviors; (2) interviewers tend to track the successful careers of those they hire, not the successful careers of those they reject; (3) interviewers presume people are what they seem to be in interviews; and (4) interviewers' preconceptions and moods color how they perceive interviewees' responses.

MODULE 38 Introduction to Emotion

1. **Christine is holding her 8-month-old baby when a fierce dog appears out of nowhere and, with teeth bared, leaps for the baby's face. Christine immediately ducks for cover to protect the baby, screams at the dog, then notices that her heart is banging in her chest and she's broken out in a cold sweat. How would the James-Lange, Cannon-Bard, and two-factor theories explain Christine's emotional reaction?**

   ANSWER: The James-Lange theory would say that Christine's emotional reaction consists of her awareness of her physiological responses to the dog attack. The Cannon-Bard theory would say that her fear experience happened simultaneously with her physiological arousal. Schacter's two-factor theory would presume that her emotional reaction stemmed from her interpreting and labeling the arousal.

2. **How do the two divisions of the autonomic nervous system help us respond to and recover from a crisis, and why is this relevant to the study of emotions?**

   ANSWER: The sympathetic division of the ANS arouses us in a crisis, and the parasympathetic division of the ANS calms us when the crisis has passed. Researchers study these physiological responses, in combination with brain pattern indicators, to reach a more complete understanding of the feeling component of emotions.

MODULE 39 Expressed Emotion

1. **Who tends to express more emotion—men or women? How do we know the answer to that question?**

   ANSWER: Women tend to surpass men not only as emotion detectors but also at expressing certain emotions (though men have slightly surpassed women in conveying anger). Researchers discovered this by showing people brief, silent clips of men's and women's faces expressing various emotions and by observing who is most skilled at reading and sending emotions.

MODULE 40 Experienced Emotion

1. **What things do (and do not) predict self-reported happiness?**
   ANSWER: People's age, gender, education level, parenthood, and physical attractiveness are not closely related to their happiness. Predictors of happiness include high self-esteem; optimism and an agreeable, outgoing personality; close friendships or a satisfying marriage; satisfying work and leisure activities; a meaningful religious faith; and adequate sleep and exercise.

MODULE 41 Stress and Illness

1. **What are the basic links in our stress response system?**
   ANSWER: When alerted to a threat (to negative, uncontrollable events), our sympathetic nervous system arouses us. Heart rate and respiration increase. Blood is diverted from digestion to the skeletal muscles. The body releases sugar and fat to prepare for fight or flight. Simultaneously, the brain (via the hypothalamus and adjacent pituitary gland) orders the adrenal glands to secrete the stress hormone cortisol. The system is wonderfully adaptive. But if stress is continuous, health consequences and exhaustion may result.

MODULE 42 Coping With Stress

1. **What are some ways that social support can help us cope with stress?**
   ANSWER: Several large studies show that social support can buffer stress and predict health. Social support seems to foster stronger immune functioning and to lower blood pressure. These effects may stem from a healthier life style, as well as an opportunity to confide in others.

MODULE 43 Modifying Illness-Related Behaviors

1. **Nonsmokers, the text reports, are less likely to become depressed and get divorced. What type of research finding is this, and what explanations might it have?**
   ANSWER: This is a correlational finding. Like other correlational findings, it can be interpreted in several ways:
   - Not smoking may be just one part of a generally healthy life-style that includes healthy emotions and relationships.
   - Depressed people and those with troubled relationships may be drawn to smoking.
   - Smoking, depression, and divorce may share common roots. Perhaps certain genes predispose a temperament that is prone to smoking, depression, and divorce. Or perhaps a certain upbringing or peer environment is conducive to smoking, depression, and divorce.

MODULE 44 The Psychoanalytic Perspective

1. **What, according to Freud, were some of the important defense mechanisms, and what do they defend against? How many of these find support in modern research?**
   ANSWER: Freud believed repression to be the basic defense mechanism. Others include regression, reaction formation, projection, rationalization, and displacement. All supposedly serve to reduce anxiety. Modern research supports the phenomenon Freud called *projection* and current researchers call the *false consensus effect*. Some evidence also supports self-esteem defenses, such as reaction formation. But there is little support for the others.

MODULE 45 The Humanistic Perspective

1. What does it mean to be "empathic"? To be "self-actualized"?

ANSWER: To be *empathic* is to share and mirror another person's feelings. Carl Rogers believed that people nurture growth in others by being empathic. Abraham Maslow viewed *self-actualization* as the ultimate psychological need—the motivation to fulfill one's potential.

MODULE 46 Contemporary Research on Personality

1. How many trait dimensions are currently used to describe personality, and what are those dimensions?

ANSWER: "The Big Five" trait dimensions—*emotional stability, extraversion, openness, agreeableness,* and *conscientiousness*—provide a reasonably complete personality description.

2. How do learned helplessness and optimism influence behavior?

ANSWER: Learned helplessness produces passive resignation after organisms find themselves unable to avoid aversive events. Nursing homes, prisons, colleges, and autocratic companies and countries have all been observed to produce symptoms of learned helplessness. Optimism has the opposite effect, leading to better moods, more persistence, and better health. Excessive optimism, however, can expose us to risks.

3. In a 1997 Gallup poll, white Americans estimated 44 percent of their fellow white Americans to be high in prejudice (scoring them 5 or higher on a 10-point scale). How many rated themselves similarly high in prejudice? Just 14 percent. What phenomenon does this illustrate?

ANSWER: This illustrates the general tendency to see oneself as superior to the average other, which is one example of the *self-serving bias.*

MODULE 47 Introduction to Psychological Disorders

1. What is the biopsychosocial approach, and why is it important in our understanding of psychological disorders?

ANSWER: This contemporary approach assumes that biological, psychological, and social-cultural influences combine to produce psychological disorders. Genes matter. The brain matters. Inner thoughts and feelings matter. Social and cultural influences matter. To get the whole integrated picture, a biopsychosocial perspective helps.

2. Does poverty cause psychological disorders? Explain.

ANSWER: Poverty-related stresses can indeed help trigger disorders. But disabling disorders can also contribute to poverty. Thus, poverty and disorders are often a chicken-and-egg situation, and it's hard to know which came first.

MODULE 48 Anxiety Disorders

1. How do generalized anxiety disorder, phobias, and obsessive-compulsive disorder differ?

ANSWER: *Generalized anxiety disorder* is unfocused tension, apprehension, and arousal. *Phobias* focus anxiety on specific feared objects or situations. *Obsessive-compulsive disorders* express anxiety through unwanted repetitive thoughts (obsessions) or actions (compulsions).

MODULE 49 Dissociative and Personality Disorders

1. Is antisocial personality disorder an inherited condition?

ANSWER: *Antisocial personality disorder*—in which a person exhibits a lack of conscience for wrongdoing—seems to have both biological and psychological components. Twin and adoption studies show that biological relatives of people with this disorder are at increased risk for antisocial behavior. But the tendency to be fearless, when combined with a sense of social responsibility, can lead to heroism, adventurism, or athletic success.

MODULE 50 Mood Disorders

1. **What does it mean to say that "depression is the common cold of psychological disorders"?**
ANSWER: Saying that "depression is the common cold of psychological disorders" is a quick way to state that this serious disorder is the most common condition in those seeking mental health treatment—with almost 6 percent of men and nearly 10 percent of women reporting a depressive episode each year. Worldwide, depression is the leading cause of disability.

MODULE 51 Schizophrenia

1. **What are the five subtypes of schizophrenia?**
ANSWER: They are *paranoid* (marked by delusions or hallucinations), *disorganized* (disorganized speech, flat emotion), *catatonic* (immobility or repetitive purposeless movements), *undifferentiated* (varied symptoms), and *residual* (withdrawal, after hallucinations and delusions have disappeared).

MODULE 52 The Psychological Therapies

1. **What is the major distinction between the underlying assumption in psychoanalytic and humanistic therapies and the underlying assumption in behavior therapies?**
ANSWER: Psychoanalytic and humanistic therapies seek to relieve problems by providing insight into their origins. Behavior therapies assume the problem behavior *is* the problem and treat it directly, paying less attention to its origins.

MODULE 53 Evaluating Psychotherapies

1. **How does the placebo effect bias clients' appraisals of the effectiveness of psychotherapies?**
ANSWER: The *placebo effect* is the healing power of *belief* in a treatment. Patients who expect a treatment to be effective may believe it was.

2. **What are the influences to keep in mind for successful therapeutic intervention?**
ANSWER: Successful therapeutic intervention—or prevention—can intervene at many different levels because biological, psychological, and social-cultural influences can combine and interact to produce psychological disorders. Bodily (for example, neurochemical) imbalances can affect mental states, and both biochemical and mental states may be affected by environmental conditions.

MODULE 54 The Biomedical Therapies

1. **How do researchers evaluate the effectiveness of particular drug therapies?**
ANSWER: Ideally, researchers assign people to treatment and no-treatment conditions to see if those who receive therapy improve more than those who don't. In many studies, the no-treatment comparison includes a placebo condition, which allows a double-blind controlled study. If neither the therapist nor the client knows for sure whether the client has received the experimental treatment (for example, a drug), then any difference between the treated and untreated groups will reflect the treatment's actual effect.

MODULE 55   Social Thinking

1. **Driving to school one wintry day, Marco narrowly misses a car that slides through a red light. "Slow down! What a terrible driver," he thinks to himself. Moments later, Marco himself slips through an intersection and yelps, "Wow! These roads are awful. The city snow plows need to get out here." What social psychology principle has Marco just demonstrated? Explain.**

   ANSWER: By attributing the other person's behavior to the person ("he's a terrible driver") and his own to the situation ("these roads are awful"), Marco has exhibited the *fundamental attribution error*.

MODULE 56   Social Influence

1. **You are organizing a Town Hall–style meeting of fiercely competitive political candidates. To add to the fun, friends have suggested handing out masks of the candidates' faces for supporters to wear. What phenomenon might these masks engage?**

   ANSWER: The anonymity provided by the masks, combined with the arousal of the contentious setting, might create *deindividuation* (lessened self-awareness and self-restraint in a group setting).

MODULE 57   Antisocial Relations

1. **Horace says, "I have no prejudice within me toward anyone. I believe everyone deserves equal opportunity in housing and employment." Even if Horace indeed expresses no obvious prejudice, what sort of prejudice might nonetheless exist?**

   ANSWER: Horace exhibited no overt, conscious prejudice. He could nevertheless harbor implicit, unconscious prejudice that surfaces in subtle and automatic ways, including assumed racial associations, race-influenced perceptions, and telltale bodily responses to encountering someone of a different race.

MODULE 58   Prosocial Relations

1. **Why didn't anybody help Kitty Genovese? What social relations principle did this incident illustrate?**

   ANSWER: The incident illustrated the *bystander effect*. In the presence of others, an individual is less likely to notice a situation, correctly interpret it as an emergency, and then take responsibility for offering help. Many of Kitty Genovese's neighbors noticed the situation and recognized it as an emergency but they apparently assumed others would help, and they did not feel responsible for offering help.

Glossary

absolute threshold the minimum stimulation needed to detect a particular stimulus 50 percent of the time.

accommodation adapting one's current understandings (schemas) to incorporate new information.

accommodation the process by which the eye's lens changes shape to focus near or far objects on the retina.

acetylcholine [ah-seat-el-KO-leen] **(ACh)** a neurotransmitter that enables learning and memory and also triggers muscle contraction.

achievement motivation a desire for significant accomplishment: for mastery of things, people, or ideas; for attaining a high standard.

achievement test a test designed to assess what a person has learned.

acoustic encoding the encoding of sound, especially the sound of words.

acquisition the initial stage in classical conditioning; the phase associating a neutral stimulus with an unconditioned stimulus so that the neutral stimulus comes to elicit a conditioned response. In operant conditioning, the strengthening of a reinforced response.

action potential a neural impulse; a brief electrical charge that travels down an axon. The action potential is generated by the movement of positively charged atoms in and out of channels in the axon's membrane.

active listening empathic listening in which the listener echoes, restates, and clarifies. A feature of Rogers' client-centered therapy.

acuity the sharpness of vision.

adaptation-level phenomenon our tendency to form judgments (of sounds, of lights, of income) relative to a neutral level defined by our prior experience.

addiction compulsive drug craving and use.

adolescence the transition period from childhood to adulthood, extending from puberty to independence.

adrenal [ah-DREEN-el] **glands** a pair of endocrine glands just above the kidneys. The adrenals secrete the hormones epinephrine (adrenaline) and norepinephrine (noradrenaline), which help to arouse the body in times of stress.

aerobic exercise sustained exercise that increases heart and lung fitness; may also alleviate depression and anxiety.

aggression any physical or verbal behavior intended to hurt or destroy.

algorithm a methodical, logical rule or procedure that guarantees solving a particular problem. Contrasts with the usually speedier—but also more error-prone—use of *heuristics*.

alpha waves the relatively slow brain waves of a relaxed, awake state.

altruism unselfish regard for the welfare of others.

Alzheimer's disease a progressive and irreversible brain disorder characterized by gradual deterioration of memory, reasoning, language, and, finally, physical functioning.

amnesia the loss of memory.

amphetamines drugs that stimulate neural activity, causing speeded-up body functions and associated energy and mood changes.

amygdala [uh-MIG-duh-la] two lima bean-sized neural clusters that are components of the limbic system and are linked to emotion.

anorexia nervosa an eating disorder in which a normal-weight person (usually an adolescent female) diets and becomes significantly (15 percent or more) underweight, yet, still feeling fat, continues to starve.

antisocial personality disorder a personality disorder in which the person (usually a man) exhibits a lack of conscience for wrongdoing, even toward friends and family members. May be aggressive and ruthless or a clever con artist.

anxiety disorders psychological disorders characterized by distressing, persistent anxiety or maladaptive behaviors that reduce anxiety.

aphasia impairment of language, usually caused by left hemisphere damage either to Broca's area (impairing speaking) or to Wernicke's area (impairing understanding).

applied research scientific study that aims to solve practical problems.

aptitude test a test designed to predict a person's future performance; *aptitude* is the capacity to learn.

assimilation interpreting one's new experience in terms of one's existing schemas.

association areas areas of the cerebral cortex that are not involved in primary motor or sensory functions; rather, they are involved in higher mental functions such as learning, remembering, thinking, and speaking.

associative learning learning that certain events occur together. The events may be two stimuli (as in classical conditioning) or a response and its consequences (as in operant conditioning).

attachment an emotional tie with another person; shown in young children by their seeking closeness to the caregiver and showing distress on separation.

attention-deficit hyperactivity disorder (ADHD) a psychological disorder marked by the appearance by age 7 of one or more of three key symptoms: extreme inattention, hyperactivity, and impulsivity.

attitude feelings, often based on our beliefs, that predispose us to respond in a particular way to objects, people, and events.

attribution theory suggests how we explain someone's behavior—by crediting either the situation or the person's disposition.

audition the sense or act of hearing.

autism a disorder that appears in childhood and is marked by deficient communication, social interaction, and understanding of others' states of mind.

automatic processing unconscious encoding of incidental information, such as space, time, and frequency, and of well-learned information, such as word meanings.

autonomic [aw-tuh-NAHM-ik] **nervous system** the part of the peripheral nervous system that controls the glands and the muscles of the internal organs (such as the heart). Its sympathetic division arouses; its parasympathetic division calms.

availability heuristic estimating the likelihood of events based on their availability in memory; if instances come readily to mind (perhaps because of their vividness), we presume such events are common.

aversive conditioning a type of counterconditioning that associates an unpleasant state (such as nausea) with an unwanted behavior (such as drinking alcohol).

axon the extension of a neuron, ending in branching terminal fibers, through which messages pass to other neurons or to muscles or glands.

babbling stage at about 4 months, the stage of speech development in which the infant spontaneously utters various sounds at first unrelated to the household language.

barbiturates drugs that depress the activity of the central nervous system, reducing anxiety but impairing memory and judgment.

basal metabolic rate the body's resting rate of energy expenditure.

basic research pure science that aims to increase the scientific knowledge base.

basic trust according to Erik Erikson, a sense that the world is predictable and trustworthy; said to be formed during infancy by appropriate experiences with responsive caregivers.

behavior genetics the study of the relative power and limits of genetic and environmental influences on behavior.

behavior therapy therapy that applies learning principles to the elimination of unwanted behaviors.

behavioral medicine an interdisciplinary field that integrates behavioral and medical knowledge and applies that knowledge to health and disease.

behaviorism the view that psychology (1) should be an objective science that (2) studies behavior without reference to mental processes. Most research psychologists today agree with (1) but not with (2).

belief bias the tendency for one's preexisting beliefs to distort logical reasoning, sometimes by making invalid conclusions seem valid, or valid conclusions seem invalid.

belief perseverance clinging to one's initial conceptions after the basis on which they were formed has been discredited.

binocular cues depth cues, such as retinal disparity and convergence, that depend on the use of two eyes.

biofeedback a system for electronically recording, amplifying, and feeding back information regarding a subtle physiological state, such as blood pressure or muscle tension.

biological psychology a branch of psychology concerned with the links between biology and behavior. (Some biological psychologists call themselves *behavioral neuroscientists, neuropsychologists, behavior geneticists, physiological psychologists,* or *biopsychologists*.)

biological rhythms periodic physiological fluctuations.

biomedical therapy prescribed medications or medical procedures that act directly on the patient's nervous system.

biopsychosocial approach an integrated perspective that incorporates biological, psychological, and social-cultural levels of analysis.

bipolar disorder a mood disorder in which the person alternates between the hopelessness and lethargy of depression and the overexcited state of mania. (Formerly called manic-depressive disorder.)

blind spot the point at which the optic nerve leaves the eye, creating a "blind" spot because no receptor cells are located there.

bottom-up processing analysis that begins with the sensory receptors and works up to the brain's integration of sensory information.

brainstem the oldest part and central core of the brain, beginning where the spinal cord swells as it enters the skull; the brainstem is responsible for automatic survival functions.

Broca's area controls language expression—an area of the frontal lobe, usually in the left hemisphere, that directs the muscle movements involved in speech.

bulimia nervosa an eating disorder characterized by episodes of overeating, usually of high-calorie foods, followed by vomiting, laxative use, fasting, or excessive exercise.

bystander effect the tendency for any given bystander to be less likely to give aid if other bystanders are present.

Cannon-Bard theory the theory that an emotion-arousing stimulus simultaneously triggers (1) physiological responses and (2) the subjective experience of emotion.

case study an observation technique in which one person is studied in depth in the hope of revealing universal principles.

catharsis emotional release. In psychology, the catharsis hypothesis maintains that "releasing" aggressive energy (through action or fantasy) relieves aggressive urges.

central nervous system (CNS) the brain and spinal cord.

cerebellum [sehr-uh-BELL-um] the "little brain" attached to the rear of the brainstem; its functions include processing sensory input and coordinating movement output and balance.

cerebral [seh-REE-bruhl] **cortex** the intricate fabric of interconnected neural cells that covers the cerebral hemispheres; the body's ultimate control and information-processing center.

chromosomes threadlike structures made of DNA molecules that contain the genes.

chunking organizing items into familiar, manageable units; often occurs automatically.

circadian [ser-KAY-dee-an] **rhythm** the biological clock; regular bodily rhythms (for example, of temperature and wakefulness) that occur on a 24-hour cycle.

classical conditioning a type of learning in which an organism comes to associate stimuli. A neutral stimulus that signals an unconditioned stimulus (US) begins to produce a response that anticipates and prepares for the unconditioned stimulus. Also called *Pavlovian* or *respondent conditioning*.

client-centered therapy a humanistic therapy, developed by Carl Rogers, in which the therapist uses techniques such as active listening within a genuine, accepting, empathic environment to facilitate clients' growth. (Also called *person-centered therapy*.)

clinical psychology a branch of psychology that studies, assesses, and treats people with psychological disorders.

cochlea [KOHK-lee-uh] a coiled, bony, fluid-filled tube in the inner ear through which sound waves trigger nerve impulses.

cochlear implant a device for converting sounds into electrical signals and stimulating the auditory nerve through electrodes threaded into the cochlea

cognition all the mental activities associated with thinking, knowing, remembering, and communicating.

cognitive-behavior therapy a popular integrated therapy that combines cognitive therapy (changing self-defeating thinking) with behavior therapy (changing behavior).

cognitive dissonance theory the theory that we act to reduce the discomfort (dissonance) we feel when two of our thoughts (cognitions) are inconsistent. For example, when our awareness of our attitudes and of our actions clash, we can reduce the resulting dissonance by changing our attitudes.

cognitive map a mental representation of the layout of one's environment. For example, after exploring a maze, rats act as if they have learned a cognitive map of it.

cognitive therapy therapy that teaches people new, more adaptive ways of thinking and acting; based on the assumption that thoughts intervene between events and our emotional reactions.

collective unconscious Carl Jung's concept of a shared, inherited reservoir of memory traces from our species' history.

collectivism giving priority to the goals of one's group (often one's extended family or work group) and defining one's identity accordingly.

color constancy perceiving familiar objects as having consistent color, even if changing illumination alters the wavelengths reflected by the object.

companionate love the deep affectionate attachment we feel for those with whom our lives are intertwined.

complementary and alternative medicine Unproven health care treatments not taught widely in medical schools, not used in hospitals, and not usually reimbursed by insurance companies.

concept a mental grouping of similar objects, events, ideas, or people.

concrete operational stage in Piaget's theory, the stage of cognitive development (from about 6 or 7 to 11 years of age) during which children gain the mental operations that enable them to think logically about concrete events.

conditioned reinforcer a stimulus that gains its reinforcing power through its association with a primary reinforcer; also known as *secondary reinforcer*.

conditioned response (CR) in classical conditioning, the learned response to a previously neutral (but now conditioned) stimulus (CS).

conditioned stimulus (CS) in classical conditioning, an originally irrelevant stimulus that, after association with an unconditioned stimulus (US), comes to trigger a conditioned response.

conduction hearing loss hearing loss caused by damage to the mechanical system that conducts sound waves to the cochlea.

cones retinal receptor cells that are concentrated near the center of the retina and that function in daylight or in well-lit conditions. The cones detect fine detail and give rise to color sensations.

confirmation bias a tendency to search for information that confirms one's preconceptions.

conflict a perceived incompatibility of actions, goals, or ideas.

conformity adjusting one's behavior or thinking to coincide with a group standard.

consciousness our awareness of ourselves and our environment.

conservation the principle (which Piaget believed to be a part of concrete operational reasoning) that properties such as mass, volume, and number remain the same despite changes in the forms of objects.

content validity the extent to which a test samples the behavior that is of interest (such as a driving test that samples driving tasks).

continuous reinforcement reinforcing the desired response every time it occurs.

control condition the condition of an experiment that contrasts with the experimental condition and serves as a comparison for evaluating the effect of the treatment.

convergence a binocular cue for perceiving depth; the extent to which the eyes converge inward when looking at an object. The greater the inward strain, the closer the object.

coping alleviating stress using emotional, cognitive, or behavioral methods.

coronary heart disease the clogging of the vessels that nourish the heart muscle; the leading cause of death in many developed countries.

corpus callosum [KOR-pus kah-LOW-sum] the large band of neural fibers connecting the two brain hemispheres and carrying messages between them.

correlation a measure of the extent to which two factors vary together, and thus of how well either factor predicts the other. The *correlation coefficient* is the mathematical expression of the relationship, ranging from −1 to +1.

counseling psychology a branch of psychology that assists people with problems in living (often related to school, work, or marriage) and in achieving greater well-being.

counterconditioning a behavior therapy procedure that conditions new responses to stimuli that trigger unwanted behaviors; based on classical conditioning. Includes *exposure therapies* and *aversive conditioning*.

creativity the ability to produce novel and valuable ideas.

criterion the behavior (such as future college grades) that a test (such as the SAT) is designed to predict; thus, the measure used in defining whether the test has predictive validity.

critical period an optimal period shortly after birth when an organism's exposure to certain stimuli or experiences produces proper development.

critical thinking thinking that does not blindly accept arguments and conclusions. Rather, it examines assumptions, discerns hidden values, evaluates evidence, and assesses conclusions.

cross-sectional study a study in which people of different ages are compared with one another.

crystallized intelligence one's accumulated knowledge and verbal skills; tends to increase with age.

culture the enduring behaviors, ideas, attitudes, and traditions shared by a large group of people and transmitted from one generation to the next.

defense mechanisms in psychoanalytic theory, the ego's protective methods of reducing anxiety by unconsciously distorting reality.

deindividuation the loss of self-awareness and self-restraint occurring in group situations that foster arousal and anonymity.

déjà vu that eerie sense that "I've experienced this before." Cues from the current situation may subconsciously trigger retrieval of an earlier experience.

delta waves the large, slow brain waves associated with deep sleep.

delusions false beliefs, often of persecution or grandeur, that may accompany psychotic disorders.

dendrite the bushy, branching extensions of a neuron that receive messages and conduct impulses toward the cell body.

dependent variable the outcome factor; the variable that may change in response to manipulations of the independent variable.

depressants drugs (such as alcohol, barbiturates, and opiates) that reduce neural activity and slow body functions.

depth perception the ability to see objects in three dimensions although the images that strike the retina are two-dimensional; allows us to judge distance.

developmental psychology a branch of psychology that studies physical, cognitive, and social change throughout the life span.

difference threshold the minimum difference between two stimuli required for detection 50 percent of the time. We experience the difference threshold as a just noticeable difference. (Also called *just noticeable difference* or *jnd*.)

discrimination in classical conditioning, the learned ability to distinguish between a conditioned stimulus and stimuli that do not signal an unconditioned stimulus.

discrimination unjustifiable negative behavior toward a group or its members.

displacement psychoanalytic defense mechanism that shifts sexual or aggressive impulses toward a more acceptable or less threatening object or person, as when redirecting anger toward a safer outlet.

dissociation a split in consciousness, which allows some thoughts and behaviors to occur simultaneously with others.

dissociative disorders disorders in which conscious awareness becomes separated (dissociated) from previous memories, thoughts, and feelings.

dissociative identity disorder (DID) a rare dissociative disorder in which a person exhibits two or more distinct and alternating personalities. Also called *multiple personality disorder*.

DNA (deoxyribonucleic acid) a complex molecule containing the genetic information that makes up the chromosomes.

double-blind procedure an experimental procedure in which both the research participants and the research staff are ignorant (blind) about whether the research participants have received the treatment or a placebo. Commonly used in drug-evaluation studies.

Down syndrome a condition of retardation and associated physical disorders caused by an extra chromosome in one's genetic makeup.

dream a sequence of images, emotions, and thoughts passing through a sleeping person's mind. Dreams are notable for their hallucinatory imagery, discontinuities, and incongruities, and for the dreamer's delusional acceptance of the content and later difficulties remembering it.

drive-reduction theory the idea that a physiological need creates an aroused tension state (a drive) that motivates an organism to satisfy the need.

DSM-IV the American Psychiatric Association's *Diagnostic and Statistical Manual of Mental Disorders* (Fourth Edition), a widely used system for classifying psychological disorders. Presently distributed in an updated "text revision" (DSM-IV-TR).

dualism the presumption that mind and body are two distinct entities that interact.

echoic memory a momentary sensory memory of auditory stimuli; if attention is elsewhere, sounds and words can still be recalled within 3 or 4 seconds.

eclectic approach an approach to psychotherapy that, depending on the client's problems, uses techniques from various forms of therapy.

Ecstasy (MDMA) a synthetic stimulant and mild hallucinogen. Produces euphoria and social intimacy, but with short-term health risks and longer-term harm to serotonin-producing neurons and to mood and cognition.

effortful processing encoding that requires attention and conscious effort.

ego the largely conscious, "executive" part of personality that, according to Freud, mediates among the demands of the id, superego, and reality. The ego operates on the *reality principle*, satisfying the id's desires in ways that will realistically bring pleasure rather than pain.

egocentrism in Piaget's theory, the preoperational child's difficulty in taking another's point of view.

electroconvulsive therapy (ECT) a biomedical therapy for severely depressed patients in which a brief electric current is sent through the brain of an anesthetized patient.

electroencephalogram (EEG) an amplified recording of the waves of electrical activity that sweep across the brain's surface. These waves are measured by electrodes placed on the scalp.

embryo the developing human organism from about 2 weeks after fertilization through the second month.

emotion a response of the whole organism, involving (1) physiological arousal, (2) expressive behaviors, and (3) conscious experience.

emotion-focused coping attempting to alleviate stress by avoiding or ignoring a stressor and attending to emotional needs related to one's stress reaction.

emotional intelligence the ability to perceive, understand, manage, and use emotions.

empirically derived test a test (such as the MMPI) developed by testing a pool of items and then selecting those that discriminate between groups.

empiricism the view that (a) knowledge comes from experience via the senses, and (b) science flourishes through observation and experiment.

encoding the processing of information into the memory system—for example, by extracting meaning.

endocrine [EN-duh-krin] **system** the body's "slow" chemical communication system; a set of glands that secrete hormones into the bloodstream.

endorphins [en-DOR-fins] "morphine within"—natural, opiatelike neurotransmitters linked to pain control and to pleasure.

environment every nongenetic influence, from prenatal nutrition to the people and things around us.

equity a condition in which people receive from a relationship in proportion to what they give to it.

estrogen a sex hormone, secreted in greater amounts by females than by males. In nonhuman female mammals, estrogen levels peak during ovulation, promoting sexual receptivity.

evolutionary psychology the study of the evolution of behavior and the mind, using principles of natural selection.

experiment a research method in which an investigator manipulates one or more factors (independent variables) to observe the effect on some behavior or mental process (the dependent variable). By random assignment of participants, the experimenter aims to control other relevant factors.

experimental condition the condition of an experiment that exposes participants to the treatment, that is, to one version of the independent variable.

explicit memory memory of facts and experiences that one can consciously know and "declare." (Also called *declarative memory*.)

exposure therapies behavioral techniques, such as systematic desensitization, that treat anxieties by exposing people (in imagination or actuality) to the things they fear and avoid.

external locus of control the perception that chance or outside forces beyond one's personal control determine one's fate.

extinction the diminishing of a conditioned response; occurs in classical conditioning when an unconditioned stimulus (US) does not follow a conditioned stimulus (CS); occurs in operant conditioning when a response is no longer reinforced.

extrasensory perception (ESP) the controversial claim that perception can occur apart from sensory input. Said to include *telepathy, clairvoyance,* and *precognition.*

extrinsic motivation a desire to perform a behavior due to promised rewards or threats of punishment.

factor analysis a statistical procedure that identifies clusters of related items (called *factors*) on a test; used to identify different dimensions of performance that underlie one's total score.

false consensus effect the tendency to overestimate the extent to which others share our beliefs and behaviors.

family therapy therapy that treats the family as a system. Views an individual's unwanted behaviors as influenced by or directed at other family members; attempts to guide family members toward positive relationships and improved communication.

farsightedness a condition in which faraway objects are seen more clearly than near objects because the image of near objects is focused behind the retina.

feature detectors nerve cells in the brain that respond to specific features of the stimulus, such as shape, angle, or movement.

feel-good, do-good phenomenon people's tendency to be helpful when already in a good mood.

fetal alcohol syndrome (FAS) physical and cognitive abnormalities in children caused by a pregnant woman's heavy drinking. In severe cases, symptoms include noticeable facial misproportions.

fetus the developing human organism from 9 weeks after conception to birth.

figure-ground the organization of the visual field into objects (the *figures*) that stand out from their surroundings (the *ground*).

fixation according to Freud, a lingering focus of pleasure-seeking energies at an earlier psychosexual stage in which conflicts were unresolved.

fixation the inability to see a problem from a new perspective; an impediment to problem solving.

fixed-interval schedule in operant conditioning, a reinforcement schedule that reinforces a response only after a specified time has elapsed.

fixed-ratio schedule in operant conditioning, a reinforcement schedule that reinforces a response only after a specified number of responses.

flashbulb memory a clear memory of an emotionally significant moment or event.

flow a completely involved, focused state of consciousness, with diminished awareness of self and time, resulting from optimal engagement of one's skills.

fluid intelligence one's ability to reason speedily and abstractly; tends to decrease during late adulthood.

fMRI (functional magnetic resonance imaging) a technique for revealing blood flow and, therefore, brain activity by comparing successive MRI scans. MRI scans show brain anatomy; fMRI scans show brain function.

foot-in-the-door phenomenon the tendency for people who have first agreed to a small request to comply later with a larger request.

formal operational stage in Piaget's theory, the stage of cognitive development (normally beginning about age 12) during which people begin to think logically about abstract concepts.

fovea the central focal point in the retina, around which the eye's cones cluster.

framing the way an issue is posed; how an issue is framed can significantly affect decisions and judgments.

fraternal twins twins who develop from separate fertilized eggs. They are genetically no closer than brothers and sisters, but they share a fetal environment.

free association in psychoanalysis, a method of exploring the unconscious in which the person relaxes and says whatever comes to mind, no matter how trivial or embarrassing.

frequency the number of complete wavelengths that pass a point in a given time (for example, per second).

frequency theory in hearing, the theory that the rate of nerve impulses traveling up the auditory nerve matches the frequency of a tone, thus enabling us to sense its pitch.

frontal lobes the portion of the cerebral cortex lying just behind the forehead; involved in speaking and muscle movements and in making plans and judgments.

frustration-aggression principle the principle that frustration—the blocking of an attempt to achieve some goal—creates anger, which can generate aggression.

functional fixedness the tendency to think of things only in terms of their usual functions; an impediment to problem solving.

functionalism a school of psychology that focused on how mental and behavioral processes function—how they enable the organism to adapt, survive, and flourish.

fundamental attribution error the tendency for observers, when analyzing another's behavior, to underestimate the impact of the situation and to overestimate the impact of personal disposition.

gate-control theory the theory that the spinal cord contains a neurological "gate" that blocks pain signals or allows them to pass on to the brain. The "gate" is opened by the activity of pain signals traveling up small nerve fibers and is closed by activity in larger fibers or by information coming from the brain.

gender in psychology, the biologically and socially influenced characteristics by which people define *male* and *female*.

gender-typing the acquisition of a traditional masculine or feminine role.

gender identity one's sense of being male or female.

gender role a set of expected behaviors for males and for females.

gender schema theory the theory that children learn from their cultures a concept of what it means to be male and female and that they adjust their behavior accordingly.

general adaptation syndrome (GAS) Selye's concept of the body's adaptive response to stress in three stages—alarm, resistance, exhaustion.

general intelligence (g) a general intelligence factor that according to Spearman and others underlies specific mental abilities and is therefore measured by every task on an intelligence test.

generalization the tendency, once a response has been conditioned, for stimuli similar to the conditioned stimulus to elicit similar responses.

generalized anxiety disorder an anxiety disorder in which a person is continually tense, apprehensive, and in a state of autonomic nervous system arousal.

genes the biochemical units of heredity that make up the chromosomes; a segment of DNA capable of synthesizing a protein.

genome the complete instructions for making an organism, consisting of all the genetic material in that organism's chromosomes.

gestalt an organized whole. Gestalt psychologists emphasized our tendency to integrate pieces of information into meaningful wholes.

glial cells (glia) cells in the nervous system that support, nourish, and protect neurons.

glucose the form of sugar that circulates in the blood and provides the major source of energy for body tissues. When its level is low, we feel hunger.

grammar in a language, a system of rules that enables us to communicate with and understand others.

GRIT Graduated and Reciprocated Initiatives in Tension-Reduction—strategy designed to decrease international tensions.

group polarization the enhancement of a group's prevailing inclinations through discussion within the group.

grouping the perceptual tendency to organize stimuli into coherent groups.

groupthink the mode of thinking that occurs when the desire for harmony in a decision-making group overrides a realistic appraisal of alternatives.

habituation decreasing responsiveness with repeated stimulation. As infants gain familiarity with repeated exposure to a visual stimulus, their interest wanes and they look away sooner.

hallucinations false sensory experiences, such as seeing something in the absence of an external visual stimulus.

hallucinogens psychedelic ("mind-manifesting") drugs, such as LSD, that distort perceptions and evoke sensory images in the absence of sensory input.

health psychology the application of psychological concepts and research to illness prevention and treatment and to health advancement.

heritability the proportion of variation among individuals that we can attribute to genes. The heritability of a trait may vary, depending on the range of populations and environments studied.

heuristic a simple thinking strategy that often allows us to make judgments and solve problems efficiently; usually speedier but also more error-prone than *algorithms*.

hierarchy of needs Maslow's pyramid of human needs, beginning at the base with physiological needs that must first be satisfied before higher-level safety needs and then psychological needs become active.

hindsight bias the tendency to believe, after learning an outcome, that one would have foreseen it. (Also known as the I-knew-it-all-along phenomenon.)

hippocampus a neural center located in the limbic system that helps process explicit memories for storage.

homeostasis a tendency to maintain a balanced or constant internal state; the regulation of any aspect of body chemistry, such as blood glucose, around a particular level.

hormones chemical messengers, mostly those manufactured by the endocrine glands, that are produced in one tissue and affect another.

hue the dimension of color that is determined by the wavelength of light; what we know as the color names *blue*, *green*, and so forth.

human factors psychology a branch of psychology that explores how people and machines interact and how machines and physical environments can be made safe and easy to use.

humanistic psychology historically significant perspective that emphasized the growth potential of healthy people; used personalized methods to study personality in hopes of fostering personal growth.

hypnosis a social interaction in which one person (the hypnotist) suggests to another (the subject) that certain perceptions, feelings, thoughts, or behaviors will spontaneously occur.

hypothalamus [hi-po-THAL-uh-muss] a neural structure lying below (hypo) the thalamus; it directs several maintenance activities (eating, drinking, body temperature), helps govern the endocrine system via the pituitary gland, and is linked to emotion.

hypothesis a testable prediction, often implied by a theory.

iconic memory a momentary sensory memory of visual stimuli; a photographic or picture-image memory lasting no more than a few tenths of a second.

id contains a reservoir of unconscious psychic energy that, according to Freud, strives to satisfy basic sexual and aggressive drives. The id operates on the pleasure principle, demanding immediate gratification.

identical twins twins who develop from a single fertilized egg that splits in two, creating two genetically identical organisms.

identification the process by which, according to Freud, children incorporate their parents' values into their developing superegos.

identity one's sense of self; according to Erikson, the adolescent's task is to solidify a sense of self by testing and integrating various roles.

illusory correlation the perception of a relationship where none exists.

imagery mental pictures; a powerful aid to effortful processing, especially when combined with semantic encoding.

implicit memory retention independent of conscious recollection. (Also called *procedural memory*.)

imprinting the process by which certain animals form attachments during a critical period very early in life.

inattentional blindness failing to see visible objects when our attention is directed elsewhere.

incentive a positive or negative environmental stimulus that motivates behavior.

independent variable the experimental factor that is manipulated; the variable whose effect is being studied.

individualism giving priority to one's own goals over group goals, and defining one's identity in terms of personal attributes rather than group identifications.

industrial-organizational (I/O) psychology the application of psychological concepts and methods to optimizing human behavior in workplaces.

informational social influence influence resulting from one's willingness to accept others' opinions about reality.

ingroup "Us"—people with whom one shares a common identity.

ingroup bias the tendency to favor one's own group.

inner ear the innermost part of the ear, containing the cochlea, semicircular canals, and vestibular sacs

insight a sudden and often novel realization of the solution to a problem; it contrasts with strategy-based solutions.

insomnia recurring problems in falling or staying asleep.

instinct a complex behavior that is rigidly patterned throughout a species and is unlearned.

intelligence mental quality consisting of the ability to learn from experience, solve problems, and use knowledge to adapt to new situations.

intelligence quotient (IQ) defined originally as the ratio of mental age (*ma*) to chronological age (*ca*) multiplied by 100 (thus, IQ = *ma*/*ca* × 100). On contemporary intelligence tests, the average performance for a given age is assigned a score of 100.

intelligence test a method for assessing an individual's mental aptitudes and comparing them with those of others, using numerical scores.

intensity the amount of energy in a light or sound wave, which we perceive as brightness or loudness, as determined by the wave's amplitude.

interaction the effect of one factor (such as environment) depends on another factor (such as heredity).

internal locus of control the perception that one controls one's own fate.

interneurons central nervous system neurons that internally communicate and intervene between the sensory inputs and motor outputs.

interpretation in psychoanalysis, the analyst's noting supposed dream meanings, resistances, and other significant behaviors and events in order to promote insight.

intimacy in Erikson's theory, the ability to form close, loving relationships; a primary developmental task in late adolescence and early adulthood.

intrinsic motivation a desire to perform a behavior for its own sake.

iris a ring of muscle tissue that forms the colored portion of the eye around the pupil and controls the size of the pupil opening.

James-Lange theory the theory that our experience of emotion is our awareness of our physiological responses to emotion-arousing stimuli.

just-world phenomenon the tendency of people to believe the world is just and that people therefore get what they deserve and deserve what they get.

kinesthesis [kin-ehs-THEE-sehs] the system for sensing the position and movement of individual body parts.

language our spoken, written, or signed words and the ways we combine them to communicate meaning.

latent content according to Freud, the underlying meaning of a dream (as distinct from its manifest content). Freud believed that a dream's latent content functions as a safety valve.

latent learning learning that occurs but is not apparent until there is an incentive to demonstrate it.

law of effect Thorndike's principle that behaviors followed by favorable consequences become more likely, and that behaviors followed by unfavorable consequences become less likely.

learned helplessness the hopelessness and passive resignation an animal or human learns when unable to avoid repeated aversive events.

learning a relatively permanent change in an organism's behavior due to experience.

lens the transparent structure behind the pupil that changes shape to help focus images on the retina.

lesion [LEE-zhuhn] tissue destruction. A brain lesion is a naturally or experimentally caused destruction of brain tissue.

levels of analysis the differing complementary views, from biological to psychological to social-cultural, for analyzing any given phenomenon.

limbic system a doughnut-shaped system of neural structures at the border of the brainstem and cerebral hemispheres; associated with emotions such as fear and aggression and drives such as those for food and sex. Includes the hippocampus, amygdala, and hypothalamus.

linguistic determinism Whorf's hypothesis that language determines the way we think.

lobotomy a now-rare psychosurgical procedure once used to calm uncontrollably emotional or violent patients. The procedure cut the nerves that connect the frontal lobes to the emotion-controlling centers of the inner brain.

long-term memory the relatively permanent and limitless storehouse of the memory system. Includes knowledge, skills, and experiences.

long-term potentiation (LTP) an increase in a synapse's firing potential after brief, rapid stimulation. Believed to be a neural basis for learning and memory.

longitudinal study research in which the same people are restudied and retested over a long period.

LSD a powerful hallucinogenic drug; also known as *acid* (*lysergic acid diethylamide*).

lymphocytes the two types of white blood cells that are part of the body's immune system: *B lymphocytes* form in the *bone marrow* and release antibodies that fight bacterial infections; *T lymphocytes* form in the *thymus* and other lymphatic tissue and attack cancer cells, viruses, and foreign substances.

major depressive disorder a mood disorder in which a person experiences, in the absence of drugs or a medical condition, two or more weeks of significantly depressed moods, feelings of worthlessness, and diminished interest or pleasure in most activities.

mania a mood disorder marked by a hyperactive, wildly optimistic state.

manifest content according to Freud, the remembered story line of a dream (as distinct from its latent, or hidden, content).

maturation biological growth processes that enable orderly changes in behavior, relatively uninfluenced by experience.

mean the arithmetic average of a distribution, obtained by adding the scores and then dividing by the number of scores.

median the middle score in a distribution; half the scores are above it and half are below it.

medical model the concept that diseases have physical causes that can be diagnosed, treated, and, in most cases, cured. When applied to psychological disorders, the medical model assumes that these *mental illnesses* can be diagnosed on the basis of their symptoms and cured through therapy, which may include treatment in a psychiatric hospital.

medulla [muh-DUL-uh] the base of the brainstem; controls heartbeat and breathing.

memory the persistence of learning over time through the storage and retrieval of information.

menarche [meh-NAR-key] the first menstrual period.

menopause the time of natural cessation of menstruation; also refers to the biological changes a woman experiences as her ability to reproduce declines.

mental age a measure of intelligence test performance devised by Binet; the chronological age that most typically corresponds to a given level of performance. Thus, a child who does as well as the average 8-year-old is said to have a mental age of 8.

mental retardation a condition of limited mental ability, indicated by an intelligence score of 70 or below and difficulty in adapting to the demands of life; varies from mild to profound.

mental set a tendency to approach a problem in a particular way, often a way that has been successful in the past.

mere exposure effect the phenomenon that repeated exposure to novel stimuli increases liking of them.

meta-analysis a procedure for statistically combining the results of many different research studies.

methamphetamine a powerfully addictive drug that stimulates the central nervous system, with speeded-up body functions and associated energy and mood changes; over time, appears to reduce baseline dopamine levels.

middle ear the chamber between the eardrum and cochlea containing three tiny bones (hammer, anvil, and stirrup) that concentrate the vibrations of the eardrum on the cochlea's oval window.

Minnesota Multiphasic Personality Inventory (MMPI) the most widely researched and clinically used of all personality tests. Originally developed to identify emotional disorders (still considered its most appropriate use), this test is now used for many other screening purposes.

mirror neurons frontal lobe neurons that fire when performing certain actions or when observing another doing so. The brain's mirroring of another's action may enable imitation, language learning, and empathy.

misinformation effect incorporating misleading information into one's memory of an event.

mnemonics [nih-MON-iks] memory aids, especially those techniques that use vivid imagery and organizational devices.

mode the most frequently occurring score(s) in a distribution.

modeling the process of observing and imitating a specific behavior.

molecular genetics the subfield of biology that studies the molecular structure and function of genes.

monism the presumption that mind and body are different aspects of the same thing.

monocular cues depth cues, such as interposition and linear perspective, available to either eye alone.

mood-congruent memory the tendency to recall experiences that are consistent with one's current good or bad mood.

mood disorders psychological disorders characterized by emotional extremes. See *major depressive disorder, mania,* and *bipolar disorder.*

morpheme in a language, the smallest unit that carries meaning; may be a word or a part of a word (such as a prefix).

motivation a need or desire that energizes and directs behavior.

motor cortex an area at the rear of the frontal lobes that controls voluntary movements.

motor neurons neurons that carry outgoing information from the central nervous system to the muscles and glands.

MRI (magnetic resonance imaging) a technique that uses magnetic fields and radio waves to produce computer-generated images that distinguish among different types of soft tissue; allows us to see structures within the brain.

mutation a random error in gene replication that leads to a change.

myelin [MY-uh-lin] **sheath** a layer of fatty tissue segmentally encasing the fibers of many neurons; enables vastly greater transmission speed of neural impulses as the impulse hops from one node to the next.

narcolepsy a sleep disorder characterized by uncontrollable sleep attacks. The sufferer may lapse directly into REM sleep, often at inopportune times.

natural selection the principle that, among the range of inherited trait variations, those that lead to increased reproduction and survival will most likely be passed on to succeeding generations.

naturalistic observation observing and recording behavior in naturally occurring situations without trying to manipulate and control the situation.

nature-nurture issue the longstanding controversy over the relative contributions that genes and experience make to the development of psychological traits and behaviors.

near-death experience an altered state of consciousness reported after a close brush with death (such as through cardiac arrest); often similar to drug-induced hallucinations.

nearsightedness a condition in which nearby objects are seen more clearly than distant objects because distant objects focus in front of the retina.

negative reinforcement increasing behaviors by stopping or reducing negative stimuli, such as shock. A negative reinforcer is any stimulus that, when *removed* after a response, strengthens the response. (*Note:* Negative reinforcement is *not* punishment.)

nerves neural "cables" containing many axons. These bundled axons, which are part of the peripheral nervous system, connect the central nervous system with muscles, glands, and sense organs.

nervous system the body's speedy, electrochemical communication network, consisting of all the nerve cells of the peripheral and central nervous systems.

neural networks interconnected neural cells. With experience, networks can learn, as feedback strengthens or inhibits connections that produce certain results. Computer simulations of neural networks show analogous learning.

neuron a nerve cell; the basic building block of the nervous system.

neurotransmitters chemical messengers that traverse the synaptic gaps between neurons. When released by the sending neuron, neurotransmitters travel across the synapse and bind to receptor sites on the receiving neuron, thereby influencing whether that neuron will generate a neural impulse.

night terrors a sleep disorder characterized by high arousal and an appearance of being terrified; unlike nightmares, night terrors occur during Stage 4 sleep, within two or three hours of falling asleep, and are seldom remembered.

norm an understood rule for accepted and expected behavior. Norms prescribe "proper" behavior.

normal curve the symmetrical bell-shaped curve that describes the distribution of many physical and psychological attributes. Most scores fall near the average, and fewer and fewer scores lie near the extremes.

normative social influence influence resulting from a person's desire to gain approval or avoid disapproval.

object permanence the awareness that things continue to exist even when not perceived.

observational learning learning by observing others.

obsessive-compulsive disorder (OCD) an anxiety disorder characterized by unwanted repetitive thoughts (obsessions) and/or actions (compulsions).

occipital [ahk-SIP-uh-tuhl] **lobes** the portion of the cerebral cortex lying at the back of the head; includes the visual areas, which receive visual information from the opposite visual field.

Oedipus [ED-uh-puss] **complex** according to Freud, a boy's sexual desires toward his mother and feelings of jealousy and hatred for the rival father.

one-word stage the stage in speech development, from about age 1 to 2, during which a child speaks mostly in single words.

operant behavior behavior that operates on the environment, producing consequences.

operant chamber a chamber also known as a *Skinner box*, containing a bar or key that an animal can manipulate to obtain a food or water reinforcer, with attached devices to record the animal's rate of bar pressing or key pecking. Used in operant conditioning research.

operant conditioning a type of learning in which behavior is strengthened if followed by a reinforcer or diminished if followed by a punisher.

operational definition a statement of the procedures (operations) used to define research variables. For example, *human intelligence* may be operationally defined as what an intelligence test measures.

opiates opium and its derivatives, such as morphine and heroin; they depress neural activity, temporarily lessening pain and anxiety.

opponent-process theory the theory that opposing retinal processes (red-green, yellow-blue, white-black) enable color vision. For example, some cells are stimulated by green and inhibited by red; others are stimulated by red and inhibited by green.

optic nerve the nerve that carries neural impulses from the eye to the brain.

organizational psychology a subfield of I/O psychology that examines organizational influences on worker satisfaction and productivity and facilitates organizational change.

outgroup "Them"—those perceived as different or apart from one's ingroup.

overconfidence the tendency to be more confident than correct—to overestimate the accuracy of one's beliefs and judgments.

panic disorder an anxiety disorder marked by unpredictable minutes-long episodes of intense dread in which a person experiences terror and accompanying chest pain, choking, or other frightening sensations.

parallel processing the processing of several aspects of a problem simultaneously; the brain's natural mode of information processing for many functions, including vision. Contrasts with the step-by-step (serial) processing of most computers and of conscious problem solving.

parapsychology the study of paranormal phenomena, including ESP and psychokinesis.

parasympathetic nervous system the division of the autonomic nervous system that calms the body, conserving its energy.

parietal [puh-RYE-uh-tuhl] **lobes** the portion of the cerebral cortex lying at the top of the head and toward the rear; receives sensory input for touch and body position.

partial (intermittent) reinforcement reinforcing a response only part of the time; results in slower acquisition of a response but much greater resistance to extinction than does continuous reinforcement.

passionate love an aroused state of intense positive absorption in another, usually present at the beginning of a love relationship.

perception the process of organizing and interpreting sensory information, enabling us to recognize meaningful objects and events.

perceptual adaptation in vision, the ability to adjust to an artificially displaced or even inverted visual field.

perceptual constancy perceiving objects as unchanging (having consistent lightness, color, shape, and size) even as illumination and retinal images change.

perceptual set a mental predisposition to perceive one thing and not another.

peripheral nervous system (PNS) the sensory and motor neurons that connect the central nervous system (CNS) to the rest of the body.

personal control our sense of controlling our environment rather than feeling helpless.

personal space the buffer zone we like to maintain around our bodies.

personality an individual's characteristic pattern of thinking, feeling, and acting.

personality disorders psychological disorders characterized by inflexible and enduring behavior patterns that impair social functioning.

personality inventory a questionnaire (often with true-false or agree-disagree items) on which people respond to items designed to gauge a wide range of feelings and behaviors; used to assess selected personality traits.

personnel psychology a subfield of I/O psychology that focuses on employee recruitment, selection, placement, training, appraisal, and development.

PET (positron emission tomography) scan a visual display of brain activity that detects where a radioactive form of glucose goes while the brain performs a given task.

phi phenomenon an illusion of movement created when two or more adjacent lights blink on and off in quick succession.

phobia an anxiety disorder marked by a persistent, irrational fear and avoidance of a specific object or situation.

phoneme in a language, the smallest distinctive sound unit.

physical dependence a physiological need for a drug, marked by unpleasant withdrawal symptoms when the drug is discontinued.

pitch a tone's experienced highness or lowness; depends on frequency.

pituitary gland the endocrine system's most influential gland. Under the influence of the hypothalamus, the pituitary regulates growth and controls other endocrine glands.

place theory in hearing, the theory that links the pitch we hear with the place where the cochlea's membrane is stimulated.

placebo [pluh-SEE-bo; Latin for "I shall please"] **effect** experimental results caused by expectations alone; any effect on behavior caused by the administration of an inert substance or condition, which is assumed to be an active agent.

plasticity the brain's capacity for modification, as evident in brain reorganization following damage (especially in children) and in experiments on the effects of experience on brain development.

polygraph a machine, commonly used in attempts to detect lies, that measures several of the physiological responses accompanying emotion (such as perspiration and cardiovascular and breathing changes).

population all the cases in a group, from which samples may be drawn for a study. (*Note:* Except for national studies, this does not refer to a country's whole population.)

positive psychology the scientific study of optimal human functioning; aims to discover and promote strengths and virtues that enable individuals and communities to thrive.

positive reinforcement increasing behaviors by presenting positive stimuli, such as food. A positive reinforcer is any stimulus that, when *presented* after a response, strengthens the response.

post-traumatic stress disorder (PTSD) an anxiety disorder characterized by haunting memories, nightmares, social withdrawal, jumpy anxiety, and/or insomnia that lingers for four weeks or more after a traumatic experience.

posthypnotic suggestion a suggestion, made during a hypnosis session, to be carried out after the subject is no longer hypnotized; used by some clinicians to help control undesired symptoms and behaviors.

predictive validity the success with which a test predicts the behavior it is designed to predict; it is assessed by computing the correlation between test scores and the criterion behavior. (Also called *criterion-related validity.*)

prejudice an unjustifiable (and usually negative) attitude toward a group and its members. Prejudice generally involves stereotyped beliefs, negative feelings, and a predisposition to discriminatory action.

preoperational stage in Piaget's theory, the stage (from about 2 to 6 or 7 years of age) during which a child learns to use language but does not yet comprehend the mental operations of concrete logic.

primary reinforcer an innately reinforcing stimulus, such as one that satisfies a biological need.

primary sex characteristics the body structures (ovaries, testes, and external genitalia) that make sexual reproduction possible.

priming the activation, often unconsciously, of certain associations, thus predisposing one's perception, memory, or response.

proactive interference the disruptive effect of prior learning on the recall of new information.

problem-focused coping attempting to alleviate stress directly—by changing the stressor or the way we interact with that stressor.

projection psychoanalytic defense mechanism by which people disguise their own threatening impulses by attributing them to others.

projective test a personality test, such as the Rorschach or TAT, that provides ambiguous stimuli designed to trigger projection of one's inner dynamics.

prosocial behavior positive, constructive, helpful behavior. The opposite of antisocial behavior.

prototype a mental image or best example of a category. Matching new items to the prototype provides a quick and easy method for including items in a category (as when comparing feathered creatures to a prototypical bird, such as a robin).

psychiatry a branch of medicine dealing with psychological disorders; practiced by physicians who sometimes provide medical (for example, drug) treatments as well as psychological therapy.

psychoactive drug a chemical substance that alters perceptions and mood.

psychoanalysis Freud's theory of personality and therapeutic technique that attributes thoughts and actions to unconscious motives and conflicts. Freud believed the patient's free associations, resistances, dreams, and transferences—and the therapist's interpretations of them—released previously repressed feelings, allowing the patient to gain self-insight.

psychological dependence a psychological need to use a drug, such as to relieve negative emotions.

psychological disorder deviant, distressful, and dysfunctional behavior patterns.

psychology the scientific study of behavior and mental processes.

psychopharmacology the study of the effects of drugs on mind and behavior.

psychophysics the study of relationships between the physical characteristics of stimuli, such as their intensity, and our psychological experience of them.

psychophysiological illness literally, "mind-body" illness; any stress-related physical illness, such as hypertension and some headaches. *Note:* This is distinct from *hypochondriasis*—misinterpreting normal physical sensations as symptoms of a disease.

psychosexual stages the childhood stages of development (oral, anal, phallic, latency, genital) during which, according to Freud, the id's pleasure-seeking energies focus on distinct erogenous zones.

psychosurgery surgery that removes or destroys brain tissue in an effort to change behavior.

psychotherapy an emotionally charged, confiding interaction between a trained therapist and someone who suffers from psychological difficulties.

puberty the period of sexual maturation, during which a person becomes capable of reproducing.

punishment an event that *decreases* the behavior that it follows.

pupil the adjustable opening in the center of the eye through which light enters.

random assignment assigning participants to experimental and control conditions by chance, thus minimizing preexisting differences between those assigned to the different groups.

random sample a sample that fairly represents a population because each member has an equal chance of inclusion.

range the difference between the highest and lowest scores in a distribution.

rationalization defense mechanism that offers self-justifying explanations in place of the real, more threatening, unconscious reasons for one's actions.

reaction formation psychoanalytic defense mechanism by which the ego unconsciously switches unacceptable impulses into their opposites. Thus, people may express feelings that are the opposite of their anxiety-arousing unconscious feelings.

recall a measure of memory in which the person must retrieve information learned earlier, as on a fill-in-the-blank test.

reciprocal determinism the interacting influences between personality and environmental factors.

reciprocity norm an expectation that people will help, not hurt, those who have helped them.

recognition a measure of memory in which the person need only identify items previously learned, as on a multiple-choice test.

reflex a simple, automatic, inborn response to a sensory stimulus, such as the knee-jerk response.

refractory period a resting period after orgasm, during which a man cannot achieve another orgasm.

regression psychoanalytic defense mechanism in which an individual faced with anxiety retreats to a more infantile psychosexual stage, where some psychic energy remains fixated.

regression toward the mean the tendency for extremes of unusual scores to fall back (regress) toward their average.

rehearsal the conscious repetition of information, either to maintain it in consciousness or to encode it for storage.

reinforcer in operant conditioning, any event that *strengthens* the behavior it follows.

relative deprivation the perception that one is worse off relative to those with whom one compares oneself.

relearning a memory measure that assesses the amount of time saved when learning material for a second time.

reliability the extent to which a test yields consistent results, as assessed by the consistency of scores on two halves of the test, on alternate forms of the test, or on retesting.

REM rebound the tendency for REM sleep to increase following REM sleep deprivation (created by repeated awakenings during REM sleep).

REM sleep rapid eye movement sleep, a recurring sleep stage during which vivid dreams commonly occur. Also known as *paradoxical sleep,* because the muscles are relaxed (except for minor twitches) but other body systems are active.

repetitive transcranial magnetic stimulation (rTMS) the application of repeated pulses of magnetic energy to the brain; used to stimulate or suppress brain activity.

replication repeating the essence of a research study, usually with different participants in different situations, to see whether the basic finding extends to other participants and circumstances.

representativeness heuristic judging the likelihood of things in terms of how well they seem to represent, or match, particular prototypes; may lead one to ignore other relevant information.

repression in psychoanalytic theory, the basic defense mechanism that banishes anxiety-arousing thoughts, feelings, and memories from consciousness.

resistance in psychoanalysis, the blocking from consciousness of anxiety-laden material.

respondent behavior behavior that occurs as an automatic response to some stimulus; Skinner's term for behavior learned through classical conditioning.

reticular formation a nerve network in the brainstem that plays an important role in controlling arousal.

retina the light-sensitive inner surface of the eye, containing the receptor rods and cones plus layers of neurons that begin the processing of visual information.

retinal disparity a binocular cue for perceiving depth: By comparing images from the two eyeballs, the brain computes distance—the greater the disparity (difference) between the two images, the closer the object.

retrieval the process of getting information out of memory storage.

retroactive interference the disruptive effect of new learning on the recall of old information.

rods retinal receptors that detect black, white, and gray; necessary for peripheral and twilight vision, when cones don't respond.

role a set of expectations (norms) about a social position, defining how those in the position ought to behave.

rooting reflex a baby's tendency, when touched on the cheek, to turn toward the touch, open the mouth, and search for the nipple.

Rorschach inkblot test the most widely used projective test, a set of 10 inkblots, designed by Hermann Rorschach; seeks to identify people's inner feelings by analyzing their interpretations of the blots.

savant syndrome a condition in which a person otherwise limited in mental ability has an exceptional specific skill, such as in computation or drawing.

scapegoat theory the theory that prejudice offers an outlet for anger by providing someone to blame.

scatterplot a graphed cluster of dots, each of which represents the values of two variables. The slope of the points suggests the direction of the relationship between the two variables. The amount of scatter suggests the strength of the correlation (little scatter indicates high correlation). (Also called a *scattergram* or *scatter diagram*.)

schema a concept or framework that organizes and interprets information.

schizophrenia a group of severe disorders characterized by disorganized and delusional thinking, disturbed perceptions, and inappropriate emotions and actions.

secondary sex characteristics nonreproductive sexual characteristics, such as female breasts and hips, male voice quality, and body hair.

selective attention the focusing of conscious awareness on a particular stimulus, as in the cocktail party effect.

self-actualization according to Maslow, the ultimate psychological need that arises after basic physical and psychological needs are met and self-esteem is achieved; the motivation to fulfill one's potential.

self-concept (1) a sense of one's identity and personal worth. (2) all our thoughts and feelings about ourselves, in answer to the question, "Who am I?"

self-disclosure revealing intimate aspects of oneself to others.

self-esteem one's feelings of high or low self-worth.

self-serving bias a readiness to perceive oneself favorably

semantic encoding the encoding of meaning, including the meaning of words.

semantics the set of rules by which we derive meaning from morphemes, words, and sentences in a given language; also, the study of meaning.

sensation the process by which our sensory receptors and nervous system receive and represent stimulus energies from our environment.

sensorimotor stage in Piaget's theory, the stage (from birth to about 2 years of age) during which infants know the world mostly in terms of their sensory impressions and motor activities.

sensorineural hearing loss hearing loss caused by damage to the cochlea's receptor cells or to the auditory nerves; also called *nerve deafness*.

sensory adaptation diminished sensitivity as a consequence of constant stimulation.

sensory cortex the area at the front of the parietal lobes that registers and processes body touch and movement sensations.

sensory interaction the principle that one sense may influence another, as when the smell of food influences its taste.

sensory memory the immediate, very brieg recording of sensory information in the memory system.

sensory neurons neurons that carry incoming information from the sense receptors to the central nervous system.

serial position effect our tendency to recall best the last and first items in a list.

set point the point at which an individual's "weight thermostat" is supposedly set. When the body falls below this weight, an increase in hunger and a lowered metabolic rate may act to restore the lost weight.

sexual disorder a problem that consistently impairs sexual arousal or functioning.

sexual orientation an enduring sexual attraction toward members of either one's own sex (homosexual orientation) or the other sex (heterosexual orientation).

sexual response cycle the four stages of sexual responding described by Masters and Johnson—excitement, plateau, orgasm, and resolution.

shaping an operant conditioning procedure in which reinforcers guide behavior toward closer and closer approximations of the desired behavior.

short-term memory activated memory that holds a few items briefly, such as the seven digits of a phone number while dialing, before the information is stored or forgotten.

signal detection theory a theory predicting how and when we detect the presence of a faint stimulus ("signal") amid background stimulation ("noise"). Assumes there is no single absolute threshold and detection depends partly on a person's experience, expectations, motivation, and level of fatigue.

sleep periodic, natural, reversible loss of consciousness—as distinct from unconsciousness resulting from a coma, general anesthesia, or hibernation. (Adapted from Dement, 1999.)

sleep apnea a sleep disorder characterized by temporary cessations of breathing during sleep and repeated momentary awakenings.

social-cognitive perspective views behavior as influenced by the interaction between persons (and their thinking) and their social context.

social-responsibility norm an expectation that people will help those dependent upon them.

social clock the culturally preferred timing of social events such as marriage, parenthood, and retirement.

social exchange theory the theory that our social behavior is an exchange process, the aim of which is to maximize benefits and minimize costs.

social facilitation stronger responses on simple or well-learned tasks in the presence of others.

social leadership group-oriented leadership that builds teamwork, mediates conflict, and offers support.

social learning theory the theory that we learn social behavior by observing and imitating and by being rewarded or punished.

social loafing the tendency for people in a group to exert less effort when pooling their efforts toward attaining a common goal than when individually accountable.

social psychology the scientific study of how we think about, influence, and relate to one another.

social trap a situation in which the conflicting parties, by each rationally pursuing their self-interest, become caught in mutually destructive behavior.

somatic nervous system the division of the peripheral nervous system that controls the body's skeletal muscles. Also called the *skeletal nervous system.*

source amnesia attributing to the wrong source an event we have experienced, heard about, read about, or imagined. (Also called *source misattribution.*) Source amnesia, along with the misinformation effect, is at the heart of many false memories.

spacing effect the tendency for distributed study or practice to yield better long-term retention than is achieved through massed study or practice.

split brain a condition in which the two hemispheres of the brain are isolated by cutting the connecting fibers (mainly those of the corpus callosum) between them.

spontaneous recovery the reappearance, after a pause, of an extinguished conditioned response.

spotlight effect overestimating others' noticing and evaluating our appearance, performance, and blunders (as if we presume a spotlight shines on us).

standard deviation a computed measure of how much scores vary around the mean score.

standardization defining meaningful scores by comparison with the performance of a pretested standardization group.

Stanford-Binet the widely used American revision (by Terman at Stanford University) of Binet's original intelligence test.

statistical significance a statistical statement of how likely it is that an obtained result occurred by chance.

stereotype a generalized (sometimes accurate but often overgeneralized) belief about a group of people.

stereotype threat a self-confirming concern that one will be evaluated based on a negative stereotype.

stimulants drugs (such as caffeine, nicotine, and the more powerful amphetamines, cocaine, and Ecstasy) that excite neural activity and speed up body functions.

storage the retention of encoded information over time.

stranger anxiety the fear of strangers that infants commonly display, beginning by about 8 months of age.

structuralism an early school of psychology that used introspection to explore the elemental structure of the human mind.

stress the process by which we perceive and respond to certain events, called *stressors*, that we appraise as threatening or challenging.

structured interviews interview process that asks the same job-relevant questions of all applicants, each of whom is rated on established scales.

subjective well-being self-perceived happiness or satisfaction with life. Used along with measures of objective well-being (for example, physical and economic indicators) to evaluate people's quality of life.

subliminal below one's absolute threshold for conscious awareness.

superego the part of personality that, according to Freud, represents internalized ideals and provides standards for judgment (the conscience) and for future aspirations.

superordinate goals shared goals that override differences among people and require their cooperation.

survey a technique for ascertaining the self-reported attitudes or behaviors of people, usually by questioning a representative, random sample of them.

sympathetic nervous system the division of the autonomic nervous system that arouses the body, mobilizing its energy in stressful situations.

synapse [SIN-aps] the junction between the axon tip of the sending neuron and the dendrite or cell body of the receiving neuron. The tiny gap at this junction is called the *synaptic gap* or *cleft.*

syntax the rules for combining words into grammatically sensible sentences in a given language.

systematic desensitization a type of counterconditioning that associates a pleasant relaxed state with gradually increasing anxiety-triggering stimuli. Commonly used to treat phobias.

tardive dyskinesia involuntary movements of the facial muscles, tongue, and limbs; a possible neurotoxic side effect of long-term use of antipsychotic drugs that target D2 dopamine receptors.

task leadership goal-oriented leadership that sets standards, organizes work, and focuses attention on goals.

telegraphic speech early speech stage in which a child speaks like a telegram—"go car"—using mostly nouns and verbs and omitting auxiliary words.

temperament a person's characteristic emotional reactivity and intensity.

temporal lobes the portion of the cerebral cortex lying roughly above the ears; includes the auditory areas, each of which receives auditory information primarily from the opposite ear.

teratogens agents, such as chemicals and viruses, that can reach the embryo or fetus during prenatal development and cause harm.

terror-management theory proposes that faith in one's worldview and the pursuit of self-esteem provide protection against a deeply rooted fear of death.

testosterone the most important of the male sex hormones. Both males and females have it, but the additional testosterone in males stimulates the growth of the male sex organs in the fetus and the development of the male sex characteristics during puberty.

thalamus [THAL-uh-muss] the brain's sensory switchboard, located on top of the brainstem; it directs messages to the sensory receiving areas in the cortex and transmits replies to the cerebellum and medulla.

THC the major active ingredient in marijuana; triggers a variety of effects, including mild hallucinations.

Thematic Apperception Test (TAT) a projective test in which people express their inner feelings and interests through the stories they make up about ambiguous scenes.

theory an explanation using an integrated set of principles that organizes and predicts observations.

theory of mind people's ideas about their own and others' mental states—about their feelings, perceptions, and thoughts and the behavior these might predict.

threshold the level of stimulation required to trigger a neural impulse.

token economy an operant conditioning procedure in which people earn a token of some sort for exhibiting a desired behavior and can later exchange the tokens for various privileges or treats.

tolerance the diminishing effect with regular use of the same dose of a drug, requiring the user to take larger and larger doses before experiencing the drug's effect.

top-down processing information processing guided by higher-level mental processes, as when we construct perceptions drawing on our experience and expectations.

trait a characteristic pattern of behavior or a disposition to feel and act, as assessed by self-report inventories and peer reports.

transduction conversion of one form of energy into another. In sensation, the transforming of stimulus energies, such as sights, sounds, and smells, into neural impulses our brains can interpret.

transference in psychoanalysis, the patient's transfer to the analyst of emotions linked with other relationships (such as love or hatred for a parent).

two-factor theory Schachter-Singer's theory that to experience emotion one must (1) be physically aroused and (2) cognitively label the arousal.

two-word stage beginning about age 2, the stage in speech development during which a child speaks mostly two-word statements.

Type A Friedman and Rosenman's term for competitive, hard-driving, impatient, verbally aggressive, and anger-prone people.

Type B Friedman and Rosenman's term for easygoing, relaxed people.

unconditional positive regard according to Rogers, an attitude of total acceptance toward another person.

unconditioned response (UR) in classical conditioning, the unlearned, naturally occurring response to the unconditioned stimulus (US), such as salivation when food is in the mouth.

unconditioned stimulus (US) in classical conditioning, a stimulus that unconditionally—naturally and automatically—triggers a response.

unconscious according to Freud, a reservoir of mostly unacceptable thoughts, wishes, feelings, and memories. According to contemporary psychologists, information processing of which we are unaware.

validity the extent to which a test measures or predicts what it is supposed to. (See also *content validity* and *predictive validity*.)

variable-interval schedule in operant conditioning, a reinforcement schedule that reinforces a response at unpredictable time intervals.

variable-ratio schedule in operant conditioning, a reinforcement schedule that reinforces a response after an unpredictable number of responses.

vestibular sense the sense of body movement and position, including the sense of balance.

virtual reality exposure therapy An anxiety treatment that progressively exposes people to simulations of their greatest fears, such as airplane flying, spiders, or public speaking.

visual capture the tendency for vision to dominate the other senses.

visual cliff a laboratory device for testing depth perception in infants and young animals.

visual encoding the encoding of picture images.

wavelength the distance from the peak of one light or sound wave to the peak of the next. Electromagnetic wavelengths vary from the short blips of cosmic rays to the long pulses of radio transmission.

Weber's law the principle that, to be perceived as different, two stimuli must differ by a constant minimum percentage (rather than a constant amount).

Wechsler Adult Intelligence Scale (WAIS) the WAIS is the most widely used intelligence test; contains verbal and performance (nonverbal) subtests.

Wernicke's area controls language reception—a brain area involved in language comprehension and expression; usually in the left temporal lobe.

withdrawal the discomfort and distress that follow discontinuing the use of an addictive drug.

working memory a newer understanding of short-term memory that involves conscious, active processing of incoming auditory and visual-spatial information, and of information retrieved from long-term memory.

X chromosome the sex chromosome found in both men and women. Females have two X chromosomes; males have one. An X chromosome from each parent produces a female child.

Y chromosome the sex chromosome found only in males. When paired with an X chromosome from the mother, it produces a male child.

Young-Helmholtz trichromatic (three-color) theory the theory that the retina contains three different color receptors—one most sensitive to red, one to green, one to blue—which when stimulated in combination can produce the perception of any color.

zygote the fertilized egg; it enters a 2-week period of rapid cell division and develops into an embryo.

References

Aas, H., & Klepp, K-I. (1992). Adolescents' alcohol use related to perceived norms. *Scandinavian Journal of Psychology, 33,* 315–325.

Abbey, A. (1987). Misperceptions of friendly behavior as sexual interest: A survey of naturally occurring incidents. *Psychology of Women Quarterly, 11,* 173–194.

Abbey, A. (1991). Acquaintance rape and alcohol consumption on college campuses: How are they linked? *Journal of American College Health, 39,* 165–169.

Abbott, R. D., White, L. R., Ross, G. W., Masaki, K. H., Curb, J. D., & Petrovitch, H. (2004). Walking and dementia in physically capable elderly men. *Journal of the American Medical Association, 292,* 1447–1453.

Abrams, D. (1991). AIDS: What young people believe and what they do. Paper presented at the British Association for the Advancement of Science conference.

Abrams, D. B., & Wilson, G. T. (1983). Alcohol, sexual arousal, and self-control. *Journal of Personality and Social Psychology, 45,* 188–198.

Abrams, M. (2002, June). Sight unseen—Restoring a blind man's vision is now a real possibility through stem-cell surgery. But even perfect eyes cannot see unless the brain has been taught to use them. *Discover, 23,* 54–60.

Abramson, L. Y., Metalsky, G. I., & Alloy, L. B. (1989). Hopelessness depression: A theory-based subtype. *Psychological Review, 96,* 358–372.

Ackerman, D. (2004). *An alchemy of mind: The marvel and mystery of the brain.* New York: Scribner.

Adelmann, P. K., Antonucci, T. C., Crohan, S. F., & Coleman, L. M. (1989). Empty nest, cohort, and employment in the well-being of midlife women. *Sex Roles, 20,* 173–189.

Adelson, R. (2004, August). Detecting deception. *APA Monitor,* pp. 70–73.

Ader, R., & Cohen, N. (1985). CNS-immune system interactions: Conditioning phenomena. *Behavioral and Brain Sciences, 8,* 379–394.

Adolphs, R., Tranel, D., & Damasio, A. R. (1998). The human amygdala in social judgment. *Nature, 393,* 470–474.

Affleck, G., Tennen, H., Urrows, S., & Higgins, P. (1994). Person and contextual features of daily stress reactivity: Individual differences in relations of undesirable daily events with mood disturbance and chronic pain intensity. *Journal of Personality and Social Psychology, 66,* 329–340.

Aggleton, J. P., Kentridge, R. W., & Neave, N. J. (1993). Evidence for longevity differences between left handed and right handed men: An archival study of cricketers. *Journal of Epidemiology and Community Health, 47,* 206–209.

Agid, O., Shapira, B., Zislin, J., Ritsner, M., Hanin, B., Murad, H., Troudart, T., Bloch, M., Heresco-Levy, U., & Lerer, B. (1999). Environment and vulnerability to major psychiatric illness: A case control study of early parental loss in major depression, bipolar disorder and schizophrenia. *Molecular Psychiatry, 4,* 163–172.

Agnati, L. F., Bjelke, B., & Fuxe, K. (1992). Volume transmission in the brain. *American Scientist, 80,* 362–373.

Aiello, J. R., Thompson, D. D., & Brodzinsky, D. M. (1983). How funny is crowding anyway? Effects of room size, group size, and the introduction of humor. *Basic and Applied Social Psychology, 4,* 193–207.

Ainsworth, M. D. S. (1973). The development of infant-mother attachment. In B. Caldwell & H. Ricciuti (Eds.), *Review of child development research* (Vol. 3). Chicago: University of Chicago Press.

Ainsworth, M. D. S. (1979). Infant-mother attachment. *American Psychologist, 34,* 932–937.

Ainsworth, M. D. S. (1989). Attachments beyond infancy. *American Psychologist, 44,* 709–716.

Albee, G. W. (1986). Toward a just society: Lessons from observations on the primary prevention of psychopathology. *American Psychologist, 41,* 891–898.

Albert, B., Brown, S., & Flanigan, C. M. (Eds.) (2003). *14 and younger: The sexual behavior of young adolescents.* Washington, DC: National Campaign to Prevent Teen Pregnancy.

Alcock, J. E. (1981). *Parapsychology: Science or magic?* Oxford: Pergamon.

Alcock, J. E. (1985, Spring). Parapsychology: The "spiritual" science. *Free Inquiry,* pp. 25–35.

Aldrich, M. S. (1989). Automobile accidents in patients with sleep disorders. *Sleep, 12,* 487–494.

Aldridge-Morris, R. (1989). *Multiple personality: An exercise in deception.* Hillsdale, NJ: Erlbaum.

Aleman, A., Kahn, R. S., & Selten, J-P. (2003). Sex differences in the risk of schizophrenia: Evidence from meta-analysis. *Archives of General Psychiatry, 60,* 565–571.

Alexander, C. N., Langer, E. J., Newman, R. I., Chandler, H. M., & Davies, J. L. (1989). Transcendental meditation, mindfulness, and longevity: An experimental study with the elderly. *Journal of Personality and Social Psychology, 57,* 950–964.

Alexander, K. W., Quas, J. A., Goodman, G. S., Ghetti, S., Edelstein, R. S., Redlich, A. D., Cordon, I. M., & Jones, D. P. H. (2005). Traumatic impact predicts long-term memory for documented child sexual abuse. *Psychological Science, 16,* 33–40.

Allard, F., & Burnett, N. (1985). Skill in sport. *Canadian Journal of Psychology, 39,* 294–312.

Allen, J. B., Repinski, D. J., Ballard, J. C., & Griffin, B. W. (1996). Beliefs about the etiology of homosexuality may influence attitudes toward homosexuals. Paper presented to the American Psychological Society convention.

Allen, K. (2003). Are pets a healthy pleasure? The influence of pets on blood pressure. *Current Directions in Psychological Science, 12,* 236–239.

Allen, L. S., & Gorski, R. A. (1992). Sexual orientation and the size of the anterior commisure in the human brain. *Proceedings of the National Academy of Sciences, 89,* 7199–7202.

Allen, N. B., & Badcock, P. B. T. (2003). The social risk hypothesis of depressed mood: Evolutionary, psychosocial, and neurobiological perspectives. *Psychological Bulletin, 129,* 887–913.

Alloy, L. B., Abramson, L. Y., Whitehouse, W. G., Hogan, M. E., Tashman, N. A., Steinberg, D. L., Rose, D. T., & Donovan, P. (1999). Depressogenic cognitive styles: Predictive validity, information processing and personality characteristics, and developmental origins. *Behaviour Research and Therapy, 37,* 503–531.

Allport, G. W. (1954). *The nature of prejudice.* New York: Addison-Wesley.

Allport, G. W. (1967). Gordon W. Allport. In E. G. Boring & G. Lindzey (Eds.), *A history of psychology in autobiography* (Vol. V). New York: Appleton-Century-Crofts.

Allport, G. W., & Odbert, H. S. (1936). Trait-names: A psycho-lexical study. *Psychological Monographs, 47*(1).

Altman, L. K. (2004, November 24). Female cases of HIV found rising worldwide. *New York Times* (www.nytimes.com).

Altmeyer, B. (2001). Changes in attitudes toward homosexuals. *Journal of Homosexuality, 42,* 63–75.

Alvarez, L. (2004, December 21). Therapy? or pills? A quandary in Britain. *New York Times* (www.nytimes.com).

Alwin, D. F. (1990). Historical changes in parental orientations to children. In N. Mandell (Ed.), *Sociological studies of child development* (Vol. 3). Greenwich, CT: JAI Press.

Amabile, T. M. (1983). *The social psychology of creativity.* New York: Springer-Verlag.

Amabile, T. M. (1987). The motivation to be creative. In S. Isaksen (Ed.), *Frontiers in creativity: Beyond the basics.* Buffalo, NY: Bearly Limited.

Amabile, T. M. (1988). From individual creativity to organizational innovation. In K. Gronhaug & G. Kaufmann (Eds.), *Innovation: A crossdisciplinary perspective.* Oslo: Norwegian University Press.

Amabile, T. M., & Hennessey, B. A. (1992). The motivation for creativity in children. In A. K. Boggiano & T. S. Pittman (Eds.), *Achievement and motivation: A social-developmental perspective.* New York: Cambridge University Press.

Ambadar, Z., Schooler, J. W., & Cohn, J. F. (2005). Deciphering the enigmatic face: The importance of facial dynamics in interpreting subtle facial expressions. *Psychological Science, 16,* 403–410.

Ambady, N., Hallahan, M., & Rosenthal, R. (1995). On judging and being judged accurately in zero-acquaintance situations. *Journal of Personality and Social Psychology, 69,* 518–529.

Ambady, N., LaPlante, D., Nguyen. T., Rosenthal, R., & Levinson, W. (2002). Surgeon's tone of voice: A clue to malpractice history. *Surgery, 132,* 5–9.

Ambady, N., & Rosenthal, R. (1992). Thin slices of expressive behavior as predictors of interpersonal consequences: A meta-analysis. *Psychological Bulletin, 111,* 256–274.

Ambady, N., & Rosenthal, R. (1993). Half a minute: Predicting teacher evaluations from thin slices of nonverbal behavior and physical attractiveness. *Journal of Personality and Social Psychology, 64,* 431–441.

Amedi, A., Floel, A., Knect, S., Zohary, E., & Cohen, L. (2004). Transcranial magnetic stimulation of the occipital pole interferes with verbal processing in blind subjects. *Nature Neuroscience, 7,* 1266–1270.

Amen, D. G., Stubblefield, M., Carmichael, B., & Thisted, R. (1996). Brain SPECT findings and aggressiveness. *Annals of Clinical Psychiatry, 8,* 129–137.

American Enterprise (1992, January/February). Women, men, marriages & ministers, p.106.

American Psychiatric Association. (1994). *Diagnostic and statistical manual of mental disorders (Fourth Edition).* Washington, DC: American Psychiatric Press.

American Psychological Association. (1991). Medical cost offset. Washington, DC: American Psychological Association Practice Directorate.

American Psychological Association. (1992). Ethical principles of psychologists and code of conduct. *American Psychologist, 47,* 1597–1611.

American Psychological Association. (2002). *Ethical principles of psychologists and code of conduct.* Washington, DC: American Psychological Association.

American Psychological Association. (2003). *Careers for the twenty-first century.* Washington, DC: Author.

American Psychological Association. (2004). Roper v. Simmons. Synopsis at http://www.apa.org/psyclaw/roper-v-simmons.html.

American Psychological Association. (2005). *Graduate study in psychology.* Washington, DC: Author.

Andersen, R. E., Crespo, C. J., Bartlett, S. J., Cheskin, L. J., & Pratt, M. (1998). Relationship of physical activity and television watching with body weight and level of fatness among children. *Journal of the American Medical Association, 279,* 938–942.

Andersen, S. M. (1998). Service Learning: A National Strategy for Youth Development. A position paper issued by the Task Force on Education Policy. Washington, DC: Institute for Communitarian Policy Studies, George Washington University.

Anderson, A. K., & Phelps, E. A. (2000). Expression without recognition: Contributions of the human amygdala to emotional communication. *Psychological Science, 11,* 106–111.

Anderson, B. L. (2002). Biobehavioral outcomes following psychological interventions for cancer patients. *Journal of Consulting and Clinical Psychology, 70,* 590–610.

Anderson, C. A. (2004). An update on the effects of playing violent video games. *Journal of Adolescence, 27,* 113–122.

Anderson, C. A., & Anderson, D. C. (1984). Ambient temperature and violent crime: Tests of the linear and curvilinear hypotheses. *Journal of Personality and Social Psychology, 46,* 91–97.

Anderson, C. A., Anderson, K. B., Dorr, N., DeNeve, K. M., & Flanagan, M. (2000). Temperature and aggression. In M. P. Zanna (Ed.), *Advances in Experimental Social Psychology.* San Diego: Academic Press.

Anderson, C. A., Berkowitz, L., Donnerstein, E., Huesmann, L. R., Johnson, J. D., Linz, D., Malamuth, N. M., & Wartella, E. (2003). The influence of media violence on youth. *Psychological Science in the Public Interest, 4*(3), 81–110.

Anderson, C. A., Carnagey, N. L., Flanagan, M., Benjamin, A. J., Jr., Eubanks, J., & Valentine, J. C. (2004). Violent video games: Specific effects of violent content on aggressive thoughts and behavior. *Advances in Experimental Social Psychology, 36,* 199–249.

Anderson, C. A., & Dill, K. E. (2000). Video games and aggressive thoughts, feelings, and behavior in the laboratory and in life. *Journal of Personality and Social Psychology, 78,* 772–790.

Anderson, C. A., Lindsay, J. J., & Bushman, B. J. (1999). Research in the psychological laboratory: Truth or triviality? *Current Directions in Psychological Science, 8,* 3–9.

Anderson, I. M. (2000). Selective serotonin reuptake inhibitors versus tricyclic antidepressants: A meta-analysis of efficacy and tolerability. *Journal of Affective Disorders, 58,* 19–36.

Anderson, J. R., Myowa-Yamakoshi, M., & Matsuzawa, T. (2004). Contagious yawning in chimpanzees. *Biology Letters, 271,* S468–S470.

Anderson, R. C., Pichert, J. W., Goetz, E. T., Schallert, D. L., Stevens, K. V., & Trollip, S. R. (1976). Instantiation of general terms. *Journal of Verbal Learning and Verbal Behavior, 15,* 667–679.

Anderson, S. R. (2004). *Doctor Dolittle's delusion: Animals and the uniqueness of human language.* New Haven: Yale University Press.

Andreasen, N. C. (1997). Linking mind and brain in the study of mental illnesses: A project for a scientific psychopathology. *Science, 275,* 1586–1593.

Andreasen, N. C. (2001). *Brave new brain: Conquering mental illness in the era of the genome.* New York: Oxford University Press.

Andreasen, N. C., Arndt, S., Swayze, V., II, Cizadlo, T., & Flaum, M. (1994). Thalamic abnormalities in schizophrenia visualized through magnetic resonance image averaging. *Science, 266,* 294–298.

Andrews, G., Hall, W., Teesson, M., & Henderson, S. (1999, April). *The mental health of Australians.* Canberra: Mental Health Branch, Commonwealth Department of Health and Aged Care.

Angell, M., & Kassirer, J. P. (1998). Alternative medicine: The risks of untested and unregulated remedies. *New England Journal of Medicine, 17,* 839–841.

Angelsen, N. K., Vik, T., Jacobsen, G., & Bakketeig, L. S. (2001). Breast feeding and cognitive development at age 1 and 5 years. *Archives of Disease in Childhood, 85,* 183–188.

Angoff, W. H. (1987). The nature-nurture debate, aptitudes, and group differences. Presidential address to American Psychological Association Division 5.

Angoff, W. H. (1988, Winter). A philosophical discussion: The issues of test and item bias. *ETS Developments,* pp. 10–11.

Anthony, J. C., Warner, L. A., & Kessler, R. C. (1994). Comparative epidemiology of dependence on tobacco, alcohol, controlled substances, and inhalants: Basic findings from the national comorbidity survey. *Experimental and Clinical Psychopharmacology, 2,* 244–268.

Antony, M. M., Brown, T. A., & Barlow, D. H. (1992). Current perspectives on panic and panic disorder. *Current Directions in Psychological Science, 1,* 79–82.

Antrobus, J. (1991). Dreaming: Cognitive processes during cortical activation and high afferent thresholds. *Psychological Review, 98,* 96–121.

APA. (2003, November). *Psychology careers for the twenty-first century.* Washington, DC: American Psychological Association.

Appleby, D. C. (2002). *The savvy psychology major.* Dubuque, IA: Kendall/Hunt.

Archer, J. (2004). Sex differences in aggression in real-world settings: A meta-analytic review. *Review of General Psychology, 8,* 291–322.

Arendt, H. (1963). *Eichmann in Jerusalem: A report on the banality of evil.* New York: Viking Press.

Arenson, K. W. (1997, May 4). Romanian woman breaks male grip on top math prize. *New York Times* News Service (in *Grand Rapids Press,* p. A7).

Arent, S. M., Landers, D. M., & Etnier, J. L. (2000). The effects of exercise on mood in older adults: A meta-analytic review. *Journal of Aging and Physical Activity, 8,* 407–430.

Aries, E. (1987). Gender and communication. In P. Shaver & C. Henrick (Eds.), *Review of Personality and Social Psychology, 7,* 149–176.

Armel, K. C., & Ramachandran, V. S. (2003). Projecting sensations to external objects: Evidence from skin conductance response. *Proceedings of the Royal Society of London. Series B. Biological Sciences, 270,* 1499–1506.

Armony, J. L., Quirk, G. J., & LeDoux, J. E. (1998). Differential effects of amygdala lesions on early and late plastic components of auditory cortex spike trains during fear conditioning. *Journal of Neuroscience, 18,* 2592–2601.

Arnett, J. J. (1999). Adolescent storm and stress, reconsidered. *American Psychologist, 54,* 317–326.

Arnett, J. J. (2000). Emerging adulthood: A theory of development from the late teens through the twenties. *American Psychologist, 55,* 469–480.

Arnold, K., & Horrigan, K. (2002). Gaining admission into the graduate program of your choice. *Eye on Psi Chi,* 30–33.

Aron, A., Melinat, E., Aron, E. N., Vallone, R. D., & Bator, R. J. (1997). The experimental generation of interpersonal closeness: A procedure and some preliminary findings. *Personality and Social Psychology Bulletin, 23,* 363–377.

Aronow, E., Reznikoff, M., & Moreland, K. (1995). The Rorschach: Projective technique or psychometric test? *Journal of Personality Assessment, 64,* 213–228.

Aronson, E. (2001, April 13). Newsworthy violence. E-mail to SPSP discussion list, drawing from *Nobody Left to Hate.* New York: Freeman, 2000.

Arrigo, J. M., & Pezdek, K. (1997). Lessons from the study of psychogenic amnesia. *Current Directions in Psychology, 6,* 148–152.

Arseneault, L., Cannon, M., Poulton, R., Murray, R., Caspi, A., & Moffitt, T. E. (2002). Cannabis use in adolescence and risk for adult psychosis: Longitudinal prospective study. *British Medical Journal, 325,* 1212–1213.

Asch, S. E. (1955). Opinions and social pressure. *Scientific American, 193,* 31–35.

Aserinsky, E. (1988, January 17). Personal communication.

ASHA. (2003). STD statistics. American Social Health Association (www.ashastd.org/stdfaqs/statistics.html).

Ashtari, M., Kumra, S., Clarke, T., Ardekani, B., Bhaskar, S., & Rhinewine, J. (2004, November 29). Diffusion tensor imaging of children with attention deficit/hyperactivity disorder. Paper presented to the Radiological Society of North America convention.

Ashton, M. C., Lee, K., & Goldberg, L. R. (2004). A hierarchical analysis of 1,710 English personality-descriptive adjectives. *Journal of Personality and Social Psychology, 87,* 707–721.

Assanand, S., Pinel, J. P. J., & Lehman, D. R. (1998). Personal theories of hunger and eating. *Journal of Applied Social Psychology, 28,* 998–1015.

Associated Press. (1999, April 26). Airline passengers mistakenly told plane would crash. *Grand Rapids Press,* p. A3.

Astin, A. W., Parrott, S. A., Korn, W. S., & Sax, L. J. (1997). *The American freshman: Thirty-year trends, 1966–1996.* Los Angeles, CA: Higher Education Research Institute, UCLA.

Atkinson, R. (1988). *The teenage world: Adolescent self-image in ten countries.* New York: Plenum Press.

Atkinson, R. C., & Shiffrin, R. M. (1968). Human memory: A control system and its control processes. In K. Spence (Ed.), *The psychology of learning and motivation* (Vol. 2). New York: Academic Press.

Atkinson, T. (2000). Master's and myths. *Eye on Psi Chi,* 19–25.

Atwell, R. H. (1986, July 28). Drugs on campus: A perspective. *Higher Education & National Affairs,* p. 5.

Atwood, K. C., IV (2003, September/October). The ongoing problem with the National Center for Complementary and Alternative Medicine. *Skeptical Inquirer,* pp. 23–29.

Au, T. K., Knightly, L. M., Jun, S-A., & Oh, J. S. (2002). Overhearing a language during childhood. *Psychological Science, 13,* 238–242.

Aubrecht, L. (2001). What can you do with a BA in psychology? *Eye on Psi Chi,* 29–31.

August, D., & Hakuta, K. (Ed.) (1998). *Educating language-minority children.* Washington, DC: National Academy of Sciences.

Austin, E. J., Deary, I. J., Whiteman, M. C., Fowkes, F. G. R., Pedersen, N. L., Rabbitt, P., Bent, N., & McInnes, L. (2002). Relationships between ability and personality: Does intelligence contribute positively to personal and social adjustment? *Personality and Individual Differences, 32,* 1391–1411.

Australian Bureau of Statistics. (1999). *Australia now—A statistical profile: Health—overweight and obesity* (www.abs.gov.au).

Australian Social Trends, (1995). Health risk factors: Alcohol use. Australian Bureau of Statistics, 4102.

Averill, J. R. (1983). Studies on anger and aggression: Implications for theories of emotion. *American Psychologist, 38,* 1145–1160.

Averill, J. R. (1993). William James's other theory of emotion. In M. E. Donnelly (Ed.), *Reinterpreting the legacy of William James.* Washington, DC: American Psychological Association.

Avery, R. D., & others. (1994, December 13). Mainstream science on intelligence. *Wall Street Journal,* p. A-18.

Avis, N. E. (2003). Depression during the menopausal transition. *Psychology of Women Quarterly, 27,* 91–100.

Ax, A. F. (1953). The physiological differentiation of fear and anger in humans. *Psychosomatic Medicine, 15,* 433–442.

Azar, B. (1998, June). Why can't this man feel whether or not he's standing up? *APA Monitor* (www.apa.org/monitor/jun98/touch.html).

Babad, E., Bernieri, F., & Rosenthal, R. (1991). Students as judges of teachers' verbal and nonverbal behavior. *American Educational Research Journal, 28,* 211–234.

Babyak, M., Blumenthal, J. A., Herman, S., Khatri, P., Doraiswamy, M., Moore, K., Craighead, W. W., Baldewics, T. T., & Krishnan, K. R. (2000). Exercise treatment for major depression: Maintenance of therapeutic benefit at ten months. *Psychosomatic Medicine, 62,* 633–638.

Bachman, J., Wadsworth, K., O'Malley, P., Johnston, L., & Schulenberg, J. (1997). *Smoking, drinking, and drug use in young adulthood: The impact of new freedoms and new responsibilities.* Mahwah, NJ: Erlbaum.

Backman, L., & Dixon, R. A. (1992). Psychological compensation: A theoretical framework. *Psychological Bulletin, 112,* 259–283.

Backus, J. (1977). *The acoustical foundations of music* (2nd ed.). New York: Norton.

Baddeley, A. (1992). Working memory. *Science, 255,* 556–569.

Baddeley, A. (1998). *Human memory: Theory and practice, revised edition.* Boston: Allyn and Bacon.

Baddeley, A. D. (1982). *Your memory: A user's guide.* New York: Macmillan.

Baddeley, A. D. (2001). Is working memory still working? *American Psychologist, 56,* 849–864.

Baddeley, A. D. (2002, June). Is working memory still working? *European Psychologist, 7,* 85–97.

Bagemihl, B. (1999). *Biological exuberance: Animal homosexuality and natural diversity.* New York: St. Martins.

Bahrick, H. P. (1984). Semantic memory content in permastore: 50 years of memory for Spanish learned in school. *Journal of Experimental Psychology: General, 111,* 1–29.

Bahrick, H. P., Bahrick, L. E., Bahrick, A. S., & Bahrick, P. E. (1993). Maintenance of foreign language vocabulary and the spacing effect. *Psychological Science, 4,* 316–321.

Bahrick, H. P., Bahrick, P. O., & Wittlinger, R. P. (1975). Fifty years of memory for names and faces: A cross-sectional approach. *Journal of Experimental Psychology: General, 104,* 54–75.

Bailey, J. M., Gaulin, S., Agyei, Y., & Gladue, B. A. (1994). Effects of gender and sexual orientation on evolutionary relevant aspects of human mating psychology. *Journal of Personality and Social Psychology, 66,* 1081–1093.

Bailey, J. M., Kirk, K. M., Zhu, G., Dunne, M. P., & Martin, N. G. (2000). Do individual differences in sociosexuality represent genetic or environmentally contingent strategies? Evidence from the Australian twin registry. *Journal of Personality and Social Psychology, 78,* 537–545.

Bailey, J. M., & Zucker, K. J. (1995). Childhood sex-typed behavior and sexual orientation: A conceptual analysis and quantitative review. *Developmental Psychology, 31,* 43–55.

Baillargeon, R. (1995). A model of physical reasoning in infancy. In C. Rovee-Collier & L. P. Lipsitt (Eds.), *Advances in infancy research* (Vol. 9). Stamford, CT: Ablex.

Baillargeon, R. (1998). Infants' understanding of the physical world. In M. Sabourin, F. I. M. Craik, & M. Roberts (Eds.), *Advances in psychological science, Vol. 2: Biological and cognitive aspects.* Hove, England: Psychology Press.

Baillargeon, R. (2004). Infants' physical world. *Current Directions in Psychological Science, 13,* 89–94.

Bairagi, R. (1987). Food crises and female children in rural Bangladesh. *Social Science, 72,* 48–51.

Baker, E. L. (1987). The state of the art of clinical hypnosis. *International Journal of Clinical and Experimental Hypnosis, 35,* 203–214.

Baker, M. C. (2001). *The atoms of language: The mind's hidden rules of grammar.* New York: Basic Books.

Baker, T. B., Piper, M. E., McCarthy, D. E., Majeskie, M. R., & Fiore, M. C. (2004). Addiction motivation reformulated: An affective processing model of negative reinforcement. *Psychological Review, 111,* 33–51.

Baker-Ward, L., Gordon, B. N., Ornstein, P. A., Larus, D. M., & Clubb, P. A. (1993). Young children's long-term retention of a pediatric examination. *Child Development, 64,* 1519–1533.

Bakermans-Kranenburg, M. J., van Ijzendoorn, M. H., & Juffer, F. (2003). Less is more: Meta-analyses of sensitivity and attachment interventions in early childhood. *Psychological Bulletin, 129,* 195–215.

Ballard, M. E., & Wiest, J. R. (1998). Mortal Kombat: The effects of violent videogame play on males' hostility and cardiovascular responding. *Journal of Applied Social Psychology, 26,* 717–730.

Baltes, P. B. (1993). The aging mind: Potential and limits. *The Gerontologist, 33,* 580–594.

Baltes, P. B. (1994). Life-span developmental psychology: On the overall landscape of human development. Invited address, American Psychological Association convention.

Baltes, P. B., & Baltes, M. M. (1999, September-October). Harvesting the fruits of age: Growing older, growing wise. *Science and the Spirit,* pp. 11–14.

Bancroft, J., Loftus, J., & Long, J. S. (2003). Distress about sex: A national survey of women in heterosexual relationships. *Archives of Sexual Behavior, 32,* 193–208.

Bandura, A. (1982). The psychology of chance encounters and life paths. *American Psychologist, 37,* 747–755.

Bandura, A. (1986). *Social foundations of thought and action: A social-cognitive theory.* Englewood Cliffs, NJ: Prentice-Hall.

Bandura, A. (2001). Social cognitive theory: An agentic perspective. *Annual Review of Psychology, 52,* 1–26.

Bandura, A. (2005). The evolution of social cognitive theory. In K. G. Smith & M. A. Hitt (Eds.), *Great minds in management: The process of theory development.* Oxford: Oxford University Press.

Bandura, A., Ross, D., & Ross, S. A. (1961). Transmission of aggression through imitation of aggressive models. *Journal of Abnormal and Social Psychology, 63,* 575–582.

Barber, T. X. (2000). A deeper understanding of hypnosis: Its secrets, its nature, its essence. *American Journal of Clinical Hypnosis, 42,* 208–272.

Barbour, D. L., & Wang, X. (2003). Contrast tuning in auditory cortex. *Science, 299,* 1073–1075.

Barinaga, M. (1991). How long is the human life-span? *Science, 254,* 936–938.

Barinaga, M. (1992a). The brain remaps its own contours. *Science, 258,* 216–218.

Barinaga, M. (1992b). How scary things get that way. *Science, 258,* 887–888.

Barinaga, M. (1997). Visual system provides clues to how the brain perceives. *Science, 275,* 1583–1585.

Barinaga, M. (1999). Salmon follow watery odors home. *Science, 286,* 705–706.

Barinaga, M. B. (1997). How exercise works its magic. *Science, 276,* 1325.

Barker, S. L., Funk, S. C., & Houston, B. K. (1988). Psychological treatment versus nonspecific factors: A meta-analysis of conditions that engender comparable expectations for improvement. *Clinical Psychology Review, 8,* 579–594.

Barkley, R. A., & 74 others (2002). International consensus statement (January 2002). *Clinical Child and Family Psychology Review, 5,* 2.

Barlow, D. H. (1988). *Anxiety and its disorders: The nature and treatment of anxiety and panic.* New York: Guilford.

Barnes, M. L., & Sternberg, R. J. (1989). Social intelligence and decoding of nonverbal cues. *Intelligence, 13,* 263–287.

Barnett, P. A., & Gotlib, I. H. (1988). Psychosocial functioning and depression: Distinguishing among antecedents, concomitants, and consequences. *Psychological Bulletin, 104,* 97–126.

Barnier, A. J., & McConkey, K. M. (2004). Defining and identifying the highly hypnotizable person. In M. Heap, R. J. Brown, & D. A. Oakley (Eds.), *High hypnotisability: Theoretical, experimental and clinical issues.* London: Brunner-Routledge.

Baron, R. A. (1988). Negative effects of destructive criticism: Impact on conflict, self-efficacy, and task performance. *Journal of Applied Psychology, 73,* 199–207.

Baron, R. S., Cutrona, C. E., Hicklin, D., Russell, D. W., & Lubaroff, D. M. (1990). Social support and immune function among spouses of cancer patients. *Journal of Personality and Social Psychology, 59,* 344–352.

Baron, R. S., Vandello, J. A., & Brunsman, B. (1996). The forgotten variable in conformity research: Impact of task importance on social influence. *Journal of Personality and Social Psychology, 71,* 915–927.

Baron-Cohen, S. (2004). *The essential difference: Men, women, and the extreme male brain.* London: Penguin Books.

Baron-Cohen, S. (2005, April 6 and May 19). The assortative mating theory: A talk with Simon Baron-Cohen. *The Edge* (www.edge.org).

Baron-Cohen, S., Leslie, A. M., & Frith, U. (1985). Does the autistic child have a "theory of mind"? *Cognition, 21,* 37–46.

Barr, R. (1991, October). In *The Evening Standard,* 9.

Barrett, L. F., Lane, R. D., Sechrest, L., & Schwartz, G. E. (2000). Sex differences in emotional awareness. *Personality and Social Psychology Bulletin, 26,* 1027–1035.

Barry, D. (1995, September 17). Teen smokers, too, get cool, toxic, waste-blackened lungs. *Asbury Park Press,* p. D3.

Barry, D. (1996, August 11). The power to embarrass (syndicated column).

Bartoshuk, L. M. (1993). The wisdom of the body: Using case studies to teach sensation and perception. Paper presented to the National Institute on the Teaching of Psychology, St. Petersburg Beach, Florida.

Baruch, G. K., & Barnett, R. (1986). Role quality, multiple role involvement, and psychological well-being in midlife women. *Journal of Personality and Social Psychology, 51,* 578–585.

Bashore, T. R., Ridderinkhof, K. R., & van der Molen, M. W. (1997). The decline of cognitive processing speed in old age. *Current Directions in Psychological Science, 6,* 163–169.

Baskind, D. E. (1997, December 14). Personal communication, from Delta College.

Bass, L. E., & Kane-Williams, E. (1993). Stereotype or reality: Another look at alcohol and drug use among African American children. U.S. Department of Health and Human Services, *Public Health Reports, 108* (Supplement 1), 78–84.

Bassett, D. R., Schneider, P. L., & Huntington, G. E. (2004). Physical activity in an Old Order Amish community. *Medicine and Science in Sports and Exercise, 36,* 79–85.

Bat-Chava, Y. (1993). Antecedents of self-esteem in deaf people: A meta-analytic review. *Rehabilitation Psychology, 38*(4), 221–234.

Bat-Chava, Y. (1994). Group identification and self-esteem of deaf adults. *Personality and Social Psychology Bulletin, 20,* 494–502.

Bauer, P. J. (2002). Long-term recall memory: Behavioral and neuro-developmental changes in the first 2 years of life. *Current Directions in Psychology, 11,* 137–141.

Baum, A., & Posluszny, D. M. (1999). Health psychology: Mapping biobehavioral contributions to health and illness. *Annual Review of Psychology, 50,* 137–163.

Baumeister, R. (2005). *The cultural animal: Human nature, meaning, and social life.* New York: Oxford University Press.

Baumeister, R. F. (1989). The optimal margin of illusion. *Journal of Social and Clinical Psychology, 8,* 176–189.

Baumeister, R. F. (1996). Should schools try to boost self-esteem? Beware the dark side. *American Educator, 20,* 14019, 43.

Baumeister, R. F. (2000). Gender differences in erotic plasticity: The female sex drive as socially flexible and responsive. *Psychological Bulletin, 126,* 347–374.

Baumeister, R. F. (2001, April). Violent pride: Do people turn violent because of self-hate, or self-love? *Scientific American,* pp. 96–101.

Baumeister, R. F., & Bratslavsky, E. (1999). Passion, intimacy, and time: Passionate love as a function of change in intimacy. *Personality and social Psychology Review, 3,* 49–67.

Baumeister, R. F., Bratslavsky, E., Finkenauer, C., & others. (2001). Bad is stronger than good. *Review of General Psychology, 5,* 323–370.

Baumeister, R. F., Campbell, J., Krueger, J. I., & Vohs, K. D. (2003). Does high self-esteem cause better performance, interpersonal success, happiness, or healthier lifestyles? *Psychological Science in the Public Interest, 4*(1), 1–44.

Baumeister, R. F., Campbell, J. D., Krueger, J. I., & Vohs, K. D. (2005, January). Exploding the self-esteem myth. *Scientific American,* pp. 84–91.

Baumeister, R. F., Catanese, K. R., & Vohs, K. D. (2001). Is there a gender difference in strength of sex drive? Theoretical views, conceptual distinctions, and a review of relevant evidence. *Personality and Social Psychology Review, 5,* 242–273.

Baumeister, R. F., Dale, K., & Sommer, K. L. (1998). Freudian defense mechanisms and empirical findings in modern personality and social psychology: Reaction formation, projection, displacement, undoing, isolation, sublimation, and denial. *Journal of Personality, 66,* 1081–1125.

Baumeister, R. F., & Exline, J. J. (2000). Self-control, morality, and human strength. *Journal of Social and Clinical Psychology, 19,* 29–42.

Baumeister, R. F., & Leary, M. R. (1995). The need to belong: Desire for interpersonal attachments as a fundamental human motivation. *Psychological Bulletin, 117,* 497–529.

Baumeister, R. F., Stillwell, A., & Wotman, S. R. (1990). Victim and perpetrator accounts of interpersonal conflict: Autobiographical narratives about anger. *Journal of Personality and Social Psychology, 59,* 994–1005.

Baumeister, R. F., & Tice, D. M. (1986). How adolescence became the struggle for self: A historical transformation of psychological development. In J. Suls & A. G. Greenwald (Eds.), *Psychological perspectives on the self* (Vol. 3). Hillsdale, NJ: Erlbaum.

Baumeister, R. F., Twenge, J. M., & Nuss, C. K. (2002). Effects of social exclusion on cognitive processes: Anticipated aloneness reduces intelligent thought. *Journal of Personality and Social Psychology, 83,* 817–827.

Baumgardner, A. H., Kaufman, C. M., & Levy, P. E. (1989). Regulating affect interpersonally: When low esteem leads to greater enhancement. *Journal of Personality and Social Psychology, 56,* 907–921.

Baumrind, D. (1982). Adolescent sexuality: Comment on Williams' and Silka's comments on Baumrind. *American Psychologist, 37,* 1402–1403.

Baumrind, D. (1996). The discipline controversy revisited. *Family Relations, 45,* 405–414.

Baumrind, D., Larzelere, R. E., & Cowan, P. A. (2002). Ordinary physical punishment: Is it harmful? Comment on Gershoff (2002). *Psychological Bulletin, 128,* 602–611.

Bavelier, D., Newport, E. L., & Supalla, T. (2003). Children need natural languages, signed or spoken. *Cerebrum, 5*(1), 19–32.

Bavelier, D., Tomann, A., Hutton, C., Mitchell, T., Corina, D., Liu, G., & Neville, H. (2000). Visual attention to the periphery is enhanced in congenitally deaf individuals. *Journal of Neuroscience, 20,* 1–6.

Bayley, P. J., Gold, J. J., Hopkins, R. O., & Squire, L. R. (2005). The neuroanatomy of remote memory. *Neuron, 46,* 799–810.

BBC. (2005, July). Japanese breaks pi memory record. http://news.bbc.co.uk/2/hi/asia-pacific/4644103.stm.

Beaman, A. L., & Klentz, B. (1983). The supposed physical attractiveness bias against supporters of the women's movement: A meta-analysis. *Personality and Social Psychology Bulletin, 9,* 544–550.

Beardsley, L. M. (1994). Medical diagnosis and treatment across cultures. In W. J. Lonner & R. Malpass (Eds.), *Psychology and culture.* Boston: Allyn & Bacon.

Beardsley, T. (1996, July). Waking up. *Scientific American,* pp. 14, 18.

Beauchamp, G. K. (1987). The human preference for excess salt. *American Scientist, 75,* 27–33.

Beck, A. J., Kline, S. A., & Greenfeld, L. A. (1988). Survey of youth in custody, 1987. U.S. Department of Justice, Bureau of Justice Statistics Special Report.

Beck, A. T., Rush, A. J., Shaw, B. F., & Emery, G. (1979). *Cognitive therapy of depression.* New York: Guilford Press.

Beck, A. T., & Steer, R. A. (1989). Clinical predictors of eventual suicide: A 5- to 10-year prospective study of suicide attempters. *Journal of Affective Disorders, 17,* 203–209.

Becklen, R., & Cervone, D. (1983). Selective looking and the noticing of unexpected events. *Memory and Cognition, 11,* 601–608.

Beckman, M. (2004). Crime, culpability, and the adolescent brain. *Science, 305,* 596–599.

Beeman, M. J., & Chiarello, C. (1998). Complementary right- and left-hemisphere language comprehension. *Current Directions in Psychological Science, 7,* 2–8.

Beitman, B. D., Goldfried, M. R., & Norcross, J. C. (1989). The movement toward integrating the psychotherapies: An overview. *American Journal of Psychiatry, 146,* 138–147.

Bell, A. P., Weinberg, M. S., & Hammersmith, S. K. (1981). *Sexual preference: Its development in men and women.* Bloomington: Indiana University Press.

Bell, R. Q., & Waldrop, M. F. (1989). Achievement and cognitive correlates of minor physical anomalies in early development. In M. G. Bornstein & N. A. Krasnegor (Eds.), *Stability and continuity in mental development: Behavioral and biological perspectives.* Hillsdale, NJ: Erlbaum.

Bellugi, U. (1994, August). Quoted in P. Radetsky, Silence, signs, and wonder. *Discover,* pp. 60–68.

Beloff, J. (1985, Spring). Science, religion and the paranormal. *Free Inquiry,* pp. 36–41

Belsher, G., & Costello, C. G. (1988). Relapse after recovery from unipolar depression: A critical review. *Psychological Bulletin, 104,* 84–96.

Belsky, J. (1990). Parental and nonparental child care and children's socioemotional development: A decade in review. *Journal of Marriage and the Family, 52,* 885–903.

Belsky, J. (2003). The politicized science of day care: A personal and professional odyssey. *Family Policy Review 1*(2), 23–40.

Bem, D. J. (1984). Quoted in *The Skeptical Inquirer, 8,* 194.

Bem, D. J. (1996). Exotic becomes erotic: A developmental theory of sexual orientation. *Psychological Review, 103,* 320–335.

Bem, D. J. (1998). Is EBE theory supported by the evidence? Is it androcentric? A reply to Peplau et al. (1998). *Psychological Review, 105,* 395–398.

Bem, D. J. (2000). Exotic becomes erotic: Interpreting the biological correlates of sexual orientation. *Archives of Sexual Behavior, 29,* 531–548.

Bem, D. J., & Honorton, C. (1994). Does psi exist? Replicable evidence for an anomalous process of information transfer. *Psychological Bulletin, 115,* 4–18.

Bem, D. J., Palmer, J., & Broughton, R. S. (2001). Updating the Ganzfeld database: A victim of its own success? *Journal of Parapsychology, 65,* 207–218.

Bem, S. L. (1987). Masculinity and femininity exist only in the mind of the perceiver. In J. M. Reinisch, L. A. Rosenblum, & S. A. Sanders (Eds.), *Masculinity/femininity: Basic perspectives.* New York: Oxford University Press.

Bem, S. L. (1993). *The lenses of gender.* New Haven: Yale University Press.

Ben-Shakhar, G., & Elaad, E. (2003). The validity of psychophysiological detection of information with the guilt knowledge test: A meta-analytic review. *Journal of Applied Psychology, 88,* 131–151.

Benbow, C. P., Lubinski, D., Shea, D. L., & Eftekhari-Sanjani, H. (2000). Sex differences in mathematical reasoning ability at age 13: Their status 20 years later. *Psychological Science, 11,* 474–2000.

Bennett, R. (1991, February). Pornography and extrafamilial child sexual abuse: Examining the relationship. Unpublished manuscript, Los Angeles Police Department Sexually Exploited Child Unit.

Bennett, W. I. (1995). Beyond overeating. *New England Journal of Medicine, 332,* 673–674.

Benson, H. (1996). *Timeless healing: The power and biology of belief.* New York: Scribner.

Benson, K., & Feinberg, I. (1977). The beneficial effect of sleep in an extended Jenkins and Dallenbach paradigm. *Psychophysiology, 14,* 375–384.

Benson, P. L. (1992, Spring). Patterns of religious development in adolescence and adulthood. *PIRI Newsletter,* 2–9.

Benson, P. L., Sharma, A. R., & Roehlkepartain, E. C. (1994). *Growing up adopted: A portrait of adolescents and their families.* Minneapolis: Search Institute.

Berenbaum, S. A., & Bailey, J. M. (2003). Effects on gender identity of prenatal androgens and genital appearance: Evidence from girls with congenital adrenal hyperplasia. *Journal of Clinical Endocrinology and Metabolism, 88,* 1102–1106.

Berenbaum, S. A., & Hines, M. (1992). Early androgens are related to childhood sex-typed toy preferences. *Psychological Science, 3,* 203–206.

Berenbaum, S. A., Korman, K., & Leveroni, C. (1995). Early hormones and sex differences in cognitive abilities. *Learning and Individual Differences, 7,* 303–321.

Berger, B. G., & Motl, R. W. (2000). Exercise and mood: A selective review and synthesis of research employing the profile of mood states. *Journal of Applied Sports Psychology, 12,* 69–92.

Bergin, A. E. (1980). Psychotherapy and religious values. *Journal of Consulting and Clinical Psychology, 48,* 95–105.

Bergsholm, P., Larsen, J. L., Rosendahl, K., & Holsten, F. (1989). Electroconvulsive therapy and cerebral computed tomography. *Acta Psychiatrica Scandinavia, 80,* 566–572.

Berk, L. E. (1994, November). Why children talk to themselves. *Scientific American,* pp. 78–83.

Berk, L. S., Felten, D. L., Tan, S. A., Bittman, B. B., & Westengard, J. (2001). Modulation of neuroimmune parameters during the eustress of humor-associated mirthful laughter. *Alternative Therapies, 7,* 62–76.

Berkel, J., & de Waard, F. (1983). Mortality pattern and life expectancy of Seventh-Day Adventists in the Netherlands. *International Journal of epidemiology, 12,* 455–459.

Berkowitz, L. (1983). Aversively stimulated aggression: Some parallels and differences in research with animals and humans. *American Psychologist, 38,* 1135–1144.

Berkowitz, L. (1989). Frustration-aggression hypothesis: Examination and reformulation. *Psychological Bulletin, 106,* 59–73.

Berkowitz, L. (1990). On the formation and regulation of anger and aggression: A cognitive-neoassociationistic analysis. *American Psychologist, 45,* 494–503.

Berman, M., Gladue, B., & Taylor, S. (1993). The effects of hormones, Type A behavior pattern, and provocation on aggression in men. *Motivation and Emotion, 17,* 125–138.

Berndt, T. J. (1992). Friendship and friends' influence in adolescence. *Current Directions in Psychological Science, 1,* 156–159.

Bernhardt, P. C., Dabbs, J. M., Jr., Fielden, J. A., & Lutter, C. D. (1998). Testosterone changes during vicarious experiences of winning and losing among fans at sporting events. *Physiology and Behavior, 65,* 59–62.

Bernstein, D. M., Atance, C., Loftus, G. R., & Meltzoff, A. (2004). We saw it all along: Visual hindsight bias in children and adults. *Psychological Science, 15,* 264–267.

Berntsen, D., & Thomsen, D. K. (2005). Personal memories for remote historical events: Accuracy and clarity of flashbulb memories related to World War II. *Journal of Experimental Psychology: General, 134,* 242–257.

Berridge, K. C., & Winkielman, P. (2003). What is an unconscious emotion? (The case of unconscious "liking"). *Cognition and Emotion, 17,* 181–211.

Berry, D. S., & McArthur, L. Z. (1986). Perceiving character in faces: The impact of age-related craniofacial changes on social perception. *Psychological Bulletin, 100,* 3–18.

Berscheid, E. (1981). An overview of the psychological effects of physical attractiveness and some comments upon the psychological effects of knowledge of the effects of physical attractiveness. In G. W. Lucker, K. Ribbens, & J. A. McNamara (Eds.), *Psychological aspects of facial form* (Craniofacial growth series). Ann Arbor: Center for Human Growth and Development, University of Michigan.

Berscheid, E. (1985). Interpersonal attraction. In G. Lindzey & E. Aronson (Eds.), *The handbook of social psychology.* New York: Random House.

Berscheid, E., Gangestad, S. W., & Kulakowski, D. (1984). Emotion in close relationships: Implications for relationship counseling. In S. D. Brown & R. W. Lent (Eds.), *Handbook of counseling psychology.* New York: Wiley.

Bértolo, H., Paiva, T., Pessoa, L., Mestre, T., Marques, R., & Santos, R. (2003). Visual dream content, graphical representation and EEG alpha activity in congenitally blind subjects. *Cognitive Brain Research, 15,* 277–284.

Besson, M., Faita, F., Peretz, I., Bonnel, A.-M., & Requin, J. (1998). Singing in the brain: Independence of lyrics and tunes. *Psychological Science, 9,* 494–498.

Bettencourt, B. A., & Dorr, N. (1997). Collective self-esteem as a mediator of the relationship between allocentrism and subjective well-being. *Personality and Social Psychology Bulletin, 23,* 955–964.

Bettencourt, B. A., & Kernahan, C. (1997). A meta-analysis of aggression in the presence of violent cues: Effects of gender differences and aversive provocation. *Aggressive Behavior, 23,* pp. 447–457.

Beyerstein, B., & Beyerstein, D. (Eds.) (1992). *The write stuff: Evaluations of graphology.* Buffalo, NY: Prometheus Books.

Bhatt, R. S., Wasserman, E. A., Reynolds, W. F., Jr., & Knauss, K. S. (1988). Conceptual behavior in pigeons: Categorization of both familiar and novel examples from four classes of natural and artificial stimuli. *Journal of Experimental Psychology: Animal Behavior Processes, 14,* 219–234.

Bialystok, E. (2001). *Bilingualism in development, language, literacy, and cognition.* New York: Cambridge University Press.

Bickman, L. (1999). Practice makes perfect and other myths about mental health services. *American Psychologist, 54,* 965–978.

Biederman, J., Wilens, T., Mick, E., Spencer, T., & Faraone, S. V. (1999). Pharmacotherapy of Attention-Deficit/Hyperactivity Disorder reduces risk for substance use disorder. *Pediatrics, 104,* 1–5.

Biello, S. M., & Dafters, R. I. (2001). MDMA and fenfluramine alter the response of the circadian clock to a serotonin agonist in vitro. *Brain Research, 920,* 202–209.

Biggs, V. (2001, April 13). Murder suspect captured in Grand Marais. *Cook County News-Herald.*

Bigler, E. D., Johnson, S. C., Jackson, C., & Blatter, D. D. (1995). Aging, brain size, and IQ. *Intelligence, 21,* 109–119.

Binet, A., & Simon, T. (1905; reprinted 1916). New methods for the diagnosis of the intellectual level of subnormals. In A. Binet & T. Simon, *The development of intelligence in children.* Baltimore: Williams & Wilkins.

Birch, S. A. J. (2005). When knowledge is a curse: Children's and adults' reasoning about mental states. *Current Directions in Psychological Science, 14,* 25–29.

Birnbaum, S. G., Yuan, P. X., Wang, M., Vijayraghavan, S., Bloom, A. K., Davis, D. J., Gobeski, K. T., Sweatt, J. D., Manhi, H. K., & Arnsten, A. F. T. (2004). Protein kinase C overactivity impairs prefrontal cortical regulation of working memory. *Science, 306,* 882–884.

Bishop, B. (2004, November 22). Personal correspondence, and earlier articles on "The great divide" in the *Austin Statesman.*

Bishop, G. D. (1991). Understanding the understanding of illness: Lay disease representations. In J. A. Skelton & R. T. Croyle (Eds.), *Mental representation in health and illness.* New York: Springer-Verlag.

Biswas-Diener, R., & Diener, E. (2001). Making the best of a bad situation: Satisfaction in the slums of Calcutta. *Social Indicators Research, 55,* 329–352.

Bjork, R. A. (1999). Assessing our own competence: Heuristics and illusions. In D. Gopher & A. Koriat (Eds.), *Attention and performance XVII. Cognitive regulation of performance: Interaction of theory and application.* Cambridge, MA: MIT Press.

Bjork, R. A. (2000, July/August). Toward one world of psychological science. *APS Observer,* p. 3.

Bjorklund, D. F., & Green, B. L. (1992). The adaptive nature of cognitive immaturity. *American Psychologist, 47,* 46–54.

Blackmore, S. (1991, Fall). Near-death experiences: In or out of the body? *Skeptical Inquirer,* pp. 34–45.

Blackmore, S. (1993). *Dying to live.* Amherst, NY: Prometheus Books.

Blackmore, S. (1999). *The meme machine.* Oxford: Oxford University Press.

Blackmore, S. (2000, October). The power of memes. *Scientific American,* pp. 63–73.

Blakemore, S-J., Wolpert, D. M., & Frith, C. D. (1998). Central cancellation of self-produced tickle sensation. *Nature Neuroscience, 1,* 635–640.

Blakeslee, S. (2005, February 8). Focus narrows in search for autism's cause. *New York Times* (www.nytimes.com).

Blanchard, R. (1997). Birth order and sibling sex ratio in homosexual versus heterosexual males and females. *Annual Review of Sex Research, 8,* 27–67.

Blanchard, R. (2001). Fraternal birth order and the maternal immune hypothesis of male homosexuality. *Hormones and Behavior, 40,* 105–114.

Blanke, O., Landis, T., & Spinelli, L. (2004). Out-of-body experience and autoscopy of neurological origin. *Brain: Journal of Neurology, 127,* 243–258.

Blanke, O., Ortigue, S., Landis, T., & Seeck, M. (2002). Stimulating illusory own-body perceptions. *Nature, 419,* 269–270.

Blankenburg, F., Taskin, B., Ruben, J., Moosmann, M., Ritter, P., Curio, G., & Villringer, A. (2003). Imperceptive stimuli and sensory processing impediment. *Science, 299,* 1864.

Blascovich, J., Seery, M. D., Mugridge, C. A., Norris, R. K., & Weisbuch, M. (2004). Predicting athletic performance from cardiovascular indexes of challenge and threat. *Journal of Experimental Social Psychology, 40,* 683–688.

Blass, T. (1996). Stanley Milgram: A life of inventiveness and controversy. In G. A. Kimble, C. A. Boneau, & M. Wertheimer (Eds.), *Portraits of pioneers in psychology* (Vol. II). Washington, DC, and Mahwah, NJ: American Psychological Association and Lawrence Erlbaum Publishers.

Blass, T. (1999). The Milgram paradigm after 35 years: Some things we now know about obedience to authority. *Journal of Applied Social Psychology, 29,* 955–978.

Blatt, S. J., Sanislow, C. A., III, Zuroff, D. C., & Pilkonis, P. (1996). Characteristics of effective therapists: Further analyses of data from the National Institute of Mental Health Treatment of Depression Collaborative

Research Program. *Journal of Consulting and Clinical Psychology, 64,* 1276–1284.

Bleustein, J. (2002, June 15). Quoted in "Harley retooled," by S. S. Smith, *American Way Magazine.*

Blizzard, R. (2004, August 31). Smoking: Will education overpower addiction? Gallup Poll (www.gallup.com).

Blom, J. M. C., Tamarkin, L., Shiber, J. R., & Nelson, R. J. (1995). Learned immunosuppression is associated with an increased risk of chemically-induced tumors. *Neuroimmunomodulation, 2,* 92–99.

Bloom, B. J. (1964). *Stability and change in human characteristics.* New York: Wiley.

Bloom, B. S. (Ed.). (1985). *Developing talent in young people.* New York: Ballantine.

Bloom, F. E. (1993, January/February). What's new in neurotransmitters. *BrainWork,* pp. 7–9.

Bloom, P. (2000). *How children learn the meanings of words.* Cambridge, MA: MIT Press.

Bloom, S. R. (2002, September/October). Quoted in Researchers identify natural appetite suppressant. *Brain Work.*

Blum, K., Cull, J. G., Braverman, E. R., & Comings, D. E. (1996). Reward deficiency syndrome. *American Scientist, 84,* 132–145.

Boahen, K. (2005, May). Neuromorphic microchips. *Scientific American,* pp. 56–63.

Bock, B. C., Marcus, B. H., King. T. E., Borrelli, B., & Roberts, M. R. (1999). Exercise effects on withdrawal and mood among women attempting smoking cessation. *Addictive Behavior, 24,* 399–410.

Bodenhausen, G. V., Sheppard, L. A., & Kramer, G. P. (1994). Negative affect and social judgment: The differential impact of anger and sadness. *European Journal of Social Psychology, 24,* 45–62.

Bodkin, J. A., & Amsterdam, J. D. (2002). Transdermal selegiline in major depression: A double-blind, placebo-controlled, parallel-group study in outpatients. *American Journal of Psychiatry, 159,* 1869–1875.

Boehm, K. E., Schondel, C. K., Marlowe, A. L., & Manke-Mitchell, L. (1999). Teens' concerns: A national evaluation. *Adolescence, 34,* 523–528.

Boesch-Achermann, H., & Boesch, C. (1993). Tool use in wild chimpanzees: New light from dark forests. *Current Directions in Psychological Science, 2,* 18–21.

Bogaert, A. F. (2003). Number of older brothers and sexual orientation: New texts and the attraction/behavior distinction in two national probability samples. *Journal of Personality and Social Psychology, 84,* 644–652.

Bogaert, A. F. (2004). Asexuality: Prevalence and associated factors in a national probability sample. *Journal of Sex Research, 41,* 279–287.

Bogaert, A. F., Friesen, C., & Klentrou, P. (2002). Age of puberty and sexual orientation in a national probability sample. *Archives of Sexual Behavior, 31,* 73–81.

Boggiano, A. K., Barrett, M., Weiher, A. W., McClelland, G. H., & Lusk, C. M. (1987). Use of the maximal-operant principle to motivate children's intrinsic interest. *Journal of Personality and Social Psychology, 53,* 866–879.

Boggiano, A. K., Harackiewicz, J. M., Bessette, M. M., & Main, D. S. (1985). Increasing children's interest through performance-contingent reward. *Social Cognition, 3,* 400–411.

Bogin, B. (1998, February). The tall and the short of it (range of height in humans demonstrates plasticity of human species). *Discover.*

Bohman, M., & Sigvardsson, S. (1990). Outcome in adoption: Lessons from longitudinal studies. In D. Brodzinsky & M. Schechter (Eds.), *The psychology of adoption.* New York: Oxford University Press.

Bolger, N., DeLongis, A., Kessler, R. C., & Schilling, E. A. (1989). Effects of daily stress on negative mood. *Journal of Personality and Social Psychology, 57,* 808–818.

Bonanno, G. A. (2001). Grief and emotion: Experience, expression, and dissociation. In M. Stroebe, W. Stroebe, R. O. Hansson, & H. Schut (Eds.), *New handbook of bereavement: Consciousness, coping, and care.* Cambridge: Cambridge University Press.

Bonanno, G. A. (2004). Loss, trauma, and human resilience: Have we underestimated the human capacity to thrive after extremely aversive events? *American Psychologist, 59,* 20–28.

Bonanno, G. A. (2005). Adult resilience to potential trauma. *Current Directions in Psychological Science, 14,* 135–137.

Bonanno, G. A., & Kaltman, S. (1999). Toward an integrative perspective on bereavement. *Psychological Bulletin, 125,* 760–777.

Bond, C. F., Jr., & DePaulo, B. M. (in press). Accuracy of deception judgments. Unpublished manuscript, Texas Christian University.

Bond, C. F., Jr., Pitre, U., & Van Leeuwen, M. D. (1991). Encoding operations and the next-in-line effect. *Personality and Social Psychology Bulletin, 17,* 435–441.

Bond, M. H. (1988). Finding universal dimensions of individual variation in multi-cultural studies of values: The Rokeach and Chinese values surveys. *Journal of Personality and Social Psychology, 55,* 1009–1015.

Bond, R., & Smith, P. B. (1996). Culture and conformity: A meta-analysis of studies using Asch's (1952b, 1956) line judgment task. *Psychological Bulletin, 119,* 111–137.

Boneva, B. S., & Frieze, I. H. (2001). Toward a concept of a migrant personality. *Journal of Social Issues, 57,* 477–491.

Bono, J. E., & Judge, T. A. (2004). Personality and transformational and transactional leadership: A meta-analysis. *Journal of Applied Psychology, 89,* 901–910.

Bookheimer, S. H., Strojwas, M. H., Cohen, M. S., Saunders, A. M., Pericak-Vance, M. A., Mazziotta, J. C., & Small, G. W. (2000). Patterns of brain activation in people at risk for Alzheimer's disease. *New England Journal of Medicine, 343,* 450–456.

Booth, F. W., & Neufer, P. D. (2005). Exercise controls gene expression. *American Scientist, 93,* 28–35.

Boring, E. G. (1930). A new ambiguous figure. *American Journal of Psychology, 42,* 444–445.

Borkenau, P., Mauer, N., Riemann, R., Spinath, F. M., & Angleitner, A. (2004). Thin slices of behavior as cues of personality and intelligence. *Journal of Personality and Social Psychology, 86,* 599–614.

Bornstein, M. H., Cote, L. R., Maital, S., Painter, K., Park, S-Y., Pascual, L., Pecheux, M-G., Ruel, J., Venute, P., & Vyt, A. (2004). Cross-linguistic analysis of vocabulary in young children: Spanish, Dutch, French, Hebrew, Italian, Korean, and American English. *Child Development, 75,* 1115–1139.

Bornstein, M. H., Tal, J., Rahn, C., Galperin, C. Z., Pecheux, M-G., Lamour, M., Toda, S., Azuma, H., Ogino, M., & Tamis-LeMonda, C. S. (1992a). Functional analysis of the contents of maternal speech to infants of 5 and 13 months in four cultures: Argentina, France, Japan, and the United States. *Developmental Psychology, 28,* 593–603.

Bornstein, M. H., Tamis-LeMonda, C. S., Tal, J., Ludemann, P., Toda, S., Rahn, C. W., Pecheux, M-G., Azuma, H., Vardi, D. (1992b). Maternal responsiveness to infants in three societies: The United States, France, and Japan. *Child Development, 63,* 808–821.

Bornstein, R. F. (1989). Exposure and affect: Overview and meta-analysis of research, 1968–1987. *Psychological Bulletin, 106,* 265–289.

Bornstein, R. F. (1999). Source amnesia, misattribution, and the power of unconscious perceptions and memories. *Psychoanalytic Psychology, 16,* 155–178.

Bornstein, R. F. (2001). The impending death of psychoanalysis. *Psychoanalytic Psychology, 18,* 3–20.

Bornstein, R. F., Galley, D. J., Leone, D. R., & Kale, A. R. (1991). The temporal stability of ratings of parents: Test-retest reliability and influence of parental contact. *Journal of Social Behavior and Personality, 6,* 641–649.

Boroditsky, R., Fisher, W., & Sand, M. (1995, July). Teenagers and contraception. Section of The Canadian contraception study. *Journal of the Society of Obstetricians and Gynaecologists of Canada*, Special Supplement, pp. 22–25.

Bortfeld, H., Morgan, J. L., Golinkoff, R. M., & Rathbun, K. (2005). Mommy and me: Familiar names help launch babies into speech-stream segmentation. *Psychological Science, 16*, 298–304.

Boscarino, J. A. (1997). Diseases among men 20 years after exposure to severe stress: Implications for clinical research and medical care. *Psychosomatic Medicine, 59*, 605–614.

Bosma, H., Marmot, M. G., Hemingway, H., Nicolson, A. C., Brunner, E., & Stansfeld, S. A. (1997). Low job control and risk of coronary heart disease in Whitehall II (prospective cohort) study. *British Medical Journal, 314*, 558–565.

Bosma, H., Peter, R., Siegrist, J., & Marmot, M. (1998). Two alternative job stress models and the risk of coronary heart disease. *American Journal of Public Health, 88*, 68–74.

Bostwick, J. M., & Pankratz, V. S. (2000). Affective disorders and suicide risk: A re-examination. *American Journal of Psychiatry, 157*, 1925–1932.

Bosworth, R. G., & Dobkins, K. R. (1999). Left-hemisphere dominance for motion processing in deaf signers. *Psychological Science, 10*, 256–262.

Bothwell, R. K., Brigham, J. C., & Malpass, R. S. (1989). Cross-racial identification. *Personality and Social Psychology Bulletin, 15*, 19–25.

Bothwell, R. K., Deffenbacher, K. A., & Brigham, J. C. (1987). Correlation of eyewitness accuracy and confidence: Optimality hypothesis revised. *Journal of Applied Psychology, 72*, 691–695.

Botwin, M. D., Buss, D. M., & Shackelford, T. K. (1997). Personality and mate preferences: Five factors in mate selection and marital satisfaction. *Journal of Personality, 65*, 107–136.

Bouchard, T. J., Jr. (1981, December 6). Interview on *Nova: Twins* [program broadcast by the Public Broadcasting Service].

Bouchard, T. J., Jr. (1995). Longitudinal studies of personality and intelligence: A behavior genetic and evolutionary psychology perspective. In D. H. Saklofske & M. Zeidner (Eds.), *International handbook of personality and intelligence.* New York: Plenum.

Bouchard, T. J., Jr. (1996a). IQ similarity in twins reared apart: Finding and responses to critics. In R. Sternberg & C. Grigorenko (Eds.), *Intelligence: Heredity and environment.* New York: Cambridge University Press.

Bouchard, T. J., Jr. (1996b). Behavior genetic studies of intelligence, yesterday and today: The long journey from plausibility to proof. *Journal of Biosocial Science, 28*, 527–555.

Bouchard, T. J., Jr. (2004). Genetic influence on human psychological traits. *Current Directions in Psychological Science, 13*, 148–151.

Bouchard, T. J., Jr., & McGue, M. (1990). Genetic and rearing environmental influences on adult personality: An analysis of adopted twins reared apart. *Journal of Personality, 58*, 263.

Bouton, M. E., Mineka, S., & Barlow, D. H. (2001). A modern learning theory perspective on the etiology of panic disorder. *Psychological Review, 108*, 4–32.

Bowden, E. M., & Beeman, M. J. (1998). Getting the right idea: Semantic activation in the right hemisphere may help solve insight problems. *Psychological Science, 9*, 435–440.

Bower, B. (2003, November 22). Vision seekers. *Science News, 164*, pp. 331, 332.

Bower, G. H. (1983). Affect and cognition. *Philosophical Transaction: Royal Society of London, Series B, 302*, 387–402.

Bower, G. H. (1986). Prime time in cognitive psychology. In P. Eelen (Ed.), *Cognitive research and behavior therapy: Beyond the conditioning paradigm.* Amsterdam: North Holland Publishers.

Bower, G. H., Clark, M. C., Lesgold, A. M., & Winzenz, D. (1969). Hierarchical retrieval schemes in recall of categorized word lists. *Journal of Verbal Learning and Verbal Behavior, 8*, 323–343.

Bower, G. H., & Morrow, D. G. (1990). Mental models in narrative comprehension. *Science, 247*, 44–48.

Bower, J. E., Kemeny, M. E., Taylor, S. E., & Fahey, J. L. (1998). Cognitive processing, discovery of meaning, CD4 decline, and AIDS-related mortality among bereaved HIV-seropositive men. *Journal of Consulting and Clinical Psychology, 66*, 979–986.

Bower, J. M., & Parsons, L. M. (2003, August). Rethinking the "lesser brain." *Scientific American*, pp. 50–57.

Bowers, K. S. (1984). Hypnosis. In N. Endler & J. M. Hunt (Eds.), *Personality and behavioral disorders* (2nd ed.). New York: Wiley.

Bowers, K. S. (1987, July). Personal communication.

Bowers, T. G., & Clum, G. A. (1988). Relative contribution of specific and nonspecific treatment effects: Meta-analysis of placebo-controlled behavior therapy research. *Psychological Bulletin, 103*, 315–323.

Bowlby, J. (1973). *Separation: Anxiety and anger.* New York: Basic Books.

Bowles, S., & Kasindorf, M. (2001, March 6). Friends tell of picked-on but "normal" kid. *USA Today*, p. 4A.

Bowman, H. (2003, Fall). Interactions between chimpanzees and their human caregivers in captive settings: The effects of gestural communication on reciprocity. *Friends of Washoe, 25*(1), 7–16.

Boyatzis, C. J., Matillo, G. M., & Nesbitt, K. M. (1995). Effects of the "Mighty Morphin Power Rangers" on children's aggression with peers. *Child Study Journal, 25*, 45–55.

Boynton, R. M. (1979). *Human color vision.* New York: Holt, Rinehart & Winston.

Braden, J. P. (1994). *Deafness, deprivation, and IQ.* New York: Plenum.

Bradley, D. R., Dumais, S. T., & Petry, H. M. (1976). Reply to Cavonius. *Nature, 261*, 78.

Bradshaw, J. (1990). *Homecoming: Reclaiming and championing your inner child.* New York: Bantam Books.

Brainerd, C. J. (1996). Piaget: A centennial celebration. *Psychological Science, 7*, 191–195.

Brainerd, C. J., & Poole, D. A. (1997). Long-term survival of children's memories: A review. *Learning and Individual Differences, 9*, 125–151.

Brainerd, C. J., & Reyna, V. F. (1998). When things that were never experienced are easier to "remember" than things that were. *Psychological Science, 9*, 484–489.

Brainerd, C. J., & Reyna, V. F. (2002). Fuzzy-trace theory and false memory. *Current Directions in Psychological Science, 11*, 164–169.

Brainerd, C. J., Reyna, V. F., & Brandse, E. (1995). Are children's false memories more persistent than their true memories? *Psychological Science, 6*, 359–364.

Brandon, S., Boakes, J., Glaser, & Green, R. (1998). Recovered memories of childhood sexual abuse: Implications for clinical practice. *British Journal of Psychiatry, 172*, 294–307.

Brannon, L. A., & Brock, T. C. (1994). Perilous underestimation of sex partners' sexual histories in calculating personal AIDS risk. Paper presented to the American Psychological Society convention.

Bransford, J. D., & Johnson, M. K. (1972). Contextual prerequisites for understanding: Some investigations of comprehension and recall. *Journal of Verbal Learning and Verbal Behavior, 11*, 717–726.

Braun, S. (1996). New experiments underscore warnings on maternal drinking. *Science, 273*, 738–739.

Braun, S. (2001, Spring). Seeking insight by prescription. *Cerebrum*, pp. 10–21.

Bray, D. W., & Byham, W. C. (1991, Winter). Assessment centers and their derivatives. *Journal of Continuing Higher Education*, pp. 8–11.

Bray, D. W., Byham, W. (1997). Insights into the history and future of assessment centers: An interview with Dr. Douglas W. Bray and Dr. William Byham. *Journal of Social Behavior and Personality, 12*, 3–12.

Bray, G. A. (1969). Effect of caloric restriction on energy expenditure in obese patients. *Lancet, 2,* 397–398.

Brayne, C., Spiegelhalter, D. J., Dufouil, C., Chi, L-Y., Dening, T. R., Paykel, E. S., O'Connor, D. W., Ahmed, A., McGee, M. A., & Huppert, F. A. (1999). Estimating the true extent of cognitive decline in the old old. *Journal of the American Geriatrics Society, 47,* 1283–1288.

Breedlove, S. M. (1997). Sex on the brain. *Nature, 389,* 801.

Brehm, S., & Brehm, J. W. (1981). *Psychological reactance: A theory of freedom and control.* New York: Academic Press.

Breland, K., & Breland, M. (1961). The misbehavior of organisms. *American Psychologist, 16,* 661–664.

Brenner, M. (1973). The next-in-line effect. *Journal of Verbal Learning and Verbal Behavior, 12,* 320–323.

Breslau, N., & Klein, D. F. (1999). Smoking and panic attacks: An epidemiologic investigation. *Archives of General Psychiatry, 56,* 1141–1147.

Bressan, P., & Dal Martello, M. F. (2002). Talis pater, talis filius: Perceived resemblance and the belief in genetic relatedness. *Psychological Science, 13,* 213–218.

Bretz, R. D. (1989). College grade point average as a predictor of adult success: A meta-analytic review and some additional evidence. *Public Personnel Management, 18,* 11–22.

Brewer, C. L. (1990). Personal correspondence.

Brewer, C. L. (1996). Personal communication.

Brewer, W. F. (1977). Memory for the pragmatic implications of sentences. *Memory & Cognition, 5,* 673–678.

Brewin, C. R., Andrews, B., Rose, S., & Kirk, M. (1999). Acute stress disorder and posttraumatic stress disorder in victims of violent crime. *American Journal of Psychiatry, 156,* 360–366.

Brewin, C. R., Andrews, B., & Valentine, J. D. (2000). Meta-analysis of risk factors for posttraumatic stress disorder in trauma-exposed adults. *Journal of Consulting and Clinical Psychology, 68,* 748–766.

Brickman, P., Coates, D., & Janoff-Bulman, R. J. (1978). Lottery winners and accident victims: Is happiness relative? *Journal of Personality and Social Psychology, 36,* 917–927.

Brief, A. P., & Weiss, H. M. (2002). Organizational behavior: Affect in the workplace. *Annual Review of Psychology, 53,* 279–307.

Brinson, S. L. (1992). The use and opposition of rape myths in prime-time television dramas. *Sex Roles, 27,* 359–375.

Briscoe, D. (1997, February 16). Women lawmakers still not in charge. Associated Press (in *Grand Rapids Press*, p. A23).

Brislin, R. (1993). *Understanding culture's influence on behavior.* Fort Worth, TX: Harcourt Brace.

Brislin, R. W. (1988). Increasing awareness of class, ethnicity, culture, and race by expanding on students' own experiences. In I. Cohen (Ed.), *The G. Stanley Hall Lecture Series.* Washington, DC: American Psychological Association.

Brissette, I., & Cohen, S. (2002). The contribution of individual differences in hostility to the associations between daily interpersonal conflict, affect, and sleep. *Personality and Social Psychology Bulletin, 28,* 1265–1274.

Brissette, I., Scheier, M. F., & Carver, C. S. (2002). The role of optimism in social network development, coping, and psychological adjustment during a life transition. *Journal of Personality and Social Psychology, 82,* 102–111.

British Psychological Society. (1993). Ethical principles for conducting research with human participants. *The Psychologist: Bulletin of the British Psychological Society, 6,* 33–36.

Britton, W. B., & Bootzin, R. R. (2004). Near-death experiences and the temporal lobe. *Psychological Science, 15,* 254–258.

Broadbent, D. E. (1978). The current state of noise research: Reply to Poulton. *Psychological Bulletin, 85,* 1052–1067.

Brody, J. E. (1999, November 30). Yesterday's precocious puberty is norm today. *New York Times* (www.nytimes.com).

Brody, J. E. (2000, March 21). When post-traumatic stress grips youth. *New York Times* (www.nytimes.com).

Brody, J. E. (2001, December 11). An old enemy, smoking, hangs tough. *New York Times* (www.nytimes.com).

Brody, J. E. (2002, November 26). When the eyelids snap shut at 65 miles an hour. *New York Times* (www.nytimes.com).

Brody, J. E. (2003, August 19). Skipping a college course: Weight gain 101. *New York Times* (www.nytimes.com).

Brody, J. E. (2003, September). Addiction: A brain ailment, not a moral lapse. *New York Times* (www.nytimes.com).

Brody, J. E. (2003, December 23). Stampede of diabetes as U.S. races to obesity. *New York Times* (www.nytimes.com).

Brody, N. (1992). *Intelligence,* 2nd ed. San Diego: Academic Press.

Brody, N. (1997). Dispositional paradigms: Comment on Eysenck (1997) and the biosocial science of individual differences. *Journal of Personality and Social Psychology, 73*(6), 1242–1245.

Brody, N. (2001). Inspection time: Past, present, and future. *Intelligence, 29,* 537–541.

Brody, N. (2003). Construct validation of the Sternberg Triarchic Abilities Test: Comment and reanalysis. *Intelligence, 31,* 319–329.

Brodzinsky, D. M., & Schechter, M. D. (Eds.) (1990). *The psychology of adoption.* New York: Oxford University Press.

Broman, S. H. (1989). Infant physical status and later cognitive development. In M. G. Bornstein & N. A. Krasnegor (Eds.), *Stability and continuity in mental development: Behavioral and biological perspectives.* Hillsdale, NJ: Erlbaum.

Bronner, E. (1998, February 25). U.S. high school seniors among worst in math and science. *New York Times* (www.nytimes.com).

Brooke, J. (2000, January 20). Canada proposes scaring smokers with pictures on the pack. *New York Times* (www.nytimes.com)

Brooks, D. (2005, April 28). Mourning Mother Russia. *New York Times* (www.nytimes.com).

Brooks, D. J. (2002, October 8). Running down the road to happiness. *Gallup Tuesday Briefing* (www.gallup.com).

Brooks, G. (1960). "The Bean Eaters," *The World of Gwendolyn Brooks,* Harper & Row.

Brown, A. S. (2003). A review of the déjà vu experience. *Psychological Bulletin, 129,* 394–413.

Brown, A. S. (2004). *The déjà vu experience.* Hove, England: Psychology Press.

Brown, A. S., Begg, M. D., Gravenstein, S., Schaefer, C. A., Wyatt, R. J., Bresnahan, M., Babulas, V. P., & Susser, E. S. (2004). Serologic evidence of prenatal influenza in the etiology of schizophrenia. *Archives of General Psychiatry, 61,* 774–780.

Brown, A. S., Bracken, E., Zoccoli, S., & Douglas, K. (2004). Generating and remembering passwords. *Applied Cognitive Psychology, 18,* 641–651.

Brown, A. S., Schaefer, C. A., Wyatt, R. J., Goetz, R., Begg, M. D., Gorman, J. M., & Susser, E. S. (2000). Maternal exposure to respiratory infections and adult schizophrenia spectrum disorders: A prospective birth cohort study. *Schizophrenia Bulletin, 26,* 287–295.

Brown, E. L., & Deffenbacher, K. (1979). *Perception and the senses.* New York: Oxford University Press.

Brown, G. K., Ten Have, T., Henriques, G. R., Xie, S. X., Hollander, J. E., & Beck, A. T. (2005). Cognitive therapy for the prevention of suicide attempts. *JAMA: Journal of the American Medical Association, 294,* 563–570.

Brown, J. D. (1991). Accuracy and bias in self-knowledge. In C. R. Snyder & D. F. Forsyth (Eds.), *Handbook of social and clinical psychology: The health perspective.* New York: Pergamon Press.

Brown, J. D., Steele, J. R., & Walsh-Childers, K. (2002). Sexual teens, sexual media: Investigating media's influence on adolescent sexuality. Mahwah, NJ: Erlbaum.

Brown, J. L., & Pollitt, E. (1996, February). Malnutrition, poverty and intellectual development. *Scientific American*, pp. 38–43.

Brown, L. R., Kane, H., & Ayres, E. (1993). *Vital signs 1993: The trends that are shaping our future.* New York: Norton.

Brown, R. (1965). *Social psychology.* New York: Free Press.

Brown, R. (1973). *A first language: The early stages.* Cambridge, MA: Harvard University Press.

Brown, R. (1986). Linguistic relativity. In S. H. Hulse & B. F. Green, Jr. (Eds.), *One hundred years of psychological research in America.* Baltimore: Johns Hopkins University Press.

Brown, R., & Kulik, J. (1982). Flashbulb memories. In U. Neisser (Ed.), *Memory observed.* San Francisco: Freeman.

Brown, S. L., Nesse, R. M., Vinokur, A. D., & Smith, D. M. (2003). Providing social support may be more beneficial than receiving it: Results from a prospective study of mortality. *Psychological Science, 14,* 320–327.

Brown, S. W., Garry, M., Loftus, E., Silver, B., DuBois, K., & DuBreuil, S. (1996). People's beliefs about memory: Why don't we have better memories? Paper presented at the American Psychological Society convention.

Brownell, K. D. (1997, March). We must be more militant about food. *APA Monitor,* p. 48.

Brownell, K. D. (2002). Public policy and the prevention of obesity. In C. G. Fairburn & K. D. Brownell (Eds.), *Eating disorders and obesity: A comprehensive handbook* (2nd ed.). New York: Guilford.

Brownell, K. D., & Wadden, T. A. (1992). Etiology and treatment of obesity: Understanding a serious, prevalent, and refractory disorder. *Journal of Consulting and Clinical Psychology, 60,* 505–517.

Browning, C. (1992). *Ordinary men: Reserve police battalion 101 and the final solution in Poland.* New York: HarperCollins.

Brownmiller, S. (1975). *Against our will: Men, women, and rape.* New York: Simon and Schuster.

Bruce, D., Dolan, A., & Phillips-Grant, K. (2000). On the transition from childhood amnesia to the recall of personal memories. *Psychological Science, 11,* 360–364.

Bruck, M., & Ceci, S. J. (1999). The suggestibility of children's memory. *Annual Review of Psychology, 50,* 419–439.

Bruck, M., & Ceci, S. J. (2004). Forensic developmental psychology: Unveiling four common misconceptions. *Current Directions in Psychological Science, 15,* 229–232.

Bruer, J. T. (1999). *The myth of the first three years: A new understanding of early brain development and lifelong learning.* New York: Free Press.

Brumberg, J. J. (2000). *Fasting girls: The history of anorexia nervosa.* New York: Vintage.

Brune, K., & Handwerker, H. (2004). *Hyperalgesia: Molecular mechanisms and clinical implications.* Special issue of *Progress in Pain Research and Management, 30.* Seattle, WA: International Association for the Study of Pain, IASP Press.

Bryant, R. A. (2001). Posttraumatic stress disorder and traumatic brain injury: Can they co-exist? *Clinical Psychology Review, 21,* 931–948.

Buchel, C., Morris, J., Dolan, R. J., & Friston, K. J. (1998). Brain systems mediating aversive conditioning: An event-related fMRI study. *Neuron, 20,* 947–957.

Buck, L., & Axel, R. (1991). A novel multigene family may encode odorant receptors: A molecular basis for odor recognition. *Cell, 65,* 175–187.

Buckingham, M. (2001, August). Quoted by P. LaBarre, "Marcus Buckingham thinks your boss has an attitude problem." *The Magazine* (fastcompany.com/online/49/buckingham.html).

Buckingham, M., & Clifton, D. O. (2001). *Now, discover your strengths.* New York: Free Press.

Buckley, K. E., & Leary, M. R. (2001). Perceived acceptance as a predictor of social, emotional, and academic outcomes. Paper presented at the Society of Personality and Social Psychology annual convention.

Buehler, R., Griffin, D., & Ross, M. (1994). Exploring the "planning fallacy": Why people underestimate their task completion times. *Journal of Personality and Social Psychology, 67,* 366–381.

Bugelski, B. R., Kidd, E., & Segmen, J. (1968). Image as a mediator in one-trial paired-associate learning. *Journal of Experimental Psychology, 76,* 69–73.

Bugental, D. B. (1986). Unmasking the "polite smile": Situational and personal determinants of managed affect in adult-child interaction. *Personality and Social Psychology Bulletin, 12,* 7–16.

Buka, S. L., Goldstein, J. M., Seidman, L. J., Zornberg, G., Donatelli, J-A. A., Denny, L. R., & Tsuang, M. T. (1999). Prenatal complications, genetic vulnerability, and schizophrenia: The New England longitudinal studies of schizophrenia. *Psychiatric Annals, 29,* 151–156.

Buka, S. L., Tsuang, M. T., Torrey, E. F., Klebanoff, M. A., Wagner, R. L., & Yolken, R. H. (2001). Maternal infections and subsequent psychosis among offspring. *Archives of General Psychiatry, 58,* 1032–1037.

Bullough, V. (1990). The Kinsey scale in historical perspective. In D. P. McWhirter, S. A. Sanders, & J. M. Reinisch (Eds.), *Homosexuality/heterosexuality: Concepts of sexual orientation.* New York: Oxford University Press.

Buquet, R. (1988). Le rêve et les déficients visuels (Dreams and the visually impaired). *Psychanalyse-à-l'Université, 13,* 319–327.

Bureau of the Census. (2004). *Statistical abstract of the United States 2004.* Washington, DC: U.S. Government Printing Office.

Bureau of Labor Statistics. (2004, September 14). American time-user survey summary. Washington, DC: United States Department of Labor (www.bls.gov).

Bureau of Labor Statistics, U.S. Department of Labor. (2004–2005). Occupational Outlook Handbook, 2004-05 Edition.

Bureau of the Census. (2004). *Statistical abstract of the United States 2004.* Washington, DC: U.S. Government Printing Office.

Burger, J. M. (1987). Increased performance with increased personal control: A self-presentation interpretation. *Journal of Experimental Social Psychology, 23,* 350–360.

Burger, J. M., & Burns, L. (1988). The illusion of unique invulnerability and the use of effective contraception. *Personality and Social Psychology Bulletin, 14,* 264–270.

Burgess, M., Enzle, M. E., & Schmaltz, R. (2004). Defeating the potentially deleterious effects of externally imposed deadlines: Practitioners' rules-of-thumb. *Personality and Social Psychology Bulletin, 30,* 868–877.

Buri, J. R., Louiselle, P. A., Misukanis, T. M., & Mueller, R. A. (1988). Effects of parental authoritarianism and authoritativeness on self-esteem. *Personality and Social Psychology Bulletin, 14,* 271–282.

Burish, T. G., & Carey, M. P. (1986). Conditioned aversive responses in cancer chemotherapy patients: Theoretical and developmental analysis. *Journal of Counseling and Clinical Psychology, 54,* 593–600.

Burke, D. M., & Shafto, M. A. (2004). Aging and language production. *Current Directions in Psychological Science, 13,* 21–24.

Burkholder, R. (2005a, January 11). Chinese far wealthier than a decade ago—but are they happier? *Gallup Poll News Service* (www.gallup.com).

Burkholder, R. (2005b, January 18). China's citizens optimistic, yet not entirely satisfied. *Gallup Poll News Service* (www.gallup.com).

Burns, B. C. (2004). The effects of speed on skilled chess performance. *Psychological Science, 15,* 442–447.

Burrell, B. (2005). *Postcards from the brain museum: The improbable search for meaning in the matter of famous minds.* New York: Broadway Books.

Burt, D. M., & Perrett, D. I. (1995). Perception of age in adult Caucasian male faces: Computer graphic manipulation of shape and colour information. *Proceedings of the Royal Society, 259,* 137–143.

Bush, G. W. (2001, May 1). Speech to the National Defense University, Washington, DC.

Bushman, B. J. (1993). Human aggression while under the influence of alcohol and other drugs: An integrative research review. *Current Directions in Psychological Science, 2,* 148–152.

Bushman, B. J. (2002). Does venting anger feed or extinguish the flame? Catharsis, rumination, distraction, anger, and aggressive responding. *Personality and Social Psychology Bulletin, 28,* 724–731.

Bushman, B. J., & Anderson, C. A. (2001). Media violence and the American public: Scientific facts versus media misinformation. *American Psychologist, 56,* 477–489.

Bushman, B. J., & Baumeister, R. F. (1998). Threatened egotism, narcissism, self-esteem, and direct and displaced aggression: Does self-love or self-hate lead to violence? *Journal of Personality and Social Psychology, 75,* 219–229.

Bushman, B. J., Baumeister, R. F., & Stack, A. D. (1999). Catharsis, aggression, and persuasive influence: Self-fulfilling or self-defeating prophecies? *Journal of Personality and Social Psychology, 76,* 367–376.

Bushman, B. J., & Bonaci, A. M. (2002). Violence and sex impair memory for television ads. *Journal of Applied Psychology, 87,* 557–564.

Busnel, M. C., Granier-Deferre, C., & Lecanuet, J. P. (1992, October). Fetal audition. *New York Academy of Sciences, 662,* 118–134.

Buss, A. H. (1989). Personality as traits. *American Psychologist, 44,* 1378–1388.

Buss, D. M. (1991). Evolutionary personality psychology. *Annual Review of Psychology, 42,* 459–491.

Buss, D. M. (1994). The strategies of human mating: People worldwide are attracted to the same qualities in the opposite sex. *American Scientist, 82,* 238–249.

Buss, D. M. (1995). Evolutionary psychology: A new paradigm for psychological science. *Psychological Inquiry, 6,* 1–30.

Buss, D. M. (1996). Sexual conflict: Evolutionary insights into feminism and the "battle of the sexes." In D. M. Buss & N. M. Malamuth (Eds.), *Sex, power, conflict: Evolutionary and feminist perspectives.* New York: Oxford University Press.

Buss, D. M. (1996). Sexual conflict: Evolutionary insights into feminism and the "battle of the sexes." In D. M. Buss & N. M. Malamuth (Eds.), *Sex, power, conflict: Evolutionary and feminist perspectives.* New York: Oxford University Press.

Butler, A. C., Hokanson, J. E., & Flynn, H. A. (1994). A comparison of self-esteem lability and low trait self-esteem as vulnerability factors for depression. *Journal of Personality and Social Psychology, 66,* 166–177.

Butler, J., & Rovee-Collier, C. (1989). Contextual gating of memory retrieval. *Developmental Psychobiology, 22,* 533–552.

Butler, R. A. (1954, February). Curiosity in monkeys. *Scientific American,* pp. 70–75.

Butterfield, F. (1999, July 12). Experts say study confirms prison's new role as mental hospital. *New York Times* (www.nytimes.com).

Butterworth, G. (1992). Origins of self-perception in infancy. *Psychological Inquiry, 3,* 103–111.

Byne, W., & Parsons, B. (1993). Human sexual orientation: The biologic theories reappraised. *Archives of General Psychiatry, 50,* 228–239.

Bynum, R. (2004, November 1). Associated Press article.

Byrne, D. (1971). *The attraction paradigm.* New York: Academic Press.

Byrne, D. (1982). Predicting human sexual behavior. In A. G. Kraut (Ed.), *The G. Stanley Hall Lecture Series* (Vol. 2). Washington, DC: American Psychological Association.

Byrne, J. (2003, September 21). From correspondence reported by Michael Shermer, "E-Skeptic for September 21, 2003, from The Skeptics Society."

Byrne, R. W. (1991, May/June). Brute intellect. *The Sciences,* pp. 42–47.

Byrne, R. W., & Russon, A. E. (1998). Learning by imitation: A hierarchical approach. *Behavioral and Brain Sciences, 21,* 667–721.

Byrnes, J. P., Miller, D. C., & Schafer, W. C. (1999). Gender differences in risk taking: A meta-analysis. *Psychological Bulletin 125,* 367–383.

Cable, D. M., & Gilovich, T. (1998). Looked over or overlooked? Prescreening decisions and postinterview evaluations. *Journal of Personality and Social Psychology, 83,* 501–508.

Cacioppo, J. T., Berntson, G. G., Klein, D. J., & Poehlmann, K. M. (1997). The psychophysiology of emotion across the lifespan. *Annual Review of Gerontology and Geriatrics, 17,* 27.

Cahill, L. (1994). (Beta)-adrenergic activation and memory for emotional events. *Nature, 371,* 702–704.

Cahill, L. (2005, May). His brain, her brain. *Scientific American,* pp. 40–47.

Cale, E. M., & Lilienfeld, S. O. (2002). Sex differences in psychopathy and antisocial personality disorder: A review and integration. *Clinical Psychology Review, 22,* 1179–1207.

Call, K. T., Riedel, A. A., Hein, K., McLoyd, V., Petersen, A., & Kipke, M. (2002). Adolescent health and well-being in the twenty-first century: A global perspective. *Journal of Research on Adolescence, 12,* 69–98.

Callaghan, T., Rochat, P., Lillard, A., Claux, M. L., Odden, H., Itakura, S., Tapanya, S., & Singh, S. (2005). Synchrony in the onset of mental-state reasoning. *Psychological Science, 16,* 378–384.

Calle, E. E., Thun, M. J., Petrelli, J. M., Rodriguez, C., & Health, C. W., Jr. (1999). Body-mass index and mortality in a prospective cohort of U.S. adults. *New England Journal of Medicine, 341,* 1097–1105.

Callicott, J. H., & 11 others (2005). Variation in DISC1 affects hippocampal structure and function and increased risk for schizophrenia. *Proceedings of the National Academy of Sciences, 102,* 8627–8632.

Calvin, W. H. (1996). *The cerebral code: Thinking a thought in the mosaics of the mind.* Cambridge, MA: MIT Press.

Calvo-Merino, B., Glaser, D. E., Grèzes, J., Passingham, R. E., & Haggard, P. (2004). Action observation and acquired motor skills: An fMRI study with expert dancers. *Cerebral Cortex, 15,* 1243–1249.

Camerer, C. F., Loewenstein, G., & Weber, M. (1989). The curse of knowledge in economic settings: An experimental analysis. *Journal of Political Economy, 97,* 1232–1254.

Campbell, D. T. (1975). On the conflicts between biological and social evolution and between psychology and moral tradition. *American Psychologist, 30,* 1103–1126.

Campbell, D. T., & Specht, J. C. (1985). Altruism: Biology, culture, and religion. *Journal of Social and Clinical Psychology, 3*(1), 33–42.

Campbell, S. (1986). *The Loch Ness Monster: The evidence.* Willingborough: Acquarian Press.

Camper, J. (1990, February 7). Drop pompom squad, U. of I. rape study says. *Chicago Tribune,* p. 1.

Camperio-Ciani, A., Corna, F., & Capiluppi, C. (2004). Evidence for maternally inherited factors favouring male homosexuality and promoting female fecundity. *Proceedings of the Royal Society of London B, 271,* 2217–2221.

Campos, J. J., Bertenthal, B. I., & Kermoian, R. (1992). Early experience and emotional development: The emergence of wariness and heights. *Psychological Science, 3,* 61–64.

Canli, T., Desmond, J. E., Zhao, Z., & Gabrieli, J. D. E. (2002). Sex differences in the neural basis of emotional memories. *Proceedings of the National Academy of Sciences, 99,* 10789–10794.

Cannon, J. (2005). Career planning and opportunities: The bachelor's degree in psychology. *Eye on Psi Chi, 26–28.*

Cannon, W. B. (1929). *Bodily changes in pain, hunger, fear, and rage.* New York: Branford.

Cannon, W. B., & Washburn, A. (1912). An explanation of hunger. *American Journal of Physiology, 29,* 441–454.

Cantor, N., & Kihlstrom, J. F. (1987). *Personality and social intelligence.* Englewood Cliffs, NJ: Prentice Hall.

Cantril, H., & Bumstead, C. H. (1960). *Reflections on the human venture.* New York: New York University Press.

Caplan, N., Choy, M. H., & Whitmore, J. K. (1992, February). Indochinese refugee families and academic achievement. *Scientific American,* pp. 36–42.

Caputo, D., & Dunning, D. (2005). What you don't know: The role played by errors of omission in imperfect self-assessments. *Journal of Experimental Social Psychology,* 488–505.

Carducci, B. J., Cosby, P. C., & Ward, D. D. (1978). Sexual arousal and interpersonal evaluations. *Journal of Experimental Social Psychology, 14,* 449–457.

Carey, G. (1990). Genes, fears, phobias, and phobic disorders. *Journal of Counseling and Development, 68,* 628–632.

Carlezon, W. A., Jr., Mague, S. D., & Andersen, S. L. (2003). Enduring behavioral effects of early exposure to methylphenidate in rats. *Biological Psychiatry, 54,* 1330–1337.

Carli, L. L., & Leonard, J. B. (1989). The effect of hindsight on victim derogation. *Journal of Social and Clinical Psychology, 8,* 331–343.

Carlson, C. L. (2000). ADHD is overdiagnosed. In R. L. Atkinson, R. C. Atkinson, E. E. Smith, D. J. Bem, & S. Nolen-Hoeksema (Eds.), *Hilgard's introduction to psychology,* 13th ed. Fort Worth: Harcourt.

Carlson, D. K. (2002, February 19). Acceptance of homosexuality: A youth movement. The Gallup Organization (www.gallup.com/poll/tb/educaYouth/200220219.asp).

Carlson, M. (1995, August 29). Quoted by S. Blakeslee, In brain's early growth, timetable may be crucial. *New York Times,* pp. C1, C3.

Carlson, M., Charlin, V., & Miller, N. (1988). Positive mood and helping behavior: A test of six hypotheses. *Journal of Personality and Social Psychology, 55,* 211–229.

Carlson, R. (1984). What's social about social psychology? Where's the person in personality research? *Journal of Personality and Social Psychology, 47,* 1304–1309.

Carlson, S. (1985). A double-blind test of astrology. *Nature, 318,* 419–425.

Carnegie Council on Adolescent Development. (1989, June). *Turning points: Preparing American youth for the 21st century.* (The report of the Task Force on Education of Young Adolescents.) New York: Carnegie Corporation.

Carrière, G. (2003). Parent and child factors associated with youth obesity. *Statistics Canada, Catalogue 82-003, Supplement to Health Reports, 2003.*

Carroll, D., Davey Smith, G., & Bennett, P. (1994, March). Health and socio-economic status. *The Psychologist,* pp. 122–125.

Carroll, J. (2005, January 14). Terrorism concerns fade. *The Gallup Organization* (www.gallup.com).

Carroll, J. M., & Russell, J. A. (1996). Do facial expressions signal specific emotions? Judging emotion from the face in context. *Journal of Personality and Social Psychology, 70,* 205–218.

Carskadon, M. (2002). *Adolescent sleep patterns: Biological, social, and psychological influences.* New York: Cambridge University Press.

Carter, R. (1998). *Mapping the mind.* Berkeley, CA: University of California Press.

Carter, S., & Snow, C. (2004, May). Helping singles enter better marriages using predictive models of marital success. Presented to the American Psychological Society convention.

Cartwright, R. D. (1978). *A primer on sleep and dreaming.* Reading, MA: Addison-Wesley.

Caryl, P. G. (1994). Early event-related potentials correlate with inspection time and intelligence. *Intelligence, 18,* 15–46.

CASA. (2003). *The formative years: Pathways to substance abuse among girls and young women ages 8–22.* New York: National Center on Addiction and Substance Use, Columbia University.

Case, R. B., Moss, A. J., Case, N., McDermott, M., & Eberly, S. (1992). Living alone after myocardial infarction: Impact on prognosis. *Journal of the American Medical Association, 267,* 515–519.

Cash, T., & Janda, L. H. (1984, December). The eye of the beholder. *Psychology Today,* pp. 46–52.

Cash, T. F., & Henry, P. E. (1995). Women's body images: The results of a national survey in the U.S.A. *Sex Roles, 33,* 19–28.

Caspi, A. (2000). The child is father of the man: Personality continuities from childhood to adulthood. *Journal of Personality and Social Psychology, 78,* 158–172.

Caspi, A., Harrington, H., Milne, B., Amell, J. W., Theodore, R. F., & Moffitt, T. E. (2003). Children's behavioral styles at age 3 are linked to their adult personality traits at age 26. *Journal of Personality, 71,* 496–513.

Caspi, A., McClay, J., Moffitt, T., Mill, J., Martin, J., Craig, I. W., Taylor, A., & Poulton, R. (2002). Role of genotype in the cycle of violence in maltreated children. *Science, 297,* 851–854.

Caspi, A., Moffitt, T. E., Newman, D. L., & Silva, P. A. (1996). Behavioral observations at age 3 years predict adult psychiatric disorders: Longitudinal evidence from a birth cohort. *Archives of General Psychiatry, 53,* 1033–1039.

Caspi, A., Sugden, K., Moffitt, T. E., Taylor, A., Craig, I. W., Harrington, H., McClay, J., Mill, J., Martin, J., Braithwaite, A., & Poulton, R. (2003). Influence of life stress on depression: Moderation by a polymorphism in the 5-HTT gene. *Science, 30,* 386–389.

Cassandro, V. J., & Simonton, D. K. (2003). Creativity and genius. In C. L. M. Keyes & J. Haidt (Eds.), *Flourishing: Positive psychology and the life well-lived.* Washington, DC: American Psychological Association.

Cassidy, J., & Shaver, P. R. (1999). *Handbook of attachment.* New York: Guilford.

Castillo, R. J. (1997). *Culture and mental illness: A client-centered approach.* Pacific Grove, CA: Brooks/Cole.

Castonguay, L. G., & Goldfried, M. R. (1994). Psychotherapy integration: An idea whose time has come. *Applied & Preventive Psychology, 3,* 159–172.

Catanese, K. R., & Tice, D. M. (2005). The effect of rejection on anti-social behaviors: Social exclusion produces aggressive behaviors. In K. D. Williams, J. P. Forgas, & W. Von Hippel (Eds.), *The social outcast: Ostracism, social exclusion, rejection, and bullying.* New York: Psychology Press.

Cattell, R. B. (1963). Theory of fluid and crystallized intelligence: A critical experiment. *Journal of Educational Psychology, 54,* 1–22.

Cavalli-Sforza, L., Menozzi, P., & Piazza, A. (1994). *The history and geography of human genes.* Princeton, NJ: Princeton University Press.

Cavigelli, S. A., & McClintock, M. K. (2003). Fear of novelty in infant rats predicts adult corticosterone dynamics and an early death. *Proceedings of the National Academy of Sciences, 100,* 16131–16136.

CDC. (2004). Teenagers in the United States: Sexual activity, contraceptive use, and childbearing, 2002. A fact sheet for series 23, number 24. DHHS Publication (PHS) 2005-1976.

CDC. (2004, December 16). Prevalence of overweight and obesity among adults: United States, 1999–2002. Centers for Disease Control and Prevention, National Center for Health Statistics (www.cdc.gov).

Ceci, S. J. (1993). Cognitive and social factors in children's testimony. Master Lecture, American Psychological Association convention.

Ceci, S. J., & Bruck, M. (1993). Child witnesses: Translating research into policy. *Social Policy Report* (Society for Research in Child Development), *7*(3), 1–30.

Ceci, S. J., & Bruck, M. (1995). *Jeopardy in the courtroom: A scientific analysis of children's testimony.* Washington, DC: American Psychological Association.

Ceci, S. J., Huffman, M. L. C., Smith, E., & Loftus, E. F. (1994). Repeatedly thinking about a non-event: Source misattributions among preschoolers. *Consciousness and Cognition, 3,* 388–407.

Ceci, S. J., & Liker, J. K. (1986). A day at the races: A study of IQ, expertise, and cognitive complexity. *Journal of Experimental Psychology: General, 115,* 255–266.

Ceci, S. J., & Williams, W. M. (1997). Schooling, intelligence, and income. *American Psychologist, 52,* 1051–1058.

Centers for Disease Control. (1992, September 16). Serious mental illness and disability in the adult household population: United States, 1989. *Advance Data* No. 218 from *Vital and Health Statistics,* National Center for Health Statistics.

Centers for Disease Control. (2003). Who should get a flu shot (influenza vaccine). National Center for Infectious Diseases (http://www.cdc.gov/ncidod/diseases/flu/who.htm).

Centers for Disease Control Vietnam Experience Study. (1988). Health status of Vietnam veterans. *Journal of the American Medical Association, 259,* 2701–2709.

Centerwall, B. S. (1989). Exposure to television as a risk factor for violence. *American Journal of Epidemiology, 129,* 643–652.

Cerella, J. (1985). Information processing rates in the elderly. *Psychological Bulletin, 98,* 67–83.

CFI. (2003, July). International developments. *Report.* Amherst, NY: Center for Inquiry International.

Chambless, D. L., Baker, M. J., Baucom, D. H., Beutler, L. E., Calhoun, K. S., Crits-Christoph, P., Daiuto, A., DeRubeis, R., Detweiler, J., Haaga, D. A. F., Johnson, S. B., McCurry, S., Mueser, K. T., Pope, K. S., Sanderson, W. C., Shoham, V., Stickle, T., Williams, D. A., & Woody, S. R. (1997). Update on empirically validated therapies, II. *The Clinical Psychologist, 51*(1), 3–16.

Chamove, A. S. (1980). Nongenetic induction of acquired levels of aggression. *Journal of Abnormal Psychology, 89,* 469–488.

Chance News (1999, July 15). National Lottery and death rates. From *Daily Express,* 13 August 1998.

Chang, E. C. (2001). Cultural influences on optimism and pessimism: Differences in Western and Eastern construals of the self. In E. C. Chang (Ed.), *Optimism and pessimism.* Washington, DC: APA Books.

Chang, P. P., Ford, D. E., Meoni, L. A., Wang, N.-Y., & Klag, M. J. (2002). Anger in young men and subsequent premature cardiovascular disease: The precursors study. *Archives of Internal Medicine, 162,* 901–906.

Chaplin, W. F., Phillips, J. B., Brown, J. D., Clanton, N. R., & Stein, J. L. (2000). Handshaking, gender, personality, and first impressions. *Journal of Personality and Social Psychology, 79,* 110–117.

Charles, S. T., Reynolds, C. A., & Gatz, M. (2001). Age-related differences and change in positive and negative affect over 23 years. *Journal of Personality and Social Psychology, 80,* 136–151.

Charpak, G., & Broch, H. (2004). *Debunked! ESP, telekinesis, and other pseudoscience.* Baltimore, MD: Johns Hopkins University Press.

Chartrand, T. L., & Bargh, J. A. (1999). The chameleon effect: The perception-behavior link and social interaction. *Journal of Personality and Social Psychology, 76,* 893–910.

Chase, M. H., & Morales, F. R. (1983). Subthreshold excitatory activity and motorneuron discharge during REM periods of active sleep. *Science, 221,* 1195–1198.

Chase, W. G., & Simon, H. A. (1973). Perception in chess. *Cognitive Psychology, 4,* 55–81.

Chase-Lansdale, P. L., Moffitt, R. A., Lohman, B. J., Cherlin, A. J., Coley, R. L., Pittman, L. D., Roff, J., & Votruba-Drzal, E. (2003). Mothers' transitions from welfare to work and the well-being of preschoolers and adolescents. *Science, 299,* 1548–1552.

Chassin, L., Presson, C. C., Sherman, S. J., & McGrew, J. (1987). The changing smoking environment for middle and high school students: 1980–1983. *Journal of Behavioral Medicine, 10,* 581–593.

Chaudhari, N., Landin, A. M., & Roper, S. D. (2000). A metabotropic glutamate receptor variant functions as a taste receptor. *Nature Neuroscience, 3,* 113–119.

Chaves, J. F. (1989). Hypnotic control of clinical pain. In N. P. Spanos & J. F. Chaves (Eds.), *Hypnosis: The cognitive-behavioral perspective.* Buffalo, NY: Prometheus Books.

Cheek, J. M., & Melchior, L. A. (1990). Shyness, self-esteem, and self-consciousness. In H. Leitenberg (Ed.), *Handbook of social and evaluation anxiety.* New York: Plenum.

Cheit, R. E. (1998). Consider this, skeptics of recovered memory. *Ethics & Behavior, 8,* 141–160.

Chen, E. (2004). Why socioeconomic status affects the health of children: A psychosocial perspective. *Current Directions in Psychological Science, 13,* 112–115.

Cheng, C. (2001). Assessing coping flexibility in real-life and laboratory settings: A multimethod approach. *Journal of Personality and Social Psychology, 80,* 814–833.

Cheng, T. O. (1999). Teenage smoking in China. *Journal of Adolescence, 22,* 607–620.

Chess, S., & Thomas, A. (1987). *Know your child: An authoritative guide for today's parents.* New York: Basic Books.

Child Trends. (2001, August). Facts at a glance. (www.childtrends.org).

Chiles, J. A., Lambert, M. J., & Hatch, A. L. (1999). The impact of psychological interventions on medical cost offset: A meta-analytic review. *Clinical Psychology: Science and Practice, 6,* 204–220.

Chisholm, K. (1998). A three year follow-up of attachment and indiscriminate friendliness in children adopted from Romanian orphanages. *Child Development, 69,* 1092–1106.

Choi, I., & Choi, Y. (2002). Culture and self-concept flexibility. *Personality and Social Psychology Bulletin, 28,* 1508–1517.

Chomsky, N. (1959). Review of B. F. Skinner's *Verbal behavior. Language, 35,* 26–58.

Chomsky, N. (1972). *Language and mind.* New York: Harcourt Brace Jovanovich.

Chomsky, N. (1987). Language in a psychological setting. Sophia Linguistic Working Papers in Linguistics, No. 22, Sophia University, Tokyo.

Chorpita, B. F., & Barlow, D. H. (1998). The development of anxiety: The role of control in the early environment. *Psychological Bulletin, 124,* 3–21.

Christakis, D. S., Zimmerman, F. J., DiGiuseppe, D. L., & McCarty, C. A. (2004). Early television exposure and subsequent attentional problems in children. *Pediatrics, 113,* 708–713.

Christensen, A., & Jacobson, N. S. (1994). Who (or what) can do psychotherapy: The status and challenge of nonprofessional therapies. *Psychological Science, 5,* 8–14.

Christophersen, E. R., & Edwards, K. J. (1992). Treatment of elimination disorders: State of the art 1991. *Applied & Preventive Psychology, 1,* 15–22.

Chugani, H. T., & Phelps, M. E. (1986). Maturational changes in cerebral function in infants determined by ^{18}FDG Positron Emission Tomography. *Science, 231,* 840–843.

CIA. (2005). Life expectancy at birth. *The world fact book.* www.cia.gov.

Cialdini, R. B. (1993). *Influence: Science and practice* (3rd ed.). New York: HarperCollins.

Cialdini, R. B., & Richardson, K. D. (1980). Two indirect tactics of image management: Basking and blasting. *Journal of Personality and Social Psychology, 39,* 406–415.

Citrome, L., & Volavka, J. (1999). Schizophrenia: Violence and comorbidity. *Current Opinion in Psychiatry, 12,* 47–51.

Clack, B., Dixon, J., & Tredoux, C. (2005). Eating together apart: Patterns of segregation in a multi-ethnic cafeteria. *Journal of Community and Applied Social Psychology, 15*, 1–16.

Clancy, S. A., McNally, R. J., Schachter, D. L., Lenzenweger, M. F., & Pitman, R. K. (2002). Memory distortion in people reporting abduction by aliens. *Journal of Abnormal Psychology, 111*, 455–461.

Clancy, S. A., Schacter, D. L., McNally, R. J., & Pitman, R. K. (2000). False recognition in women reporting recovered memories of sexual abuse. *Psychological Science, 11*, 26–31.

Clark, A., Seidler, A., & Miller, M. (2001). Inverse association between sense of humor and coronary heart disease. *International Journal of Cardiology, 80*, 87–88.

Clark, K. B., Chein, I., & Cook, S. W. (1952; reprinted 2004). The effects of segregation and the consequences of desegregation: A (September 1952) social science statement in the *Brown v Board of Education of Topeka* Supreme Court Case. *American Psychologist, 59*, 495–501.

Clark, K. B., & Clark, M. P. (1947). Racial identification and preference in Negro children. In T. M.. Newcomb and E. L. Hartley (Eds.), *Readings in social psychology*. New York: Holt.

Clark, R., Anderson, N. B., Clark, V. R., & Williams, D. R. (1999). Racism as a stressor for African Americans: A biopsychosocial model. *American Psychologist, 54*, 805–816.

Clark, R. D. (1990, May). The impact of AIDS on gender differences in willingness to engage in casual sex. *Journal of Applied Social Psychology, 20*, 771–782.

Clark, R. D., III, & Hatfield, E. (1989). Gender differences in willingness to engage in casual sex. *Journal of Psychology and Human Sexuality, 2*, 39–55.

Coats, E. J., & Feldman, R. S. (1996). Gender differences in nonverbal correlates of social status. *Personality and Social Psychology Bulletin, 22*, 1014–1022.

Cofer, J. O., (1992). *The Latin Deli*, New York: W. W. Norton and Company.

Coffey, C. E. (Ed.) (1993). *Clinical science of electroconvulsive therapy*. Washington, DC: American Psychiatric Press.

Coffey, C. E., Lucke, J. F., Saxton, J. A., Ratcliff, G., Unitas, L. J., Billig, B., & Bryan, R. N. (1998). Sex differences in brain aging: A quantitative magnetic resonance imagine study. *Archives of Neurology, 55*, 169–179.

Coffey, C. E., Wilkinson, W. E., Weiner, R. D., Parashos, I. A., Djang, W. T., Webb, M. C., Figiel, G. S., & Spritzer, C. E. (1993). Quantitative cerebral anatomy in depression: A controlled magnetic resonance imaging study. *Archives of General Psychiatry, 50*, 7–16.

Cogan, J. C., Bhalla, S. K., Sefa-Dedeh, A., & Rothblum, E. D. (1996). A comparison study of United States and African students on perceptions of obesity and thinness. *Journal of Cross-Cultural Psychology, 27*, 98–113.

Cogan, J. C., & Ernsberger, P. (1999). Dieting, weight, and health: Reconceptualizing research and policy. *Journal of Social Issues, 55*, 187–205.

Cohen, D. (1995, June 17). Now we are one, or two, or three. *New Scientist*, pp. 14–15.

Cohen, G., Conway, M. A., & Maylor, E. A. (1994, September). Flashbulb memories in older adults. *Psychology & Aging, 9*(3), 454–463.

Cohen, H., Kaplan, Z., Kotler, M., Kouperman, I., Moisa, R., & Grisaru, N. (2005). Repetitive transcranial magnetic stimulation of the right dorsolaterial prefrontal cortex in posttraumatic stress disorder: A double-blind, placebo-controlled study. *American Journal of Psychiatry, 16*, 515–524.

Cohen, K. M. (2002). Relationships among childhood sex-atypical behavior, spatial ability, handedness, and sexual orientation in men. *Archives of Sexual Behavior, 31*, 129–143.

Cohen, S. (1988). Psychosocial models of the role of social support in the etiology of physical disease. *Health Psychology, 7*, 269–297.

Cohen, S. (2004). Social relationships and health. *American Psychologist, 59*, 676–684.

Cohen, S., Doyle, W. J., Skoner, D. P., Rabin, B. S., & Gwaltney, J. M., Jr. (1997). Social ties and susceptibility to the common cold. *Journal of the American Medical Association, 277*, 1940–1944.

Cohen, S., Doyle, W. J., Turner, R., Alper, C. M., & Skoner, D. P. (2003). Sociability and susceptibility to the common cold. *Psychological Science, 14*, 389–395.

Cohen, S., Kaplan, J. R., Cunnick, J. E., Manuck, S. B., & Rabin, B. S. (1992). Chronic social stress, affiliation, and cellular immune response in nonhuman primates. *Psychological Science, 3*, 301–304.

Cohen, S., Line, S., Manuck, S. B., Rabin, B. S., Heise, E. R., & Kaplan, J. R. (1997). Chronic social stress, social status, and susceptibility to upper respiratory infections in nonhuman primates. *Psychosomatic Medicine, 59*, 213–221.

Cohen, S., Tyrrell, D. A. J., & Smith, A. P. (1991). Psychological stress and susceptibility to the common cold. *New England Journal of Medicine, 325*, 606–612.

Colangelo, N., Assouline, S. G., & Gross, M. U. M. (2004). *A nation deceived: How schools hold back America's brightest students*, Volumes I and II. *The Templeton National Report on Acceleration*. Iowa City, IA: College of Education, University of Iowa.

Colapinto, J. (2000). *As nature made him: The boy who was raised as a girl*. New York: HarperCollins.

Colarelli, S. M., & Dettman, J. R. (2003). Intuitive evolutionary perspectives in marketing. *Psychology and Marketing, 20*, 837–865.

Colarelli, S. M., Spranger, J. L., & Hechanova, M. R. (2006). Women, power, and sex composition in small groups: An evolutionary perspective. *Journal of Organizational Behavior, 27*, 163–184.

Colcombe, S., & Kramer, A. F. (2003). Fitness effects on the cognitive function of older adults: A meta-analytic study. *Psychological Science, 14*, 125–130.

Colcombe, S. J., Kramer, A. F., Erickson, K. I., Scalf, P., McAuley, E., Cohen, N. J., Webb, A., Jerome, G. J., Marquex, D. X., & Elavsky, S. (2004). Cardiovascular fitness, cortical plasticity, and aging. *Proceedings of the National Academy of Sciences, 101*, 3316–3321.

Cole, K. C. (1998). *The universe and the teacup: The mathematics of truth and beauty*. New York: Harcourt Brace.

Coleman, J. (1997, June 30). Cigarette industry thriving in Japan. Associated Press (in *Grand Rapids Press*, p. A14).

Coleman, J. C. (1980). *The nature of adolescence*. London: Methuen.

Coleman, P. D., & Flood, D. G. (1986). Dendritic proliferation in the aging brain as a compensatory repair mechanism. In D. F. Swaab, E. Fliers, M. Mirmiram, W. A. Van Gool, & F. Van Haaren (Eds.), *Progress in brain research* (Vol. 20). New York: Elsevier.

Collins, D. W., & Kimura, D. (1997). A large sex difference on a two-dimensional mental rotation task. *Behavioral Neuroscience, 111*, 845–849.

Collins, N. L., & Miller, L. C. (1994). Self-disclosure and liking: A meta-analytic review. *Psychological Bulletin, 116*, 457–475.

Collins, R. L., Elliott, M. N., Berry, S. H., Danouse, D. E., Kunkel, D., Hunter, S. B., & Miu, A. (2004). Watching sex on television predicts adolescent initiation of sexual behavior. *Pediatrics, 114*, 280–289.

Collins, W. A., Maccoby, E. E., Steinberg, L., Hetherington, E. M., & Bornstein, M. H. (2000). Contemporary research on parenting: The case for nature and nurture. *American Psychologist, 55*, 218–232.

Collinson, S. L., MacKay, C. E., James, A. C., Quested, D. J., Phillips, T., Roberts, N., & Crow, T. J. (2003). Brain volume, asymmetry and intellectual impairment in relation to sex in early-onset schizophrenia. *British Journal of Psychiatry, 183*, 114–120.

Colom, R., Lluis-Font, J. M., & Andrés-Pueyo, A. (2005). The generational intelligence gains are caused by decreasing variance in the lower half of the distribution: Supporting evidence for the nutrition hypothesis. *Intelligence, 33,* 83–91.

Colombo, J. (1982). The critical period concept: Research, methodology, and theoretical issues. *Psychological Bulletin, 91,* 260–275.

Colon, E. A., Callies, A. L., Popkin, M. K., & McGlave, P. B. (1991). Depressed mood and other variables related to bone marrow transplantation survival in acute leukemia. *Psychosomatics, 32,* 420–425.

Comer, R. J. (2004). *Abnormal psychology.,* 5th ed. New York: Worth Publishers.

Commissioner of Official Languages. (1999). *Annual Report 1998.* Minister of Public Works and Government Services Canada, Cat. No. SF1–1998.

Conner, M., & McMillan, B. (1999). Interaction effects in the theory of planned behaviour: Studying cannabis use. *British Journal of Social Psychology, 38,* 195–222.

Consensus Conference. (1985). Electroconvulsive therapy. *Journal of the American Medical Association, 254,* 2103–2108.

Consumer Reports. (1995, November). Does therapy help? Pp. 734–739.

Conway, M., & Ross, M. (1984). Getting what you want by revising what you had. *Journal of Personality and Social Psychology, 47,* 738–748.

Conway, M. A., Wang, Q., Hanyu, K., & Haque, S. (2005). A cross-cultural investigation of autobiographical memory. On the universality and cultural variation of the reminiscence bump. *Journal of Cross-Cultural Psychology, 36,* 739–749.

Cook, E. W., III, Hodes, R. L., & Lang, P. J. (1986). Preparedness and phobia: Effects of stimulus content on human visceral conditioning. *Journal of Abnormal Psychology, 95,* 195–207.

Cook, M., & Mineka, S. (1991). Selective associations in the origins of phobic fears and their implications for behavior therapy. In P. Martin (Ed.), *Handbook of behavior therapy and psychological science: An integrative approach.* New York: Pergamon Press.

Cooke, L. J., Wardle, J., & Gibson, E. L. (2003). Relationship between parental report of food neophobia and everyday food consumption in 2–6-year-old children. *Appetite, 41,* 205–206.

Cooper, K. J. (1999, May 1). This time, copycat wave is broader. *Washington Post* (www.washingtonpost.com).

Coopersmith, S. (1967). *The antecedents of self-esteem.* San Francisco: Freeman.

Corballis, M. C. (1989). Laterality and human evolution. *Psychological Review, 96,* 492–505.

Corballis, M. C. (2002). *From hand to mouth: The origins of language.* Princeton: Princeton University Press.

Corballis, M. C. (2003). From mouth to hand: Gesture, speech, and the evolution of right-handedness. *Behavioral and Brain Sciences, 26,* 199–260.

Coren, S. (1993a). Failure to find statistical significance in left-handedness and pathology studies: A forgotten consideration. *Bulletin of the Psychonomic Society, 31,* 443–446.

Coren, S. (1993b). *The left-hander syndrome: The causes and consequences of left-handedness.* New York: Vintage Books.

Coren, S. (1996). *Sleep thieves: An eye-opening exploration into the science and mysteries of sleep.* New York: Free Press.

Corey, D. P., & 15 others (2004). TRPA1 is a candidate for the mechanosensitive transduction channel of vertebrate hair cells. *Nature* (advance online publication, October 13, at www.nature.com).

Corina, D. P. (1998). The processing of sign language: Evidence from aphasia. In B. Stemmer & H. A. Whittaker (Eds.), *Handbook of neurolinguistics.* San Diego: Academic Press.

Corina, D. P., Vaid, J., & Bellugi, U. (1992). The linguistic basis of left hemisphere specialization. *Science, 255,* 1258–1260.

Corneille, O., Huart, J., Becquart, E., & Brédart, S. (2004). When memory shifts toward more typical category exemplars: Accentuation effects in the recollection of ethnically ambiguous faces. *Journal of Personality and Social Psychology, 86,* 236–250.

Correll, J., Park, B., Judd, C. M., & Wittenbrink, B. (2002). The police officer's dilemma: Using ethnicity to disambiguate potentially threatening individuals. *Journal of Personality and Social Psychology, 83,* 1314–1329.

Costa, P. T., Jr., Terracciano, A., & McCrae, R. R. (2001). Gender differences in personality traits across cultures: Robust and surprising findings. *Journal of Personality and Social Psychology, 81,* 322–331.

Costa, P. T., Jr., Zonderman, A. B., McCrae, R. R., Cornoni-Huntley, J., Locke, B. Z., & Barbano, H. E. (1987). Longitudinal analyses of psychological well-being in a national sample: Stability of mean levels. *Journal of Gerontology, 42,* 50–55.

Costanzo, M. (1997). *Just revenge: Costs and consequences of the death penalty.* New York: St. Martins.

Costello, E. J., Compton, S. N., Keeler, G., & Angold, A. (2003). Relationships between poverty and psychopathology: A natural experiment. *Journal of the American Medical Association, 290,* 2023–2029.

Coughlin, J. F., Mohyde, M., D'Ambrosio, L. A., & Gilbert, J. (2004). Who drives older driver decisions? Cambridge, MA: MIT Age Lab.

Couli, J. T., Vidal, F., Nazarian, B., & Macar, F. (2004). Functional anatomy of the attentional modulation of time estimation. *Science, 303,* 1506–1508.

Courage, M. L., & Howe, M. L. (2002). From infant to child: The dynamics of cognitive change in the second year of life. *Psychological Bulletin, 128,* 250–277.

Courneya, K. S., & Carron, A. V. (1992). The home advantage in sports competitions: A literature review. *Journal of Sport and Exercise Psychology, 14,* 13–27.

Courtney, J. G., Longnecker, M. P., Theorell, T., & de Verdier, M. G. (1993). Stressful life events and the risk of colorectal cancer. *Epidemiology, 4,* 407–414.

Cousins, N. (1989). *Head first: The biology of hope.* New York: Dutton.

Covington, M. V., & Omelich, C. L. (1988). I can resist anything but temptation: Adolescent expectations for smoking cigarettes. *Journal of Applied Social Psychology, 18,* 203–227.

Cowan, G., Lee, C., Levy, D., & Snyder, D. (1988). Dominance and inequality in X-rated videocassettes. *Psychology of Women Quarterly, 12,* 299–311.

Cowan, N. (1988). Evolving conceptions of memory storage, selective attention, and their mutual constraints within the human information-processing system. *Psychological Bulletin, 104,* 163–191.

Cowan, N. (1994). Mechanisms of verbal short-term memory. *Current Directions in Psychological Science, 3,* 185–189.

Cowan, N. (2001). The magical number 4 in short-term memory: A reconsideration of mental storage capacity. *Behavioral and Brain Sciences, 24,* 87–185.

Cowart, B. J. (1981). Development of taste perception in humans: Sensitivity and preference throughout the life span. *Psychological Bulletin, 90,* 43–73.

Crabbe, J. C. (2002). Genetic contributions to addiction. *Annual Review of Psychology, 53,* 435–462.

Crabtree, S. (2002, January 22). Gender roles reflected in teen tech use. *Gallup Tuesday Briefing* (www.gallup.com).

Crabtree, S. (2005, January 13). Engagement keeps the doctor away. *Gallup Management Journal* (gmj.gallup.com).

Craig, M. E., Kalichman, S. C., & Follingstad, D. R. (1989). Verbal coercive sexual behavior among college students. *Archives of Sexual Behavior, 18,* 421–434.

Craik, F. I. M. (1986). A functional account of age differences in memory. In F. Klix & H. Hagendorf (Eds.), *Human memory and cognitive capabilities.* Amsterdam: Elsevier.

Craik, F. I. M., & Tulving, E. (1975). Depth of processing and the retention of words in episodic memory. *Journal of Experimental Psychology: General, 104,* 268–294.

Craik, F. I. M., & Watkins, M. J. (1973). The role of rehearsal in short-term memory. *Journal of Verbal Learning and Verbal Behavior, 12,* 599–607.

Crain-Thoreson, C., & Dale, P. S. (1992). Do early talkers become early readers? Linguistic precocity, preschool language, and emergent literacy. *Developmental Psychology, 28,* 421–429.

Crandall, C. S. (1988). Social contagion of binge eating. *Journal of Personality and Social Psychology, 55,* 588–598.

Crandall, C. S. (1994). Prejudice against fat people: Ideology and self-interest. *Journal of Personality and Social Psychology, 66,* 882–894.

Crandall, C. S. (1995). Do parents discriminate against their heavyweight daughters? *Personality and Social Psychology Bulletin, 21,* 724–735.

Crandall, J. E. (1984). Social interest as a moderator of life stress. *Journal of Personality and Social Psychology, 47,* 164–174.

Crawford, M., Chaffin, R., & Fitton, L. (1995). *Learning and Individual Differences, 7,* 341–362.

Crews, F. (Ed.) (1998). *Unauthorized Freud: Doubters confront a legend.* New York: Viking.

Crocker, J., & Major, B. (1989). Social stigma and self-esteem: The self-protective properties of stigma," *Psychological Review, 89,* 608–630.

Crocker, J., & Park, L. E. (2004). The costly pursuit of self-esteem. *Psychological Bulletin, 130,* 392–414.

Crocker, J., Thompson, L. L., McGraw, K. M., & Ingerman, C. (1987). Downward comparison, prejudice, and evaluation of others: Effects of self-esteem and threat. *Journal of Personality and Social Psychology, 52,* 907–916.

Crocker, J., & Wolfe, C. (1999). Rescuing self-esteem: A contingencies of worth perspective. Unpublished manuscript, University of Michigan.

Croft, R. J., Klugman, A., Baldeweg, T., & Gruzelier, J. H. (2001). Electrophysiological evidence of serotonergic impairment in long-term MDMA ("Ecstasy") users. *American Journal of Psychiatry, 158,* 1687–1692.

Crombie, A. C. (1964, May). Early concepts of the senses and the mind. *Scientific American,* pp. 108–116.

Crook, T. H., & West, R. L. (1990). Name recall performance across the adult life-span. *British Journal of Psychology, 81,* 335–340.

Cross, S., & Markus, H. (1991). Possible selves across the life span. *Human Development, 34,* 230–255.

Cross-National Collaborative Group. (1992). The changing rate of major depression. *Journal of the American Medical Association, 268,* 3098–3105.

Crossen, C. (1994). *Tainted truth: The manipulation of fact in America.* New York: Simon & Schuster.

Crowell, J. A., & Waters, E. (1994). Bowlby's theory grown up: The role of attachment in adult love relationships. *Psychological Inquiry, 5,* 1–22.

Croyle, R. T., & Ditto, P. H. (1990). Illness cognition and behavior: An experimental approach. *Journal of Behavioral Medicine, 13,* 31–52.

Csikszentmihalyi, M. (1990). *Flow: The psychology of optimal experience.* New York: Harper & Row.

Csikszentmihalyi, M. (1999). If we are so rich, why aren't we happy? *American Psychologist, 54,* 821–827.

Csikszentmihalyi, M., & Hunter, J. (2003). Happiness in everyday life: The uses of experience sampling. *Journal of Happiness Studies, 4,* 185–199.

Csikszentmihalyi, M., & Larson, R. (1984). *Being adolescent: Conflict and growth in the teenage years.* New York: Basic Books.

Cunningham, M. R., Roberts, A. R., Barbee, A. P., Druen, P. B., & Wu", C. H. (1995). "Their ideas of beauty are, on the whole, the same as ours": Consistency and variability in the cross-cultural perception of female physical attractiveness. *Journal of Personality and Social Psychology, 68,* 261–279.

Cunningham, W. A., Johnson, M. K., Raye, C. L., Gatenby, J. C., Gore, J. C., & Banaji, M. R. (2004). Separable neural components in the processing of Black and White faces. *Psychological Science, 15,* 806–813.

Curtis, G. C., Magee, W. J., Eaton, W. W., Wittchen, H-U., & Kessler, R. C. (1998). Specific fears and phobias: Epidemiology and classification. *British Journal of Psychiatry, 173,* 212–217.

Curtis, R. C., & Miller, K. (1986). Believing another likes or dislikes you: Behaviors making the beliefs come true. *Journal of Personality and Social Psychology, 51,* 284–290.

Cutler, B. L., & Penrod, S. D. (1989). Forensically relevant moderators of the relation between eyewitness identification accuracy and confidence. *Journal of Applied Psychology, 74,* 650–652.

Czeisler, C. A., Allan, J. S., Strogatz, S. H., Ronda, J. M., Sanchez, R., Rios, C. D., Freitag, W. O., Richardson, G. S., & Kronauer, R. E. (1986). Bright light resets the human circadian pacemaker independent of the timing of the sleep-wake cycle. *Science, 233,* 667–671.

Czeisler, C. A., Duffy, J. F., Shanahan, T. L., Brown, E. N., Mitchell, J. F., Rimmer, D. W., Ronda, J. M., Silva, E. J., Allan, J. S., Emens, J. S., Dijk, D-J., & Kronauer, R. E. (1999). Stability, precision, and near-24-hour period of the human circadian pacemaker. *Science, 284,* 2177–2181.

Czeisler, C. A., Kronauer, R. E., Allan, J. S., & Duffy, J. F. (1989). Bright light induction of strong (type O) resetting of the human circadian pacemaker. *Science, 244,* 1328–1333.

Dabbs, J. M., Jr. (2000). Heroes, rogues, and lovers: Testosterone and behavior. New York: McGraw-Hill.

Dabbs, J. M., Jr., Bernieri, F. J., Strong, R. K., Campo, R., & Milun, R. (2001b). Going on stage: Testosterone in greetings and meetings. *Journal of Research in Personality, 35,* 27–40.

Dabbs, J. M., Jr., & Morris, R. (1990). Testosterone, social class, and antisocial behavior in a sample of 4,462 men. *Psychological Science, 1,* 209–211.

Dabbs, J. M., Jr., Riad, J. K., & Chance, S. E. (2001a). Testosterone and ruthless homicide. *Personality and Individual Differences, 31,* 599–603.

Dabbs, J. M., Jr., Ruback, R. B., & Besch, N. F. (1987). Male saliva testosterone following conversations with male and female partners. Paper presented at the American Psychological Association convention.

Daley, T. C., Whaley, S. E., Sigman, M. D., Espinosa, M. P., & Neumann, C. (2003). IQ on the rise: The Flynn effect in rural Kenyan children. *Psychological Science, 14,* 215–219.

Dalton, M. A., Ahrens, M. B., Sargent, J. D., Mott, L. A., Beach, M. L., Tickle, J. J., & Heatherton, T. F. (2002). Relation between parental restrictions on movies and adolescent use of tobacco and alcohol. *Effective Clinical Practice, 5,* 1–9.

Damasio, A. (2003). *Looking for Spinoza: Joy, sorrow, and the feeling brain.* New York: Harcourt.

Damasio, A. R. (1994). *Descartes' error: Emotion, reason, and the human brain.* New York: Grossett/Putnam & Sons.

Damasio, H., Grabowski, T., Frank, R., Galaburda, A. M., & Damasio, A. R. (1994). The return of Phineas Gage: Clues about the brain from the skull of a famous patient. *Science, 264,* 1102–1105.

Damon, W. (1995). *Greater expectations: Overcoming the culture of indulgence in America's homes and schools.* New York: Free Press.

Damon, W., & Hart, D. (1982). The development of self-understanding from infancy through adolescence. *Child Development, 53,* 841–864.

Damon, W., & Hart, D. (1988). *Self-understanding in childhood and adolescence.* Cambridge: Cambridge University Press.

Damon, W., Menon, J., & Bronk, K. (2003). The development of purpose during adolescence. *Applied Developmental Science, 7,* 119–128.

Dannenberg, A. L., Burton, D., & Jackson, R. J. (2004). Economic and environmental costs of obesity: The impact on airlines. *American Journal of Preventive Medicine, 27,* 264.

Danner, D. D., Snowdon, D. A., & Friesen, W. V. (2001). Positive emotions in early life and longevity: Findings from the Nun Study. *Journal of Personality and Social Psychology, 80,* 804–813.

Danso, H., & Esses, V. (2001). Black experimenters and the intellectual test performance of white participants: The tables are turned. *Journal of Experimental Social Psychology, 37,* 158–165.

Darley, J. M., & Latané, B. (1968a). Bystander intervention in emergencies: Diffusion of responsibility. *Journal of Personality and Social Psychology, 8,* 377–383.

Darley, J. M., & Latané, B. (1968b, December). When will people help in a crisis? *Psychology Today,* pp. 54–57, 70–71.

Darley, J. M., Seligman, C., & Becker, L. J. (1979, April). The lesson of twin rivers: Feedback works. *Psychology Today,* pp. 16, 23–24.

Darrach, B., & Norris, J. (1984, August). An American tragedy. *Life,* pp. 58–74.

Daum, I., & Schugens, M. M. (1996). On the cerebellum and classical conditioning. *Psychological Science, 5,* 58–61.

Dauvilliers, Y., Carlander, B., Moinari, N., Desautels, A., Okun, M., Tafti, M., Montplaisir, J., Mignot, E., & Billard, M. (2003). Month of birth as a risk factor for narcolepsy. *Sleep, 26,* 663–665.

Davey, G. C. L. (1992). Classical conditioning and the acquisition of human fears and phobias: A review and synthesis of the literature. *Advances in Behavior Research and Therapy, 14,* 29–66.

Davey, G. C. L. (1995). Preparedness and phobias: Specific evolved associations or a generalized expectancy bias? *Behavioral and Brain Sciences, 18,* 289–297.

Davidoff, J. (2004). Coloured thinking. *The Psychologist, 17,* 570–572.

Davidson, R. (2000). Affective style, psychopathology, and resilience: Brain mechanisms and plasticity. *American Psychologist, 55,* 1196–1209.

Davidson, R. J. (2003). Affective neuroscience and psychophysiology: Toward a synthesis. *Psychophysiology, 40,* 655–665.

Davidson, R. J., Kabat-Zinn, J., Schumacher, J., Rosenkranz, M., Muller, D., Santorelli, S. F., Urbanowski, F., Harrington, A., Bonus, K., & Sheridan, J. F. (2003). Alterations in brain and immune function produced by mindfulness meditation. *Psychosomatic Medicine, 65,* 564–570.

Davidson, R. J., Pizzagalli, D., Nitschke, J. B., & Putnam, K. (2002). Depression: Perspectives from affective neuroscience. *Annual Review of Psychology, 53,* 545–574.

Davidson, R. J., Putnam, K. M., & Larson, C. L. (2000). Dysfunction in the neural circuitry of emotion regulation—a possible prelude to violence. *Science, 289,* 591–594.

Davies, D. R., Matthews, G., & Wong, C. S. K. (1991). Aging and work. *International Review of Industrial and Organizational Psychology, 6,* 149–211.

Davies, M. F. (1997). Positive test strategies and confirmatory retrieval processes in the evaluation of personality feedback. *Journal of Personality and Social Psychology, 73,* 574–583.

Davies, P. (1992). *The mind of God: The scientific basis for a rational world.* New York: Simon & Schuster.

Davies, P. (1999). *The fifth miracle: The search for the origin and meaning of life.* New York: Simon & Schuster.

Davies, P. (2004, April 14). Into the 21st century. *Metaviews* (www.metanexus.net).

Davis, B. E., Moon, R. Y., Sachs, H. C., & Ottolini, M. C. (1998). Effects of sleep position on infant motor development. *Pediatrics, 102,* 1135–1140.

Davis, J. O., & Phelps, J. A. (1995a). Twins with schizophrenia: Genes or germs? *Schizophrenia Bulletin, 21,* 13–18.

Davis, J. O., Phelps, J. A., & Bracha, H. S. (1995b). Prenatal development of monozygotic twins and concordance for schizophrenia. *Schizophrenia Bulletin, 21,* 357–366.

Davis, S., Rees, M., Ribot, J., Moufarege, A., Rodenberg, C., & Purdie, D. (2003). Efficacy and safety of testosterone patches for the treatment of low sexual desire in surgically menopausal women. Presented to the American Society for Reproductive Medicine, San Antonio, October 11–15.

Davison, K. P., Pennebaker, J. W., & Dickerson, S. S. (2000). Who talks? The social psychology of illness support groups. *American Psychologist, 55,* 205–217.

Dawes, R. M. (1980). Social dilemmas. *Annual Review of Psychology, 31,* 169–193.

Dawes, R. M. (1994). *House of cards: Psychology and psychotherapy built on myth.* New York: Free Press.

Dawkins, R. (1998). *Unweaving the rainbow.* Boston: Houghton Mifflin.

Dawkins, R. (1999, April 8). Is science killing the soul (a discussion with Richard Dawkins and Steven Pinker). www.edge.org

Dawkins, R. (2004). edge.org.

Dawson, N. V., Arkes, H. R., Siciliano, C., Blinkhorn, R., Lakshmanan, M., & Petrelli, M. (1988). Hindsight bias: An impediment to accurate probability estimation in clinicopathologic conferences. *Medical Decision Making, 8,* 259–264.

Deacon, B. J., & Abramowitz, J. S. (2004). Cognitive and behavioral treatments for anxiety disorders: A review of meta-analytic findings. *Journal of Clinical Psychology, 60,* 429–441.

Dean, G. A., Kelly, I. W., Saklofske, D. H., & Furnham, A. (1992). Graphology and human judgment. In B. Beyerstein & D. Beyerstein (Eds.), *The write stuff: Evaluations of graphology.* Buffalo, NY: Prometheus Books.

Deary, I. J., & Caryl, P. G. (1993). Intelligence, EEG and evoked potentials. In P. A. Vernon (Ed.), *Biological approaches to the study of human intelligence.* Norwood, NJ: Ablex.

Deary, I. J., & Der, G. (2005). Reaction time explains IQ's association with death. *Psychological Science, 16,* 64–69.

Deary, I. J., & Matthews, G. (1993). Personality traits are alive and well. *The Psychologist: Bulletin of the British Psychological Society, 6,* 299–311.

Deary, I. J., & Stough, C. (1997). Looking down on human intelligence. *American Psychologist, 52,* 1148–1149.

Deary, I. J., Thorpe, G., Wilson, V., Starr, J. M., & Whalley, L. J. (2003). Population sex differences in IQ at age 11: The Scottish mental survey 1932. *Intelligence, 31,* 533–541.

Deary, I. J., Whiteman, M. C., Starr, J. M., Whalley, L. J., & Fox, H. C. (2004). The impact of childhood intelligence on later life: Following up the Scottish mental surveys of 1932 and 1947. *Journal of Personality and Social Psychology, 86,* 130–147.

de Beyer, J. (1999). Why is tobacco control a public health priority around the world? Washington, DC: World Bank.

de Beyer, J. (2005, February 4). Tobacco: How trade policy affects health. Annual Conference: Health in Foreign Policy. Panel II: Global Commerce and Health.

de Boysson-Bardies, B., Halle, P., Sagart, L., & Durand, C. (1989). A cross linguistic investigation of vowel formats in babbling. *Journal of Child Language, 16,* 1–17.

DeBruine, L. M. (2002). Facial resemblance enhances trust. *Proceedings of the Royal Society of London, 269,* 1307–1312.

DeBruine, L. M. (2004). Facial resemblance increases the attractiveness of same-sex faces more than other-sex faces. *Proceedings of the Royal Society of London B, 271,* 2085–2090.

DeCasper, A. J., Lecanuet, J-P., Busnel, M-C., & others. (1994). Fetal reactions to recurrent maternal speech. *Infant Behavior and Development, 17,* 159–164.

DeCasper, A. J., & Prescott, P. A. (1984). Human newborns' perception of male voices: Preference, discrimination and reinforcing value. *Developmental Psychobiology, 17,* 481–491.

DeCasper, A. J., & Spence, M. J. (1986). Prenatal maternal speech influences newborns' perception of speech sounds. *Infant Behavior and Development, 9*, 133–150.

Deci, E. L., Koestner, R., & Ryan, R. M. (1999, November). A meta-analytic review of experiments examining the effects of extrinsic rewards on intrinsic motivation. *Psychological Bulletin, 125*(6), 627–668.

Deci, E. L., & Ryan, R. M. (1985). *Intrinsic motivation and self-determination in human behavior.* New York: Plenum Press.

Deci, E. L., & Ryan, R. M. (1992). The initiation and regulation of intrinsically motivated learning and achievement. In A. K. Boggiano & T. S. Pittman (Eds.), *Achievement and motivation: A social-developmental perspective.* New York: Cambridge University Press.

Deci, E. L., & Ryan, R. M. (2000). The "what" and "why" of goal pursuits: Human needs and the self-determination of behavior. *Psychological Inquiry, 11*, 227–268.

de Courten-Myers, G. (2005, February 4). Personal correspondence (estimating total brain neurons, extrapolating from her carefully estimated 20 to 23 billion cortical neurons).

de Courten-Myers, G. M. (2002, May 9). Personal correspondence.

de Cuevas, J. (1990, September–October). "No, she holded them loosely." *Harvard Magazine*, pp. 60–67.

de Hoogh, A. H. B., den Hartog, D. N., Koopman, P. L., Thierry, H., van den Berg, P. T., van der Weide, J. G., & Wilderom, C. P. M. (2004). Charismatic leadership, environmental dynamism, and performance. *European Journal of Work and Organisational Psychology, 13*, 447–471.

De Houwer, J., Thomas, S., & Baeyens, F. (2001). Associative learning of likes and dislikes: A review of 25 years of research on human evaluative conditioning. *Psychological Bulletin, 127*, 853–869.

De Koninck, J. (2000). Waking experiences and dreaming. In M. Kryger, T. Roth, & W. Dement (Eds.), *Principles and practice of sleep medicine, 3rd ed.* Philadelphia: Saunders.

Delaney, P. F., Ericsson, K. A., Weaver, G. E., & Mahadevan, S. (1999). Accounts of the memorist Rajan's exceptional performance: Comparing three theoretical proposals. Paper presented to the American Psychological Society convention.

Delgado, J. M. R. (1969). *Physical control of the mind: Toward a psychocivilized society.* New York: Harper & Row.

DeLoache, J. S. (1995). Early understanding and use of symbols: The model model. *Current Directions in Psychological Science, 4*, 109–113.

DeLoache, J. S., & Brown, A. L. (1987, October–December). Differences in the memory-based searching of delayed and normally developing young children. *Intelligence, 11*(4), 277–289.

DeLoache, J. S., Uttal, D. H., & Rosengren, K. S. (2004). Scale errors offer evidence for a perception-action dissociation early in life. *Science, 304*, 1027–1029.

Dement, W. (1997, September). What all undergraduates should know about how their sleeping lives affect their waking lives. Stanford University: www.leland.stanford.edu/~dement/sleepless.html

Dement, W. C. (1978). *Some must watch while some must sleep.* New York: Norton.

Dement, W. C. (1999). *The promise of sleep.* New York: Delacorte Press.

Dement, W. C., & Wolpert, E. A. (1958). The relation of eye movements, body mobility, and external stimuli to dream content. *Journal of Experimental Psychology, 55*, 543–553.

Demir, E., & Dickson, B. J. (2005). *Fruitless* splicing specifies male courtship behavior in *Drosophila. Cell, 121*, 785–794.

Dempster, F. N. (1988). The spacing effect: A case study in the failure to apply the results of psychological research. *American Psychologist, 43*, 627–634.

Denes-Raj, V., Epstein, S., & Cole, J. (1995). The generality of the ratio-bias phenomenon. *Personality and Social Psychology Bulletin, 21*, 1083–1092.

DeNeve, K. M., & Cooper, H. (1998). The happy personality: A meta-analysis of 137 personality traits and subjective well-being. *Psychological Bulletin, 124*, 197–229.

Dennerstein, L., Dudley, E., Guthrie, J., & Barrett-Connor, E. (2000). Life satisfaction, symptoms, and the menopausal transition. *Medscape Women's Health, 5*(4) (www.medscape.com).

Dennett, D. (1996, September 9). Quoted by Ian Parker, Richard Dawkins' evolution. *The New Yorker,* pp. 41–45.

Denton, K., & Krebs, D. (1990). From the scene to the crime: The effect of alcohol and social context on moral judgment. *Journal of Personality and Social Psychology, 59*, 242–248.

D'Eon, J. L. (1989). Hypnosis in the control of labor pain. In N. P. Spanos & J. F. Chaves (Eds.), *Hypnosis: The cognitive-behavioral perspective.* Buffalo, NY: Prometheus Books.

DePaulo, B. M. (1994). Spotting lies: Can humans learn to do better? *Current Directions in Psychological Science 3*, 83–86.

DePaulo, B. M., Blank, A. L., Swaim, G. W., & Hairfield, J. G. (1992). Expressiveness and expressive control. *Personality and Social Psychology Bulletin, 18*, 276–285.

De Quervain, D. J.-F., Roozendaal, B., & McGaugh, J. L. (1998). Stress and glucocorticoids impair retrieval of long-term spatial memory. *Nature, 394*, 787–790.

Deregowski, J. (1972, November). Pictorial perception and culture. *Scientific American,* pp. 82–88.

Dermer, M., Cohen, S. J., Jacobsen, E., & Anderson, E. A. (1979). Evaluative judgments of aspects of life as a function of vicarious exposure to hedonic extremes. *Journal of Personality and Social Psychology, 37*, 247–260.

Dermer, M., & Pyszczynski, T. A. (1978). Effects of erotica upon men's loving and liking responses for women they love. *Journal of Personality and Social Psychology, 36*, 1302–1309.

Deroche-Garmonet, V., Belin, D., & Piazza, P. V. (2004). Evidence for addiction-like behavior in the rat. *Science, 305*, 1014–1017.

DeRubeis, R. J., & 10 others. (2005). Cognitive therapy vs. medications in the treatment of moderate to severe depression. *Archives of General Psychiatry, 62*, 409–416.

DeSteno, D., Dasgupta, N., Bartlett, M. Y., & Cajdric, A. (2004). Prejudice from thin air: The effect of emotion on automatic intergroup attitudes. *Psychological Science, 15*, 319–324.

DeSteno, D., Petty, R. E., Wegener, D. T., & Rucker, D. D. (2000). Beyond valence in the perception of likelihood: The role of emotion specificity. *Journal of Personality and Social Psychology, 78*, 397–416.

Deutsch, J. A. (1972, July). Brain reward: ESP and ecstasy. *Psychology Today,* 46–48.

Deutsch, M. (1991). Egalitarianism in the laboratory and at work. In R. Vermunt & H. Steensma (Eds.), *Social justice in human relations.* New York: Plenum.

DeValois, R. L., & DeValois, K. K. (1975). Neural coding of color. In E. C. Carterette & M. P. Friedman (Eds.), *Handbook of perception: Vol. V. Seeing.* New York: Academic Press.

Devilly, G. J. (2003). Eye movement desensitization and reprocessing: A chronology of its development and scientific standing. *Scientific Review of Mental Health Practice, 1*, 113–118.

Devine, P. G. (1995). Prejudice and outgroup perception. In A. Tesser (Ed.), *Advanced social psychology.* New York: McGraw-Hill.

Devlin, B., Daniels, M., & Roeder, K. (1997). The heritability of IQ. *Nature, 388*, 468–471.

Dew, M. A., Hoch, C. C., Buysse, D. J., Monk, T. H., Begley, A. E., Houck, P. R., Hall, M., Kupfer, D. J., Reynolds, C. F., III (2003). Healthy older adults' sleep predicts all-cause mortality at 4 to 19 years of follow-up. *Psychosomatic Medicine, 65*, 63–73.

de Waal, F. B. M. (1999, December). The end of nature versus nurture. *Scientific American,* pp. 94–99.

de Waal, F. B. M., Dindo, M., Freeman, C. A., & Hall, M. J. (2005). The monkey in the mirror: Hardly a stranger. *Proceedings of the National Academy of Sciences, 102*, 11140–11147.

de Waal, F. B. M., & Johanowicz, D. L. (1993). Modification of reconciliation behavior through social experience: An experiment with two macaque species. *Child Development, 64*, 897–908.

De Wolff, M. S., & van IJzendoorn, M. H. (1997). Sensitivity and attachment: A meta-analysis on parental antecedents of infant attachment. *Child Development, 68*, 571–591.

Dey, E. L., Astin, A. W., & Korn, W. S. (1991). *The American freshman: Twenty-five year trends.* Los Angeles: Higher Education Research Institute, UCLA.

Dhawan, N., Roseman, I. J., Naidu, R. K., Thapa, K., & Rettek, S. I. (1995). Self-concepts across two cultures: India and the United States. *Journal of Cross-Cultural Psychology, 26*, 606–621.

Diaconis, P. (2002, August 11). Quoted by L. Belkin, The odds of that. *New York Times* (www.nytimes.com).

Diaconis, P., & Mosteller, F. (1989). Methods for studying coincidences. *Journal of the American Statistical Association, 84*, 853–861.

Diamond, J. (1989, May). The great leap forward. *Discover*, pp. 50–60.

Diamond, J. (2001, February). A tale of two reputations: Why we revere Darwin and give Freud a hard time. *Natural History*, pp. 20–24.

Diamond, L. M. (2000). Sexual identity, attractions, and behavior among young sexual-minority women over a 2-year period. *Developmental Psychology, 36*, 241–250.

Diamond, L. M. (2003). Was it a phase? Young women's relinquishment of lesbian/bisexual identities over a 5-year period. *Journal of Personality and Social Psychology, 84*, 352–364.

Diamond, R. (1993). Genetics and male sexual orientation (letter). *Science, 261*, 1258.

Dickerson, S. S., & Kemeny, M. E. (2004). Acute stressors and cortisol responses: A theoretical integration and synthesis of laboratory research. *Psychological Bulletin, 130*, 355–391.

Dickson, B. (2005, June 3). Quoted in E. Rosenthal, For fruit flies, gene shift tilts sex orientation. *New York Times* (www.nytimes.com).

Diener, E., & Biswas-Diener, R. (2002). Will money increase subjective well-being? A literature review and guide to needed research. *Social Indicators Research, 57*, 119–169.

Diener, E., Diener, M., & Diener, C. (1995). Factors predicting the subjective well-being of nations. *Journal of Personality and Social Psychology, 69*, 851–864.

Diener, E., Emmons, R. A., & Sandvik, E. (1986). The dual nature of happiness: Independence of positive and negative moods. Unpublished manuscript, University of Illinois.

Diener, E., & Oishi, S. (2000). Money and happiness: Income and subjective well-being across nations. In E. Diener & E. M. Suh (Eds.), *Subjective well-being across cultures.* Cambridge, MA: MIT Press.

Diener, E., Oishi, S., & Lucas, R. E. (2003). Personality, culture, and subjective well-being: Emotional and cognitive evaluations of life. *Annual Review of Psychology, 54*, 403–425.

Diener, E., & Seligman, M. E. P. (2002). Very happy people. *Psychological Science, 13*, 81–84.

Diener, E., & Seligman, M. E. P. (2004). Beyond money: Toward an economy of well-being. *Psychological Science in the Public Interest, 5*, 1–31.

Diener, E., Wirtz, D., & Oishi, S. (2001). End effects of rated life quality: The James Dean effect. *Psychological Science, 12*, 124–128.

Diener, E., Wolsic, B., & Fujita, F. (1995). Physical attractiveness and subjective well-being. *Journal of Personality and Social Psychology, 69*, 120–129.

Diener, M. L., & Lucas, R. E. (2004). Adults' desires for children's emotions across 48 countries: Associations with individual and national characteristics. *Journal of Cross-Cultural Psychology, 35*, 525–547.

Dietz, W. H., Jr., & Gortmaker, S. L. (1985). Do we fatten our children at the television set? Obesity and television viewing in children and adolescents. *Pediatrics, 75*, 807–812.

Dijksterhuis, A., & Aarts, H. (2003). On wildebeests and humans: The preferential detection of negative stimuli. *Psychological Science, 14*, 14–18.

DiLalla, D. L., Carey, G., Gottesman, I. I., & Bouchard, T. J., Jr. (1996). Heritability of MMPI personality indicators of psychopathology in twins reared apart. *Journal of Abnormal Psychology, 105*, 491–499.

Dimberg, U., Thunberg, M., & Elmehed, K. (2000). Unconscious facial reactions to emotional facial expressions. *Psychological Science, 11*, 86–89.

Dimberg, U., Thunberg, M., & Grunedal, S. (2002). Facial reactions to emotional stimuli: Automatically controlled emotional responses. *Cognition and Emotion, 16*, 449–472.

Dindia, K., & Allen, M. (1992). Sex differences in self-disclosure: A meta-analysis. *Psychological Bulletin, 112*, 106–124.

Dinges, N. G., & Hull, P. (1992). Personality, culture, and international studies. In D. Lieberman (Ed.), *Revealing the world: An interdisciplinary reader for international studies.* Dubuque, IA: Kendall-Hunt.

Dion, K. K., & Dion, K. L. (1993). Individualistic and collectivistic perspectives on gender and the cultural context of love and intimacy. *Journal of Social Issues, 49*, 53–69.

Dion, K. K., & Dion, K. L. (2001). Gender and cultural adaptation in immigrant families. *Journal of Social Issues, 57*, 511–521.

DiPietro, J. A. (2004). The role of prenatal maternal stress in child development. *Current Directions in Psychological Science, 13*, 71–74.

Discover (1996, May). A fistful of risks. Pp. 82–83.

Dishion, T. J., McCord, J., & Poulin, F. (1999). When interventions harm: Peer groups and problem behavior. *American Psychologist, 54*, 755–764.

Di Tella, R., MacCulloch, R. J., & Oswald, A. J. (2001). The macroeconomics of happiness. Warwick Economic Research Paper No. 615, Department of Economics, University of Warwick.

Doherty, E. W., & Doherty, W. J. (1998). Smoke gets in your eyes: Cigarette smoking and divorce in a national sample of American adults. *Families, Systems, and Health, 16*, 393–400.

Dohrenwend, B. P., Levav, I., Shrout, P. E., Schwartz, S., Naveh, G., Link, B. G., Skodol, A. E., & Stueve, A. (1992). Socioeconomic status and psychiatric disorders: The causation-selection issue. *Science, 255*, 946–952.

Dohrenwend, B., Pearlin, L., Clayton, P., Hamburg, B., Dohrenwend, B. P., Riley, M., & Rose, R. (1982). Report on stress and life events. In G. R. Elliott & C. Eisdorfer (Eds.), *Stress and human health: Analysis and implications of research* (A study by the Institute of Medicine/National Academy of Sciences). New York: Springer.

Dolan, R. J. (1999). On the neurology of morals. *Nature Neuroscience, 2*, 927–929.

Dolcos, F., LaBar, K. S., & Cabeza, R. (2004). Interaction between the amygdala and the medial temporal lobe memory system predicts better memory for emotional events. *Neuron, 42*, 855–863.

Dole, R. (1996, April 20). Quoted by M. Duffy, Look who's talking. *Time*, p. 48.

Dolezal, H. (1982). *Living in a world transformed.* New York: Academic Press.

Domhoff, G. W. (1996). *Finding meaning in dreams: A quantitative approach.* New York: Plenum.

Domhoff, G. W. (1999). New directions in the study of dream content using the Hall and Van de Castle coding system. *Dreaming, 9*, 115–137.

Domhoff, G. W. (2000). Moving dream theory beyond Freud and Jung. Paper presented to the symposium "Beyond Freud and Jung?" Graduate Theological Union, Berkeley, CA, 9/23/2000.

Domhoff, G. W. (2003). *The scientific study of dreams: Neural networks, cognitive development, and content analysis.* Washington, DC: APA Books.

Domjan, M. (1992). Adult learning and mate choice: Possibilities and experimental evidence. *American Zoologist, 32,* 48–61.

Domjan, M. (1994). Formulation of a behavior system for sexual conditioning. *Psychonomic Bulletin & Review, 1,* 421–428.

Domjan, M. (2005). Pavlovian conditioning: A functional perspective. *Annual Review of Psychology, 56.*

Domjan, M., Blesbois, E., & Williams, J. (1998). The adaptive significance of sexual conditioning: Pavlovian control of sperm release. *Psychological Science, 9,* 411–415.

Domjan, M., Cusato, B., & Krause, M. (2004). Learning with arbitrary versus ecological conditioned stimuli: Evidence from sexual conditioning. *Psychonomic Bulletin & Review, 11,* 232–246.

Donahoe, J. W., & Vegas, R. (2004). Pavlovian conditioning: The CS-UR relation. *Journal of Experimental Psychology: Animal Behavior, 30,* 17–33.

Donnellan, M. B., Conger, R. D., & Bryant, C. M. (2004). The Big Five and enduring marriages. *Journal of Research in Personality, 38,* 481–504.

Donnellan, M. B., Trzesniewski, K. H., Robins, R. W., Moffitt, T. E., & Caspi, A. (2005). Low self-esteem is related to aggression, antisocial behavior, and delinquency. *Psychological Science, 16,* 328–335.

Donnerstein, E. (1998). Why do we have those new ratings on television? Invited address to the National Institute on the Teaching of Psychology.

Donnerstein, E., Linz, D., & Penrod, S. (1987). *The question of pornography.* New York: Free Press.

Dorman, M. F., & Wilson, B. S. (2004). The design and function of cochlear implants. *American Scientist, 92,* 436–445.

Dorner, G. (1976). *Hormones and brain differentiation.* Amsterdam: Elsevier Scientific.

Dorner, G. (1988). Neuroendocrine response to estrogen and brain differentiation in heterosexuals, homosexuals, and transsexuals. *Archives of Sexual Behavior, 17,* 57–75.

Dorozyaski, A. (1993, January/February). Maternal alcoholism: Grapes of wrath. *Psychology Today,* p. 18.

Dorris, M. (1989). *The Broken Cord.* New York: HarperCollins.

Doty, R. L. (2001). Olfaction. *Annual Review of Psychology, 52,* 423–452.

Doty, R. L., Shaman, P., Applebaum, S. L., Giberson, R., Siksorski, L., & Rosenberg, L. (1984). Smell identification ability: Changes with age. *Science, 226,* 1441–1443.

Doty, R. W. (1998). The five mysteries of the mind, and their consequences. *Neuropsychologia, 36,* 1069–1076.

Dovidio, J. F., & Gaertner, S. L. (1999). Reducing prejudice: Combating intergroup biases. *Current Directions in Psychological Science, 8,* 101–105.

Dovidio, J. F., ten Vergert, M., Stewart, T. L., Gaertner, S. L., Johnson, J. D., Esses, V. M., Riek, B. M., & Pearson, A. R. (2004). Perspective and prejudice: Antecedents and mediating mechanisms. *Personality and Social Psychology Bulletin, 30,* 1537–1549.

Downing, P. E., Jiang, Y., & Shuman, M. (2001). A cortical area selective for visual processing of the human body. *Science, 293,* 2470–2473.

Doyle, R. (2005, March). Gay and lesbian census. *Scientific American,* p. 28.

Draguns, J. G. (1990a). Normal and abnormal behavior in cross-cultural perspective: Specifying the nature of their relationship. *Nebraska Symposium on Motivation 1989, 37,* 235–277.

Draguns, J. G. (1990b). Applications of cross-cultural psychology in the field of mental health. In R. W. Brislin (Ed.), *Applied cross-cultural psychology.* Newbury Park, CA: Sage.

Draguns, J. G. (1997). Abnormal behavior patterns across cultures: Implications for counseling and psychotherapy. *International Journal of Intercultural Relations, 21,* 213–248.

Druckman, D., & Bjork, R. A. (1991). *In the mind's eye: Enhancing human performance.* National Academy Press: Washington, DC.

Druckman, D., & Bjork, R. A. (Eds.) (1994). *Learning, remembering, believing: Enhancing human performance.* Washington, DC: National Academy Press.

Duckworth, A. L., & Seligman, M. E. P. (2005). Discipline outdoes talent: Self-discipline predicts academic performance in adolescents. *Psychological Science, 12,* 939–944.

Duclos, S. E., Laird, J. D., Sexter, M., Stern, L., & Van Lighten, O. (1989). Emotion-specific effects of facial expressions and postures on emotional experience. *Journal of Personality and Social Psychology, 57,* 100–108.

Duenwald, M. (2004, October 26). The dorms may be great, but how's the counseling? *New York Times* (www.nytimes.com).

Duffy, M. (2003, June 9). Weapons of mass disappearance. *Time,* pp. 28–33.

Dugatkin, L. A. (2002, Winter). Watching culture shape even guppy love. *Cerebrum,* pp. 51–66.

Duggan, J. P., & Booth, D. A. (1986). Obesity, overeating, and rapid gastric emptying in rats with ventromedial hypothalamic lesions. *Science, 231,* 609–611.

Dugger, C. W. (2005, January 18). U.N. proposes doubling of aid to cut poverty. *New York Times* (www.nytimes.com).

Duncan, B. L. (1976). Differential social perception and attribution of intergroup violence: Testing the lower limits of stereotyping of blacks. *Journal of Personality and Social Psychology, 34,* 590–598.

Duncan, G. J., Hill, M. S., & Hoffman, S. D. (1988). Welfare dependence within and across generations. *Science, 239,* 467–471.

Duncan, J. (2000, July 21). Quoted by N. Angier, Study finds region of brain may be key problem solver. *New York Times* (www.nytimes.com).

Duncan, J., Seitz, R. J., Kolodny, J., Bor, D., Herzog, H., Ahmed, A., Newell, F. N., & Emslie, H. (2000). A neural basis of general intelligence. *Science, 289,* 457–460.

Duncker, K. (1945). On problem solving. *Psychological Monographs, 58* (Whole no. 270).

Dunn, A. L., Trivedi, M. H., Kampert, J. B., Clark, C. G., & Chambliss, H. O. (2005). Exercise treatment for depression: Efficacy and dose response. *American Journal of Preventive Medicine, 28,* 1–8.

Dunson, D. B., Colombo, B., & Baird, D. D. (2002). Changes with age in the level and duration of fertility in the menstrual cycle. *Human Reproduction, 17,* 1399–1403.

Durston, S., Hulshoff, P., Hilleke, E., Casey, B. J., Giedd, J. N., Buitelaar, J. K., & van Engeland, H. (2001). Anatomical MRI of the developing human brain: What have we learned? *Journal of the American Academy of Child and Adolescent Psychiatry, 40,* 1012–1020.

Dush, C. M. K, Cohan, C. L., & Amato, P. R. (2003). The relationship between cohabitation and marital quality and stability: Change across cohorts? *Journal of Marriage and Family, 65,* 539–549.

Dutton, D. G., & Aron, A. (1989). Romantic attraction and generalized liking for others who are sources of conflict-based arousal. *Canadian Journal of Behavioural Sciences, 21,* 246–257.

Dutton, D. G., & Aron, A. P. (1974). Some evidence for heightened sexual attraction under conditions of high anxiety. *Journal of Personality and Social Psychology, 30,* 510–517.

Dye, D. A., & Reck, M. (1989). College grade point average as a predictor of adult success: A reply. *Public Personnel Management, 18,* 235–241.

Eagly, A. (1994). Are people prejudiced against women? Donald Campbell Award invited address, American Psychological Association convention.

Eagly, A. H., Ashmore, R. D., Makhijani, M. G., & Kennedy, L. C. (1991). What is beautiful is good, but . . .: A meta-analytic review of research on the physical attractiveness stereotype. *Psychological Bulletin, 110,* 109–128.

Eagly, A. H., & Crowley, M. (1986). Gender and helping behavior: A meta-analytic review of the social psychological literature. *Psychological Bulletin, 100,* 283–308.

Eagly, A. H., & Johnson, B. T. (1990). Gender and leadership style: A meta-analysis. *Psychological Bulletin, 108,* 233–256.

Eagly, A. H., & Wood, W. (1999). The origins of sex differences in human behavior: Evolved dispositions versus social roles. *American Psychologist, 54,* 408–423.

Eastman, C. L., Boulos, Z., Terman, M., Campbell, S. S., Dijk, D-J., & Lewy, A. J. (1995). Light treatment for sleep disorders: Consensus report. VI. Shift work. *Journal of Biological Rhythms, 10,* 157–164.

Eastman, C. L., Young, M. A., Fogg, L. F., Liu, L., & Meaden, P. M. (1998). Bright light treatment of winter depression: A placebo-controlled trial. *Archives of General Psychiatry, 55,* 883–889.

Ebbesen, E. B., Duncan, B., & Konecni, V. J. (1975). Effects of content of verbal aggression on future verbal aggression: A field experiment. *Journal of Experimental Social Psychology, 11,* 192–204.

Ebbinghaus, H. (1885). *Über das Gedächtnis.* Leipzig: Duncker & Humblot. Cited in R. Klatzky (1980), *Human memory: Structures and processes.* San Francisco: Freeman.

Ebbinghaus, H. (1885/1964). *Memory: A contribution to experimental psychology* (tr. by H. A. Ruger & C. E. Bussenius). New York: Dover.

Eberhardt, J. L. (2005). Imaging race. *American Psychologist, 60,* 181–190.

Eberhardt, J. L., Goff, P. A., Purdie, V. J., & Davies, P. G. (2004). Seeing Black: Race, crime, and visual processing. *Journal of Personality and Social Psychology, 87,* 876–893.

Eccles, J. S., Jacobs, J. E., & Harold, R. D. (1990). Gender role stereotypes, expectancy effects, and parents' socialization of gender differences. *Journal of Social Issues, 46,* 183–201.

Eckensberger, L. H. (1994). Moral development and its measurement across cultures. In W. J. Lonner & R. Malpass (Eds.), *Psychology and culture.* Boston: Allyn and Bacon.

Eckersley, R. (2000). The mixed blessings of material progress: Diminishing returns in the pursuit of happiness. *Journal of Happiness Studies, 1,* 267–292.

Eckersley, R. (2001, March 23). Wealthier, but poorer for all that. *The Australian,* p. 13.

Eckersley, R., & Dear, K. (2002). Correlates of youth suicide. *Social Science and Medicine, 55,* 1891–1935.

Eckert, E. D., Heston, L. L., & Bouchard, T. J., Jr. (1981). MZ twins reared apart: Preliminary findings of psychiatric disturbances and traits. In L. Gedda, P. Paris, & W. D. Nance (Eds.), *Twin research: Vol. 3. Pt. B. Intelligence, personality, and development.* New York: Alan Liss.

Ecklund-Flores, L. (1992). The infant as a model for the teaching of introductory psychology. Paper presented to the American Psychological Association annual convention.

Economist. (2001, December 20). An anthropology of happiness. *The Economist* (www.economist.com/world/asia).

Economist. (2004, September 16). Supercharging the brain (www.economist.co.uk).

Edelman, S., & Kidman, A. D. (1997). Mind and cancer: Is there a relationship? A review of the evidence. *Australian Psychologist, 32,* 1–7.

Edison, T. A. (1948). *The diary and sundry observations of Thomas Alva Edison,* edited by D. D. Runes. New York: Philosophical Library. Cited by S. Coren (1996). *Sleep Thieves.* New York: Free Press.

Edwards, C. P. (1981). The comparative study of the development of moral judgment and reasoning. In R. H. Munroe, R. L. Munroe, & B. B. Whiting (Eds.), *Handbook of cross-cultural human development.* New York: Garland Press.

Edwards, C. P. (1982). Moral development in comparative cultural perspective. In D. A. Wagner & H. W. Stevenson (Eds.), *Cultural perspectives on child development.* San Francisco: Freeman.

Edwards, R., Peet, M., Shay, J., & Horrobin, D. (1998). Omega-3 polyunsaturated fatty acid levels in the diet and in red blood cell membranes of depressed patients. *Journal of Affective Disorders, 48,* 149–155.

Egan, M. F., & 16 others. (2004). Variation in *GRM3* affects cognition, prefrontal glutamate, and risk for schizophrenia. *Proceedings of the National Academy of Sciences, 101,* 12604–12609.

Ehrhardt, A. A. (1987). A transactional perspective on the development of gender differences. In J. M. Reinisch, L. A. Rosenblum, & S. A. Sanders (Eds.), *Masculinity/femininity: Basic perspectives.* New York: Oxford University Press.

Ehrlichman, H., & Halpern, J. N. (1988). Affect and memory: Effects of pleasant and unpleasant odors on retrieval of happy and unhappy memories. *Journal of Personality and Social Psychology, 55,* 769–779.

Eibl-Eibesfeldt, I. (1971). *Love and hate: The natural history of behavior patterns.* New York: Holt, Rinehart & Winston.

Eich, E. (1990). Learning during sleep. In R. B. Bootzin, J. F. Kihlstrom, & D. L. Schacter (Eds.), *Sleep and cognition.* Washington, DC: American Psychological Association.

Eich, E., Macaulay, D., Loewenstein, R. J., & Dihle, P. H. (1997). Memory, amnesia, and dissociative identity disorder. *Psychological Science, 8,* 417–422.

Einstein, G. O., & McDaniel, M. A. (1990). Normal aging and prospective memory. *Journal of Experimental Psychology: Learning, Memory, and Cognition, 16,* 717–726.

Einstein, G. O., McDaniel, M. A., Richardson, S. L., Guynn, M. J., & Cunfer, A. R. (1995). Aging and prospective memory: Examining the influences of self-initiated retrieval processes. *Journal of Experimental Psychology: Learning, Memory, and Cognition, 21,* 996–1007.

Einstein, G. O., McDaniel, M. A., Smith, R. E., & Shaw, P. (1998). Habitual prospective memory and aging: Remembering intentions and forgetting actions. *Psychological Science, 9,* 284–288.

Eisenberg, N., Cumberland A., & Spinrad, T. L. (1998a). Parental socialization of emotion. *Psychological Inquiry, 9,* 241–271.

Eisenberg, N., & Lennon, R. (1983). Sex differences in empathy and related capacities. *Psychological Bulletin, 94,* 100–131.

Eisenberg, N., Spinrad, T. L., & Cumberland, A. (1998b). The socialization of emotion: Reply to commentaries. *Psychological Inquiry, 9,* 317–333.

Eisenberger, N. I., Lieberman, M. D., & Williams, K. D. (2003). Does rejection hurt? An fMRI study of social exclusion. *Science, 302,* 290–292.

Eisenberger, R., & Rhoades, L. (2001). Incremental effects of reward on creativity. *Journal of Personality and Social Psychology, 81,* 728–741.

Eiser, J. R. (1985). Smoking: The social learning of an addiction. *Journal of Social and Clinical Psychology, 3,* 446–457.

Ekman, P. (1994). Strong evidence for universals in facial expressions: A reply to Russell's mistaken critique. *Psychological Bulletin, 115,* 268–287.

Ekman, P. (2003). *Emotions revealed: Recognizing faces and feelings to improve communication and emotional life.* New York: Times Books.

Ekman, P., Friesen, W. V., O'Sullivan, M., Chan, A., Diacoyanni-Tarlatzis, I., Heider, K., Krause, R., LeCompte, W. A., Pitcairn, T., Ricci-Bitti, P. E., Scherer, K., Tomita, M., & Tzavaras, A. (1987). Universals and cultural differences in the judgments of facial expressions of emotion. *Journal of Personality and Social Psychology, 53,* 712–717.

Ekman, P., & O'Sullivan, M. (1991). Who can catch a liar? *American Psychologist, 46,* 913–920.

Ekman, P., O'Sullivan, M. O., & Frank, M. G. (1999). A few can catch a liar. *Psychological Science, 10,* 263–266.

Elbert, T., Pantev, C., Wienbruch, C., Rockstroh, B., & Taub, E. (1995). Increased cortical representation of the fingers of the left hand in string players. *Science, 270,* 305–307.

Elfenbein, H. A., & Ambady, N. (1999). Does it take one to know one? A meta-analysis of the universality and cultural specificity of emotion recognition. Unpublished manuscript, Harvard University.

Elfenbein, H. A., & Ambady, N. (2002). On the universality and cultural specificity of emotion recognition: A meta-analysis. *Psychological Bulletin, 128,* 203–235.

Elfenbein, H. A., & Ambady, N. (2003a). When familiarity breeds accuracy: Cultural exposure and facial emotion recognition. *Journal of Personality and Social Psychology, 85,* 276–290.

Elfenbein, H. A., & Ambady, N. (2003b). Universals and cultural differences in recognizing emotions. *Current Directions in Psychological Science, 12,* 159–164.

Elkin, I., Shea, T., Watkins, J. T., Imber, S. D., Sotsky, S. M., Collins, J. F., Glass, D. R., Pilkonis, P. A., Leber, W. R., Docherty, J. P., Fiester, S. J., & Parloff, M. B. (1989). National Institute of Mental Health treatment of depression collaborative research program. *Archives of General Psychiatry, 46,* 971–983.

Elkind, D. (1970). The origins of religion in the child. *Review of Religious Research, 12,* 35–42.

Elkind, D. (1978). *The child's reality: Three developmental themes.* Hillsdale, NJ: Erlbaum.

Ellis, A. (1980). Psychotherapy and atheistic values: A response to A. E. Bergin's "Psychotherapy and religious values." *Journal of Consulting and Clinical Psychology, 48,* 635–639.

Ellis, A., & Becker, I. M. (1982). *A guide to personal happiness.* North Hollywood, CA: Wilshire Book Co.

Ellis, B. J. (2004). Timing of pubertal maturation in girls: An integrated life history approach. *Psychological Bulletin, 130,* 920–958.

Ellis, B. J., Bates, J. E., Dodge, K. A., Fergusson, D. M., John, H. L., Pettit, G. S., & Woodward, L. (2003). Does father absence place daughters at special risk for early sexual activity and teenage pregnancy? *Child Development, 74,* 801–821.

Ellis, L., & Ames, M. A. (1987). Neurohormonal functioning and sexual orientation: A theory of homosexuality-heterosexuality. *Psychological Bulletin, 101,* 233–258.

Emde, R. N., Plomin, R., Robinson, J., Corley, R., DeFries, J., Fulker, D. W., Reznick, J. S., Campos, J., Kagan, J., & Zahn-Waxler, C. (1992). Temperament, emotion, and cognition at fourteen months: The MacArthur Longitudinal Twin Study. *Child Development, 63,* 1437–1455.

EMDR. (2002, September 19). Description for professionals. (www.emdr.org).

Emerging Trends. (1997, September). Teens turn more to parents than friends on whether to attend church. Princeton, NJ: Princeton Religion Research Center, p. 5.

Emery, G. (2004). Psychic predictions 2004. Committee for the Scientific Investigation of Claims of the Paranormal (www.csicop.org).

Emery, N. J., & Clayton, N. S. (2004). The mentality of crows: Convergent evolution of intelligence in corvids and apes. *Science, 306,* 1903–1907.

Emmons, S., Geisler, C., Kaplan, K. J., & Harrow, M. (1997). *Living with schizophrenia.* Muncie, IN: Taylor and Francis (Accelerated Development).

Emmorey, K., Allen, J. S., Bruss, J., Schenker, N., & Damasio, H. (2003). A morphometric analysis of auditory brain regions in congenitally deaf adults. *Proceedings of the National Academy of Sciences, 100,* 10049–10054.

Empson, J. A. C., & Clarke, P. R. F. (1970). Rapid eye movements and remembering. *Nature, 227,* 287–288.

Emslie, C., Hunt, K., & Macintyre, S. (2001). Perceptions of body image among working men and women. *Journal of Epidemiology and Community Health, 55,* 406–407.

Endler, N. S. (1982). *Holiday of darkness: A psychologist's personal journey out of his depression.* New York: Wiley.

Endler, N. S., & Speer, R. L. (1998). Personality psychology: Research trends for 1993–1995. *Journal of Personality, 66,* 621–669.

Engemann, K. M., & Owyang, M. T. (2005, April). So much for that merit raise: The link between wages and appearance. *Regional Economist* (www.stlouisfed.org).

Engen, T. (1987). Remembering odors and their names. *American Scientist, 75,* 497–503.

Engle, R. W. (2002). Working memory capacity as executive attention. *Current Directions in Psychological Science, 11,* 19–23.

Epel, E. S., Blackburn, E. H., Lin, J., Dhabhar, F. S., Adler, N. E., Morrow, J. D., & Cawthon, R. M. (2004). Accelerated telomere shortening in response to life stress. *Proceedings of the National Academy of Sciences, 101,* 17312–17315.

Epley, N., & Dunning, D. (2000). Feeling "holier than thou": Are self-serving assessments produced by errors in self- or social prediction? *Journal of Personality and Social Psychology, 79,* 861–875.

Epley, N., Keysar, B., Van Boven, L., & Gilovich, T. (2004). Perspective taking as egocentric anchoring and adjustment. *Journal of Personality and Social Psychology, 87,* 327–339.

EPOCH. (2000). *Legal reforms: Corporal punishment of children in the family* (www.stophitting.com/laws/legalReform.php).

Epstein, J., Stern, E., & Silbersweig, D. (1998). Mesolimbic activity associated with psychosis in schizophrenia: Symptom-specific PET studies. In J. F. McGinty (Ed.), *Advancing from the ventral striatum to the extended amygdala: Implications for neuropsychiatry and drug use: In honor of Lennart Heimer. Annals of the New York Academy of Sciences, 877,* 562–574.

Epstein, S. (1983a). Aggregation and beyond: Some basic issues on the prediction of behavior. *Journal of Personality, 51,* 360–392.

Epstein, S. (1983b). The stability of behavior across time and situations. In R. Zucker, J. Aronoff, & A. I. Rabin (Eds.), *Personality and the prediction of behavior.* San Diego: Academic Press.

Epstein, S., & Meier, P. (1989). Constructive thinking: A broad coping variable with specific components. *Journal of Personality and Social Psychology, 57,* 332–350.

Erdberg, P. (1990). Rorschach assessment. In G. Goldstein & M. Hersen (Eds.), *Handbook of psychological assessment,* 2nd ed. New York: Pergamon.

Erdelyi, M. H. (1985). *Psychoanalysis: Freud's cognitive psychology.* New York: Freeman.

Erdelyi, M. H. (1988). Repression, reconstruction, and defense: History and integration of the psychoanalytic and experimental frameworks. In J. Singer (Ed.), *Repression: Defense mechanism and cognitive style.* Chicago: University of Chicago Press.

Erel, O., & Burman, B. (1995). Interrelatedness of marital relations and parent-child relations: A meta-analytic review. *Psychological Bulletin, 118,* 108–132.

Erel, O., Oberman, Y., & Yirmiya, N. (2000). Maternal versus nonmaternal care and seven domains of children's development. *Psychological Bulletin, 126,* 727–747.

Erickson, M. F., & Aird, E. G. (2005). *The motherhood study: Fresh insights on mothers' attitudes and concerns.* New York: The Motherhood Project, Institute for American Values.

Ericsson, K. A. (2001). Attaining excellence through deliberate practice: Insights from the study of expert performance. In M. Ferrari (Ed.), *The pursuit of excellence in education.* Hillsdale, NJ: Erlbaum.

Ericsson, K. A. (2002). Attaining excellence through deliberate practice: Insights from the study of expert performance. In C. Desforges & R. Fox (Eds.), *Teaching and learning: The essential readings.* Malden, MA: Blackwell Publishers.

Ericsson, K. A., & Chase, W. G. (1982). Exceptional memory. *American Scientist, 70,* 607–615.

Ericsson, K. A., Krampe, R. T., & Heizman, S. (1993). Can we create gifted people? In G. R. Bock & K. Ackrill (Eds.), *Ciba Foundation Symposium 178: The origins and development of high ability.* New York: Wiley. Cited by M. J. A. Howe, J. W. Davison, & J. A. Sioboda (1998). Innate talents: Reality or myth? *Behavioral and Brain Sciences, 21,* 399–442.

Ericsson, K. A., & Lehmann, A. C. (1996). Expert and exceptional performance: Evidence of maximal adaptations to task constraints. *Annual Review of Psychology, 47,* 273–305.

Erikson, E. H. (1963). *Childhood and society.* New York: Norton.

Erikson, E. H. (1983, June). A conversation with Erikson (by E. Hall). *Psychology Today,* pp. 22–30.

Ernsberger, P., & Koletsky, R. J. (1999). Biomedical rationale for a wellness approach to obesity: An alternative to a focus on weight loss. *Journal of Social Issues, 55,* 221–260.

Eron, L. D. (1987). The development of aggressive behavior from the perspective of a developing behaviorism. *American Psychologist, 42,* 435–442.

ESPAD. (2003). Summary of the 2003 findings. European School Survey Project on Alcohol and Other Drugs (www.espad.org).

Esser, J. K., & Lindoerfer, J. S. (1989). Groupthink and the space shuttle *Challenger* accident: Toward a quantitative case analysis. *Journal of Behavioral Decision Making, 2,* 167–177.

Esterson, A. (2001). The mythologizing of psychoanalytic history: Deception and self-deception in Freud's accounts of the seduction theory episode. *History of Psychiatry, 12,* 329–352.

Esty, A. (2004). The new wealth of nations. *American Scientist, 92,* 513.

Eszterhas, J. (2002, August 9). Hollywood's responsibility for smoking deaths. *New York Times* (www.nytimes.com).

Etcoff, N. L., Ekman, P., Magee, J. J., & Frank, M. G. (2000). Lie detection and language comprehension. *Nature, 405,* 139.

Etnier, J. L., Salazar, W., Landers, D. M., Petruzzello, S. J., Han, M., & Nowell, P. (1997). The influence of physical fitness and exercise upon cognitive functioning: A meta-analysis. *Journal of Sport & Exercise Psychology, 19,* 249–277.

ETS. (1992). Three reports shed new light on gender differences in testing. *ETS Developments, 37*(3), 4–7.

Etzioni, A. (1999). The monochrome society. *The Public Interest, 137* (Fall), 42–55.

Evans, C. R., & Dion, K. L. (1991). Group cohesion and performance: A meta-analysis. *Small Group Research, 22,* 175–186.

Evans, G. W. (2004). The environment of childhood poverty. *American Psychologist, 59,* 77–92.

Evans, G. W., Hygge, S., & Bullinger, M. (1995). Chronic noise and psychological stress. *Psychological Science, 6,* 333–338.

Evans, G. W., Palsane, M. N., & Carrere, S. (1987). Type A behavior and occupational stress: A cross-cultural study of blue-collar workers. *Journal of Personality and Social Psychology, 52,* 1002–1007.

Evans, G. W., Palsane, M. N., Lepore, S. J., & Martin, J. (1989). Residential density and psychological health: The mediating effects of social support. *Journal of Personality and Social Psychology, 57,* 994–999.

Evans, R. I., Dratt, L. M., Raines, B. E., & Rosenberg, S. S. (1988). Social influences on smoking initiation: Importance of distinguishing descriptive versus mediating process variables. *Journal of Applied Social Psychology, 18,* 925–943.

Ewing, R., Schmid, T., Killingsworth, R., Zlot, A., & Raudenbush, S. (2003). Relationship between urban sprawl and physical activity, obesity, and morbidity. *American Journal of Health Promotion, 18,* 47–57.

Exner, J. E. (2003). *The Rorschach: A comprehensive system,* 4th edition. Hoboken, NJ: Wiley.

Eysenck, H. J. (1952). The effects of psychotherapy: An evaluation. *Journal of Consulting Psychology, 16,* 319–324.

Eysenck, H. J. (1990, April 30). An improvement on personality inventory. *Current Contents: Social and Behavioral Sciences, 22*(18), 20.

Eysenck, H. J. (1992). Four ways five factors are *not* basic. *Personality and Individual Differences, 13,* 667–673.

Eysenck, H. J., & Grossarth-Maticek, R. (1991). Creative novation behaviour therapy as a prophylactic treatment for cancer and coronary heart disease: Part II—Effects of treatment. *Behaviour Research and Therapy, 29,* 17–31.

Eysenck, H. J., Wakefield, J. A., Jr., & Friedman, A. F. (1983). Diagnosis and clinical assessment: The DSM-III. *Annual Review of Psychology, 34,* 167–193.

Eysenck, M. W., MacLeod, C., & Mathews, A. (1987). Cognitive functioning and anxiety. *Psychological Research, 49,* 189–195.

Eysenck, S. B. G., & Eysenck, H. J. (1963). The validity of questionnaire and rating assessments of extraversion and neuroticism, and their factorial stability. *British Journal of Psychology, 54,* 51–62.

Faber, N. (1987, July). Personal glimpse. *Reader's Digest,* p. 34.

Fagan, J. F., III (1992). Intelligence: A theoretical viewpoint. *Current Directions in Psychological Science, 1,* 82–86.

Fairburn, C. G., Cowen, P. J., & Harrison, P. J. (1999). Twin studies and the etiology of eating disorders. *International Journal of Eating Disorders, 26,* 349–358.

Fantz, R. L. (1961, May). The origin of form perception. *Scientific American,* pp. 66–72.

Farah, M. J., Rabinowitz, C., Quinn, G. E., & Liu, G. T. (2000). Early commitment of neural substrates for face recognition. *Cognitive Neuropsychology, 17,* 117–124.

Farina, A. (1982). The stigma of mental disorders. In A. G. Miller (Ed.), *In the eye of the beholder.* New York: Praeger.

Farina, A., & Fisher, J. D. (1982). Beliefs about mental disorders: Findings and implications. In G. Weary & H. L. Mirels (Eds.), *Integrations of clinical and social psychology.* New York: Oxford University Press.

Farley, M, Baral, I., Kiremire, M., & Sezgin, U. (1998). Prostitution in five countries: Violence and post-traumatic stress disorder. *Feminism and Psychology, 8,* 405–426.

Farley, T., & Cohen, D. (2001, December). Fixing a fat nation. *Washington Monthly* (www.washingtonmonthly.com/features/2001/0112.farley.cohen.html).

Faro, S. (2004). Presentation to the Radiological Society of North America, Chicago.

Farrington, D. P. (1991). Antisocial personality from childhood to adulthood. *The Psychologist: Bulletin of the British Psychological Society, 4,* 389–394.

Farwell, L. A., & Smith, S. S. (2001). Using brain MERMER testing to detect concealed knowledge despite efforts to conceal. *Journal of Forensic Sciences, 46* (1), 1–9.

FBI. (2004). Crime in the United States 2003, Five-Year Arrest Trends by Sex, 1999–2003. Table 35.

Feder, H. H. (1984). Hormones and sexual behavior. *Annual Review of Psychology, 35,* 165–200.

Feeney, J. A., & Noller, P. (1990). Attachment style as a predictor of adult romantic relationships. *Journal of Personality and Social Psychology, 58,* 281–291.

Feigenson, L., Carey, S., & Spelke, E. (2002). Infants' discrimination of number vs. continuous extent. *Cognitive psychology, 44,* 33–66.

Feingold, A. (1990). Gender differences in effects of physical attractiveness on romantic attraction: A comparison across five research paradigms. *Journal of Personality and Social Psychology, 59,* 981–993.

Feingold, A. (1992). Good-looking people are not what we think. *Psychological Bulletin, 111,* 304–341.

Feingold, A., & Mazzella, R. (1998). Gender differences in body image are increasing. *Psychological Science, 9,* 190–195.

Feminist Psychologist. (2002, Winter). Justice for Mary Whiton Calkins, p. 11.

Fenn, K. M., Nusbaum, H. C., & Margoliash, D. (2003). Consolidation during sleep of perceptual learning of spoken language. *Nature, 425,* 614–616.

Fenton, W. S., & McGlashan, T. H. (1991). Natural history of schizophrenia subtypes: II. Positive and negative symptoms and long-term course. *Archives of General Psychiatry, 48,* 978–986.

Fenton, W. S., & McGlashan, T. H. (1994). Antecedents, symptom progression, and long-term outcome of the deficit syndrome in schizophrenia. *American Journal of Psychiatry, 151,* 351–356.

Ferguson, E. D. (1989). Adler's motivational theory: An historical perspective on belonging and the fundamental human striving. *Individual Psychology, 45,* 354–361.

Fergusson, D. M., & Woodward, L. G. (2002). Mental health, educational, and social role outcomes of adolescents with depression. *Archives of General Psychiatry, 59,* 225–231.

Fernandez, E., & Turk, D. C. (1989). The utility of cognitive coping strategies for altering pain perception: A meta-analysis. *Pain, 38,* 123–135.

Fernández-Ballesteros, R., & Caprara, M. (2003). Psychology of aging in Europe. *European Psychologist, 8,* 129–130.

Ferris, C. F. (1996, March). The rage of innocents. *The Sciences,* pp. 22–26.

Fiedler, F. E. (1981). Leadership effectiveness. *American Behavioral Scientist, 24,* 619–632.

Fiedler, F. E. (1987, September). When to lead, when to stand back. *Psychology Today,* pp. 26–27.

Fiedler, K., Nickel, S., Muehlfriedel, T., & Unkelbach, C. (2001). Is mood congruency an effect of genuine memory or response bias? *Journal of Experimental Social Psychology, 37,* 201–214.

Field, T. (1996). Attachment and separation in young children. *Annual Review of Psychology, 47,* 541–561.

Field, T. (2001). Massage therapy facilitates weight gain in preterm infants. *Current Directions in Psychological Science, 10,* 51–54.

Field, T., Hernandez-Reif, M., Diego, M., Feijo, L., Vera, Y., & Gil, K. (2004). Massage therapy by parents improves early growth and development. *Infant Behaviour and Development, 27,* 435–442.

Fields, R. D. (2004, April). The other half of the brain. *Scientific American,* pp. 54–61.

Fields, R. D. (2005, February). Making memories stick. *Scientific American,* pp. 75–81.

Fincham, F. D., & Bradbury, T. N. (1993). Marital satisfaction, depression, and attributions: A longitudinal analysis. *Journal of Personality and Social Psychology, 64,* 442–452.

Fink, G. R., Markowitsch, H. J., Reinkemeier, M., Bruckbauer, T., Kessler, J., & Heiss, W-D. (1996). Cerebral representation of one's own past: Neural networks involved in autobiographical memory. *Journal of Neuroscience, 16,* 4275–4282.

Fink, M. (1998). ECT and managed care. *Journal Watch Psychiatry, 4,* 73, 76.

Finkel, L. H., & Sajda, P. (1994). Constructing visual perception. *American Scientist, 82,* 224–237.

Finlay, S. W. (2000). Influence of Carl Jung and William James on the origin of alcoholics anonymous. *Review of General Psychology, 4,* 3–12.

Finney, E. M., Fine, I., & Dobkins, K. R. (2001). Visual stimuli activate auditory cortex in the deaf. *Nature Neuroscience, 4,* 1171–1173.

Finucci, J. M., & Childs, B. (1981). Are there really more dyslexic boys than girls? In A. Ansara, N. Geschwind, A. Galaburda, M. Albert, & N. Gartrell (Eds.), *Sex differences in dyslexia.* Towson, MD: The Orton Dyslexia Society.

Fischhoff, B. (1982). Debiasing. In D. Kahneman, P. Slovic, & A. Tversky (Eds.), *Judgment under uncertainty: Heuristics and biases.* New York: Cambridge University Press.

Fischhoff, B., Slovic, P., & Lichtenstein, S. (1977). Knowing with certainty: The appropriateness of extreme confidence. *Journal of Experimental Psychology: Human Perception and Performance, 3,* 552–564.

Fisher, H. E. (1993, March/April). After all, maybe it's biology. *Psychology Today,* pp. 40–45.

Fisher, H. E., Aron, A., Mashek, D., Li, H., & Brown, L. L. (2002). Defining the brain systems of lust, romantic attraction, and attachment. *Archives of Sexual Behavior, 31,* 413–419.

Fisher, H. T. (1984). Little Albert and Little Peter. *Bulletin of the British Psychological Society, 37,* 269.

Fisher, R. P., & Geiselman, R. E. (1992). *Memory-enhancing techniques for investigative interviewing: The cognitive interview.* Springfield, IL: Charles C. Thomas.

Fisher, R. P., Geiselman, R. E., & Raymond, D. S. (1987). Critical analysis of police interview techniques. *Journal of Police Science and Administration, 15,* 177–185.

Fisher, S., & Greenberg, R. (Eds.) (1997). *From placebo to panacea: Putting psychiatric drugs to the test.* New York: Wiley.

Fiske, S. T., Harris, L. T., & Cuddy, A. J. C. (2004). Why ordinary people torture enemy prisoners. *Science, 306,* 1482–1483.

Flack, W. F., Jr., Laird, J. D., & Cavallaro, L. A. (1999). Separate and combined effects of facial expressions and bodily postures on emotional feelings. *European Journal of Social Psychology, 29,* 203–217.

Flavell, J. H., Flavell, E. R., & Green, F. L. (2001). Development of children's understanding of connections between thinking and feeling. *Psychological Science, 12,* 430–432.

Fleming, I., Baum, A., & Weiss, L. (1987). Social density and perceived control as mediator of crowding stress in high-density residential neighborhoods. *Journal of Personality and Social Psychology, 52,* 899–906.

Fleming, J. H. (2001, Winter/Spring). Introduction to the special issue on linkage analysis. *The Gallup Research Journal,* pp. i–vi.

Fleming, J. H., & Scott, B. A. (1991). The costs of confession: The Persian Gulf War POW tapes in historical and theoretical perspective. *Contemporary Social Psychology, 15,* 127–138.

Fletcher, G. J. O., Fitness, J., & Blampied, N. M. (1990). The link between attributions and happiness in close relationships: The roles of depression and explanatory style. *Journal of Social and Clinical Psychology, 9,* 243–255.

Fletcher, P. C., Zafiris, O., Frith, C. D., Honey, R. A. E., Corlett, P. R., Zilles, K., & Fink, G. R. (2005). On the benefits of not trying: Brain activity and connectivity reflecting the interactions of explicit and implicit sequence learning. *Cerebral Cortex, 7,* 1002–1015.

Flora, S. R. (2004). *The power of reinforcement.* Albany, NY: SUNY Press.

Flouri, E., & Buchanan, A. (2004). Early father's and mother's involvement and child's later educational outcomes. *British Journal of Educational Psychology, 74,* 141–153.

Flynn, J. R. (1987). Massive IQ gains in 14 nations: What IQ tests really measure. *Psychological Bulletin, 101,* 171–191.

Flynn, J. R. (1999). Searching for justice: The discovery of IQ gains over time. *American Psychologist, 54,* 5–20.

Flynn, J. R. (2003). Movies about intelligence: The limitations of *g. Current Directions in Psychological Science, 12,* 95–99.

Foa, E. B., & Kozak, M. J. (1986). Emotional processing of fear: Exposure to corrective information. *Psychological Bulletin, 99,* 20–35.

Fogg, N. P., Harrington P. E., & Harrington T. F. (1999). *The College Majors Handbook.* Indianapolis, IN: JIST Works, Inc.

Fong, G. T., Frantz, D. H., & Nisbett, R. E. (1986). The effects of statistical training on thinking about everyday problems. *Cognitive Psychology, 18,* 253–292.

Ford, E. S. (2002). Does exercise reduce inflammation? Physical activity and C-reactive protein among U.S. adults. *Epidemiology, 13,* 561–569.

Foree, D. D., & LoLordo, V. M. (1973). Attention in the pigeon: Differential effects of food-getting versus shock-avoidance procedures. *Journal of Comparative and Physiological Psychology, 85,* 551–558.

Forer, B. R. (1949). The fallacy of personal validation: A classroom demonstration of gullibility. *Journal of Abnormal and Social Psychology, 44,* 118–123.

Forgas, J. P., Bower, G. H., & Krantz, S. E. (1984). The influence of mood on perceptions of social interactions. *Journal of Experimental Social Psychology, 20,* 497–513.

Forge, A., Li, L., Corwin, J. T., & Nevill, G. (1993). Ultrastructural evidence for hair cell regeneration in the mammalian inner ear. *Science, 259,* 1616–1619.

Forman, D. R., Aksan, N., & Kochanska, G. (2004). Toddlers' responsive imitation predicts preschool-age conscience. *Psychological Science, 15,* 699–704.

Foss, D. J., & Hakes, D. T. (1978). *Psycholinguistics: An introduction to the psychology of language.* Englewood Cliffs, NJ: Prentice-Hall.

Fosse, R., Stickgold, R., & Hobson, J. A. (2001). Brain-mind states: Reciprocal variation in thoughts and hallucinations. *Psychological Science, 12,* 30–36.

Foster, J. D., Campbell, W. K., & Twenge, J. M. (2003). Individual differences in narcissism: Inflated self-views across the lifespan and around the world. *Journal of Research in Personality, 37,* 469–486.

Foster, R. G. (2004). Are we trying to banish biological time? *Cerebrum, 6*(2), 7–26.

Foulkes, D. (1999). *Children's dreaming and the development of consciousness.* Cambridge, MA: Harvard University Press.

Fouts, R. S. (1992). Transmission of a human gestural language in a chimpanzee mother-infant relationship. *Friends of Washoe, 12/13,* pp. 2–8.

Fouts, R. (1997). *Next of kin: What chimpanzees have taught me about who we are.* New York: Morrow.

Fouts, R. S., & Bodamer, M. (1987). Preliminary report to the National Geographic Society on: "Chimpanzee intrapersonal signing." *Friends of Washoe, 7*(1), 4–12.

Fowler, M. J., Sullivan, M. J., & Ekstrand, B. R. (1973). Sleep and memory. *Science, 179,* 302–304.

Fowler, R. C., Rich, C. L., & Young, D. (1986). San Diego suicide study: II. Substance abuse in young cases. *Archives of General Psychiatry, 43,* 962–965.

Fowler, R. D. (1986, May). Howard Hughes: A psychological autopsy. *Psychology Today,* pp. 22–33.

Fowles, D. C. (1992). Schizophrenia: Diathesis-stress revisited. *Annual Review of Psychology, 43,* 303–336.

Fox, B. H. (1998). Psychosocial factors in cancer incidence and prognosis. In P. M. Cinciripini & others (Eds.), *Psychological and behavioral factors in cancer risk.* New York: Oxford University Press.

Fox, E., Lester, V., Russo, R., Bowles, R. J., Pichler, A., & Dutton, K. (2000). Facial expression of emotion: Are angry faces detected more efficiently? *Cognition and Emotion, 14,* 61–92.

Fox, J. L. (1984). The brain's dynamic way of keeping in touch. *Science, 225,* 820–821.

Fox, N. C., Crum, W. R., Scahill, R. I., Stevens, J. M., Janssen, J. C., Rossor, M. N. (2001). Imaging of onset and progression of Alzheimer's disease with voxel-compression mapping of serial magnetic resonance images. *Lancet, 358,* 201–205.

Fozard, J. L., & Popkin, S. J. (1978). Optimizing adult development: Ends and means of an applied psychology of aging. *American Psychologist, 33,* 975–989.

Fracassini, C. (2000, August 27). Holidaymakers led by the nose in sales quest. *Scotland on Sunday.*

Fraley, R. C. (2002). Attachment stability from infancy to adulthood: Meta-analysis and dynamic modeling of developmental mechanisms. *Personality and Social Psychology Review, 6,* 123–151.

Francis, D., Diorio, J., Liu, D., & Meaney, M. J. (1999). Nongenomic transmission across generations of maternal behavior and stress responses in the rat. *Science, 286,* 1155–1158.

Frank, J. D. (1982). Therapeutic components shared by all psychotherapies. In J. H. Harvey & M. M. Parks (Eds.), *The Master Lecture Series: Vol. 1. Psychotherapy research and behavior change.* Washington, DC: American Psychological Association.

Frank, R. (1999). *Luxury fever: Why money fails to satisfy in an era of excess.* New York: Free Press.

Frank, S. J. (1988). Young adults' perceptions of their relationships with their parents: Individual differences in connectedness, competence, and emotional autonomy. *Developmental Psychology, 24,* 729–737.

Frankel, A., Strange, D. R., & Schoonover, R. (1983). CRAP: Consumer rated assessment procedure. In G. H. Scherr & R. Liebmann-Smith (Eds.), *The best of The Journal of Irreproducible Results.* New York: Workman Publishing.

Frankenburg, W., Dodds, J., Archer, P., Shapiro, H., & Bresnick, B. (1992). The Denver II: A major revision and restandardization of the Denver Developmental Screening Test. *Pediatrics, 89,* 91–97.

Franz, E. A., Waldie, K. E., & Smith, M. J. (2000). The effect of callosotomy on novel versus familiar bimanual actions: A neural dissociation between controlled and automatic processes? *Psychological Science, 11,* 82–85.

Frasure-Smith, N., & Lespérance, F. (2005). Depression and coronary heart disease: Complex synergism of mind, body, and environment. *Current Directions in Psychological Science, 14,* 39–43.

Fredrickson, B. L. (2002). Positive emotions. In C. R. Snyder & S. J. Lopez (Eds.), *Handbook of positive psychology.* New York: Oxford.

Fredrickson, B. L. (2003). The value of positive emotions. *American Scientist, 91,* 330–335.

Fredrickson, B. L., & Kahneman, D. (1993). Duration neglect in retrospective evaluations of affective episodes. *Journal of Personality and Social Psychology, 65,* 45–55.

Fredrickson, B. L., Roberts, T-A., Noll, S. M., Quinn, D. M., & Twenge, J. M. (1998). That swimsuit becomes you: Sex differences in self-objectification, restrained eating, and math performance. *Journal of Personality and Social Psychology, 75,* 269–284.

Freedman, D. J., Riesenhuber, M., Poggio, T., & Miller, E. K. (2001). Categorical representation of visual stimuli in the primate prefrontal cortex. *Science, 291,* 312–316.

Freedman, J. L. (1978). *Happy people.* San Diego: Harcourt Brace Jovanovich.

Freedman, J. L. (1988). Television violence and aggression: What the evidence shows. In S. Oskamp (Ed.), *Television as a social issue.* Newbury Park, CA: Sage.

Freedman, J. L., & Fraser, S. C. (1966). Compliance without pressure: The foot-in-the-door technique. *Journal of Personality and Social Psychology, 4,* 195–202.

Freedman, J. L., & Perlick, D. (1979). Crowding, contagion, and laughter. *Journal of Experimental Social Psychology, 15,* 295–303.

Freedman, L. R., Rock, D., Roberts, S. A., Cornblatt, B. A., & Erlenmeyer-Kimling, L. (1998). The New York high-risk project: Attention, anhedonia and social outcome. *Schizophrenia Research, 30,* 1–9.

Freeman, W. J. (1991, February). The physiology of perception. *Scientific American,* pp. 78–85.

Frensch, P. A., & Rünger, D. (2003). Implicit learning. *Current Directions in Psychological Science, 12,* 13–18.

Freud, S. (1933). *New introductory lectures on psychoanalysis.* New York: Carlton House.

Freud, S. (1935; reprinted 1960). *A general introduction to psychoanalysis.* New York: Washington Square Press.

Frey, M. C., & Detterman, D. K. (2004). Scholastic assessment or *g*? The relationship between the Scholastic Assessment Test and general cognitive ability. *Psychological Science, 15*, 373–378.

Freyd, J. J., Putnam, F. W., Lyon, T. D., Becker-Blease, K. A., Cheit, R. E., Siegel, N. B., & Pezdek, K. (2005). The science of child sexual abuse. *Science, 308*, 501.

Friedman, M., & Ulmer, D. (1984). *Treating Type A behavior—and your heart.* New York: Knopf.

Friedrich, O. (1987, December 7). New age harmonies. *Time,* pp. 62–72.

Friend, T. (2004). *Animal talk: Breaking the codes of animal language.* New York: Free Press.

Frith, U., & Frith, C. (2001). The biological basis of social interaction. *Current Directions in Psychological Science, 10*, 151–155.

Fritsch, G., & Hitzig, E. (1870; reprinted 1960). On the electrical excitability of the cerebrum. In G. Von Bonin (Trans.), *Some papers on the cerebral cortex.* Springfield, IL: Charles C. Thomas.

Fromkin, V., & Rodman, R. (1983). *An introduction to language* (3rd ed.). New York: Holt, Rinehart & Winston.

Fry, A. F., & Hale, S. (1996). Processing speed, working memory, and fluid intelligence: Evidence for a developmental cascade. *Psychological Science, 7*, 237–241.

Fuhriman, A., & Burlingame, G. M. (1994). Group psychotherapy: Research and practice. In A. Fuhriman & G. M. Burlingame (Eds.), *Handbook of group psychotherapy.* New York: Wiley.

Fujiki, N., Yoshida, Y., Ripley, B., Mignot, E., & Nishino, S. (2003). Effects of IV and ICV hypocretin-1 (Orexin A) in hypocretin receptor-2 gene mutated narcoleptic dogs and IV hypocretin-1 replacement therapy in a hypocretin-ligand-deficient narcoleptic dog. *Sleep, 26*, 953–959.

Fujita, F., & Diener, E. (2005). Life satisfaction set point: Stability and change. *Journal of Personality and Social Psychology, 88*, 158–164.

Fuller, M. J., & Downs, A. C. (1990). Spermarche is a salient biological marker in men's development. Poster presented at the American Psychological Society convention.

Fulmer, I. S., Gerhart, B., & Scott, K. S. (2003). Are the 100 best better? An empirical investigation fo the relationship between being a "great place to work" and firm performance. *Personnel Psychology, 56*, 965–993.

Funder, D. C. (2001). Personality. *Annual Review of Psychology, 52*, 197–221.

Funder, D. C., & Block, J. (1989). The role of ego-control, ego-resiliency, and IQ in delay of gratification in adolescence. *Journal of Personality and Social Psychology, 57*, 1041–1050.

Furlow, F. B., & Thornhill, R. (1996, January/February). The orgasm wars. *Psychology Today,* pp. 42–46.

Furnham, A. (1982). Explanations for unemployment in Britain. *European Journal of Social Psychology, 12*, 335–352.

Furnham, A. (2001). Self-estimates of intelligence: Culture and gender difference in self and other estimates of both general (g) and multiple intelligences. *Personality and Individual Differences, 31*, 1381–1405.

Furnham, A., & Baguma, P. (1994). Cross-cultural differences in the evaluation of male and female body shapes. *International Journal of Eating Disorders, 15*, 81–89.

Furnham, A., Callahan, I., & Akande, D. (2004). Self-estimates of intelligence: A study in two African countries. *Journal of Psychology, 138*, 265–285.

Furnham, A., Callahan, I., & Rawles, R. (2003). Adults' knowledge of general psychology. *European Psychologist, 8*, 101–116.

Furnham, A., Hosoe, T., & Tang, T. L-P. (2002a). Male hubris and female humility? A cross-cultural study of ratings of self, parental, and sibling multiple intelligence in American, Britain, and Japan. *Intelligence, 30*, 101–115.

Furnham, A., & Mottabu, R. (2004). Sex and culture differences in the estimates of general and multiple intelligence: A study comparing British and Egyptian students. *Individual Differences Research, 3*, 82–96.

Furnham, A., & Rawles, R. (1995). Sex differences in the estimation of intelligence. *Journal of Social Behavior and Personality, 10*, 741–748.

Furnham, A., Reeves, E., & Bughani, S. (2002b). Parents think their sons are brighter than their daughters: Sex differences in parental self-estimations and estimations of their children's multiple intelligences. *Journal of Genetic Psychology, 163*, 24–39.

Furnham, A., & Taylor, L. (1990). Lay theories of homosexuality: Aetiology, behaviours, and 'cures.' *British Journal of Social Psychology, 29*, 135–147.

Furnham, A., & Thomas, C. (2004). Parents' gender and personality and estimates of their own and their children's intelligence. *Personality and Individual Differences, 37*, 887–903.

Furr, R. M., & Funder, D. C. (1998). A multimodal analysis of personal negativity. *Journal of Personality and Social Psychology, 74*, 1580–1591.

Gabbay, F. H. (1992). Behavior-genetic strategies in the study of emotion. *Psychological Science, 3*, 50–55.

Gabrieli, J. D. E., Desmond, J. E., Demb, J. E., Wagner, A. D., Stone, M. V., Vaidya, C. J., & Glover, G. H. (1996). Functional magnetic resonance imaging of semantic memory processes in the frontal lobes. *Psychological Science, 7*, 278–283.

Gaertner, L., & Iuzzini, J. (2005). Rejection and entitativity: A synergistic model of mass violence. In K. D. Williams, J. P. Forgas, & W. von Hippel (Eds.). *The social outcast: Ostracism, social exclusion, rejection, and bullying.* New York: Psychology Press.

Gage, F. H. (2003, September). Repair yourself. *Scientific American,* pp. 46–53.

Galambos, N. L. (1992). Parent-adolescent relations. *Current Directions in Psychological Science, 1*, 146–149.

Galanter, E. (1962). Contemporary psychophysics. In R. Brown, E. Galanter, E. H. Hess, & G. Mandler (Eds.), *New directions in psychology.* New York: Holt Rinehart, & Winston.

Galati, D., Scherer, K. R., & Ricci-Bitti, P. E. (1997). Voluntary facial expression of emotion: Comparing congenitally blind with normally sighted encoders. *Journal of Personality and Social Psychology, 73*, 1363–1379.

Galea, S., Boscarino, J., Resnick, H., & Vlahov, D. (2002). Mental health in New York City after the September 11 terrorist attacks: Results from two population surveys. Chapter 7. In *Mental-Health, United States, 2001*, R. W. Manderscheid, & M. J. Henderson (Eds.). Washington, DC: Superintendent of Documents, U.S. Government Printing Office.

Gallup. (2002, February 21). Homosexual relations. The Gallup Organization (www.gallup.com/poll/topics/homosexual.asp).

Gallup. (2002, June 11). Poll insights: The gender gap—post Sept. 11th fear. The Gallup Organization (www.gallup.com/poll/pollInsights).

Gallup. (2002). Alcohol and drinking (results of November 8–11, 2001 survey) (www.gallup.com/poll/topics/alcohol.asp).

Gallup. (2005, May 5). The gender gap: President Bush's handling of Iraq. The Gallup Poll (www.gallup.com).

Gallup, G., Jr. (1982). *Adventures in immortality.* New York: McGraw-Hill.

Gallup, G., Jr. (1998). Can animals empathize? *Scientific American, 4*, 66.

Gallup, G., Jr. (2002, April 30). Education and youth. *Gallup Tuesday Briefing* (www.gallup.com/poll/tb/educaYouth/20020430.asp).

Gallup, G. G., Jr., & Suarez, S. D. (1986). Self-awareness and the emergence of mind in humans and other primates. In J. Suls & A. G. Greenwald (Eds.), *Psychological perspectives on the self* (Vol. 3.). Hillsdale, NJ: Erlbaum.

Gallup, G. H. (1972). *The Gallup poll: Public opinion 1935-1971* (Vol. 3). New York: Random House.

Gallup, G. H., Jr. (1994, October). Millions finding care and support in small groups. *Emerging Trends*, pp. 2-5.

Gallup Organization. (1993). Other hemispheres may think our religion is alien and exotic. *PRRC Emerging Trends, 15*, 1-3.

Gallup Organization. (2003, July 8). American public opinion about Iraq. Gallup Poll News Service (www.gallup.com)

Gallup Organization. (2004, August 16). 65% of Americans receive NO praise or recognition in the workplace. E-mail from Tom Rath: bucketbook@gallup.com.

Gangestad, S. W., & Simpson, J. A. (2000). The evolution of human mating: Trade-offs and strategic pluralism. *Behavioral and Brain Sciences, 23*.

Garb, H. N., Wood, J. M., Lilienfeld, S. O., & Nezworski, M. T. (2005). Roots of the Rorschach controversy. *Clinical Psychology Review, 25*, 97-118.

Garbarino, J., Dubrow, N., & Kostelny, K. (1992). *Children in danger: Coping with the consequences of community violence.* San Francisco: Jossey-Bass Inc.

Garbarino, J., Kostelny, K., & Dubrow, N. (1991). What children can tell us about living in danger. *American Psychologist, 46*, 376-383.

Garcia, J., & Gustavson, A. R. (1997, January). Carl R. Gustavson (1946-1996): Pioneering wildlife psychologist. *APS Observer*, pp. 34-35.

Garcia, J., & Koelling, R. A. (1966). Relation of cue to consequence in avoidance learning. *Psychonomic Science, 4*, 123-124.

Gardner, H. (1983). *Frames of mind: The theory of multiple intelligences.* New York: Basic Books.

Gardner, H. (1998, March 19). An intelligent way to progress. *The Independent* (London), p. E4.

Gardner, H. (1998, November 5). Do parents count? *New York Review of Books* (www.nybooks.com).

Gardner, H. (1999, February). Who owns intelligence? *Atlantic Monthly*, pp. 67-76.

Gardner, H. (1999). *Multiple views of multiple intelligence.* New York: Basic Books.

Gardner, J., & Oswald, A. (2001). Does money buy happiness? A longitudinal study using data on windfalls. Working paper, Department of Economics, Cambridge University.

Gardner, R. A., & Gardner, B. I. (1969). Teaching sign language to a chimpanzee. *Science, 165*, 664-672.

Gardner, R. M., & Tockerman, Y. R. (1994). A computer-TV video methodology for investigating the influence of somatotype on perceived personality traits. *Journal of Social Behavior and Personality, 9*, 555-563.

Garfield, C. (1986). *Peak performers: The new heroes of American business.* New York: Morrow.

Garlick, D. (2002). Understanding the nature of the general factor of intelligence: The role of individual differences in neural plasticity as an explanatory mechanism. *Psychological Review, 109*, 116-136.

Garlick, D. (2003). Integrating brain science research with intelligence research. *Current Directions in Psychological Science, 12*, 185-189.

Garner, D. M., & Wooley, S. C. (1991). Confronting the failure of behavioral and dietary treatments for obesity. *Clinical Psychology Review, 11*, 729-780.

Garnets, L., & Kimmel, D. (1990). Lesbian and gay dimensions in the psychological study of human diversity. Master lecture, American Psychological Association convention.

Garry, M., & Loftus, E. F., & Brown, S. W. (1994). Memory: A river runs through it. *Consciousness and Cognition, 3*, 438-451.

Garry, M., Manning, C. G., Loftus, E. F., & Sherman, S. J. (1996). Imagination inflation: Imagining a childhood event inflates confidence that it occurred. *Psychonomic Bulletin & Review, 3*, 208-214.

Garza, D. L., & Feltz, D. L. (1998). Effects of selected mental practice on performance, self-efficacy, and competition confidence of figure skaters. *The Sports Psychologist, 12*, 1-15.

Gates, G. A., & Miyamoto, R. T. (2003). Cochlear implants. *New England Journal of Medicine, 349*, 421-423.

Gates, W. (1998, July 20). Charity begins when I'm ready (interview). *Fortune* (www.pathfinder.com/fortune/1998/980720/bil7.html).

Gawande, A. (1998, September 21). The pain perplex. *The New Yorker*, pp. 86-94.

Gawin, F. H. (1991). Cocaine addiction: Psychology and neurophysiology. *Science, 251*, 1580-1586.

Gazzaniga, M. S. (1967, August). The split brain in man. *Scientific American*, pp. 24-29.

Gazzaniga, M. S. (1983). Right hemisphere language following brain bisection: A 20-year perspective. *American Psychologist, 38*, 525-537.

Gazzaniga, M. S. (1988). Organization of the human brain. *Science, 245*, 947-952.

Gazzaniga, M. S. (1992). *Nature's mind: The biological roots of thinking, emotions, sexuality, language, and intelligence.* New York: Basic Books.

Gazzaniga, M. S. (1997). Brain, drugs, and society. *Science, 275*, 459.

Geary, D. C. (1995). Sexual selection and sex differences in spatial cognition. *Learning and Individual Differences, 7*, 289-301.

Geary, D. C. (1996). Sexual selection and sex differences in mathematical abilities. *Behavioral and Brain Sciences, 19*, 229-247.

Geary, D. C. (1998). *Male, female: The evolution of human sex differences.* Washington, DC: American Psychological Association.

Geary, D. C., Salthouse, T. A., Chen, G-P., & Fan, L. (1996). Are East Asian versus American differences in arithmetical ability a recent phenomenon? *Developmental Psychology, 32*, 254-262.

Geen, R. G., & Quanty, M. B. (1977). The catharsis of aggression: An evaluation of a hypothesis. In L. Berkowitz (Ed.), *Advances in experimental social psychology* (Vol. 10). New York: Academic Press.

Geen, R. G., & Thomas, S. L. (1986). The immediate effects of media violence on behavior. *Journal of Social Issues, 42*(3), 7-28.

Gehring, W. J., Wimke, J., & Nisenson, L. G. (2000). Action monitoring dysfunction in obsessive-compulsive disorder. *Psychological Science, 11*(1), 1-6.

Geldard, F. A. (1972). *The human senses* (2nd ed.). New York: Wiley.

Gelman, D. (1989, May 15). Voyages to the unknown. *Newsweek*, pp. 66-69.

Genesee, F., & Gándara, P. (1999). Bilingual education programs: A cross-national perspective. *Journal of Social Issues, 55*, 665-685.

Genevro, J. L. (2003). *Report on bereavement and grief research.* Washington, DC: Center for the Advancement of Health.

Genovese, J. E. C. (2004). The ten percent solution. *Skeptic, 10*(4), 55-57.

Gentile, D. A., Lynch, P. J., Linder, J. R., & Walsh, D. A. (2004). The effects of violent video game habits on adolescent hostility, aggressive behaviors, and school performance. *Journal of Adolescence, 27*, 5-22.

Gentile, D. A., Walsh, D. A., Ellison, P. R., Fox, M., & Cameron, J. (2004). Media violence as a risk factor for children: A longitudinal study. Paper presented at the American Psychological Society Convention.

Gentry, J., & Eron, L. D. (1993). American Psychological Association Commission on Violence and Youth. *American Psychological Association, 48*, 89.

George, L. K., Ellison, C. G., & Larson, D. B. (2002). Explaining the relationships between religious involvement and health. *Psychological Inquiry, 13*, 190-200.

George, L. K., Larson, D. B., Koenig, H. G., & McCullough, M. E. (2000). Spirituality and health: What we know, what we need to know. *Journal of Social and Clinical Psychology, 19*, 102-116.

George, M. S. (2003, September). Stimulating the brain. *Scientific American*, pp. 67–73.

Gerard, R. W. (1953, September). What is memory? *Scientific American*, pp. 118–126.

Gerbner, G. (1990). Stories that hurt: Tobacco, alcohol, and other drugs in the mass media. In H. Resnik (Ed.), *Youth and drugs: Society's mixed messages*. Rockville, MD: Office for Substance Abuse Prevention, U.S. Department of Health and Human Services.

Gerbner, G. (1993, June). Women and minorities on television: A study in casting and fate. A report to the Screen Actors Guild and the American Federation of Radio and Television Artists.

Gerbner, G., Gross, L., Morgan, M., & Signorielli, N. (1994). Growing up with television: The cultivation perspective. In J. Bryant, & D. Zillman (Eds.), *Media Effects: Advances in theory and research* . Hillsdale, NJ: Erlbaum.

Gerbner, G., Morgan, M., & Signorielli, N. (1993). Television violence profile No. 16: The turning point from research to action. Annenberg School for Communication, University of Pennsylvania.

Gerhart, K. A., Koziol-McLain, J., Lowenstein, S. R., & Whiteneck, G. G. (1994). Quality of life following spinal cord injury: Knowledge and attitudes of emergency care providers. *Annals of Emergency Medicine, 23*, 807–812.

Gerrard, M., & Luus, C. A. E. (1995). Judgments of vulnerability to pregnancy: The role of risk factors and individual differences. *Personality and Social Psychology Bulletin, 21*, 160–171.

Gershoff, E. T. (2002). Parental corporal punishment and associated child behaviors and experiences: A meta-analytic and theoretical review. *Psychological Bulletin, 128*, 539–579.

Gershon, J., Anderson, P., Graap, K., Zimand, E., Hodges, L., & Rothbaum, B. O. (2002). Virtual reality exposure therapy in the treatment of anxiety disorders, *Scientific Review of Mental Health Practice, 1*, 76–81.

Geschwind, N. (1979, September). Specializations of the human brain. *Scientific American*, pp. 180–199.

Geschwind, N., & Behan, P. O. (1984). Laterality, hormones, and immunity. In N. Geschwind & A. M. Galaburda (Eds.), *Cerebral dominance: The biological foundations*. Cambridge, MA: Harvard University Press.

Gfeller, J. D., Lynn, S. J., & Pribble, W. E. (1987). Enhancing hypnotic susceptibility: Interpersonal and rapport factors. *Journal of Personality and Social Psychology, 52*, 586–595.

Gibbons, F. X. (1986). Social comparison and depression: Company's effect on misery. *Journal of Personality and Social Psychology, 51*, 140–148.

Gibbs, W. W. (1996, June). Mind readings. *Scientific American*, pp. 34–36.

Gibbs, W. W. (2002, August). Saving dying languages. *Scientific American*, pp. 79–85.

Gibbs, W. W. (2005, June). Obesity: An overblown epidemic? *Scientific American*, pp. 70–77.

Gibson, E. J., & Walk, R. D. (1960, April). The "visual cliff." *Scientific American*, pp. 64–71.

Gibson, H. B. (1995, April). Recovered memories. *The Psychologist*, pp. 153–154.

Gigerenzer, G. (2004). Dread risk, September 11, and fatal traffic accidents. *Psychological Science, 15*, 286–287.

Gigerenzer, G. (2004). Fast and frugal heuristics: The tools of bounded rationality. In D. Koehler & N. Harvey (Eds.), *Handbook of judgment and decision making*. Oxford, UK: Blackwell.

Gignac, G., Vernon, P. A., & Wickett, J. C. (2003). Factors influencing the relationship between brain size and intelligence. In H. Nyborg, *The scientific study of general intelligence*. Amsterdam: Pergamon.

Gilbert, D. T., Pelham, B. W., & Krull, D. S. (2003). The psychology of good ideas. *Psychological Inquiry, 14*, 258–260.

Gilbert, D. T., Pinel, E. C., Wilson, T. D., Blumberg, S. J., & Wheatley, T. P. (1998). Immune neglect: A source of durability bias in affective forecasting. *Journal of Personality and Social Psychology, 75*, 617–638.

Giles, D. E., Dahl, R. E., & Coble, P. A. (1994). Childbearing, developmental, and familial aspects of sleep. In J. M. Oldham & M. B. Riba (Eds.), *Review of Psychiatry*, (Vol. 13). Washington, DC: American Psychiatric Press.

Gillham, J. E., Reivich, K. J., Jaycox, L. H., & Seligman, M. E. P. (1995). Preventing depressive symptoms in schoolchildren: Two year follow-up. *Psychological Science, 6*, 343–351.

Gilligan, C. (1982). *In a different voice: Psychological theory and women's development*. Cambridge, MA: Harvard University Press.

Gilligan, C., Lyons, N. P., & Hanmer, T. J. (Eds.). (1990). *Making connections: The relational worlds of adolescent girls at Emma Willard School*. Cambridge, MA: Harvard University Press.

Gilovich, T. (1991). *How we know what isn't so: The fallibility of human reason in everyday life*. New York: Free Press.

Gilovich, T. D. (1996). The spotlight effect: Exaggerated impressions of the self as a social stimulus. Unpublished manuscript, Cornell University.

Gilovich, T., Kruger, J., & Medvec, V. H. (2002). The spotlight effect revisited: Overestimating the manifest variability of our actions and appearance. *Journal of Experimental Social Psychology, 38*, 93–99.

Gilovich, T., & Medvec, V. H. (1995). The experience of regret: What, when, and why. *Psychological Review, 102*, 379–395.

Gilovich, T., & Savitsky, K. (1999). The spotlight effect and the illusion of transparency: Egocentric assessments of how we are seen by others. *Current Directions in Psychological Science, 8*, 165–168.

Gilovich, T., Vallone, R., & Tversky, A. (1985). The hot hand in basketball: On the misperception of random sequences. *Cognitive Psychology, 17*, 295–314.

Gingerich, O. (1999, February 6). Is there a role for natural theology today? *The Real Issue* (www.origins.org/real/n9501/natural.html).

Giuliano, T. A., Barnes, L. C., Fiala, S. E., & Davis D. M. (1998a). An empirical investigation of male answer syndrome. Paper presented at the Southwestern Psychological Association convention.

Giuliano, T. A., Fiala, S. E., Davis, D. M., Barnes, L. C., & Patrick, E. C. (1998b). The reluctance to admit "I don't know": Exploring "male answer syndrome." Paper presented to the American Psychological Society convention.

Gladue, B. A. (1990). Hormones and neuroendocrine factors in atypical human sexual behavior. In J. R. Feierman (Ed.), *Pedophilia: Biosocial dimensions*. New York: Springer-Verlag.

Gladue, B. A. (1994). The biopsychology of sexual orientation. *Current Directions in Psychological Science, 3*, 150–154.

Gladwell, M. (2000, May 9). The new-boy network: What do job interviews really tell us? *New Yorker*, pp. 68–86.

Gladwell, M. (2004, September 20). Personality plus. *New Yorker*, pp. 42–48.

Gladwell, M. (2005). *Blink: The power of thinking without thinking*. New York: Little Brown.

Glass, D. C., & Singer, J. E. (1972). *Urban stress*. New York: Academic Press.

Glass, R. I. (2004). Perceived threats and real killers. *Science, 304*, 927.

Glass, R. M. (2001). Electroconvulsive therapy: Time to bring it out of the shadows. *Journal of the American Medical Association, 285*, 1346–1348.

Glater, J. D. (2001, March 26). Women are close to being majority of law students. *New York Times* (www.nytimes.com).

Gleaves, D. H. (1996). The sociocognitive model of dissociative identity disorder: A reexamination of the evidence. *Psychological Bulletin, 120*, 42–59.

Glenn, N. D. (1975). Psychological well-being in the postparental stage: Some evidence from national surveys. *Journal of Marriage and the Family, 37,* 105–110.

Glick, P., & 15 others (2004). Bad but bold: Ambivalent attitudes toward men predict gender inequality in 16 nations. *Journal of Personality and Social Psychology, 86,* 713–728.

Glick, P., Gottesman, D., & Jolton, J. (1989). The fault is not in the stars: Susceptibility of skeptics and believers in astrology to the Barnum effect. *Personality and Social Psychology Bulletin, 15,* 572–583.

Gluhoski, V. L., & Wortman, C. B. (1996). The impact of trauma on world views. *Journal of Social and Clinical Psychology, 15,* 417–429.

Godden, D. R., & Baddeley, A. D. (1975). Context-dependent memory in two natural environments: On land and underwater. *British Journal of Psychology, 66,* 325–331.

Goel, M. S., McCarthy, E. P., Phillips, R. S., & Wee, C. C. (2004). Obesity among U.S. immigrant subgroups by duration of residence. *Journal of the American Medical Association, 292,* 2860–2867.

Goel, V., & Dolan, R. J. (2001). The functional anatomy of humor: Segregating cognitive and affective components. *Nature Neuroscience, 4,* 237–238.

Goff, D. C. (1993). Reply to Dr. Armstrong. *Journal of Nervous and Mental Disease, 181,* 604–605.

Goff, D. C., & Simms, C. A. (1993). Has multiple personality disorder remained consistent over time? *Journal of Nervous and Mental Disease, 181,* 595–600.

Goff, L. M., & Roediger, III, H. L. (1998). Imagination inflation for action events: Repeated imaginings lead to illusory recollections. *Memory and Cognition, 26,* 20–33.

Gold, M., & Yanof, D. S. (1985). Mothers, daughters, and girlfriends. *Journal of Personality and Social Psychology, 49,* 654–659.

Goldapple, K., Segal, Z., Garson, C., Lau, M., Bieling, P., Kennedy, S., & Mayberg, H. (2004). Modulation of cortical-limbic pathways in major depression. *Archives of General Psychiatry, 61,* 34–41.

Golden, R. N., Gaynes, B. N., Ekstrom, R. D., Hamer, R. M., Jacobsen, F. M., Suppes, T., Wisner, K. L., & Nemeroff, C. B. (2005). The efficacy of light therapy in the treatment of mood disorders: A review and meta-analysis of the evidence. *American Journal of Psychiatry, 162,* 656–662.

Goldfried, M. R. (2001). Integrating gay, lesbian, and bisexual issues into mainstream psychology. *American Psychologist, 56,* 977–988.

Goldfried, M. R., & Padawer, W. (1982). Current status and future directions in psychotherapy. In M. R. Goldfried (Ed.), *Converging themes in psychotherapy: Trends in psychodynamic, humanistic, and behavioral practice.* New York: Springer.

Goldfried, M. R., Raue, P. J., & Castonguay, L. G. (1998). The therapeutic focus in significant sessions of master therapists: A comparison of cognitive-behavioral and psychodynamic-interpersonal interventions. *Journal of Consulting and Clinical Psychology, 66,* 803–810.

Goldin-Meadow, S., Nusbaum, H., Kelly, S. D., & Wagner, S. (2001). Explaining math: Gesturing lightens the load. *Psychological Science, 12,* 516–522.

Golding, J. M. (1996). Sexual assault history and women's reproductive and sexual health. *Psychology of Women Quarterly, 20,* 101–121.

Golding, J. M. (1999). Sexual-assault history and the long-term physical health problems: Evidence from clinical and population epidemiology. *Current Directions in Psychological Science, 8,* 191–194.

Goldstein, A. P., Glick, B., & Gibbs, J. C. (1998). *Aggression replacement training: A comprehensive intervention for aggressive youth* (rev. ed.). Champaign, IL: Research Press.

Goldstein, I. (2000, August). Male sexual circuitry. *Scientific American,* pp. 70–75.

Goldstein, I., Lue, T. F., Padma-Nathan, H., Rosen, R. C., Steers, W. D., & Wicker, P. A. (1998). Oral sildenafil in the treatment of erectile dysfunction. *New England Journal of Medicine, 338,* 1397–1404.

Goleman, D. (1980, February). 1,528 little geniuses and how they grew. *Psychology Today,* pp. 28–53.

Goleman, D. (1995). *Emotional intelligence.* New York: Bantam.

Gonsalves, B., Reber, P. J., Gitelman, D. R., Parrish, T. B., Mesulam, M-M., & Paller, K. A. (2004). Neural evidence that vivid imagining can lead to false remembering. *Psychological Science, 15,* 655–659.

Goodall, J. (1968). The behaviour of free-living chimpanzees in the Gombe Stream Reserve. *Animal Behaviour Monographs, 1,* 161–311.

Goodall, J. (1986). *The chimpanzees of Gombe: Patterns of behavior.* Cambridge, MA: Harvard University Press.

Goodall, J. (1998). Learning from the chimpanzees: A message humans can understand. *Science, 282,* 2184–2185.

Goodchilds, J. (1987). Quoted by Carol Tavris, Old age is not what it used to be. *The New York Times Magazine: Good Health Magazine,* September 27, pp. 24–25, 91–92.

Goode, E. (1999, February 16). Tales of midlife crisis found greatly exaggerated. *New York Times* (www.nytimes.com).

Goode, E. (1999, April 13). If things taste bad, 'phantoms' may be at work. *New York Times* (www.nytimes.com).

Goode, E. (2002, June 30). Antidepressants life clouds, but lose 'miracle drug' label. *New York Times* (www.nytimes.com).

Goode, E. (2003, January 28). Even in the age of Prozac, some still prefer the couch. *New York Times* (www.nytimes.com).

Goodhart, D. E. (1986). The effects of positive and negative thinking on performance in an achievement situation. *Journal of Personality and Social Psychology, 51,* 117–124.

Goodman, E. (2000). Depressive symptoms and cigarette smoking among teens. *Pediatrics, 106,* 4. 748–756.

Goodman, G. S., Ghetti, S., Quas, J. A., Edelstein, R. S., Alexander, K. W., Redlich, A. D., Cordon, I. M., & Jones, D. P. H. (2003). A prospective study of memory for child sexual abuse: New findings relevant to the repressed-memory controversy. *Psychological Science, 14,* 113–118.

Goodman, G. S., Rudy, L., Bottoms, B. L., & Aman, B. (1990). Children's concerns and memory: Issues of ecological validity in the study of children's eyewitness testimony. In R. Fivush & J. A. Hudson (Eds.), *Knowing and remembering in young children.* New York: Cambridge University Press.

Goodman, L. A., Koss, M. P., & Russo, N. F. (1993). Violence against women: Mental health effects. Part II. Conceptualizations of posttraumatic stress. *Applied & Preventive Psychology, 2,* 123–130.

Goodnough, A. (2002, May 2). Post-9/11 pain found to linger in young minds. *New York Times* (www.nytimes.com).

Goodson, P., McCormick, D., & Evans, A. (2001). Searching for sexually explicit materials on the Internet: An exploratory study of college students' behavior and attitudes. *Archives of Sexual Behavior, 30,* 101–118.

Goodstein, L., & Glaberson, W. (2000, April 9). The well-marked roads to homicidal rage. *New York Times* (www.nytimes.com).

Goodwin, F. K., & Morrison, A. R. (1999). Scientists in bunkers: How appeasement of animal rights activism has failed. *Cerebrum, 1*(2), 50–62.

Goodwin, R., & Hamilton, S. P. (2002). Cigarette smoking and panic: The role of neuroticism. *American Journal of Psychiatry, 159,* 1208–1213.

Gopnik, A., & Meltzoff, A. N. (1986). Relations between semantic and cognitive development in the one-word stage: The specificity hypothesis. *Child Development, 57,* 1040–1053.

Goranson, R. E. (1978). *The hindsight effect in problem solving.* Unpublished manuscript, cited by G. Wood (1984), Research methodology: A decision-making perspective. In A. M. Rogers & C. J. Scheirer (Eds.), *The G. Stanley Hall Lecture Series* (Vol. 4). Washington, DC: American Psychological Association.

Gordon, P. (2004). Numerical cognition without words: Evidence from Amazonia. *Science, 306,* 496–499.

Gore, A., Jr. (1992). *Earth in the balance: Ecology and the human spirit.* Boston: Houghton-Mifflin.

Gore-Felton, C., Koopman, C., Thoresen, C., Arnow, B., Bridges, E., & Spiegel, D. (2000). Psychologists' beliefs and clinical characteristics: Judging the veracity of childhood sexual abuse memories. *Professional Psychology: Research and Practice, 31,* 372–377.

Gortmaker, S. L., Must, A., Perrin, J. M., Sobol, A. M., & Dietz, W. H. (1993). Social and economic consequences of overweight in adolescence and young adulthood. *New England Journal of Medicine, 329,* 1008–1012.

Gosling, S. D., Ko, S. J., Mannarelli, T., & Morris, M. E. (2002). A room with a cue: Personality judgments based on offices and bedrooms. *Journal of Personality and Social Psychology, 82,* 379–398.

Gosling, S. D., Kwan, V. S. Y., & John, O. P. (2003). A dog's got personality: A cross-species comparative approach to personality judgments in dogs and humans. *Journal of Personality and Social Psychology, 85,* 1161–1169.

Gotlib, I. H., & Hammen, C. L. (1992). *Psychological aspects of depression: Toward a cognitive-interpersonal integration.* New York: Wiley.

Gottesman, I. I. (1991). *Schizophrenia genesis: The origins of madness.* New York: Freeman.

Gottesman, I. I. (2001). Psychopathology through a life span—genetic prism. *American Psychologist, 56,* 867–881.

Gottfredson, L. S. (2002a). Where and why *g* matters: Not a mystery. *Human Performance, 15,* 25–46.

Gottfredson, L. S. (2002b). *g:* Highly general and highly practical. In R. J. Sternberg & E. L. Grigorenko (Eds.), *The general factor of intelligence: How general is it?* Mahwah, NJ: Erlbaum.

Gottfredson, L. S. (2003a). Dissecting practical intelligence theory: Its claims and evidence. *Intelligence, 31,* 343–397.

Gottfredson, L. S. (2003b). On Sternberg's "Reply to Gottfredson." *Intelligence, 31,* 415–424.

Gottfried, J. A., O'Doherty, J., & Dolan, R. J. (2003). Encoding predictive reward value in human amygdala and orbitofrontal cortex. *Science, 301,* 1104–1108.

Gottman, J., with Silver N. (1994). *Why marriages succeed or fail.* New York: Simon & Schuster.

Gougoux, F., Zatorre, R., Lassonde, M., Voss, P., & Lepore, F. (2005). A functional neuroimaging study of sound localization: Visual cortex activity predicts performance in early-blind individuals. *PloS Biology, 3*(2): e27.

Gould, E., Reeves, A. J., Graziano, M. S. A., & Gross, C. G. (1999). Neurogenesis in the neocortex of adult primates. *Science, 286,* 548–552.

Gould, S. J. (1981). *The mismeasure of man.* New York: Norton.

Gould, S. J. (1997, June 12). Darwinian fundamentalism. *The New York Review of Books, XLIV*(10), 34–37.

Grady, C. L., & McIntosh, A. R., Horwitz, B., Maisog, J. M., Ungeleider, L. G., Mentis, M. J., Pietrini, P., Schapiro, M. B., & Haxby, J. V. (1995). Age-related reductions in human recognition memory due to impaired encoding. *Science, 269,* 218–221.

Graf, P. (1990). Life-span changes in implicit and explicit memory. *Bulletin of the Psychonomic Society, 28,* 353–358.

Graham, J. W., Marks, G., & Hansen, W. B. (1991). Social influence processes affecting adolescent substance use. *Journal of Applied Psychology, 76,* 291–298.

Grant, B. F., & Dawson, D. A. (1998). Age of onset of drug use and its association with DSM-IV drug abuse and dependence: Results from the national Longitudinal Alcohol Epidemiologic Survey. *Journal of Substance Abuse, 10,* 163–173.

Grant, B. F., Stinson, F. S., Hasin, D. S., Dawson, D. A., Chou, S. P., & Anderson, K. (2004). Immigration and lifetime prevalence of DSM-IV psychiatric disorders among Mexican Americans and non-Hispanic Whites in the United States. *Archives of General Psychiatry, 61,* 1226–1233.

Gray-Little, B., & Burks, N. (1983). Power and satisfaction in marriage: A review and critique. *Psychological Bulletin, 93,* 513–538.

Gray-Little, B., & Hafdahl, A. R. (2000). Factors influencing racial comparisons of self-esteem: A quantitative review. *Psychological Bulletin, 126,* 26–54.

GRE. (1990). *GRE guide to the use of the Graduate Record Examinations Program.* Princeton, NJ: Graduate Record Examinations Board, Educational Testing Service.

Green, B. (2002). Listening to leaders: Feedback on 360-degree feedback one year later. *Organizational Development Journal, 20,* 8–16.

Green, C. S., & Bavelier, D. (2003). Action video game modifies visual selective attention. *Nature, 423,* 534–537.

Green, J. T., & Woodruff-Pak, D. S. (2000). Eyeblink classical conditioning: Hippocampal formation is for neutral stimulus associations as cerebellum is for association-response. *Psychological Bulletin, 126,* 138–158.

Greenberg, D. L. (2004). President Bush's false 'flashbulb' memory of 9/11/01. *Applied Cognitive Psychology, 18,* 363–370.

Greenberg, J., Solomon, S., & Pyszczynski, T. (1997). Terror management theory of self-esteem and cultural worldviews: Empirical assessments and conceptual refinements. *Advances in Social Psychology, 29,* 61–142.

Greene, J., Sommerville, R. B., Nystrom, L. E., Darley, J. M., & Cohen, J. D. (2001). An fMRI investigation of emotional engagement in moral judgment. *Science, 293,* 2105.

Greene, R. L. (1987). Effects of maintenance rehearsal on human memory. *Psychological Bulletin, 102,* 403–413.

Greenfeld, L. A. (1998). *Alcohol and crime: An analysis of national data on the prevalence of alcohol involvement in crime.* Washington, DC: Document NCJ-168632, Bureau of Justice Statistics (www.ojp.usdoj.gov/bjs).

Greenough, W. T., Black, J. E., & Wallace, C. S. (1987). Experience and brain development. *Child Development, 58,* 539–559.

Greenwald, A. G. (1992). New look 3: Unconscious cognition reclaimed. *American Psychologist, 47,* 766–779.

Greenwald, A. G. (1992). Subliminal semantic activation and subliminal snake oil. Paper presented to the American Psychological Association Convention, Washington, DC.

Greenwald, A. G., McGhee, D. E., & Schwartz, J. L. K. (1998). Measuring individual differences in implicit cognition: The implicit association test. *Journal of Personality and Social Psychology, 74,* 1464–1480.

Greenwald, A. G., Oakes, M. A., & Hoffman, H. (2003). Targets of discrimination: Effects of race on responses to weapons holders. *Journal of Experimental Social Psychology, 39,* 399.

Greenwald, A. G., Spangenberg, E. R., Pratkanis, A. R., & Eskenazi, J. (1991). Double-blind tests of subliminal self-help audiotapes. *Psychological Science, 2,* 119–122.

Greenwood, M. R. C. (1989). Sexual dimorphism and obesity. In A. J. Stunkard & A. Baum (Eds.). *Perspectives in behavioral medicine: Eating, sleeping, and sex.* Hillsdale, NJ: Erlbaum.

Greers, A. E. (2004). Speech, language, and reading skills after early cochlear implantation. *Archives of Otolaryngology—Head & Neck Surgery, 130,* 634–638.

Gregory, R. L. (November, 1968). Visual illusions. *Scientific American, 219*(5), 66–76.

Gregory, R. L. (1978). *Eye and brain: The psychology of seeing* (3rd ed.). New York: McGraw-Hill.

Gregory, R. L., & Gombrich, E. H. (Eds.). (1973). *Illusion in nature and art.* New York: Charles Scribner's Sons.

Greif, E. B., & Ulman, K. J. (1982). The psychological impact of menarche on early adolescent females: A review of the literature. *Child Development, 53,* 1413–1430.

Greist, J. H., Jefferson, J. W., & Marks, I. M. (1986). *Anxiety and its treatment: Help is available.* Washington, DC: American Psychiatric Press.

Grewal, D., & Salovey, P. (2005). Feeling smart: The science of emotional intelligence. *American Scientist, 93,* 330–339.

Grèzes, J., & Decety, J. (2001). Function anatomy of execution, mental simulation, observation, and verb generation of actions: A meta-analysis. *Human Brain Mapping, 12,* 1–19.

Griffiths, M. (2001). Sex on the Internet: Observations and implications for Internet sex addiction. *Journal of Sex Research, 38,* 333–342.

Grill-Spector, K., & Kanwisher, N. (2005). Visual recognition: As soon as you know it is there, you know what it is. *Psychological Science, 16,* 152–160.

Grilo, C. M., & Pogue-Geile, M. F. (1991). The nature of environmental influences on weight and obesity: A behavior genetic analysis. *Psychological Bulletin, 110,* 520–537.

Grobstein, C. (1979, June). External human fertilization. *Scientific American,* pp. 57–67.

Groothuis, T. G. G., & Carere, C. (2005). Avian personalities: Characterization and epigenesis. *Neuroscience and Biobehavioral Reviews, 29,* 137–150.

Gross, A. E., & Crofton, C. (1977). What is good is beautiful. *Sociometry, 40,* 85–90.

Grossberg, S. (1995). The attentive brain. *American Scientist, 83,* 438–449.

Grossman, M., & Wood, W. (1993). Sex differences in intensity of emotional experience: A social role interpretation. *Journal of Personality and Social Psychology, 65,* 1010–1022.

Gruder, C. L. (1977). Choice of comparison persons in evaluating oneself. In J. M. Suls & R. L. Miller (Eds.), *Social comparison processes.* New York: Hemisphere.

Grudnik, J., & Kranzler, J. H. (2001). Meta-analysis of the relationship between intelligence and inspection time. *Intelligence, 13,* 523–537.

Grunebaum, M. F., Ellis, S. P., Li, S., O(quendo, M. A., Mann, J. J. (2004). Antidepressants and suicide risk in the United States, 1985–1999. *Journal of Clinical Psychiatry, 65,* 1456–1462.

Guerin, B. (1986). Mere presence effects in humans: A review. *Journal of Personality and Social Psychology, 22,* 38–77.

Guerin, B. (2003). Language use as social strategy: A review and an analytic framework for the social sciences. *Review of General Psychology, 7,* 251–298.

Guilbault, R. L., Bryant, F. B., Brockway, J. H., & Posavac, E. J. (2004). A meta-analysis of research on hindsight bias. *Basic and Applied Social Psychology, 26,* 103–117.

Guisinger, S. (2004). Adapted to flee famine: Adding an evolutionary perspective on anorexia nervosa. *Psychological Review, 110,* 745–761.

Gundersen, E. (2001, August 1). MTV is a many splintered thing. *USA Today,* pp. D1, D2.

Güntürkün, O. (2003). Adult persistence of head-turning asymmetry. *Nature, 421,* 711.

Gura, T. (2004). New data on appetite-suppressing peptide challenges critics. *Science, 306,* 1453–1454.

Gustafson, D., Lissner, L., Bengtsson, C., Björkelund, C., & Skoog, I. (2004). A 24-year follow-up of body mass index and cerebral atrophy. *Neurology, 63,* 1876–1881.

Gustafson, D., Rothenberg, E., Blennow, K., Steen, B., & Skoog, I. (2003). An 18-year follow-up of overweight and risk of Alzheimer disease. *Archives of Internal Medicine, 163,* 1524–1528.

Gustavson, C. R., Garcia, J., Hankins, W. G., & Rusiniak, K. W. (1974). Coyote predation control by aversive conditioning. *Science, 184,* 581–583.

Gustavson, C. R., Kelly, D. J., & Sweeney, M. (1976). Prey-lithium aversions I: Coyotes and wolves. *Behavioral Biology, 17,* 61–72.

Guttmacher Institute. (1994). *Sex and America's teenagers.* New York: Alan Guttmacher Institute.

Guttmacher Institute. (2000). *Fulfilling the promise: Public policy and U.S. family planning clinics.* New York: Alan Guttmacher Institute.

H., Sally (1979, August). Videotape recording number T-3, Fortunoff Video Archive of Holocaust Testimonies. New Haven, CT: Yale University Library.

Haber, R. N. (1970, May). How we remember what we see. *Scientific American,* pp. 104–112.

Haddock, G., & Zanna, M. P. (1994). Preferring "housewives" to "feminists." *Psychology of Women Quarterly, 18,* 25–52.

Haidt, J. (2000). The positive emotion of elevation. *Prevention and Treatment, 3,* article 3 (journals.apa.org/prevention/volume3).

Haidt, J. (2001). The emotional dog and its rational tail: A social intuitionist approach to moral judgment. *Psychological Review, 108,* 814–834.

Haidt, J. (2002). The moral emotions. In R. J. Davidson, K. Scherer, & H. H. Goldsmith (Eds.), *Handbook of Affective Sciences.* New York: Oxford University Press.

Haier, R. J., Jung, R. E., Yeo, R. A., Head, K., & Alkire, M. T. (2004). Structural brain variation and general intelligence. *NeuroImage, 23,* 425–433.

Haines, R. F. (1991). A breakdown in simultaneous information processing. In G. Obrecht & L. W. Stark (Eds.), *Presbyopia research.* New York: Plenum Press.

Hakuta, K., Bialystok, E., & Wiley, E. (2003). Critical evidence: A test of the critical-period hypothesis for second-language acquisition. *Psychological Science, 14,* 31–38.

Halberstadt, J. B., & Niedenthal, P. M. (2001). Effects of emotion concepts on perceptual memory for emotional expressions. *Journal of Personality and Social Psychology, 81,* 587–598.

Halberstadt, J. B., & Niedenthal, P. M., & Kushner, J. (1995). Resolution of lexical ambiguity by emotional state. *Psychological Science, 6,* 278–281.

Haldeman, D. C. (1994). The practice and ethics of sexual orientation conversion therapy. *Journal of Consulting and Clinical Psychology, 62,* 221–227.

Haldeman, D. C. (2002). Gay rights, patient rights: The implications of sexual orientation conversion therapy. *Professional Psychology: Research and Practice, 33,* 260–264.

Hall, C. S. (1984). "A ubiquitous sex difference in dreams" revisited. *Journal of Personality and Social Psychology, 46,* 1109–1117.

Hall, C. S., Dornhoff, W., Blick, K. A., & Weesner, K. E. (1982). The dreams of college men and women in 1950 and 1980: A comparison of dream contents and sex differences. *Sleep, 5,* 188–194.

Hall, C. S., & Lindzey, G. (1978). *Theories of personality* (2nd ed.). New York: Wiley.

Hall, G. (1997). Context aversion, Pavlovian conditioning, and the psychological side effects of chemotherapy. *European Psychologist, 2,* 118–124.

Hall, G. S. (1904). *Adolescence: Its psychology and its relations to physiology, anthropology, sex, crime, religion and education* (Vol. I). New York: Appleton-Century-Crofts.

Hall, J. A. (1984). *Nonverbal sex differences: Communication accuracy and expressive style.* Baltimore: Johns Hopkins University Press.

Hall, J. A. (1987). On explaining gender differences: The case of nonverbal communication. In P. Shaver & C. Hendrick (Eds.), *Review of Personality and Social Psychology, 7,* 177–200.

Hall, J. A. Y., & Kimura, D. (1994). Dermatoglyphic assymetry and sexual orientation in men. *Behavioral Neuroscience, 108,* 1203–1206.

Hall, J. G. (2003). Twinning. *Lancet, 362,* 735–743.

Hall, S. S. (2004, May). The good egg. *Discover,* pp. 30–39.

Halpern, C. T., Joyner, K., Udry, J. R., & Suchindran, C. (2000). Smart teens don't have sex (or kiss much either). *Journal of Adolescent Health, 26,* 213–225.

Halpern, D. F. (1991). Cognitive sex differences: Why diversity is a critical research issue. Paper presented to the American Psychological Association convention.

Halpern, D. F. (2000). *Sex-related ability differences: Changing perspectives, changing minds.* Mahwah, NJ: Erlbaum.

Halpern, D. F. (2005, May 20). Response to Drs. Pinker and Spelke. www.edge.org.

Halpern, D. F., & Coren, S. (1988). Do right-handers live longer? *Nature, 333,* 213.

Halpern, D. F., & Coren, S. (1990). Laterality and longevity: Is left-handedness associated with a younger age at death? In S. Coren (Ed.), *Left-handedness: Behavioral implications and anomalies.* Amsterdam: North-Holland.

Halpern, D. F., & Coren, S. (1991). Lateral preference and life span. *New England Journal of Medicine, 324,* 998.

Halpern, D. F., & Coren, S. (1993). Left-handedness and life span: A reply to Harris. *Psychological Bulletin, 114,* 235–241.

Halpern, D. F., Gilbert, R., & Coren, S. (1996). PC or not-PC? Contemporary challenges to unpopular research. *Journal of Social Distress and the Homeless, 5,* 251–271.

Halsey, A. H., & Webb, J. (2000). *Twentieth-century British social trends.* Basingstoke: Macmillan.

Hamann, S., Herman, R. A., Nolan, C. L., & Wallen, K. (2004). Men and women differ in amygdala response to visual sexual stimuli. *Nature Neuroscience, 7,* 411–416.

Hamann, S., Monarch, E. S., & Goldstein, F. C. (2002). Impaired fear conditioning in Alzheimer's disease. *Neuropsychologica, 40,* 1187–1195.

Hamill, R., Wilson, T. D., & Nisbett, R. E. (1980). Insensitivity to sample bias: Generalizing from atypical cases. *Journal of Personality and Social Psychology, 39,* 578–589.

Hamilton, G. (2001, July 11). Family sues Coca-Cola over son's death. *National Post.*

Hamilton, R. H. (2000, November). Increased prevalence of absolute pitch in blind musicians (Abstract 739.13). Society for Neuroscience meeting, New Orleans.

Hammer, E. (2003). How lucky you are to be a psychology major. *Eye on Psi Chi,* 4–5.

Hammersmith, S. K. (1982, August). *Sexual preference: An empirical study from the Alfred C. Kinsey Institute for Sex Research.* Paper presented at the meeting of the American Psychological Association, Washington, DC.

Hampson, R. (2000, April 10). In the end, people just need more room. *USA Today,* p. 19A.

Haney, C., & Logan, D. D. (1994). Broken promise: The Supreme Court's response to social science research on capital punishment. *Journal of Social Issues, 50,* 75–101.

Hankin, B. L., & Abramson, L. Y. (2001). Development of gender differences in depression: An elaborated cognitive vulnerability-transactional stress theory. *Psychological Bulletin, 127,* 773–796.

Hansen, C. H., & Hansen, R. D. (1988). Finding the face-in-the-crowd: An anger superiority effect. *Journal of Personality and Social Psychology, 54,* 917–924.

Harber, K. D. (1998), Feedback to minorities: Evidence of a positive bias. *Journal of Personality and Social Psychology, 74,* 622–628.

Hardin, C., & Banaji, M. R. (1993). The influence of language on thought. *Social Cognition, 11,* 277–308.

Hare, R. D. (1975). Psychophysiological studies of psychopathy. In D. C. Fowles (Ed.), *Clinical applications of psychophysiology.* New York: Columbia University Press.

Hariri, A. R., Mattay, V. S., Tessitore, A., Kolachana, B., Fera, F., Goldman, D., Egan, M. F., & Weinberger, D. R. (2002). Serotonin transporter genetic variation and the response of the human amygdala. *Science, 297,* 400–403.

Harkins, S. G., & Szymanski, K. (1989). Social loafing and group evaluation. *Journal of Personality and Social Psychology, 56,* 934–941.

Harlow, H. F., Harlow, M. K., & Suomi, S. J. (1971). From thought to therapy: Lessons from a primate laboratory. *American Scientist, 59,* 538–549.

Harlow, R. E., & Cantor, N. (1996). Still participating after all these years: A study of life task participation in later life. *Journal of Personality and Social Psychology, 71,* 1235–1249.

Harmon-Jones, E., Abramson, L. Y., Sigelman, J., Bohlig, A., Hogan, M. E., & Harmon-Jones, C. (2002). Proneness to hypomania/mania symptoms or depression symptoms and asymmetrical frontal cortical responses to an anger-evoking event. *Journal of Personality and Social Psychology, 82,* 610–618.

Harris, B. (1979). Whatever happened to Little Albert? *American Psychologist, 34,* 151–160.

Harris, J. A. (1999). Review and methodological considerations in research on testosterone and aggression. *Aggression and Violent Behavior, 4,* 273–291.

Harris, J. R. (1998). *The nurture assumption.* New York: Free Press.

Harris, J. R. (2000b). Socialization, personality development, and the child's environments: Comment on Vandell (2000). *Developmental Psychology, 36,* 711–723.

Harris, J. R. (2006). *No two are alike: Human nature and human individuality.* New York: Norton.

Harris, L. J. (1993). Do left-handers die sooner than right-handers? Commentary on Coren and Halpern's (1991) "Left-handedness: A marker for decreased survival fitness." *Psychological Bulletin, 114,* 203–234.

Harris, R. J. (1994). The impact of sexually explicit media. In J. Brant & D. Zillmann (Eds.), *Media effects: Advances in theory and research.* Hillsdale, NJ: Erlbaum.

Harrison, Y., & Horne, J. A. (2000). The impact of sleep deprivation on decision making: A review. *Journal of Experimental Psychology: Applied, 6,* 236–249.

Harriston, K. A. (1993, December 24). 1 shakes, 1 snoozes; both win $45 million. *Washington Post* release (in *Tacoma News Tribune*).

Hart, C. L., Taylor, M. D., Smith, G. D., Whalley, L. J., Starr, J. M., Hole, D. J., Wilson, V., & Deary, I. J. (2003). Childhood IQ, social class, deprivation, and their relationships with mortality and morbidity risk in later life: Prospective observational study linking the Scottish Mental Survey 1932 and the Midspan Studies. *Psychosomatic Medicine, 65,* 877–883.

Hart, D. (1988). The development of personal identity in adolescence: A philosophical dilemma approach. *Merrill-Palmer Quarterly, 34,* 105–114.

Harter, J. K. (2000, Winter/Spring). The linkage of employee perceptions to outcomes in a retail environment—cause and effect? *Gallup Research Journal,* pp. 25–38.

Harter, J. K., Schmidt, F. L., & Hayes, T. L. (2002). Business-unit-level relationship between employee satisfaction, employee engagement, and business outcomes: A meta-analysis. *Journal of Applied Psychology, 87,* 268–279.

Hartmann, E. (1981, April). The strangest sleep disorder. *Psychology Today,* pp. 14, 16, 18.

Hartmann, E. (1984). *The nightmare: The psychology and biology of terrifying dreams.* New York: Basic Books.

Harvey, F. (2002, February). Surrounded by sound. *Scientific American,* pp. 94–95.

Hassan, R., & Carr, J. (1989). Changing patterns of suicide in Australia. *Australian and New Zealand Journal of Psychiatry, 23,* 226–234.

Hatfield, E. (1988). Passionate and companionate love. In R. J. Sternberg & M. L. Barnes (Eds.), *The psychology of love.* New Haven: Yale University Press.

Hatfield, E., & Sprecher, S. (1986). *Mirror, mirror . . . The importance of looks in everyday life.* Albany: State University of New York Press.

Hathaway, S. R. (1960). *An MMPI Handbook* (Vol. 1, Foreword). Minneapolis: University of Minnesota Press. (Revised edition, 1972).

Hauser, M. D., Chomsky, N., & Fitch, W. T. (2002). The faculty of language: What is it, who has it, and how did it evolve? *Science, 298,* 1569–1579.

Hawkes, N. (2002, September 10). Fat children may die before their parents (report on presentation to the British Association for the Advancement of Science). *Times of London,* p. 3.

Haxby, J. V. (2001, July 7). Quoted by B. Bower, Faces of perception. *Science News,* pp. 10–12. See also J. V. Haxby, M. I. Gobbini, M. L. Furey, A. Ishai, J. L. Schouten & P. Pietrini, Distributed and overlapping representations of faces and objects in ventral temporal cortex. *Science, 293,* 2425–2430.

Hayne, H. (2004). Infant memory development: Implications for childhood amnesia. *Developmental Review, 24,* 33–73.

Hazan, C., & Shaver, P. R. (1994). Attachment as an organizational framework for research on close relationships. *Psychological Inquiry, 5,* 1–22.

Hazelrigg, M. D., Cooper, H. M., & Borduin, C. M. (1987). Evaluating the effectiveness of family therapies: An integrative review and analysis. *Psychological Bulletin, 101,* 428–442.

Head Start. (2005). Head Start program fact sheet. www.acf.hhs.gov/programs/hsb/research/2005.htm

Healey, J. (2004). *Overweight and obesity.* Thirroul, NSW, Australia: Spinney Press.

Heaps, C. M., & Nash, M. (2001). Comparing recollective experience in true and false autobiographical memories. *Journal of Experimental Psychology: Learning, Memory, and Cognition, 27,* 920–930.

Heath, A. C., & Madden, P. A. F. (1995). Genetic influences on smoking behavior. In J. R. Turner & L. R. Cardon (Eds.), *Behavior genetic approaches in behavioral medicine.* New York: Plenum Press, 45–66.

Hebb, D. O. (1980). *Essay on mind.* Hillsdale, NJ: Erlbaum. 9–16.

Hebert, R. (2001, September). Doing a number on memory. *APS Observer,* pp. 1, 7–11.

Hebl, M. R., & Mannix, L. M. (2003). The weight of obesity in evaluating others: A mere proximity effect. *Personality and Social Psychology Bulletin, 29,* 28–38.

Hedges, L. V., & Nowell, A. (1995). Sex differences in mental test scores, variability, and numbers of high-scoring individuals. *Science, 269,* 41–45.

Heider, F. (1958). *The psychology of interpersonal relations.* New York: Wiley.

Heiman, J. R. (1975, April). The physiology of erotica: Women's sexual arousal. *Psychology Today,* 90–94.

Heinrichs, R. W. (2005). The primacy of cognition in schizophrenia. *American Psychologist, 60,* 229–242.

Heins, M. (2004, December 14). Quoted by B. Kloza, Violent Christmas games. *ScienCentralNews* (www.sciencecentral.com).

Heishman, S. J., Kozlowski, L. T., & Henningfield, J. E. (1997). Nicotine addiction: Implications for public health policy. *Journal of Social Issues, 53,* 13–33.

Hejmadi, A., Davidson, R. J., & Rozin, P. (2000). Exploring Hindu Indian emotion expressions: Evidence for accurate recognition by Americans and Indians. *Psychological Science, 11,* 183–187.

Helgeson, V. S., Cohen, S., & Fritz, H. L. (1998). Social ties and cancer. In P. M. Cinciripini & others (Eds.), *Psychological and behavioral factors in cancer risk.* New York: Oxford University Press.

Heller, W. (1990, May/June). Of one mind: Second thoughts about the brain's dual nature. *The Sciences,* pp. 38–44.

Helmreich, W. B. (1992). *Against all odds: Holocaust survivors and the successful lives they made in America.* New York: Simon & Schuster.

Helmreich, W. B. (1994). Personal correspondence. Department of Sociology, City University of New York.

Helms, J. E., Jernigan, M., & Mascher, J. (2005). The meaning of race in psychology and how to change it: A methodological perspective. *American Psychologist, 60,* 27–36.

Helmuth, L. (2001). Boosting brain activity from the outside in. *Science, 292,* 1284–1286.

Helweg-Larsen, M. (1999). (The lack of) optimistic biases in response to the 1994 Northridge earthquake: The role of personal experience. *Basic and Applied Social Psychology, 21,* 119–129.

Hembree, R. (1988). Correlates, causes, effects, and treatment of test anxiety. *Review of Educational Research, 58,* 47–77.

Hemenover, S. H. (2003). The good, the bad, and the healthy: Impacts of emotional disclosure of trauma on resilient self-concept and psychological distress. *Personality and Social Psychology Bulletin, 29,* 1236–1244.

Henderlong, J., & Lepper, M. R. (2002). The effects of praise on children's intrinsic motivation: A review and synthesis. *Psychological Bulletin, 128,* 774–795.

Henkel, L. A., Franklin, N., & Johnson, M. K. (2000, March). Cross-modal source monitoring confusions between perceived and imagined events. *Journal of Experimental Psychology: Learning, Memory, & Cognition, 26,* 321–335.

Henley, N. M. (1989). Molehill or mountain? What we know and don't know about sex bias in language. In M. Crawford & M. Gentry (Eds.), *Gender and thought: Psychological perspectives.* New York: Springer-Verlag.

Henninger, P. (1992). Conditional handedness: Handedness changes in multiple personality disordered subject reflect shift in hemispheric dominance. *Consciousness and Cognition, 1,* 265–287.

Henry, J. D., MacLeod, M. S., Phillips, L. H., & Crawford, J. R. (2004). A meta-analytic review of prospective memory and aging. *Psychology and Aging, 19,* 27–39.

Hepper, P. G., Shahidullah, S., & White, R. (1990). Origins of fetal handedness. *Nature, 347,* 431.

Hepper, P. G., Wells, D. L., & Lynch, C. (2004). Prenatal thumb sucking is related to postnatal handedness. *Neuropsychologia, 43,* 313–315.

Herbert, B. (2001, July 23). Economics 202 at Big Tobacco U. *New York Times* (www.nytimes.com).

Herbert, J. D., Lilienfeld, S. O., Lohr, J. M., Montgomery, R. W., O'Donohue, W. T., Rosen, G. M., & Tolin, D. F. (2000). Science and pseudoscience in the development of eye movement desensitization and reprocessing: Implications for clinical psychology. *Clinical Psychology Review, 20,* 945–971.

Herek, G. M., & Capitanio, J. P. (1996). "Some of my best friends": Intergroup contact, concealable stigma, and heterosexuals' attitudes toward gay men and lesbians. *Personality and Social Psychology Bulletin, 22,* 412–424.

HERI. (2005, April 13). Spirituality in higher education: A national study of college students' search for meaning and purpose. Press release from Higher Education Research Institute, UCLA.

Herman, C. P., & Polivy, J. (1980). Restrained eating. In A. J. Stunkard (Ed.), *Obesity.* Philadelphia: Saunders.

Herman, C. P., & Polivy, J. (2003). Realistic and unrealistic self-change efforts. *American Psychologist, 58,* 823.

Herman-Giddens, M. E., Wang, L., & Koch, G. (2001). Secondary sexual characteristics in boys: Estimates from the National Health and Nutrition Examination Survey III, 1988–1994. *Archives of Pediatrics and Adolescent Medicine, 155,* 1022–1028.

Herrmann, D. (1982). Know thy memory: The use of questionnaires to assess and study memory. *Psychological Bulletin, 92,* 434–452.

Herrnstein, R. J., & Loveland, D. H. (1964). Complex visual concept in the pigeon. *Science, 146,* 549–551.

Hershenson, M. (1989). *The moon illusion.* Hillsdale, NJ: Erlbaum.

Hertenstein, M. J. (2002). Touch: Its communicative functions in infancy. *Human Development, 45,* 70–94.

Herz, R. S. (2001). Ah sweet skunk! Why we like or dislike what we smell. *Cerebrum, 3*(4), 31–47.

Herz, R. S., Schankler, C., & Beland, S. (2004). Olfaction, emotion and associative learning: Effects on motivated behavior. *Motivation and Emotion, 28*(4), 363–383.

Hess, E. H. (1956, July). Space perception in the chick. *Scientific American,* pp. 71–80.

Hettema, J. M., Neale, M. C., & Kendler, K. S. (2001). A review and meta-analysis of the genetic epidemiology of anxiety disorders. *American Journal of Psychiatry, 158,* 1568–1578.

Hewlett, B. S. (1991). *Intimate fathers: The nature and context of Aka Pygmy.* Ann Arbor: University of Michigan Press.

Hibbeln, J. R. (1998). Fish consumption and major depression. *Lancet, 351,* 1213.

Hickok, G., Bellugi, U., & Klima, E. S. (2001, June). Sign language in the brain. *Scientific American,* pp. 58–65.

Higgins, E. T., & Bargh, J. A. (1987). Social cognition and social perception. *Annual Review of Psychology, 38,* 369–425.

Hilgard, E. R. (1986). *Divided consciousness: Multiple controls in human thought and action.* New York: Wiley.

Hilgard, E. R. (1992). Dissociation and theories of hypnosis. In E. Fromm & M. R. Nash (Eds.), *Contemporary hypnosis research.* New York: Guilford.

Hill, C. E., & Nakayama, E. Y. (2000). Client-centered therapy: Where has it been and where is it going? A comment on Hathaway. *Journal of Clinical Psychology, 56,* 961–875.

Hill, H., & Johnston, A. (2001). Categorizing sex and identity from the biological motion of faces. *Current Biology, 11,* 880–885.

Hines, M. (2004). *Brain gender.* New York: Oxford University Press.

Hines, M., & Green, R. (1991). Human hormonal and neural correlates of sex-typed behaviors. *Review of Psychiatry, 10,* 536–555.

Hingson, R. W., Heeren, T., Zakocs, R. C., Kopstein, A., & Wechsler, H. (2002). Magnitude of alcohol-related mortality and morbidity among U.S. college students ages 18–24. *Journal of Studies on Alcohol, 63,* 136–144.

Hintzman, D. L. (1978). *The psychology of learning and memory.* San Francisco: Freeman.

Hinz, L. D., & Williamson, D. A. (1987). Bulimia and depression: A review of the affective variant hypothesis. *Psychological Bulletin, 102,* 150–158.

Hirsch, J. (2003). Obesity: Matter over mind? *Cerebrum, 5*(1), 7–18.

Hirst, W., Neisser, U., & Spelke, E. (1978, June). Divided attention. *Human Nature,* pp. 54–61.

Hirt, E. R., Zillmann, D., Erickson, G. A., & Kennedy, C. (1992). Costs and benefits of allegiance: Changes in fans' self-ascribed competencies after team victory versus defeat. *Journal of Personality and Social Psychology, 63,* 724–738.

HMHL. (2001, February). How schizophrenia develops: New evidence and new ideas. *Harvard Mental Health Letter,* pp. 1–4.

HMHL. (2002, January). Disaster and trauma. *Harvard Mental Health Letter,* pp. 1–5.

HMHL. (2002, August). Smoking and depression. *Harvard Mental Health Letter,* pp. 6–7.

Hobfoll, S. E., Johnson, R. J., Ennis, E., & Jackson, A. P. (2003). Resource loss, resource gain, and emotional outcomes among inner city women. *Journal of Personality, 84,* 632–643.

Hobson, J. A. (1989). *Sleep.* New York: Scientific American Library.

Hobson, J. A. (1995, September). Quoted by C. H. Colt, The power of dreams. *Life,* pp. 36–49.

Hobson, J. A. (2003). *Dreaming: An introduction to the science of sleep.* New York: Oxford.

Hobson, J. A. (2004). *13 dreams Freud never had: The new mind science.* New York: Pi Press.

Hodgkinson, V. A., & Weitzman, M. S. (1992). *Giving and volunteering in the United States.* Washington, DC: Independent Sector.

Hoebel, B. G., & Teitelbaum, P. (1966). Effects of forcefeeding and starvation on food intake and body weight in a rat with ventromedial hypothalamic lesions. *Journal of Comparative and Physiological Psychology, 61,* 189–193.

Hoffman, C., & Hurst, N. (1990). Gender stereotypes: Perception or rationalization? *Journal of Personality and Social Psychology, 58,* 197–208.

Hoffman, D. D. (1998). *Visual intelligence: How we create what we see.* New York: Norton.

Hoffman, H. G. (2004, August). Virtual-reality therapy. *Scientific American,* pp. 58–65.

Hofstede, G. (1980). *Culture's consequences: International differences in work-related values.* Beverly Hills: Sage.

Hogan, J. (1995, November). Get smart, take a test. *Scientific American,* pp. 12, 14.

Hogan, R. (1998). Reinventing personality. *Journal of Social and Clinical Psychology, 17,* 1–10.

Hoge, C. W., Castro, C. A., Messer, S. C., McGurk, D., Cotting, D. I., & Koffman, R. L. (2004). Combat duty in Iraq and Afghanistan, mental health problems, and barriers to care. *New England Journal of Medicine, 35,* 13–22.

Hogg, M. A. (1996). Intragroup processes, group structure and social identity. In W. P. Robinson (Ed.), *Social groups and identities: Developing the legacy of Henri Tajfel.* Oxford: Butterworth Heinemann.

Hohmann, G. W. (1966). Some effects of spinal cord lesions on experienced emotional feelings. *Psychophysiology, 3,* 143–156.

Hokanson, J. E., & Edelman, R. (1966). Effects of three social responses on vascular processes. *Journal of Personality and Social Psychology, 3,* 442–447.

Holahan, C. K., & Sears, R. R. (1995). *The gifted group in later maturity.* Stanford, CA: Stanford University Press.

Holden, C. (1980a). Identical twins reared apart. *Science, 207,* 1323–1325.

Holden, C. (1980b, November). Twins reunited. *Science, 80,* 55–59.

Holden, C. (1986b). Researchers grapple with problems of updating classic psychological test. *Science, 233,* 1249–1251.

Holden, C. (1993). Wake-up call for sleep research. *Science, 259,* 305.

Holden, G. W., & Miller, P. C. (1999). Enduring and different: A meta-analysis of the similarity in parents' child rearing. *Psychological Bulletin, 125,* 223–254.

Holliday, R. E., & Albon, A. J. (2004). Minimizing misinformation effects in young children with cognitive interview mnemonics. *Applied Cognitive Psychology, 18,* 263–281.

Hollis, K. L. (1997). Contemporary research on Pavlovian conditioning: A "new" functional analysis. *American Psychologist, 52,* 956–965.

Hollon, S. D., & 10 others (2005). Prevention of relapse following cognitive therapy vs. medications in moderate to severe depression. *Archives of General Psychiatry, 62,* 417–422.

Hollon, S. D., Thase, M. E., & Markowitz, J. C. (2002). Treatment and prevention of depression. *Psychological Science in the Public Interest, 3,* 39–77.

Holloway, K. (2000, June 22). Among the deaf, sign language faces a challenge. *New York Times* (www.nytimes.com).

Holmes, D. (1990). The evidence for repression: An examination of sixty years of research. In J. Singer (Ed.), *Repression and dissociation: Implications for personality theory, psychopathology, and health.* Chicago: University of Chicago Press.

Holmes, D. S. (1994). Is there evidence for repression? No. (Unexpurgated version on an article which was rewritten by the *Harvard Mental Health Letter* and published as "Is there evidence for repression? Doubtful," June, 1994, pp. 4–6.)

Holstege, G., Georgiadis, J. R., Paans, A. M. J., Meiners, L. C., van der Graaf, F. H. C. E., & Reinders, A. A. T. S. (2003a). Brain activation during male ejaculation. *Journal of Neuroscience, 23,* 9185–9193.

Holstege, G., Reinders, A. A. T., Paans, A. M. J., Meiners, L. C., Pruim, J., & Georgiadis, J. R. (2003b). Brain activation during female sexual orgasm. Program No. 727.7. Washington, DC: Society for Neuroscience.

Holt, L. (2002, August). Reported in "Sounds of speech," p. 26, and in personal correspondence, July 18, 2002.

Holzman, P. S., & Matthysse, S. (1990). The genetics of schizophrenia: A review. *Psychological Science, 1,* 279–286.

Home Office. (2003). Prevalence of drug use: Key findings from the 2002/2003 British Crime Survey. London: Research, Development and Statistics Directorate, Home Office.

Hooper, J., & Teresi, D. (1986). *The three-pound universe.* New York: Macmillan.

Hooykaas, R. (1972). *Religion and the rise of modern science.* Grand Rapids, MI: Eerdmans.

Hopkins, W. D., Russell, J., Freeman, H., Buehler, N., Reynolds, E., & Schapiro, S. J. (2005). The distribution and development of handedness for manual gestures in captive chimpanzees *(Pan troglodytes). Psychological Science, 16,* 487–493.

Horn, J. L. (1982). The aging of human abilities. In J. Wolman (Ed.), *Handbook of developmental psychology.* Englewood Cliffs, NJ: Prentice-Hall.

Horowitz, T. S., Cade, B. E., Wolfe, J. M., & Czeisler, C. A. (2003). Searching night and day: A dissociation of effects of circadian phase and time awake on visual selective attention and vigilance. *Psychological Science, 14,* 549–557.

Horwood, L. J., & Fergusson, D. M. (1998). Breastfeeding and later cognitive and academic outcomes. *Pediatrics, 101*(1).

Hötting, K, & Röder, B. (2004). Hearing cheats touch, but less in congenitally blind than in sighted individuals. *Psychological Science, 15,* 60–64.

House, J. S., Landis, K. R., & Umberson, D. (1988). Social relationships and health. *Science, 241,* 540–545.

House, R. J., & Singh, J. V. (1987). Organizational behavior: Some new directions for I/O psychology. *Annual Review of Psychology, 38,* 669–718.

Houts, A. C., Berman, J. S., & Abramson, H. (1994). Effectiveness of psychological and pharmacological treatments for nocturnal enuresis. *Journal of Consulting and Clinical Psychology, 62,* 737–745.

Howe, M. L. (1997). Children's memory for traumatic experiences. *Learning and Individual Differences, 9,* 153–174.

Howe, M. L. (2003). Memories from the cradle. *Current Directions in Psychological Science, 12,* 62–65.

Hoyer, G., & Lund, E. (1993). Suicide among women related to number of children in marriage. *Archives of General Psychiatry, 50,* 134–137.

Hróbjartsson, A., & Gøtzsche, P. C. (2001). Is the placebo powerless? An analysis of clinical trials comparing placebo with no treatment. *New England Journal of Medicine, 344,* 1594–602.

Hu, F. B., Li, T. Y., Colditz, G. A., Willett, W. C., & Manson, J. E. (2003). Television watching and other sedentary behaviors in relation to risk of obesity and type 2 diabetes mellitus in women. *Journal of the American Medical Association, 289,* 1785–1791.

Huart, J., Corneille, O., & Becquart, E. (2005). Face-based categorization, context-based categorization, and distortions in the recollection of gender ambiguous faces. *Journal of Experimental Social Psychology, 41,* 598–608.

Hubbard, E. M., Arman, A. C., Ramachandran, V. S., & Boynton, G. M. (2005). Individual differences among grapheme-color synesthetes: Brain-behavior correlations. *Neuron, 45,* 975–985.

Hubel, D. H. (1979, September). The brain. *Scientific American,* pp. 45–53.

Hubel, D. H., & Wiesel, T. N. (1979, September). Brian mechanisms of vision. *Scientific American,* pp. 150–162.

Hublin, C., Kaprio, J., Partinen, M., Heikkila, K., & Koskenvuo, M. (1997). Prevalence and genetics of sleepwalking—A population-based twin study. *Neurology, 48,* 177–181.

Hublin, C., Kaprio, J., Partinen, M., & Koskenvuo, M. (1998). Sleeptalking in twins: Epidemiology and psychiatric comorbidity. *Behavior Genetics, 28,* 289–298.

Hucker, S. J., & Bain, J. (1990). Androgenic hormones and sexual assault. In W. Marshall, R. Law, & H. Barbaree (Eds.), *The handbook on sexual assault.* New York: Plenum.

Hudson, W. (1960). Pictorial depth perception in sub-cultural groups in Africa. *Journal of Social Psychology, 52,* 183–208.

Huffcutt, A. I., Conway, J. M., Roth, P. L., & Stone, N. J. (2001). Identification and meta-analytic assessment of psychological constructs measured in employment interviews. *Journal of Applied Psychology, 86,* 897–913.

Hugenberg, K., & Bodenhausen, G. V. (2003). Facing prejudice: Implicit prejudice and the perception of facial threat. *Psychological Science, 14,* 640–643.

Hughes, H. C. (1999). *Sensory exotica: A world beyond human experience.* Cambridge, MA: MIT Press.

Hugick, L. (1989, July). Women play the leading role in keeping modern families close. *Gallup Report,* No. 286, pp. 27–34.

Huizink, A. C., Mulder, E. J. H., & Buitelaar, J. K. (2004). Prenatal stress and risk for psychopathology: Specific effects or indication of general susceptibility? *Psychological Bulletin, 130,* 115–142.

Hull, J. G., & Bond, C. F., Jr. (1986). Social and behavioral consequences of alcohol consumption and expectancy: A meta-analysis. *Psychological Bulletin, 99,* 347–360.

Hull, J. G., Young, R. D., & Jouriles, E. (1986). Applications of the self-awareness model of alcohol consumption: Predicting patterns of use and abuse. *Journal of Personality and Social Psychology, 51,* 790–796.

Hull, J. M. (1990). *Touching the rock: An experience of blindness.* New York: Vintage Books.

Hulme, C., & Tordoff, V. (1989). Working memory development: The effects of speech rate, word length, and acoustic similarity on serial recall. *Journal of Experimental Child Psychology, 47,* 72–87.

Hummer, R. A., Rogers, R. G., Nam, C. B., & Ellison, C. G. (1999). Religious involvement and U.S. adult mortality. *Demography, 36,* 273–285.

Humphreys, L. G., & Davey, T. C. (1988). Continuity in intellectual growth from 12 months to 9 years. *Intelligence, 12,* 183–197.

Hunsley, J., & Bailey, J. M. (1999). The clinical utility of the Rorschach: Unfulfilled promises and an uncertain future. *Psychological Assessment, 11*(3), 266–277.

Hunsley, J., & Di Giulio, G. (2002). Dodo bird, phoenix, or urban legend? The question of psychotherapy equivalence. *Scientific Review of Mental Health Practice, 1,* 11–22.

Hunt, C., Slade, T., & Andrews, G. (2004). Generalized anxiety disorder and major depressive disorder comorbidity in the National Survey of Mental Health and Well-Being. *Depression and Anxiety, 20,* 23–31.

Hunt, E. (1983). On the nature of intelligence. *Science, 219,* 141–146.

Hunt, J. M. (1982). Toward equalizing the developmental opportunities of infants and preschool children. *Journal of Social Issues, 38*(4), 163–191.

Hunt, M. (1974). *Sexual behavior in the 1970s.* Chicago: Playboy Press.

Hunt, M. (1982). *The universe within.* New York: Simon and Schuster.

Hunt, M. (1990). *The compassionate beast: What science is discovering about the humane side of humankind.* New York: William Morrow.

Hunt, M. (1993). *The story of psychology.* New York: Doubleday.

Hunter, J. E. (1997). Needed: A ban on the significance test. *Psychological Science, 8,* 3–7.

Hunter, S., & Sundel, M. (Eds.). (1989). *Midlife myths: Issues, findings, and practice implications.* Newbury Park, CA: Sage.

Huss, M. (1996). Secrets to standing out from the pile: Getting into graduate school. *Psi Chi Newsletter, 6–7.*

Hussein, S. (2002, July 17 and August 28). Speeches to the Iraqi people as reported by various media.

Huston, A. C., & Aronson, S. R. (2005). Mothers' time with infant and time in employment as predictors of mother-child relationships and children's early development. *Child Development, 76,* 467–482.

Huston, A. C., Donnerstein, E., Fairchild, H., Feshbach, N. D., Katz, P. A., & Murray, J. P. (1992). *Big world, small screen: The role of television in American society.* Lincoln, NE: University of Nebraska Press.

Hyde, J. S. (1983, November). *Bem's gender schema theory.* Paper presented at GLCA Women's Studies Conference, Rochester, IN.

Hyde, J. S., Fennema, E., & Lamon, S. J. (1990). Gender differences in mathematics performance: A meta-analysis. *Psychological Bulletin, 107,* 139–155.

Hygge, S., Evans, G. W., & Bullinger, M. (2002). A prospective study of some effects of aircraft noise on cognitive performance in schoolchildren. *Psychological Science, 13,* 469–474.

Hyler, S., Gabbard, G. O., & Schneider, I. (1991). Homicidal maniacs and narcissistic parasites: Stigmatization of mentally ill persons in the movies. *Hospital and Community Psychiatry, 42,* 1044–1048.

Hyman, R. (1981). Cold reading: How to convince strangers that you know all about them. In K. Frazier (Ed.), *Paranormal borderlands of science.* Buffalo, NY: Prometheus.

Hyman, S. (1999). Quoted by M. Enserink, Can the placebo be the cure? *Science, 284,* 238–240.

Iacono, W. G., & Lykken, D. T. (1997). The validity of the lie detector: Two surveys of scientific opinion. *Journal of Applied Psychology, 82,* 426–433.

Ickes, W., Snyder, M., & Garcia, S. (1997). Personality influences on the choice of situations. In R. Hogan, J. Johnson, & S. Briggs (Eds.). *Handbook of Personality Psychology.* San Diego, CA: Academic Press.

ICR. (2001, October 12). Women fear flying; pill sales rise (survey by ICR of Media, PA). Associated Press (in *Grand Rapids Press*), p. A3.

Idson, L. C., & Mischel, W. (2001). The personality of familiar and significant people: The lay perceiver as a social-cognitive theorist. *Journal of Personality and Social Psychology, 80,* 585–596.

Ikonomidou, C., Bittigau, P., Ishimaru, M. J., Wozniak, D. F., Koch, C., Genz, K., Price, M. T., Stefovska, V., Hoerster, F., Tenkova, T., Dikranian, K., & Olney, J. W. (2000). Ethanol-induced apoptotic neurodegeneration and fetal alcohol syndrome. *Science, 287,* 1056–1060.

Illes, J. (2004, Fall). A fish story? Brain maps, lie detection, and personhood. *Cerebrum,* pp. 73–80.

Immen, W. (1995, July 16). Canadians ignore 'safe sex' warning. *Toronto Globe and Mail* (in *Grand Rapids Press,* p. A22).

Independent Sector. (2002). *Faith and philanthropy: The connection between charitable giving behavior and giving to religion.* Washington, DC: Independent Sector.

Ingham, A. G., Levinger, G., Graves, J., & Peckham, V. (1974). The Ringelmann effect: Studies of group size and group performance. *Journal of Experimental Social Psychology, 10,* 371–384.

Inglehart, R. (1990). *Culture shift in advanced industrial society.* Princeton, NJ: Princeton University Press.

Inglehart, R., Basañez, M., Diez-Medrano, J., Halman, L., & Luijkx, R. (Eds.). (2004). *Human beliefs and values: A sourcebook based on the 1999-2001 values surveys.* Mexico City: Siglo XXI.

Ingram, V. (2003). Alzheimer's disease. *American Scientist, 91,* 312–321.

Inman, M. L., & Baron, R. S. (1996). Influence of prototypes on perceptions of prejudice. *Journal of Personality and Social Psychology, 70,* 727–739.

Insana, R. (2005, February 21). Coach says honey gets better results than vinegar (interview with Larry Brown). *USA Today,* p. 4B.

Inzlicht, M., & Ben-Zeev, T. (2000). A threatening intellectual environment: Why females are susceptible to experiencing problem-solving deficits in the presence of males. *Psychological Science, 11,* 365–371.

IPU. (2005). Women in national parliaments: Situation as of 28 February 2005. Inter-Parliamentary Union (www.ipu.org).

Ireland, T. O., Smith, C. A., & Thornberry, T. P. (2002). Developmental issues in the impact of child maltreatment on later delinquency and drug use. *Criminology, 40,* 359–399.

Ironson, G., Solomon, G. F., Balbin, E. G., O'Cleirigh, C., George, A., Kumar, M., Larson, D., & Woods, T. E. (2002). The Ironson-Woods spiritual/religiousness index is associated with long survival, health behaviors, less distress, and low cortisol in people with HIV/AIDS. *Annals of Behavioral Medicine, 24,* 34–48.

Irwin, M., Mascovich, A., Gillin, J. C., Willoughby, R., Pike, J., & Smith, T. L. (1994). Partial sleep deprivation reduces natural killer cell activity in humans. *Psychosomatic Medicine, 56,* 493–498.

Isensee, B., Wittchen, H-U., Stein, M. B., Hofler, M., & Lieb, R. (2003). Smoking increases the risk of panic: Findings from a prospective community study. *Archives of General Psychiatry, 60,* 692–700.

Isham, W. P., & Kamin, L. J. (1993). Blackness, deafness, IQ, and *g. Intelligence, 17,* 37–46.

ISR. (2003, Spring). Drug use: Religion plays role for White as well as Black teens (data from 70,000 seniors surveyed 1997-2001, *ISR Monitoring the Future Study*). Ann Arbor, MI: Institute for Social Research Newsletter, University of Michigan.

Ito, T. A., Miller, N., & Pollock, V. E. (1996). Alcohol and aggression: A meta-analysis on the moderating effects of inhibitory cues, triggering events, and self-focused attention. *Psychological Bulletin, 120,* 60–82.

Iversen, L. L. (2000). *The science of marijuana.* New York: Oxford.

Iverson, J. M., & Goldin-Meadow, S. (1998). Why people gesture when they speak. *Nature, 396,* 228.

Iyengar, S. S., & Lepper, M. R. (2000). When choice is demotivating: Can one desire too much of a good thing? *Journal of Personality and Social Psychology, 79,* 995–1006.

Iyer, P. (1993, April). The soul of an intercontinental wanderer. *Harper's, 286,* 13–17.

Izard, C. E. (1977). *Human emotions.* New York: Plenum Press.

Izard, C., Fine, S., Schultz, D., Mostow, A., Ackerman, B., & Younstrom, E. (2001). Emotion knowledge as a predictor of social behavior and academic competence in children at risk. *Psychological Science, 12,* 18–23.

Izzetoglu, K., Yurtsever, G., Bozkurt, A., Yazici, B., Bunce, S., Pourrezaei, K., Onaral, B. (2003). NIR spectroscopy measurements of cognitive load elicited by GKT and target categorization. System Sciences, Proceedings of the 36th Hawaii International Conference on System Sciences, 129–134.

Jablensky, A. (1999). Schizophrenia: Epidemiology. *Current Opinion in Psychiatry, 12,* 19–28.

Jackson, J. M., & Williams, K. D. (1988). Social loafing: A review and theoretical analysis. Unpublished manuscript, Fordham University.

Jackson, J. S., Brown, K. T., Brown, T. N., & Marks, B. (2001). Contemporary immigration policy orientations among dominant-group members in western Europe. *Journal of Social Issues, 57,* 431–456.

Jackson, L. A., & Gerard, D. A. (1996). Diurnal types, the "Big Five" personality factors and other personal characteristics. *Journal of Social Behavior and Personality, 11,* 273–283.

Jackson, S. W. (1992). The listening healer in the history of psychological healing. *American Journal Psychiatry, 149,* 1623–1632.

Jacobe, D. (2003, December 2). Why the gender gap in investor optimism? Gallup Poll Tuesday Briefing (www.gallup.com).

Jacobi, C., Hayward, C., deZwaan, M., Kraemer, H. C., & Agras, W. S. (2004). Coming to terms with risk factors for eating disorders: Application of risk terminology and suggestions for a general taxonomy. *Psychological Bulletin, 130,* 19–65.

Jacobs, B. L. (1987). How hallucinogenic drugs work. *American Scientist, 75,* 386–392.

Jacobs, B. L. (1994). Serotonin, motor activity, and depression-related disorders. *American Scientist, 82,* 456–463.

Jacobs, B. L. (2004). Depression: The brain finally gets into the act. *Current Directions in Psychological Science, 13,* 103–106.

Jacobs, B., van Praag, H., & Gage, F. H. (2000). Adult brain neurogenesis and psychiatry: A novel theory of depression. *Molecular Psychiatry, 5,* 262–269.

Jacobs, W. J., & Nadel, L. (1985). Stress-induced recovery of fears and phobias. *Psychological Bulletin, 92,* 512–531.

Jacoby, L. L., Bishara, A. J., Hessels, S., & Toth, J. P. (2005). Aging, subjective experience, and cognitive control: Dramatic false remembering by older adults. *Journal of Experimental Psychology: General, 154,* 131–148.

Jaffe, E. (2004, October). Peace in the Middle East may be impossible: Lee D. Ross on naive realism and conflict resolution. *APS Observer,* pp. 9–11.

Jakicic, J. M., Winters, C., Lang, W., & Wing R. R. (1999). Effects of intermittent exercise and use of home exercise equipment on adherence, weight loss, and fitness in overweight women. *Journal of the American Medical Association, 282,* 1554–1560.

James, K. (1986). Priming and social categorizational factors: Impact on awareness of emergency situations. *Personality and Social Psychology Bulletin, 12,* 462–467.

James, W. (1890). *The principles of psychology* (Vol. 2). New York: Holt.

James, W. (1902; reprinted 1958). *Varieties of religious experience.* New York: Mentor Books.

Jameson, D. (1985). Opponent-colors theory in light of physiological findings. In D. Ottoson & S. Zeki (Eds.), *Central and peripheral mechanisms of color vision.* New York: Macmillan.

Jamison, K. R. (1993). *Touched with fire: Manic-depressive illness and the artistic temperament.* New York: Free Press.

Jamison, K. R. (1995, February). Manic-depressive illness and creativity. *Scientific American,* pp. 62–67.

Janicak, P. G. (2005). Treating psychiatric disorders using transcranial magnetic stimulation. *Psychiatric Annals, 35,* 102–108.

Janis, I. L. (1982). *Groupthink: Psychological studies of policy decisions and fiascoes.* Boston: Houghton Mifflin.

Janis, I. L. (1986). Problems of international crisis management in the nuclear age. *Journal of Social Issues, 42(2),* 201–220.

Janoff-Bulman, R., Timko, C., & Carli, L. L. (1985). Cognitive biases in blaming the victim. *Journal of Experimental Social Psychology, 21,* 161–177.

Javitt, D. C., & Coyle, J. T. (2004, January). Decoding schizophrenia. *Scientific American,* pp. 48–55.

Jeffery, R. W., Drewnowski, A., Epstein, L. H., Stunkard, A. J., Wilson, G. T., Wing, R. R., & Hill, D. R. (2000). Long-term maintenance of weight loss: Current status. *Health Psychology, 19,* No. 1 (Supplement), 5–16.

Jenkins, J. G., & Dallenbach, K. M. (1924). Obliviscence during sleep and waking. *American Journal of Psychology, 35,* 605–612.

Jenkins, J. M., & Astington, J. W. (1996). Cognitive factors and family structure associated with theory of mind development in young children. *Developmental Psychology, 32,* 70–78.

Jensen, A. R. (1980). *Bias in mental testing.* New York: The Free Press.

Jensen, A. R. (1983, August). The nature of the black-white difference on various psychometric tests: Spearman's hypothesis. Paper presented at the meeting of the American Psychological Association, Anaheim, CA.

Jensen, A. R. (1989). New findings on the intellectually gifted. *New Horizons, 30,* 73–80.

Jensen, A. R. (1998). *The g factor: The science of mental ability.* Westport, CT: Praeger/Greenwood.

Jensen, J. P., & Bergin, A. E. (1988). Mental health values of professional therapists: A national interdisciplinary survey. *Professional Psychology: Research and Practice, 19,* 290–297.

Jepson, C., Krantz, D. H., & Nisbett, R. E. (1983). Inductive reasoning: Competence or skill. *The Behavioral and Brain Sciences, 3,* 494–501.

Jervis, R. (1985, April 2). Quoted in D. Goleman, Political forces come under new scrutiny of psychology. *The New York Times,* pp. C1, C4.

Jing, H. (1999, Summer). China faces myriad psychological challenges of modernization. *Psychology International* (APA newsletter), p. 7.

Johansson, P., Hall, L., Sikström, S., & Olsson, A. (2005). Failure to detect mismatches between intention and outcome in a simple decision task. *Science, 310,* 116–119.

John, O. P., & Srivastava, S. (1999). The Big Five trait taxonomy: History, measurement, and theoretical perspectives. In L. A. Pervin & O. P. John (Eds.), *Handbook of personality: Theory and research.* New York: Guilford.

Johnson, C. B., Stockdale, M. S., & Saal, F. E. (1991). Persistence of men's misperceptions of friendly cues across a variety of interpersonal encounters. *Psychology of Women Quarterly, 15,* 463–475.

Johnson, D. F. (1997, Winter). Margaret Floy Washburn. *Psychology of Women Newsletter,* pp. 17, 22.

Johnson, D. L., Wiebe, J. S., Gold, S. M., Andreasen, N. C., Hichwa, R. D., Watkins, G. L., & Ponto, L. L. B. (1999). Cerebral blood flow and personality: A Positron Emission Tomography study. *American Journal of Psychiatry, 156,* 252–257.

Johnson, D. W., & Johnson, R. T. (1989). *Cooperation and competition: Theory and research.* Edina, MN: Interaction Book.

Johnson, D. W., & Johnson, R. T. (1994). Constructive conflict in the schools. *Journal of Social Issues, 50(1),* 117–137.

Johnson, G. (2003, November 5). Suspect admits 48 Seattle-area killings. Associated Press release.

Johnson, J. G., Cohen, P., Kotler, L., Kasen, S., & Brook, J. S. (2002). Psychiatric disorders associated with risk for the development of eating disorders during adolescence and early adulthood. *Journal of Consulting and Clinical Psychology, 70,* 1119–1128.

Johnson, J. S., & Newport, E. L. (1991). Critical period effects on universal properties of language: The status of subjacency in the acquisition of a second language. *Cognition, 39,* 215–258.

Johnson, L. C. (2001, July 10). The declining terrorist threat. *New York Times* (www.nytimes.com).

Johnson, M. E., & Hauck, C. (1999). Beliefs and opinions about hypnosis held by the general public: A systematic evaluation. *American Journal of Clinical Hypnosis, 42,* 10–20.

Johnson, M. H. (1992). Imprinting and the development of face recognition: From chick to man. *Current Directions in Psychological Science, 1,* 52–55.

Johnson, M. H., & Morton, J. (1991). *Biology and cognitive development: The case of face recognition.* Oxford: Blackwell Publishing.

Johnson, W., McGue, M., & Krueger, R. F. (2005). Personality stability in late adulthood: A behavioral genetic analysis. *Journal of Personality, 73,* 523–552.

Johnston, L. D., O'Malley, P. M., Bachman, J. G., & Schulenberg, J. E. (2005). *Monitoring the future: National results on adolescent drug use: Overview of key findings, 2004.* Bethesda, MD: National Institute on Drug Abuse.

Johnston, L. D., O'Malley, P. M., Bachman, J. G., & Schulenberg, J. E. (2005). *Teen drug use down but progress halts among youngest teens.* University of Michigan News and Information Services: Ann Arbor, MI. www.monitoringthefuture.org.

Johnstone, E. C., Ebmeier, K. P., Miller, P., Owens, D. G. C., & Lawrie, S. M. (2005). Predicting schizophrenia: Findings from the Edinburgh High-Risk Study. *British Journal of Psychiatry, 186,* 18–25.

Joiner, T. E., Jr. (1999). The clustering and contagion of suicide. *Current Directions in Psychological Science, 8,* 89–92.

Joiner, T. E., Pettit, J. W., Walker, R. L., Voelz, Z. R., Cruz, J., Rudd, M. D., & Lester, D. (2002). Perceived burdensomeness and suicidality: Two studies on the suicide notes of those attempting and those completing suicide. *Journal of Social and Clinical Psychology, 21,* 531–545.

Jones, E. E., Cumming, J. D., & Horowitz, M. J. (1988). Another look at the nonspecific hypothesis of therapeutic effectiveness. *Journal of Consulting and Clinical Psychology, 56,* 48–55.

Jones, J. M. (2003, February 12). Fear of terrorism increases amidst latest warning. *Gallup News Service* (www.gallup.com/releases/pr030212.asp).

Jones, J. M., & Moore, D. W. (2003, June 17). Generational differences in support for a woman president. The Gallup Organization (www.gallup.com).

Jones, J. T., Pelham, B. W., Carvallo, M., & Mirenberg, M. C. (2004). How do I love thee? Let me count the Js: Implicit egotism and interpersonal attraction. *Journal of Personality and Social Psychology, 87,* 665–683.

Jones, L. (2000, December). Skeptics New Year quiz. *Skeptical Briefs,* p. 11.

Jones, M. C. (1924). A laboratory study of fear: The case of Peter. *Journal of Genetic Psychology, 31,* 308–315.

Jones, M. V., Paull, G. C., & Erskine, J. (2002). The impact of a team's aggressive reputation on the decisions of association football referees. *Journal of Sports Sciences, 20,* 991–1000.

Jones, S. S., Collins, K., & Hong, H-W. (1991). An audience effect on smile production in 10-month-old infants. *Psychological Science, 2,* 45–49.

Jones, W. H., Carpenter, B. N., & Quintana, D. (1985). Personality and interpersonal predictors of loneliness in two cultures. *Journal of Personality and Social Psychology, 48,* 1503–1511.

Jonides, J., Lacey, S. C., & Nee, D. E. (2005). Processes of working memory in mind and brain. *Psychological Science, 14,* 2–5.

Jordan, C. H., Spencer, S. J., Zanna, M. P., Hoshino-Browne, E., & Correll, J. (2003). Secure and defensive high self-esteem. *Journal of Personality and Social Psychology, 85,* 969–978.

Jorgenson, D. O., & Papciak, A. S. (1981). The effects of communication, resource feedback, and identifiability on behavior in a simulated commons. *Journal of Experimental Social Psychology, 17,* 373–385.

Joseph, J. (2001). Separated twins and the genetics of personality differences: A critique. *American Journal of Psychology, 114,* 1–30.

Judge, T. A., Thoresen, C. J., Bono, J. E., & Patton, G. K. (2001). The job satisfaction/job performance relationship: A qualitative and quantitative review. *Psychological Bulletin, 127,* 376–407.

Jung-Beeman, M., Bowden, E. M., Haberman, J., Frymiare, J. L., Arambel-Liu, S., Greenblatt, R., Reber, P. J., & Kounios, J. (2004). Neural activity when people solve verbal problems with insight. *PloS Biology* 2(4): e111.

Kagan, J. (1976). Emergent themes in human development. *American Scientist, 64,* 186–196.

Kagan, J. (1984). *The nature of the child.* New York: Basic Books.

Kagan, J. (1990). Interview with M. V. Ellis & E. S. Robbins, In Celebration of nature: A dialogue with Jerome Kagan. *Journal of Counseling and Development, 68,* 623–627.

Kagan, J. (1995). On attachment. *Harvard Review of Psychiatry, 3,* 104–106.

Kagan, J. (1998). *Three seductive ideas.* Cambridge, MA: Harvard University Press.

Kagan, J., Arcus, D., Snidman, N., Feng, W. Y., Hendler, J., & Greene, S. (1994). Reactivity in infants: A cross-national comparison. *Developmental Psychology, 30,* 342–345.

Kagan, J., Lapidus, D. R., & Moore, M. (December, 1978). Infant antecedents of cognitive functioning: A longitudinal study. *Child Development, 49*(4), 1005–1023.

Kagan, J., & Snidman, N. (2004). *The long shadow of temperament.* Cambridge, MA: Belknap Press.

Kagan, J., Snidman, N., & Arcus, D. M. (1992). Initial reactions to unfamiliarity. *Current Directions in Psychological Science, 1,* 171–174.

Kahneman, D. (1985, June). Quoted by K. McKean, Decisions, decisions. *Discover,* pp. 22–31.

Kahneman, D. (1999). Assessments of objective happiness: A bottom-up approach. In D. Kahneman, E. Diener, & N. Schwartz (Eds.), *Understanding well-being: Scientific perspectives on enjoyment and suffering.* New York: Russell Sage Foundation.

Kahneman, D. (2005, January 13). What were they thinking? Q&A with Daniel Kahneman. *Gallup Management Journal* (gmj.gallup.com).

Kahneman, D. (2005, February 10). Are you happy now? *Gallup Management Journal* interview (www.gmj.gallup.com).

Kahneman, D., Fredrickson, B. L., Schreiber, C. A., & Redelmeier, D. A. (1993). When more pain is preferred to less: Adding a better end. *Psychological Science, 4,* 401–405.

Kahneman, D., Krueger, A. B., Schkade, D. A., Schwarz, N., & Stone, A. A. (2004). A survey method for characterizing daily life experience: The day reconstruction method. *Science, 306,* 1776–1780.

Kahneman, D., & Tversky, A. (1972). Subjective probability: A judgment of representativeness. *Cognitive Psychology, 3,* 430–454.

Kahneman, D., & Tversky, A. (1979). Intuitive prediction: Biases and corrective procedures. *Management Science, 12,* 313–327.

Kail, R. (1991). Developmental change in speed of processing during childhood and adolescence. *Psychological Bulletin, 109,* 490–501.

Kaiser (2001). Inside-out: A report on the experiences of lesbians, gays and bisexuals in America and the public's views on issues and policies related to sexual orientation. The Henry J. Kaiser Foundation (www.kff.org).

Kaiser Family Foundation. (2003, October 28). New study finds children age zero to six spend as much time with TV, computers and video games as playing outside. www.kff.org/entmedia/entmedia102803nr.cfm

Kalff, A. C., Kroes, M., Vles, J. S. H., Hendriksen, J. G. M., Feron, F. J. M., Steyaert, J., van Zeban, T. M. C. B., Jolles, J., & van Os, J. (2001). Neighbourhood level and individual level SES effects on child problem behaviour: a multilevel analysis. *Journal of Epidemiology and Community Health, 55,* 246–250.

Kalin, N. H. (1993, May). The neurobiology of fear. *Scientific American,* pp. 94–101.

Kamarck, T., & Jennings, J. R. (1991). Biobehavioral factors in sudden cardiac death. *Psychological Bulletin, 109,* 42–75.

Kamena, M. (1998). Repressed/false childhood sexual abuse memories: A survey of therapists. Paper presented to the Sexual Abuse memories Symposium at the American Psychological Association convention.

Kaminski, J., Cali, J., & Fischer, J. (2004). Word learning in a domestic dog: Evidence for "fast mapping." *Science, 304,* 1682–1683.

Kanaya, T., Scullin, M. H., & Ceci, S. J. (2003). The Flynn effect and U.S. policies: The impact of rising IQ scores on American society via mental retardation diagnoses. *American Psychologist, 58,* 778–790.

Kanazawa, S. (2004). General intelligence as a domain-specific adaptation. *Psychological Review, 111,* 512–523.

Kandel, D. B., & Raveis, V. H. (1989). Cessation of illicit drug use in young adulthood. *Archives of General Psychiatry, 46,* 109–116.

Kandel, E. R., & Schwartz, J. H. (1982). Molecular biology of learning: Modulation of transmitter release. *Science, 218,* 433–443.

Kann, L., Warren, W., Collins, J. L., Ross, J., Collins, B., Kolbe, L. J. (1993). Results from the national school-based 1991 Youth Risk Behavior Survey and progress toward achieving related health objectives for the nation. U.S. Department of Health and Human Services, *Public Health Reports, 108* (Supplement 1), 47–55.

Kapitza, S. (1991, August). Antiscience trends in the U.S.S.R. *Scientific American,* pp. 32–38.

Kaplan, A. (2004). Exploring the gene-environment nexus in anorexia, bulimia. *Psychiatric Times, 21* (www.psychiatrictimes.com/p040801b.html).

Kaplan, H. I., & Saddock, B. J. (Eds.). (1989). *Comprehensive textbook of psychiatry, V.* Baltimore, MD: Williams and Wilkins.

Kaprio, J., Koskenvuo, M., & Rita, H. (1987). Mortality after bereavement: A prospective study of 95,647 widowed persons. *American Journal of Public Health, 77,* 283–287.

Karacan, I., Aslan, C., & Hirshkowitz, M. (1983). Erectile mechanisms in man. *Science, 220,* 1080–1082.

Karacan, I., Goodenough, D. R., Shapiro, A., & Starker, S. (1966). Erection cycle during sleep in relation to dream anxiety. *Archives of General Psychiatry, 15,* 183–189.

Karau, S. J., & Williams, K. D. (1993). Social loafing: A meta-analytic review and theoretical integration. *Journal of Personality and Social Psychology, 65,* 681–706.

Kark, J. D., Shemi, G., Friedlander, Y., Martin, O., Manor, O., & Blondheim, S. H. (1996). Does religious observance promote health? Mortality in secular vs. religious kibbutzim in Israel. *American Journal of Public Health, 86,* 341–346.

Karni, A., Meyer, G., Rey-Hipolito, C., Jezzard, P., Adams, M. M., Turner, R., & Ungerleider, L. G. (1998). The acquisition of skilled motor performance: Fast and slow experience-driven changes in primary motor cortex. *Proceedings of the National Academy of Sciences, 95,* 861–868.

Karni, A., & Sagi, D. (1994). Dependence on REM sleep for overnight improvement of perceptual skills. *Science, 265,* 679–682.

Karno, M., Golding, J. M., Sorenson, S. B., & Burnam, A. (1988). The epidemiology of obsessive-compulsive disorder in five US communities. *Archives of General Psychiatry, 45,* 1094–1099.

Karon, P. B., & Widener, A. (1998). Repressed memories: The real story. *Professional Psychology: Research and Practice, 29,* 482–487.

Karon, P. B., & Widener, A. J. (1997). Repressed memories and World War II: Lest we forget. *Professional Psychology: Research and Practice, 28,* 338–340.

Kashima, Y., Siegal, M., Tanaka, K., & Kashima, E. S. (1992). Do people believe behaviours are consistent with attitudes? Towards a cultural psychology of attribution processes. *British Journal of Social Psychology, 31,* 111–124.

Kassel, J. D., Stroud, L. R., & Paronis, C. A. (2003). Smoking, stress, and negative affect: Correlation, causation, and context across stages of smoking. *Psychological Bulletin, 129,* 270–304.

Kasser, T. (2000). Two version of the American dream: Which goals and values make for a high quality of life? In E. Diener (Ed.), *Advances in quality of life theory and research.* Dordrecht, Netherlands: Kluwer.

Kasser, T. (2002). *The high price of materialism.* Cambridge, MA: MIT Press.

Kaufman, J. C., & Baer, J. (2002). I bask in dreams of suicide: Mental illness, poetry, and women. *Review of General Psychology, 6,* 271–286.

Kaufman, J., & Zigler, E. (1987). Do abused children become abusive parents? *American Journal of Orthopsychiatry, 57,* 186–192.

Kaufman, L., & Kaufman, J. H. (2000). Explaining the moon illusion. *Proceedings of the National Academy of Sciences, 97,* 500–505.

Kavšek, M. (2004). Predicting later IQ from infant visual habituation and dishabituation: A meta-analysis. *Journal of Applied Developmental Psychology, 25,* 369–393.

Kazdin, A. E., & Benjet, C. (2003). Spanking children: Evidence and issues. *Current Directions in Psychological Science, 12,* 99–103.

Keenan, J. P., Nelson, A., O'Connor, M., & Pascual-Leone, A. (2001). Self-recognition and the right hemisphere. *Nature, 409,* 305.

Keesey, R. E., & Corbett, S. W. (1983). Metabolic defense of the body weight set-point. In A. J. Stunkard & E. Stellar (Eds.), *Eating and its disorders.* New York: Raven Press.

Kellehear, A. (1996). *Experiences near death: Beyond medicine and religion.* New York: Oxford University Press.

Keller, H. (2003). "Before the Soul Dawn," *The World I Live In,* New York Review Books.

Keller, M. B., McCullough, J. P., Klein, D. N., Arnow, B., Dunner, D. L., Gelenberg, A. J., Markowitz, J. C., Nemeroff, C. B., Russell, J. M., Thase, M. E., Trivedi, M. H., & Zajecka J. (2000), A comparison of nefazodone, the cognitive behavioral-analysis system of psychotherapy, and their combination for the treatment of chronic depression. *New England Journal of Medicine, 342,* 1462–1470.

Kellerman, J., Lewis, J., & Laird, J. D. (1989). Looking and loving: The effects of mutual gaze on feelings of romantic love. *Journal of Research in Personality, 23,* 145–161.

Kellermann, A. L. (1997). Comment: Gunsmoke—changing public attitudes toward smoking and firearms. *American Journal of Public Health, 87,* 910–913.

Kellermann, A. L., Rivara, F. P., Rushforth, N. B., Banton, H. G., Feay, D. T., Francisco, J. T., Locci, A. B., Prodzinski, J., Hackman, B. B., & Somes, G. (1993). Gun ownership as a risk factor for homicide in the home. *New England Journal of Medicine, 329,* 1084–1091.

Kellermann, A. L., Somes, G. Rivara, F. P., Lee, R. K., & Banton, J. G. (1998). Injuries and deaths due to firearms in the home. *Journal of Trauma, 45,* 263-267.

Kelley, J., & De Graaf, N. D. (1997). National context, parental socialization, and religious belief: Results from 15 nations, *American Sociological Review, 62,* 639–659.

Kelling, S. T., & Halpern, B. P. (1983). Taste flashes: Reaction times, intensity, and quality. *Science, 219,* 412–414.

Kellner, C. H., & 15 others (2005). Relief of expressed suicidal intent by ECT: A consortium for research in ECT study. *American Journal of Psychiatry, 162,* 977–982.

Kelly, A. E. (2000). Helping construct desirable identities: A self-presentational view of psychotherapy. *Psychological Bulletin, 126,* 475–494.

Kelly, I. W. (1997). Modern astrology: A critique. *Psychological Reports, 81,* 1035–1066.

Kelly, I. W. (1998). Why astrology doesn't work. *Psychological Reports, 82,* 527–546.

Kelly, T. A. (1990). The role of values in psychotherapy: A critical review of process and outcome effects. *Clinical Psychology Review, 10,* 171–186.

Kempe, R. S., & Kempe, C. C. (1978). *Child abuse.* Cambridge, MA: Harvard University Press.

Kempermann, G., & Gage, F. H. (1999, May). New nerve cells for the adult brain. *Scientific American,* pp. 48–53.

Kempermann, G., Kuhn, H. G., & Gage, F. H. (May, 1998). *Journal of Neuroscience, 18*(9), 3206–3212.

Kendall-Tackett, K. A., Williams, L. M., & Finkelhor, D. (1993). Impact of sexual abuse on children: A review and synthesis of recent empirical studies. *Psychological Bulletin, 113,* 164–180.

Kendler, K. S. (1996). Parenting: A genetic-epidemiologic perspective. *The American Journal of Psychiatry, 153,* 11–20.

Kendler, K. S. (1997). Social support: A genetic-epidemiologic analysis. *American Journal of Psychiatry, 154,* 1398–1404.

Kendler, K. S. (1998, January). Major depression and the environment: A psychiatric genetic perspective. *Pharmacopsychiatry, 31*(1), 5–9.

Kendler, K. S., Jacobson, K. C., Myers, J., & Prescott, C. A. (2002a). Sex differences in genetic and environmental risk factors for irrational fears and phobias. *Psychological Medicine, 32,* 209–217.

Kendler, K. S., Karkowski, L. M., & Prescott, C. A. (1999). Fears and phobias: Reliability and heritability. *Psychological Medicine, 29,* 539–553.

Kendler, K. S., Myers, J., & Prescott, C. A. (2002b). The etiology of phobias: An evaluation of the stress-diathesis model. *Archives of General Psychiatry, 59,* 242–248.

Kendler, K. S., Neale, M. C., Kessler, R. C., Heath, A. C., & Eaves, L. J. (1992). Generalized anxiety disorder in women: A population-based twin study. *Archives of General Psychiatry, 49,* 267–272.

Kendler, K. S., Neale, M. C., Thornton, L. M., Aggen, S. H., Gilman, S. E., & Kessler, R. C. (2002). Cannabis use in the last year in a U.S. national sample of twin and sibling pairs. *Psychological Medicine, 32,* 551–554.

Kendler, K. S., Thornton, L. M., & Gardner, C. O. (2001). Genetic risk, number of previous depressive episodes, and stressful life events in predicting onset of major depression. *American Journal of Psychiatry, 158,* 582–586.

Kendler, K. S., Thornton, L. M., Gilman, S. E., & Kessler, R. C. (2000). Sexual orientation in a U.S. national sample of twin and nontwin sibling pairs. *American Journal of Psychiatry, 157,* 1843–1846.

Kennedy, S., & Over, R. (1990). Psychophysiological assessment of male sexual arousal following spinal cord injury. *Archives of Sexual Behavior, 19,* 15–27.

Kenrick, D. T., & Funder, D. C. (1988). Profiting from controversy: Lessons from the person-situation debate. *American Psychologist, 43,* 23–34.

Kenrick, D. T., & Gutierres, S. E. (1980). Contrast effects and judgments of physical attractiveness: When beauty becomes a social problem. *Journal of Personality and Social Psychology, 38,* 131–140.

Kenrick, D. T., Gutierres, S. E., & Goldberg, L. L. (1989). Influence of popular erotica on judgments of strangers and mates. *Journal of Experimental Social Psychology, 25,* 159–167.

Kenrick, D. T., & Trost, M. R. (1987). A biosocial theory of heterosexual relationships. In K. Kelly (Ed.), *Females, males, and sexuality.* Albany: State University of New York Press.

Keough, K. A., Zimbardo, P. G., & Boyd, J. N. (1999). Who's smoking, drinking, and using drugs? Time perspective as a predictor of substance use. *Basic and Applied Social Psychology, 2,* 149–164.

Kernis, M. H. (2003). Toward a conceptualization of optimal self-esteem. *Psychological Inquiry, 14,* 1–26.

Kerr, N. L., & Bruun, S. E. (1983). Dispensability of member effort and group motivation losses: Free-rider effects. *Journal of Personality and Social Psychology, 44,* 78–94.

Kessler, M., & Albee, G. (1975). Primary prevention. *Annual Review of Psychology, 26,* 557–591.

Kessler, R. C. (2000). Posttraumatic stress disorder: The burden to the individual and to society. *Journal of Clinical Psychiatry, 61*(suppl. 5), 4–12.

Kessler, R. C. (2001). Epidemiology of women and depression. *Journal of Affective Disorders, 74,* 5–13.

Kessler, R. C., Foster, C., Joseph, J., Ostrow, D., Wortman, C., Phair, J., & Chmiel, J. (1991). Stressful life events and symptom onset in HIV infection. *American Journal of Psychiatry, 148,* 733–738.

Kessler, R. C., Soukup, J., Davis, R. B., Foster, D. F., Wilkey, S. A., Van Rompay, M. I., & Eisenberg, D. M. (2001). The use of complementary and alternative therapies to treat anxiety and depression in the United States. *American Journal of Psychiatry, 158,* 289–294.

Kestenbaum, R. (1992). Feeling happy versus feeling good: The processing of discrete and global categories of emotional expressions by children and adults. *Developmental Psychology, 28,* 1132–1142.

Keynes, M. (1980, December 20/27). Handel's illnesses. *The Lancet,* pp. 1354–1355.

Keys, A., Brozek, J., Henschel, A., Mickelsen, O., & Taylor, H. L. (1950). *The biology of human starvation.* Minneapolis: University of Minnesota Press.

Keys, L. (2001, May 27). Once isolated nation falls for TV. Associated Press (*Grand Rapids Press,* p. A14).

Khan, A., Warner, H. A., & Brown, W. A. (2000). Symptom reduction and suicide risk inpatients treated with placebo in antidepressant clinical trials. *Archives of General Psychiatry, 57,* 311–317.

Kho, K. H., van Vreeswijk, M. F., Simpson, S., & Zwinderman, A. H. (2003). A meta-analysis of electroconvulsive therapy efficacy in depression. *Journal of ECT, 19,* 139–147.

Kiecolt-Glaser, J. K., & Glaser, R. (1995). Psychoneuroimmunology and health consequences: Data and shared mechanisms. *Psychosomatic Medicine, 57,* 269–274.

Kiecolt-Glaser, J. K., & Newton, T. L. (2001). Marriage and health: His and hers. *Psychological Bulletin, 127,* 472–503.

Kiecolt-Glaser, J. K., Page, G. G., Marucha, P. T., MacCallum, R. C., & Glaser, R. (1998). Psychological influences on surgical recovery: Perspectives from psychoneuroimmunology. *American Psychologist, 53,* 1209–1218.

Kihlstrom, J. F. (1990). Awareness, the psychological unconscious, and the self. Address to the American Psychological Association convention.

Kihlstrom, J. F. (1990). The psychological unconscious. In L. A. Pervin (Ed.), *Handbook of personality: Theory and research.* New York: Guilford Press.

Kihlstrom, J. F. (1994). The social construction of memory. Paper presented at the American Psychological Society convention.

Kihlstrom, J. F. (1997, November 11). Freud as giant pioneer on whose shoulders we should stand. Social Psychology listserv posting (spsp@stolaf.edu).

Kihlstrom, J. F. (2005). Dissociative disorders. *Annual Review of Clinical Psychology, 1,* 227–253.

Kihlstrom, J. F., & McConkey, K. M. (1990). William James and hypnosis: A centennial reflection. *Psychological Science, 1,* 174–177.

Killeen, P. R., & Nash, M. R. (2003). The four causes of hypnosis. *Internal Journal of Clinical and Experimental Hypnosis, 51,* 195–231.

Kim, B. S. K., Ng, G. F., & Ahn, A. J. (2005). Effects of client expectation for counseling success, client-counselor worldview match, and client adherence to Asian and European American cultural values on counseling process with Asian Americans. *Journal of Counseling Psychology, 52,* 67–76.

Kim, H., & Markus, H. R. (1999). Deviance or uniqueness, harmony or conformity? A cultural analysis. *Journal of Personality and Social Psychology, 77,* 785–800.

Kim, K. H. S., Relkin, N. R., Lee, K-M., & Hirsch, J. (1997). Distinct cortical areas associated with native and second languages. *Nature, 388,* 171–174.

Kim, Y., & Lee, S-H. (1994). The Confucian model of morality, justice, selfhood and society: Implications for modern society. In *The universal and particular natures of Confucianism.* The Academy of Korean Studies.

Kimata, H. (2001). Effect of humor on allergen-induced wheal reactions. *Journal of the American Medical Association, 285,* 737.

Kimball, M. M. (1989). A new perspective on women's math achievement. *Psychological Bulletin, 105,* 198–214.

Kimble, G. A. (1956). *Principles of general psychology.* New York: Ronald.

Kimble, G. A. (1981). *Biological and cognitive constraints on learning.* Washington, DC: American Psychological Association.

King, R. N., & Koehler, D. J. (2000). Illusory correlations in graphological interference. *Journal of Experimental Psychology: Applied, 6,* 336–348.

Kinnier, R. T., & Metha, A. T. (1989). Regrets and priorities at three stages of life. *Counseling and Values, 33,* 182–193.

Kinsey, A. C., Pomeroy, W., & Martin, C. (1948). *Sexual behavior in the human male.* Philadelphia: Saunders.

Kinsey, A. C., Pomeroy, W., Martin, C., & Gebhard, P. (1953). *Sexual behavior in the human female.* Philadelphia: Saunders.

Kirby, D. (2002). Effective approaches to reducing adolescent unprotected sex, pregnancy, and childbearing. *Journal of Sex Research, 39,* 51–57.

Kirkpatrick, L. (1999). Attachment and religious representations and behavior. In J. Cassidy & P. R. Shaver (Eds.), *Handbook of attachment.* New York: Guilford.

Kirsch, I. (1996). Hypnotic enhancement of cognitive-behavioral weight loss treatments: Another meta-reanalysis. *Journal of Consulting and Clinical Psychology, 64,* 517–519.

Kirsch, I., & Braffman, W. (2001). Imaginative suggestibility and hypnotizability. *Current Directions in Psychological Science, 10,* 57–61.

Kirsch, I., & Lynn, S. J. (1995). The altered state of hypnosis. *American Psychologist, 50,* 846–858.

Kirsch, I., & Lynn, S. J. (1998a). Dissociation theories of hypnosis. *Psychological Bulletin, 123,* 100–115.

Kirsch, I., & Lynn, S. J. (1998b). Social-cognitive alternatives to dissociation theories of hypnotic induction. *Review of General Psychology, 2,* 66–80.

Kirsch, I., & Lynn, S. J. (1999). Automaticity in clinical psychology. *American Psychologist, 54,* 504–515.

Kirsch, I., Montgomery, G., & Sapirstein, G. (1995). Hypnosis as an adjunct to cognitive-behavioral psychotherapy: A meta-analysis. *Journal of Consulting and Clinical Psychology, 63,* 214–220.

Kirsch, I., Moore, T. J., Scoboria, A., & Nicholls, S. S. (2002, July 15). New study finds little difference between effects of antidepressants and placebo. *Prevention and Treatment* (journals.apa.org/prevention).

Kirsch, I., & Sapirstein, G. (1998). Listening to Prozac but hearing placebo: A meta-analysis of antidepressant medication. *Prevention and Treatment, 1,* posted June 26 at (journals.apa.org/prevention/volume1).

Kisor, H. (1990). *What's that pig outdoors.* New York: Hill and Wang.

Kitayama, S., & Markus, H. R. (2000). The pursuit of happiness and the realization of sympathy: Cultural patterns of self, social relations, and well-being. In E. Diener & E. M. Suh (Eds.), *Subjective well-being across cultures.* Cambridge, MA: MIT Press.

Kite, M. E., & Whitley, B. E., Jr. (1996). Sex differences in attitudes toward homosexual persons, behaviors, and civil rights: A meta-analysis. *Personality and Social Psychology Bulletin, 22,* 336–353.

Kivimaki, M., Leino-Arjas, P., Luukkonen, R., Rihimaki, H., & Kirjonen, J. (2002). Work stress and risk of cardiovascular mortality: Prospective cohort study of industrial employees. *British Medical Journal, 325,* 857.

Klayman, J., & Ha, Y-W. (1987). Confirmation, disconfirmation, and information in hypothesis testing. *Psychological Review, 94,* 211–228.

Klein, D. N., & 16 others (2003). Therapeutic alliance in depression treatment: Controlling for prior change and patient characteristics. *Journal of Consulting and Clinical Psychology, 71,* 997–1006.

Klein, E., Kreinin, I., Chistyakov, A., Koren, D., Mecz, L., Marmur, S., Ben-Shachar, D., & Feinsod, M. (1999). Therapeutic efficacy of right prefrontal slow repetitive transcranial magnetic stimulation in major depression. *Archives of General Psychiatry, 56,* 315–320.

Klein, S. B., & Kihlstrom, J. F. (1998). On bridging the gap between social-personality psychology and neuropsychology. *Personality and Social Psychology Review, 2,* 228–242.

Kleinfeld, J. (1998). The myth that schools shortchange girls: Social science in the service of deception. Washington, DC: Women's Freedom Network. Available from ERIC, Document ED423210, and via www.uaf.edu/northern/schools/myth.html

Kleinke, C. L., Peterson, T. R., & Rutledge, T. R. (1998). Effects of self-generated facial expressions on mood. *Journal of Personality and Social Psychology, 74,* 272–279.

Kleinmuntz, B., & Szucko, J. J. (1984). A field study of the fallibility of polygraph lie detection. *Nature, 308,* 449–450.

Kleitman, N. (1960, November). Patterns of dreaming. *Scientific American,* pp. 82–88.

Klemm, W. R. (1990). Historical and introductory perspectives on brain-stem-mediated behaviors. In W. R. Klemm & R. P. Vertes (Eds.), *Brainstem mechanisms of behavior.* New York: Wiley.

Kline, D., & Schieber, F. (1985). Vision and aging. In J. E. Birren & K. W. Schaie (Eds.), *Handbook of the psychology of aging.* New York: Van Nostrand Reinhold.

Kline, G. H., Stanley, S. M., Markman, J. H., Olmos-Gallo, P. A., St. Peters, M., Whitton, S. W., & Prado, L. M. (2004). Timing is everything: Pre-engagement cohabitation and increased risk for poor marital outcomes. *Journal of Family Psychology, 18,* 311–318.

Kline, N. S. (1974). *From sad to glad.* New York: Ballantine Books.

Klineberg, O. (1938). Emotional expression in Chinese literature. *Journal of Abnormal and Social Psychology, 33,* 517–520.

Klineberg, O. (1984). Public opinion and nuclear war. *American Psychologist, 39,* 1245–1253.

Klinke, R., Kral, A., Heid, S., Tillein, J., & Hartmann, R. (1999). Recruitment of the auditory cortex in congenitally deaf cats by long-term cochlear electrostimulation. *Science, 285,* 1729–1733.

Kluft, R. P. (1991). Multiple personality disorder. In A. Tasman & S. M. Goldfinger (Eds.), *Review of Psychiatry,* (Vol. 10). Washington, DC: American Psychiatric Press.

Klüver, H., & Bucy, P. C. (1939). Preliminary analysis of functions of the temporal lobes in monkeys. *Archives of Neurology and Psychiatry, 42,* 979–1000.

Knapp, M., Mangalore, R., & Simon, J. (2004). The global costs of schizophrenia. *Schizophrenia Bulletin, 30,* 279–293.

Knapp, S., & VandeCreek, L. (2000, August). Recovered memories of childhood abuse: Is there an underlying professional consensus? *Professional Psychology: Research and Practice, 31,* 365–371.

Knecht, S., Floeel, A., Draeger, B., Breitenstein, C., Sommer, J., Henningsen, H., Ringelstein, E. F., & Pascual-Leone, A. (2002). Degree of language lateralization determines susceptibility to unilateral brain lesions. *Nature Neuroscience, 5,* 695–699.

Knickmeyer, E. (2001, August 7). In Africa, big is definitely better. Associated Press (*Seattle Times,* p. A7).

Knight, W. (2004, August 2). Animated face helps deaf with phone chat. *NewScientist.com.*

Koenig, H. (2002, October 9). Personal communication, from Director of Center for the Study of Religion/Spirituality and Health, Duke University.

Koenig, H. G., & Larson, D. B. (1998). Use of hospital services, religious attendance, and religious affiliation. *Southern Medical Journal, 91,* 925–932.

Koenig, L. B., McGue, M., Krueger, R. F., & Bouchard, T. J., Jr. (2005). Genetic and environmental influences on religiousness: Findings for retrospective and current religiousness ratings. *Journal of Personality, 73,* 471–488.

Koestner, R., Lekes, N., Powers, T. A., & Chicoine, E. (2002). Attaining personal goals: Self-concordance plus implementation intentions equals success. *Journal of Personality and Social Psychology, 83,* 231–244.

Kohlberg, L. (1981). *The philosophy of moral development: Essays on moral development* (Vol. I). San Francisco: Harper & Row.

Kohlberg, L. (1984). *The psychology of moral development: Essays on moral development* (Vol. II). San Francisco: Harper & Row.

Kohler, I. (1962, May). Experiments with goggles. *Scientific American,* pp. 62–72.

Köhler, W. (1925; reprinted 1957). *The mentality of apes.* London: Pelican.

Kohn, P. M., & Macdonald, J. E. (1992). The survey of recent life experiences: A decontaminated hassles scale for adults. *Journal of Behavioral Medicine, 15,* 221–236.

Kohout, J., & Wicherski, M. (2004). *2001 Doctorate employment survey,* Washington, DC: American Psychological Association.

Kolata, G. (1986). Youth suicide: New research focuses on a growing social problem. *Science, 233,* 839–841.

Kolata, G. (1987). Metabolic catch-22 of exercise regimens. *Science, 236,* 146–147.

Kolata, G. (2004, September 30). Health and money issues arise over who pays for weight loss. *New York Times* (www.nytimes.com).

Kolb, B. (1989). Brain development, plasticity, and behavior. *American Psychologist, 44,* 1203–1212.

Kolb, B., & Whishaw, I. Q. (1998). Brain plasticity and behavior. *Annual Review of Psychology, 49,* 43–64.

Kolb, B., & Whishaw, I. Q. (2006). *An introduction to brain and behavior,* 2nd edition. New York: Worth Publishers.

Kolker, K. (2002, December 8). Video violence disturbs some; others scoff at influence. *Grand Rapids Press,* pp. A1, A12.

Kolodziej, M. E., & Johnson, B. T. (1996). Interpersonal contact and acceptance of persons with psychiatric disorders: A research synthesis. *Journal of Consulting and Clinical Psychology, 64,* 1387–1396.

Konishi, M. (1993, April). Listening with two ears. *Scientific American,* pp. 66–73.

Koole, S., & Spijker, M. (2000). Overcoming the planning fallacy through willpower: Effects of implementation intentions on actual and predicted task-completion times. *European Journal of Social Psychology, 30,* 873–888.

Kopta, S. M., Lueger, R. J., Saunders, S. M., & Howard, K. I. (1999). Individual psychotherapy outcome and process research: Challenges leading to greater turmoil or a positive transition? *Annual Review of Psychology, 30,* 441–469.

Koriat, A., Goldsmith, M., & Pansky, A. (2000). Toward a psychology of memory accuracy. *Annual Review of Psychology, 51,* pp. 481–537.

Koss, M. P., Heise, L., & Russo, N. P. (1994). The global health burden of rape. *Psychology of Women Quarterly, 18,* 509–537.

Kosslyn, S. M., & Koenig, O. (1992). *Wet mind: The new cognitive neuroscience.* New York: Free Press.

Kosslyn, S. M., Thompson, W. L., Costantini-Ferrando, M. F., Alpert, N. M., & Spiegel, D. (2000). Hypnotic visual illusion alters color processing in the brain. *American Journal of Psychiatry, 157,* 1279–1284.

Kotchick, B. A., Shaffer, A., & Forehand, R. (2001). Adolescent sexual risk behavior: A multi-system perspective. *Clinical Psychology Review, 21,* 493–519.

Kotkin, M., Daviet, C., & Gurin, J. (1996). The *Consumer Reports* mental health survey. *American Psychologist, 51,* 1080–1082.

Kotva, H. J., & Schneider, H. G. (1990). Those "talks"—general and sexual communication between mothers and daughters. *Journal of Social Behavior and Personality, 5,* 603–613.

Kraft, C. (1978). A psychophysical approach to air safety: Simulator studies of visual illusions in night approaches. In H. L. Pick, H. W. Leibowitz, J. E. Singer, A. Steinschneider, & H. W. Stevenson (Eds.), *Psychology: From research to practice.* New York: Plenum Press.

Kraft, R. (1996, December 2, and 1994, July 20). Personal correspondence (from Otterbein College) regarding Holocaust memories.

Kraus, N., Malmfors, T., & Slovic, P. (1992). Intuitive toxicology: Expert and lay judgments of chemical risks. *Risk Analysis, 12,* 215–232.

Krauss, C. (2002, August 11). A well-rounded Canada. *New York Times* (in *Grand Rapids Press,* p. E5).

Krauss, R. M. (1998). Why do we gesture when we speak? *Current Directions in Psychology, 7,* 54–60.

Kraut, R. E., & Johnston, R. E. (1979). Social and emotional messages of smiling: An ethological approach. *Journal of Personality and Social Psychology, 37,* 1539–1553.

KRC Research & Consulting. (2001, August 7). Memory isn't quite what it used to be (survey for General Nutrition Centers). *USA Today,* p. D1.

Krebs, D. L., & Van Hesteren, F. (1994). The development of altruism: Toward an integrative model. *Developmental Review, 14,* 103–158.

Kreitner, R. (1992). *Management,* 5th ed. Boston: Houghton Mifflin.

Krijn, M., Emmelkamp, P. M. G., Olafsson, R. P., & Biemond, R. (2004). Virtual reality exposure therapy of anxiety disorders: A review. *Clinical Psychology Review, 24,* 259–281.

Kring, A. M., & Gordon, A. H. (1998). Sex differences in emotion: Expression, experience, and physiology. *Journal of Personality and Social Psychology, 74,* 686–703.

Kristof, N. D. (2004, July 21). Saying no to killers. *New York Times* (www.nytimes.com).

Kroenke, K., & Mangelsdorff, A. D. (1989). Common symptoms in ambulatory care: Incidence, evaluation, therapy, and outcome. *American Journal of Medicine, 86,* 262–266.

Kroll, R., Danis, S., Moreau, M., Waldbaum, A., Shifren, J., & Wekselman, K. (2004). Testosterone transdermal patch (TPP) significantly improved sexual function in naturally menopausal women in a large Phase III study. Presented to the American Society of Reproductive Medicine annual meeting, Philadelphia, October.

Krosnick, J. A., & Alwin, D. F. (1989). Aging and susceptibility to attitude change. *Journal of Personality and Social Psychology, 57,* 416–425.

Krosnick, J. A., Betz, A. L., Jussim, L. J., & Lynn, A. R. (1992). Subliminal conditioning of attitudes. *Personality and Social Psychology Bulletin, 18,* 152–162.

Kruger, J., & Dunning, D. (1999). Unskilled and unaware of it: How difficulties in recognizing one's own incompetence lead to inflated self-assessments. *Journal of Personality and Social Psychology, 77,* 1121–1134.

Kruger, J., Epley, N., & Gilovich, T. (1999). Egocentrism over email. Paper presented at the American Psychological Society meeting.

Krugman, P. (2003, September 14). The tax-cut con. *New York Times* (www.nytimes.com).

Krugman, P. (2005, July 4). Girth of a nation. *New York Times* (www.nytimes.com).

Krupa, D. J., Thompson, J. K., & Thompson, R. F. (1993). Localization of a memory trace in the mammalian brain. *Science, 260,* 989–991.

Krützen, M., Mann, J., Heithaus, M. R., Connor, R. C., Bejder, L., & Sherwin,, W. B. (2005). Cultural transmission of tool use in bottlenose dolphins. *Proceedings of the National Academy of Sciences, 102,* 8939–8943.

Kubey, R., & Csikszentmihalyi, M. (2002, February). Television addiction is no mere metaphor. *Scientific American,* pp. 74–80.

Kübler, A., Winter, S., Ludolph, A. C., Hautzinger, M., & Birbaumer, N. (2005). Severity of depressive symptoms and quality of life in patients with amyotrophic lateral sclerosis. *Neurorehabilitation and Neural Repair, 19*(3), 182–193.

Kubzansky, L. D., Sparrow, D., Vokanas, P., Kawachi, I. (2001). Is the glass half empty or half full? A prospective study of optimism and coronary heart disease in the normative aging study. *Psychosomatic Medicine, 63,* 910–916.

Kuhl, P. K., & Meltzoff, A. N. (1982). The bimodal perception of speech in infancy. *Science, 218,* 1138–1141.

Kujala, U. M., Kaprio, J., Sarna, S., & Koskenvuo, M. (1998). Relationship of leisure-time physical activity and mortality: The Finnish twin cohort. *Journal of the American Medical Association, 279,* 440–444.

Kulkin, H. S., Chauvin, E. A., & Percle, G. A. (2000). Suicide among gay and lesbian adolescents and young adults: A review of the literature. *Journal of Homosexuality, 40,* 1–29.

Kuncel, N. R., Nezlett, S. A., & Ones, D. S. (2004). Academic performance, career potential, creativity, and job performance: Can one construct predict them all? *Journal of Personality and Social Psychology, 86*, 148–161.

Kunkel, D. (2001, February 4). *Sex on TV.* Menlo Park, CA: Henry J. Kaiser Family Foundation (www.kff.org).

Kunkel, D., Cope-Farrar, K., Biely, E., Farinola, W. J. M., & Donnerstein, E. (2001). *Sex on TV (2): A biennial report to the Kaiser Family Foundation.* Menlo Park, CA: Kaiser Family Foundation.

Kurtz, P. (1983, Spring). Stars, planets, and people. *The Skeptical Inquirer,* pp. 65–68.

Kushner, H. (1986). Quoted by J. Viorst, *Necessary losses.* New York: Fawcett, p. 295.

Kutas, M. (1990). Event-related brain potential (ERP) studies of cognition during sleep: Is it more than a dream? In R. R. Bootzin, J. F. Kihlstrom, & D. Schacter (Eds.), *Sleep and cognition.* Washington, DC: American Psychological Association.

Kvavilashvili, L., Mirani, J., Schlagman, S., & Kornbrot, D. E. (2003). Comparing flashbulb memories of September 11 and the death of Princess Diana: Effects of time delays and nationality. *Applied Cognitive Psychology, 17,* 1017–1031.

Labouvie-Vief, G., & Schell, D. A. (1982). Learning and memory in later life. In B. B. Wolman (Ed.), *Handbook of developmental psychology.* Englewood Cliffs, NJ: Prentice-Hall.

Lacayo, R. (1995, June 12). Violent reaction. *Time,* pp. 25–39.

Lacey, M. (2004. April 9). A decade after massacres, Rwanda outlaws ethnicity. *New York Times* (www.nytimes.com).

Lachman, M. E. (2004). Development in midlife. *Annual Review of Psychology, 55,* 305–331.

Lachman, M. E., & Weaver, S. L. (1998). The sense of control as a moderator of social class differences in health and well-being. *Journal of Personality and Social Psychology, 74,* 763–773.

Ladd, E. C. (1998, August/September). The tobacco bill and American public opinion. *The Public Perspective,* pp. 5–19.

Ladd, G. T. (1887). *Elements of physiological psychology.* New York: Scribner's.

Laird, J. D. (1974). Self-attribution of emotion: The effects of expressive behavior on the quality of emotional experience. *Journal of Personality and Social Psychology, 29,* 475–486.

Laird, J. D. (1984). The real role of facial response in the experience of emotion: A reply to Tourangeau and Ellsworth, and others. *Journal of Personality and Social Psychology, 47,* 909–917.

Laird, J. D., Cuniff, M., Sheehan, K., Shulman, D., & Strum, G. (1989). Emotion specific effects of facial expressions on memory for life events. *Journal of Social Behavior and Personality, 4,* 87–98.

Lakin, J. L., & Chartrand, T. L. (2003). Using nonconscious behavioral mimicry to create affiliation and rapport. *Psychological Science, 14,* 334–339.

Lalumière, M. L., Blanchard, R., & Zucker, K. J. (2000). Sexual orientation and handedness in men and women: A meta-analysis. *Psychological Bulletin, 126,* 575–592.

Lambert, W. E. (1992). Challenging established views on social issues: The power and limitations of research. *American Psychologist, 47,* 533–542.

Lambert, W. E., Genesee, F., Holobow, N., & Chartrand, L. (1993). Bilingual education for majority English-speaking children. *European Journal of Psychology of Education, 8,* 3–22.

Lamberth, J. (1998, August 6). Driving while black: A statistician proves that prejudice still rules the road. *Washington Post,* p. C1.

Lammers, W. (2000). Quick tips for applying to graduate school in psychology. *Eye on Psi Chi, 4*(3), 40–42.

Lampinen, J. M. (2002). What exactly is déjà vu? *Scientific American* (scieam.com/askexpert/biology/biology63).

Landau, M. J., Solomon, S., Greenberg, J., Cohen, F., Pyszczynski, T., Arndt, J., Miller, C. H., Ogilvie, D. M., & Cook, A. (2004). Deliver us from evil: The effects of mortality salience and reminders of 9/11 on support for President George W. Bush. *Personality and Social Psychology Bulletin, 30,* 1136–1150.

Landauer, T. (2001, September). Quoted by R. Herbert, You must remember this. *APS Observer,* p. 11.

Landauer, T. K. (1986). How much do people remember? Some estimates of the quantity of learned information in long-term memory. *Cognitive Science, 10,* 477–493.

Landauer, T. K., & Whiting, J. W. M. (1979). Correlates and consequences of stress in infancy. In R. Munroe, B. Munroe & B. Whiting (Eds.), *Handbook of Cross-Cultural Human Development.* New York: Garland.

Landers, A. (1969, April 8). Syndicated newspaper column. Cited by L. Berkowitz, The case for bottling up rage. *Psychology Today,* September, 1973, pp. 24–31.

Landrum, E. (2001). I'm getting my bachelor's degree in psychology. What can I do with it? *Eye on Psi Chi,* 22–24.

Landry, M. J. (2002). MDMA: A review of epidemiologic data. *Journal of Psychoactive Drugs, 34,* 163–169.

Lang, E. V., Benotsch, E. G., Fick, L. J., Lutgendorf, S., Berbaum, M. L., Logan, H., & Spiegel, D. (2000). Adjunctive non-pharmacological analgesia for invasive medical procedures: A randomised trial. *Lancet, 355,* 1486–1490.

Langer, E. J. (1983). *The psychology of control.* Beverly Hills, CA: Sage.

Langer, E. J., & Abelson, R. P. (1974). A patient by any other name . . . : Clinician group differences in labeling bias. *Journal of Consulting and Clinical Psychology, 42,* 4–9.

Langer, E. J., & Imber, L. (1980). The role of mindlessness in the perception of deviance. *Journal of Personality and Social Psychology, 39,* 360–367.

Langleben, D. D., Schroeder, L., Maldjian, J. A., Gur, R. C., McDonald, S., Ragland, J. D., O'Brien, C. P., & Childress, A. R. (2002). Brain activity during simulated deception: An event-related functional magnetic resonance study. *NeuroImage, 15,* 727–732.

Langlois, J. H., Kalakanis, L., Rubenstein, A. J., Larson, A., Hallam, M., & Smoot, M. (2000). Maxims or myths of beauty? A meta-analytic and theoretical review. *Psychological Bulletin, 126,* 390–423.

Langlois, J. H., & Roggman, L. A. (1990). Attractive faces are only average. *Psychological Science, 1,* 115–121.

Langlois, J. H., Roggman, L. A., Casey, R. J., Ritter, J. M., Rieser-Danner, L. A., & Jenkins, V. Y. (1987). Infant preferences for attractive faces: Rudiments of a stereotype? *Developmental Psychology, 23,* 363–369.

Larkin, K., Resko, J. A., Stormshak, F., Stellflug, J. N., & Roselli, C. E. (2002). Neuroanatomical correlates of sex and sexual partner preference in sheep. Society for Neuroscience convention.

Larrance, D. T., & Twentyman, C. T. (1983). Maternal attributions and child abuse. *Journal of Abnormal Psychology, 92,* 449–457.

Larsen, R. J. (2004). Emotion and cognition: The case of automatic vigilance. *Psychological Science Agenda, 18* (www.apa.org/science/psa/sb-larsenprt.html).

Larsen, R. J., & Diener, E. (1987). Affect intensity as an individual difference characteristic: A review. *Journal of Research in Personality, 21,* 1–39.

Larsen, R. J., Diener, E., & Cropanzano, R. S. (1987). Cognitive operations associated with individual differences in affect intensity. *Journal of Personality and Social Psychology, 53,* 767–774.

Larsen, R. J., Kasimatis, M., & Frey, K. (1992). Facilitating the furrowed brow: An unobtrusive test of the facial feedback hypothesis applied to unpleasant affect. *Cognition and Emotion, 6,* 321–338.

Larson, R. W. (2001). How U.S. children and adolescents spend time: What it does (and doesn't) tell us about their development. *Current Directions in Psychological Science, 10,* 160–164.

Larson, R. W., & Verma, S. (1999). How children and adolescents spend time across the world: Work, play, and developmental opportunities. *Psychological Bulletin, 125,* 701–736.

Larzelere, R. E. (1996). A review of the outcomes of parental use of nonabusive or customary physical punishment. *Pediatrics, 78,* 824–828.

Larzelere, R. E. (1999). The intervention selection bias. Unpublished manuscript. Boys Town, NE: Boys Town.

Larzelere, R. E. (2000). Child outcomes of non-abusive and customary physical punishment by parents: An updated literature review. *Clinical Child and Family Psychology Review, 3,* 199–221.

Larzelere, R. E., Kuhn, B. R., & Johnson, B. (2004). The intervention selection bias: An underrecognized confound in intervention research. *Psychological Bulletin, 130,* 289–303.

Lashley, K. S. (1950). In search of the engram. In *Symposium of the Society for Experimental Biology* (Vol. 4). New York: Cambridge University Press.

Lassiter, G. D., & Irvine, A. A. (1986). Video-taped confessions: The impact of camera point of view on judgments of coercion. *Journal of Personality and Social Psychology, 16,* 268–276.

Latané, B. (1981). The psychology of social impact. *American Psychologist, 36,* 343–356.

Latané, B., & Dabbs, J. M., Jr. (1975). Sex, group size and helping in three cities. *Sociometry, 38,* 180–194.

Laudenslager, M. L., & Reite, M. L. (1984). Losses and separations: Immunological consequences and health implications. *Review of Personality and Social Psychology, 5,* 285–312.

Laumann, E. O., Gagnon, J. H., Michael, R. T., & Michaels, S. (1994). *The social organization of sexuality: Sexual practices in the United States.* Chicago: University of Chicago Press.

Lazarus, R. S. (1990). Theory-based stress measurement. *Psychological Inquiry, 1,* 3–13.

Lazarus, R. S. (1991). Progress on a cognitive-motivational-relational theory of emotion. *American Psychologist, 46,* 352–367.

Lazarus. R. S. (1998). *Fifty years of the research and theory of R. S. Lazarus: An analysis of historical and perennial issues.* Mahwah, NJ: Erlbaum.

Lea, S. E. G. (2000). Towards an ethical use of animals. *The Psychologist, 13,* 556–557.

Leach, P. (1993). Should parents hit their children? *The Psychologist: Bulletin of the British Psychological Society, 6,* 216–220.

Leach, P. (1994). *Children first.* New York: Knopf.

Leary, M. R. (1999). The social and psychological importance of self-esteem. In R. M. Kowalski & M. R. Leary (Eds.), *The social psychology of emotional and behavioral problems.* Washington, DC: APA Books.

Leary, M. R., Haupt, A. L., Strausser, K. S., & Chokel, J. T. (1998). Calibrating the sociometer: The relationship between interpersonal appraisals and state self-esteem. *Journal of Personality and Social Psychology, 74,* 1290–1299.

Leary, M. R., Schreindorfer, L. S., & Haupt, A. L. (1995). The role of low self-esteem in emotional and behavioral problems: Why is low self-esteem dysfunctional? *Journal of Social and Clinical Psychology, 14,* 297–314.

Leary, W. E. (1998, September 28). Older people enjoy sex, survey says. *New York Times* (www.nytimes.com).

LeDoux, J. (1996). *The emotional brain: The mysterious underpinnings of emotional life.* New York: Simon & Schuster.

LeDoux, J. E. (2002). *The synaptic self.* London: Macmillan.

LeDoux, J. E., & Armony, J. (1999). Can neurobiology tell us anything about human feelings? In D. Kahneman, E. Diener, & N. Schwartz (Eds.), *Well-being: The foundations of hedonic psychology.* New York: Sage.

Lee, K., Byatt, G., & Rhodes, G. (2000). Caricature effects, distinctiveness, and identification: Testing the face-space framework. *Psychological Science, 11,* 379–385.

Lefcourt, H. M. (1982). *Locus of control: Current trends in theory and research.* Hillsdale, NJ: Erlbaum.

Legrand, L. N., Iacono, W. G., & McGue, M. (2005). Predicting addiction. *American Scientist, 93,* 140–147.

Le Grand, R., Mondloch, C. J., Maurer, D., & Brent, H. P. (2004). Impairment in holistic face processing following early visual deprivation. *Psychological Science, 15,* 762–768.

Lehman, A. F., Steinwachs, D. M., Dixon, L. B., Goldman, H. H., Osher, F., Postrado, L., Scott, J. E., Thompson, J. W., Fahey, M., Fischer, P., Kasper, J. A., Lyles, A., Skinner, E. A., Buchanan, R., Carpenter, W. T., Jr., Levine, J., McGlynn, E. A., Rosenheck, R., & Zito, J. (1998). Translating research into practice: The schizophrenia patient outcomes research team (PORT) treatment recommendations. *Schizophrenia Bulletin, 24,* 1–10.

Lehman, D. R., Lempert, R. O., & Nisbett, R. E. (1988). The effects of graduate training on reasoning: Formal discipline and thinking about everyday-life events. *American Psychologist, 43,* 431–442.

Lehman, D. R., & Nisbett, R. E. (1985). Effects of higher education on inductive reasoning. Unpublished manuscript, University of Michigan.

Lehman, D. R., Wortman, C. B., & Williams, A. F. (1987). Long-term effects of losing a spouse or child in a motor vehicle crash. *Journal of Personality and Social Psychology, 52,* 218–231.

Leibowitz, H. W. (1985). Grade crossing accidents and human factors engineering. *American Scientist, 73,* 558–562.

Leigh, B. C. (1989). In search of the seven dwarves: Issues of measurement and meaning in alcohol expectancy research. *Psychological Bulletin, 105,* 361–373.

Leitenberg, H., & Henning, K. (1995). Sexual fantasy. *Psychological Bulletin, 117,* 469–496.

Lemonick, M. D. (2002, June 3). Lean and hungrier. *Time,* p. 54.

L'Engle, M. (1972). *A wind in the door.* Bantam Doubleday Dell Books for Young Readers.

Lennox, B. R., Bert, S., Park, G., Jones, P. B., & Morris, P. G. (1999). Spatial and temporal mapping of neural activity associated with auditory hallucinations. *Lancet, 353,* 644.

Lenzenweger, M. F., Dworkin, R. H., & Wethington, E. (1989). Models of positive and negative symptoms in schizophrenia: An empirical evaluation of latent structures. *Journal of Abnormal Psychology, 98,* 62–70.

Leonhardt, D. (2004, August 17). Top athletes may be running into a tall hurdle: Themselves. *New York Times* (www.nytimes.com).

Lerman, C., Caporaso, N. E., Audrain, J., Main, D., Bowman, E. D., Lockshin, B., Boyd, N. R., & Shields, P. G. (1999). Evidence suggesting the role of specific genetic factors in cigarette smoking. *Health Psychology, 18,* 14–20.

Lerner, J. S, Gonzalez, R. M., Small, D. A., & Fischhoff, B. (2002). Effects of Fear and Anger on Perceived Risks of Terrorism: A National Field Experiment. *Psychological Science, 14(2),* 144–150.

Lerner, M. J. (1980). *The belief in a just world: A fundamental delusion.* New York: Plenum Press.

Leserman, J., Jackson, E. D., Petitto, J. M., Golden, R. N., Silva, S. G., Perkins, D. O., Cai, J., Folds, J. D., & Evans, D. L. (1999). Progression to AIDS: The effects of stress, depressive symptoms, and social support. *Psychosomatic Medicine, 61,* 397–406.

Lessard, N., Pare, M., Lepore, F., & Lassonde, M. (1998). Early-blind human subjects localize sound sources better than sighted subjects. *Nature, 395,* 278–280.

Lester, W. (2004, May 26). AP polls: Nations value immigrant workers. Associated Press release.

Leucht, S., Barnes, T. R. E., Kissling, W., Engel, R. R., Correll, C., & Kane, J. M. (2003). Relapse prevention in schizophrenia with new-generation antipsychotics: A systematic review and exploratory meta-analysis of randomized, controlled trials. *American Journal of Psychiatry, 160,* 1209–1222.

LeVay, S. (1991). A difference in hypothalamic structure between heterosexual and homosexual men. *Science, 253,* 1034–1037.

LeVay, S. (1994, March). Quoted in D. Nimmons, Sex and the brain. *Discover,* pp. 64–71.

Levenson, R. W. (1992). Autonomic nervous system differences among emotions. *Psychological Science, 3,* 23–27.

Leventhal, T., & Brooks-Gunn, J. (2000). The neighborhoods they live in: The effects of neighborhood residence on child and adolescent outcomes. *Psychological Bulletin, 126,* 309–337.

Lever, J. (2003, November 11). Personal correspondence reporting data responses volunteered to *Elle/MSNBC.com* survey of weight perceptions.

Levesque, M. J., & Kenny, D. A. (1993). Accuracy of behavioral predictions at zero acquaintance: A social relations analysis. *Journal of Personality and Social Psychology, 65,* 1178–1187.

Levin, I. P., & Gaeth, G. J. (1988). How consumers are affected by the framing of attribute information before and after consuming the product. *Journal of Consumer Research, 15,* 374–378.

Levine, J. A., Eberhardt, N. L., & Jensen, M. D. (1999). Role of nonexercise activity thermogenesis in resistance to fat gain in humans. *Science, 283,* 212–214.

Levine, J. A., Lanningham-Foster, L. M., McCrady, S. K., Krizan, A. C., Olson, L. R., Kane, P. H., Jensen, M. D., & Clark, M. M. (2005). Interindividual variation in posture allocation: Possible role in human obesity. *Science, 307,* 584–586.

Levine, R., Sato, S., Hashimoto, T., & Verma, J. (1995). Love and marriage in eleven cultures. *Journal of Cross-Cultural Psychology, 26,* 554–571.

Levine, R. V., & Norenzayan, A. (1999). The pace of life in 31 countries. *Journal of Cross-Cultural Psychology, 30,* 178–205.

Levy, B., & Langer, E. (1992). Avoidance of the memory loss stereotype: Enhanced memory among the elderly deaf. American Psychological Association convention, Washington, DC.

Levy, P. E. (2003). *Industrial/organizational psychology: Understanding the workplace.* Boston: Houghton Mifflin.

Lewicki, P., Hill, T., & Czyzewska, M. (1992). Nonconscious acquisition of information. *American Psychologist, 47,* 796–801.

Lewicki, P., Hill, T., & Czyzewska, M. (1997). Hidden covariation detection: A fundamental and ubiquitous phenomenon. *Journal of Experimental Psychology: Learning, Memory, and Cognition, 23,* 221–228.

Lewinsohn, P. M., Hoberman, H., Teri, L., & Hautziner, M. (1985). An integrative theory of depression. In S. Reiss & R. Bootzin (Eds.), *Theoretical issues in behavior therapy.* Orlando, FL: Academic Press.

Lewinsohn, P. M., Rohde, P., & Seeley, J. R. (1998). Major depressive disorder in older adolescents: Prevalence, risk factors, and clinical implications. *Clinical Psychology Review, 18,* 765–794.

Lewinsohn, P. M., & Rosenbaum, M. (1987). Recall of parental behavior by acute depressives, remitted depressives, and nondepressives. *Journal of Personality and Social Psychology, 52,* 611–619.

Lewis, C. S. (1960). *Mere Christianity.* New York: Macmillan.

Lewis, C. S. (1967). *Christian reflections.* Grand Rapids, MI: Eerdmans.

Lewis, D. O., Pincus, J. H., Bard, B., Richardson, E., Prichep, L. S., Feldman, M., & Yeager, C. (1988). Neuropsychiatric, psychoeducational, and family characteristics of 14 juveniles condemned to death in the United States. *American Journal of Psychiatry, 145,* 584–589.

Lewis, D. O., Pincus, J. H., Feldman, M., Jackson, L., & Bard, B. (1986). Psychiatric, neurological, and psychoeducational characteristics of 15 death row inmates in the United States. *American Journal of Psychiatry, 143,* 838–845.

Lewis, D. O., Yeager, C. A., Swica, Y., Pincus, J. H., & Lewis, M. (1997). Objective documentation of child abuse and dissociation in 12 murderers with dissociative identity disorder. *American Journal of Psychiatry, 154,* 1703–1710.

Lewis, M. (1992). Commentary. *Human Development, 35,* 44–51.

Lewontin, R. (1976). Race and intelligence. In N. J. Block & G. Dworkin (Eds.), *The IQ controversy: Critical readings.* New York: Pantheon.

Lewontin, R. (1982). *Human diversity.* New York: Scientific American Library.

Li, J. C., Dunning, D., & Malpass, R. L. (1996). Cross-racial identification among European-Americans Basketball fandom and the contact hypothesis. Unpublished manuscript, Cornell University.

Li, J., Laursen, T. M., Precht, D. H., Olsen, J., & Mortensen, P. B. (2005). Hospitalization for mental illness among parents after the death of a child. *New England Journal of Medicine, 352,* 1190–1196.

Libet, B. (1985). Unconscious cerebral initiative and the role of conscious will in voluntary action. *Behavioral and Brain Sciences, 12,* 181–187.

Libet, B. (2004). Mind time: The temporal factor in consciousness. Cambridge, MA: Harvard University Press.

Licata, A., Taylor, S., Berman, M., & Cranston, J. (1993). Effects of cocaine on human aggression. *Pharmacology Biochemistry and Behavior, 45,* 549–552.

Lichtman, S. W., Pisarska, K., Berman, E. R., Pestone, M., Dowling, H., Offenbacher, E., Weisel, H., Heshka, S., Matthews, D. E., & Heymsfield, S. B. (1992). Discrepancy between self-reported and actual caloric intake and exercise in obese subjects. *New England Journal of Medicine, 327,* 1893–1898.

Lieberman, J. A., & 11 others (2005). Effectiveness of antipsychotic drugs in patients with chronic schizophrenia. *New England Journal of Medicine, 353,* 1209–1223.

Lilienfeld, S. O. (1998). Pseudoscience in contemporary clinical psychology: What it is and what we can do about it. *The Clinical Psychologist, 51*(4), 3–5.

Lilienfeld, S. O., Lynn, S. J., Kirsch, I., Chaves, J. F., Sarbin, T. R., Ganaway, G. K., & Powell, R. A. (1999). Dissociative identity disorder and the sociocognitive model: Recalling the lessons of the past. *Psychological Bulletin, 125,* 507–523.

Lilienfeld, S. O., Wood, J. M., & Garb, H. N. (2000). The scientific status of projective techniques. *Psychological Science in the Public Interest, 1,* 27–66.

Lilienfeld, S. O., Wood, J. M., & Garb, H. N. (2001, May). What's wrong with this picture? *Scientific American,* pp. 81–87.

Lin, L., Faraco, J., Li, R., Kadotani, H., Rogers, W., Lin, X., Qiu, X., de Jong, P. J., Nishino, S., & Mignot E. (1999). The sleep disorder canine narcolepsy is caused by a mutation in the hypocretin (orexin) receptor 2 gene. *Cell, 98,* 365–376.

Lincoln, C. (2001). *Sap Rising,* Pantheon Books.

Linde, K., & 10 others (2005). Acupuncture for patients with migraine: A randomized controlled trial. *Journal of the American Medical Association, 293,* 2118–2125.

Linder, D. (1982). Social trap analogs: The tragedy of the commons in the laboratory. In V. J. Derlega & J. Grzelak (Eds.), *Cooperative and helping behavior: Theories and research.* New York: Academic Press.

Lindskold, S. (1978). Trust development, the GRIT proposal, and the effects of conciliatory acts on conflict and cooperation. *Psychological Bulletin, 85,* 772–793.

Lindskold, S., & Han, G. (1988). GRIT as a foundation for integrative bargaining. *Personality and Social Psychology Bulletin, 14,* 335–345.

Linville, P. W., Fischer, G. W., & Fischhoff, B. (1992). AIDS risk perceptions and decision biases. In J. B. Pryor & G. D. Reeder (Eds.), *The social psychology of HIV infection.* Hillsdale, NJ: Erlbaum.

Lippa, R. A. (2002). Gender-related traits of heterosexual and homosexual men and women. *Archives of Sexual Behavior, 31,* 83–98.

Lippman, J. (1992, October 25). Global village is characterized by a television in every home. *Los Angeles Times* Syndicate (in *Grand Rapids Press*, p. F9).

Lipps, H. M. (1999). *A new psychology of women: Gender, culture, and ethnicity.* Mountain View, CA: Mayfield Publishing.

Lipsey, M. W., & Wilson, D. B. (1993). The efficacy of psychological, educational, and behavioral treatment: Confirmation from meta-analyses. *American Psychologist, 48,* 1181–1209.

Lipsitt, L. P. (2003). Crib death: A biobehavioral phenomenon? *Current Directions in Psychological Science, 12,* 164–170.

Lipton, J. S., & Spelke, E. S. (2003). Origins of number sense: Large-number discrimination in human infants. *Psychological Science, 14,* 296–401.

Livingstone, M., & Hubel, D. (1988). Segregation of form, color, movement, and depth: Anatomy, physiology, and perception. *Science, 240,* 740–749.

Lock, M. (1998). Menopause: Lessons from anthropology. *Psychosomatic Medicine, 60,* 410–419.

Locke, E. A., & Latham, G. P. (2002). Building a practically useful theory of goal setting and task motivation. *American Psychologist, 57,* 705–717.

Loehlin, J. C., McCrae, R. R., & Costa, P. T., Jr. (1998). Heritabilities of common and measure-specific components of the Big Five personality factors. *Journal of Research in Personality, 32,* 431–453.

Loehlin, J. C., & Nichols, R. C. (1976). *Heredity, environment, and personality.* Austin: University of Texas Press.

Loewenstein, G., & Furstenberg, F. (1991). Is teenage sexual behavior rational? *Journal of Applied Social Psychology, 21,* 957–986.

Loftus, E. F. (1979). The malleability of human memory. *American Scientist, 67,* 313–320.

Loftus, E. (1995, March/April). Remembering dangerously. *Skeptical Inquirer,* pp. 20–29.

Loftus, E. F. (1980). *Memory: Surprising new insights into how we remember and why we forget.* Reading, MA: Addison-Wesley.

Loftus, E. F. (1993). The reality of repressed memories. *American Psychologist, 48,* 518–537.

Loftus, E. F. (2001, November). Imagining the past. *The Psychologist, 14,* 584–587.

Loftus, E. F., Coan, J., & Pickrell, J. E. (1996). Manufacturing false memories using bits of reality. In L. Reder (Ed.), *Implicit memory and metacognition.* Mahway, NJ: Erlbaum.

Loftus, E. F., & Kaufman, L. (1992). Why do traumatic experiences sometimes produce good memory (flashbulbs) and sometimes no memory (repression)? In E. Winograd & U. Neisser (Eds.), *Affect and accuracy in recall: Studies of "flashbulb" memories.* New York: Cambridge University Press.

Loftus, E. F., & Ketcham, K. (1994). *The myth of repressed memory.* New York: St. Martin's Press.

Loftus, E. F., Levidow, B., & Duensing, S. (1992). Who remembers best? Individual differences in memory for events that occurred in a science museum. *Applied Cognitive Psychology, 6,* 93–107.

Loftus, E. F., & Loftus, G. R. (1980). On the permanence of stored information in the human brain. *American Psychologist, 35,* 409–420.

Loftus, E. F., Milo, E. M., & Paddock, J. R. (1995). The accidental executioner: Why psychotherapy must be informed by science. *The Counseling Psychologist, 23,* 300–309.

Loftus, E. F., & Palmer, J. C. (October, 1974). Reconstruction of automobile destruction: An example of the interaction between language and memory. *Journal of Verbal Learning & Verbal Behavior, 13*(5), 585–589.

Loftus, E. F. (1992). When a lie becomes memory's truth: Memory distortion after exposure to misinformation. *Current Directions in Psychological Science, 1,* 121–123.

Logan, T. K., Walker, R., Cole, J., & Leukefeld, C. (2002). Victimization and substance abuse among women: Contributing factors, interventions, and implications. *Review of General Psychology, 6,* 325–397.

Logothetis, N. K., & Schall, J. D. (1989). Neuronal correlates of subjective visual perception. *Science, 245,* 761–763.

Logue, A. W. (1998a). Laboratory research on self-control: Applications to administration. *Review of General Psychology, 2,* 221–238.

Logue, A. W. (1998b). Self-control. In W. T. O'Donohue, (Ed.), *Learning and behavior therapy.* Boston, MA: Allyn & Bacon.

London, P. (1970). The rescuers: Motivational hypotheses about Christians who saved Jews from the Nazis. In J. Macaulay & L. Berkowitz (Eds.), *Altruism and helping behavior.* New York: Academic Press.

Looy, H. (2001). Sex differences: Evolved, constructed, and designed. *Journal of Psychology and Theology, 29,* 301–313.

Lopes, P. N., Brackett, M. A., Nezlek, J. B., Sch_tz, A., Sellin, Il, & Salovey, P. (2004). Emotional intelligence and social interaction. *Personality and Social Psychology Bulletin, 30,* 1018–1034.

Lopez, A. D. (1999). Measuring the health hazards of tobacco: Commentary. *Bulletin of the World Health Organization, 77*(1), 82–83.

Lopez, D. J. (2002, January/February). Snaring the fowler: Mark Twain debunks phrenology. *Skeptical Inquirer* (www.csicop.org).

Lord, C. G., Lepper, M. R., & Preston, E. (1984). Considering the opposite: A corrective strategy for social judgment. *Journal of Personality and Social Psychology, 47,* 1231–1247.

Lord, C. G., Ross, L., & Lepper, M. (1979). Biased assimilation and attitude polarization: The effects of prior theories on subsequently considered evidence. *Journal of Personality and Social Psychology, 37,* 2098–2109.

Lorenz, K. (1937). The companion in the bird's world. *Auk, 54,* 245–273.

Los Angeles Times (1998, 14 March). Daughters give birth on same day, p. A15.

Louie, K., & Wilson, M. A. (2001). Temporally structured replay of awake hippocampal ensemble activity during rapid eye movement sleep. *Neuron, 29,* 145–156.

Lourenco, O., & Machado, A. (1996). In defense of Piaget's theory: A reply to 10 common criticisms. *Psychological Review, 103,* 143–164.

Lovaas, O. I. (1987). Behavioral treatment and normal educational and intellectual functioning in young autistic children. *Journal of Consulting and Clinical Psychology, 55,* 3–9.

Love, J. M., & 13 others (2003). Child care quality matters: How conclusions may vary with context. *Child Development, 74,* 1021–1033.

Love, S. M. (2002, July 16). Preventive medicine, properly practiced. *New York Times* (www.nytimes.com).

Lowry, P. E. (1997). The assessment center process: New directions. *Journal of Social Behavior and Personality, 12,* 53–62.

Lu, Z.-L., Williamson, S. J., & Kaufman, L. (1992). Behavioral lifetime of human auditory sensory memory predicted by physiological measures. *Science, 258,* 1668–1670.

Lubinski, D., & Benbow, C. P. (1992). Gender differences in abilities and preferences among the gifted: Implications for the math-science pipeline. *Current Directions in Psychological Science, 1,* 61–66.

Lubinski, D., & Benbow, C. P. (2000). States of excellence. *American Psychologist, 137–150.*

Luborsky, L., Rosenthal, R., Diguer, L., Andrusyna, T. P., Berman, J. S., Levitt, J. T., Seligman, D. A., & Krause, E. D. (2002). The dodo bird verdict is alive and well—mostly. *Clinical Psychology: Science and Practice, 9,* 2–34.

Lucas, A., Morley, R., Cole, T. J., Lister, G., & Leeson-Payne, C. (1998). Breast milk and subsequent intelligence quotient in children born preterm. *Lancet, 339,* 261–264.

Lucas, R. E. (2005). Long-term disability has lasting effects on subjective well-being: Evidence from two nationally representative longitudinal studies. Unpublished manuscript, Michigan State University.

Lucas, R. E., Clark, A. E., Georgellis, Y., & Diener, E. (2003). Re-examining adaptation and the setpoint model of happiness: Reactions to changes in marital status. *Journal of Personality and Social Psychology, 84*, 527–539. (Figure courtesy of R. E. Lucas.)

Lucas, R. E., Clark, A. E., Georgellis, Y., & Diener, E. (2004). Unemployment alters the set point for life satisfaction. *Psychological Science, 15*, 8–13.

Ludwig, A. M. (1995). *The price of greatness: Resolving the creativity and madness controversy.* New York: Guilford Press.

Ludwig, J. (2004, June 1). Acceptance of interracial marriage at record high. Gallup Poll Tuesday Briefing (www.gallup.com).

Lukoff, D., Lu, F., & Turner, R. (1992). Toward a more culturally sensitive DSM-IV: Psychoreligious and psychospiritual problems. *Journal of Nervous and Mental Disease, 180*, 673–682.

Lumsden, C. J., & Wilson, E. O. (1983). *Promethean fire: Reflections on the origin of mind.* Cambridge, MA: Harvard University Press.

Luntz, F. (2003, June 10). Quoted by T. Raum, "Bush insists banned weapons will be found." Associated Press (story.news.yahoo.com).

Luria, A. M. (1968). In L. Solotaroff (Trans.), *The mind of a mnemonist.* New York: Basic Books.

Lustig, C., & Buckner, R. L. (2004). Preserved neural correlates of priming in old age and dementia. *Neuron, 42*, 865–875.

Lutgendorf, S. K., Russell, D., Ullrich, P., Harris, T. B., & Wallace, R. (2004). Religious participation, Interleukin-6, and mortality in older adults. *Health Psychology, 23*, 465–475.

Luthar, S. S., & Latendresse, S. J. (2005). Children of the affluent: Challenges to well-being. *Current Directions in Psychological Science, 14*, 49–53.

Lykken, D. T. (1982, September). Fearlessness: Its carefree charm and deadly risks. *Psychology Today,* pp. 20–28.

Lykken, D. T. (1991). Science, lies, and controversy: An epitaph for the polygraph. Invited address upon receipt of the Senior Career Award for Distinguished Contribution to Psychology in the Public Interest, American Psychological Association convention.

Lykken, D. T. (1995). *The antisocial personalities.* Hillsdale, NJ: Erlbaum.

Lykken, D. T. (1999). *Happiness.* New York: Golden Books.

Lykken, D. T. (2001). Happiness—stuck with what you've got? *The Psychologist, 14*, 470–473.

Lykken, D. T., & Tellegen, A. (1993). Is human mating adventitious or the result of lawful choice? A twin study of mate selection. *Journal of Personality and Social Psychology, 65*, 56–68.

Lykken, D. T., & Tellegen, A. (1996). Happiness is a stochastic phenomenon. *Psychological Science, 7*, 186–189.

Lyman, D. R. (1996). Early identification of chronic offenders: Who is the fledgling psychopath? *Psychological Bulletin, 120*, 209–234.

Lynch, G. (2002). Memory enhancement: The search for mechanism-based drugs. *Nature Neuroscience, 5* (suppl.), 1035–1038.

Lynch, G., & Staubli, U. (1991). Possible contributions of long-term potentiation to the encoding and organization of memory. *Brain Research Reviews, 16*, 204–206.

Lyness, S. A. (1993). Predictors of differences between Type A and B individuals in heart rate and blood pressure reactivity. *Psychological Bulletin, 114*, 266–295.

Lynn, M. (1988). The effects of alcohol consumption on restaurant tipping. *Personality and Social Psychology Bulletin, 14*, 87–91.

Lynn, R. (1987). Japan: Land of the rising IQ. A reply to Flynn. *Bulletin of the British Psychological Society, 40*, 464–468.

Lynn, R. (1991, Fall/Winter). The evolution of racial differences in intelligence. *The Mankind Quarterly, 32*, 99–145.

Lynn, R. (2001). *Eugenics: A reassessment.* Westport, CT: Praeger/Greenwood.

Lynn, S. J., Rhue, J. W., & Weekes, J. R. (1990). Hypnotic involuntariness: A social cognitive analysis. *Psychological Review, 97*, 169–184.

Lyons, L. (2002, June 25). Are spiritual teens healthier? *Gallup Tuesday Briefing,* Gallup Organization (www.gallup.com/poll/tb/religValue/20020625b.asp).

Lyons, L. (2003, September 23). Oh, boy: Americans still prefer sons. *Gallup Poll Tuesday Briefing* (www.gallup.com).

Lyons, L. (2004, February 3). Growing up lonely: Examining teen alienation. Gallup Poll Tuesday Briefing (www.gallup.com).

Lyons, L. (2005, January 4). Teens stay true to parents' political perspectives. Gallup Poll News Service (www.gallup.com).

Lytton, H., & Romney, D. M. (1991). Parents' differential socialization of boys and girls: A meta-analysis. *Psychological Bulletin, 109*, 267–296.

Lyubomirsky, S. (2001). Why are some people happier than others? The role of cognitive and motivational processes in well-being. *American Psychologist, 56*, 239–249.

Lyubomirsky, S., King, L., & Diener, E. (2005). The benefits of frequent positive affect: Does happiness lead to success? *Psychological Bulletin, 131*, 803–855.

Lyubomirsky, S., Sousa, L., & Dickerhoof, R. (2006). The costs and benefits of writing, talking, and thinking about life's triumphs and defeats. *Journal of Personality and Social Psychology,* in press.

Ma, L. (1997, September). On the origin of Darwin's ills. *Discover,* p. 27.

Maas, J. B. (1999). *Power sleep. The revolutionary program that prepares your mind for peak performance.* New York: HarperCollins.

Maass, A., & Russo, A. (2003). Directional bias in the mental representation of spatial events: Nature or culture? *Psychological Science, 14*, 296–301.

Macaluso, E., Frith, C. D., & Driver, J. (2000). Modulation of human visual cortex by crossmodal spatial attention. *Science, 289*, 1206–1208.

Macan, T. H., & Dipboye, R. L. (1994). The effects of the application on processing of information from the employment interview. *Journal of Applied Social Psychology, 24*, 1291.

Macaskill, P., Pierce, J. P., Simpson, J. M., & Lyle, D. M. (1992). Mass media-led antismoking campaign can remove the education gap in quitting behavior. *American Journal of Public Health, 82*, 96–98.

Maccoby, E. (1980). *Social development: Psychological growth and the parent-child relationship.* New York: Harcourt Brace Jovanovich.

Maccoby, E. E. (1990). Gender and relationships: A developmental account. *American Psychologist, 45*, 513–520.

Maccoby, E. E. (1995). Divorce and custody: The rights, needs, and obligations of mothers, fathers, and children. *Nebraska Symposium on Motivation, 42*, 135–172.

Maccoby, E. E. (1998). *The paradox of gender.* Cambridge, MA: Harvard University Press.

Maccoby, E. E. (2002). Gender and group process: A developmental perspective. *Current Directions in Psychological Science, 11*, 54–58.

Maccoby, E. E. (2003, July 22). In Susan Gilbert, Turning a mass of data on child care into advice for parents. *New York Times* (www.nytimes.com).

MacDonald, G., & Leary, M. R. (2005). Why does social exclusion hurt? The relationship between social and physical pain. *Psychological Bulletin, 131*, 202–223.

MacDonald, N. (1960). Living with schizophrenia. *Canadian Medical Association Journal, 82*, 218–221.

MacDonald, T. K., Fong, G. T., Zanna, M. P., & Martineau, A. M. (2000). Alcohol myopia and condom use: Can alcohol intoxication be associated with more prudent behavior? *Journal of Personality and Social Psychology, 78*, 605–619.

MacDonald, T. K., Zanna, M. P., & Fong, G. T. (1995). Decision making in altered states: Effects of alcohol on attitudes toward drinking and driving. *Journal of Personality and Social Psychology, 68,* 973–985.

MacDonald, T. K., Zanna, M. P., & Fong, G. T. (1996). Why common sense goes out the window: The effects of alcohol on intentions to use condoms. *Personality and Social Psychology Bulletin, 22,* 763–775.

Macfarlane, J. W. (1964). Perspectives on personality consistency and change from the guidance study. *Vita Humana, 7,* 115–126.

MacFarlane, A. (1978, February). What a baby knows. *Human Nature,* pp. 74–81.

MacKay, D. G. (1983). Prescriptive grammar and the pronoun problem. In B. Thorne, C. Kramarae, & N. Henley (Eds.), *Language, gender and society.* Rowley, MA: Newbury House.

MacKinnon, D. W., & Hall, W. B. (1972). Intelligence and creativity. In *Proceedings, XVIIth International Congress of Applied Psychology* (Vol. 2). Brussels: Editest.

MacLeod, C., & Campbell, L. (1992). Memory accessibility and probability judgments: An experimental evaluation of the availability heuristic. *Journal of Personality and Social Psychology, 63,* 890–902.

MacNeilage, P. F., & Davis, B. L. (2000). On the origin of internal structure of word forms. *Science, 288,* 527–531.

Maddieson, I. (1984). *Patterns of sounds.* Cambridge: Cambridge University Press.

Maddox, K. B. (2004). Perspectives on racial phenotypicality bias. *Personality and Social Psychology Review, 8,* 383–401.

Maes, H. H. M., Neale, M. C., & Eaves, L. J. (1997). Genetic and environmental factors in relative body weight and human adiposity. *Behavior Genetics, 27,* 325–351.

Maes, M., Armand, C., Delanghe, J., Altamura, C., Neels, H., & Meltzer, H. Y. (1999). Lowered omega3 polyunsaturated fatty acids in serum phospholipids and cholesteryl esters of depressed patients. *Psychiatry Residency, 85,* 275–291.

Maestripieri, D. (2003). Similarities in affiliation and aggression between cross-fostered rhesus macaque females and their biological mothers. *Developmental Psychobiology, 43,* 321–327.

Magnusson, D. (1990). Personality research—challenges for the future. *European Journal of Personality, 4,* 1–17.

Maguire, E. A., Spiers, H. J., Good, C. D., Hartley, T., Frackowiak, R. S. J., & Burgess, N. (2003a). Navigation expertise and the human hippocampus: A structural brain imaging analysis. *Hippocampus, 13,* 250–259.

Maguire, E. A., Valentine, E. R., Wilding, J. M., & Kapur, N. (2003b). Routes to remembering: The brains behind superior memory. *Nature Neuroscience, 6,* 90–95.

Mahowald, M. W., & Ettinger, M. G. (1990). Things that go bump in the night: The parsomias revisited. *Journal of Clinical Neurophysiology, 7,* 119–143.

Maier, S. F., Watkins, L. R., & Fleshner, M. (1994). Psychoneuroimmunology: The interface between behavior, brain, and immunity. *American Psychologist, 49,* 1004–1017.

Major, B., Carrington, P. I., & Carnevale, P. J. D. (1984). Physical attractiveness and self-esteem: Attribution for praise from an other-sex evaluator. *Personality and Social Psychology Bulletin, 10,* 43–50.

Major, B., Schmidlin, A. M., & Williams, L. (1990). Gender patterns in social touch: The impact of setting and age. *Journal of Personality and Social Psychology, 58,* 634–643.

Malamuth, N. M. (1996). Sexually explicit media, gender differences, and evolutionary theory. *Journal of Communication, 46,* 8–31.

Malamuth, N. M., & Check, J. V. P. (1981). The effects of media exposure on acceptance of violence against women: A field experiment. *Journal of Research in Personality, 15,* 436–446.

Malamuth, N. M., Linz, D., Heavey, C. L., Barnes, G., & Acker, M. (1995). Using the confluence model of sexual aggression to predict men's conflict with women: A 10-year follow-up study. *Journal of Personality and Social Psychology, 69,* 353–369.

Malamuth, N. M., Sockloskie, R. J., Koss, M. P., & Tanaka, J. S. (1991). Characteristics of aggressors against women: Testing a model using a national sample of college students. *Journal of Consulting and Clinical Psychology, 59,* 670–681.

Malan, D. H. (1978). "The case of the secretary with the violent father." In H. Davanloo (Ed.), *Basic principles and techniques in short-term dynamic psychotherapy.* New York: Spectrum.

Malaspina, D., Harlap, S., Fennig, S., Heiman, D., Nahon, D., Feldman, D., & Susser, E. S. (2001). Advancing paternal age and the risk of schizophrenia. *Archives of General Psychiatry, 58,* 361–367.

Malinosky-Rummell, R., & Hansen, D. J. (1993). Long-term consequences of childhood physical abuse. *Psychological Bulletin, 114,* 68–79.

Malkiel, B. G. (1989). Is the stock market efficient? *Science, 243,* 1313–1318.

Malkiel, B. G. (1995, June). Returns from investing in equity mutual funds 1971 to 1991. *Journal of Finance,* pp. 549–572.

Malkiel, B. (2004). *A random walk down Wall Street* (8th ed.). New York: Norton.

Malloy, E. A. (1994, June 7). Report of the Commission on Substance Abuse at Colleges and Universities, reported by *Associated Press.*

Malmquist, C. P. (1986). Children who witness parental murder: Posttraumatic aspects. *Journal of the American Academy of Child Psychiatry, 25,* 320–325.

Malnic, B., Hirono, J., Sato, T., & Buck, L. B. (1999). Combinatorial receptor codes for odors. *Cell, 96,* 713–723.

Manber, R., Bootzin, R. R., Acebo, C., & Carskadon, M. A. (1996). The effects of regularizing sleep-wake schedules on daytime sleepiness. *Sleep, 19,* 432–441.

Mandel, D. (1983, March 13). One man's holocaust: Part II. The story of David Mandel's journey through hell as told to David Kagan. *Wonderland Magazine (Grand Rapids Press),* pp. 2–7.

Mann, J. J. (2003). Neurobiology of suicidal behaviour. *Nature Reviews Neuroscience, 4,* 819–828.

Mann, S., Vrij, A., & Bull, R. (2004). Detecting true lies: Police officers' ability to detect suspects' lies. *Journal of Applied Psychology, 89,* 137–149.

Manning, A. (2002, May 17). Teenage smoking rates drop. *USA Today* (story.news.yahoo.com).

Manson, J. E. (2002). Walking compared with vigorous exercise for the prevention of cardiovascular events in women. *New England Journal of Medicine, 347,* 716–725.

Maquet, P. (2001). The role of sleep in learning and memory. *Science, 294,* 1048–1052.

Maquet, P., Peters, J-M., Aerts, J., Delfiore, G., Degueldre, C., Luxen, A., & Franck, G. (1996). Functional neuroanatomy of human rapid-eye-movement sleep and dreaming. *Nature, 383,* 163–166.

Marangell, L. B., Rush, A. J., George, M. S., Sackeim, H. A., Johnson, C. R., Husain, M. M., Nahas, Z., & Lisanby, S. H. (2002). Vagus nerve stimulation (VNS) for major depressive episodes: One year outcomes. *Biological Psychiatry, 51,* 280–287.

Marcus, G. (2004). *The birth of the mind: How a tiny number of genes creates the complexity of human thought.* New York: Basic Books.

Marcus, G. F., Vijayan, S., Rao, S. B., & Vishton, P. M. (1999). Rule learning by seven-month-old infants. *Science, 283,* 77–80.

Margolis, M. L. (2000). Brahms' lullaby revisited: Did the composer have obstructive sleep apnea? *Chest, 118,* 210–213.

Marino, L. A., Reiss, D., & Gallup, G. G., Jr. (1994). Mirror self-recognition in bottlenose dolphins: Implications for comparative investigations of highly dissimilar species. In S. P. Parker, R. Mitchell, & M. Boccia (Eds.), *Self-awareness in animals and humans: Developmental perspectives.* New York: Cambridge University Press.

Mark, V., & Ervin, F. (1970). *Violence and the brain.* New York: Harper & Row.

Markowitsch, H. J. (1995). Which brain regions are critically involved in the retrieval of old episodic memory? *Brain Research Reviews, 21,* 117–127.

Markowitz, J. C., Svartberg, M., & Swartz, H. A. (1998). Is IPT time-limited psychodynamic psychotherapy? *Journal of Psychotherapy Practice and Research, 7,* 185–195.

Markus, G. B. (1986). Stability and change in political attitudes: Observe, recall, and "explain." *Political Behavior, 8,* 21–44.

Markus, H. (2001, October 7). Culture and the good life. Address to the Positive Psychology Summit conference, Washington, DC.

Markus, H., & Kitayama, S. (1991). Culture and the self: Implications for cognition, emotion, and motivation. *Psychological Review, 98,* 224–253.

Markus, H., & Nurius, P. (1986). Possible selves. *American Psychologist, 41,* 954–969.

Marlatt, G. A. (1991). Substance abuse: Etiology, prevention, and treatment issues. Master lecture, American Psychological Association convention.

Marley, J., & Bulia, S. (2001). Crimes against people with mental illness: Types, perpetrators and influencing factors. *Social Work, 46,* 115–124.

Marmot, M. G., Bosma, H., Hemingway, H., Brunner, E., & Stansfeld, S. (1997). Contribution of job control and other risk factors to social variations in coronary heart disease incidents. *Lancet, 350,* 235–239.

Marr, D. (1982). *Vision.* San Francisco: W. H. Freeman.

Marschark, M., Richman, C. L., Yuille, J. C., & Hunt, R. R. (1987). The role of imagery in memory: On shared and distinctive information. *Psychological Bulletin, 102,* 28–41.

Marsh, A. A., Elfenbein, H. A., & Ambady, N. (2003). Nonverbal "accents": Cultural differences in facial expressions of emotion. *Psychological Science, 14,* 373–376.

Marsh, H. W., & Parker, J. W. (1984). Determinants of student self-concept: Is it better to be a relatively large fish in a small pond even if you don't learn to swim as well? *Journal of Personality and Social Psychology, 47,* 213–231.

Marshall, E. (2004). A star-studded search for memory-enhancing drugs. *Science, 304,* 36–38.

Marshall, M. J. (2002). *Why spanking doesn't work.* Springville, UT: Bonneville Books.

Marshall, W. L. (1989). Pornography and sex offenders. In D. Zillmann & J. Bryant (Eds.), *Pornography: Research advances and policy considerations.* Hillsdale, NJ: Erlbaum.

Marteau, T. M. (1989). Framing of information: Its influences upon decisions of doctors and patients. *British Journal of Social Psychology, 28,* 89–94.

Marti, M. W., Robier, D. M., & Baron, R. S. (2000). Right before our eyes: The failure to recognize non-prototypical forms of prejudice. *Group Processes and Intergroup Relations, 3,* 403–418.

Martin, A., Wiggs, C. L., Ungerleider, L. G., & Haxby, J. V. (1996). Neural correlates of category-specific knowledge. *Nature, 379,* 649–652.

Martin, C. L., & Ruble, D. (2004). Children's search for gender cues. *Current Directions in Psychological Science, 13,* 67–70.

Martin, C. L., Ruble, D. N., & Szkrybalo, J. (2002). Cognitive theories of early gender development. *Psychological Bulletin, 128,* 903–933.

Martin, J. L. R., Barbanojh, M. J., Schlaepfer, T. E., Thompson, E., Perez, V., & Kulisevsky, J. (2003). Repetitive transcranial magnetic stimulation for the treatment of depression: Systematic review and meta-analysis. *British Journal of Psychiatry, 182,* 480–491.

Martin, R. A. (2001). Humor, laughter, and physical health: Methodological issues and research findings. *Psychological Bulletin, 127,* 504–519.

Martin, R. A. (2002). Is laughter the best medicine? Humor, laughter, and physical health. *Current Directions in Psychological Science, 11,* 216–220.

Martin, R. J., White, B. D., & Hulsey, M. G. (1991). The regulation of body weight. *American Scientist, 79,* 528–541.

Martin, S. J., Kelly, I. W., & Saklofske, D. H. (1992). Suicide and lunar cycles: A critical review over 28 years. *Psychological Reports, 71,* 787–795.

Martins, Y., Preti, G., Crabtree, C. R., & Wysocki, C. J. (2005). Preference for human body odors is influenced by gender and sexual orientation. *Psychological Science, 16,* 694–701.

Maruta, T., Colligan, R. C., Malinchoc, M., & Offord, K. P. (2002). Optimists vs. pessimists: Survival rate among medical patients over a 30-year period. *Mayo Clinic Proceedings, 75,* 140–143.

Marx, J. (2005). Preventing Alzheimer's: A lifelong commitment? *Science, 309,* 864–866.

Maslow, A. H. (1970). *Motivation and personality* (2nd ed.). New York: Harper & Row.

Maslow, A. H. (1971). *The farther reaches of human nature.* New York: Viking Press.

Mason, C., & Kandel, E. R. (1991). Central visual pathways. In E. R. Kandel, J. H. Schwartz, & T. M. Jessell (Eds.), *Principles of neural science* (3rd ed.). New York: Elsevier.

Mason, H. (2003, March 25). Wake up, sleepy teen. *Gallup Poll Tuesday Briefing* (www.gallup.com).

Mason, H. (2003, September 2). Americans, Britons at odds on animal testing. *Gallup Poll News Service* (www.gallup.com).

Mason, H. (2004, September 28). Support for smoking bans smoldering in Britain, Canada. *Gallup Poll* (www.gallup.com).

Mason, H. (2005, January 25). Who dreams, perchance to sleep? *Gallup Poll News Service* (www.gallup.com).

Mason, H. (2005, February 22). How many teens are on mood medication? *The Gallup Organization* (www.gallup.com).

Mason, R. A., & Just, M. A. (2004). How the brain processes causal inferences in text. *Psychological Science, 15,* 1–7.

Masse, L. C., & Tremblay, R. E. (1997). Behavior of boys in kindergarten and the onset of substance use during adolescence. *Archives of General Psychiatry, 54,* 62–68.

Massimini, M., Ferrarelli, F., Huber, R., Esser, S. K., Singh, H., & Tononi, G. (2005). Breakdown of cortical effective connectivity during sleep. *Science, 309,* 2228–2232.

Masten, A. S. (2001). Ordinary magic: Resilience processes in development. *American Psychologist, 56,* 227–238.

Masters, W. H., & Johnson, V. E. (1966). *Human sexual response.* Boston: Little, Brown.

Masuda, T., & Kitayama, S. (2005). Perceiver-induced constraint and attitude attribution in Japan and the US: A case for the cultural dependence of the correspondence bias. *Journal of Experimental Social Psychology, 40,* 409–416.

Mataix-Cols, D., Rosario-Campos, M. C., & Leckman, J. F. (2005). A multidimensional model of obsessive-compulsive disorder. *American Journal of Psychiatry, 162,* 228–238.

Mataix-Cols, D., Wooderson, S., Lawrence, N., Brammer, M. J., Speckens, A., & Phillips, M. L. (2004). Distinct neural correlates of washing, checking, and hoarding symptom dimensions in obsessive-compulsive disorder. *Archives of General Psychiatry, 61,* 564–576.

Mather, M., Canli, T., English, T., Whitfield, S., Wais, P., Ochsner, K., Gabrieli, J. D. E., & Carstensen, L. L. (2004). Amygdala responses to emotionally valenced stimuli in older and younger adults. *Psychological Science, 15,* 259–263.

Mather, M., & Carstensen, L. L. (2003). Aging and attentional biases for emotional faces. *Psychological Science, 14,* 409–415.

Matsumoto, D. (1994). *People: Psychology from a cultural perspective.* Pacific Grove, CA: Brooks/Cole.

Matsumoto, D., & Ekman, P. (1989). American-Japanese cultural differences in intensity ratings of facial expressions of emotion. *Motivation and Emotion, 13*, 143–157.

Maurer, D., Lewis, T. L., Brent, H. P., & Levin, A. V. (1999). Rapid improvement in the acuity of infants after visual input. *Science, 286,* 108–110.

Maurer, D., & Maurer, C. (1988). *The world of the newborn.* New York: Basic Books.

May, C., & Hasher, L. (1998). Synchrony effects in inhibitory control over thought and action. *Journal of Experimental Psychology: Human Perception and Performance, 24,* 363–380.

May, C. P., Hasher, L., & Stoltzfus, E. R. (1993). Optimal time of day and the magnitude of age differences in memory. *Psychological Science, 4,* 326–330.

May, R. (1982). The problem of evil: An open letter to Carl Rogers. *Journal of Humanistic Psychology, 22,* 10–21.

Mayberg, H. S., Lozano, A. M., Voon, V., McNeely, H. E., Seminowicz, D., Hamani, C., Schwalb, J. M., & Kennedy, S. H. (2005). Deep brain stimulation for treatment-resistant depression. *Neuron, 45,* 651–660.

Mayberry, R. I., Lock, E., & Kazmi, H. (2002). Linguistic ability and early language exposure. *Nature, 417,* 38.

Mayer, J. D. Salovey, P., & Caruso, D. (2002). *The Mayer-Salovey-Caruso emotional intelligence test (MSCEIT).* Toronto: Multi-Health Systems, Inc.

Mazur, A., & Booth, A. (1998). Testosterone and dominance in men. *Behavioral and Brain Sciences, 21,* 353–363.

Mazure, C., Keita, G., & Blehar, M. (2002). *Summit on women and depression: Proceedings and recommendations.* Washington, DC: American Psychological Association (www.apa.org/pi/wpo/women&depression.pdf).

Mazzoni, G., & Memon, A. (2003). Imagination can create false autobiographical memories. *Psychological Science, 14,* 186–188.

Mazzuca, J. (2002, July 2). Same-sex parenting: Does public back Rosie? The Gallup Organization (www.gallup.com/poll/tb/religValue/20020702.asp).

Mazzuca, J. (2002, August 20). Teens shrug off movie sex and violence. *Gallup Tuesday Briefing* (www.gallup.com/poll/tb/educayouth/20020820b.asp).

McAneny, L. (1996, September). Large majority think government conceals information about UFO's. *Gallup Poll Monthly,* pp. 23–26.

McBeath, M. K., Shaffer, D. M., & Kaiser, M. K. (1995). How baseball outfielders determine where to run to catch fly balls. *Science, 268,* 569–572.

McBurney, D. H. (1996). *How to think like a psychologist: Critical thinking in psychology.* Upper Saddle River, NJ: Prentice-Hall.

McBurney, D. H., & Collings, V. B. (1984). *Introduction to sensation and perception* (2nd ed.). Englewood Cliffs, NJ: Prentice-Hall.

McBurney, D. H., & Gent, J. F. (1979). On the nature of taste qualities. *Psychological Bulletin, 86,* 151–167.

McCall, R. B., Evahn, C., & Kratzer, L. (1992). High school underachievers. Newbury Park, CA: Sage.

McCann, I. L., & Holmes, D. S. (1984). Influence of aerobic exercise on depression. *Journal of Personality and Social Psychology, 46,* 1142–1147.

McCann, U. D., Eligulashvili, V., & Ricaurte, G. A. (2001). (+-)3,4-Methylenedioxymethamphetamine ('Ecstasy')-induced serotonin neurotoxicity: Clinical studies. *Neuropsychobiology, 42,* 11–16.

McCarthy, P. (1986, July). Scent: The tie that binds? *Psychology Today,* pp. 6, 10.

McCaul, K. D., & Malott, J. M. (1984). Distraction and coping with pain. *Psychological Bulletin, 95,* 516–533.

McCauley, C. R. (2002). Psychological issues in understanding terrorism and the response to terrorism. In C. E. Stout (Ed.), *The psychology of terrorism, Vol. 3.* Westport, CT: Praeger/Greenwood.

McCauley, C. R., & Segal, M. E. (1987). Social psychology of terrorist groups. In C. Hendrick (Ed.), *Group processes and intergroup relations.* Beverly Hills, CA: Sage.

McClearn, G. E., Johansson, B., Berg, S., Pedersen, N. L., Ahern, F., Petrill, S. A., & Plomin, R. (1997). Substantial genetic influence on cognitive abilities in twins 80 or more years old. *Science, 276,* 1560–1563.

McClintock, M. K., & Herdt, G. (December, 1996). Rethinking puberty: The development of sexual attraction. *Current Directions in Psychological Science, 5*(6), 178–183.

McClure, E. B. (2000). A meta-analytic review of sex differences in facial expression processing and their development in infants, children, and adolescents. *Psychological Bulletin, 126,* 424–453.

McClure, S. M., Laibson, D. I., Loewenstein, G., & Cohen, J. D. (2004). Separate neural systems value immediate and delayed monetary rewards. *Science, 306,* 503–507.

McConkey, K. M. (1995). Hypnosis, memory, and the ethics of uncertainty. *Australian Psychologist, 30,* 1–10.

McConnell, R. A. (1991). National Academy of Sciences opinion on parapsychology. *Journal of the American Society for Psychical Research, 85,* 333–365.

McCool, G. (1999, October 26). Mirror-gazing Venezuelans top of vanity stakes. *Toronto Star* (via web.lexis-nexis.com).

McCord, J. (1978). A thirty-year follow-up on treatment effects. *American Psychologist, 33,* 284–289.

McCord, J. (1979). Following up on Cambridge-Somerville. *American Psychologist, 34,* 727.

McCormick, C. M., & Witelson, S. F. (1991). A cognitive profile of homosexual men compared to heterosexual men and women. *Psychoneuroendocrinology, 16,* 459–473.

McCrae, R. R. (2001). Trait psychology and culture. *Journal of Personality, 69,* 819–846.

McCrae, R. R., & Costa, P. T., Jr. (1986). Clinical assessment can benefit from recent advances in personality psychology. *American Psychologist, 41,* 1001–1003.

McCrae, R. R., & Costa, P. T., Jr. (1990). *Personality in adulthood.* New York: Guilford.

McCrae, R. R., & Costa, P. T., Jr. (1994). The stability of personality: Observations and evaluations. *Current Directions in Psychological Science, 3,* 173–175.

McCrae, R. R., & Costa, P. T., Jr. (1999). A five-factor theory of personality. In L. A. Pervin & O. P. John (Eds.), *Handbook of personality: Theory and research.* New York: Guilford.

McCrae, R. R., Costa, P. T., Jr., de Lirna, M. P., Simoes, A., Ostendorf, F., Angleitner, A., Marusic, I., Bratko, D., Caprara, G. V., Barbaranelli, C., Chae, J-H., & Piedmont, R. L. (1999). Age differences in personality across the adult life span: Parallels in five cultures. *Developmental Psychology, 35,* 466–477.

McCrae, R. R., Costa, P. T., Jr., Ostendorf, F., Angleitner, A., Hrebickova, M., Avia, M. D., Sanz, J., Sanchez-Bernardos, M. L., Kusdil, M. E., Woodfield, R., Saunders, P. R., & Smith, P. B. (2000). Nature over nurture: Temperament, personality, and life span development. *Journal of Personality and Social Psychology, 78,* 173–186.

McCrae, R. R., Terracciano, A., & 78 others (2005). Universal features of personality traits from the observer's perspective: Data from 50 cultures. *Journal of Personality and Social Psychology, 88,* 547–561.

McCrink, K., & Wynn, K. (2004). Large-number addition and subtraction by 9-month-old infants. *Psychological Science, 15,* 776–781.

McCullough, M. E., Hoyt, W. T., Larson, D. B., Koenig, H. G., & Thoresen, C. (2000). Religious involvement and mortality: A meta-analytic review. *Health Psychology, 19,* 211–222.

McCullough, M. E., & Laurenceau, J-P. (2005). Religiousness and the trajectory of self-rated health across adulthood. *Personality and Social Psychology Bulletin, 31,* 560–573.

McCullough, M. E., Tsang, J-A., & Emmons, R. A. (2004). Gratitude in intermediate affective terrain: Links of grateful moods to individual differences and daily emotional experience. *Journal of Personality and Social Psychology, 86,* 295–309.

McEwen, B. S. (1998). Protective and damaging effects of stress mediators. *Seminars in Medicine of the Beth Israel Deaconess Medical Center, 338,* 171–179.

McEwen, B. S. (2002). Sex, stress and the hippocampus: Allostasis, allostatic load and the aging process. *Neurobiology of Aging, 23,* 921–939.

McFadden, D. (2002). Masculinization effects in the auditory system. *Archives of Sexual Behavior, 31,* 99–111.

McFarland, C., & Ross, M. (1987). The relation between current impressions and memories of self and dating partners. *Psychological Bulletin, 13,* 228–238.

McFarland, C., Ross, M., & DeVourville, N. (1989). Women's theories of menstruation and biases in recall of menstrual symptoms. *Journal of Personality and Social Psychology, 57,* 522–531.

McFarland, C., White, K., & Newth, S. (2003). Mood acknowledgment and correction for the mood-congruency bias in social judgment. *Journal of Experimental Social Psychology, 39,* 483–491.

McGarry-Roberts, P. A., Stelmack, R. M., & Campbell, K. B. (1992). Intelligence, reaction time, and event-related potentials. *Intelligence, 16,* 289–313.

McGaugh, J. I. (2003). *Memory and emotion: The making of lasting memories.* New York: Columbia University Press.

McGaugh, J. L. (1994). Quoted by B. Bower, Stress hormones hike emotional memories. *Science News, 146,* p. 262.

McGaugh, J. L. (2000). Memory—a century of consolidation. *Science, 287,* 248–251.

McGhee, P. E. (June, 1976). Children's appreciation of humor: A test of the cognitive congruency principle. *Child Development, 47*(2), 420–426.

McGlone, M. S., & Tofighbakhsh, J. (2000). Birds of a feather flock conjointly (?): Rhyme as reason in aphorisms. *Psychological Science, 11,* 424–428.

McGrath, J. J., & Welham, J. L. (1999). Season of birth and schizophrenia: A systematic review and meta-analysis of data from the Southern hemisphere. *Schizophrenia Research, 35,* 237–242.

McGrath, J., Welham, J., & Pemberton, M. (1995). Month of birth, hemisphere of birth and schizophrenia. *British Journal of Psychiatry, 167,* 783–785.

McGrath, M. J., & Cohen, D. B. (1978). REM sleep facilitation of adaptive waking behavior: A review of the literature. *Psychological Bulletin, 85,* 24–57.

McGue, M., & Bouchard, T. J., Jr. (1998). Genetic and environmental influences on human behavioral differences. *Annual Review of Neuroscience, 21,* 1–24.

McGue, M., Bouchard, T. J., Jr., Iacono, W. G., & Lykken, D. T. (1993). Behavioral genetics of cognitive ability: A life-span perspective. In R. Plomin & G. E. McClearn (Eds.), *Nature, nurture and psychology.* Washington, DC: American Psychological Association.

McGue, M., & Lykken, D. T. (1992). Genetic influence on risk of divorce. *Psychological Science, 3,* 368–373.

McGuire, M. T., Wing, R. R., Klem, M. L., Lang, W., & Hill, J. O. (1999). What predicts weight regain in a group of successful weight losers? *Journal of Consulting and Clinical Psychology, 67,* 177–185.

McGuire, W. J. (1986). The myth of massive media impact: Savings and salvagings. In G. Comstock (Ed.), *Public communication and behavior.* Orlando, FL: Academic Press.

McGuire, W. J., McGuire, C. V., Child, P., & Fujioka, T. (1978). Salience of ethnicity in the spontaneous self-concept as a function of one's ethnic distinctiveness in the social environment. *Journal of Personality and Social Psychology, 36,* 511–520.

McGurk, H., & MacDonald, J. (1976). Hearing lips and seeing voices. *Nature, 264,* 746–748.

McHugh, P. R. (1995a). Witches, multiple personalities, and other psychiatric artifacts. *Nature Medicine, 1*(2), 110–114.

McHugh, P. R. (1995b). Resolved: Multiple personality disorder is an individually and socially created artifact. *Journal of the American Academy of Child and Adolescent Psychiatry, 34,* 957–959.

McHugh, P. R., & Moran, T. H. (1978). Accuracy of the regulation of caloric ingestion in the rhesus monkey. *American Journal of Physiology, 235,* R29–34.

McKellar, J., Stewart, E., & Humphreys, K. (2003). Alcoholics Anonymous involvement and positive alcohol-related outcomes: Cause, consequence, or just a correlate? A prospective 2-year study of 2,319 alcohol-dependent men. *Journal of Consulting and Clinical Psychology, 71,* 302–308.

McKenna, K. Y. A., & Bargh, J. A. (1998). Coming out in the age of the Internet: Identity "demarginalization" through virtual group participation. *Journal of Personality and Social Psychology, 75,* 681–694.

McKillop, J., Lisman, S. A., Weinstein, A., & Rosenbaum, D. (2003). Controversial treatments for alcoholism. In S. O. Lilienfeld, S. J. Lynn, & J. M. Lohr (Eds.), *Science and pseudoscience in clinical psychology.* New York: Guilford Press.

McLaughlin, C. S., Chen, C., Greenberger, E., & Biermeier, C. (1997). Family, peer, and individual correlates of sexual experience among Caucasian and Asian American late adolescents. Journal of Personality and Social Psychology, *Journal of Research on Adolescence, 7,* 33–53.

McMurray, C. (2004, January 13). U.S., Canada, Britain: Who's getting in shape? *Gallup Poll Tuesday Briefing* (www.gallup.com).

McMurray, C. (2004, February 24). Current smoking trends in U.S., Canada, Britain. *Gallup Poll Tuesday Briefing* (www.gallup.com).

McNally, R. J. (1987). Preparedness and phobias: A review. *Psychological Bulletin, 101,* 283–303.

McNally, R. J. (1999). EMDR and Mesmerism: A comparative historical analysis. *Journal of Anxiety Disorders, 13,* 225–236.

McNally, R. J. (2003). *Remembering trauma.* Cambridge, MA: Harvard University Press.

McNally, R. J., Bryant, R. A., & Ehlers, A. (2003). Does early psychological intervention promote recovery from posttraumatic stress? *Psychological Science in the Public Interest, 4,* 45–79.

McNeil, B. J., Pauker, S. G., & Tversky, A. (1988). On the framing of medical decisions. In D. E. Bell, H. Raiffa, & A. Tversky (Eds.), *Decision making: Descriptive, normative, and prescriptive interactions.* New York: Cambridge, 1988.

Meador, B. D., & Rogers, C. R. (1984). Person-centered therapy. In R. J. Corsini (Ed.), *Current psychotherapies* (3rd ed.). Itasca, IL: Peacock.

Medical Institute for Sexual Health. (1994, April). Condoms ineffective against human papilloma virus. *Sexual Health Update, 2.*

Medland, S. E., Perelle, I., De Monte, V., & Ehrman, L. (2004). Effects of culture, sex, and age on the distribution of handedness: An evaluation of the sensitivity of three measures of handedness. *Laterality: Asymmetries of Body, Brain, and Cognition, 9,* 287–297.

Mednick, S. A., Huttunen, M. O., & Machon, R. A. (1994). Prenatal influenza infections and adult schizophrenia. *Schizophrenia Bulletin, 20,* 263–267.

Mehl, M. R., & Pennebaker, J. W. (2003). The sounds of social life: A psychometric analysis of students' daily social environments and natural conversations. *Journal of Personality and Social Psychology, 84,* 857–870.

Meichenbaum, D. (1977). *Cognitive-behavior modification: An integrative approach.* New York: Plenum Press.

Meichenbaum, D. (1985). *Stress inoculation training.* New York: Pergamon.

Meltzoff, A. N. (1988). Infant imitation after a 1-week delay: Long-term memory for novel acts and multiple stimuli. *Developmental Psychology, 24,* 470–476.

Meltzoff, A. N., & Moore, M. K. (1989). Imitation in newborn infants: Exploring the range of gestures imitated and the underlying mechanisms. *Developmental Psychology, 25,* 954–962.

Meltzoff, A. N., & Moore, M. K. (1997). Explaining facial imitation: A theoretical model. *Early Development and Parenting, 6,* 179–192.

Melzack, R. (1984). The myth of painless childbirth. *Pain, 19,* 321–337.

Melzack, R. (1990, February). The tragedy of needless pain. *Scientific American,* pp. 27–33.

Melzack, R. (1992, April). Phantom limbs. *Scientific American,* pp. 120–126.

Melzack, R. (1993). Distinguished contribution series. *Canadian Journal of Experimental Psychology, 47,* 615–629.

Melzack, R. (1998, February). Quoted in Phantom limbs. *Discover,* p. 20.

Melzack, R. (1999). Pain and Stress: A new perspective. In R. J. Gatchel, & D. C. Turk (Eds.), *Psychosocial factors in pain: Critical perspectives.* New York: Guilford Press.

Melzack, R., & Wall, P. D. (1965). Pain mechanisms: A new theory. *Science, 150,* 971–979.

Melzack, R., & Wall, P. D. (1983). *The challenge of pain.* New York: Basic Books.

Mendolia, M., & Kleck, R. E. (1993). Effects of talking about a stressful event on arousal: Does what we talk about make a difference? *Journal of Personality and Social Psychology, 64,* 283–292.

Merari, A. (2002). Explaining suicidal terrorism: Theories versus empirical evidence. Invited address to the American Psychological Association.

Merriman, J. (1999, May 13). These pounds aren't sterling. *Reuters* (www.abcnews.go.com).

Merskey, H. (1992). The manufacture of personalities: The production of multiple personality disorder. *British Journal of Psychiatry, 160,* 327–340.

Merton, R. K. (1938; reprinted 1970). *Science, technology and society in seventeenth-century England.* New York: Fertig.

Merton, R. K., & Kitt, A. S. (1950). Contributions to the theory of reference group behavior. In R. K. Merton & P. F. Lazarsfeld (Eds.), *Continuities in social research: Studies in the scope and method of the American soldier.* Glencoe, IL: Free Press.

Messer, D. (2000). Language acquisition. *The Psychologist, 13,* 138–143.

Messer, W. S., & Griggs, R. A. (1989). Student belief and involvement in the paranormal and performance in introductory psychology. *Teaching of Psychology, 16,* 187–191.

Mestel, R. (1997, April 26). Get real, Siggi. *New Scientist* (www.newscientist.com/ns/970426/siggi.html).

Meston, C. M., & Frohlich, P. F. (2000). The neurobiology of sexual function. *Archives of General Psychiatry, 57,* 1012–1030.

Meston, C. M., Trapnell, P. D., & Gorzalka, B. B. (1996). Ethnic and gender differences in sexuality: Variations in sexual behavior between Asian and non-Asian university students. *Archives of Sexual Behavior, 25,* 33–72.

Metcalfe, J. (1998). Cognitive optimism: Self-deception or memory-based processing heuristics. *Personality and Social Psychology Review, 2,* 100–110.

Meyer, I. H. (2003). Prejudice, social stress, and mental health in lesbian, gay, and bisexual populations: Conceptual issues and research evidence. *Psychological Bulletin, 129,* 674–697.

Meyer-Bahlburg, H. F. L. (1995). Psychoneuroendocrinology and sexual pleasure: The aspect of sexual orientation. In P. R. Abramson & S. D. Pinker-

ton (Eds.), *Sexual nature/sexual culture.* Chicago: University of Chicago Press.

Mezulis, A. M., Abramson, L. Y., Hyde, J. S., & Hankin, B. L. (2004). Is there a universal positivity bias in attributions? A meta-analytic review of individual, developmental, and cultural differences in the self-serving attributional bias. *Psychological Bulletin, 130,* 711–747.

Michaels, J. W., Bloomel, J. M., Brocato, R. M., Linkous, R. A., & Rowe, J. S. (1982). Social facilitation and inhibition in a natural setting. *Replications in Social Psychology, 2,* 21–24.

Michel, G. F. (1981). Right-handedness: A consequence of infant supine head-orientation preference? *Science, 212,* 685–687.

Middlebrooks, J. C., & Green, D. M. (1991). Sound localization by human listeners. *Annual Review of Psychology, 42,* 135–159.

Mikkelsen, T. S., & 66 others (2005). Initial sequence of the chimpanzee genome and comparison with the human genome. *Nature, 437,* 69–87.

Mikulincer, M., Babkoff, H., Caspy, T., & Sing, H. (1989). The effects of 72 hours of sleep loss on psychological variables. *British Journal of Psychology, 80,* 145–162.

Mikulincer, M., Florian, V., & Hirschberger, G. (2003). The existential function of close relationships: Introducing death into the science of love. *Personality and Social Psychology Review, 7,* 20–40.

Mikulincer, M., & Shaver, P. R. (2001). Attachment theory and intergroup bias: Evidence that priming the secure base schema attenuates negative reactions to our-groups. *Journal of Personality and Social Psychology, 81,* 97–115.

Mikulincer, M., & Shaver, P. R. (2005). Attachment theory and emotions in close relationships: Exploring the attachment-related dynamics of emotional reactions to relational events. *Personal Relationships, 12,* 149–168.

Milan, R. J., Jr., & Kilmann, P. R. (1987). Interpersonal factors in premarital contraception. *Journal of Sex Research, 23,* 289–321.

Miles, D. R., & Carey, G. (1997). Genetic and environmental architecture of human aggression. *Journal of Personality and Social Psychology, 72,* 207–217.

Milgram, S. (1963). Behavioral study of obedience. *Journal of Abnormal & Social Psychology, 67*(4), 371–378.

Milgram, S. (1974). *Obedience to authority.* New York: Harper & Row.

Miller, E. J., Smith, J. E., & Trembath, D. L. (2000). The "skinny" on body size requests in personal ads. *Sex Roles, 43,* 129–141.

Miller, G. (2004). Axel, Buck share award for deciphering how the nose knows. *Science, 306,* 207.

Miller, G. A. (1956). The magical number seven, plus or minus two: Some limits on our capacity for processing information. *Psychological Review, 63,* 81–97.

Miller, G. A. (1962). *Psychology: The science of mental life.* New York: Harper & Row.

Miller, J. G., & Bersoff, D. M. (1995). Development in the context of everyday family relationships: Culture, interpersonal morality and adaptation. In M. Killen and D. Hart (Eds.), *Morality in everyday life: A developmental perspective.* New York: Cambridge University Press.

Miller, K. I., & Monge, P. R. (1986). Participation, satisfaction, and productivity: A meta-analytic review. *Academy of Management Journal, 29,* 727–753.

Miller, L. (2005, January 4). U.S. airlines have 34 deaths in 3 years. Associated Press.

Miller, L. C., Putcha-Bhagavatula, A., & Pedersen, W. C. (2002). Men's and women's mating preferences: Distinct evolutionary mechanisms? *Current Directions in Psychological Science, 11,* 88–93.

Miller, L. K. (1999). The Savant Syndrome: Intellectual impairment and exceptional skill. *Psychological Bulletin, 125,* 31–46.

Miller, M. (2005, March 7). Effects of laughter and mental stress on endothelial function: Potential impact of entertainment. Paper presented to the Scientific Session of the American College of Cardiology, Orlando.

Miller, N. E. (1985, February). Rx: biofeedback. *Psychology Today*, pp. 54–59.

Miller, N. E. (1995). Clinical-experimental interactions in the development of neuroscience: A primer for nonspecialists and lessons for young scientists. *American Psychologist, 50*, 901–911.

Miller, N. E., & Brucker, B. S. (1979). A learned visceral response apparently independent of skeletal ones in patients paralyzed by spinal lesions. In N. Birbaumer & H. D. Kimmel (Eds.), *Biofeedback and self-regulation.* Hillsdale, NJ: Erlbaum.

Miller, P. A., Eisenberg, N., Fabes, R. A., & Shell, R. (1996). Relations of moral reasoning and vicarious emotion to young children's prosocial behavior toward peers and adults. *Developmental Psychology, 32*, 210–219.

Miller, P. C., Lefcourt, H. M., Holmes, J. G., Ware, E. E., & Saleh, W. E. (1986). Marital locus of control and marital problem solving. *Journal of Personality and Social Psychology, 51*, 161–169.

Miller, S. D., Blackburn, T., Scholes, G., White, G. L., & Mamalis, N. (1991). Optical differences in multiple personality disorder: A second look. *Journal of Nervous and Mental Disease, 179*, 132–135.

Mills, M., & Melhuish, E. (1974). Recognition of mother's voice in early infancy. *Nature, 252*, 123–124.

Milner, D. A. (2003). Visual awareness and the primate brain. In M. A. Jeeves (Ed.), *Human nature.* London: Routledge.

Milton, J., & Wiseman, R. (2001). Does psi exist? Reply to Storm and Ertel (2001). *Psychological Bulletin, 127*, 434–438.

Milton, J., & Wiseman, R. (2002). A response to Storm and Ertel (2002). *Journal of Parapsychology, 66*, 183–185.

Mineka, S. (1985). The frightful complexity of the origins of fears. In F. R. Brush & J. B. Overmier (Eds.), *Affect, conditioning and cognition: Essays on the determinants of behavior.* Hillsdale, NJ: Erlbaum.

Mineka, S., & Suomi, S. J. (1978). Social separation in monkeys. *Psychological Bulletin, 85*, 1376–1400.

Mineka, S., & Sutton, S. K. (1992). Cognitive biases and the emotional disorders. *Psychological Science, 3*, 65–69.

Mineka, S., & Zinbarg, R. (1996). Conditioning and ethological models of anxiety disorders: Stress-in-dynamic-context anxiety models. In D. Hope (Ed.), *Perspectives on anxiety, panic, and fear. Nebraska symposium on motivation.* Lincoln, NE: University of Nebraska Press.

Miner-Rubino, K., & Winter, D. G., & Stewart, A. J. (2004). Gender, social class, and the subjective experience of aging: Self-perceived personality change from early adulthood to late midlife. *Personality and Social Psychology Bulletin, 30*, 1599–1610.

Mingroni, M. A. (2004). The secular rise in IQ: Giving heterosis a closer look. *Intelligence, 32*, 65–83.

Mirescu, C., Peters, J. D., & Gould, E. (2004). Early life experience alters response of adult neurogenesis to stress. *Nature Neuroscience, 7*, 841–846.

Mischel, W. (1968). *Personality and assessment.* New York: Wiley.

Mischel, W. (1981). Current issues and challenges in personality. In L. T. Benjamin, Jr. (Ed.), *The G. Stanley Hall Lecture Series* (Vol. 1). Washington, DC: American Psychological Association.

Mischel, W. (1984). Convergences and challenges in the search for consistency. *American Psychologist, 39*, 351–364.

Mischel, W. (2004). Toward an integrative science of the person. *Annual Review of Psychology, 55*, 1–22.

Mischel, W., Shoda, Y., & Peake, P. K. (1988). The nature of adolescent competencies predicted by preschool delay of gratification. *Journal of Personality and Social Psychology, 54*, 687–696.

Mischel, W., Shoda, Y., & Rodriguez, M. L. (1989). Delay of gratification in children. *Science, 244*, 933–938.

Miserandino, M. (1991). Memory and the seven dwarfs. *Teaching of Psychology, 18*, 169–171.

Mita, T. H., Dermer, M., & Knight, J. (1977). Reversed facial images and the mere-exposure hypothesis. *Journal of Personality and Social Psychology, 35*, 597–601.

Mitchell, T. R., Thompson, L., Peterson, E., & Cronk, R. (1997). Temporal adjustments in the evaluation of events: The "rosy view." *Journal of Experimental Social Psychology, 33*, 421–448.

MMWR. (1999, April 2). Tobacco use among middle and high school students—Florida, 1998 and 1999. *Morbidity and Mortality Weekly Report, 48*, 248–253.

Moffitt, T. E. (2005). The new look of behavioral genetics in developmental psychopathology: Gene-environment interplay in antisocial behaviors. *Psychological Bulletin, 131*, 533–554.

Moffitt, T. E., Caspi, A., Harrington, H., & Milne, B. J. (2002). Males on the life-course-persistent and adolescence-limited antisocial pathways: Follow-up at age 26 years. *Development and Psychopathology, 14*, 179–207.

Moghaddam, F. M. (2005). The staircase to terrorism: A psychological exploration. *American Psychologist, 60*, 161–169.

Mohn, J. K., Tingle, L. R., & Finger, R. (2003). An analysis of the causes of the decline in non-marital birth and pregnancy rates for teens from 1991 to 1995. *Adolescent and Family Health, 3*, 39–47.

Moises, H. W., Zoega, T., & Gottesman, I. I. (2002, 3 July). The glial growth factors deficiency and synaptic destabilization hypothesis of schizophrenia. *BMC Psychiatry, 2*(8) (www.biomedcentral.com/1471-244X/2/8).

Mokdad, A. H., Marks, J. S., Stroup, D. F., & Gerberding, J. L. (2004). Actual causes of death in the United States, 2000. *Journal of the American Medical Association, 291*, 1238–1245.

Mollica, R. F., McInnes, K., Pham, T., Fawzi, M. C. S., Murphy, E., & Lin, L. (1998). The dose-effect relationships between torture and psychiatric symptoms in Vietnamese ex-political detainees and a comparison group. *Journal of Nervous and Mental Diseases, 186*, 543–553.

Monaghan, P. (1992, September 23). Professor of psychology stokes a controversy on the reliability and repression of memory. *Chronicle of Higher Education*, pp. A9–A10.

Mondloch, C. J., Lewis, T. L., Budreau, D. R., Maurer, D., Dannemiller, J. L., Stephens, B. R., & Kleiner-Gathercoal, K. A. (1999). Face perception during early infancy. *Psychological Science, 10*, 419–422.

Money, J. (1987). Sin, sickness, or status? Homosexual gender identity and psychoneuroendocrinology. *American Psychologist, 42*, 384–399.

Money, J. (1988). *Gay, straight, and in-between.* New York: Oxford University Press.

Money, J., Berlin, F. S., Falck, A., & Stein, M. (1983). *Antiandrogenic and counseling treatment of sex offenders.* Baltimore: Department of Psychiatry and Behavioral Sciences, The Johns Hopkins University School of Medicine.

Moody, R. (1976). *Life after life.* Harrisburg, PA: Stackpole Books.

Mook, D. G. (1983). In defense of external invalidity. *American Psychologist, 38*, 379–387.

Moorcroft, W. (1993). *Sleep, dreaming, and sleep disorders: An introduction* (2nd ed.). Landam, MD: University Press of America.

Moorcroft, W. H. (2003). *Understanding sleep and dreaming.* New York: Kluwer/Plenum.

Moore, D. W. (2003, November 23). Many Americans deluding themselves about weight. *Gallup Poll* (poll.gallup.com).

Moore, D. W. (2004, December 17). Sweet dreams go with a good night's sleep. Gallup News Service (www.gallup.com).

Mor, N., & Winquist, J. (2002). Self-focused attention and negative affect: A meta-analysis. *Psychological Bulletin, 128*, 638–662.

Moreland, R. L., & Beach, S. R. (1992). Exposure effects in the classroom: The development of affinity among students. *Journal of Experimental Social Psychology, 28*, 255–276.

Moreland, R. L., & Zajonc, R. B. (1982). Exposure effects in person perception: Familiarity, similarity, and attraction. *Journal of Experimental Social Psychology, 18*, 395–415.

Morell, V. (1995a). Attacking the causes of "silent" infertility. *Science, 269,* 775–776.

Morell, V. (1995b). Zeroing in on how hormones affect the immune system. *Science, 269,* 773–775.

Morelli, G. A., Rogoff, B., Oppenheim, D., & Goldsmith, D. (1992). Cultural variation in infants' sleeping arrangements: Questions of independence. *Developmental Psychology, 26,* 604–613.

Morey, R. A., Inan, S., Mitchell, T. V., Perkins, D. O., Lieberman, J. A., & Belger, A. (2005). Imaging frontostriatal function in ultra-high-risk, early, and chronic schizophrenia during executive processing. *Archives of General Psychiatry, 62,* 254–262.

Morgan, A. B., & Lilienfeld, S. O. (2000). A meta-analytic review of the relation between antisocial behavior and neuropsychological measures of executive function. *Clinical Psychology Review, 20,* 113–136.

Morgan, B., & Korschgen, A. (2001). Psychology career exploration made easy. *Eye on Psi Chi,* 35–36.

Morin, R., & Brossard, M. A. (1997, March 4). Communication breakdown on drugs. *Washington Post,* pp. A1, A6.

Morris, J. S., Ohman, A., & Dolan, R. (1998). Conscious and unconscious emotional learning in the human amygdala. *Nature, 393,* 467–470.

Morrison, A. R. (2003). The brain on night shift. *Cerebrum, 5*(3), 23–36.

Mortensen, E. L., Michaelsen, K. F., Sanders, S. A., & Reinisch, J. M. (2002). The association between duration of breastfeeding and adult intelligence. *Journal of the American Medical Association, 287,* 2365–2371.

Mortensen, P. B. (1999). Effects of family history and place and season of birth on the risk of schizophrenia. *New England Journal of Medicine, 340,* 603–608.

Moruzzi, G., & Magoun, H. W. (1949). Brain stem reticular formation and activation of the EEG. *Electroencephalography and Clinical Neurophysiology, 1,* 455–473.

Moscovici, S. (1985). Social influence and conformity. In G. Lindzey & E. Aronson (Eds.), *The handbook of social psychology* (3rd ed). Hillsdale, N.J.: Erlbaum.

Moser, P. W. (1987, May). Are cats smart? Yes, at being cats. *Discover,* pp. 77–88.

Mosher, D. L., & Anderson, R. D. (1986). Macho personality, sexual aggression, and reactions to guided imagery of realistic rape. *Journal of Research in Personality, 20,* 77–94.

Moss, A. J., Allen, K. F., Giovino, G. A., & Mills, S. L. (1992, December 2). Recent trends in adolescent smoking, smoking-update correlates, and expectations about the future. *Advance Data No. 221* (from Vital and Health Statistics of the Centers for Disease Control and Prevention).

Moss, H. A., & Susman, E. J. (1980). Longitudinal study of personality development. In O. G. Brim, Jr., & J. Kagan (Eds.), *Constancy and change in human development.* Cambridge, MA: Harvard University Press.

Moyer, K. E. (1983). The physiology of motivation: Aggression as a model. In C. J. Scheier & A. M. Rogers (Eds.), *G. Stanley Hall Lecture Series* (Vol. 3). Washington, DC: American Psychological Association.

Mroczek, D. K. (2001). Age and emotion in adulthood. *Current Directions in Psychological Science, 10,* 87–90.

Mroczek, D. K., & Kolarz, D. M. (1998). The effect of age on positive and negative affect: A developmental perspective on happiness. *Journal of Personality and Social Psychology, 75,* 1333–1349.

Mroczek, D. K., & Spiro, A., III (2005). Change in life satisfaction during adulthood: Findings from the Veterans Affairs normative aging study. *Journal of Personality and Social Psychology, 88,* 189–202.

Muhlnickel, W. (1998). Article on tinnitus processing in the brain *Proceedings of the National Academy of Sciences, 95,* 10340–10343.

Muller, J. E., Mittleman, M. A., Maclure, M., Sherwood, J. B., & Tofler, G. H. (1996). Triggering myocardial infarction by sexual activity. *Journal of the American Medical Association, 275,* 1405–1409.

Muller, J. E., & Verrier, R. L. (1996). Triggering of sudden death—Lessons from an earthquake. *New England Journal of Medicine, 334,* 461.

Mullin, C. R., & Linz, D. (1995). Desensitization and resensitization to violence against women: Effects of exposure to sexually violent films on judgments of domestic violence victims. *Journal of Personality and Social Psychology, 69,* 449–459.

Mulrow, C. D. (1999, March). Treatment of depression—newer pharmacotherapies, summary. *Evidence Report/Technology Assessment, 7.* Agency for Health Care Policy and Research, Rockville, MD. (http://www.ahrq.gov/clinic/deprsumm.htm).

Murphy, G. E., & Wetzel, R. D. (1990). The lifetime risk of suicide in alcoholism. *Archives of General Psychiatry, 47,* 383–392.

Murphy, K. R., & Cleveland, J. N. (1995). *Understanding performance appraisal: Social, organizational, and goal-based perspectives.* Thousand Oaks, CA: Sage.

Murphy, S. T., Monahan, J. L., & Miller, L. C. (1998). Inference under the influence: The impact of alcohol and inhibition conflict on women's sexual decision making. *Personality and Social Psychology Bulletin, 24,* 517–528.

Murphy, S. T., Monahan, J. L., & Zajonc, R. B. (1995). Additivity of nonconscious affect: Combined effects of priming and exposure. *Journal of Personality and Social Psychology, 69,* 589–602.

Murphy, T. N. (1982). Pain: Its assessment and management. In R. J. Gatchel, A. Baum, & J. E. Singer (Eds.), *Handbook of psychology and health: Vol. I. Clinical psychology and behavioral medicine: Overlapping disciplines.* Hillsdale, NJ: Erlbaum.

Murray, B. (1998, May). Psychology is key to airline safety at Boeing. *The APA Monitor,* p. 36.

Murray, C., & Herrnstein, R. J. (1994, October 31). Race, genes and I.Q.—An apologia. *New Republic,* pp. 27–37.

Murray, C. J., & Lopez, A. D. (Eds.) (1996). *The global burden of disease: A comprehensive assessment of mortality and disability from diseases, injuries, and risk factors in 1990 and projected to 2020.* Cambridge, MA: Harvard University Press.

Murray, H. (1938). *Explorations in personality.* New York: Oxford University Press.

Murray, H. A. (1933). The effect of fear upon estimates of the maliciousness of other personalities. *Journal of Social Psychology, 4,* 310–329.

Murray, H. A., & Wheeler, D. R. (1937). A note on the possible clairvoyance of dreams. *Journal of Psychology, 3,* 309–313.

Murray, J. E. (2000). Marital protection and marital selection: Evidence from a historical-prospective sample of American men. *Demography, 37,* 511–521.

Murray, R., Jones, P., O'Callaghan, E., Takei, N., & Sham, P. (1992). Genes, viruses, and neurodevelopmental schizophrenia. *Journal of Psychiatric Research, 26,* 225–235.

Murray, S. L., Bellavia, G. M., Rose, P., & Griffin, D. W. (2003). Once hurt, twice hurtful: How perceived regard regulates daily marital interactions. *Journal of Personality and Social Psychology, 84,* 126–147.

Murray, S. L., Rose, P., Bellavia, G. M., Holmes, J. G., & Kusche, A. G. (2002). When rejection stings: How self-esteem constrains relationship-enhancement processes. *Journal of Personality and Social Psychology, 83,* 556–573.

Musallam, S., Corneil, B. D., Greger, B., Scherberger, H., & Andersen, R. A. (2004). Cognitive control signals for neural prosthetics. *Science, 305,* 258–262.

Musick, M. A., Herzog, A. R., & House, J. S. (1999). Volunteering and mortality among older adults: Findings from a national sample. *Journals of Gerontology, 54B,* 173–180.

Mustanski, B. S., & Bailey, J. M. (2003). A therapist's guide to the genetics of human sexual orientation," *Sexual and Relationship Therapy 18,* 1468–1479.

Mustanski, B. S., Bailey, J. M., & Kaspar, S. (2002). Dermatoglyphics, handedness, sex, and sexual orientation. *Archives of Sexual Behavior, 31,* 113–122.

Mydans, S. (2002, May 17). In Pakistan, rape victims are the 'criminals.' *New York Times* (www.nytimes.com).

Myers, D. G. (1993). *The pursuit of happiness.* New York: Avon Books.

Myers, D. G. (2000). *The American paradox: Spiritual hunger in an age of plenty.* New Haven: Yale University Press.

Myers, D. G. (2001, December). Do we fear the right things? *American Psychological Society Observer,* p. 3.

Myers, D. G. (2002). *Intuition: Its powers and perils.* New Haven: Yale University Press.

Myers, D. G. (2005). *Social psychology,* 8th edition. New York: McGraw-Hill.

Myers, D. G., & Bishop, G. D. (1970). Discussion effects on racial attitudes. *Science, 169,* 78–779.

Myers, D. G., & Diener, E. (1995). Who is happy? *Psychological Science, 6,* 10–19.

Myers, D. G., & Diener, E. (1996, May). The pursuit of happiness. *Scientific American,* p. 545)

Myers, D. G., & Scanzoni, L. D. (2005). *What God has joined together? A Christian case for gay marriage.* San Francisco: HarperSanFrancisco.

Myers, I. B. (1987). *Introduction to type: A description of the theory and applications of the Myers-Briggs Type Indicator.* Palo Alto, CA: Consulting Psychologists Press.

Myerson, J., Rank, M. R., Raines, F. Q., & Schnitzler, M. A. (1998). Race and general cognitive ability: The myth of diminishing returns to education. *Psychological Science, 9,* 139–142.

Nagourney, A. (2002, September 25). For remarks on Iraq, Gore gets praise and scorn. *New York Times* (www.nytimes.com).

Napolitan, D. A., & Goethals, G. R. (1979). The attribution of friendliness. *Journal of Experimental Social Psychology, 15,* 105–113.

Narrow, W. E., Rae, D. S., Robins, L. N., & Regier, D. A. (2002). Revised prevalence estimates of mental disorders in the United States. *Archives of General Psychiatry, 59,* 115–123.

Nash, M. R. (2001, July). The truth and the hype of hypnosis. *Scientific American,* pp. 47–55.

National Academy of Sciences. (1999). *Marijuana and medicine: Assessing the science base* (by J. A. Benson, Jr. & S. J. Watson, Jr.). Washington, DC: National Academy Press.

National Academy of Sciences. (2001). *Exploring the biological contributions to human health: Does sex matter?* Washington, DC: Institute of Medicine, National Academy Press.

National Academy of Sciences. (2002). *The polygraph and lie detection.* Washington, DC: Committee to Review the Scientific Evidence on the Polygraph, National Research Council.

National Academy of Sciences, Institute of Medicine. (1982). *Marijuana and health.* Washington, DC: National Academic Press.

National Center for Health Statistics. (1990). *Health, United States, 1989.* Washington, DC: U.S. Department of Health and Human Services.

National Center for Health Statistics. (1991). Family structure and children's health: United States, 1988, *Vital and Health Statistics, Series 10, No. 178,* CHHS Publication No. PHS 91-1506 by Deborah A. Dawson.

National Center for Health Statistics. (1992, May). *Health United States 1991.* Hyattsville, MD: Department of Health and Human Services Pub. No. (PHS) 92-1232, Table 27.

National Center for Health Statistics. (2002, September 16). Deaths: Leading Causes for 2000. *National Vital Statistics Reports, 50,* 16. Hyattsville, MD: National Center for Health Statistics.

National Center for Health Statistics. (2004, December 15). Marital status and health: United States, 1999–2002 (by Charlotte A. Schoenborn). *Advance Data from Vital and Human Statistics,* number 351. Centers for Disease Control and Prevention.

National Institute of Mental Health. (1982). *Television and behavior: Ten years of scientific progress and implications for the eighties.* Washington, DC: U. S. Government Printing Office.

National Institute of Mental Health. (1999). *ADHD: Attention deficit hyperactivity disorder.* Bethesda, MD: National Institute of Health Publication No 96-3572, 1994, update July 1, 1999.

National Institute of Mental Health. (2003). *Attention deficit hyperactivity disorder.* Bethesda, MD: National Institute of Mental Health.

National Institute on Drug Abuse. (2004). NIDA InfoFacts: Marijuana. www.nida.nih.gov/Infofax/marijuana.html.

National Institutes of Health. (1998). Clinical guidelines on the identification evaluation and treatment of overweight and obesity in adults. Executive summary, Obesity Education Initiative, National Heart, Lung, and Blood Institute.

National Research Council. (1987). *Risking the future: Adolescent sexuality, pregnancy, and childbearing.* Washington, DC: National Academy Press.

National Research Council. (1990). *Human factors research needs for an aging population.* Washington, DC: National Academy Press.

National Safety Council. (2005, October 3). Passenger deaths and death rates, from *Injury Facts* (via correspondence with Kevin T. Fearn, Research & Statistical Services Department).

Naylor, T. H. (1990). Redefining corporate motivation, Swedish style. *Christian Century, 107,* 566–570.

NCTV News. (1987, July-August). More research links harmful effects to non-violent porn, p. 12.

Neeleman, J., & Persaud, R. (1995). Why do psychiatrists neglect religion? *British Journal of Medical Psychology, 68,* 169–178.

Neese, R. M. (1991, November/December). What good is feeling bad? The evolutionary benefits of psychic pain. *The Sciences,* pp. 30–37.

Neisser, U. (1979). The control of information pickup in selective looking. In A. D. Pick (Ed.), *Perception and its development: A tribute to Eleanor J. Gibson.* Hillsdale, NJ: Erlbaum.

Neisser, U. (1997). The ecological study of memory. *Philosophical Transactions of the Royal Society of London, 352,* 1697–1701.

Neisser, U. (1998). *The rising curve: Long-term gains in IQ and related measures.* Washington, DC: American Psychological Association.

Neisser, U., Boodoo, G., Bouchard, T. J., Jr., Boykin, A. W., Brody, N., Ceci, S. J., Halpern, D. F., Loehlin, J. C., Perloff, R., Sternberg, R. J., & Urbina, S. (1996). Intelligence: Knowns and unknowns. *American Psychologist, 51,* 77–101.

Neisser, U., Winograd, E., & Weldon, M. S. (1991). Remembering the earthquake: "What I experienced" vs. "How I heard the news." Paper presented at the Psychonomic Society convention.

Neitz, J., Geist, T., & Jacobs, G. H. (1989). Color vision in the dog. *Visual Neuroscience, 3,* 119–125.

Nell, V. (2002). Why young men drive dangerously: Implications for injury prevention. *Current Directions in Psychological Science, 11,* 75–79.

Nelson, E. C., Heath, A. C., Madden, P. A. F., Cooper, M. L., Dinwiddie, S. H., Bucholtz, K. K., Glowinski, A., McLaughlin, T., Dunne, M. P., Statham, D. J., & Martin, N. G. (2002). Association between self-reported childhood sexual abuse and adverse psychosocial outcomes. *Archives of General Psychiatry, 59,* 139–145.

Nelson, G., Hoon, M. A., Chandrashekar, J., Zhang, Y., Ryba, N. J., Nicholas, J. P., & Zuker, C. S. (2001). Mammalian sweet taste receptors. *Cell, 106,* 381–390.

Nelson, M. D., Saykin, A. J., Flashman, L. A., & Riordan, H. J. (1998). Hippocampal volume reduction in schizophrenia as assessed by magnetic resonance imaging. *Archives of General Psychiatry, 55,* 433–440.

Nelson, N. (1988). *A meta-analysis of the life-event/health paradigm: The influence of social support.* Philadelphia: Temple University Ph.D. dissertation.

Nephew, T. M., Williams, G. D., Stinson, F. S., Nguyen, K., & Dufour, M. C. (1999). Surveillance report #51: Apparent per capita alcohol consumption: National, state, and regional trends, 1977–1997. Bethesda, MD: National Institute on Alcohol Abuse and Alcoholism.

Nesca, M., & Koulack, D. (1994). Recognition memory, sleep and circadian rhythms. *Canadian Journal of Experimental Psychology, 48,* 359–379.

Nestler, E. J., & Malenka, R. C. (2004, March). The addicted brain. *Scientific American,* pp. 79–83.

Neubauer, P. B., & Neubauer, A. (1990). *Nature's thumbprint: The new genetics of personality.* Reading, MA: Addison-Wesley.

Neugarten, B. L., Wood, V., Kraines, R. J., & Loomis, B. (1963). Women's attitudes toward the menopause. *Vita Humana, 6,* 140–151.

Neumann, R., & Strack, F. (2000). "Mood contagion": The automatic transfer of mood between persons. *Journal of Personality and Social Psychology, 79,* 211–223.

Nevin, J. A. (1988). Behavioral momentum and the partial reinforcement effect. *Psychological Bulletin, 103,* 44–56.

Newberg, A., & D'Aquili, E. (2001). *Why God won't go away: Brain science and the biology of belief.* New York: Simon and Schuster.

Newcomb, M. D., & Harlow, L. L. (1986). Life events and substance use among adolescents: Mediating effects of perceived loss of control and meaninglessness in life. *Journal of Personality and Social Psychology, 51,* 564–577.

Newcombe, N. S., Drummey, A. B., Fox, N. A., Lie, E., & Ottinger-Alberts, W. (2000). Remembering early childhood: How much, how, and why (or why not). *Current Directions in Psychological Science, 9,* 55–58.

Newman, A. J., Bavelier, D., Corina, D., Jezzard, P., & Neville, H. J. (2002). A critical period for right hemisphere recruitment in American Sign Language processing. *Nature Neuroscience, 5,* 76–80.

Newman, L. S., & Baumeister, R. F. (1996). Toward an explanation of the UFO abduction phenomenon: Hypnotic, elaboration, extraterrestrial sadomasochism, and spurious memories. *Psychological Inquiry, 7,* 99–126.

Newman, L. S., Duff, K. J., & Baumeister, R. F. (1997). A new look at defensive projection: Thought suppression, accessibility, and biased person perception. *Journal of Personality and Social Psychology, 72,* 980–1001.

Newman, L. S., & Ruble, D. N. (1988). Stability and change in self-understanding: The early elementary school years. *Early Child Development and Care, 40,* 77–99.

Newman, M. L., Pennebaker, J. W., Berry, D. S., & Richards, J. M. (2003). Lying words: Predicting deception from linguistic style. *Personality and Social Psychology Bulletin, 29,* 665–675.

Newport, E. L. (1990). Maturational constraints on language learning. *Cognitive Science, 14,* 11–28.

Newport, F. (2001, February). Americans see women as emotional and affectionate, men as more aggressive. *The Gallup Poll Monthly,* pp. 34–38.

Newport, F. (2002, July 29). Bush job approval update. Gallup News Service (www.gallup.com/poll/releases/pr020729.asp).

Newport, F., Moore, D. W., Jones, J. M., & Saad, L. (2003, March 21). Special release: American opinion on the war. *Gallup Poll Tuesday Briefing* (www.gallup.com).

Newton, I. (1704). *Opticks, or a treatise of the reflections, refractions, inflections & colours of light.* Oxford, England Whittlesey House, McGraw-Hill, 1931.

Neylan, T. C., Metzler, T. J., Best, S. R., Weiss, D. S., Fagan, J. A., Liberman, A., Rogers, C., Vedantham, K., Brunet, A., Lipsey, T. L., & Marmar, C. R. (2002). Critical incident exposure and sleep quality in police officers. *Psychosomatic Medicine, 64,* 345–352.

Nezlek, J. B. (2001). Daily psychological adjustment and the planfulness of day-to-day behavior. *Journal of Social and Clinical Psychology, 20,* 452–475.

Ng, S. H. (1990). Androcentric coding of *man* and *his* in memory by language users. *Journal of Experimental Social Psychology, 26,* 455–464.

NHTSA. (2000). Traffic safety facts 1999: Older population. Washington, DC: National Highway Traffic Safety Administration (National Transportation Library: www.ntl.bts.gov).

Niccols, G. A. (1994). Fetal alcohol syndrome: Implications for psychologists. *Clinical Psychology Review, 14,* 91–111.

NICHHD Early Child Care Research Network. (2002). Structure/process/outcome: Direct and indirect effects of caregiving quality on young children's development. *Psychological Science, 13,* 199–206.

NICHHD Early Child Care Research Network. (2003). Does amount of time spent in child care predict socioemotional adjustment during the transition to kindergarten? *Child Development, 74,* 976–1005.

Nickell, J. (1996, May/June). A study of fantasy proneness in the thirteen cases of alleged encounters in John Mack's *Abduction. Skeptical Inquirer,* pp. 18–20, 54.

Nickerson, R. S. (1998). Applied experimental psychology. *Applied Psychology: An International Review, 47,* 155–173.

Nickerson, R. S. (1999). How we know—and sometimes misjudge—what others know: Imputing one's own knowledge to others. *Psychological Bulletin, 125,* 737–759.

Nickerson, R. S., & Adams, M. J. (1979). Long-term memory for a common object. *Cognitive Psychology, 11,* 287–307.

Nicol, S. E., & Gottesman, I. I. (1983). Clues to the genetics and neurobiology of schizophrenia. *American Scientist, 71,* 398–404.

Nicolaus, L. K., Cassel, J. F., Carlson, R. B., & Gustavson, C. R. (1983). Taste-aversion conditioning of crows to control predation on eggs. *Science, 220,* 212–214.

Nicolelis, M. A. L., & Chapin, J. K. (2002, October). Controlling robots with the mind. *Scientific American,* pp. 46–53.

NIDA. (2002). Methamphetamine abuse and addiction. *Research Report Series.* National Institute on Drug Abuse, NIH Publication Number 02-4210.

NIDA. (2005, May). Methamphetamine. *NIDA Info Facts.* National Institute on Drug Abuse.

Nier, J. A. (2004). Why does the "above average effect" exist? Demonstrating idiosyncratic trait definition. *Teaching of Psychology, 31,* 53–54.

Nightingale, F. (1860/1969). *Notes on nursing.* Mineola, NY: Dover.

Nigro, G. (1984). Cited by U. Neisser, The role of invariant structures in the control of movement. In M. Frese & J. Sabini (Eds.), *Goal directed behavior: The concept of action in psychology.* Hillsdale, NJ: Erlbaum.

NIH. (2001, July 20). Workshop summary: Scientific evidence on condom effectiveness for sexually transmitted disease (STD) prevention. Bethesda: National Institute of Allergy and Infectious Diseases, National Institutes of Health.

NIMH. (2002, April 26). U.S. suicide rates by age, gender, and racial group. National Institute of Mental Health (www.nimh.nih.gov/research/suichart.cfm).

Nisbett, R. E. (1987). Lay personality theory: Its nature, origin, and utility. In N. E. Grunberg, R. E. Nisbett, & others, *A distinctive approach to psychological research: The influence of Stanley Schachter* (Hillsdale, NJ: 1987).

Nisbett, R. E., & Borgida, E. (1975). Attribution and the psychology of prediction. *Journal of Personality and Social Psychology, 32,* 932–943.

Nisbett, R. E., & Cohen, D. (1996). *Culture of honor: The psychology of violence in the South.* Boulder, CO: Westview Press.

Nisbett, R. E., & Ross, L. (1980). *Human inference: Strategies and shortcomings of social judgment.* Englewood Cliffs, NJ: Prentice-Hall.

Noel, J. G., Forsyth, D. R., & Kelley, K. N. (1987). Improving the performance of failing students by overcoming their self-serving attributional biases. *Basic and Applied Social Psychology, 8,* 151–162.

Nolen-Hoeksema, S. (2001). Gender differences in depression. *Current Directions in Psychological Science, 10,* 173–176.

Nolen-Hoeksema, S. (2003). *Women who think too much: How to break free of overthinking and reclaim your life.* New York: Holt.

Nolen-Hoeksema, S., & Larson, J. (1999). *Coping with loss.* Mahwah, NJ: Erlbaum.

NORC (National Opinion Research Center). (1985, October/November). Images of the world. *Public Opinion,* p. 38.

NORC (National Opinion Research Center). (2002). Percent saying sex with person other than spouse is always or almost always wrong. National Opinion Research Center General Social Survey of 2000 (www.csa.berkeley.edu:7502).

Norcross, J. C. (Ed.). (2002). *Psychotherapy relationships that work: Therapist contributions and responsiveness to patient needs.* New York: Oxford University Press.

Norem, J. K. (2001). *The positive power of negative thinking: Using defensive pessimism to harness anxiety and perform at your peak.* Basic Books.

Norman, D. A. (1988). *The psychology of everyday things.* New York: Basic Books.

Norman, D. A. (2001). The perils of home theater (www.jnd.org/dn.mss/ProblemsOfHomeTheater.html).

Noroozian, M., Lofti, J., Gassemzadeh, H., Emami, H., & Mehrabi, Y. (2003). Academic achievement and learning abilities in left-handers: Guilt or gift? *Cortex, 38,* 779–785.

Norton, K. L., Olds, T. S., Olive, S., & Dank, S. (1996). Ken and Barbie at life size. *Sex Roles, 34,* 287–294.

Norton, M. B. (2002, October 31). *They called it witchcraft.* New York Times (www.nytimes.com).

Nowak, R. (1994). Nicotine scrutinized as FDA seeks to regulate cigarettes. *Science, 263,* 1555–1556.

Nowell, A., & Hedges, L. V. (1998). Trends in gender differences in academic achievement from 1960 to 1994: An analysis of differences in mean, variance, and extreme scores. *Sex Roles, 39,* 21–43.

NSF. (2001, October 24). Public bounces back after Sept. 11 attacks, national study shows. *NSF News,* National Science Foundation (www.nsf.gov/od/lpa/news/press/ol/pr0185.htm).

Nuttin, J. M., Jr. (1987). Affective consequences of mere ownership: The name letter effect in twelve European languages. *European Journal of Social Psychology, 17,* 381–402.

Oakhill, J., Garnham, A., & Johnson-Laird, P. N. (1990). Belief bias effects in syllogistic reasoning. In D. J. Gilhooly, M. T. G. Keane, R. H. Logie, & G. Erdos (Eds.), *Lines of thinking* (Vol. 1). Chichester, England: Wiley.

Oakhill, J. V., Johnson-Laird, P. N., & Garnham, A. (1989). Believability and syllogistic reasoning. *Cognition, 31,* 117–140.

O'Connor, A. (2004, February 6). Study details 30-year increase in calorie consumption. *New York Times* (www.nytimes.com).

O'Connor, A. (2004, May 14). Pressure to go along with abuse is strong, but some soldiers find strength to refuse. *New York Times* (www.nytimes.com).

O'Connor, P., & Brown, G. W. (1984). Supportive relationships: Fact or fancy? *Journal of Social and Personal Relationships, 1,* 159–175.

Oddone-Paolucci, E., Genuis, M., & Violato, C. (2000). A meta-analysis of the published research on the effects of pornography. In C. Violato, E. Oddone-Paolucci, & M. Genuis (Eds.), *The changing family and child development.* Aldershot, England: Ashgate.

O'Donnell, L., Stueve, A., O'Donnell, C., Duran, R., San Doval, A., Wilson, R. F., Haber, D., Perry, E., & Pleck, J. H. (2002). Long-term reduction in sexual initiation and sexual activity among urban middle schoolers in the reach for health service learning program. *Journal of Adolescent Health, 31,* 93–100.

Oetting, E. R., & Beauvais, F. (1987). Peer cluster theory, socialization characteristics, and adolescent drug use: A path analysis. *Journal of Counseling Psychology, 34,* 205–213.

Oetting, E. R., & Beauvais, F. (1990). Adolescent drug use: Findings of national and local surveys. *Journal of Social and Personal Relationships, 1,* 159–175.

Oettingen, G., & Mayer, D. (2002). The motivating function of thinking about the future: Expectations versus fantasies. *Journal of Personality and Social Psychology, 83,* 1198–1212.

Oettingen, G., & Seligman, M. E. P. (1990). Pessimism and behavioural signs of depression in East versus West Berlin. *European Journal of Social Psychology, 20,* 207–220.

Offer, D., Kaiz, M., Howard, K. I., & Bennett, E. S. (2000). The altering of reported experiences. *Journal of the American Academy of Child and Adolescent Psychiatry, 39,* pp. 735–742.

Offer, D., Ostrov, E., Howard, K. I., & Atkinson, R. (1988). *The teenage world: Adolescents' self-image in ten countries.* New York: Plenum.

Office of National Statistics. (2002). *The social and economic circumstances of adults with mental disorders* (report based on the analysis of the ONS Survey of Psychiatric Morbidity Among Adults in Great Britain carried out in 2000). Norwich: HMSO.

Ogden, C. L., Fryar, C. D., Carroll, M. D., & Flegal, K. M. (2004, October 27). Mean body weight, heights, and body mass index, Unites States 1960–2002. *Advance Data from Vital and Health Statistics,* No. 347.

Öhman, A. (1986). Face the beast and fear the face: Animal and social fears as prototypes for evolutionary analyses of emotion. *Psychophysiology, 23,* 123–145.

Öhman, A., Lundqvist, D., & Esteves, F. (2001). The face in the crowd revisited: A threat advantage with schematic stimuli. *Journal of Personality and Social Psychology, 80,* 381–396.

Öhman, A., & Mineka, S. (2003). The malicious serpent: Snakes as a prototypical stimulus for an evolved module of fear. *Current Directions in Psychological Science, 12,* 5–9.

Oishi, S., Diener, E. F., Lucas, R. E., & Suh, E. M. (1999). Cross-cultural variations in predictors of life satisfaction: Perspectives from needs and values. *Personality and Social Psychology Bulletin, 25,* 980–990.

O'Keeffe, C., & Wiseman, R. (2005). Testing alleged mediumship: Methods and results. *British Journal of Psychology, 96,* 165–179.

Okun, M. S., & 12 others (2004). What's in a "smile?" Intra-operative observations of contralateral smiles induced by deep brain stimulation. *Neurocase, 10,* 271–279.

Olds, J. (1958). Self-stimulation of the brain. *Science, 127,* 315–324.

Olds, J. (1975). Mapping the mind onto the brain. In F. G. Worden, J. P. Swazey, & G. Adelman (Eds.), *The neurosciences: Paths of discovery.* Cambridge, MA: MIT Press.

Olds, J., & Milner, P. (1954). Positive reinforcement produced by electrical stimulation of the septal area and other regions of rat brain. *Journal of Comparative and Physiological Psychology, 47,* 419–427.

O'Leary, V. E., & Ickovics, J. R. (1995). Resilience and thriving in response to challenge: An opportunity for a paradigm shift in women's health. *Women's Health: Research on Gender, Behavior, and Policy, 1,* 121–142.

Olfson, M., Gameroff, M. J., Marcus, S. C., & Jensen, P. S. (2003). National trends in the treatment of attention deficit hyperactivity disorder. *American Journal of Psychiatry, 160,* 1071–1077.

Olfson, M., Marcus, S. C., Wan, G. J., & Geissler, E. C. (2004). National trends in the outpatient treatment of anxiety disorders. *Journal of Clinical Psychiatry, 65,* 1166–1173.

Olfson, M., Shaffer, D., Marcus, S. C., & Greenberg, T. (2003). Relationship between antidepressant medication treatment and suicide in adolescents. *Archives of General Psychiatry, 60,* 978–982.

Olin, S. S., & Mednick, S. A. (1996). Risk factors of psychosis: Identifying vulnerable populations premorbidly. *Schizophrenia Bulletin, 22,* 223–240.

Oliner, S. P., & Oliner, P. M. (1988). *The altruistic personality: Rescuers of Jews in Nazi Europe.* New York: Free Press.

Oliver, M. B. (1994). Portrayals of crime, race, and aggression in "reality-based" police shows: A content analysis. *Journal of Broadcasting and Electronic Media, 38,* 179-192.

Olshansky, S. J., Carnes, B. A., & Cassel, C. K. (1993, April). The aging of the human species. *Scientific American,* pp. 46-52.

Olshansky, S. J., Passaro, D. J., Hershow, R. C., Layden, J., Carnes, B. A., Brody, J., Hayflick, L., Butler, R. N., Allison, D. B., & Ludwig, D. S. (2005). A potential decline in life expectancy in the United States in the 21st century. *New England Journal of Medicine, 352,* 1138-1145.

Olson, M. A., & Fazio, R. H. (2001). Implicit attitude formation through classical conditioning. *Psychological Science, 12,* 413-417.

Olson, S. (2005). Brain scans raise privacy concerns. *Science, 307,* 1548-1550.

Olsson, A., & Phelps, E. A. (2004). Learned fear of "unseen" faces after Pavlovian, observational, and instructed fear. *Psychological Science, 15,* 822-828.

Olweus, D., Mattsson, A., Schalling, D., & Low, H. (1988). Circulating testosterone levels and aggression in adolescent males: A causal analysis. *Psychosomatic Medicine, 50,* 261-272.

Oman, D., Kurata, J. H., Strawbridge, W. J., & Cohen, R. D. (2002). Religious attendance and cause of death over 31 years. *International Journal of Psychiatry in Medicine, 32,* 69-89.

O'Neil, J. (2002, September 3). Vital Signs: Behavior: Parent smoking and teenage sex. *New York Times.*

O'Neill, M. J. (1993). The relationship between privacy, control, and stress responses in office workers. Paper presented to the Human Factors and Ergonomics Society convention.

Oren, D. A., & Terman, M. (1998). Tweaking the human circadian clock with light. *Science, 279,* 333-334.

Orlovskaya, D. D., Uranova, N. A., Zimina, I. S., Kolomeets, N. S., Vikhreva, O. V., Rachmanova, V. I., Black, J. E., Klintsova, A. Y., & Greenough, W. T. (1999). Effect of professional status on the number of synapses per neuron in the prefrontal cortex of normal human and schizophrenic brain. *Society for Neuroscience Abstracts, 329.11, 25,* 818, 1999.

Orne, M. T., & Evans, F. J. (1965). Social control in the psychological experiment: Antisocial behavior and hypnosis. *Journal of Personality and Social Psychology, 1,* 189-200.

Osborne, J. W. (1997). Race and academic disidentification. *Journal of Educational Psychology, 89,* 728-735.

Osborne, L. (1999, October 27). A linguistic big bang. *New York Times Magazine* (www.nytimes.com).

Osgood, C. E. (1962). *An alternative to war or surrender.* Urbana: University of Illinois Press.

Osgood, C. E. (1980). GRIT: A strategy for survival in mankind's nuclear age? Paper presented at the Pugwash Conference on New Directions in Disarmament.

OSS Assessment Staff. (1948). *The assessment of men.* New York: Rinehart.

Ost, L. G., & Hugdahl, K. (1981). Acquisition of phobias and anxiety response patterns in clinical patients. *Behaviour Research and Therapy, 16,* 439-447.

Ostfeld, A. M., Kasl, S. V., D'Atri, D. A., & Fitzgerald, E. F. (1987). *Stress, crowding, and blood pressure in prison.* Hillsdale, NJ: Erlbaum.

Ouellette, J. A., & Wood, W. (1998). Habit and intention in everyday life: The multiple processes by which past behavior predicts future behavior. *Psychological Bulletin, 124,* 54-74.

Overmier, J. B., & Murison, R. (1997). Animal models reveal the "psych" in the psychosomatics of peptic ulcers. *Current Directions in Psychological Science, 6,* 180-184.

Owen, R. (1814). First essay in *New view of society or the formation of character.* Quoted in *The story of New Lanark.* New Lanark Mills, Lanark, Scotland: New Lanark Conservation Trust, 1993.

Oxfam (2005, March 26). Three months on: New figures show tsunami may have killed up to four times as many women as men. Oxfam Press Release (www.oxfam.org.uk).

Oyserman, D., Coon, H. M., & Kemmelmeier, M. (2002a). Rethinking individualism and collectivism: Evaluation of theoretical assumptions and meta-analyses. *Psychological Bulletin, 128,* 3-72.

Oyserman, D., Kemmelmeier, M., & Coon, H. M. (2002b). Cultural psychology, a new look: Reply to Bond (2002), Fiske (2002), Kitayama (2002), and Miller (2002). *Psychological Bulletin, 128,* 110-117.

Ozer, E. J., Best, S. R., Lipsey, T. L., & Weiss, D. S. (2003). Predictors of posttraumatic stress disorder and symptoms in adults: A meta-analysis. *Psychological Bulletin, 129,* 52-73.

Ozer, E. J., & Weiss, D. S. (2004). Who develops posttraumatic stress disorder. *Current Directions in Psychological Science, 13,* 169-172.

Özgen, E. (2004). Language, learning, and color perception. *Current Directions in Psychological Science, 13,* 95-98.

Pacifici, R., Zuccaro, P., Farre, M., Pichini, S., Di Carlo, S., Roset, P. N., Ortuno, J., Pujadas, M., Bacosi, A., Menoyo, E., Segura, J., & de la Torre, R. (2001). Effects of repeated doses of MDMA ("Ecstasy") on cell-mediated immune response in humans. *Life Sciences, 69,* 2931-2941.

Padgett, V. R. (1989). Predicting organizational violence: An application of 11 powerful principles of obedience. Paper presented to the American Psychological Association convention.

Padilla, R. V., & Benavides, A. H. (Eds.) (1992). *Critical perspectives on bilingual education research.* Tempe, AZ: Bilingual Press.

Page, S. (1977). Effects of the mental illness label in attempts to obtain accommodation. *Canadian Journal of Behavioral Science, 9,* 84-90.

Paikoff, R. L., & Brooks-Gunn, J. (1991). Do parent-child relationships change during puberty? *Psychological Bulletin, 110,* 47-66.

Paivio, A. (1986). *Mental representations: A dual coding approach.* New York: Oxford University Press.

Palace, E. M. (1995). Modification of dysfunctional patterns of sexual response through autonomic arousal and false physiological feedback. *Journal of Consulting and Clinical Psychology, 63,* 604-615.

Palladino, J. J., & Carducci, B. J. (1983). *"Things that go bump in the night": Students' knowledge of sleep and dreams.* Paper presented at the meeting of the Southeastern Psychological Association.

Paller, K. A. (2004). Electrical signals of memory and of the awareness of remembering. *Current Directions in Psychological Science, 13,* 49-55.

Pallier, C., Colomé, A., & Sebastián-Gallés, N. (2001). The influence of native-language phonology on lexical access: Exemplar-based versus abstract lexical entries. *Psychological Science, 12,* 445-448.

Palmer, S., Schreiber, C., & Box, C. (1991). Remembering the earthquake: "Flashbulb" memory for experienced vs. reported events. Paper presented to the Psychonomic Society convention.

Paltrow, S. J. (2004, March 22). Detailed picture of U.S. actions on Sept. 22 remains elusive. *Wall Street Journal,* pp. A1, A9.

Pandey, J., Sinha, Y., Prakash, A., & Tripathi, R. C. (1982). Right-left political ideologies and attribution of the causes of poverty. *European Journal of Social Psychology, 12,* 327-331.

Panksepp, J. (1982). Toward a general psychobiological theory of emotions. *Behavioral and Brain Sciences, 5,* 407-467.

Pantelis, C., Velakoulis, D., McGorry, P. D., Wood, S. J., Suckling, J., Phillips, L. J., Yung, A. R., Bullmore, E. T., Brewer, W., Soulsby, B., Desmond, P., & McGuire, P. K. (2002). Neuroanatomical abnormalities before and after onset of psychosis: A cross-sectional and longitudinal MRI comparison. *The Lancet,* published online at image.thelancet.com/extras/01art9092web.pdf.

Pantev, C., Oostenveld, R., Engelien, A., Ross, B., Roberts, L. R., & Hoke, M. (1998). Increased auditory cortical representation in musicians. *Nature, 392,* 811–814.

Park, D. C., Lautenschlager, G., Hedden, T., Davidson, N. S., Smith, A. D., & Smith, P. K. (2002). Models of visuospatial and verbal memory across the adult life span. *Psychology and Aging, 17,* 299–320.

Park, R. L. (1999). Liars never break a sweat. *New York Times,* July 12, 1999 (www.nytimes.com).

Parker, C. P., Baltes, B. B., Young, S. A., Huff, J. W., Altmann, R. A., LaCost, H. A., & Roberts, J. E. (2003). Relationships between psychological climate perceptions and work outcomes: A meta-analytic review. *Journal of Organizational Behavior, 24,* 389–416.

Parker, S., Nichter, M., Nichter, M., & Vuckovic, N. (1995). Body image and weight concerns among African American and white adolescent females: Differences that make a difference. *Human Organization, 54,* 103–114.

Passell, P. (1993, March 9). Like a new drug, social programs are put to the test. *New York Times,* pp. C1, C10.

Pate, J. E., Pumariega, A. J., Hester, C., & Garner, D. M. (1992). Cross-cultural patterns in eating disorders: A review. *Journal of the American Academy of Child and Adolescent Psychiatry, 31,* 802–809.

Patoine, B. (2005, January–February). Imagine that! Neural prosthetics harness thoughts to control computers and robotics. *Brain Work,* pp. 1–3.

Patterson, D. R. (2004). Treating pain with hypnosis. *Current Directions in Psychological Science, 13,,* 252–255.

Patterson, D. R., & Jensen, M. (2003). Hypnosis for clinical pain control. *Psychological Bulletin, 129,* 495–521.

Patterson, F. (1978, October). Conversations with a gorilla. *National Geographic,* pp. 438–465.

Patterson, G. R., Chamberlain, P., & Reid, J. B. (1982). A comparative evaluation of parent training procedures. *Behavior Therapy, 13,* 638–650.

Patterson, G. R., Reid, J. B., & Dishion, T. J. (1992). *Antisocial boys.* Eugene, OR: Castalia.

Patterson, M., Warr, P., & West, M. (2004). Organizational climate and company productivity: The role of employee affect and employee level. *Journal of Occupational and Organizational Psychology, 77,* 193–216.

Patterson, R. (1951). *The riddle of Emily Dickinson.* Boston: Houghton Mifflin.

Patton, G. C., Coffey, C., Carlin, J. B., Degenhardt, L., Lynskey, M., & Hall, W. (2002). Cannabis use and mental health of young people: Cohort study. *British Medical Journal, 325,* 1195–1198.

Patton, W., & Mannison, M. (1995). Sexual coercion in dating situations among university students: Preliminary Australian data. *Australian Journal of Psychology, 47,* 66–72.

Paulesu, E., Demonet, J-F., Fazio, F., McCrory, E., Chanoine, V., Brunswick, N., Cappa, S. F., Cossu, G., Habib, M., Frith, C. D., & Frith, U. (2001). Dyslexia: Cultural diversity and biological unity. *Science, 291,* 2165–2167.

Paulos, J. A. (1995). *A mathematician reads the newspaper.* New York: Basic Books.

Paunonen, S. V., Zeidner, M., Engvik, H. A., Oosterveld, P., & Maliphant, R. (2000). The nonverbal assessment of personality in five cultures. *Journal of Cross-Cultural Psychology, 31,* 220–239.

Paus, T., Zijdenbos, A., Worsley, K., Collins, D. L., Blumenthal, J., Giedd, J. N., Rapoport, J. L., & Evans, A. C. (1999) Structural maturation of neural pathways in children and adolescents: In vivo study. *Science, 283,* 1908–1911.

Pavlidis, G. T. (2005, January 17). Eye movements can diagnose preschoolers at high risk for attention deficit/hyperactivity disorder (ADHD). Press release, Brunel University (www.brunel.ac.uk).

Pavlov, I. (1927). *Conditioned reflexes: An investigation of the physiological activity of the cerebral cortex.* Oxford: Oxford University Press.

Pedersen, N. L., Plomin, R., McClearn, G. E., & Friberg, L. (1988). Neuroticism, extraversion, and related traits in adult twins reared apart and reared together. *Journal of Personality and Social Psychology, 55,* 950–957.

Peeters, A., Barendregt, J. J., Willekens, F., Mackenbach, J. P., & Mamum, A. A. (2003). Obesity in adulthood and its consequences for life expectancy: A life-table analysis. *Annals of Internal Medicine, 138,* 24–32.

Peigneux, P., Laureys, S., Fuchs, S., Collette, F., Perrin, F., Reggers, J., Phillips, C., Degueldre, C., Del Fiore, G., Aerts, J., Luxen, A., & Maquet, P. (2004). Are spatial memories strengthened in the human hippocampus during slow wave sleep? *Neuron, 44,* 535–545.

Pekkanen, J. (1982, June). Why do we sleep? *Science, 82,* p. 86.

Pelham, B. W. (1993). On the highly positive thoughts of the highly depressed. In R. F. Baumeister (Ed.), *Self-esteem: The puzzle of low self-regard.* New York: Plenum.

Pendick, D. (1994, January/February). The mind of violence. *Brain Work: The Neuroscience Newsletter,* pp. 1–3, 5.

Penfield, W. (1969). Consciousness, memory, and man's conditioned reflexes. In K. Pigram (Ed.), *On the biology of learning.* New York: Harcourt, Brace & World.

Penhune, V. B., Cismaru, R., Dorsaint-Pierre, R., Petitto, L-A., & Zatorre, R. J. (2003). The morphometry of auditory cortex in the congenitally deaf measured using MRI. *NeuroImage, 20,* 1215–1225.

Pennebaker, J. (1990). *Opening up: The healing power of confiding in others.* New York: William Morrow.

Pennebaker, J. W. (2002, January 28). Personal communication.

Pennebaker, J. W., Barger, S. D., & Tiebout, J. (1989). Disclosure of traumas and health among Holocaust survivors. *Psychosomatic Medicine, 51,* 577–589.

Pennebaker, J. W., & O'Heeron, R. C. (1984). Confiding in others and illness rate among spouses of suicide and accidental death victims. *Journal of Abnormal Psychology, 93,* 473–476.

Pennebaker, J. W., & Stone, L. D. (2003). Words of wisdom: Language use over the life span. *Journal of Personality and Social Psychology, 85,* 291–301.

Peplau, L. A. (1982). Research on homosexual couples: An overview. *Journal of Homosexuality, 8*(2), 3–8.

Peplau, L. A., & Garnets, L. D. (2000). A new paradigm for understanding women's sexuality and sexual orientation. *Journal of Social Issues, 56,* 329–350.

Pepperberg, I. M. (2002). Cognitive and communicative abilities of grey parrots. *Current Directions in Psychological Science, 11,* 83–87.

Perkins, A., & Fitzgerald, J. A. (1997). Sexual orientation in domestic rams: Some biological and social correlates. In L. Ellis and L. Ebertz (Eds.), *Sexual orientation: Toward biological understanding.* Westport, CT: Praeger Publishers.

Perkins, H. W. (1991). Religious commitment, Yuppie values, and well-being in post-collegiate life. *Review of Religious Research, 32,* 244–251.

Perlmutter, M. (1983). Learning and memory through adulthood. In M. W. Riley, B. B. Hess, & K. Bond (Eds.), *Aging in society: Selected reviews of recent research.* Hillsdale, NJ: Erlbaum.

Perls, T., & Silver, M. H., with Lauerman, J. F. (1999). *Living to 100: Lessons in living to your maximum potential.* Thorndike, ME: Thorndike Press.

Perrett, D. (2002, October 1). Perception laboratory, Department of Psychology, University of St. Andrews, Scotland (www.perception.st-and.ac.uk).

Perrett, D. I., Harries, M., Misflin, A. J., & Chitty, A. J. (1988). Three stages in the classification of body movements by visual neurons. In H. B. Barlow, C. Blakemore, & M. Weston Smith (Eds.), *Images and understanding.* Cambridge: Cambridge University Press.

Perrett, D. I., Hietanen, J. K., Oram, M. W., & Benson, P. J. (1992). Organization and functions of cells responsive to faces in the temporal cortex.

Philosophical Transactions of the Royal Society of London: Series B, 335, 23–30.

Perrett, D. I., Lee, K. J., Penton-Voak, I., Rowland, D., Yoshikawa, S., Burt, D. M., Henzi, S. P., Castles, D. L., Akamatsu, S. (1998, August). Effects of sexual dimorphism on facial attractiveness. *Nature, 394,* 884–887.

Perrett, D. I., May, K. A., & Yoshikawa, S. (1994). Facial shape and judgments of female attractiveness. *Nature, 368,* 239–242.

Persky, S., & Blascovich, J. (2005). Consequences of playing violent video games in immersive virtual environments, In A. Axelsson & Ralph Schroeder (Eds.). *Work and Play in Shared Virtual Environments.* New York: Springer.

Persons, J. B. (1986). The advantages of studying psychological phenomena rather than psychiatric diagnoses. *American Psychologist, 41,* 1252–1260.

Pert, C. (1986). Quoted in J. Hooper & D. Teresi, *The three-pound universe.* New York: Macmillan.

Pert, C. B. (1986, Summer). The wisdom of the receptors: Neuropeptides, the emotions, and bodymind. *Advances* (Institute for the Advancement of Health), *3,* 8–16.

Pert, C. B., & Snyder, S. H. (1973). Opiate receptor: Demonstration in nervous tissue. *Science, 179,* 1011–1014.

Perugini, E. M., Kirsch, I., Allen, S. T., Coldwell, E., Meredith, J., Montgomery, G. H., & Sheehan, J. (1998). Surreptitious observation of responses to hypnotically suggested hallucinations: A test of the compliance hypothesis. *International Journal of Clinical and Experimental Hypnosis, 46,* 191–203.

Peschel, E. R., & Peschel, R. E. (1987). Medical insights into the castrati in opera. *American Scientist, 75,* 578–583.

Peters, T. J., & Waterman, R. H., Jr. (1982). *In search of excellence: Lessons from America's best-run companies.* New York: Harper & Row.

Peterson, C., & Barrett, L. C. (1987). Explanatory style and academic performance among university freshmen. *Journal of Personality and Social Psychology, 53,* 603–607.

Peterson, C., Peterson, J., & Skevington, S. (1986). Heated argument and adolescent development. *Journal of Social and Personal Relationships, 3,* 229–240.

Peterson, C., & Seligman, M. E. P. (2004). *Character strengths and virtues: A handbook and classification.* New York: Oxford.

Peterson, C. C., & Siegal, M. (1999). Representing inner worlds: Theory of mind in autistic, deaf, and normal hearing children. *Psychological Science, 10,* 126–129.

Peterson, L. R., & Peterson, M. J. (1959). Short-term retention of individual verbal items. *Journal of Experimental Psychology, 58,* 193–198.

Petitto, L. A., & Marentette, P. F. (1991). Babbling in the manual mode: Evidence for the ontogeny of language. *Science, 251,* 1493–1496.

Petrosino, A., Turpin-Petrosino, C., & Finckenauer, J. O. (2000). Well-meaning programs can have harmful effects! Lessons from experiments of programs such as Scared Straight. *Crime and Delinquency, 46,* 354–379.

Pettegrew, J. W., Keshavan, M. S., & Minshew, N. J. (1993). 31P nuclear magnetic resonance spectroscopy: Neurodevelopment and schizophrenia. *Schizophrenia Bulletin, 19,* 35–53.

Petticrew, C., Bell, R., & Hunter, D. (2002). Influence of psychological coping on survival and recurrence in people with cancer: Systematic review. *British Medical Journal, 325,* 1066.

Petticrew, M., Fraser, J. M., & Regan, M. F. (1999). Adverse life events and risk of breast cancer: A meta-analysis. *British Journal of Health Psychology, 4,* 1–17.

Pettigrew, T. F. (1969). Racially separate or together? *Journal of Social Issues, 25,* 43–69.

Pettigrew, T. F. (1998). Reactions toward the new minorities of western Europe. *Annual Review of Sociology, 24,* 77–103.

Pettigrew, T. F. (2004). Justice deferred a half century after Brown v. Board of Education. *American Psychologist, 59,* 521–529.

Pew. (2003). Views of a changing world 2003. The Pew Global Attitudes Project. Washington, DC: Pew Research Center for the People and the Press (http://people-press.org/reports/pdf/185.pdf).

Phelps, J. A., Davis J. O., & Schartz, K. M. (1997). Nature, nurture, and twin research strategies. *Current Directions in Psychological Science 6,* 117–120.

Philip Morris. (2003). Philip Morris USA youth smoking prevention. Teenage attitudes and behavior study, 2002. In "Raising kids who don't smoke," vol. 1(2).

Phillips, D. P. (1985). Natural experiments on the effects of mass media violence on fatal aggression: Strengths and weaknesses of a new approach. In L. Berkowitz (Ed.), *Advances in experimental social psychology* (Vol. 19). Orlando, FL: Academic Press.

Phillips, D. P., Carstensen, L. L., & Paight, D. J. (1989). Effects of mass media news stories on suicide, with new evidence on the role of story content. In D. R. Pfeffer (Ed.), *Suicide among youth: Perspectives on risk and prevention.* Washington, DC: American Psychiatric Press.

Phillips, J. L. (1969). *Origins of intellect: Piaget's theory.* San Francisco: Freeman.

Phillips, T. (2004, April 3). Quoted by T. Baldwin & G. Rozenberg, Britain 'must scrap multiculturalism.' *The Times,* p. 1.

Piaget, J. (1932). *The moral judgment of the child.* New York: Harcourt, Brace & World.

Picchioni, D., Mignot, E. J., & Harsh, J. R. (2004). The month-of-birth pattern in narcolepsy is moderated by cataplexy severity and may be independent of HLA-DQB1*0602. *Sleep, 27,* 1471–1475.

Pickar, D., Labarca, R., Linnoila, M., Roy, A., Hommer, D., Everett, D., & Payl, S. M. (1984). Neuroleptic-induced decrease in plasma homovanillic acid and antipsychotic activity in schizophrenic patients. *Science, 225,* 954–957.

Pike, K. M., & Rodin, J. (1991). Mothers, daughters, and disordered eating. *Journal of Abnormal Psychology, 100,* 198–204.

Piliavin, J. A. (2003). Doing well by doing good: Benefits for the benefactor. In C. L. M. Keyes & J. Haidt (Eds.), *Flourishing: Positive psychology and the life well-lived.* Washington, DC: American Psychological Association.

Pillemer, D. (1998). *Momentous events, vivid memories.* Cambridge: Harvard University Press, 1998.

Pillemer, D. G. (1995). What is remembered about early childhood events? Invited paper presentation to the American Psychological Society convention.

Pillsworth, M. G., Haselton, M. G., & Buss, D. M. (2004). Ovulatory shifts in female desire. *Journal of Sex Research, 41,* 55–65.

Pincus, H. A. (1997) Commentary: Spirituality, religion, and health: Expanding, and using the knowledge base. *Mind/Body Medicine, 2,* 49.

Pinel, J. P. J. (1993). *Biopsychology* (2nd ed). Boston: Allyn & Bacon.

Pingitore, R., Dugoni, B. L., Tindale, R. S., & Spring, B. (1994). Bias against overweight job applicants in a simulated employment interview. *Journal of Applied Psychology, 79,* 909–917.

Pinker, S. (1990, September-October). Quoted by J. de Cuevas, "No, she holded them loosely." *Harvard Magazine,* pp. 60–67.

Pinker, S. (1995). The language instinct. *The General Psychologist, 31,* 63–65.

Pinker, S. (1998). Words and rules. *Lingua, 106,* 219–242.

Pinker, S. (1999, June 24). His brain measured up. *New York Times* (www.nytimes.com).

Pinker, S. (2002, September 9). A biological understanding of human nature: A talk with Steven Pinker. The Edge Third Culture Mail List (www.edge.org).

Pinker, S. (2002). *The blank slate.* New York: Viking.

Pinker, S. (2005, April 22). The science of gender and science: A conversation with Elizabeth Spelke. Harvard University (www.edge.org).

Pinkerton, S. D., & Abramson, P. R. (1997). Condoms and the prevention of AIDS. *American Scientist, 85,* 364–373.

Pipe, M-E. (1996). Children's eyewitness memory. *New Zealand Journal of Psychology, 25,* 36–43.

Pipe, M-E., Lamb, M. E., Orbach, Y., & Esplin, P. W. (2004). Recent research on children's testimony about experienced and witnessed events. *Developmental Review, 24,* 440–468.

Piper, A., Jr. (1998, Winter). Multiple personality disorder: Witchcraft survives in the twentieth century. *Skeptical Inquirer,* pp. 44–50.

Pipher, M. (2002). *The middle of everywhere: The world's refugees come to our town.* New York: Harcourt Brace.

Pittenger, D. J. (1993). The utility of the Myers-Briggs Type Indicator. *Review of Eduational Research, 63,* 467–488.

Pleck, J. H., Sonenstein, F. L., & Ku, L. C. (1993). Masculinity ideology: Its impact on adolescent males' heterosexual relationships. *Journal of Social Issues, 49,* 11–29.

Pliner, P. (1982). The effects of mere exposure on liking for edible substances. *Appetite: Journal for Intake Research, 3,* 283–290.

Pliner, P., & Pelchat, M. L. (1991). Neophobia in humans and the special status of foods of animal origin. *Appetite, 16,* 205–218.

Plomin, R. (1997). Identifying genes for cognitive abilities and disabilities. In R. Sternberg, & E. Grigorenko (Eds.), *Intelligence, heredity, and environment.* New York: Cambridge University Press.

Plomin, R. (1999). Genetics and general cognitive ability. *Nature, 402* (Suppl), C25–C29.

Plomin, R. (2001). Genetics and behaviour. *The Psychologist, 14,* 134–139.

Plomin, R. (2003). General cognitive ability. In R. Plomin, J. C. DeFries, I. W. Craig, & P. McGuffin (Eds.), *Behavioral genetics in a postgenomic world.* Washington, DC: APA Books.

Plomin, R., & Bergeman, C. S. (1991). The nature of nurture: Genetic influence on "environmental" measures. *Behavioral and Brain Sciences, 14,* 373–427.

Plomin, R., Corley, R., Caspi, A., Fulker, D. W., & DeFries, J. (1998). Adoption results for self-reported personality: Evidence for nonadditive genetic effects? *Journal of Personality and Social Psychology, 75,* 211–219.

Plomin, R., & Crabbe, J. (2000). DNA. *Psychological Bulletin, 126,* 806–828.

Plomin, R., & Daniels, D. (1987). Why are children in the same family so different from one another? *Behavioral and Brain Sciences, 10,* 1–60.

Plomin, R., & DeFries, J. C. (1998, May). The genetics of cognitive abilities and disabilities. *Scientific American,* pp. 62–69.

Plomin, R., DeFries, J. C., McClearn, G. E., & Rutter, M. (1997a). *Behavioral genetics.* New York: Freeman.

Plomin, R., Fulker, D. W., Corley, R., & DeFries, J. C. (1997b). Nature, nurture and cognitive development from 1 to 16 years: A parent-offspring adoption study. *Psychological Science, 8,* 442–447.

Plomin, R., McClearn, G. E., Pedersen, N. L., Nesselroade, J. R., & Bergeman, C. S. (1988). Genetic influence on childhood family environment perceived retrospectively from the last half of the life span. *Developmental Psychology, 24,* 37–45.

Plomin, R., & McGuffin, P. (2003). Psychopathology in the postgenomic era. *Annual Review of Psychology, 54,* 205–228.

Plomin, R., Reiss, D., Hetherington, E. M., & Howe, G. W. (January, 1994). Nature and nurture: Genetic contributions to measures of the family environment. *Developmental Psychology, 30*(1), 32–43.

Plous, S. (1993). Psychological mechanisms in the human use of animals. *Journal of Social Issues, 49*(1), 11–52.

Plous, S., & Herzog, H. A. (2000). Poll shows researchers favor lab animal protection. *Science, 290,* 711.

Poldrack, R. A., & Wagner, A. D. (2004). What can neuroimaging tell us about the mind? *Current Directions in Psychological Science, 13,* 177–181.

Polivy, J., & Herman, C. P. (1985). Dieting and binging: A causal analysis. *American Psychologist, 40,* 193–201.

Polivy, J., & Herman, C. P. (1987). Diagnosis and treatment of normal eating. *Journal of Personality and Social Psychology, 55,* 635–644.

Polivy, J., & Herman, C. P. (2002). Causes of eating disorders. *Annual Review of Psychology, 53,* 187–213.

Pollack, A. (2004, April 13). With tiny brain implants, just thinking may make it so. *New York Times* (www.nytimes.com).

Pollak, S., Cicchetti, D., & Klorman, R. (1998). Stress, memory, and emotion: Developmental considerations from the study of child maltreatment. *Developmental Psychopathology, 10,* 811–828.

Pollak, S. D., & Kistler, D. J. (2002). Early experience is associated with the development of categorical representations for facial expressions of emotion. *Proceedings of the National Academy of Sciences, 99,* 9072–9076.

Pollak, S. D., & Tolley-Schell, S. A. (2003). Selective attention to facial emotion in physically abused children. *Journal of Abnormal Psychology, 112,* 323–328.

Pollard, R. (1992). 100 years in psychology and deafness: A centennial retrospective. Invited address to the American Psychological Association convention, Washington, DC.

Polusny, M. A., & Follette, V. M. (1995). Long-term correlates of child sexual abuse: Theory and review of the empirical literature. *Applied & Preventive Psychology, 4,* 143–166.

Pomerleau, O. F., Collins, A. C., Shiffman, S., & Pomerleau, C. S. (1993). Why some people smoke and others do not: New perspectives. *Journal of Consulting and Clinical Psychology, 61,* 723–731.

Poole, D. A., & Lindsay, D. S. (1995). Interviewing preschoolers: Effects of nonsuggestive techniques, parental coaching and leading questions on reports of nonexperienced events. *Journal of Experimental Child Psychology, 60,* 129–154.

Poole, D. A., & Lindsay, D. S. (2001). Children's eyewitness reports after exposure to misinformation from parents. *Journal of Experimental Psychology: Applied, 7,* 27–50.

Poole, D. A., & Lindsay, D. S. (2002). Reducing child witnesses' false reports of misinformation from parents. *Journal of Experimental Child Psychology, 81,* 117–140.

Poole, D. A., Lindsay, D. S., Memon, A., & Bull, R. (1995). Psychotherapy and the recovery of memories of childhood sexual abuse: U.S. and British practitioners' opinions, practices, and experiences. *Journal of Consulting and Clinical Psychology, 63,* 426–437.

Poon, L. W. (1987). Myths and truisms: Beyond extant analyses of speed of behavior and age. Address to the Eastern Psychological Association convention.

Pope, H. G., & Yurgelun-Todd, D. (1996). The residual cognitive effects of heavy marijuana use in college students. *Journal of the American Medical Association, 275,* 521–527.

Popenoe, D. (1993). The evolution of marriage and the problem of stepfamilies: A biosocial perspective. Paper presented at the National Symposium on Stepfamilies, Pennsylvania State University.

Popenoe, D., & Whitehead, B. D. (2002). *Should We Live Together?,* 2nd Ed. New Brunswick, NJ: The National Marriage Project, Rutgers University.

Porac, C., Coren, S., & Duncan, P. (1980). Life-span age trends in laterality. *Journal of Gerontology, 35,* 715–721.

Poremba, A., & Gabriel, M. (2001). Amygdalar efferents initiate auditory thalamic discriminative training-induced neuronal activity. *Journal of Neuroscience, 21,* 270–278.

Porkka-Heiskanen, T., Strecker, R. E., Thakkar, M., Bjorkum, A. A., Greene, R. W., & McCarley, R. W. (1997). Adenosine: A mediator of the sleep-inducing effects of prolonged wakefulness. *Science, 276,* 1265–1268.

Porter, D., & Neuringer, A. (1984). Music discriminations by pigeons. *Journal of Experimental Psychology: Animal Behavior Processes, 10,* 138–148.

Porter, R. P. (1998). Twisted tongues: The failure of bilingual education. Washington, DC: The Communitarian Network (www.gwu.edu/~ccps/pop_biling.html).

Porter, S., Birt, A. R., Yuille, J. C., & Lehman, D. R. (2000, Nov.). Negotiating false memories: Interviewer and rememberer characteristics relate to memory distortion. *Psychological Science, 11,* 507–510.

Porter, S., Yuille, J. C., & Lehman, D. R. (1999). The nature of real, implanted, and fabricated memories for childhood events: Implications for the recovered memory debate. *Law and Human Behavior, 23,* 517–537.

Posavac, H. D., Posavac, S. S., & Posavac, E. J. (1998). Exposure to media images of female attractiveness and concern with body weight among young women. *Sex Roles, 38,* 187–201.

Posner, M. I., & Carr, T. H. (1992). Lexical access and the brain: Anatomical constraints on cognitive models of word recognition. *American Journal of Psychology, 105,* 1–26.

Poulton, R., & Milne, B. J. (2002). Low fear in childhood is associated with sporting prowess in adolescence and young adulthood. *Behaviour Research and Therapy, 40,* 1191–1197.

Povinelli, D. J., & Bering, J. M. (2002). The mentality of apes revisited. *Current Directions in Psychological Science, 11,* 115–119.

Powell, J. (1989). *Happiness is an inside job.* Valencia, CA: Tabor.

Powell, K. E., Thompson, P. D., Caspersen, C. J., & Kendrick, J. S. (1987). Physical activity and the incidence of coronary heart disease. *Annual Review of Public Health, 8,* 253–287.

Powell, L. H., Schahabi, L., & Thoresen, C. E. (2003). Religion and spirituality: Linkages to physical health. *American Psychologist, 58,* 36–52.

Powell, R. A., & Boer, D. P. (1994). Did Freud mislead patients to confabulate memories of abuse? *Psychological Reports, 74,* 1283–1298.

Prairie Home Companion. (1999). *The Prairie Home Companion's Pretty Good Joke Book* (Vol. 4). St. Paul, MN: Prairie Home Companion.

Pratkanis, A. R. (1992). The cargo-cult science of subliminal persuasion. *Skeptical Inquirer, 16,* 260–272.

Pratkanis, A. R., & Greenwald, A. G. (1988). Recent perspectives on unconscious processing: Still no marketing applications. *Psychology and Marketing, 5,* 337–353.

PRB. (2002). *2002 Women of our World.* Population Reference Bureau (www.prb.org).

PRB. (2004). *2004 world population data sheet.* Washington, DC: Population Reference Bureau.

Prentice, D. A., & Miller, D. T. (1993). Pluralistic ignorance and alcohol use on campus: Some consequences of misperceiving the social norm. *Journal of Personality and Social Psychology, 64,* 243–256.

Presley, C. A., Meilman, P. W., & Lyerla, R. (1997). *Alcohol and drugs on American college campuses: Issues of violence and harrassment.* Carbondale, IL: Core Institute, Southern Illinois University.

Presson, P. K., & Benassi, V. A. (1996). Locus of control orientation and depressive symptomatology: A meta-analysis. *Journal of Social Behavior and Personality, 11,* 201–212.

Pringle, P. J., Geary, M. P., Rodeck, C. H., Kingdom, J. C., Kayamba-Kay's, S., & Hindmarsh, P. C. (2005). The influence of cigarette smoking on antenatal growth, birth size, and the insulin-like growth factor axis. *Journal of Clinical Endocrinology and Metabolism, 90,* 2556–2562.

Prioleau, L., Murdock, M., & Brody, N. (1983). An analysis of psychotherapy versus placebo studies. *The Behavioral and Brain Sciences, 6,* 275–310.

Project Match Research Group. (1997). Matching alcoholism treatments to client heterogeneity: Project MATCH posttreatment drinking outcomes. *Journal of Studies on Alcohol, 58,* 7–29.

Project on Redefining the Meaning and Purpose of Baccalaureate Degrees. (1985). *Integrity in the college curriculum.* Washington, DC: Association of American Colleges.

Pronin, E., Gilovich, T., & Ross, L. (2004). Objectivity in the eye of the beholder: Divergent perceptions of bias in self versus others. *Psychological Review, 111,* 781–799.

Pronin, E., Lin, D. Y., & Ross, L. (2002). The bias blind spot: Perceptions of bias in self versus others. *Personality and Social Psychology Bulletin, 28,* 369–381.

Provine, R. R. (2001). *Laughter: A scientific investigation.* New York: Penguin.

Psychologist (2003, April). Who's the greatest? *The Psychologist, 16,* 17.

Psychologist (2005, August). Description or explanation? *The Psychologist, 18,* 460–461.

Puchalski, C. (2005, March 12). Personal correspondence from Director, George Washington Institute for Spirituality and Health.

Putnam, F. W. (1991). Recent research on multiple personality disorder. *Psychiatric Clinics of North America, 14,* 489–502.

Putnam, F. W. (1995). Rebuttal of Paul McHugh. *Journal of the American Academy of Child and Adolescent Psychiatry, 34,* 963.

Putnam, R. (2000). *Bowling alone.* New York: Simon and Schuster.

Pyszczynski, T., Hamilton, J. C., Greenberg, J., & Becker, S. E. (1991). Self-awareness and psychological dysfunction. In C. R. Snyder & D. O. Forsyth (Eds.), *Handbook of social and clinical psychology: The health perspective.* New York: Pergamon.

Pyszczynski, T. A., Solomon, S., & Greenberg, J. (2002). *In the wake of 9/11: The psychology of terror.* Washington, DC: American Psychological Association.

Qirko, H. N. (2004). "Fictive kin" and suicide terrorism. *Science, 304,* 49–50.

Quasha, S. (1980). *Albert Einstein: An intimate portrait.* New York: Forest.

Quinn, P. C. (2002). Category representation in young infants. *Current Directions in Psychological Science, 11,* 66–70.

Quinn, P. C., Bhatt, R. S., Brush, D., Grimes, A., & Sharpnack, H. (2002). Development of form similarity as a Gestalt grouping principle in infancy. *Psychological Science, 13,* 320–328.

Quinn, P. J., Williams, G. M., Najman, J. M., Andersen, M. J., & Bor, W. (2001). The effect of breastfeeding on child development at 5 years: A cohort study. *Journal of Pediatrics & Child Health, 3,* 465–469.

Rabin, A. S., Kaslow, N. J., & Rehm, L. P. (1986). Aggregate outcome and follow-up results following self-control therapy for depression. Paper presented at the American Psychological Association convention.

Rabinowicz, T., Dean, D. E., Petetot, J. M., & de Courten-Myers, G. M. (1999). Gender differences in the human cerebral cortex: More neurons in males; more processes in females. *Journal of Child Neurology, 14,* 98–107.

Rabinowicz, T., de Courten-Myers, G. M., Petetot, J. M., Xi, G., & de los Reyes, E. (1996). Human cortex development: Estimates of neuronal numbers indicate major loss late during gestation. *Journal of Neuropathology and Experimental Neurology, 55,* 320–328.

Radford, B. (2002, November/December). Psychics wrong about Chandra Levy. *Skeptical Inquirer,* p. 9.

Raglin, J. S. (1992). Anxiety and sport performance. In J. O. Holloszy (Ed.), *Exercise and sports sciences reviews* (Vol. 20). Baltimore: Williams & Wilkins.

Rahman, Q., & Wilson, G. D. (2003). Born gay? The psychobiology of human sexual orientation. *Personality and Individual Differences, 34,* 1337–1382.

Rahman, Q., Wilson, G. D., & Abrahams, S. (2004). Biosocial factors, sexual orientation and neurocognitive functioning. *Psychoneuroendocrinology, 29,* 867–881.

Raine, A. (1999). Murderous minds: Can we see the mark of Cain? *Cerebrum: The Dana Forum on Brain Science 1*(1), 15–29.

Raine, A., Brennan, P., Mednick, B., & Mednick, S. A. (1996). High rates of violence, crime, academic problems, and behavioral problems in males with both early neuromotor deficits and unstable family environments. *Archives of General Psychiatry, 53,* 544–549.

Raine, A., Lencz, T., Bihrle, S., LaCasse, L., & Colletti, P. (2000). Reduced prefrontal gray matter volume and reduced autonomic activity in antisocial personality disorder. *Archives of General Psychiatry, 57,* 119–127.

Rainville, P., Duncan, G. H., Price, D. D., Carrier, B., & Bushnell, M. C. (1997). Pain affect encoded in human anterior cingulate but not somatosensory cortex. *Science, 277,* 968–971.

Raison, C. L., Klein, H. M., & Steckler, M. (1999). The mood and madness reconsidered. *Journal of Affective Disorders, 53,* 99–106.

Ralston, A. (2004). Enough rope. Interview for ABC TV, Australia, by Andrew Denton (www.abc.net.au/enoughrope/stories/s1227885.htm).

Ramachandran, V. S., & Blakeslee, S. (1998). *Phantoms in the brain: Probing the mysteries of the human mind.* New York: Morrow.

Ramey, S. L., & Ramey, C. T. (1992). Early educational intervention with disadvantaged children—To what effect? *Applied and Preventive Psychology, 1,* 131–140.

Rand, C. S. W., & Macgregor, A. M. C. (1990). Morbidly obese patients' perceptions of social discrimination before and after surgery for obesity. *Southern Medical Journal, 83,* 1390–1395.

Rand, C. S. W., & Macgregor, A. M. C. (1991). Successful weight loss following obesity surgery and perceived liability or morbid obesity. *Internal Journal of Obesity, 15,* 577–579.

Randi, J. (1999, February 4). 2000 Club mailing list e-mail letter.

Rapoport, J. L. (1989, March). The biology of obsessions and compulsions. *Scientific American,* pp. 83–89.

Räsänen, S., Pakaslahti, A., Syvalahti, E., Jones, P. B., & Isohanni, M. (2000). Sex differences in schizophrenia: A review. *Nordic Journal of Psychiatry, 54,* 37–45.

Ray, J. (2005, April 12). U.S. teens walk away from anger: Boys and girls manage anger differently. The Gallup Organization (www.gallup.com).

Ray, O., & Ksir, C. (1990). *Drugs, society, and human behavior* (5ᵗʰ ed.). St. Louis: Times Mirror/Mosby.

Raynor, H. A., & Epstein, L. H. (2001). Dietary variety, energy regulation, and obesity. *Psychological Bulletin, 127,* 325–341.

Reason, J. (1987). The Chernobyl errors. *Bulletin of the British Psychological Society, 40,* 201–206.

Reason, J., & Mycielska, K. (1982). *Absent-minded? The psychology of mental lapses and everyday errors.* Englewood Cliffs, NJ: Prentice-Hall.

Redelmeier, D. A., & Tversky, D. A. (1996). On the belief that arthritis pain is related to the weather. *Proceedings of the National Academy of Sciences, 93,* 2895–2896.

Redish, A. D. (2004). Addiction as a computational process gone awry. *Science, 306,* 1944–1947.

Reed, P. (2000). Serial position effects in recognition memory for odors. *Journal of Experimental Psychology: Learning, Memory, and Cognition, 26,* 411–422.

Reed, T. E., & Jensen, A. R. (1992). Conduction velocity in a brain nerve pathway of normal adults correlates with intelligence level. *Intelligence, 16,* 259–272.

Reeve, C. L., & Hakel, M. D. (2002). Asking the right questions about g. *Human Performance, 15,* 47–74.

Regier, D. A., Kaelber, C. T., Rae, D. S., Farmer, M. E., Knauper, B., Kessler, R. C., & Norquist, G. S. (1998). Limitations of diagnostic criteria and assessment instruments for mental disorders: Implications for research and policy. *Archives of General Psychiatry, 55,* 109–115.

Reichman, J. (1998). *I'm not in the mood: What every woman should know about improving her libido.* New York: Morrow.

Reiner, W. G., & Gearhart, J. P. (2004). Discordant sexual identity in some genetic males with cloacal exstrophy assigned to female sex at birth. *New England Journal of Medicine, 350,* 333–341.

Reisenzein, R. (1983). The Schachter theory of emotion: Two decades later. *Psychological Bulletin, 94,* 239–264.

Reiser, M. (1982). *Police psychology.* Los Angeles: LEHI.

Reiss, D., & Marino, L. (2001). Mirror self-recognition in the bottlenose dolphin: A case of cognitive convergence. *Proceedings of the National Academy of Sciences, 98,* 5937–5942.

Relman, A. S. (1998, December 14). A trip to stonesville. *New Republic* (www.thenewrepublic.com).

Remafedi, G. (1999). Suicide and sexual orientation: Nearing the end of controversy? *Archives of General Psychiatry, 56,* 885–886.

Remley, A. (1988, October). From obedience to independence. *Psychology Today,* pp. 56–59.

Remondes, M., & Schuman, E. M. (2004). Role for a cortical input to hippocampal area CA1 in the consolidation of a long-term memory. *Nature, 431,* 699–703.

Reneman, L., Lavalaye, J., Schmand, B., De Wolff, F. A., Van Den Brink, W., Den Heeten, G., & Booij, J. (2001). Cortical serotonin transporter density and verbal memory in individuals who stopped using 3, 4-methylenedioxy-methampamine. *Archives of General Psychiatry, 58,* 901–908.

Renner, M. J. (1992). Curiosity and exploration. In L. R. Squire (Ed.), *Encyclopedia of Learning and Memory.* New York: Macmillan.

Renner, M. J., & Renner, C. H. (1993). Expert and novice intuitive judgments about animal behavior. *Bulletin of the Psychonomic Society, 31,* 551–552.

Renner, M. J., & Rosenzweig, M. R. (1987). *Enriched and impoverished environments: Effects on brain and behavior.* New York: Springer-Verlag.

Rentfrow, P. J., & Gosling, S. D. (2003). The Do Re Mi's of everyday life: The structure and personality correlates of music preferences. *Journal of Personality and Social Psychology, 84,* 1236–1256.

Repetti, R. L., Taylor, S. E., & Seeman, T. E. (2002). Risky families: Family social environments and the mental and physical health of offspring. *Psychological Bulletin, 128,* 330–366.

Rescorla, R. A. (1988, March). Pavlovian conditioning: It's not what you think it is. *American Psychologist, 43,* 151–160.

Rescorla, R. A., & Wagner, A. R. (1972). A theory of Pavlovian conditioning: Variations in the effectiveness of reinforcement and nonreinforcement. In A. H. Black & W. F. Perokasy (Eds.), *Classical conditioning II: Current theory.* New York: Appleton-Century-Crofts.

Resnick, M. D., Bearman, P. S., Blum, R. W., Bauman, K. E., Harris, K. M., Jones, J., Tabor, J., Beuhring, T., Sieving, R., Shew, M., Bearinger, L. H., & Udry, J. R. (1997). Protecting adolescents from harm: Findings from the National Longitudinal Study on Adolescent Health. *Journal of the American Medical Association, 278,* 823–832.

Resnick, R. A., O'Regan, J. K., & Clark, J. J. (1997). To see or not to see: The need for attention to perceive changes in scenes. *Psychological Science, 8,* 368–373.

Resnick, S. M. (1992). Positron emission tomography in psychiatric illness. *Current Directions in Psychological Science, 1,* 92–98.

Responsive Community. (1996, Fall). Age vs. weight. Page 83 (reported from a *Wall Street Journal* survey).

Ressler, R. K., Burgess, A. W., & Douglas, J. E. (1988). *Sexual homicide patterns.* Boston: Lexington Books.

Reynolds, A. J., Temple, J. A., Robertson, D. L., & Manri, E. A. (2001). Long-term effects of an early childhood intervention on educational achievement and juvenile arrest. *Journal of the American Medical Association, 285,* 2339–2346.

Rhee, S. H., & Waldman, I. D. (2002). Genetic and environmental influences on antisocial behavior: A meta-analysis of twin and adoption studies. *Psychological Bulletin, 128,* 490–529.

Rhodes, G., Sumich, A., & Byatt, G. (1999). Are average facial configurations attractive only because of their symmetry? *Psychological Science, 10,* 52–58.

Rhodes, S. R. (1983). Age-related differences in work attitudes and behavior: A review and conceptual analysis. *Psychological Bulletin, 93,* 328–367.

Rholes, W. S., & Simpson, J. A. (Eds.) (2004). *Adult attachment: Theory, research, and clinical implications.* New York: Guilford.

Ribeio, S., Gervasoni, D., Soares, E. S., Zhou, Y., & Lin S-C., Pantoja, J., Lavine, M., & Nicolelis, M. A. L. (2004). Long-lasting novelty-induced neuronal reverberation during slow-wave sleep in multiple forebrain areas. *PloS Biology, 2*(1), e37 (www.plosbiology.org).

Ricciardelli, L. A., & McCabe, M. P. (2004). A biopsychosocial model of disordered eating and the pursuit of muscularity in adolescent boys. *Psychological Bulletin, 130,* 179–205.

Riccio, D. C., Millin, P. M., & Gisquet-Verrier, P. (2003). Retrograde amnesia: Forgetting back. *Current Directions in Psychological Science, 12,* 41–44.

Rice, B. (1985, September). Performance review: The job nobody likes. *Psychology Today,* pp. 30–36.

Rice, M. E., & Grusec, J. E. (1975). Saying and doing: Effects on observer performance. *Journal of Personality and Social Psychology, 32,* 584–593.

Rich, F. (2001, May 20). Naked capitalists: there's no business like porn business. *New York Times* (www.nytimes.com).

Richards, J. M., & Gross, J. J. (2000). Emotion regulation and memory: The cognitive costs of keeping one's cool. *Journal of Personality and Social Psychology, 79,* 410–424.

Richardson, J. (1993). The curious case of coins: Remembering the appearance of familiar objects. *The Psychologist: Bulletin of the British Psychological Society, 6,* 360–366.

Richardson, J. T. E., & Zucco, G. M. (1989). Cognition and olfaction: A review. *Psychological Bulletin, 105,* 352–360.

Rieff, P. (1979). *Freud: The mind of a moralist* (3rd ed.). Chicago: University of Chicago Press.

Rieger, G., Chivers, M. L., & Bailey, J. M. (2005). Sexual arousal patterns of bisexual men. *Psychological Science, 16,* 579–584.

Riis, J., Loewenstein, G., Baron, J., Jepson, C., Fagerlin, A., & Ubel, P. A. (2005). Ignorance of hedonic adaptation to hemodialysis: A study using ecological momentary assessment. *Journal of Experimental Psychology: General, 134,* 3–9.

Ring, K. (1980). *Life at death: A scientific investigation of the near-death experience.* New York: Coward, McCann & Geoghegan.

Ripple, C. H., & Zigler, E. (2003). Research, policy, and the federal role in prevention initiatives for children. *American Psychologist, 58,* 482–490.

Riskind, J. H., Beck, A. T., Berchick, R. J., Brown, G., & Steer, R. A. (1987). Reliability of DSM-III diagnoses for major depression and generalized anxiety disorder using the structured clinical interview for DSM-III. *Archives of General Psychiatry, 44,* 817–820.

Rizzolatti, G., Fadiga, L., Fogassi, L., & Gallese, V. (2002). From mirror neurons to imitation: Facts and speculations. In A. N. Meltzoff & W. Prinz (Eds.), *The imitative mind: Development, evolution, and brain bases.* Cambridge: Cambridge University Press, 2002.

Roberson, D., Davidoff, J., Davies, I. R. L., & Shapiro, L. R. (2004). The development of color categories in two languages: A longitudinal study. *Journal of Experimental Psychology: General, 133,* 554–571.

Roberts, A. H., Kewman, D. G., Mercier, L., & Hovell, M. (1993). The power of nonspecific effects in healing: Implications for psychosocial and biological treatments. *Clinical Psychology Review, 13,* 375–391.

Roberts, B. W., Caspi, A., & Moffitt, T. E. (2001). The kids are alright: Growth and stability in personality development from adolescence to adulthood. *Journal of Personality and Social Psychology, 81,* 670–683.

Roberts, B. W., Caspi, A., & Moffitt, T. E. (2003). Work experiences and personality development in young adulthood. *Journal of Personality and Social Psychology, 84,* 582–593.

Roberts, B. W., & DelVecchio, W. F. (2000). The rank-order consistency of personality traits from childhood to old age: A quantitative review of longitudinal studies. *Psychological Bulletin, 126,* 3–25.

Roberts, B. W., O'Donnell, M., & Robins, R. W. (2004). Goal and personality trait development in emerging adulthood. *Journal of Personality and Social Psychology, 87,* 541–550.

Roberts, L. (1988). Beyond Noah's ark: What do we need to know? *Science, 242,* 1247.

Roberts, T-A. (1991). Determinants of gender differences in responsiveness to others' evaluations. *Dissertation Abstracts International, 51*(8-B).

Robins, L. N., Davis, D. H., & Goodwin, D. W. (1974). Drug use by U.S. Army enlisted men in Vietnam: A follow-up on their return home. *American Journal of Epidemiology, 99,* 235–249.

Robins, L., & Regier, D. (Eds.). (1991). *Psychiatric disorders in America.* New York: Free Press.

Robins, R. W., Gosling, S. D., & Craik, K. H. (1999). An empirical analysis of trends in psychology. *American Psychologist, 54,* 117–128.

Robins, R. W., & Trzesniewski, K. H. (2005). Self-esteem development across the lifespan. *Current Directions in Psychological Science, 14*(3), 158–162.

Robins, R. W., Trzesniewski, K. H., Tracy, J. L., Gosling, S. D., & Potter, J. (2002). Global self-esteem across the lifespan. *Psychology and Aging, 17,* 423–434.

Robinson, J. (2002, October 8). What percentage of the population is gay? *Gallup Tuesday Briefing* (www.gallup.com/poll/tb/religValue/20021008b.asp).

Robinson, J. L., Kagan, J., Reznick, J. S., & Corley, R. (1992). The heritability of inhibited and uninhibited behavior: A twin study. *Developmental Psychology, 28,* 1030–1037.

Robinson, T. E., & Berridge, K. C. (2003). Addiction. *Annual Review of Psychology, 54,* 25–53.

Robinson, T. N. (1999). Reducing children's television viewing to prevent obesity. *Journal of the American Medical Association, 282,* 1561–1567.

Robinson, V. M. (1983). Humor and health. In P. E. McGhee & J. H. Goldstein (Eds.), *Handbook of humor research: Vol. II. Applied studies.* New York: Springer-Verlag.

Robison, J., & Mason, H. (2002, July 2). Getting between teens and tobacco. *Gallup Tuesday Briefing,* Gallup Organization (www.gallup.com/poll/tb/healthcare/20020702.asp).

Robison, L. (1999). Why our MENTALLY ILL son is on DEATH ROW. www.swuuc.org/fjuuc/Courier/robison.htm. See also www.larryrobison.org

Rochat, F. (1993). How did they resist authority? Protecting refugees in Le Chambon during World War II. Paper presented at the American Psychological Association convention.

Rock, I., & Palmer, S. (1990, December). The legacy of Gestalt psychology. *Scientific American,* pp. 84–90.

Rodin, J. (1986). Aging and health: Effects of the sense of control. *Science, 233,* 1271–1276.

Rodriguez, E., George, N., Lachaux, J-P., Martinerie, J., Renault, B., & Varela, F. J. (1999). Perception's shadow: Long-distance synchronization of human brain activity. *Nature, 297*, 430–433.

Roediger, H. (2001, September). Quoted by R. Herbert, Doing a number on memory. *APS Observer,* pp. 1, 7–11.

Roediger, H. L., III, & McDermott, K. B. (1995). Creating false memories: Remembering words not presented in lists. *Journal of Experimental Psychology: Learning, Memory, and Cognition, 21*, 803–814.

Roediger, H. L., III, Wheeler, M. A., & Rajaram, S. (1993). Remembering, knowing, and reconstructing the past. In D. L. Medin (Ed.), *The psychology of learning and motivation: Advances in research and theory* (Vol. 30). Orlando, FL: Academic Press.

Roehling, M. V. (1999). Weight-based discrimination in employment: Psychological and legal aspects. *Personnel Psychology, 52*, 969–1016.

Roehling, P. V., Roehling, M. V., & Moen, P. (2001). The relationship between work-life policies and practices and employee loyalty: A life course perspective. *Journal of Family and Economic Issues, 22*, 141–170.

Roenneberg, T., Kuehnle, T., Pramstaller, P. P., Ricken, J., Havel, M., Guth, A., Merrow, M. (2004). A marker for the end of adolescence. *Current Biology, 14*, R1038–9.

Roesser, R. (1998). What you should know about hearing conservation. Better Hearing Institute (www.betterhearing.org).

Rogers, C. R. (1958). Reinhold Niebuhr's *The self and the dramas of history:* A criticism. *Pastoral Psychology, 9*, 15–17.

Rogers, C. R. (1961). *On becoming a person: A therapist's view of psychotherapy.* Boston: Houghton Mifflin.

Rogers, C. R. (1980). *A way of being.* Boston: Houghton Mifflin.

Rogers, C. R. (1981, Summer). Notes on Rollo May. *Perspectives, 2*(1), p. 16.

Rogers, L. J. (2003, Fall). Seeking the right answers about right brain-left brain. *Cerebrum, 5*(4), 55–68.

Rogers, S. (1992–1993, Winter). How a publicity blitz created the myth of subliminal advertising. *Public Relations Quarterly,* pp. 12–17.

Rogers, S. (1994). Subliminal advertising: Grand scam of the 20th century. Paper presented to the American Academy of Advertising convention.

Rogerson, P. A. (1994). On the relationship between handedness and longevity. *Social Biology, 40*, 283–287.

Rohan, M. J., & Zanna, M. P. (1996). Value transmission in families," in C. Seligman, J. M. Olson, & M. P. Zanna (Eds.), *The psychology of values: The Ontario Symposium* (Vol. 8). Malwah, NJ: Erlbaum.

Rohner, R. P. (1986). *The warmth dimension: Foundations of parental acceptance-rejection theory.* Newbury Park, CA: Sage.

Rohner, R. P., & Veneziano, R. A. (2001). The importance of father love: History and contemporary evidence. *Review of General Psychology, 5*, 382–405.

Roiser, J. P., Cook, L. J., Cooper, J. D., Rubinsztein, D. C., & Sahakian, B. J. (2005). Association of a functional polymorphism in the serotonin transporter gene with abnormal emotional processing in ecstasy users. *American Journal of Psychiatry, 162*, 609–612.

Rokach, A., Orzeck, T., Moya, M., & Exposito, F. (2002). Causes of loneliness in North America and Spain. *European Psychologist, 7*, 70–79.

Rosch, E. (1974). Linguistic relativity. In A. Silverstein (Ed.), *Human communication: Theoretical perspectives.* New York: Halsted Press.

Rosch, E. (1978). Principles of categorization. In E. Rosch & B. L. Lloyd (Eds.), *Cognition and categorization.* Hillsdale, NJ: Erlbaum.

Rose, J. S., Chassin, L., Presson, C. C., & Sherman, S. J. (1999). Peer influences on adolescent cigarette smoking: A prospective sibling analysis. *Merrill-Palmer Quarterly, 45*, 62–84.

Rose, R. J., Kaprio, J., Winter, T., Dick, D. M., Viken, R. J., Pulkkinen, L., & Koskenvuo, M. (2002). Femininity and fertility in sisters with twin brothers: Prenatal androgenization? Cross-sex socialization? *Psychological Science, 13*, 263–266.

Rose, R. J., Viken, R. J., Dick, D. M., Bates, J. E., Pulkkinen, L., & Kaprio, J. (2003a). It *does* take a village: Nonfamiliar environments and children's behavior. *Psychological Science, 14*, 273–277.

Rose, S. (1999). Precis of *Lifelines: Biology, freedom, determinism. Behavioral and Brain Sciences, 22*, 871–921.

Rose, S., Bisson, J., & Wessely, S. (2003b). A systematic review of single-session psychological interventions ('debriefing') following trauma. *Psychotherapy and Psychosomatics, 72*, 176–184.

Roselli, C. E., Resko, J. A., & Stormshak, F. (2002). Hormonal influences on sexual partner preference in rams. *Archives of Sexual Behavior, 31*, 43–9.

Rosenbaum, M. (1986). The repulsion hypothesis: On the nondevelopment of relationships. *Journal of Personality and Social Psychology, 51*, 1156–1166.

Rosenberg, N. A., Pritchard, J. K., Weber, J. L., Cann, H. M., Kidd, K. K., Zhivotosky, L. A., & Feldman, M. W. (2002). Genetic structure of human populations. *Science, 298*, 2381–2385.

Rosenhan, D. L. (1973). On being sane in insane places. *Science, 179*, 250–258.

Rosenthal, R., Hall, J. A., Archer, D., DiMatteo, M. R., & Rogers, P. L. (1979). The PONS test: Measuring sensitivity to nonverbal cues. In S. Weitz (Ed.), *Nonverbal communication* (2nd ed.). New York: Oxford University Press.

Rosenzweig, M. R. (1984). Experience, memory, and the brain. *American Psychologist, 39*, 365–376.

Ross, L., Greene, D., & House, P. (1977). The false consensus effect: An egocentric bias in social perception and attribution process. *Journal of Experimental Social Psychology, 13*, 279–301.

Ross, M., McFarland, C., & Fletcher, G. J. O. (1981). The effect of attitude on the recall of personal histories. *Journal of Personality and Social Psychology, 40*, 627–634.

Ross, M., Xun, W. Q. E., & Wilson, A. E. (2002). Language and the bicultural self. *Personality and Social Psychology Bulletin, 28*, 1040–1050.

Rossi, A. S., & Rossi, P. H. (1993). *Of human bonding: Parent-child relations across the life course.* Hawthorne, NY: Aldine de Gruyter.

Rossi, P. J. (1968). Adaptation and negative after effect to lateral optical displacement in newly hatched chicks. *Science, 160*, 430–432.

Rostosky, S. S., Wilcox, B. L., Wright, M. L. C., & Randall, B. A. (2004). The impact of religiosity on adolescent sexual behavior: A review of the evidence. *Journal of Adolescent Research, 19*, 677–697.

Roth, T., Roehrs, T., Zwyghuizen-Doorenbos, A., Stpeanski, E., & Witting, R. (1988). Sleep and memory. In I. Hindmarch & H. Ott (Eds.), *Benzodiazepine receptor ligans, memory and information processing.* New York: Springer-Verlag.

Rothbart, M., Fulero, S., Jensen, C., Howard, J., & Birrell, P. (1978). From individual to group impressions: Availability heuristics in stereotype formation. *Journal of Experimental Social Psychology, 14*, 237–255.

Rothbart, M. K., Ahadi, S. A., & Evans, D. E. (2000). Temperament and personality: Origins and outcomes. *Journal of Personality and Social Psychology, 78*, 122–135.

Rothbaum, B. O., Hodges, L., Anderson, P. L., Price, L., & Smith, S. (2002). Twelve-month followup of virtual reality and standard exposure therapies for the fear of flying. *Journal of Consulting and Clinical Psychology, 70*, 428–432.

Rothbaum, F., & Tsang, B. Y-P. (1998). Lovesongs in the United States and China: On the nature of romantic love. *Journal of Cross-Cultural Psychology, 29*, 306–319.

Rothman, A. J., & Salovey, P. (1997). Shaping perceptions to motivate healthy behavior: The role of message framing. *Psychological Bulletin, 121*, 3–19.

Rothstein, W. G. (1980). The significance of occupations in work careers: An empirical and theoretical review. *Journal of Vocational Behavior, 17,* 328–343.

Rotton, J., & Kelly, I. W. (1985). Much ado about the full moon: A meta-analysis of lunar-lunacy research. *Psychological Bulletin, 97,* 286–306.

Rovee-Collier, C. (1989). The joy of kicking: Memories, motives, and mobiles. In P. R. Solomon, G. R. Goethals, C. M. Kelley, & B. R. Stephens (Eds.), *Memory: Interdisciplinary approaches.* New York: Springer-Verlag.

Rovee-Collier, C. (1993). The capacity for long-term memory in infancy. *Current Directions in Psychological Science, 2,* 130–135.

Rovee-Collier, C. (1997). Dissociations in infant memory: Rethinking the development of implicit and explicit memory. *Psychological Review, 104,* 467–498.

Rowe, D. C. (1990). As the twig is bent? The myth of child-rearing influences on personality development. *Journal of Counseling and Development, 68,* 606–611.

Rowe, D. C. (2005). Under the skin: On the impartial treatment of genetic and environmental hypotheses of racial differences. *American Psychologist, 60,* 60–70.

Rowe, D. C., Almeida, D. M., & Jacobson, K. C. (1999). School context and genetic influences on aggression in adolescence. *Psychological Science, 10,* 277–280.

Rowe, D. C., Jacobson, K. C., & Van den Oord, E. J. C. G. (1999). Genetic and environmental influences on vocabulary IQ: Parental education level as moderator. *Child Development, 70*(5), 1151–1162.

Rowe, D. C., Vazsonyi, A. T., & Flannery, D. J. (1994). No more than skin deep: Ethnic and racial similarity in developmental process. *Psychological Review, 101*(3), 396.

Rowe, D. C., Vazsonyi, A. T., & Flannery, D. J. (1995). Ethnic and racial similarity in developmental process: A study of academic achievement. *Psychological Science, 6,* 33–38.

Rozin, P., Dow, S., Mosovitch, M., & Rajaram, S. (1998). What causes humans to begin and end a meal? A role for memory for what has been eaten, as evidenced by a study of multiple meal eating in amnesic patients. *Psychological Science, 9,* 392–396.

Rozin, P., Millman, L., & Nemeroff, C. (1986). Operation of the laws of sympathetic magic in disgust and other domains. *Journal of Personality and Social Psychology, 50,* 703–712.

Ruback, R. B., Carr, T. S., & Hopper, C. H. (1986). Perceived control in prison: Its relation to reported crowding, stress, and symptoms. *Journal of Applied Social Psychology, 16,* 375–386.

Rubenstein, J. S., Meyer, D. E., & Evans, J. E. (2001). Executive control of cognitive processes in task switching. *Journal of Experimental Psychology: Human Perception and Performance, 27,* 763–797.

Rubin, D. C., Rahhal, T. A., & Poon, L. W. (1998). Things learned in early adulthood are remembered best. *Memory and Cognition, 26,* 3–19.

Rubin, J. Z., Pruitt, D. G., & Kim, S. H. (1994). *Social conflict: Escalation, stalemate, and settlement.* New York: McGraw-Hill.

Rubin, L. B. (1985). *Just friends: The role of friendship in our lives.* New York: Harper & Row.

Rubin, Z. (1970). Measurement of romantic love. *Journal of Personality and Social Psychology, 16,* 265–273.

Rubonis, A. V., & Bickman, L. (1991). Psychological impairment in the wake of disaster: The disaster-psychopathology relationship. *Psychological Bulletin, 109,* 384–399.

Ruchlis, H. (1990). *Clear thinking: A practical introduction.* Buffalo, NY: Prometheus Books.

Rudman, L. A., & Goodwin, S. A. (2004). Gender differences in automatic in-group bias: Why do women like women more than men like men? *Journal of Personality and Social Psychology, 87,* 494–509.

Ruffin, C. L. (1993). Stress and health—little hassles vs. major life events. *Australian Psychologist, 28,* 201–208.

Rule, B. G., & Ferguson, T. J. (1986). The effects of media violence on attitudes, emotions, and cognitions. *Journal of Social Issues, 42*(3), 29–50.

Rumbaugh, D. M. (1977). *Language learning by a chimpanzee: The Lana project.* New York: Academic Press.

Rumbaugh, D. M. (1994, February 15). Remarks on *Nova: Can chimps talk?* PBS Television.

Rumbaugh, D. M., & Savage-Rumbaugh, S. (1978). Chimpanzee language research: Status and potential. *Behavior Research Methods & Instrumentation, 10,* 119–131.

Rumbaugh, D. M., & Savage-Rumbaugh, S. (1994, January/February). Language and apes. *Psychology Teacher Network,* pp. 2–5, 9.

Rumbaugh, D. M., & Washburn, D. A. (2003). *Intelligence of apes and other rational beings.* New Haven, CT: Yale University Press.

Rupp, R. (1998). *How we remember and why we forget.* New York: Three Rivers Press.

Rush, A. J., & 15 others (2005). Vagus nerve stimulation for treatment-resistant depression: A randomized, controlled acute phase trial. *Biological Psychiatry, 58,* 347–354.

Rushton, J. P. (1975). Generosity in children: Immediate and long-term effects of modeling, preaching, and moral judgment. *Journal of Personality and Social Psychology, 31,* 459–466.

Rushton, J. P. (1998). The "Jensen effect" and the "Spearman-Jensen hypothesis" of black-white IQ differences. *Intelligence, 26,* 217–225.

Rushton, J. P. (2003). Race, brain size, and IQ: The case for consilience. *Behavioral and Brain Sciences, 26,* 648–649.

Rushton, J. P., & Ankney, C. D. (1996). Brain size and cognitive ability: Correlations with age, sex, social class, and race. *Psychonomic Bulletin & Review, 3,* 21–36.

Russell, B. (1930/1985). *The conquest of happiness.* London: Unwin Paperbacks.

Russell, J. A., & Carroll, J. M. (January, 1999a). On the bipolarity of positive and negative affect. *Psychological Bulletin, 125,* 3–30.

Russell, J. A., & Carroll, J. M. (1999b). The phoenix of bipolarity: Reply to Watson and Tellegan (1999). *Psychological Bulletin, 125,* 611–614.

Russell, J. A., Lewicka, M., & Niit, T. (1989). A cross-cultural study of a circumplex model of affect. *Journal of Personality and Social Psychology, 57,* 848–856.

Rusting, C. L., & Nolen-Hoeksema, S. (1998). Regulating responses to anger: Effects of rumination and distraction on angry mood. *Journal of Personality and Social Psychology, 74,* 790–803.

Rutter, M., and the English and Romanian Adoptees (ERA) study team. (1998). Developmental catch-up, and deficit, following adoption after severe global early privation. *Journal of Child Psychology and Psychiatry, 39,* 465–476.

Ryan, L., Hatfield, C., & Hofstetter, M. (2002). Caffeine reduces time-of-day effects on memory performance in older adults. *Psychological Science, 13,* 68–71.

Ryan, R. (1999, February 2). Quoted by Alfie Kohn, In pursuit of affluence, at a high price. *New York Times* (www.nytimes.com).

Ryan, R. M., & Deci, E. L. (2004). Avoiding death or engaging life as accounts of meaning and culture: Comment on Pyszczynski et al. (2004). *Psychological Bulletin, 130,* 473–477.

Ryckman, R. M., Robbins, M. A., Kaczor, L. M., & Gold J. A. (1989). Male and female raters' stereotyping of male and female physiques. *Personality and Social Psychology Bulletin, 15,* 244–251.

Saad, L. (2001, December 17). Americans' mood: Has Sept. 11 made a difference? Gallup Poll News Service (www.gallup.com/poll/releases/pr011217.asp).

Saad, L. (2002, July 30). Dieter's dilemma: Bagel or bacon? *Gallup Tuesday Briefing,* Gallup Organization (www.gallup.com/poll/tb/healthcare/20020730.asp).

Saad, L. (2002, November 21). Most smokers wish they could quit. Gallup News Service (www.gallup.com).

Saad, L. (2003, December 9). Religion is very important to majority of Americans. Gallup News Service (www.gallup.com).

Sabini, J. (1986). Stanley Milgram (1933–1984). American Psychologist, 41, 1378–1379.

Sabol, S. Z., Nelson, M. L., Fisher, C., Gunzerath, L., Brody, C. L., Hu, S., Sirota, L. A., Marcus, S. E., Greenberg, B. D., Lucas, F. R., IV, Benjamin, J. Murphy, D. L., & Hamer, D. H. (1999). A genetic association for cigarette smoking behavior. Health Psychology, 18, 7–13.

Sachdev, P., & Sachdev, J. (1997). Sixty years of psychosurgery: Its present status and its future. Australian and New Zealand Journal of Psychiatry, 31, 457–464.

Sacks, O. (1985). The man who mistook his wife for a hat. New York: Summit Books.

Sacks, O. (1990). Seeing voices: A journey into the world of the deaf. New York: HarperCollins.

Sadato, N., Pascual-Leone, A., Grafman, J., Ibanez, V., Deiber, M-P., Dold, G., & Hallett, M. (1996). Activation of the primary visual cortex by Braille reading in blind subjects. Nature, 380, 526–528.

Saffran, J. R., Aslin, R. N., & Newport, E. L. (1996). Statistical learning by 8-month-old infants. Science, 274, 1926–1928.

Sagan, C. (1979). Broca's brain. New York: Random House.

Sagan, C. (1987, February 1). The fine art of baloney detection. Parade.

Sagan, C., & Druyan, A. (1992). Shadows of forgotten ancestors: A search for who we are. New York: Random House.

Sage, C., Huang, M., Karimi, K., Gutierrez, G., Vollrath, M. A., Zhang, D-S., Garcia-Anoveros, J., Hinds, P. W., Corwin, J. T., Coren, D. P., & Chen, Z-Y. (2005). Proliferation of functional hair cells in vivo in the absence of the retinoblastoma protein. Science, 307, 1114–1118.

Sakurai, T., Amemiya, A., Ishii, M., Matsuzaki, I., Chemelli, R. M., Tanaka, H., Williams, S. C., Richardson, J. A., Kozlowski, G. P., Wilson, S., Arch, J. R. S., Buckingham, R. E., Haynes, A. C., Carr, S. A., Annan, R. S., McNulty, D. E., Liu, W-S., Terrett, J. A., Elshourbagy, N. A., Bergsma, D. J., Yanagisawa, M. (1998). Orexins and orexin receptors: A family of hypothalamic neuropeptides and G protein-coupled receptors that regulate feeding behavior. Cell, 92, 573–585.

Salive, M. E., Guralnik, J. M., & Glynn, R. J. (1993). Left-handedness and mortality. American Journal of Public Health, 83, 265–267.

Salmon, P. (2001). Effects of physical exercise on anxiety, depression, and sensitivity to stress: A unifying theory. Clinical Psychology Review, 21, 33–61.

Salovey, P. (1990, January/February). Interview. American Scientist, pp. 25–29.

Salovey, P., & Birnbaum, D. (1989). Influence of mood on health-relevant cognitions. Journal of Personality and Social Psychology, 57, 539–551.

Salovey, P., & Mayer, J. D. (1990). Emotional intelligence. Imagination, Cognition, and Personality, 9, 185–211.

Salovey, P., Mayer, J. D., & Caruso, D. (2002). The positive psychology of emotional intelligence. In C. R. Snyder & S. J. Lopez (Eds.), Handbook of positive psychology. New York: Oxford.

Salthouse, T. A. (2004). What and when of cognitive aging. Current Directions in Psychological Science, 13, 140–144.

Sampson, E. E. (2000). Reinterpreting individualism and collectivism: Their religious roots and monologic versus dialogic person–other relationship. American Psychologist, 55, 1425–1432.

Samuels, J., & Nestadt, G. (1997). Epidemiology and genetics of obsessive-compulsive disorder. International Review of Psychiatry, 9, 61–71.

Samuels, S., & McCabe, G. (1989). Quoted by P. Diaconis & F. Mosteller, Methods for studying coincidences. Journal of the American Statistical Association, 84, 853–861.

Sandberg, G. G., Jackson, T. L., & Petretic-Jackson, P. (1985). Sexual aggression and courtship violence in dating relationships. Paper presented at the meeting of the Midwestern Psychological Association.

Sanders, G., Sjodin, M., & de Chastelaine, M. (2002). On the elusive nature of sex differences in cognition hormonal influences contributing to within-sex variation. Archives of Sexual Behavior, 31, 145–152.

Sanders, G., & Wright, M. (1997). Sexual orientation differences in cerebral asymmetry and in the performance of sexually dimorphic cognitive and motor tasks. Archives of Sexual Behavior, 26, 463–479.

Sandfort, T. G. M., de Graaf, R., Bijl, R., & Schnabel, P. (2001). Same-sex sexual behavior and psychiatric disorders. Archives of General Psychiatry, 58, 85–91.

Sandler, W., Meir, I., Padden, C., & Aronoff, M. (2005). The emergence of grammar: Systematic structure in a new language. Proceedings of the National Academy of Sciences, 102, 2261–2265.

Sanford, A. J., Fray, N., Stewart, A., & Moxey, L. (2002). Perspective in statements of quantity, with implications for consumer psychology. Psychological Science, 13, 130–134.

Santarelli, L., & 11 others (2003). Requirement of hippocampal neurogenesis for the behavioral effects of antidepressants. Science, 301, 805–809.

Sanz, C., Blicher, A., Dalke, K., Gratton-Fabri, L., McClure-Richards, T., & Fouts, R. (1998, Winter-Spring). Enrichment object use: Five chimpanzees' use of temporary and semi-permanent enrichment objects. Friends of Washoe, 19(1,2), 9–14.

Sanz, C., Morgan, D., Gulick, S. (2004). New insights into chimpanzees, tools, and termites from the Congo Basin. American Naturalist, 164, 567–581.

Sapadin, L. A. (1988). Friendship and gender: Perspectives of professional men and women. Journal of Social and Personal Relationships, 5, 387–403.

Sapolsky, B. S., & Tabarlet, J. O. (1991). Sex in primetime television: 1979 versus 1989. Journal of Broadcasting and Electronic Media, 35, 505–516.

Sapolsky, R. (1999, March). Stress and your shrinking brain. Discover, pp. 116–120.

Sapolsky, R. (2003, September). Taming stress. Scientific American, pp. 87–95.

Sapolsky, R. (2005). The influence of social hierarchy on primate health. Science, 308, 648–652.

Sapolsky, R. M., & Finch, C. E. (1991, March/April). On growing old. The Sciences, pp. 30–38.

Sato, K. (1987). Distribution of the cost of maintaining common resources. Journal of Experimental Social Psychology, 23, 19–31.

Saudino, K. J., Wertz, A. E., Gagne, J. R., & Chawla, S. (2004). Night and day: Are siblings as different in temperament as parents say they are? Journal of Personality and Social Psychology, 87, 698–706.

Savage-Rumbaugh, E. S., Murphy, J., Sevcik, R. A., Brakke, K. E., Williams, S. L., & Rumbaugh, D. M., with commentary by Bates, E. (1993). Language comprehension in ape and child. Monographs of the Society for Research in Child Development, 58 (no. 233), 1–254.

Savic, I., Berglund, H., & Lindstrom, P. (2005). Brain response to putative pheromones in homosexual men. Proceedings of the National Academy of Sciences, 102, 7356–7361.

Savitsky, K., Epley, N., & Gilovich, T. (2001). Do others judge us as harshly as we think? Overestimating the impact of our failures, shortcomings, and mishaps. Journal of Personality and Social Psychology, 81, 44–56.

Savitsky, K., & Gilovich, T. (2003). The illusion of transparency and the alleviation of speech anxiety. Journal of Experimental Social Psychology, 39, 618–625.

Savoy, C., & Beitel, P. (1996). Mental imagery for basketball. *International Journal of Sport Psychology, 27*, 454–462.

Sawyer, M. G., Arney, F. M., Baghurst, P. A., Clark, J. J., Graetz, B. W., Kosky, R. J., Nurcombe, B., Patton, G. C., Prior, M. R., Raphael, B., Rey, J., Whaites, L. C., & Zubrick, S. R. (2000). *The mental health of young people in Australia.* Canberra: Mental Health and Special Programs Branch, Commonwealth Department of Health and Aged Care.

Sax, L. J., Hurtado, S., Lindholm, J A., Astin, A. W., Korn, W. S., & Mahoney, K. M. (2004). *The American freshman: National norms for Fall, 2004.* Los Angeles: Cooperative Institutional Research Program, UCLA.

Sax, L. J., Lindholm, J. A., Astin, A. W., Korn, W. S., & Mahoney, K. M. (2002). *The American freshman: National norms for Fall 2002.* Los Angeles, CA: Higher Education Research Institute, UCLA.

Sayre, R. F. (1979). The parents' last lessons. In D. D. Van Tassel (Ed.), *Aging, death, and the completion of being.* Philadelphia: University of Pennsylvania Press.

Sbraga, T. P., & O'Donohue, W. (2003). Post hoc reasoning in possible cases of child sexual abuse: Symptoms of inconclusive origins. *Clinical Psychology: Science and Practice, 10*, 320–334.

Scarborough, E., & Furumoto, L. (1987). *Untold lives: The first generation of American women psychologists.* New York: Columbia University Press.

Scarr, S. (1984, May). What's a parent to do? A conversation with E. Hall. *Psychology Today*, pp. 58–63.

Scarr, S. (1986). *Mother care/other care.* New York: Basic Books.

Scarr, S. (1989). Protecting general intelligence: Constructs and consequences for interventions. In R. J. Linn (Ed.), *Intelligence: Measurement, theory, and public policy.* Champaign: University of Illinois Press.

Scarr, S. (1990). Back cover comments on J. Dunn & R. Plomin (1990). *Separate lives: Why siblings are so different.* New York: Basic Books.

Scarr, S. (1993, May/June). Quoted by *Psychology Today,* Nature's thumbprint: So long, superparents, p. 16.

Scarr, S. (1997). Why child care has little impact on most children's development. *Current Directions in Psychological Science, 6*, 143–148.

Schab, F. R. (1991). Odor memory: Taking stock. *Psychological Bulletin, 109*, 242–251.

Schachter, S. (1982). Recidivism and self-cure of smoking and obesity. *American Psychologist, 37*, 436–444.

Schachter, S., & Singer, J. E. (1962). Cognitive, social and physiological determinants of emotional state. *Psychological Review, 69*, 379–399.

Schacter, D. L. (1992). Understanding implicit memory: A cognitive neuroscience approach. *American Psychologist, 47*, 559–569.

Schacter, D. L. (1996). *Searching for memory: The brain, the mind, and the past.* New York: Basic Books.

Schacter, D. L. (1999). The seven sins of memory: Insights from psychology and cognitive neuroscience. *American Psychologist, 54*, 182–201.

Schafer, G. (2005). Infants can learn decontextualized words before their first birthday. *Child Development, 76*, 87–96.

Schaie, K. W. (1994). The life course of adult intellectual abilities. *American Psychologist, 49*, 304–313.

Schaie, K. W., & Geiwitz, J. (1982). *Adult development and aging.* Boston: Little, Brown.

Schall, T., & Smith, G. (2000, Fall). Career trajectories in baseball. *Chance*, pp. 35–38.

Scheier, M. F., & Carver, C. S. (1992). Effects of optimism on psychological and physical well-being: Theoretical overview and empirical update. *Cognitive Therapy and Research, 16*, 201–228.

Schein, E. H. (1956). The Chinese indoctrination program for prisoners of war: A study of attempted brainwashing. *Psychiatry, 19*, 149–172.

Schelling, T. C. (1992). Addictive drugs: The cigarette experience. *Science, 255*, 430–433.

Scherer, K. R., Banse, R., & Wallbott, H. G. (2001). Emotion inferences from vocal expression correlate across languages and cultures. *Journal of Cross-Cultural Psychology, 32*, 76–92.

Schiavi, R. C., & Schreiner-Engel, P. (1988). Nocturnal penile tumescence in healthy aging men. *Journal of Gerontology: Medical Sciences, 43*, M146–150.

Schiffenbauer, A., & Schiavo, R. S. (1976). Physical distance and attraction: An intensification effect. *Journal of Experimental Social Psychology, 12*, 274–282.

Schimel, J., Arndt, J., Pyszczynski, T., & Greenberg, J. (2001). Being accepted for who we are: Evidence that social validation of the intrinsic self reduces general defensiveness. *Journal of Personality and Social Psychology, 80*, 35–52.

Schimel, J., Greenberg, J., & Martens, A. (2003). Evidence that projection of a feared trait can serve a defensive function. *Personality and Social Psychology Bulletin, 29*, 969–979.

Schlaug, G., Jancke, L., Huang, Y., & Steinmetz, H. (1995). In vivo evidence of structural brain asymmetry in musicians. *Science, 267*, 699–701.

Schmidt, F. L. (2002). The role of general cognitive ability and job performance: Why there cannot be a debate. *Human Performance, 15*, 187–210.

Schmidt, F. L., & Hunter, J. E. (1998). The validity and utility of selection methods in personnel psychology: Practical and theoretical implications of 85 years of research findings. *Psychological Bulletin, 124*, 262–274.

Schmidt, F. L., & Zimmerman, R. D. (2004). A counterintuitive hypothesis about employment interview validity and some supporting evidence. *Journal of Applied Psychology, 89*, 553–561.

Schmitt, D. P., & Pilcher, J. J. (2004). Evaluating evidence of psychological adaptation: How do we know one when we see one? *Psychological Science, 15*, 643–649.

Schnaper, N. (1980). Comments germane to the paper entitled "The reality of death experiences" by Ernst Rodin. *Journal of Nervous and Mental Disease, 168*, 268–270.

Schneider, R. H., Alexander, C. N., Staggers, F., Rainforth, M., Salerno, J. W., Hartz, A., Arndt, S., Barnes, V. A., & Nidich, S. (2005). Long-term effects of stress reduction on mortality in persons > or = 55 years of age with systemic hypertension. *American Journal of Cardiology, 95*, 1060–1064.

Schneider, S. L. (2001). In search of realistic optimism: Meaning, knowledge, and warm fuzziness. *American Psychologist, 56*, 250–263.

Schneiderman, N. (1999). Behavioral medicine and the management of HIV/AIDS. *International Journal of Behavioral Medicine, 6*, 3–12.

Schneiderman, N., Chesney, M. A., & Krantz, D. S. (1989). Biobehavioral aspects of cardiovascular disease: Progress and prospects. *Health Psychology, 8*, 649–676.

Schoeneman, T. J. (1994). *Individualism.* In V. S. Ramachandran (Ed.), *Encyclopedia of Human Behavior.* San Diego: Academic Press.

Schofield, J. W. (1986). Black-White contact in desegregated schools. In M. Hewstone & R. Brown (Eds.), *Contact and conflict in intergroup encounters.* Oxford: Basil Blackwell.

Schonfield, D., & Robertson, B. A. (1966). Memory storage and aging. *Canadian Journal of Psychology, 20*, 228–236.

Schooler, J. W., Gerhard, D., & Loftus, E. F. (1986). Qualities of the unreal. *Journal of Experimental Psychology: Learning, Memory, and Cognition, 12*, 171–181.

Schulenberg, J., Bachman, J. G., O'Malley, P. M., & Johnston, L. D. (March, 1994). High school educational success and subsequent substance use: A panel analysis following adolescents into young adulthood. *Journal of Health & Social Behavior, 35*(1), 45–62.

Schuman, H., & Scott, J. (June, 1989). Generations and collective memories. *American Sociological Review, 54*(3), 359–381.

Schwartz, B. (1984). *Psychology of learning and behavior* (2nd ed.). New York: Norton.

Schwartz, B. (2000). Self-determination: The tyranny of freedom. *American Psychologist, 55,* 79–88.

Schwartz, B. (2004). *The paradox of choice: Why more is less.* New York: Ecco/HarperCollins.

Schwartz, J., & Estrin, J. (2004, November 7). Living for today, locked in a paralyzed body. *New York Times* (www.nytimes.com).

Schwartz, J., & Pomfret, J. (1998, November 20). Smoking-related deaths in China are up sharply. *Washington Post* (www.washingtonpost.com).

Schwartz, J. M., Stoessel, P. W., Baxter, L. R., Jr., Martin, K. M., & Phelps, M. E. (1996). Systematic changes in cerebral glucose metabolic rate after successful behavior modification treatment of obsessive-compulsive disorder. *Archives of General Psychiatry, 53,* 109–113.

Schwarz, N., Strack, F., Kommer, D., & Wagner, D. (1987). Soccer, rooms, and the quality of your life: Mood effects on judgments of satisfaction with life in general and with specific domains. *European Journal of Social Psychology, 17,* 69–79.

Science (2004). Obesity drugs. *Science, 306,* 2014.

Sclafani, A. (1995). How food preferences are learned: Laboratory animal models. *Proceedings of the Nutrition Society, 54,* 419–427.

Scott, D. J., & others. (2004, November 9). U-M team reports evidence that smoking affects human brain's natural "feel good" chemical system (press release by Kara Gavin). University of Michigan Medical School (www.med.umich.edu).

Scott, W. A., Scott, R., & McCabe, M. (1991). Family relationships and children's personality: A cross-cultural, cross-source comparison. *British Journal of Social Psychology, 30,* 1–20.

Sechrest, L., Stickle, T. R., & Stewart, M. (1998). The role of assessment in clinical psychology. In A. Bellack, M. Hersen (Series eds.) & C. R. Reynolds (Vol. ed.), *Comprehensive clinical psychology: Vol 4: Assessment.* New York: Pergamon.

Seeman, P., Guan, H-C., & Van Tol, H. H. M. (1993). Dopamine D4 receptors elevated in schizophrenia. *Nature, 365,* 441–445.

Segal, N. L. (1999). *Entwined lives: Twins and what they tell us about human behavior.* New York: Dutton.

Segal, N. L. (2000). Virtual twins: New findings on within-family environmental influences on intelligence. *Journal of Educational Psychology, 92,* 442–448.

Segall, M. H., Dasen, P. R., Berry, J. W., & Poortinga, Y. H. (1990). *Human behavior in global perspective: An introduction to cross-cultural psychology.* New York: Pergamon.

Segerstrom, S. C., McCarthy, W. J., Caskey, N. H., Gross, T. D., & Jarvik, M. E. (1993). Optimistic bias among cigarette smokers. *Journal of Applied Social Psychology, 23,* 1606–1618.

Segerstrom, S. C., Taylor, S. E., Kemeny, M. E., & Fahey, J. L. (1998). Optimism is associated with mood, coping, and immune change in response to stress. *Journal of Personality and Social Psychology, 74,* 1646–1655.

Segerstrom, S., & Miller, G. E. (2004). Psychological stress and the human immune system: A meta-analytic study of 30 years of inquiry. *Psychological Bulletin, 130,* 601–630.

Seidlitz, L., & Diener, E. (1998). Sex differences in the recall of affective experiences. *Journal of Personality and Social Psychology, 74,* 262–271.

Self, C. E. (1994). *Moral culture and victimization in residence halls.* Dissertation: Thesis (M.A.). Bowling Green University.

Seligman, M. E. P. (1974, May). Submissive death: Giving up on life. *Psychology Today,* pp. 80–85.

Seligman, M. E. P. (1975). *Helplessness: On depression, development and death.* San Francisco: Freeman.

Seligman, M. E. P. (1991). *Learned optimism.* New York: Knopf.

Seligman, M. E. P. (1994). *What you can change and what you can't.* New York: Knopf.

Seligman, M. E. P. (1995). The effectiveness of psychotherapy: The Consumer Reports study. *American Psychologist, 50,* 965–974.

Seligman, M. E. P. (2002). *Authentic happiness: Using the new positive psychology to realize your potential for lasting fulfillment.* New York: Free Press.

Seligman, M. E. P. (2004). Eudaemonia, the good life. A talk with Martin Seligman. www.edge.org.

Seligman, M. E. P., & Schulman, P. (1986). Explanatory style as a predictor of productivity and quitting among life insurance sales agents. *Journal of Personality and Social Psychology, 50,* 832–838.

Seligman, M. E. P., Steen, T. A., Park, N., & Peterson, C. (2005). Positive psychology progress: Empirical validation of interventions. *American Psychologist, 60,* 410–421.

Seligman, M. E. P., & Yellen, A. (1987). What is a dream? *Behavior Research and Therapy, 25,* 1–24.

Selye, H. (1936). A syndrome produced by diverse nocuous agents. *Nature, 138,* 32.

Selye, H. (1976). *The stress of life.* New York: McGraw-Hill.

Sen, A. (2003). Missing women—revisited. *British Medical Journal, 327,* 1297–1298.

Senghas, A., & Coppola, M. (2001). Children creating language: How Nicaraguan Sign Language acquired a spatial grammar. *Psychological Science, 12,* 323–328.

Sengupta, S. (2001, October 10). Sept. 11 attack narrows the racial divide. *New York Times* (www.nytimes.com).

Serdula, M. K., Mokdad, A., Williamson, D. F., Galuska, D. A., Mendlein, J. M., & Heath, G. W. (1999). Prevalence of attempting weight loss and strategies for controlling weight. *Journal of the American Medical Association, 282,* 1353–1358.

Sergent, C., & Dehaene, S. (2004). Is consciousness a gradual phenomenon? *Psychological Science, 15,* 720–728.

Serruya, M. D., Hatsopoulos, N. G., Paninski, L., Fellow, M. R., & Donoghue, J. P. (2002). Instant neural control of a movement signal. *Nature, 416,* 141–142.

Service, R. F. (1994). Will a new type of drug make memory-making easier? *Science, 266,* 218–219.

Seto, M. C., & Barbaree, H. E. (1995). The role of alcohol in sexual aggression. *Clinical Psychology Review, 15,* 545–566.

Shadish, W. R., Baldwin, S. A. (2005). Effects of behavioral marital therapy: A meta-analysis of randomized controlled trials. *Journal of Consulting and Clinical Psychology, 73,* 6–14.

Shadish, W. R., Matt, G. E., Navarro, A. M., & Phillips, G. (2000). The effects of psychological therapies under clinically representative conditions: A meta-analysis. *Psychological Bulletin, 126,* 512–529.

Shadish, W. R., Montgomery, L. M., Wilson, P., Wilson, M. R., Bright, I., & Okwumabua, T. (1993). Effects of family and marital psychotherapies: A meta-analysis. *Journal of Consulting and Clinical Psychology, 61,* 992–1002.

Shaffer, D. M., Krauchunas, S. M., Eddy, M., & McBeath, M. K. (2004). How dogs navigate to catch frisbees. *Psychological Science, 15,* 437–441.

Shafir, E., & LeBoeuf, R. A. (2002). Rationality. *Annual Review of Psychology, 53,* 491–517.

Shamir, B., House, R. J., & Arthur, M. B. (1993). The motivational effects of charismatic leadership: A self-concept based theory. *Organizational Science, 4*(4), 577–594.

Shapiro, F. (1989). Efficacy of the eye movement desensitization procedure in the treatment of traumatic memories. *Journal of Traumatic Stress, 2,* 199–223.

Shapiro, F. (1995). *Eye movement desensitization and reprocessing: Basic principles, protocols, and procedures.* New York: Guilford.

Shapiro, F. (1999). Eye movement desensitization and reprocessing (EMDR) and the anxiety disorders: Clinical and research implications of an integrated psychotherapy treatment. *Journal of Anxiety Disorders, 13*, 35–67.

Shapiro, F. (Ed.) (2002). *EMDR as an integrative psychotherapy approach: Experts of diverse orientations explore the paradigm prism.* Washington, DC: APA Books.

Sharma, A. R., McGue, M. K., & Benson, P. L. (1998). The psychological adjustment of United States adopted adolescents and their nonadopted siblings. *Child Development, 69*, 791–802.

Shaughnessy, J., & Zechmeister, E. (1992). Memory monitoring accuracy as influenced by the distribution of retrieval practice. *Bulletin of the Psychonomic Society, 30*, 125–128.

Shaver, P. R., Morgan, H. J., & Wu, S. (1996). Is love a basic emotion? *Personal Relationships, 3*, 81–96.

Shaw, H. L. (1989–90). Comprehension of the spoken word and ASL translation by chimpanzees (Pan troglodytes). *Friends of Washoe, 9*(1/2), 8–19.

Sheehan, S. (1982). *Is there no place on earth for me?* Boston: Houghton Mifflin.

Sheldon, K. M., Elliot, A. J., Kim, Y., & Kasser, T. (2001). What is satisfying about satisfying events? Testing 10 candidate psychological needs. *Journal of Personality and Social Psychology, 80*, 325–339.

Shelton, J. N., & Richeson, J. A. (2005). Intergroup contact and pluralistic ignorance. *Journal of Personality and Social Psychology, 88*, 91–107.

Shenton, M. E. (1992). Abnormalities of the left temporal lobe and thought disorder in schizophrenia: A quantitative magnetic resonance imaging study. *New England Journal of Medicine, 327*, 604–612.

Shepard, R. N. (1990). *Mind sights.* New York: Freeman.

Shepherd, C. (1997, April). News of the weird. *Funny Times*, p. 15.

Shepherd, C. (1999, June). News of the weird. *Funny Times*, p. 21.

Shepherd, C., Kohut, J. J., & Sweet, R. (1990). *More news of the weird.* New York: Penguin/Plume Books.

Sheridan, E. P. (1999). Psychology's future in medical schools and academic health care centers. *American Psychologist, 54*, 267–271.

Sherif, M. (1966). *In common predicament: Social psychology of intergroup conflict and cooperation.* Boston: Houghton Mifflin.

Sherman, D. (2004, May 30). Doctors peer into brains to gauge antidepressants. Reuters News Service.

Sherman, P. W., & Flaxman, S. M. (2001). Protecting ourselves from food. *American Scientist, 89*, 142–151.

Shermer, M. (1999). *How we believe: The search for God in an age of science.* New York: Freeman.

Sherry, D., & Vaccarino, A. L. (1989). Hippocampus and memory for food caches in black-capped chickadees. *Behavioral Neuroscience, 103*, 308–318.

Shettleworth, S. J. (1973). Food reinforcement and the organization of behavior in golden hamsters. In R. A. Hinde & J. Stevenson-Hinde (Eds.), *Constraints on learning.* London: Academic Press.

Shettleworth, S. J. (1993). Where is the comparison in comparative cognition? Alternative research programs. *Psychological Science, 4*, 179–184.

Shneidman, E. (1987, March). At the point of no return. *Psychology Today*, pp. 54–58.

Shobe, K. K., & Kihlstrom, J. F. (June, 1997). Is traumatic memory special? *Current Directions in Psychological Science, 6*(3), 70–74.

Shotland, R. L. (1984, March 12). Quoted in Maureen Dowd, 20 years after the murder of Kitty Genovese, the question remains: Why? *The New York Times*, p. B1.

Showers, C. (1992). The motivational and emotional consequences of considering positive or negative possibilities for an upcoming event. *Journal of Personality and Social Psychology, 63*, 474–484.

Shulman, P. (2000, June). The girl who loved math. *Discover*, pp. 67–70.

Sieff, E. M., Dawes, R. M., & Loewenstein, G. (1999). Anticipated versus actual reaction to HIV test results. *The American Journal of Psychology, 112*, 297–313.

Siegel, J. M. (1990). Stressful life events and use of physician services among the elderly: The moderating role of pet ownership. *Journal of Personality and Social Psychology, 58*, 1081–1086.

Siegel, J. (2000, Winter). Recent developments in narcolepsy research: An explanation for patients and the general public. *Narcolepsy Network Newsletter*, pp. 1–2.

Siegel, J. M. (2002). Sleep. *Encarta encyclopedia* (www.bol.ucla.edu/~jsiegel/encarta/Article.htm).

Siegel, J. M. (2003, November). Why we sleep. *Scientific American*, pp. 92–97.

Siegel, R. K. (1977, October). Hallucinations. *Scientific American*, pp. 132–140.

Siegel, R. K. (1980). The psychology of life after death. *American Psychologist, 35*, 911–931.

Siegel, R. K. (1982, October). Quoted by J. Hooper, Mind tripping. *Omni*, pp. 72–82, 159–160.

Siegel, R. K. (1984, March 15). Personal communication.

Siegel, R. K. (1990). *Intoxication.* New York: Pocket Books.

Siegler, R. S., & Ellis, S. (1996). Piaget on childhood. *Psychological Science, 7*, 211–215.

Silbersweig, D. A., Stern, E., Frith, C., Cahill, C., Holmes, A., Grootoonk, S., Seaward, J., McKenna, P., Chua, S. E., Schnorr, L., Jones, T., & Frackowiak, R. S. J. (1995). A functional neuroanatomy of hallucinations in schizophrenia. *Nature, 378*, 176–179.

Silva, A. J., Stevens, C. F., Tonegawa, S., & Wang, Y. (1992). Deficient hippocampal long-term potentiation in alpha-calcium-calmodulin kinase II mutant mice. *Science, 257*, 201–206.

Silva, C. E., & Kirsch, I. (1992). Interpretive sets, expectancy, fantasy proneness, and dissociation as predictors of hypnotic response. *Journal of Personality and Social Psychology, 63*, 847–856.

Silver, M., & Geller, D. (1978). On the irrelevance of evil: The organization and individual action. *Journal of Social Issues, 34*, 125–136.

Silverman, I., & Eals, M. (1992). Sex differences in spatial abilities: Evolutionary theory and data. In J. H. Barkow, L. Cosmides, & J. Tooby (Eds.), *The adapted mind: Evolutionary psychology and the generation of culture.* New York: Oxford University Press.

Silverman, I., & Phillips, K. (1998). The evolutionary psychology of spatial sex differences. In C. Crawford & D. L. Krebs (Eds.), *Handbook of Evolutionary Psychology: Ideas, Issues, and Applications.* Mahwah, NJ: Erlbaum.

Silverman, K., Evans, S. M., Strain, E. C., & Griffiths, R. R. (1992). Withdrawal syndrome after the double-blind cessation of caffeine consumption. *New England Journal of Medicine, 327*, 1109–1114.

Silverman, P. S., & Retzlaff, P. D. (1986). Cognitive stage regression through hypnosis: Are earlier cognitive stages retrievable? *International Journal of Clinical and Experimental Hypnosis, 34*, 192–204.

Simek, T. C., & O'Brien, R. M. (1981). *Total golf: A behavioral approach to lowering your score and getting more out of your game.* Huntington, NY: B-MOD Associates.

Simek, T. C., & O'Brien, R. M. (1988). A chaining-mastery, discrimination training program to teach Little Leaguers to hit a baseball. *Human Performance, 1*, 73–84.

Simon, H. (1998, November 16). Flash of genius (interview with P. E. Ross). *Forbes*, pp. 98–104.

Simon, H. (2001, February). Quoted by A. M. Hayashi, "When to trust your gut." *Harvard Business Review*, pp. 59–65.

Simons, D. J. (1996). In sight, out of mind: When object representations fail. *Psychological Science, 7,* 301-305.

Simons, D. J., & Ambinder, M. S. (2005). Change blindness: Theory and consequences. *Current Directions in Psychological Science, 14,* 44-48.

Simons, D. J., & Chabris, C. F. (1999). Gorillas in our midst: Sustained inattentional blindness for dynamic events. *Perception, 28,* 1059-1074.

Simonton, D. K. (1988). Age and outstanding achievement: What do we know after a century of research? *Psychological Bulletin, 104,* 251-267.

Simonton, D. K. (1990). Creativity in the later years: Optimistic prospects for achievement. *The Gerontologist, 30,* 626-631.

Simonton, D. K. (1992). The social context of career success and course for 2,026 scientists and inventors. *Personality and Social Psychology Bulletin, 18,* 452-463.

Simonton, D. K. (2000). Creativity: Cognitive, personal, developmental, and social aspects. *American Psychologist, 55,* 151-158.

Sinclair, R. C., Hoffman, C., Mark, M. M., Martin, L. L., & Pickering, T. L. (1994). Construct accessibility and the misattribution of arousal: Schachter and Singer revisited. *Psychological Science, 5,* 15-18.

Singelis, T. M., Bond, M. H., Sharkey, W. F., & Lai, C. S. Y. (1999). Unpackaging culture's influence on self-esteem and embarrassability: The role of self-construals. *Journal of Cross-Cultural Psychology, 30,* 315-341.

Singelis, T. M., & Sharkey, W. F. (1995). Culture, self-construal, and embarrassability. *Cross-Cultural Psychology, 26,* 622-644.

Singer, J. L. (1981). Clinical intervention: New developments in methods and evaluation. In L. T. Benjamin, Jr. (Ed.), *The G. Stanley Hall Lecture Series* (Vol. 1). Washington, DC: American Psychological Association.

Singer, T., Seymour, B., O'Doherty, J., Kaube, H., Dolan, R. J., & Frith, C. (2004). Empathy for pain involves the affective but not sensory components of pain. *Science, 303,* 1157-1162.

Singh, D. (1993). Adaptive significance of female physical attractiveness: Role of waist-to-hip ratio. *Journal of Personality and Social Psychology, 65,* 293-307.

Singh, D. (1995). Female health, attractiveness, and desirability for relationships: Role of breast asymmetry and waist-to-hip ratio. *Ethology and Sociobiology, 16,* 465-481.

Singh, S. (1997). *Fermat's enigma: The epic quest to solve the world's greatest mathematical problem.* New York: Bantam Books.

Singh, S., & Riber, K. A. (1997, November). Fermat's last stand. *Scientific American,* pp. 68-73.

Singleton, D., Tate, A., & Kohout, J. (2003). *2002 Master's, specialist's, and related degrees employment survey.* Washington, DC: American Psychological Association.

Sipski, M. L., & Alexander, C. J. (1999). Sexual response in women with spinal cord injuries: Implications for our understanding of the able bodied. *Journal of Sex and Marital Therapy, 25,* 11-22.

Sirenteanu, R. (1999). Switching on the infant brain. *Science, 286,* 59, 61.

Sivard, R. L. (1996). *World military and social expenditures 1996,* 16th edition. Washington, DC: World Priorities.

Sjöstrum, L. (1980). Fat cells and body weight. In A. J. Stunkard (Ed.), *Obesity.* Philadelphia: Saunders.

Skinner, B. F. (1953). *Science and human behavior.* New York: Macmillan.

Skinner, B. F. (1956). A case history in scientific method. *American Psychologist, 11,* 221-233.

Skinner, B. F. (1957). *Verbal behavior.* Englewood Cliffs, NJ: Prentice-Hall.

Skinner, B. F. (1961, November). Teaching machines. *Scientific American,* pp. 91-102.

Skinner, B. F. (1983, September). Origins of a behaviorist. *Psychology Today,* pp. 22-33.

Skinner, B. F. (1985). *Cognitive science and behaviorism.* Unpublished manuscript, Harvard University.

Skinner, B. F. (1986). What is wrong with daily life in the western world? *American Psychologist, 41,* 568-574.

Skinner, B. F. (1988). The school of the future. Address to the American Psychological Association convention.

Skinner, B. F. (1989). Teaching machines. *Science, 243,* 1535.

Skinner, B. F. (1990). Address to the American Psychological Association convention.

Skitka, L. J., Bauman, C. W., & Mullen, E. (2004). Political tolerance and coming to psychological closure following the September 11, 2001, terrorist attacks: An integrative approach. *Personality and Social Psychology Bulletin, 30,* 743-756.

Sklar, L. S., & Anisman, H. (1981). Stress and cancer. *Psychological Bulletin, 89,* 369-406.

Skoog, G., & Skoog, I. (1999). A 40-year follow-up of patients with obsessive-compulsive disorder. *Archives of General Psychiatry, 56,* 121-127.

Skov, R. B., & Sherman, S. J. (1986). Information-gathering processes: Diagnosticity, hypothesis-confirmatory strategies, and perceived hypothesis confirmation. *Journal of Experimental Social Psychology, 22,* 93-121.

Slater, A. (1994, February 15). Personal correspondence.

Slater, E., & Meyer, A. (1959). *Confinia Psychiatra.* Basel: S. Karger AG.

Slater, L. (2000, November 19). How do you cure a sex addict? *New York Times Magazine* (www.nytimes.com).

Slavin, R. E., & Braddock, J. H., III (1993, Summer). Ability grouping: On the wrong track. *The College Board Review,* pp. 11-18.

Slavin, R. E., Hurley, E. A., & Chamberlain, A. (2003). Cooperative learning and achievement: Theory and research. In W. M. Reynolds & G. E. Miller (Eds.), *Handbook of psychology: Educational psychology, Vol. 7.* New York: Wiley.

Sloan, R. P. (2005). Field analysis of the literature on religion, spirituality, and health. Columbia University (available at www.metanexus.net/tarp).

Sloan, R. P., & Bagiela E. (2002). Claims about religious involvement and health outcomes. *Annals of Behavioral Medicine, 24,* 14-21.

Sloan, R. P., Bagiella, E., & Powell, T. (1999). Religion, spirituality, and medicine. *Lancet, 353,* 664-667.

Sloan, R. P., Bagiella, E., VandeCreek, L., & Poulos, P. (2000). Should physicians prescribe religious activities? *New England Journal of Medicine, 342,* 1913-1917.

Slovic, P. (2000). What does it mean to know a cumulative risk? Adolescents' perceptions of short-term and long-term consequences of smoking. *Journal of Behavioral Decision Making, 13,* 259-266.

Slovic, P. (2001). Cigarette smokers: Rational actors or rational fools? In P. Slovic (Ed.), *Smoking risk, perception and policy.* Thousand Oaks, CA: Sage.

Slovic, P., Finucane, M., Peters, E., & MacGregor, D. G. (2002). The affect heuristic. In T. Gilovich, D. Griffin, & D. Kahneman (Eds.), *Intuitive judgment: Heuristics and biases.* New York: Cambridge University Press.

Slovic, P., & Fischhoff, B. (1977). On the psychology of experimental surprises. *Journal of Experimental Psychology: Human Perception and Performance, 3,* 544-551.

Slutske, W. S. (2005). Alcohol use disorders among U.S. college students and their non-college-attending peers. *Archives of General Psychiatry, 62,* 321-327.

Small, M. F. (1997). Making connections. *American Scientist, 85,* 502-504.

Small, M. F. (2002, July). What you can learn from drunk monkeys. *Discover,* pp. 40-45.

Smart, R. G., Adlaf, E. M., & Walsh, G. W. (1991). The Ontario student drug use survey: Trends between 1977 and 1991. Toronto: Addiction Research Foundation.

Smedley, A., & Smedley, B. D. (2005). Race as biology is fiction, racism as a social problem is real: Anthropological and historical perspectives on the social construction of race. *American Psychologist, 60,* 16–26.

Smelser, N. J., & Mitchell, F. (Eds.) (2002). *Terrorism: Perspectives from the behavioral and social sciences.* Washington, DC: National Research Council, National Academies Press.

Smith, A. (1983). Personal correspondence.

Smith, D. V., & Margolskee, R. F. (2001, March). Making sense of taste. *Scientific American,* pp. 32–39.

Smith, E., & Delargy, M. (2005). Locked-in syndrome. *British Medical Journal, 330,* 406–409.

Smith, J. E., Waldorf, V. A., & Trembath, D. L. (1990). "Single white male looking for thin, very attractive . . ." *Sex Roles, 23,* 675–685.

Smith, M. B. (1978). Psychology and values. *Journal of Social Issues, 34,* 181–199.

Smith, M., Franz, E. A., Joy, S. M., & Whitehead, K. (2005). Superior performance of blind compared with sighted individuals on bimanual estimations of object size. *Psychological Science, 16,* 11–14.

Smith, M. L., & Glass, G. V. (1977). Meta-analysis of psychotherapy outcome studies. *American Psychologist, 32,* 752–760.

Smith, M. L., Glass, G. V., & Miller, R. L. (1980). *The benefits of psychotherapy.* Baltimore: Johns Hopkins Press.

Smith, P. B., & Tayeb, M. (1989). Organizational structure and processes. In M. Bond (Ed.), *The cross-cultural challenge to social psychology.* Newbury Park, CA: Sage.

Smith, P. F. (1995). Cannabis and the brain. *New Zealand Journal of Psychology, 24,* 5–12.

Smith, S. B. (1999). *Diana in search of herself: Portrait of a troubled princess.* New York: Times Books.

Smith, S. M., McIntosh, W. D., & Bazzini, D. G. (1999). Are the beautiful good in Hollywood? An investigation of the beauty-and-goodness stereotype on film. *Basic and Applied Social Psychology, 21,* 69–80.

Smith, T. W. (1998, December). American sexual behavior: Trends, sociodemographic differences, and risk behavior. National Opinion Research Center GSS Topical Report No. 25.

Smith, T. W., & Ruiz, J. M. (2002). Psychosocial influences on the development and course of coronary heart disease: Current status and implications for research and practice. *Journal of Consulting and Clinical Psychology, 70,* 548–568.

Smolak, L., & Murnen, S. K. (2002). A meta-analytic examination of the relationship between child sexual abuse and eating disorders. *International Journal of Eating Disorders, 31,* 136–150.

Smoreda, Z., & Licoppe, C. (2000). Gender-specific use of the domestic telephone. *Social Psychology Quarterly, 63,* 238–252.

Snarey, J. R. (1985). Cross-cultural universality of social-moral development: A critical review of Kohlbergian research. *Psychological Bulletin, 97,* 202–233.

Snarey, J. R. (1987, June). A question of morality. *Psychology Today,* pp. 6–7.

Snodgrass, S. E., Higgins, J. G., & Todisco, L. (1986). The effects of walking behavior on mood. Paper presented at the American Psychological Association convention.

Snowdon, D. A., Kemper, S. J., Mortimer, J. A., Greiner, L. H., Wekstein, D. R., & Markesbery, W. R. (1996). Linguistic ability in early life and cognitive function and Alzheimer's disease in late life: Finds from the Nun Study. *Journal of the American Medical Association, 275,* 528–532.

Snyder, F., & Scott, J. (1972). The psychophysiology of sleep. In N. S. Greenfield & R. A. Sterbach (Eds.), *Handbook of psychophysiology.* New York: Holt, Rinehart & Winston.

Snyder, M. (1984). When belief creates reality. In L. Berkowitz (Ed.), *Advances in experimental social psychology* (Vol. 18). New York: Academic Press.

Snyder, S. H. (1984). Neurosciences: An integrative discipline. *Science, 225,* 1255–1257.

Snyder, S. H. (1986). *Drugs and the brain.* New York: Scientific American Library.

Society for Personality Assessment. (2005). The status of the Rorschach in clinical and forensic practice: An official statement by The Board of Trustees of the Society for Personality Assessment (www.personality.org).

Sokol, D. K., Moore, C. A., Rose, R. J., Williams, C. J., Reed, T., & Christian, J. C. (1995). Intrapair differences in personality and cognitive ability among young monozygotic twins distinguished by chorion type. *Behavior Genetics, 25,* 457–466.

Sokoll, G. R., & Mynatt, C. R. (1984). *Arousal and free throw shooting.* Paper presented at the meeting of the Midwestern Psychological Association.

Solomon, D. A., Keitner, G. I., Miller, I. W., Shea, M. T., & Keller, M. B. (1995). Course of illness and maintenance treatments for patients with bipolar disorder. *Journal of Clinical Psychiatry, 56,* 5–13.

Solomon, J. (1996, May 20). Breaking the silence. *Newsweek,* pp. 20–22.

Solomon, M. (1987, December). Standard issue. *Psychology Today,* pp. 30–31.

Sommer, R. (1969). *Personal space.* Englewood Cliffs, NJ: Prentice-Hall.

Sonenstein, F. L. (1992). Condom use. *Science, 257,* 861.

Sontag, S. (1978). *Illness as metaphor.* New York: Farrar, Straus, & Giroux.

Soussignan, R. (2001). Duchenne smile, emotional experience, and autonomic reactivity: A test of the facial feedback hypothesis. *Emotion, 2,* 52–74.

Sowell, T. (1991, May/June). Cultural diversity: A world view. *American Enterprise,* pp. 44–55.

Spanos, N. P. (1982). A social psychological approach to hypnotic behavior. In G. Weary & H. L. Mirels (Eds.), *Integrations of clinical and social psychology.* New York: Oxford.

Spanos, N. P. (1986). Hypnosis, nonvolitional responding, and multiple personality: A social psychological perspective. *Progress in Experimental Personality Research, 14,* 1–62.

Spanos, N. P. (1991). Hypnosis, hypnotizability, and hypnotherapy. In C. R. Snyder & D. R. Forsyth (Eds.), *Handbook of social and clinical psychology: The health perspective.* New York: Pergamon Press.

Spanos, N. P. (1994). Multiple identity enactments and multiple personality disorder: A sociocognitive perspective. *Psychological Bulletin, 116,* 143–165.

Spanos, N. P. (1996). *Multiple identities and false memories: A sociocognitive perspective.* Washington, DC: American Psychological Association Books.

Spanos, N. P., & Coe, W. C. (1992). A Social-psychological approach to hypnosis. In E. Fromm & M. R. Nash (Eds.), *Contemporary hypnosis research.* New York: Guilford.

Spector, P. E. (1986). Perceived control by employees: A meta-analysis of studies concerning autonomy and participation at work. *Human Relations, 39,* 1005–1016.

Spelke, E. (2005, April 22). The science of gender and science. Harvard University (www.edge.org).

Spelke, E. S. (2000). Core knowledge. *American Psychologist, 55,* 1233–1243.

Spencer, J., Quinn, P. C., Johnson, M. H., & Karmiloff-Smith, A. (1997). Heads you win, tails you lose: Evidence for young infants categorizing mammals by head and facial attributes. *Early Development & Parenting, 6,* 113–126.

Spencer, K. M., Nestor, P. G., Perlmutter, R., Niznikiewicz, M. A., Klump, M. C., Frumin, M., Shenton, M. E., & McCarley, R. W. (2004). Neural synchrony indexes disordered perception and cognition in schizophrenia. *Proceedings of the National Academy of Sciences, 101,* 17288–17293.

Spencer, S. J., Steele, C. M., & Quinn, D. M. (1997). Stereotype threat and women's math performance. Unpublished manuscript, Hope College.

Sperling, G. (1960). The information available in brief visual presentations. *Psychological Monographs, 74* (Whole No. 498).

Sperry, R. W. (1964). *Problems outstanding in the evolution of brain function.* James Arthur Lecture, American Museum of Natural History, New York. Cited by R. Ornstein (1977), *The psychology of consciousness* (2nd ed.). New York: Harcourt Brace Jovanovich.

Sperry, R. W. (1982). Some effects of disconnecting the cerebral hemispheres. *Science, 217,* 1223–1226.

Sperry, R. W. (1985). Changed concepts of brain and consciousness: Some value implications. *Zygon, 20,* 41–57.

Sperry, R. W. (1992, Summer). Turnabout on consciousness: A mentalist view. *Journal of Mind & Behavior, 13*(3), 259–280.

Spiegel, K., Leproult, R., & Van Cauter, E. (1999). Impact of sleep debt on metabolic and endrocrine function. *Lancet, 354,* 1435–1439.

Spielberger, C., & London, P. (1982). Rage boomerangs. *American Health, 1,* 52–56.

Spradley, J. P., & Phillips, M. (1972). Culture and stress: A quantitative analysis. *American Anthropologist, 74,* 518–529.

Sprecher, S. (1989). The importance to males and females of physical attractiveness, earning potential, and expressiveness in initial attraction. *Sex Roles, 21,* 591–607.

Sprecher, S., & Sedikides, C. (1993). Gender differences in perceptions of emotionality: The case of close heterosexual relationships. *Sex Roles, 28,* 511–530.

Spring, B., Pingitore, R., Bourgeois, M., Kessler, K. H., & Bruckner, E. (1992). The effects and non-effects of skipping breakfast: Results of three studies. Paper presented at the American Psychological Association convention.

Springer, S. P., & Deutsch, G. (1985). *Left brain, right brain.* San Francisco: Freeman.

Spychalski, A., Quinones, M. A., & Gaugler, B. B. (1997). A survey of assessment center practices in the United States. *Personnel Psychology, 50,* 71–90.

Squire, L. R. (1992). Memory and the hippocampus: A synthesis from findings with rats, monkeys, and humans. *Psychological Review, 99,* 195–231.

Srivastava, S., John, O. P., Gosling, S. D., & Potter, J. (2003). Development of personality in early and middle adulthood: Set like plaster or persistent change? *Journal of Personality & Social Psychology, 84,* 1041–1053.

Srivastava, A., Locke, E. A., & Bartol, K. M. (2001). Money and subject well-being: It's not the money, it's the motives. *Journal of Personality and Social Psychology, 80,* 959–971.

St. Clair, D., Xu, M., Wang, P., Yu, Y., Fang, Y., Zhang, F., Zheng, X., Gu, N., Feng, G., Sham, P., & He, L. (2005). Rates of adult schizophrenia following prenatal exposure to the Chinese famine of 1959-1961. *Journal of the American Medical Association, 294,* 557–562.

Stack, S. (1992). Marriage, family, religion, and suicide. In R. Maris, A. Berman, J. Maltsberger, & R. Yufit (Eds.), *Assessment and prediction of suicide.* New York: Guilford Press.

Stafford, R. S., MacDonald, E. A., & Finkelstein, S. N. (2001). National patterns of medication treatment for depression, 1987 to 2001. *Primary Care Companion Journal of Clinical Psychiatry, 3,* 232–235.

Stanford University Center for Narcolepsy. (2002). Narcolepsy is a serious medical disorder and a key to understanding other sleep disorders (www.med.stanford.edu/school/Psychiatry/narcolepsy).

Stanley, J. C. (1997). Varieties of intellectual talent. *Journal of Creative Behavior, 31,* 93–119.

Stanovich, K. (1996). *How to think straight about psychology.* New York: HarperCollins.

Staples, B. (1999a, May 2). When the 'paranoids' turn out to be right. *New York Times* (www.nytimes.com).

Staples, B. (1999b, May 24). Why 'racial profiling' will be tough to fight. *New York Times* (www.nytimes.com).

Stark, R. (2002). Physiology and faith: Addressing the "universal" gender difference in religious commitment. *Journal for the Scientific Study of Religion, 41,* 495–507.

Stark, R. (2003a). *For the glory of God: How monotheism led to reformations, science, witch-hunts, and the end of slavery.* Princeton, NJ: Princeton University Press.

Stark, R. (2003b, October-November). False conflict: Christianity is not only compatible with science—it created it. *American Enterprise,* pp. 27–33.

Starr, J. M., Deary, I. J., Lemmon, H., & Whalley, L. J. (2000). Mental ability age 11 years and health status age 77 years. *Age and Ageing, 29,* 523–528.

Statistics Canada. (1999). *Statistical report on the health of Canadians.* Prepared by the Federal, Provincial and Territorial Advisory Committee on Population Health for the Meeting of Ministers of Health, Charlottetown, PEI, September 16–17, 1999.

Statistics Canada. (2002). (www.statcan.ca).

Statistics Canada. (2003). Victims and persons accused of homicide, by age and sex. Table 253-0003. www.statcan.ca

Staub, E. (1989). *The roots of evil: The psychological and cultural sources of genocide.* New York: Cambridge University Press.

Steadman, H. J., Mulvey, E. P., Monahan, J., Robbins, P. C., Appelbaum, P. S., Grisso, T., Roth, L. H., & Silver, E. (1998). Violence by people discharged from acute psychiatric inpatient facilities and by others in the same neighborhoods. *Archives of General Psychiatry, 55,* 393–401.

Steel, P., & Ones, D. S. (2002). Personality and happiness: A national-level analysis. *Journal of Personality and Social Psychology, 83,* 767–781.

Steele, C. (1990, May). A conversation with Claude Steele. *APS Observer,* pp. 11–17.

Steele, C. M. (1995, August 31). Black students live down to expectations. *New York Times.*

Steele, C. M. (1997). A threat in the air: How stereotypes shape intellectual identity and performance. *American Psychologist, 52,* 613–629.

Steele, C. M., & Josephs, R. A. (1990). Alcohol myopia: Its prized and dangerous effects. *American Psychologist, 45,* 921–933.

Steele, C. M., Spencer, S. J., & Aronson, J. (2002). Contending with group image: The psychology of stereotype and social identity threat. *Advances in Experimental Social Psychology, 34,* 379–440.

Steele, J. (2000). Handedness in past human population: Skeletal markers. *Laterality, 5,* 193–220.

Steenhuysen, J. (2002, May 8). Bionic retina gives six patients partial sight. Reuters News Service. (See also www.optobionics.com/artificialretina.htm.)

Steinberg, L. (1987, September). Bound to bicker. *Psychology Today,* pp. 36–39.

Steinberg, L., & Morris, A. S. (2001). Adolescent development. *Annual Review of Psychology, 52,* 83–110.

Steinberg, L., & Scott, E. S. (2003). Less guilty by reason of adolescence: Developmental immaturity, diminished responsibility, and the juvenile death penalty. *American Psychologist, 58,* 1009–1018.

Steinberg, N. (1993, February). Astonishing love stories (from an earlier United Press International report). *Games,* p. 47.

Steinem, G. (1988). Six great ideas that television is missing. In G. Comstock (Ed.), *Public communication and behavior.* New York: Academic Press.

Steinhauer, J. (1999). More traffic in the double-stroller lane: Twin births surge, and the parents face special, and costly challenges. *New York Times* (www.nytimes.com).

Steinhauer, J. (1999, November 29). Number of twins rises; so does parental stress. *New York Times* (www.nytimes.com).

Steinmetz, J. E. (1999). The localization of a simple type of learning and memory: The cerebellum and classical eyeblink conditioning. *Contemporary Psychology, 7,* 72–77.

Stengel, E. (1981). Suicide. In *The new encyclopaedia britannica, macropaedia* (Vol. 17, pp. 777–782). Chicago: Encyclopaedia Britannica.

Stern, M., & Karraker, K. H. (1989). Sex stereotyping of infants: A review of gender labeling studies. *Sex Roles, 20,* 501–522.

Stern, S. L., Dhanda, R., & Hazuda, H. P. (2001). Hopelessness predicts mortality in older Mexican and European Americans. *Psychosomatic Medicine, 63,* 344–351.

Sternbach, H. (1998). Age-associated testosterone decline in men: Clinical issues for psychiatry. *American Journal of Psychiatry, 155,* 1310–1318.

Sternberg, E. M. (2001). *The balance within: The science connecting health and emotions.* New York: Freeman.

Sternberg, R. (Ed.), (2002). *Career paths in psychology: Where your degree can take you.* Washington, DC: APA.

Sternberg, R. J. (1985). *Beyond IQ: A triarchic theory of human intelligence.* New York: Cambridge University Press.

Sternberg, R. J. (1988). Applying cognitive theory to the testing and teaching of intelligence. *Applied Cognitive Psychology, 2,* 231–255.

Sternberg, R. J. (1998). Principles of teaching for successful intelligence. *Educational Psychologist, 33,* 65–72.

Sternberg, R. J. (1999). The theory of successful intelligence. *Review of General Psychology, 3,* 292–316.

Sternberg, R. J. (2000). Presidential aptitude in Science.

Sternberg, R. J. (2003). Our research program validating the triarchic theory of successful intelligence: Reply to Gottfredson. *Intelligence, 31,* 399–413.

Sternberg, R. J., & Grajek, S. (1984). The nature of love. *Journal of Personality and Social Psychology, 47,* 312–329.

Sternberg, R. J., & Grigorenko, E. L. (2000). Theme-park psychology: A case study regarding human intelligence and its implications for education. *Educational Psychology Review, 12,* 247–268.

Sternberg, R. J., Grigorenko, E. L., & Kidd, K. K. (2005). Intelligence, race, and genetics. *American Psychologist, 60,* 46–59.

Sternberg, R. J., & Kaufman, J. C. (1998). Human abilities. *Annual Review of Psychology, 49,* 479–502.

Sternberg, R. J., & Lubart, T. I. (1991). An investment theory of creativity and its development. *Human Development,* 1–31.

Sternberg, R. J., & Lubart, T. I. (1992). Buy low and sell high: An investment approach to creativity. *Psychological Science, 1,* 1–5.

Sternberg, R. J., & Wagner, R. K. (1993). The *g*-ocentric view of intelligence and job performance is wrong. *Current Directions in Psychological Science, 2,* 1–5.

Sternberg, R. J., Wagner, R. K., Williams, W. M., & Horvath, J. A. (1995). Testing common sense. *American Psychologist, 50,* 912–927.

Stetter, F., & Kupper, S. (2002). Autogenic training: A meta-analysis of clinical outcome studies. *Applied Psychophysiology and Biofeedback, 27,* 45–98.

Stevenson, H. W. (1992, December). Learning from Asian schools. *Scientific American,* pp. 70–76.

Stevenson, H. W., & Lee, S-Y. (1990). Contexts of achievement: A study of American, Chinese, and Japanese children. *Monographs of the Society for Research in Child Development, 55* (Serial No. 221, Nos. 1–2).

Stewart, B. (2002, April 6). Recall of the wild. *New York Times* (www.nytimes.com).

Stewart, D. (2000, February). Driving the wrong way. *The Psychologist,* pp. 64–65.

Stice, E. (2002). Risk and maintenance factors for eating pathology: A meta-analytic review. *Psychological Bulletin, 128,* 825–848.

Stice, E., & Shaw, H. E. (1994). Adverse effects of the media portrayed thin-ideal on women and linkages to bulimic symptomatology. *Journal of Social and Clinical Psychology, 13,* 288–308.

Stice, E., Spangler, D., & Agras, W. S. (2001). Exposure to media-portrayed thin-ideal images adversely affects vulnerable girls: A longitudinal experiment. *Journal of Social and Clinical Psychology, 20,* 270–288.

Stickgold, R. (2000, March 7). Quoted by S. Blakeslee, For better learning, researchers endorse "sleep on it" adage. *New York Times,* p. F2.

Stickgold, R., Hobson, J. A., Fosse, R., & Fosse, M. (2001). Sleep, learning, and dreams: Off-line memory processing. *Science, 294,* 1052–1057.

Stickgold, R., James, L., & Hobson, J. A. (2000). Visual discrimination learning requires sleep after training. *Nature Neuroscience, 3,* 1237–1238.

Stickgold, R., Malia, A., Maquire, D., Roddenberry, D., & O'Connor, M. (2000, October 13). Replaying the game: Hypnagogic images in normals and amnesics. *Science, 290,* 350–353.

Stipek, D. (1992). The child at school. In M. H. Bornstein & M. E. Lamb (Eds.), *Developmental psychology: An advanced textbook.* Hillsdale, NJ: Erlbaum.

Stith, S. M., Rosen, K. H., Middleton, K. A., Busch, A. L., Lunderberg, K., & Carlton, R. P. (2000). The intergenerational transmission of spouse abuse: A meta-analysis. *Journal of Marriage and the Family, 62,* 640–654.

Stockton, M. C., & Murnen, S. K. (1992). Gender and sexual arousal in response to sexual stimuli: A meta-analytic review. Presented at the American Psychological Society convention.

Stone, A. A., & Neale, J. M. (1984). Effects of severe daily events on mood. *Journal of Personality and Social Psychology, 46,* 137–144.

Stoolmiller, M. (1999). Implications of the restricted range of family environments for estimates of heritability and nonshared environment in behavior-genetic adoption studies. *Psychological Bulletin, 125,* 392–409.

Stoppard, J. M., & Gruchy, C. D. G. (1993). Gender, context, and expression of positive emotion. *Personality and Social Psychology Bulletin, 19,* 143–150.

Storm, L. (2000). Research note: Replicable evidence of psi: A revision of Milton's (1999) meta-analysis of the ganzfeld data bases. *Journal of Parapsychology, 64,* 411–416.

Storm, L. (2003). Remote viewing by committee: RV using a multiple agent/multiple percipient design. *Journal of Parapsychology, 67,* 325–342.

Storms, M. D. (1973). Videotape and the attribution process: Reversing actors' and observers' points of view. *Journal of Personality and Social Psychology, 27,* 165–175.

Storms, M. D. (1981). A theory of erotic orientation development. *Psychological Review, 88,* 340–353.

Storms, M. D. (1983). *Development of sexual orientation.* Washington, DC: Office of Social and Ethical Responsibility, American Psychological Association.

Storms, M. D., & Thomas, G. C. (1977). Reactions to physical closeness. *Journal of Personality and Social Psychology, 35,* 412–418.

Strack, F., Martin, L., & Stepper, S. (1988). Inhibiting and facilitating conditions of the human smile: A nonobtrusive test of the facial feedback hypothesis. *Journal of Personality and Social Psychology, 54,* 768–777.

Strack, S., & Coyne, J. C. (1983). Social confirmation of dysphoria: Shared and private reactions to depression. *Journal of Personality and Social Behavior, 44,* 798–806.

Strahan, E. J., Spencer, S. J., & Zanna, M. P. (2002). Subliminal priming and persuasion: Striking while the iron is hot. *Journal of Experimental Social Psychology, 38,* 556–568.

Strange, B. A., & Dolan, R. J. (2004). b-Adrenergic modulation of emotional memory-evoked human amygdala and hippocampal responses. *Proceedings of the National Academy of Sciences, 101,* 11454–11458.

Stratton, G. M. (1896). Some preliminary experiments on vision without inversion of the retinal image. *Psychological Review, 3,* 611–617.

Straub, R. O., Seidenberg, M. S., Bever, T. G., & Terrace, H. S. (1979). Serial learning in the pigeon. *Journal of the Experimental Analysis of Behavior, 32,* 137–148.

Straus, M. A., & Gelles, R. J. (1980). *Behind closed doors: Violence in the American family.* New York: Anchor/Doubleday.

Straus, M. A., Sugarman, D. B., & Giles-Sims, J. (1997). Spanking by parents and subsequent antisocial behavior of children. *Archives of Pediatric Adolescent Medicine, 151,* 761–767.

Strawbridge, W. J. (1999). Mortality and religious involvement: A review and critique of the results, the methods, and the measures. Paper presented at a Harvard University conference on religion and health, sponsored by the National Instititue for Healthcare Research and the John Templeton Foundation.

Strawbridge, W. J., Cohen, R. D., & Shema, S. J. (1997). Frequent attendance at religious services and mortality over 28 years. *American Journal of Public Health, 87,* 957–961.

Strawbridge, W. J., Shema, S. J., Cohen, R. D., & Kaplan, G. A. (2001). Religious attendance increases survival by improving and maintaining good health behaviors, mental health, and social relationships. *Annals of Behavioral Medicine, 23,* 68–74.

Strayer, D. L., Drews, F. A., & Johnston, W. A. (2003). Cell phone-induced failures of visual attention during simulated driving. *Journal of Experimental Psychology: Applied, 9,* 23–32.

Strayer, D. L., & Johnston, W. A. (2001). Driven to distraction: Dual-task studies of simulated driving and conversing on a cellular telephone. *Psychological Science, 12,* 462–466.

Streissguth, A. P., Aase, J. M., Clarren, S. K., Randels, S. P., LaDue, R. A., & Smith, D. F. (1991). Fetal alcohol syndrome in adolescents and adults. *Journal of the American Medical Association, 265,* 1961–1967.

Strickland, B. (1992, February 20). Gender differences in health and illness. Sigma Xi national lecture delivered at Hope College.

Striegel-Moore, R. H., Silberstein, L. R., & Rodin, J. (1993). The social self in bulimia nervosa: Public self-consciousness, social anxiety, and perceived fraudulence. *Journal of Abnormal Psychology, 102,* 297–303.

Stroebe, M., Stroebe, W., & Schut, H. (2001). Gender differences in adjustment to bereavement: An empirical and theoretical review. *Review of General Psychology, 5,* 62–83.

Stroebe, M., Stroebe, W., Schut, H., Zech, E., & van den Bout, J. (2002). Does disclosure of emotions facilitate recovery from bereavement? Evidence from two prospective studies. *Journal of Consulting and Clinical Psychology, 70,* 169–178.

Stroebe, W., Schut, H., & Stroebe, M. S. (2005). Grief work, disclosure and counseling: Do they help the bereaved? *Clinical Psychology Review, 25,* 395–414.

Strupp, H. H. (1982). The outcome problem in psychotherapy: Contemporary perspectives. In J. H. Harvey & M. M. Parks (Eds.), *The master lecture series: Vol. 1. Psychotherapy research and behavior change.* Washington, DC: American Psychological Association.

Strupp, H. H. (1986). Psychotherapy: Research, practice, and public policy (How to avoid dead ends). *American Psychologist, 41,* 120–130.

Stumpf, H., & Jackson, D. N. (1994). Gender-related differences in cognitive abilities: Evidence from a medical school admissions testing program. *Personality and Individual Differences, 17,* 335–344.

Stumpf, H., & Stanley, J. C. (1998). Stability and change in gender-related differences on the college board advanced placement and achievement tests. *Current Directions in Psychology, 7,* 192–196.

Stunkard, A. J., Harris, J. R., Pedersen, N. L., & McClearn, G. E. (1990). A separated twin study of the body mass index. *New England Journal of Medicine, 322,* 1483–1487.

Sturm, R. (2003). Increases in clinically severe obesity in the United States, 1986–2000. *Archives of Internal Medicine, 163,* 2146–2148.

Subiaul, F., Cantlon, J. F., Holloway, R. L., & Terrace, H. S. (2004). Cognitive imitation in rhesus macaques. *Science, 305,* 407–410.

Suddath, R. L., Christison, G. W., Torrey, E. F., Casanova, M. F., & Weinberger, D. R. (1990). Anatomical abnormalities in the brains of monozygotic twins discordant for schizophrenia. *New England Journal of Medicine, 322,* 789–794.

Suddendorf, T., & Whiten, A. (2001). Mental evolution and development: Evidence for secondary representation in children, great apes, and other animals. *Psychological Bulletin, 137,* 629–650.

Sue, D. W. (1990). Culture-specific strategies in counseling: A conceptual framework. *Professional Psychology: Research and Practice, 21,* 424–433.

Suedfeld, P. (1998). Homo invictus: The indomitable species. *Canadian Psychology, 38,* 164–173.

Suedfeld, P. (2000). Reverberations of the Holocaust fifty years later: Psychology's contributions to understanding persecution and genocide. *Canadian Psychology, 41,* 1–9.

Suedfeld, P., & Mocellin, J. S. P. (1987). The "sensed presence" in unusual environments. *Environment and Behavior, 19,* 33–52.

Sugita, Y. (2004). Experience in early infancy is indispensable for color perception. *Current Biology. 14,* 1267–1271.

Suhail, K., & Chaudry, H. R. (2004). Predictors of subjective well-being in an Eatern Muslim Cultre. *Journal of Social and Clinical Psychology, 23,* 359.

Suinn, R. M. (1997). Mental practice in sports psychology: Where have we been, Where do we go? *Clinical Psychology: Science and Practice.*

Sullivan, P. F., Neale, M. C., & Kendler, K. S. (2000). Genetic epidemiology of major depression: Review and meta-analysis. *American Journal of Psychiatry, 157,* 1552–1562.

Suls, J. M., & Tesch, F. (1978). Students' preferences for information about their test performance: A social comparison study. *Journal of Experimental Social Psychology, 8,* 189–197.

Summers, M. (1996, December 9). Mister clean. *People Weekly,* pp. 139–142.

Sundet, J. M., Barlaug, D. G., & Torjussen, T. M. (2004). The end of the Flynn effect? A study of secular trends in mean intelligence test scores of Norwegian conscripts during half a century. *Intelligence, 32,* 349–362.

Sundstrom, E., De Meuse, K. P., & Futrell, D. (1990). Work teams: Applications and effectiveness. *American Psychologist, 45,* 120–133.

Suomi, S. J. (1986). Anxiety-like disorders in young nonhuman primates. In R. Gettleman (Ed.), *Anxiety disorders of childhood.* New York: Guilford Press.

Suomi, S. J. (1987). Genetic and maternal contributions to individual differences in rhesus monkey biobehavioral development. In N. A. Krasnegor & others (Eds.), *Perinatal development: A psychobiological perspective.* Orlando, FL: Academic Press.

Super, C., & Super, D. (2001). Education and Training. *Opportunities in psychology careers* (pp. 68–80). Chicago, IL: VGM Career Books.

Suppes, P. Quoted by R. H. Ennis (1982). Children's ability to handle Piaget's propositional logic: A conceptual critique. In S. Modgil & C. Modgil (Eds.), *Jean Piaget: Consensus and controversy.* New York: Praeger.

Surgeon General. (1986). *The Surgeon General's workshop on pornography and public health,* June 22–24. Report prepared by E. P. Mulvey & J. L. Haugaard and released by Office of the Surgeon General on August 4, 1986.

Surgeon General. (1999). *Mental health: A report of the Surgeon General.* Rockville, MD: U.S. Department of Health and Human Services.

Susser, E. (1999). Life course cohort studies of schizophrenia. *Psychiatric Annals, 29,* 161–165.

Susser, E., Neugenbauer, R., Hoek, H. W., Brown, A. S., Lin, S., Labovitz, D., & Gorman, J. M. (1996). Schizophrenia after prenatal famine. *Archives of General Psychiatry, 53*(1), 25–31

Susser, E. S., Herman, D. B., & Aaron, B. (2002, August). Combating the terror of terrorism. *Scientific American*, pp. 70–77.

Svirsky, M. A., Robbins, A. M., Kirk, K. I., Pisoni, D. B., & Miyamoto, R. T. (2000). Language development in profoundly deaf children with cochlear implants. *Psychological Science, 11*, 153–158.

Sweat, J. A., & Durm, M. W. (1993). Psychics: Do police departments really use them? *Skeptical Inquirer, 17*, 148–158.

Swerdlow, N. R., & Koob, G. F. (1987). Dopamine, schizophrenia, mania, and depression: Toward a unified hypothesis of cortico-stiato-pallido-thalamic function (with commentary). *Behavioral and Brain Sciences, 10*, 197–246.

Swim, J. K. (1994). Perceived versus meta-analytic effect sizes: An assessment of the accuracy of gender stereotypes. *Journal of Personality and Social Psychology, 66*, 21–36.

Swindle, R., Jr., Heller, K., Bescosolido, B., & Kikuzawa, S. (2000). Responses to nervous breakdowns in America over a 40-year period: Mental health policy implications. *American Psychologist, 55*, 740–749.

Symbaluk, D. G., Heth, C. D., Cameron, J., & Pierce, W. D. (1997). Social modeling, monetary incentives, and pain endurance: The role of self-efficacy and pain perception. *Personality and Social Psychology Bulletin, 23*, 258–269.

Symond, M. B., Harris, A. W. F., Gordon, E., & Williams, L. M. (2005). "Gamma synchrony" in first-episode schizophrenia: A disorder of temporal connectivity? *American Journal of Psychiatry, 162*, 459–465.

Symons, C. S., & Johnson, B. T. (1997). The self-reference effect in memory: A meta-analysis. *Psychological Bulletin, 121*(3), 371–394.

TADS (Treatment for Adolescents with Depression Study Team). (2004). Fluoxetine, cognitive-behavioral therapy, and their combination for adolescents with depression: Treatment for adolescents with depression study (TADS) randomized controlled trial. *Journal of the American Medical Association, 292*, 807–820.

Taha, F. A. (1972). A comparative study of how sighted and blind perceive the manifest content of dreams. *National Review of Social Sciences, 9*(3), 28.

Taheri, S. (2004). The genetics of sleep disorders. *Minerva Medica, 95*, 203–212.

Taheri, S., Lin, L., Austin, D., Young, T., & Mignot, E. (2004). Short sleep duration is associated with reduced leptin, elevated ghrelin, and increased body mass index. *PloS Medicine, 1*(3), e62 (www.plosmedicine.org).

Taheri, S., Zeitzer, J. M., & Mignot, E. (2002). The role of hypocretins (orexins) in sleep regulation and narcolepsy. *Annual Review of Neuroscience, 25*, 283–313.

Tajfel, H. (Ed.). (1982). *Social identity and intergroup relations*. New York: Cambridge University Press.

Talal, N. (1995). Quoted by V. Morell, Zeroing in on how hormones affect the immune system. *Science, 269*, 773–775.

Talarico, J. M., & Rubin, D. C. (2003). Confidence, not consistency, characterizes flashbulb memories. *Psychological Science, 14*, 455–461.

Talbot, M. (1999, October 31). The Rorschach chronicles. *New York Times* (www.nytimes.com).

Talbot, M. (2002, June 2). Hysteria hysteria. *New York Times* (www.nytimes.com).

Talwar, S. K., Xu, S., Hawley, E. S., Weiss, S. A., Moxon, K. A., & Chapin, J. K. (2002). Rat navigation guided by remote control. *Nature, 417*, 37–38.

Tamres, L. K., Janicki, D., & Helgeson, V. S. (2002). Sex differences in coping behavior: A meta-analytic review and an examination of relative coping. *Personality and Social Psychology Review, 6*, 2–30.

Tang, S-H., & Hall, V. C. (1995). The overjustification effect: A meta-analysis. *Applied Cognitive Psychology, 9*, 365–404.

Tangney, J. P., Baumeister, R. F., & Boone, A. L. (2004). High self-control predicts good adjustment, less pathology, better grades, and interpersonal success. *Journal of Personality, 72*, 271–324.

Tannen, D. (1990). *You just don't understand: Women and men in conversation*. New York: Morrow.

Tannenbaum, P. (2002, February). Quoted by R. Kubey & M. Csikszentmihalyi, Television addiction is no mere metaphor. *Scientific American*, pp. 74–80.

Tanner, J. M. (1978). *Fetus into man: Physical growth from conception to maturity*. Cambridge, MA: Harvard University Press.

Tarbert, J. (2004, May 14). Bad apples, bad command, or both? Dart Center for Journalism and Trauma (www.dartcenter.org).

Tarmann, A. (2002, May/June). Out of the closet and onto the Census long form. *Population Today, 30*, pp. 1, 6.

Tasbihsazan, R., Nettelbeck, T., & Kirby, N. (2003). Predictive validity of the Fagan Test of Infant Intelligence. *British Journal of Developmental Psychology, 21*, 585–597.

Tatarkiewicz, W. (1976). *Analysis of happiness*. The Hague: Martinus Nijhoff, 1976.

Taubes, G. (1994). Will new dopamine receptors offer a key to schizophrenia? *Science, 265*, 1034–1035.

Taubes, G. (2001). The soft science of dietary fat. *Science, 291*, 2536–2545.

Taubes, G. (2002, July 7). What if it's all been a big fat lie? *New York Times* (www.nytimes.com).

Tavris, C. (1982, November). Anger defused. *Psychology Today*, pp. 25–35.

Taylor, H. (2003, February 26). The religious and other beliefs of Americans 2003. *The Harris Poll #11* (www.harrisinteracctive.com).

Taylor, K. M., Shepperd, J. A. (1998). Bracing for the worst: Severity, testing, and feedback timing as moderators of the optimistic bias. *Personality and Social Psychology Bulletin, 24*, 915–926.

Taylor, S. E. (1989). *Positive illusions*. New York: Basic Books.

Taylor, S. E. (2002). *The tending instinct: How nurturing is essential to who we are and how we live*. New York: Times Books.

Taylor, S. E., Cousino, L. K., Lewis, B. P., Gruenewald, T. L., Gurung, R. A. R., & Updegraff, J. A. (2000). Biobehavioral responses to stress in females: Tend-and-befriend, not fight-or-flight. *Psychological Review, 107*, 411–430.

Taylor, S. E., Lerner, J. S., Sherman, D. K., Sage, R. M., & McDowell, N. K. (2003). Portrait of the self-enhancer: Well adjusted and well liked or maladjusted and friendless? *Journal of Personality and Social Psychology, 84*, 165–176.

Taylor, S. E., Pham, L. B., Rivkin, I. D., & Armor, D. A. (1998). Harnessing the imagination: Mental simulation, self-regulation, and coping. *American Psychologist, 53*, 429–439.

Taylor, S., Kuch, K., Koch, W. J., Crockett, D. J., & Passey, G. (1998). The structure of posttraumatic stress symptoms. *Journal of Abnormal Psychology, 107*, 154–160.

Taylor, S. P., & Chermack, S. T. (1993). Alcohol, drugs and human physical aggression. *Journal of Studies on Alcohol*, Supplement No. 11, 78–88.

Teasdale, T. W., & Owen, D. R. (2000). Forty-year secular trends in cognitive abilities. *Intelligence, 28*, 115–120.

Tedeschi, R. G., & Calhoun, L. G. (2004). Posttraumatic growth: Conceptual foundations and empirical evidence. *Psychological Inquiry, 15*, 1–18.

Teerlink, R., & Ozley, L. (2000). *More than a motorcycle: The leadership journey at Harley-Davidson*. Cambridge, MA: Harvard Business School Press.

Teghtsoonian, R. (1971). On the exponents in Stevens' law and the constant in Ekinan's law. *Psychological Review, 78,* 71-80.

Teicher, M. (2002). McLean motion and attention test (M-MAT): A new test to diagnose a troubling disorder. McLean Hospital Annual Report (www.mclean.harvard.edu).

Teicher, M. H. (2002, March). The neurobiology of child abuse. *Scientific American,* pp. 68-75.

Tenopyr, M. L. (1997). Improving the workplace: Industrial/organizational psychology as a career. In R. J. Sternberg (Ed.), *Career paths in psychology: Where your degree can take you.* Washington, DC: American Psychological Association.

Teran-Santos, J., Jimenez-Gomez, A., & Cordero-Guevara, J. (1999). The association between sleep apnea and the risk of traffic accidents. *New England Journal of Medicine, 340,* 847-851.

Terman, J. S., Terman, M., Lo, E-S., & Cooper, T. B. (2001). Circadian time of morning light administration and therapeutic response in winter depression. *Archives of General Psychiatry, 58,* 69-73.

Terman, L. M. (1916). *The measurement of intelligence.* Boston: Houghton Mifflin.

Terman, M., Terman, J. S., & Ross, D. C. (1998). A controlled trial of timed bright light and negative air ionization for treatment of winter depression. *Archives of General Psychiatry, 55,* 875-882.

Terrace, H. S. (1979, November). How Nim Chimpsky changed my mind. *Psychology Today,* pp. 65-76.

Terre, L., & Stoddart, R. (2000). Cutting edge specialties for graduate study in psychology. *Eye on Psi Chi,* 23-26.

Tesser, A., Forehand, R., Brody, G., & Long, N. (1989). Conflict: The role of calm and angry parent-child discussion in adolescent development. *Journal of Social and Clinical Psychology, 8,* 317-330.

Tetlock, P. E. (1988). Monitoring the integrative complexity of American and Soviet policy rhetoric: What can be learned? *Journal of Social Issues, 44,* 101-131.

Tetlock, P. E. (1998). Close-call counterfactuals and belief-system defenses: I was not almost wrong but I was almost right. *Journal of Personality and Social Psychology, 75,* 639-652.

Thannickal, T. C., Moore, R. Y., Nienhuis, R., Ramanathan, L., Gulyani, S., Aldrich, M., Cornford, M., & Siegel, J. M. (2000). Reduced number of hypocretin neurons in human narcolepsy. *Neuron, 27,* 469-474.

Thatcher, R. W., Walker, R. A., & Giudice, S. (1987). Human cerebral hemispheres develop at different rates and ages. *Science, 236,* 1110-1113.

Thayer, R. E. (1987). Energy, tiredness, and tension effects of a sugar snack versus moderate exercise. *Journal of Personality and Social Psychology, 52,* 119-125.

Thayer, R. E. (1993). Mood and behavior (smoking and sugar snacking) following moderate exercise: A partial test of self-regulation theory. *Personality and Individual Differences, 14,* 97-104.

Thomas, A., & Chess, S. (1986). The New York Longitudinal Study: From infancy to early adult life. In R. Plomin & J. Dunn (Eds.), *The study of temperament: Changes, continuities, and challenges.* Hillsdale, NJ: Erlbaum.

Thomas, L. (1974). *The lives of a cell.* New York: Viking Press.

Thomas, L. (1979). *The medusa and the snail.* New York: Viking.

Thomas, L. (1983). *The youngest science: Notes of a medicine watcher.* New York: Viking Press.

Thomas, L. (1992). *The fragile species.* New York : Scribner's.

Thomas, W. P., & Collier, V. P. (1998). Two languages are better than one. *Educational Leadership, 55,* 23-36.

Thompson, C. P., Frieman, J., & Cowan, T. (1993). Rajan's memory. Paper presented to the American Psychological Society convention.

Thompson, G. (1998, December 14). As obesity in children increases, so do cases of adult-onset diabetes. *New York Times* (www.nytimes.com).

Thompson, J. K., Jarvie, G. J., Lahey, B. B., & Cureton, K. J. (1982). Exercise and obesity: Etiology, physiology, and intervention. *Psychological Bulletin, 91,* 55-79.

Thompson, J. K., & Stice, E. (2001). Thin-ideal internalization: Mounting evidence for a new risk factor for body-image disturbance and eating pathology. *Current Directions in Psychological Science, 10,* 181-183.

Thompson, P. (1980). Margaret Thatcher: A new illusion. *Perception, 9,* 483-484.

Thompson, P. M., Cannon, T. D., Narr, K. L., van Erp, T., Poutanen, V-P., Huttunen, M., Lönnqvist, J., Standerskjöld-Nordenstam, C-G., Kaprio, J., Khaledy, M., Dail, R., Zoumalan, C. I., & Toga, A. W. (2001). Genetic influences on brain structure. *Nature Neuroscience, 4,* 1253-1258.

Thompson, P. M., Giedd, J. N., Woods, R. P., MacDonald, D., Evans, A. C., & Toga, A. W. (2000). Growth patterns in the developing brain detected by using continuum mechanical tensor maps. *Nature, 404,* 190-193.

Thompson, R., Emmorey, K., & Gollan, T. H. (2005). "Tip of the fingers" experiences by Deaf signers. *Psychological Science, 16,* 856-860.

Thomson, R., & Murachver, T. (2001). Predicting gender from electronic discourse. *British Journal of Social Psychology, 40,* 193-208 (and personal correspondence from T. Murachver, May 23, 2002).

Thorndike, A. L., & Hagen, E. P. (1977). *Measurement and evaluation in psychology and education.* New York: Macmillan.

Thorndike, E. L. (1898). Animal intelligence: An experimental study of associative processes in animals. *Psychological Review Monograph Supplements, 2,* 4-160.

Thorne, J., with Larry Rothstein (1993). *You are not alone: Words of experience and hope for the journey through depression.* New York: HarperPerennial.

Thornhill, R., & Gangestad, S. W. (1994). Human fluctuating asymmetry and sexual behavior. *Psychological Science, 5,* 297-302.

Thornton, B., & Moore, S. (1993). Physical attractiveness contrast effect: Implications for self-esteem and evaluations of the social self. *Personality and Social Psychology Bulletin, 19,* 474-480.

Thorpe, W. H. (1974). *Animal nature and human nature.* London: Metheun.

Tiedens, L. Z. (2001). Anger and advancement versus sadness and subjugation: The effect of negative emotion expressions on social status conferral. *Journal of Personality and Social Psychology, 80,* 86-94.

Tiihonen, J., Isohanni, M., Rasanen, P, Koiranen, M., & Moring, J. (1997). Specific major mental disorders and criminality: A 26-year prospective study of the 1966 northern Finland birth cohort. *American Journal of Psychiatry, 154,* 840-845.

Tikkanen, T. (2001). Psychology in Europe: A growing profession with high standards and a bright future. *European Psychologist, 6,* 144-146.

Time. (1997, December 22). Greeting card association data, p.19.

Tinbergen, N. (1951). *The study of instinct.* Oxford: Clarendon.

Tirrell, M. E. (1990). Personal communication.

Tjaden, P., & Thoennes, N. (2000b). Full report of the prevalence, incidence, and consequences of violence against women: Findings from the National Violence Against Women Survey (NCJ 183781). Washington, DC: U.S. Department of Justice, National Institute of Justice.

Todes, D. P. (1997). From the machine to the ghost within: Pavlov's transition from digestive physiology to conditional reflexes. *American Psychologist, 52,* 947-955.

Tolchin, M. (1994, April 17). Major airlines go two years without a fatality. *New York Times* report (in *Grand Rapids Press,* p. A10).

Tolkien, J. R. R. (1965). *The fellowship of the ring.* Boston: Houghton Mifflin Co.

Tollefson, G. D., Fawcett, J., Winokur, G., Beasley, C. M., et al. (1993). Evaluation of suicidality during pharmacologic treatment of mood and non-mood disorders. *Annals of Clinical Psychiatry, 5*(4), 209-224.

Tollefson, G. D., Rampey, A. H., Beasley, C. M., & Enas, G. G. (1994). Absence of a relationship between adverse events and suicidality during pharmacotherapy for depression. *Journal of Clinical Psychopharmacology, 14,* 163–169.

Tolman, E. C., & Honzik, C. H. (1930). Introduction and removal of reward, and maze performance in rats. *University of California Publications in Psychology, 4,* 257–275.

Tolstoy, L. (1904). *My confessions.* Boston: Dana Estes.

Tondo, L., Jamison, K. R., & Baldessarini, R. J. (1997). Effect of lithium maintenance on suicidal behavior in major mood disorders. In D. M. Stoff & J. J. Mann (Eds.), *The neurobiology of suicide: From the bench to the clinic.* New York: New York Academy of Sciences.

Toni, N., Buchs, P.-A., Nikonenko, I., Bron, C. R., & Muller, D. (1999). LTP promotes formation of multiple spine synapses between a single axon terminal and a dendrite. *Nature, 402,* 421–42.

Torrey, E. F. (1986). *Witchdoctors and psychiatrists.* New York: Harper & Row.

Torrey, E. F. (1998, February 22). Quoted by M. Winerip, Schizophrenia's most zealous foe. *New York Times Magazine,* pp. 26–28.

Torrey, E. F., & Miller, J. (2002). The invisible plague: The rise of mental illness from 1750 to the present. New Brunswick, NJ: London: Rutgers University Press.

Torrey, E. F., Miller, J., Rawlings, R., & Yolken, R. H. (1997). Seasonality of births in schizophrenia and bipolar disorder: A review of the literature. *Schizophrenia Research, 28,* 1–38.

Totterdell, P., Kellett, S., Briner, R. B., & Teuchmann, K. (1998). Evidence of mood linkage in work groups. *Journal of Personality and Social Psychology, 74,* 1504–1515.

Tovee, M. J., Mason, S. M., Emery, J. L., McCluskey, S. E., & Cohen-Tovee, E. M. (1997). Supermodels: Stick insects or hourglasses? *The Lancet, 350,* 1474–1475.

Towler, G. (1986). From zero to one hundred: Coaction in a natural setting. *Perceptual and Motor Skills, 62,* 377–378.

Tracey, J. L., & Robins, R. W. (2004). Show your pride: Evidence for a discrete emotion expression. *Psychological Science, 15,* 194–197.

Tramontana, M. G., Hooper, S. R., & Selzer, S. C. (1988). Research on the preschool prediction of later academic achievement: A review. *Developmental Review, 8,* 89–146.

Tranel, D., Bechara, A., & Denburg, N. L. (2002). Asymmetric functional roles of right and left ventromedial prefrontal cortices in social conduct, decision-making and emotional processing. *Cortex, 38,* pp. 589–613.

Travis, J. (1994). Glia: The brain's other cells. *Science, 266,* 970–972.

Treffert, D. A., & Wallace, G. L. (2002). Island of genius—The artistic brilliance and dazzling memory that sometimes accompany autism and other disorders hint at how all brains work. *Scientific American, 286,* 76–86.

Treisman, A. (1987). Properties, parts, and objects. In K. R. Boff, L. Kaufman, & J. P. Thomas (Eds.), *Handbook of perception and human performance.* New York: Wiley.

Tremblay, R. E., Pihl, R. O., Vitaro, F., & Dobkin, P. L. (1994). Predicting early onset of male antisocial behavior from preschool behavior. *Archives of General Psychiatry, 51,* 732–739.

Trewin, D. (2001). *Australian social trends 2001.* Canberra: Australian Bureau of Statistics.

Triandis, H. C. (1981). Some dimensions of intercultural variation and their implications for interpersonal behavior. Paper presented at the American Psychological Association convention.

Triandis, H. C. (1989a). The self and social behavior in differing cultural contexts. *Psychological Review, 96,* 506–520.

Triandis, H. C. (1989b). Cross-cultural studies of individualism and collectivism. In J. J. Berman (Ed.), *Nebraska symposium on motivation 1989* (Vol. 37). Lincoln, NE: University of Nebraska Press.

Triandis, H. C. (1994). *Culture and social behavior.* New York: McGraw-Hill.

Triandis, H. C., Bontempo, R., Villareal, M. J., Asai, M., & Lucca, N. (1988). Individualism and collectivism: Cross-cultural perspectives on self-ingroup relationships. *Journal of Personality and Social Psychology, 54,* 323–338.

Trickett, P. K., & McBride-Chang, C. (1995). The developmental impact of different forms of child abuse and neglect. *Developmental Review, 15,* 311–337.

Trimble, J. E. (1994). Cultural variations in the use of alcohol and drugs. In W. J. Lonner & R. Malpass (Eds.), *Psychology and culture.* Boston: Allyn & Bacon.

Triplett, N. (1898). The dynamogenic factors in pacemaking and competition. *American Journal of Psychology, 9,* 507–533.

Trolier, T. K., & Hamilton, D. L. (1986). Variables influencing judgments of correlational relations. *Journal of Personality and Social Psychology, 50,* 879–888.

Trut, L. N. (1999). Early canid domestication: The farm-fox experiment. *American Scientist, 87,* 160–169.

Tsai, J. L., & Chentsova-Dutton, Y. (2003). Variation among European Americans in emotional facial expression. *Journal of Cross-Cultural Psychology, 34,* 650–657.

Tsang, Y. C. (1938). Hunger motivation in gastrectomized rats. *Journal of Comparative Psychology, 26,* 1–17.

Tsien, J. Z. (April, 2000). Building a brainier mouse. *Scientific American,* 62–68.

Tsuang, M. T., & Faraone, S. V. (1990). *The genetics of mood disorders.* Baltimore, MD: Johns Hopkins University Press.

Tuber, D. S., Miller, D. D., Caris, K. A., Halter, R., Linden, F., & Hennessy, M. B. (1999). Dogs in animal shelters: Problems, suggestions, and needed expertise. *Psychological Science, 10,* 379–386.

Tucker, K. A. (2002). I believe you can fly. *Gallup Management Journal* (www.gallupjournal.com/CA/st/20020520.asp).

Tuerk, P. W. (2005). Research in the high-stakes era: Achievement, resources, and no child left behind. *Psychological Science, 16,* 419–425.

Tulving, E. (1996, August 18). Quoted in J. Gatehouse, Technology revealing brain's secrets. *Montreal Gazette,* p. A3.

Turkheimer, E., Haley, A., Waldron, M., D'Onofrio, B., & Gottesman, I. I. (2003). Socioeconomic status modifies heritability of IQ in young mothers. *Psychological Science, 14,* 623–628.

Turner, C. W., Hesse, B. W., & Peterson-Lewis, S. (1986). Naturalistic studies of the long-term effects of television violence. *Journal of Social Issues, 42*(3), 7–28.

Turner, J. C. (1987). *Rediscovering the social group: A self-categorization theory.* New York: Basil Blackwell.

Turner, N., Barling, J., & Zacharatos, A. (2002). Positive psychology at work. In C. R. Snyder & S. J. Lopez (Eds.), *The handbook of positive psychology.* New York: Oxford University Press.

Turpin, A. (2005, April 3). The science of psi. *FT Weekend,* pp. W1, W2.

Tutu, D. (1999). *No future without forgiveness.* New York: Doubleday.

Tversky, A. (1985, June). Quoted in K. McKean, Decisions, decisions. *Discover,* pp. 22–31.

Tversky, A., & Kahneman, D. (1974). Judgment under uncertainty: Heuristics and biases. *Science, 185,* 1124–1131.

Twenge, J. M. (1997). Changes in masculine and feminine traits over time: A meta-analysis. *Sex Roles 36*(5–6), 305–325.

Twenge, J. M. (2000). The age of anxiety? Birth cohort change in anxiety and neuroticism, 1952–1993. *Journal of Personality and Social Psychology, 79,* 1007–1021.

Twenge, J. M. (2001). Changes in women's assertiveness in response to status and roles: A cross-temporal meta-analysis, 1931–1993. *Journal of Personality and Social Psychology, 8,* 133–145.

Twenge, J. M., Baumeister, R. F., Tice, D. M., & Stucke, T. S. (2001). If you can't join them, beat them: Effects of social exclusion on aggressive behavior. *Journal of Personality and Social Psychology, 81,* 1058–1069.

Twenge, J. M., & Campbell, W. K. (2001). Age and birth cohort differences in self-esteem: A cross-temporal meta-analysis. *Personality and Social Psychology Review, 5,* 321–344.

Twenge, J. M., Catanese, K. R., & Baumeister, R. F. (2002). Social exclusion causes self-defeating behavior. *Journal of Personality and Social Psychology, 83,* 606–615.

Twenge, J. M., Catanese, K. R., & Baumeister, R. F. (2003). Social exclusion and the deconstructed state: Time perception, meaninglessness, lethargy, lack of emotion, and self-awareness. *Journal of Personality and Social Psychology, 85,* 409–423.

Twenge, J. M., & Crocker, J. (2002). Race and self-esteem: Meta-analyses comparing Whites, Blacks, Hispanics, Asians, and American Indians and comment on Gray-Little and Hafdahl (2000). *Psychological Bulletin, 128,* 371–408.

Twenge, J. M., & Nolen-Hoeksema, S. (2002). Age, gender, race, socioeconomic status, and birth cohort differences on the children's depression inventory: A meta-analysis. *Journal of Abnormal Psychology, 111,* 578–588.

Twenge, J. M., Zhang, L., & Im, C. (2004). It's beyond my control: A cross-temporal meta-analysis of increasing externality in locus of control, 1960–2002. *Personality and Social Psychology Review, 8,* 308–319.

Twiss, C., Tabb, S., & Crosby, F. (1989). Affirmative action and aggregate data: The importance of patterns in the perception of discrimination. In F. Blanchard & F. Crosby (Eds.), *Affirmative action: Social psychological perspectives.* New York: Springer-Verlag.

Tyler, C. (1998). An eye-placement principle in 500 years of portraits. San Francisco: Smith-Kettlewell Eye Reseach Institute (http://www.ski.org/CWTyler_lab/ARVO/cwtarvo.html).

Tyler, K. A. (2002). Social and emotional outcomes of childhood sexual abuse: A review of recent research. *Aggression and Violent Behavior, 7,* 567–589.

Uchino, B. N., Cacioppo, J. T., & Kiecolt-Glaser, J. K. (1996). The relationship between social support and physiological processes: A review with emphasis on underlying mechanisms and implications for health. *Psychological Bulletin, 119,* 488–531.

Uchino, B. N., Uno, D., & Holt-Lunstad, J. (1999). Social support, physiological processes, and health. *Current Directions in Psychological Science, 8,* 145–148.

Udry, J. R. (2000). Biological limits of gender construction. *American Sociological Review, 65,* 443–457.

Uehling, M. C. (1998, August). A brief history of Stephen Hawking. *Biography Magazine,* pp. 61–65, 116–117.

UK ECT Review Group. (2003). Efficacy and safety of electroconvulsive therapy in depressive disorders: A systematic review and meta-analysis. *Lancet, 361,* 799–808.

Ullman, E. (2005, October 19). The boss in the machine. *New York Times* (www.nytimes.com).

Ulrich, R. E. (1991). Animal rights, animal wrongs and the question of balance. *Psychological Science, 2,* 197–201.

Ulrich, R. S. (1984). View through a window may influence recovery from surgery. *Science, 224,* 420–421.

UNAIDS. (2004, July). *UNAIDS 2004 report on the global AIDS epidemic* (www.unaids.org).

UNAIDS. (2004). *AIDS epidemic update 2004.* United Nations (www.unaids.org).

UNAIDS. (2004). Sub-Saharan Africa. Joint United Nations Programme on HIV/AIDS (www.unaids.org).

UNAIDS. (2005). *AIDS epidemic update, December 2005.* United Nations (www.unaids.org).

UNAIDS. (2005). *AIDS in Africa: Three scenarios to 2025.* United Nations (www.unaids.org).

UNAIDS. (2005). Epidemiology. Joint United Nations Programme on HIV/AIDS (www.unaids.org).

Underwood, B. J. (1957). Interference and forgetting. *Psychological Review, 64,* 49–60.

United Nations. (1992). *1991 demographic yearbook.* New York: United Nations.

Urbany, J. E., Bearden, W. O., & Weilbaker, D. C. (1988). The effect of plausible and exaggerated reference prices on consumer perceptions and price search. *Journal of Consumer Research, 15,* 95–110.

Urry, H. L., Nitschke, J. B., Dolski, I., Jackson, D. C., Dalton, K. M., Mueller, C. J., Rosenkranz, M. A., Ryff, C. D., Singer, B. H., & Davidson, R. J. (2004). Making a life worth living: Neural correlates of well-being. *Psychological Science, 15,* 367–372.

Ursu, S., Stenger, V. A., Shear, M. K., Jones, M. R., & Carter, C. S. (2003). Overactive action monitoring in obsessive-compulsive disorder: Evidence from functional magnetic resonance imaging. *Psychological Science, 14,* 347–353.

USAID. (2004, January). The ABCs of HIV prevention. www.usaid.gov.

U.S. News & World Report. (1997, March 31). Oprah: A heavenly body? Survey finds talk-show host a celestial shoo-in. P. 18.

U.S. Senate Select Committee on Intelligence (2004, July 9). *Report of the U.S. Intelligence Community's prewar intelligence assessments on Iraq.* www.gpoaccess.gov/serialset/creports/iraq.html

Vaidya, J. G., Gray, E. K., Haig, J., & Watson, D. (2002). On the temporal stability of personality: Evidence for differential stability and the role of life experiences. *Journal of Personality and Social Psychology, 83,* 1469–1484.

Vaillant, G. E. (1977). *Adaptation to life.* New York: Little, Brown.

Vaillant, G. E. (2002). *Aging well: Surprising guideposts to a happier life from the landmark Harvard study of adult development.* Boston: Little, Brown.

Vaitl, D., & 14 others (2005). Psychobiology of altered states of consciousness. *Psychological Bulletin, 131,* 98–127.

Valenstein, E. (1998). *Blaming the brain: The truth about drugs and mental health.* Free Press.

Valenstein, E. S. (1986). *Great and desperate cures: The rise and decline of psychosurgery.* New York: Basic Books.

Vallone, R. P., Griffin, D. W., Lin, S., & Ross, L. (1990). Overconfident prediction of future actions and outcomes by self and others. *Journal of Personality and Social Psychology, 58,* 582–592.

van Boxtel, H. W., Orobio de Castro, B., & Goossens, F. A. (2004). High self-perceived social competence in rejected children is related to frequent fighting. *European Journal of Developmental Psychology, 1,* 205–214.

Vance, E. B., & Wagner, N. N. (1976). Written descriptions of orgasm: A study of sex differences. *Archives of Sexual Behavior, 5,* 87–98.

Vandell, D. L. (2000). Parents, peer groups, and other socializing influences. *Developmental Psychology, 36,* 699–710.

Vandello, J. A., & Cohen, D. (1999). Patterns of individualism and collectivism across the United States. *Journal of Personality and Social Psychology, 77,* 279–292.

Vandenberg, S. G., & Kuse, A. R. (1978). Mental rotations: A group test of three-dimensional spatial visualization. *Perceptual and Motor Skills, 47,* 599–604.

van den Boom, D. (1990). Preventive intervention and the quality of mother-infant interaction and infant exploration in irritable infants. In W. Koops, H. J. G. Soppe, J. L. van der Linden, P. C. M. Molenaar, & J. J. F. Schroots (Eds.), *Developmental psychology behind the dikes: An outline of developmental psychology research in The Netherlands.* The Netherlands: Uitgeverij Eburon. Cited by C. Hazan & P. R. Shaver (1994). Deeper into attachment theory. *Psychological Inquiry, 5,* 68–79.

van den Bos, K., & Spruijt, N. (2002). Appropriateness of decisions as a moderator of the psychology of voice. *European Journal of Social Psychology, 32,* 57–72.

VanderStoep, S. W., & Shaughnessy, J. J. (1997). Taking a course in research methods improves reasoning about real-life events. *Teaching of Psychology, 24,* 122–124.

Van Dyke, C., & Byck, R. (1982, March). Cocaine. *Scientific American,* pp. 128–141.

van Engen, M. L., & Willemsen, T. M. (2004). Sex and leadership styles: A meta-analysis of research published in the 1990s. *Psychological Reports, 94,* 3–18.

van IJzendoorn, M. H., & De Wolff, M. S. (1997). In search of the absent father—Meta-analyses of infant-father attachment: A rejoinder to our discussants. *Child Development, 68,* 604–610.

van IJzendoorn, M. H., & Kroonenberg, P. M. (1988). Cross-cultural patterns of attachment: A meta-analysis of the strange situation. *Child Development, 59,* 147–156.

Van Leeuwen, M. S. (1978). A cross-cultural examination of psychological differentiation in males and females. *International Journal of Psychology, 13,* 87–122.

Van Leeuwen, M. S. (1982). IQism and the just society: Historical background. *Journal of the American Scientific Affiliation, 34,* 193–201.

van Lommel, P., van Wees, R., Meyers, V., & Elfferich, I. (2001). Near-death experience in survivors of cardiac arrest: A prospective study in the Netherlands. *Lancet, 358,* 2039–2045.

Vanman, E. J., Saltz, J. L., Nathan, L. R., & Warren, J. A. (2004). Racial discrimination by low-prejudiced Whites. *Psychological Science, 15,* 711–714.

Van Praag, H., Schinder, A. F., Christie, B. R., Toni, N., Palmer, T. D., & Gage, F. H. (2002). Neurogenesis: Functional neurons in adult hippocampus. *Nature, 415,* 1030–1034.

Van Rooy, D. L., & Viswesvaran, C. (2004). Emotional intelligence: A meta-analytic investigation of predictive validity and nomological net. *Journal of Vocational Behavior, 65,* 71–95.

van Schaik, C. P., Ancrenaz, M., Borgen, G., Galdikas, B., Knott, C. D., Singleton, I., Suzuki, A., Utami, S. S., & Merrill, M. (2003). Orangutan cultures and the evolution of material culture. *Science, 299,* 102–105.

VanTassel-Baska, J. (1983). Profiles of precocity: The 1982 Midwest Talent Search finalists. *Gifted Child Quarterly, 27,* 139–145.

Van Yperen, N. W., & Buunk, B. P. (1990). A longitudinal study of equity and satisfaction in intimate relationships. *European Journal of Social Psychology, 20,* 287–309.

Vaughn, K. B., & Lanzetta, J. T. (1981). The effect of modification of expressive displays on vicarious emotional arousal. *Journal of Experimental Social Psychology, 17,* 16–30.

Vazire, S., & Gosling, S. D. (2004). e-Perceptions: Personality impressions based on personal websites. *Journal of Personality and Social Psychology, 87,* 123–132.

Vecera, S. P., Vogel, E. K., & Woodman, G. F. (2002). Lower region: A new cue for figure-ground assignment. *Journal of Experimental Psychology: General, 13,* 194–205.

Vega, W. A., Kolody, B., Aguilar-Gaxiola, S., Alderete, E., Catalano, R., & Caraveo-Anduaga, J. (1998). Lifetime prevalence of DSM-III-R psychiatric disorders among urban and rural Mexican Americans in California. *Archives of General Psychiatry, 55,* 771–778.

Vekassy, L. (1977). Dreams of the blind. *Magyar Pszichologiai Szemle, 34,* 478–491.

Vemer, E., Coleman, M., Ganong, L. H., & Cooper, H. (1989). Marital satisfaction in remarriage: A meta-analysis. *Journal of Marriage and the Family, 51,* 713–725.

Venn, J. (1986). Hypnosis and the Lamaze method: A reply to Wideman and Singer. *American Psychologist, 41,* 475–476.

Verbeek, M. E. M., Drent, P. J., & Wiepkema, P. R. (1994). Consistent individual differences in early exploratory behaviour of male great tits. *Animal Behaviour, 48,* 1113–1121.

Verhaeghen, P., & Salthouse, T. A. (1997). Meta-analyses of age-cognition relations in adulthood: Estimates of linear and nonlinear age effects and structural models. *Psychological Bulletin, 122,* 231–249.

Vernon, P. A. (1983). Speed of information processing and general intelligence. *Intelligence, 7,* 53–70.

Viding, E., Blair, R., James, R., Moffitt, T. E., & Plomin, R. (2005). Evidence for substantial genetic risk for psychopathy in 7-year-olds. *Journal of Child Psychology & Psychiatry, 46,* 592–597.

Vigliocco, G., & Hartsuiker, R. J. (2002). The interplay of meaning, sound, and syntax in sentence production. *Psychological Bulletin, 128,* 442–472.

Vining, E. P. G., Freeman, J. M., Pillas, D. J., Uematsu, S., Carson, B. S., Brandt, J., Boatman, D., Pulsifer, M. B., & Zukerberg, A. (1997). Why would you remove half a brain? The outcome of 58 children after hemispherectomy—The Johns Hopkins Experience: 1968 to 1996. *Pediatrics, 100,* 163–171.

Vita, A. J., Terry, R. B., Hubert, H. B., & Fries, J. F. (1998). Aging, health risks, and cumulative disability. *New England Journal of Medicine, 338,* 1035–1041.

Vitaliano, P. P., Zhang, J., & Scanlan, J. M. (2003). Is caregiving hazardous to one's physical health? A meta-analysis. *Psychological Bulletin, 129,* 946–972.

Vitevitch, M. S. (2003). Change deafness: The inability to detect changes between two voices. *Journal of Experimental Psychology: Human Perception and Performance, 29,* 333–342.

Vogel, S. (1999). *The skinny on fat: Our obsession with weight control.* New York: W. H. Freeman.

Vohs, K., Voelz, Z., Pettit, J., Bardone, A., Katz, J., Abramson, L., Heatherton, T., & Joiner, T. (2001). Perfectionism, body dissatisfaction, and self-esteem: An interactive model of bulimic symptom development. *Journal of Social and Clinical Psychology, 20,* 476–497.

Vokey, J. R. (2002). Subliminal messages. In J. R. Vokey and S.W. Allen (Eds.), *Psychological sketches* (6th Edition). Lethbridge, Alberta: Psyence Ink, pp. 223–246.

von Békésy, G. (1957, August). The ear. *Scientific American,* pp. 66–78.

von Senden, M. (1932; reprinted 1960). In P. Heath (Trans.), *Space and sight: The perception of space and shape in the congenitally blind before and after operation.* Glencoe, IL: Free Press.

Vreeland, C. N., Gallagher, B. J., III, & McFalls, J. A., Jr. (1995). The beliefs of members of the American Psychiatric Association on the etiology of male homosexuality: A national survey. *Journal of Psychology, 129,* 507–517.

Wadden, T. A., Vogt, R. A., Foster, G. D., & Anderson, D. A. (1998). Exercise and the maintenance of weight loss: 1-year follow-up of a controlled clinical trial. *Journal of Consulting and Clinical Psychology, 66,* 429–433.

Wager, T. D., Rilling, J. K., Smith, E. E., Sokolik, A., Casey, K. L., Davidson, R. J., Kosslyn, S. M., Rose, R. M., & Cohen, J. D. (2004). Placebo-induced changes in fMRI in the anticipation and experience of pain. *Science, 303,* 1162–1167.

Wagner, A. D., Schacter, D. L., Rotte, M., Koutstaal, W., Maril, A., Dale, A. M., Rosen, B. R., & Buckner, R. L. (1998). Building memories: Remembering and forgetting of verbal experiences as predicted by brain activity. *Science, 281,* 1188–1191.

Wagner, U., Gais, S., Haider, H., Verleger, R., & Born, J. (2004). Sleep inspires insight. *Nature, 427,* 352–355.

Wagstaff, G. (1982). Attitudes to rape: The "just world" strikes again? *Bulletin of the British Psychological Society, 13,* 275–283.

Wahl, O. F. (1992). Mass media images of mental illness: A review of the literature. *Journal of Community Psychology, 20,* 343–352.

Wahlberg, D. (2001, October 11). We're more depressed, patriotic, poll finds. *Grand Rapids Press,* p. A15.

Wakefield, J. C., & Spitzer, R. L. (2002). Lowered estimates—but of what? *Archives of General Psychiatry, 59,* 129–130.

Waldrop, M. M. (1987). The workings of working memory. *Science, 237,* 1564–1567.

Walker, W. R., Skowronski, J. J., Gibbons, J. A., Vogl, R. J., & Thompson, C. P. (2003). On the emotions that accompany autobiographical memories: Dysphoria disrupts the fading affect bias. *Cognition and Emotion, 17,* 703–723.

Walker, W. R., Skowronski, J. J., & Thompson, C. P. (2003). Life is pleasant—and memory helps to keep it that way! *Review of General Psychology, 7,* 203–210.

Wall, B. (2002, August 24–25). Profit matures along with baby boomers. *International Herald Tribune,* p. 13.

Wall, P. (2000). *Pain: The science of suffering.* New York: Columbia University Press.

Wall Street Journal. (1999, December 17). Money and misery. Editorial, p. A14.

Wallace, D. S., Paulson, R. M., Lord, C. G., & Bond, C. F., Jr. (2005). Which behaviors do attitudes predict? Meta-analyzing the effects of social pressure and perceived difficulty. *Review of General Psychology, 9*(3), 214–227.

Wallach, M. A., & Wallach, L. (1983). *Psychology's sanction for selfishness: The error of egoism in theory and therapy.* New York: Freeman.

Wallach, M. A., & Wallach, L. (1985, February). How psychology sanctions the cult of the self. *Washington Monthly,* pp. 46–56.

Wallbott, H. G. (1988). In and out of context: Influences of facial expression and context information on emotion attributions. *British Journal of Social Psychology, 27,* 357–369.

Wallis, C. (1983, June 6). Stress: Can we cope? *Time,* pp. 48–54.

Walster (Hatfield), E., Aronson, V., Abrahams, D., & Rottman, L. (1966). Importance of physical attractiveness in dating behavior. *Journal of Personality and Social Psychology, 4,* 508–516.

Wampold, B. E. (2001). *The great psychotherapy debate: Models, methods, and findings.* Mahwah, NJ: Erlbaum.

Wampold, B. E., Mondin, G. W., Moody, M., & Ahn, H. (1997). The flat earth as a metaphor for the evidence for uniform efficacy of bona fide psychotherapies: Reply to Crits-Christoph (1997) and Howard et al. (1997). *Psychological Bulletin, 122,* 226–230.

Wang, Y., Liu, D., & Wang, Y. (2003). Discovering the capacity of human memory. *Brain and Mind, 4,* 189–198.

Wansink, B., & van Ittersum, K. (2003). Bottoms up! The influence of elongation on pouring and consumption volume. *Journal of Consumer Research, 30,* 455–464.

Warchol, M. E., Lambert, P. R., Goldstein, B. J., Forge, A., & Corwin, J. T. (1993). Regenerative proliferation in inner ear sensory epithelia from adult guinea pigs and humans. *Science, 259,* 1619–1622.

Ward, A., & Mann, T. (2000). Don't mind if I do: Disinhibited eating under cognitive load. *Journal of Personality and Social Psychology, 78,* 753–763.

Ward, C. (1994). Culture and altered states of consciousness. In W. J. Lonner & R. Malpass (Eds.), *Psychology and culture.* Boston: Allyn & Bacon.

Ward, J. (2003). State of the art synaesthesia. *The Psychologist, 16,* 196–199.

Ward, K. D., Klesges, R. C., & Halpern, M. T. (1997). Predictors of smoking cessation and state-of-the-art smoking interventions. *Journal of Socies Issues, 53,* 129–145.

Wardle, J., Cooke, L. J., Gibson, L., Sapochnik, M., Sheiham, A., Lawson, M. (2003). Increasing children's acceptance of vegetables; a randomized trial of parent-led exposure. *Appetite, 40,* 155–162.

Warm, J. S., & Dember, W. N. (1986, April). Awake at the switch. *Psychology Today,* pp. 46–53.

Warner, J., McKeown, E., Johnson, K., Ramsay, A., Cort, C., & King, M. (2004). Rates and predictors of mental illness in gay men, lesbians and bisexual men and women. *British Journal of Psychiatry, 185,* 479–485.

Warr, P., & Payne, R. (1982). Experiences of strain and pleasure among British adults. *Social Science and Medicine, 16,* 1691–1697.

Warren, N. C. (2005, March 4). Personal correspondence from founder of eHarmony.com.

Wason, P. C. (1960). On the failure to eliminate hypotheses in a conceptual task. *Quarterly Journal of Experimental Psychology, 12,* 129–140.

Wason, P. C. (1981). The importance of cognitive illusions. *The Behavioral and Brain Sciences, 4,* 356.

Wasserman, E. A. (1993). Comparative cognition: Toward a general understanding of cognition in behavior. *Psychological Science, 4,* 156–161.

Wasserman, E. A. (1995). The conceptual abilities of pigeons. *American Scientist, 83,* 246–255.

Wastell, C. A. (2002). Exposure to trauma: The long-term effects of suppressing emotional reactions. *Journal of Nervous and Mental Disorders, 190,* 839–845.

Watamura, S. E., Donzella, B., Alwin, J., & Gunnar, M. R. (2003). Morning-to-afternoon increases in cortisol concentrations for infants and toddlers at child care: Age differences and behavioral correlates. *Child Development, 74,* 1006–1020.

Waterhouse, R. (1993, July 19). Income for 62 percent is below average pay. *The Independent,* p. 4.

Waterman, A. S. (1988). Identity status theory and Erikson's theory: Commonalities and differences. *Developmental Review, 8,* 185–208.

Watkins, C. E., Campbell, V. L., Nieberding, R., & Hallmark, R. (1995). Contemporary practice of psychological assessment by clinical psychologists. *Professional Psychology: Research and Practice, 26,* 54–60.

Watkins, J. G. (1984). The Bianchi (L. A. Hillside Strangler) case: Sociopath or multiple personality? *International Journal of Clinical and Experimental Hypnosis, 32,* 67–101.

Watkins, P. C. (2004). Gratitude and subjective well-being. In R. A. Emmons and M. E. McCullough (Eds.), *The psychology of gratitude.* New York: Oxford University Press.

Watson, D. (2000). *Mood and temperament.* New York: Guilford Press.

Watson, D. (2003). To dream, perchance to remember: Individual differences in dream recall. *Personality and Individual Differences, 34,* 1271–1286.

Watson, D., Suls, J., & Haig, J. (2002). Global self-esteem in relation to structural models of personality and affectivity. *Journal of Personality and Social Psychology, 83,* 185–197.

Watson, D., Wiese, D., Vaidya, J., & Tellegen, A. (1999). The two general activation systems of affect: Structured findings, evolutionary considerations, and psychobiological evidence. *Journal of Personality and Social Psychology, 76,* 820–838.

Watson, J. B. (1913). Psychology as the behaviorist views it. *Psychological Review, 20,* 158–177.

Watson, J. B. (1924). The unverbalized in human behavior. *Psychological Review, 31,* 339–347.

Watson, J. B., & Rayner, R. (1920). Conditioned emotional reactions. *Journal of Experimental Psychology, 3,* 1–14.

Watson, R. I., Jr. (1973). Investigation into deindividuation using a cross-cultural survey technique. *Journal of Personality and Social Psychology, 25,* 342–345.

Watson, S. J., Benson, J. A., Jr., & Joy, J. E. (2000). NEWS AND VIEWS—Marijuana and medicine: Assessing the science base: A summary of the 1999 Institute of Medicine report. *Archives of General Psychiatry, 57,* 547–553.

Wayment, H. A., & Peplau, L. A. (1995). Social support and well-being among lesbian and heterosexual women: A structural modeling approach. *Personality and Social Psychology Bulletin, 21,* 1189–1199.

Weaver, J. B., Masland, J. L., & Zillmann, D. (1984). Effect of erotica on young men's aesthetic perception of their female sexual partners. *Perceptual and Motor Skills, 58,* 929–930.

Webb, W. B. (1992). *Sleep: The gentle tyrant.* Bolton, MA: Anker Publishing.

Webb, W. B., & Campbell, S. S. (1983). Relationships in sleep characteristics of identical and fraternal twins. *Archives of General Psychiatry, 40,* 1093–1095.

Wechsler, D. (1972). "Hold" and "Don't Hold" tests. In S. M. Chown (Ed.), *Human aging.* New York: Penguin.

Wechsler, H., Davenport, A., Dowdall, G., Moeykens, B., & Castillo, S. (1994). Health and behavioral consequences of binge drinking in college. *Journal of the American Medical Association, 272,* 1672–1677.

Wechsler, H., Lee, J. E., Kuo, M., Seibring, M., Nelson, T. F., & Lee, H. (2002). Trends in college binge drinking during a period of increased prevention efforts. *Journal of American College Health, 50,* 203–217.

Wee, C. C., Phillips, R. S., Legedza, A. T. R., Davis, R. B., Soukup, J. R., Colditz, G. A., & Hamel, M. B. (2005). Health care expenditures associated with overweight and obesity among US adults: Importance of age and race. *American Journal of Public Health, 95,* 159–165.

Weed, W. S. (2001, May). Can we go to Mars without going crazy? *Discover,* pp. 31–43.

Wegner, D. M. (1990). *White bears and other unwanted thoughts: Suppression, obsession, and the psychology of mental control.* New York: Penguin Books.

Wegner, D. M. (2002). *The illusion of conscious will.* Cambridge, MA: MIT Press.

Weigel, G. (2005, March–April). Is Europe dying? Notes on a crisis of civilizational morale. *New Atlantic Initiative,* American Enterprise Institute for Public Policy Research (www.aei.org/nai).

Weinberg, M. S., & Williams, C. (1974). *Male homosexuals: Their problems and adaptations.* New York: Oxford University Press.

Weinberger, N. M. (2004, November). Music and the brain. *Scientific American,* pp. 89–95.

Weiner, B. (1985). An attributional theory of achievement motivation and emotion. *Psychological Review, 92,* 548–573.

Weingarten, G. (2002, March 10). Below the beltway. *Washington Post,* p. WO3.

Weinstein, N. D. (1980). Unrealistic optimism about future life events. *Journal of Personality and Social Psychology, 39,* 806–820.

Weinstein, N. D. (1982). Unrealistic optimism about susceptibility to health problems. *Journal of Behavioral Medicine, 5,* 441–460.

Weinstein, N. D. (1987). Unrealistic optimism about susceptibility to health problems: Conclusions from a community-wide sample. *Journal of Behavioral Medicine, 10,* 481–500.

Weinstein, N. D. (1996, October 4). 1996 optimistic bias bibliography. Distributed via internet (weinstein_c@aesop.rutgers.edu).

Weiskrantz, L. (1986). *Blindsight: A case study and implications.* Oxford, UK: Oxford University Press.

Weiss, A., King, J. E., & Enns, R. M. (2002). Subjective well-being is heritable and genetically correlated with dominance in chimpanzees (*Pan troglodytes*). *Journal of Personality and Social Psychology, 83,* 1141–1149.

Weiss, A., King, J. E., & Figueredo, A. J. (2000). The heritability of personality factors in chimpanzees (*Pan troglodytes*). *Behavior Genetics, 30,* 213–221.

Weiss, J. M. (1977). Psychological and behavioral influences on gastrointestinal lesions in animal models. In J. D. Maser & M. E. P. Seligman (Eds.), *Psychopathology: Experimental models.* San Francisco: Freeman.

Weissman, M. M. (1999). Interpersonal psychotherapy and the health care scene. In D. S. Janowsky (Ed.), *Psychotherapy indications and outcomes.* Washington, DC: American Psychiatric Press.

Weissman, M. M., Bland, R. C., Canino, G. J., Faravelli, C., Greenwald, S., Hwu, H-G., Joyce, P. R., Karam, E. G., Lee, C-K., Lellouch, J., Lepine, J-P., Newman, S. C., Rubio-Stepic, M., Wells, J. E., Wickramaratne, P. J., Wittchen, H-U., & Yeh, E-K. (1996). Cross-national epidemiology of major depression and bipolar disorder. *Journal of the American Medical Association, 276,* 293–299.

Weisz, J. R., Rothbaum, F. M., & Blackburn, T. C. (1984). Standing out and standing in: The psychology of control in America and Japan. *American Psychologist, 39,* 955–969.

Wellman, H. M., Cross, D., & Watson, J. (2001). Meta-analysis of theory-of-mind development: The truth about false belief. *Child Development, 72,* 655–684.

Wellman, H. M., & Gelman, S. A. (1992). Cognitive development: Foundational theories of core domains. *Annual Review of Psychology, 43,* 337–375.

Wells, B. L. (1986). Predictors of female nocturnal orgasms: A multivariate analysis. *Journal of Sex Research, 22,* 421–437.

Wells, C. (1983, March). Teaching the brain new tricks. *Esquire,* 49–57.

Wells, G. L. (1981). Lay analyses of causal forces on behavior. In J. Harvey (Ed.), *Cognition, social behavior and the environment.* Hillsdale, NJ: Erlbaum.

Wells, G., & Murray, D. M. (1984). Eyewitness confidence. In G. L. Wells & E. F. Loftus (Eds.), *Eyewitness testimony: Psychological perspectives.* New York: Cambridge University Press.

Wender, P. H., Kety, S. S., Rosenthal, D., Schulsinger, F., Ortmann, J., & Lunde, I. (1986). Psychiatric disorders in the biological and adoptive families of adopted individuals with affective disorders. *Archives of General Psychiatry, 43,* 923–929.

Wener, R., Frazier, W., & Farbstein, J. (1987, June). Building better jails. *Psychology Today,* pp. 40–49.

Wessely, S., & Kerwin, R. (2004). Suicide risk and the SSRIs. *Journal of the American Medical Association, 292,* 379–381.

West, P. D. B., & Evans, E. F. (1990). Early detection of hearing damage in young listeners resulting from exposure to amplified music. *British Journal of Audiology, 24,* 89–103.

Westen, D. (1996). Is Freud really dead? Teaching psychodynamic theory to introductory psychology. Presentation to the Annual Institute on the Teaching of Psychology, St. Petersburg Beach, Florida.

Westen, D. (1998). The scientific legacy of Sigmund Freud: Toward a psychodynamically informed psychological science. *Psychological Bulletin, 124,* 333–371.

Westen, D., & Morrison, K. (2001). A multidimensional meta-analysis of treatments for depression, panic, and generalized anxiety disorder: An empirical examination of the status of empirically supported therapies. *Journal of Consulting and Clinical Psychology, 69,* 875–899.

Wetter, D. W., Fiore, M. C., Gritz, E. R., Lando, H. A., Stitzer, M. L., Hasselblad, V., & Baker, T. B. (1998). The Agency for Health Care Policy and Research. *Smoking cessation clinical practice guideline: Findings and implications for psychologists. American Psychologist, 53,* 657–669.

Weuve, J., Kang, J. H., Manson, J. E., Breteler, M. M. B., Ware, J. H., & Grodstein, F. (2004). Physical activity, including walking, and cognitive function in older women. *Journal of the American Medical Association, 292,* 1454–1460.

Wever, E. G. (1949). Theory of hearing. New York: Wiley.

Whalen, P. J., Kagan, J., Cook, R. G., Davis, F. C., Kim, H., Polis, S., McLaren, D. G., Somerville, L. H., McLean, A. A., Maxwell, J. S., & Johnstone, T. (2004). Human amygdala responsibility to masked fearful eye whites. Science, 302, 2061.

Whalen, P. J., Shin, L. M., McInerney, S. C., Fisher, H., Wright, C. I., & Rauch, S. L. (2001). A functional MRI study of human amygdala responses to facial expressions of fear versus anger. Emotion, 1, 70–83.

Whaley, S. E., Sigman, M., Beckwith, L., Cohen, S. E., & Espinosa, M. P. (2002). Infant-caregiver interaction in Kenya and the United States: The importance of multiple caregivers and adequate comparison samples. Journal of Cross-Cultural Psychology, 33, 236–247.

Whalley, L. J., & Deary, I. J. (2001). Longitudinal cohort study of childhood IQ and survival up to age 76. British Medical Journal, 322, 1–5.

Whalley, L., Starr, J. M. Athawes, R., Hunter, D., Pattie, A., & Deary, I. J. (2000). Childhood mental ability and dementia. Neurology, 55, 1455–1459.

Wheelwright, J. (2004, August). Study the clones first. Discover, pp. 44–50.

White, G. L., & Kight, T. D. (1984). Misattribution of arousal and attraction: Effects of salience of explanations for arousal. Journal of Experimental Social Psychology, 20, 55–64.

White, H. R., Brick, J., & Hansell, S. (1993). A longitudinal investigation of alcohol use and aggression in adolescence. Journal of Studies on Alcohol, Supplement No. 11, 62–77.

White House. (1999, June 7). White House fact sheet on myths and facts about mental illness. Washington, DC: White House Press Office.

White, K. M. (1983). Young adults and their parents: Individuation to mutuality. New Directions for Child Development, 22, 61–76.

White, L., & Edwards, J. (1990). Emptying the nest and parental well-being: An analysis of national panel data. American Sociological Review, 55, 235–242.

White, P. H., Kjelgaard, M. M., & Harkins, S. G. (1995). Testing the contribution of self-evaluation to goal-setting effects. Journal of Personality and Social Psychology, 69, 69–79.

White, R. A. (1998). Intuition, heart knowledge, and parapsychology. Journal of the American Society for Psychical Research, 92, 158–171.

Whitehead, B. D., & Popenoe, D. (2001). The state of our unions 2001: The social health of marriage in America. Rutgers University: The National Marriage Project.

Whiten, A., & Boesch, C. (2001, January). Cultures of chimpanzees. Scientific American, pp. 60–67.

Whiten, A., & Byrne, R. W. (1988). Tactical deception in primates. Behavioral and Brain Sciences, 11, 233–244, 267–273.

Whiting, B. B., & Edwards, C. P. (1988). Children of different worlds: The formation of social behavior. Cambridge, MA: Harvard University Press.

Whitley, B. E., Jr. (1990). The relationships of heterosexuals' attributions for the causes of homosexuality to attitudes toward lesbians and gay men. Personality and Social Psychology Bulletin, 16, 369–377.

Whitley, B. E., Jr. (1999). Right-wing authoritarianism, social dominance orientation, and prejudice. Journal of Personality and Social Psychology, 77, 126–134.

Whitley, B. E., Jr. (2002). Gender-role variables and attitudes toward homosexuality. Sex Roles, 45, 691–720.

Whittington, C. J., Kendall, T., Fonagy, P., Cottrell, D., Cotgrove, A., & Boddington, E. (2004). Selective serotonin reuptake inhibitors in childhood depression: Systematic review of published versus unpublished data. Lancet, 363, 1341–1345.

WHO. (2002). The global burden of disease. Geneva: World Health Organization (www.who.int/msa/mnh/ems/dalys/intro.htm).

WHO. (2002a, September 4). Suicide rates. World Health Organization (www5.who.int/mental_health).

WHO. (2002c, December 9). China: WHO lauds launch of nation's first suicide prevent center: Xinhua news. World Health Organization (www5.who.int/mental_health).

WHO. (2002d). Schizophrenia. World Health Organization (www5.who.int/mental_health).

WHO. (2004). Prevalence, severity, and unmet need for treatment of mental disorders in the World Health Organization World Mental Health Surveys. Journal of the American Medical Association, 291, 2581–2590.

WHO. (2005, February 24). Global tobacco treaty enters into force with 57 countries already committed. World Health Organization media centre (www.who.int).

Whooley, M. A., & Browner, W. S. (1998). Association between depressive symptoms and mortality in older women. Archives of Internal Medicine, 158, 2129–2135.

Whorf, B. L. (1956). Science and linguistics. In J. B. Carroll (Ed.), Language, thought, and reality: Selected writings of Benjamin Lee Whorf. Cambridge, MA: MIT Press.

Wichman, H. (1992). Human factors in the design of spacecraft. Stony Brook, NY: State University of New York.

Wickelgren, I. (2005). Autistic brains out of sync? Science, 308, 1856–1858.

Wickelgren, W. A. (1977). Learning and memory. Englewood Cliffs, NJ: Prentice-Hall.

Widom, C. S. (1989a). Does violence beget violence? A critical examination of the literature. Psychological Bulletin, 106, 3–28.

Widom, C. S. (1989b). The cycle of violence. Science, 244, 160–166.

Wiens, A. N., & Menustik, C. E. (1983). Treatment outcome and patient characteristics in an aversion therapy program for alcoholism. American Psychologist, 38, 1089–1096.

Wierson, M., & Forehand, R. (1994). Parent behavioral training for child noncompliance: Rationale, concepts, and effectiveness. Current Directions in Psychological Science, 3, 146–149.

Wiertelak, E. P., Smith K. P., Furness, L., Mooney-Heiberger, K., Mayr, T., Maier, S. F., & Watkins, L. R. (1994). Acute and conditioned hyperalgesic responses to illness. Pain, 56, 227–234.

Wierzbicki, M. (1993). Psychological adjustment of adoptees: A meta-analysis. Journal of Clinical Child Psychology, 22, 447–454.

Wiesel, T. N. (1982). Postnatal development of the visual cortex and the influence of environment. Nature, 299, 583–591.

Wiesner, W. H., & Cronshow, S. P. (1988). A meta-analytic investigation of the impact of interview format and degree of structure on the validity of the employment interview. Journal of Occupational Psychology, 61, 275–290.

Wigdor, A. K., & Garner, W. R. (1982). Ability testing: Uses, consequences, and controversies. Washington, DC: National Academy Press.

Wilcox, A. J., Baird, D. D., Dunson, D. B., McConnaughey, D. R., Kesner, J. S., & Weinberg, C. R. (2004). On the frequency of intercourse around ovulation: Evidence for biological influences. Human Reproduction, 19, 1539–1543.

Wilder, D. A. (1981). Perceiving persons as a group: Categorization and intergroup relations. In D. L. Hamilton (Ed.), Cognitive processes in stereotyping and intergroup behavior. Hillsdale, NJ: Erlbaum.

Wildman, D. E., Uddin, M., Liu, G., Grossman, L. I., & Goodman, M. (2003). Implications of natural selection in shaping 99.4% nonsynonymous DNA identity between humans and chimpanzees: Enlarging genus Homo. Proceedings of the National Academy of Sciences, 100, 7181–7188.

Wilford, J. N. (1999, February 9). New findings help balance the cosmological books. New York Times (www.nytimes.com).

Williams, C. L., & Berry, J. W. (1991). Primary prevention of acculturative stress among refugees. American Psychologist, 46, 632–641.

Williams, J. E., & Best, D. L. (1990). Measuring sex stereotypes: A multination study. Newbury Park, CA: Sage.

Williams, J. E., Paton, C. C., Siegler, I. C., Eigenbrodt, M. L., Nieto, F. J., & Tyroler, H. A. (2000). Anger proneness predicts coronary heart disease risk: Prospective analysis from the artherosclerosis risk in communities (ARIC) study. *Circulation, 101,* 17, 2034-2040.

Williams, K. D. (2002). *Ostracism: The power of silence.* New York: Guilford.

Williams, K. D., & Zadro, L. (2001). Ostracism: On being ignored, excluded and rejected. In M. Leary (Ed.), *Rejection.* New York: Oxford University Press.

Williams, R. (1989). *The trusting heart: Great news about Type A behavior.* New York: Random House.

Williams, R. (1993). *Anger kills.* New York: Times Books.

Williams, R. B., Barefoot, J. C., Califf, R. M., Haney, T. L., Saunders, W. B., Pryor, D. B., Hlatky, M. A., Siegler, I. C., & Mark, D. B. (1992). Prognostic importance of social and economic resources among medically treated patients with angiographically documented coronary artery disease. *Journal of the American Medical Association, 267,* 520-524.

Williams, S., & Kohut, J. L. (1999). Psychologists in medical schools in 1997: Research brief. *American Psychologist, 54,* 272-276.

Williams, S. L. (1987). Self-efficacy and mastery-oriented treatment for severe phobias. Paper presented to the American Psychological Association convention.

Willingham, W. W., Lewis, C., Morgan, R., & Ramist, L. (1990). *Predicting college grades: An analysis of institutional trends over two decades.* Princeton: Educational Testing Service.

Willmuth, M. E. (1987). Sexuality after spinal cord injury: A critical review. *Clinical Psychology Review, 7,* 389-412.

Wilson, A. E., & Ross, M. (2001). From chump to champ: People's appraisals of their earlier and present selves. *Journal of Personality and Social Psychology, 80,* 572-584.

Wilson, C. M., & Oswald, A. J. (2002). How does marriage affect physical and psychological health? A survey of the longitudinal evidence. Working paper, University of York and Warwick University.

Wilson, J. P., Harel, Z., & Kahana, B. (1988). *Human adaptation to extreme stress: From the Holocaust to Vietnam.* New York: Plenum Press.

Wilson, R. C., Gaft, J. G., Dienst, E. R., Wood, L., & Bavry, J. L. (1975). *College professors and their impact on students.* New York: Wiley.

Wilson, R. S. (1979). Analysis of longitudinal twin data: Basic model and applications to physical growth measures. *Acta Geneticae medicae et Gemellologiae, 28,* 93-105.

Wilson, R. S., & Bennett, D. A. (2003). Cognitive activity and risk of Alzheimer's disease. *Current Directions in Psychological Science, 12,* 87-91.

Wilson, R. S., & Matheny, A. P., Jr. (1986). Behavior-genetics research in infant temperament: The Louisville twin study. In R. Plomin & J. Dunn (Eds.), *The study of temperament: Changes, continuities, and challenges.* Hillsdale, NJ: Erlbaum.

Wilson, T. D. (2002). *Strangers to ourselves: Discovering the adaptive unconscious.* Cambridge: Harvard University Press.

Windholz, G. (1989, April-June). The discovery of the principles of reinforcement, extinction, generalization, and differentiation of conditional reflexes in Pavlov's laboratories. *Pavlovian Journal of Biological Science, 26,* 64-74.

Windholz, G. (1997). Ivan P. Pavlov: An overview of his life and psychological work. *American Psychologist, 52,* 941-946.

Wingo, P. A., Ries, L. A. G., Giovino, G. A., Miller, D. S., Rosenberg, H. M., Shopland, D. R., Thun, M. J., & Edwards, B. K. (1999) The annual report to the nation on the status of cancer, 1973-1996, with a special section on lung cancer and tobacco smoking. *Journal of the National Cancer Institute, 91,* 675-690.

Wink, P., & Dillon, M. (2002). Spiritual development across the adult life course: Findings from a longitudinal study. *Journal of Adult Development, 9,* 79-94.

Winner, E. (2000). The origins and ends of giftedness. *American Psychologist, 55,* 159-169.

Wirtz, D., Kruger, J., Scollon, C. N., & Diener, E. (2003). What to do on Spring break? The role of predicted, on-line, and remembered experience in future choice. *Psychological Science, 14,* 520-524.

Wiseman, R. (2002). Laugh Lab—final results. University of Hertfordshire (www.laughlab.co.uk).

Wiseman, R., Jeffreys, C., Smith, M., & Nyman, A. (1999). The psychology of the seance. *The Skeptical Inquirer, 23*(2), 30-33.

Wisman, A., & Goldenberg, J. L. (2005). From the grave to the cradle: Evidence that mortality salience engenders a desire for offspring. *Journal of Personality and Social Psychology, 89,* 46-61.

Witelson, S. F., Kigar, D. L., & Harvey, T. (1999). The exceptional brain of Albert Einstein. *The Lancet, 353,* 2149-2153.

Witvliet, C. V. O., Ludwig, T., & Vander Laan, K. (2001). Granting forgiveness or harboring grudges: Implications for emotions, physiology, and health. *Psychological Science, 12,* 117-123.

Witvliet, C. V. O., & Vrana, S. R. (1995). Psychophysiological responses as indices of affective dimensions. *Psychophysiology, 32,* 436-443.

Wixted, J. T., & Ebbesen, E. B. (1991). On the form of forgetting. *Psychological Science, 2,* 409-415.

Woehr, D. J., & Cavell, T. A. (1993). Self-report measures of ability, effort, and nonacademic activity as predictors of introductory psychology test scores. *Teaching of Psychology, 20,* 156-160.

Woerlee, G. M. (2004, May/June). Darkness, tunnels, and light. *Skeptical Inquirer,* pp. 28-32.

Wolfson, A. R., & Carskadon, M. A. (1998). Sleep schedules and daytime functioning in adolescents. *Child Development, 69,* 875-887.

Woll, S. (1986). So many to choose from: Decision strategies in videodating. *Journal of Social and Personal Relationships, 3,* 43-52.

Wolpe, J. (1958). *Psychotherapy by reciprocal inhibition.* Stanford, CA: Stanford University Press.

Wolpe, J., & Plaud, J. J. (1997). Pavlov's contributions to behavior therapy: The obvious and the not so obvious. *American Psychologist, 52,* 966-972.

Wong, D. F., Wagner, H. N., Tune, L. E., Dannals, R. F., & others. (1986). Positron emission tomography reveals elevated D_2 dopamine receptors in drug-naive schizophrenics. *Science, 234,* 1588-1593.

Wong, M. M., & Csikszentmihalyi, M. (1991). Affiliation motivation and daily experience: Some issues on gender differences. *Journal of Personality and Social Psychology, 60,* 154-164.

Wood, C. J, & Aggleton, J. P. (1989). Handedness in "fast ball' sports: Do left-handers have an innate advantage? *British Journal of Psychology, 80,* 227-240.

Wood, J. (2003, May 19). Quoted by R. Mestel, Rorschach tested: Blot out the famous method? Some experts say it has no place in psychiatry. *Los Angeles Times* (www.latimes.com).

Wood, J. M., Bootzin, R. R., Kihlstrom, J. F., & Schacter, D. L. (1992). Implicit and explicit memory for verbal information presented during sleep. *Psychological Science, 3,* 236-239.

Wood, J. M., Nezworski, M. T., Garb, H. N., & Lilienfeld, S. O. (2006). The controversy over the Exner Comprehensive System and the Society for Personality Assessment's white paper on the Rorschach. *Independent Practitioner,* in press.

Wood, J. V., Heimpel, S. A., & Michela, J. L. (2003). Savoring versus dampening: Self-esteem differences in regulating positive affect. *Journal of Personality and Social Psychology, 85,* 566-580.

Wood, J. V., Saltzberg, J. A., & Goldsamt, L. A. (1990a). Does affect induce self-focused attention? *Journal of Personality and Social Psychology, 58,* 899-908.

Wood, J. V., Saltzberg, J. A., Neale, J. M., Stone, A. A., & Rachmiel, T. B. (1990b). Self-focused attention, coping responses, and distressed mood in everyday life. *Journal of Personality and Social Psychology, 58,* 1027-1036.

Wood, W. (1987). Meta-analytic review of sex differences in group performance. *Psychological Bulletin, 102,* 53–71.

Wood, W., & Eagly, A. (2002). A cross-cultural analysis of the behavior of women and men: Implications for the origins of sex differences. *Psychological Bulletin, 128,* 699–727.

Wood, W., Lundgren, S., Ouellette, J. A., Busceme, S., & Blackstone, T. (1994). Minority influence: A meta-analytic review of social influence processes. *Psychological Bulletin, 115,* 323–345.

Woodruff-Pak, D. S. (1989). Aging and intelligence: Changing perspectives in the twentieth century. *Journal of Aging Studies, 3,* 91–118.

Woods, N. F., Dery, G. K., & Most, A. (1983). Recollections of menarche, current menstrual attitudes, and premenstrual symptoms. In S. Golub (Ed.), *Menarche: The transition from girl to woman.* Lexington, MA: Lexington Books.

Woody, E. Z., & McConkey, K. M. (2003). What we don't know about the brain and hypnosis, but need to: A view from the Buckhorn Inn. *International Journal of Clinical and Experimental Hypnosis, 51,* 309–338.

Woolcock, N. (2004, September 3). Driver thought everyone else was on wrong side. *The Times,* p. 22.

World Federation for Mental Health. (2005). ADHD: The hope behind the hype. www.wfmh.org

World Health Organization. (1979). *Schizophrenia: An international follow-up study.* Chicester, England: Wiley.

World Health Organization. (2004a). *Prevention of mental disorders: Effective interventions and policy options. Summary report.* Geneva: World Health Organization, Department of Mental Health and Substance Abuse.

World Health Organization. (2004b). *Promoting mental health: Concepts, emerging evidence, practice. Summary report.* Geneva: World Health Organization, Department of Mental Health and Substance Abuse.

Worobey, J., & Blajda, V. M. (1989). Temperament ratings at 2 weeks, 2 months, and 1 year: Differential stability of activity and emotionality. *Developmental Psychology, 25,* 257–263.

Worthington, E. L., Jr. (1989). Religious faith across the life span: Implications for counseling and research. *The Counseling Psychologist, 17,* 555–612.

Worthington, E. L., Jr., Kurusu, T. A., McCullogh, M. E., & Sandage, S. J. (1996). Empirical research on religionand psychotherapeutic processes and outcomes: A 10-year review and research prospectus. *Psychological Bulletin, 119,* 448–487.

Wortman, C. B., & Silver, R. C. (1989). The myths of coping with loss. *Journal of Consulting and Clinical Psychology, 57,* 349–357.

Wren, C. S. (1999, April 8). Drug survey of children finds middle school a pivotal time. *New York Times* (www.nytimes.com).

Wright, I. C., Rabe-Hesketh, S., Woodruff, P. W. R., David, A. S., Murray, R. M., & Bullmore, E. T. (2000). Meta-analysis of regional brain volumes in schizophrenia. *American Journal of Psychiatry, 157,* 16–25.

Wright, K. (November, 1996). The Tarzan syndrome. *Discover, 17*(11), 88–94, 96, 98.

Wright, P. H. (1989). Gender differences in adults' same- and cross-gender friendships. In R. G. Adams & R. Blieszner (Eds.), *Older adult friendships: Structure and process.* Newbury Park, CA: Sage.

Wright, P., Takei, N., Rifkin, L., & Murray, R. M. (1995). Maternal influenza, obstetric complications, and schizophrenia. *American Journal of Psychiatry, 152,* 1714–1720.

Wright, R. (1999, January 11). Who gets the good genes? *Time,* p. 67.

Wright, W. (1998). *Born that way: Genes, behavior, personality.* New York: Knopf.

Wrzesniewski, A., & Dutton, J. E. (2001). Crafting a job: Revisioning employees as active crafters of their work. *Academy of Management Review, 26,* 179–201.

Wrzesniewski, A., McCauley, C. R., Rozin, P., & Schwartz, B. (1997). Jobs, careers, and callings: People's relations to their work. *Journal of Research in Personality, 31,* 21–33.

Wuethrich, B. (2001, March). Features—GETTING STUPID—Surprising new neurological behavioral research reveals that teenagers who drink too much may permanently damage their brains and seriously compromise their ability to learn. *Discover, 56,* 56–64.

Wulsin, L. R., Vaillant, G. E., & Wells, V. E. (1999). A systematic review of the mortality of depression. *Psychosomatic Medicine, 61,* 6–17.

Wyatt, J. K., & Bootzin, R. R. (1994). Cognitive processing and sleep: Implications for enhancing job performance. *Human Performance, 7,* 119–139.

Wyatt, R. J., Henter, I., & Sherman-Elvy, E. (2001). Tantalizing clues to preventing schizophrenia. *Cerebrum: The Dana Forum on Brain Science, 3,* pp. 15–30.

Wynn, K. (1992). Addition and subtraction by human infants. *Nature, 358,* 749–759.

Wynn, K. (2000). Findings of addition and subtraction in infants are robust and consistent: reply to Wakeley, Rivera, and Langer. *Child Development, 71,* 1535–1536.

Wynn, K., Bloom, P., & Chiang, W-C. (2002). Enumeration of collective entities by 5-month-old infants. *Cognition, 83,* B55–B62.

Wynn, V., & Gilhooly, K. (1999). The veracity of memories for what you were doing and who you were with when you heard of the death of Diana. *British Psychological Society 1999 Proceedings, 71,* p. 47.

Wynne, C. D. L. (2004). *Do animals think?* Princeton, NJ: Princeton University Press.

Wysocki, C. J., & Gilbert, A. N. (1989). *National Geographic* survey: Effects of age are heterogeneous. *Annals of the New York Academy of Sciences, 561,* 12–28.

Xu, Y., & Corkin, S. (2001). H.M. revisits the Tower of Hanoi puzzle. *Neuropsychology, 15,* 69–79.

Yalom, I. D. (1985). *The theory and practice of group psychotherapy* (3rd ed.). New York: Basic Books.

Yang, N., & Linz, D. (1990). Movie ratings and the content of adult videos: The sex-violence ratio. *Journal of Communication, 40*(2), 28–42.

Yankelovich Partners. (1995, May/June). Growing old. *American Enterprise,* p. 108.

Yankelovich Partners. (1997, December 15). Ability of spirituality to help people who are sick. (Press release.)

Yardley, J. (2005, January 31). Fearing future, China starts to give girls their due. *New York Times* (www.nytimes.com).

Yarnell, P. R., & Lynch, S. (1970, April 25). Retrograde memory immediately after concussion. *Lancet,* pp. 863–865.

Yarrow, L. J., Goodwin, M. S., Manheimer, H., & Milowe, I. D. (1973). Infancy experience and cognitive and personality development at ten years. In L. J. Stone, H. T. Smith, & L. B. Murphy (Eds.), *The competent infant.* New York: Basic Books.

Yates, A. (1989). Current perspectives on the eating disorders: I. History, psychological and biological aspects. *Journal of the American Academy of Child and Adolescent Psychiatry, 28,* 813–828.

Yates, A. (1990). Current perspectives on the eating disorders: II. Treatment, outcome, and research directions. *Journal of the American Academy of Child and Adolescent Psychiatry, 29,* 1–9.

Yates, W. R. (2000). Testosterone in psychiatry. *Archives of General Psychiatry, 57,* 155–156.

Ybarra, O. (1999). Misanthropic person memory when the need to self-enhance is absent. *Personality and Social Psychology Bulletin, 25,* 261–269.

Yip, P. S. F. (1998). Age, sex, marital status and suicide: An empirical study of east and west. *Psychological Reports, 82,* 311–322.

Yirmiya, N., Erel, O., Shaken, M., & Solomonica-Levi, D. (1998). Meta-analyses comparing theory of mind abilities of individuals with autism, individuals with mental retardation, and normally developing individuals. *Psychological Bulletin, 124,* 283–307.

Zajonc, R. B. (1965). Social facilitation. *Science, 149,* 269–274.

Zajonc, R. B. (1980). Feeling and thinking: Preferences need no inferences. *American Psychologist, 35,* 151–175.

Zajonc, R. B. (1984a). On the primacy of affect. *American Psychologist, 39,* 117–123.

Zajonc, R. B. (1984b, July 22). Quoted by D. Goleman, Rethinking IQ tests and their value. *The New York Times,* p. D22.

Zajonc, R. B. (1998). Emotions. In D. Gilbert, S. T. Fiske, & G. Lindzey (Eds.), *Handbook of social psychology,* 4th ed. New York: McGraw-Hill.

Zajonc, R. B. (2001). Mere exposure: A gateway to the subliminal. *Current Directions in Psychological Science, 10,* 224–228.

Zajonc, R. B., & Markus, G. B. (1975). Birth order and intellectual development. *Psychological Review, 82,* 74–88.

Zajonc, R. B., Murphy, S. T., & Inglehart, M. (1989). Feeling and facial efference: Implications of the vascular theory of emotions. *Psychological Review, 96,* 395–416.

Zammit, S., Allebeck, P., Andreasson, S., Lundberg, I., & Lewis, G. (2002). Self reported cannabis use as a risk factor for schizophrenia in Swedish conscripts of 1969: Historical cohort study. *British Medical Journal, 325,* 1199.

Zauberman, G., & Lynch, J. G., Jr. (2005). Resource slack and propensity to discount delayed investments of time versus money. *Journal of Experimental Psychology: General, 134,* 23–37.

Zeidner, M. (1990). Perceptions of ethnic group modal intelligence: Reflections of cultural stereotypes or intelligence test scores? *Journal of Cross-Cultural Psychology, 21,* 214–231.

Zeineh, M. M., Engel, S. A., Thompson, P. M., & Bookheimer, S. Y. (2003). Dynamics of the hippocampus during encoding and retrieval of face-name pairs. *Science, 299,* 577–580.

Zigler, E. F. (1987). Formal schooling for four-year-olds? No. *American Psychologist, 42,* 254–260.

Zigler, E., & Styfco, S. J. (2001). Extended childhood intervention prepared children for school and beyond. *Journal of the American Medical Association, 285,* 2378–2380.

Zilbergeld, B. (1983). *The shrinking of America: Myths of psychological change.* Boston: Little, Brown.

Zillmann, D. (1986). Effects of prolonged consumption of pornography. Background paper for *The Surgeon General's workshop on pornography and public health,* June 22–24. Report prepared by E. P. Mulvey & J. L. Haugaard and released by Office of the Surgeon General on August 4, 1986.

Zillmann, D. (1989). Effects of prolonged consumption of pornography. In D. Zillmann & J. Bryant (Eds.), *Pornography: Research advances and policy considerations.* Hillsdale, NJ: Erlbaum.

Zillmann, D., & Bryant, J. (1984). Effects of massive exposure to pornography. In N. Malamuth & E. Donnerstein (Eds.), *Pornography and sexual aggression.* Orlando, FL: Academic Press.

Zimbardo, P. G. (1970). The human choice: Individuation, reason, and order versus deindividuation, impulse, and chaos. In W. J. Arnold & D. Levine (Eds.), *Nebraska Symposium on Motivation, 1969.* Lincoln, NE: University of Nebraska Press.

Zimbardo, P. G. (1972, April). Pathology of imprisonment. *Transaction/Society,* pp. 4–8.

Zimbardo, P. G. (2001, September 16). Fighting terrorism by understanding man's capacity for evil. Op Ed Essay distributed by spsp-discuss@stolaf.edu.

Zimbardo, P. G. (2004, May 25). Journalist interview re: Abu Ghraib prison abuses: Eleven answers to eleven questions. Unpublished manuscript, Stanford University.

Zimbardo, P. G. (2005, January 18). You can't be a sweet cucumber in a vinegar barrel. *The Edge* (www.edge.org).

Zimmer, C. (2003). How the mind reads other minds. *Science, 300,* 1079–1080.

Zornberg, G. L., Buka, S. L., & Tsuang, M. T. (2000). At issue: The problem of obstetrical complications and schizophrenia. *Schizophrenia Bulletin, 26,* 249–256.

Zubieta, J-K., Heitzeg, M. M., Smith, Y. R., Bueller, J. A., Xu, K., Xu, Y., Koeppe, R. A., Stohler, C. S., & Goldman, D. (2003). COMT val[158]met genotype affects μ-opioid neurotransmitter responses to a pain stressor. *Science, 299,* 1240–1243.

Zucco, G. M. (2003). Anomalies in cognition: Olfactory memory. *European Psychologist, 8,* 77–86.

Zucker, G. S., & Weiner, B. (1993). Conservatism and perceptions of poverty: An attributional analysis. *Journal of Applied Social Psychology, 23,* 925–943.

Zuckerman, M. (1979). *Sensation seeking: Beyond the optimal level of arousal.* Hillsdale, NJ: Erlbaum.

NAME INDEX

SUBJECT INDEX

Timeline

The Story of Psychology: A Timeline

by Charles L. Brewer, Furman University

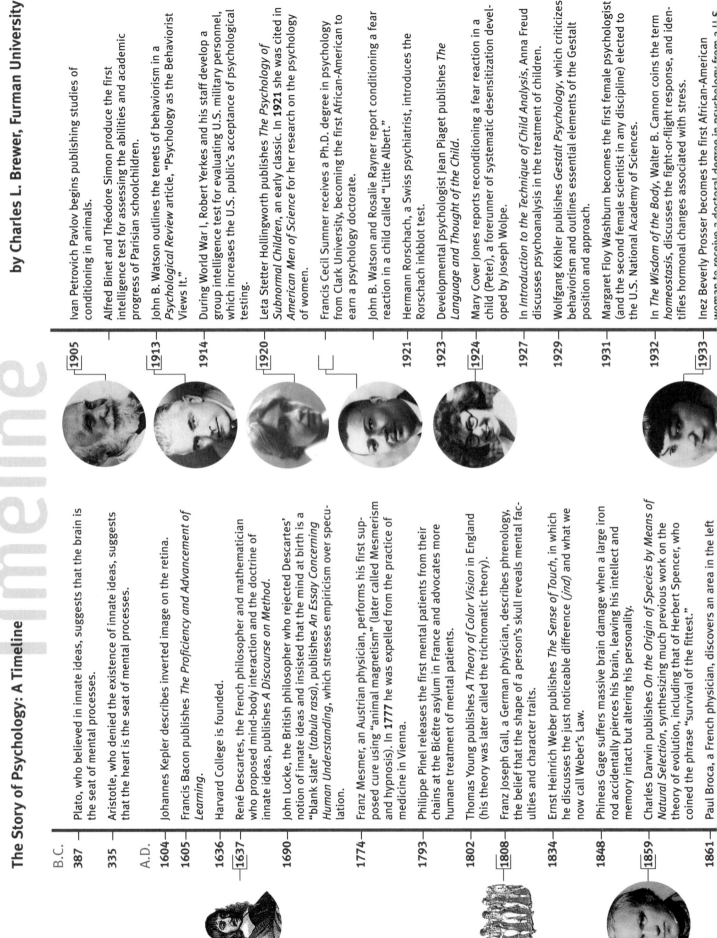

B.C.

387 — Plato, who believed in innate ideas, suggests that the brain is the seat of mental processes.

335 — Aristotle, who denied the existence of innate ideas, suggests that the heart is the seat of mental processes.

A.D.

1604 — Johannes Kepler describes inverted image on the retina.

1605 — Francis Bacon publishes *The Proficiency and Advancement of Learning.*

1636 — Harvard College is founded.

1637 — René Descartes, the French philosopher and mathematician who proposed mind-body interaction and the doctrine of innate ideas, publishes *A Discourse on Method.*

1690 — John Locke, the British philosopher who rejected Descartes' notion of innate ideas and insisted that the mind at birth is a "blank slate" (*tabula rasa*), publishes *An Essay Concerning Human Understanding,* which stresses empiricism over speculation.

1774 — Franz Mesmer, an Austrian physician, performs his first supposed cure using "animal magnetism" (later called Mesmerism and hypnosis). In **1777** he was expelled from the practice of medicine in Vienna.

1793 — Philippe Pinel releases the first mental patients from their chains at the Bicêtre asylum in France and advocates more humane treatment of mental patients.

1802 — Thomas Young publishes *A Theory of Color Vision* in England (his theory was later called the trichromatic theory).

1808 — Franz Joseph Gall, a German physician, describes phrenology, the belief that the shape of a person's skull reveals mental faculties and character traits.

1834 — Ernst Heinrich Weber publishes *The Sense of Touch,* in which he discusses the just noticeable difference (*jnd*) and what we now call Weber's Law.

1848 — Phineas Gage suffers massive brain damage when a large iron rod accidentally pierces his brain, leaving his intellect and memory intact but altering his personality.

1859 — Charles Darwin publishes *On the Origin of Species by Means of Natural Selection,* synthesizing much previous work on the theory of evolution, including that of Herbert Spencer, who coined the phrase "survival of the fittest."

1861 — Paul Broca, a French physician, discovers an area in the left

1905 — Ivan Petrovich Pavlov begins publishing studies of conditioning in animals.

Alfred Binet and Théodore Simon produce the first intelligence test for assessing the abilities and academic progress of Parisian schoolchildren.

1913 — John B. Watson outlines the tenets of behaviorism in a *Psychological Review* article, "Psychology as the Behaviorist Views It."

1914 — During World War I, Robert Yerkes and his staff develop a group intelligence test for evaluating U.S. military personnel, which increases the U.S. public's acceptance of psychological testing.

1920 — Leta Stetter Hollingworth publishes *The Psychology of Subnormal Children,* an early classic. In **1921** she was cited in *American Men of Science* for her research on the psychology of women.

Francis Cecil Sumner receives a Ph.D. degree in psychology from Clark University, becoming the first African-American to earn a psychology doctorate.

John B. Watson and Rosalie Rayner report conditioning a fear reaction in a child called "Little Albert."

1921 — Hermann Rorschach, a Swiss psychiatrist, introduces the Rorschach inkblot test.

1923 — Developmental psychologist Jean Piaget publishes *The Language and Thought of the Child.*

1924 — Mary Cover Jones reports reconditioning a fear reaction in a child (Peter), a forerunner of systematic desensitization developed by Joseph Wolpe.

1927 — In *Introduction to the Technique of Child Analysis,* Anna Freud discusses psychoanalysis in the treatment of children.

1929 — Wolfgang Köhler publishes *Gestalt Psychology,* which criticizes behaviorism and outlines essential elements of the Gestalt position and approach.

1931 — Margaret Floy Washburn becomes the first female psychologist (and the second female scientist in any discipline) elected to the U.S. National Academy of Sciences.

1932 — In *The Wisdom of the Body,* Walter B. Cannon coins the term *homeostasis,* discusses the fight-or-flight response, and identifies hormonal changes associated with stress.

1933 — Inez Beverly Prosser becomes the first African-American

Apperception Test to elicit fantasies from people undergoing psychoanalysis.

1936 — Egas Moniz, Portuguese physician, publishes work on the first frontal lobotomies performed on humans.

1938 — B. F. Skinner publishes *The Behavior of Organisms*, which describes operant conditioning of animals.

In *Primary Mental Abilities*, Louis L. Thurstone proposes seven such abilities.

Ugo Cerletti and Lucino Bini use electroshock treatment with a human patient.

1939 — David Wechsler publishes the Wechsler-Bellevue intelligence test, forerunner of the Wechsler Intelligence Scale for Children (WISC) and the Wechsler Adult Intelligence Scale (WAIS).

Mamie Phipps Clark receives a master's degree from Howard University. In collaboration with Kenneth B. Clark, she later extended her thesis, "The Development of Consciousness of Self in Negro Preschool Children," providing joint research cited in the U.S. Supreme Court's **1954** decision to end racial segregation in public schools.

Edward Alexander Bott helps found the Canadian Psychological Association. He becomes its first president in **1940.**

World War II provides many opportunities for psychologists to enhance the popularity and influence of psychology, especially in applied areas.

1943 — Psychologist Starke Hathaway and physician J. Charnley McKinley publish the Minnesota Multiphasic Personality Inventory (MMPI).

1945 — Karen Horney, who criticized Freud's theory of female sexual development, publishes *Our Inner Conflicts*.

1946 — Benjamin Spock's first edition of *The Commonsense Book of Baby and Child Care* appears; the book will influence child rearing in North America for several decades.

1948 — Alfred Kinsey and his colleagues publish *Sexual Behavior in the Human Male*.

B. F. Skinner's novel, *Walden Two*, describes a Utopian community based on positive reinforcement, which becomes a clarion call for applying psychological principles in everyday living, especially communal living.

Ernest R. Hilgard publishes *Theories of Learning*, which was required reading for several generations of psychology students in North America.

1949 — Raymond B. Cattell publishes the Sixteen Personality Factor Questionnaire (16PF).

Genius, in which he claims that intelligence is inherited. In **1876** he coined the expression "nature and nurture" to correspond with "heredity and environment."

1874 — Carl Wernicke, a German neurologist and psychiatrist, shows that damage to a specific area in the left temporal lobe (now called Wernicke's area) disrupts ability to comprehend or produce spoken or written language.

1878 — G. Stanley Hall receives from Harvard University the first Ph.D. degree in psychology awarded in the United States.

1879 — Wilhelm Wundt establishes at the University of Leipzig, Germany, the first psychology laboratory, which becomes a Mecca for psychology students from all over the world.

1883 — G. Stanley Hall, student of Wilhelm Wundt, establishes the first formal U.S. psychology laboratory at Johns Hopkins University.

1885 — Hermann Ebbinghaus publishes *On Memory*, summarizing his extensive research on learning and memory, including the "forgetting curve."

1889 — Alfred Binet and Henri Beaunis establish the first psychology laboratory in France at the Sorbonne, and the first International Congress of Psychology meets in Paris.

1890 — William James, Harvard University philosopher and psychologist, publishes *The Principles of Psychology*, describing psychology as "the science of mental life."

1891 — James Mark Baldwin establishes the first psychology laboratory in the British Commonwealth at the University of Toronto.

1892 — G. Stanley Hall spearheads the founding of the American Psychological Association (APA) and becomes its first president.

1893 — Mary Whiton Calkins (pictured) and Christine Ladd-Franklin are the first women elected to membership in the APA.

1894 — Margaret Floy Washburn is the first woman to receive a Ph.D. degree in psychology (Cornell University).

Harvard University denies Mary Whiton Calkins admission to doctoral candidacy because of her gender, despite Hugo Münsterberg's claim that she was the best student he had ever had there.

1896 — John Dewey publishes "The Reflex Arc Concept in Psychology," helping to formalize the school of psychology called functionalism.

1898 — In "Animal Intelligence," Edward L. Thorndike, Columbia University, describes his learning experiments with cats in "puzzle boxes." In **1905,** he proposed the "law of effect."

1900 — Sigmund Freud publishes *The Interpretation of Dreams*, his major theoretical work on psychoanalysis.

1901 — Ten founders establish the British Psychological Society.

1905 — Mary Whiton Calkins becomes the first woman president of the APA.

Continued on inside back cover

The Story of Psychology: A Timeline   (continued from inside front cover)

1949 In *The Organization of Behavior: A Neuropsychological Theory*, Canadian psychologist Donald O. Hebb outlines a new and influential conceptualization of how the nervous system functions.

1950 Solomon Asch publishes studies of effects of conformity on judgments of line length.

In *Childhood and Society*, Erik Erikson outlines his stages of psychosocial development.

1951 Carl Rogers publishes *Client-Centered Therapy*.

1952 The American Psychiatric Association publishes *Diagnostic and Statistical Manual of Mental Disorders*, an influential book that will be updated periodically.

1953 Eugene Aserinski and Nathaniel Kleitman describe rapid eye movements (REM) that occur during sleep.

Janet Taylor's Manifest Anxiety Scale appears in the *Journal of Abnormal Psychology*.

1954 In *Motivation and Personality*, Abraham Maslow proposes a hierarchy of motives ranging from physiological needs to self-actualization.

James Olds and Peter Milner, McGill University neuropsychologists, describe rewarding effects of electrical stimulation of the hypothalamus in rats.

Gordon Allport publishes *The Nature of Prejudice*.

1956 In his *Psychological Review* article titled "The Magical Number Seven, Plus or Minus Two: Some Limits on Our Capacity for Processing Information," George Miller coins the term *chunk* for memory researchers.

1957 Robert Sears, Eleanor Maccoby, and Harry Levin publish *Patterns of Child Rearing*.

Charles Ferster and B. F. Skinner publish *Schedules of Reinforcement*.

1959 Noam Chomsky's critical review of B. F. Skinner's *Verbal Behavior* appears in the journal *Language*.

Eleanor Gibson and Richard Walk report their research on infants' depth perception in "The Visual Cliff."

Harry Harlow outlines "The Nature of Love," his work on attachment in monkeys.

Lloyd Peterson and Margaret Peterson in the *Journal of Experimental Psychology* article, "Short-Term Retention of Individual Verbal Items," highlight the importance of rehearsal in memory.

John Thibaut and Harold Kelley publish *The Social Psychology of Groups*.

1969 In his APA presidential address, "Psychology as a Means of Promoting Human Welfare," George Miller emphasizes the importance of "giving psychology away."

1971 Kenneth B. Clark becomes the first African-American president of the American Psychological Association.

Albert Bandura publishes *Social Learning Theory*.

Allan Paivio publishes *Imagery and Verbal Processes*.

B. F. Skinner publishes *Beyond Freedom and Dignity*.

Elliot Aronson publishes *The Social Animal*.

1972 Fergus Craik and Robert Lockhart's "Levels of Processing: A Framework for Memory Research" appears in the *Journal of Verbal Learning and Verbal Behavior*.

Robert Rescorla and Allan Wagner publish their associative model of Pavlovian conditioning.

Under the leadership of Derald Sue and Stanley Sue, the Asian-American Psychological Association is founded.

1973 Ethologists Karl von Frisch, Konrad Lorenz, and Nikolaas Tinbergen receive the Nobel Prize for their research on animal behavior.

1974 APA's Division 2 first publishes its journal, *Teaching of Psychology*, with Robert S. Daniel as editor.

Eleanor Maccoby (pictured) and Carol Jacklin publish *The Psychology of Sex Differences*.

1975 Biologist Edward O. Wilson's *Sociobiology* appears; it will be a controversial precursor to evolutionary psychology.

1976 Sandra Wood Scarr and Richard A. Weinberg publish "IQ Test Performance of Black Children Adopted by White Families" in *American Psychologist*.

1978 Psychologist Herbert A. Simon, Carnegie-Mellon University, wins a Nobel Prize for pioneering research on computer simulations of human thinking and problem solving.

1979 James J. Gibson publishes *The Ecological Approach to Visual Perception*.

Elizabeth Loftus publishes *Eyewitness Testimony*.

Ellen Langer is the first woman to be granted tenure in Harvard University's Department of Psychology.

1981 David Hubel and Torsten Wiesel receive a Nobel Prize for research on single-cell recordings that identified feature detector cells in the visual cortex.

Roger Sperry receives a Nobel Prize for research on split-brain patients.